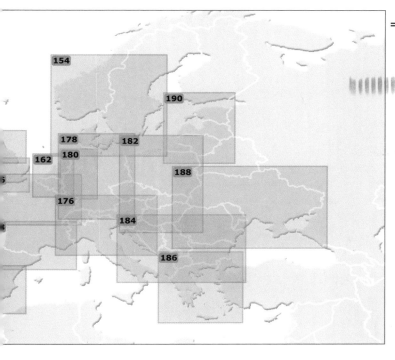

City plans

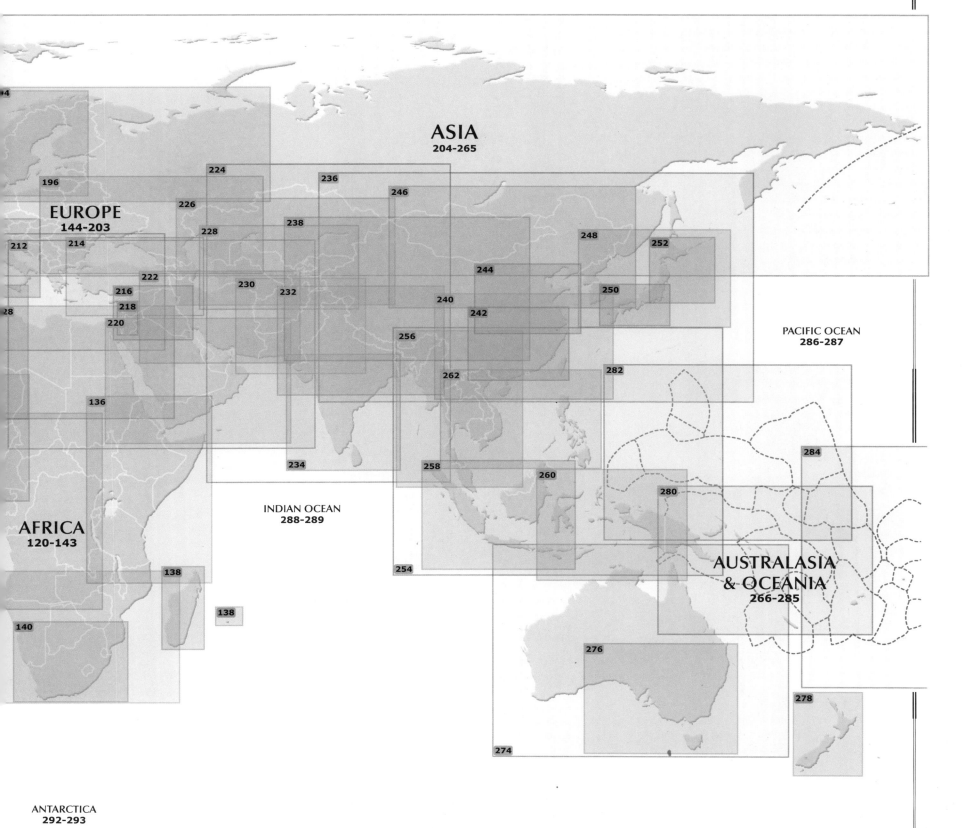

COMPLETE ATLAS

OF THE WORLD

COMPLETE ATLAS

OF THE WORLD

LONDON, NEW YORK, MELBOURNE, MUNICH AND DELHI

FOR THE SECOND EDITION

Publishing Director Jonathan Metcalf

Art Director Philip Ormerod

Associate Publishing Director Liz Wheeler

Associate Publisher Andrew Macintyre

Senior Cartographic Editor Simon Mumford

Cartographers Encompass Graphics Ltd, Brighton, UK

Jacket Designer Silke Spingles

Production Controller Mandy Inness   **Production Editor** Joanna Byrne

Cartographic Editors
Tony Chambers, John Dear, Ruth Hall, Andrew Johnson, Belinda Kane, Lynn Neal, Ann Stephenson

Cartographers
Paul Eames, Edward Merritt, John Plumer, Rob Stokes, Iorwerth Watkins

Digital Map Suppliers
Advanced Illustration, Congleton, UK • Cosmographics, Watford, UK
Encompass Graphics, Brighton, UK • Lovell Johns Ltd., Long Hanborough, UK
Netmaps, Barcelona, Spain

Digital Terrain Data
Digital terrain data and continental panoramic images created by Planetary Visions Ltd, Farnham, UK

Editor
Robert Dinwiddie

Designers
Nicola Liddiard, Yak El-Droubie

Picture Research
Louise Thomas, Jenny Baskaya

Indexing and Database
T-Kartor, Sweden
Francesca Albini, Eleanor Arkwright, Renata Dyntarova, Edward Heelas, Britta Hansesgaard

Systems Coordinator
Philip Rowles

Flags courtesy of The Flag Institue, Cheshire, UK

First American Edition, 2007
This revised edition 2012

Published in the United States by DK Publishing, 375 Hudson Street, New York, New York 10014

12 13 14 15 16 10 9 8 7 6 5 4 3 2 1
175654—May 2012

Reprinted with revisions 2009, Second edition 2012
Copyright © 2007, 2009, 2012 Dorling Kindersley Limited. All rights reserved.

Published in Great Britain by Dorling Kindersley Limited

A catalog record for this book is available from the Library of Congress

ISBN: 978-0-7566-8972-8

DK books are available at special discounts when purchased in bulk for sales promotions, premiums, fund-raising, or educational use.
For details, contact: DK Publishing Special Markets, 375 Hudson Street, New York, New York 10014 or SpecialSales@dk.com

Color reproduction by MDP Ltd, Wiltshire, UK
Printed and bound by Tien Wah Press, Singapore

Discover more at **www.dk.com**

Introduction

The World at the beginning of the 21st Century would be a place of unimaginable change to our forefathers. Since 1900 the human population has undergone a fourfold growth coupled with an unparalleled development in the technology at our disposal. The last vestiges of the unknown World are gone, and previously hostile realms claimed for habitation. The advent of aviation technology and the growth of mass tourism have allowed people to travel further and more frequently than ever before

Allied to this, the rapid growth of global communication systems mean that World events have become more accessible than ever before and their knock on effects quickly ripple across the whole planet. News broadcasts bring the far-flung corners of the world into everyone's lives, and with it, a view of the people and places that make up that region. The mysteries of the World that once fueled global exploration and the quest to discover the unknown are behind us; we inhabit a world of mass transportation, a world where even the most extreme regions have been mapped, a world with multi faceted view points on every event, a World of communication overload.

However, does this help us make sense of the World? It is increasingly important for us to have a clear vision of the World in which we live and such a deluge of information can leave us struggling to find some context and meaning. It has never been more important to own an atlas; the *DK Complete Atlas of the World* has been conceived to meet this need. At its core, like all atlases, it seeks to define where places are, to describe their main characteristics, and to locate them in relation to other places. By gathering a spectacular collection of satellite imagery and draping it with carefully selected and up-to-date geographic information this atlas filters the World's data into clear, meaningful and user-friendly maps.

The World works on different levels and so does the *DK Complete Atlas of the World*. Readers can learn about global issues of many kinds or they can probe in a little further for the continental context. Delving even further they can explore at regional, national or even sub-national level. The very best available satellite data has been used to create topography and bathymetry that reveal the breathtaking texture of landscapes and sea-floors. These bring out the context of the places and features selected to appear on top of them.

This second edition of the *DK Complete Atlas of the World* incorporates hundreds of revisions and updates affecting every map and every page, distilling the burgeoning mass of information available through modern technology into an extraordinarily detailed and reliable view of our World.

Contents

The atlas is organized by continent, moving eastward from the International Date Line. The opening section describes the world's structure, systems and its main features. The Atlas of the World which follows, is a continent-by-continent guide to today's world, starting with a comprehensive insight into the physical, political, and economic structure of each continent, followed by detailed maps of carefully selected geopolitical regions.

WORLD

NORTH AMERICA

SOUTH AMERICA

AFRICA

EUROPE

Key to regional maps

Physical features

elevation

6000m / 19,686ft
4000m / 13,124ft
3000m / 9843ft
2000m / 6562ft
1000m / 3281ft
500m / 1640ft
250m / 820ft
100m / 328ft
sea level
below sea level

▲ elevation above sea level (mountain height)

▲ volcano

✕ pass

▼ elevation below sea level (depression depth)

sand desert

lava flow

coastline

reef

atoll

sea depth

sea level
-250m / -820ft
-2000m / -6562ft
-4000m / -13,124ft

▲ seamount / guyot symbol

▼ undersea spot depth

Drainage features

main river

secondary river

tertiary river

minor river

main seasonal river

secondary seasonal river

canal

waterfall

rapids

dam

perennial lake

seasonal lake

perennial salt lake

seasonal salt lake

reservoir

salt flat / salt pan

marsh / salt marsh

mangrove

wadi

○ spring / well / waterhole / oasis

Ice features

ice cap / sheet

ice shelf

glacier / snowfield

summer pack ice limit

winter pack ice limit

Graticule features

lines of latitude and longitude / Equator

Tropics / Polar circles

45° degrees of longitude / latitude

Communications

motorway / highway

motorway / highway (under construction)

major road

minor road

tunnel (road)

main railroad

minor railroad

tunnel (railroad)

✈ international airport

Borders

full international border

undefined international border

disputed de facto border

disputed territorial claim border

indication of country extent (Pacific only)

indication of dependent territory extent (Pacific only)

demarcation/ cease fire line

autonomous / federal region border

other 1st order internal administrative border

2nd order internal administrative border

Miscellaneous features

ancient wall

◇ site of interest

◦ scientific station

Settlements

built up area

settlement population symbols

■ more than 5 million

◉ 1 million to 5 million

◉ 500,000 to 1 million

◎ 100,000 to 500,000

⊕ 50,000 to 100,000

○ 10,000 to 50,000

○ fewer than 10,000

■●● country/dependent territory capital city

■●● autonomous / federal region / other 1st order internal administrative center

■●⊕ 2nd order internal administrative center

Typographic key

Physical features

landscape features ... *Namib Desert*
Massif Central
ANDES

headland .... *Nordkapp*

elevation / volcano / pass .... Mount Meru 4556 m

drainage features ... *Lake Geneva*

rivers / canals spring / well / waterhole / oasis / waterfall / rapids / dam .... *Mekong*

ice features .... *Vatnajökull*

Physical features (continued)

sea features .... *Golfe de Lion*
Andaman Sea
INDIAN OCEAN

undersea features ... *Barracuda Fracture Zone*

Regions

country .... **ARMENIA**

dependent territory with parent state ..... NIUE (to NZ)

autonomous / federal region .... MINAS GERAIS

other 1st order internal administrative region .... MINSKAYA VOBLASTS'

2nd order internal administrative region .... Vaucluse

cultural region .... New England

Settlements

capital city .... **BEIJING**

dependent territory capital city .... FORT-DE-FRANCE

other settlements ... Chicago
Adana
Tizi Ozou
Yonezawa
Farnham

Miscellaneous

sites of interest / miscellaneous .... *Valley of the Kings*

Tropics / Polar circles .... *Antarctic Circle*

The Solar System

The Solar System consists of our local star, the Sun, and numerous objects that orbit the Sun – eight planets, five currently recognized dwarf planets, over 165 moons orbiting these planets and dwarf planets, and countless smaller bodies such as comets and asteroids. Including a vast outer region that is populated only by comets, the Solar System is about 9,300 billion miles (15,000 billion km) across. The much smaller region containing just the Sun and planets is about 7.5 billion miles (12 billion km) across. The Sun, which contributes over 99 percent of the mass of the entire Solar System, creates energy from nuclear reactions deep within its interior, providing the heat and light that make life on Earth possible.

THE MOON'S PHASES

As the Moon orbits Earth, the relative positions of Moon, Sun and Earth continuously change. Thus, the angle at which the Moon's sunlit face is seen by an observer on Earth varies in a cyclical fashion, producing the Moon's phases, as shown at right. Each cycle takes 29.5 days.

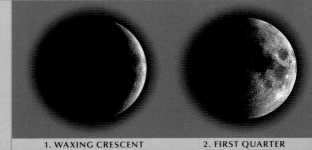

1. WAXING CRESCENT   2. FIRST QUARTER

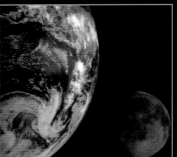

The Earth and Moon's relative sizes are clear in this long-range image from space.

The Moon

Earth's only satellite, the Moon, is thought to have formed 4.5 billion years ago from a cloud of debris produced when a large asteroid hit the young Earth. The Moon is too small to have retained an atmosphere, and is therefore a lifeless, dusty and dead world. However, although the Moon has only about 1 percent of the mass of the Earth, its gravity exerts an important influence on Earth's oceans, manifest in the ebb and flow of the tides.

What is a Planet?

The International Astronomical Union defines a Solar System planet as a near-spherical object that orbits the Sun (and no other body) and has cleared the neighborhood around its orbit of other bodies. A dwarf planet is a planet that is not big enough to have cleared its orbital neighborhood. Extra-solar planets are objects orbiting stars other than the Sun.

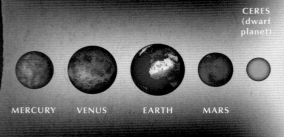

MERCURY   VENUS   EARTH   MARS

CERES (dwarf planet)

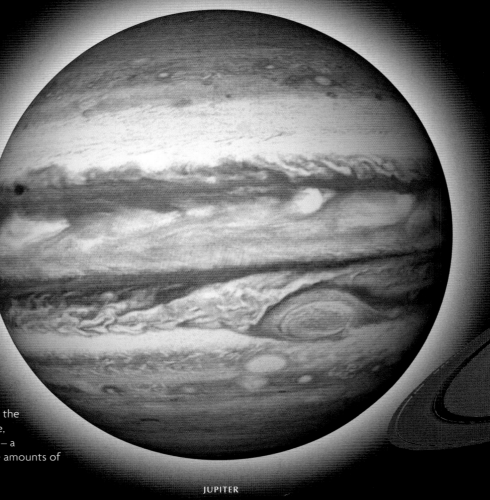

JUPITER

The Sun

The Sun is a huge sphere of exceedingly hot plasma (ionized gas), consisting mainly of the elements hydrogen and helium. It formed about 4.6 billion years ago, when a swirling cloud of gas and dust began to contract under the influence of gravity. When the center of this cloud reached a critically high temperature, hydrogen nuclei started combining to form helium nuclei – a process called nuclear fusion – with the release of massive amounts of energy. This process continues to this day.

SOLAR ECLIPSE

A solar eclipse occurs when the Moon passes between Earth and the Sun, casting its shadow on Earth's surface. During a total eclipse (below), viewers along a strip of Earth's surface, called the area of totality, see the Sun totally blotted out for a short time, as the umbra (Moon's full shadow) sweeps over them. Outside this area is a larger one, where the Sun appears only partly obscured, as the penumbra (partial shadow) passes over.

INSIDE THE SUN

The Sun has three internal layers. At its center is the core, where temperatures reach 27 million°F (15 million°C) and nuclear fusion occurs. The radiative zone is a slightly cooler region through which energy radiates away from the core. Further out, in the convective zone, plumes of hot plasma carry the energy towards the Sun's visible surface layer, called the photosphere. Once there, the energy escapes as light, heat and other forms of radiation.

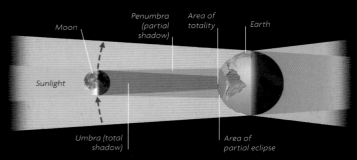

Moon

Penumbra (partial shadow)

Area of totality

Earth

Sunlight

Umbra (total shadow)

Area of partial eclipse

Photosphere

Core

Radiative zone

Convective zone

Sunspots mark cooler areas of surface

Prominences are loops of gas arching above the photosphere

| 3. WAXING GIBBOUS | 4. FULL MOON | 5. WANING GIBBOUS | 6. LAST QUARTER | 7. WANING CRESCENT | 8. NEW MOON |

PLANETS | MAIN DWARF PLANETS

	MERCURY	VENUS	EARTH	MARS	JUPITER	SATURN	URANUS	NEPTUNE	CERES	PLUTO	ERIS
DIAMETER	3029 miles (4875 km)	7521 miles (12,104 km)	7928 miles (12,756 km)	4213 miles (6780 km)	88,846 miles (142,984 km)	74,898 miles (120,536 km)	31,763 miles (51,118 km)	30,775 miles (49,528 km)	590 miles (950 km)	1432 miles (2304 km)	1429-1553 miles (2300-2500 km)
AVERAGE DISTANCE FROM THE SUN	36 mill. miles (57.9 mill. km)	67.2 mill. miles (108.2 mill. km)	93 mill. miles (149.6 mill. km)	141.6 mill. miles (227.9 mill. km)	483.6 mill. miles (778.3 mill. km)	889.8 mill. miles (1431 mill. km)	1788 mill. miles (2877 mill. km)	2795 mill. miles (4498 mill. km)	257 mill. miles (414 mill. km)	3675 mill. miles (5,915 mill. km)	6344 mill. miles (10,210 mill. km)
ROTATION PERIOD	58.6 days	243 days	23.93 hours	24.62 hours	9.93 hours	10.65 hours	17.24 hours	16.11 hours	9.1 hours	6.38 days	not known
ORBITAL PERIOD	88 days	224.7 days	365.26 days	687 days	11.86 years	29.37 years	84.1 years	164.9 years	4.6 years	248.6 years	557 years
SURFACE TEMPERATURE	-292°F to 806°F (-180°C to 430°C)	896°F (480°C)	-94°F to 131°F (-70°C to 55°C)	-184°F to 77 °F (-120°C to 25°C)	-160°F (-110°C)	-220°F (-140°C)	-320°F (-200°C)	-320°F (-200°C)	-161°F (-107°C)	-380°F (-230°C)	-405°F (-243°C)

DWARF PLANETS

In 2006 a new type of dwarf planet was defined in an attempt to classify the numerous smaller bodies within the solar system that behave like planets physically but which are only a fraction of the size of the major planets. Currently, there are five dwarf planets recognized under this new system, Ceres, Pluto, Haumea, Makemake, and Eris.

ERIS (dwarf planet)

PLUTO (dwarf planet)

URANUS

NEPTUNE

THE OUTER PLANETS

SATURN

Orbits

All the Solar System's planets and dwarf planets orbit the Sun in the same direction and (apart from Pluto) roughly in the same plane. All the orbits have the shapes of ellipses (stretched circles). However in most cases, these ellipses are close to being circular: only Pluto and Eris have very elliptical orbits. Orbital period (the time it takes an object to orbit the Sun) increases with distance from the Sun. The more remote objects not only have further to travel with each orbit, they also move more slowly.

THE OUTER PLANETS

The four gigantic outer planets – Jupiter, Saturn, Uranus and Neptune – consist mainly of gas, liquid and ice. All have rings and many moons. The dwarf planet Pluto is made of rock and ice.

THE INNER PLANETS

The four planets closest to the Sun – Mercury, Venus, Earth and Mars – are composed mainly of rock and metal. They are much smaller than the outer planets, have few or no moons, and no rings.

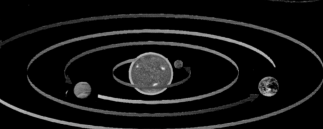

THE INNER PLANETS

AVERAGE DISTANCE FROM THE SUN

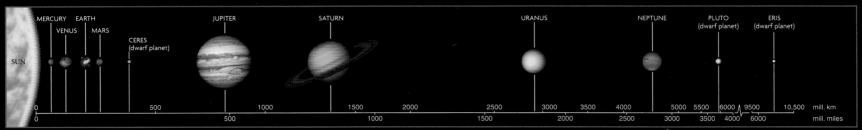

| SUN | MERCURY VENUS EARTH MARS | CERES (dwarf planet) | JUPITER | SATURN | URANUS | NEPTUNE | PLUTO (dwarf planet) | ERIS (dwarf planet) |

0   500   1000   1500   2000   2500   3000   3500   4000   5000 5500 6000 9500   10,500 mill. km

0   500   1000   1500   2000   2500   3000   3500 4000 6000 mill. miles

The Physical World

Earth's surface is constantly being transformed. Movements of the rigid tectonic plates that make up this surface are continuously, if slowly, shifting its landmasses around, while the land itself is constantly weathered and eroded by wind, water, and ice. Sometimes change is dramatic, the spectacular results of earthquakes or floods. More often it is a slow process lasting for millions of years. A physical map of the world represents a snapshot of Earth's ever-evolving architecture. The terrain maps below and at right show the planet's whole surface, including variations in ocean depth as well as the mountain-rippled texture of Earth's continents.

THE WORLD'S OCEANS

Earth's surface is dominated by water. The hemisphere shown here, centered around the southwest Pacific, is nearly all ocean, with the waters interrupted only by Antarctica, a part of South America, Australia, and the numerous islands of Australasia & Oceania, and southeast Asia.

NORTH AMERICA
Arctic Circle
Tropic of Cancer
PACIFIC OCEAN
Equator
ATLANTIC OCEAN
SOUTH AMERICA
Tropic of Capricorn
Antarctic Circle
SOUTHERN

Mendocino Fracture Zone
Murray Fracture Zone
Molokai Fracture Zone
Hawaiian Islands
Hawai'i
Clarion Fracture Zone
Tropic of Cancer
Shatskiy Rise
Mapmaker Seamounts
Mid-Pacific Mountains
Johnston Atoll
Central Pacific Basin
Marshall Islands
PACIFIC OCEAN
Micronesia
Polynesia
Shikoku Basin
West Mariana Basin
Mariana Islands -10,920m
Mariana Trench
Philippine Sea
Central Basin Trough
Caroline Ridge
Melanesian Basin
Kiritimati
Clipperton Fracture Zone
Line Islands
Phoenix Islands
Eauripik Rise
Ontong Java Rise
Manihiki Plateau
Galapagos Fracture Zone
Palau
Philippine Islands
Melanesia
Bismarck Archipelago
Samoa
Penrhyn Basin
Cook Islands
Marquesas Islands
Marquesas Fracture Zone
South China Basin
Sulu Sea
Celebes Sea Celebes Basin
Bismarck Sea
Solomon Sea
Solomon Islands
New Guinea
Mount Wilhelm 4509m
Fiji
North Fiji Basin
Vanuatu
Tuamotu Islands
Tubuai Islands
South China Sea
Borneo
East Indies
Celebes
Arafura Sea
Torres Strait
Cape York
Coral Sea
New Caledonia
South Fiji Basin
Tonga
Kermadec Trench
Tonga Trench
Southwest Pacific Basin
Pitcairn Islands
East Pacific Rise
Gulf of Thailand
Timor
Timor Sea
Arnhem Land
Gulf of Carpentaria
Kimberley Plateau
Simpson Desert
Great Sandy Desert
Great Dividing Range
Great Barrier Reef
Lord Howe Rise
North Island
New Zealand
Bauer Basin
Galapagos Islands
Malay Peninsula
Strait of Malacca
Java Sea
Java
Ashmore & Cartier Islands
Gibson Desert
AUSTRALIA
Great Victoria Desert
Darling
Mount Kosciuszko 2228m
Tasman Sea
Cook Strait
South Island
Campbell Plateau
Chatham Islands
Southeast Pacific Basin
Easter Island
Galapagos Rise
Sala y Gomez
Sumatra
Equator
Nullarbor Plain
Bass Strait
Tasmania
Auckland Islands
Menard Fracture Zone
Challenger Fracture Zone
Sala y Gomez Ridge
Cocos Basin
Investigator Ridge
Perth Basin
South Australian Basin
Great Australian Bight
Campbell Island
Eltanin Fracture Zone
Udintsev Fracture Zone
San Felix Island
Peru Basin
Ninetyeast Ridge
INDIAN OCEAN
Ceylon Plain
Broken Ridge
South Indian Basin
SOUTHERN OCEAN
Antarctic Circle
Pacific-Antarctic Ridge
San Ambrosio Island
Nazca Ridge
Chile Basin
Juan Fernandez Islands
Roggeveen Basin
Chile Trench
Peru-Chile Trench
Tropic of Capricorn
Southeast Indian Ridge
Amsterdam Island
St Paul Island
Davis Sea
Ross Sea
Mt Erebus 3794m
Amundsen Plain
Amundsen Sea
Andes
Kerguelen Plateau
Dronning Maud Land
Wilkes Land
Ross Ice Shelf
Marie Byrd Land
Bellingshausen Sea
Strait of Magellan
Golfo Corcovado
Patagonia
SOUTH AMERICA
Heard Island
South Pole
ANTARCTICA
Ronne Ice Shelf
Antarctic Peninsula
Tierra del Fuego
Cape Horn
Gulf of San Jorge
Bahía Blanca
Pampas
Kerguelen
Enderby Plain
Weddell Sea
Falkland Islands
Río de la Plata
Southwest Indian Ridge
Crozet Islands
Maud Rise
Antarctic Circle
Scotia Sea
Drake Passage
South Georgia
Argentine Basin
Prince Edward Islands
Bouvet Island
South Sandwich Islands
America-Antarctic Ridge
South Sandwich Trench
Falkland Fracture Zone
Agulhas Basin
Gough Island

Scale 1:87,000,000

(projection: Azimuthal Equidistant)

Km
0 250 500 1000 1500 2000
0 250 500 1000 1500 2000
Miles

6000m
4000m
3000m
2000m
1000m
500m
250m
100m
Sea Level
-250m
-2000m
-4000m

THE WORLD

10

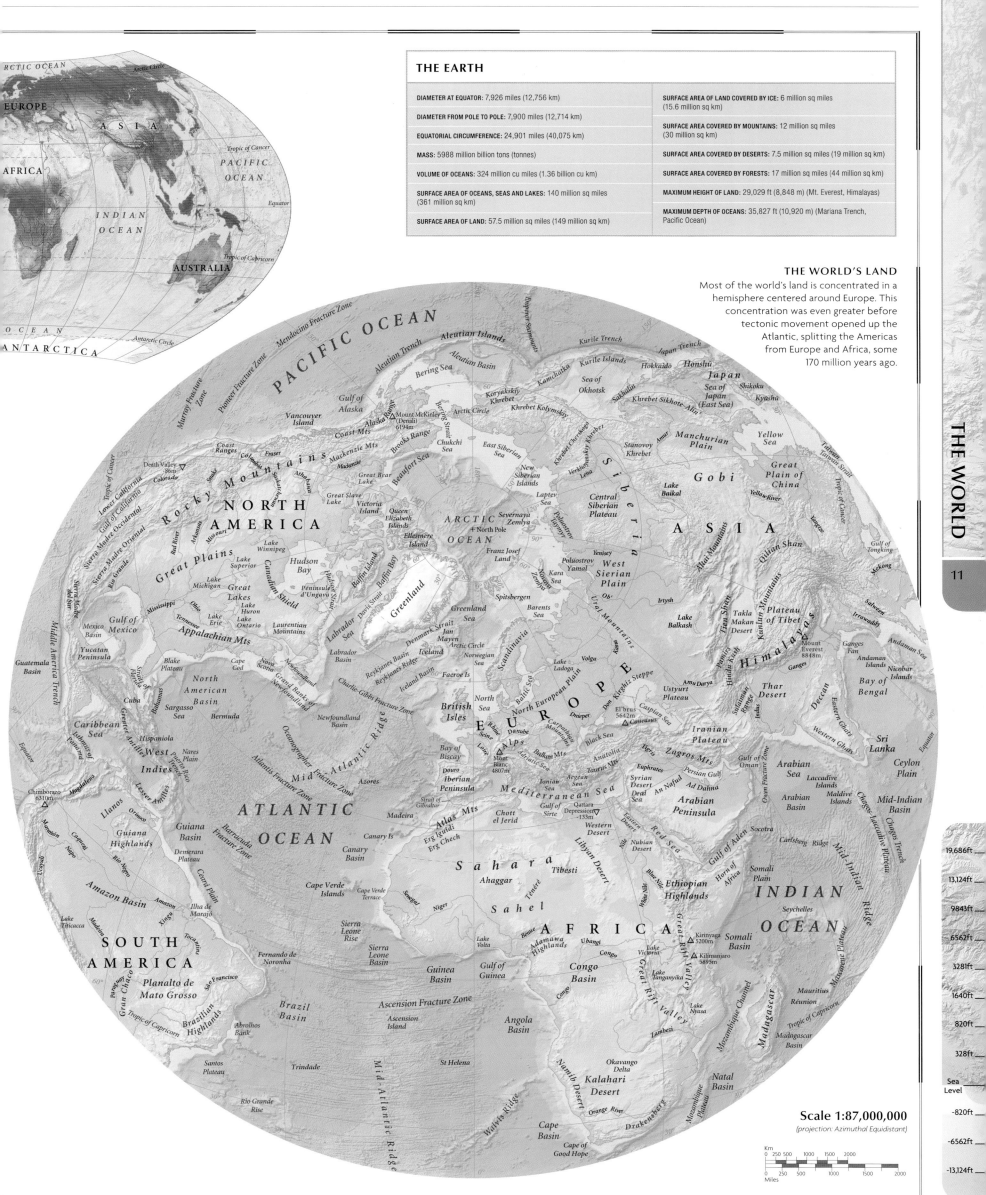

THE EARTH

DIAMETER AT EQUATOR: 7,926 miles (12,756 km)	**SURFACE AREA OF LAND COVERED BY ICE:** 6 million sq miles (15.6 million sq km)
DIAMETER FROM POLE TO POLE: 7,900 miles (12,714 km)	**SURFACE AREA COVERED BY MOUNTAINS:** 12 million sq miles (30 million sq km)
EQUATORIAL CIRCUMFERENCE: 24,901 miles (40,075 km)	**SURFACE AREA COVERED BY DESERTS:** 7.5 million sq miles (19 million sq km)
MASS: 5988 million billion tons (tonnes)	**SURFACE AREA COVERED BY FORESTS:** 17 million sq miles (44 million sq km)
VOLUME OF OCEANS: 324 million cu miles (1.36 billion cu km)	**MAXIMUM HEIGHT OF LAND:** 29,029 ft (8,848 m) (Mt. Everest, Himalayas)
SURFACE AREA OF OCEANS, SEAS AND LAKES: 140 million sq miles (361 million sq km)	**MAXIMUM DEPTH OF OCEANS:** 35,827 ft (10,920 m) (Mariana Trench, Pacific Ocean)
SURFACE AREA OF LAND: 57.5 million sq miles (149 million sq km)	

THE WORLD'S LAND

Most of the world's land is concentrated in a hemisphere centered around Europe. This concentration was even greater before tectonic movement opened up the Atlantic, splitting the Americas from Europe and Africa, some 170 million years ago.

Scale 1:87,000,000
(projection: Azimuthal Equidistant)

19,686ft
13,124ft
9843ft
6562ft
3281ft
1640ft
820ft
328ft
Sea Level
-820ft
-6562ft
-13,124ft

The Structure of the Earth

Earth is an almost perfect sphere consisting of a partly liquid core overlain by a deep, semisolid layer, called the mantle, and two types of surface crust, known as continental and oceanic crust. Our planet has constantly evolved since it formed some 4.5 billion years ago. Its continents are neither fixed nor stable. Over the course of history, gradual movements of rocky material within Earth's mantle, resulting from massive internal flows of heat, have caused the great slabs of material that make up the planet's surface, known as tectonic plates, to shift around. The plates have moved, collided, joined together, and sometimes split apart. These processes continue to mold Earth's surface, causing earthquakes and volcanic eruptions, and creating oceans, mountain ranges, rift valleys, deep ocean trenches, and island chains.

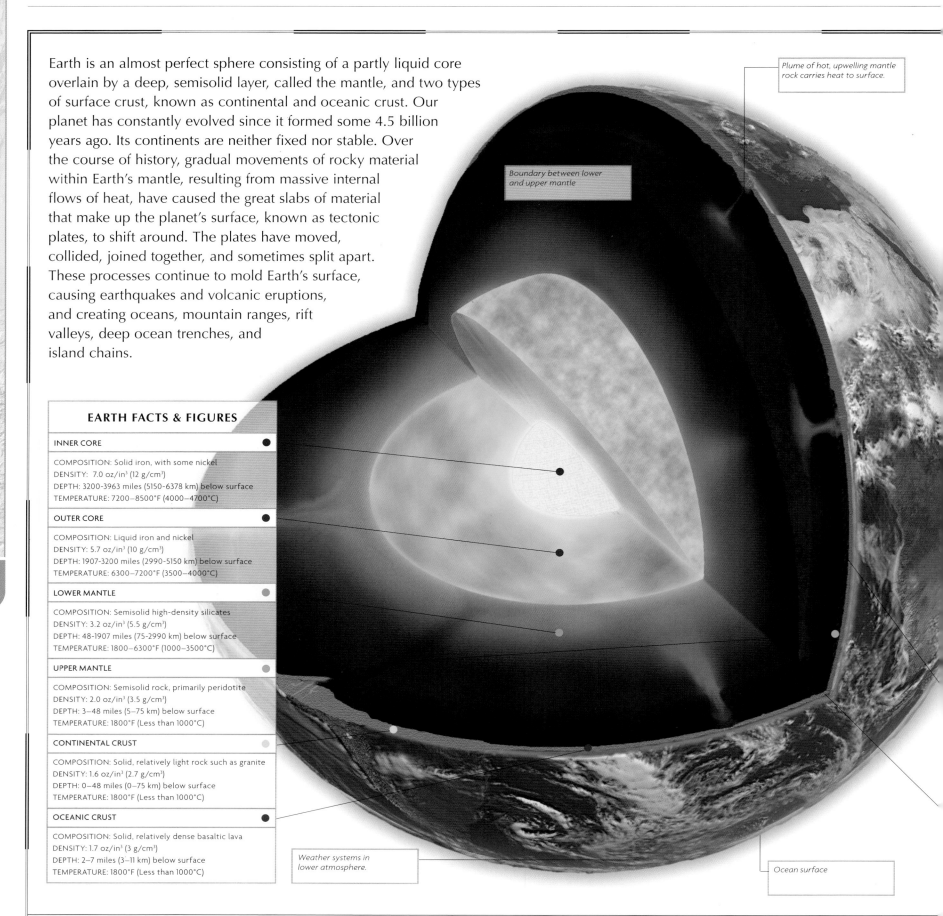

Plume of hot, upwelling mantle rock carries heat to surface.

Boundary between lower and upper mantle

Weather systems in lower atmosphere.

Ocean surface

EARTH FACTS & FIGURES

INNER CORE
COMPOSITION: Solid iron, with some nickel
DENSITY: 7.0 oz/in³ (12 g/cm³)
DEPTH: 3200-3963 miles (5150-6378 km) below surface
TEMPERATURE: 7200–8500°F (4000–4700°C)

OUTER CORE
COMPOSITION: Liquid iron and nickel
DENSITY: 5.7 oz/in³ (10 g/cm³)
DEPTH: 1907-3200 miles (2990-5150 km) below surface
TEMPERATURE: 6300–7200°F (3500–4000°C)

LOWER MANTLE
COMPOSITION: Semisolid high-density silicates
DENSITY: 3.2 oz/in³ (5.5 g/cm³)
DEPTH: 48-1907 miles (75-2990 km) below surface
TEMPERATURE: 1800–6300°F (1000–3500°C)

UPPER MANTLE
COMPOSITION: Semisolid rock, primarily peridotite
DENSITY: 2.0 oz/in³ (3.5 g/cm³)
DEPTH: 3–48 miles (5–75 km) below surface
TEMPERATURE: 1800°F (Less than 1000°C)

CONTINENTAL CRUST
COMPOSITION: Solid, relatively light rock such as granite
DENSITY: 1.6 oz/in³ (2.7 g/cm³)
DEPTH: 0–48 miles (0–75 km) below surface
TEMPERATURE: 1800°F (Less than 1000°C)

OCEANIC CRUST
COMPOSITION: Solid, relatively dense basaltic lava
DENSITY: 1.7 oz/in³ (3 g/cm³)
DEPTH: 2–7 miles (3–11 km) below surface
TEMPERATURE: 1800°F (Less than 1000°C)

FROM THE BIG BANG TO THE PRESENT DAY

The Big Bang | first galaxies form | Milky Way galaxy forms

13,700 million years ago (mya) | 12,000 mya | 11,000 mya | 10,000 mya

1000 mya | 2000 mya first multi-celled organisms | 3000 mya first landmasses

Phanerozoic Eon

543 mya | present day

Phanerozoic Eon (right) has been enlarged to show geological eras, periods and epochs

ERA		Paleozoic - age of ancient life					
PERIOD	Cambrian	Ordovician	Silurian	Devonian	Carboniferous		Permian
EPOCH					Mississippian	Pennsylvanian	
	543	490	443	418	354	323	290

Continental drift

Although Earth's tectonic plates move only a few inches (centimeters) each year, over hundreds of millions of years, its landmasses have moved many thousands of miles (kilometers), to create new continents, oceans, and mountain chains.

Cambrian 543–490 million years ago

LAURENTIA Greenland BALTICA Australia
North America Siberia Antarctica
Northern Europe India South America
Arabia
Africa GONDWANALAND

Devonian 418–354 million years ago

SIBERIA
Greenland
LAURENTIA/ BALTICA Northern Europe South Asia
North America Africa Kazakhstania
Arabia Australia
South America India
GONDWANALAND Antarctica

Carboniferous 354–290 million years ago

ANGARALAND Siberia
LAURENTIA Greenland Northwest China
North America Northern Europe Australia Antarctica
South America Arabia
Africa
GONDWANALAND

Dynamic Earth

Earth's surface is split up into several rigid, closely-fitting sections, called tectonic plates. Each of the plates contains some oceanic crust, and most also contain some continental crust. The plates constantly move relative to one another. Movements at different types of plate boundary produce various types of geological structure and activity.

Tectonic activity and geological regions

Plate boundaries
— Convergent
— Divergent
— Transform
- - - Uncertain

Tectonic activity
▲ volcanic zone
● earthquake zone
○ hot spot
≡ rift valley
Sedimentary cover
Mesozoic & Cenozoic volcanic rock
Cenozoic (65 mya – present)
Mesozoic (252 mya – 65 mya)
Paleozoic (543 mya – 252 mya)
pre-Cambrian Shields

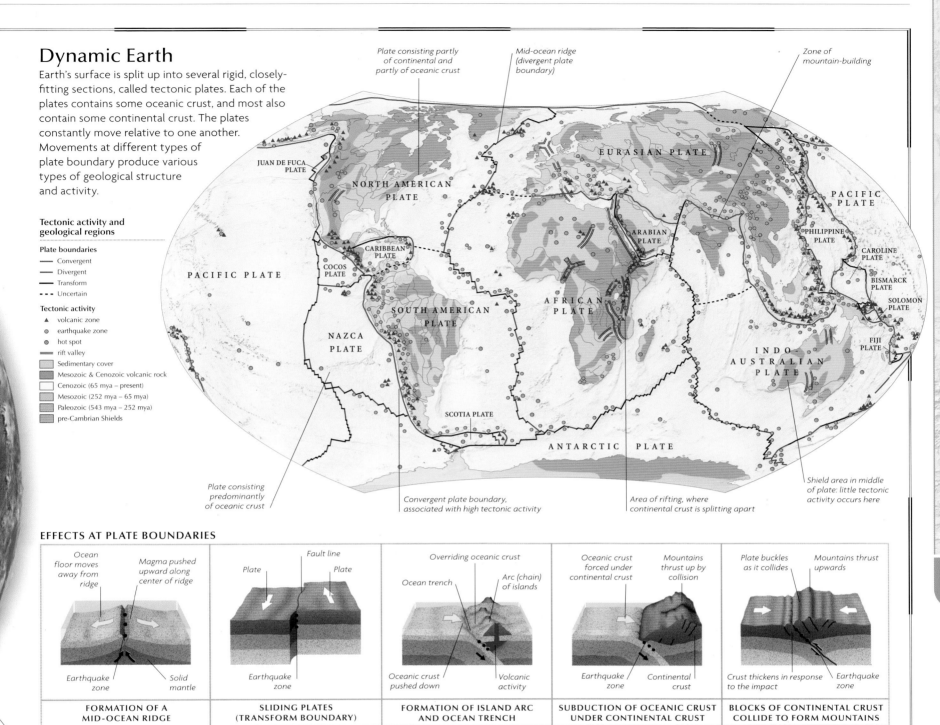

Plate consisting partly of continental and partly of oceanic crust

Mid-ocean ridge (divergent plate boundary)

Zone of mountain-building

EURASIAN PLATE

JUAN DE FUCA PLATE

NORTH AMERICAN PLATE

PACIFIC PLATE

ARABIAN PLATE

PHILIPPINE PLATE

CARIBBEAN PLATE

CAROLINE PLATE

PACIFIC PLATE

COCOS PLATE

BISMARCK PLATE

SOLOMON PLATE

SOUTH AMERICAN PLATE

AFRICAN PLATE

FIJI PLATE

NAZCA PLATE

INDO AUSTRALIAN PLATE

SCOTIA PLATE

ANTARCTIC PLATE

Plate consisting predominantly of oceanic crust

Convergent plate boundary, associated with high tectonic activity

Area of rifting, where continental crust is splitting apart

Shield area in middle of plate: little tectonic activity occurs here

EFFECTS AT PLATE BOUNDARIES

Ocean floor moves away from ridge

Magma pushed upward along center of ridge

Earthquake zone

Solid mantle

FORMATION OF A MID-OCEAN RIDGE

Plate

Fault line

Plate

Earthquake zone

SLIDING PLATES (TRANSFORM BOUNDARY)

Overriding oceanic crust

Ocean trench

Arc (chain) of islands

Oceanic crust pushed down

Volcanic activity

FORMATION OF ISLAND ARC AND OCEAN TRENCH

Oceanic crust forced under continental crust

Mountains thrust up by collision

Earthquake zone

Continental crust

SUBDUCTION OF OCEANIC CRUST UNDER CONTINENTAL CRUST

Plate buckles as it collides

Mountains thrust upwards

Crust thickens in response to the impact

Earthquake zone

BLOCKS OF CONTINENTAL CRUST COLLIDE TO FORM MOUNTAINS

Boundary between upper mantle and crust

Sea floor made of oceanic crust

CONVECTION CURRENTS

Deep within Earth's core, temperatures may exceed 8100°F (4500°C). The heat from the core warms rocks in the mantle, which become semimolten and rise upwards, displacing cooler rock below the solid oceanic and continental crust. This rock sinks and is warmed again by heat given off from the core. The process continues in a cyclical fashion, producing convection currents below the crust. These currents lead, in turn, to gradual movements of the tectonic plates over the planet's surface.

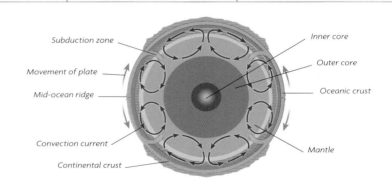

Subduction zone

Movement of plate

Mid-ocean ridge

Convection current

Continental crust

Inner core

Outer core

Oceanic crust

Mantle

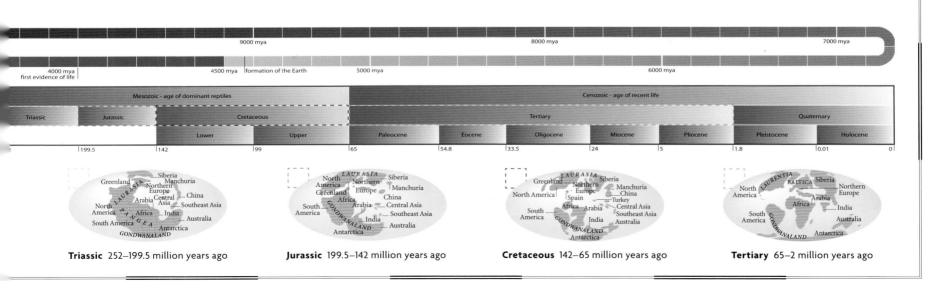

9000 mya

8000 mya

7000 mya

4000 mya first evidence of life

4500 mya formation of the Earth

5000 mya

6000 mya

Mesozoic - age of dominant reptiles

Cenozoic - age of recent life

Triassic

Jurassic

Cretaceous

Tertiary

Quaternary

Lower

Upper

Paleocene

Eocene

Oligocene

Miocene

Pliocene

Pleistocene

Holocene

199.5 142 99 65 54.8 33.5 24 5 1.8 0.01 0

Greenland Siberia Manchuria
LAURASIA
Northern Europe
North America Central Asia China
PANGEA Arabia Southeast Asia
Africa India Australia
South America Antarctica
GONDWANALAND

Triassic 252–199.5 million years ago

North America
LAURASIA
Greenland Northern Europe Siberia Manchuria
China
Central Asia
South America GONDWANALAND Arabia Southeast Asia
Africa India Australia
Antarctica

Jurassic 199.5–142 million years ago

Greenland
LAURASIA
Northern Europe Siberia Manchuria
North America China
Turkey
Central Asia
South America Arabia Southeast Asia
Africa India Australia
GONDWANALAND Antarctica

Cretaceous 142–65 million years ago

North America
LAURENTIA BALTICA Siberia
Northern Europe
South America Arabia India
Africa
GONDWANALAND

Tertiary 65–2 million years ago

Shaping the Landscape

The basic material of Earth's surface is solid rock: valleys, deserts, soil, and sand are all evidence of the powerful agents of weathering, erosion and deposition that constantly transform Earth's landscapes. Water, whether flowing in rivers or grinding the ground in the form of glaciers, has the most clearly visible impact on Earth's surface. Also, wind can transport fragments of rock over huge distances and strip away protective layers of vegetation, exposing rock surfaces to the impact of extreme heat and cold. Many of the land-shaping effects of ice and water can be seen in northern regions such as Alaska *(below)*, while the effects of heat and wind are clearly visible in the Sahara *(far right)*.

● FJORD
A valley carved by an ancient glacier and later flooded by the sea is called a fiord.

Ice and water

Some of the most obvious and striking features of Earth's surface are large flows and bodies of liquid water, such as rivers, lakes, and seas. In addition to these are landforms caused by the erosional or depositional power of flowing water, which include gullies, river valleys, and coastal features such as headlands and deltas. Ice also has had a major impact on Earth's appearance. Glaciers—rivers of ice formed by the compaction of snow—pick up and carry huge amounts of rocks and boulders as they pass over the landscape, eroding it as they do so. Glacially-sculpted landforms range from mountain *cirques* and U-shaped valleys to fiords and glacial lakes.

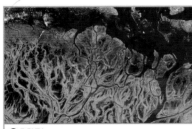

● DELTA
A delta, such as that of the Yukon River (above), is a roughly triangular or fan-shaped area of sediment deposited by a river at its mouth.

● PINGO
These blister-like mounds, seen in regions of Arctic tundra, are formed by the upward expansion of water as it freezes in the soil.

● TIDEWATER GLACIER
Glaciers of this type flow to the sea, where they calve (disgorge) icebergs. Like all glaciers, they erode huge amounts of rock from the landscape.

● LANDSLIDE
The freezing and later thawing of water, which occurs in a continuous cycle, can shatter and crumble rocks, eventually causing landslides.

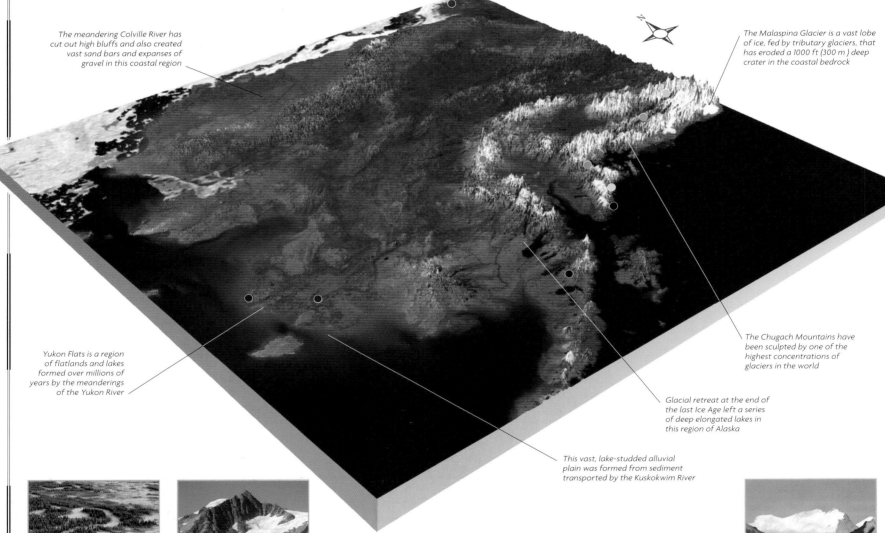

The meandering Colville River has cut out high bluffs and also created vast sand bars and expanses of gravel in this coastal region

The Malaspina Glacier is a vast lobe of ice, fed by tributary glaciers, that has eroded a 1000 ft (300 m) deep crater in the coastal bedrock

Yukon Flats is a region of flatlands and lakes formed over millions of years by the meanderings of the Yukon River

The Chugach Mountains have been sculpted by one of the highest concentrations of glaciers in the world

Glacial retreat at the end of the last Ice Age left a series of deep elongated lakes in this region of Alaska

This vast, lake-studded alluvial plain was formed from sediment transported by the Kuskokwim River

● MEANDERING RIVER
In their lower courses, some rivers carve out a series of looping bends called meanders.

● CIRQUE
A cirque is a hollow formed high on a mountain by glacial action. It may be ice-filled.

● POSTGLACIAL FEATURES
Glacially-polished cliffs like these are a tell-tale sign of ancient glacial action. Other signs include various forms of sculpted ridge and hummock.

● RIVER VALLEY
Over thousands of years, rivers erode uplands to form characteristic V-shaped valleys, with flat narrow floors and steeply-rising sides.

● GULLIES
Gullies are deep channels cut by rapidly flowing water, as here below Alaska's Mount Denali.

Heat and wind

Marked changes in temperature—rapid heating caused by fierce solar radiation during the day, followed by a sharp drop in temperature at night—cause rocks at the surface of hot deserts to continually expand and contract. This can eventually result in cracking and fissuring of the rocks, creating thermally-fractured desert landscapes. The world's deserts are also swept and scoured by strong winds. The finer particles of sand are shaped into surface ripples, dunes, or sand mountains, which can rise to a height of 650 ft (200 m). In other areas, the winds sweep away all the sand, leaving flat, gravelly areas called desert pavements.

DESERT LANDSCAPES

In desert areas, wind picks up loose sand and blasts it at the surface, creating a range of sculpted landforms from faceted rocks to large-scale features such as *yardangs*. Individually sculpted-rocks are called ventifacts. Where the sand abrasion is concentrated near the ground, it can turn these rocks into eccentrically-shaped "stone mushrooms." Other desert features are produced by thermal cracking and by winds continually redistributing the vast sand deposits.

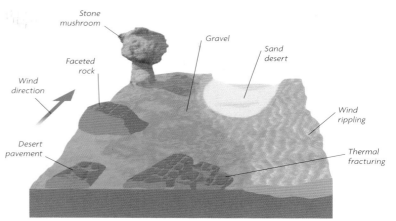

Stone mushroom

Faceted rock

Wind direction

Desert pavement

Gravel

Sand desert

Wind rippling

Thermal fracturing

FEATURES OF A DESERT SURFACE

● **DUST STORM**
A common phenomenon in some deserts, dust storms result from intense heating of the ground creating strong convection currents.

● **LOESS DEPOSIT**
A deposit of silt that has been transported over long distances by wind, then compacted. Loess is found in a few marginal areas of the Sahara.

● **YARDANG**
A yardang is a ridge of rock produced by wind erosion, usually in a desert. Large yardangs can be many miles long.

● **DESERT PAVEMENT**
Dark, gravelly surfaces like this result from wind removing all the sand from an area of desert.

Part of the Grand Erg Oriental, this region is a vast wind-sculpted sea of sand, much affected by sand storms

This area of complex dune morphology has resulted from two different types of dunes overlapping and coalescing

Wind erosion of the sandstone rocks in this area (the Tassili n'Ajjer) has created nearly 300 natural rock arches

The Tefedest is an impressive, sun-baked, wind-eroded, granite massif located in southern Algeria

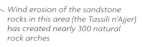

This highland region, called the Ahaggar Mountains, has largely been blasted free of sand and is heavily eroded throughout

● **TRANSVERSE DUNES**
This series of parallel sand ridges lies at right angles to the prevailing wind direction.

● **VENTIFACT**
A ventifact is a rock that has been heavily sculpted and abraded by wind-driven sand.

● **CRACKED DESERT**
Intensely heated and dried-out desert areas often developed geometrically-patterned surface cracking.

● **WADI**
Wadis are dried out stream beds, found in some desert regions, that carry water only during occasional periods of heavy rain.

● **BARCHAN DUNE**
This arc-shaped type of dune migrates across the desert surface, blown by the wind.

The World's Oceans

Two-thirds of Earth's surface is covered by the five oceans: the Pacific, Atlantic, Indian, Southern (or Antarctic), and Arctic. The basins that form these oceans, and the ocean floor landscape, have formed over the past 200 million years through volcanic activity and gradual movements of the Earth's crust. Surrounding the continents are shallow flat regions called continental shelves. These shelves extend to the continental slope, which drops steeply to the ocean floor. There, vast submarine plateaus, known as abyssal plains, are interrupted by massive ridges, chains of seamounts, and deep ocean trenches.

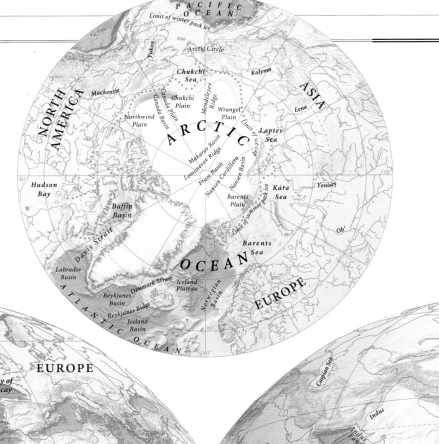

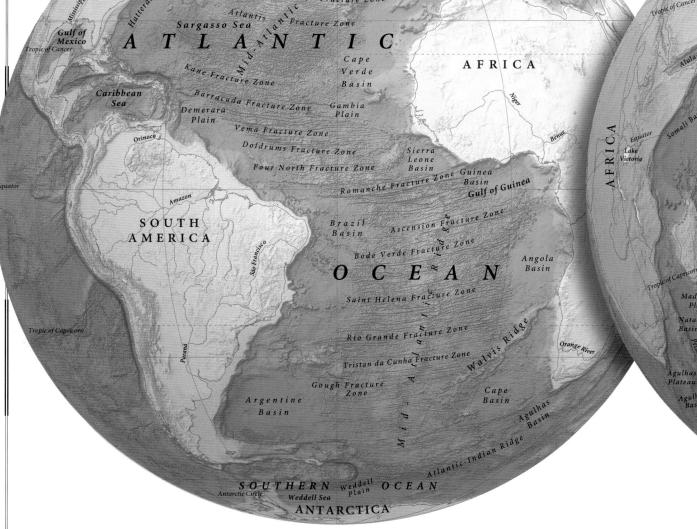

Ocean currents

Surface currents are driven by winds and by the Earth's rotation. Together these cause large circular flows of water over the surface of the oceans, called gyres. Deep sea currents are driven by changes in the salinity or temperature of surface water. These changes cause the water to become denser and sink, forcing horizontal movements of deeper water.

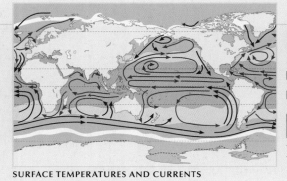

Surface temperature and currents

- - - - - ice-shelf (below 32°F / 0°C)
sea-ice* (average) below 28°F / -2°C
sea-water 28–32°F / -2 to 0°C * sea-water freezes at 28.4°F / -1.9°C
32–50°F / 0–10°C
50–68°F / 10–20°C
68–86°F / 20–30°C
→ warm current
→ cold current

SURFACE TEMPERATURES AND CURRENTS

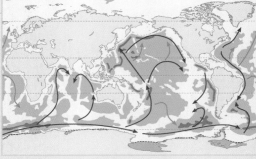

DEEP SEA TEMPERATURES AND CURRENTS

The ocean floor

The ages of seafloor rocks increase in parallel bands outward from central ocean ridges. At these ridges, new oceanic crust is continuously created from lava that erupts from below the seafloor and then cools to form solid rock. As this new crust forms, it gradually pushes older crust away from the ridge.

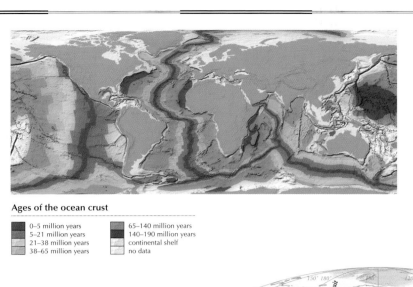

Ages of the ocean crust

- 0–5 million years
- 5–21 million years
- 21–38 million years
- 38–65 million years
- 65–140 million years
- 140–190 million years
- continental shelf
- no data

Tides

Tides are caused by gravitational interactions between the Earth, Moon, and Sun. The strongest tides occur when the three bodies are aligned and the weakest when the Sun and Moon align at right angles

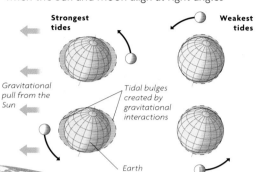

Strongest tides

Weakest tides

Gravitational pull from the Sun

Tidal bulges created by gravitational interactions

Earth

Moon

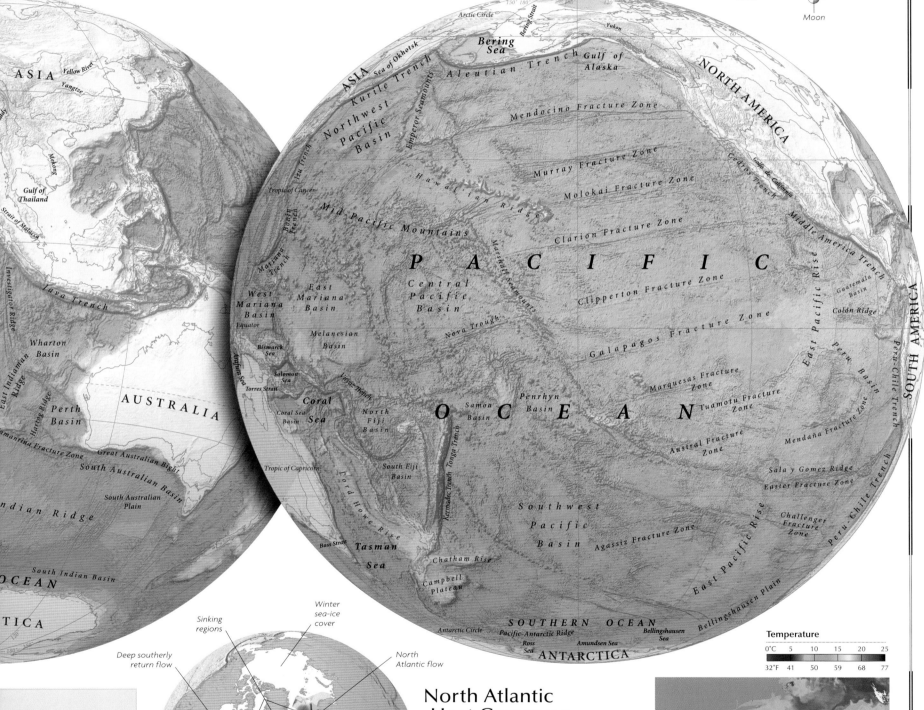

Arctic Circle
Bering Strait
Yukon

Bering Sea

NORTH AMERICA

ASIA

Yellow River
Yangtze

Weddy

Mekong

Gulf of Thailand

Strait of Malacca

ASIA
Sea of Okhotsk
Kurile Trench
Aleutian Trench
Gulf of Alaska

Northwest Pacific Basin

Emperor seamounts

Mendocino Fracture Zone

Izu Trench

Bonin Trench

Murray Fracture Zone

Hawaiian Ridge

Tropic of Cancer

Molokai Fracture Zone

Golfo de California

Gorda Trench

MIDDLE AMERICA TRENCH

Mid-Pacific Mountains

Clarion Fracture Zone

East Pacific Rise

Guatemala Basin

P A C I F I C

Mariana Trench

West Mariana Basin

East Mariana Basin

Central Pacific Basin

Equator

Clipperton Fracture Zone

Colón Ridge

Investigator Ridge

Java Trench

Melanesian Basin

Marshall seamounts

Galapagos Fracture Zone

Peru Basin

Peru–Chile Trench

SOUTH AMERICA

Wharton Basin

Nova Trough

Marquesas Fracture Zone

Tuamotu Fracture Zone

Mendaña Fracture Zone

East Indiaman Ridge

Bismarck Sea

Solomon Sea

Samoa Basin

Penrhyn Basin

O C E A N

Austral Fracture Zone

Sala y Gomez Ridge

Perth Basin

Arafura Sea

Coral Sea Basin

North Fiji Basin

Coral Sea

Easter Fracture Zone

Tamanrfha Fracture Zone

Hjertz Ridge

AUSTRALIA

Great Australian Bight

Torres Strait

Vityaz trench

Challenger Fracture Zone

Peru–Chile Trench

South Australian Basin

South Fiji Basin

Agassiz Fracture Zone

Southwest Pacific Basin

East Pacific Rise

n d i a n R i d g e

South Australian Plain

Lord Howe Rise

Kermadec Trench

Tonga Trench

South Indian Basin

OCEAN

Bass Strait

Tasman Sea

Chatham Rise

Bellingshausen Plain

TICA

Campbell Plateau

SOUTHERN OCEAN

Antarctic Circle
Pacific–Antarctic Ridge
Amundsen Sea
Bellingshausen Sea

Ross Sea

ANTARCTICA

Temperature

0°C	5	10	15	20	25
32°F	41	50	59	68	77

Winter sea-ice cover

Sinking regions

Deep southerly return flow

North Atlantic flow

Subtropical recirculation

Gulf Stream

Deep sea temperature and currents

- ice-shelf (below 32°F / 0°C)
- sea-water 28–32°F / -2 to 0°C (below 16,400 ft / 5000 m)
- sea-water 32–41°F / 0–5°C (below 13,120 ft / 4000 m)
- → primary currents
- → secondary currents

North Atlantic Heat Conveyor

The North Atlantic Heat Conveyor is a system of heat flows in the Atlantic that keeps western Europe relatively warm. Surface currents, notably the Gulf Stream and its extension, the North Atlantic Drift, carry warm water from the tropical Atlantic into the northeastern Atlantic. There, the heat they supply is released, warming Europe, while the water itself cools and sinks. This cold water then returns at depth towards the equator.

A key part of the North Atlantic Heat Conveyor is the warm Gulf Stream, visible as the dark red ribbon in this Atlantic sea-surface temperature map.

Global Climate

The climates of different regions on Earth are the typical long-term patterns of temperature and humidity in those regions. By contrast, weather consists of short-term variations in factors such as wind, rainfall, and sunshine. Climates are determined primarily by the Sun's variable heating of different parts of Earth's atmosphere and oceans, and by Earth's rotation. These factors drive the ocean currents and prevailing winds, which in turn redistribute heat energy and moisture between the equator and poles, and between sea and land. Most scientists think that major changes are currently occurring in global climate due to the effects of rising carbon dioxide levels in the atmosphere.

Global air circulation

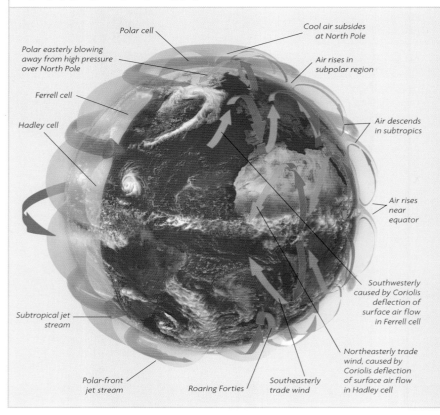

Polar cell

Polar easterly blowing away from high pressure over North Pole

Ferrell cell

Hadley cell

Cool air subsides at North Pole

Air rises in subpolar region

Air descends in subtropics

Air rises near equator

Southwesterly caused by Coriolis deflection of surface air flow in Ferrell cell

Northeasterly trade wind, caused by Coriolis deflection of surface air flow in Hadley cell

Subtropical jet stream

Polar-front jet stream

Roaring Forties

Southeasterly trade wind

The atmosphere

Earth's atmosphere is a giant ocean of air that surrounds the planet. It extends to a height of about 625 miles (1000 km) but has no distinct upper boundary. The Sun's rays pass through the atmosphere and warm Earth's surface, causing the air to move and water to evaporate from the oceans.

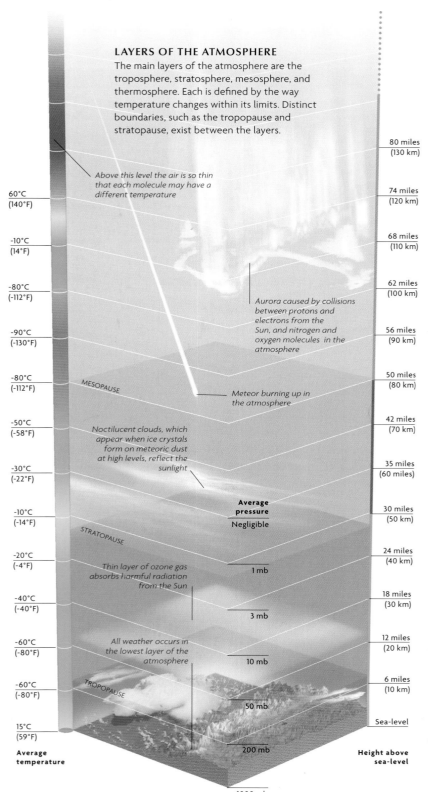

LAYERS OF THE ATMOSPHERE
The main layers of the atmosphere are the troposphere, stratosphere, mesosphere, and thermosphere. Each is defined by the way temperature changes within its limits. Distinct boundaries, such as the tropopause and stratopause, exist between the layers.

Above this level the air is so thin that each molecule may have a different temperature

Aurora caused by collisions between protons and electrons from the Sun, and nitrogen and oxygen molecules in the atmosphere

MESOPAUSE

Meteor burning up in the atmosphere

Noctilucent clouds, which appear when ice crystals form on meteoric dust at high levels, reflect the sunlight

STRATOPAUSE

Thin layer of ozone gas absorbs harmful radiation from the Sun

All weather occurs in the lowest layer of the atmosphere

TROPOPAUSE

Average temperature		Height above sea-level
60°C (140°F)		80 miles (130 km)
-10°C (14°F)		74 miles (120 km)
-80°C (-112°F)		68 miles (110 km)
-90°C (-130°F)		62 miles (100 km)
-80°C (-112°F)		56 miles (90 km)
-50°C (-58°F)		50 miles (80 km)
-30°C (-22°F)		42 miles (70 km)
-10°C (-14°F)	Average pressure Negligible	35 miles (60 miles)
-20°C (-4°F)	1 mb	30 miles (50 km)
-40°C (-40°F)	3 mb	24 miles (40 km)
-60°C (-80°F)	10 mb	18 miles (30 km)
-60°C (-80°F)	50 mb	12 miles (20 km)
15°C (59°F)	200 mb	6 miles (10 km)
	1000 mb	Sea-level

Winds, currents, and climate

Earth has 12 climatic zones, ranging from ice-cap and tundra to temperate, arid (desert), and tropical zones. Each of these zones features a particular combination of temperature and humidity. The effects of prevailing winds, ocean currents of both the warm and cold variety, as well as latitude and altitude, all have an important influence on a region's climate. For example, the climate of western Europe is influenced by the effects of the warm North Atlantic Drift current.

● **THERMOSPHERE**
This layer extends from a height of 50 miles (80 km) upward. Its temperature increases rapidly above a height of 60 miles (90 km), due to absorption of highly energetic solar radiation.

● **MESOSPHERE**
The temperature of the lower part of this layer stays constant with height; but above 35 miles (55 km), it drops, reaching -112°F (80°C) at the mesopause.

● **STRATOSPHERE**
The temperature of the stratosphere is a fairly constant -76° F (-60°C) up to an altitude of about 12 miles (20 km), then increases, due to absorption of ultraviolet radiation.

● **TROPOSPHERE**
This layer extends from Earth's surface to a height of about 10 miles (16 km) at the equator and 5 miles (8 km) at the poles. Air temperature in this layer decreases with height.

Arctic Circle January

Chinook January

July

Alaska Current

WESTERLIES

North Pacific Current

North Atlantic Current

California Current

Decem

Norther January

Tornadoes May–Ju

Tropic of Cancer

NORTH

EAST

TRADES

Northern Equatorial Current

January

Equatorial Counter Current

July

Doldrums · El Niño

Equator

South Equatorial Current

SOUTH

EAST

TRADES

Tropic of Capricorn

WESTERLIES

West Wind Dri

Antarctic Circle

Air moves within giant atmospheric cells called
Hadley, Ferrell, and polar cells. These cells are
caused by air being warmed and rising in some
latitudes, such as near the equator, and sinking in
other latitudes. This north-south circulation
combined with the Coriolis effect *(below)*
produces the prevailing surface winds.

THE CORIOLIS EFFECT

Air moving over Earth's surface is deflected in a
clockwise direction in the northern hemisphere and
counterclockwise in the south. Known as the Coriolis
effect, and caused by Earth's spin,
these deflections to the air
movements produce
winds such as the
trade winds and
westerlies.

Direction of Earth's spin

Deflected clockwise

Deflected counterclockwise

Initial direction

Temperature and precipitation

The world divides by latitude into three major
temperature zones: the warm tropics, the cold
polar regions; and an intermediate temperate
zone. In addition, temperature is strongly
influenced by height above sea level.
Precipitation patterns are related to factors
such as solar heating, atmospheric pressure,
winds, and topography. Most equatorial
areas have high rainfall, caused by moist air
being warmed and rising, then cooling to form
rain clouds. In areas of the subtropics and
near the poles, sinking air causes high pressure
and low precipitation. In temperate regions
rainfall is quite variable.

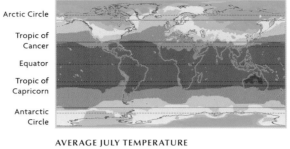

AVERAGE JANUARY TEMPERATURE

Arctic Circle
Tropic of Cancer
Equator
Tropic of Capricorn
Antarctic Circle

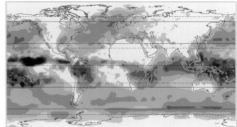

AVERAGE JANUARY RAINFALL

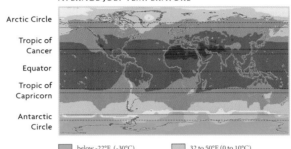

AVERAGE JULY TEMPERATURE

Arctic Circle
Tropic of Cancer
Equator
Tropic of Capricorn
Antarctic Circle

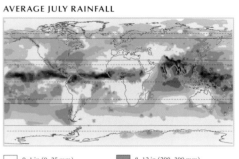

AVERAGE JULY RAINFALL

 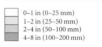 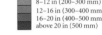

below -22°F (-30°C)	32 to 50°F (0 to 10°C)
-22 to -4°F (-30 to -20°C)	50 to 68°F (10 to 20°C)
-4 to 14°F (-20 to -10°C)	68 to 86°F (20 to 30°C)
14 to 32°F (-10 to 0°C)	above 86°F (30°C)

0–1 in (0–25 mm)	8–12 in (200–300 mm)
1–2 in (25–50 mm)	12–16 in (300–400 mm)
2–4 in (50–100 mm)	16–20 in (400–500 mm)
4–8 in (100–200 mm)	above 20 in (500 mm)

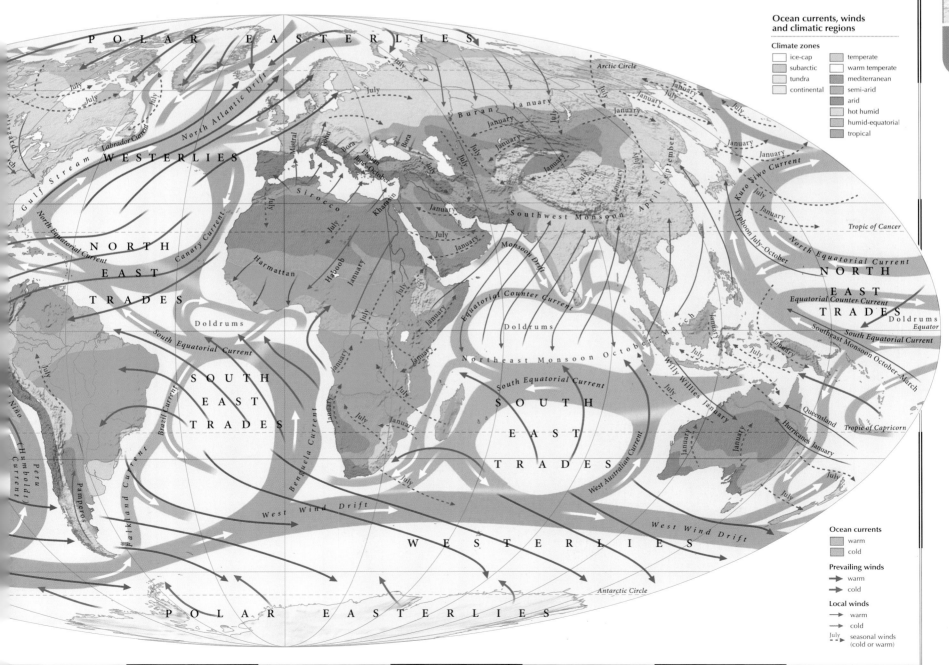

Ocean currents, winds
and climatic regions

Climate zones

ice-cap	temperate
subarctic	warm temperate
tundra	mediterranean
continental	semi-arid
	arid
	hot humid
	humid-equatorial
	tropical

Ocean currents
warm
cold

Prevailing winds
→ warm
→ cold

Local winds
→ warm
→ cold
July seasonal winds (cold or warm)

Life on Earth

A unique combination of an oxygen-rich atmosphere and plentiful surface water is the key to life on Earth, where few areas have not been colonized by animals, plants, or smaller life-forms. An important determinant of the quantity of life in a region is its level of primary production—the amount of energy-rich substances made by organisms living there, mainly through the process of photosynthesis. On land, plants are the main organisms responsible for primary production; in water, algae fulfil this role. These primary producers supply food for animals. Primary production is affected by climatic, seasonal, and other local factors. On land, cold and aridity restrict the quantity of life in a region, whereas warmth and regular rainfall allow a greater diversity of species. In the oceans, production is mainly affected by sunlight levels, which reduce rapidly with depth, and by nutrient availability.

POLAR REGIONS
Ice restricts life in these regions to just a few species, such as polar bears in the Arctic.

Biogeographical regions

Earth's biogeographical regions, or biomes, are communities where certain species of plants and animals coexist within the constraints of particular climatic conditions. They range from tundra to various types of grassland, forest, desert, and marine biomes such as coral reefs. Factors like soil richness, altitude, and human activities such as deforestation can affect the local distribution of living species in each biome.

TEMPERATE GRASSLAND
Also known as steppe or prairie, grassland of this type occurs mainly in the northern hemisphere and in South America (the Pampas).

NEEDLELEAF FOREST
These vast forests of coniferous trees cover huge areas of Canada, Siberia, and Scandinavia.

TROPICAL GRASSLAND
This type of grassland is widespread in Africa and South America, supporting large numbers of grazing animals and their predators.

World biomes

- ice
- tundra
- temperate coniferous forest
- temperate broadleaf mixed forest
- temperate grassland
- mediterranean
- desert and shrubland
- boreal forest/taiga

Animal diversity

The number of animal species, and the range of genetic diversity within the populations of those species, determines the level of animal diversity within each country or other region of the world. The animals that are endemic to a region—that is, those found nowhere else on the planet—are also important in determining its level of animal diversity.

Number of animal species per country

- more than 2,000
- 1000–1999
- 700–999
- 400–699
- 200–399
- 100–199
- 0–99
- data not available

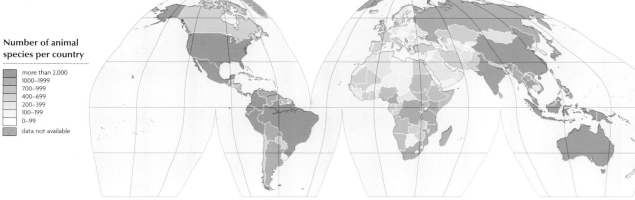

TUNDRA
With little soil and large areas of frozen ground, the tundra is largely treeless, though briefly clothed by small flowering plants in summer.

TEMPERATE RAIN FOREST
Occurring in mid-latitudes in areas of high rainfall, these forests may be predominantly coniferous or mixed with deciduous species.

CORAL REEFS
Occurring in clear tropical waters, coral reefs support an extraordinary diversity of species, especially fish and many types of invertebrate.

MOUNTAINS
In high mountain areas only a few hardy species of plant will grow above the tree-line.

TROPICAL RAINFOREST
Characterized by year-round warmth and high rainfall, tropical rainforests contain the highest diversity of plant and animal species on Earth.

HOT DESERT
Only a few highly adapted species can survive in hot deserts, which occur mainly in the tropics.

OPEN OCEAN
Earth's largest biome, the oceans are home to a vast diversity of fish, mammals, invertebrates, and algae.

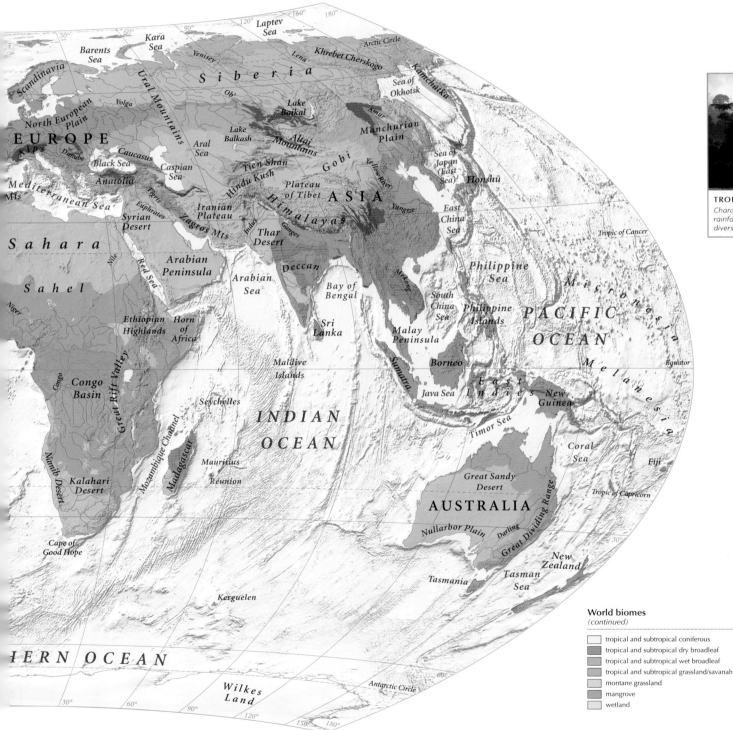

World biomes
(continued)

- ☐ tropical and subtropical coniferous
- ☐ tropical and subtropical dry broadleaf
- ☐ tropical and subtropical wet broadleaf
- ☐ tropical and subtropical grassland/savanah
- ☐ montane grassland
- ☐ mangrove
- ☐ wetland

Number of plant species per country

- ☐ more than 50,000
- ☐ 7000–49,999
- ☐ 3000–6999
- ☐ 2000–2999
- ☐ 1000–1999
- ☐ 600–999
- ☐ 0–599
- ☐ data not available

Plant diversity

Environmental conditions, particularly climate, soil type, and the extent of competition with other living organisms, influence the development of plants into distinctive forms and thus also the extent of plant diversity. Human settlement and intervention has considerably reduced the diversity of plant species in many areas.

Man and the Environment

The impact of human activity on the environment has widened from being a matter of local concern (typically over the build-up of urban waste, industrial pollution, and smog) to affect whole ecosystems and, in recent decades, the global climate. Problems crossing national boundaries first became a major issue over acid rain, toxic waste dumping at sea, and chemical spillages polluting major rivers. Current concerns center on loss of biodiversity and vital habitat including wetlands and coral reefs, the felling and clearance of great tropical and temperate forests, overexploitation of scarce resources, the uncontrolled growth of cities and, above all, climate change.

OZONE HOLE
Man-made chlorofluorocarbons (CFCs), used in refrigeration and aerosols, damaged the ozone layer in the stratosphere which helps filter out the sun's harmful ultraviolet rays. When a seasonal ozone hole first appeared in 1985 over Antarctica, a shocked world agreed to phase out CFC use.

1980   1985

CO₂ emissions in 2008
(million tons)

- over 4000
- 1000–4000
- 500–1000
- 100–500
- 50–100
- 10–50
- 2–10
- 0–2
- no data

Kyoto Protocol

- △ countries that have reached targets
- ▽ countries that have not reached targets
- ⊗ countries without targets

Only the US has not ratified the Kyoto Protocol

Climate change

Global warming is happening much faster than Earth's normal long-term cycles of climate change. The consequences include unpredictable extreme weather and potential disruption of ocean currents. Melting ice-caps and glaciers, and warmer oceans, will raise average sea levels and threaten coastlines and cities. Food crops like wheat are highly vulnerable to changes in temperature and rainfall. Such changes can also have a dramatic affect on wildlife habitats.

Since 1800 the amount of CO₂ in the atmosphere has risen sharply. Urgent worldwide action to control emissions is vital to stabilize the level by the mid 21st century.

THE GREENHOUSE EFFECT
Some solar energy, reflected from the Earth's surface as infra red radiation, is reflected back as heat by "greenhouse gases" (mainly carbon dioxide and methane) in the atmosphere. Nearly all scientists now agree that an upsurge in emissions caused by humans burning fossil fuel has contributed to making the resultant warming effect a major problem.

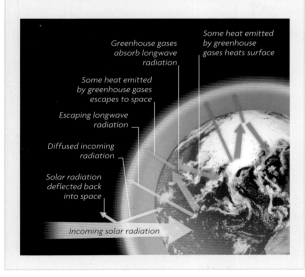

FOOD AND LAND USE
The world has about five billion hectares of agriculturally useful land, well under one hectare per person. The majority of this is pasture for grazing. Crops are grown on about 30 percent (and nearly a fifth of cropland is artificially irrigated). Mechanized farming encouraged vast single crop "monocultures," dependent on fertilizers and pesticides. North America's endless prairies of wheat and corn, huge soybean plantations, and southern cotton fields are mirrored in Ukraine (wheat), Brazil and Argentina (soya) and Uzbekistan (cotton). Elsewhere, scarce farmland can be squeezed by the housing needs of growing urban populations. Current interest in crop-derived "biofuels" means further pressure to grow food more productively on less land.

Intensive farming. Satellite photography picks up the greenhouses that now cover almost all the land in this Spanish coastal area southwest of Almeria.

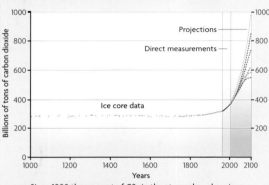

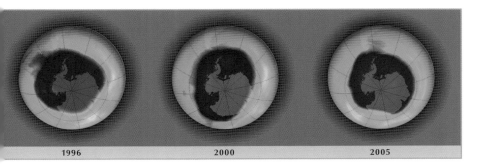

1996   2000   2005

DEFORESTATION

At current rates of destruction, all tropical forests, and most old-growth temperate forest, will be gone by 2090. The Amazon rain forest is a valuable genetic resource, containing innumerable unique plants and animals, as well as acting as a crucial natural "sink" for absorbing climate-damaging carbon dioxide. Stemming the loss of these precious assets to logging and farming is one of the major environmental challenges of modern times.

Over 25,000 sq miles (60,000 sq km) of virgin rain forest are cleared annually by logging and agricultural activities, destroying an irreplaceable natural resource.

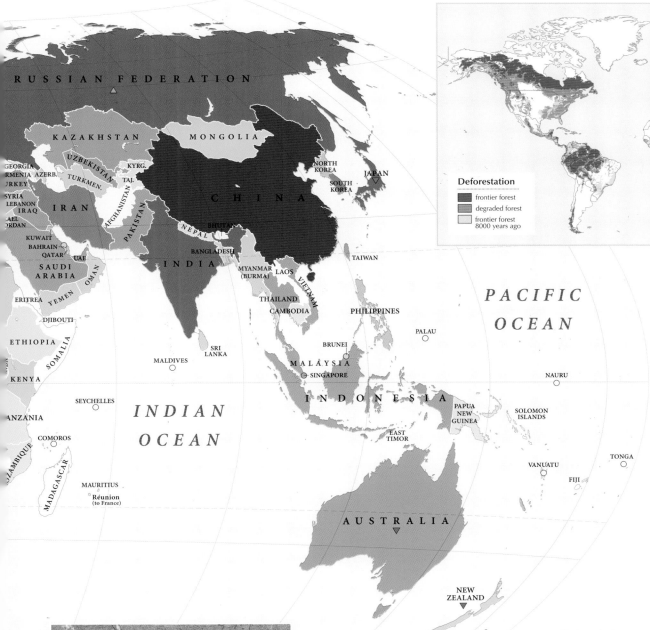

Deforestation
- frontier forest
- degraded forest
- frontier forest 8000 years ago

GLACIATION

The world's glaciers and ice sheets have been in retreat for decades, forming less new ice at high altitudes than they lose by melting lower down. The loss of ice from Greenland doubled between 1996 and 2005, with alarming implications for rising sea levels. Other dramatic evidence of global warming includes the rapid thinning of ice in the Himalayas, and the highly symbolic loss of the snowcap on Africa's Mount Kilimanjaro.

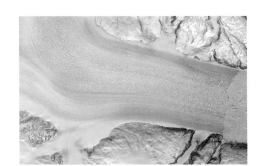

Helheim Glacier 2001
The Helheim glacier (above) almost completely fills this image, with the leading edge visible on the righthand side, and was in a relatively stable condition.

Helheim Glacier 2005
By 2005 (right) it had retreated by 2.5 miles (4 km).

Delhi 1971
In 1971 Delhi (above) occupied an area of about 190 sq miles (500 sq km).

Delhi 1999
By 1999 (right) it had sprawled to cover 500 sq miles (1300 sq km). It vies with Mumbai in the southwest to be the sub-continent's most populous city, fast approaching 20 million people.

CITY GROWTH

The world in 2006 had five cities with populations over 20 million—Tokyo, Mexico City, Seoul, New York City, and São Paulo. The number of cities with populations between 10 and 20 million has reached 20 and continues to rise. The search for work, and the hope of escape from rural poverty, drives migration from rural to urban areas across the developing world. Urban dwellers now amount to more than half the world's population, and consume more resources than their rural counterparts.

Population and Settlement

Earth's human population is projected to rise from its current level of 6.9 billion to between 7.6 and 11 billion by the year 2050. The distribution of this population is very uneven and is dictated by climate, terrain, and by natural and economic resources. Most people live in coastal zones and along the valleys of great rivers such as the Ganges, Indus, Nile, and Yangtze. Deserts cover over 20 percent of Earth's surface but support less than 5 percent of its human population. Over half the world's population live in cities—most of them in Asia, Europe, and North America—as a result of mass migrations that have occurred from rural areas as people search for jobs. Many of these people live in so-called "megacities"—sprawling urban areas that have populations higher than 10 million.

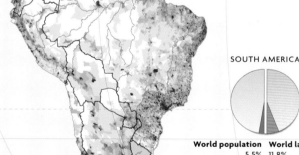

Population density by country (population per sq mile)

over 2600	260-389	65–129
775-2599	195–259	26–64
390-774	130–194	0–25

Population density

A few regions, including Europe, India, and much of eastern Asia, have extremely high population densities. Within these areas, a few spots, such as Monaco and Hong Kong, have densities of over 12,900 per sq mile (5000 people per sq km). Other regions (mostly desert, mountain, ice cap, tundra, or thickly forested areas) have densities close to zero —examples include large areas of Australia, western China, Siberia, North Africa, Canada, Greenland, and much of the Amazon rain forest region.

NORTH AMERICA

World population   World land area
9%   17.0%

EUROPE

World population   World land area
14%   7.1%

Million-person cities

In the year 1900 there were fewer than 20 cities in the world with a population that exceeded one million. By 1950 there were 75 such cities, and by the year 2000 there were more than 300 such cities, 40 of them in China alone, with another 30 in India, 14 in Brazil, and 10 in Japan.

Million-cities in 1900

• Cities over 1 million in population

Million-cities in 1950

Million-cities in 2006

Population density
(persons per sq mile)

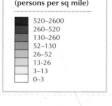

	520–2600
	260–520
	130–260
	52–130
	26–52
	13-26
	3–13
	0–3

SOUTH AMERICA

World population   World land area
5.5%   11.8%

ANTARCTICA

World population   World land area
0.0%   8.9%

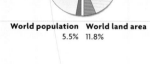

Tokyo urban sprawl

—— City boundary, 1860   —— City boundary, 1964

GREATER TOKYO
The Greater Tokyo Area is the most populous urban area in the world, with an estimated head count in 2011 of 35.6 million. It includes Tokyo City, which has a population of about 12 million, and adjoining cities such as Yokohama. This satellite photograph shows the Greater Tokyo Area today, and also the boundaries of Tokyo City in 1860 (red) and 1964 (yellow).

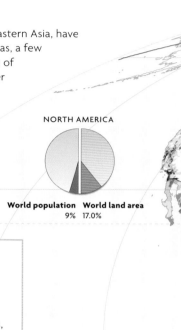

Migration

Every year about 200 million people – 3 percent of the global population – change their country of residence. Emigration rates are generally highest in countries affected by wars or that have suffered economic woes, natural disasters, or where groups of people have been oppressed or persecuted. Immigration rates are generally highest in stable, developed countries, such as the USA, Spain and Canada, which usually have low birth rates and need immigrants to provide economic support to their ageing populations.

NET MIGRATION

The map at right shows the net migration rate for each country. A positive value means more people are entering the country than leaving it (net immigration) and a negative value the reverse (net emigration).

Net migration
average annual migration (thousands)

- over 300
- 200 to 300
- 100 to 200
- 0 to 100
- -100 to 0
- -200 to -100
- -300 to -200
- -400 to -300
- data unavailable

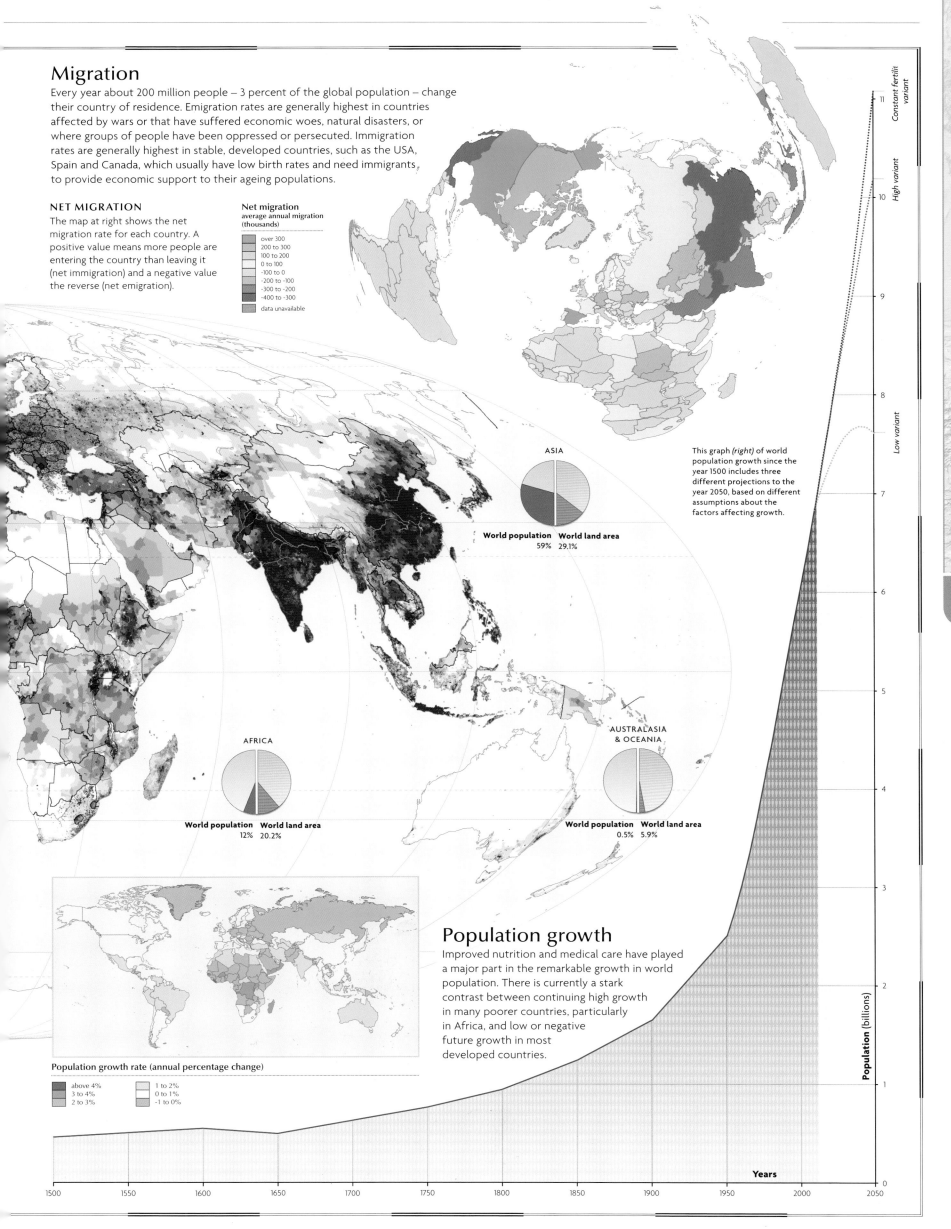

ASIA

World population 59% **World land area** 29.1%

AFRICA

World population 12% **World land area** 20.2%

AUSTRALASIA & OCEANIA

World population 0.5% **World land area** 5.9%

This graph *(right)* of world population growth since the year 1500 includes three different projections to the year 2050, based on different assumptions about the factors affecting growth.

Population growth

Improved nutrition and medical care have played a major part in the remarkable growth in world population. There is currently a stark contrast between continuing high growth in many poorer countries, particularly in Africa, and low or negative future growth in most developed countries.

Population growth rate (annual percentage change)

- above 4%
- 3 to 4%
- 2 to 3%
- 1 to 2%
- 0 to 1%
- -1 to 0%

Constant fertility variant

High variant

Low variant

Population (billions)

Years

1500 1550 1600 1650 1700 1750 1800 1850 1900 1950 2000 2050

Language

Over 6800 different languages exist throughout the world, each one with its own unique evolutionary history and cultural connotations. Most of these languages are spoken only by small groups of people in remote regions. Sadly these minority tongues are dying out—it is estimated that about a third will have disappeared by the year 2100. The relatively small number of widely-spoken languages have gained their current predominance and pattern of distribution through a variety of historical factors. Among these have been the economic, military, or technological success of certain peoples and cultures, differing population growth rates, and the effects of migrations and colonization.

The European Union (EU) embraces the diversity of its 27 countries and 23 official languages by providing a translation and interpretation service for the majority of its meetings and documentation. This costs around US$ 650 million per year, which equates to 1 percent of the EU budget.

Main international languages

- Chinese
- Spanish
- Arabic
- Hindi
- English
- French
- Russian
- Portuguese
- English/Spanish
- Spanish/other
- Arabic/French
- French/other
- English/other
- Arabic/other
- Hindi/English/other
- Chinese/other
- Russian/other
- English/French
- Portuguese/other
- other language

Bantu language group
Mari other language

- uninhabited land

The colonial powers

Colonialism between the 15th and 20th centuries had a major influence in establishing the world prevalence of various, mainly European, languages. Britain, for example, was the colonial power in Canada, the USA (until 1776), the Indian subcontinent, Australia, and parts of Africa and the Caribbean. Hence, English is still the main (or a major) language in these areas. The same applies to France and the French language in parts of Africa and southeast Asia, and to Spain and the Spanish language in much of Latin America. For similar reasons, Portuguese is the main language in Brazil and parts of Africa, and there are many Dutch speakers in Indonesia.

This dual language sign, written in both in Hindi and English, stands outside Shimla railway station in northern India. The sign reflects India's past—the British used Shimla as their summer capital during the colonial period.

TOP TEN LANGUAGES

About 45 percent of people speak one of just ten languages as their native tongue. Mandarin Chinese is spoken by far the largest number—a situation likely to persist, as minority language speakers in China are encouraged to switch to Mandarin. English usage is also increasing, as it is the most favored language on the internet and in business circles. Wherever English is not the mother tongue, it is often the second language.

THE TEN MOST SPOKEN LANGUAGES
(number of native speakers)

- Mandarin Chinese (1.1 billion)
- English (330 million)
- Spanish (300 million)
- Hindi/Urdu (250 million)
- Arabic (200 million)
- Bengali (185 million)
- Portuguese (160 million)
- Russian (160 million)
- Japanese (125 million)
- German (100 million)

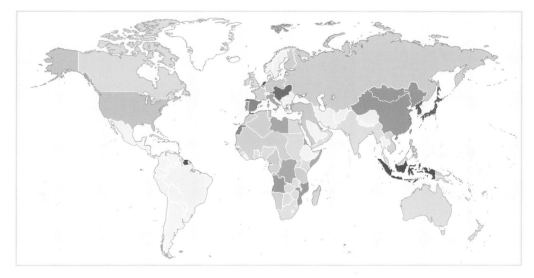

Colonial Empires in 1914

- Austro-Hungarian
- Belgian
- British
- Chinese
- Danish
- Dutch
- French
- German
- Italian
- Japanese
- Ottoman
- Portuguese
- Russian
- Spanish
- United States
- Independent
- Disputed

Religion

The spread of religion

By their nature, religions usually start off in small geographical areas and then spread. For Christianity and Islam, this spread was rapid and extensive. Buddhism diffused more slowly from around 500 BCE into a large part of Asia. The oldest religion, Hinduism, has always been concentrated in the Indian subcontinent, although its adherents in other parts of the world now number millions following migrations from India.

1ST– 7TH CENTURY

During this period, Christianity spread from its origins in the eastern Mediterranean, while Hinduism and forms of Buddhism spread in Asia. Islam became established in Arabia.

Rise and spread of the classical religions to 650 CE

- Buddhist heartland
- Chinese Confucianism/ Daoism and indigenous primal traditions
- Converted to Christianity by 600 CE
- Hinduism
- Islam under Muhammad
- Mahayana Buddhism
- Shintoism
- Zoroastrianism
- → spread of Buddhism
- → spread of Christianity
- → spread of Hinduism
- → dispersion of Jews, to 500 CE

7TH–16TH CENTURY

Islam later spread further through Asia and into parts of Africa and Europe. Christianity diffused through Europe and was then carried to many other parts of the world by colonialists and missionaries. Buddhism spread further in Asia.

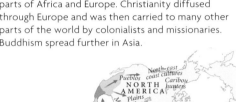

World religions c.1500 CE

- Catholic Christianity
- area converted to Catholic Christianity
- Hinduism
- Islam
- Mahayana Buddhism and Confucianism, Daoism and Shinto
- Mahayana Buddhism and Confucianism, Daoism
- Russian Orthodox
- Theravada Buddhism
- Tibetan Buddhism
- Aztec Empire
- Inca Empire
- → spread of Catholicism
- → spread of Islam
- → spread of Protestantism
- → spread of Russian Orthodoxy

About 83 percent of the world's population adheres to a religion. The remainder adopt irreligious stances such as atheism. In terms of broad similarities of belief, there are about 20 different religions in the world with more than 1 million adherents. However, the larger of these are split into several denominations, which differ in their exact beliefs and practices. Christianity, for example, includes three major groupings that have historically been in conflict—Roman Catholicism, Protestantism, and Orthodox Christianity—as well as hundreds of separate smaller groups. Many of the world's other main religious, such as Islam and Buddhism, are also subdivided.

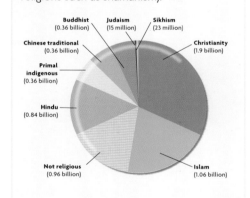

Each year millions of Muslims visit Mecca during the the Islamic pilgrimage known as the *Hajj*

RELIGION AROUND THE WORLD

About 72 percent of humanity adheres to one of five religions: Christianity, Islam, Hinduism, Buddhism, and Chinese traditional religion (which includes Daoism and Confucianism). Of the remainder, many are adherents of primal indigenous religions (a wide range of tribal or folk religions such as shamanism).

Buddhist (0.36 billion)
Judaism (15 million)
Sikhism (23 million)
Chinese traditional (0.36 billion)
Christianity (1.9 billion)
Primal indigenous (0.36 billion)
Hindu (0.84 billion)
Not religious (0.96 billion)
Islam (1.06 billion)

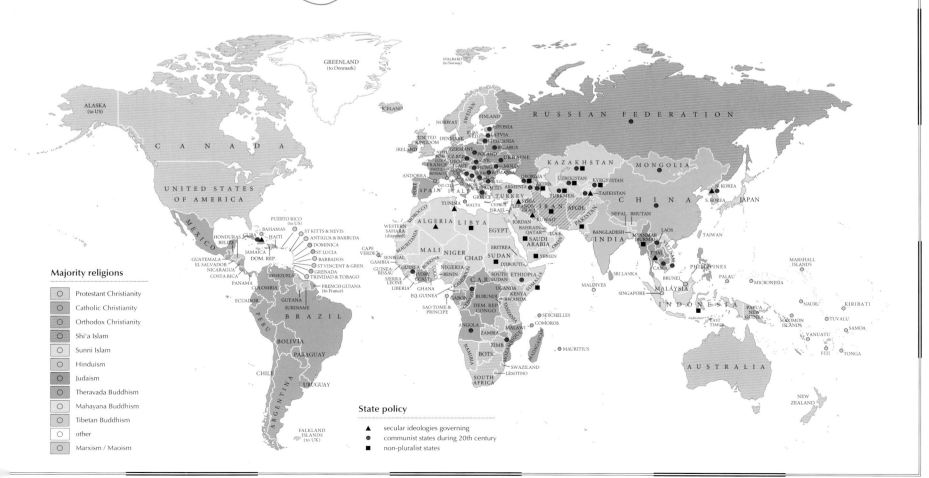

Majority religions

- ○ Protestant Christianity
- ○ Catholic Christianity
- ○ Orthodox Christianity
- ○ Shi'a Islam
- ○ Sunni Islam
- ○ Hinduism
- ○ Judaism
- ○ Theravada Buddhism
- ○ Mahayana Buddhism
- ○ Tibetan Buddhism
- ○ other
- ○ Marxism / Maoism

State policy

- ▲ secular ideologies governing
- ● communist states during 20th century
- ■ non-pluralist states

Health

On most health parameters, the countries of the world split into two distinct groups. The first of these encompass the richer, developed, countries, where medical care is good to excellent, infant mortality and the incidence of deadly infectious diseases is low, and life expectancy is high and rising. Some of the biggest health problems in these countries arise from overeating, while the two main causes of death are heart disease and cancer. The second region consists of the poorer developing countries, where medical care is much less adequate, infant mortality is high, many people are undernourished, and infectious diseases such as malaria are major killers. Life expectancy in these countries is much lower and in some cases is falling.

Life expectancy

Life expectancy has risen remarkably in developed countries over the past 50 years and has now topped 80 years in many of them. In contrast, life expectancy in many of the countries of sub-Saharan Africa has fallen well below 50, in large part due to the high prevalence of HIV/AIDS.

Many people in developed countries are now living for 15–20 years after retirement, putting greater pressure on welfare and health services.

Infant deaths and births

Infant mortality is still high in many developing nations, especially some African countries, due in part to stretched medical services. As well as lower infant mortality, the world's developed countries have much lower birth rates—greater female emancipation and easier access to contraceptives are two causative factors.

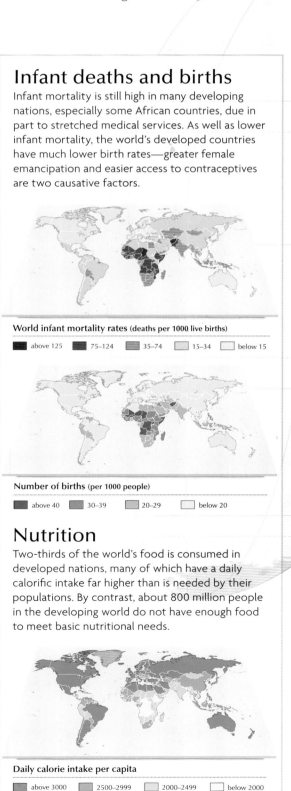

World infant mortality rates (deaths per 1000 live births)

■ above 125   ■ 75–124   ■ 35–74   □ 15–34   □ below 15

Number of births (per 1000 people)

■ above 40   ■ 30–39   ■ 20–29   □ below 20

Nutrition

Two-thirds of the world's food is consumed in developed nations, many of which have a daily calorific intake far higher than is needed by their populations. By contrast, about 800 million people in the developing world do not have enough food to meet basic nutritional needs.

Daily calorie intake per capita

■ above 3000   ■ 2500–2999   ■ 2000–2499   □ below 2000

Healthcare

An indicator of the strength of healthcare provision in a country is the number of doctors per 1000 population. Some communist and former communist countries such as Cuba and Russia score well in this regard. In general, healthcare provision is good or adequate in most of the world's richer countries but scanty throughout much of Africa and in parts of Asia and Latin America.

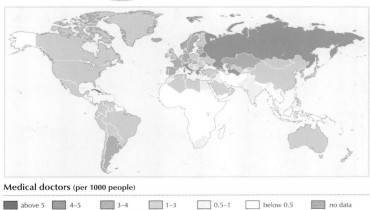

The extensive public healthcare system in Cuba provides for around 6 doctors per 1000 people, one of the highest ratios in the world.

Medical doctors (per 1000 people)

■ above 5   ■ 4–5   ■ 3–4   □ 1–3   □ 0.5–1   □ below 0.5   ■ no data

Map labels

USA (Alaska)

CANADA

UNITED STATES OF AMERICA

MEXICO

ATLANTIC OCEAN

Greenland (to Denmark)

Life expectancy

○ above 80 years
○ 75–80 years
○ 70–75 years
○ 60–70 years
○ 50–60 years
● below 50 years

BAHAMAS
CUBA   HAITI   DOMINICAN REPUBLIC
JAMAICA
BELIZE
GUATEMALA   HONDURAS
EL SALVADOR   NICARAGUA
COSTA RICA   PANAMA
ANTIGUA & BARBUDA
DOMINICA
SAINT LUCIA
ST VINCENT & THE GRENADINES
GRENADA
ST KITTS & NEVIS
BARBADOS
TRINIDAD & TOBAGO
VENEZUELA
COLOMBIA
GUYANA
SURINAME
French Guiana (to France)
ECUADOR
PERU
BRAZIL
BOLIVIA
PARAGUAY
CHILE
ARGENTINA
URUGUAY

ATLANTIC OCEAN

ICELAND
NORWAY   SWEDEN
UNITED KINGDOM   DENMARK
IRELAND
NETH.   POLAND
BELG.   GERMANY
LUX.   CZECH REP.
LIECH.
FRANCE   SWITZ.   AUS.   HUN.
SLOVENIA   CRO.
MONACO   B-H.
SAN MARINO   MON.
PORTUGAL   SPAIN   ANDORRA   ITALY
ALBANIA   GRE.
MALTA
MOROCCO   TUNISIA
WESTERN SAHARA (occupied by Morocco)   ALGERIA   LIBYA
CAPE VERDE
MAURITANIA   MALI   NIGER
SENEGAL
GAMBIA   BURKINA   CHAD
GUINEA-BISSAU   GUINEA
SIERRA LEONE   IVORY COAST   GHANA   BENIN   NIGERIA
LIBERIA   TOGO   CAMEROON   CENTRAL AFRICAN REPUBLIC
EQUATORIAL GUINEA
SAO TOME & PRINCIPE   GABON   CONGO   DEM. REP. CONGO
ANGOLA (Cabinda)
ANGOLA
NAMIBIA
SOUTH AFRICA

United States of America: has an average life expectancy of about 78 years, with women living about 5 years longer than men.

Liberia: currently has one of the lowest life expectancies in West Africa, at about 45 years, owing to factors such as high rates of infectious disease, recent conflict, and poverty.

Smoking

Cigarette smoking—one of the most harmful activities to health—is common throughout much of the world. Smoking prevalence is generally highest in the richer, developed countries. However, awareness of the health risks has seen cigarette consumption in most of these countries stabilize or begin to fall. By contrast, more and more people, especially males, are taking up the habit in poorer developing countries.

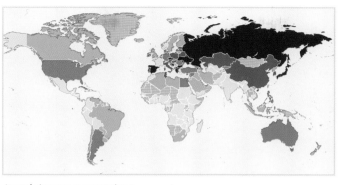

Annual cigarette consumption (per person)

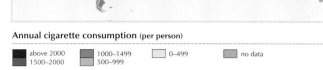

- above 2000
- 1500–2000
- 1000–1499
- 500–999
- 0–499
- no data

Japan: has one of the world's highest life expectancies, at over 81 years—a fact commonly put down to the typical Japanese low-fat diet of rice, fish, and soy products.

Swaziland: currently has the lowest life expectancy in the world, at about 40 years, due to widespread HIV/AIDS.

Communicable diseases

Despite advances in their treatment and prevention, infectious diseases remain a huge problem, especially in developing countries. Three of the most common and deadly are tuberculosis (TB), HIV/AIDS, and malaria. Of these, active TB affects about 25 million people (often as a complication of AIDS), with a particularly high prevalence in parts of Africa. HIV/AIDS has spread since 1981 to become a global pandemic. Malaria affects about 225 million people every year.

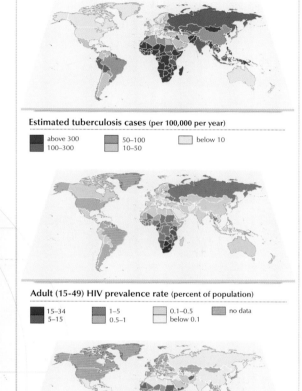

Estimated tuberculosis cases (per 100,000 per year)

- above 300
- 100–300
- 50–100
- 10–50
- below 10

Adult (15-49) HIV prevalence rate (percent of population)

- 15–34
- 5–15
- 1–5
- 0.5–1
- 0.1–0.5
- below 0.1
- no data

Malaria cases (per 100,000 per year)

- above 25,000
- 10,000–25,000
- 1000–10,000
- 100–1000
- 10–100
- below 10
- low risk

Preventive medicine

Throughout the world, doctors recognize that the prevention of disease and disease transmission is just as important as the treatment of illness. Preventive medicine has many aspects and includes advice about diet and nutrition; education about the avoidance of health-threatening behaviors such as smoking, excess alcohol consumption, and unprotected sex; and the use of vaccines against diseases such as typhoid, polio and cholera. In developing countries, some of the main priorities in preventive medicine are the provision of pure water supplies and proper sanitation, as well as measures against malaria, including the use of antimalarial drugs and mosquito nets.

The use of mosquito nets greatly reduces the transmission of malaria and the risk of infection.

TOP TEN KILLER DISEASES, 2004

The world's biggest killer diseases fall into two main groups. One group, which includes HIV/AIDS, malaria, tuberculosis, and childhood diseases such as measles, mainly kills people in poor countries. The other group includes cardiovascular diseases and cancer, the big killers in rich countries.

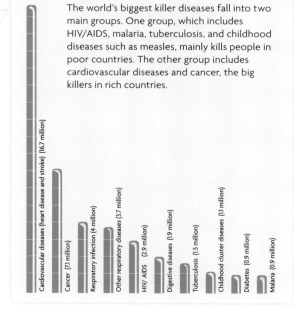

- Cardiovascular diseases (heart disease and stroke) (16.7 million)
- Cancer (7.1 million)
- Respiratory infection (4 million)
- Other respiratory diseases (3.7 million)
- HIV/ AIDS (2.9 million)
- Digestive diseases (1.9 million)
- Tuberculosis (1.5 million)
- Childhood cluster diseases (1.1 million)
- Diabetes (0.9 million)
- Malaria (0.9 million)

Water Resources

Water covers 71 percent of Earth's surface, but only 2.5 percent of this is fresh water, and two thirds of that is locked up in glaciers and polar ice sheets. Patterns of human settlement have developed around fresh water availability, but increasing numbers of people are now vulnerable to chronic shortage or interruptions in supply. Worldwide, fresh water consumption multiplied more than sixfold during the 20th century as populations increased and agriculture became more dependent on irrigation, much of it hugely wasteful because of evaporation and run-off. Industrial water demand also rose, as did use in the home, for washing, flushing, cooking, and gardening.

Amid the desert of Wadi Rum, Jordan, crops grow on circular patches of land irrigated with water from an underground aquifer.

Water withdrawal

Agriculture accounts for 70 percent of water consumption worldwide. Industry and domestic use each account for 15 percent. Excessive withdrawal of water affects the health of rivers and the needs of people. China's Yellow River now fails to reach the sea for most of the year.

Percentage of freshwater withdrawal by agriculture

79–100	66–79	47–66	31–47	16–31	0–16

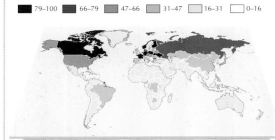

Percentage of freshwater withdrawal by industry

79–100	66–79	47–66	31–47	16–31	0–16

Percentage of freshwater withdrawal by domestic use

60–81	45–60	30–45	15–30	0–15	no data

Availability of fresh water
total renewable (cubic yards/capita/per year)

- less than 1300 (water scarcity)
- 1300–2221 (water stress)
- 2222–3921 (insufficient water)
- 3922–12,999 (relatively sufficient)
- 13,000 or more (plentiful supplies)
- major drainage basin
- ▼ over 50% of water resource originating from outside country

Drought

The disruption of normal rainfall patterns can cause drought problems even in temperate zones, with consequences ranging from domestic water usage restrictions to low crop yields to forest fires. In regions of the developing world where monsoon rains fail, or water is perennially scarce, drought is a life or death issue. Parts of central and east Africa, for instance, have suffered severe and recurring droughts in recent decades, with disastrous results including destruction of livestock, desertification, famine, and mass migration.

In a severe drought, river beds may dry up *(above left)*, leaving stranded fish to die, as here in Florida.

A Chinese farmer waters dry fields *(above)* in China's southern province of Guangdong. This picture was taken in May 2002, but the image is timeless; it could be August 2006 in Sichuan province, to the northwest of here—or almost any year in water-stressed northern China.

Water stress

A region is under "water stress" when the rate of water withdrawal from its rivers and aquifers exceeds their natural replenishment, so that people living there are subject to frequent shortages. Currently 1.7 billion people live in "highly stressed" river basins worldwide. This is a major potential cause of conflict, particularly when several countries share one river; the Euphrates, running through Turkey, Syria, and Iraq, or the rivers of southern China running south into Korea, are just two examples.

Freshwater stress in 1995 Water withdrawal (% of total available)

| above 40 | 20–40 | 10–20 | below 10 |

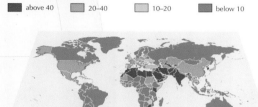

Freshwater stress in 2025 Water withdrawal (% of total available)

| above 40 | 20–40 | 10–20 | below 10 |

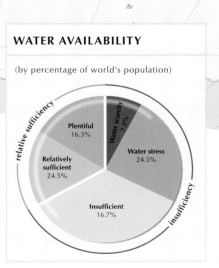

WATER AVAILABILITY

(by percentage of world's population)

relative sufficiency

Plentiful 16.3%

Water scarcity 7.8%

Water stress 24.5%

Relatively sufficient 24.5%

Insufficient 16.7%

insufficiency

Mozambican children *(above)* fetch precious water in metal pans.

Gujarati villagers gather to draw water from a huge well *(above left)* in Natwarghad, western India. Many wells and village ponds ran dry in the severe drought of 2003, leaving local people to wait for irregular supplies brought in by state-run tankers.

Clean drinking water

Sub-Saharan Africa is among the most deprived regions for lack of access to safe drinking water. Worldwide, this terrible health hazard affects over a billion people—at least 15 percent of the population. One of the agreed United Nations "millennium goals" for international development is to halve this proportion by 2015, by tackling chemical pollution from agriculture and industry, and by introducing essential purification facilities and local supply systems. In the industrialized world, people have come to expect clean drinking water on tap, even if they face rising prices for its treatment and supply.

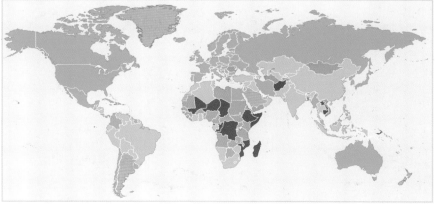

Access to safe drinking water source (percentage of population)

91%–100%	below 50%
76%–90%	no data
50%–75%	

Economic Systems

The world economy is now effectively a single global system based on "free market" capitalist principles. Few countries still cling, like North Korea, to the "command economy" formula developed in the former communist bloc, where centralized state plans set targets for investment and production. In the West, state ownership of companies has greatly diminished thanks to the wave of privatization in the last 25 years. Major companies move capital and raw materials around the globe to take advantage of different labor costs and skills. The World Trade Organization (WTO) promotes free trade, but many countries still use subsidies, and protect their markets with import tariffs or quotas, to favor their own producers.

Enormous volumes of trade pass through the world's stock markets making them key indicators of the strength of the global economy.

Balance of trade

Few countries earn from their exports exactly as much as they spend on imports. If the imbalance is persistently negative, it creates a potentially serious problem of indebtedness. The European Union's (EU) external trade is broadly in balance, but the US balance of trade has been in deficit since the 1970s, partly because it imports so many consumer goods. This deficit now stands at around US$ 500 billion a year.

Balance of trade
(million US$)

over 30,000	
10,000–29,000	
1000–9999	Surplus
0-999	
0-999	
1000-9999	
10,000–29,999	Deficit
over 30,000	
data unavailable	

TOP TEN GLOBAL COMPANIES (2010)

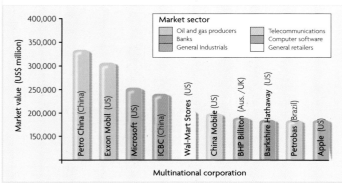

Market sector
- Oil and gas producers
- Banks
- General Industrials
- Telecommunications
- Computer software
- General retailers

Energy

Countries with oil and gas to sell (notably in the Middle East and Russia) can charge high prices; trade in fuel was worth US$ 1.4 trillion in 2005. The US and others are turning back to nuclear power (despite safety fears) for generating electricity. China relies heavily on (polluting) coal. Renewable technologies promise much, but so far make relatively minor contributions.

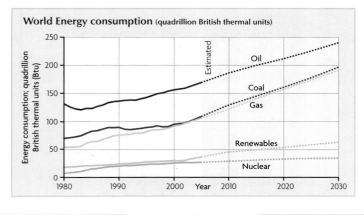

World Energy consumption (quadrillion British thermal units)

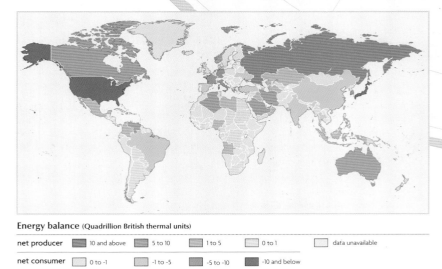

Energy balance (Quadrillion British thermal units)

net producer	10 and above	5 to 10	1 to 5	0 to 1	data unavailable
net consumer	0 to -1	-1 to -5	-5 to -10	-10 and below	

International debt

International debt
(as percentage of GNI)

- above 100%
- 75–100%
- 50–74%
- 25–49%
- 15–24%
- below 15%
- no data

Saddled with crippling debts from past borrowing, the world's poorest countries are still paying off US $100 million a day. This is despite recent successful campaigns to get some of their debts cancelled to allow them to use their limited resources for development. Most international debt, however, is owed by developed countries to one another. The US owes just over a trillion dollars, around 7% of its total debt, to China.

Trade sector

World trade in merchandise tops US$ 10 trillion a year. The global pattern is uneven. Latin America, Africa, the Middle East, and Russia principally export "primary" goods (agricultural produce, mining and fuel). The "secondary" manufacturing sector includes iron and steel, machine tools, chemicals, clothing and textiles, cars and other consumer goods. The West still dominates the "tertiary" or non-merchandise sector, worth US$ 2.4 trillion, in services such as insurance and banking.

Gross Domestic Product (GDP) by continent (US$ billion)

- Europe
- North America
- Asia
- South America
- Africa
- Australia, Oceania

Primary sector
Value added to the economy (percentage of GDP)

- above 50
- 26–50
- 16–25
- 6–15
- below 5
- no data

Secondary sector
Value added to the economy (percentage of GDP)

- above 50
- 40–49
- 30–39
- 20–29
- below 20
- no data

Tertiary sector
Value added to the economy (percentage of GDP)

- above 65
- 55–64
- 54–45
- 35–44
- below 35
- no data

NORTH AMERICA

ASIA

AUSTRALIA

Tokyo

Gross Domestic Product (GDP*)
(nominal per capita US$)

- 40,001–90,000
- 10,001–40,000
- 6251–10,000
- 2501–6250
- 1501–2500
- 501–1500
- 251–500
- 0–250
- data unavailable

*Gross Domestic Product (GDP) is defined as the total market value of all final goods and services produced in a country.

Direct Foreign Investment

- from USA
- from Europe
- from Japan
- major stock exchange
- stock exchange

Average monthly salary
(US$)

- above 3000
- 2000–3000
- 1000–2000
- 500–1000
- 250–500
- below 250
- no data

Labor

China's huge low-cost labor force promotes its conquest of world markets for manufactured goods. India's educated workforce attracts call centers and other service sector jobs, while the more economically developed countries's (MEDC) caring professions, and low-wage agriculture, draw in immigrant labor.

Travel

Mass travel is now a ubiquitous feature of all developed countries, and the provision of transport and tourism facilities one of the world's biggest industries, employing well over 100 million people. The travel explosion has come about, first, through major improvements in transportation technology; and second, as a result of increasing amounts of disposable income and leisure time in the world's wealthier countries. The main reasons for travel today include leisure pursuits and tourism (accounting for well over half of the total financial outlay), work and business, pilgrimage, migration, and visits to family and friends.

There are currently around 4.2 billion air travelers a year passing through over 1600 international and domestic airports. This figure is forecast to grow by 4 percent each year, leading to increased pressure on air traffic control and ground handling systems that, in many areas, are already close to maximum capacity.

Major modes of transportation

The major transport modes for people in the 21st century are road, rail, and air travel. The most popular air routes are highly concentrated within and between the USA, western Europe, and Asia. Major roads and railroads are more evenly spread, following the general distribution of the world's population.

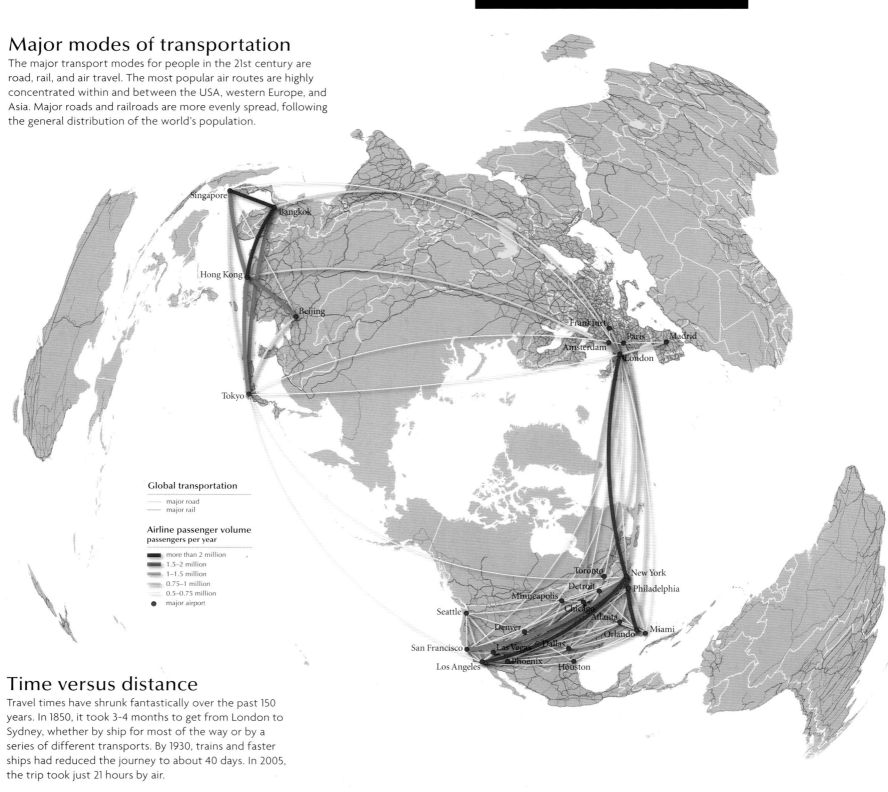

Global transportation

— major road
— major rail

Airline passenger volume
passengers per year

- more than 2 million
- 1.5–2 million
- 1–1.5 million
- 0.75–1 million
- 0.5–0.75 million
- ● major airport

Time versus distance

Travel times have shrunk fantastically over the past 150 years. In 1850, it took 3-4 months to get from London to Sydney, whether by ship for most of the way or by a series of different transports. By 1930, trains and faster ships had reduced the journey to about 40 days. In 2005, the trip took just 21 hours by air.

Media and Communications

Over the past 50 years, the term "media" has come to denote various means of communicating information between people at a distance. These include mass media—methods such as newspapers, radio, and television that can be used to rapidly disseminate information to large numbers of people—and two-way systems, such as telephones and e-mail. Currently, the communication systems undergoing the most rapid growth worldwide include mobile telephony and various Internet-based applications, such as web sites, blogs, and podcasting, which can be considered forms of mass media.

Internet usage

Internet usage has grown extremely rapidly since the early 1990s, largely as a result of the invention of the World Wide Web. Usage rates are highest in the USA (where about 80 percent of people were using the Internet in 2006), Australia, Japan, South Korea, and Finland. They are lowest in Africa, where on average less than 5 percent of the population were Internet users in 2006.

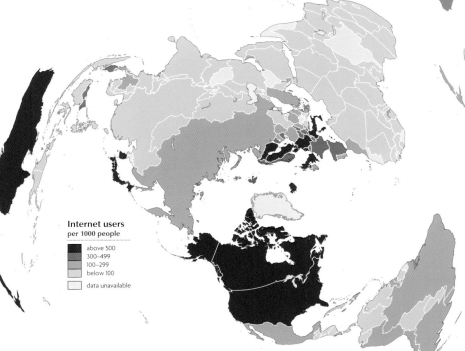

Internet users
per 1000 people

- above 500
- 300–499
- 100–299
- below 100
- data unavailable

Mobile phone usage

By 2006, there were more than 2.5 billion mobile phone users worldwide. In some parts of Europe, such as Italy, almost everyone owns and uses a mobile—many possess more than one phone. In contrast, throughout much of Southern Asia and Africa, less than 10 percent of the population are users. As well as utilizing them as telephones, most users now employ the devices for the additional functions they offer, such as text messaging and e-mail.

Mobile phone users
per 1000 people

- above 900
- 700–899
- 500–699
- 300–499
- 100–299
- below 100
- data unavailable

The internet emerged in the early 1990s as a computer-based global communication system. Since then massive growth has seen user numbers increase to around 1.1 billion people, or roughly 17 percent of the world's population.

Satellite Communications

Modern communications satellites are used extensively for international telephony, for television and radio broadcasting, and to some extent for transmitting Internet data. Many of these satellites are deployed in clusters or arrays, often in geostationary orbits—that is, in positions that appear fixed to Earth-based observers.

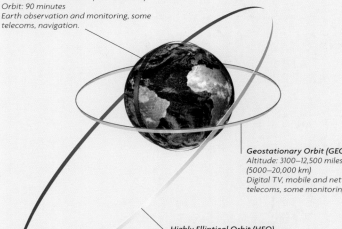

Low Earth Orbit (LEO)
Altitudes: 375–1250 miles (600–2000 km)
Orbit: 90 minutes
Earth observation and monitoring, some telecoms, navigation.

Geostationary Orbit (GEO)
Altitude: 3100–12,500 miles (5000–20,000 km)
Digital TV, mobile and net telecoms, some monitoring.

Highly Elliptical Orbit (HEO)
Altitude: 25,000 miles (40,000 km)
Orbit: 5–6 hours
Russian communications satellites

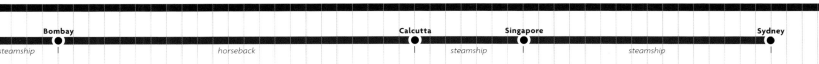

Sydney

Bombay | Calcutta | Singapore | Sydney

steamship | horseback | steamship | steamship

58 59 60 61 62 63 64 65 66 67 68 69 70 71 72 73 74 75 76 77 78 79 80 81 82 83 84 85 86 87 88 89 90 91 92 93 94 95 96 97 98 99 100 101 102 103 104 105 106 107 108 109 110 111 112 113 114 115

The Political World

Today's world map shows nearly 200 independent states, compared with about 80 after World War II. The transformation is mainly due to the withdrawal of European powers from huge colonial empires; their remaining overseas dependencies are tiny by comparison. The late 20th century also saw the collapse of communism, realignment in Europe, and fragmentation in former Yugoslavia. Globally, the Soviet Union's demise left the USA as the sole superpower, though with fast-growing China and India emerging as economic giants of the future. US security preoccupations switched to combating terrorism, while looming oil and other resource shortages, and environmental constraints, underlined the need for more effective international cooperation.

CONTINENTAL FACTFILE

	Total area: sq miles	Total area: sq km	Total population
North & Central America	9,358,340	24,238,000	516.8 million
South America	6,886,000	17,835,000	380.2 million
Africa	11,712,434	30,335,000	924.6 million
Europe	4,053,309	10,498,000	711.5 million
Asia	16,838,365	43,608,000	3978.2 million
Australia & Oceania	3,285,048	8,508,238	32.7 million

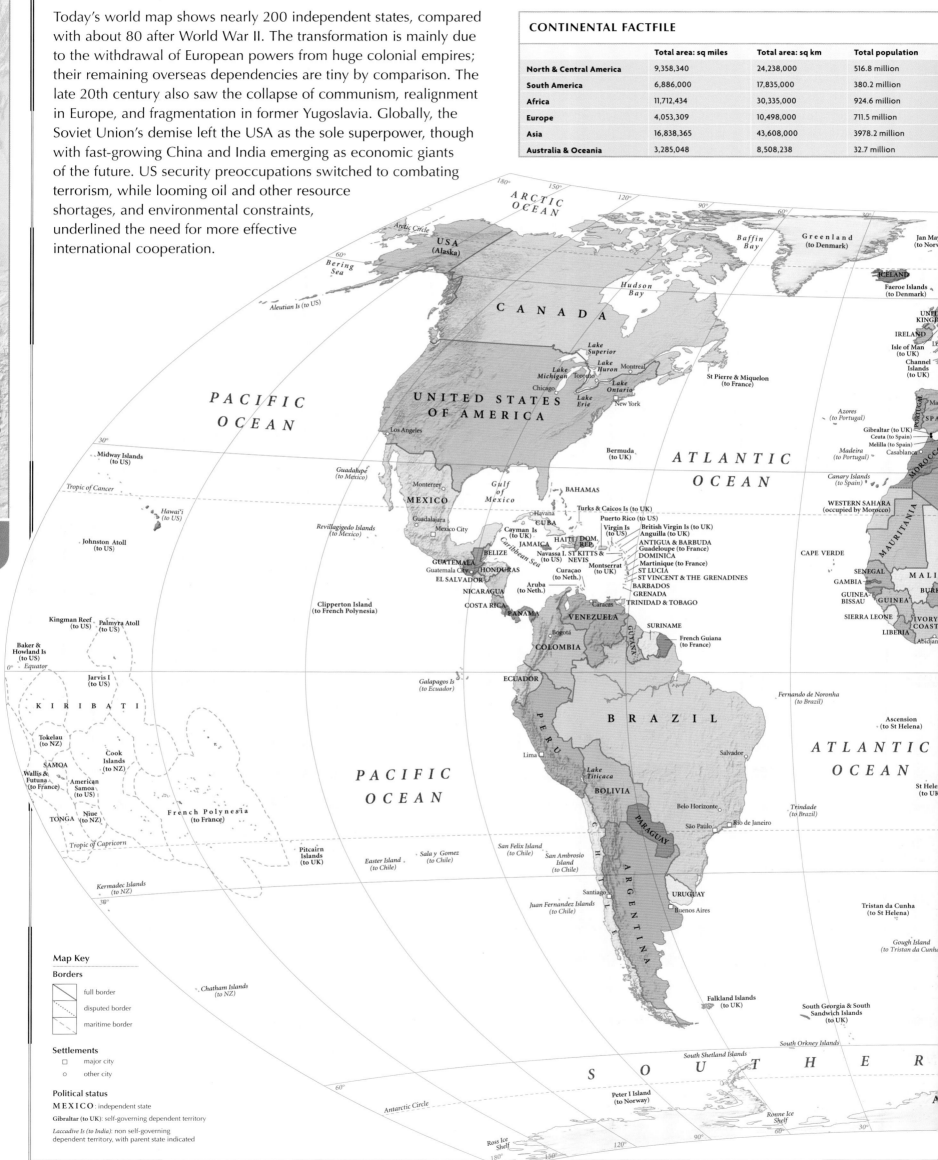

Map Key

Borders

full border

disputed border

maritime border

Settlements

□ major city

○ other city

Political status

MEXICO: independent state

Gibraltar (to UK): self-governing dependent territory

Laccadive Is (to India): non self-governing dependent territory, with parent state indicated

Countries	Largest country	Country with largest population
23	Canada 3,855,171 sq miles (9,984,670 sq km)	United States 318 million
12	Brazil 3,286,470 sq miles (8,511,965 sq km)	Brazil 195 million
54	Algeria 919,590 sq miles (2,381,740 sq km)	Nigeria 158 million
46	European Russia 1,527,341 sq miles (3,955,818 sq km)	European Russia 110 million
49	Asiatic Russia 5,065,394 sq miles (13,119,382 sq km)	China 1350 million
14	Australia 2,967,893 sq miles (7,686,850 sq km)	Australia 21 million

International borders

The world political map of today displays a complex pattern of boundaries that has evolved through history, and is still constantly changing as new countries emerge and disputes and territorial claims are slowly resolved. The map shows two main types of border. Full borders represent internationally agreed and recognized territorial boundaries. A disputed border is indicated where a *de facto* territorial boundary exists, which is not agreed or is still subject to arbitration.

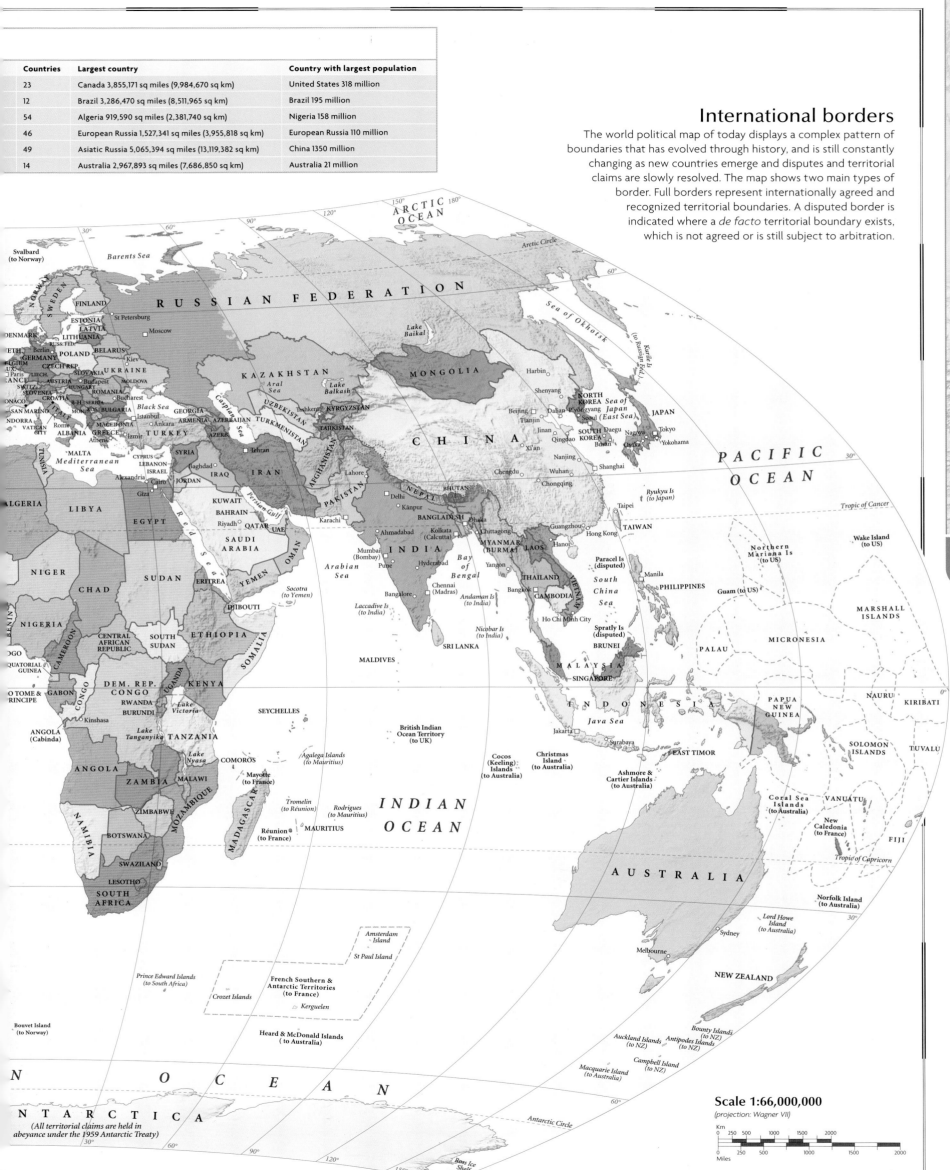

Scale 1:66,000,000

(projection: Wagner VII)

Borders, conflicts and disputes

Conflict evolved in the 20th century from conventional land- or sea-based warfare to increasingly long-range airborne attacks. Nuclear arms from 1945 took this to the intercontinental scale. The Cold War presented a new type of conflict, underlined by the race for weapons capabilities between the US and the Soviet Union. In Korea, Vietnam, the Middle East and elsewhere, soldiers and civilians were exposed to deadly chemicals. International treaties aimed to prevent the spread of nuclear, biological and chemical "weapons of mass destruction". Intercommunal conflict and "ethnic cleansing" reminded the world that horror needed no sophisticated weaponry. After 9/11, the US-led "war on terror" perceived conflict in a new light, where international terrorism knew no borders.

THE PEACEKEEPERS

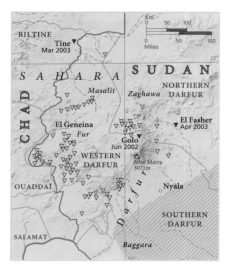

Over 130 countries have contributed around a million troops to UN missions to monitor peace processes and help implement peace accords since 1948. Regional alliances such as NATO and the African Union (AU) are increasingly deploying their own multinational forces in trouble-spots, while Australia has intervened in a similar manner in nearby Pacific island states. Peacekeepers oversaw East Timor's elections in 2001 and subsequent celebration of independence *(above)*. The US defines many of its activities as peacekeeping, despite the confrontational nature of some of its interventions.

DARFUR

African ethnic minorities in Darfur in western Sudan have suffered appalling violence since 2003 at the hands of genocidal Arab Janjaweed militias, for which the government in Khartoum denies responsibility. Displaced in their hundreds of thousands, refugees receive inadequate protection and aid from an international community unwilling to commit to full-scale intervention.

Darfur conflict

Fur ethnic group

▨ arabic speaking area

▽ villages destroyed by Janjaweed

▼ towns that have been attacked by rebels opposing the Sudanese government

ISRAEL

Since its creation in 1948, Israel has been at war with its Arab neighbors. The Palestinians are fighting for a separate, viable state, comprising of at least East Jerusalem, and the West Bank and Gaza Strip, territories occupied by Israel in 1967. Their struggle *(intifada)* has attracted international support, but has been met by a hard-line response from Israel, which is backed by the US.

Arab-Israeli Wars 1947-2006

MAIN MAP: Arab-Israeli Wars

▨ Israel in 1949

▨ occupied by Israel after 1967 war

▨ occupied by Israel after 1973 war

▨ occupied by Israel after 1967 war reoccupied by Egypt after 1973 war

▭ demilitarized zone held by UN after Israel-Syria agreement, 1974, and 2nd Sinai agreement, 1975

▽ Hezbollah rocket attacks 2006

▼ Israeli rocket attacks 2006

—·— disputed border

INSET MAP 1: UN Partition plan in 1947

— border of British mandate 1923

▨ proposed Arab State

▨ proposed Jewish State

▨ proposed international zone

INSET MAP 2: West Bank security

▨ Palestinian responsibility for civil affairs and internal security

▨ Palestinian responsibility for civil affairs; Israel responsible for security

— Security Wall (existing and planned)

Conflicts and international disputes

- Major active territorial or border disputes
- Countries involved in internal conflict
- Active territorial or border disputes and internal conflict

Types of government

- Multiparty democracy for more than 10 yrs
- Multiparty democracy within last 10 yrs
- Single-party government
- Military regime
- Theocracy
- Monarchy
- Non-party system
- Transitional regime

Lines on the map

The determination of international boundaries can use a variety of criteria. Many borders between older states follow physical boundaries, often utilizing natural defensive features. Others have been determined by international agreement or arbitration, or simply ended up where the opposing forces stood at the end of a conflict.

WORLD BOUNDARIES

Dates from which current boundaries have existed

- 1990–present
- 1966–1989
- 1946–1965
- 1915–1945
- 1850–1914
- 1800–1849
- Pre-1800

POST-COLONIAL BORDERS

Independent African countries have largely inherited the earlier carve up of the continent by European colonial powers. These often arbitrarily divided or grouped differing ethnic and religious groups which has, in turn, contributed to the tensions that underlie the many civil conflicts that have plagued post-colonial Africa.

ENCLAVES

Changes to international boundaries occasionally create pockets of land cut off from the main territory of the country they belong to. In Europe, Kaliningrad has been separated from the rest of the Russian Federation since the independence of the Baltic States. Likewise, when Morocco was granted independence, Spain retained the coastal enclaves of Ceuta and Melilla.

GEOMETRIC BORDERS

Straight lines and lines of longitude and latitude have occasionally been used to determine international boundaries: the 49th Parallel forms a large section of the Canada–US border, while the 38th Parallel roughly divides the Korean Peninsula. Internal administrative divisions within Canada, the US, and Australia also use geometric boundaries.

PHYSICAL BORDERS

Rivers account for one-sixth of the world's borders: the Danube forms part of the boundaries for nine European nations. Changes in a river's course or disruption of its flow can lead to territorial disputes. Lakes and mountains also form natural borders.

Lake border *(right)*
Mountain border *(below left)*
River border *(below right)*

RUSSIAN FEDERATION

KAZAKHSTAN

MONGOLIA

CHINA

NORTH KOREA

SOUTH KOREA

JAPAN

PACIFIC OCEAN

UZBEKISTAN
KYRG.
TURKMEN.
GEORGIA
ARMENIA AZERB.
TURKEY
CYPRUS
SYRIA LEBANON
AZA TRIP
ISRAEL JORDAN
WEST BANK
KUWAIT
BAHRAIN
QATAR
UAE
SAUDI ARABIA
IRAN
AFGHANISTAN
PAKISTAN
NEPAL
BHUTAN
INDIA
BANGLADESH
MYANMAR (BURMA)
LAOS
THAILAND
CAMBODIA
VIETNAM
TAIWAN
PHILIPPINES
SRI LANKA
MALDIVES
MALAYSIA
SINGAPORE
BRUNEI
INDONESIA
EAST TIMOR
PAPUA NEW GUINEA
MICRONESIA
MARSHALL ISLANDS
PALAU
NAURU
KIRIBATI
SOLOMON ISLANDS
TUVALU
SAMOA
VANUATU
FIJI
TONGA

EGYPT
UDAN
ERITREA
YEMEN
OMAN
DJIBOUTI
ETHIOPIA
SOUTH UDAN
SOMALIA
UGANDA
KENYA
RWANDA
BURUNDI
TANZANIA
SEYCHELLES
COMOROS
AMBIA
MALAWI
MOZAMBIQUE
TIMBABWE
MADAGASCAR
MAURITIUS
SWAZILAND
LESOTHO

INDIAN OCEAN

AUSTRALIA

NEW ZEALAND

THE WORLD

39

GULF CONFLICTS

Although the West armed Saddam Hussein in the brutal 1980s Iran-Iraq War, his unprovoked invasion of Kuwait in 1990 was decried the world over. A US-led coalition, including Arab states, repelled his troops but left him in power. A decade of sanctions followed until, in 2003, Saddam was finally toppled by US-led forces. Following elections in 2005, Iraq has struggled to contain a violent insurgency.

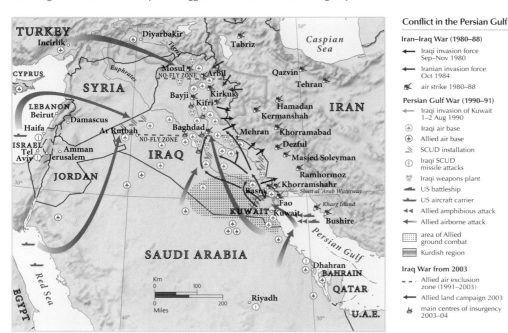

Conflict in the Persian Gulf

Iran–Iraq War (1980–88)
- ← Iraqi invasion force Sep–Nov 1980
- ← Iranian invasion force Oct 1984
- ✷ air strike 1980–88

Persian Gulf War (1990–91)
- ← Iraqi invasion of Kuwait 1–2 Aug 1990
- Iraqi air base
- Allied air base
- SCUD installation
- Iraqi SCUD missile attacks
- Iraqi weapons plant
- US battleship
- US aircraft carrier
- Allied amphibious attack
- Allied airborne attack
- area of Allied ground combat
- Kurdish region

Iraq War from 2003
- Allied air exclusion zone (1991–2003)
- ← Allied land campaign 2003
- main centres of insurgency 2003–04

The World's Time Zones

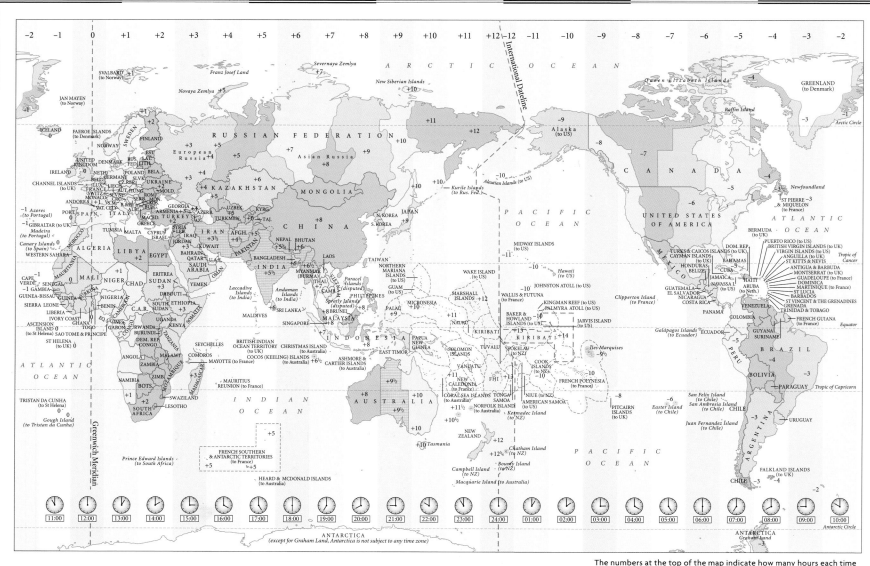

The numbers at the top of the map indicate how many hours each time zone is ahead or behind Coordinated Universal Time (UTC). The row of clocks indicate the time in each zone when it is 12:00 noon UTC.

TIME ZONES

Because Earth is a rotating sphere, the Sun shines on only half of its surface at any one time. Thus, it is simultaneously morning, evening and night time in different parts of the world (see diagram below). Because of these disparities, each country or part of a country adheres to a local time. A region of Earth's surface within which a single local time is used is called a time zone. There are 24 one hour time zones around the world, arranged roughly in longitudinal bands.

STANDARD TIME

Standard time is the official local time in a particular country or part of a country. It is defined by the time zone or zones associated with that country or region. Although time zones are arranged roughly in longitudinal bands, in many places the borders of a zone do not fall exactly on longitudinal meridians, as can be seen on the map (above), but are determined by geographical factors or by borders between countries or parts of countries. Most countries have just one time zone and one standard time, but some large countries (such as the USA, Canada and Russia) are split between several time zones, so standard time varies across those countries. For example, the coterminous United States straddles four time zones and so has four standard times, called the Eastern, Central, Mountain and Pacific standard times. China is unusual in that just one standard time is used for the whole country, even though it extends across 60° of longitude from west to east.

COORDINATED UNIVERSAL TIME (UTC)

Coordinated Universal Time (UTC) is a reference by which the local time in each time zone is set. For example, Australian Western Standard Time (the local time in Western Australia) is set 8 hours ahead of UTC (it is UTC+8) whereas Eastern Standard Time in the United States is set 5 hours behind UTC (it is UTC-5). UTC is a successor to, and closely approximates, Greenwich Mean Time (GMT). However, UTC is based on an atomic clock, whereas GMT is determined by the Sun's position in the sky relative to the 0° longitudinal meridian, which runs through Greenwich, UK.

In 1884 the Prime Meridian (0° longitude) was defined by the position of the cross-hairs in the eyepiece of the "Transit Circle" telescope in the Meridian Building at the Royal Observatory, Greenwich, UK.

DAY AND NIGHT AROUND THE WORLD

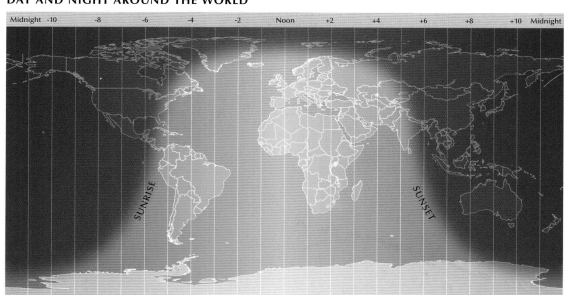

THE INTERNATIONAL DATELINE

The International Dateline is an imaginary line from pole to pole that roughly corresponds to the 180° longitudinal meridian. It is an arbitrary marker between calendar days. The dateline is needed because of the use of local times around the world rather than a single universal time. When moving from west to east across the dateline, travelers have to set their watches back one day. Those traveling in the opposite direction, from east to west, must add a day.

DAYLIGHT SAVING TIME

Daylight saving is a summertime adjustment to the local time in a country or region, designed to cause a higher proportion of its citizens' waking hours to pass during daylight. To follow the system, timepieces are advanced by an hour on a pre-decided date in spring and reverted back in the fall. About half of the world's nations use daylight saving.

COMPLETE
ATLAS

OF THE WORLD

THE MAPS IN THIS ATLAS ARE ARRANGED CONTINENT BY CONTINENT, STARTING FROM THE INTERNATIONAL DATE LINE, AND MOVING EASTWARD. THE MAPS PROVIDE A UNIQUE VIEW OF TODAY'S WORLD, COMBINING TRADITIONAL CARTOGRAPHIC TECHNIQUES WITH THE LATEST REMOTE-SENSED AND DIGITAL TECHNOLOGY.

North America is the world's third largest continent with
a total area of 9,358,340 sq miles (24,238,000 sq km)
including Greenland and the Caribbean islands.
It lies wholly within the Northern Hemisphere.

FACTFILE

N **Most Northerly Point:** Kap Morris Jesup, Greenland 83° 38' N
S **Most Southerly Point:** Peninsula de Azuero, Panama 7° 15' N
E **Most Easterly Point:** Nordostrundingen, Greenland 12° 08' W
W **Most Westerly Point:** Attu, Aleutian Islands, USA 172° 30' E

Largest Lakes:
1 Lake Superior, Canada/USA 31,151 sq miles (83,270 sq km)
2 Lake Huron, Canada/USA 23,436 sq miles (60,700 sq km)
3 Lake Michigan, USA 22,402 sq miles (58,020 sq km)
4 Great Bear Lake, Canada 12,274 sq miles (31,790 sq km)
5 Great Slave Lake, Canada 10,981 sq miles (28,440 sq km)

Longest Rivers:
1 Mississippi-Missouri, USA 3710 miles (5969 km)
2 Mackenzie, Canada 2640 miles (4250 km)
3 Yukon, Canada/USA 1978 miles (3184 km)
4 St Lawrence/Great Lakes, Canada/USA 1900 miles (3058 km)
5 Rio Grande, Mexico/USA 1900 miles (3057 km)

Largest Islands:
1 Greenland 849,400 sq miles (2,200,000 sq km)
2 Baffin Island, Canada 183,800 sq miles (476,000 sq km)
3 Victoria Island, Canada 81,900 sq miles (212,000 sq km)
4 Ellesmere Island, Canada 75,700 sq miles (196,000 sq km)
5 Newfoundland, Canada 42,031 sq miles (108,860 sq km)

Highest Points:
1 Mount McKinley (Denali), USA 20,332 ft (6194 m)
2 Mount Logan, Canada 19,550 ft (5959 m)
3 Volcán Pico de Orizaba, Mexico 18,700 ft (5700 m)
4 Mount St Elias, USA 18,008 ft (5489 m)
5 Popocatépetl, Mexico 17,887 ft (5452 m)

Lowest Point:
▼ Death Valley, USA -282 ft (-86 m) below sea level

Highest recorded temperature:
✛ Death Valley, USA 135°F (57°C)

Lowest recorded temperature:
⊖ Northice, Greenland -87°F (-66°C)

Wettest Place:
≋ Vancouver, Canada 183 in (4645 mm)

Driest Place:
⊖ Death Valley, USA 2 in (50 mm)

Cross-section from San Francisco to Washington DC

line of cross-section

0   500   1000 Km
0   500   1000 Miles

Political

Democracy is well established in some parts of the continent but is a recent phenomenon in others. The economically dominant nations of Canada and the USA have a long democratic tradition but elsewhere, notably in the countries of Central America, political turmoil has been more common. In Nicaragua and Haiti, harsh dictatorships have only recently been superseded by democratically-elected governments. North America's largest countries—Canada, Mexico, and the USA—have federal state systems, sharing political power between national and state or provincial governments. The USA has intervened militarily on several occasions in Central America and the Caribbean to protect its strategic interests.

Transportation

In the 19th century, railroads were used to open up the North American continent. Air transport is now more common for long distance passenger travel, although railroads are still extensively used for bulk freight transport. Waterways, like the Mississippi River, are important for the transport of bulk materials, and the Panama Canal is a vital link between the Pacific Ocean and the Caribbean. In the 20th century, road transportation increased massively in North America, with the introduction of cheap, mass-produced cars and extensive highway construction.

Transportation
- major roads and motorways
- major railroads
- major canals
- international borders
- transport intersections
- international airports
- major ports

Standard of living
(UN human development index)
high — low

Standard of living

The USA and Canada have one of the highest overall standards of living in the world. However, many people still live in poverty, especially in inner city ghettos and some rural areas. Central America and the Caribbean are markedly poorer than their wealthier northern neighbors Haiti is the poorest country in the western hemisphere.

UNITED STATES OF AMERICA
Scale 1:13,000,000

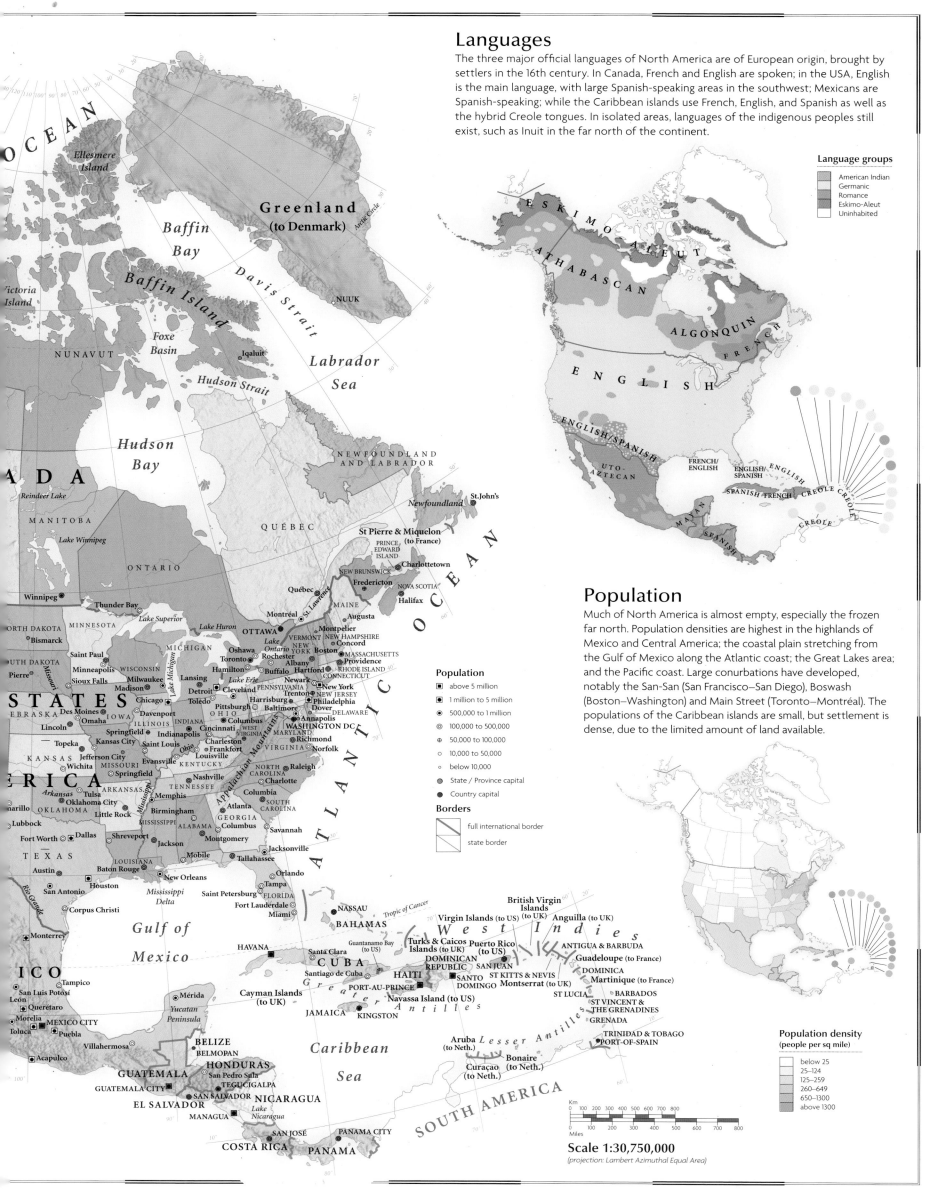

Languages

The three major official languages of North America are of European origin, brought by settlers in the 16th century. In Canada, French and English are spoken; in the USA, English is the main language, with large Spanish-speaking areas in the southwest; Mexicans are Spanish-speaking; while the Caribbean islands use French, English, and Spanish as well as the hybrid Creole tongues. In isolated areas, languages of the indigenous peoples still exist, such as Inuit in the far north of the continent.

Language groups
- American Indian
- Germanic
- Romance
- Eskimo-Aleut
- Uninhabited

Population

Much of North America is almost empty, especially the frozen far north. Population densities are highest in the highlands of Mexico and Central America; the coastal plain stretching from the Gulf of Mexico along the Atlantic coast; the Great Lakes area; and the Pacific coast. Large conurbations have developed, notably the San-San (San Francisco–San Diego), Boswash (Boston–Washington) and Main Street (Toronto–Montréal). The populations of the Caribbean islands are small, but settlement is dense, due to the limited amount of land available.

Population
- ■ above 5 million
- ■ 1 million to 5 million
- ⊙ 500,000 to 1 million
- ⊙ 100,000 to 500,000
- ⊕ 50,000 to 100,000
- ○ 10,000 to 50,000
- ○ below 10,000
- □ State / Province capital
- ● Country capital

Borders
- full international border
- state border

Population density
(people per sq mile)
- below 25
- 25–124
- 125–259
- 260–649
- 650–1300
- above 1300

Km 0 100 200 300 400 500 600 700 800

Miles 0 100 200 300 400 500 600 700 800

Scale 1:30,750,000
(projection: Lambert Azimuthal Equal Area)

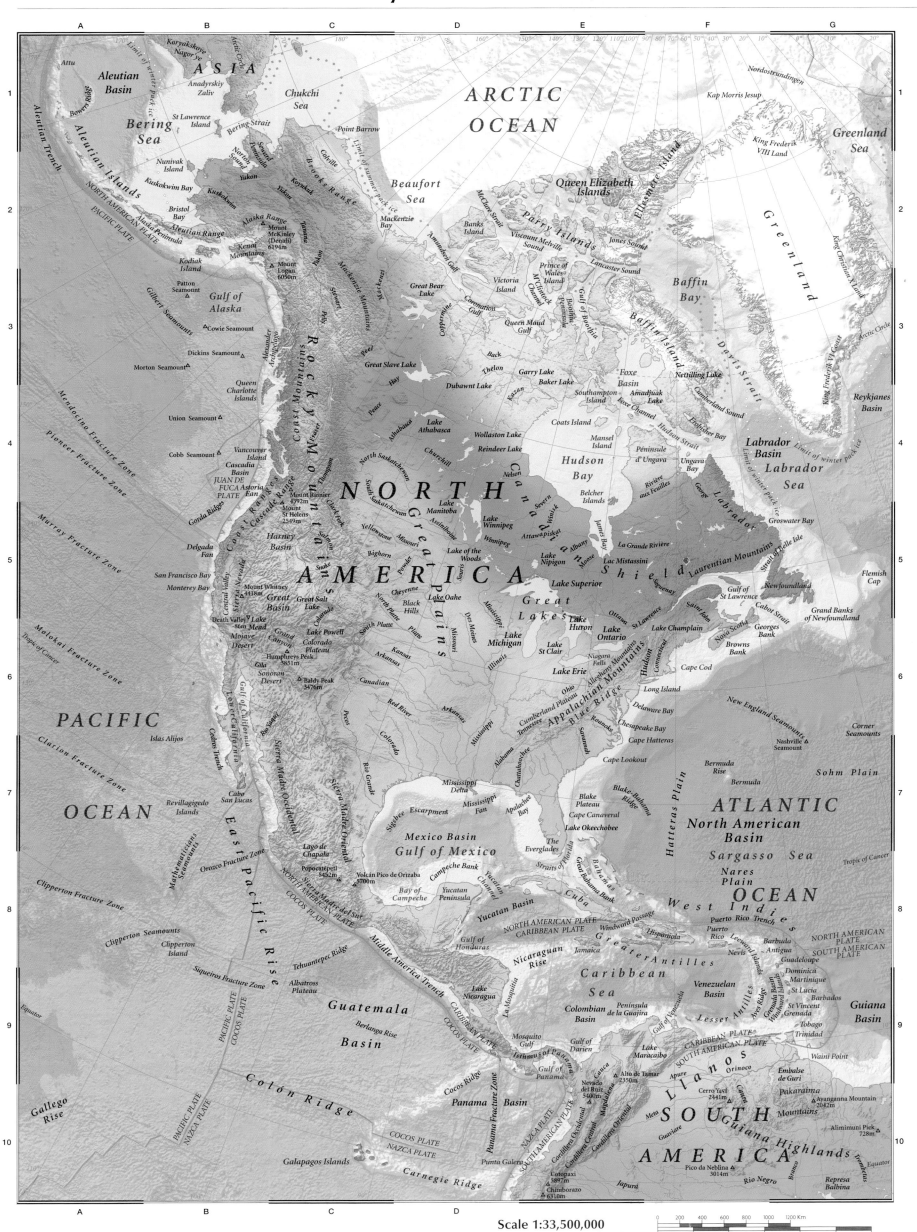

Scale 1:33,500,000
(projection: Lambert Conformal Conic)

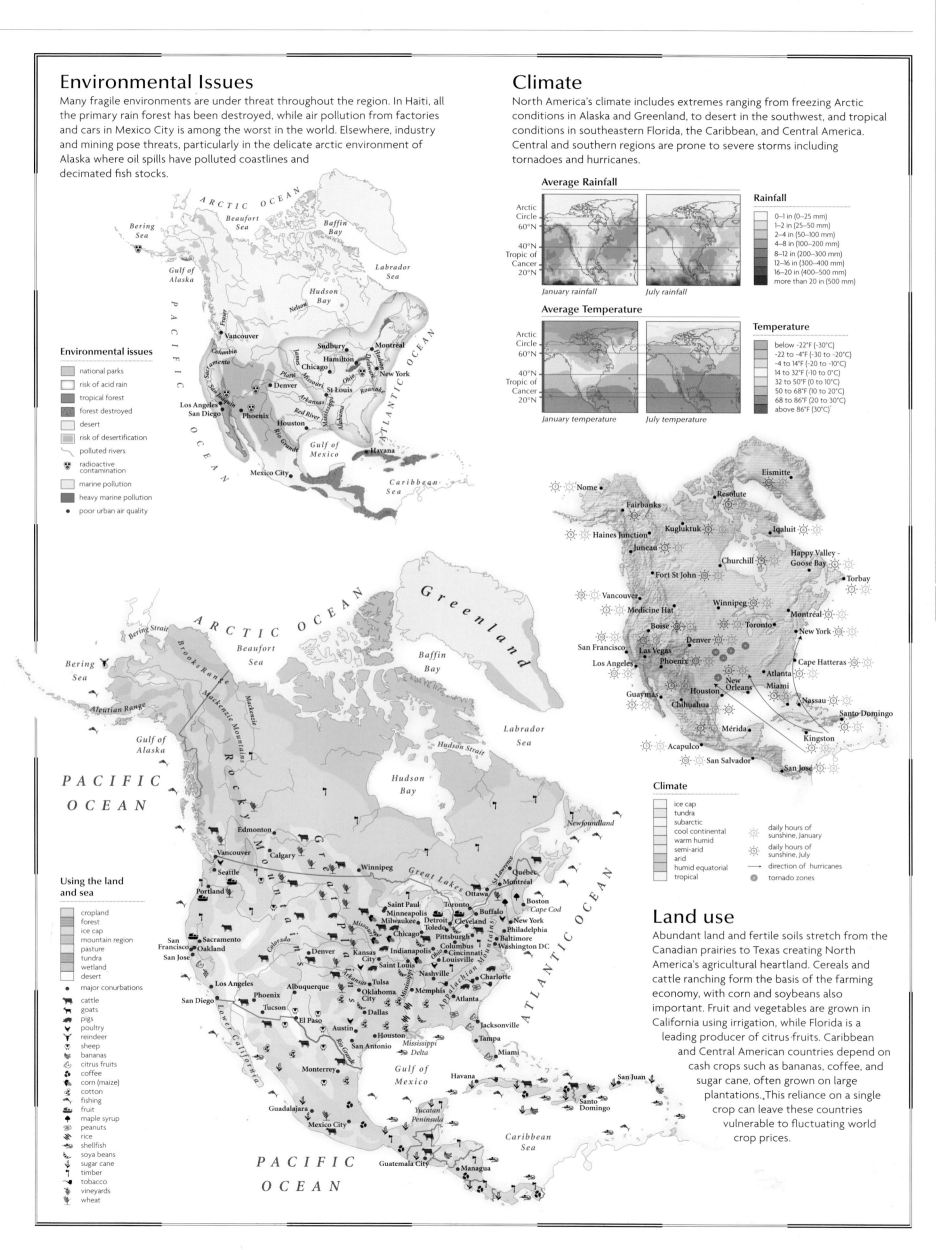

Environmental Issues

Many fragile environments are under threat throughout the region. In Haiti, all the primary rain forest has been destroyed, while air pollution from factories and cars in Mexico City is among the worst in the world. Elsewhere, industry and mining pose threats, particularly in the delicate arctic environment of Alaska where oil spills have polluted coastlines and decimated fish stocks.

Environmental issues

- national parks
- risk of acid rain
- tropical forest
- forest destroyed
- desert
- risk of desertification
- polluted rivers
- radioactive contamination
- marine pollution
- heavy marine pollution
- poor urban air quality

Map labels: ARCTIC OCEAN, Beaufort Sea, Baffin Bay, Bering Sea, Gulf of Alaska, Hudson Bay, Labrador Sea, Nelson, Fraser, Vancouver, Columbia, Sudbury, Hamilton, Montréal, Sacramento, James, Chicago, Missouri, Platte, Denver, St Louis, Ohio, Roanoke, New York, Los Angeles, San Diego, Arkansas, Red River, Phoenix, Rio Grande, Houston, Alabama, Mississippi, Gulf of Mexico, Havana, Mexico City, Caribbean Sea, PACIFIC OCEAN, ATLANTIC OCEAN

Climate

North America's climate includes extremes ranging from freezing Arctic conditions in Alaska and Greenland, to desert in the southwest, and tropical conditions in southeastern Florida, the Caribbean, and Central America. Central and southern regions are prone to severe storms including tornadoes and hurricanes.

Average Rainfall

January rainfall — *July rainfall*

Arctic Circle, 60°N, 40°N, Tropic of Cancer, 20°N

Rainfall

- 0–1 in (0–25 mm)
- 1–2 in (25–50 mm)
- 2–4 in (50–100 mm)
- 4–8 in (100–200 mm)
- 8–12 in (200–300 mm)
- 12–16 in (300–400 mm)
- 16–20 in (400–500 mm)
- more than 20 in (500 mm)

Average Temperature

January temperature — *July temperature*

Arctic Circle, 60°N, 40°N, Tropic of Cancer, 20°N

Temperature

- below -22°F (-30°C)
- -22 to -4°F (-30 to -20°C)
- -4 to 14°F (-20 to -10°C)
- 14 to 32°F (-10 to 0°C)
- 32 to 50°F (0 to 10°C)
- 50 to 68°F (10 to 20°C)
- 68 to 86°F (20 to 30°C)
- above 86°F (30°C)

Climate

- ice cap
- tundra
- subarctic
- cool continental
- warm humid
- semi-arid
- arid
- humid equatorial
- tropical
- daily hours of sunshine, January
- daily hours of sunshine, July
- direction of hurricanes
- tornado zones

Climate map labels: Nome, Fairbanks, Resolute, Eismitte, Haines Junction, Kugluktuk, Iqaluit, Juneau, Churchill, Happy Valley - Goose Bay, Fort St John, Torbay, Vancouver, Winnipeg, Montréal, Medicine Hat, Toronto, New York, Boise, Denver, San Francisco, Las Vegas, Cape Hatteras, Los Angeles, Phoenix, Atlanta, Guaymas, Houston, New Orleans, Miami, Chihuahua, Nassau, Mérida, Santo Domingo, Acapulco, Kingston, San Salvador, San José, San Juan

Land use

Abundant land and fertile soils stretch from the Canadian prairies to Texas creating North America's agricultural heartland. Cereals and cattle ranching form the basis of the farming economy, with corn and soybeans also important. Fruit and vegetables are grown in California using irrigation, while Florida is a leading producer of citrus fruits. Caribbean and Central American countries depend on cash crops such as bananas, coffee, and sugar cane, often grown on large plantations. This reliance on a single crop can leave these countries vulnerable to fluctuating world crop prices.

Using the land and sea

- cropland
- forest
- ice cap
- mountain region
- pasture
- tundra
- wetland
- desert
- major conurbations
- cattle
- goats
- pigs
- poultry
- reindeer
- sheep
- bananas
- citrus fruits
- coffee
- corn (maize)
- cotton
- fishing
- fruit
- maple syrup
- peanuts
- rice
- shellfish
- soya beans
- sugar cane
- timber
- tobacco
- vineyards
- wheat

Land use map labels: ARCTIC OCEAN, Greenland, Bering Strait, Beaufort Sea, Baffin Bay, Bering Sea, Brooks Range, Mackenzie Mountains, Mackenzie, Gulf of Alaska, Aleutian Range, Rocky Mountains, Hudson Strait, Labrador Sea, Hudson Bay, Newfoundland, PACIFIC OCEAN, Edmonton, Vancouver, Calgary, Winnipeg, Great Lakes, Québec, St Lawrence, Montréal, Ottawa, Seattle, Portland, Saint Paul, Minneapolis, Milwaukee, Toronto, Buffalo, Boston, Cape Cod, Detroit, Cleveland, New York, Chicago, Toledo, Pittsburgh, Philadelphia, Columbus, Baltimore, Washington DC, Sacramento, San Francisco, Oakland, San Jose, Colorado, Denver, Kansas City, Indianapolis, Cincinnati, Louisville, Saint Louis, Nashville, Charlotte, Appalachian Mountains, Los Angeles, Albuquerque, Tulsa, Memphis, Atlanta, Phoenix, Oklahoma City, Arkansas, San Diego, Tucson, Dallas, Lower California, El Paso, Austin, Jacksonville, Houston, San Antonio, Mississippi Delta, Tampa, Rio Grande, Miami, Guadalajara, Monterrey, Havana, Mexico City, Gulf of Mexico, Yucatan Peninsula, San Juan, Santo Domingo, Caribbean Sea, Guatemala City, Managua, PACIFIC OCEAN, ATLANTIC OCEAN

NORTH AMERICA

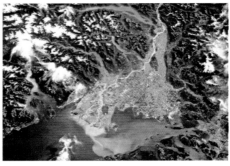

1 VANCOUVER, BRITISH COLUMBIA, CANADA
Canada's premier west coast city occupies the delta of the Fraser river, formed among the Coast Mountains.

2 MOUNT SAINT HELENS, WASHINGTON, USA
In 1980, this volcano's catastrophic eruption devastated 270 sq miles (700 sq km) of forest almost instantly.

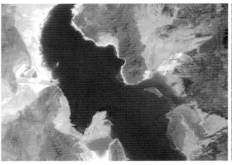

3 GREAT SALT LAKE, UTAH, USA
A causeway carries a railroad, blocking circulation between the northern and southern parts, the water reddened by bacteria in the more saline north.

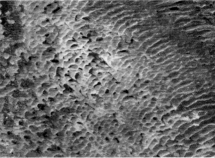

4 SAND HILLS, NEBRASKA, USA
Forming the largest sand sea in the Western Hemisphere, these hills are not classified as desert because today's relatively wet climate has allowed grasses to take hold.

9 LOS ANGELES AND LONG BEACH, CALIFORNTIA, USA
Taken together, these west coast cities constitute the busiest seaport in the United States.

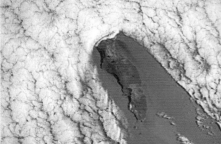

10 ISLA GUADALUPE, MEXICO
The volcanic island, 186 miles (300 km) off the west coast of Mexico, is a protected wildlife reserve.

11 GRAND CANYON, ARIZONA, USA
The 5250 ft (1600 m) deep canyon cuts through the Kaibab Plateau in this southwest-looking view.

12 DENVER, COLORADO, USA
Colorado's state capital nestles under the Rocky Mountains with the South Platte River running through its center.

BELCHER ISLANDS, NUNAVUT, CANADA 5
These low-lying, treeless, and sparsely-
populated islands lie icebound in Hudson Bay
for much of the year.

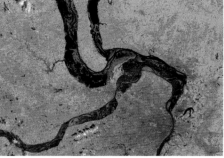

MISSISSIPPI, MISSOURI, AND ILLINOIS RIVERS, USA 6
This infrared image shows how these rivers burst their
banks in many places after heavy rains in the summer
of 1993, leading to the area's worst floods on record.

RÉSERVOIR MANICOUAGAN, QUÉBEC, CANADA 7
This unusual 62 mile (100 km) diameter annular
lake occupies the low ground between the rim
and central uplift of an ancient meteorite crater.

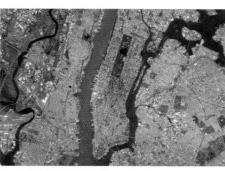

NEW YORK CITY, USA 8
The largest city in the United States, with
a population of over 8 million, it is also the
country's main financial center.

MISSISSIPPI RIVER DELTA, LOUISIANA, USA 13
This delta has developed a "bird's foot" shape
due to the shifting course of the river over
the last 6000 years.

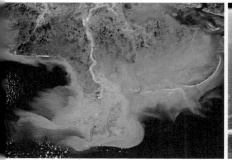

FLORIDA, USA 14
This low-lying, subtropical peninsula is home to
thousands of lakes that have formed among its
limestone "karst" topography.

HAVANA, CUBA 15
Cuba's capital city is home to 2 million
people and was founded by the Spanish in
1519 around a natural harbor.

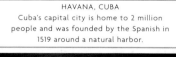

BARRIER REEF, BELIZE 16
The world's second-longest barrier reef lies
about 12 miles (20 km) off the coast of Belize.

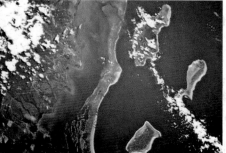

Canada

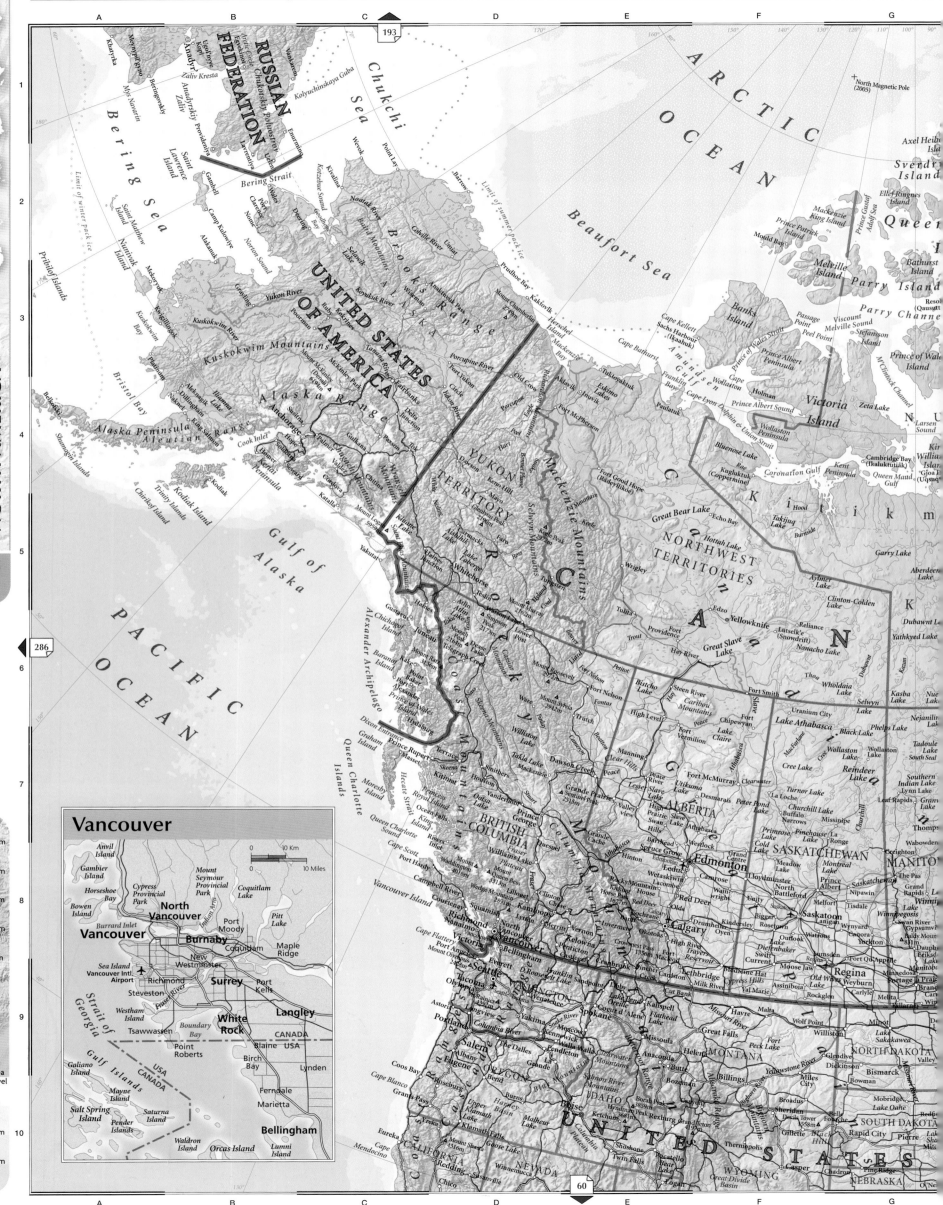

Northern Canada

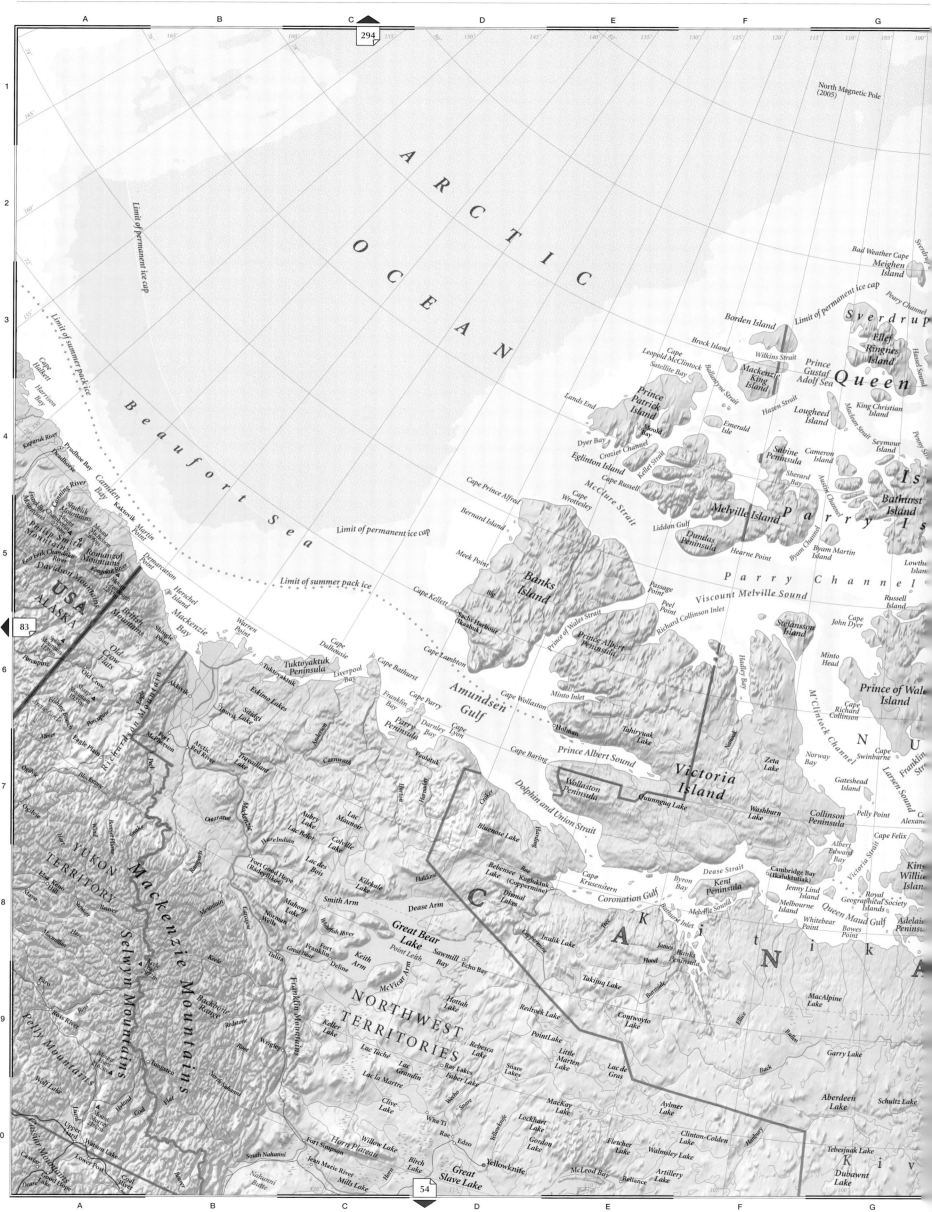

Scale 1:7,500,000
(projection: Lambert Conformal Conic)

0 25 50 75 100 125 150 175 200 Km
0 25 50 75 100 125 150 175 200 Miles

Population
■ above 5 million   ▣ 1 million to 5 million   ◉ 500,000 to 1 million
◎ 100,000 to 500,000   ⊕ 50,000 to 100,000   ○ 10,000 to 50,000   ∘ below 10,000

19,686ft
13,124ft
9843ft
6562ft
3281ft
1640ft
820ft
328ft
Sea Level
-820ft
-6562ft
-13,124ft

H   I   J   K   L   M   N

Cape Columbia
Cape Hecla
Cape Discovery
Alert
Cape Bicknor
British Empire Range
Hall Basin
Lake Hazen
Alert Point
Victoria and Albert Mountains
Kennedy Channel
Cape Bourne
Otto Fiord
Greely Fiord
North Geomagnetic Pole (2005)
Nares Strait
Kane Bassin
Cape Stallworthy
Nansen Sound
Agassiz Ice Cap
Princess Marie Bay
Bache Peninsula
Buchanan Bay
Cape Herschel
AVANNAARSUA
Knud Rasmussen Land
GREENLAND
(to Denmark)
TUNU

Axel Heiberg Island
Eureka
Fosheim Peninsula
Ellesmere Island
Qaanaaq
KITAA
Amund Ringnes Island
Elizabeth
Norwegian Bay
Bjorne Peninsula
Cape Dunsterville
Savissivik
Qimusseriarsuaq
Kullorsuaq
Cornwall Island
Smith Bay
Innaanganeq
Buckingham Island
Simmons Peninsula
Clarence Head
Belcher Channel
Grinnell Peninsula
Cape Norton Shaw
Grise Fiord (Aujuittuq)
Coburg Island
Upernavik
Queens Channel
Cape Storm
Jones Sound
Lady Ann Strait
Uummannaq
Baillie-Hamilton Island
Bear Bay
Cape Parker
lands
Cornwallis Island
Devon Island
Cape Sherard
Wellington Channel
Cape Warrender
Baffin Bay
Qeqertarsuaq
Resolute (Qausuittuq)
Barrow Strait
Lancaster Sound
Qeqertarsuaq Tunua
Qasigiannguit
Somerset Island
Cape York
Cape Crawford
Cape Byam Martin
Bylot Island
Cape Graham Moore
Sisimiut
Kong Frederik IX Land
Prince Regent Inlet
Admiralty Inlet
Arctic Bay
Navy Board Inlet
Pond Inlet
Pond Inlet (Mittimatalik)
Nova Zembla Island
N
Creswell Bay
Brodeur Peninsula
Borden Peninsula
Milne Inlet
Buchan Gulf
Cape Hunter
Cape Adair
Limit of summer pack ice
Gulf of Boothia
McBean Bay
Jungersen Bay
Gifford
Clyde River (Kangiqtugaapik)
Arctic Circle
Cape Scoresby
Bernier Bay
Berlinguet Inlet
Nina Bang Lake
Com Lake
Barnes Ice Cap
Bieler Lake
Cape Raper
Baffin Island
Bellot Strait
Boothia Peninsula
Cape Palmerston
Neergaard Lake
Lake Gillian
Cape Henry Kater
Home Bay
Kekertaluk Island
Davis Strait
Limit of winter pack ice
Krusenstern Lake
Cape Margaret
Crown Prince Frederick Island
Murray Maxwell Bay
Koch Island
Kangeeak Point
Qikiqtarjuaq
Auyuittuq National Park
Cape Dyer
Fury and Hecla Strait
Cape Englefield
Jens Munk Island
Bray Island
Baird Peninsula
Qikiqtarjuaq (Broughton Island)
Exeter Sound
Spence Bay
Taloyoak (Spence Bay)
Cape Kjer
Igloolik
Rowley Island
South Tweedsmuir Island
Cumberland Peninsula
Angijak Island
Matty Island
Cape Chapman
Hall Beach (Sanirajak)
Spicer Islands
Pangnirtung
Hoare Bay
Gjoa Haven (Uqsuqtuuq)
Lady Melville Lake
Simpson Peninsula
Parry Bay
Prince Charles Island
Air Force Island
Kingnait Fiord
Rasmussen Basin
Kugaaruk (Pelly Bay)
Committee Bay
Hall Lake
Taverner Bay
Nettilling Fiord
Cumberland Sound
Murchison
Wales Island
Melville Peninsula
Lemieux Islands
CANADA
Lefroy Bay
Koukdjuak
Nettilling Lake
Brevoort Island
Franklin Lake
Curtis
Rae Isthmus
Foxe Basin
Cape Dominion
Amadjuak Lake
Brown Lake
Repulse Bay
Lyon Inlet
Winter Island
Bowman Bay
Aukpar
Sylvia Grinnell Lake
Hall Peninsula
Buck
Wager Bay
Vansittart Island
Mingo Lake
Iqaluit (Frobisher Bay)
Frobisher Bay
Tehek Lake
Hansine Lake
White Island
Prescott Strait
Cape Dorchester
Finnie Bay
Foxe Peninsula
Blunt Peninsula
Loks Land
Southampton Island
Cape Bylot
Shukbuk Bay
Meta Incognita Peninsula
Edgell Island
Baker Lake
Cape Comfort
Foxe Channel
Cape Dorset (Kingait)
Markham Bay
Fair Ness
Kimmirut (Lake Harbour)
Big Island
Resolution Island
Quoich
Kivalliq
Seahorse Point
Salisbury Island
Gabriel Strait
Armit Lake
Southampton Island
Coral Harbour
Nottingham Island
Button Islands
Qamanittuaq
Duke Bay
Native Bay
Evans Strait
Digges Islands
Charles Island
Hudson Strait
Cape Chidley
Port Burwell
Killinek Island
Baker Lake
Chesterfield Inlet (Igluligaarjuk)
Cape Kendall
Fisher Strait
Nuvuk Islands
Deception
Kangiqsujuaq
Diana Bay
Cap Hopes Advance
Torngat Mountains
Peter Lake
Chesterfield Inlet
Bay of Gods Mercy
Coats Island
Cape Pembroke
Mansel Island
Ivujivik
Salluit
Whitley Bay
Quaqtaq
Akpatok Island
Ungava Bay
Cape Low
Péninsule d'Ungava   QUEBEC

295
58
Arctic Circle
295

Western Canada

Scale 1:7,500,000
(projection: Lambert Conformal Conic)

0 25 50 75 100 125 150 175 200 Km
0 25 50 75 100 125 150 175 200 Miles

Population
- ■ above 5 million
- ◎ 100,000 to 500,000
- ■ 1 million to 5 million
- ◎ 50,000 to 100,000
- ◉ 500,000 to 1 million
- ○ 10,000 to 50,000
- ○ below 10,000

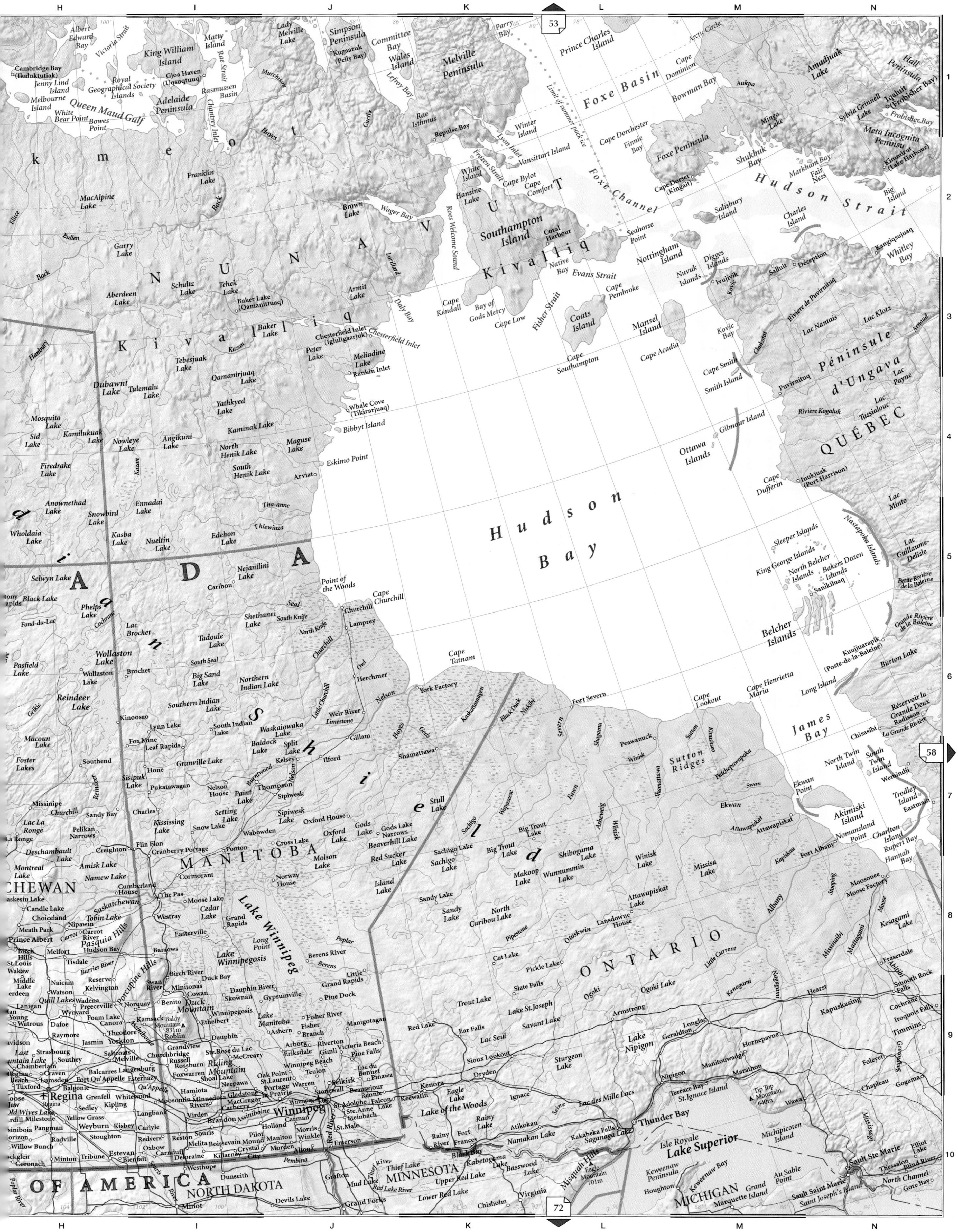

Elevation scale:
19,686ft · 13,124ft · 9843ft · 6562ft · 3281ft · 1640ft · 820ft · 328ft · Sea Level · -820ft · -6562ft · -13,124ft

Major water bodies and regions:
Hudson Bay · James Bay · Foxe Basin · Foxe Channel · Hudson Strait · Foxe Peninsula · Melville Peninsula · Southampton Island · Coats Island · Mansel Island · Belcher Islands · Queen Maud Gulf · Victoria Strait · Committee Bay · Roes Welcome Sound · Chesterfield Inlet · Péninsule d'Ungava

Territories / Provinces:
NUNAVUT · Kivalliq · CANADA · MANITOBA · ONTARIO · SASKATCHEWAN · QUÉBEC · UNITED STATES OF AMERICA · NORTH DAKOTA · MINNESOTA · MICHIGAN

Selected place names:
Cambridge Bay (Ikaluktutiak) · Melbourne Island · Gjoa Haven (Uqsuqtuuq) · King William Island · Repulse Bay · Coral Harbour · Rankin Inlet · Arviat · Eskimo Point · Churchill · Gillam · Thompson · Flin Flon · The Pas · Lynn Lake · Norway House · Gods Lake · Oxford House · Cross Lake · Island Lake · Red Lake · Pickle Lake · Sioux Lookout · Dryden · Kenora · Fort Severn · Attawapiskat · Fort Albany · Moosonee · Moose Factory · Kuujjuarapik (Poste-de-la-Baleine) · Inukjuak (Port Harrison) · Puvirnituq · Salluit · Kangiqsujuaq · Iqaluit (Frobisher Bay) · Kimmirut (Lake Harbour) · Cape Dorset (Kingait)

Regina · Winnipeg · Prince Albert · Portage la Prairie · Selkirk · Thunder Bay · Lake Superior · Lake Winnipeg · Lake Winnipegosis · Lake Manitoba · Lake of the Woods · Lake Nipigon · Reindeer Lake · Wollaston Lake · Lake Athabasca · Dubawnt Lake · Baker Lake (Qamanittuaq) · Southern Indian Lake · Sault Ste Marie

53 · 58 · 72

287

54

76

A **B** **C** **D** **E** **F** **G**

1
2
3
4
5
6
7
8
9
10

6000m
4000m
3000m
2000m
1000m
500m
250m
100m
Sea Level
-250m
-2000m
-4000m

Wrangell
Ketchikan
Mountain Point
Annette Island
Metlakatla
Duke Island
Revillagigedo Island
USA
ALASKA
Hyder
Stewart
Mount Pattullo 2776m
Meziadin Junction
Cranberry Junction
Prince Rupert
Port Edward
Porcher Island
Terrace
Skeena
Kitwanga
Hazelton
New Hazelton
Seven Sisters Peaks 2755m
Smithers
Telkwa
Granisle
Babine Lake
Houston
Burns Lake
Stuart Lake
Fort St.James
Kitimat
Banks Island
Kemano
Ootsa Lake
Fraser Lake
Vanderhoof
Nechako
Pitt Island
Princess Royal Island
Aristazabal Island
Eutsuk Lake
Prince George
Nazko
BRITISH COLUMBIA
Fraser Plateau
Quesnel
Barkerville
Ocean Falls
Bella Bella
King Island
Hagensborg
Bella Coola
Mount Saugstad 2908m
Anahim Lake
Likely
Marguerite
Namu
Monarch Mountain 3533m
Kleena Kleene
Alexis Creek
Burke Channel
Williams Lake
Rivers Inlet
Dawsons Landing
Rivers Inlet
Tatla Lake
Hanceville
Cariboo Mountains
Cape Caution
Mount Waddington 4016m
100 Mile House
Clearwater
Cape Scott
Mount Queen Bess 3313m
Little Fort
Queen Charlotte Strait
Port Hardy
Winter Harbour
Port McNeill
Port Alice
Knight Inlet
Telegraph Cove
Clinton
Barriere
Sayward
Mount Gilbert 3109m
Bute Inlet
Lillooet
Ashcroft
Cache Creek Thompson
Kamloops
Chase
Salmon Arm
Enderby
Cape Cook
Tahsis
Gold River
Campbell River
Courtenay
Comox
Powell River
Pemberton
Whistler
Wedge Mountain 2891m
Lytton
Merritt
Logan Lake
Armstrong
Vernon
Coldstream
Nootka Sound
Vancouver Island
Parksville
Strait of Georgia
Sechelt
Gibsons
Squamish
Boston Bar
Okanagan Lake
Westbank
Kelowna
Tofino
Port Alberni
Nanaimo
Richmond
North Vancouver
Vancouver
Burnaby
Hope
Princeton
Peachland
Summerland
Penticton
Ucluelet
Ladysmith
Lake Cowichan
Langley
Chilliwack
Bamfield
Barkley Sound
Duncan
Swartz Bay
Blaine
Lynden
Sumas
Abbotsford
Deming
Ferndale
Oliver
Osoyoos
Port Renfrew
Cape Flattery
Neah Bay
Victoria
Esquimalt
San Juan Islands
Friday Harbor
Newhalem
Grand Forks
Rossland
Trail
Northport
Clallam Bay
Strait of Juan de Fuca
Bellingham
Anacortes
Skagit River
Rockport
Mount Logan 2770m
Mazama
Winthrop
Republic
Oroville
Tonasket
Mount Bonaparte 2212m
Orient
PACIFIC OCEAN
Forks
Olympic Mountains
Mount Olympus 2428m
Oak Harbor
Port Angeles
Port Townsend
Sequim
Coupeville
Mount Vernon
Stanwood
Arlington
Darrington
Glacier Peak 3213m
UNITED ST
Lake Chelan
Pateros
Franklin D. Roosevelt Lake
Hunters
Queets
Quinault River
Marysville
WASHINGTON
Chewelah
Colville
Deer Park
Moclips
Quinault
Bremerton
Port Orchard
Bellevue
Seattle
Edmonds
Redmond
Kent
Auburn
Skykomish
Leavenworth
Entiat
Columbia River
Grand Coulee
Banks Lake
Wilbur
Spokane River
Spokane
Tahola
Humptulips
Seattle-Tacoma
Tacoma
Puyallup
Shelton
Monroe
Green River
Wenatchee
Coulee City
Davenport
Cheney
Pacific Beach
Copalis Beach
Crab Creek
Ephrata
Roslyn
Odessa
Sprague
COAST
Skeena Mountains
Omineca Mountains
Williston Lake
ROCKY
Great Snow Mountain 2896m
Tuchit
Beatton River
Sikanni Chief
Sikanni Chief
Pink Mountain
Clear Hills
Chinchaga
Twin Rivers
Manning
Sustut Peak 2470m
Mackenzie
Ping Pass 869m
Finlay
Findlay
Ware
Wonowon
Cameron
Fort St.John
Hudson's Hope
Chetwynd
Taylor
Peace
Hines Creek
Grimshaw
McLeod Lake
Beatton
Dawson Creek
Spirit River
Fairview
Tupper
Hythe
Beaverlodge
Wembley
Sexsmith
Grande Prairie
Sentinel Peak 2515m
Tumbler Ridge
Wapiti
Sinclair Mills
Mount Sir Alexander 3274m
Grande Cache
Smoky
Little Smoky
Stuart
Columbia
McBride
Fraser
Mount Robson 3954m
Tete Jaune Cache
Mount Sir Wilfrid Laurier 3505m
Yellowhead Pass 1131m
Jasper
Jasper National Park
Hinton
Valemount
Kinbasket Lake
Mount Columbia 3741m
Blue River
Mica Creek
SELKIRK
MOUNTAINS
Rogers Pass 1327m
Glacier
Revelstoke
Sicamous
Nakusp
New Denver
Nelson
Castlegar
Kettle Falls
McCall Falls
Grand Coulee
Davenport
Columbia
Mountains

A **B** **C** **D** **E** **F** **G**

Scale 1:3,750,000
(projection: Lambert Azimuthal Equal Area)

0 20 40 60 80 100 Km
0 20 40 60 80 100 Miles

Population
■ above 5 million
◉ 100,000 to 500,000
◙ 1 million to 5 million
⊕ 50,000 to 100,000
◉ 500,000 to 1 million
◉ 10,000 to 50,000
○ below 10,000

Elevation scale:
19,686ft
13,124ft
9843ft
6562ft
3281ft
1640ft
820ft
328ft
Sea Level
-820ft
-6562ft
-13,124ft

CANADA

ALBERTA

SASKATCHEWAN

Great Plains

Birch Mountains
Peace River
Wabasca
Athabasca
Richardson
Clearwater
Fort MacKay
Fort McMurray
La Loche
Turnor Lake
Cree Lake
Reindeer Lake
Foster Lakes
Macoun Lake
Southend

Donnelly
McLennan
Gift Lake
Utikuma Lake
Desmarais
Sandy Lake
Conklin
Peter Pond Lake
Churchill Lake
Buffalo Narrows
Ile-a-la-Crosse
Pinehouse Lake
Missinipe
Churchill
Pelikan Narrows

High Prairie
Kinuso
Lesser Slave Lake
Faust
Slave Lake
Smith
Hondo
Calling Lake
Primrose Lake
Beauval
La Ronge
Lac La Ronge
Deschambault Lake

Valleyview
Little Smoky
Wallace Mountain 1259m
Swan Hills
Athabasca
Boyle
Lac La Biche
Cold Lake
Doré Lake
Green Lake
Montreal Lake

Fox Creek
Whitecourt
Barrhead
Westlock
Smoky Lake
Grand Centre
Bonnyville
Cold Lake
Pierceland
Meadow Lake
Big River
Waskesiu Lake
Candle Lake
Choiceland
Nipawin
Tobin Lake

Mayerthorpe
Redwater
Morinville
Willingdon
St.Paul
Elk Point
St.Walburg
Meath Park
Carrot River

Edson
Evansburg
Spruce Grove
Fort Saskatchewan
St.Albert
Two Hills
Marwayne
Turtleford
Glaslyn
Spiritwood
Shellbrook
Prince Albert
Birch Hills
Melfort
Tisdale

Edmonton
Stony Plain
Devon
Sherwood Park
Mundare
Vegreville
Vermilion
Lloydminster
Lashburn
Maidstone
Blaine Lake
St.Louis
Carrot

Drayton Valley
Leduc
Tofield
Mannville
North Saskatchewan
Rosthern
Waldheim

Little Smoky
Wetaskiwin
Camrose
Viking
Wainwright
Marsden
Cut Knife
Battleford
North Battleford
Hafford
Duck Lake
Wakaw
Middle Lake
Naicam
Watson

Nordegg
Rimbey
Ponoka
Bashaw
Daysland
Killam
Hardisty
Unity
Wilkie
Borden
Martensville
Aberdeen
Quill Lakes

Rocky Mountain House
Bentley
Sylvan Lake
Lacombe
Battle
Provost
Macklin
Saskatoon
Lanigan

Red Deer
Stettler
Castor
Coronation
Consort
Biggar
Delisle
Allan
Young
Dafoe
Wynyard

Innisfail
Delburne
Kerrobert
Smiley
Kindersley
Rosetown
Dundurn
Watrous
Raymore

Sundre
Olds
Trochu
Three Hills
Hanna
Youngstown
Alsask
Outlook
Davidson
Last Mountain Lake
Strasbourg

Red Deer
Kicking Horse Pass 1627m
Lake Louise
Didsbury
Carstairs
Morrin
Drumheller
Oyen
Eatonia
Eston
Elrose
Elbow
Chamberlain
Southey

Golden
Crossfield
Beiseker
Airdrie
Calgary
Strathmore
Red Deer
Riverhurst
Regina Beach
Craven
Lumsden

Calgary
Banff
Canmore
Cochrane
Leader
South Saskatchewan
Lake Diefenbaker
Tuxford
Moose Jaw
Regina
Qu'Appelle
Balgonie

Mount Assiniboine 3618m
Turner Valley
Okotoks
Bassano
Fox Valley
Cabri
Stewart Valley
Herbert
Chaplin

Regina

Radium Hot Springs
Invermere
Black Diamond
High River
Brooks
Swift Current
Hodgeville
Ardill
Milestone

Kaslo
Crawford Bay
Nanton
Vulcan
Bow City
Suffield
Tompkins
Gull Lake
Gravelbourg
Assiniboia
Horizon
Pangman

Elkford
Sparwood
Claresholm
Vauxhall
Redcliff
Walsh
Maple Creek
Cadillac
Ponteix
Lafleche
Willow Bunch
Minton

Kimberley
Crowsnest Pass 1356m
Coleman
Fort Macleod
Taber
Bow Island
Medicine Hat
Shaunavon
Val Marie
Rockglen
Coronach

Cranbrook
Fernie
Pincher Creek
Coaldale
Lethbridge
Cypress Hills
Eastend
Mankota
Robsart

Creston
Kingsgate
Roosville
Raymond
Magrath
Foremost
Climax

Purcell Mountains
Rocky Mountains
Columbia Icefield

Cardston
Milk River
Wild Horse
Loring
Opheim
Scobey

UNITED STATES OF AMERICA

MONTANA

IDAHO

Mount Cleveland 3190m
Babb
Sweetgrass
Sunburst
Mount Brown 2121m
Rudyard
Gildford
Havre
Harlem
Malta
Glasgow
Nashua
Wolf Point
Poplar

Bonners Ferry
Moyie Springs
Eureka
Logan Pass 2026m
Cut Bank
Shelby
Chester
Lothair
Chinook
Dodson
Milk River
Fort Peck

Priest Lake
Libby
Whitefish
Columbia Falls
Browning
Marias River
Big Sandy
Baldy Mountain 2018m
Fort Peck Lake
Vida

Sandpoint
Snowshoe Peak 2655m
Kalispell
Lake Elwell
Conrad
Missouri River
Circle

Coeur d'Alene
Cabinet Mountains
Trout Creek
Somers
Bigfork
Rocky Mountain 2863m
Choteau
Teton River
Fort Benton
Piney Buttes

Coeur d'Alene Lake
Flathead Lake
Hungry Horse Reservoir
Winifred
Jordan

Kellogg
Wallace
Mullan
Thompson Falls
Plains
Ronan
Polson
Fairfield

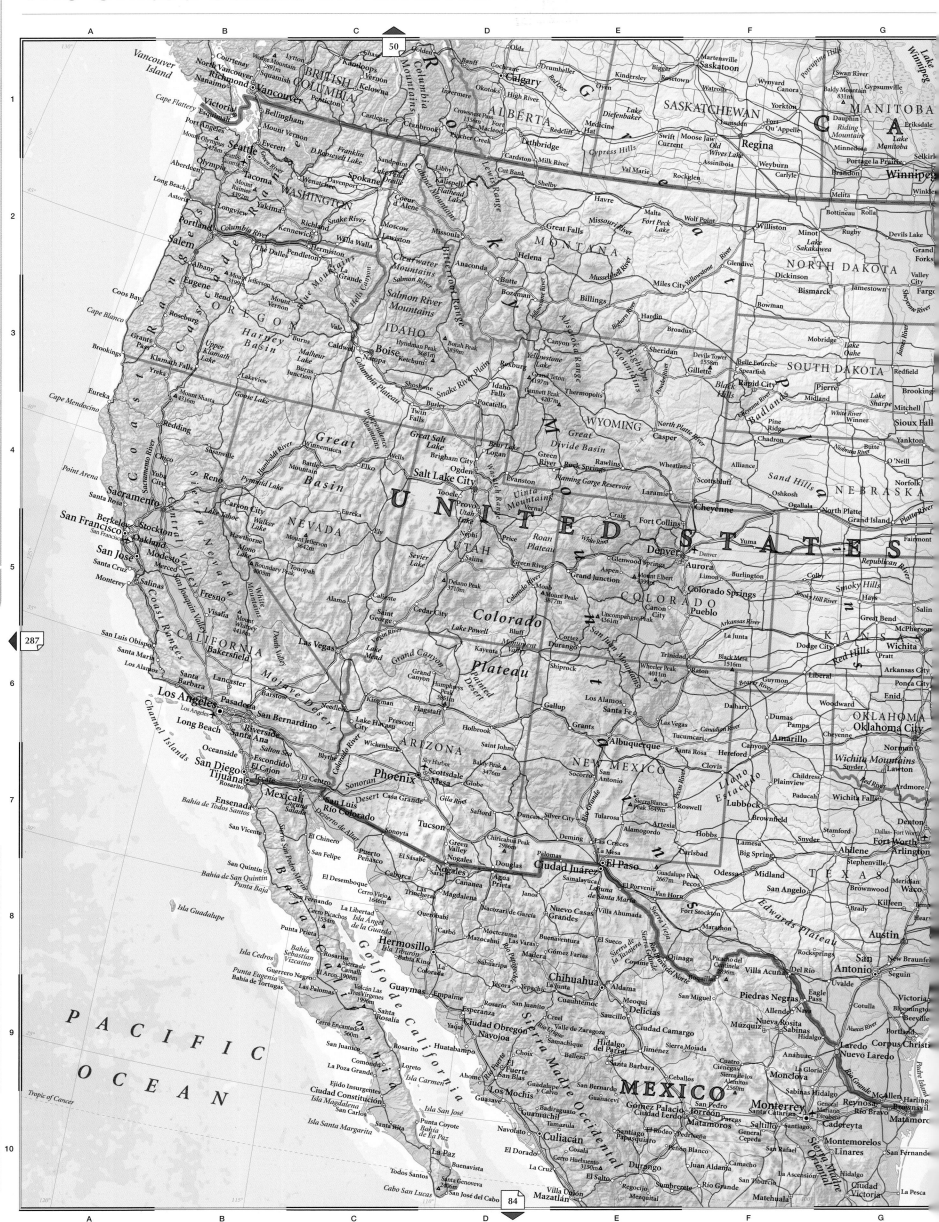

Scale 1:3,000,000
(projection: Lambert Conformal Conic)

0 20 40 60 80 100 Km
0 20 40 60 80 100 Miles

Population
■ above 5 million
◉ 100,000 to 500,000
□ 1 million to 5 million
⊕ 50,000 to 100,000
◉ 500,000 to 1 million
○ 10,000 to 50,000
○ below 10,000

NORTH AMERICA

63

H I J K L M N

Québec

QUÉBEC

Laurentian Mountains

Monts Notre Dame

Reservoir Blanc
Lac Manouane
Lac Devenyns
Lac Mékinac
La Croche
Lac-Édouard
La Tuque
St-Hilarion
Lac Pohénégamook
Rivière-Bleue
Dégelis
Édmundston
Baie-St-Paul
Petite-Rivière-St-François
La Pocatière
St-Pacôme
Madawaska
St-Léonard
Fort Kent
Van Buren
Grand Falls
Plaster Rock

NEW BRUNSWICK

Miramichi
Newcastle
Chatham
Laketon
Tignish
Neguac
Mount Carleton 820m
Nepisiguit
Bouctouche
Sackville
Amherst
Shediac
Moncton
Riverview
Fredericton

NOVA SCOTIA

Bay of Fundy
Minas Basin
Digby
Bridgetown
Middleton
Kentville
Berwick
Springhill
Lake Rossignol
Liverpool
Shelburne
Cape Sable
Clark's Harbour
Yarmouth
Port Maitland
Church Point
Glenwood

MAINE

Mount Katahdin 1605m
Moosehead Lake
Chamberlain Lake
Eagle Lake
Churchill Lake
Fish River Lake
Chesuncook Lake
Caribou
Presque Isle
Fort Fairfield
Houlton
Millinocket
Lincoln
Bangor
Brewer
Hampden
Augusta
Waterville
Skowhegan
Old Town
Milford
Ellsworth
Bar Harbor
Mount Desert Island
Machias
Eastport
Lubec
Calais
St. Stephen
West Grand Lake
Big Lake
Grand Manan Island

Gulf of Maine

NEW HAMPSHIRE
Mount Washington 1917m
White Mountains
Concord
Manchester
Nashua
Portsmouth
Keene
Berlin

VERMONT
Green Mountains
Mount Mansfield 1339m
Montpelier
Burlington
Rutland
Lake Champlain

Montréal
Laval
Sorel
Trois-Rivières
Drummondville
Sherbrooke
Granby
St-Hyacinthe
Victoriaville
Thetford-Mines

MASSACHUSETTS
Boston
Cambridge
Worcester
Springfield
Lowell
Lawrence
Pittsfield
Massachusetts Bay

Cape Cod
Cape Cod Bay
Provincetown
Nantucket Island
Martha's Vineyard
Nantucket
Buzzards Bay
New Bedford
Fall River
Plymouth

RHODE ISLAND
Providence
Newport
Warwick

CONNECTICUT
Hartford
New Haven
Bridgeport
Waterbury
Stamford
Norwalk
New London

Long Island Sound
Long Island
NEW YORK
New York
New Rochelle
Yonkers
Jersey City
Newark
Albany
Troy
Schenectady

ATLANTIC OCEAN

Lake Champlain
Lake George

Boston (inset)

Pinehurst
Reading
Wakefield
Peabody
Salem
Salem Maritime N.H.S.
Beverly
Marblehead
Woburn
Melrose
Saugus
Lynn
Lynn Woods Reserve
Swampscott
Tinkers Island
Winchester
Middlesex Park Reserve
Medford
Malden
Revere
Nahant Bay
Lexington
Arlington
Everett
Chelsea
Winthrop
Broad Sound
East Point
Lincoln
Somerville
Bunker Hill Monument
Logan International Airport
Massachusetts Bay
Waltham
Watertown
Cambridge
Quincy Market
Boston Harbor
John F. Kennedy N.H.S.
Newton
Boston
Brewster Islands
Brookline
Franklin Park
Point Allerton
Wellesley
Quincy Bay
Hingham Bay
Needham
Charles River
Milton
Neponset
Quincy
Adams N.H.S.
Dedham
Weymouth
Norwood
Braintree

0 4 Km
0 4 Miles

19,686ft
13,124ft
9843ft
6562ft
3281ft
1640ft
820ft
328ft
Sea Level
-820ft
-6562ft
-13,124ft

59
290
91

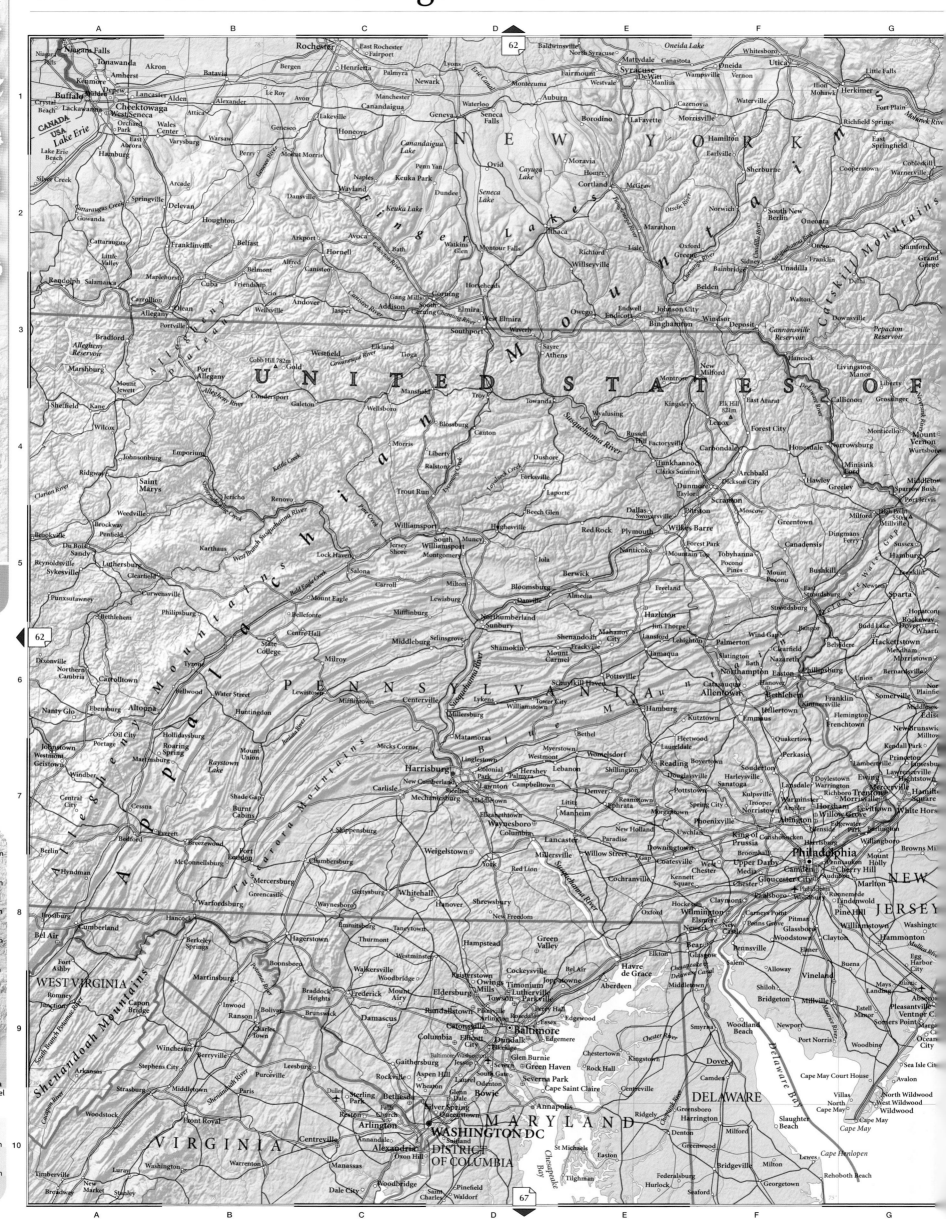

Scale 1:3,000,000
(projection: Lambert Conformal Conic)

0 20 40 60 80 100 Km
0 20 40 60 80 100 Miles

Population
- ■ above 5 million
- ■ 1 million to 5 million
- ◉ 500,000 to 1 million
- ◎ 100,000 to 500,000
- ● 50,000 to 100,000
- ● 10,000 to 50,000
- ○ below 10,000

PENNSYLVANIA

OHIO

WEST VIRGINIA

VIRGINIA

MARYLAND

DELAWARE

NEW JERSEY

DISTRICT OF COLUMBIA

WASHINGTON DC

Baltimore

Philadelphia

Pittsburgh

Harrisburg

Richmond

NORTH CAROLINA

Raleigh

Charlotte

Greensboro

Winston Salem

Durham

Asheville

SOUTH CAROLINA

Columbia

Charleston

GEORGIA

Savannah

APPALACHIAN MOUNTAINS

UNITED STATES OF AMERICA

Chesapeake Bay

Albemarle Sound

Pamlico Sound

Cape Hatteras

Hatteras Island

Ocracoke Island

Roanoke Island

Cape Lookout

Cape Fear

Long Bay

Raleigh Bay

Onslow Bay

ATLANTIC OCEAN

Assateague Island

Delaware Bay

Cape May

Cape Henlopen

BERMUDA (to UK)

St George's Island
St Catherine Point
St George
Kindley Field
Castle Harbour
St David's Island
Ireland Island North
Commissioner's Point
Harrington Sound
Tucker's Town
Ireland Island South
Spanish Point
Flatts Village
Somerset Island
Great Sound
Little Sound
Somerset
HAMILTON
Gibbs Hill 73m

Scale 1:500,000
0 2.5 5 Km
0 2.5 5 Miles

ATLANTIC OCEAN

19,686ft
13,124ft
9843ft
6562ft
3281ft
1640ft
820ft
328ft
Sea Level
-820ft
-6562ft
-13,124ft

62

69

290

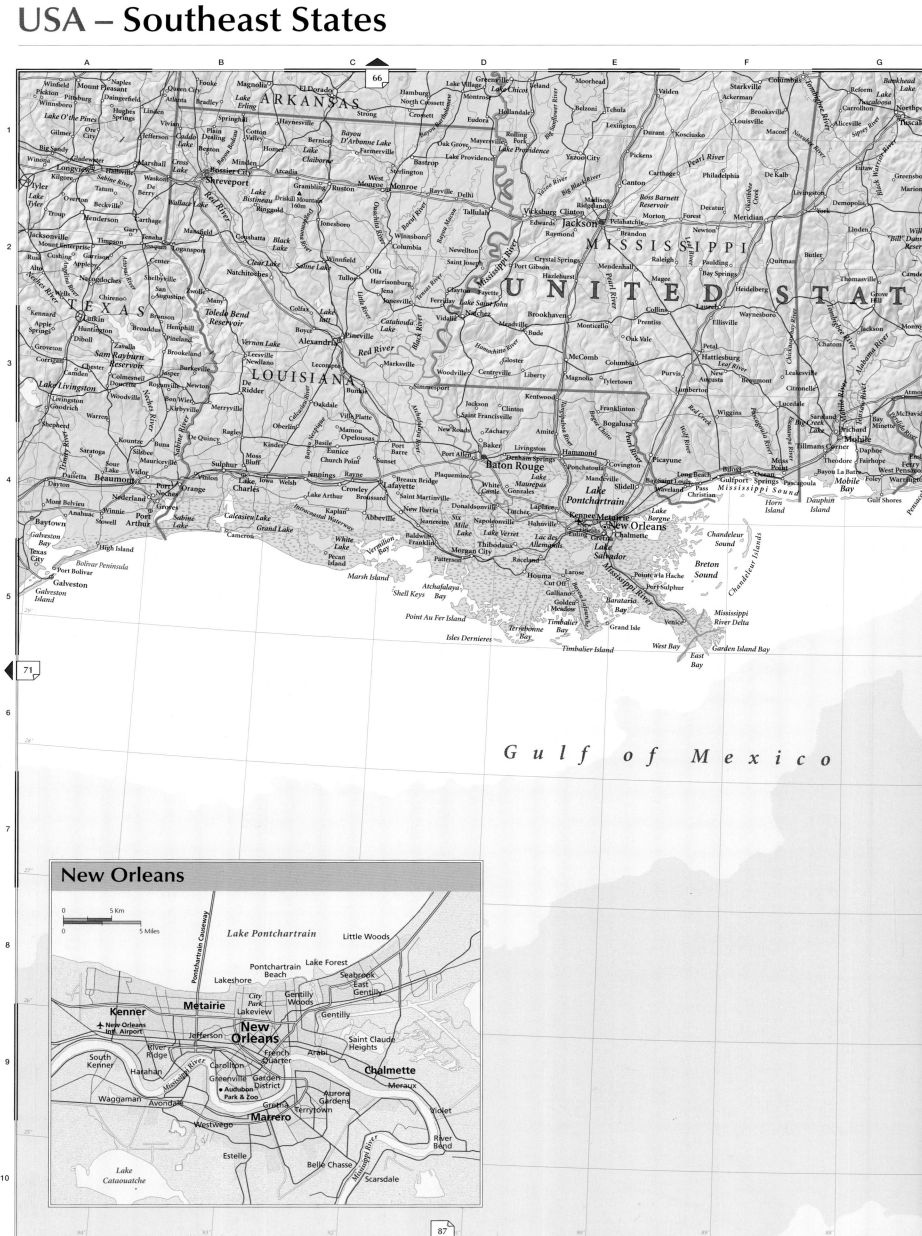

NORTH AMERICA

New Orleans

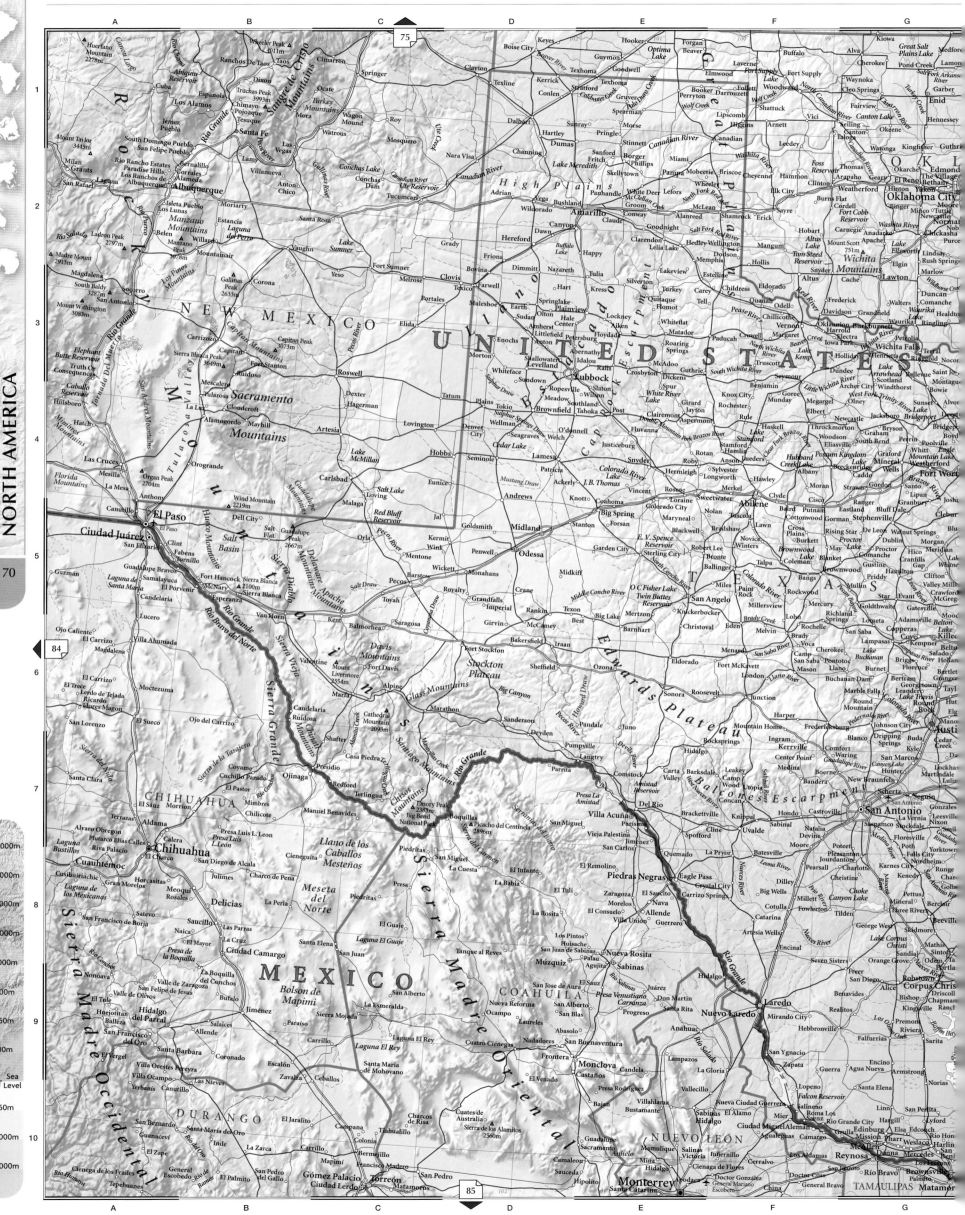

Scale 1:3,750,000
(projection: Lambert Conformal Conic)

0 20 40 60 80 100 Km
0 20 40 60 80 100 Miles

Population
- ■ above 5 million
- ▣ 1 million to 5 million
- ◉ 500,000 to 1 million
- ◎ 100,000 to 500,000
- ⊕ 50,000 to 100,000
- ⊙ 10,000 to 50,000
- ○ below 10,000

Gulf of Mexico

State labels: MISSOURI, TENNESSEE, ARKANSAS, MISSISSIPPI, ALABAMA, LOUISIANA, OKLAHOMA, OF AMERICA

Physiographic labels: Ozark Plateau, Boston Mountains, Ouachita Mountains, Kiamichi Mountains, Caddo Mountains, Crowley's Ridge, Mississippi River, Red River, Arkansas River, White River

Major cities: Tulsa, Dallas, Fort Worth, Little Rock, Memphis, Nashville, Shreveport, Jackson, Monroe, Baton Rouge, New Orleans, Houston, Galveston, Beaumont, Lafayette, Lake Charles, Corpus Christi, Victoria

Houston (inset)

Houston Intl. Airport, Lake Houston, North Houston, Mount Houston, Alexander Deusen Park, San Jacinto River, George Bush Park, Bunker Hill Village, Antique Car Museum, Anheuser-Busch Brewery, Jacinto City, Channelview, Highlands, Contemporary Art Museum, Museum of Fine Arts, Houston, Galena Park, Buffalo Bayou, Battleship Texas, Baytown, Bellaire West, Bellaire, Zoo, Pasadena, Sugar Land, South Houston, La Porte, William P. Hobby Airport, Missouri City, Pearland, Johnson Space Ctr. & Space Center Houston, Seabrook, Clear Lake, Friendswood, Galveston Bay

Elevation scale: 19,686ft, 13,124ft, 9843ft, 6562ft, 3281ft, 1640ft, 820ft, 328ft, Sea Level, -820ft, -6562ft, -13,124ft

75   79   87

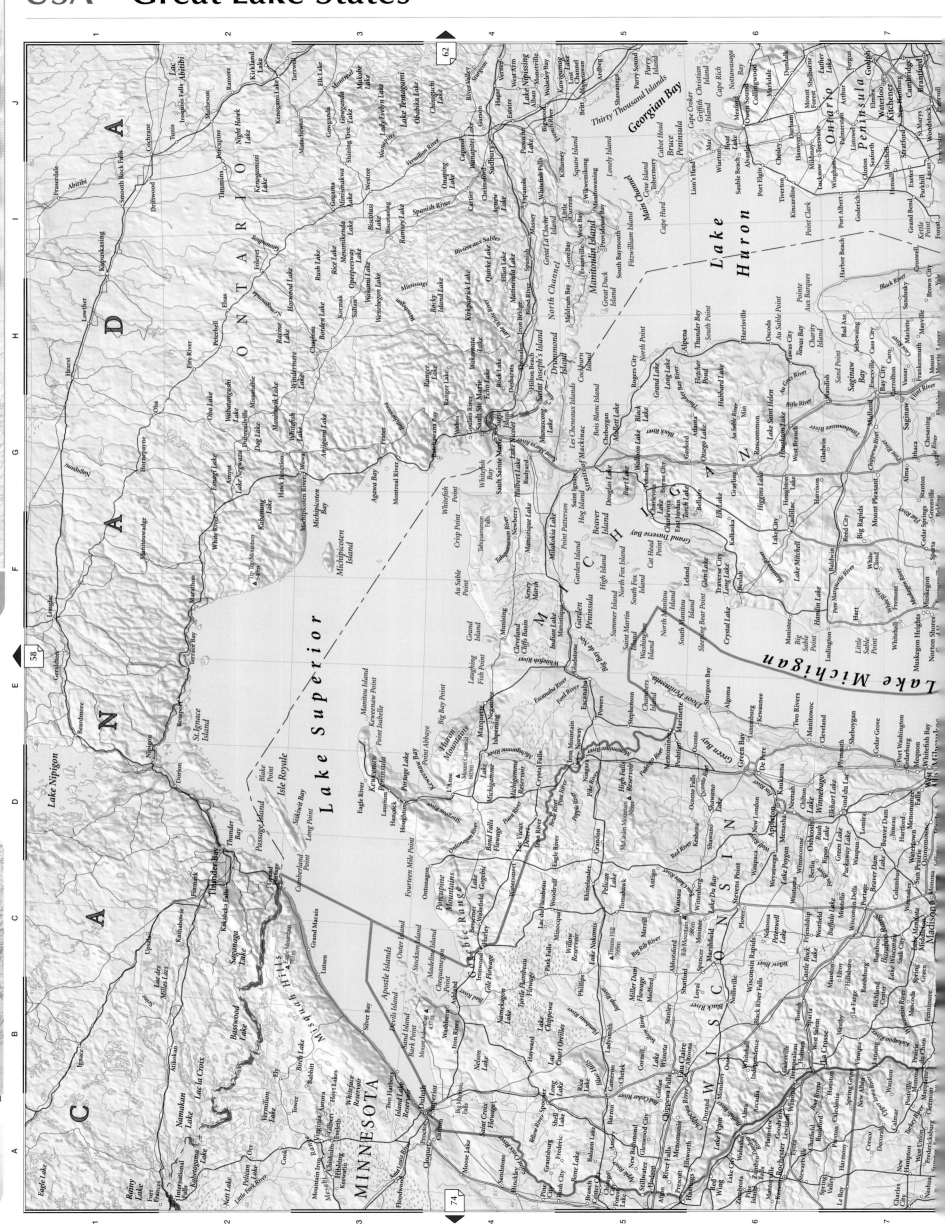

Scale 1:3,000,000
(projection: Lambert Conformal Conic)

Population
- above 5 million
- 1 million to 5 million
- 500,000 to 1 million
- 100,000 to 500,000
- 50,000 to 100,000
- 10,000 to 50,000
- below 10,000

NORTH AMERICA

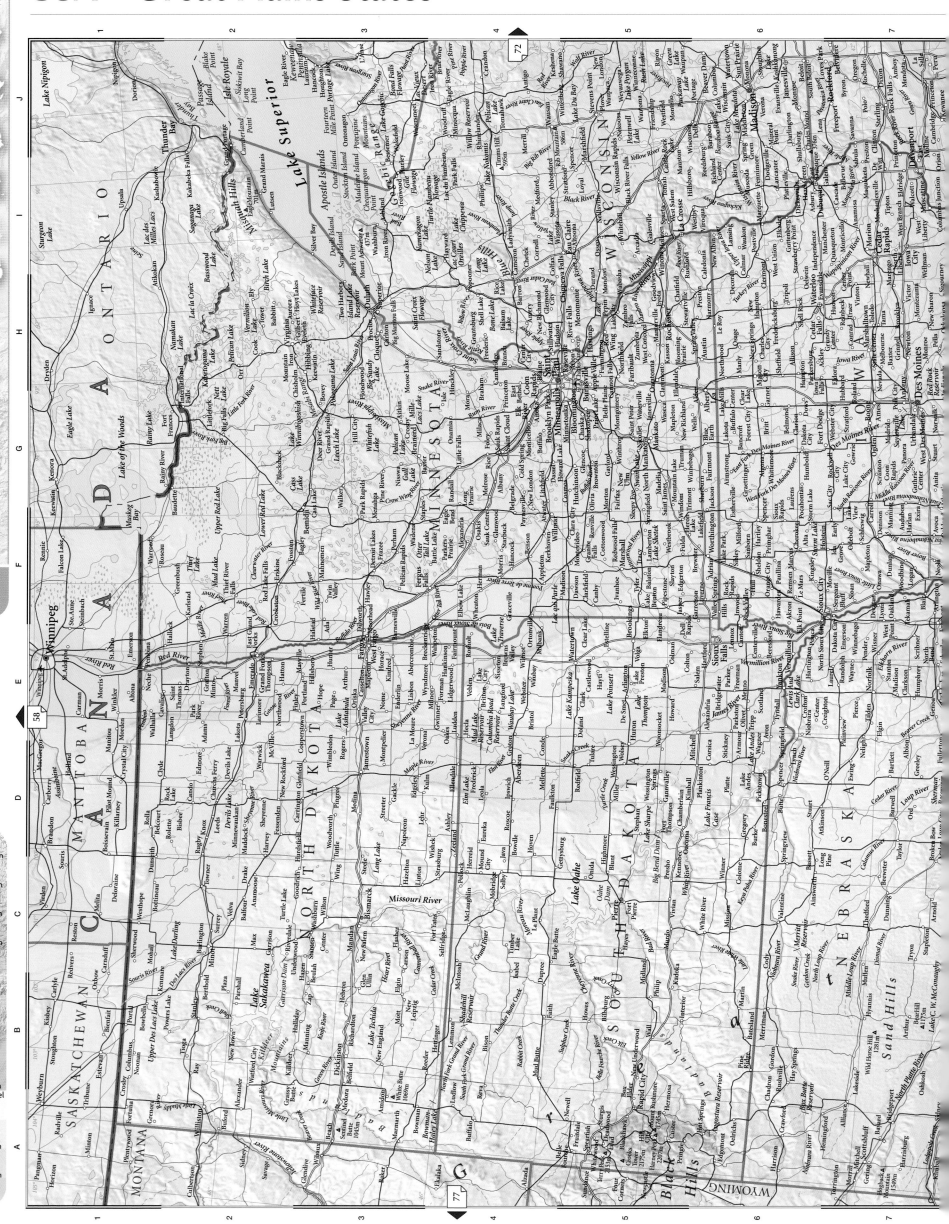

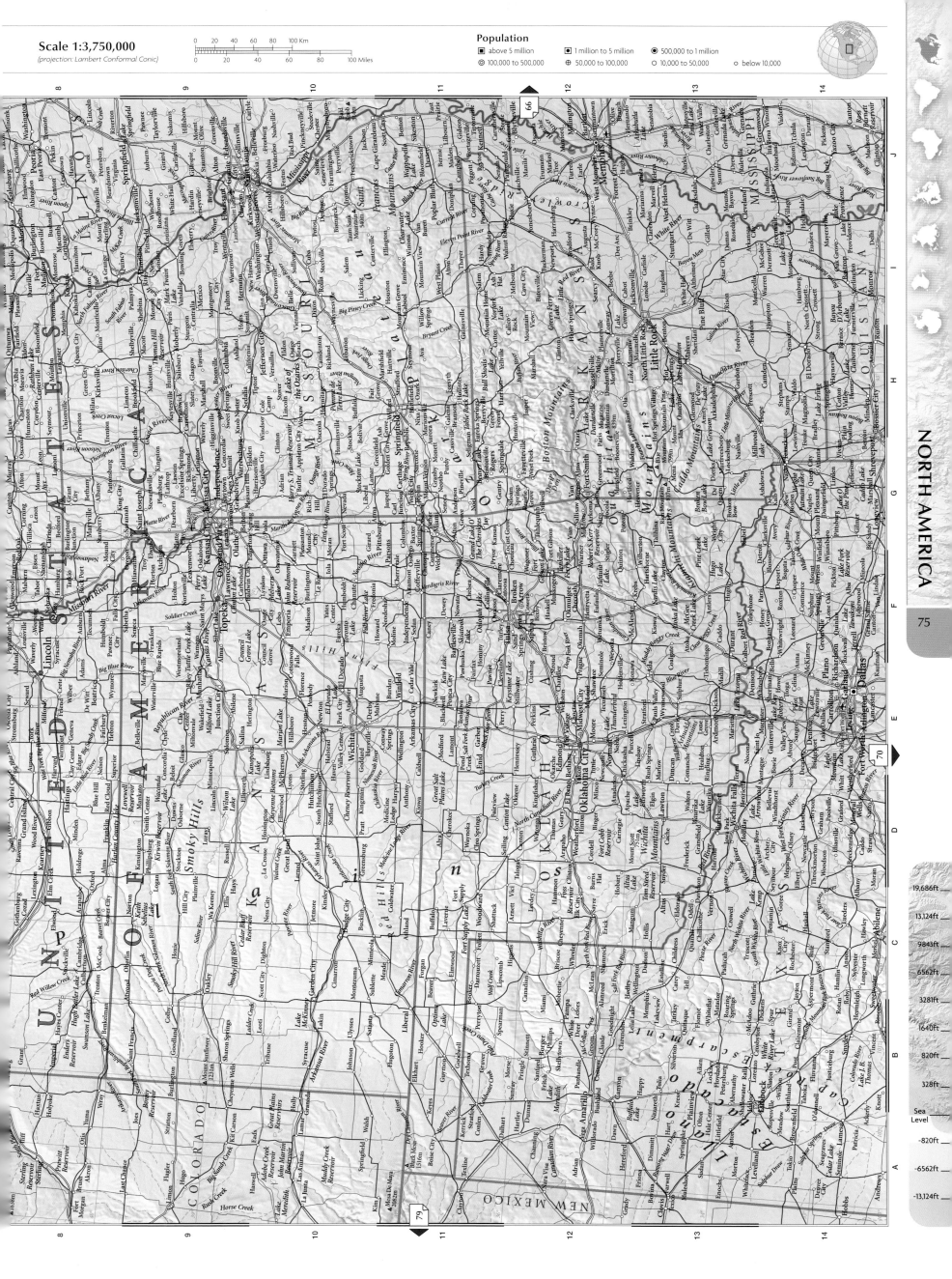

Scale 1:3,750,000
(projection: Lambert Conformal Conic)

0 20 40 60 80 100 Km
0 20 40 60 80 100 Miles

Population

■ above 5 million   ■ 1 million to 5 million   ◉ 500,000 to 1 million
◎ 100,000 to 500,000   ⊕ 50,000 to 100,000   ○ 10,000 to 50,000   ○ below 10,000

19,686ft
13,124ft
9843ft
6562ft
3281ft
1640ft
820ft
328ft
Sea
Level
-820ft
-6562ft
-13,124ft

56
78
287

NORTH AMERICA

76

PACIFIC OCEAN

BRITISH COLUMBIA

WASHINGTON

OREGON

IDAHO

CALIFORNIA

NEVADA

UNITED STATES

Vancouver Island

Coast Mountains

Columbia Basin

Cascade Range

Coast Range

Olympic Mountains

Salmon River Mountains

Clearwater Mountains

Blue Mountains

Harney Basin

Great Basin

Snake River Plateau

Sierra Nevada

Klamath Mountains

Siskiyou Mountains

Cabinet Mountains

Selkirk Mountains

Purcell Mountains

Sawtooth Range

Santa Rosa Range

Independence Mountains

Ruby Mountains

Warner Mountains

Trinity Range

Stillwater Range

Sacramento Valley

Major cities and towns:

Calgary, Vancouver, Victoria, Seattle, Tacoma, Olympia, Spokane, Portland, Salem, Eugene, Boise, Redding

Strait of Georgia, Strait of Juan de Fuca, Puget Sound, Columbia River, Snake River, Willamette River, Humboldt River

Mount Baker 3285m, Mount Rainier 4392m, Mount Saint Helens 2549m, Mount Adams 3741m, Mount Hood 3424m, Mount Jefferson 3199m, Three Sisters 3157m, Mount Shasta 4316m, Lassen Peak 3187m, Glacier Peak 3213m

Scale 1:3,750,000
(projection: Lambert Conformal Conic)

0 20 40 60 80 100 Km
0 20 40 60 80 100 Miles

Population

- above 5 million
- 1 million to 5 million
- 500,000 to 1 million
- 100,000 to 500,000
- 50,000 to 100,000
- 10,000 to 50,000
- below 10,000

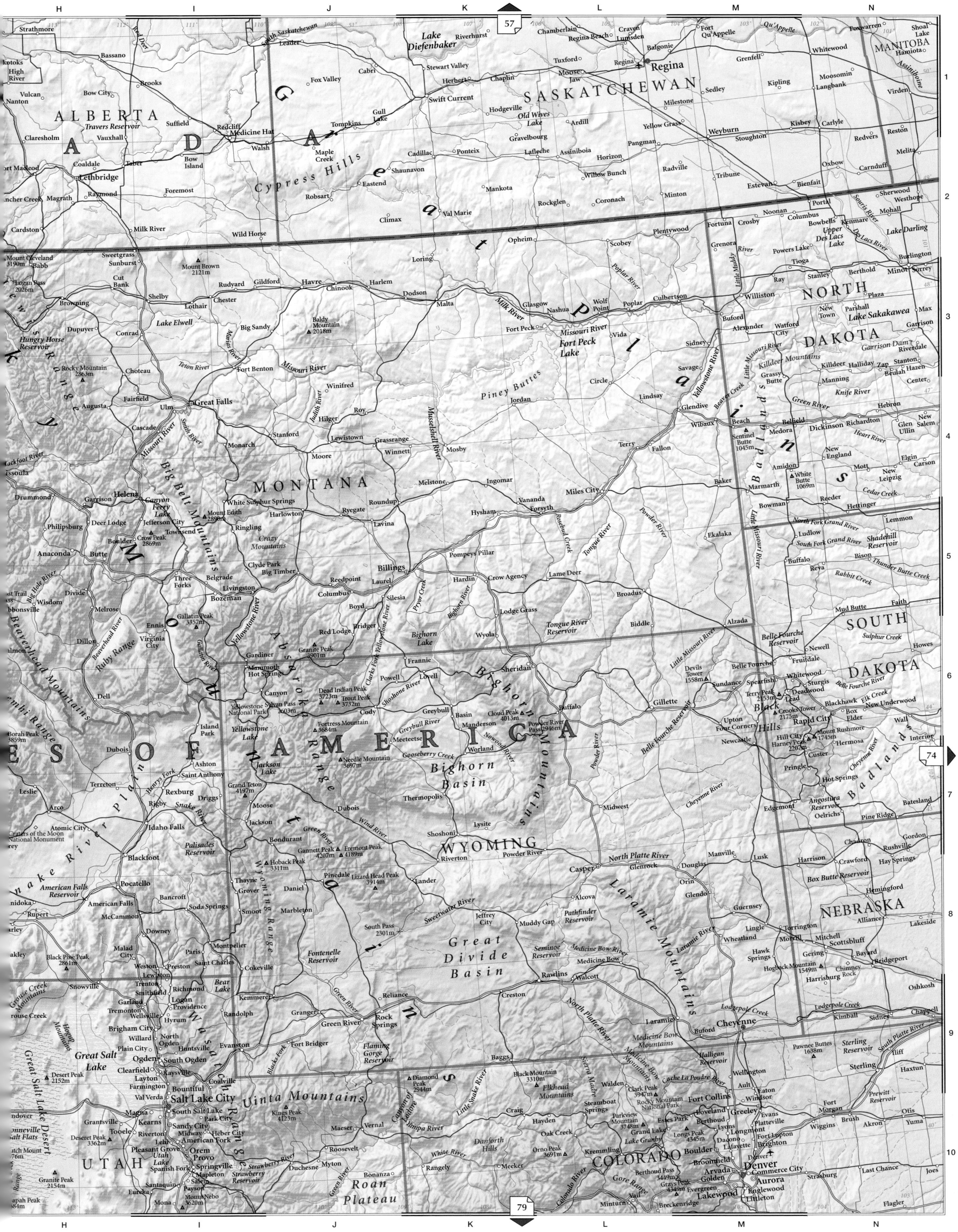

H I J K L M N
57
74
79
1 2 3 4 5 6 7 8 9 10
ALBERTA
SASKATCHEWAN
MANITOBA
MONTANA
NORTH DAKOTA
SOUTH DAKOTA
WYOMING
NEBRASKA
COLORADO
UTAH
G r e a t P l a i n s
C A N A D A
U N I T E D S T A T E S O F A M E R I C A
R o c k y M o u n t a i n s
Regina
Moose Jaw
Swift Current
Medicine Hat
Lethbridge
Lake Diefenbaker
Cypress Hills
Weyburn
Estevan
Great Falls
Helena
Butte
Bozeman
Billings
Miles City
Glendive
Williston
Minot
Lake Sakakawea
Fort Peck Lake
Missouri River
Milk River
Yellowstone River
Badlands
Black Hills
Rapid City
Bighorn Basin
Bighorn Mountains
Absaroka Range
Yellowstone Lake
Yellowstone National Park
Grand Teton 4197m
Wind River
Gannett Peak 4207m
Casper
Laramie Mountains
North Platte River
Great Divide Basin
Rawlins
Rock Springs
Laramie
Cheyenne
Fort Collins
Boulder
Denver
Aurora
Lakewood
Great Salt Lake
Great Salt Lake Desert
Ogden
Salt Lake City
Provo
Uinta Mountains
Wasatch Range
Idaho Falls
Pocatello
Snake River Plain
Roan Plateau
Medicine Bow Mountains
Scottsbluff
Sidney
Devils Tower 1558m
Crazy Mountains
Big Belt Mountains
Piney Buttes
19,686ft
13,124ft
9843ft
6562ft
3281ft
1640ft
820ft
328ft
Sea Level
-820ft
-6562ft
-13,124ft

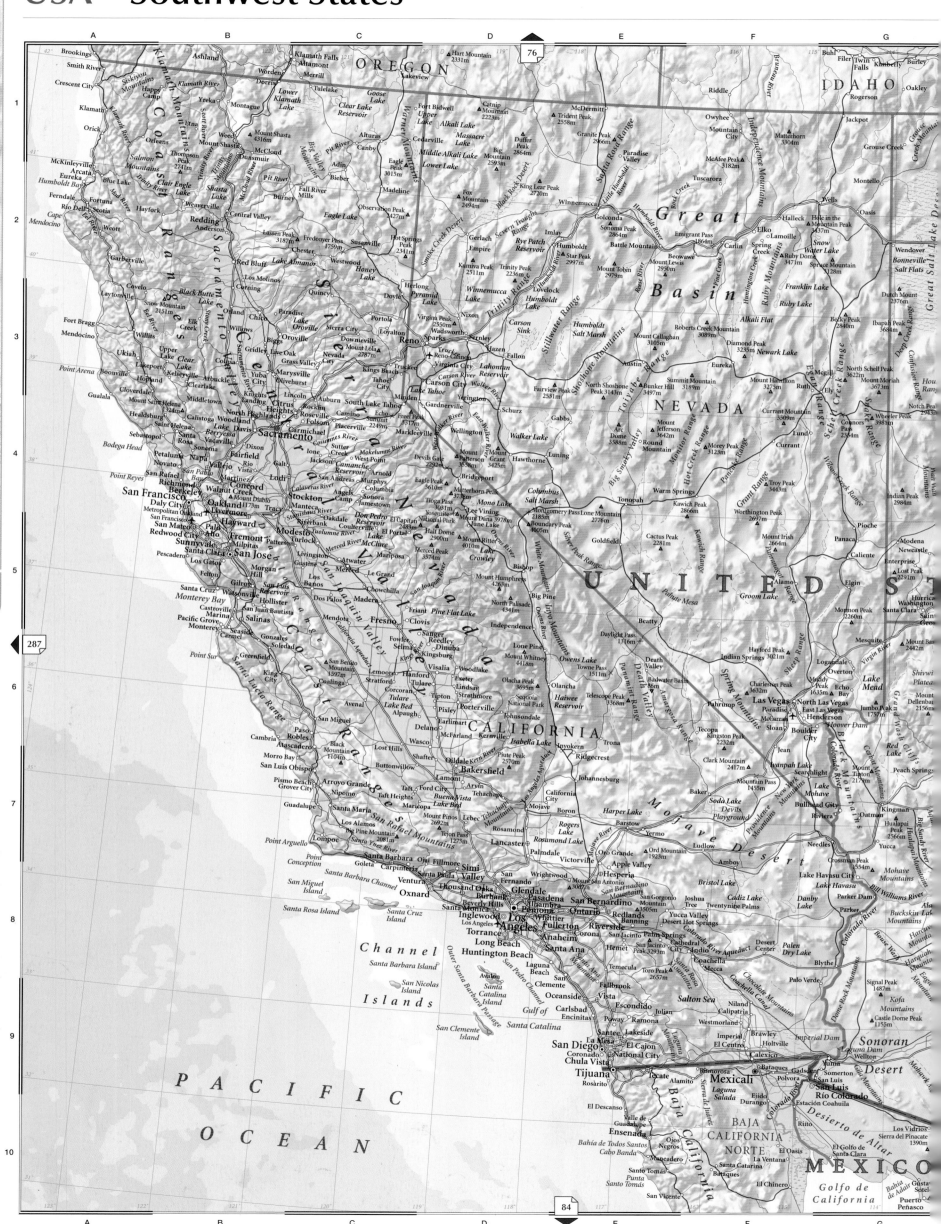

Scale 1:3,750,000
(projection: Lambert Conformal Conic)

0 20 40 60 80 100 Km
0   20   40   60   80   100 Miles

Population
■ above 5 million   ■ 1 million to 5 million   ◉ 500,000 to 1 million
◎ 100,000 to 500,000   ⊕ 50,000 to 100,000   ○ 10,000 to 50,000   ○ below 10,000

Elevation scale

19,686ft
13,124ft
9843ft
6562ft
3281ft
1640ft
820ft
328ft
Sea Level
-820ft
-6562ft
-13,124ft

Map labels

WYOMING

McCammon, Downey, Montpelier, Marbleton, Jeffrey City, Muddy Gap, Pathfinder Reservoir, Guernsey, Lingle, Wheatland, Torrington, Morrill, Scottsbluff, Lakeside, Hyannis, Alliance

Malad City, Black Pine Peak, Snowville, Garland, Paris, Saint Charles, Cokeville, South Pass 2301m, Sweetwater River, Seminoe Reservoir, Medicine Bow River, Medicine Bow, Hawk Springs, Mitchell, Gering, Hogback Mountain 1549m, Bridgeport, Sand Hills, Arthur

Weston, Lewiston, Richmond, Smithfield, Logan, Providence, Hyrum, Kemmerer, Reliance, Rawlins, Walcott, North Platte River, Laramie, Lodgepole Creek, Harrisburg, Lodgepole Creek, Sidney, Chappell, Ogallala

Great Divide Basin, Creston, ROCKY

Brigham City, Willard, Plain City, Ogden, North Ogden, Huntsville, South Ogden, Evanston, Fort Bridger, Granger, Green River, Rock Springs, Baggs, Sierra Madre, Cheyenne, Buford, Halligan Reservoir, Wellington, Ault, Pawnee Buttes 1638m, Eaton, Sterling Reservoir, Sterling, Iliff, Haxtun, Holyoke, Grant

Great Salt Lake, Clearfield, Layton, Farmington, Val Verda, Bountiful, Coalville, Kings Peak 4123m, Diamond Peak 2944m, Black Mountain 3310m, Elkhead Mountains, Walden, Clark Peak 3947m, Rocky Mountain National Park, Fort Collins, Windsor, Jackson Reservoir, Prewitt Reservoir, Akron, Otis, Yuma, Wray

UTAH

Salt Lake City, South Salt Lake, Kearns, Magna, Sandy City, Park City, Heber City, Midway, Pleasant Grove, Maeser, Vernal, Craig, Hayden, Steamboat Springs, Parkview Mountain 3781m, Estes Park, Loveland, Greeley, Evans, Riverside Reservoir, Fort Morgan, Wiggins, Brush

Grantsville, Tooele, Deseret Peak 3362m, Riverton, American Fork, Orem, Provo, Springville, Mapleton, Roosevelt, Duchesne, Danforth Hills, Oak Creek, Kremmling, Grand Lake, Lake Granby, Granby, Longs Peak 4345m, Longmont, Lyons, Dacono, Fort Lupton, Brighton, Strasburg, Last Chance

Stockton, Lehi, Santaquin, Mount Nebo 3620m, Spanish Fork, Myton, Bonanza, White River, Rangely, Meeker, Orno Peak 3691m, Green Mountain Reservoir 3449m, Berthoud Pass, Boulder, Lafayette, Broomfield, Arvada, Wheat Ridge, Denver, Aurora, Englewood, Limon

Eureka, Payson, Strawberry Reservoir, Strawberry River, Roan Cliffs, Roan Plateau, Rifle, Glenwood Springs, Mount Of The Holy Cross 4269m, Carbondale, Mount Powell 4125m, Minturn, Vail, Grays Peak 4349m, Lakewood, Littleton, Mount Evans 4138m, Castle Rock, Flagler, Stratton, Burlington

Nephi, Fountain Green, Fairview, Mount Pleasant, Price, Sunnyside, Helper, Book Cliffs, Collbran, Somerset, Snowmass Mountain 4295m, Aspen, Leadville, Fairplay, Tennessee Pass 3177m, Cheesman Lake, Palmer Lake, Woodland Park, Manitou Springs, Calhan, Hugo, Big Sandy Creek, Cheyenne Wells, Kit Carson

Monroe, Delta, Scipio, Ephraim, Manti, Orangeville, Castle Dale, Ferron, Green River, Grand Junction, Orchard Mesa, Grand Mesa, Paonia, Crested Butte, Pyramid Peak 4273m, Castle Peak 4348m, Mount Elbert 4399m, Mount Harvard 4395m, Antero Reservoir, Elevenmile Reservoir, Pikes Peak 4300m, Fountain, Colorado Springs

COLORADO

Salina, Redmond, Mayfield, Emery, Hotchkiss, Delta, West Elk Peak 3973m, Gunnison River, Gunnison, Taylor Park Reservoir, Buena Vista, Salida, Canon City, Florence, Pueblo, Ordway, Lake Meredith, Eads, Haswell

Richfield, Glenwood, Mount Marvine 3539m, Loa, Bicknell, Hanksville, Moab, Mount Peale 3877m, Montrose, Uncompahgre Plateau, Uncompahgre Peak 4361m, Cochetopa Hills, Saguache, Center, Crestone Peak 4357m, Greenhorn Mountain 3763m, Wet Mountains, Sangre de Cristo, Rocky Ford, La Junta, John Martin Reservoir, Granada, Holly

Beaver, Junction, Otter Creek Reservoir, Blue Bell Knoll 3453m, Fremont River, Mount Ellen 3512m, Dirty Devil River, La Sal, Lake City, Handies Peak 4282m, La Garita Mountains, Creede, Blanca Peak 4372m, Walsenburg, Huerfano River, Fowler, Las Animas, Lamar, Springfield, Walsh

Circleville, Antimony, Mount Hillers 3268m, Abajo Peak 3463m, Blanding, Telluride, Ouray, Silverton, Mount Wilson 4342m, Windom Peak 4292m, San Juan Mountains, Del Norte, Monte Vista, Alamosa, Fort Garland, San Luis, Culebra Peak 4282m, Trinidad, Fishers Peak 2934m, Mesa De Maya 2082m, Kim, Black Mesa 1516m, Branson

Paragonah, Panguitch, Mount Dutton 3365m, Escalante, Monticello, Hesperus Mountain 4033m, Electra Lake, Cortez, Durango, Vallecito Reservoir, Wolf Creek Pass 3327m, Summit Peak 4054m, La Jara, San Luis Valley, Manassa, Costilla, Raton

Cedar City, Hatch, Tropic, Colorado River, Lake Powell, Bluff, San Juan River, Chama, Dulce, Rio Grande, Questa, Raton

STATES OF AMERICA

Kanab, Fredonia, Glen Canyon Dam, Rainbow Bridge, Monument Valley, Navajo Mount 3166m, Page, Navajo Reservoir, Tierra Amarilla, El Vado Reservoir, Rio Chama, Wheeler Peak 4011m, Eagle Nest Lake, Cimarron, Springer, Texline, Clayton, Dalhart

Kaibab Plateau, Colorado River, Marble Canyon, Echo Cliffs, Kaibito Plateau, Kayenta, Pastora Peak 2869m, Ship Rock 2188m, Shiprock, Kirtland, Aztec, Bloomfield, Farmington, Abiquiu Reservoir, Ranchos De Taos, Taos, Ocate, Turkey Mountains, Wagon Mound, Roy, Nara Visa

Grand Canyon, Coconino Plateau, Tuba City, Moenkopi Wash, Painted Desert, Chinle, Chuska Mountains, Huerfano Mountain 2278m, Canyon Largo, Cuba, Los Alamos, Espanola, Pojoaque, Tesuque, Chimayo, Truchas Peak 3993m, Dixon, Mora, Watrous, Mosquero, Adrian

Aubrey Cliffs, Grand Canyon, Little Colorado River, Moenkopi Wash, Keams, Ganado, Fort Defiance, Window Rock, Gamerco, Santa Fe, Pecos River, Las Vegas, Mina, Conchas Lake, Conchas Dam, Canadian River, Tucumcari, Ute Reservoir

Seligman, Ash Fork, Picacho Butte 2210m, Williams, Bill Williams Mountain 2821m, Winslow, Joseph City, Holbrook, Chambers, Sanders, Zuni, Gallup, Thoreau, Mount Taylor 3445m, Milan, Grants, Laguna, Isleta Pueblo, San Felipe Pueblo, Bernalillo, Corrales, Rio Rancho Estates, Paradise Hills, Alameda, Albuquerque, Moriarty, Santa Rosa, Grady, Friona, Bovina

Chino Valley, Flagstaff, Humphreys Peak 3851m, Meteor Crater, Petrified Forest, Zuni Mountains, San Rafael, Los Ranchos de Albuquerque, Los Lunas, Manzano Mountains, Estancia, Laguna del Perro, Vaughn, Lake Sumner, Melrose, Clovis, Texico, Portales

Clarkdale, Jerome, Sedona, Mormon Lake, Hutch Mountain 2601m, Snowflake, Silver Creek, Show Low, Lakeside, Concho, Saint Johns, Quemado, Belen, Willard, Mountainair, Fort Sumner, Yeso, Portales

ARIZONA

Granite Mountain 2324m, Prescott, Camp Verde, Baker Butte 2462m, Mogollon Rim, McNary, Eagar, Greens Peak 3089m, Alegres Mountain 3118m, Gallo Mountains, Magdalena, Socorro, Manzano Peak 3078m, Los Pinos Mountains, Corona, Gallinas Peak 2633m, Elida

Wickenburg, Mayer, Payson, Mazatzal Mountains, Aztec Peak 2345m, Whiteriver, Baldy Peak 3476m, Eagle Peak 2983m, Horse Mount 2911m, Plains of San Agustin, Mount Withington 3083m, South Baldy 3287m, San Antonio, Carrizozo, Capitan, Capitan Peak 3073m, Capitan Mountains, Capitan Peak 3073m

Horseshoe Reservoir, Theodore Roosevelt Lake, Salt River, Black River, San Carlos, Globe, Tularosa Mountains, Reserve, Pelona Mountain 2808m, Magdalena, Elephant Butte Reservoir, Truth Or Consequences, Mescalero, Ruidoso, Sierra Blanca Peak 3649m, Roswell, Dexter, Hagerman, Lovington, Tatum

NEW MEXICO

McDowell Mountains, Sun City, El Mirage, Peoria, Paradise Valley, Scottsdale, Superstition Mountains, Apache Junction, Mesa, Miami, Superior, Claypool, Whitewater Baldy 3321m, Caballo Reservoir, Alamogordo, Cloudcroft, La Luz, Tularosa, Mayhill, Artesia, Hobbs

Phoenix, Tempe, Guadalupe, Gila River, Chandler, Florence, Coolidge, Winkelman, Hayden, San Carlos Reservoir, Clifton, Morenci, Mogollon Mountains, Hillsboro, Bayard, Central, Sacramento Mountains, Lake McMillan, Eunice

Glendale, Litchfield Park, Avondale, Tolleson, Buckeye, Gila Bend, Casa Grande, Eloy, Marana, Mammoth, Oracle, San Manuel, Pinaleno Mountains, Mount Graham 3267m, Pima, Thatcher, Safford, Duncan, Silver City, Cookes Peak 2563m, Hatch, Mayhill, Carlsbad, Loving, Malaga, Jal

Gila Bend Mountains, Sand Tank Mountains, Table Top 1333m, Tucson, South Tucson, Bassett Peak 2336m, Reiley Peak 2326m, Mount Lemmon 2791m, Willcox, Willcox Playa, Cochise Head 2472m, Lordsburg, Deming, Florida Mountains, Las Cruces, Mesilla, Organ Mountains, Organ Peak 2704m, Orogrande, Wind Mountain 2219m, Guadalupe Mountains, Guadalupe Peak 2667m, Salt Flat, Dell City, Red Bluff Reservoir, Kermit

Ajo, Growler Mountains, Sauceda Mountains, Sells, Sahuarita, Green Valley, Babaquivari Peak 2357m, Benson, Tombstone, Pyramid Peak, Animas Peak, Columbus, Anthony, El Paso, Salt Basin, Orla, Pecos River, Mentone, Wink

Quitovac, Costa Rica 1243m, Cerro Cozón, Sonoyta, El Sásabe, Nogales, Mormon Lake, Patagonia, Mount Wrightson 2881m, Sierra Vista, Miller Peak 2885m, Bisbee, Douglas, Agua Prieta, Naco, Santa Cruz, Chiricahua Mountains, Cochise Head, Animas Peak 2597m, Big Hatchet Peak 2550m, Playas Lake, Palomas, Rio Casas Grandes, San Elizario, Socorro, Fabens, Fort Hancock, Sierra Blanca 2100m, Van Horn, Kent, Toyah

CHIHUAHUA, **TEXAS**, **SONORA**

Ciudad Juárez, El Paso, Zaragoza, Rio Bravo del Norte, Guadalupe Bravos, Laguna de Guzmán, Samalayuca, Laguna de Santa María, Guzmán, Candelaria, Esperanza, Sierra Blanca, Apache Mountains, Delaware Mountains, Sierra Diablo, Pecos River, Saragosa, Balmorhea

NEBRASKA

Lake C.W. McConaughy, Bear Hill 1175m, Big Springs, Julesburg, Sedgwick, Crook, Ovid, Sterling, Fleming, Yuma, Joes, Cope, Anton, Bethune, Arikaree River, Bonny Reservoir, Idalia, Vernon, Kirk

Denver, Lakewood, Aurora, Thornton, Commerce City, Northglenn, Westminster, Golden, Morrison, Conifer, Bailey, Grant, Como, Hartsel, Guffey, Cripple Creek, Victor, Florissant, Divide, Green Mountain Falls, Cascade

Scale 1:1,875,000
(projection: Lambert Conformal Conic)

0 10 20 30 40 50 Km
0 10 20 30 40 50 Miles

Population

- ■ above 5 million
- ■ 1 million to 5 million
- ◉ 500,000 to 1 million
- ◎ 100,000 to 500,000
- ⊕ 50,000 to 100,000
- ○ 10,000 to 50,000
- ∘ below 10,000

Elevation scale:
19,686ft
13,124ft
9843ft
6562ft
3281ft
1640ft
820ft
328ft
Sea Level
-820ft
-6562ft
-13,124ft

ARIZONA

MEXICO

BAJA CALIFORNIA NORTE

CALIFORNIA

PACIFIC OCEAN

Los Angeles · San Diego · Las Vegas · Bakersfield · Tijuana · Mexicali · Santa Barbara · Oxnard · Ventura · Santa Clarita · Palmdale · Lancaster · Victorville · Barstow · Needles · Kingman · Bullhead City · Laughlin · Lake Havasu City · Parker · Blythe · El Centro · Calexico · Ensenada · Rosarito · Oceanside · Carlsbad · Escondido · Riverside · San Bernardino · Fontana · Ontario · Pomona · Anaheim · Santa Ana · Irvine · Long Beach · Pasadena · Glendale · Burbank · Inglewood · Torrance · Palm Springs · Indio · Coachella · Hemet · Temecula · Murrieta · Moreno Valley · Redlands · Hesperia · Apple Valley · Boulder City · Henderson · North Las Vegas

Death Valley · **Mojave Desert** · **Sonoran Desert** · **Colorado Desert**

San Gabriel Mountains · **San Bernardino Mountains** · **Tehachapi Mountains** · **Panamint Range** · **Argus Range** · **Chocolate Mountains** · **Kofa Mountains** · **Whipple Mountains** · **San Rafael Mountains** · **Santa Catalina Mountains**

Salton Sea · **Lake Mead** · **Lake Mohave** · **Lake Havasu** · **Colorado River** · **Gulf of Santa Catalina** · **San Pedro Channel** · **Santa Barbara Channel** · **Outer Santa Barbara Passage** · **Channel Islands**

Santa Cruz Island · Santa Rosa Island · San Miguel Island · Santa Catalina Island · San Clemente Island · San Nicolas Island · Santa Barbara Island

Point Conception · Point Arguello · Purisima Point · Point Dume

Hoover Dam · Parker Dam · Imperial Dam

Charleston Peak 3632m · Telescope Peak 3366m · Clark Mountain 2417m · Mount San Gorgonio 3506m · Mount San Jacinto 3291m · Toro Peak 2657m

79 · 84 · 287

USA – Alaska

Scale 1:4,250,000
(projection: Lambert Conformal Conic)

0 20 40 60 80 100 Km
0 20 40 60 80 100 Miles

Population
- ■ above 5 million
- ◉ 100,000 to 500,000
- ■ 1 million to 5 million
- ◉ 50,000 to 100,000
- ◉ 500,000 to 1 million
- ○ 10,000 to 50,000
- ○ below 10,000

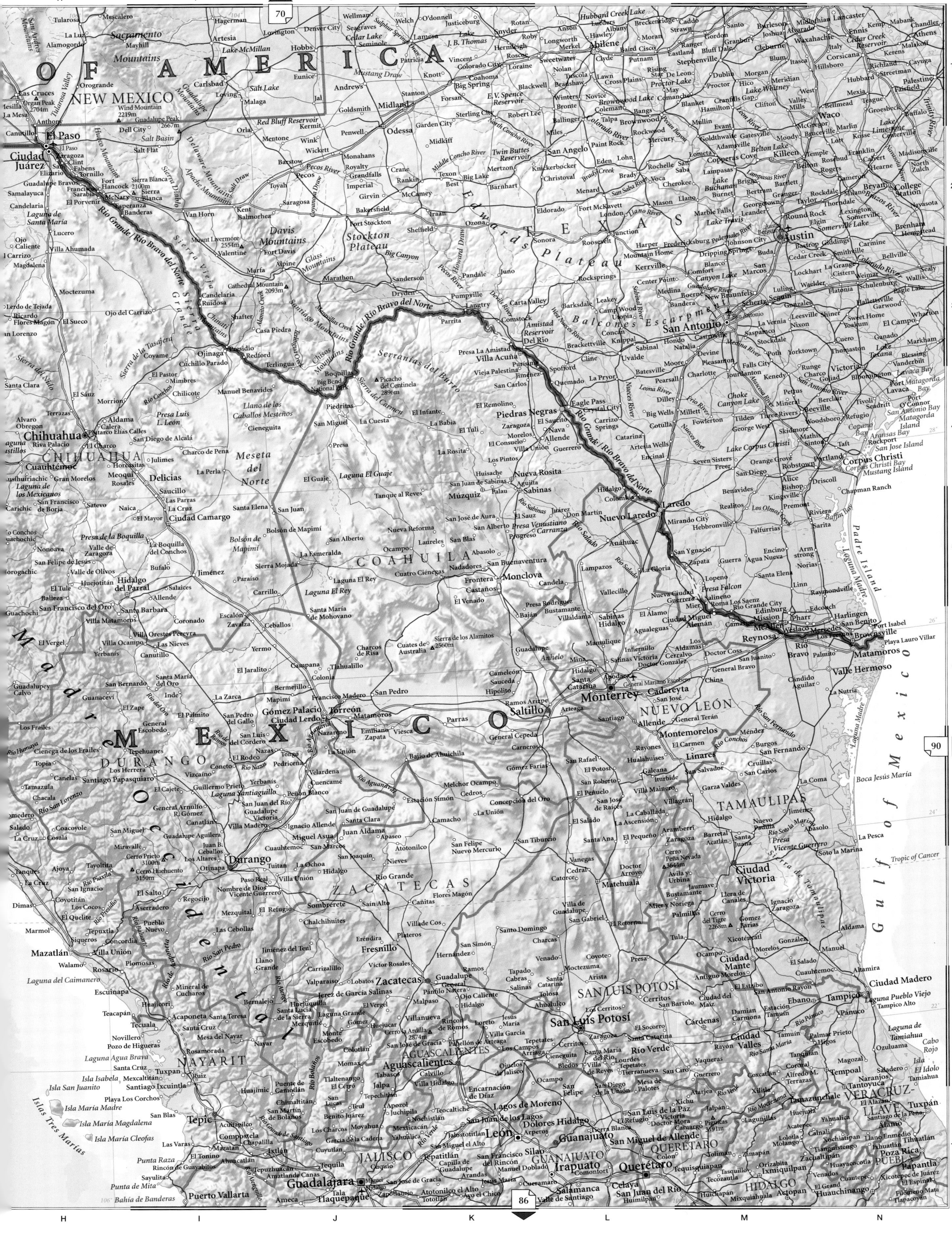

85

19,686ft
13,124ft
9843ft
6562ft
3281ft
1640ft
820ft
328ft
Sea Level
-820ft
-6562ft
-13,124ft

Southern Mexico

Scale 1:4,250,000
(projection: Lambert Conformal Conic)

0 20 40 60 80 100 Km
0 20 40 60 80 100 Miles

Population

■ above 5 million   ■ 1 million to 5 million   ◉ 500,000 to 1 million
◎ 100,000 to 500,000   ◉ 50,000 to 100,000   ○ 10,000 to 50,000   ○ below 10,000

90

JAMAICA

Montego Bay
Lucea
Sangster
Falmouth
The Cockpit
Country
Grange Hill
Christiana
Ocho Rios
Port Maria
Annotto Bay
Port Antonio
North East Point
South Negril Point
Mount Denham
886m
Mandeville
Spanish
Town
Blue
Mountain
Peak
2256m
KINGSTON
Savanna-La-Mar
Crab Pond Point
Black River
May Pen
Old
Harbour
Norman
Manley
Morant Bay
Great Pedro Bluff
Malvern
Long Bay
Lionel
Town
Wreck Point
Portland
Point

Jamaica Channel

Caribbean

Sea

Laguna de
Caratasca
Puerto Lempira
GRACIAS A DIOS
Cabo de Gracias a Dios
Río Coco
Boom
Waspam
Río Wawa
Yablis
Dákura
REGIÓN
AUTÓNOMA
Río Kukalaya
San Luis
La Rosita
ATLÁNTICO
Wounta
NORTE
Makantaka
Alamikamba
Río Bambana
Prinzapolka
La Cruz
de Río Grande
Barra de Río Grande
Kara
Río Kurinwás
REGIÓN
UTÓNOMA
TLÁNTICO
SUR
Laguna de Perlas
Río Escondido
Punta de Perlás
El
Rama
Bahía
de Bluefields
El Bluff
Bluefields
Nueva Guinea
Monkey Point
Punta Gorda
o Punta Gorda

Arrecifes de la Media Luna
Arrecife Edinburgh
Cayo Muerto
Cayos Miskitos
Tuapi
Cayos Londres
Puerto Cabezas
Isla Santa Catalina
Isla de Providencia
Cayos Guerrero
SAN ANDRÉS Y
PROVIDENCIA
(to Colombia)
Cayos King
Cayos de Perlas
Isla de San Andrés
Cayos del
Este Sudeste
Cayos de
Albuquerque

El Castillo de
La Concepción
Río San Juan
San Juan del Norte
Barra del Colorado
San
rlos
HEREDIA
Río Colorado
amira
Puerto Viejo
LIMÓN
esada
Volcán
Poás
2704m
Guápiles
COSTA
RICA
Volcán
Barva
2906m
Siquirres
Matina
Heredia
Volcán
Irazú
3339m
Limón
rcia
ón
AN JOSÉ
SAN JOSÉ
Turrialba
Cerro Chirripó Grande
3819m
Punta Mona
Paraíso
CARTAGO
Cerro La
Muerte
3491m
Cerro
Kamuk
3554m
San Isidro
Bribri
 Quepos
Dominical
Río General
UNTARENAS
Cortés
Buenos
Aires
Guabito
Changuinola
Bocas del Toro
Archipiélago de Bocas del Toro
Palmar Sur
Bahía de Coronado
Río Grande de Terraba
Volcán
Barú
3475m
Boquete
BOCAS
DEL TORO
Almirante
Río Teribe
Laguna
de Chiriquí
Península
Valiente
Peninsula
de Osa
San Vito
Volcán
Golfito
Cerro Chorcha
2238m
Golfo
Dulce
Río Chiriquí
David
NGÖBE
BUGLE
Miguel de la Borda
Península
de Osa
Pedregal
Cerro
Santiago
2125m
Quebrada
Guabo
Concepción
CHIRIQUÍ
Alanje
Puerto Armuelles
Isla Sevilla
Remedios
Isla Parida
Horconcitos
VERAGUAS
Soná
Santiago
Palmas
Punta Burica
Golfo de Chiriquí
Isla de Coiba
Isla Cébaco
Montijo
Río de Jesús
Ponuga
HERRERA
Guararal
Parita
Chitré
Los Santos
Monagrillo
Bahía
de Parita
Macaracas
Las Tablas
Península
de Azuero
LOS SANTOS
Cerro
Hoya
1560m
Ocú
Pedasí
Tonosí
Punta Mala

Portobelo
Santa Isabel
Archipiélago
de San Blas
El Porvenir
KUNA DE WARGANDÍ
Colón
Cristobal
Nuevo Chagres
Istmo de Panamá
PANAMÁ
Ailigandi
SAN BLAS
Punta Mosquito
Coclé del Norte
Lago
Gatún
Río Chagres
Panama City
KUNA DE
MADUNGANDÍ
Lago
Bayano
Punta Escocés
Gulf of
Darien
Lorica
COLÓN
La Chorrera
Balboa
PANAMÁ
(PANAMA CITY)
San Miguelito
Capira
Chepo
Río Bayano
Cerro
Chucantí
1439m
Río Chucunaque
Puerto
Obaldía
Acandí
Arboletes
Montería
Golfo de los Mosquitos
Río Indio
Santa Catalina
Cerro Peña Blanca
1314m
COCLÉ
El Valle
Cerro
Gaital
1173m
Punta Chame
Bahía de
Panamá
Chimán
Archipiélago
de las Perlas
San Miguel
Punta
Brava
La Palma
EMBERÁ
WOUNAAN
Yaviza
El Real
Serranía del Darién
Tierralta
CÓRDOBA
Santa Fé
Río Santa María
Calobre
Antón
Penonomé
Aguadulce
Río Hato
San Carlos
Isla San José
Bahía de
San Miguel
DARIÉN
Cerro Tacarcuna
1875m
Unión
Chocó
Turbo
Golfo de Urabá
PANAMA
Golfo de Panamá
Punta Garachiné
Garachiné
Cerro Pirre
1200m
Cerro Seteale
1220m
EMBERÁ
WOUNAAN
Chigorodó
ANTIOQUIA
Jaqué
Ríosucio
Río Atrato
CHOCÓ
Jurado
Mutatá
Cerro Musinga
3850m
Dabeiba
Frontino

COLOMBIA

Panama City

Sara Sotillo
San
Miguelito
Santa
Clara
Villa
Caceres
Miraflores
Juan Díaz
Río Abajo
Río
Abajo
Nuevo
Paitilla
Reparto
Nuevo
Panamá
Villa de
Fuentes
Pueblo
Nuevo
El Cangrejo
Clayton
Curundú
Los
Angeles
Parque
Omar Torrijos
Herrera
San
Francisco
Coco de
Mar
Parque
Nacional
Metropolitano
Lo Locería
Bahía de
Panamá
Corozal
Iglesia
del Carmen
**Panamá
(Panama City)**
Marcos A.
Gelabert
International
Airport
Museo de las
Ciencias Naturales
Bella
Vista
Altos de
Diablo
Calidonia
Bahía de
Panamá
Pacific
Ocean
Canal de Panamá
Anacón
Museo Reina
Torres de Araúz
Balboa
Santa
Ana
Palacio Presidencial
Iglesia de San José

0   1 Km
0   1 Miles

90

Pacific Ocean

19,686ft
13,124ft
9843ft
6562ft
3281ft
1640ft
820ft
328ft
Sea
Level
-820ft
-6562ft
-13,124ft

102

NORTH AMERICA

90

UNITED STATES OF AMERICA

Gulf of Mexico

FLORIDA

Saint Petersburg · Bradenton · Sarasota · Venice · Port Charlotte · Punta Gorda · Fort Myers · Cape Coral · Bonita Springs · Naples · Marathon · Key West · Key Largo · Islamorada · Homestead · Kendall · Miami · Miami Beach · North Miami · Hollywood · Fort Lauderdale · Pompano Beach · Boca Raton · West Palm Beach · Lake Worth · Boynton Beach · Belle Glade · Hobe Sound · Stuart · Jensen Beach · Fort Pierce · Vero Beach · Sebastian · Indiantown · Okeechobee · Avon Park · Lake Wales · Wauchula · Arcadia · La Belle · Immokalee · Big Cypress Swamp · The Everglades · Everglades City · Cape Sable · Cape Romano · Florida Bay · Dry Tortugas · Marquesas Keys · Florida Keys

Straits of Florida

BAHAMAS

Grand Bahama Island · West End · Freeport · Eight Mile Rock · Great Sale Cay · Little Abaco · Coopers Town · Marsh Harbour · Great Abaco · Cherokee Sound · Moores Island · Pelican Point · Northwest Providence Channel · Bimini Islands · Berry Islands · Nicholls Town · Northeast Providence Channel · Current · NASSAU · New Providence · Adelaide · Linden Pindling · Andros Town · Behring Point · Andros Island · Governor's Harbour · Eleuthera Island · Rock Sound · Cat Island · Arthur's Town · Bannerman Town · Exuma Sound · Exuma Cays · Kemp's Bay · Great Guana Cay · Cockburn Town · San Salvador · Columbus Point · Conception Island · Santa Maria Cape · George Town · Great Exuma Island · Little Exuma · Deadman's Cay · Long Island · Clarence Town · Samana Cay · Crooked Island Passage · Cape Verde · Colonel Hill · Crooked Island · Northeast Point · Plana Cays · Snug Corner · Long Cay · Mayaguana · The Carlton · Acklins Island · Salina Point · Ragged Island Range · Mayaguana Passage · Southeast Point · West Caicos · Caicos Passage · Little Inagua · Northeast Point · Great Inagua · Lake Rosa · Matthew Town

Tropic of Cancer

MEXICO

Cabo Catoche · Isla Mujeres · Cancún · Puerto Juárez · Leona Vicario · Puerto Morelos · Playa del Carmen · Cozumel · Punta Molas del Norte · Isla Cozumel · *Yucatan Channel* · Cabo de San Antonio · Cabo Corrientes

LA HABANA (HAVANA) · Mariel · Guanabacoa · Artemisa · Matanzas · Cárdenas · Jovellanos · Colón · Güira de Melena · Güines · Jagüey Grande · San Cristóbal · Consolación del Sur · Los Palacios · Pinar del Río · Minas de Matahambre · Sierra de los Organos · Guane · Archipiélago de los Colorados · Nueva Gerona · Santa Fé · Isla de la Juventud · Cayos de San Felipe · Golfo de Batabanó · Península de Zapata · Aguada de Pasajeros · Cruces · Cienfuegos · Santo Domingo · Sagua la Grande · Cayo Fragoso · Caibarién · Placetas · Santa Clara · Cabaiguán · Jatibonico · Morón · Sancti Spíritus · Trinidad · Cayo Coco · Cayo Romano · Ciego de Ávila · Esmeralda · Cayo Guajaba · Florida · Nuevitas · Vertientes · Camagüey · Puerto Padre · Gibara · Las Tunas · Holguín · Banes · Cabo Lucrecia · Santa Cruz del Sur · Bayamo · Jiguaní · Cueto · Mayarí · Moa · Punta Guarico · Manzanillo · Guacanayabo · Campechuela · Palma Soriano · Sierra del Cristal · Sagua de Tánamo · Baracoa · Pilón · La Maya · Sierra Maestra · Pico Turquino 1944m · Santiago de Cuba · Maisí · Punta de Quemado · Cabo Cruz · Bahía de Guantánamo (to US) · Guantánamo

CUBA

Great · *Archipiélago de los Jardines de la Reina* · *Golfo de Ana María* · *Golfo de Guacanayabo*

Pico San Juan 1156m

Nicholas Channel · *Archipiélago de Sabana* · *Archipiélago de Camagüey* · *Old Bahama Channel* · *Santaren Channel* · *Tongue of the Ocean*

er · *Grea* · *t* · *er* · *A* · *n*

CAYMAN ISLANDS (to UK) · Little Cayman · Cayman Brac · Owen Roberts · GEORGE TOWN · Bodden Town · Grand Cayman

JAMAICA · Sangster · Montego Bay · Port Maria · Port Antonio · South Negril Point · Savanna-La-Mar · Christiana · Spanish Town · Black River · Mandeville · May Pen · KINGSTON · Norman Manley · Port Royal · Blue Mountain Peak 2256m · Morant Bay · Portland Point

Windward Passage · *Jamaica Channel*

NAVASSA ISLAND (to US)

HAITI · Port-de-Paix · Jean-Rabel · Môle St-Nicolas · Gros-Morne · Gonaïves · Golfe de la Gonâve · St-Marc · Canal de St-Marc · Cap Dame Marie · Dame-Marie · Jérémie · Corail · Miragoâne · Léogâne · Chardonnières · Massif de la Hotte · Aquin · Cayes · Port Salut · Pointe à Gravois · Île à Vache · Arcahaie · Canal de la Gonâve · Île de la Gonâve · Petit-Goâve · Jacmel

HONDURAS · ISLAS DE LA BAHÍA · Isla de Guanaja · Roatán · Isla de Roatán · Punta Caxinas · Trujillo · Balfate · Limón · Iriona · COLÓN · Río Aguán · Sierra de Agalta · Catacamas · Juticalpa · OLANCHO · GRACIAS A DIOS · Brus Laguna · Puerto Lempira · Río Coco · Laguna de Caratasca · Cabo de Gracias a Dios · Arrecifes de la Media Luna · Arrecife Edinburgh · Río Patuca · Cayo Muerto · Cayos Miskitos · Cayos Londres · Río Tinto · Río Sico · Sava · San Esteban · Gualaco · San Luis · Río Patuca · Boom · Waspam · Ulmukhuás · Bocay · Río Bocay · Wina · Río Coco · La Rosita · Siuna · Bonanza · Dákura · Tuapi · Puerto Cabezas · Wounta · Prinzapolka

NICARAGUA · REGIÓN AUTÓNOMA ATLÁNTICO NORTE · Jinotega · Matagalpa · MATAGALPA · May May · BOACO · Boaco · Juigalpa · CHONTALES · Santo Tomás · Muelle de los Bueyes · Lago de Nicaragua · El Rama · Bluefields · REGIÓN AUTÓNOMA ATLÁNTICA SUR · Río Escondido · Río Punta Gorda · Monkey Point · Punta Gorda · Morrito · Volcán Concepción 1610m · Isla de Ometepe · Rivas · San Carlos · Río San Juan · San Juan del Sur · Barra de Río Grande · Cayos Guerrero · Kara · Cayos King · Isla Santa Catalina · Isla de Providencia · Cayos de Perlas · Isla de San Andrés · "Islas del Maíz" · Cayos de Albuquerque · Cayos del Este Sudeste

SAN ANDRÉS Y PROVIDENCIA (to Colombia)

Caribbean Sea

COSTA RICA · GUANACASTE · Liberia · Upala · Volcán Miravalles 2028m · Volcán Arenal · Cañas · ALAJUELA · HEREDIA · Quesada · Puntarenas · PUNTARENAS · Santa Cruz · Puerto Viejo · Siquirres · Guápiles · LIMÓN · Barra del Colorado · El Castillo de la Concepción · Río San Juan · San Juan del Norte · SAN JOSÉ · Heredia · Limón

COLOMBIA · Santa Marta · Ríohacha · Dibulla · MAGDALENA · Ciénaga · Pico Cristóbal Colón 5775m · Sierra Nevada de Santa Marta · Barranquilla · Puerto Colombia · Soledad · Sabanalarga · ATLÁNTICO · Santo Tomé · Sitionuevo · Salamina · Piviiay · Aracataca · Fundación · Cartagena · Turbaco · Campo de la Cruz · San Juan del Cesar · Valledupar · Villanueva · Robles

Caribbean Sea

Inset map:

JAMAICA · Montego Bay · Sangster · Lucea · Falmouth · Discovery Bay · St Ann's Bay · Clark's Town · Browns Town · Ocho Rios · Port Maria · Don Christophers Point · Dolphin Head 545m · Birchs Hill · Grange Hill · The Cockpit Country · Cambridge · Alexandria · Claremont · Highgate · Annotto Bay · Buff Bay · Port Antonio · Negril · Little London · Savanna-La-Mar · Mount Denham 888m · Frankfield · Ewarton · Bog Walk · Blue Mountain · Crab Pond Point · Maggotty · Christiana · Linstead · Chapelton · Spanish Town · Blue Mountain Peak 2258m · Black River · Santa Cruz · Mandeville · May Pen · KINGSTON · Malvern 725m · Alligator Pond · Old Harbour · Portmore · Norman Manley · Bath · Golden Grove · Great Pedro Bluff · Lionel Town · Long Bay · Portland Bight · Yallahs Hill 730m · Port Royal · Port Morant · Morant Bay · Wreck Point · Portland Point · North East Point · Jamaica Channel

Caribbean Sea

Scale 1:2,500,000
0 5 10 20 Km
0 5 10 20 Miles

Elevation scale: 6000m · 4000m · 3000m · 2000m · 1000m · 500m · 250m · 100m · Sea Level · -250m · -2000m · -4000m

Scale 1:6,250,000
(projection: Lambert Conformal Conic)

0 25 50 75 100 125 150 175 200 Km
0 25 50 75 100 125 150 175 200 Miles

Population
- ■ above 5 million
- ▣ 1 million to 5 million
- ◉ 500,000 to 1 million
- ◎ 100,000 to 500,000
- ◌ 50,000 to 100,000
- ○ 10,000 to 50,000
- · below 10,000

GUADELOUPE (to France)

Pointe de la Grande Vigie
Anse-Bertrand
Port-Louis
le Moule
Morne-à-l'Eau
Guadeloupe Passage
Grand Cul-de-Sac Marin
Ste-Rose
Baie-Mahault
Lamentin
Pointe-à-Pitre
les Abymes
Ste-Anne
St-François
Grande Terre
Pointe des Colibris
Pointe Noire
Caribbean Sea
Basse Terre
Petit-Bourg
Petit Cul-de-Sac Marin
Vieux-Habitants
Soufrière 1467m
Capesterre-Belle-Eau
St-Claude
BASSE-TERRE
Canal des Saintes
Canal de Marie-Galante
ATLANTIC OCEAN
Scale 1:2,500,000
0 5 10 20 Km
0 5 10 20 Miles

DOMINICA

Dominica Passage
Pointe Jaco
Vieille Case
Portsmouth
Melville Hill
Marigot
Morne Diablotins 1447m
Castle Bruce
Salisbury
St. Joseph
Canefield
ROSEAU
La Plaine
Rosalie
Berekua
Scotts Head Village
Martinique Passage
ATLANTIC OCEAN
Caribbean Sea
Scale 1:2,000,000
0 5 10 Km
0 5 10 Miles

MARTINIQUE (to France)

Martinique Passage
Grand' Rivière
Basse-Pointe
le Prêcheur
Montagne Pelée 1397m
Ste-Marie
St-Pierre
la Trinité
le Robert
Schoelcher
le Lamentin
FORT-DE-FRANCE
le François
Baie de Fort-de-France
José César
Rivière-Pilote
les Anses-d'Arlets
le Diamant
Ste-Anne
Saint Lucia Channel
ATLANTIC OCEAN
Caribbean Sea
Scale 1:2,500,000
0 5 10 20 Km
0 5 10 20 Miles

ST LUCIA

Pointe Du Cap
Gros Islet
George F.L Charles
CASTRIES
Anse La Raye
Dennery
Soufrière
Mount Gimie 950m
Petit Piton 743m
Micoud
Gros Piton 798m
Laborie
Hewanorra
Vieux Fort
Caribbean Sea
ATLANTIC OCEAN
Saint Vincent Passage
Scale 1:2,000,000
0 5 10 Km
0 5 10 Miles

BARBADOS

North Point
Crab Hill
Speightstown
Mount Hillaby 340m
Bathsheba
Holetown
Welchman Hall
BRIDGETOWN
The Crane
Oistins
Grantley Adams
ATLANTIC OCEAN
Scale 1:2,000,000
0 5 10 Km
0 5 10 Miles

ST VINCENT & THE GRENADINES

Saint Vincent Passage
Porter Point
Fancy
Soufrière 1234m
Chateaubelair
Georgetown
St Vincent
Layou
Barrouallie
North Union
KINGSTOWN
Stubbs
Arnos Vale
Caribbean Sea
ATLANTIC OCEAN
Scale 1:2,000,000
0 5 10 Km
0 5 10 Miles

GRENADA

Caribbean Sea
Sauteurs
Victoria
Mont St Catherine 840m
Gouyave
Grenville
ST.GEORGE'S
St. David's
Grand Anse
Point Salines
ATLANTIC OCEAN
Scale 1:2,000,000
0 5 10 Km
0 5 10 Miles

ATLANTIC OCEAN

Tropic of Cancer

TURKS & CAICOS ISLANDS (to UK)
North Caicos
Caicos Islands
Kew
Grand Caicos
Providenciales
East Caicos
South Caicos
Grand Turk Island
COCKBURN TOWN
Cockburn Harbour
Turks Islands

Mouchoir Passage

Hispaniola
DOMINICAN REPUBLIC
Monte Cristi
Cabo Isabela
Puerto Plata
Cap-Haïtien
Port-Liberté
Mao
Sosúa
Cabo Francés Viejo
Dajabón
Sabaneta
Santiago
Cabrera
Moca
Salcedo
Nagua
La Vega
San Francisco de Macorís
Bahía Escocesa
Artibonite
Bonao
Río Yuma
Bahía de Samaná
Pico Duarte 3175m
Monte Plata
Hato Mayor
El Seibo
Hinche
Cordillera Central
Villa Altagracia
Las Américas
Higüey
Cabo Engaño
San Juan
Azua
San Cristóbal
San Pedro de Macorís
PORT-AU-PRINCE
SANTO DOMINGO
La Romana
Isla Saona
Lago Enriquillo
Neiba
Baní
Punta Salinas
Punta Palenque
Barahona
Enriquillo
Pedernales
Oviedo
Isla Beata
Cabo Beata

Mona Passage
Cabo Rojo
Isla Mona

PUERTO RICO (to US)
Aguadilla
Arecibo
SAN JUAN
Luis Muñoz Marín
Carolina
Utuado
Bayamón
Caguas
Mayagüez
Cordillera Central
Yauco
Ponce
Guayama
Guayama

BRITISH VIRGIN ISLANDS (to UK)
Anegada
Sombrero (to Anguilla)
ANGUILLA (to UK)
THE VALLEY
Anguilla
Clayton J. Lloyd
St-Martin (to France)
ROAD TOWN
St Thomas
Tortola
Virgin Gorda
Beef Island
PHILIPSBURG
Sint Maarten (to Netherlands)
St-Barthélemy (to France)
Codrington
Barbuda
CHARLOTTE AMALIE
VIRGIN ISLANDS (to US)
Isla de Vieques
Sint Eustatius (to Neth.)
Saba (to Neth.)
Frederiksted
Christiansted
St Croix
Robert L. Bradshaw
Nevis
V.C. Bird
BASSETERRE
St Kitts
ANTIGUA & BARBUDA
Charlestown
John A. Osborne
ST. JOHN'S
Redonda
Antigua
Falmouth
ST KITTS & NEVIS
BRADES
MONTSERRAT (to UK)
Guadeloupe Passage
le Raizet
Pointe-à-Pitre
Port-Louis
la Désirade
Ste-Rose
Soufrière 1467m
Basse Terre
BASSE-TERRE
GUADELOUPE (to France)
Marie-Galante
Grand-Bourg
les Saintes
Dominica Passage
Portsmouth
Melville Hall
Marigot
ROSEAU
La Plaine
DOMINICA
Martinique Passage
Montagne Pelée 1397m
Ste-Marie
St-Pierre
le Lamentin
MARTINIQUE (to France)
FORT-DE-FRANCE
Rivière-Pilote
Aimé Césaire
Saint Lucia Channel
CASTRIES
ST LUCIA
Mount Gimie 950m
Hewanorra
Vieux Fort
Saint Vincent Passage
BARBADOS
St Vincent
Speightstown
Chateaubelair
Soufrière 1234m
Arnos Vale
KINGSTOWN
BRIDGETOWN
Grantley Adams
ST VINCENT & THE GRENADINES
Port Elizabeth
Bequia
Mustique
Canouan
The Grenadines
Union Island
Hillsborough
Carriacou
GRENADA
Victoria
ST GEORGE'S
Grenville
Point Salines
Charlotteville
Scarborough
Tobago
Galera Point
TRINIDAD & TOBAGO
PORT-OF-SPAIN
Sangre Grande
Trinidad
San Fernando
Point Fortin
Gulf of Paria
Galeota Point
The Serpent's Mouth

Lesser Antilles
Leeward Islands
Windward Islands
Antilles

PUERTO RICO (to US)

ATLANTIC OCEAN
Isabela
Aguadilla
Arecibo
Laguna Tortuguero
Manatí
Vega Baja
SAN JUAN
Luis Muñoz Marín
Río Grande
Fajardo
Punta Higüero
San Sebastián
Lago Dos Bocas
Bayamón
Cataño
Carolina
Cabezas de San Juan
Sonda de Vieques
Culebra
Isla de Culebra
Bahía de Mayagüez
Adjuntas
Utuado
Orocovis
Sierra de Cayey
Guaynabo
Caguas
Humacao
Isla de Vieques
Yabucoa
Punta Puerca
Mayagüez
El Yunque 1065m
San Germán
Cordillera Central
Cerro de Punta 1338m
Toa Vaca
Juana Díaz
Cayey
Yauco
Ponce
Salinas
Guayama
Cabo Rojo
Punta Brea
Punta Petrona
Punta Guayanés
Caribbean Sea
Scale 1:2,500,000
0 5 10 20 Km
0 5 10 20 Miles

TRINIDAD & TOBAGO

Caribbean Sea
Galera Point
Blanchisseuse
Matelot
Redhead
The Dragon's Mouth
PORT-OF-SPAIN
Arima
Tunapuna
Piarco
Sangre Grande
Chaguanas
Caroni River
Couva
Caroni Arena Dam
Gulf of Paria
La Brea
Trinidad
Guatuaro Point
San Fernando
Point Fortin
Princes Town
Río Claro
Bonasse
Siparia
Rushville
Galeota Point
Moruga
The Serpent's Mouth
VENEZUELA
Scale 1:2,500,000
0 5 10 20 Km
0 5 10 20 Miles

Lesser Antilles

ARUBA (to Netherlands)
ORANJESTAD
Reina Beatrix
Sint Nicolaas
CURAÇAO (to Netherlands)
Noordpunt
Hato Airport
Santa Catherina
Curaçao
WILLEMSTAD
BONAIRE (to Netherlands)
Malmok
Bonaire
KRALENDIJK
Islas Las Aves
Islas Los Roques
Isla La Orchila
Isla La Tortuga
Isla Blanquilla
Islas Los Testigos
Charlotteville
Scarborough
Tobago
TRINIDAD & TOBAGO
PORT-OF-SPAIN

Punta Gallinas
Peninsula de la Guajira
URIBIA
Puerto López
Cabo San Román
Pueblo Nuevo
Los Taques
Punta Fijo
Puerto Cumarebo
San Juan de los Cayos
Tucacas
Golfo de Venezuela
La Vela de Coro
Mirimire
Tocuyo de la Costa
Chichiriviche
Paraguaná
Coro
La Cruz de Taratara
NUEVA ESPARTA
Juangriego
Asunción
Pampatar
Porlamar
Isla de Margarita
Punta de Piedras
Puerto La Cruz
ZULIA
Sabaneta
Capatárida
Dabajuro
Pedregal
Río Caribe
Araya
Güiria
Irapa
Maracaibo
Concepción
San Rafael
San Francisco
La Concepción
Cabimas
La Juana
FALCÓN
Churuguara
Maparari
Yaracal
Puerto Cabello
La Guaira
Morón
CARACAS
VENEZUELA
SUCRE
Cumaná
Cumanacoa
San Antonio de Maturín
Cariaco
Casanay
Araya
Carúpano
San Fernando
Point Fortin
Gulf of Paria
Trinidad
Galeota Point
The Serpent's Mouth
Punta Baja
LARA
Duaca
Aroa
San Felipe
Valencia
YARACUY
Maracay
Cua
Cagua
Villa de Cura
Los Teques
MIRANDA
Petare
Ocumare
Barcelona
ANZOÁTEGUI
Clarines
Valle de Guanape
MONAGAS
Caicara
Maturín
Caripito
Quiriquire
DELTA AMACURO
Río Chico

19,686ft
13,124ft
9843ft
6562ft
3281ft
1640ft
820ft
328ft
Sea Level
-820ft
-6562ft
-13,124ft

290

102

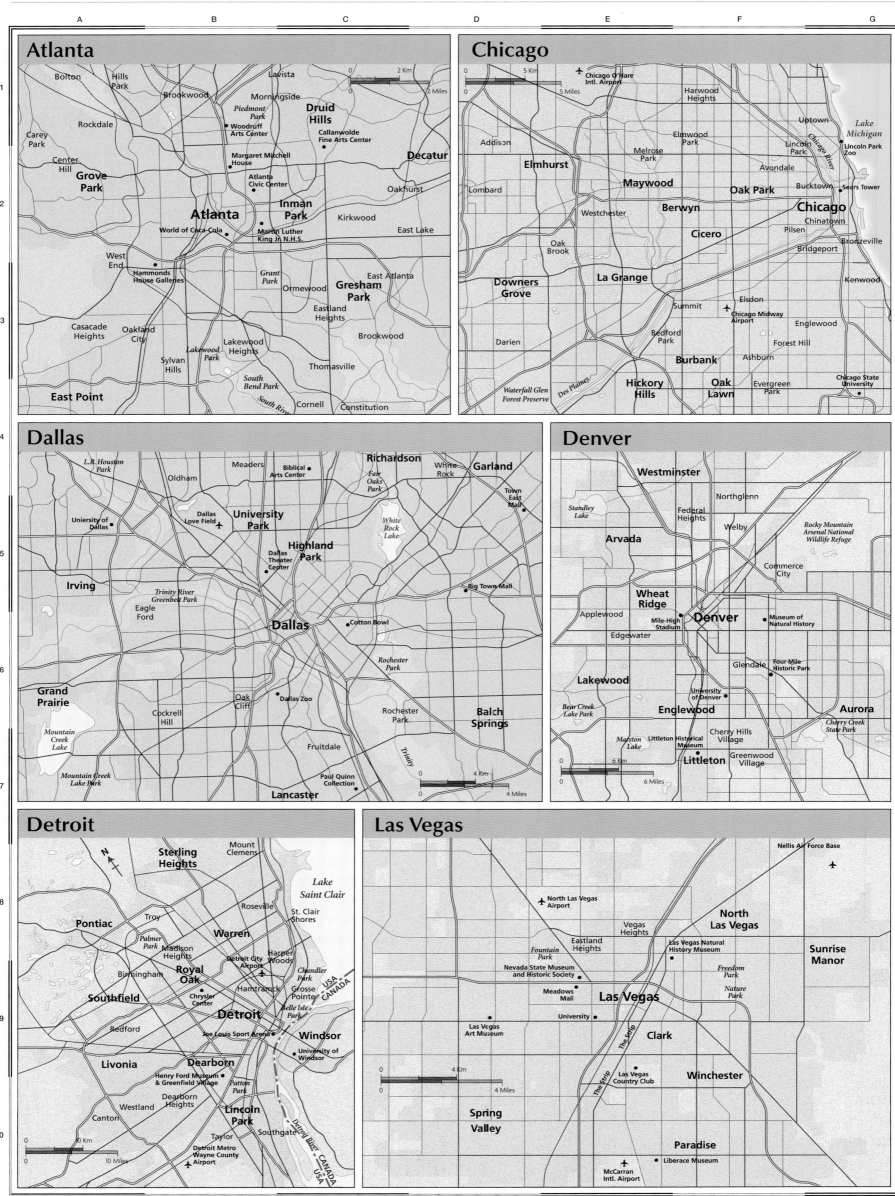

Atlanta

Bolton
Hills Park
LaVista
Brookwood
Morningside
Piedmont Park
Druid Hills
Woodruff Arts Center
Rockdale
Callanwolde Fine Arts Center
Carey Park
Decatur
Center Hill
Margaret Mitchell House
Grove Park
Atlanta Civic Center
Oakhurst
Atlanta
Inman Park
Kirkwood
World of Coca-Cola
East Lake
Martin Luther King Jr N.H.S.
West End
East Atlanta
Hammonds House Galleries
Grant Park
Gresham Park
Casacade Heights
Ormewood
Oakland City
Eastland Heights
Brookwood
Lakewood Park
Lakewood Heights
Sylvan Hills
Thomasville
East Point
South Bend Park
Cornell
Constitution
South River

Chicago

Chicago O'Hare Intl. Airport
Harwood Heights
Uptown
Lake Michigan
Addison
Elmwood Park
Lincoln Park
Lincoln Park Zoo
Melrose Park
Elmhurst
Avondale
Maywood
Oak Park
Bucktown
Sears Tower
Lombard
Chicago
Westchester
Berwyn
Chinatown
Oak Brook
Cicero
Pilsen
Bronzeville
Bridgeport
La Grange
Kenwood
Downers Grove
Summit
Elsdon
Chicago Midway Airport
Englewood
Darien
Bedford Park
Forest Hill
Burbank
Ashburn
Waterfall Glen Forest Preserve
Des Plaines
Hickory Hills
Oak Lawn
Evergreen Park
Chicago State University

Dallas

L.B. Houston Park
Meaders
Biblical Arts Center
Richardson
White Rock
Garland
Oldham
Fair Oaks Park
Town East Mall
University of Dallas
Dallas Love Field
University Park
White Rock Lake
Highland Park
Irving
Dallas Theater Center
Big Town Mall
Trinity River Greenbelt Park
Eagle Ford
Dallas
Cotton Bowl
Rochester Park
Grand Prairie
Oak Cliff
Dallas Zoo
Cockrell Hill
Rochester Park
Balch Springs
Mountain Creek Lake
Fruitdale
Trinity
Mountain Creek Lake Park
Paul Quinn Collection
Lancaster

Denver

Westminster
Northglenn
Standley Lake
Federal Heights
Welby
Rocky Mountain Arsenal National Wildlife Refuge
Arvada
Commerce City
Wheat Ridge
Mile-High Stadium
Denver
Museum of Natural History
Applewood
Edgewater
Lakewood
Glendale
Four Mile Historic Park
Bear Creek Lake Park
University of Denver
Englewood
Aurora
Marston Lake
Littleton Historical Museum
Cherry Hills Village
Cherry Creek State Park
Littleton
Greenwood Village

Detroit

Sterling Heights
Mount Clemens
Roseville
Lake Saint Clair
Troy
St. Clair Shores
Pontiac
Palmer Park
Warren
Madison Heights
Detroit City Airport
Harper Woods
Birmingham
Chandler Park
Grosse Pointe
Royal Oak
Hamtramck
USA CANADA
Southfield
Chrysler Center
Belle Isle Park
Detroit
Joe Louis Sport Arena
Windsor
Redford
University of Windsor
Livonia
Dearborn
Henry Ford Museum & Greenfield Village
Patton Park
Dearborn Heights
Canton
Westland
Lincoln Park
Taylor
Southgate
Detroit River
CANADA USA
Detroit Metro Wayne County Airport

Las Vegas

Nellis Air Force Base
North Las Vegas Airport
Vegas Heights
North Las Vegas
Fountain Park
Eastland Heights
Las Vegas Natural History Museum
Sunrise Manor
Nevada State Museum and Historic Society
Freedom Park
Meadows Mall
Nature Park
Las Vegas
Las Vegas Art Museum
University
The Strip
Clark
Las Vegas Country Club
Winchester
The Strip
Spring Valley
Paradise
Liberace Museum
McCarran Intl. Airport

Los Angeles

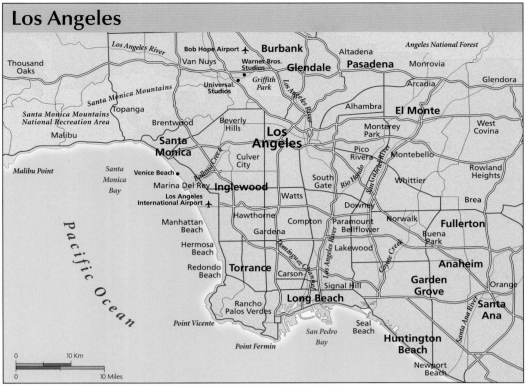

Thousand Oaks • Los Angeles River • Bob Hope Airport • Burbank • Altadena • Angeles National Forest • Van Nuys • Warner Bros. Studios • Glendale • Pasadena • Monrovia • Santa Monica Mountains • Universal Studios • Griffith Park • Arcadia • Glendora • Topanga • Alhambra • El Monte • West Covina • Brentwood • Beverly Hills • Los Angeles • Santa Monica Mountains National Recreation Area • Malibu • Santa Monica • Culver City • Monterey Park • Pico Rivera • Montebello • Rowland Heights • Malibu Point • Santa Monica Bay • Venice Beach • Marina Del Rey • Inglewood • Watts • South Gate • Downey • Whittier • Brea • Los Angeles International Airport • Hawthorne • Compton • Paramount • Norwalk • Fullerton • Manhattan Beach • Gardena • Bellflower • Buena Park • Anaheim • Hermosa Beach • Lakewood • Garden Grove • Redondo Beach • Torrance • Carson • Signal Hill • Orange • Santa Ana • Rancho Palos Verdes • Long Beach • Point Vicente • Seal Beach • Huntington Beach • Point Fermin • San Pedro Bay • Newport Beach • Pacific Ocean

10 Km / 10 Miles

Montréal

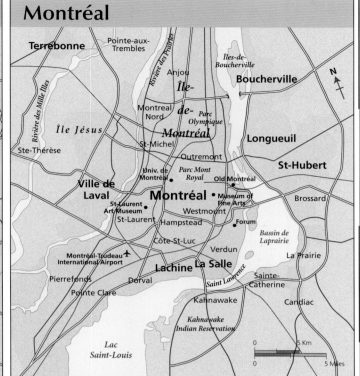

Terrebonne • Pointe-aux-Trembles • Îles-de-Boucherville • Anjou • Boucherville • Île-de-Montréal • Rivière des Prairies • Montreal Nord • Longueuil • Ste-Thérèse • St-Michel • Outremont • St-Hubert • Rivière des Mille Îles • Univ. de Montréal • Parc Mont Royal • Île Jésus • Ville de Laval • St-Laurent Art Museum • Montréal • Museum of Fine Arts • Brossard • Westmount • St-Laurent • Hampstead • Forum • Côte-St-Luc • Verdun • Bassin de Laprairie • Montréal-Trudeau International Airport • Lachine • La Salle • La Prairie • Pierrefonds • Dorval • Saint Lawrence • Sainte-Catherine • Pointe Claire • Kahnawake • Candiac • Kahnawake Indian Reservation • Lac Saint-Louis

5 Km / 5 Miles

Philadelphia

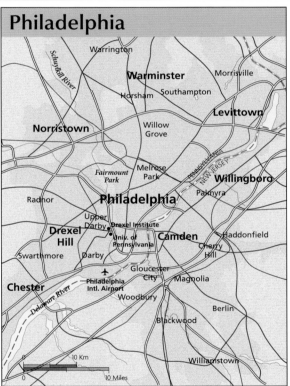

Warrington • Schuylkill River • Warminster • Morrisville • Horsham • Southampton • Norristown • Willow Grove • Levittown • Fairmount Park • Melrose Park • Willingboro • Radnor • Philadelphia • Palmyra • NEW JERSEY • Drexel Hill • Upper Darby • Drexel Institute • Camden • Swarthmore • Univ. of Pennsylvania • Darby • Cherry Hill • Haddonfield • Chester • Gloucester City • Magnolia • Philadelphia Intl. Airport • Woodbury • Berlin • Delaware River • Blackwood • Williamstown

10 Km / 10 Miles

Seattle

Whidbey Island • Everett • Clinton • Mukilteo • Puget Sound • Snohomish • Port Gamble • Kingston • Lynnwood • Monroe • Edmonds • Bothell • Woodinville • Shoreline • Hollywood • Duvall • Poulsbo • Suquamish Museum • Redmond • Keyport • Bainbridge Island • Kirkland • Marymoor Park • Sammamish • Seattle Center • Lake Washington • Bellevue • Lake Sammamish • Winslow • Seattle • Bremerton • Mercer Is. • Monohon • Port Orchard • Fauntleroy • Newcastle • Issaquah • Southworth • White Center • Renton • Fairwood • Issaquah Alps • Vashon Heights • Burien • Tukwila • Seattle-Tacoma International Airport • Kent • Vashon Island • Des Moines • Cedar • Herndon Bay • Gig Harbor • East Passage • Covington • Black Diamond • Ruston • Auburn • Tacoma

10 Km / 10 Miles

Toronto

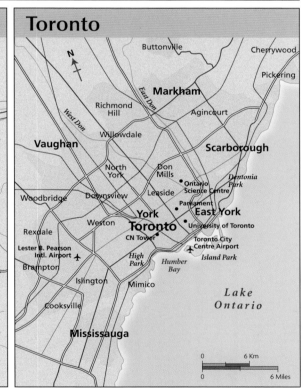

Buttonville • Cherrywood • Richmond Hill • Markham • Pickering • East Don • West Don • Agincourt • Vaughan • Willowdale • Scarborough • North York • Don Mills • Dentonia Park • Woodbridge • Downsview • Leaside • Ontario Science Centre • Weston • Parliament • East York • Rexdale • York • Toronto • University of Toronto • Lester B. Pearson Intl. Airport • CN Tower • Toronto City Centre Airport • Brampton • High Park • Humber Bay • Island Park • Islington • Mimico • Cooksville • Lake Ontario • Mississauga

6 Km / 6 Miles

San Francisco

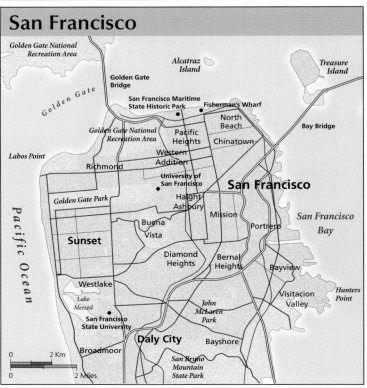

Golden Gate National Recreation Area • Alcatraz Island • Treasure Island • Golden Gate Bridge • San Francisco Maritime State Historic Park • Fisherman's Wharf • Golden Gate • North Beach • Bay Bridge • Golden Gate National Recreation Area • Pacific Heights • Chinatown • Labos Point • Western Addition • Richmond • University of San Francisco • San Francisco • Golden Gate Park • Haight Ashbury • Mission • San Francisco Bay • Pacific Ocean • Bugna Vista • Portrero • Sunset • Diamond Heights • Bernal Heights • Bayview • Hunters Point • Westlake • Lake Merced • Visitacion Valley • John McLaren Park • San Francisco State University • Daly City • Broadmoor • San Bruno Mountain State Park • Bayshore

2 Km / 2 Miles

Washington D.C.

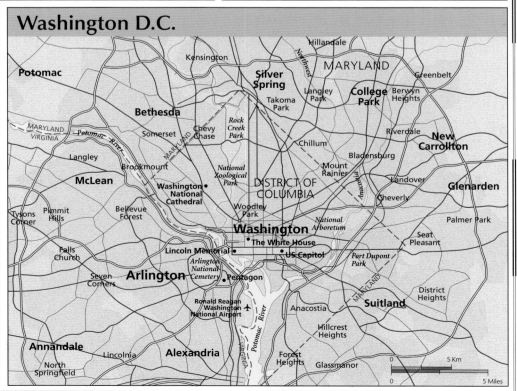

Hillandale • Kensington • Silver Spring • MARYLAND • Greenbelt • Potomac • Langley Park • College Park • Berwyn Heights • Takoma Park • Bethesda • Chevy Chase • Rock Creek Park • Riverdale • MARYLAND VIRGINIA • Potomac River • Somerset • Chillum • Bladensburg • New Carrollton • Langley • Brookmount • National Zoological Park • Mount Rainier • Vandover • McLean • DISTRICT OF COLUMBIA • Glenarden • Tysons Corner • Washington National Cathedral • Woodley Park • Cheverly • National Arboretum • Pimmit Hills • Bellevue Forest • Washington • Palmer Park • Falls Church • Lincoln Memorial • The White House • US Capitol • Fort Dupont Park • Seat Pleasant • Seven Corners • Arlington National Cemetery • Arlington • Pentagon • District Heights • Ronald Reagan Washington National Airport • Anacostia • Suitland • Hillcrest Heights • Annandale • Lincolnia • Alexandria • Forest Heights • North Springfield • Glassmanor

5 Km / 5 Miles

South America reaches from the humid tropics down into the cold South Atlantic, with a total area of 6,886,000 sq miles (17,835,000 sq km). It comprises 12 separate countries, with the largest, Brazil, covering almost half the continent.

FACTFILE

N **Most Northerly Point:** Punta Gallinas, Colombia 12° 28′ N
S **Most Southerly Point:** Cape Horn, Chile 55° 59′ S
E **Most Easterly Point:** Ilhas Martin Vaz, Brazil 28° 51′ W
W **Most Westerly Point:** Galapagos Islands, Ecuador 92° 00′ W

Largest Lakes:
1 Lake Titicaca, Bolivia/Peru 3141 sq miles (8135 sq km)
2 Mirim Lagoon, Brazil/Uruguay 1158 sq miles (3000 sq km)
3 Lago Poopó, Bolivia 976 sq miles (2530 sq km)
4 Lago Buenos Aires, Argentina/Chile 864 sq miles (2240 sq km)
5 Laguna Mar Chiquita, Argentina 695 sq miles (1800 sq km)

Longest Rivers:
1 Amazon, Brazil/Colombia/Peru 4049 miles (6516 km)
2 Paraná, Argentina/Brazil/Paraguay 2920 miles (4700 km)
3 Madeira, Bolivia/Brazil 2100 miles (3379 km)
4 Purus, Brazil/Peru 2013 miles (3239 km)
5 São Francisco, Brazil 1802 miles (2900 km)

Largest Islands:
1 Tierra del Fuego, Argentina/Chile 18,302 sq miles (47,401 sq km)
2 Ilha de Marajo, Brazil 15,483 sq miles (40,100 sq km)
3 Isla de Chiloé, Chile 3241 sq miles (8394 sq km)
4 East Falkland, Falkland Islands 2550 sq miles (6605 sq km)
5 Isla Wellington, Chile 2145 sq miles (5556 sq km)

Highest Points:
1 Cerro Aconcagua, Argentina 22,831 ft (6959 m)
2 Cerro Ojos del Salado, Argentina/Chile 22,572 ft (6880 m)
3 Cerro Bonete, Argentina 22,546 ft (6872 m)
4 Monte Pissis, Argentina 22,224 ft (6774 m)
5 Cerro Mercedario, Argentina 22,211 ft (6768 m)

Lowest Point:
▼ Península Valdés -131 ft (-40 m) below sea level

Highest recorded temperature:
Rivadavia, Argentina 120°F (49°C)

Lowest recorded temperature:
— Sarmiento, Argentina -27°F (-33°C)

Wettest Place:
Quibdó, Colombia 354 in (8990 mm)

Driest Place:
— Arica, Chile 0.03 in (0.8 mm)

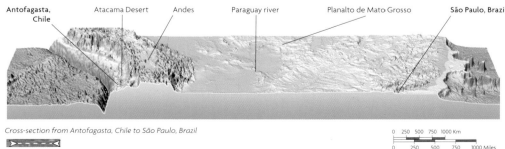

Antofagasta, Chile   Atacama Desert   Andes   Paraguay river   Planalto de Mato Grosso   São Paulo, Brazil

Cross-section from Antofagasta, Chile to São Paulo, Brazil

⟫－－－－⟪
line of cross-section

0 250 500 750 1000 Km
0 250 500 750 1000 Miles

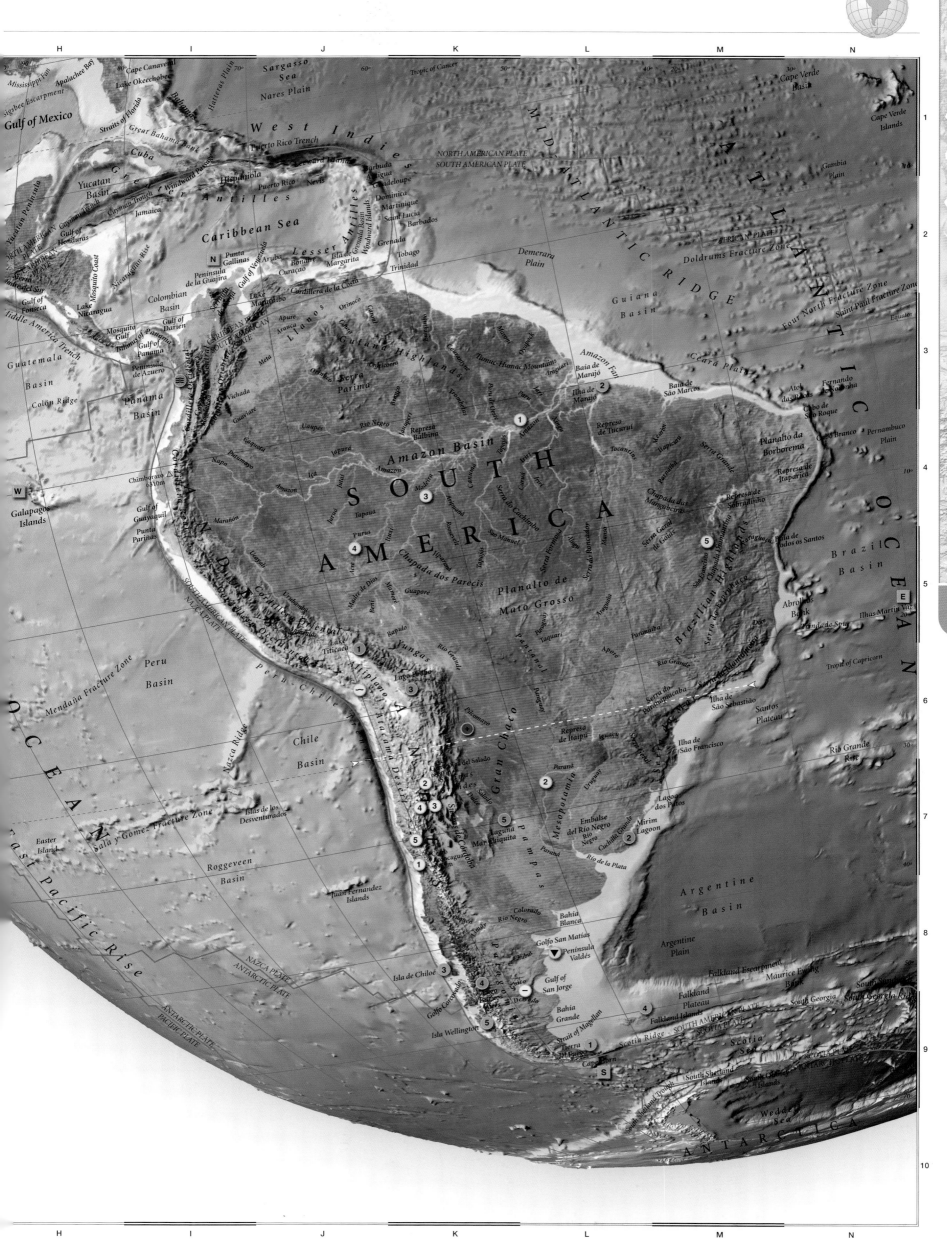

H I J K L M N

H I J K L M N

Gulf of Mexico

Sigsbee Escarpment
Apalachee Bay
Cape Canaveral
Lake Okeechobee
Hatteras plain
Sargasso Sea
Nares Plain
Tropic of Cancer
Cape Verde Basin

West Indies

Straits of Florida
Great Bahama Bank
Bahamas
Puerto Rico Trench
Cuba
Greater Antilles
Jamaica
Hispaniola
Puerto Rico
Windward Passage
Leeward Islands
Barbuda
Antigua
Guadeloupe
Dominica
Martinique
Saint Lucia
Barbados
Gambia Plain
Cape Verde Islands

NORTH AMERICAN PLATE
SOUTH AMERICAN PLATE

MID-ATLANTIC RIDGE

ATLANTIC

AFRICAN PLATE
Doldrums Fracture Zone
Four North Fracture Zone
Saint-Paul Fracture Zone
Equator

Yucatan Peninsula
Yucatan Basin
Cayman Trough
Gulf of Honduras
Mosquito Coast
Nicaraguan Rise
Caribbean Sea
Peninsula de la Guajira
Punta Gallinas
Gulf of Venezuela
Aruba
Curaçao
Bonaire
Isla de Margarita
Windward Islands
Grenada
Tobago
Trinidad
Lesser Antilles
Demerara Plain

Guatemala Basin
Middle America Trench
Gulf of Fonseca
Lake Nicaragua
Mosquito Gulf
Isthmus of Panama
Gulf of Panama
Peninsula de Azuero
Colón Ridge
Panama Basin
Colombian Basin
Cordillera de la Costa
Lake Maracaibo
Cordillera Oriental
Llanos
Apure
Orinoco
Arauca
Meta
Guaviare
Vichada
Orinoco
Guiana Highlands
Serra Parima
Tumuc-Humac Mountains
Guiana Basin
Ceara Plain
Amazon Fan
Baía de Marajó
Ilha de Marajó

Chimborazo 6310m
Galápagos Islands
Gulf of Guayaquil
Punta Parinas
Marañón
Uaupés
Caqueta
Napo
Putumayo
Ica
Rio Negro
Japurá
Amazon Basin
Amazon
Madeira
SOUTH AMERICA
Represa Balbina
Tocantins
Araguaia
Represa de Tucuruí
Baía de São Marcos
Planalto da Borborema
Cabo de São Roque
Pernambuco Plain
Cabo Branco

Peru Basin
Mendaña Fracture Zone
NAZCA PLATE
SOUTH AMERICAN PLATE
Cordillera Occidental
Juruá
Purus
Madre de Dios
Beni
Guaporé
Chapada dos Parecis
Planalto de Mato Grosso
Serra do Cachimbo
Chapada dos Mangabeiras
Serra Geral de Goiás
Represa de Itaparica
Represa de Sobradinho
Brazilian Highlands
Serra do Espinhaço
Baía de Todos os Santos
Brazil Basin
Abrolhos Bank
Ilhas Martin Vaz

Chile Basin
Nazca Ridge
Islas de los Desventurados
Lake Titicaca
Altiplano
Yungas
Lago Poopó
ANDES
Pantanal
Rio Grande
Apore
Paranaíba
São Francisco
Serra do Paranapiacaba
Ilha de São Sebastião
Santos Plateau
Tropic of Capricorn
Rio Grande Rise

Easter Island
Sala y Gómez Fracture Zone
Roggeveen Basin
Juan Fernández Islands
Atacama Desert
Llullaillaco
Salar de Atacama
Gran Chaco
Represa de Itaipu
Iguaçu
Uruguay
Paraná
Mesopotamia
Embalse del Río Negro
Río Negro
Mirim Lagoon
Lagoa dos Patos

Laguna Mar Chiquita
Sierra de Córdoba
Pampas
Paraná
Cuchilla Grande
Río de la Plata

Isla de Chiloé
Aconcagua
Colorado
Río Negro
Bahía Blanca
Golfo San Matías
Península Valdés
Argentine Basin
Argentine Plain

NAZCA PLATE
ANTARCTIC PLATE
Golfo Corcovado
Isla Wellington
Gulf of San Jorge
Bahía Grande
Falkland Escarpment
Maurice Ewing Bank
South Georgia
South Sandwich Trench

ANTARCTIC PLATE
PACIFIC PLATE
Strait of Magellan
Tierra del Fuego
Cape Horn
Falkland Plateau
Scotia Ridge
SOUTH AMERICAN PLATE
Scotia Sea
South Shetland Islands
South Orkney Islands
ANTARCTIC PLATE

Weddell Sea

ANTARCTICA

OCEAN

PACIFIC

East Pacific Rise

SOUTH ATLANTIC OCEAN

Km
0 100 200 300 400 500 600 700 800
Miles
0 100 200 300 400 500 600 700 800

Scale 1:24,000,000
(projection: Lambert Azimuthal Equal Area)

Caribbean Sea

TRINIDAD & TOBAGO

ATLANTIC OCEAN

Santa Marta
Barranquilla
Cartagena
Valledupar
Maracaibo
Valencia
CARACAS
Maracay
Cumaná
Gulf of Darien
Montería
Cabimas
Barquisimeto
Lake Maracaibo
Cúcuta
San Cristóbal
Barinas
Ciudad Guayana
Venezuelan territorial claim

PANAMA
Gulf of Panama
Medellín
Bucaramanga
Manizales
Pereira
Armenia
Ibagué
BOGOTÁ
Cali

VENEZUELA

GUYANA
GEORGETOWN
Linden
PARAMARIBO
SURINAME
CAYENNE
French Guiana (to France)
Surinamese territorial claims

COLOMBIA

Llanos
Orinoco
Río Negro
Boa Vista
RORAIMA
Guiana Highlands

AMAPÁ
Macapá

Esmeraldas
Pasto
QUITO
Equator

ECUADOR
Ambato
Riobamba
Portoviejo
Guayaquil
Babahoyo
Machala
Cuenca

Caquetá
Putumayo
Japurá
Amazon
Amazon
Belém
São Luís
Santarém
Manaus

AMAZONAS

Iquitos
Marañón
Ucayali
Juruá
Purús
Madeira
Tapajós

Basin

PARÁ
Tocantins
MARANHÃO
Teresina

Piura
Chiclayo
Trujillo

PERU

ACRE
Rio Branco
Porto Velho
RONDONIA

CEARÁ
Fortaleza
RIO GRANDE DO NORTE
Natal
PIAUÍ
PARAÍBA
João Pessoa
PERNAMBUCO
Jaboatão
Recife
ALAGOAS
Maceió

Callao
Huancayo
LIMA
Cusco
Madre de Dios

BRAZIL

TOCANTINS
Palmas do Tocantins
Juazeiro
Represa de Sobradinho
SERGIPE
Aracaju

BOLIVIA

MATO GROSSO
Planalto de Mato Grosso
Cuiabá

BAHIA
Brazilian Highlands
Salvador
São Francisco

Arequipa
Lake Titicaca
LA PAZ
Cochabamba
Santa Cruz
Tacna
Oruro
Arica
Lago Poopó
SUCRE

BRASÍLIA
DISTRITO FEDERAL
Goiânia
GOIÁS
MINAS GERAIS
Belo Horizonte

Iquique
Tocopilla

Pilcomayo
Paraguay

MATO GROSSO DO SUL
Campo Grande
Ribeirão Preto
SÃO PAULO
Londrina
Campinas
Osasco
São Paulo
Sorocaba
Santos
PARANÁ
Curitiba

Vitória
ESPÍRITO SANTO
Juiz de Fora
Nova Iguaçu
RIO DE JANEIRO
Niterói
Rio de Janeiro
Tropic of Capricorn

Tropic of Capricorn
Antofagasta

PARAGUAY
San Salvador de Jujuy
Salta
Gran Chaco
ASUNCIÓN
Ciudad del Este
Formosa
Villarrica

Atacama Desert
San Miguel de Tucumán
Santiago del Estero
La Rioja

Resistencia
Corrientes
Posadas
SANTA CATARINA
Florianópolis
Paraná

RIO GRANDE DO SUL
Santa Maria
Porto Alegre

La Serena
Coquimbo

Córdoba
Santa Fe
Paraná
Rosario
Uruguay
Tacuarembó
Melo

San Juan
Mendoza
Viña del Mar
Valparaíso
SANTIAGO
San Luis
BUENOS AIRES
La Plata
Río de la Plata
MONTEVIDEO

URUGUAY

Population
■ above 5 million
▣ 1 million to 5 million
◉ 500,000 to 1 million
◎ 100,000 to 500,000
⊕ 50,000 to 100,000
◌ 10,000 to 50,000
○ below 10,000
● Country capital
◦ State capital

Concepción
Lota
Temuco
Valdivia
Linares
Santa Rosa
Colorado
Bahía Blanca
Mar del Plata
Río Negro
Neuquén

CHILE
ARGENTINA

Pampas

PACIFIC OCEAN

ATLANTIC OCEAN

Borders
— full international border
-·- disputed de facto border
-··- disputed territorial claim border
— state border

Puerto Montt
Lago Colhué Huapí
Rawson
Chico
Gulf of San Jorge
Deseado
Golfo de Penas

Patagonia

Bahía Grande
STANLEY
Falkland Islands
(Islas Malvinas)
(to UK)
Río Gallegos
Strait of Magellan
Punta Arenas
Ushuaia
Beagle Channel
Cape Horn

Political

Modern South America's political boundaries have their origins in the territorial endeavors of explorers during the 16th century, who claimed almost the entire continent for Portugal and Spain. The Portuguese land in the east later evolved into the federal states of Brazil, while the Spanish vice-royalties eventually emerged as separate independent nation-states in the early 19th century. South America's growing population has become increasingly urbanized, with the expansion of coastal cities into large conurbations like Rio de Janeiro and Buenos Aires. In Brazil, Argentina, Chile, and Uruguay, a succession of military dictatorships has given way to fragile, but strengthening, democracies.

Languages

Prior to European exploration in the 16th century, a diverse range of indigenous languages were spoken across the continent. With the arrival of Iberian settlers, Spanish became the dominant language, with Portuguese spoken in Brazil, and Native American languages, such as Quechua and Guaraní, becoming concentrated in the continental interior. Today this pattern persists, although successive European colonization has led to Dutch being spoken in Suriname, English in Guyana, and French in French Guiana, while in large urban areas, Japanese and Chinese are increasingly common.

Language groups

- American Indian
- Germanic
- Romance

Standard of living

Wealth disparities throughout the continent create a wide gulf between affluent landowners and those afflicted by chronic poverty in inner-city slums. The illicit production of cocaine, and the hugely influential drug barons who control its distribution, contribute to the violent disorder and corruption which affect northwestern South America, destabilizing local governments and economies.

Standard of living
(UN human development index)

- low
- high

Population

Almost half of South America's population lives in Brazil but, due to the large uninhabited expanses of the Amazon Basin, its overall population density is much lower than in other countries. During the 20th century the most important population trend was the movement from rural to urban areas, giving rise to great population concentrations in cities like São Paulo, Rio de Janeiro, Caracas, Lima, Bogotá, and Buenos Aires.

Population density
(people per sq mile)

- below 10
- 11–23
- 24–36
- 37–49
- 50–75
- above 75

Transportation

- major roads and motorways
- major railroads
- international borders
- • transport intersections
- ⊕ international airports
- ⊕ major ports

Transportation

Most major road and rail routes are confined to the coastal regions by the forbidding natural barriers of the Andes mountains and the Amazon Basin. Few major cross-continental routes exist, although Buenos Aires serves as a transport center for the main rail links to La Paz and Valparaíso, while the construction of the Trans-Amazon and Pan-American Highways have made direct road travel possible from Recife to Lima and from Puerto Montt up the coast into central America. A new waterway project is proposed to transform the Paraguay river into a major shipping route, although it involves considerable wetland destruction.

SOUTH AMERICA – Physical

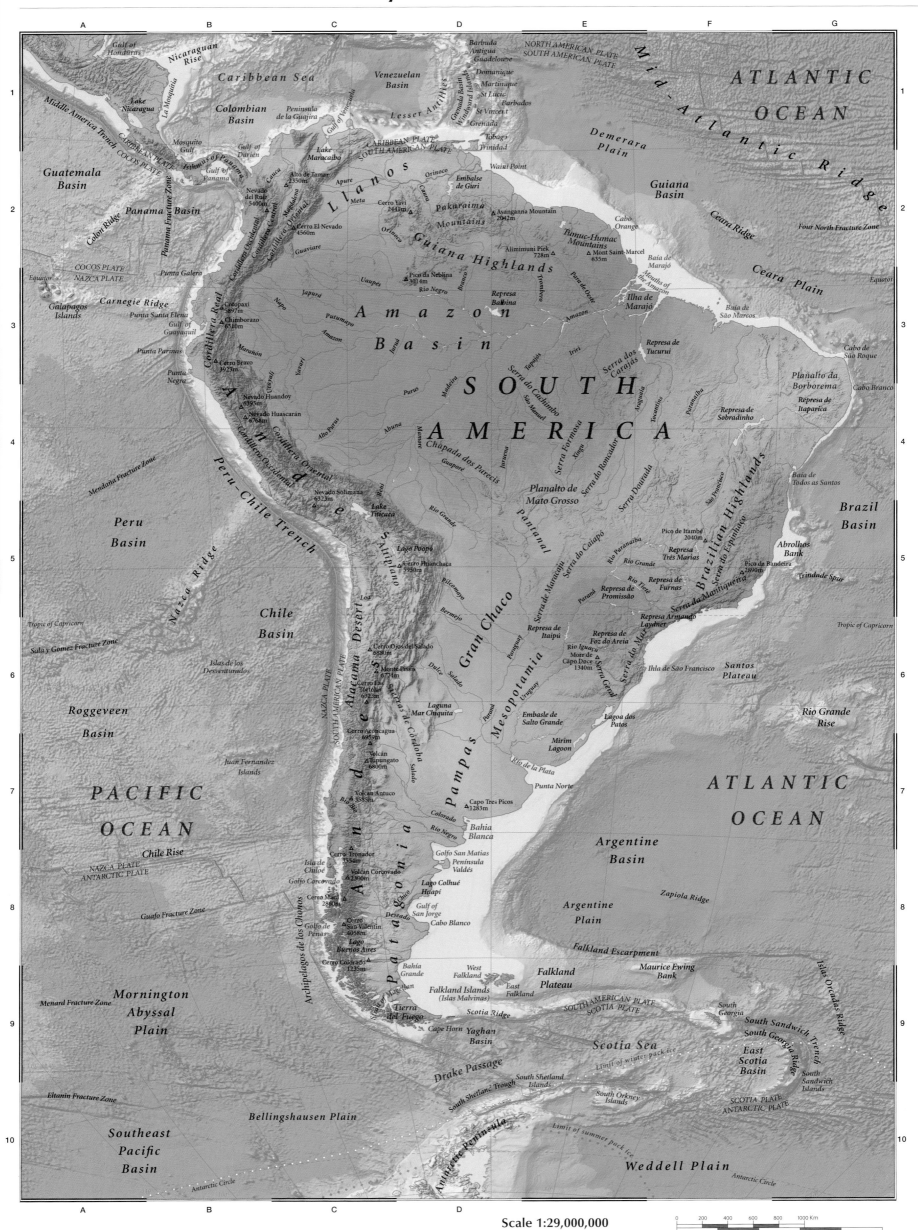

Gulf of Honduras
Nicaraguan Rise
Caribbean Sea
Barbuda
Antigua
Guadeloupe
NORTH AMERICAN PLATE
SOUTH AMERICAN PLATE
ATLANTIC OCEAN
Mid-Atlantic Ridge

Lake Nicaragua
La Mosquitia
Colombian Basin
Peninsula de la Guajira
Venezuelan Basin
Lesser Antilles
Grenada Basin
Windward Islands
Dominique
Martinique
St Lucia
Barbados
St Vincent
Grenada
Tobago
Trinidad

Middle America Trench
COCOS PLATE
Mosquito Gulf
Isthmus of Panama
Gulf of Darién
Lake Maracaibo
Gulf of Venezuela
CARIBBEAN PLATE
SOUTH AMERICAN PLATE
Demerara Plain

Guatemala Basin
Gulf of Panama
Alto de Tamar 2350m
Cauca
Cordillera Oriental
Cordillera Central
Apure
Orinoco
Embalse de Guri
Waini Point
Guiana Basin
Ceara Ridge

Colón Ridge
Panama Fracture Zone
Panama Basin
Nevado del Ruiz 5400m
Magdalena
Meta
Cerro Yavi 2441m
Pakaraima Mountains
Asanganna Mountain 2042m
Cabo Orange
Four North Fracture Zone

COCOS PLATE
NAZCA PLATE
Cerro El Nevado 4560m
Llanos
Orinoco
Guiana Highlands
Alimimuni Peak 728m
Tumuc-Humac Mountains
Mont Saint-Marcel 635m
Baía de Marajó
Ceara Plain

Equator
Punta Galera
Cordillera Occidental
Guaviare
Pico da Neblina 3014m
Rio Negro
Branco
Trombetas
Mouths of the Amazon
Ilha de Marajó
Equator

Galapagos Islands
Carnegie Ridge
Punta Santa Elena
Cotopaxi 5897m
Guarico
Japurá
Napo
Putumayo
Amazon
Amazon Basin
Para de Oeste
Amazon
Baía de São Marcos

Gulf of Guayaquil
Chimborazo 6310m
Cordillera Real
Marañón
Putumayo
Amazon
Juruá
Purus
Madeira
Tapajós
SOUTH
Iriri
Xingu
Serra do Cachimbo
São Manuel
Represa Balbina
Represa de Tucuruí

Punta Parinas
Cerro Bravo 3923m
Yavari
Ucayali
Amazon
Serra dos Carajás
Tocantins
Araguaia
Represa de Sobradinho

Punta Negra
Nevado Huandoy 6395m
Cordillera Oriental
Alto Purus
AMERICA
Serra Formosa
Serra do Roncador
Planalto da Borborema
Cabo de São Roque
Cabo Branco

Nevado Huascarán 6768m
Abuná
Chapada dos Parecis
Guaporé
Serra Dourada
São Francisco
Represa de Itaparica

Mendaña Fracture Zone
Cordillera Occidental
Mamoré
Chapada dos Parecis
Planalto de Mato Grosso
Serra da Canastra
Pico de Itambé 2040m
Baía de Todos os Santos

Peru Basin
Nazca Ridge
Nevado Solimana 6323m
Beni
Lago Poopó
Pantanal
Serra de Maracaju
Serra do Caiapó
Represa Três Marias
Brazilian Highlands
Serra do Espinhaço
Brazil Basin

Lake Titicaca
Rio Grande
Rio Paranaíba
Rio Grande
Represa de Furnas
Pico da Bandeira 2890m
Abrolhos Bank

Tropic of Capricorn
Peru-Chile Trench
Altiplano
Cerro Huanchaca 5950m
Pilcomayo
Rio Tietê
Represa de Promissão
Serra da Mantiqueira
Trindade Spur

Salá y Gomez Fracture Zone
Chile Basin
Loa
Bermejo
Gran Chaco
Paraná
Represa de Itaipú
Represa de Foz do Areia
Rio Iguaçu
Morro de Capo Doce 1340m
Serra Geral
Ilhe de São Francisco
Santos Plateau

Islas de los Desventurados
Cerro Ojos del Salado 6880m
Atacama Desert
Dulce
Salado
Mesopotamia
Uruguay
Embalse de Salto Grande
Lagoa dos Patos

Roggeveen Basin
Monte Pissis 6774m
Sierras de Córdoba
Laguna Mar Chiquita
Paraná
Mirim Lagoon
Rio Grande Rise

Juan Fernandez Islands
Cerro Las Tórtolas 6323m
NAZCA PLATE
SOUTH AMERICAN PLATE
Cerro Aconcagua 6959m
Salado
Pampas
Rio de la Plata
Punta Norte

Volcán Tupungato 6800m
Colorado
PACIFIC OCEAN
Volcán Antuco 3585m
Biobío
Río Negro
Bahía Blanca
Capo Tres Picos 1283m
ATLANTIC OCEAN

Chile Rise
NAZCA PLATE
ANTARCTIC PLATE
Golfo San Matías
Península Valdés
Argentine Basin
Argentine Plain

Isla de Chiloé
Cerro Tronador 3554m
Volcán Corcovado 2300m
Lago Colhué Huapí
Gulf of San Jorge
Cabo Blanco
Zapiola Ridge

Guafo Fracture Zone
Golfo Corcovado
Archipiélagos de los Chonos
Cerro Macá 2960m
Patagonia
Deseado
Falkland Escarpment
Maurice Ewing Bank
Islas Orcadas Ridge

Golfo de Penas
Cerro San Valentín 4058m
Lago Buenos Aires
Andes
West Falkland
East Falkland
Falkland Plateau
South Georgia
South Sandwich Trench
South Georgia Ridge

Menard Fracture Zone
Mornington Abyssal Plain
Cerro Colorado 1235m
Bahía Grande
Magellan
Falkland Islands (Islas Malvinas)
Scotia Ridge
SOUTH AMERICAN PLATE
SCOTIA PLATE
East Scotia Basin
South Sandwich Islands

Tierra del Fuego
Cape Horn
Yaghan Basin
Scotia Sea
Limit of winter pack ice
SCOTIA PLATE
ANTARCTIC PLATE

Eltanin Fracture Zone
Drake Passage
South Shetland Trough
South Shetland Islands
South Orkney Islands

Southeast Pacific Basin
Bellingshausen Plain
Antarctic Circle
Antarctic Peninsula
Limit of summer pack ice
Weddell Plain
Antarctic Circle

Tropic of Capricorn
Equator

Scale 1:29,000,000
(projection: Lambert Azimuthal Equal Area)

0 200 400 600 800 1000 Km
0 200 400 600 800 1000 Miles

Climate

The climate of South America is influenced by three principal factors: the seasonal shift of high pressure air masses over the tropics, cold ocean currents along the western coast, affecting temperature and precipitation, and the mountain barrier produced by by the Andes, which creates a rain shadow over much of the south.

Climate

- tundra
- cool continental
- warm humid
- semi-arid
- arid
- humid equatorial
- tropical

☼ daily hours of sunshine, January

☼ daily hours of sunshine, July

→ cold wind

Average Rainfall

January rainfall

July rainfall

Rainfall

- 0–1 in (0–25 mm)
- 1–2 in (25–50 mm)
- 2–4 in (50–100 mm)
- 4–8 in (100–200 mm)
- 8–12 in (200–300 mm)
- 12–16 in (300–400 mm)
- 16–20 in (400–500 mm)
- more than 20 in (500 mm)

Average Temperature

January temperature

July temperature

Temperature

- below -22°F (-30°C)
- -22 to -4°F (-30 to -20°C)
- -4 to 14°F (-20 to -10°C)
- 14 to 32°F (-10 to 0°C)
- 32 to 50°F (0 to 10°C)
- 50 to 68°F (10 to 20°C)
- 68 to 86°F (20 to 30°C)
- above 86°F (30°C)

Land use

Many foods now common worldwide originated in South America. These include the potato, tomato, squash, and cassava. Today, large herds of beef cattle roam the temperate grasslands of the Pampas, supporting an extensive meat-packing trade in Argentina, Uruguay and Paraguay. Corn (maize) is grown as a staple crop across the continent and coffee is grown as a cash crop in Brazil and Colombia. Coca plants grown in Bolivia, Peru and Colombia provide most of the western world's cocaine. Fish and shellfish are caught off the western coast, especially anchovies off Peru, shrimps off Ecuador and sardines off Chile.

Environmental Issues

The Amazon Basin is one of the last great wilderness areas left on Earth. The tropical rainforests which grow there are a valuable genetic resource, containing innumerable unique plants and animals. The forests are increasingly under threat from new and expanding settlements and "slash and burn" farming techniques, which clear land for the raising of beef cattle, causing land degradation and soil erosion.

Environmental Issues

- national parks
- tropical forest
- forest destroyed
- desert
- desertification
- polluted rivers
- marine pollution
- heavy marine pollution
- • poor urban air quality

Using the Land and Sea

- barren land
- cropland
- desert
- forest
- mountain region
- pasture
- • major conurbations
- cattle
- pigs
- sheep
- bananas
- corn (maize)
- citrus fruits
- cocoa
- cotton
- coffee
- fishing
- oil palms
- peanuts
- rubber
- shellfish
- soya beans
- sugar cane
- vineyards
- wheat

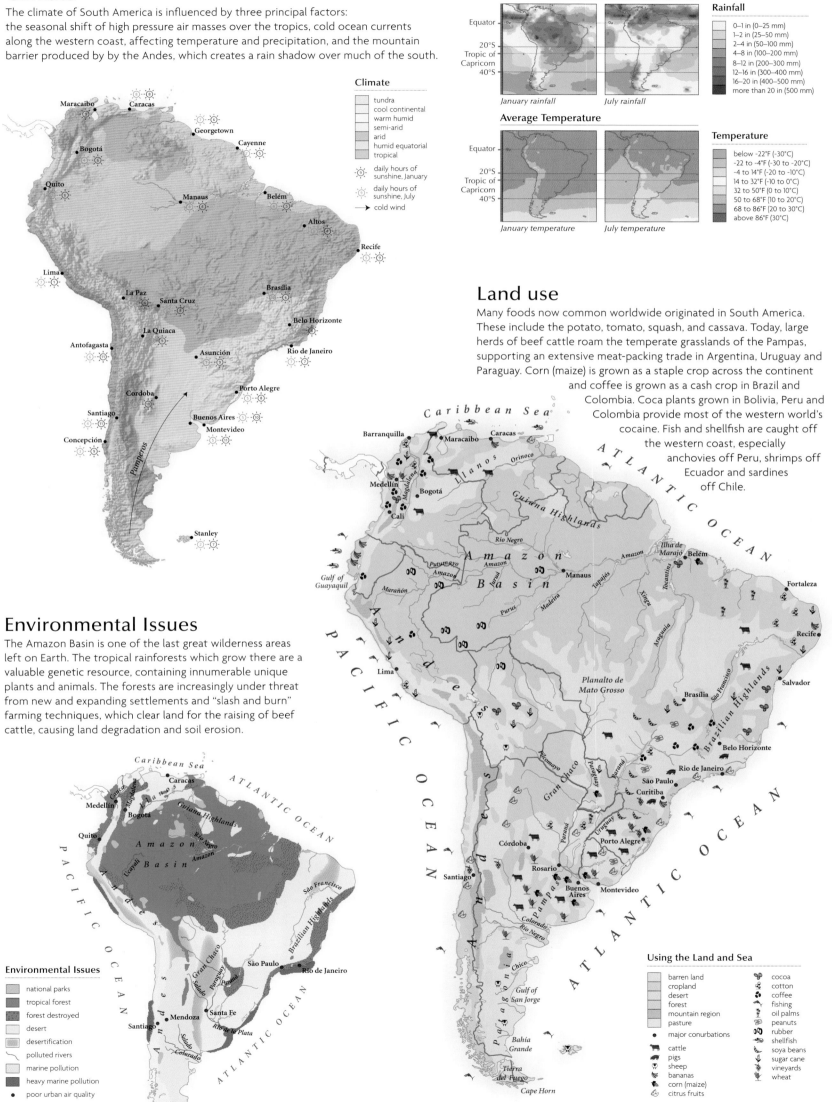

SOUTH AMERICA

1 SANTIAGO, CHILE
Chile's capital city was founded in 1541 by Pedro de Valdivia who chose the location because it had a Mediterranean climate and was easy to defend.

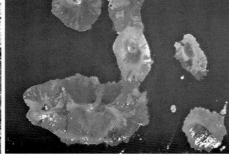

2 GALAPAGOS ISLANDS, ECUADOR
These islands are a collection of volcanoes rising from the ocean floor 621 miles (1000 km) west of the South American mainland.

3 SALAR DE UYUNI, BOLIVIA
Occupying a depression high up on the Altiplano between the volcanoes of the western Andes and the fold belts of the eastern Andes, this is the world's largest salt flat.

4 MACHU PICCHU, PERU
Perched precariously above the Urubamba valley, the lost Inca retreat was rediscovered in 1911 by Hiram Bingham, an American archaeologist.

9 LAGO VIEDMA, ARGENTINA
Lago Viedma enjoys a milky-blue appearance due to the glacial sediment suspended in its waters.

10 LOS LAGOS, CHILE
A region of many lakes at the foothills of the Andes in south-central Chile, this area is an attraction for many tourists.

11 ROSARIO, ARGENTINA
Located on the west bank of the Paraná river, Rosario lies at that heart of Argentina's industrial corridor, centered on the river.

12 RIVER PLATE, ARGENTINA/URUGUAY
Fed by the Paraná and Uruguay rivers, this Atlantic Ocean inlet separates Argentina and Uruguay.

RONDÔNIA, BRAZIL
Pale strips of forest clearance can be seen along perpendicular tracks in this region of the Amazon Basin.

5

MARACAIBO, VENEZUELA
Maracaibo is the center of Venezuela's oil industry and its second largest city with a population of 1.6 million.

6

AMAZON RIVER/RIO NEGRO, BRAZIL
The dark, plant debris-stained waters of the Rio Negro join the beige Amazon near the city of Manaus.

7

EMBALSE DE GURI, VENEZUELA
This enormous reservoir, on the Caroni river, was completed in 1986 and its hydroelectric plant was the first to produce more than 10 gigawatts of electricity.

8

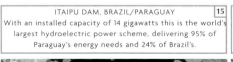

FOREST CLEARANCE IN SANTA CRUZ STATE, BOLIVIA
This infrared image shows the distinctive radial clearance patterns of original tropical dry forest with a small settlement at each center.

13

LAGOA DOS PATOS AND MIRIM LAGOON, BRAZIL/URUGUAY
These two lagoons are separated from the Atlantic Ocean by 248 miles (400 km) of sandbar.

14

ITAIPU DAM, BRAZIL/PARAGUAY
With an installed capacity of 14 gigawatts this is the world's largest hydroelectric power scheme, delivering 95% of Paraguay's energy needs and 24% of Brazil's.

15

POINT BALEIA, BRAZIL
This headland has built up through steady accumulation of silt and sediment, shaped by tides and ocean currents.

16

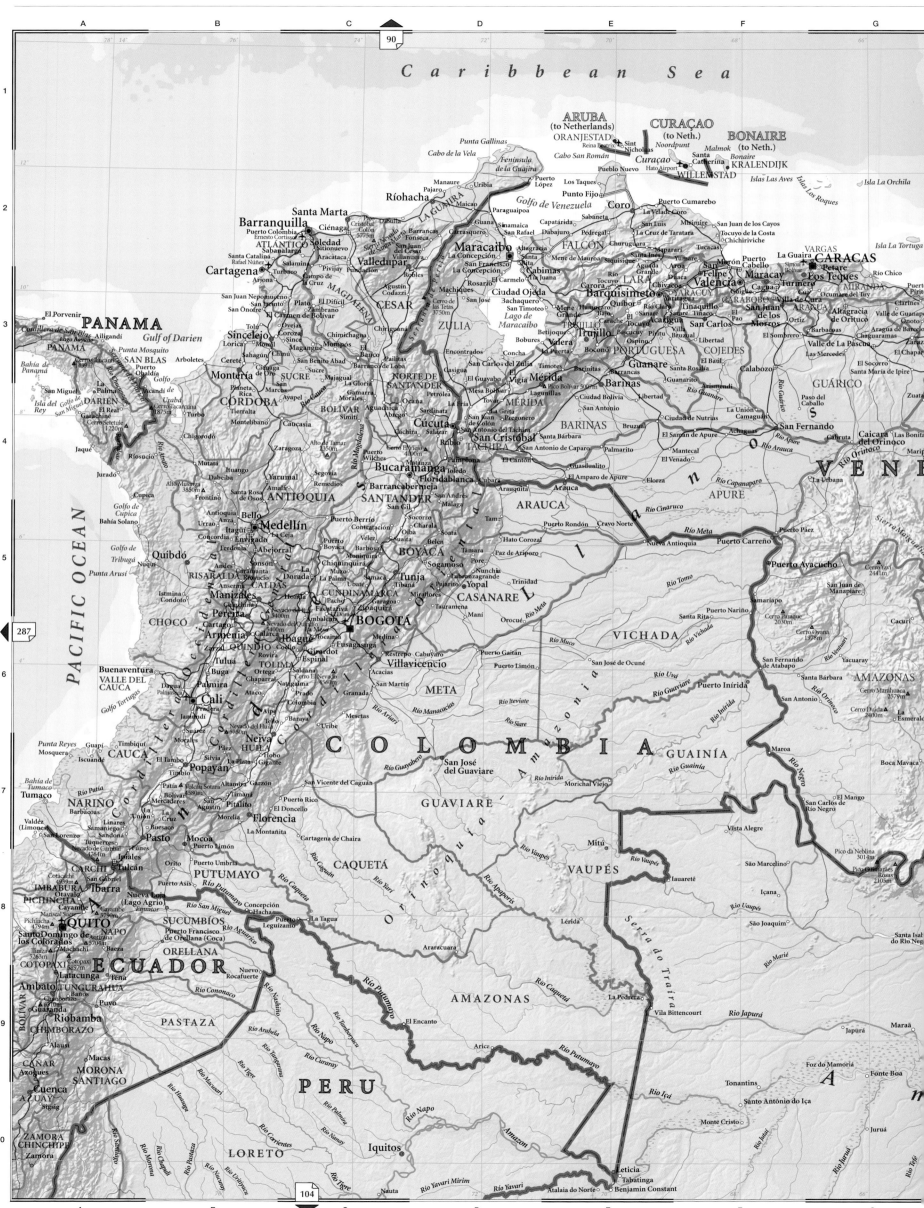

Scale 1:6,500,000
(projection: Lambert Azimuthal Equal Area)

0 25 50 75 100 125 150 175 200 Km
0 25 50 75 100 125 150 175 200 Miles

Population
- ■ above 5 million
- ■ 1 million to 5 million
- ◉ 500,000 to 1 million
- ◎ 100,000 to 500,000
- ⊕ 50,000 to 100,000
- ○ 10,000 to 50,000
- ○ below 10,000

290

Bogotá

N

Usaquén

Molinos

Canal de Guaymaral

Río Juan Amarillo

Monumento Lara Bonita

Aeropuerto Internacional El Dorado

Barrios Unidos

Chapinero

Engativá

Teusaquillo

Fontibón

Bogotá

Puente Aranda

Museo Nacional de Colombia

Kennedy

Río Fucha

Los Mártires

Catedral La Candelaria

Santa Fe

Antonio Marino

San Cristóbal

Tunjuelito

Rafael Uribe

0   1 Km
0   1 Miles

George F.L. Charles
CASTRIES
Mount Gimie
950m
ST LUCIA
Hewanorra
Vieux Fort

Saint Vincent Passage

St Vincent
KINGSTOWN
ST VINCENT & THE GRENADINES
Arnos Vale
Bequia
Mustique
Canouan
Union Island
Carriacou
The Grenadines

BARBADOS
BRIDGETOWN
Grantley Adams

ST. GEORGE'S
Point Salines
GRENADA

Isla Blanquilla

Isla de Margarita
Islas los Testigos
NUEVA ESPARTA
Juangriego La Asunción
Pampatar
Porlamar
Punta de Piedras
Boca de Pozo

Tobago
Charlotteville
Scarborough
Galera Point

ATLANTIC OCEAN

Río Caribe
PORT-OF-SPAIN
Arima

Puerto La Cruz
Cumaná
Araya
Carúpano
El Pilar
Irapa
Güiria
Puerto de Hierro
Casanay
SUCRE
Cariaco
San Antonio
Cumanacoa
Caripe
Quiriquire
Caripito
San Fernando
Point Fortin
Bonasse
Siparia
Rushville
Galeota Point

Sangre Grande
Piarco
Trinidad
TRINIDAD & TOBAGO

Gulf of Paria

Cerro Turimiquire
1957m

Barcelona
San Mateo
Aragua de Maturín
Caicara
San Joaquín
Anaco Aguasay
Cantaura
MONAGAS
Punta de Mata
Santa Rosa
Maturín
Temblador
Tucupita

Pedernales

Punta Baja

El Tigre
San Tomé
San José de Guanipa
ANZOÁTEGUI
Pariaguán
Barrancas
DELTA AMACURO
La Horqueta

Cano Mariusa
Cano Manamo

Waini Point
Guayabones
Curiapo
Waini

Ciudad Guayana
Soledad
Río Orinoco
Ciudad Bolívar
El Pao
El Palmar
Upata

Port Kaituma

Borbón
Mapire
Caicara

Ciudad Piar
Embalse de Guri
El Manteco
El Callao
Tumeremo

Arakaka
Matthews Ridge

Barama River
Charity

Spring Garden
Aurora
Kuracki

Essequibo Islands
Parika
GEORGETOWN
Bartica
Cheddi Jagan

New Amsterdam
Rosa Hall

Cuyuni River

Z U E L A
Cerro Guaiquinima
2100m
BOLÍVAR
Salto Ángel
Auyán Tepuy
2950m
Uruyén
Cerro Venamo
1563m
Canaima
El Casabe
Caño Negro
El Dorado

Kamarang
Imbaimadai
Mahdia
Issano

Peters Mine
Rockstone
Linden

Mazaruni River

Demerara River

Corriverton

Nieuw Nickerie
Wageningen
Friendship
Totness
Paramaribo
WANICA
COMMEWIJNE

Nieuw Amsterdam

Essequibo River

Santa Maria de Erebato
G u
Cabadisocaña

Mount Roraima
2810m
Ayangganna Mountain
2042m

Orealla
Wasjabo
Apoera

Nieuw Nickerie
Groningen
SARA-MACCA
PARA
Onverwacht
PARAMARIBO
Leidydorp
Mana
NICKERIE
CORONIE
Corneliskondre
Kaaimanston
Kwakoegron
Brownsweg
Brokopondo
Bergen Dal
Albina
St-Laurent-du-Maroni
Sinnamary
Iracoubo
Kourou

Ilu du Salut
Ile du Diable
Centre Spatial Guyanais

GUYANA
G u i a n a
Uonán
Santa Elena de Uairén

Glendor Mountains
Kaieteur Falls
Ituni

Coppename River

Hendrik Top
957m
Tafelberg
1026m

Pokigron
Boti-Pasi
BROKOPONDO
Poeketi

St-Jean
Apatou
Herminadorp
Citron
Délices
Cacao
Tonate
Cayenne
Roura
CAYENNE
Rémire
Matoury
Pointe Béhague

Pakaraima Mountains
Caruana de Montana
Normandia

Kurupukari

Kanuku Mountains
Saurwaunawa

Lucie River

W.J. van Blommesteinmeer
Bergi

Grand-Santi
Apetina
Djoemoe

St-Élie
Régina

Baie de l'Oyapok

Cabo Orange

Catisimina

Conceição do Maú
Lethem

Rupununi River

Coppename River

SURINAME
Juliana Top
1230m

Maripasoula
Saül

FRENCH GUIANA
(to France)
Saül

Oyapock

St-Georges

Oiapoque

Uaiacás

Santa Rosa

Río Uraricoera

Jacobs Ladder Falls

Kuyuwini Landing

Johi Village

New River

(Claimed by Suriname)

Appikalo

SIPALIWINI

Alimimuni Pick
728m
Juliana Top

Massif du Mitaraka
Mont Saint-Marcel
635m
Trois Sauts

Montagnes Bellevue de l'Inini

Oyapock-Fleuve
Camopi

Río Oiapoque

Calçoene

Río Orinoco
Horqueta Minas
Serra de Unturán

Boa Vista

RORAIMA
Caracaraí
Missão Catrimani

Río Catrimani

Río Demini

Caroebe

Conceição do Maú

H i g h l a n d s

Acarai Mountains

Essequibo River

T u m u c - H u m a c   M o u n t a i n s

(Claimed by Suriname)

Amapá

AMAPÁ

Sete Ilhas

Río Araguari

Macapá
Equator

Ilha Grande de Gurupá

Río Negro
Tapuruquara

Barcelos

Barcelona

Catrimani

Moura
Carvoeiro

Serra do Jatapu

Represa Balbina

Río Nhamundá

Río Jatapu

Río Trombetas

Río Para de Oeste

Planalto Maracanaquará

Río Cuminá

Río Paru

Oriximiná
Óbidos

Alenquer

PARÁ

Monte Dourado

Amazon

Porto de Moz

Portel

Río Solimões
Tefé
varzés

Novo Airão
Eduardo Gomes
Manaus
Manacapuru
Iranduba
Caldeirão
Manaquiri

B R A Z I L
A M A Z O N A S
A m a z o n   B a s i n

Itacoatiara
Autazes
Careiro
Codajás
Beruri

Parintins
Urucará

Santarém

Coari

Río Purus

Itaituba

Río Iriri

Rurópolis Presidente
Pimenta

Altamira

107

19,686ft
13,124ft
9843ft
6562ft
3281ft
1640ft
820ft
328ft
Sea Level
-820ft
-6562ft
-13,124ft

Western South America

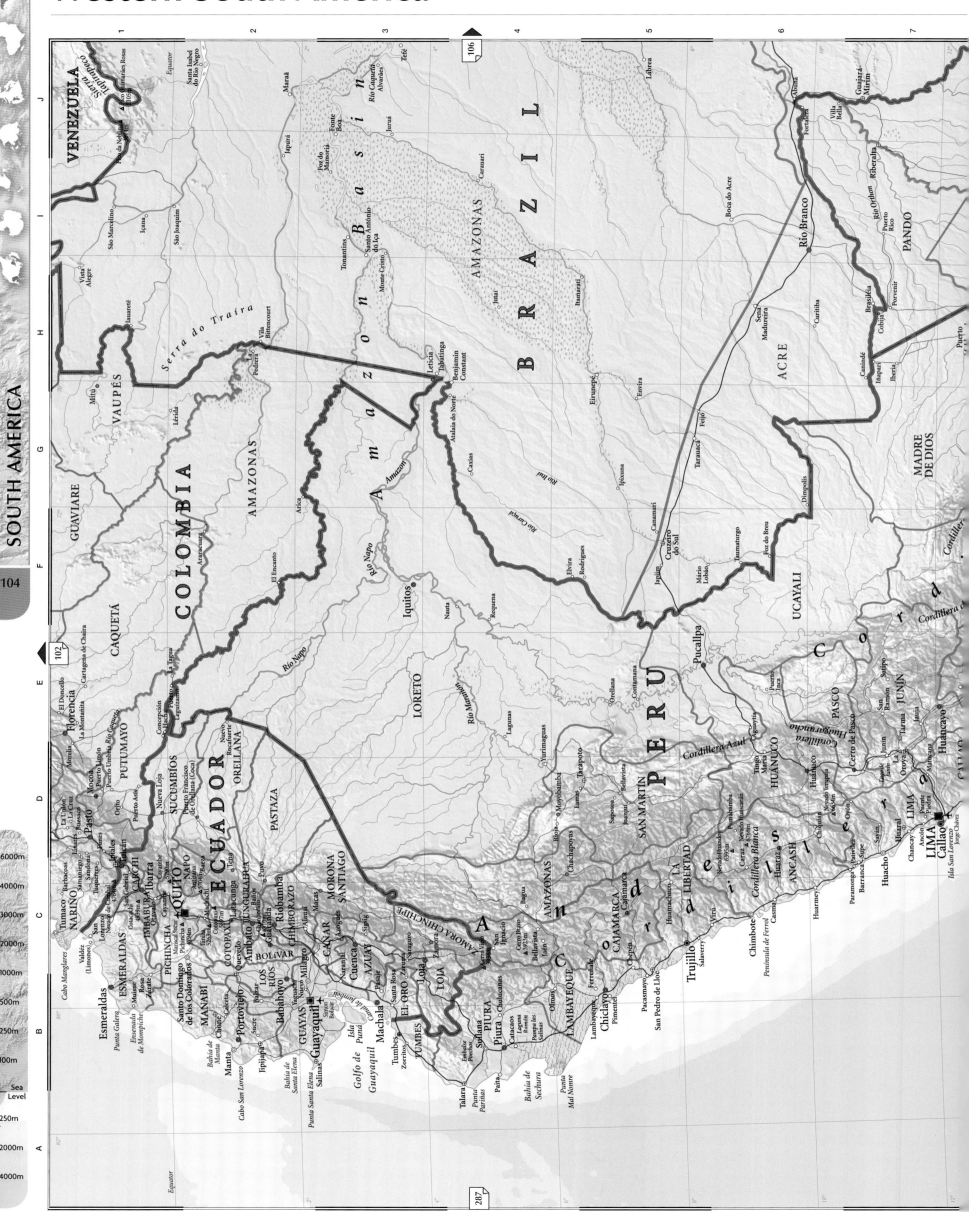

SOUTH AMERICA

VENEZUELA

BRAZIL

Basin

AMAZONAS

Amazon

COLOMBIA

AMAZONAS

VAUPÉS

GUAVIARE

CAQUETÁ

PUTUMAYO

ECUADOR

ESMERALDAS

MANABÍ

PICHINCHA

IMBABURA

COTOPAXI

TUNGURAHUA

NAPO

CHIMBORAZO

BOLÍVAR

LOS RÍOS

GUAYAS

CAÑAR

AZUAY

EL ORO

LOJA

MORONA SANTIAGO

PASTAZA

ORELLANA

SUCUMBÍOS

ZAMORA CHINCHIPE

PERU

LORETO

UCAYALI

ACRE

PANDO

MADRE DE DIOS

AMAZONAS

SAN MARTÍN

LA LIBERTAD

CAJAMARCA

LAMBAYEQUE

PIURA

TUMBES

ANCASH

HUÁNUCO

PASCO

JUNÍN

LIMA

CALLAO

Cordillera de los Andes

Cordillera Blanca

Cordillera Azul

Cordillera Huayhuash

Iquitos

Quito

Guayaquil

Lima

Callao

Trujillo

Chiclayo

Chimbote

Pucallpa

Leticia

Benjamin Constant

Tabatinga

Río Branco

Cobija

Brasiléia

Guajará-Mirim

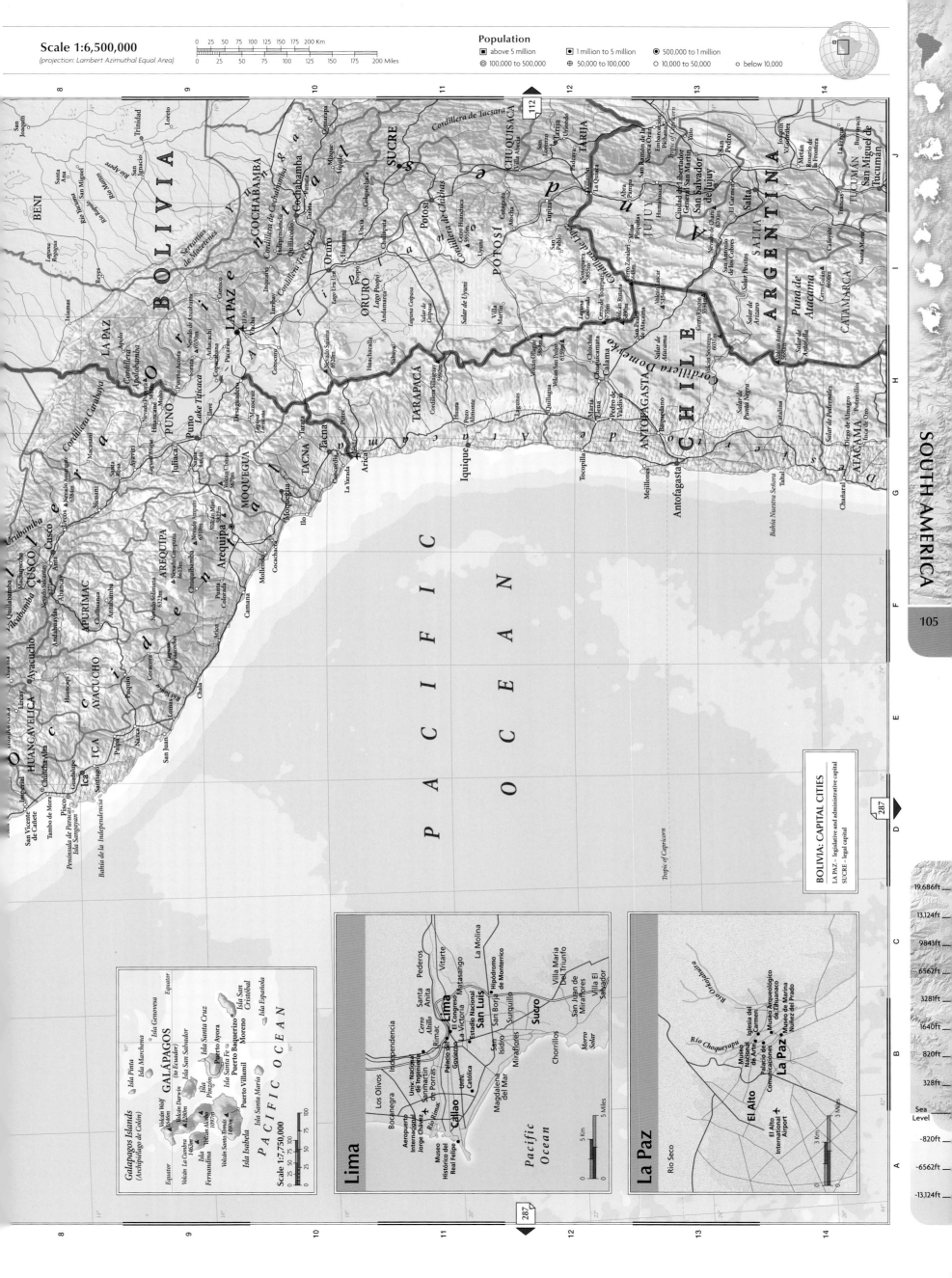

Amazon Basin

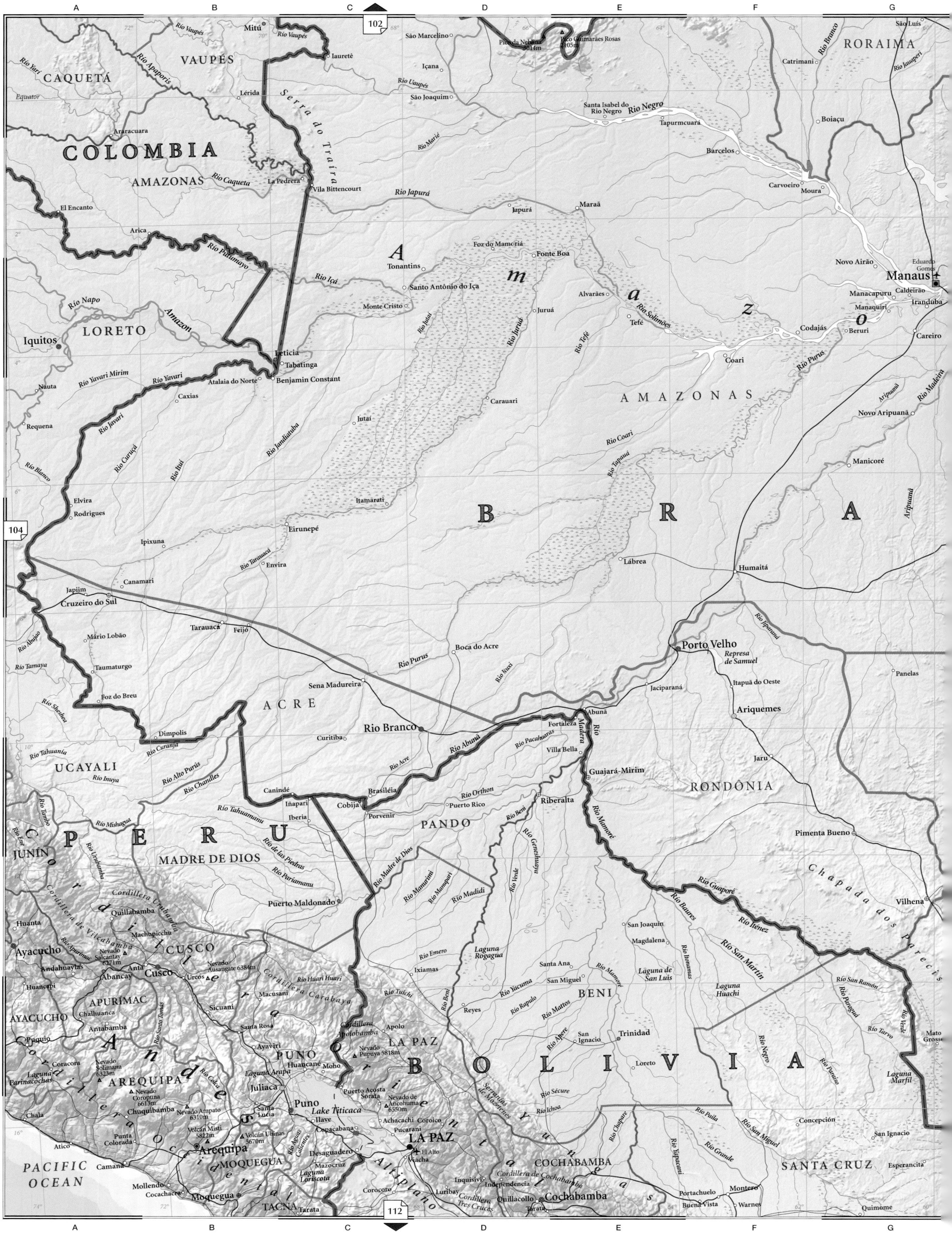

102
104
112

COLOMBIA

CAQUETÁ

VAUPÉS

AMAZONAS

LORETO

PERU

BRAZIL

AMAZONAS

ACRE

UCAYALI

MADRE DE DIOS

PANDO

RONDÔNIA

BENI

LA PAZ

BOLIVIA

SANTA CRUZ

RORAIMA

JUNIN

APURÍMAC

AYACUCHO

CUSCO

PUNO

AREQUIPA

MOQUEGUA

TACNA

COCHABAMBA

PACIFIC OCEAN

Manaus

Iquitos

Porto Velho

LA PAZ

Cochabamba

Arequipa

Cusco

Rio Branco

Equator

Sea Level

6000m
4000m
3000m
2000m
1000m
500m
250m
100m
-250m
-2000m
-4000m

Scale 1:6,500,000
(projection: Lambert Azimuthal Equal Area)

0 25 50 75 100 125 150 175 200 Km

0 25 50 75 100 125 150 175 200 Miles

Population
- ■ above 5 million
- ■ 1 million to 5 million
- ◉ 500,000 to 1 million
- ◉ 100,000 to 500,000
- ○ 50,000 to 100,000
- ○ 10,000 to 50,000
- ○ below 10,000

103

108

113

Serra do Jatapu
Represa Balbina
Rio Nhamundá
Rio Canumã
Rio Abacaxis
Autazes
Itacoatiara
Urucará
Parintins
Rio Paru de Oeste
Rio Trombetas
Rio Curuá
Oriximiná
Óbidos
Alenquer
Santarém
Planalto Maracanaquará
Monte Dourado
Ilha Grande de Gurupá
Amazon
Porto de Moz
Portel

AMAPÁ
Sete Ilhas
Rio Araguari
Ilha Bailique
Ilha do Curuá
Ilha Janaucu
Macapá
Ilha Caviana de Fora
Ilha Mexiana
Mouths of the Amazon

ATLANTIC OCEAN
Equator

Ilha de Marajó
Baía de Marajó
Vigia
Marudá
Belém
Ilha Sirituba
Castanhal
Capanema
Viseu
Carutapera
Alto Bonito
Turiaçu

Rio Jari
Rio Iriri
Altamira
PARÁ
Tomé-Açu
Rio Tocantins
Represa de Tucuruí
São Félix
Marabá
Dom Eliseu
Açailândia
MARANHÃO
Imperatriz
Grajaú
Serra do Tiracambu
Rio Gurupi
Rio Grajaú

Itaituba
Rurópolis Presidente Medici
Pimenta
Rio Tapajós
Tucunaré
Rio Jamanxim
Jacaré-a-Canga
Araras
Bom Futuro
Manuel Zinho
José Rodrigues
Serra dos Carajás
Parauapebas
São Félix do Xingu
Rio Xingu
Estreito
São Raimundo das Mangabeiras
Carolina
Balsas
Craolândia
Araguaína

BRAZIL

Barra do São Manuel
Serra do Cachimbo
Recreio
Pereirinha
Rio São Manuel
Colniza
Bandeirantes
Cachimbo
Paranaíta
Serra dos Gradaús
Conceição do Araguaia
Rio Araguaia
Rio Tocantins
Tasso Fragoso
Chapada das Mangabeiras
Alto Parnaíba
PIAUÍ
Santa Filomena
Corrente

Vila Rica
Juruena
Rio Juruena
Juará
Novo Horizonte
Porto dos Gaúchos
Peixoto de Azevedo
Marcelândia
Campo de Diauarum
São Félix do Araguaia
Ilha do Bananal
TOCANTINS
Palmas do Tocantins
Porto Nacional
Gurupi
Serra Geral de Goiás
Espigão Mestre

Rio do Sangue
Rio Arinos
Sinop
Serra Formosa
Pôsto Jacaré
Serra do Roncador
Rio das Mortes
Taguatinga
BAHIA

MATO GROSSO
Arenápolis
Nobres
Rosário Oeste
Rio Manso
Planalto de Mato Grosso
Porangatu
Campos Belos
Pontes e Lacerda
Cáceres
Várzea Grande
Cuiabá
Jaciara
Cocalinho
Itacaiu
Uruaçu
Tupiraçaba
Alto Paraíso de Goiás
Serra Dourada

San Matías
Pantanal
Rio Catiabá
Rio Piquiri
Rondonópolis
Aragarças
Piranhas
Santa Rita de Araguaia
Mineiros
Alto Araguaia
Goiás
Pirenópolis
Ceres
Rialma
Goianésia
Barro Alto
GOIÁS
BRASILIA
Planaltina
DISTRITO FEDERAL
Anápolis
MINAS GERAIS
Unaí

Laguna Uberaba
Rio Santa Corazón
Goiânia
Indiara
Cristalina
Planalto Central
Rio São Francisco
Paracatu

6000m
4000m
3000m
2000m
1000m
500m
250m
100m
Sea Level
-250m
-2000m
-4000m

291

290

107

Equator

ATLANTIC OCEAN

Atol das Rocas

Cabo de São Roque

Touros

Ceará Mirim

Natal

João Pessoa

Olinda

Recife

Campina Grande

Jaboatão

Cabedelo

Maceió

RIO GRANDE DO NORTE

PARAÍBA

Macau

Areia Branca

Mossoró

Assu

Currais Novos

Caicó

Arcoverde

Garanhuns

Arapiraca

ALAGOAS

SERGIPE

Aracaju

São Cristóvão

Estância

Planalto da Borborema

PERNAMBUCO

Açude de Itaparica

Represa de Itaparica

Paulo Afonso

Camocim

Cascavel

Aracati

Fortaleza

Caucaia

Itapipoca

Acaraú

Sobral

Araras

Crateús

Tauá

CEARÁ

Quixadá

Senador Pompeu

Açude Banabuiú

Açude Orós

Campos Sales

Juazeiro do Norte

Marcolândia

Ouricuri

Salgueiro

Afrânio

Petrolina

Juazeiro

Sobradinho

Represa de Sobradinho

Sento Sé

Xique-Xique

Monte Santo

Camoés

Tucano

Queimadas

Serrinha

Paranaíba

Piripiri

Campo Maior

Teresina

Timon

Caxias

Codó

Bacabal

Presidente Dutra

Colinas

Barro Duro

Valença do Piauí

Floriano

Oeiras

Picos

São João do Piauí

Canto do Buriti

PIAUÍ

Serra Grande do Piauí

Rio Parnaíba

Chapadinha

Itapecuru-Mirim

São Luís

Baía de São Marcos

Baía de São José

Recife do Silva

Recife Manuel Luís

Ilha de São Luís

Ilha do Caju

São João de Cortês

Cururupu

Cedral

Turiaçu

Viseu

Cametá

Capanema

Alto Bonito

Tomé-Açu

Castanhal

Belém

Ilha de Marajó

Baía de Marajó

Ilha Mexiana

Ilha Caviana de Fora

Ilha Janaucu

Ilha do Curuá

Ilha Bailique

Ilha de Maracá

Sucuriju

Calçoene

Amapá

Macapá

Sete Ilhas

Ilha Grande de Gurupá

Porto de Moz

Almeirim

Rio Jari

Equator

AMAPÁ

Mouths of the Amazon

Amazon Basin

PARÁ

Porto de Moz

Bom Bisco

José Rodrigues

Parauapebas

Serra dos Carajás

São Félix do Xingu

Rio Xingu

Marabá

São Félix

Represa de Tucuruí

Rio Tocantins

Araguaína

TOCANTINS

Palmas

Porto Nacional

Conceição do Araguaia

Rio Araguaia

Vila Rica

São Félix do Araguaia

Gurupi

Ilha do Bananal

Serra dos Gradaús

MARANHÃO

Rio Mearim

Rio Grajaú

Rio Itapicuru

Serra do Tiracambu

Rio Gurupi

Roncador

São João dos Patos

São Raimundo das Mangabeiras

Grajaú

Imperatriz

Açailândia

Estreito

Carolina

Carolândia

Balsas

Tasso Fragoso

Santa Filomena

Alto Parnaíba

Corrente

Chapada das Mangabeiras

Campo Alegre de Lourdes

Mansidão

Santa Rita de Cássia

Barra

Espigão

Serra Geral de Goiás

BRAZIL

Rio Gurgueia

Rio Tocantins

Rio Tocantins

Amazon Basin

109

291

Represa Três Marias

Sete Lagoas

MINAS GE

Represa dos Peixotos

Represa de Furnas

B R A

SÃO PAULO

Serra do Paranapiacaba

Tropic of Capricorn

6000m
4000m
3000m
2000m
1000m
500m
250m
100m
Sea Level
-250m
-2000m
-4000m

Ilha Grande

Ilha de São Sebastião

Scale 1:2,000,000
(projection: Lambert Conformal Conic)

0 10 20 30 40 50 60 70 80 Km
0 10 20 30 40 50 60 70 80 Miles

SOUTH AMERICA

111

Population
- ■ above 5 million
- ◙ 100,000 to 500,000
- ▣ 1 million to 5 million
- ⊕ 50,000 to 100,000
- ◉ 500,000 to 1 million
- ○ 10,000 to 50,000
- ∘ below 10,000

H   I   J   K   L   M   N

109

Congonhas · Guanhães · Gonzaga · Sardoa · São Geraldo da Piedade · Governador Valadares · Central de Minas · São João de Manteninha · Barra de S. Francisco · Nova Venécia · São Mateus

Dom Joaquim · Virginópolis · Santa Efigênia · Divino das Laranjeiras · São Geraldo do Baixio · Goiabeira · Águia Branca · São Gabriel da Palha · Barra Nova

Conceição do Mato Dentro · Carmésia · Açucena · Alpercata · Itanhomi · Galiléia · Alto Rio Novo · Pancas · São Domingos

Morro do Pilar · Santo Antônio do Rio Abaixo · Ferros · Joanésia · Mesquita · Periquito · Sobrália · Conselheiro Pena · Resplendor · Governador Lindenberg · Rio Bananal · Marilândia · Linhares

Jaboticatubas · Passabém · São Sebastião do Rio Prêto · Belo Oriente · Naque · São João do Oriente · Tarumirim · Santa Rita do Itueto · Itueta · Rio Doce

Lagoa Santa · Vespasiano · Itabira · Antônio Dias · Ipaba · Bugre · Iapu · Dom Cavati · Inhapim · Imbé · Baixo Guandu · Colatina · ESPÍRITO · Jacupemba · Regência

Santa Luzia · São Gonçalo do Rio Abaixo · Nova Era · São Domingos do Prata · Bom Jesus do Galho · Ipanema · Pocrane · Itaguaçu · João Neiva · São Roque · Aracruz

Sabará · Caeté · João Monlevade · Rio Piracicaba · Córrego Novo · Caratinga · Santa Rita de Minas · Conceição de Ipanema · Mutum · Laranja da Terra · Itarana · Santa Teresa · Nova Almeida

Belo Horizonte · Raposos · Nova Lima · Barão de Cocais · Santa Bárbara · Alvinópolis · Vermelho Novo · Santa Bárbara do Leste · São José do Mantimento · Afonso Cláudio · Santa Maria · SANTO · Serra

Rio Acima · Calas Altas · Dom Silvério · Simonésia · Caputira · Reduto · Martins Soares · Ibatiba · Brejetuba · Domingos Martins · Cariacica · Vitória · Vila Velha

Itabirito · Barra Longa · Rio Casca · Rio Doce · Abre Campo · Matipó · Manhuaçu · Irupi · Iúna · Pico da Bandeira 2890m · Conceição do Castelo · Marechal Floriano · Aracitaba

Belo Vale · Mariana · Acaiaca · Urucânia · Santo Antônio do Grama · Santa Margarida · São João do Manhuaçu · Caparaó Velho · Conceição do Castelo · Castelo · Alfredo Chaves · Anchieta

Ouro Preto · Ponte Nova · Jequeri · Oratórios · Pedra Bonita · Espera Feliz · Castelo · Jerônimo Monteiro · Iconha · Guarapari

Ouro Branco · Diogo de Vasconcelos · Guaraciaba · Amparo da Serra · Teixeiras · Pedra do Anta · Araponga · Dores do Rio Preto · Guaçuí · Cachoeiro de Itapemirim · Vargem Alta · Piúma

Conselheiro Lafaiete · Itaverava · Catas Altas da Noruega · Lamim · Piranga · Senhora de Oliveira · Viçosa · São Francisco da Glória · Carangola · Caiana · Faria Lemos · Varre-Sai · Muqui · Itapemirim

São Brás do Suaçuí · Rio Espera · Bras Pires · Paula Cândido · Coimbra · Pedra Dourada · Tombos · Castelo · Maratazes

Z I L · Capela Nova · Cipotânea · São Geraldo · Belisario · Vieiras · Porciúncula · São José do Calçado · Mimoso

Alto Rio Doce · Dores do Turvo · Rosário da Limeira · Guiricema · Antônio Prado · Natividade

Barbacena · Mercês · Silveirânia · Tocantins · Ubá · Guidoval · Rodeiro · Eugenópolis · Bom Jesus do Itabapoana · Barra de Itabapoana

Santa Bárbara do Tugúrio · Piraúba · Paiva · Dona Eusébia · Mirai · Muriaé · Laje de Muriaé · Itaperuna

Antônio Carlos · Aracitaba · Astolfo Dutra · Itamarati · Palma · Miracema · Italva · Cardoso Moreira

Ibertioga · Tabuleiro · Descoberto · Laranjal · Santo Antônio de Pádua · Cambuci · Travessão · São João da Barra

Rio Novo · Cataguases · Recreio · São Fidélis · Rio Itabapoana

Bias Fortes · Goiana · São João Nepomuceno · Argirita · Leopoldina · Itaocara · Campos dos Goytacazes

Pedro Teixeira · Coronel Pacheco · Chácara · Bicas · Maripá · Guarará · Volta Grande · Pirapetinga

Juiz de Fora · Matias Barbosa · Além Paraíba · Carmo · Cantagalo · Santa Maria Madalena · Carapebus

Lima Duarte · Santana do Deserto · Mar de Espanha · Barra de São Francisco · Santa Bárbara do Monte Verde · Comendador Levy Gasparian · Sapucaia · Sumidouro · Duas Barras · Cordeiro · São Sebastião do Alto · Trajano de Morais

Rio Preto · Três Rios · Bom Jardim

Paraíba do Sul · Areal · Nova Friburgo · Macaé

Rio Preto · Rio das Flores · Pedro do Rio · M a r · R I O D E J A N E I R O · Teresópolis · Cachoeiras de Macacu · Casimiro de Abreu · Rio das Ostras

Vassouras · Barra do Piraí · Miguel Pereira · Petrópolis · Guapimirim · Silva Jardim · São Vicente de Paula · Armação dos Búzios

Pinheiral · Engenheiro Paulo de Frontin · Mendes · Imbariê · Majé · Tanguá · Rio Bonito · São Pedro da Aldeia

Paracambi · Japeri · Queimados · Belford Roxo · Caxias · São Gonçalo · Itaboraí · Iguaba Grande · Cabo Frio

Seropédica · Nova Iguaçu · Nilópolis · Niterói · Maricá · Araruama · Saquarema

Itaguaí · Rio de Janeiro · Mangaratiba · Arraial do Cabo · Cabo Frio

A T L A N T I C   O C E A N

Tropic of Capricorn

291

Rio de Janeiro

Olinda · Mesquita · Coelho da Rocha · Duque de Caxias

Nilópolis · São João de Meriti · Rio de Janeiro Galeão · Ilha do Governador · Cocotá

Guadalupe · Cordovil · Galeão

Bangu · Magalhães · Rocha Miranda · Olaria · Ramos · Baía de Guanabara

Padre Miguel · Inhaúma · Benefica · Novos

Taquara · Praça Seca · Rio de Janeiro · Engenho Novo · São Cristóvão · Museu Nacional · Gámboa · Niterói

Pechincha · Vila Isabel · Catedral Metropolitana · Santos Dumont

Jacarepaguá · Tijuca · Botafogo

Gruta Paulo e Virginia · Monumento Cristo Redentor · Gávea · Copacabana · Pão de Açúcar (Sugarloaf Mt.)

Lagoa de Jacarepauá · Parque Nacional da Tijuca · Lagoa Rodrigo de Freitas

Barra de Tijuca · Niemeyer · Ipanema

Tijucamar

Atlantic Ocean

0   2 Km
0   2 Miles

291

H   I   J   K   L   M   N

19,686ft · 13,124ft · 9843ft · 6562ft · 3281ft · 1640ft · 820ft · 328ft · Sea Level · -820ft · -6562ft · -13,124ft

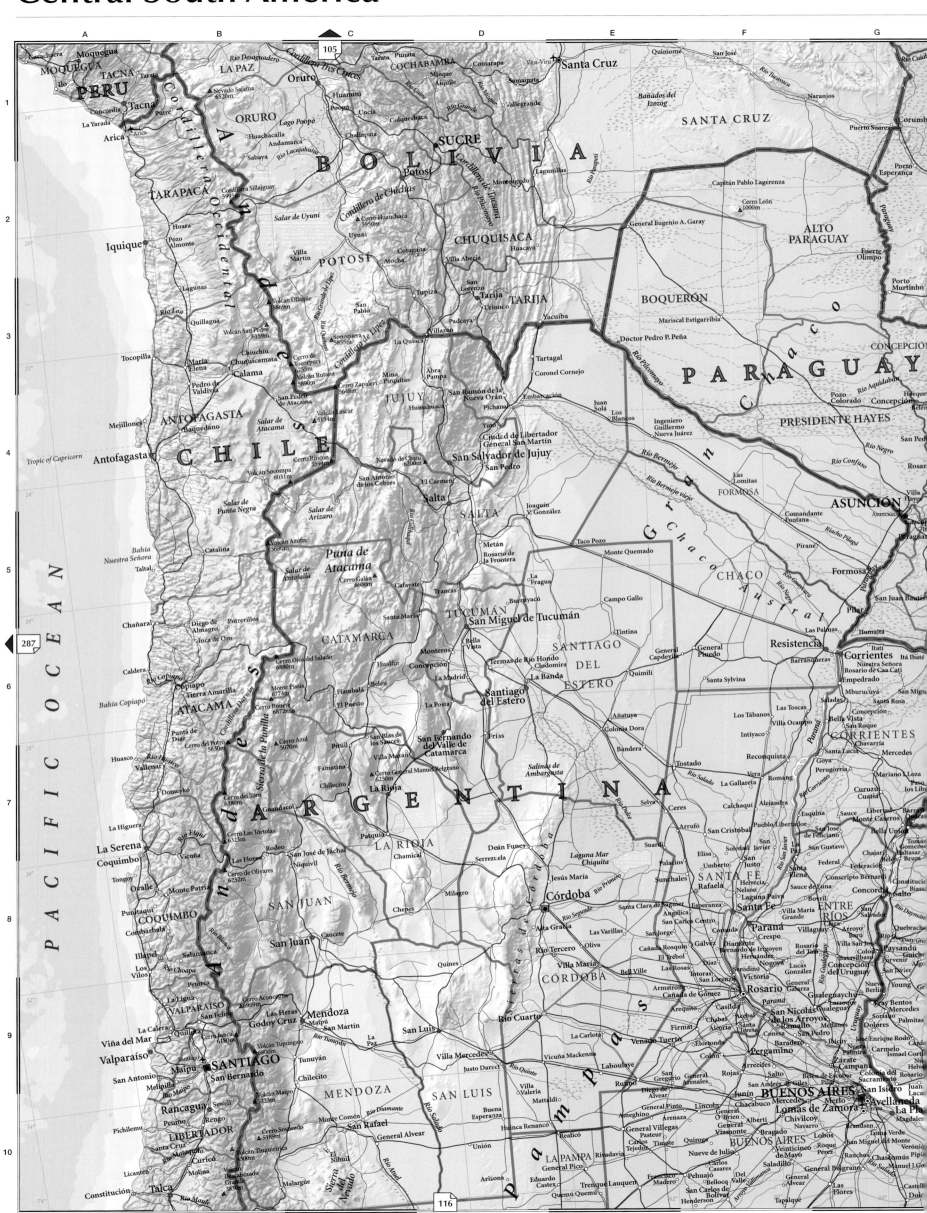

SOUTH AMERICA

PACIFIC OCEAN

6000m
4000m
3000m
2000m
1000m
500m
250m
100m
Sea Level
-250m
-2000m
-4000m

Scale 1:6,500,000
(projection: Lambert Azimuthal Equal Area)

0 25 50 75 100 125 150 175 200 Km
0 25 50 75 100 125 150 175 200 Miles

Population
- ■ above 5 million
- ▣ 1 million to 5 million
- ◉ 500,000 to 1 million
- ◎ 100,000 to 500,000
- ○ 50,000 to 100,000
- ◉ 10,000 to 50,000
- ○ below 10,000

109

291

291

Pantanal

GOIÁS
Jataí · Rio Verde · Itumbiara · Anhanguera · Piraporá
Luislândia do Oeste · Diamantina
Araguari · Uberlândia · Patos de Minas · Curvelo · Pico de Itambé 2040m · Serro · Guanhães · Governador Valadares
Coxim · Rio Apore · Rio Grande · Represa Três Marias · Abaeté · Ibiá · Araxá · Uberaba · Sete Lagoas · Itabira · Ipatinga

MINAS GERAIS
Belo Horizonte · Betim · Divinópolis · Ouro Preto · Ponte Nova · Manhuaçu · Pico da Bandeira 2890m · Conselheiro Lafaiete · Bom Jesus do Itabapoana · Itaperuna

Aquidauana · Água Clara · Santa Fé do Sul · Fernandópolis · Igarapava · Franca · Passos · Batatais · Represa de Furnas · São João del Rei · Barbacena · Juiz de Fora · Miracema · Nova Macaé

Campo Grande
MATO GROSSO DO SUL
Três Lagoas · Jales · Votuporanga · São José do Rio Preto · Barretos · Ituverava · São Joaquim da Barra · Sertãozinho · Ribeirão Preto · Mococa · Poços de Caldas · Três Pontas · Casa Branca · Pouso Alegre · Campos do Jordão · Vassouras · Três Rios · Teresópolis · Nova Friburgo · Petrópolis

BRAZIL

SÃO PAULO
Araraquara · São Carlos · Rio Claro · Araras · Limeira · Americana · Piracicaba · Campinas · Jundiaí · São José dos Campos · Taubaté · Jacareí · Guaratinguetá · Angra dos Reis · Volta Redonda · Barra Mansa · Barra do Piraí · Nova Iguaçu · **Rio de Janeiro** · São Gonçalo · Niterói
RIO DE JANEIRO

São Paulo · Osasco · São Bernardo do Campo · São Caetano do Sul · Santo André · São Vicente · Santos · Guarujá · Caraguatatuba · Ubatuba · Ilha Grande · Cabo Frio · Arraial do Cabo

Dourados · Navirai · Pedro Juan Caballero · Cordillera de Amambai · Ivinheima · Presidente Epitácio · Presidente Venceslau · Presidente Prudente · Marília · Bauru · Botucatu · Itapetininga · Sorocaba · Itararé

PARANÁ
Maringá · Apucarana · Londrina · Cornélio Procópio · Curitiba · Ponta Grossa · Campo Largo · Paranaguá · Antonina

SANTA CATARINA
Joinville · Jaraguá do Sul · Blumenau · Itajaí · Brusque · Florianópolis · São José · Lages · Tubarão · Laguna · Criciúma · Araranguá

RIO GRANDE DO SUL
Caxias do Sul · Novo Hamburgo · Canoas · Gravataí · Porto Alegre · Pelotas · Rio Grande · Passo Fundo · Santa Maria · Santa Cruz do Sul · Cachoeira do Sul · Bagé · Santana do Livramento

URUGUAY
MONTEVIDEO · Melo · Minas · Maldonado · Punta del Este · Rivera · Durazno

ATLANTIC OCEAN

Tropic of Capricorn

Rio de la Plata

Buenos Aires
Tigre · Las Conchas · San Isidro · Vicente López · San Miguel · General San Martín · Belgrano · Hippodrome · Palermo · Zoo · **Buenos Aires** · Teatro Colón · Cathedral · Plaza de Mayo · Morón · Sáenz Peña · Floresta · Barracas · San Justo · Villa Madero · Lanús · Avellaneda · Villa Alsina · Quilmes · Lomas de Zamora · Moreno · Merlo · Pontevedra · Mariano Acosta · González Catán · Almirante Brown · Berazategui · Aeropuerto Internacional de Ezeiza

0 10 Km
0 10 Miles

19,686ft
13,124ft
9843ft
6562ft
3281ft
1640ft
820ft
328ft
Sea Level
-820ft
-6562ft
-13,124ft

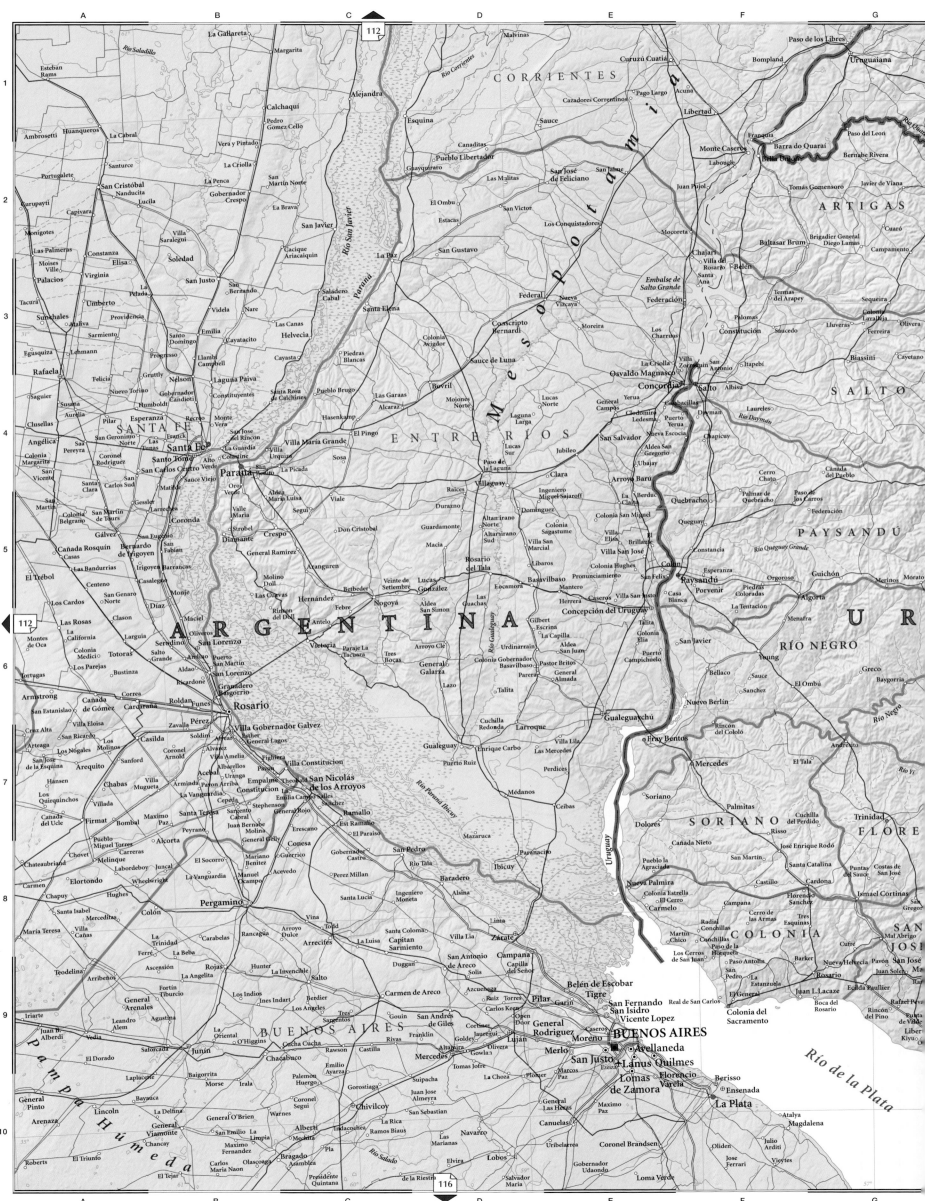

Scale 1:2,000,000
(projection: Lambert Conformal Conic)

0 10 20 30 40 50 60 70 80 Km
0 10 20 30 40 50 60 70 80 Miles

Population
- ■ above 5 million
- ◉ 100,000 to 500,000
- ■ 1 million to 5 million
- ⊕ 50,000 to 100,000
- ◉ 500,000 to 1 million
- ○ 10,000 to 50,000
- ○ below 10,000

113

116

291

BRAZIL

RIO GRANDE DO SUL

Serra das Encantadas

URUGUAY

RIVERA

TACUAREMBÓ

DURAZNO

FLORIDA

CANELONES

LAVALLEJA

MALDONADO

ROCHA

TREINTA Y TRES

CERRO LARGO

MONTEVIDEO

ATLANTIC OCEAN

Lagoa dos Patos

Mirim Lagoon

Lagoa Mangueira

Embalse del Río Negro

Santa Maria
Santa Cruz do Sul
Plano Alto
Passo Novo
Jacaquá
Loreto
São Vicente do Sul
Silveira Martins
Agudo
Candelária
Alegrete
Cacequi
Restinga Seca
Três Vendas
Azevedo Sodré
Formigueiro
Ferreira
Cachoeira do Sul
Rio Pardo
Passo do Sobrado
General Câmara
São Jerônimo
Triunfo
Charqueadas
Quaraí
Rosário do Sul
Itaraju
São Sépe
Barro Vermelho
Capane
Cordilheira
Mina do Loao
Arroio dos Ratos
Butiá
Artigas
Pintado Grande
Pampeiro
Vacacaí
Pântano Grande
Capivarita
Mariana Pimentel
Barão do Triunfo
Quitéria
Palomas
Santana do Livramento
Rivera
Dom Pedrito
Lavras do Sul
Santana da Boa Vista
Rio Camaquã
Encruzilhada do Sul
Barão do Triunfo
Sertão de Santana
Cerro Grande
Camaquã
Masoller
Tranqueiras
Zanja Honda
Bagé
Pinheiro Machado
Boqueirão
São Lourenço do Sul
Pacheca
Rio Arapey Grande
Quintana
Paso del Cerro
Cerro Pelado del Este
Lapuente
Cerrillada
Piratini
Candiota
Canguçu
Quilombo
Cerrito Alegre
Matojo
Banado de Rocha
Minas de Corrales
Arroyo Blanco
Pedras Altas
Alegrias
Capão do Leão
Pelotas
Quiebra Yugos
Zapara
Pueblo de Arriba
Abrojal
Vichadero
Cerrito
Tacuarembó
Los Rosanos
Ansina
Caraguatá
Acegua
Maria Isabel
Pedreiras
Quinta
São José do Norte
Tambores
Pueblo del Barro
Coronilla
Zanja Honda
Isidoro Noblia
Cruz de Piedra
Cassino
Rio Grande
Piedra Sola
Las Arenas
Buena Vista
Passo del Centurión
Quilombo
Arroio Grande
Estreito
Arbolito
Curtina
Larrayos
Las Toscas
La Pedrera
Taim
Cuchilla de Peralta
Clara
Cuchilla Caraguatá
Melo
Uruguay
Jaguarão
Rio Branco
Achar
Blanquillo
Banado de Medina
Peralta
Cerro Convento
Paso Pereira
Fraile Muerto
Carlos Reyes
Blanquillo
Cerro de las Cuentas
Arbolito
Rincón del Bonete
Capilla Farruco
Toledo
Placido Rosas
Carpinteria
Santa Clara de Olimar
Arévalo
Rincón
Cerro Chato
Tupambaé
Vergara
Arrozal Treinta y Tres
de los Toros
Durazno
Santa Bernardina
Ombúes de Oribe
Sarandí del Yí
Valentines
Mendizabal
Julio Maria Sanz
Treinta y Tres
General Enrique Martínez
Cebollatí
Santa Vitória do Palmar
Villa Sara
José Batlle y Ordoñez
Maria Albina
José Pedro Varela
Arrozal Victoria
Capilla del Sauce
Nico Pérez
La Coronilla
Polanco del Yí
Zapicán
Diez y Ocho de Julio
Chuí
Sarandí Grande
Illescas
Pirarajá
Lascano
Chuy
Pintado
Polanco Gallinal
Polanco Sur
Maria Isabel
La Cruz
Reboledo
Mariscala
Florida
Mendoza Chico
Casupá
Los Talas
Velázquez
La Coronilla
Veinticinco de Mayo
Fray Marcos
Aiguá
Castillos
Cardal
Mendoza
Chamizo
Bolívar
Parallé
Independencia
San Ramón
Tala
Villa Serrana
La Barra
Rodríguez
Veinticinco de Agosto
San Antonio
San Bautista
Solís
Minas
Rocha
Cabo Polonio
Santa Lucía
Jacinto
Tapia
Solís de Mataojo
La Querencia
Gregorio Aznarez
Nueva Carrara
La Paloma
Canelones
San Ramón
Santa Rosa
Migues
Montes
Piedra del Toro
Soca
Pan de Azúcar
Los Cerrillos
Cruz de los Caminos
Toledo
Totoral
Sauce
Piedras de Afilar
Las Flores
San Carlos
Las Piedras
Joaquín Suárez
Pando
La Paz
Carrasco
Piriápolis
Maldonado
Delta del Tigre
Barra de Carrasco
Punta del Este

Cordillera

Cuchilla de Santa Ana

Río Ibicuí
Rio Ibirapuitã
Río Cuareim
Río Santa María
Río Tacuarembó
Río Negro
Río Yaguarón
Río Jaguarão
Cuchilla Grande
Río Cebollati
Río Arapey Grande

Elevation
19,686ft
13,124ft
9843ft
6562ft
3281ft
1640ft
820ft
328ft
Sea Level
-820ft
-6562ft
-13,124ft

Southern South America

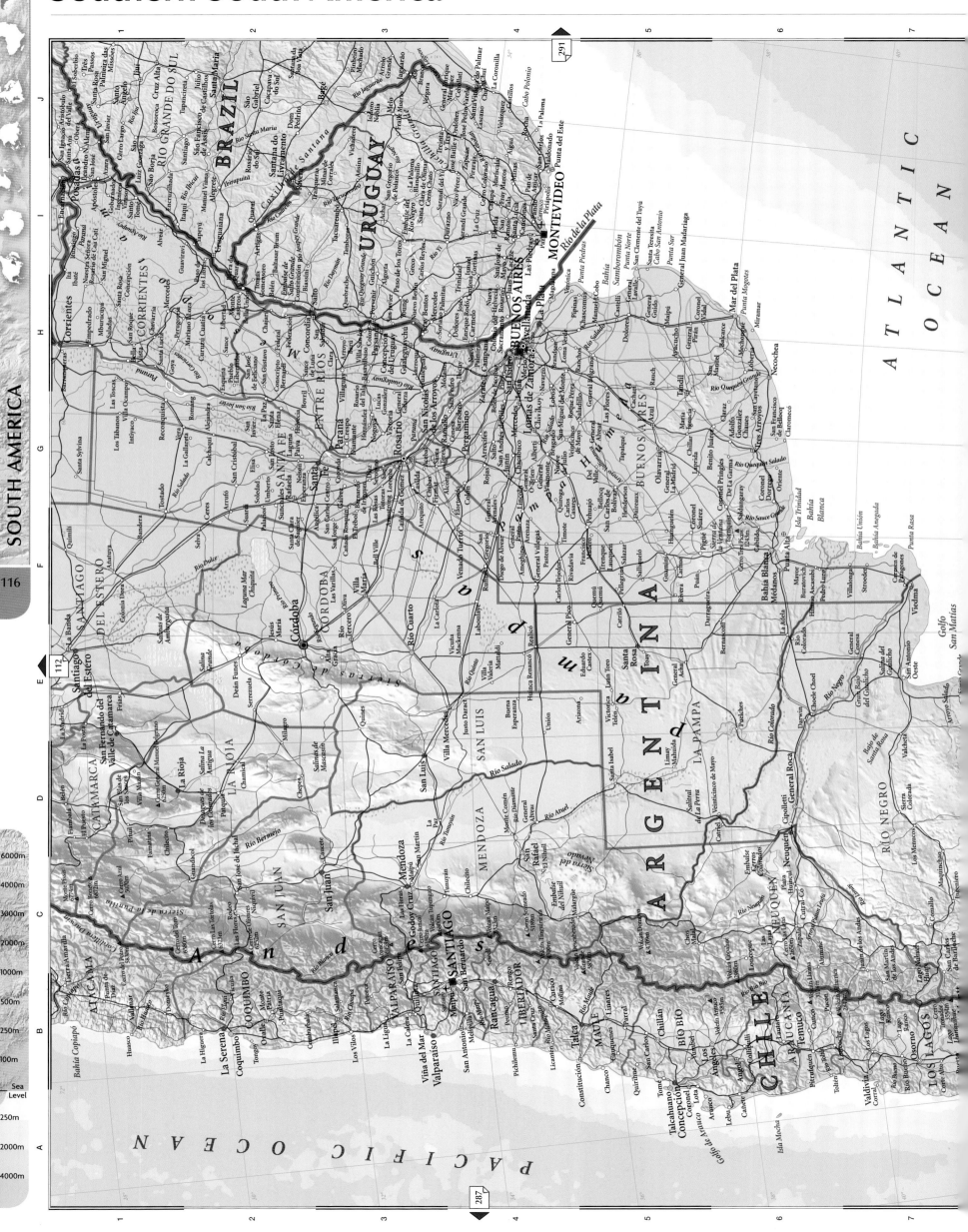

Scale 1:6,500,000
(projection: Lambert Azimuthal Equal Area)

0 25 50 75 100 125 150 175 200 Km
0 25 50 75 100 125 150 175 200 Miles

Population

- ■ above 5 million
- ◉ 100,000 to 500,000
- ■ 1 million to 5 million
- ⊕ 50,000 to 100,000
- ◉ 500,000 to 1 million
- ○ 10,000 to 50,000
- ○ below 10,000

Montevideo

Joaquín Suárez
Toledo
Ciudad de la Costa
Villa García
Las Piedras
La Paz
Villa Española
Flor de Maroñas
Santiago Vázquez
Aerodromo de Melilla
Cerro
Kel
Caburú
Montevideo
Ciudad Vieja
Punta Carretas
Río de la Plata
Delta del Tigre
Pajas Blancas
Punta Yeguas
Punta Pajas Blancas

5 km
5 Miles

FALKLAND ISLANDS
(to UK)

Cape Dolphin
Cape Bougainville
Macbride Head
Salvador
Port Salvador
Berkeley Sound
Menguera Point
North Fitz Roy
STANLEY
Pebble Island
Keppel Island
Sedge Island
Carcass Island
Jason Islands
Grand Jason
New Island
Beaver Settlement
Beaver Island
Port Stephens Settlement
Port Stephens
Cape Meredith
West Falkland
East Falkland
Darwin
Goose Green
Mount Pleasant
Fox Bay East
Bleaker Island
Bay of Harbours
Sea Lion Islands
Speedwell Island
George Island
Eagle Passage
ATLANTIC OCEAN

Scale 1:3,000,000

FALKLAND ISLANDS
(to UK)

Jason Islands
West Falkland
Keppel Island
King George Bay
Weddell Island
Cape Meredith
STANLEY
Mt Usborne 705m
Bluff Cove
Choiseul Sound
East Falkland
Darwin
Goose Green
Mt Adam 700m
Glorious Hill

ATLANTIC OCEAN

Península Valdés
Salinas Grandes
Punta Delgada
Golfo San José
Golfo Nuevo
Puerto Lobos
Puerto Madryn
Rawson
Trelew
Gaimán
Dolavon
CHUBUT
Río Chubut
Bahía Vera
Bahía Camarones
Camarones
Cabo Blanco
Puerto Deseado
Punta Pozos
Bahía de los Nodales
Golfo San Jorge
Comodoro Rivadavia
Rada Tilly
Caleta Olivia
Pico Truncado
Río Deseado
Gran Bajo
Puerto San Julián
Gran Bajo de San Julián
Laguna del Carbón
Comandante Luis Piedra Buena
Bahía Grande
Punta Sur
Río Chico
Río Santa Cruz
SANTA CRUZ
Río Coig
Río Gallegos
Punta Dungeness
Punta Arenas
Bahía San Sebastián
Río Grande
TIERRA DEL FUEGO
Isla de los Estados
Estrecho de Le Maire
Cabo de Hornos
Lago Fagnano
Ushuaia
Beagle Channel
Isla Navarino
Isla Nueva
Isla Lennox
Isla Wollaston
Estrecho de Magallanes
Strait of Magellan
Punta Arenas
MAGALLANES
Puerto Natales
Isla Riesco
Isla Santa Inés
Isla Desolación
Isla Londonderry
Isla Stewart
Isla Hoste
Península Brecknock

ANDES
AISÉN
Coyhaique
Balmaceda
Cochrane
El Calafate
Lago Argentino
Lago Viedma
Lago Buenos Aires
Lago Cochrane
Lago General Carrera
Golfo de Penas
Isla Wellington
Golfo Trinidad
Archipiélago de los Chonos
Isla de Chiloé
Castro
Ancud
Golfo de Ancud
Canal Moraleda
Península de Taitao
Isla Madre de Dios
Archipiélago Reina Adelaida

19,686ft
13,124ft
9843ft
6562ft
3281ft
1640ft
820ft
328ft
Sea Level
-820ft
-6562ft
-13,124ft

291
292
287

Central Chile & Argentina

Scale 1:2,600,000
(projection: Lambert Conformal Conic)

0 10 20 30 40 50 Km
0 10 20 30 40 50 Miles

Easter Island (Isla de Pascua) (to Chile)

Punta San Juan
Cabo Norte
Maunga Terevaka 506m
Motu Tautara
Hanga Roa
Mataveri
Vaihu
Rano Kau
Motu Nui
Orongo
Ahu Tepeu
Naunau
Ahu Akivi
Maunga Tangaroa 270m
Punta Baja
Ahu Vinapu
Playa de Anakena
Punta Rosalia
Bahia de La Pérouse
Maunga Pukatikei 370m
Cabo O'Higgins
Cabo Roggewein
Punta Akahanga
Punta Cuidado

Scale 1:500,000
0 2.5 5 Km
0 2.5 5 Miles

PACIFIC OCEAN

PACIFIC OCEAN

CHILE

ARGENTINA

SAN JUAN

MENDOZA

NEUQUÉN

LA PAMPA

COQUIMBO
VALPARAÍSO
SANTIAGO
LIBERTADOR
MAULE
BIO BIO
ARAUCANÍA

Matancilla
Auco
Carén
Huentelauquén
Mincha
Illapel
Zapallar
Caleta Huentelauquén
Punta Loberia
Choapa
Pintacura
Cunlagua
Chalinguita
Río Blanco
San Agustín
Tamberías
Hilario
San Juan
Rivadavia
Villa San Isidro
Santa Lucia
Pie de Palo
Los Vilos
Caimanes
Tilama
COQUIMBO
Almendrillo
Cerro Mercedario 6769m
Sierra del Tontal
Villa Aberastain
Villa Krause
Carpinteria
Las Casuarinas
Villa Media Agua
Quilimari
Guanguali
La Vega
Petorca
Retamito
Jocoli
Lavalle
Costa de Araujo
Ingeniero Gustavo André
Nueva California
Pampa del Salado
Alto del Cuero
Encón
Río San Juan
Longotoma
Pedegua
Valle Hermoso
Resguardo de los Patos
Uspallata
Puente del Inca
Cerro Aconcagua 6959m
El Borbollón
Las Heras
Villa Nueva
Tres Porteñas
El Melón
Quillota
La Calera
San Felipe
Jahuel
Cerro Juncal 6180m
Polvaredas
Punta de Vacas
Cacheuta
Luján de Cuyo
Godoy Cruz
Mendoza
Maipú
San Martín
Ingeniero Giagnoni
Rivadavia
Santa Rosa
Las Catitas
La Dormida
Viña del Mar
Valparaíso
Quintay
Rungue
Casas de Chacabuco
Chicureo
Planchada
Farellones
Corral Quemado
Villa Seca
San José
Tunuyán
Tupungato
Eugenio Bustos
San Carlos
Chilecito
La Paz
Pichi Ciego
Alto Conzapampa
SANTIAGO
Maipú
Los Maitenes
Guayacán
Sewell
Volcán Maipo 5323m
Refugio Lo Valdés
Paredites
Estancia El Puma
Nacunan
San Antonio
Leyda
Calera de Tango
San Bernardo
Los Morros
Valdivia de Paine
Las Melosas Refugio
El Manzanito
El Prado
Longovilo
Laguna de Aculeo
La Leonera
La Compañía
Rancagua
Volcán Maipo
MENDOZA
Tumán
Coipue
Las Chacras
Los Cardillos
Los Lingues
Rengo
Los Maquis
Las Nieves
Polonia
Cerro Sosneado 5189m
La Jaula
Resolana
Pedro Vargas
San Rafael
Rama Caida
Río Diamante
Monte Comán
Pichilemu
Marchant
Santa Cruz
Nerquihue
Codegua
Volcán Tinguiririca 4300m
Las Malvinas
General Alvear
Bucalemu
Boyeruca
La Palma
El Membrillo
Morza
Río Teno
El Sosneado
Estancia Coihueco
El Nihuil
Río Diamante
Laguna Vichuquén
Lipimávida
Pichibudi
Licantén
Curicó
Santa Lucia
Los Quenes
Lagunas de Teno
Embalse del Nihuil
Molina
Itahue
Los Niches Pobres
Upeo
Los Molles
Huaquén
Rapilermo
Camarico
El Bolsico
Carrizal
Junquillar
Batuco
Río Lircay
Panguilemu
Río Pinos de San Pedro
Malargüe
Bardas Blancas
Constitución
Río Maule
Toconey
El Morro
Colín
Talca
Volcán Descabezado Grande 3830m
Laguna de la Invernada
Laguna Llancanelo
Cerro Nevado 3810m
Sierra del Nevado
Pichamán
Curtiduria
Santa Ana de Queri
Maitenes
Tres Esquinas
Cerro Campanario 4049m
Chanco
Sauzal
Putagán
Abranquil
Rari
Los Rabones
Río Puelche
Pueblo Hundido
Villa Seca
Linares
Llepo
Laguna del Maule
Río La Puente
Cauquenes
Quella
Unicaven
Parral
Agua Escondida
Punta Pullay
Punta Los Maquis
Coronel
Quinchamávida
Pocillas
Terquilauquén
San Gregorio
Lago Vervazo Carapos
Cerro Payún 3680m
La Cortadera
Colmuyao
Quirihue
Las Raices
Santa Cruz
Torrecilla
Niquén
San Carlos
Cachapoal
Nahueltoro
Volcán Domuyo 4709m
Buli
Tres Esquinas
Río Cato
Ranquil del Norte
Vegas de Itata
Punta Burca
Huape
Chillán
Río Ñuble
Barrancas
Punta Lobera
Punta Tumbes
Tomé
San Miguel
Recinto
Buta Ranquil
Tricao Malal
Matancilla
Talcahuano
Punta Gualpen
Santa Clara
Lúcura
Los Puquios
Chos Malal
La Salada
LA PAMPA
Concepción
Paso Hondo
Tomeco
San Pedro
Andacollo
Cerro Bayo
Chacay Melehue
Lihueo
La Copelina
Coronel
Lota
Golfo de Arauco
Yumbel
Río Laja
Campanario
Cholguan
Polcura
Isla Santa Maria
BIO BIO
La Salada
Rio Colorado
Punta Lavapie
Llico
Arauco
Laraquete
Diuquin
Millantu
Canteras
El Cholar
Tres Chorros
Naunauco
Cortaderas
Sierra Auca Mahuida
Gobernador Ayala
Salitral de La Perra
Punta Carnero
Ramadillas
Los Ángeles
Volcán Antuco 3585m
Laguna de la Laja
El Huecu
Catriel
Veinticinco de Mayo
Colonia Chica
Punta Millonhue
Lebu
Los Cambuchos
Antihuala
Caramávida
Loncopangue
Hualcupen
Auca Mahuida
Río Colorado
Punta Morguilla
Cañete
Cayucupil
Lago Lanalhue
Tijeral
Angol
Trintre
Collipulli
Volcán Copahue 2980m
Loncopue
NEUQUÉN
Río Neuquén
Quidico
Tirúa
Isla Mocha
Quillem
Rarirruca
Manzanat
Laguna Conguillío
Lúgura
Laguna Guallería
Cerro Las Lajas 2650m
Bajada del Agrio
Añelo
Tratayen
Lago Pellegrini
Lautaro
Refugio Llaima
General López
Melipeuco
Laguna de Icalma
Lago Aluminé
Las Lajas
Paso de los Indios
Mariano Moreno
Ramón M. Castro
Embalse Cerros Colorados
Barda del Medio
Cinco Saltos
Temuco
Quepe
Río Imperial
Lago del Budi
Puerto Domínguez
Río Quepe
Quepe
Zapala
Cutral Co
Plaza Huincul
Neuquén
Plottier
Cipolletti
Allen

6000m
4000m
3000m
2000m
1000m
500m
250m
100m
Sea Level
-250m
-2000m
-4000m

SOUTH AMERICA – Cities

Brazília

Parque Nacional de Brasília
Península Norte
Brazlandia
Asa Norte
Universida de Brasília
Estadio
Retiro de Barra Alta
Lago do Paranoá
Brasília
Palacio de Justicia
Palacio de Alvorada
Taguatinga
Guará
Asa Sul
Catedral Metropolitana
Rasgado
Cellândia
Jardim Zoológico de Brasília
Dom Bosco
Paranoá
Sto. Antonio do Descoberto
Aeroporto Internacional do Brasília
Lago Sul
Recanto das Emas
Jardim Botânico do Brasília
Nucleo Bandeirante

Caracas

Catia La Mar
Caribbean Sea
Caraballeda
El Caribe
Simón Bolívar Airport
Mamo
El Palmar
Quebrada Tácagua
Maiquetía
La Guaira
Río Carabilleda
Parque Nacional Ávila
Cordillera de la Costa
Quebrada Topo
Catia
Nueva Caracas
El Retiro
Caracas
Sarria
La Florida
Palacio Miraflores
Capitolio Nacional
Chacao
Los Dos Caminos
Artigas
El Silencio
Jardín Botánico
Algodonal
Estadio Nacional
Las Acacias
Univ. Central de Venezuela
Parque Nacional del Este
Petare
La Vega
Las Mercedes
Antimano
El Valle
Cochecito
Baruta
El Hatillo
Río Guaire

Havana

N
Castillo de los Tres Reyes del Morro
Castillo de San Carlos de la Cabaña
Castillo de San Salvador de la Punta
Catedral
Bahía de la Habana
Guanabacoa
Straits of Florida
La Habana (Havana)
Regla
Castillo del Príncipe
Cerro
Vedado
Castillo de Atares
Jacomino
Río Almendares
Zoo
Diez de Octubre
San Miguel de Padrón
Miramar
Nuevo Vedado
Jesus del Monte
Lawton
Lucero
Almendares
La Vibora
Mantilla
La Playa
Ciudad Libertad
Bello
Los Pinos
Rosario
El Calvario
Barlovento
Marianao
Collazo
Santa Fé
Siboney
Arroyo Arenas
Arroyo Naranjo
Embalse Ejército Revelde
Cangrejeras
La Lisa
Punta Brava
Cantarranas
El Cano

Quito

El Condado
Carcelen
Cotocollao
Ponceano
Cordillera Pichincha
Concepcion
Aeropuerto Mariscal Sucre
San Isidro de Inca
Jipijapa
Cumbaya
Volcán Guagua Pichincha 4794m
Cochapamba
Rumipamba
Estadio Olímpico
Tumbaco
Belisario Quevedo
Quito
San Juan
Plaza y Convento de Santo Domingo
Palacio del Gobierno
Palacio Arzobispal
Teatro Sucre
Museo de la Ciudad
Río Machángara
Cerro Ilaló 3188m
Chilibulo
Puengasi
Chillogallio
La Argelia
Conocoto
La Ecuatoriana
Quitumbe
Río de San Nicolás
Guamani
Turubamba
Sangolqui

Santiago

El Carmen
Lo Barnechea
Quilicura
El Cortijo
Huechuraba
Vitacura
Conchali
Santa Emilia
Las Condes
Renca
Recoleta
Río Mapocho
Carrascal
San Cristóbal
Cerro Navia
Sta. Rosa de Locobe
Quinta Normal
Barrancas
Congreso Nacional
Providencia
La Reina
Lo Prado Arriba
Palacio de la Moneda
Catedral
Las Rejas
Universidad de Chile
Santiago
Club Hípico
Parque O'Higgins
La Aguada
Ñuñoa
Cerrillos
Santa Julia
Maipu
San Miguel
La Blanca
Bellavista
Lo Espejo
La Granja
San Ramón
San Bernardo
El Bosque
La Florida

São Paulo

Congo
Aeroporto Internacional de Guarulhos
Pirituba
Itaberaba
Guarulhos
Mutinga
Jaguara
Casa Verde
Mandaqui
Río Guapira
Río Tietê
N. Senhora Do O.
Santana
Ermelino Matarazzo
Osasco
Alto da Lapa
Lapa
Vila Maria
Jardim Munhoz
Cangaiba
Cidade de Dèus
Vila Madalena
Perdizes
Teatro Municipal
Belènzinho
Tatuapé
Penha
Vila Ré
Butantã
Cerqueira Cesar
Consolação
Brás
Instituto Butantã
Jardim Paulista
São Paulo
Mooca
Vila Formosa
Jardim Ouro Preto
Vila Sonia
Estadio do Morumbi
Museu Iparanga
Vila Mariana
Alto da Móoca
Cidade Lider
Vila Iasi
Campo Belo
Indianápolis
Ipiranga
Vila Prudente
Vila Ema
Pirajussara
Vila Andrade
Ibirapuera
Brooklin
Bosque da Saúde
Iguassú
Jardim Sapopemba
Taboão da Serra
Alto de Boa Vista
São Paulo Congonhas
Santo Amaro
Zoológico
São Caetano do Sul
Utinga
Capelinha
Parque do Estado
Parque das Naçoes
Capuava
Itupu
Cupacé
Jurubatuba
Santo André
Mauá
Interagos
Zuvuvús
Diadema
Vila Tereza
Pedreira
Vila Goncales
Jardim do Mar
Santa Tereza
Vila Pires
Represa de Guarapiranga
São Bernardo do Campo
Represa Billings

SOUTH AMERICA

119

19,686ft
13,124ft
9843ft
6562ft
3281ft
1640ft
820ft
328ft
Sea Level
-820ft
-6562ft
-13,124ft

Africa is the world's second largest continent with a total area of 11,712,434 sq miles (30,335,000 sq km). It has 54 separate countries, including Madagascar in the Indian Ocean. It straddles the equator and is the only continent to stretch from the northern to southern temperate zones.

FACTFILE

N Most Northerly Point: Jalta, Tunisia 37° 31′ N
S Most Southerly Point: Cape Agulhas, South Africa 34° 52′ S
E Most Easterly Point: Raas Xaafuun, Somalia 51° 24′ E
W Most Westerly Point: Santo Antão, Cape Verde, 25° 11′ W

Largest Lakes:
1 Lake Victoria, Kenya/Tanzania/Uganda 26,828 sq miles (69,484 sq km)
2 Lake Tanganyika, Dem. Rep. Congo/Tanzania 12,703 sq miles (32,900 sq km)
3 Lake Nyasa, Malawi/Mozambique/Tanzania 11,600 sq miles (30,044 sq km)
4 Lake Turkana, Ethiopia/Kenya 2473 sq miles (6405 sq km)
5 Lake Albert, Dem. Rep. Congo/Uganda 2046 sq miles (5299 sq km)

Longest Rivers:
1 Nile, NE Africa 4160 miles (6695 km)
2 Congo, Angola/Congo/Dem. Rep. Congo 2900 miles (4667 km)
3 Niger, W Africa 2589 miles (4167 km)
4 Zambezi, Southern Africa 1673 miles (2693 km)
5 Ubangi-Uele, C Africa 1429 miles (2300 km)

Largest Islands:
1 Madagascar, 229,300 sq miles (594,000 sq km)
2 Réunion, 970 sq miles (2535 sq km)
3 Tenerife, Canary Islands 785 sq miles (2034 sq km)
4 Isla de Bioco, Equatorial Guinea 779 sq miles (2017 sq km)
5 Mauritius, 709 sq miles (1836 sq km)

Highest Points:
1 Kilimanjaro, Tanzania 19,340 ft (5895 m)
2 Kirinyaga, Kenya 17,058 ft (5199 m)
3 Mount Stanley, Dem. Rep. Congo/Uganda 16,762 ft (5109 m)
4 Mount Speke, Uganda 16,043 ft (4890 m)
5 Mount Baker, Uganda 15,892 ft (4844 m)

Lowest Point:
▼ Lac 'Assal, Djibouti -512 ft (-156 m) below sea level

Highest recorded temperature:
⊕ Al'Aziziyah, Libya 136°F (58°C)

Lowest recorded temperature:
⊖ Ifrane, Morocco -11°F (-24°C)

Wettest Place:
≋ Cape Debundsha, Cameroon 405 in (10,290 mm)

Driest Place:
⊖ Wadi Halfa, Sudan <0.1 in (<2.5 mm)

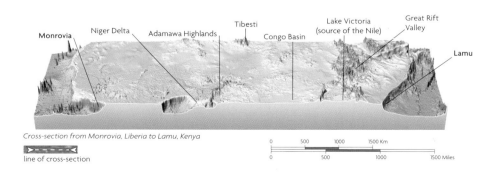

Cross-section from Monrovia, Liberia to Lamu, Kenya

◁▭▭▭▭◁
line of cross-section

Political

The political map of modern Africa only emerged following the end of World War II. Over the next half-century, all of the countries formerly controlled by European powers gained independence from their colonial rulers—only Liberia and Ethiopia were never colonized. The post-colonial era has not been an easy period for many countries, but there have been moves toward multi-party democracy across much of the continent. In South Africa, democratic elections replaced the internationally-condemned apartheid system only in 1994. Other countries have still to find political stability; corruption in government and ethnic tensions are serious problems. National infrastructures, based on the colonial transportation systems built to exploit Africa's resources, are often inappropriate for independent economic development.

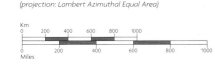

Scale 1:30,500,000
(projection: Lambert Azimuthal Equal Area)

Population

- ■ above 5 million
- ▣ 1 million to 5 million
- ◉ 500,000 to 1 million
- ◎ 100,000 to 500,000
- ⊕ 50,000 to 100,000
- ○ 10,000 to 50,000
- ● Country capital

Borders

- full international border
- disputed de facto border
- ceasefire line

Standard of living

Since the 1960s most countries in Africa have seen significant improvements in life expectancy, healthcare, and education. However, 28 of the 30 most deprived countries in the world are African, and the continent as a whole lies well behind the rest of the world in terms of meeting many basic human needs.

Standard of living
(UN human development index)

high
low

Transportation

African railroads were built to aid the exploitation of natural resources, and most offer passage only from the interior to the coastal cities, leaving large parts of the continent untouched—five land-locked countries have no railroads at all. The Congo, Nile, and Niger river networks offer limited access to land within the continental interior, but have a number of waterfalls and cataracts which prevent navigation from the sea. Many roads were developed in the 1960s and 1970s, but economic difficulties are making the maintenance and expansion of the networks difficult.

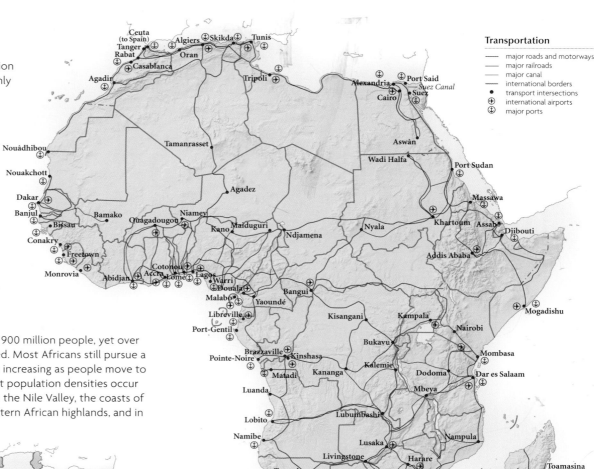

Transportation
- major roads and motorways
- major railroads
- major canal
- international borders
- transport intersections
- ⊕ international airports
- ⊕ major ports

Population

Africa has a rapidly-growing population of over 900 million people, yet over 75% of the continent remains sparsely populated. Most Africans still pursue a traditional rural lifestyle, though urbanization is increasing as people move to the cities in search of employment. The greatest population densities occur where water is more readily available, such as in the Nile Valley, the coasts of North and West Africa, along the Niger, the eastern African highlands, and in South Africa.

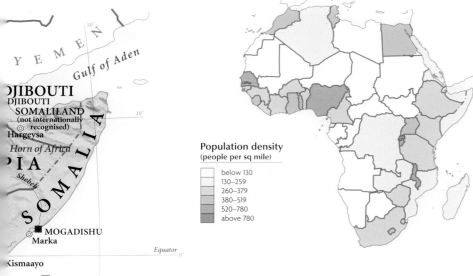

Population density
(people per sq mile)
- below 130
- 130–259
- 260–379
- 380–519
- 520–780
- above 780

Languages

Three major world languages act as *lingua francas* across the African continent: Arabic in North Africa; English in southern and eastern Africa and Nigeria; and French in Central and West Africa, and in Madagascar. A huge number of African languages are spoken as well—over 2000 have been recorded, with more than 400 in Nigeria alone—reflecting the continuing importance of traditional cultures and values. In the north of the continent, the extensive use of Arabic reflects Middle Eastern influences while Bantu is widely-spoken across much of southern Africa.

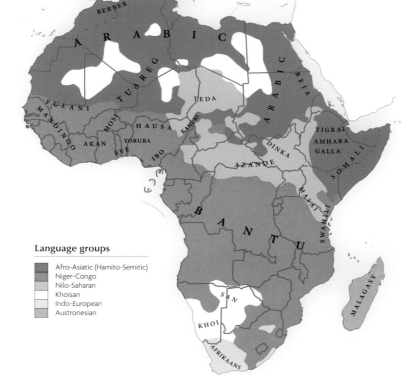

Language groups
- Afro-Asiatic (Hamito-Semitic)
- Niger-Congo
- Nilo-Saharan
- Khoisan
- Indo-European
- Austronesian

Official African Languages

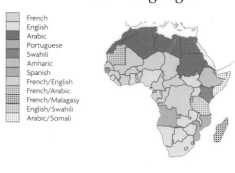

- French
- English
- Arabic
- Portuguese
- Swahili
- Amharic
- Spanish
- French/English
- French/Arabic
- French/Malagasy
- English/Swahili
- Arabic/Somali

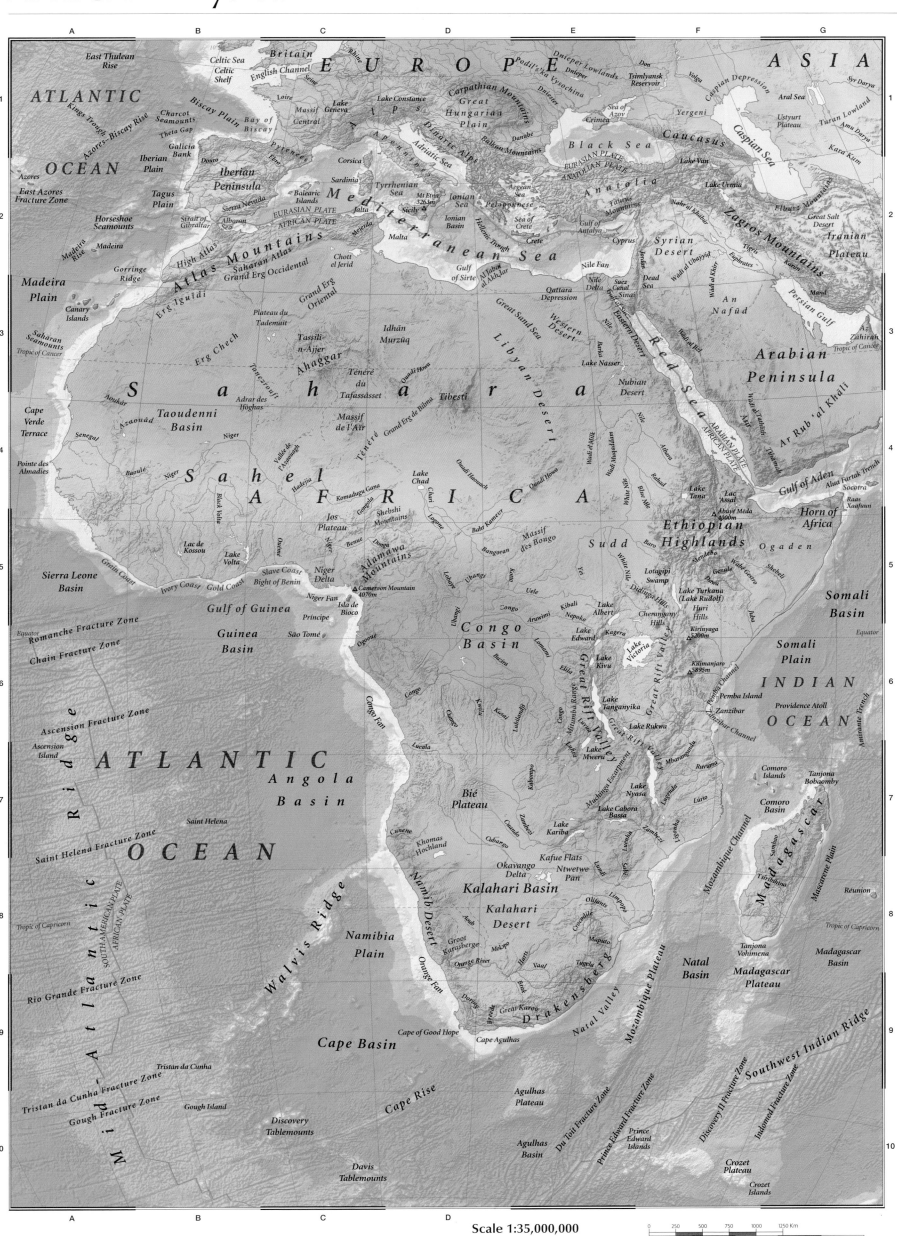

Scale 1:35,000,000
(projection: Lambert Azimuthal Equal Area)

0 250 500 750 1000 1250 Km
0 250 500 750 1000 1250 Miles

Climate

The climates of Africa range from mediterranean to arid, dry savannah and humid equatorial. In East Africa, where snow settles at the summit of volcanoes such as Kilimanjaro, climate is also modified by altitude. The winds of the Sahara export millions of tons of dust a year both northward and eastward.

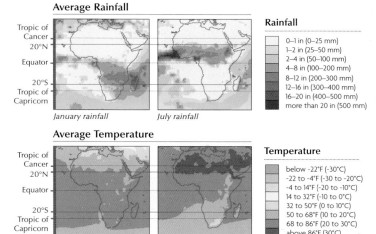

Average Rainfall

January rainfall *July rainfall*

Rainfall
- 0–1 in (0–25 mm)
- 1–2 in (25–50 mm)
- 2–4 in (50–100 mm)
- 4–8 in (100–200 mm)
- 8–12 in (200–300 mm)
- 12–16 in (300–400 mm)
- 16–20 in (400–500 mm)
- more than 20 in (500 mm)

Average Temperature

January temperature *July temperature*

Temperature
- below -22°F (-30°C)
- -22 to -4°F (-30 to -20°C)
- -4 to 14°F (-20 to -10°C)
- 14 to 32°F (-10 to 0°C)
- 32 to 50°F (0 to 10°C)
- 50 to 68°F (10 to 20°C)
- 68 to 86°F (20 to 30°C)
- above 86°F (30°C)

Climate
- arid
- humid equatorial
- mediterranean
- semi-arid
- tropical
- warm humid
- ☼ daily hours of sunshine, January
- ☼ daily hours of sunshine, July
- → cold wind
- → hot wind

Land use

Some of Africa's most productive agricultural land is found in the eastern volcanic uplands, where fertile soils support a wide range of valuable export crops including vegetables, tea, and coffee. The most widely-grown grain is corn and peanuts (groundnuts) are particularly important in West Africa. Without intensive irrigation, cultivation is not possible in desert regions and unreliable rainfall in other areas limits crop production. Pastoral herding is most commonly found in these marginal lands. Substantial local fishing industries are found along coasts and in vast lakes such as Lake Nyasa and Lake Victoria.

Environmental issues

One of Africa's most serious environmental problems occurs in marginal areas such as the Sahel where scrub and forest clearance, often for cooking fuel, combined with overgrazing, are causing desertification. Game reserves in southern and eastern Africa have helped to preserve many endangered animals, although the needs of growing populations have led to conflict over land use, and poaching is a serious problem.

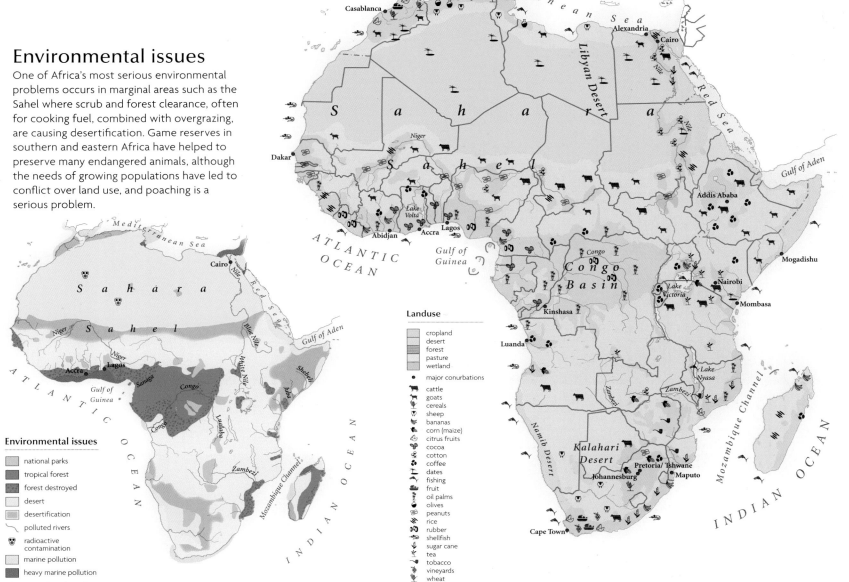

Landuse
- cropland
- desert
- forest
- pasture
- wetland
- • major conurbations
- cattle
- goats
- cereals
- sheep
- bananas
- corn (maize)
- citrus fruits
- cocoa
- cotton
- coffee
- dates
- fishing
- fruit
- oil palms
- olives
- peanuts
- rice
- rubber
- shellfish
- sugar cane
- tea
- tobacco
- vineyards
- wheat

Environmental issues
- national parks
- tropical forest
- forest destroyed
- desert
- desertification
- polluted rivers
- ☢ radioactive contamination
- marine pollution
- heavy marine pollution
- • poor urban air quality

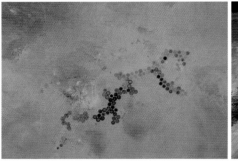

1
AL KHUFRAH, LIBYA
The circular irrigation patterns at this oasis have developed through the use of sprinkler units sweeping around a central point.

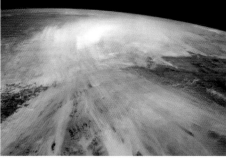

2
ERG DU DJOURAB, CHAD
Looking southwest, the pale area, just south of the darker Tibesti mountains on the right and the Ennedi plateau on the left, shows a desert sandstorm in motion.

3
ASWAN HIGH DAM, EGYPT
Completed in 1970 the dam controls flooding along the lower stretches of the Nile river.

4
KHARTOUM, SUDAN
The capital of Sudan lies at the junction of the Blue Nile, flowing from the east, and the broad White Nile, flowing from the south.

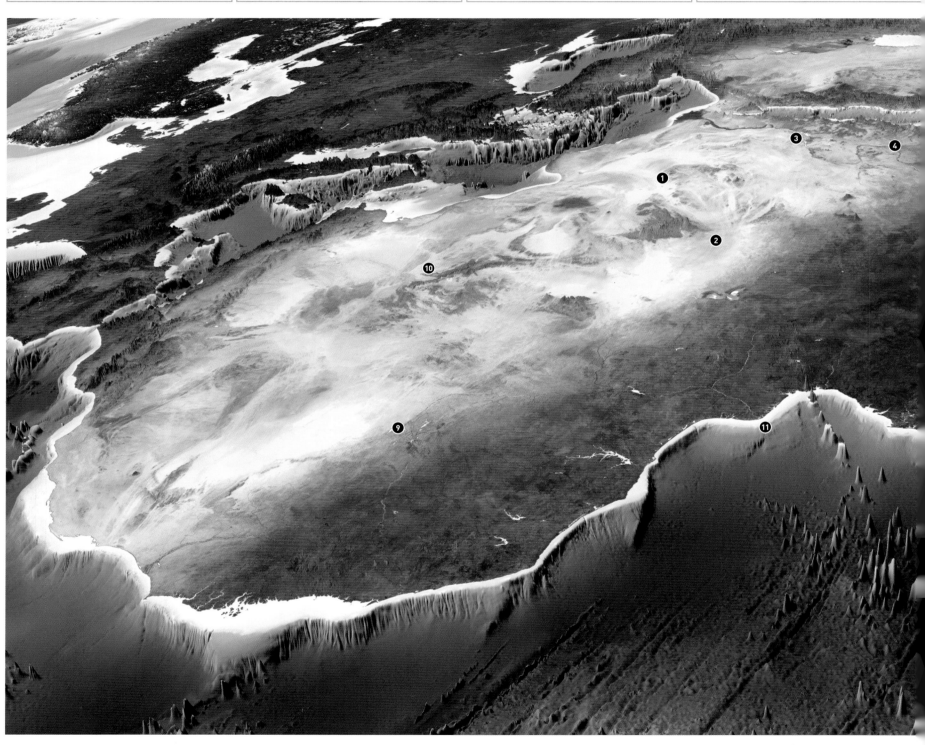

9
LAKE FAGUIBINE, MALI
Part of the Niger river's "inland delta," a region of lakes, creeks and backwaters near Tombouctou.

10
TASSILI-N-AJJER, ALGERIA
These sand dunes, one of a variety found in the Sahara, overlie the darker sandstone bedrock of the Tassili-n-Ajjer plateau.

11
NIGER DELTA, NIGERIA
At this point lies the vast, low-lying region through which the waters of the Niger river drain into the Gulf of Guinea.

12
CONGO/UBANGI RIVERS, DR CONGO
The confluence of these two rivers lies at the heart of the Congo Basin.

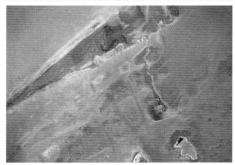

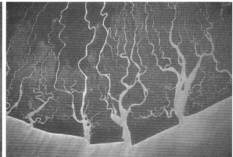

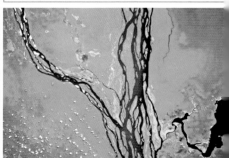

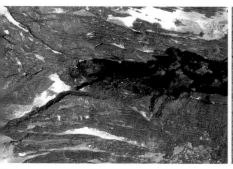

AFAR DEPRESSION, DJIBOUTI | 5
This low point is located at the junction of three tectonic plates—the Gulf of Aden to the east, the Red Sea to the north and the Great Rift Valley to the south.

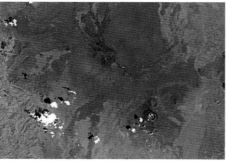

NYIRAGONGO AND NYAMURAGIRA VOLCANOES, DR CONGO | 6
These two volcanoes, lying to the west of the Great Rift Valley, last erupted in 2002 and 2001 respectively.

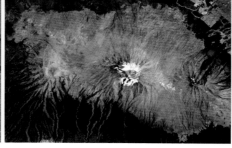

KILIMANJARO, TANZANIA | 7
An extinct volcano, its great height modifies the local climate, forcing moist air streams from the Indian Ocean to rise, inducing rain and, higher up, snow.

BETSIBOKA RIVER, MADAGASCAR | 8
The waters of Madagascar's second longest river are red with sediment as it carries eroded topsoil from the interior and deposits it in the Indian Ocean.

MALEBO POOL, CONGO/DR CONGO | 13
A lake in the lower reaches of the Congo river, it hosts two capital cities on its banks, Brazzaville, Congo to the north and Kinshasa, DR Congo to the south.

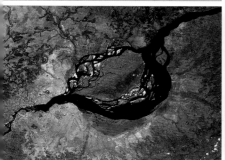

ZAMBEZI RIVER, ZAMBIA | 14
Seasonal flooding of the river and its tributaries turned the Mulonga and Liuwa plains on the Zambia-Angola border into a vast wetland in April 2004

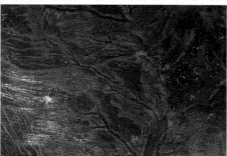

BEIRA, MOZAMBIQUE | 15
This port and beach resort lies on the north side of the mouth of the Pungoé river.

CAPE TOWN, SOUTH AFRICA | 16
South Africa's third largest city with a population of 2.9 million, it is also the seat of the country's parliament.

AFRICA

128

GREECE

Mediterranean

TUNISIA

ṬARĀBULUS (TRIPOLI)

ALGERIA

Tripolitania

L I B Y A

Cyrenaica

Libyan Plateau

Khalīj Surt (Gulf of Sirte)

Banghāzī (Benghazi)

Al Jabal al Akhḍar

Khalīj al Bumbah

Khalīj as Sallūm

Saḥrā' al (Western

Great Sand Sea

Jabal as Sawdā'

Al Hārūj al Aswad

Fezzan

Ramlat Rabyānah

S a h a r a

Idhān Awbārī

Ḥamādat Murzuq

Idhān Murzuq

Jabal Bin Ghunaymah

Sarīr Tībistī

Tassili-n-Ajjer

L i b y a n   D e s e r t

Ḥadabat al Jilf al Kabīr

Tropic of Cancer

Jabal al 'Uwaynāt 1907m

NIGER

Plateau du Manguéni

Plateau du Djado

Plateau du Tchigaï

Massif de l'Aïr

Ténéré

Grand Erg de Bilma

Erg du Ténéré

AGADEZ

Massif du Tibesti

Picco Bette 2286m

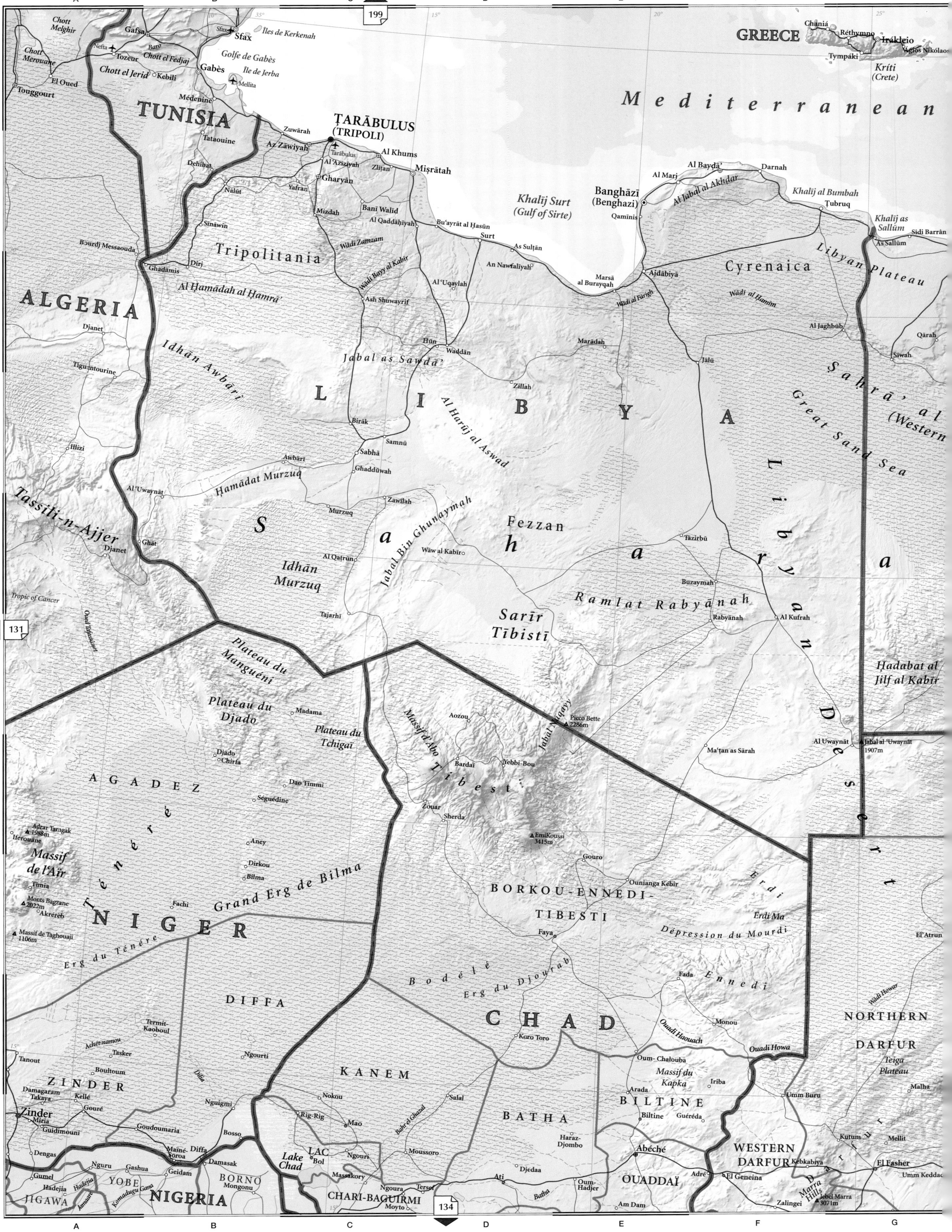

Jabal Nuqay

Emi Koussi 3415m

Erdi

Erdi Ma

Dépression du Mourdi

BORKOU-ENNEDI-TIBESTI

Ennedi

CHAD

Bodélé

Erg du Djourab

DIFFA

KANEM

BATHA

BILTINE

ZINDER

Lake Chad

LAC Bol

BORNO

NIGERIA

YOBE

JIGAWA

CHARI-BAGUIRMI

OUADDAÏ

NORTHERN DARFUR

WESTERN DARFUR

Teiga Plateau

Jebel Marra 3071m

Marra Hills

Sea Level
6000m
4000m
3000m
2000m
1000m
500m
250m
100m
-250m
-2000m
-4000m

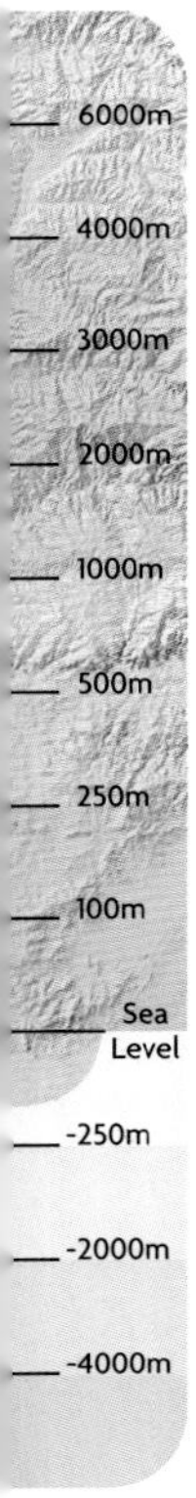

Scale 1:8,000,000

(projection: Lambert Azimuthal Equal Area)

| 0 | 25 | 50 | 75 | 100 | 125 | 150 | 175 | 200 Km |

| 0 | 25 | 50 | 75 | 100 | 125 | 150 | 175 | 200 Miles |

Population

■ above 5 million
⬛ 1 million to 5 million
◉ 500,000 to 1 million
◎ 100,000 to 500,000
⊕ 50,000 to 100,000
⊙ 10,000 to 50,000
○ below 10,000

216

220

136

19,686ft
13,124ft
9843ft
6562ft
3281ft
1640ft
820ft
328ft
Sea Level
-820ft
-6562ft
-13,124ft

Kárpathos

TURKISH REPUBLIC OF NORTHERN CYPRUS
(recognized only by Turkey)

Olýmpos 1951m

NICOSIA
Kerýneia (Keryneia)
Girne (Kyrenia)
Ammóchostos (Famagusta)
Gazimağusa
CYPRUS
Páfos (Paphos)
Lárnaka
Lemesós (Limassol)

Al Lādhiqīyah (Latakia)
Ţarţūs
Tripoli
Ḩamāh
Ḩimş (Homs)
Jabal Abū Rahbah

SYRIA

Al Jazīrah
Tikrīt
Tigris

Kermānshāh (Bākhtarān)
KERMĀNSHĀH (BĀKHTARĀN)
IRAN
LORESTĀN
ILĀM

LEBANON
BEYROUTH (BEIRUT)
DIMASHQ (DAMASCUS)
Dūmā
Al Quнayţirah
Naharriyya
Hefa (Haifa)
ISRAEL
Netanya
Tel Aviv-Yafo
Holon
Ashdod
JERUSALEM
Gaza Strip Gaza
Be'ér Sheva'
Ha'Negev
Be'ér Menuha

West Bank
Irbid
Az Zarqā'
AMMAN
Ma'daba
Dead Sea
Al Karak
As Suwaydā'

Syrian Desert

JORDAN

Al Quţayfah
Turayf
Jabal al 'Amūd 1076m
Jabal 'Unayzah 940m
Al Qurayyāt
'Ar'ar
Al Isāwīyah
Al Jarāwī
Al Murayr
Sakākah
Al Labbah
Al Jawf

Umm ar Raşāş
Ar Ruthīyah

Umm Qaşr
Al Fallūjah
BAGHDAD
Ba'qūbah
Buhayrat ath Tharthār
Al Hillah
Al Kūt
Karbalā'
An Najaf
Al 'Amārah
As Samāwah
Ar Rihāb
An Nāşirīyah
Hawr al Hammar

Zaghrat al Baţn
Rafhah
Bi'r Junayбīyāt
Niṣāb
Hafar al Bāţin
Ath Thumāmī

EGYPT

Marsā Matruh
Alexandria (Al Iskandarīyah)
Rashīd (Rosetta)
Kafr ash Shaykh
Damanhūr
Tanta
Az Zaqāzīq
Al Manşūrah
Dumyāt (Damietta)
Būr Sa'īd (Port Said)
Al 'Arīsh
Al Isma'īliyya
Suez Canal (Qanāt as Suways)
Banhā
Shibin al Kawm
Al 'Alamayn
Al Fayyūm
Banī Suwayf
Al Fashn
Banī Mazār
Bawiti
Al Minyā
Mallawi
Dayrūt
Asyūţ
Abnūb
Al Khārijah
Al Qaşr
Mūt
Tahtā
Sawhāj
Akhmīm
Irja
Qinā
Baris
Kom Ombo (Kawm Umbū)
Aswān
Aswan Dam (Khazzān Aswān)
Abu Simbel (Abū Sunbul)

CAIRO (AL QĀHIRAH)
Giza (Al Jizah)
Pyramids of Giza
Hilwān
As Saff
Suez (As Suways)
Za'faranah

Sinai (Sīnā)
Jabal Mūsā 2285m
Aţ Ţūr
Ra's Ghārib
Sharm ash Shaykh
Jabal Dabbagh 2350m
Jazīrat Tīrān
Ra's Muhammad

Gulf of Aqaba
Al 'Aqabah
Ḩaql
Al Bad'
Jabal al Lawz 2580m
Ash Sharmah
Al Muwaylih
Dubā

TABŪK
Tabūk
Al Bi'r
Al Qalībah
Al Akhdar
Taymā'
Ad Dār al Hamrā'
Bi'r al Murār

Jabal 'Unayzah
Al Mayyāh
Al Hamūdīyah

Al Qubbah
Jabal 'Unayzah
HĀ'IL
Hā'il
Al Ghazālah
Az Zilfi
Al Artāwīyah
Al Majma'ah
Jalājil

SAUDI ARABIA

Al 'Ulā
Al 'Ifanākiyah
Hadīyah
Khaybar
Uqlat as Suqūr
Wādi ar Rimah
AL QAŞĪM
Najd
Shaqrā'
Marāh
Durmā
Az Zulfi
Buraydah
'Unayzah

AL MADĪNAH
Al Madīnah (Medina)
Jabal Radwā 1814m
Mahd adh Dhahab
Ar Ruwaydah
Ad Dawādimī
Al Quwayyīyah

Yanbu' al Bahr
Badr Ḩunayn
Rābigh
Budayyi'ah
Halabān

Tropic of Cancer

AR RIYĀḌ

King Abdul Aziz
Makkah (Mecca)
JIDDAH (JEDDA)
Aţ Ţā'if
MAKKAH
Turabah
Ar Rawdah
Al Khurmah
'Afif
Al Mīshah
Zalim

Al Lith
Al Bāḩah
AL BĀḤAH
Al Qunfudhah
'ASĪR
Al Birk
Muḩāyil
Khamīs Mushayţ
Abhā
Jabal Sawdā 3133m
Jizān
JĪZĀN
Sabyā
Najrān
NAJRĀN
Ad Darb
Tathlith
Sa'dah
'Abs
Khamir
Ḩūth
Al Luhayyah
'Amrān
SAN'Ā (SANA)
YEMEN

Red Sea

RED SEA

Lake Nasser (Buhayrat Naşir)

(Administrative border)
(Administered by Egypt claimed by Sudan)
(Political border)
Halaib
Ras Abu Shagara
Muhammad Qol
Dungunab
Salala

Port Sudan
Sallom
Suakin
Sinkat
Ekowit
Tokar
Ras Shakal

Wadi Halfa
Selima Oasis
Akasha
Laqīya Arba 'in
Abu Hamed
Wadi 'Amur
NORTHERN
Argo
Dongola
Delgo
El Khandaq
Merowe
Shereik
Korti
RIVER NILE
Berber
Atbara
Ed Damer
Musmar
Haiya
Derudeb

Nubian Desert

SUDAN

KHARTOUM
Omdurman
Khartoum North
KHARTOUM
Umm Inderab
NORTHERN KORDOFAN
Hamrat esh Sheikh
Sodiri
El Obeid
Khuwei
Wad Banda
Umm Ruwaba
Bara
Tendelti
WESTERN KORDOFAN
WHITE NILE
GEZIRA
Wad Medani
Ed Dueim
Kosti
Rabak
Singa
Sennar
El Hawata
SINNAR
Gedaref
GEDAREF
Doka
Hag 'Abdullah
El Manaqil
Barakat
El Kamlin
Rufa'a
Wad Nimr
Shendi
Kabushiya
Adarama
Eilei
Wadi el Milk
Wadi Muqaddam
Kashm el Girba
Khashm el Girba
Teseney
KASSALA
Kassala
Mendefera
Barentu
Om Hajer
Tekeze
Gedaref
Aykel
Gallabat
Metema
Gonder

ERITREA
Keren
Massawa
Akurdet
Zula
ASMARA
Massawa Channel
Mersa Fatma
Dahlak Archipelago
Adīgrat
TIGRAY
Adi Ark'ay
Aksum
Adwa
Mek'elē
Sek'ot'a
AMHARA
AFAR
Korem
Maych'ew
Soyra 3018m
Simēn 4620m
Ras Dashen 4620m
Enghershatu 2570m

ETHIOPIA

Musawwa'
Jazīrat Farasān
Al Qahmah
Kamarān
Bayt al Faqih
Al Hudaydah (Hodeida)
Zabīd
Ibb
Ta'izz
Al Mukhā
Zula
Mersa
Bab el Mandeb
Jazīrat Hanish al Kabir
Jazīrat Zuqar
DJIBOUTI

Danakil Desert

Beylul
Aseb
Ed
Moulhoule
Obock
DJIBOUTI

AFRICA

130

290

290

132

ATLANTIC OCEAN

PORTUGAL

Sines
Beja
Azuaga
Córdoba
Montoro
Linares
Valverde del Camino
Guadalquivir
SPAIN
Jaén
Cabo de São Vicente
Lagos
Faro
Huelva (Seville)
Sevilla
Dos Hermanas
Osuna
Lucena
Guadix
Loja
Granada
Béticas
Almería
Mojácar
1481m
Lebrija
Jerez de la Frontera
Golfo de Cádiz
Cádiz
San Fernando
Ronda
Málaga
Marbella
Costa del Sol
Vejer de la Frontera
Algeciras
GIBRALTAR
Strait of Gibraltar (to UK)
Cap Spartel
Ceuta (to Spain)
Tanger
Cap des Trois Fourches
Asilah
Boukhalef
Larache
Tétouan
Al-Hoceïma
Melilla (to Spain)
Beni Sa
Ghazaouet
Chefchaouen
Nador
Oujda
Ksar-el-Kebir
Moulay-Bousselham
Rif
El Aïoun
Souk-el-Arba- Rharb
Kénitra
Salé
Sidi- Kacem
Taounate
Jerada
RABAT
Sais
Fès
Oujad
Taza
Tendrara
Casablanca
Khemisset
Meknès
Sefrou
Mohammed V
Mohammedia
Azrou
Afrane
El-Jadida
Berrechid
Settat
Oued- Zem
Khénifra
Jbel Ayachi
Ma
Safi
Cap Beddouza
Sidi-Bennour
Khouribga
Oum er Rbia
Béchar
Tensift
El Kelaa Srarhna
Beni-Mellal
Azilal
Haut Atlas
Er-Rachidia
Hamada du Guir
Essaouira
Marrakech
Menara
Moyen Atlas
Erfoud
Abadla
Jbel Toubkal 4165m
Ouarzazate
MOROCCO Atlas
Cap Rhir
Agadir
Inezgane
Taroudannt
Anti Atlas
Beni Ab
Sidi-Ifni
Tiznit
Tata
'Erg er Raoui
Bou-Izakarn
Guelmime
Dráa
Hamada du Dra
Tabelbala
Tan-Tan
Hamada Tounassine
Tarfaya
Sebkha de Tindouf
A L G E
El Mahbas
Tindouf
S
LAÂYOUNE
Saguia al Hamra
Smara
'Aïn Ben Tili
El Eglab
Bou Craa
WESTERN SAHARA (occupied by Morocco)
Yetti
'Erg Iguidi
Boujdour
Galtat-Zemmour
Bir Mogrein
Chegga
Ch
Tropic of Cancer
TIRIS
'Ayoûn 'Abd el Mâlek
'Erg el Ahmar
Ad Dakhla
Sebkhet Aghzoumal
ZEMMOUR
El Mreïti
Erg
Kâghet
El Hank
Erg
Ch
Cap Barbas
Adrar Souttouf
Aousard
Zouérat
El Hammâmi
Taoudenni
Fdérik
Tourine
Touâjil
Touîrat
Malqteïr
El Guettâra
Bir- Gandouz
Char
Ouarâne
El Mrayer
'Erg Atouila
Techla
Azeffâl
Choûm
Nouâdhibou
Bou Lanouâr
'Erg I-n-Sâkâr
Lagouira
Akchâr
Ouadâne
'Erîgât
1-n-Échaï
Râs Nouâdhibou
Nouâdhibou
Atâr
Ouadâne
TOMBOUCTOU
Dakhlet Nouâdhibou
Chinguetti
ADRAR
MA
DAKHLET NOUÂDHIBOU
Ouadâne
Oujeft
El Mreyyé
Araouane
Et Tîdra
INCHIRI
Akjoujt
Boû Djébéha
Nouâmghâr
Bennichchâb
Râs Timîris
MAURITANIA
NOUAKCHOTT
Boû Rjeïmât
Sebkhet Te-n-Dghâmcha
Rachid
'Erg Azaouâ
Beïla
Nouakchott
Tîdjîkja
TAGANT
Jîchît
HODH
Azaoua
Idini
TRARZA
Moudjéria
Aoukâr
Boutilimit
ECH CHARGUI
Tiguent
Magta' Lahjar
Boûmdeïd
Lac Faguibine
Mederdra
Rkiz
BRAKNA
Jâmchekket
Boû Djébéha
Rosso
Sénégal
Aleg
Guérou
Qualâta
Tombouctou
Dagana
Podor
Bababé
Kiffa
Néma
Oudeïka
Richard Toll
Bogué
Kaédi
Mônguel
ASSABA
'Ayoûn el 'Atroûs
Gourr Rharo
Lac de Guier
Saint Louis
Matam
Mbout
Timânê
Timbedgha
Ladam
Gorgol
Maghama
Kankossa
HODH EL GHARBI
Amourj
Ould Yenjé
Louga
Dara
GORGOL
Kobenni
'Adel Bagrou
Bassikounou
Niafounké
Diré
Lac Niangay
Kébémèr
Linguère
Ranérou
Goundam
Lac Garou
Mékhé
GUIDIMAKA
Sélibabi
Yélimané
Nioro
Néma
Lac Aougoundou
Tivaouane
Vallée de Felo
Vélingara
Bakel
Youvarou
DAKAR
SENEGAL
KAYES
SÉGOU
MOPTI
Pointe des Almadies
Diourbel
Baké
Ballé
KOULIKORO
Nampala
Thiès
Bambey
Rufisque
Mbour
Fatick

Madeira (to Portugal)
Funchal
Ilhas Desertas
Porto Santo

La Palma
Santa Cruz de la Palma
Tenerife
Santa Cruz de Tenerife
Lanzarote
Arrecife
Gomera
Fuerteventura
Puerto del Rosario
Hierro
Islas Canarias (Canary Islands) (to Spain)
Las Palmas de Gran Canaria
Gran Canaria
Cap Juby

6000m
4000m
3000m
2000m
1000m
500m
250m
100m
Sea Level
-250m
-2000m
-4000m

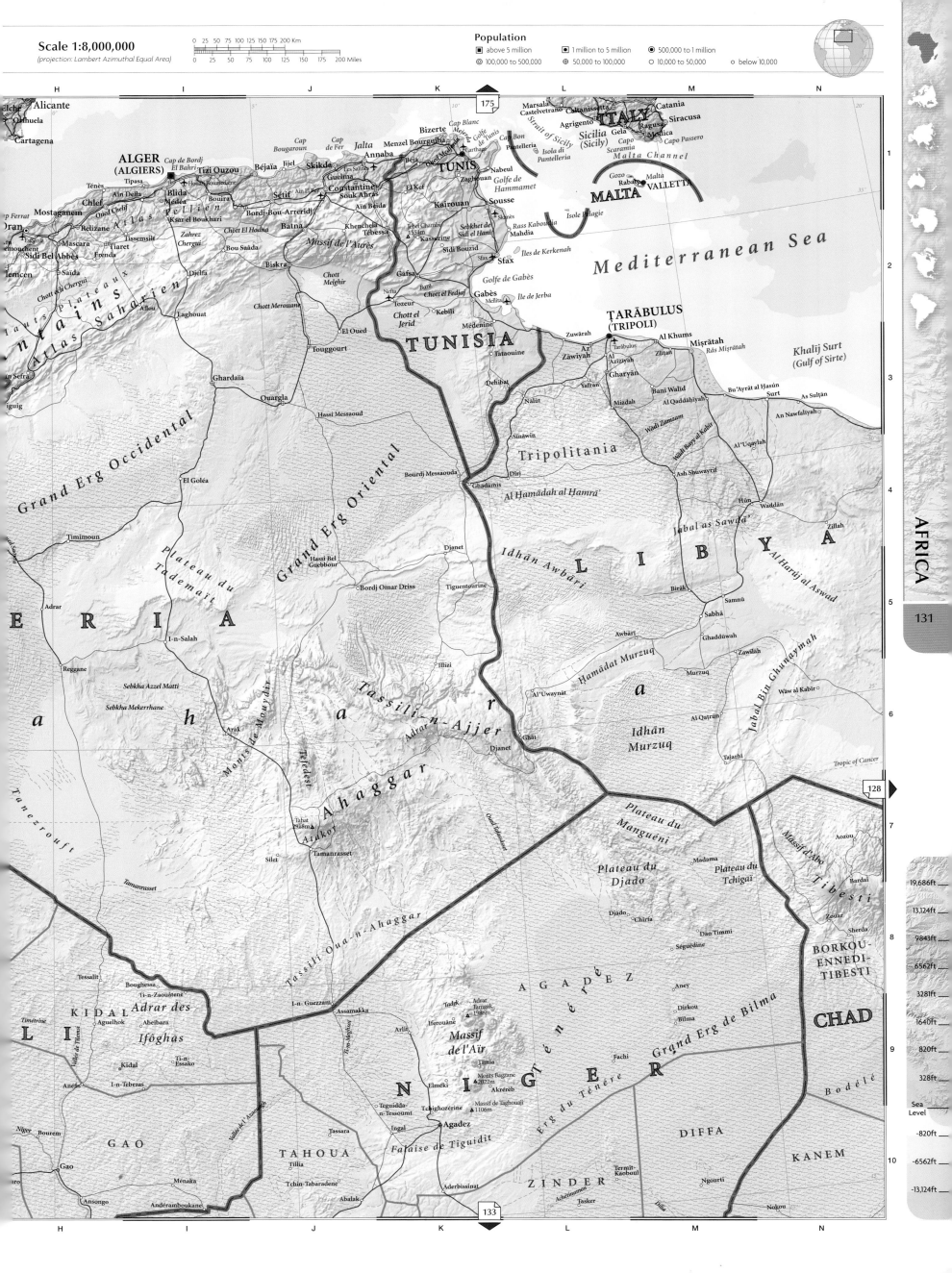

Scale 1:8,000,000
(projection: Lambert Azimuthal Equal Area)

0 25 50 75 100 125 150 175 200 Km
0 25 50 75 100 125 150 175 200 Miles

Population
■ above 5 million
⊚ 100,000 to 500,000
□ 1 million to 5 million
⊕ 50,000 to 100,000
⦿ 500,000 to 1 million
○ 10,000 to 50,000
∘ below 10,000

19,686ft
13,124ft
9843ft
6562ft
3281ft
1640ft
820ft
328ft
Sea Level
-820ft
-6562ft
-13,124ft

AFRICA

132

290

130

291

Map labels

TIRIS ZEMMOUR

MAURITANIA

Cap Barbas
Bir-Gandouz
Aghouinit
Touâjil
Tourine
Techla
Char
Choûm
Ouadâne
Chinguetti
Atâr
Oujeft

Nouâdhibou
Lagouira
Râs Nouâdhibou
Dakhlet Nouâdhibou
Boû Lanouâr

DAKHLET NOUÂDHIBOU
INCHIRI
ADRAR

El Mrâyer
El Guettâra
Taoudenni

'Erg Atouila
'Erg I-n-Sâkâne
'Erîgât
I-n-Echaï

Nouâmghâr
Râs Timirist
Bennichâb
Akjoujt
Boû Rjeïmat

El Mreyyé

S
a
h

TOMBOUCTOU
Araouane
Boû Djébéha

Azaouâd

NOUAKCHOTT
Bella
Nouakchott
Idini
Sebkhet Te-n-Dghâmcha

Rachid
Tidjikja
TAGANT
Itchit
Aoukâr
HODH
ECH CHARGUI

Moudjéria
Boûmdeïd
Tâmchekket
Néma
Oualâta
'Adel Bagrou

TRARZA
Boutilimit
Tiguent
Mederdra
Rkiz
BRAKNA
Aleg
Magta' Lahjar
Guérou
Kiffa
Tintane
'Ayoûn el 'Atroûs
Oudeïka

Rosso
Dagana
Richard Toll
Podor
Bogué
Bababé
Kaédi
Mônguel
ASSABA
Kankossa
Ballé
Lac Faguibine
Tombouctou
Gourma-Rharous
Goundam
Diré
Lac Garou
Lac Niangay

Saint Louis
Louga
Vallée de Ferlo
Matam
Maghama
GORGOL
Sélibabi
HODH EL GHARBI
Kobenni
Timbedgha
Amourj
Bassikounou
Nampala
Youvarou
Niafunké
Lac Aougoundou

Pointe des Almadies
Dakar
Méhké
Tivaouane
Thiès
Touba
Dara
Vélingara
Linguère
Ranérou
Nioro
Yélimané
Nara
Sokolo
Niono
Dioura
Diaka
MOPTI
Konna
Douenza
Hombori

DAKAR
Rufisque
Bambey
Diourbel
Mbaké
Kidira
Bakel
Ambidédi
Kayes
Matéra
Sandaré
Diéma
Mourdiah
Massina
Ténenkou
Diafarabé
Mopti
Sévaré
Bandiagara
Koro

SENEGAL
Mbour
Joal-Fadiout
Fatick
Saloum
Goudiri
Diamou
Sadiola
KAYES
Bafoulabé
Kolokani
Banamba
Niger
SÉGOU
Djenné
Bankass
Tiou

Kaolack
Sokone
Kaffrine
Koungheul
Maka
Tambacounda
Bafing
Toukoto
Kita
Sebekoro
KOULIKORO
Fana
Ségou
Bla
San
Bénéna
Tougan
Gourcy
Yako
Ouahigouya
Koungou

GAMBIA
BANJUL
Banjul
Mansa Konko
Basse Santa Su
Brikama
Dialakoto
Saraya
Lac de Manantali
Kéniéba
Satadougou
Kokofata
Koulikoro
Kati
BAMAKO
Dioïla
Koutiala
Yorosso
Kouri
Nouna
Toma
Déodougou
Réo
Koudougou
QUAGADOUGOU
Kombissiri

Dioulouloû
Bignona
Sédhiou
Farim
Médina Gonnas
Gambia
Kolda
Kédougou
Mali
Tambgue 1538m
Maléa
Doko
Kangaba
Bougouni
SIKASSO
Garalo
Kolondiéba
Kadiolo
Orodara
Banfora
Sidéradougou
Diébougou
Lawra
Nadawli
Tumu
Léo
Sapouli
Gaoua
Kampti

Ziguinchor
Cacheu
Bissorã
Mansôa
Bafatá
Gabú
Vélingara
Koundara
Labé
Télimélé
Kavendou
Pha
1421m
Dalaba
Dinguiraye
Tikinso
Siguiri
Yanfolila
Kouroussa
Manankoro
Niélé
Sîkasso
Koloko
Bobo-Dioulasso
Ouessa
Boundoukui
Boromo
Houndé
Tangoloko
Kouto
Boundiali
Korhogo
Ferkessédougou
Tehini
Wa
Black Volta

BISSAU
Quinhámel
Bissau
Bolama
Fulacunda
Buba
Catió
GUINEA-BISSAU
Boké
Kamsar
Cap Verga
Boffa
Fouta Djallon
Friâ
FOUTA DJALLON
Dabola
Manou
Dabola
Niger
GUINEA
Mandiana
Kankan
Kangaré
Samatigula
Madinani
Odienné
Buko
Borotou
Samatiguila
Orodara
BURK
Medj Idri (Niabérri)
Sapouli

Dubréka
Coyah
Kindia
Mongo
Kabala
Bintimani 1948m
Falaba
Faranah
Tokounou
Kérouané
Kissidougou
Nzérékoré
Lola
Man's Nimba
Sifié
Séguéla
Kounahiri
Mankono
Katiola
Dabakala
Bondoukou
Sawla
Bole
Damongo
Techimani
Wenchi
Kintampo

CONAKRY
Forécariah
Kambia
Pendembu
Port Loko
Makéni
Lunsar
Magburaka
Koidu
Guékédou
Macenta
Beyla
Boola
Touba
Kani
Biankouma
Vavoua
Daloa
Séguéla
Béoumi
Bouaké
Tiébissou
Mbahiakro
Bongouanou
Berekum
Sunyani
Fiura
Mampong

FREETOWN
Pepel
SIERRA LEONE
Moyamba
Bo
Kenema
Mano
Lofa
Zorzor
Yomou
Danané
Sassandra
Bouaflé
Zuénoula
Lac de Buyo
Zoukougbeu
IVORY COAST
Duékoué
Gagnoa
Soubré
Lakota
Divo
Adzopé
Agboville
Bibiani
Awaso
Obuasi
Dunk
Kumasi
GHA

ATLANTIC OCEAN

Shenge
Mafru
Bonthe
Pujehún
Sulima
Robertsports
Tubmanburg
Kakata
Harbel
MONROVIA
Monrovia
Marshall
Buchanan
LIBERIA
Tapeta
Ganta
Saniquellie
Yekepa
Gbanga
Toulépleu
Guiglo
Issia
Oumé
YAMOUSSOUKRO
San Pédro
Dimbokro
Toumodi
Abengourou
Bongouanou
Goaso
Enchi

Greenville
Grand Cess
Plibo
River Cess
Zwedru
Cavalla
Grabo
San Pédro
Sassandra
Grand-Lahou
Fresco
Abidjan
Port-Bouet
Grand-Bassam
Half Assini
Axim
Prestea
Tarkwa
Sekon
Takora
Cape Three Points

Harper
Cape Palmas

Pic de Tibé 1501m
Guékédou
Kolahun
Voinjama
Macenta
Boola

Scale (elevation legend)

6000m
4000m
3000m
2000m
1000m
500m
250m
100m
Sea Level
-250m
-2000m
-4000m

Inset: CAPE VERDE

CAPE VERDE

Santo Antão
Pombas
Mindelo
São Vicente
Ribeira Brava
São Nicolau
Ilhas de Barlavento
Pedra Lume
Sal
Amílcar Cabral

Boa Vista
João Barrosa

ATLANTIC OCEAN

Tarrafal
Maio
Fogo
São Filipe
Santiago
PRAIA
Maio
Ilhas de Sotavento

Scale 1:8,000,000
0   50   100 Km
0   50   100 Miles

Inset: ASCENSION ISLAND

ASCENSION ISLAND
(to Saint Helena)

North Point
Sisters Peak 446m
Porpoise Point
North East Bay
Clarence Bay
The Peak 859m
South East Point
GEORGETOWN
South West Bay
Portland Point
Mars Bay
South Point
Wideawake Airfield
South East Bay
Pillar Bay
ATLANTIC OCEAN

Scale 1:750,000
0   5   10 Km
0   5   10 Miles

Inset: TRISTAN DA CUNHA

TRISTAN DA CUNHA
(to Saint Helena)

ATLANTIC OCEAN
Big Point
Rookery Point
EDINBURGH
Anchorstock Point
Queen Mary's Peak 2060m
Sandy Point
Longbluff
Lyon Point
Cave Point
Stonybeach Bay
Stonyhill Point

Scale 1:750,000
0   5   10 Km
0   5   10 Miles

Inset: SAINT HELENA

SAINT HELENA
(to UK)

Sugar Loaf Point
Flagstaff Bay
JAMESTOWN
Horse Pasture Point
The Haystack
Longwood
Egg Island
Diana's Peak 820m
Gill Point
South West Point
Long Range Point
Speery Island
Castle Rock Point
ATLANTIC OCEAN

Scale 1:750,000
0   5   10 Km
0   5   10 Miles

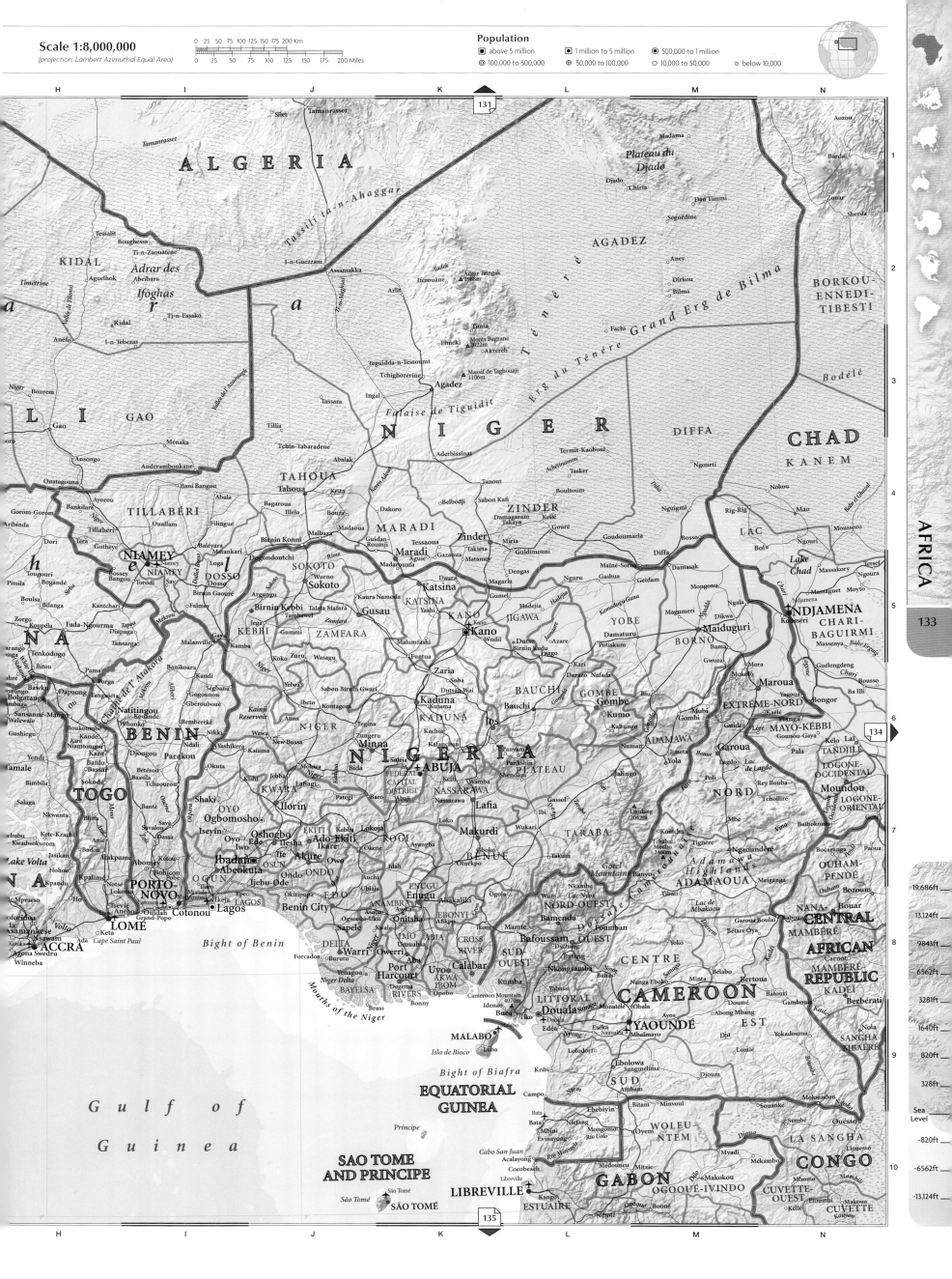

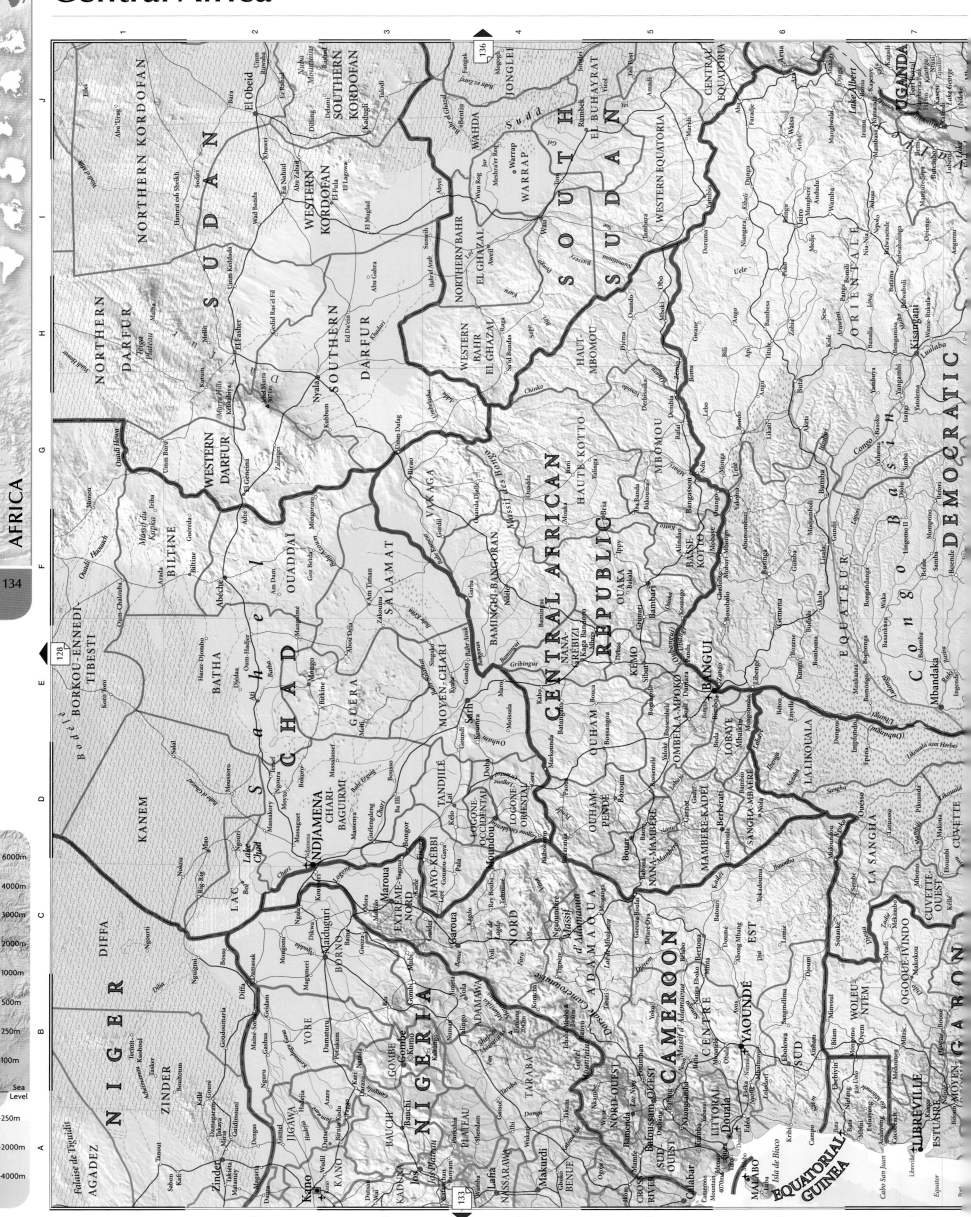

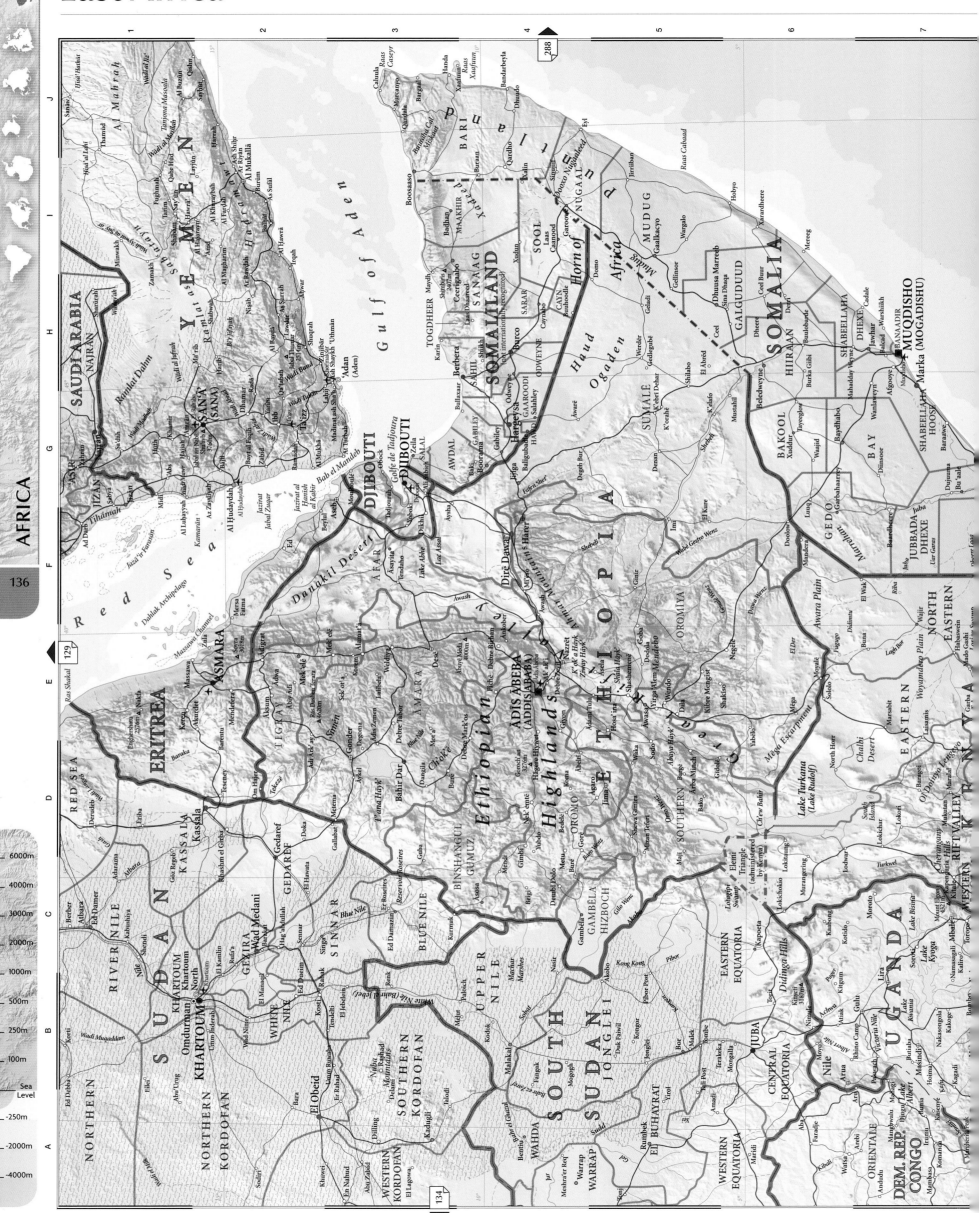

Scale 1:8,000,000
(projection: Lambert Azimuthal Equal Area)

0 25 50 75 100 125 150 175 200 Km
0 25 50 75 100 125 150 175 200 Miles

Population
- ■ above 5 million
- ■ 1 million to 5 million
- ◉ 500,000 to 1 million
- ◎ 100,000 to 500,000
- ⊕ 50,000 to 100,000
- ○ 10,000 to 50,000
- ∘ below 10,000

SEYCHELLES

Inner Islands
Île Aride, Curieuse, Les Sœurs, Grand Sœur, Félicité, Marianne, Praslin, Cousin, Cousine, La Digue, Île aux Récifs, Silhouette, Mamelles, North Point, Sainte Anne, Île au Cerf, VICTORIA, Morne Seychellois 905m, Île Thérèse, Anse Boileau, Île au Cerf, Pointe Lazare, Quatre Bornes, Mahé, Pointe Police, Pointe Bornée

Scale 1:2,000,000
0 10 20 30 Miles / 0 10 20 30 Km

RÉUNION (to France)
ST-DENIS, Ste-Marie, Ste-Suzanne, St-André, Le Port, Ste-Rose, St-Paul, St-Benoît, St-Gilles-les-Bains, Salazie, La Plaine-des-Palmistes, St-Leu, Cilaos, Le Piton, Piton de la Fournaise, St-Louis, St-Pierre, St-Joseph, St-Philippe, Pointe de la Table
Scale 1:2,000,000
0 10 20 30 Km

MAURITIUS
PORT LOUIS, Triolet, Pamplemousses, Goodlands, Round Island, Flat Island, Gunner's Quoin, Rivière du Rempart, Centre de Flacq, Beau Bassin, Rose Hill, Bel Air, Quatre Bornes, Curepipe, Vacoas, Mahebourg, Chemin Grenier, Souillac, Pointe Sud Ouest
Scale 1:2,000,000
0 10 20 30 Km

INDIAN OCEAN

SEYCHELLES
Providence Atoll, Farquhar Group, Cosmoledo Group, Astove Island, Aldabra Group, Assumption Island

COMOROS / Comoro Islands
Ngazidja, MORONI, Le Karthala 2361m, Dembéni, Mwali, Mutsamudu, Nzwani
MAYOTTE (to France), MAMOUDZOU, Pamandzi

Mozambique Channel

MADAGASCAR
ANTSIRANANA, Maroantsetra, MAHAJANGA, Mahajanga, TOAMASINA, Nosy Sainte Marie, Ambositra

Mainland
JUBBADA HOOSE, Kismaayo, COAST, Mombasa, Malindi, Lamu, NAIROBI, CENTRAL, Nyeri, Nakuru, Kisumu, NYANZA, Lake Victoria, Entebbe, Bukoba, KAGERA, RWANDA, KIGALI, BURUNDI, BUJUMBURA, KIGOMA, TANZANIA, DODOMA, Zanzibar, DAR ES SALAAM, PWANI, Mafia, Morogoro, MOROGORO, Iringa, IRINGA, SINGIDA, TABORA, Tabora, Mwanza, MWANZA, SHINYANGA, MARA, ARUSHA, Arusha, Moshi, KILIMANJARO, TANGA, Tanga, PEMBA NORTH, PEMBA SOUTH, ZANZIBAR NORTH, ZANZIBAR SOUTH, LINDI, MTWARA, RUVUMA, MBEYA, Mbeya, Great Rift Valley, Lake Tanganyika, Lake Nyasa, MALAWI, LILONGWE, Blantyre, NORTHERN, CENTRAL, SOUTHERN, ZAMBIA, LUAPULA, NORTHERN, MOZAMBIQUE, Nampula, NAMPULA, NIASSA, Lichinga, CABO DELGADO, Pemba, ZAMBÉZIA, TETE, Tete, MANICA, ZIMBABWE, MASHONALAND CENTRAL, MASHONALAND WEST, LUSAKA

Elevation: 19,686ft / 13,124ft / 9843ft / 6562ft / 3281ft / 1640ft / 820ft / 328ft / Sea Level / -820ft / -6562ft / -13,124ft

SOUTH AFRICA: CAPITAL CITIES

PRETORIA / TSHWANE – administrative capital
CAPE TOWN – legislative capital
BLOEMFONTEIN – judicial capital

Scale 1:8,000,000
(projection: Lambert Azimuthal Equal Area)

0 25 50 75 100 125 150 175 200 Km
0 25 50 75 100 150 175 200 Miles

Population
- above 5 million
- 1 million to 5 million
- 500,000 to 1 million
- 100,000 to 500,000
- 50,000 to 100,000
- 10,000 to 50,000
- below 10,000

COMOROS

MAMOUDZOU
MAYOTTE
(to France)

Comoro Islands

Mutsamudu   Mwali   Nzwani

CABO DELGADO
Pemba
Mecúfi
Montepuez
Ancuabi
Balama
Muidumbe
Namuno
Lúrio
Memba
Baía de Memba
Nacala
Minguri
Baía de Fernão Veloso
Lumbo

NIASSA
Lichinga
Metangula
Macaloge
Mataca
Unango
Marrupa
Maúa
Lalaua
Ribáuè
Mutuáli
Malema
Mont Namúli 2419m
Molumbo

NAMPULA
Nampula
Murrupula
Quixaxe
Angoche
Moma
Mualama
Nova Nabúri
Gilé

Mahajanga   Boriziny

MAHAJANGA
Mitsinjo   Marovoay   Mampikony
Soalala
Besalampy
Kandreho
Tsaratanana
Morafenobe
Maevatanana
Ambatomainty
Maintirano

Mozambique Channel

Île Juan de Nova
(to France)

Nosy Glorieuses

Tanjona Bobaomby
Antsiraŭana

Tanjona Anorontany

ANTSIRAŬANA
Maromokotro 2876m
Sambava
Bealanana
Andapa
Antalaha
Ambohitralanana

MADAGASCAR

Nosy Be
Ambilobe
Ambanja
Analalava
Antsohihy
Befandriana Avaratra
Maroantsetra
Mandritsara
Tanjona Masoala
Mananara Avaratra

Mahajanga
Mahajanga
Marovoay
Mampikony
Soalala
Besalampy
Borizïny
Andilamena
Maevatanana
Kandreho

TOAMASINA
Soanierana-Ivongo
Nosy Sainte Marie
Fenoarivo Atsinanana
Ambodifotatra
Vavatenina
Ankazobe
Anjozorobe
Toamasina
Ampasimanolotra
Moramanga

ANTANANARIVO
Antananarivo
Tsiroanomandidy
Ambohidratrimo
Arivonimamo
Soavinandriana
Miarinarivo
Manjakandriana
Anosibe An'ala
Antsalova
Miandrivazo
Ambatolampy
Faratsiho
Antanambao Manampotsy
Mahanoro
Belo Tsiribihina
Betafo
Morondava
Mahabo
Ambato Finandrahana
Fandriana
Marolambo
Ambositra
Ambohimahasoa
Nosy Varika
Mandabe
Makay
Ikalamavony
Ifanadiana
Mananjary
Fianarantsoa
Fianarantsoa
Ambalavao
Ikongo
Manakara
Beroroha
FIANARANTSOA
Morombe
Ivohibe
Vohipeno
Ankazoabo
Ihosy
Ivato
Farafangana
Sakaraha
Betroka
Midongy Atsimo
Vangaindrano
Befotaka
Benenitra
Iakora
Toliara
Betioky
TOLIARA
Bekily
Mandrare
Ampanihy
Amboasary
Ambovombe
Beloha
Tôlañaro
Tsiombe

Tanjona Vohimena

Tropic of Capricorn

MOZAMBIQUE
Mozambique Channel

INDIAN OCEAN

INDIAN OCEAN

MALAWI
LILONGWE
Blantyre
Lake Nyasa
Lake Chilwa

Zambezi
Tete
Quelimane
ZAMBÉZIA
SOFALA
MANICA
Beira
Baía de Sofala
INHAMBANE
GAZA
Inhambane
Xai-Xai

HARARE
Chitungwiza
Mutare
Chimoio

MASVINGO
Beitbridge
Musina

MAPUTO
MAPUTO
Matola
MBABANE
SWAZILAND
MANZINI

Pietermaritzburg
Durban
KWAZULU/NATAL

Comoros inset
(Scale 1:4,500,000)

0 20 40 60 80 Km
0 20 40 60 80 Miles

Grande Comore
Saondzou 1087m
Mitsamiouli
Hahaya
Mbéni
MORONI
Koimbani
Ikartala 2361m
Mitsoudjé
Dembéni
Foumbouni

COMOROS

INDIAN OCEAN

Mohéli
Nioumachoua
Miringoni
Fomboni Sima
Ouanani
Anjouan
Moutsamudu
Ouani
Domoni
Moya
Mramani

MAYOTTE
(to France)
Comoro Islands
MAMOUDZOU
Dzaoudzi
Pamandzi
Bandrélé

Mozambique Channel

Scale 1:8,000,000
0 25 50 75 100 125 150 Km
0 25 50 75 100 150 Miles

19,686ft
13,124ft
9843ft
6562ft
3281ft
1640ft
820ft
328ft
Sea Level
-820ft
-6562ft
-13,124ft

AFRICA

140

138

291

293

SOUTH AFRICA: CAPITAL CITIES

PRETORIA / TSHWANE – administrative capital
CAPE TOWN – legislative capital
BLOEMFONTEIN – judicial capital

ATLANTIC

OCEAN

6000m
4000m
3000m
2000m
1000m
500m
250m
100m
Sea Level
-250m
-2000m
-4000m

Scale 1:4,650,000
(projection: Lambert Azimuthal Equal Area)

0 20 40 60 80 100 Km
0 20 40 60 80 100 Miles

Population
- ■ above 5 million
- ◉ 100,000 to 500,000
- ■ 1 million to 5 million
- ⊕ 50,000 to 100,000
- ◉ 500,000 to 1 million
- ○ 10,000 to 50,000
- ∘ below 10,000

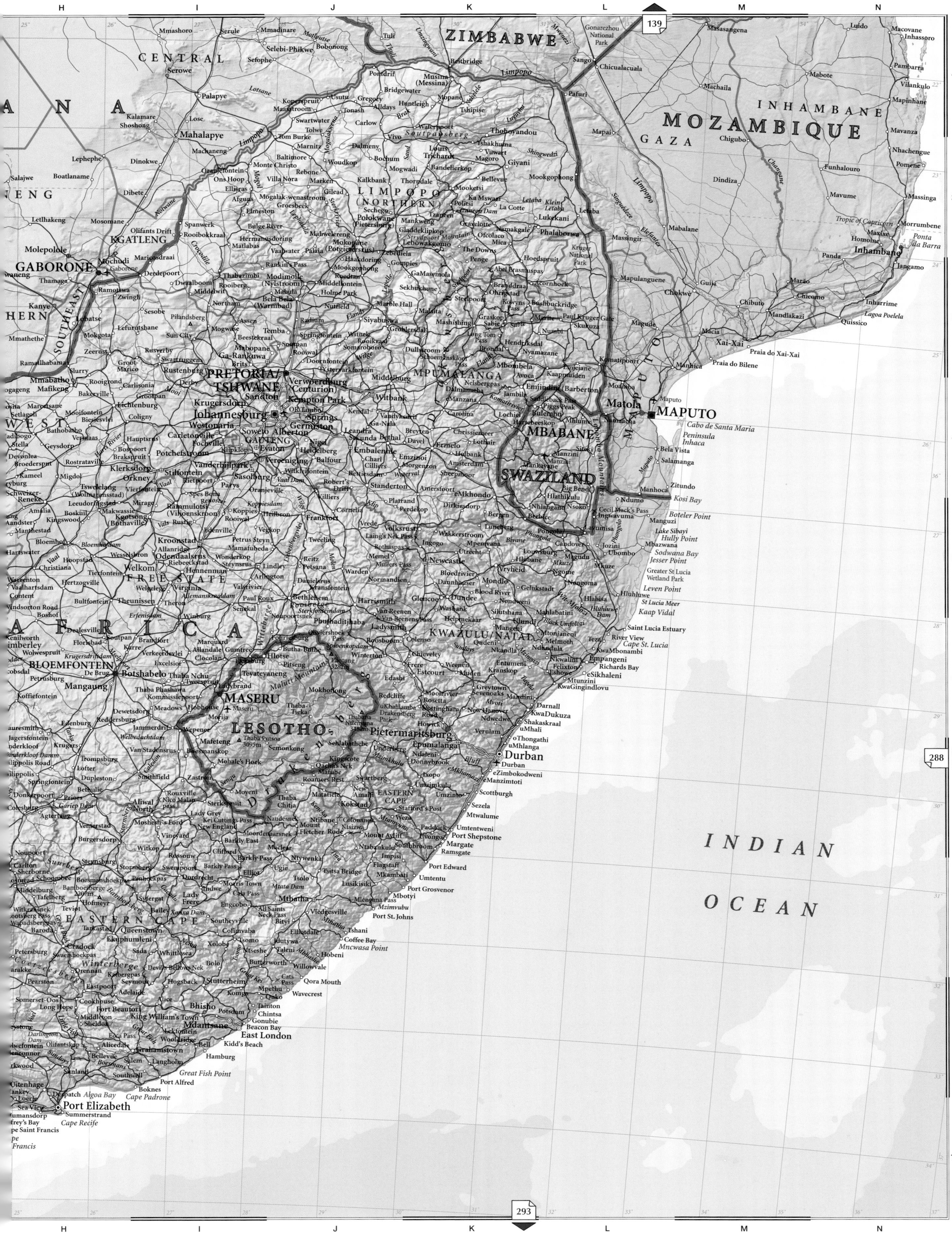

ZIMBABWE

MOZAMBIQUE

GAZA

INHAMBANE

BOTSWANA

LIMPOPO (NORTHERN)

MPUMALANGA

GAUTENG

FREE STATE

KWAZULU / NATAL

EASTERN CAPE

SWAZILAND

LESOTHO

NORTH WEST

GABORONE

PRETORIA / TSHWANE

Johannesburg

BLOEMFONTEIN

MASERU

MBABANE

Maputo

MATOLA

Durban

Pietermaritzburg

East London

Port Elizabeth

Kruger National Park

INDIAN OCEAN

Tropic of Capricorn

19,686ft
13,124ft
9843ft
6562ft
3281ft
1640ft
820ft
328ft
Sea Level
-820ft
-6562ft
-13,124ft

139
288
293

Algiers

Mediterranean Sea

L'Ermitage
Cap de Bordj
Grande Mosquée
Bab El Oued
Kasbah
Bordj El Bahri
Alger (Algiers)
El Biar
Palais du Gouvernement
Chéraga
Ben Aknoûn
Agha
Hussein-Dey
Bordj El Kiffan
Musée des Beaux Arts
Birmandreïs
Kouba
Cité Olympique
Dar El Beïda
Birkhadem
Draria
El Harrach
Oued Smar
Algiers Airport
Douera
Oued Harrach
Baraki

0   3 Km
0   3 Miles

Cairo

Abu Al Ghayt
Bahtîm
El Matarîya
Cairo International Airport
Shubra Al Amiriya
Nile
El Zeitûn
Masr el Gedida (Heliopolis)
Warrâq el Hadr
Shubra Al Khaymah
Warrâq el'Arab
Mâdinet Nasr
Imbâbah
Bûlâq
El Ezbekiya
Aguza
CAIRO (AL QÂHIRAH)
Egyptian Antiquities Museum
Âbdin
El Dûqqi
The Citadel
Central Government Building
Garden City
Zoological Gardens
Giza (Al Jîzah)
Masr el Qadima
El Basâlîn
Cheops
Sphinx
Pyramids of Giza
Nile
El Ma'âdi

0   3 Km
0   3 Miles

Cape Town

Atlantic Ocean
Table Bay
Granger Bay
Paarden Eiland
Mouille Point
Ben Schoeman Dock
Fort Wynyard
South Africa Maritime Museum
Duncan Dock
Green Point
Foreshore
Salt River
Three Anchor Bay
Woodstock
Cape Town
Three Anchor Bay
De Waterkant
Central
Signal Hill
Malay Quarter
Castle
Sea Point
Schotsche Kloof
Botanical Gardens
Houses of Parliament
Tamboerskloof
Zonnebloem
Bantry Bay
Gardens Toine
Vredehoek
Devils Peak Estate
Clifton
Lions Head
Clifton Bay

0   1 Km
0   1 Miles

Casablanca

Atlantic Ocean
El Hank
Mosquée Hassan II
Aïn Harrounda
Old Médina
Aïn Diab
Aïn Sebaa
Marchée Centrale
Essoukour Assawda
Hay Mohammadi
Casablanca
Anfa
Palais du Roi
Sidi Moumen Ahl Ahl Loughlam
Casablanca Airport
El Maarif
El Fida Drissia
Moulay Rachid
Mohamed V
Sidi Othmâne
Notre Dame de Lourdes
Ben Msick
Ain Clock Sidi Maarouf
Sbata-Salmia
L'Oasis

0   3 Km
0   3 Miles

Dakar

Industrial Zone
Grand Dakar
Fass
Colobane
Gouye Salane
Darou Kipp
Point E
Medina
Gibraltar
Dakar-Marine
Grande Mosquée
Fann Hok
Abattoirs
Claudel
Rebeus
Dakar
Pointe de Dakar
Théâtre Daniel Sorano
Palais Présidentiel
Musée Dakar
Atlantic Ocean
Le Plateau
Pointe Bernard

0   1 Km
0   1 Miles

Harare

Belgravia
Kensington
Milton Park
Avondale
Greenwood Park
Gun Hill
Eastlea North
Harare Gardens
Newlands
National Art Gallery
Belvedere North
Cathedral
Parliament
Eastlea
Cecil Square
Civic Centre
Harare
Town House
National Sports Centre
Eastlea South
Kopje
Mukuvisi
Hillside
Braeside
Arcadia

0   0.5 Km
0   0.5 Miles

Johannesburg

Diepsloot N.R.

Tembisa

Sandton

Modderfontein

Kempton Park

Randburg

Alexandra

Krugersdorp

Wits University

Edenvale

O.R. Tambo International Airport

Johannesburg

National School of Arts

Photographic Museum

Museum of Africa

Johannesburg Library

Bedfordview

Boksburg

Germiston

National Exhibition Centre

Elsburg

Soweto

Klipriviersberg N.R.

Alberton

Lenasia

Klip

10 Km

10 Miles

Kinshasa

Congo

Palais de Nation

Palace de Justice

Gombe

Kinshasa

Mont Ngaliema

Lingwala

Barumbu

Ngaliema

Kintambo

Musée de Kinshasa

Binza Ozone

Bandalungwa

Kasa-Vubu

Binza Meteo

Kalamu

Ngiri-Ngiri

Limete

Selembao

Makala

Bumbu

Ngaba

Binza Delvaux

Matete

Masina

Kinsenso

Ndjili

Ngafula

Kimbanseke

3 Km

3 Miles

Lagos

Yaba

Lagos Lagoon

Ebute-Metta

Iganmu

National Theatre

Ijora

Oba's Palace

Central Mosque

Bamgboshe

Lagos Island

Lagos

Onikan National Museum

Moba

Obalende

Ikoyi

Lagos Harbour

Apapa

Apapa Warf

Falomo

Five Cowrie Creek

Lekki Peninsula

Porto Novo Creek

Ogogoro

Victoria Island

Maroko

Ogoyo

Tamaro

Alaguntan

Okeogbe

Tarqua Bay

Atlantic Ocean

2 Km

2 Miles

Nairobi

Kasarani

Parklands

Groganville

Westlands

Komarock Estate

Chiromo

Jeevanjee

Art Gallery

Kenya National Theatre

Pumwani

Makongeni

Kileleshwa

Nairobi

Umoja

Nairobi Hill

Nairobi

Embakasi

Onyoka

City Square

All Saints Cathedral

Parliament Buildings

Makadara

Upper Hill Estate

Nairobi Airport

Nairobi Hill

Nairobi National Park

Golf Course Estate

2 Km

2 Miles

Tripoli

Mediterranean Sea

Gurji Mosque

Harbour

Assaraya Al Hamra

Al Madinah

People's Palace

Ṭarābulus (Tripoli)

Sidi al Mašri

Suq al Juma'a

Annasr Forest

Al Fatah University

Abu Salim

Janzur

Wadi al Migņnin

Wadi Aşîrat

5 Km

5 Miles

Tunis

Sebkhet Ariana

La Marsa

Bou Saïd

Tunis-Carthage Airport

El Manar

Parc Archéologique

Cité Olympique

El Aouine

Musée Océanographique

Université

Parc du Belvédère

Carthage

Tunis

Cité El Zhadra

Lac du Tunis

Musée du Barde

La Médina

La Goulette

Bardo

El Bhira

Mediterranean Sea

Mégrine

Rades

Golfe de Tunis

Sebkhet Sejoumi

Ben Arous

Oued Méliane

Ez Zahra

Hammamet

Habeuf

Hammam Lif

5 Km

5 Miles

Europe is the world's second smallest continent with a total area of 4,053,309 sq miles (10,498,000 sq km). It comprises 46 separate countries, including Turkey and the Russian Federation, although the greater parts of these nations lie in Asia.

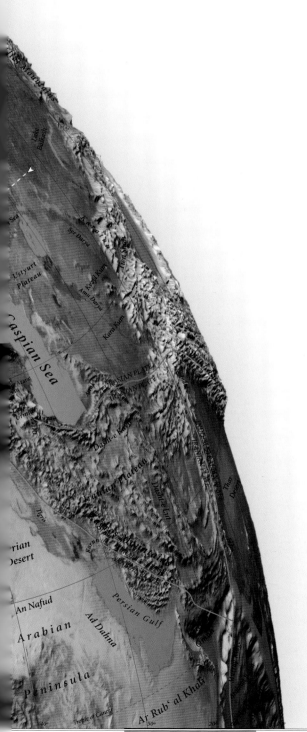

FACTFILE

N **Most Northerly Point:** Ostrov Rudol'fa, Russian Federation 81° 47′ N

S **Most Southerly Point:** Gávdos, Greece 34° 51′ N

E **Most Easterly Point:** Mys Flissingskiy, Novaya Zemlya, Russian Federation 69° 03′ E

W **Most Westerly Point:** Bjargtangar, Iceland 24° 33′ W

Largest Lakes:
1. Lake Ladoga, Russian Federation 7100 sq miles (18,390 sq km)
2. Lake Onega, Russian Federation 3819 sq miles (9891 sq km)
3. Vänern, Sweden 2141 sq miles (5545 sq km)
4. Lake Peipus, Estonia/Russian Federation 1372 sq miles (3555 sq km)
5. Vättern, Sweden 737 sq miles (1910 sq km)

Longest Rivers:
1. Volga, Russian Federation 2265 miles (3645 km)
2. Danube, C Europe 1771 miles (2850 km)
3. Dnieper, Belarus/Russian Federation/Ukraine 1421 miles (2287 km)
4. Don, Russian Federation 1162 miles (1870 km)
5. Pechora, Russian Federation 1124 miles (1809 km)

Largest Islands:
1. Britain, 88,700 sq miles (229,800 sq km)
2. Iceland, 39,315 sq miles (101,826 sq km)
3. Ireland, 31,521 sq miles (81,638 sq km)
4. Ostrov Severny, Novaya Zemlya, Russian Federation 18,177 sq miles (47,079 sq km)
5. Spitsbergen, Svalbard 15,051 sq miles (38,981 sq km)

Highest Points:
1. El'brus, Russian Federation 18,510 ft (5642 m)
2. Dykhtau, Russian Federation 17,077 ft (5205 m)
3. Koshtantau, Russian Federation 16,877 ft (5144 m)
4. Gora Kazbek, Georgia/Russian Federation 16,647 ft (5074 m)
5. Gora Dzhangitau, Georgia/Russian Federation 16,571 ft (5051 m)

Lowest Point:
▼ Caspian Depression, Russian Federation -92 ft (-28 m) below sea level

Highest recorded temperature:
Seville, Spain 122°F (50°C)

Lowest recorded temperature:
Ust'-Shchuger, Russian Federation -72.6°F (-58.1°C)

Wettest Place:
Crkvice, Bosnia and Herzegovina 183 in (4648 mm)

Driest Place:
Astrakhan', Russian Federation 6.4 in (162.5 mm)

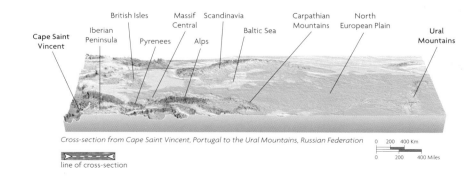

Cross-section from Cape Saint Vincent, Portugal to the Ural Mountains, Russian Federation

line of cross-section

0   200   400 Km
0   200   400 Miles

Political

The political boundaries of Europe have changed many times, especially during the 20th century in the aftermath of two world wars, the break-up of the empires of Austria-Hungary, Nazi Germany, and, toward the end of the century, the collapse of communism in eastern Europe. The fragmentation of Yugoslavia has again altered the political map of Europe, highlighting a trend towards nationalism and devolution. In contrast, economic federalism is growing. In 1958, the formation of the European Economic Community (now the European Union or EU) started a move toward economic and political union and increasing internal migration. This process is still ongoing and the accession of Bulgaria and Romania in January 2007 brought the number of EU member states to twenty seven. Of these, seventeen have joined the Eurozone by adopting the Euro as their official currency.

Population
- ■ above 5 million
- ◪ 1 million to 5 million
- ◉ 500,000 to 1 million
- ◎ 100,000 to 500,000
- ⊕ 50,000 to 100,000
- ○ 10,000 to 50,000
- ● Country capital

Borders
- ⬡ full international border

Scale 1:17,250,000
(projection: Lambert Azimuthal Equal Area)

Languages

There are three main European language groups: Germanic languages predominate in central and northern Europe; Romance languages in western and Mediterranean Europe and Romania; while Slavic languages are spoken in eastern Europe and the Russian Federation. Isolated pockets of local languages, such as Basque and Gaelic, persist and frequently provide a focus for national identity.

Language groups

- Turkic
- Albanian
- Finno-Ugric/Samoyed
- Germanic
- Slavic
- Romance
- Basque
- Baltic
- Celtic
- Greek
- Caucasian
- Iranian
- Mongol

Population

Europe is a densely populated, urbanized continent; in Belgium over 90% of people live in urban areas. The highest population densities are found in an area stretching east from southern Britain and northern France, into Germany. The northern fringes are only sparsely populated.

Population density
(people per sq mile)

- below 130
- 130–259
- 260–379
- 380–519
- 520–780
- above 780

Standard of living

Living standards in western Europe are among the highest in the world, although there is a growing sector of homeless, jobless people. Eastern Europeans have lower overall standards of living—a legacy of stagnated economies.

Standard of living
(UN human development index)

- low
- high
- data not available

Transportation

Despite its fragmented geography and many natural frontiers, communications in Europe are well developed. Extensive motorway links allow rapid road transportation, while high-speed rail connections like France's TGV (Train à Grande Vitesse), and the Channel Tunnel have improved rail travel. Outdated communication infrastructures in parts of eastern Europe, and insufficient transport links across the Alps, however, remain weak parts of the network.

Transportation

- major roads and motorways
- major railroads
- international borders
- transport intersections
- major international airports
- major ports

Scale 1:22,500,000
(projection: Lambert Conformal Conic)

Climate

Europe experiences few extremes in either rainfall or temperature, with the exception of the far north and south. Along the west coast, the warm currents of the North Atlantic Drift moderate temperatures. Although east–west air movement is relatively unimpeded by relief, the Alpine Uplands halt the progress of north–south air masses, protecting most of the Mediterranean from cold, north winds.

Average Rainfall

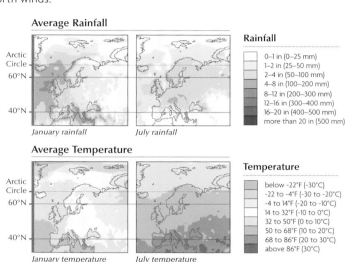

January rainfall   *July rainfall*

Rainfall

	0–1 in (0–25 mm)
	1–2 in (25–50 mm)
	2–4 in (50–100 mm)
	4–8 in (100–200 mm)
	8–12 in (200–300 mm)
	12–16 in (300–400 mm)
	16–20 in (400–500 mm)
	more than 20 in (500 mm)

Average Temperature

January temperature   *July temperature*

Temperature

	below -22°F (-30°C)
	-22 to -4°F (-30 to -20°C)
	-4 to 14°F (-20 to -10°C)
	14 to 32°F (-10 to 0°C)
	32 to 50°F (0 to 10°C)
	50 to 68°F (10 to 20°C)
	68 to 86°F (20 to 30°C)
	above 86°F (30°C)

Climate

	tundra
	subarctic
	cool continental
	warm humid
	mediterranean
	semi-arid

- daily hours of sunshine, January
- daily hours of sunshine, July
- cold wind
- hot wind

Environmental issues

The partially enclosed waters of the Baltic and Mediterranean seas have become heavily polluted, while the Barents Sea is contaminated with spent nuclear fuel from Russia's navy. Acid rain, caused by emissions from factories and power stations, is actively destroying northern forests. As a result, pressure is growing to safeguard Europe's natural environment and prevent further deterioration.

Environmental issues

	national parks
	Risk of acid rain
	polluted rivers
	radioactive contamination

	marine pollution
	heavy marine pollution
	poor urban air quality

Land use

Europe's swelling urban population and the outward expansion of many cities has created acute competition for land. Despite this, European resourcefulness has maximized land potential, and over half of Europe's land is still used for a wide variety of agricultural purposes. Land in northern Europe is used for cattle-rearing, pasture, and arable crops. Towards the Mediterranean, the mild climate allows the growing of grapes for wine; olives, sunflowers, tobacco and citrus fruits. EU subsidies, however, have resulted in massive overproduction and a land "set-aside" policy has been introduced.

Using the land and sea

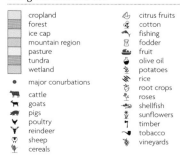

	cropland		citrus fruits
	forest		cotton
	ice cap		fishing
	mountain region		fodder
	pasture		fruit
	tundra		olive oil
	wetland		potatoes
	major conurbations		rice
	cattle		root crops
	goats		roses
	pigs		shellfish
	poultry		sunflowers
	reindeer		timber
	sheep		tobacco
	cereals		vineyards

1
VATNAJÖKULL, ICELAND
Europe's largest ice cap is located in the
southeast of this Atlantic island.

2
ORESUND LINK, DENMARK/SWEDEN
This link was opened to traffic in 2000, joining the
Danish capital, Copenhagen, with the Swedish town of
Malmö across the waters of the Oresund Strait.

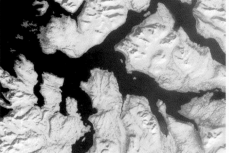

3
BALSFJORD, NORWAY
Fjords were cut into Norway's west coast by glaciers
during the last ice age but as the ice retreated rising
sea-levels flooded the valleys left behind.

4
PRAGUE, CZECH REPUBLIC
In August 2002 some parts of the capital
were still under water after the worst
floods in living memory.

9
GIBRALTAR
A British colony since 1713, this rocky
promontory commands a strategic position at
the southern end of the Iberian Peninsula.

10
BORDEAUX, FRANCE
Famous for its wines, this city sits on the west
bank of the Garonne river, which is joined from
the east by the Dordogne river.

11
SOUTH FLEVOLAND, NETHERLANDS
This polder was reclaimed from the sea in
the early 1970s and is now home to extensive
farmland and small towns.

12
RHINE, GERMANY
The Rhine has been straightened in places, such
as here, just south of Mannheim,
to ease navigation.

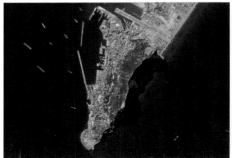

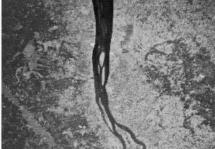

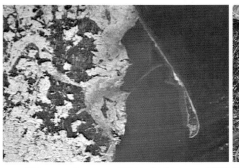

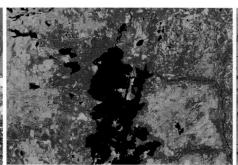

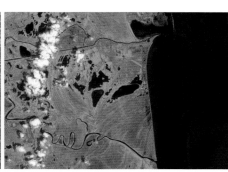

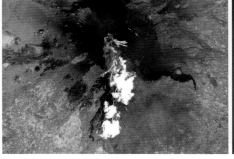

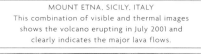

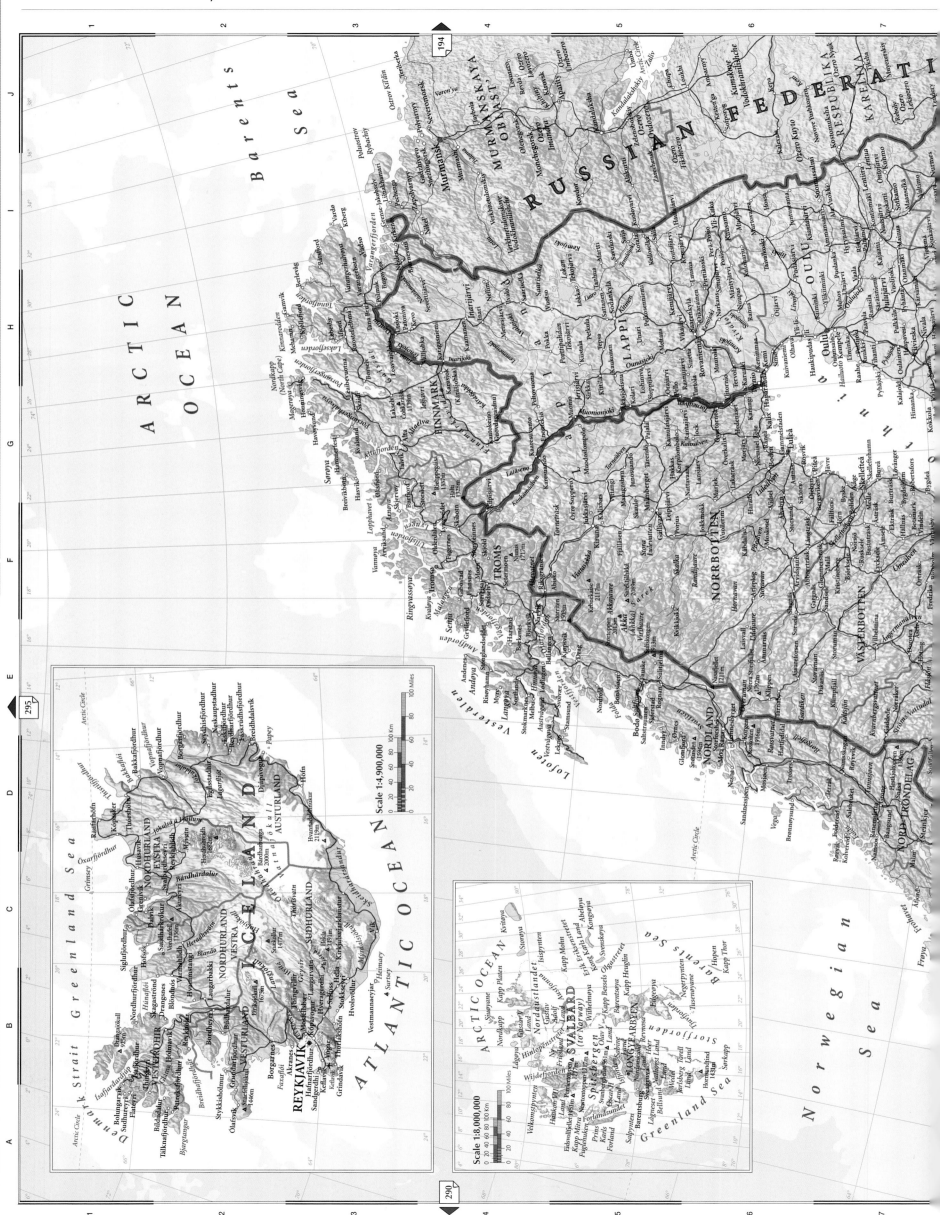

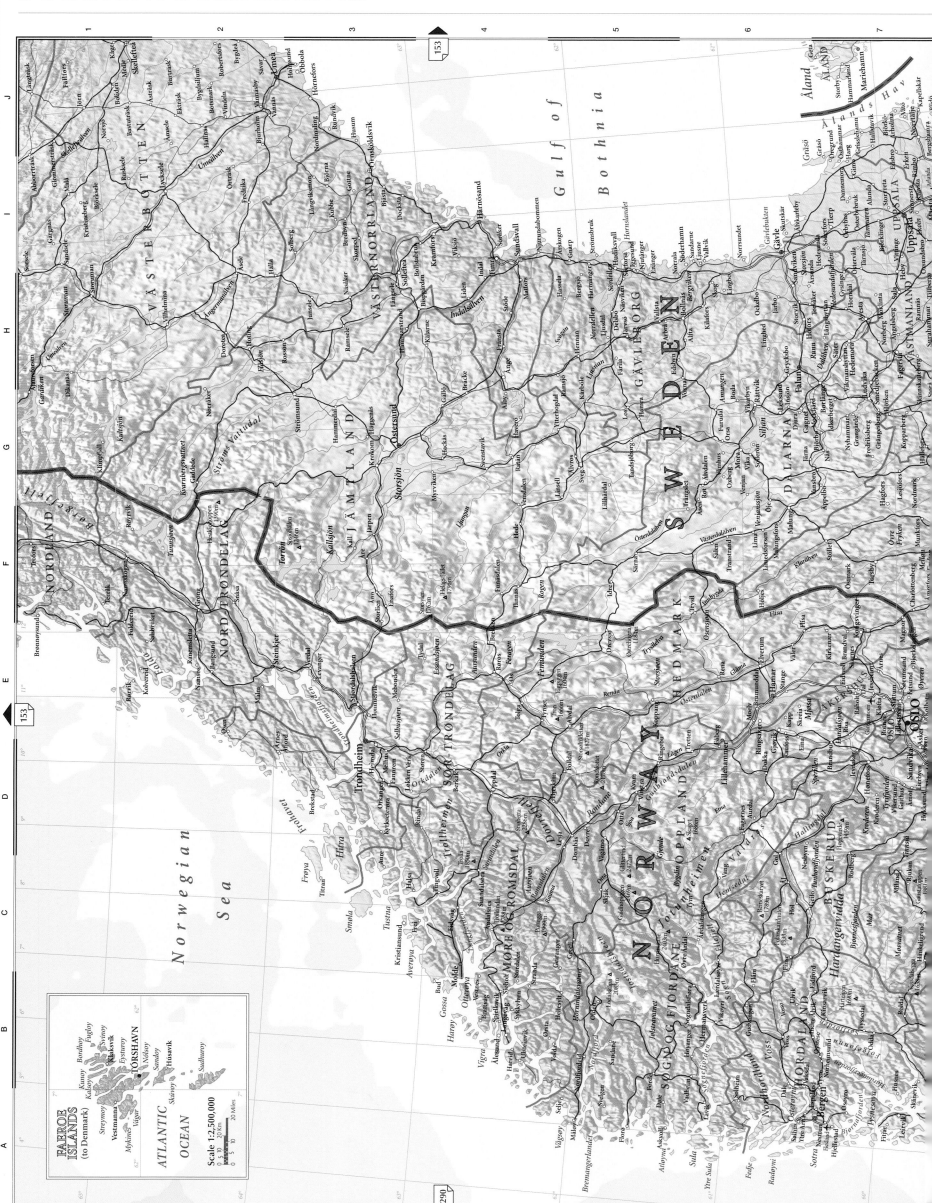

United Kingdom & Ireland

155
290

UNITED KINGDOM

North Sea

SCOTLAND

North West Highlands

Grampian Mountains

Southern Uplands

ATLANTIC OCEAN

Outer Hebrides

Inner Hebrides

Shetland Islands
Herma Ness
Unst
Fetlar
Yell
Out Skerries
Yell Sound
Whalsay
Bressay
Lerwick
Hillswick
St Magnus Bay
Sullom Voe
Mainland
Scalloway
West Burra
Papa Stour
Foula
Fitful Head
Sumburgh Head
Fair Isle

Orkney Islands
Papa Westray
Westray
The North Ronaldsay
North Ronaldsay
Rousay
Sanday
Eday
Stronsay
Mainland
Stenness
Stromness
Scapa Flow
Kirkwall
Shapinsay
Hoy
Burray
St Margaret's Hope
South Ronaldsay
Pentland Firth
Duncansby Head
John o'Groats
Noss Head
Wick

Dunnet Head
Strathy Point
Thurso
Halkirk
Helmsdale
Halladale
Brora
Golspie
Dornoch
Tarbat Ness
Loch Eriboll
Cape Wrath
Durness
Tongue
Bettyhill
Kinbrace
Ben Klibreck
Lairg
Dornoch Firth
Ben Hope
Brora
Loch Shin
Bonar Bridge
Beauly Firth
Scourie
Ben More Assynt
Lochinver
Ullapool
Invergordon
Cromarty
Nairn
Elgin
Lossiemouth
Buckie
Macduff
Banff
Moray Firth
Ben Wyvis
Strathpeffer
Dingwall
Forres
Fraserburgh
Peterhead
Kinnaird Head
Buchan Ness
Aberdeen
Girdle Ness
Stonehaven

Edrachillis Bay
Enard Bay
Loch Maree
Gairloch
Loch Torridon
Inner Sound
Beinn Eighe
Kyle of Lochalsh
Broadford
Canna
Loch Carron
Loch Alsh
Inverness
Loch Ness
Beauly
Loch Lochy
Fort Augustus
Aviemore
Cairn Gorm
Grantown-on-Spey
Ben Macdui
Loch Laggan
Huntly
Keith
Turriff
Oldmeldrum
Inverurie
Alford
Ellon
Dyce
Don
Dee
Ben Avon
Banchory
Braemar
Brechin
Montrose
Arbroath
Carnoustie
Dundee
St Andrews
Fife Ness
Perth
Firth of Tay
Cupar
Loch Tay
Crieff
Callander
Dunfermline
Kirkcaldy
North Berwick
Firth of Forth
Edinburgh
Haddington
Berwick-upon-Tweed
St Abb's Head
Holy Island

Butt of Lewis
Port of Ness
Eye Peninsula
Broad Bay
Carloway
Stornoway
Isle of Lewis
Tarbert
Harris
Scarp
Taransay
Pabbay
Loch Roag
Loch Seaforth
Shiant Islands
The Minch
Sound of Harris
The Little Minch
Sea of the Hebrides
North Uist
Benbecula
Lochmaddy
Monach Islands
Flannan Isles
Sula Sgeir
North Rona
Sule Skerry
Stack Skerry
St Kilda
South Uist
Lochboisdale
Eriskay
Barra
Barra Head

Isle of Skye
Uig
Portree
Raasay
Rhum
Eigg
Muck
Coll
Tiree
Point of Ardnamurchan
Ben More
Tobermory
Isle of Mull
Iona
Colonsay
Jura
Islay
Port Askaig
Port Ellen
Mull of Oa

Oban
Loch Linnhe
Fort William
Ben Nevis
Glen Coe
Loch Leven
Loch Etive
Loch Awe
Sound of Jura
Loch Fyne
Inveraray
Lochgilphead
Tarbert
Campbeltown
Mull of Kintyre
Gigha Island
Arran
Brodick
Isle of Bute
Rothesay
Firth of Clyde
Ailsa Craig
Ballantrae
Girvan
Maybole
Ayr
Troon
Irvine
Kilmarnock
Cumnock
Dalmellington
Greenock
Port Glasgow
Dumbarton
Loch Lomond
GLASGOW
Paisley
Largs
East Kilbride
Hamilton
Motherwell
Lanark
Coatbridge
Airdrie
Cumbernauld
Falkirk
Stirling
Alloa
Grangemouth
Bo'ness

Kyle of Tongue

Dumfries
Lockerbie
Moffat
Merrick
Thornhill
Sanquhar
New Galloway
Newton Stewart
Stranraer
Loch Ryan

Peebles
Galashiels
Selkirk
Melrose
Hawick
Kelso
Jedburgh
Duns
Eyemouth
Coldstream
Lauder

Newcastle upon Tyne
Tynemouth
South Shields
Blyth
Morpeth
Alnwick
Bamburgh
Bellingham
Hexham

Malin Head
Inishtrahull
Bloody Foreland
Tory Island
Carndonagh
Dunfanaghy
Gweedore
Dungloe
Lough Swilly
Sheep Haven
Errigal Mountain
Letterkenny
Giant's Causeway
Portrush
Portstewart
Coleraine
Ballymoney
Ballycastle
Rathlin Island
Larne
Carrickfergus

Lough

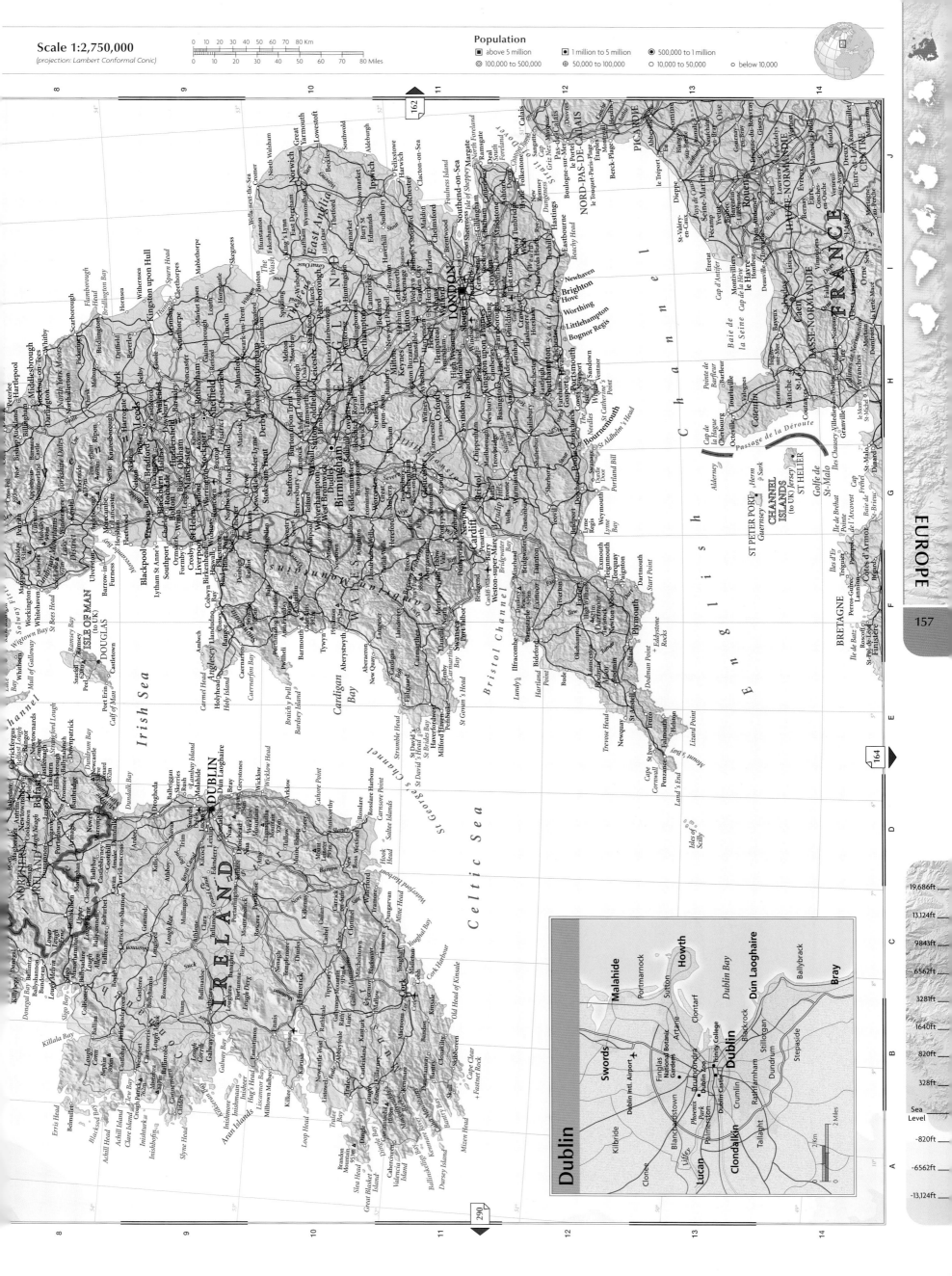

Northern Britain & Ireland

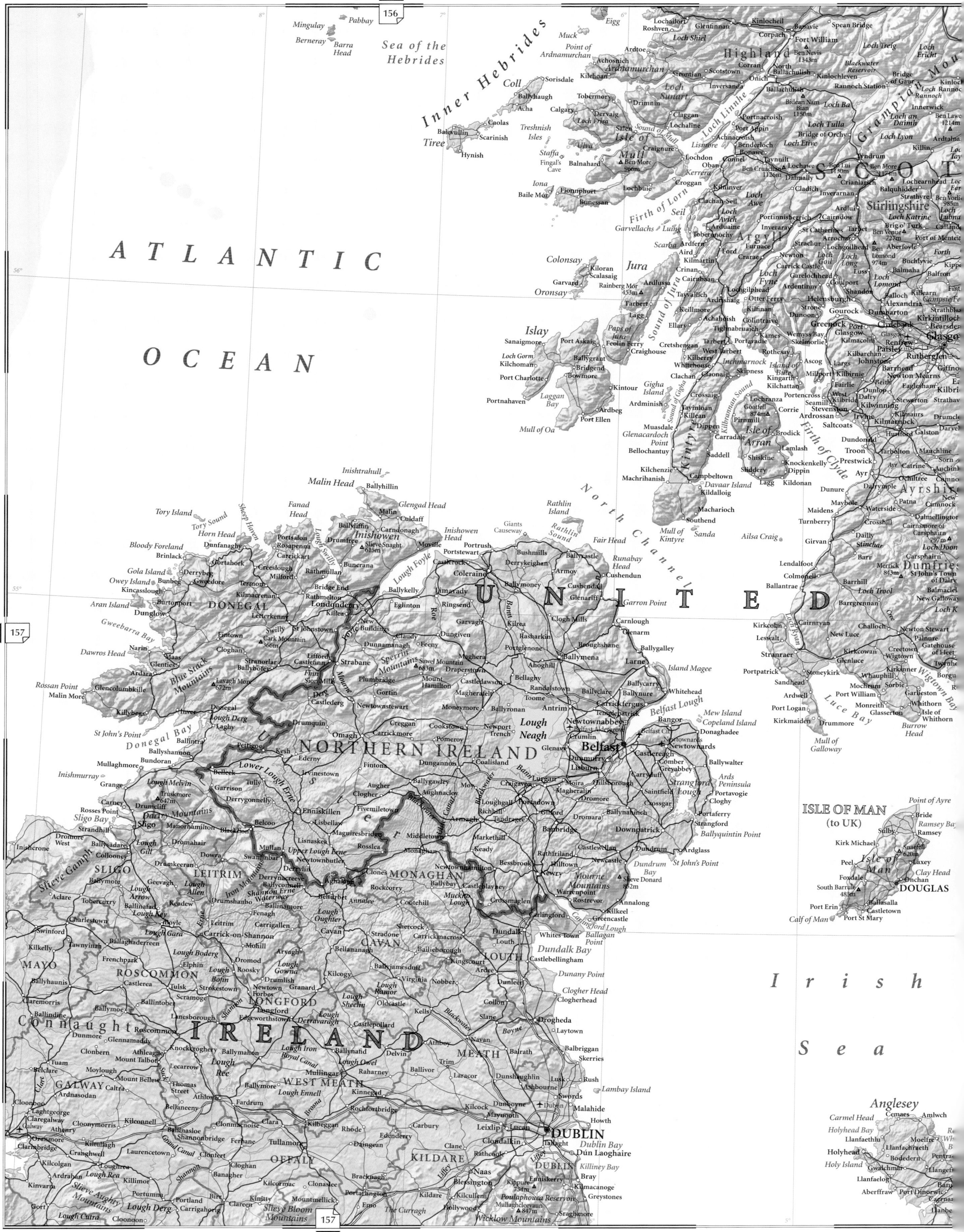

ATLANTIC

OCEAN

Sea of the Hebrides

Inner Hebrides

North Channel

Irish

Sea

UNITED

NORTHERN IRELAND

IRELAND

SCOT

Highland

Grampian Mou

Stirlingshire

Argyll

Ayrshir

Dumfrie

DONEGAL

SLIGO

MAYO

ROSCOMMON

LEITRIM

CAVAN

MONAGHAN

LONGFORD

WEST MEATH

MEATH

LOUTH

KILDARE

OFFALY

GALWAY

CONNAUGHT

Belfast

DUBLIN

ISLE OF MAN
(to UK)

DOUGLAS

Anglesey

156

157

6000m
4000m
3000m
2000m
1000m
500m
250m
100m
Sea
Level
-250m
-2000m
-4000m

Scale 1:1,300,000
(projection: Lambert Conformal Conic)

Population
■ above 5 million
■ 1 million to 5 million
◉ 500,000 to 1 million
◎ 100,000 to 500,000
⊕ 50,000 to 100,000
● 10,000 to 50,000
○ below 10,000

Southern Britain

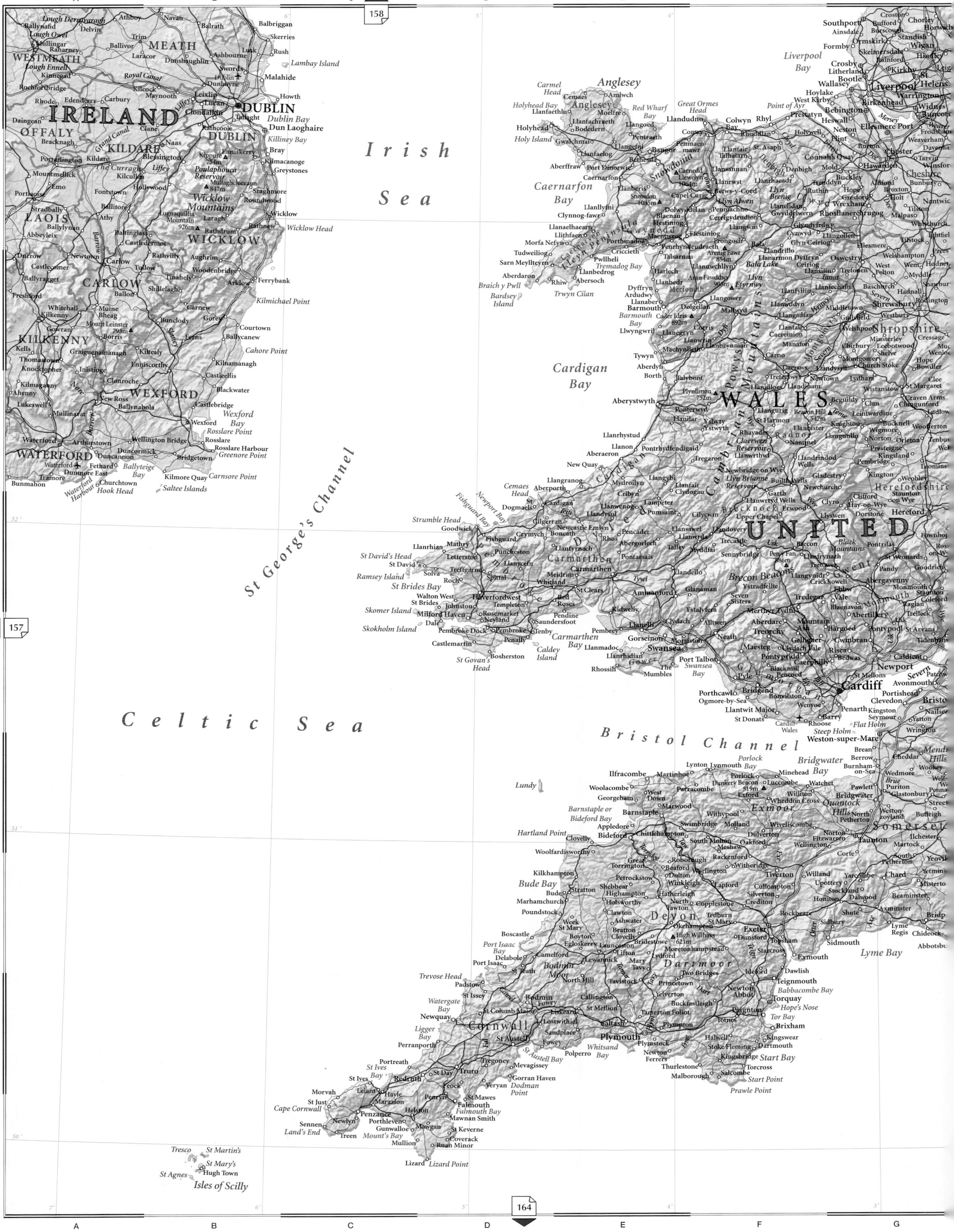

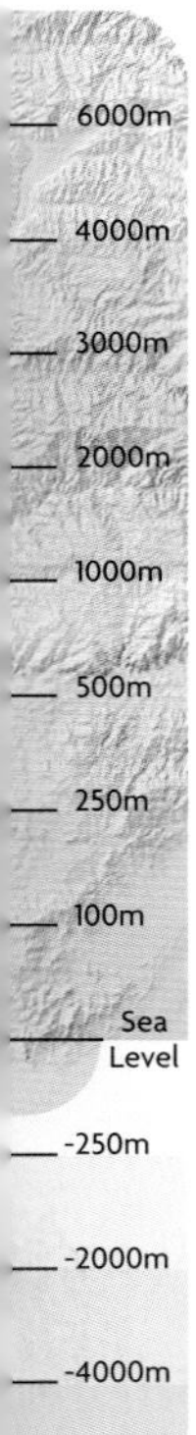

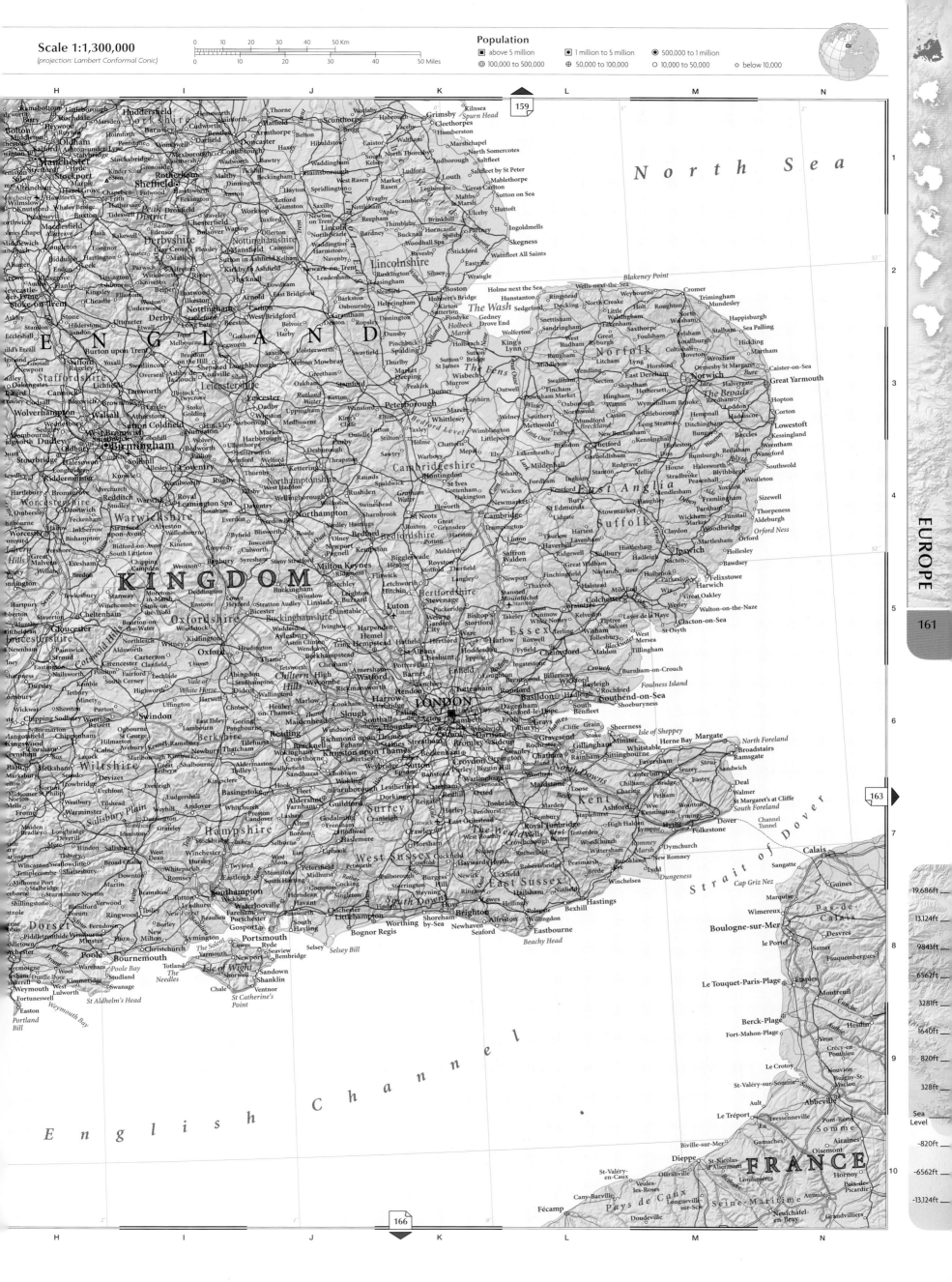

The Low Countries

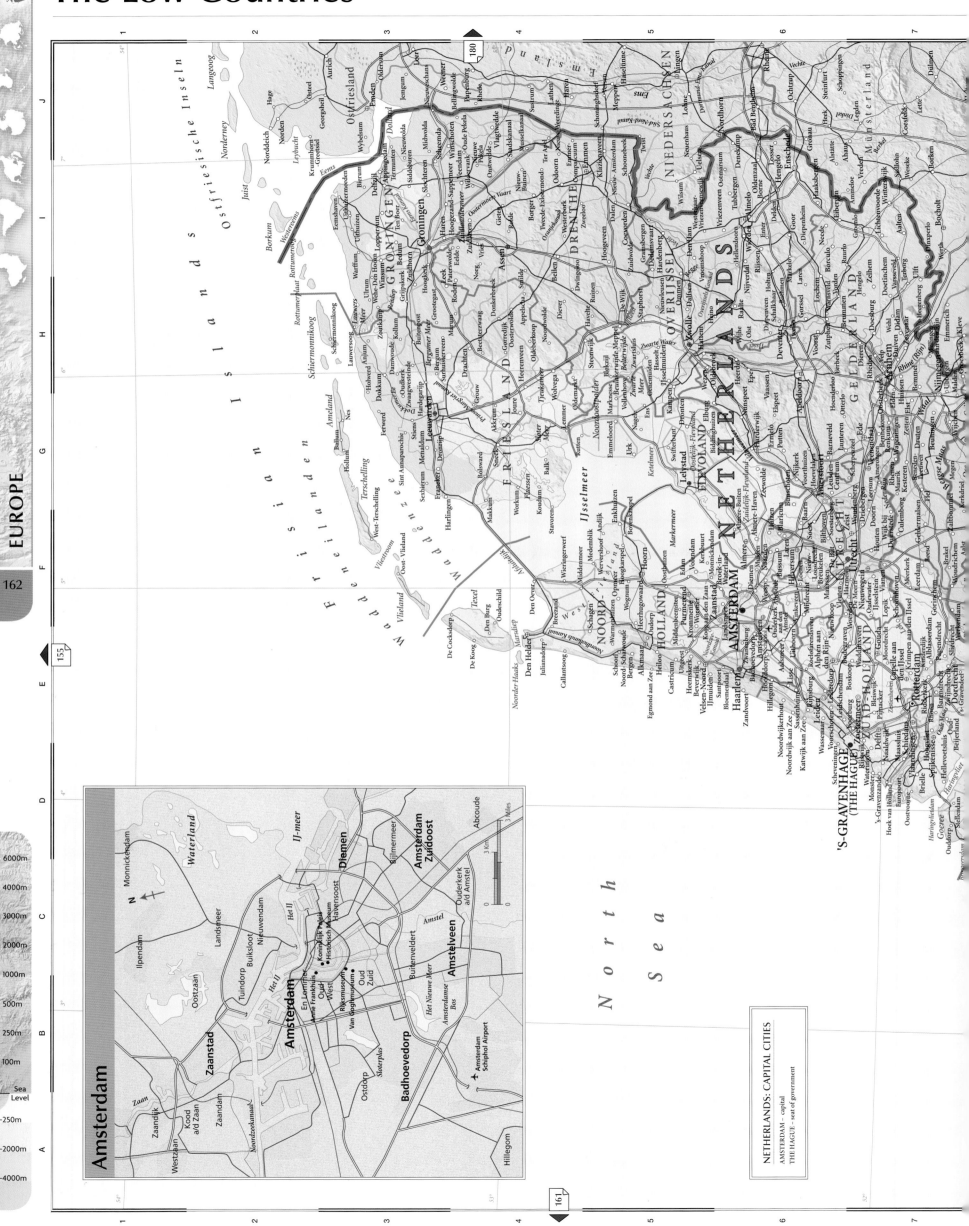

France

160

UNITED KINGDOM

Hartland Point • Bideford • Barnstaple • Taunton • Bridgwater • Salisbury • Andover • Guildford • Reigate • Royal Tunbridge Wells • Ashford
Tiverton • Yeovil • Sherborne • Shaftesbury • Winchester • Crawley • Haywards Heath • Hastings
Okehampton • Exeter • Lyme Regis • Bridport • Dorchester • Eastleigh • Southampton • Gosport • Littlehampton • Hove • Bexhill • Rye
High Willhays • Torquay • Paignton • Weymouth • Poole • Bournemouth • Portsmouth • Bognor Regis • Worthing • Brighton • Eastbourne • Beachy Head
Bodmin Moor • Dartmouth • Start Point • Isle of Wight • St Catherine's Point • Sandown • Ventnor
Newquay • Bodmin • Truro • St Austell • Plymouth • Portland Bill
St Ives • Saltash
Cape Cornwall • Penzance • Helston • Falmouth
Land's End • Helston • Lizard Point
Isles of Scilly • Mount's Bay

ATLANTIC OCEAN

English Channel

Alderney • Cap de la Hague • Cherbourg • Barfleur • Pointe de Barfleur • Cap d'Antifer • St-Valéry-en-Caux • Fécamp • Pays de Caux
Guernsey • Herm • Sark • Octeville • Tourlaville • Valognes • Montivilliers • Bolbec • Yvetot • Lillebonne
ST PETER PORT • Cotentin • Manche • Isigny-sur-Mer • le Havre • Cap de la Hève • Harfleur
CHANNEL ISLANDS (to UK) • Jersey • ST HELIER • Carentan • Bayeux • Calvados • Trouville • Deauville • Honfleur • Pont-Audemer
Passage de la Déroute • St-Lô • Coutances • Caen • Lisieux • Bernay • Conches-en-Ouche
Îles d'Er • Île de Bréhat • Perros-Guirec • Tréguier • Golfe de St-Malo • Îles Chausey • Villedieu-les-Poêles • BASSE-NORMANDIE • Falaise
Île de Batz • Roscoff • St-Pol-de-Léon • Pointe de l'Arcovest • Baie de St-Malo • Granville • Vire • Flers • Argentan • l'Aigle
Lesneven • Lannion • Paimpol • St-Brieuc • Le Mont St-Michel • Avranches • Collines de Normandie • Sées • Vernon
Île d'Ouessant • Landivisiau • Morlaix • Bégard • Plérin • Dinard • Dol-de-Bretagne • Mortain • Domfront • Mamers
Landerneau • Brest • Monts d'Arrée • Callac • Dinan • Combourg • 417m • Alençon • Nogent-le-Rotrou • la Ferté-Bernard
Crozon • Châteaulin • Guingamp • Loudéac • BRETAGNE • Rance • Fougères • Mayenne • Beaumont-sur-Sarthe
Pointe St-Mathieu • Iroise • Douarnenez • Carhaix-Plouguer • Pontivy • Ille-et-Vilaine • Vitré • Évron • Mondoubleau • Le Mans
Pointe du Raz • Audierne • Quimper • Scaer • Gourin • Josselin • Ploërmel • Rennes • Laval • St-Calais
Baie d'Audierne • Pont-l'Abbé • Quimperlé • Rosporden • Morbihan • Guer • Guichen • Mayenne • Craon • Château-Gontier • Château-du-Loir • Vendôme
Pointe de Penmarch • Concarneau • Hennebont • Landes de Lanvaux • Questembert • Redon • Segré • Sablé-sur-Sarthe • la Flèche • Azay-le-Rideau
Îles Glénan • Lorient • Auray • Vannes • Muzillac • Châteaubriant • Angers • Maine-et-Loire • Tours
Île de Groix • Quiberon • Blain • Loire-Atlantique • Ingrandes • Loire • Montreuil-Bellay • Loches
Baie de Quiberon • Belle Île • le Palais • Guérande • Nozay • Beaupréau • Chemillé • Saumur • Indre-et-Loire • Richelieu
Pointe du Croisic • St-Nazaire • Nantes • Vertou • Cholet • Montaigu • Château-Gontier • Thouars • Descartes
Pointe du St-Gildas • Pornic • PAYS DE LA LOIRE • Rezé • Vihiers • Argenton • Mauléon • Parthenay • Châtellerault
Noirmoutier-en-l'Île • Lac de Grand-Lieu • Sèvre • Bressuire • Airvault • Deux-Sèvres
Île de Noirmoutier • Beauvoir-sur-Mer • la Roche-sur-Yon • les Herbiers • Poitiers
St-Jean-de-Monts • Challans • Chantonnay • Fontenay-le-Comte • Lusignan • Lussac-les-Châteaux
Île d'Yeu • St-Gilles-Croix-de-Vie • Luçon • St-Maixent-l'École • Niort • Civray • Montmorillon
les Sables-d'Olonne • Marans • POITOU-CHARENTES • Ruffec • Confolens
Île de Ré • la Rochelle • Surgères • Charente • St-Jean-d'Angély • Mansle • St-Junien
Pertuis Breton • Rochefort • Matha • Rochechouart
Pertuis d'Antioche • Île d'Oléron • Saintes • Cognac • Jarnac • la Rochefoucauld
le Château-d'Oléron • Marennes • Jonzac • Barbezieux-St-Hilaire • Angoulême
Pointe de la Coubre • Royan • Saujon • Pons • Thiviers
Pointe de Grave • Lesparre-Médoc • Blaye • Chalais • Brantôme • Nontron
Lac d'Hourtin-Carcans • St-Laurent-Médoc • Mirambeau • Montmoreau • Périgueux
Lacanau • St-André-de-Cubzac • Coutras • Dordogne
St-Médard-en-Jalles • Libourne • Castillon-la-Bataille • Lalinde • Bergerac
Bassin d'Arcachon • Mérignac • Bordeaux • Branne • Ste-Foy-la-Grande
Arcachon • le Teste • Pessac • Talence • Gironde • Sauveterre-de-Guyenne • Mussidan • Montpon-Ménestérol
Cap Ferret • AQUITAINE • Langon • Marmande • Villeneuve-sur-Lot
Étang de Biscarrosse et de Parentis • Bazas • Casteljaloux • Agen
Mimizan • Parentis-en-Born • Captieux • Houeillès • Nérac
Labouheyre • Labrit • Roquefort • Mézin • Lauzerte
Morcenx • Mont-de-Marsan • Lectoure • Auch
Léon • St-Paul-lès-Dax • Villeneuve-de-Marsan

Bay of Biscay

Costa Verde

Cabo Ortegal • Punta de Estaca de Bares
Cabo Prior • Cedeira • Ortigueira
Cabo Peñas • Lluanco • Luarca • Pravia • Avilés • Candás • Gijón (Xixón)
Santander • Cabo de Ajo • Castro-Urdiales • Donostia-San Sebastián
A Coruña (La Coruña) • Ferrol • Narón • Viveiro • Cervo • Ribadeo • Tapia de Casariego • Navia • Villaviciosa • Llanes • Torrelavega • Santoña • Laredo • Bilbao • Hendaye • Biarritz • Bayonne • Anglet
Carballo • Mondoñedo • Oviedo • Cangas de Onís • Santurtzi • Barakaldo • Irún • Hasparren
Lugo • ASTURIAS • Mieres del Camino • CANTABRIA • Portugalete • Arrasate • Cambo-les-Bains
Santiago de Compostela • Sarria • Puerto de Leitariegos • Reinosa • Guernica • Bermeo • Mondragón • Mauléon-Licharre
Pontevedra • Ourense (Orense) • Ponferrada • León • Aguilar de Campoo • Miranda de Ebro • Pamplona (Iruña) • Pau • Tarbes
Vigo • GALICIA • Monforte de Lemos • Astorga • Sahagún • Guardo • Cervera de Pisuerga • Vitoria-Gasteiz • Estella • PAÍS VASCO • Navarra • Lourdes
Tui • Quiroga • La Bañeza • Carrión de los Condes • Burgos • Logroño • Jaca
PORTUGAL • Verín • Benavente • Villadiego • NAVARRA • Tafalla
Braga • Chaves • Puebla de Sanabria • Valladolid • Palencia • CASTILLA Y LEÓN • Aranda de Duero • Soria • LA RIOJA • Tudela • Huesca • ARAGÓN • Barbastro • Monzón
VILA REAL • Bragança • Zamora • Toro • Medina de Rioseco • Valoria la Buena • El Burgo de Osma • Calahorra • Zaragoza • Lleida (Lérida)
PORTO (Oporto) • Vila Real • Lamego • Duero • Rueda • Cuéllar • Segovia • Medinaceli • Ejea de los Caballeros • Fraga

170

Paris inset map

Seine
Montmorency
Forêt de St-Germain
Enghien
Aéroport Charles de Gaulle
Poissy
Argenteuil
Asnières
St-Denis
Drancy
Tremblay-en-France
Aulnay-sous-Bois
St-Germain-en-Laye
Nanterre
Aubervilliers
Le Raincy
Marly-le-Roi
Montmartre
Sacré-Coeur
Arc de Triomphe
Paris
Montreuil
Lagny
Rueil-Malmaison
Musée du Louvre
Bastille
Marne
Boulogne-Billancourt
Tour Eiffel
Notre Dame
Vincennes
Marne-la-Vallée
Château de Versailles
Meudon
Seine
Champigny-sur-Marne
Versailles
Trappes
Vitry-sur-Seine
Créteil
Sceaux
Orly
Chevreuse
Palaiseau
Antony
Aéroport d'Orly
Brie-Comte-Robert
Orsay
Mortgeron

0   5 Km
0   5 Miles

Elevation scale

6000m
4000m
3000m
2000m
1000m
500m
250m
100m
Sea Level
-250m
-2000m
-4000m

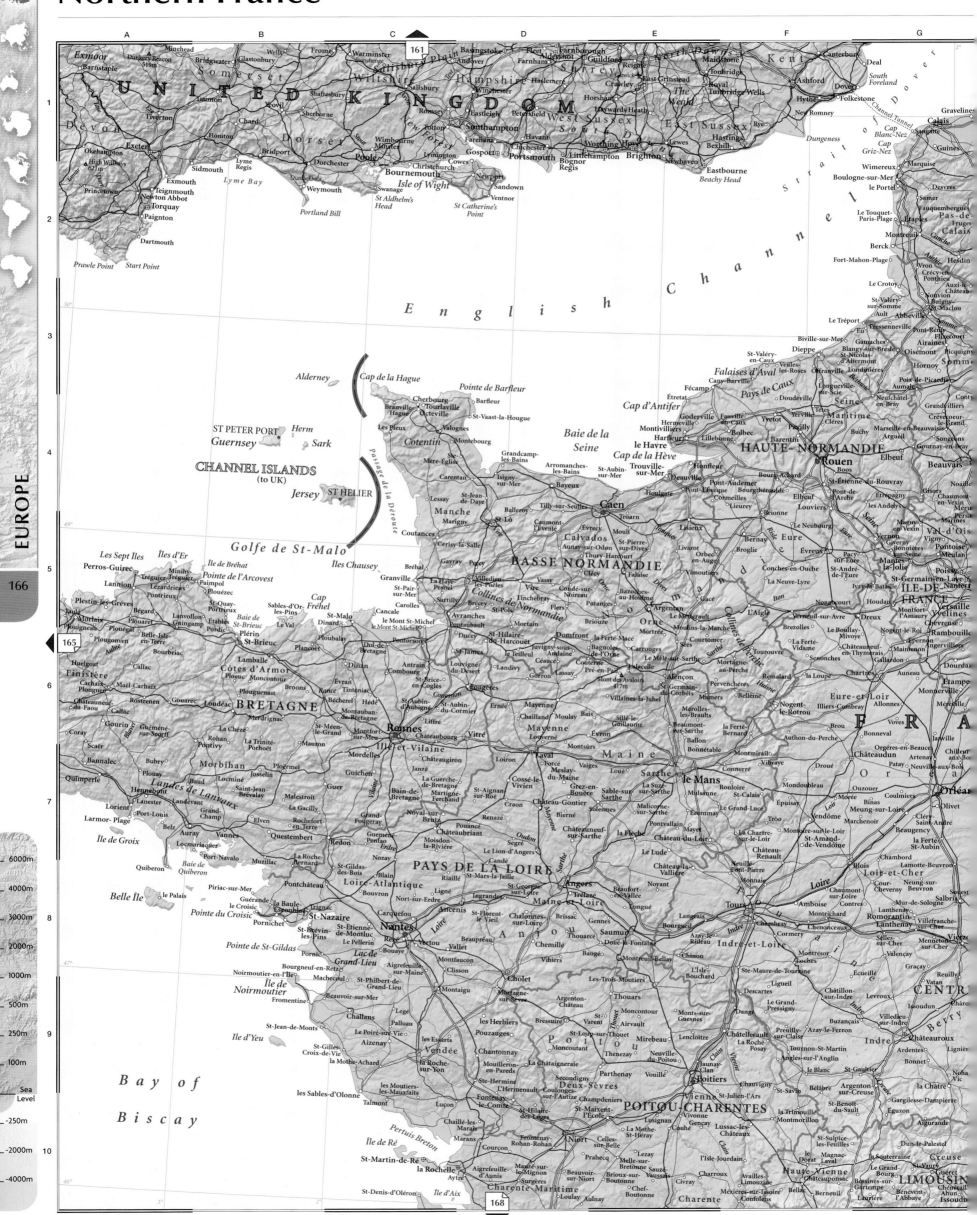

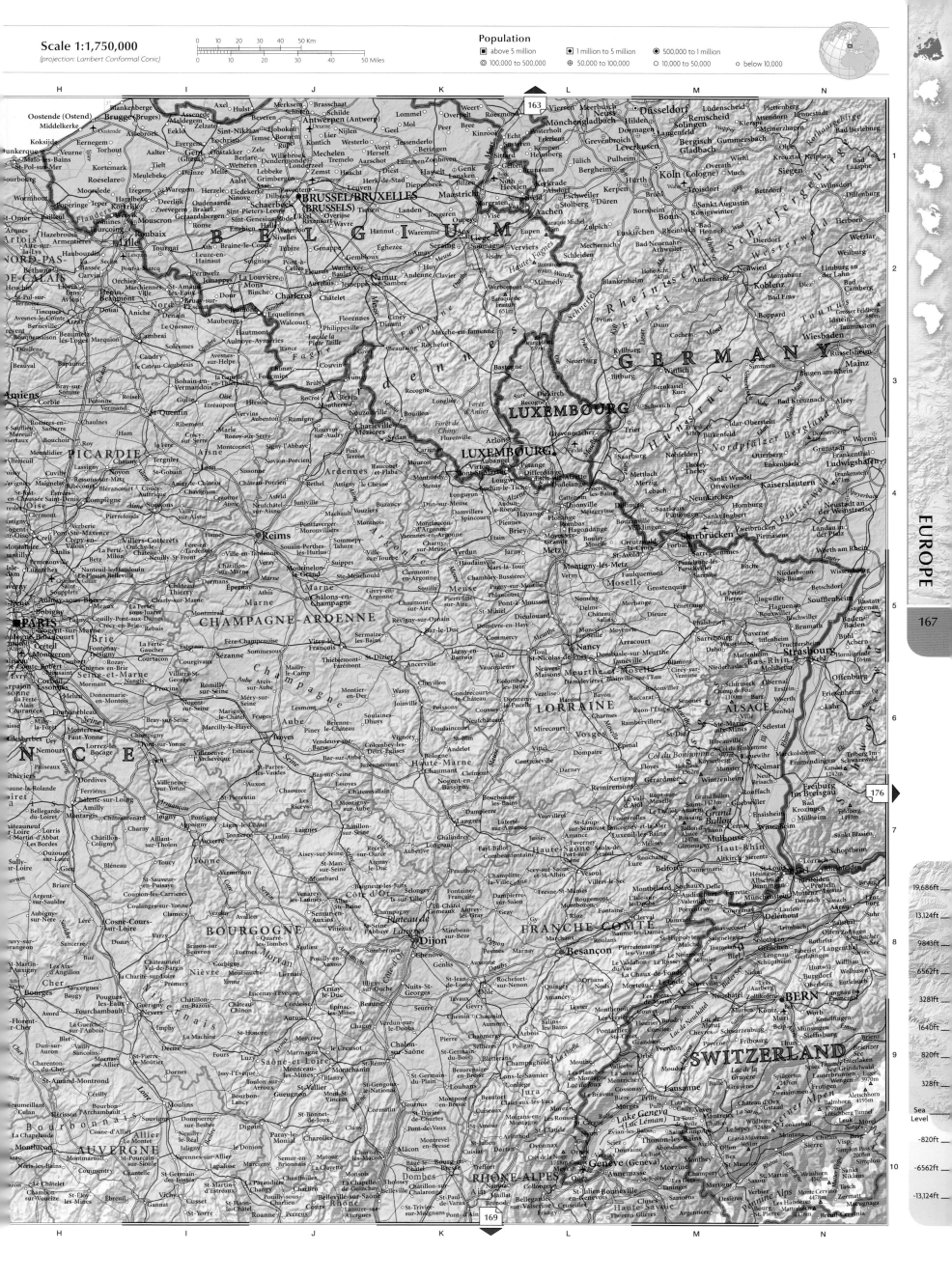

Southern France & the Pyrenees

Scale 1:1,750,000

(projection: Lambert Conformal Conic)

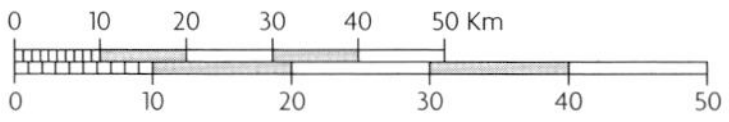

0 10 20 30 40 50 Km
0 10 20 30 40 50 Miles

Population

- ■ above 5 million
- ▣ 1 million to 5 million
- ◉ 500,000 to 1 million
- ◎ 100,000 to 500,000
- ⊕ 50,000 to 100,000
- ○ 10,000 to 50,000
- ○ below 10,000

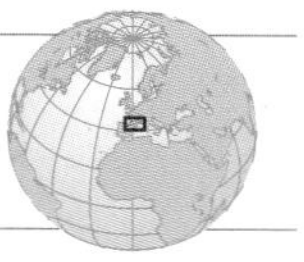

H
I
J
K
L
M
N
167
174
198
Clermont-Ferrand
AUVERGNE
Massif Central
Lyon
Villeurbanne
RHÔNE-ALPES
St-Étienne
Grenoble
Chambéry
Annecy
Haute-Savoie
Savoie
Isère
Vercors
Massif de la Vanoise
Hautes-Alpes
Drôme
Ardèche
Lozère
Valence
Avignon
Nîmes
LANGUEDOC-ROUSSILLON
Montpellier
Hérault
Béziers
Narbonne
Perpignan
PROVENCE-ALPES-CÔTE D'AZUR
Vaucluse
Bouches-du-Rhône
Aix-en-Provence
Marseille
Toulon
Camargue
Nice
Cannes
MONACO
Torino (Turin)
ITALY
Maritime Alps
Côte d'Azur
Golfe du Lion
Ligurian Sea
Golfo di Genova
Mediterranean Sea
Costa Brava
Girona
Figueres

19,686ft
13,124ft
9843ft
6562ft
3281ft
1640ft
820ft
328ft
Sea Level
-820ft
-6562ft
-13,124ft

The Iberian Peninsula

EUROPE

170

Bay of Biscay

ATLANTIC OCEAN

Costa Verde

CORDILLERA CANTÁBRICA

GALICIA

ASTURIAS

CANTABRIA

CASTILLA-LEÓN

A Coruña (La Coruña)

Santiago de Compostela

Pontevedra

Vigo

Ourense (Orense)

Oviedo

Gijón (Xixón)

Santander

Bilbao

León

Burgos

Valladolid

Zamora

Salamanca

Palencia

PORTUGAL

Porto (Oporto)

Vila Nova de Gaia

VILA REAL

BRAGANÇA

BRAGA

Braga

Guimarães

Viana do Castelo

VIANA DO CASTELO

Aveiro

VISEU

Viseu

Coimbra

COIMBRA

GUARDA

Guarda

CASTELO BRANCO

Castelo Branco

LEIRIA

Leiria

SANTARÉM

Santarém

LISBOA

LISBOA (LISBON)

Setúbal

SETÚBAL

ÉVORA

Évora

PORTALEGRE

Portalegre

BEJA

Beja

FARO

Faro

Sistema Central

MADRID

MADRID

Guadalajara

Segovia

Ávila

Toledo

Toledo

SPAIN

EXTREMADURA

Cáceres

Cáceres

Mérida

Badajoz

Badajoz

Sierra Morena

Sierra de Gredos

Ciudad Real

Ciudad Real

ANDALUCÍA

Sevilla (Seville)

Córdoba

Huelva

Jaén

Granada

Málaga

Cádiz

Sistemas Béticos

Sierra Nevada

Mulhacén 3481m

Costa del Sol

GIBRALTAR

GIBRALTAR (to UK)

Strait of Gibraltar

Ceuta (to Spain)

Tanger

Alboran Sea

Golfo de Cádiz

Baía de Setúbal

MOROCCO

Rif

Tétouan

Larache

Ksar-el-Kebir

Chefchaouen

Al-Hoceima

Cabo de São Vicente

MADEIRA (to Portugal)

Madeira

Funchal

Porto Santo

Ilhas Desertas

Scale 1:2,500,000

0 5 10 20 Km
0 5 10 20 Miles

ATLANTIC OCEAN

ISLAS CANARIAS (CANARY ISLANDS) (to Spain)

Scale 1:6,500,000

0 25 50 75 Km
0 25 50 75 Miles

La Palma

Santa Cruz de la Palma

Gomera

Hierro

Valverde

Santa Cruz de Tenerife

Tenerife

Pico del Teide 3718m

Las Palmas de Gran Canaria

Gran Canaria

Lanzarote

Arrecife

Fuerteventura

Puerto del Rosario

Alegranza

Graciosa

ATLANTIC OCEAN

6000m
4000m
3000m
2000m
1000m
500m
250m
100m
Sea Level
−250m
−2000m
−4000m

290

ATLANTIC OCEAN

PORTUGAL

PORTO
VILA REAL
BRAGANÇA
AVEIRO
VISEU
GUARDA
COIMBRA
CASTELO BRANCO
LEIRIA
SANTARÉM
PORTALEGRE
LISBOA (LISBON)
ÉVORA
SETÚBAL
BEJA
FARO

CASTILLA-LEON
Salamanca
Ávila
EXTREMADURA
Cáceres
Mérida
Badajoz
ANDALUCÍA
Sevilla (Seville)
Huelva
Córdoba
Cádiz
MÁLAGA
Jerez de la Frontera
Algeciras
GIBRALTAR (to UK)
Europa Point

Sierra Morena
Guadalquivir
Golfo de Cádiz
Bahía de Cádiz
Costa de la Luz
Strait of Gibraltar
Cabo de Trafalgar
Ceuta (to Spain)

MOROCCO
Tanger
Cap Spartel

Cabo de São Vicente
Sagres
Algarve
Cabo de Santa Maria
Ilha de Tavira

Cabo de São Vicente

AZORES (to Portugal)

Corvo
Flores
Graciosa
Terceira
Vila da Praia da Vitória
Angra do Heroísmo
São Jorge
Faial
Horta
Ponta do Pico 2351m
Pico
Ponta Delgada
Ribeira Grande
São Miguel
Santa Maria
Vila do Porto

Scale 1:6,500,000
0 25 50 75 km
0 25 50 75 Miles

6000m
4000m
3000m
2000m
1000m
500m
250m
100m
Sea Level
-250m
-2000m
-4000m

The Italian Peninsula

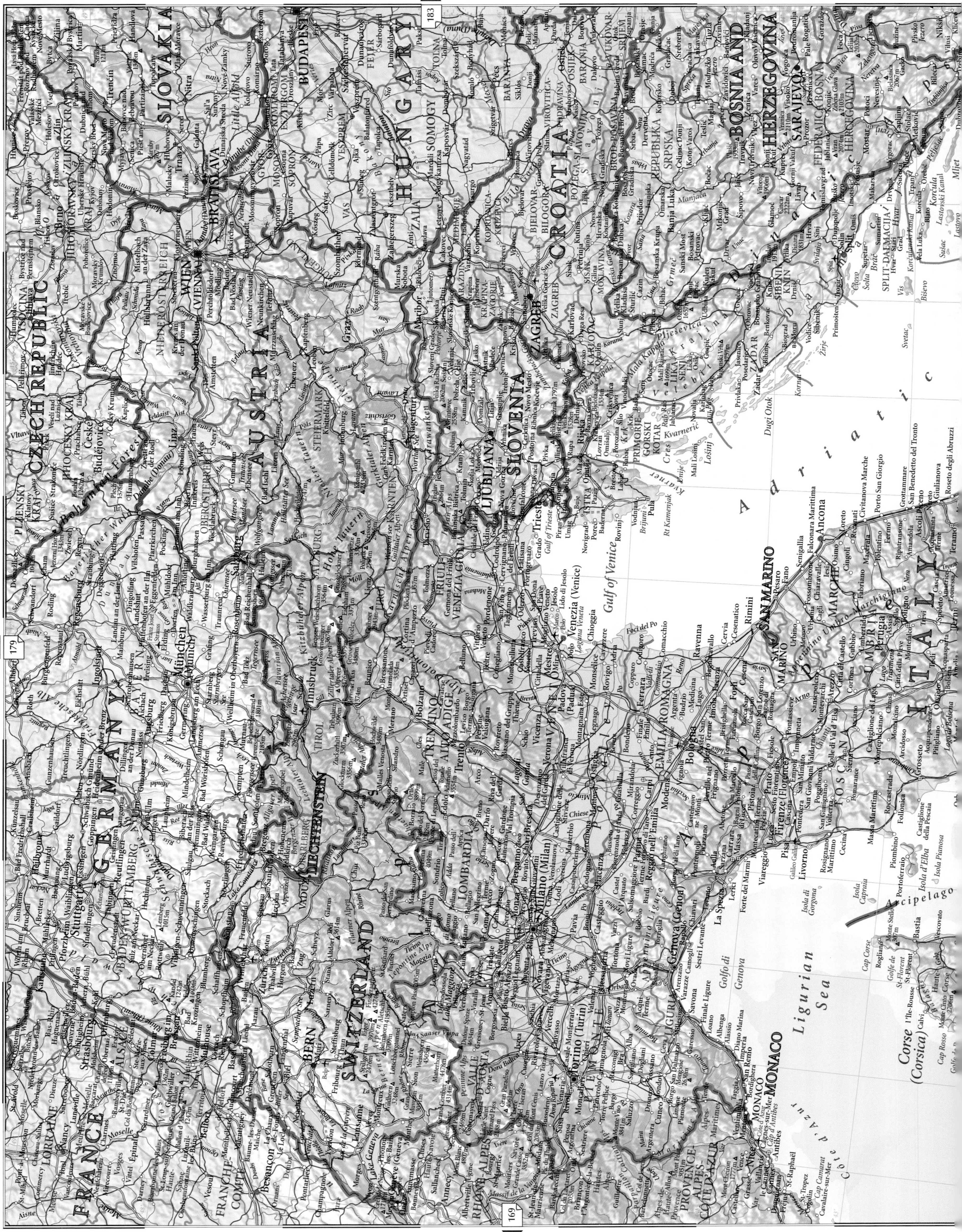

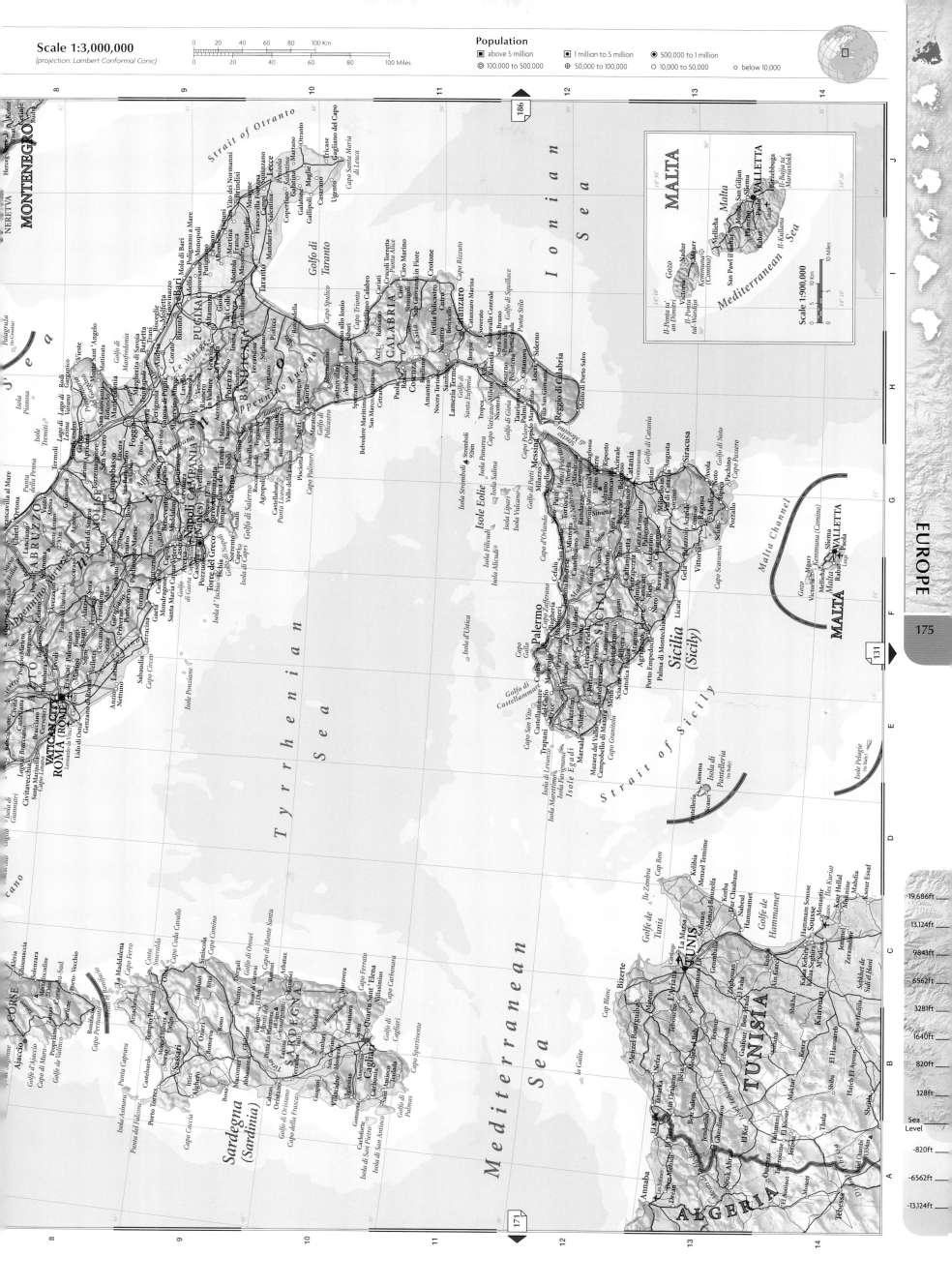

181

169

198

6000m
4000m
3000m
2000m
1000m
500m
250m
100m
Sea Level
-250m
-2000m
-4000m

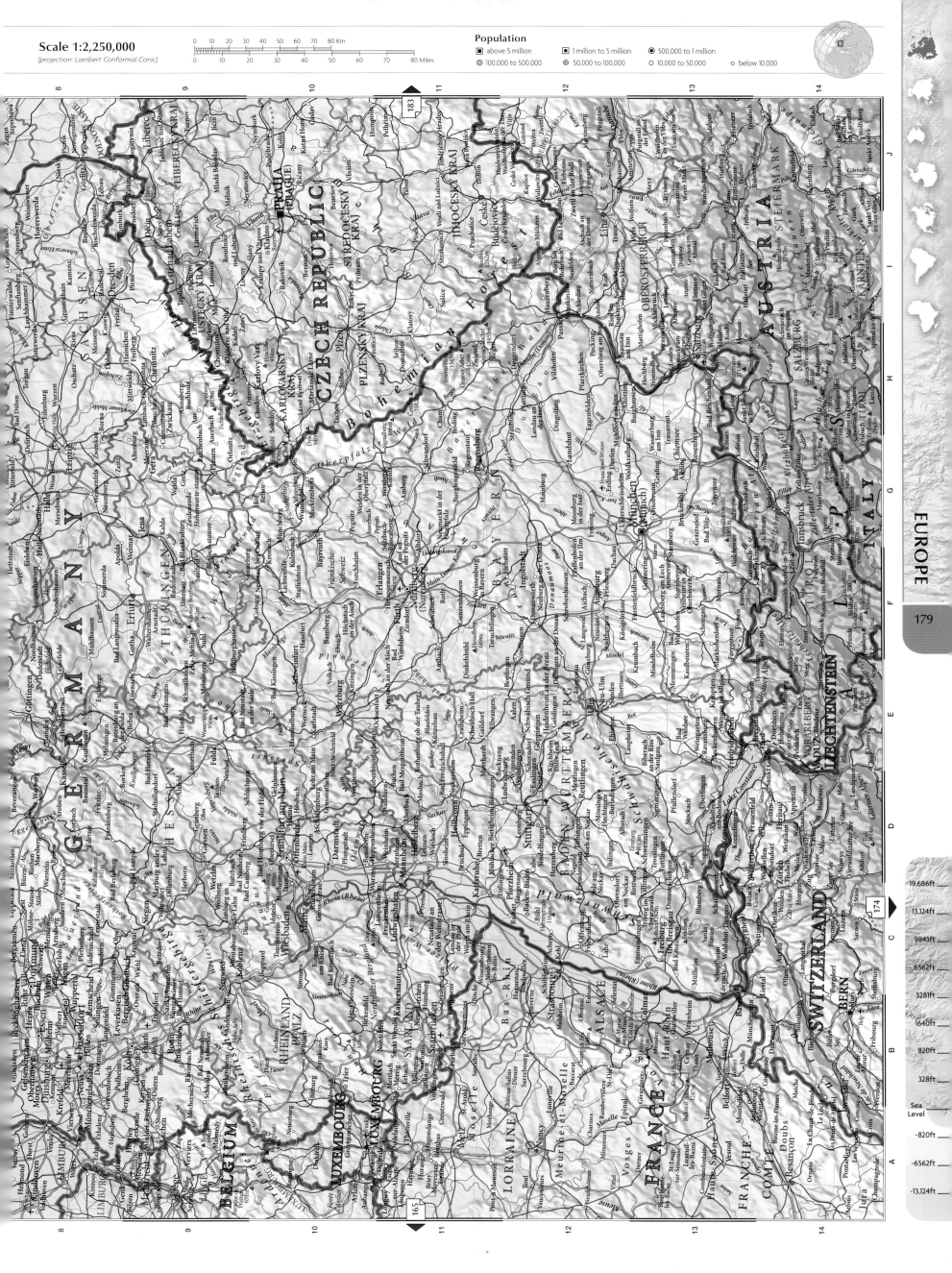

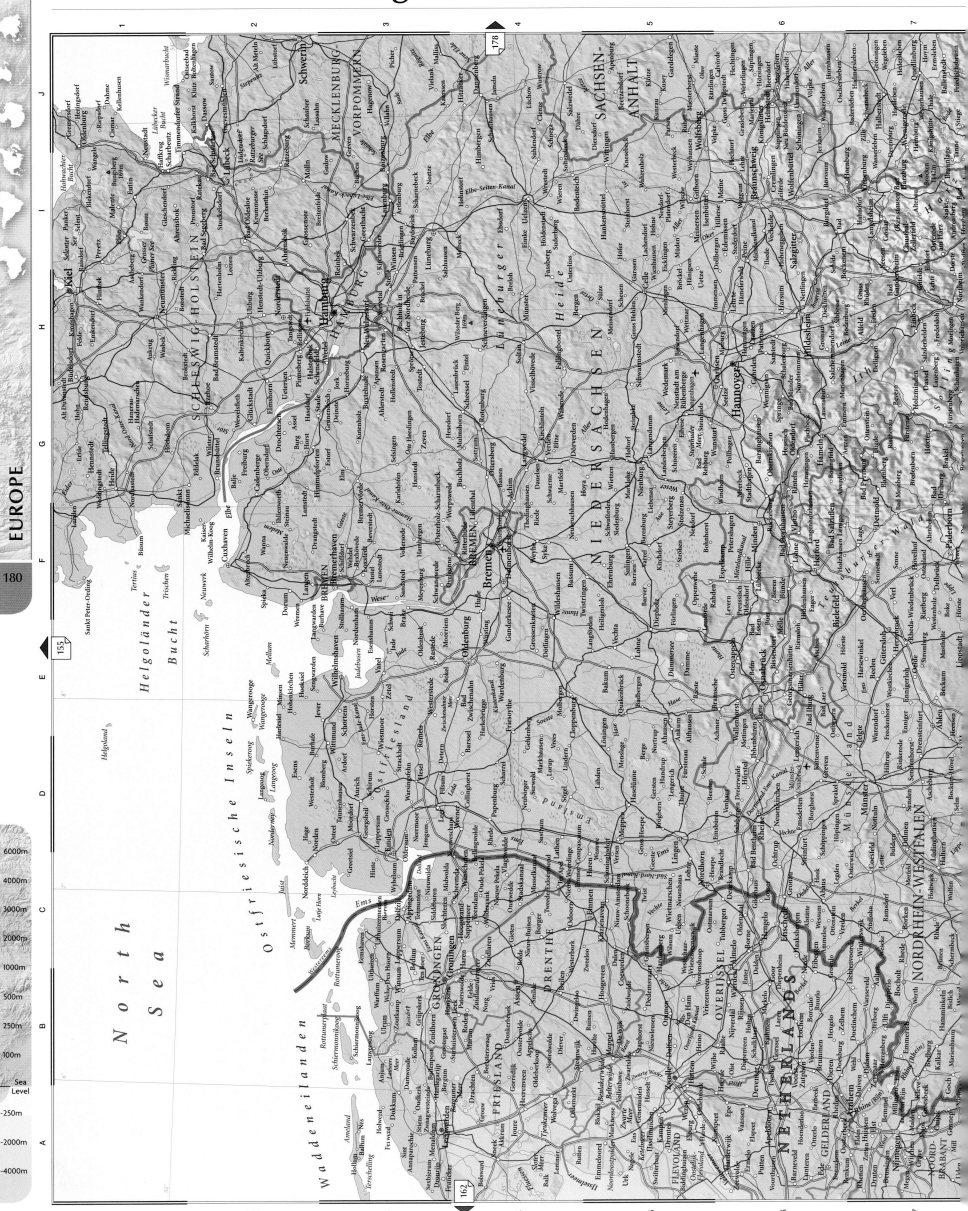

LATVIA

LITHUANIA

BELARUS

RUSSIAN FEDERATION

KALININGRADSKAYA OBLAST'

DENMARK

SWEDEN

GERMANY

POLAND

BALTIC SEA

Gulf of Danzig

BORNHOLM

Öland

Kattegat

Pomeranian Bay

KØBENHAVN (COPENHAGEN)

Malmö

KALMAR

BLEKINGE

SKÅNE

Liepāja

Klaipėda

Kaliningrad

Gdańsk

Gdynia

WARSZAWA (WARSAW)

Łódź

Wrocław

Poznań

Bydgoszcz

Berlin

Dresden

Potsdam

Schwerin

MECKLENBURG-VORPOMMERN

BRANDENBURG

SACHSEN

SACHSEN-ANHALT

THÜRINGEN

POMORSKIE

ZACHODNIO-POMORSKIE

KUJAWSKO-POMORSKIE

WIELKOPOLSKIE

LUBUSKIE

DOLNOŚLĄSKIE

OPOLSKIE

ŁÓDZKIE

MAZOWIECKIE

PODLASKIE

WARMIŃSKO-MAZURSKIE

LUBELSKIE

ŚWIĘTOKRZYSKIE

TELŠIAI

ŽemaitijaSIAULIAI

TAURAGĖ

MARIJAMPOLĖ

KAUNAS

ALYTUS

Białystok

Olsztyn

Elbląg

Hel

6000m
4000m
3000m
2000m
1000m
500m
250m
100m
Sea Level
-250m
-2000m
-4000m

Scale 1:2,500,000
(projection: Lambert Conformal Conic)

0 10 20 30 40 50 Km
0 10 20 30 40 50 Miles

Population
- above 5 million
- 1 million to 5 million
- 500,000 to 1 million
- 100,000 to 500,000
- 50,000 to 100,000
- 10,000 to 50,000
- below 10,000

19,686ft
13,124ft
9843ft
6562ft
3281ft
1640ft
820ft
328ft
Sea Level
-820ft
-6562ft
-13,124ft

EUROPE

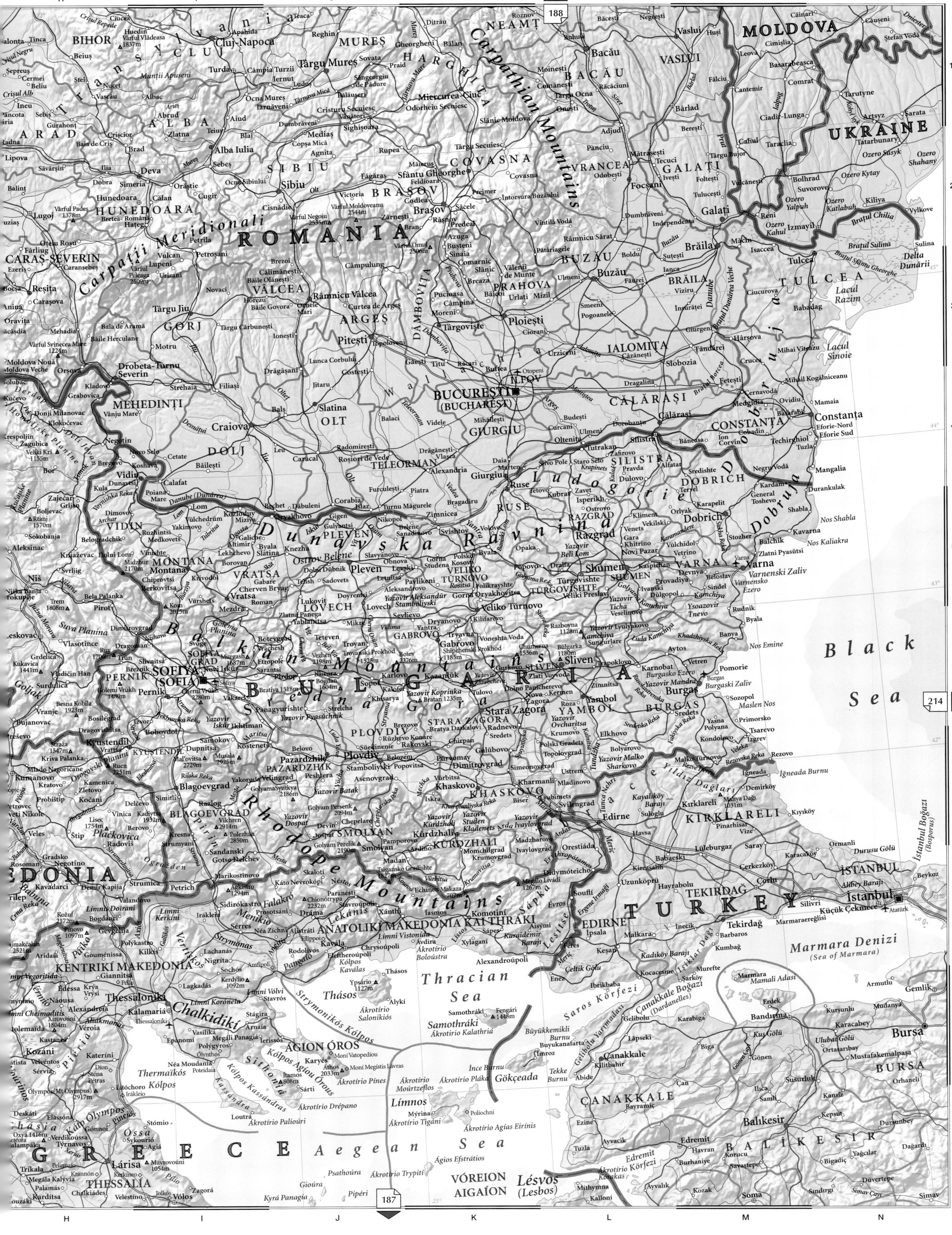

EUROPE

186

A B C D E F G

Adriatic Sea

Strait of Otranto

ITALY

PUGLIA
Le Murge
BASILICATA
CALABRIA

Lago di Lesina
Lago di Varano
Rodi Garganico
Viestec
Apricena
Sannicandro Garganico
Promontorio del Gargano
Monte Sant' Angelo
Mattinata
Torremaggiore
San Severo
San Giovanni Rotondo
Lucera
Manfredonia
Foggia
Golfo di Manfredonia
Troia
Bovino
Ascoli
Satriano
Orta Nova
Cerignola
Canosa di Puglia
Andria
Barletta
Margherita di Savoia
Trani
Bisceglie
Molfetta
Giovinazzo
Mola di Bari
Bari
Bitonto
Adelfia
Conversano
Monopoli
Polignano a Mare
Melfi
Venosa
Spinazzola
Rionero in Vulture
Minervino Murge
Corato
Gravina in Puglia
Altamura
Santeramo in Colle
Gioia del Colle
Putignano
Alberobello
Fasano
Mottola
Grottaglie
Castellaneta
Massafra
Martina Franca
San Vito dei Normanni
Brindisi
Mesagne
Francavilla Fontana
Oria
San Severo
Muro Lucano
Potenza
Acerenza
Tricarico
Matera
Ferrandina
Taranto
Manduria
Squinzano
Campi Salentina
Lecce
Penisola Salentina
Copertino
Galatina
Martano
Maglie
Otranto
Casarano
Gallipoli
Galatone
Ugento
Tricase
Gagliano del Capo
Capo Santa Maria di Leuca
Golfo di Taranto
Capo Spulico
Cassano allo Ionio
Sibari
Spezzano Albanese
Capo Trionto
Corigliano Calabro
Rossano
Cariati
Acri
Crucoli Torretta
Punta Alice
Ciro
Ciro Marino
San Giovanni in Fiore
Neto
Strongoli
Crotone
La Sila
Roglian
Petilia Policastro
Cutro
Catanzaro
Capo Rizzuto
Golfo di Squillace
Soverato
Punta Stilo
Siderno
Locri
Taurianova
Cittanova
Oppido Mamertina
Reggio di Calabria
Villa San Giovanni
Melito di Porto Salvo

Ionian Sea

IÓNIOI NÍSOI (Ionian Islands)

Kérkyra (Corfu)
Lefkimmi
Akrotírio Asprókavos
Paxoí
Antípaxoi
Lefkáda
Kefalloniá
Akrotírio Athéras
Lixoúri
Argostóli
Zákynthos
Akrotírio Skinári
Vrachíonas
Akrotírio Marathiá
Strofádes

ALBANIA
SHKODËR
LEZHË
DURRËS
TIRANË (TIRANA)
ELBASAN
FIER
BERAT
VLORË
GJIROKASTËR

MACEDONIA
KOSOVO
SKOPJE

Shkodër
Lezhë
Durrës
Tiranë
Elbasan
Fier
Berat
Vlorë
Gjirokastër
Korçë
Sarandë

KOSOVO
Prizren
Kumanovo

Lake Ohrid
Lake Prespa

Bitola
Florina
Kastoria
Kozáni
Grevená
Ioánnina
Préveza
Árta
Agrínio
Mesolóngi
Pátra
Pýrgos
Olympía
Kalamáta
Pylos
Spárti
Trípoli
Árgos
Náfplio

ÍPEIROS
DYTIKÍ MAKEDONÍA
KENTRIKÍ MAKEDONÍA
THESSALÍA
STEREÁ ELLÁDA
DYTIKÍ ELLÁDA
PELOPÓNNISOS

Lárisa
Thessaloníki
Kateríni
Olympós (Mt Olympus)
Óssa
Pineiós
Vólos
Pagasitikós Kólpos

Patraïkós Kólpos
Korinthiakós Kólpos (Gulf of Corinth)

Mediterranean Sea

Kýthira

Athens

N

Acharnés
Kifisiá
Pikérmi
Néa Liósia
Néa Ionía
Chalándri
Spáta
Asprópyrgos
Patísia
Olympiako Stadio
Cholargos
Peristéri
Arheol. Moussío
Likavittós
Athína (Athens)
Zográfou
Eleftherios Venizelos Intl. Airport
Agorá
Parthenón
Akrópoli
Panathinaïko Stadio
Výronas
Aigáleo
Távros
Paianía
Kallithéa
Néa Smýrni
Ymittós
Iroúpoli
Nikaía
Palaió Fáliro
Peiraías (Piraeus)
Kalamáki
Saronikós Kólpos
Argyroúpoli
Voúla
Várkiza

Oros Aigáleo
Oros Ymittós

0   4 Km
0   4 Miles

6000m
4000m
3000m
2000m
1000m
500m
250m
100m
Sea Level
-250m
-2000m
-4000m

A B C D E F G

Scale 1:2,500,000
(projection: Lambert Conformal Conic)

0 10 20 30 40 50 Km
0   10   20   30   40   50 Miles

Population
■ above 5 million
◉ 1 million to 5 million
◉ 500,000 to 1 million
◎ 100,000 to 500,000
⊕ 50,000 to 100,000
○ 10,000 to 50,000
○ below 10,000

BULGARIA

TURKEY

GREECE

Black Sea

Thracian Sea

Aegean Sea

Aegean Islands

VÓREION AIGAÍON

NÓTION AIGAÍON

Marmara Denizi (Sea of Marmara)

Mirtóo Pélagos

Kritikó Pélagos (Sea of Crete)

Mediterranean Sea

Anatolia

Rhodope Mountains

PAZARDZHIK · PLOVDIV · SMOLYAN · KURDZHALI · BLAGOEVGRAD

KIRKLARELI · TEKIRDAG · ISTANBUL · KOCAELI · SAKARYA · YALOVA · BURSA · BILECIK · ESKIŞEHIR · BALIKESIR · KÜTAHYA · MANISA · AFYON · IZMIR · UŞAK · AYDIN · DENIZLI · MUĞLA · BURDUR · ANTALYA · ÇANAKKALE

ANATOLIKI MAKEDONÍA KAI THRÁKI

Athína (Athens) · Peiraiás (Piraeus)

İstanbul · Bursa · İzmit · Adapazarı · İzmir · Manisa · Bandırma · Balıkesir · Kütahya · Eskişehir · Uşak · Aydın · Denizli · Muğla · Burdur · Edirne

Kríti (Crete) · KRÍTI · Irákleio · Réthymno · Chaniá

Lésvos (Lesbos) · *Chíos* · *Sámos* · *Ikaría* · *Ándros* · *Tínos* · *Mýkonos* · *Náxos* · *Páros* · *Kárpathos* · *Ródos (Rhodes)* · *Kos* · *Astypálaia* · *Santoríni* · *Amorgós* · *Mílos* · *Kýthira* · *Skýros* · *Évvoia (Euboea)* · *Thásos* · *Samothráki* · *Límnos* · *Gökçeada* · *Kárystos*

Kykládes (Cyclades)

Dodekánisos · Karpáthio Pélagos

Vóreies Sporádes

Çanakkale Boğazı (Dardanelles)

Sea Level · 19,686ft · 13,124ft · 9843ft · 6562ft · 3281ft · 1640ft · 820ft · 328ft · -820ft · -6562ft · -13,124ft

Romania, Moldova & Ukraine

EUROPE

BELARUS

POLAND

SLOVAKIA

HUNGARY

ROMANIA

MOLDOVA

SERBIA

BULGARIA

6000m
4000m
3000m
2000m
1000m
500m
250m
100m
Sea Level
-250m
-2000m
-4000m

Scale 1:3,000,000
(projection: Lambert Conformal Conic)

0 20 40 60 80 100 Km

0 20 40 60 80 100 Miles

Population

- ■ above 5 million
- ◉ 1 million to 5 million
- ◎ 100,000 to 500,000
- ◉ 500,000 to 1 million
- ○ 50,000 to 100,000
- ○ 10,000 to 50,000
- ○ below 10,000

196

214

196

19,686ft
13,124ft
9843ft
6562ft
3281ft
1640ft
820ft
328ft
Sea Level
-820ft
-6562ft
-13,124ft

RUSSIAN FEDERATION

ORLOVSKAYA OBLAST'

LIPETSKAYA OBLAST'

KURSKAYA OBLAST'

BELGORODSKAYA OBLAST'

VORONEZHSKAYA OBLAST'

UKRAINE

CHERNIHIVS'KA OBLAST'

SUMS'KA OBLAST'

KYYIVS'KA OBLAST'

POLTAVS'KA OBLAST'

KHARKIVS'KA OBLAST'

LUHANS'KA OBLAST'

CHERKAS'KA OBLAST'

KIROVOHRADS'KA OBLAST'

DNIPROPETROVS'KA OBLAST'

DONETS'KA OBLAST'

MYKOLAYIVS'KA OBLAST'

ODES'KA OBLAST'

KHERSONS'KA OBLAST'

ZAPORIZ'KA OBLAST'

KRASNODARSKIY KRAY

AVTONOMNA RESPUBLIKA KRYM

Krym's'kyy Pivostriv

Kyyiv (Kiev)
Chernihiv
Sumy
Kharkiv
Poltava
Cherkasy
Kirovohrad
Dnipropetrovs'k
Donets'k
Luhans'k
Zaporizhzhya
Mykolayiv
Kherson
Odesa
Simferopol'
Sevastopol'
Voronezh
Belgorod
Kursk
Rostov-na-Donu
Krasnodar

Black Sea

Sea of Azov

Gulf of Taganrog

Kerch Strait

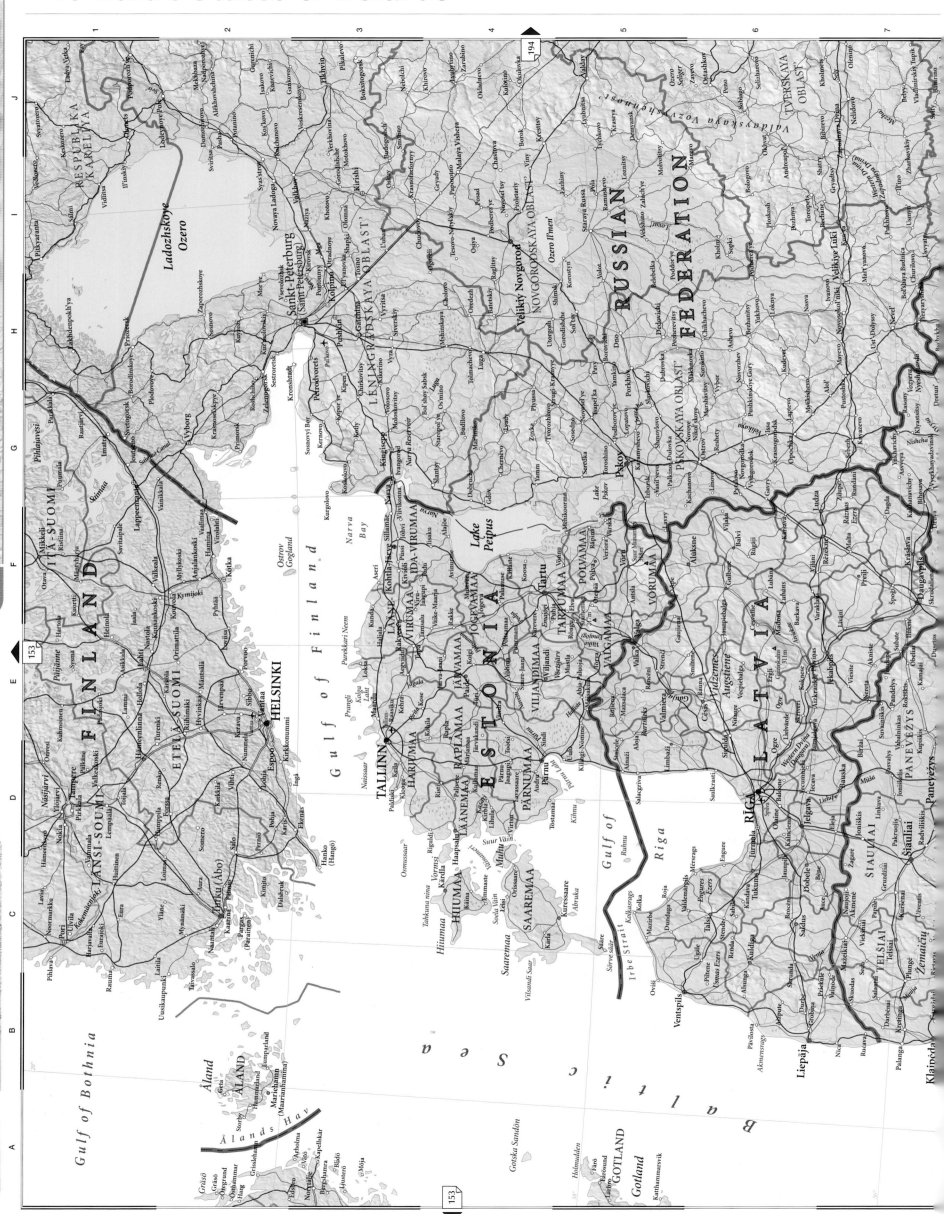

Scale 1:2,750,000
(projection: Lambert Conformal Conic)

0 10 20 30 40 50 60 70 80 Km
0 10 20 30 40 50 60 70 80 Miles

Population

■ above 5 million	■ 1 million to 5 million	◉ 500,000 to 1 million
◎ 100,000 to 500,000	⊕ 50,000 to 100,000	○ 10,000 to 50,000
		○ below 10,000

19,686ft
13,124ft
9843ft
6562ft
3281ft
1640ft
820ft
328ft
Sea Level
−820ft
−6562ft
−13,124ft

RUSSIAN FEDERATION
LITHUANIA
BELARUS
POLAND
UKRAINE
KALININGRADSKAYA OBLAST'

Major cities: VILNIUS, KAUNAS, MINSK, Smolensk, Homyel', Mahilyow, Hrodna, Brest, Bialystok, WARSZAWA (WARSAW), Lublin, L'viv, Rivne, Luts'k, Ternopil', Zhytomyr, KYIV (KIEV), Chernihiv, Kaliningrad, Vitsyebsk

Oblasts: SMOLENSKAYA OBLAST', BRYANSKAYA OBLAST', VITSYEBSKAYA VOBLASTS', MAHILYOWSKAYA VOBLASTS', MINSKAYA VOBLASTS', HOMYEL'SKAYA VOBLASTS', HRODZYENSKAYA VOBLASTS', BRESTSKAYA VOBLASTS', CHERNIHIVS'KA OBLAST', KYIVS'KA OBLAST', ZHYTOMYRS'KA OBLAST', RIVNENS'KA OBLAST', VOLYNS'KA OBLAST', L'VIVS'KA OBLAST', TERNOPIL'S'KA OBLAST', KHMEL'NYTS'KA OBLAST', VINNYTS'KA OBLAST', PODLASKIE, MAZOWIECKIE, LUBELSKIE, WARMIŃSKO-MAZURSKIE, ŚWIĘTOKRZYSKIE, MAŁOPOLSKIE, PODKARPACKIE, UTENA, TAURAGE, MARIJAMPOLE, ALYTUS

Physical features: Pripet Marshes, Gulf of Danzig, Curonian Spit, Curonian Lagoon, Carpathian Mountains, Dnieper (Dnyapro), Wisła, Bug, San

The Russian Federation

THE RUSSIAN FEDERATION: ADMINISTRATIVE REGIONS

The administrative area names in European Russia have been omitted west of the Ural Mountains. Please refer to pages 194-195 and 196-197 where these areas are shown at a larger scale.

6000m
4000m
3000m
2000m
1000m
500m
250m
100m
Sea Level
-250m
-2000m
-4000m

199

Population
- ■ above 5 million
- ◉ 100,000 to 500,000
- ■ 1 million to 5 million
- ⊕ 50,000 to 100,000
- ◉ 500,000 to 1 million
- ○ 10,000 to 50,000
- ○ below 10,000

EUROPE

195

192

19,686ft
13,124ft
9843ft
6562ft
3281ft
1640ft
820ft
328ft
Sea Level
-820ft
-6562ft
-13,124ft

H I J K L M N

1 2 3 4 5 6 7 8 9 10

s s   S e a

Novaya Zemlya
Ostrov Mezhdusharskiy

Proliv Karskiye Vorota

Ostrov Vaygach

Pechorskoye More

Ostrov Dolgiy

Khaypudyrskaya Guba

Yugorskiy Poluostrov

Khrebet Pay-Khoy

Baydaratskaya Guba

Poluostrov Yamal

Ostrov Kolguyev

Amderma

Morrasale

Yuribey

Mys Kamennyy

Obskaya Guba

Ozero Yarato Pervoye

Tazovskaya Guba

Bugrino

Pomorskiy Proliv

Pechorskaya Guba

Tobseda

Varandey

Chernaya

Chernaya

More-Yu

Khal'mer-Yu

Shchuch'ya

YAMALO-NENETSKIY AVTONOMNYY OKRUG

Nyda

Arctic Circle

Nori

Kutop'yugan

Kanin Nos

Shoyna

Mys Mikulkin

Kanin Kamen

Poluostrov Kanin

Chizha

Chëshskaya Guba

Indiga

Nosovaya

Malozemel'skaya Tundra

Nar'yan-Mar

Oksino

Shapkina

Korey-Ver

Bol'shezemel'skaya Tundra

Gryada Chernyshëva

Adz'vavom

Usa

Promyshlennyy Komsomol'skiy

Severnyy Mul'da

Vorkuta

Yeletskiy

Gora Payer 1472m

Labytnangi

Salekhard

Poluy

Beloyarsk

Oktyabr'skiy

Aksarka

Starvy Nadym

Nadym

NENETSKIY AVTONOMNYY OKRUG

Mezen'

Kamenka

Velikovisochnoye

Yermitsa

Khorey-Ver

Mezen

Peza

Oma

Timanskiy Kryazh

Nizhnyaya Pësha

Shoyna

Indiga

Sula

Pechora

Khabarikha

Ust'-Tsil'ma

Mylva

Il'ya

Kolva

Usa

Kochmes

Inta

Kos'yu

Verkhnyaya Inta

Kos'yu

Khosedayu

Bol'shaya Rogovaya

Siyomaskinskiy

Abez'

Polyarnyy Ural

Ural'skiye Gory

Gora Narodnaya 1895m

Ob'

Pitlyar

Pospoluy

Chuprovo

Vazhgort

Karpogory

Pinega

Mezen

Leshukonskoye

Vashka

Vym'

RESPUBLIKA

Izhma

Pechora

Gora Sablya 1497m

Labytnangi

Lopkhari

Kunovat

Kazym-Mys

Azovy

Kuloy

Mezen'

Vodlanka

Yertom

Nyukhcha

Koslan

Meshchura

Vym'

Kozhva

Kadzherom

Irayel'

Kyrta

Gora Telpoziz 1617m

Zapadno-Sibirskaya

Kazym

Kazym

Yuil'sk

Numto

Karpogory

Pinega

Ida

Pinega

Chuprovo

Nyukhcha

Vendinga

Onega

Mezen'

Yorga

Sula

Ust'-Shchuger

Podcher'ye

Dutovo

Vuktyl

Gora Kozhymiz 1195m

Berezovo

Beloyarskiy

Sibirskiye Uvaly

Sos'va

Igrim

Sherkaly

Ob'

Priob'ye

Oktyabr'skoye

Karymkary

Ravnina

KHANTY-MANSIYSKIY

OBLAST'

FEDERATION

Verkhnyaya Toyma

Mikun'

Chasovo

Yarensk

Storozhevsk

Vychegda

Ust'-Kulom

Myyeldino

Kur'ya

Pechora

Ukhta

Vodnyy

Sosnogorsk

Yarega

KOMI

Voyvozh

Pomozdino

Troitsko-Pechorsk

Severnyy Ural

Vizhay

Khotpriya

Severnyy

Tayezhnyy

Pionerskiy

Oshmar'y

Uray

Nyagan'

AVTONOMNYY OKRUG

Soyevatpaul'

Yugorsk

Sovetskiy

Zelenoborsk

Konda

Kondinskoye

Mezhdurechenskiy

Khanty-Mansiysk

Gora Isherim 1331m

Polunochnoye

Ivdel'

Pelym

Pelym

Ozero Tursuntskiy Tuman

Ozero Pelymskiy Tuman

Mortka

Yemva

Cherevkovo

Krasnoborsk

Syktyvkar

Krasnozatonskiy

Ezhva

Vizinga

Nyrob

Mysy

Cherdyn

Krasnovishersk

Severoural'sk

Gora Vogul'skiy Kamen' 1066m

Pokrovsk-Ural'skiy

Volchansk

Karpinsk

Pavda

Lobva

SVERDLOVSKAYA

Sos'va

Andryushkino

Kuminskiy

Bestuzhevo

Kizema

Oktyabr'skiy

Kotlas

Koryazhma

Krasavino

Velikiy Ustyug

Nikol'sk

Kichmengskiy Gorodok

Nyuksenitsa

Tarnogskiy Gorodok

Luza

Podosinovets

Pinyug

Yug

Luza

Sysola

Kazhym

Gayny

Kama

Kosa

Kochevo

PERMSKIY KRAY

Solikamsk

Berezniki

Krasnovishersk

Severnyy Ural

Krasnotur'insk

Serov

Shaburovo

Gari

Tavda

Tavda

Srednesalymskiy

Ozero

Nikol'sk

Kologriv

Pavino

Vetluga

Sharya

Kichmengskiy Gorodok

Kirs

Lesnoy

Voyno

Rudnichnyy

Peskovka

Yur'ya

Belaya Kholunitsa

Omutninsk

Afanas'yevo

Yug'va

Kudymkar

Kama

Kamskoye Vodokhranilishche

Yayva

Aleksandrovsk

Kizel

Gubakha

Gremyachinsk

Gornozavodsk

Chusovoy

Pavda

Krasnoural'sk

Kushva

Verkhnyaya Salda

Nizhnyaya Salda

Alapayevsk

Makhnevo

Verkhotur'ye

Novaya Lyalya

Lesnoy

Murakovo

Fabrichnoye

Turinsk

Nizhnyaya Tavda

OBLAST'

Kostroma

Manturovo

Sharya

Makar'yev

Uren'

Vakhtan

Shakhun'ya

Shabalino

Svecha

Kotel'nich

Orlov

Kirovo-Chepetsk

Kirov

Slobodskoy

Nagorsk

Murashi

Zuyevka

Falenki

Glazov

Balezino

Kez

KIROVSKAYA OBLAST'

Dobryanka

Krasnokamsk

Perm

Nytva

Ocher

Yug

Kungur

Shamary

Kyn

Lys'va

Kirovgrad Rezh

Verkh-Neyvinskiy

Nizhniy Tagil

Nev'yansk

Artemovskiy

Irbit

Kirovgrad

Sukhoy Log

Kamyshlov

Talitsa

Tugulym

Botkin

Tyumen'

Vinzili

TYUMENSKAYA OBLAST'

Iyevlevo

Yalutorovsk

Zavodoukovsk

Nizhegorodskaya Oblast'

Semenov

Uren'

Vetluga

Tonkino

Shakhun'ya

Tuzha

Yaransk

Sovetsk

Nolinsk

Urzhum

Malmyzh

Nema

Medvedok

Vyatskiye Polyany

UDMURTSKAYA RESPUBLIKA

Glazov

Debesy

Zura

Votkinsk

Votkinskoye Vodokhranilishche

Chaykovskiy

Osa

Chernushka

Orda

Suksun

Achit

Nizhniye Sergi

Krasnoufimsk

Arti

Mikhaylovsk

Pervoural'sk

Revda

Yekaterinburg

Degtyarsk

Sysert'

Polevskoy

Kamensk-Ural'skiy

Kataysk

Dalmatovo

Shadrinsk

Uksyanskoye

Isetskoye

Yalutorovsk

Kurgan

KURGANSKAYA OBLAST'

Nizhniy Novgorod

Dzerzhinsk

Kstovo

RESPUBLIKA MARIY EL

Yoshkar-Ola

Cheboksary

Novocheboksarsk

Mariinskiy Posad

RESPUBLIKA TATARSTAN

Izhevsk

Sarapul

Kambarka

Neftekamsk

Dyurtyuli

Nizhnekamskoye Vodokhranilishche

RESPUBLIKA BASHKORTOSTAN

CHELYABINSKAYA OBLAST'

Verkhniy Ufaley

Kyshtym

Ozersk

Karabash

Miass

Zlatoust

Chelyabinsk

Kopeysk

Korkino

Yuzhno-Ural'skiy

Yuzhnyye Ural'skiye Gory

295

197

192

Scale 1:5,750,000
(projection: Lambert Conformal Conic)

0 25 50 75 100 125 150 175 200 Km
0 25 50 75 100 125 150 175 200 Miles

Population

■ above 5 million
■ 1 million to 5 million
◉ 500,000 to 1 million
◎ 100,000 to 500,000
◉ 50,000 to 100,000
◉ 10,000 to 50,000
○ below 10,000

195

226

222

RUSSIAN FEDERATION

KAZAKHSTAN

ZAPADNYY KAZAKHSTAN

AKTYUBINSK

ATYRAU

MANGYSTAU

UZBEKISTAN

QORAQALPOG'ISTON RESPUBLIKASI

TURKMENISTAN

GEORGIA

AZERBAIJAN

ARMENIA

Caspian Sea

Aral Sea

Caspian Depression

Ustyurt Plateau

RESPUBLIKA KALMYKIYA

RESPUBLIKA TATARSTAN

RESPUBLIKA BASHKORTOSTAN

RESPUBLIKA MORDOVIYA

RESPUBLIKA MARIY EL

ORENBURGSKAYA OBLAST'

SAMARSKAYA OBLAST'

SARATOVSKAYA OBLAST'

VOLGOGRADSKAYA OBLAST'

ASTRAKHANSKAYA OBLAST'

PENZENSKAYA OBLAST'

TAMBOVSKAYA OBLAST'

ULYANOVSKAYA OBLAST'

UDMURTSKAYA RESPUBLIKA

KIROVSKAYA OBLAST'

CHELYABINSKAYA OBLAST'

KURGANSKAYA OBLAST'

KOSTANAY

NIZHEGORODSKAYA OBLAST'

IVANOVSKAYA OBLAST'

STAVROPOL'SKIY KRAY

CHECHENSKAYA RESPUBLIKA

RESPUBLIKA DAGESTAN

Nizhniy Novgorod
Kazan'
Ufa
Chelyabinsk
Yekaterinburg
Izhevsk
Samara
Tol'yatti
Saratov
Volgograd
Orenburg
Astrakhan'
Atyrau
Aktobe (Aktyubinsk)
Aktau
Nukus
Makhachkala
Groznyy
Vladikavkaz
T'BILISI
BAKI

19,686ft
13,124ft
9843ft
6562ft
3281ft
1640ft
820ft
328ft
Sea Level
-820ft
-6562ft
-13,124ft

The Mediterranean

ATLANTIC OCEAN

Bay of Biscay

English Channel

UNITED KINGDOM
NETHERLANDS
'S-GRAVENHAGE
BERLIN
GERMANY
BELGIUM
BRUXELLES (BRUSSEL)
LUXEMBOURG
PRAHA (PRAGUE)
CZECH
PARIS
FRANCE
BERN
SWITZ.
LIECHTENSTEIN
AUSTRIA
LJUBLJANA
SLOVENIA
MONACO
Venezia (Venice)
SAN MARINO
ITALY
VATICAN CITY
ROMA (ROME)
ANDORRA
Barcelona

PORTUGAL
LISBOA (LISBON)
SPAIN
MADRID

Corse (Corsica)
Sardegna (Sardinia)

Islas Baleares (Balearic Islands)
Mallorca (Majorca)
Menorca (Minorca)
Ibiza

Ligurian Sea
Tyrrhenian Sea

Mediterranean Sea

GIBRALTAR (to UK)
Tánger
Ceuta (to Spain)
Melilla (to Spain)

RABAT
Casablanca
MOROCCO
Marrakech

ALGER (ALGIERS)
Oran

Atlas Saharien
Hauts Plateaux
Moyen Atlas
Haut Atlas

TUNIS
MALTA
VALLETTA

Sicilia (Sicily)
Palermo
Messina
Catania
Siracusa

TUNISIA

ṬARĀBULUS (TRIPOLI)

ALGERIA

Grand Erg Occidental
Grand Erg Oriental

Hamada du Dra
Hamada Tounassine
'Erg Iguidi
Erg Chech
Erg el Aḥmar

Plateau du Tademaït

Tripolitania

Idhān Awbārī

6000m
4000m
3000m
2000m
1000m
500m
250m
100m
Sea Level
-250m
-2000m
-4000m

Scale 1:8,750,000
(projection: Lambert Conformal Conic)

0 25 50 75 100 125 150 175 200 Km
0 25 50 75 100 125 150 175 200 Miles

Population
■ above 5 million
◨ 1 million to 5 million
◉ 500,000 to 1 million
◎ 100,000 to 500,000
⊕ 50,000 to 100,000
○ 10,000 to 50,000
○ below 10,000

19,686ft
13,124ft
9843ft
6562ft
3281ft
1640ft
820ft
328ft
Sea Level
-820ft
-6562ft
-13,124ft

POLAND
WARSZAWA (WARSAW)
BELARUS
UKRAINE
KYYIV (KIEV)
RUSSIAN FEDERATION
SLOVAKIA
BRATISLAVA
WIEN
HUNGARY
BUDAPEST
ZAGREB
CROATIA
ROMANIA
BUCUREŞTI (BUCHAREST)
MOLDOVA
CHIŞINĂU
BOSNIA AND HERZEGOVINA
SARAJEVO
SERBIA
BEOGRAD (BELGRADE)
MONTENEGRO
PODGORICA
KOSOVO
PRISHTINË (PRISTINA)
BULGARIA
SOFIYA (SOFIA)
SKOPJE
MACEDONIA
TIRANË (TIRANA)
ALBANIA
GREECE
ATHÍNA (ATHENS)
Peiraías (Piraeus)
GEORGIA
Black Sea
Sea of Azov
TURKEY
ANKARA
İstanbul
İzmir
Bursa
CYPRUS
NICOSIA
TURKISH REPUBLIC OF NORTHERN CYPRUS
(recognised only by Turkey)
SYRIA
DIMASHQ (DAMASCUS)
LEBANON
BEYROUTH (BEIRUT)
ISRAEL
JERUSALEM
Tel Aviv-Yafo
WEST BANK
GAZA STRIP
JORDAN
AMMAN
IRAQ
Syrian Desert
Ionian Sea
Mediterranean Sea
Aegean Sea
Kríti (Crete)
Ródos (Rhodes)
LIBYA
Banghāzī (Benghazi)
Khalīj Surt (Gulf of Sirte)
Cyrenaica
Libyan Plateau
Libyan Desert
EGYPT
CAIRO (AL QĀHIRAH)
Alexandria (Al Iskandarīyah)
Giza (Al Jīzah)
Nile Delta
Sinai (Sinā')
Red Sea
SAUDI ARABIA

EUROPE – Cities

Barcelona

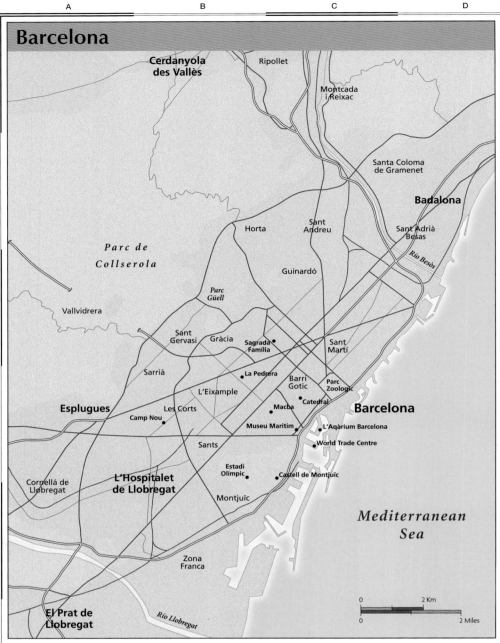

Cerdanyola des Vallès
Ripollet
Montcada i Reixac
Santa Coloma de Gramenet
Badalona
Horta
Sant Andreu
Sant Adrià Besàs
Guinardó
Río Besòs
Parc de Collserola
Parc Güell
Vallvidrera
Sant Gervasi
Gràcia
Sagrada Familia
Sant Martí
Sarrià
La Pedrera
Barri Gòtic
Parc Zoològic
L'Eixample
Macba
Catedral
Esplugues
Les Corts
Camp Nou
Museu Marítim
L'Aqàrium Barcelona
Barcelona
World Trade Centre
Sants
Cornellá de Llobregat
L'Hospitalet de Llobregat
Estadi Olímpic
Castell de Montjuïc
Montjuïc
Mediterranean Sea
Zona Franca
El Prat de Llobregat
Río Llobregat

0   2 Km
0   2 Miles

Belgrade

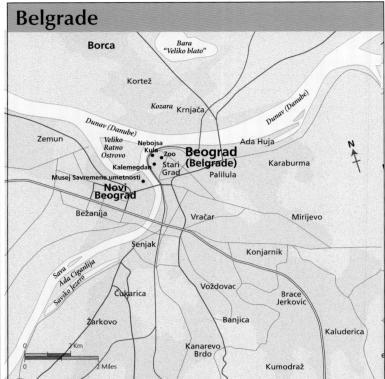

Borca
Bara "Veliko blato"
Kortež
Kozara
Krnjača
Dunav (Danube)
Zemun
Dunav (Danube)
Veliko Ratno Ostrovo
Nebojsa
Ada Huja
Kula
Zoo
Beograd (Belgrade)
Kalemegdan
Stari Grad
Karaburma
Musej Savremene umetnosti
Novi Beograd
Palilula
Bežanija
Vračar
Mirijevo
Senjak
Konjarnik
Ada Ciganlija
Sava
Savsko Jezero
Čukarica
Voždovac
Brace Jerkovic
Žarkovo
Banjica
Kaluderica
Kanarevo Brdo
Kumodraž

0   2 Km
0   2 Miles

Bucharest

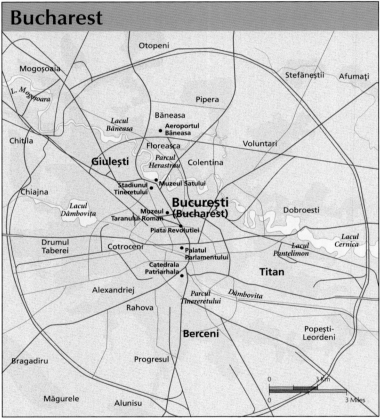

Otopeni
Mogoşoaia
Stefăneştii
Afumaţi
L. Mogoşoara
Pipera
Lacul Băneasa
Băneasa
Chitila
Aeroportul Băneasa
Voluntari
Floreasca
Giuleşti
Parcul Herastrau
Colentina
Chiajna
Stadionul Tineretului
Muzeul Satului
Lacul Dâmbovita
Bucureşti (Bucharest)
Muzeul Taranului Roman
Dobroesti
Piata Revolutiei
Lacul Cernica
Drumul Taberei
Cotroceni
Palatul Parlamentului
Lacul Pantelimon
Catedrala Patriarhala
Titan
Alexandriej
Parcul Tineretului
Dâmbovita
Rahova
Popeşti-Leordeni
Bragadiru
Berceni
Progresul
Măgurele
Alunisu

0   3 Km
0   3 Miles

Berlin

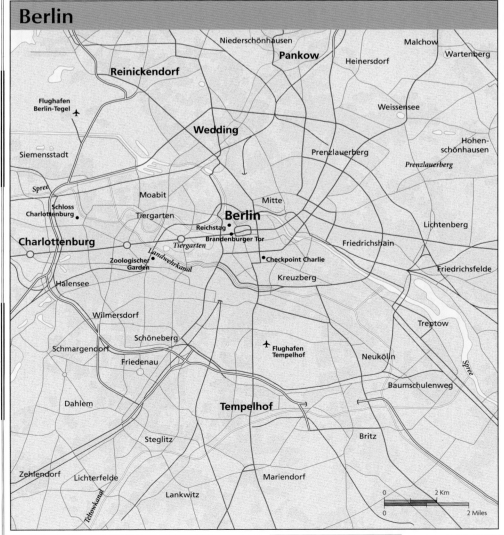

Niederschönhausen
Malchow
Pankow
Heinersdorf
Wartenberg
Reinickendorf
Flughafen Berlin-Tegel
Weissensee
Wedding
Höhen-schönhausen
Siemensstadt
Prenzlauerberg
Prenzlauerberg
Spree
Moabit
Mitte
Schloss Charlottenburg
Tiergarten
Berlin
Lichtenberg
Reichstag
Brandenburger Tor
Charlottenburg
Tiergarten
Friedrichshain
Zoologischer Garten
Landwehrkanal
Checkpoint Charlie
Friedrichsfelde
Halensee
Kreuzberg
Wilmersdorf
Treptow
Schöneberg
Spree
Schmargendorf
Friedenau
Flughafen Tempelhof
Neukölln
Dahlem
Baumschulenweg
Tempelhof
Britz
Steglitz
Zehlendorf
Lichterfelde
Mariendorf
Teltowkanal
Lankwitz

0   2 Km
0   2 Miles

Budapest

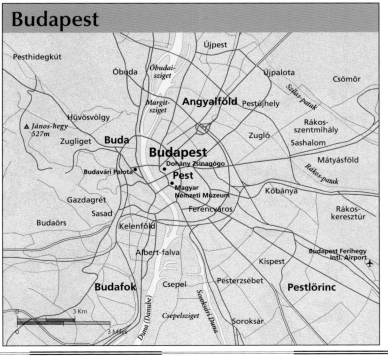

Újpest
Pesthidegkút
Óbuda
Óbudai-sziget
Újpalota
Csömör
Angyalföld
Pestújhely
Margit-sziget
Szilas-patak
Hüvösvölgy
Rákos-szentmihály
△ János-hegy 527m
Zugló
Sashalom
Zugliget
Buda
Budapest
Mátyásföld
Budavári Palota
Dohány Zsinagóga
Pest
Rákos-patak
Magyar Nemzeti Múzeum
Kőbánya
Gazdagrét
Rákos-keresztúr
Sasad
Ferencváros
Budaörs
Kelenföld
Budapest Ferihegy Intl. Airport
Albert-falva
Kispest
Pestlőrinc
Budafok
Csepel
Pesterzsébet
Dunav (Danube)
Soroksári Duna
Csepelsziget
Soroksár

0   3 Km
0   3 Miles

Copenhagen

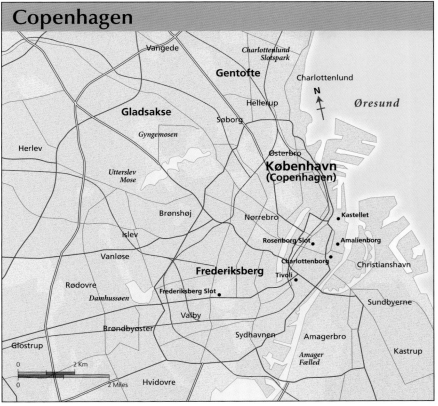

Vangede
Charlottenlund Slotspark
Gentofte
Charlottenlund
 Øresund
Hellerup
Gladsakse
Søborg
N
Herlev
Gyngemosen
Østerbro
Uttersley Mose
Islev
København (Copenhagen)
Brønshøj
Kastellet
Nørrebro
Rosenborg Slot
Amalienborg
Vanløse
Charlottenborg
Rødovre
Christianshavn
Frederiksberg
Tivoli
Frederiksberg Slot
Damhussøen
Valby
Sundbyerne
Brøndbyøster
Sydhavnen
Amagerbro
Glostrup
Amager Fælled
Kastrup
0   2 Km
0   2 Miles
Hvidovre

Kiev

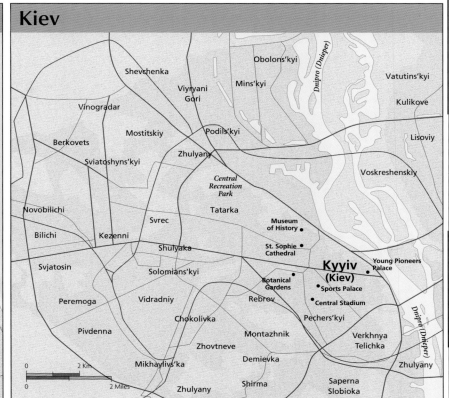

Obolons'kyi
Dnipro (Dnieper)
Shevchenka
Vatutins'kyi
Mins'kyi
Viynyani Gori
Kulikove
Vinogradar
Mostitskiy
Podils'kyi
Lisoviy
Berkovets
Zhulyany
Voskreshens'kiy
Sviatoshyns'kyi
Central Recreation Park
Novobilichi
Tatarka
Svrec
Museum of History
Bilichi
Kezenni
St. Sophie Cathedral
Shulyaka
Kyyiv (Kiev)
Young Pioneers Palace
Svjatosin
Solomians'kyi
Botanical Gardens
Sports Palace
Peremoga
Vidradniy
Rebrov
Central Stadium
Chokolivka
Pechers'kyi
Pivdenna
Montazhnik
Verkhnya Telichka
Zhovtneve
Demievka
Mikhaylivs'ka
Shirma
Saperna Slobioka
0   2 Km
0   2 Miles
Zhulyany
Zhulyany

London

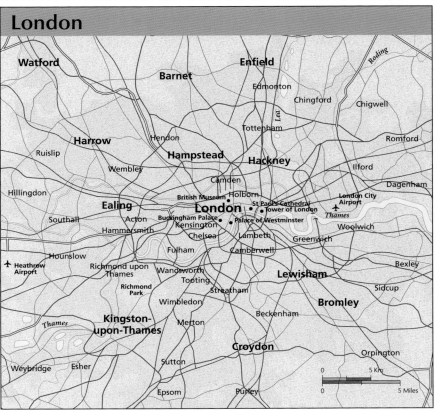

Watford
Enfield
Roding
Barnet
Edmonton
Chingford
Chigwell
Harrow
Tottenham
Romford
Ruislip
Hendon
Hampstead
Hackney
Ilford
Wembley
Camden
Dagenham
Hillingdon
British Museum
Holborn
London City Airport
Ealing
St. Paul's Cathedral
Tower of London
Southall
Acton
Buckingham Palace
London
Woolwich
Kensington
Palace of Westminster
Thames
Hammersmith
Chelsea
Lambeth
Greenwich
Hounslow
Fulham
Camberwell
Heathrow Airport
Bexley
Richmond upon Thames
Wandsworth
Lewisham
Richmond Park
Tooting
Streatham
Sidcup
Wimbledon
Bromley
Thames
Kingston-upon-Thames
Merton
Beckenham
Croydon
Weybridge
Esher
Sutton
Orpington
Epsom
Purley
0   5 Km
0   5 Miles

Lisbon

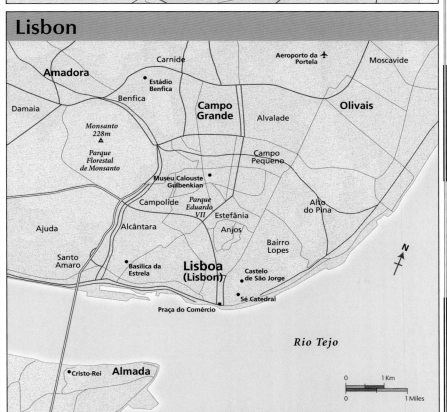

Aeroporto da Portela
Carnide
Moscavide
Amadora
Estádio Benfica
Benfica
Campo Grande
Olivais
Damaia
Monsanto 228m
Alvalade
Parque Florestal de Monsanto
Campo Pequeno
Museu Calouste Gulbenkian
Alto do Pina
Campolide
Parque Eduardo VII
Ajuda
Estefânia
Alcântara
Anjos
Bairro Lopes
Santo Amaro
N
Basílica da Estrela
Lisboa (Lisbon)
Castelo de São Jorge
Sé Catedral
Praça do Comércio
Rio Tejo
Cristo-Rei
Almada
0   1 Km
0   1 Miles

Madrid

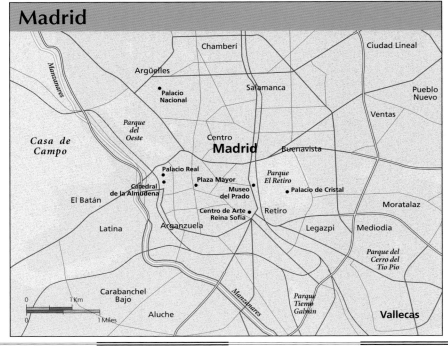

Chamberí
Ciudad Lineal
Argüelles
Manzanares
Palacio Nacional
Salamanca
Pueblo Nuevo
Parque del Oeste
Centro
Ventas
Casa de Campo
Madrid
Buenavista
Palacio Real
Catedral de la Almudena
Plaza Mayor
Parque El Retiro
Palacio de Cristal
Museo del Prado
El Batán
Centro de Arte Reina Sofía
Retiro
Moratalaz
Latina
Arganzuela
Legazpi
Mediodía
Manzanares
Parque del Cerro del Tío Pío
Carabanchel Bajo
Parque Tierno Galván
0   1 Km
Aluche
Vallecas
0   1 Miles

Minsk

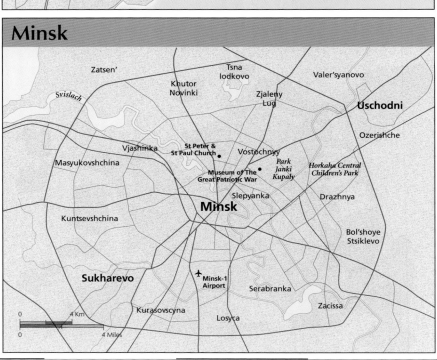

Zatsen'
Tsna Iodkovo
Valer'syanovo
Khutor Novinki
Svislach
Zjaleny Lug
Uschodni
Vjashinka
Ozerishche
St Peter & St Paul Church
Vostochnyy
Masyukovshchina
Park Janki Kupaly
Horkaha Central Children's Park
Museum of The Great Patriotic War
Slepyanka
Drazhnya
Minsk
Kuntsevshchina
Bol'shoye Stsiklevo
Sukharevo
Minsk-1 Airport
Serabranka
Zacissa
Kurasovscyna
0   4 Km
Losyca
0   4 Miles

EUROPE – Cities

Moscow

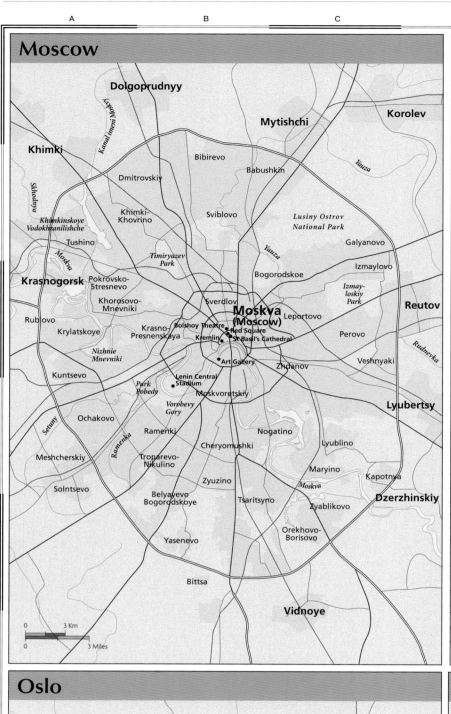

Dolgoprudnyy
Mytishchi
Korolev
Khimki
Bibirevo
Babushkin
Dmitrovskiy
Khimki-Khovrino
Sviblovo
Yauza
Lusiny Ostrov National Park
Khimkinskoye Vodokhranilishche
Tushino
Galyanovo
Skhodnya
Timiryazev Park
Yauza
Izmaylovo
Moskva
Krasnogorsk
Pokrovsko-Stresnevo
Bogorodskoe
Izmayloskiy Park
Reutov
Khorosovo-Mnevniki
Sverdlov
Leportovo
Rublovo
Krasno-Presnenskaya
Bolshoy Theatre
Moskva (Moscow)
Red Square
St Basil's Cathedral
Kremlin
Perovo
Krylatskoye
Nizhnie Mnevniki
Art Gallery
Zhdanov
Veshnyaki
Kuntsevo
Lenin Central Stadium
Park Pobedy
Moskvoretskiy
Lyubertsy
Setuny
Vorobevy Gory
Ochakovo
Ramenka
Ramenki
Nogatino
Lyublino
Meshcherskiy
Troparevo-Nikulino
Cheryomushki
Maryino
Kapotnya
Solntsevo
Zyuzino
Moskva
Zyablikovo
Dzerzhinskiy
Belyayevo Bogorodskoye
Tsaritsyno
Orekhovo-Borisovo
Yasenevo
Bittsa
Vidnoye

0   3 Km
0   3 Miles

Munich

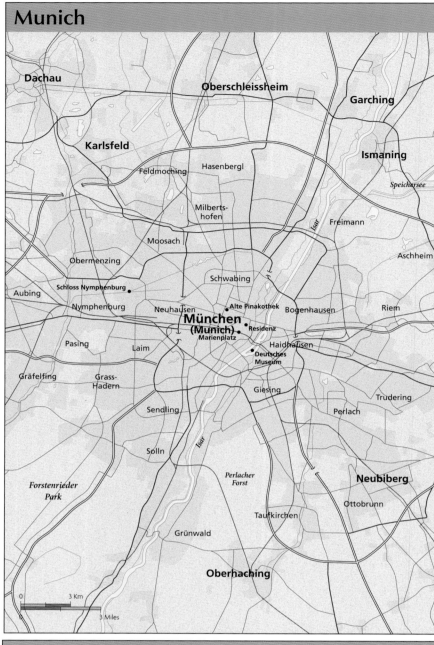

Dachau
Oberschleissheim
Garching
Karlsfeld
Ismaning
Feldmoching
Hasenbergl
Speichersee
Milberts-hofen
Moosach
Freimann
Isar
Obermenzing
Schwabing
Aschheim
Aubing
Schloss Nymphenburg
Alte Pinakothek
Bogenhausen
Riem
Nymphenburg
Neuhausen
München (Munich)
Residenz
Pasing
Marienplatz
Haidhausen
Laim
Deutsches Museum
Gräfelfing
Grass-Hadern
Giesing
Trudering
Sendling
Perlach
Isar
Solln
Neubiberg
Perlacher Forst
Forstenrieder Park
Taufkirchen
Ottobrunn
Grünwald
Oberhaching

0   3 Km
0   3 Miles

Oslo

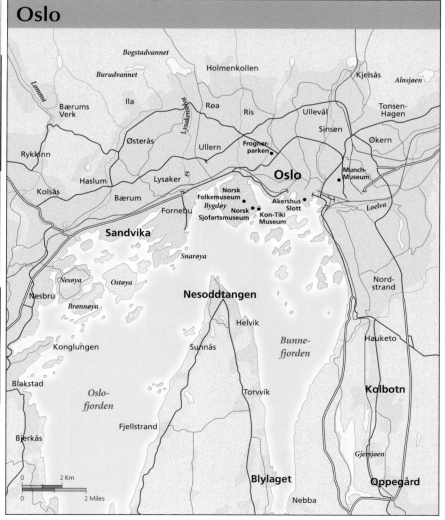

Bogstadvannet
Holmenkollen
Kjelsås
Burudvannet
Alnsjøen
Ila
Røa
Ris
Ullevål
Tonsen-Hagen
Bærums Verk
Sinsen
Lomma
Økern
Østerås
Ullern
Frogner-parken
Rykkinn
Munch-Museum
Haslum
Lysaker
Oslo
Kolsås
Norsk Folkemuseum
Bærum
Bygdøy
Akershus Slott
Fornebu
Norsk Sjofartsmuseum
Kon-Tiki Museum
Loelva
Sandvika
Snarøya
Nesøya
Ostøya
Nord-strand
Nesbru
Brønnøya
Nesoddtangen
Helvik
Blakstad
Bunne-fjorden
Hauketo
Konglungen
Sunnås
Bjerkås
Oslo-fjorden
Torvvik
Kolbotn
Fjellstrand
Gjersjøen
Blylaget
Oppegård
Nebba

0   2 Km
0   2 Miles

Prague

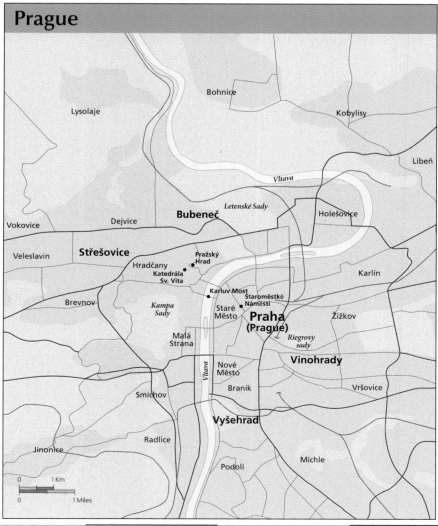

Bohnice
Lysolaje
Kobylisy
Vltava
Libeň
Letenské Sady
Vokovice
Dejvice
Bubeneč
Holešovice
Veleslavin
Střešovice
Prazský Hrad
Karlín
Hradčany
Katedrála Sv. Vita
Brevnov
Karluv Most
Staroměstké Náměstí
Žižkov
Kampa Sady
Staré Město
Malá Strana
Riegrovy sady
Nové Město
Vinohrady
Vltava
Smíchov
Branik
Vršovice
Jinonice
Vyšehrad
Radlice
Podolí
Michle

0   1 Km
0   1 Miles

Rome

Tor di Quinto
Tufello
Villa Ada
Torrevécchia
Stadio Olimpico
Flaminio
Trieste
Monte Sacro
Primavalle
Trionfale
Parioli
Pietralata
Nomentano
Villa Borghese
Roma (Rome)
Montespaccato
Cappella Sistina
Castel Sant' Angelo
CITTÀ DEL VATICANO
Basilica di San Pietro
Fontana di Trevi
Aurelio
Pantheon
Palazzo di Quirinale
Tiburtino
Foro Romano
Trastevere
Colosseo
Tor Pignattara
Fiume Tévere
Valcannuta
Tuscolano
Monteverde Nuovo
Cinecittà
Corviale
Garbatella
Catacombe di Domitilla
Ostiense
Magliana
0 1 Km
0 1 Miles

St Petersburg

Olgino
Ozero Lakhtinskiy Razliv
Vdelnoe
Grazhdanka
Rzhevká
0 3 Km
0 3 Miles
Ostrova Krestovskiye
Petrogradskaya Storona
Stoyka
Polyustrovo
Zhernovka
Vasilyevskiy Ostrov
Hermitage and Winter Palace
Cruiser Aurora
Neva
Bolshaya-Okhta
Smolnvy Cathedral
Kirov Palace of Culture
Admiralty
Finskiy Zaliv
St Isaac's Cathedral
Malaya-Okhta
Sankt-Peterburg (St Petersburg)
Alexander Nevsky Abbey
Ostrov Gutuyevskiy
Volynkina Derevnya
Volodanskoye
Vesolyy Posolok
Utkina Zavod
Avtovo
Obukhovo
Neva
Ulyanka
Aleksandrovskoye
Kupchino
Ligovo
Srednaya Rogatka
Novoaleksandrovskoye

Sofia

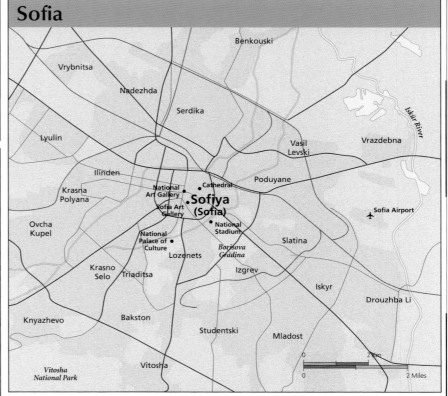

Benkouski
Vrybnitsa
Iskár River
Nadezhda
Serdika
Vasil Levski
Vrazdebna
Lyulin
Ilinden
Poduyane
Krasna Polyana
National Art Gallery
Cathedral
Sofiya (Sofia)
Sofia Airport
Sofia Art Gallery
Ovcha Kupel
National Palace of Culture
National Stadium
Slatina
Lozenets
Borisova Gradina
Krasno Selo
Triaditsa
Izgrev
Iskyr
Knyazhevo
Bakston
Studentski
Drouzhba Li
Mladost
Vitosha National Park
Vitosha
0 2 Km
0 2 Miles

Stockholm

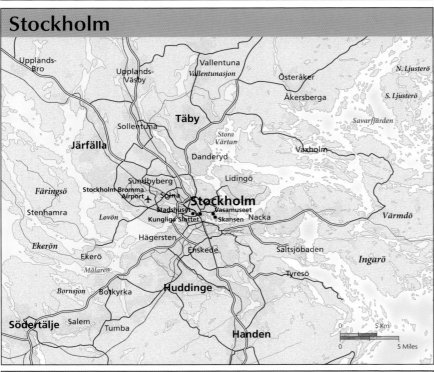

Upplands-Bro
Vallentuna
Vallentunasjön
N. Ljusterö
Upplands-Väsby
Österåker
Åkersberga
S. Ljusterö
Täby
Savarfjärden
Järfälla
Sollentuna
Stora Värtan
Vaxholm
Danderyd
Färingsö
Sundbyberg
Lidingö
Värmdö
Stockholm Bromma Airport
Solna
Stadshuset
Stockholm
Vasamuseet
Stenhamra
Lovön
Kungliga Slottet
Skansen
Nacka
Ekerön
Ekerö
Hägersten
Ingarö
Mälaren
Enskede
Saltsjöbaden
Bornsjön
Botkyrka
Tyresö
Huddinge
Södertälje
Salem
Tumba
Handen
0 5 Km
0 5 Miles

Warsaw

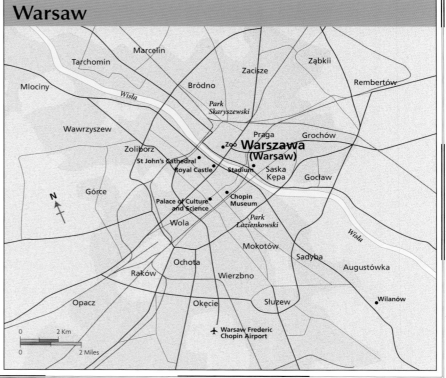

Marcelin
Ząbkii
Tarchomin
Zacisze
Mlociny
Bródno
Rembertów
Wisla
Park Skaryszewski
Wawrzyszew
Praga
Grochów
Zoliborz
Zoo
Warszawa (Warsaw)
Górce
St John's Cathedral
Royal Castle
Stadium
Saska Kępa
N
Goclaw
Palace of Culture and Science
Chopin Museum
Wola
Park Łazienkowski
Wisla
Mokotów
Ochota
Sadyba
Augustówka
Raków
Wierzbno
Opacz
Służew
Okęcie
Wilanów
0 2 Km
0 2 Miles
Warsaw Frederic Chopin Airport

Zagreb

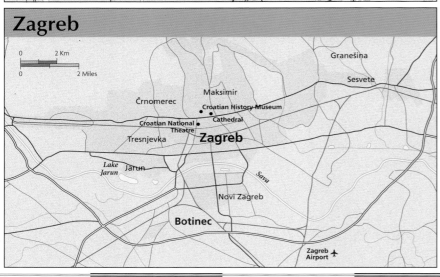

0 2 Km
0 2 Miles
Granešina
Sesvete
Maksimir
Crnomerec
Croatian History Museum
Croatian National Theatre
Cathedral
Tresnjevka
Zagreb
Lake Jarun
Jarun
Sava
Novi Zagreb
Botinec
Zagreb Airport

ASIA

Asia is the world's largest continent with a total area of 16,838,365 sq miles (43,608,000 sq km). It comprises 49 separate countries, including 97% of Turkey and 72% of the Russian Federation. Almost 60% of the world's population lives in Asia.

FACTFILE

N **Most Northerly Point:** Mys Articheskiy, Russia 81° 12′ N
S **Most Southerly Point:** Pulau Pamana, Indonesia 11° S
E **Most Easterly Point:** Mys Dezhneva, Russia 169° 40′ W
W **Most Westerly Point:** Bozzcaada, Turkey 26° 2′ E

Largest Lakes:
1. Caspian Sea, Asia/Europe 143,243 sq miles (371,000 sq km)
2. Lake Baikal, Russian Federation 11,776 sq miles (30,500 sq km)
3. Lake Balkhash, Kazakhstan/China 7115 sq miles (18,428 sq km)
4. Aral Sea, Kazakhstan/Uzbekistan 6625 sq miles (17,160 sq km)
5. Tonlé Sap, Cambodia 3861 sq miles (10,000 sq km)

Longest Rivers:
1. Yangtze, China 3915 miles (6299 km)
2. Yellow River, China 3395 miles (5464 km)
3. Mekong, SE Asia 2749 miles (4425 km)
4. Lena, Russian Federation 2734 miles (4400 km)
5. Yenisey, Russian Federation 2541 miles (4090 km)

Largest Islands:
1. Borneo, Brunie/Indonesia/Malaysia 292,222 sq miles (757,050 sq km)
2. Sumatra, Indonesia 202,300 sq miles (524,000 sq km)
3. Honshu, Japan 88,800 sq miles (230,000 sq km)
4. Sulawesi, Indonesia 73,057 sq miles (189,218 sq km)
5. Java, Indonesia 53,589 sq miles (138,794 sq km)

Highest Points:
1. Mount Everest, China/Nepal 29,029 ft (8848 m)
2. K2, China/Pakistan 28,253 ft (8611 m)
3. Kangchenjunga I, India/Nepal 28,210 ft (8598 m)
4. Lhotse, Nepal 27,939 ft (8516 m)
5. Makalu, China/Nepal 27,767 ft (8463 m)

Lowest Point:
▼ Dead Sea, Israel/Jordan -1388 ft (-423 m) below sea level

Highest recorded temperature:
➕ Tirat Zevi, Israel 129°F (54°C)

Lowest recorded temperature:
➖ Verkhoyansk, Russian Federation -90°F (-68°C)

Wettest Place:
≋ Cherrapunji, India 450 in (11,430 mm)

Driest Place:
⌢ Aden, Yemen 1.8 in (46 mm)

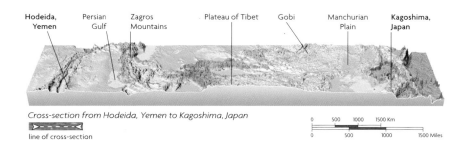

Cross-section from Hodeida, Yemen to Kagoshima, Japan

line of cross-section

0   500   1000   1500 Km
0   500   1000   1500 Miles

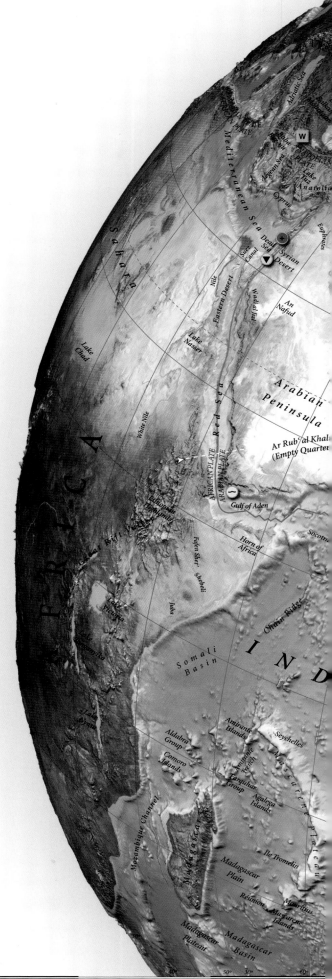

ARCTIC OCEAN

North Pole

NORTH AMERICAN PLATE
EURASIAN PLATE

EUROPE

ASIA

Norwegian Sea
North Sea
Baltic Sea
Gulf of Bothnia
North Cape
Barents Sea
White Sea
Novaya Zemlya
Kara Sea
Severnaya Zemlya
Mys Chelyuskin
Laptev Sea
New Siberian Islands
East Siberian Sea
Long Strait
Bering Strait
Bering Sea

Scandinavia
Gulf of Finland
North European Plain
Central Russian Upland
Ural Mountains
West Siberian Plain
North Siberian Lowland
Central Siberian Plateau
Siberia

Black Sea
Sea of Azov
Caspian Depression
Caspian Sea
Kirghiz Steppe
Lake Chany
Altai Mountains
Plateau of Mongolia
Sea of Okhotsk

Aral Sea
Ustyurt Plateau
Turan Lowland
Kara Kum
Lake Balkhash
Lake Zaysan
Dzungaria
Gobi
Manchurian Plain

Iranian Plateau
Tien Shan
Tarim Basin
Takla Makan Desert
Nan Shan
Ordos Desert
Yellow River
Sea of Japan (East Sea)
Japan

Zagros Mountains
Great Salt Desert
Hindu Kush
Karakoram Range
Kunlun Mountains
Plateau of Tibet
Korea Bay
Bo Hai
Korea Strait
Yellow Sea
Cheju-do

Hamun Jaz Murian
Suleiman Range
Punjab Plains
Mount Everest 8848m
Plain of China
East China Sea

Gulf of Oman
Thar Desert
Vindhya Range
Satpura Range
Ganges
Brahmaputra
Khasi Hills
Taiwan Strait
Taiwan

Arabian Sea
Arabian Basin
Deccan
Western Ghats
Eastern Ghats
Mouths of the Ganges
Philippine Sea

Laccadive Islands
Malabar Coast
Coromandel Coast
Bay of Bengal
Andaman Islands
Gulf of Martaban
Gulf of Tongking
Hainan
Luzon Strait
Luzon

Cape Comorin
Gulf of Mannar
Sri Lanka
Maldives
Andaman Sea
Gulf of Thailand
South China Sea
Philippine Basin

INDIAN OCEAN
Ceylon plain
Nicobar Islands
Mouths of the Mekong
South China Basin
Sulu Sea
Mindanao

Mid-Indian Basin
Cocos Basin
Sunda Shelf
Natuna Islands
Celebes Sea

Greater Sunda Islands
Java Sea
Bali
Lesser Sunda Islands
Arafura Sea
Timor Trough

Java Trench
Sunda Trough

AUSTRALIA

PACIFIC OCEAN

Political

Asia is the world's largest continent, encompassing many different and discrete realms, from the desert Arab lands of the southwest to the subtropical archipelago of Indonesia; from the vast barren wastes of Siberia to the fertile river valleys of China and South Asia, seats of some of the world's most ancient civilizations. The collapse of the Soviet Union has fragmented the north of the continent into the Siberian portion of the Russian Federation, and the new republics of Central Asia. Strong religious traditions heavily influence the politics of South and Southwest Asia. Hindu and Muslim rivalries threaten to upset the political equilibrium in South Asia where India—in terms of population—remains the world's largest democracy. China, another population giant, is reasserting its position as a world political and economic power, while on its doorstep, the dynamic Pacific Rim countries, led by Japan, continue to assert their worldwide economic force.

Population density
(people per sq mile)

below 25
25–124
125–259
260–649
650–10,400
above 10,400

Population

Some of the world's most populous and least populous regions are in Asia. The plains of eastern China, the Ganges River plains in India, Japan, and the Indonesian island of Java, all have very high population densities; by contrast parts of Siberia and the Plateau of Tibet are virtually uninhabited. China has the world's greatest population—20% of the globe's total—while India, with the second largest, has more than one billion.

Map labels

ARCTIC OCEAN
East Siberian Sea
Bering Sea
Laptev Sea
Kara Sea
Kolyma Range
Anadyr
Magadan
Sea of Okhotsk
Arctic Circle
Central Siberian Plateau
Siberia
Noril'sk
Yakutsk
RUSSIAN FEDERATION
West Siberian Plain
Lake Baikal
Khabarovsk
Yekaterinburg
Chelyabinsk
Omsk
Tomsk
Novosibirsk
Krasnoyarsk
Irkutsk
Ural'sk
Rudnyy
Novokuznetsk
Istanbul
Black Sea
ANKARA
Sokhumi
GEORGIA
Bat'umi
K'ut'aisi
T'BILISI
ARMENIA
YEREVAN
AZERB.
BAKU
ASTANA
Karagandy
Suhbaatar
Choybalsan
Erdenet
ULAN BATOR
Harbin
Vladivostok
Jilin
Changchun
TURKEY
Anatolia
CYPRUS
NICOSIA
Adana
Gaziantep
Aleppo
LEBANON
Tripoli
SYRIA
DAMASCUS
Haifa
Tel Aviv-Yafo
JERUSALEM
Gaza
ISRAEL
AMMAN
JORDAN
BAGHDAD
Mosul
Kirkuk
An Najaf
IRAQ
KUWAIT
KUWAIT
SAUDI ARABIA
RIYADH
JEDDA
At Ta'if
MANAMA
BAHRAIN
QATAR
DOHA
ABU DHABI
UAE
Ar Rustaq
MUSCAT
Sur
Arabian Peninsula
Ar Rub' al Khali (Empty Quarter)
SANA
YEMEN
Ta'izz
Aden
Gulf of Aden
Socotra (to Yemen)
Red Sea
AFRICA
Tropic of Cancer
KAZAKHSTAN
Zhezkazgan
Semey
Aktau
Aral Sea
Syr Darya
Amu Darya
Kyzylorda
Balkash
Lake Balkash
UZBEKISTAN
Taraz
BISHKEK
KYRGYZSTAN
Karakol
Osh
TASHKENT
Dasoguz
TURKMENISTAN
ASGABAT
DUSHANBE
TAJIKISTAN
Balkh
Qal'eh-ye Now
Herat
Mashhad
Gorgan
Qom
TEHRAN
Esfahan
IRAN
Iranian Plateau
Ahvaz
Shiraz
Kerman
Zahedan
Bandar-e 'Abbas
Basra
Persian Gulf
Gulf of Oman
Euphrates
Tigris
Caspian Sea
Tabriz
Güncä
Gobi
MONGOLIA
Inner Mongolia
Altai Mountains
Urumqi
Tien Shan
Tarim He
Takla Makan Desert (claimed by India)
Kunlun Mountains
CHINA
Shenyang
Anshan
Wonsan
NORTH KOREA
PYONGYANG
Dalian
Datong
BEIJING
SEOUL
Incheon
SOUTH KOREA
Baotou
Tangshan
Tianjin
Shijiazhuang
Baoding
Taiyuan
Handan
Jinan
Qingdao
Yellow Sea
Lanzhou
Zhengzhou
Xuzhou
Luoyang
Huainan
Nanjing
Shanghai
Xi'an
Hefei
Wuhan
Hangzhou
Ningbo
Jinhua
Mianyang
Chengdu
Changsha
Nanchang
Fuzhou
Chongqing
Leshan
Hengyang
TAIPEI
T'aichung
TAIWAN
Guiyang
Shantou
Liuzhou
Guangzhou
Kaohsiung
Kunming
Nanning
Hong Kong (Xianggang)
Hainan Dao
South China Sea
AFGHANISTAN
KABUL
Jalalabad
Srinagar
Jammu
Kandahar
Peshawar
ISLAMABAD
Gujranwala
Faisalabad
Lahore
Multan
Ludhiana
(line of control)
(administered by China, claimed by India)
Plateau of Tibet
(Much of Arunachal Pradesh is claimed by China)
Lhasa
Brahmaputra
Salween
Mekong
Himalayas
PAKISTAN
Quetta
Shikarpur
Larkana
Indus
Karachi
Hyderabad
Thar Desert
NEW DELHI
Delhi
Jaipur
Agra
Bareilly
Lucknow
Kanpur
NEPAL
KATHMANDU
THIMPHU
BHUTAN
Varanasi
Patna
Rangpur
Guwahati
Ganges
INDIA
Ahmadabad
Bhopal
Vadodara
Narmada
Indore
Jamshedpur
BANGLADESH
DHAKA
Rajshahi
Brahmanbaria
Khulna
Chittagong
MYANMAR (BURMA)
Mandalay
HANOI
Hai Phong
Surat
Nagpur
Kolkata (Calcutta)
Bhubaneshwar
Taunggyi
Pakokku
NAY PYI TAW
Louangphabang
Vinh
Mumbai (Bombay)
Pune
Solapur
Hyderabad
Godavari
Krishna
Vijayawada
Bay of Bengal
Prome
Chiang Mai
VIENTIANE
Da Nang
LAOS
VIETNAM
Hubli
Rangoon
Pegu
Bassein
Bogale
THAILAND
Pakxe
Hyderabad
Andaman Islands (to India)
Bangalore
Mysore
Chennai (Madras)
BANGKOK
CAMBODIA
Batdambang
Da Lat
Coimbatore
PHNOM PENH
Ho Chi Minh City
Kochi / Cochin
Jaffna
Andaman Sea
Gulf of Thailand
Thiruvananthapuram/ Trivandrum
SRI LANKA
COLOMBO
SRI JAYAWARDENAPURA KOTTE
Nicobar Islands (to India)
BANDAR SERI BEGAWAN
BRUNEI
Kota Bharu
MALAYSIA
Borneo
Taiping
Medan
KUALA LUMPUR
PUTRAJAYA
SINGAPORE
SINGAPORE
Balikpapan
Pontianak
Banjarmasin
Equator
Padang
Jambi
Palembang
Sumatra
JAKARTA
Bandung
Java
Semarang
Surabaya
Malang
Java Sea
INDIAN OCEAN
Arabian Sea
EUROPE
Ural Mountains
Ob'
Tobol
Ishim
Irtysh
Zhayyk
Kheta
Olenek
Anabar
Lena
Kureyka
Vilyuy
Aldan
Yenisey
Stony Tunguska
Chulym
Angara
Yana
Indigirka
Kolyma
Amur
Argun
Amga
Vitim
Yellow River
Yangtze
Irriwaddy
Salween

Transportation

The transportation system varies enormously in extent and quality across Asia. Early trade routes included the Silk Route, from Beijing across Central Asia, and the sea routes around the coastline of southern Asia. Today, transportation networks often radiate from coastal ports, reflecting the continuing importance of sea and river travel for trade and external communications. In the interior, high mountain barriers such as the Himalayas, the Altai Mountains, and the Tien Shan, deserts like the Gobi, Takla Makan, and Ar Rub' al Khali, remain virtually impenetrable to most modern terrestrial transportation. Major engineering feats are necessary to conquer these hostile frontier territories, although the success of the Trans-Siberian Railway in overcoming the harsh Siberian landscape, proves that cross-continental transportation, if not economically viable, is physically possible.

Languages

During the 19th century, Russian was introduced into Central Asia and Siberia. Under the Soviets, Russian-speaking became mandatory—replacing the indigenous Ural-Altaic languages in many urban areas—although today the use of Central Asian languages is being revived in the new republics. India's linguistic mosaic comprises Dravidian languages, such as Tamil, in the south, and the Indo-Aryan languages of the north such as Hindi. In China, three main languages, Mandarin Chinese, Wu Chinese, and Cantonese, share the same written form but their spoken dialects are mutually unintelligible.

Standard of living

Despite Japan's high standards of living, and Southwest Asia's oil-derived wealth, immense disparities exist across the continent. Afghanistan remains one of the world's most underdeveloped nations, as do the mountain states of Nepal and Bhutan. Further rapid population growth is exacerbating poverty and overcrowding in many parts of India and Bangladesh.

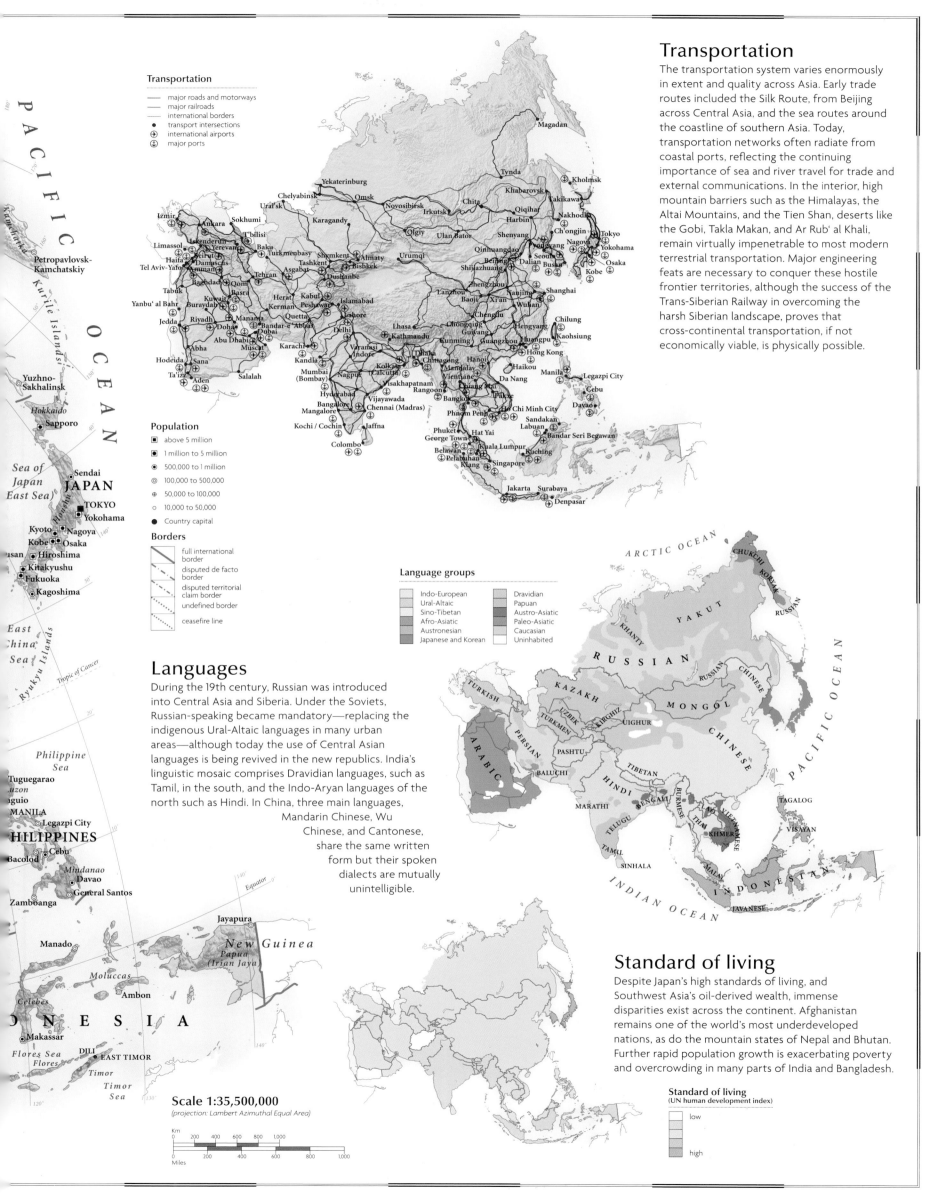

Transportation

— major roads and motorways
— major railroads
— international borders
• transport intersections
⊕ international airports
⊕ major ports

Population

■ above 5 million
▪ 1 million to 5 million
◉ 500,000 to 1 million
⊚ 100,000 to 500,000
⊕ 50,000 to 100,000
○ 10,000 to 50,000
● Country capital

Borders

full international border
disputed de facto border
disputed territorial claim border
undefined border
ceasefire line

Language groups

Indo-European
Ural-Altaic
Sino-Tibetan
Afro-Asiatic
Austronesian
Japanese and Korean
Dravidian
Papuan
Austro-Asiatic
Paleo-Asiatic
Caucasian
Uninhabited

Standard of living
(UN human development index)

low
high

Scale 1:35,500,000
(projection: Lambert Azimuthal Equal Area)

Km
0   200 400 600 800 1,000

Miles
0   200   400   600   800   1,000

ASIA – Physical

ASIA

208

Scale 1:47,500,000
(projection: Gall Stereographic)

| 0 | 500 | 1000 | 1500 Km |
| 0 | 500 | 1000 | 1500 Miles |

Climate

The climate of Asia exhibits marked differences from region to region, with freezing polar conditions in the north, hot and cold deserts in central regions and subtropical conditions throughout the south. Much of this variation can be attributed to enormous mountain barriers and internal depressions found across the continent. Monsoon winds, which reverse semi-annually, cause alternate wet and dry seasons across southern Asia. These air masses moving north from the ocean are stripped of their moisture over the Himalayas causing arid conditions across the Plateau of Tibet. Both the south and east are susceptible to tropical cyclones or typhoons.

Average Rainfall

January rainfall

July rainfall

Rainfall

- 0–1 in (0–25 mm)
- 1–2 in (25–50 mm)
- 2–4 in (50–100 mm)
- 4–8 in (100–200 mm)
- 8–12 in (200–300 mm)
- 12–16 in (300–400 mm)
- 16–20 in (400–500 mm)
- more than 20 in (500 mm)

Average Temperature

January temperature

July temperature

Temperature

- below -22°F (-30°C)
- -22 to -4°F (-30 to -20°C)
- -4 to 14°F (-20 to -10°C)
- 14 to 32°F (-10 to 0°C)
- 32 to 50°F (0 to 10°C)
- 50 to 68°F (10 to 20°C)
- 68 to 86°F (20 to 30°C)
- above 86°F (30°C)

Climate

- tundra
- subarctic
- cool continental
- warm humid
- mediterranean
- semi-arid
- arid
- humid equatorial
- tropical
- daily hours of sunshine, January
- daily hours of sunshine, July
- cyclone
- typhoon
- cold/dry monsoon
- warm/wet monsoon
- cold wind

Environmental issues

The transformation of Uzbekistan by the former Soviet Union into the world's fifth largest producer of cotton led to the diversion of several major rivers for irrigation. Starved of this water, the Aral Sea diminished in volume by over 75% since 1960, irreversibly altering the ecology of the area. Heavy industries in eastern China have polluted coastal waters, rivers and urban air, while in Myanmar (Burma), Malaysia and Indonesia, ancient hardwood rainforests are felled faster than they can regenerate.

Environmental issues

- tropical forest
- forest destroyed
- desert
- desertification
- acid rain
- polluted rivers
- marine pollution
- heavy marine pollution
- radioactive contamination
- poor urban air quality

Using the land and sea

- cropland
- desert
- forest
- mountain region
- pasture
- tundra
- wetland
- major conurbations
- cattle
- pigs
- goats
- sheep
- coconuts
- corn (maize)
- cotton
- dates
- fishing
- fruit
- jute
- peanuts
- rice
- rubber
- shellfish
- soya beans
- sugar beet
- sugar cane
- tea
- timber
- wheat

Land use

Vast areas of Asia remain uncultivated as a result of unsuitable climatic and soil conditions. In favourable areas such as river deltas, farming is intensive. Rice is the staple crop of most Asian countries, grown in paddy fields on waterlogged alluvial plains and terraced hillsides, and often irrigated for higher yields. Across the black earth region of the Eurasian steppe in southern Siberia and Kazakhstan, wheat farming is the dominant activity. Cash crops, like tea in Sri Lanka and dates in the Arabian Peninsula, are grown for export, and provide valuable income. The sovereignty of the rich fishing grounds in the South China Sea is disputed by China, Malaysia, Taiwan, the Philippines and Vietnam, because of potential oil reserves.

ASIA

1   BOSPORUS, TURKEY
The Bosporus provides the only outlet for the Black Sea, linking it with the Sea of Marmara to the south and then with the Mediterranean Sea via the Dardanelles.

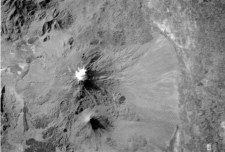

2   MOUNT ARARAT, TURKEY
Said to be the resting place for Noah's Ark, this extinct volcanic massif lies in the far east of Turkey.

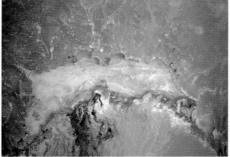

3   LAKE BALKASH, KAZAKHSTAN
Still covered in winter ice in this image, this lakes lies in a dry desert region and has no outlet.

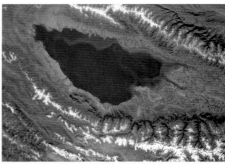

4   OZERO ISSYK-KUL', KYRGYZSTAN
Against the dry slopes of the Tien Shan mountains to the south this lake appears bright blue.

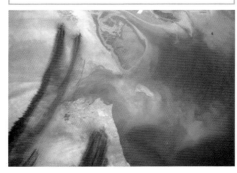

9   KUWAIT'S OILFIELDS, KUWAIT
The dark plumes are smoke rising from the 700 wells set alight by Iraqi forces during the Gulf War of 1991.

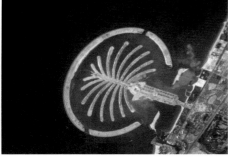

10   PALM ISLAND, UNITED ARAB EMIRATES
This luxury housing development and tourist resort, one mile (1.6 km) off the seafront of Dubai, is built from sediments dredged from the nearby port of Jebel Ali.

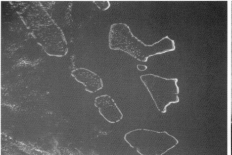

11   MALDIVES
The Maldives consist of 1300 coral formations in 19 atolls and stretch over 1491 miles (2400 km).

12   KARACHI, PAKISTAN
Pakistan's main seaport and former capital lies to the northwest of the delta of the Indus river.

THREE GORGES DAM, CHINA [5]
Seen here during its construction in 2000, the world's largest dam is designed to tame the Yangtze river which has regularly flooded.

BEIJING, CHINA [6]
China's ancient capital was laid out on a grid pattern centred on the Forbidden City and its streets are picked out in this winter image by snowfall.

MOUNT FUJI, JAPAN [7]
The steep, symmetrical, snow-capped volcano last erupted in 1707.

VULKAN KLYUCHEVSKAYA SOPKA, RUSSIAN FEDERATION [8]
The Kamchatka Peninsula's highest and most active volcano last erupted in 1994.

MOUNT EVEREST, CHINA/NEPAL [13]
The world's highest mountain at 29,029 ft (8848 m) straddles the border between China and Nepal.

MOUTHS OF THE GANGES, BANGLADESH/INDIA [14]
Stretching across the northern end of the Bay of Bengal, this river delta contains the Sundarbans, the world's largest mangrove forest, which appears as a rich green area.

MEKONG DELTA, VIETNAM [15]
The Mekong river flows over 2494 miles (4000 km) from the Plateau of Tibet before crossing Vietnam to reach the South China Sea.

HONG KONG, CHINA [16]
Handed back to China by the British in 1997, this city remains east Asia's trade and finance center.

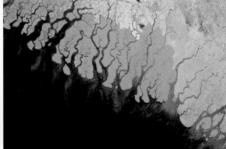
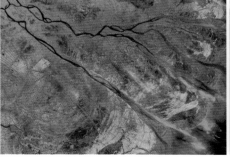

185

131

136

Elevation scale:
6000m
4000m
3000m
2000m
1000m
500m
250m
100m
Sea Level
-250m
-2000m
-4000m

Seas and Water Bodies

Adriatic Sea
Tyrrhenian Sea
Ionian Sea
Ionian Nísia (Ionian Islands)
Aegean Sea
Thracian Sea (Thrakikó Pélagos)
Mirtóo Pélagos
Kritikó Pélagos (Sea of Crete)
Sea of Marmara (Marmara Denizi)
Black Sea
Mediterranean Sea
Khalij Surt (Gulf of Sirte)
Red Sea
Gulf of Suez (Khalij as Suways)
Gulf of Aqaba
Dead Sea
Lake Nasser (Buhayrat Nāsir)
Suez Canal (Qanāt as Suways)
Buhayrat ath Tharthar
Roseires Reservoir

Countries

BOSNIA & HERZEGOVINA
CROATIA
SERBIA
MONTENEGRO
ALBANIA
MACEDONIA
BULGARIA
ROMANIA
GREECE
TURKEY
CYPRUS
TURKISH REPUBLIC OF NORTHERN CYPRUS (recognised only by Turkey)
SYRIA
LEBANON
ISRAEL
JORDAN
IRAQ
SAUDI ARABIA
EGYPT
LIBYA
CHAD
SUDAN
SOUTH SUDAN
CENTRAL AFRICAN REPUBLIC
ERITREA
ETHIOPIA
DJIBOUTI
RUSSIAN FEDERATION
GEORGIA
ARMENIA

Selected Cities and Places

Perugia, Terni, Pescara, L'Aquila, Campobasso, Napoli (Naples), Foggia, Bari, Salerno, Potenza, Taranto, Lecce, Cosenza, Catanzaro, Reggio di Calabria, Messina, Etna 3340m, Catania, Siracusa, Ragusa, Sicilia (Sicily), Stromboli 926m (Isole Eolie), Golfo di Taranto, Split, Kraljevo, Vidin, Niš, Pleven, Vratsa, Pristina, Prizren, Skopje, Sofiya, Plovdiv, Stara Zagora, Sliven, Burgas, Varna, Dobrich, Constanța, Giurgiu, Razgrad, Ruse, Veliko Tarnovo, Shumen, Tirane, Podgorica, Shkodër, Kavála, Thessaloníki (Saloníca), Chalkidikí, Mount Olympus (Ólympos) 2917m, Lárisa, Vólos, Kozáni, Édessa, Bitola, Pátra, Kérkyra, Lefkáda, Kefallonía, Zákynthos, Athína (Athens), Korinthos, Peloponnísos, Évvoia (Euboea), Lésvos (Lesbos), Límnos, Kykládes (Cyclades), Dodekánisa (Dodecanese), Ródos (Rhodes), Iráklio, Ágios Nikólaos, Kríti (Crete), Istanbul, Tekirdağ, İzmit, Bursa, Adapazarı, Eskişehir, Kütahya, Afyon, Akşehir, Konya, Ankara, Kırıkkale, Çorum, Tokat, Sivas, Kayseri, Niğde, Aksaray, Ereğli, Adana, Mersin, Tarsus, İskenderun, Antakya, Osmaniye, Gaziantep, Şanlıurfa, Adıyaman, Malatya, Kahramanmaraş, Elazığ, Diyarbakır, Mardin, Batman, Siirt, Muş, Bingöl, Erzurum, Erzincan, Ağrı, Van, Van Gölü, Tatvan, İzmir, Manisa, Denizli, Aydın, Uşak, Isparta, Antalya, Alanya, Finike, Marmaris, Bafra, Samsun, Ordu, Giresun, Trabzon, Rize, Hopa, Bat'umi, Zonguldak, Karabük, Kastamonu, Sinop, İnebolu, Çankırı, Yalta, Sevastopol, Sochi, Maykop, Tuapse, Novorossiysk, Nal'chik, Kislovodsk, Nevinnomyssk, Prokhladny, Groznyy, Vladikavkaz, El'brus 5642m, Kazbek 5047m, K'ut'aisi, Tbilisi, Rust'avi, Gyumri, Yerevan, Mount Ararat (Büyükağrı Dağı) 5165m, Khoy, Orūmīyeh, Tabriz, Banghāzī (Benghazi), Al Bayda', Al Jabal al Akhdar, Tubruq, Sīdī Barrānī, Alexandria (Al Iskandarīyah), Marsá Matrūh, El 'Alamein, Tanta, Az Zaqāzīq, Dumyāt (Damietta), Būr Sa'īd (Port Said), Cairo (Al Qāhirah), Giza (Al Jīzah), Banī Suwayf, Al Minyā, Mallawī, Asyūt, Sawhāj, Qinā, Luxor (Al 'Uqşur), Al Khārijah, Aswān, Bawīṭī, Al Farāfirah, Qaşr al Farāfirah, Siwah, Jaghbūb, Jālū, Marādah, Ajdābiyā, Surt, Al Kufrah, Al 'Uwaynāt, Jabal al 'Uwaynāt 1907m, Picco Bette 2286m, Faya, Fada, Ennedi, Emi Koussi 3415m, Ounianga Kébir, Erg du Djourab, Biltine, Abéché, Am Timan, Birao, Abou-Déïa, Goz-Beïda, Wadi Halfa, Akasha, Delgo, Dongola, El 'Atrun, Nubian Desert, Abu Hamed, Atbara, Ed Damer, Shendi, Omdurman, Khartoum, Khartoum North, Wad Medani, Kassala, Gedaref, Sennar, El Obeid, En Nahud, Er Rahad, Umm Ruwaba, Sodiri, Nyala, El Fasher, El Geneina, Kebkabiya, El Da'ein, El Muglad, Kadugli, Rabak, Kosti, Ed Damazin, Paloich, Sumeih, Port Sudan, Suakin, Haiya, Tokar, Halaib, Keren, Asmara, Aksum, Mek'ele, Teseney, Gonder, Bahir Dar, Gedaref, Ras Dashen Terara 4620m, Ethiopian Highlands, Addis Ababa, Desē, Weldiya, Obock, Djibouti, Berbera, San'ā (Sana), Al Hudaydah (Hodeida), Zabid, Ta'izz, Najrān, Sa'dah, Jīzān, Abhā, Al Bāhah, Tathlith, Khaybar, Al Madīnah (Medina), Buraydah, Al Majma'ah, Hā'il, An Nafūd, Taymā', Tabūk, Al Wajh, Yanbu' al Bahr, Jiddah (Jedda), Makkah (Mecca), Aţ Tā'if, Al Qunfudhah, Halabān, Zalim, Halahān, At Tubayq, Al Jawf, Ḥalāt 'Ammār, Ḥaql, 'Ar'ar, Ḥafar al Bāṭin, An Najaf, As Samāwah, Al Hillah, Karbalā', Baghdad, Ba'qūbah, Bayji, Kirkūk, As Sulaymānīyah, Arbīl, Al Mawşil (Mosul), Ar Raqqah, Al Ḥasakah, Dayr az Zawr, Tudmur (Palmyra), Al Fuḥaymī, Halab (Aleppo), Al Lādhiqīyah (Latakia), Ḥamāh, Ḥimş (Homs), Tarṭūs, Tripoli, Beyrouth (Beirut), Dimashq (Damascus), Dūmā, Ma'an, Az Zarqā', Amman, Jerusalem, Tel Aviv-Yafo, Haifa (Hefa), Netanya, Ashdod, Ashqelon, Gaza Strip, Be'ér Sheva', Mizpé Ramon, Elat, 'Aqaba, Al Karak, Nicosia, Lemesós, Lárnaka, Paphos, Tróodos.

(projection: Lambert Azimuthal Equal Area)

0   50 100 150 200 250 300 Km
0   50   100   150   200   250   300 Miles

Population
■ above 5 million
◉ 100,000 to 500,000
▣ 1 million to 5 million
● 50,000 to 100,000
◎ 500,000 to 1 million
○ 10,000 to 50,000
· below 10,000

ASIA

213

KAZAKHSTAN
Aktau
Zhanaozen
Makhachkala
Derbent
uynaksk
Ustyurt Plateau
UZBEKISTAN
Kyzyl Kum
Turkistan
Taraz
KAZAKHSTAN
Shymkent
BISHKEK
Balykchy
Karakol
KYRGYZSTAN
Kirghiz Range
Talas
Naryn
Tien Shan
Kashi
CHINA

Sumqayit
BAKI
(BAKU)
AZERBAIJAN
Qazimämmäd
Türkmenbaşy
Nukus
Uchquduq
Daşoguz
Urganch
Lebap
TOSHKENT
(TASHKENT)
Chirchiq
Angren
Olmaliq
Qo'qon
Namangan
Andijon
Osh
Art
Artux

TURKMENISTAN
Garabogaz Aylagy
Garagum
Balkanabat
Serdar
Merkezi Garagumy
Sėydi
Türkmenabat
Mary
Bojnūrd
Navoiy
Buxoro
Gazli
Kattaqo'rg'on
Qarshi
Samarqand
DUSHANBE
TAJIKISTAN
Kūlob
Khorugh
Pamir
Kashi

Mingačevir
Tabrīz
Marāgheh
Rasht
Zanjān
Qazvīn
Bābol
Amol
Sārī
Gorgān
Shahrud
Aşgabat
Denov
Termiz
Āqchah
Balkh
Mazār-e Sharīf
Eshkāshem
Gilgit
Indus

Ardabīl
Lānkarān
Sanandaj
Hamadān
TEHRĀN
Qom
Semnān
Mashhad
Sabzevār
Meymaneh
Marghī
Chārikār
Asadābād
Asmar
Sandu
Srinagar

Kermānshāh
(Bākhtarān)
Malāyer
Arāk
Borūjerd
Kāshān
Dasht-e Kavīr
Gonābād
Kūshk
Qal'eh-ye Now
Herāt
Shahrak
KĀBOL
(KABUL)
Jalālābād
Peshāwar
ISLĀMĀBĀD
Rāwalpindi
Jhelum

Khorramābād
Najafābād
Eşfahān
Shahreza
Yazd
Ābādeh
Kermānshāh
Anār
Robāṭ-e Khān
Rāvar
Shindand
Anār Darreh
Delārām
Orūzgān
Ghaznī
Gardēz
Khōst
Miānwāli
Gujrānwāla
Amritsar
Jammu

Al Kūt
Al 'Amārah
Dezfūl
Ahvāz
Masjed Soleymān
Kāzerūn
Shīrāz
Dārāb
Sīrjān
Kermān
Dasht-e Lūt
Chakhānsūr
Zābol
Dasht-e Mārgow
Darvīshān
Sūn Buldak
Chaman
Kandahār
Faisalābād
Sāhīwāl
Okāra
Lahore

An Nāṣirīyah
Al Başrah
(Basra)
Khorramshahr
Ābādān
Bam
Zāhedān
Daryā-ye Helmand
Deh Shū
Rīgestān
Quetta
Dera Ghāzi Khān
Multān
Bahāwalnagar

KUWAIT
AL KUWAYT
(KUWAIT)
Bandar-e Būshehr
Ḥafar al Bāṭin
An Nu'ayrīyah
Bandar-e Kangān
Gāvbandi
Hāmūn-e Jaz Mūriān
Īrānshahr
Shāhān Range
Central Makrān Range
Dālbandīn
Sūrāb
Jacobābād
Shikārpur
Sukkur
Lārkāna
Rahīmyār Khān
Bīkāner
Jodhpur
Bārmer
Pāli

AD DAMMĀM
BAHRAIN
AL MANĀMAH
(MANAMA)
Al Hufūf
AD DAWḤAH
(DOHA)
QATAR
ABŪ ZABY
(ABU DHABI)
Dubayy
(Dubai)
Ash Shāriqah
OMAN
Bandar-e'Abbās
Strait of Hormuz
Makran Coast
Konārak
Gulf of Oman
Turbat
Bela
Nawābshāh
Mīrpur Khās
Hyderābād
Karāchi
Mouths of the Indus
Rann of Kachchh
Pālanpur

AR RIYĀḌ
(RIYADH)
Harad
Al 'Ayn
Tarīf
Al Ḥajar al Gharbī
Ṣuḥār
As Suwayq
Ar Rustāq
Abrī
MASQAT
(MUSCAT)
Ṣūr
Adam
Tropic of Cancer
Gulf of Kachchh
Jāmnagar
Gāndhīdhām
Surendranagar
Ahmadābād
Mahesāna
Rājkot
Vadodara
Bhāvnagar
Porbandar
Kāthiāwār Peninsula
Bharuch
Verāval
Surat
Gulf of Khambhāt

Layla
Ramlat Al Wahībah
Al Ghābah
UNITED ARAB EMIRATES

Sulayyil
insula
OMAN
Khalīj Maşīrah
Duqm
Masīrah

Ar Rub' al Khālī
(Empty Quarter)
Al 'Urūq al Mu'tariḍah
Mughshin
Jiddat al Ḥarāsīs
Ṣawqirah

Thamarit
Jabal al Qamar
Ṣalālah
Zufār
Sanāw
Al Mahrah
Damqawt

Riyadh

Ad Dir'iyah
Al Marooj
Al Mursalat
Al Hamra
King Khaled Intl. Airport
Al Roudah Park
Al Ulayah
Al Rawabi Park
Al Quds
Ar Riyāḍ
(Riyadh)
Zoo
Al Malaz
Al Murabba
Al Amir Fahad Park
Al Noor
Dhratal Badiah
Al Masmak Fortress
Al Nasiriyah Gate
Al Hamrah Palace
Main Juma'a Mosque
King Abdul Aziz Manakh Park
Hijrat Laban
Al Madinah As Sinaiiyah
Yamamah
Al Masanya
Al Dar Al Baida
Nammar
Jiza

0   3 Km
0   3 Miles

YEMEN
Ramlat as Sab'atayn
Tarim
Ḥaḍramawt
Ash Shiḥr
Sayhūt
Ar Rawdah
Al Mukallā
huqrah

Arabian

Sea

Gulf of Aden
Caluula
Boosaaso
Shimbiris 2407m
Ceerigaabo
Karin
SOMALIA
OMALILAND
ot internationally recognized)
Raas Xaafuun
Suquṭrā
(Socotra)

19,686ft
13,124ft
9843ft
6562ft
3281ft
1640ft
820ft
328ft
Sea Level
-820ft
-6562ft
-13,124ft

226
232
288

H   I   J   K   L   M   N
1   2   3   4   5   6   7   8   9   10

189

187

129

ROMANIA

BUCUREŞTI
(BUCHAREST)

BULGARIA

UKRAINE

AVTONOMNA
RESPUBLIKA KRYM

Simferopol'
Sevastopol'
Yalta

Sea of Azov

Kerch

Novorossiysk

B l a c k   S e a

İSTANBUL

TEKIRDAĞ

EDIRNE

KIRKLARELİ

ÇANAKKALE

Thracian Sea

Aegean Islands

Lésvos (Lesbos)

Chíos

İZMIR

MANISA

BALIKESIR

BURSA

KOCAELİ

YALOVA

SAKARYA

BILECIK

ESKIŞEHIR

KÜTAHYA

DÜZCE

BOLU

ÇANKIRI

ANKARA

KIRIKKALE

ÇORUM

AMASYA

TOKAT

SIVAS

KIRŞEHIR

NEVŞEHIR

KAYSERI

YOZGAT

AKSARAY

KONYA

KARAMAN

NIĞDE

ADANA

MERSİN

ANTALYA

ISPARTA

BURDUR

DENIZLI

AYDIN

MUĞLA

AFYON

UŞAK

GAZIANTEP

KAHRAMANMARAŞ

HATAY

Antakya

HALAB
Halab
(Aleppo)

AL LĀDHIQĪYAH

IDLIB

HAMAH

ṬARṬŪS

Ḥimṣ
(Homs)

T   U   R   K   E   Y

Anatolia

GREECE

Dodekánisa

Ródos
(Rhodes)

Kárpathos

Kríti

CYPRUS

TURKISH REPUBLIC OF
NORTHERN CYPRUS
(recognised only by Turkey)

NICOSIA

Lemesós (Limassol)

Larnaka

Gazimağusa
(Ammóchostos, Famagusta)

Girne
(Kerynia)

LEBANON

BEYROUTH
(BEIRUT)

DIMASHQ
(DAMASCUS)

M e d i t e r r a n e a n   S e a

6000m
4000m
3000m
2000m
1000m
500m
250m
100m
Sea
Level
-250m
-2000m
-4000m

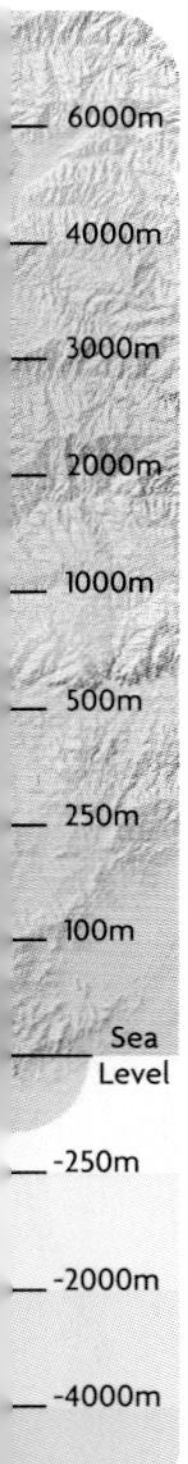

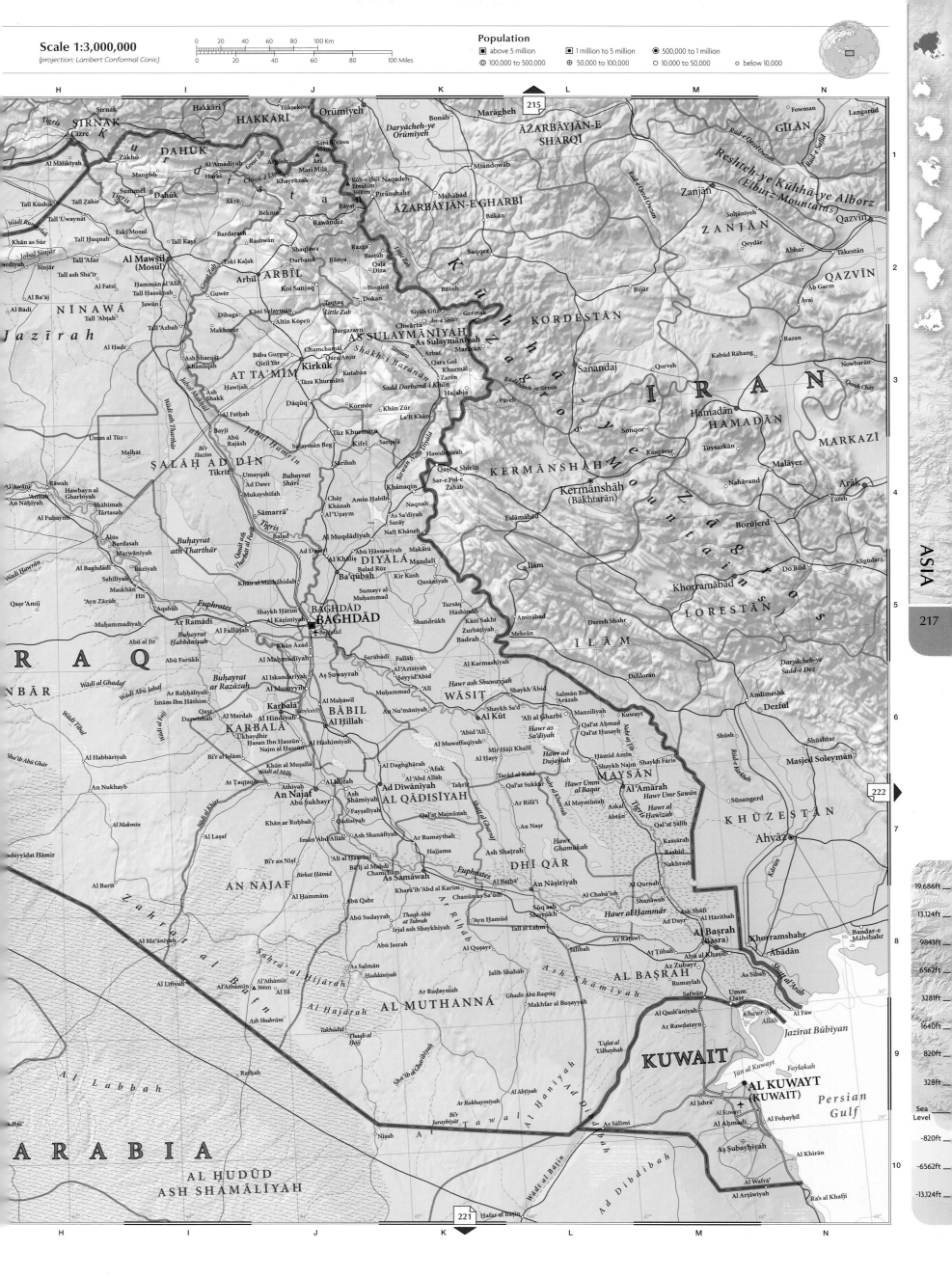

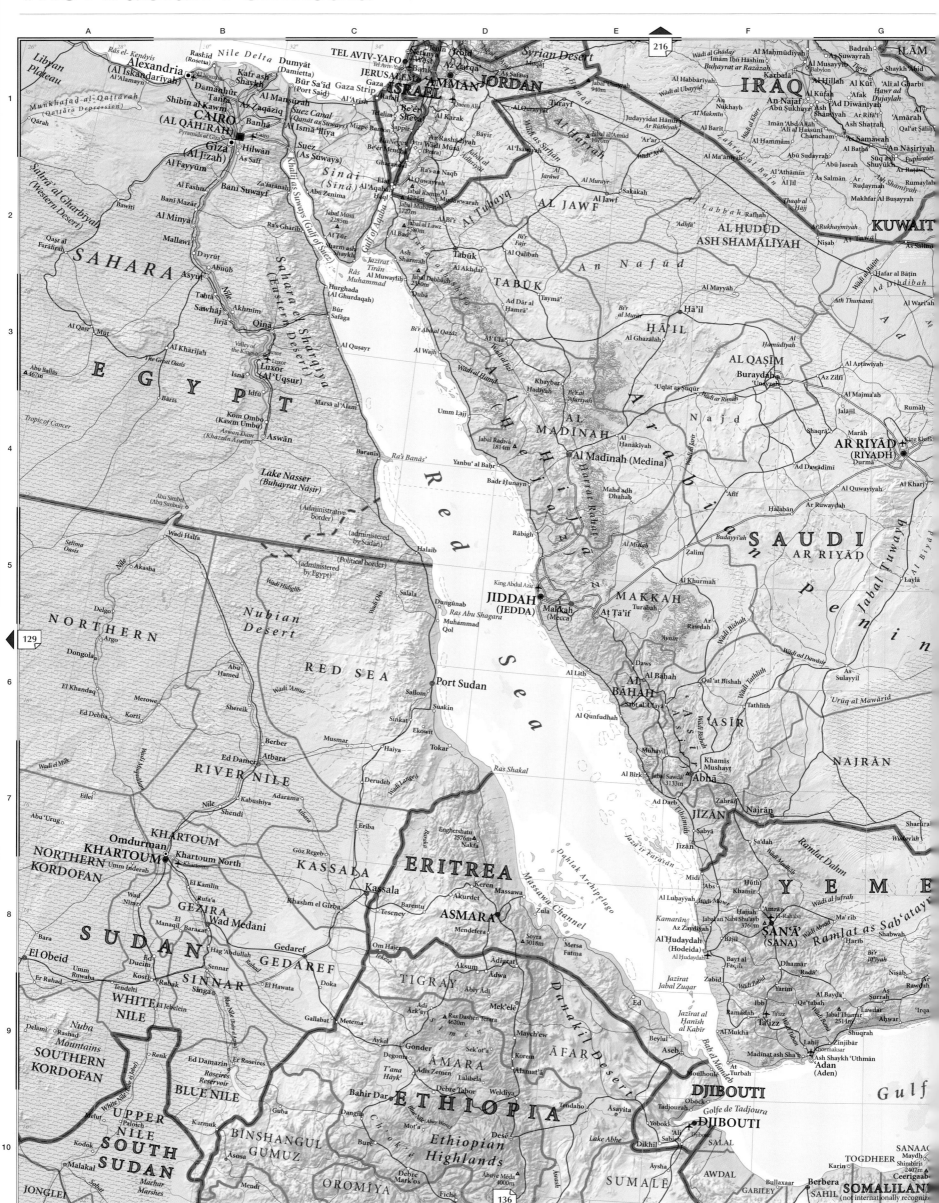

ASIA

222

6000m
4000m
3000m
2000m
1000m
500m
250m
100m
Sea Level
-250m
-2000m
-4000m

TURKEY

ARMENIA

AZERBAIJAN

BAKI (BAKU)

Caspian Sea

SYRIA

IRAQ

BAGHDAD

Syrian Desert

KUWAIT

AL KUWAYT (KUWAIT)

SAUDI ARABIA

An Nafud

AL HUDUD ASH SHAMALIYAH

AL JAWF

HA'IL

AL QASIM

AR RIYAD (RIYADH)

Najd

ASH SHARQIYAH

Ad Dammam

AL MANAMAH (MANAMA)

BAHRAIN

QATAR

AD DAWHAH (DOHA)

UNITED ARAB EMIRATES

ABU ZABY (ABU DHABI)

Persian Gulf

Gulf of Bahrain

IRAN

ESFAHAN

Esfahan

TEHRAN

Shiraz

FARS

Tabriz

Rasht

HAMADAN

MARKAZI

KERMANSHAH

LORESTAN

KHUZESTAN

Ahvaz

Al Basrah (Basra)

Abadan

Tropic of Cancer

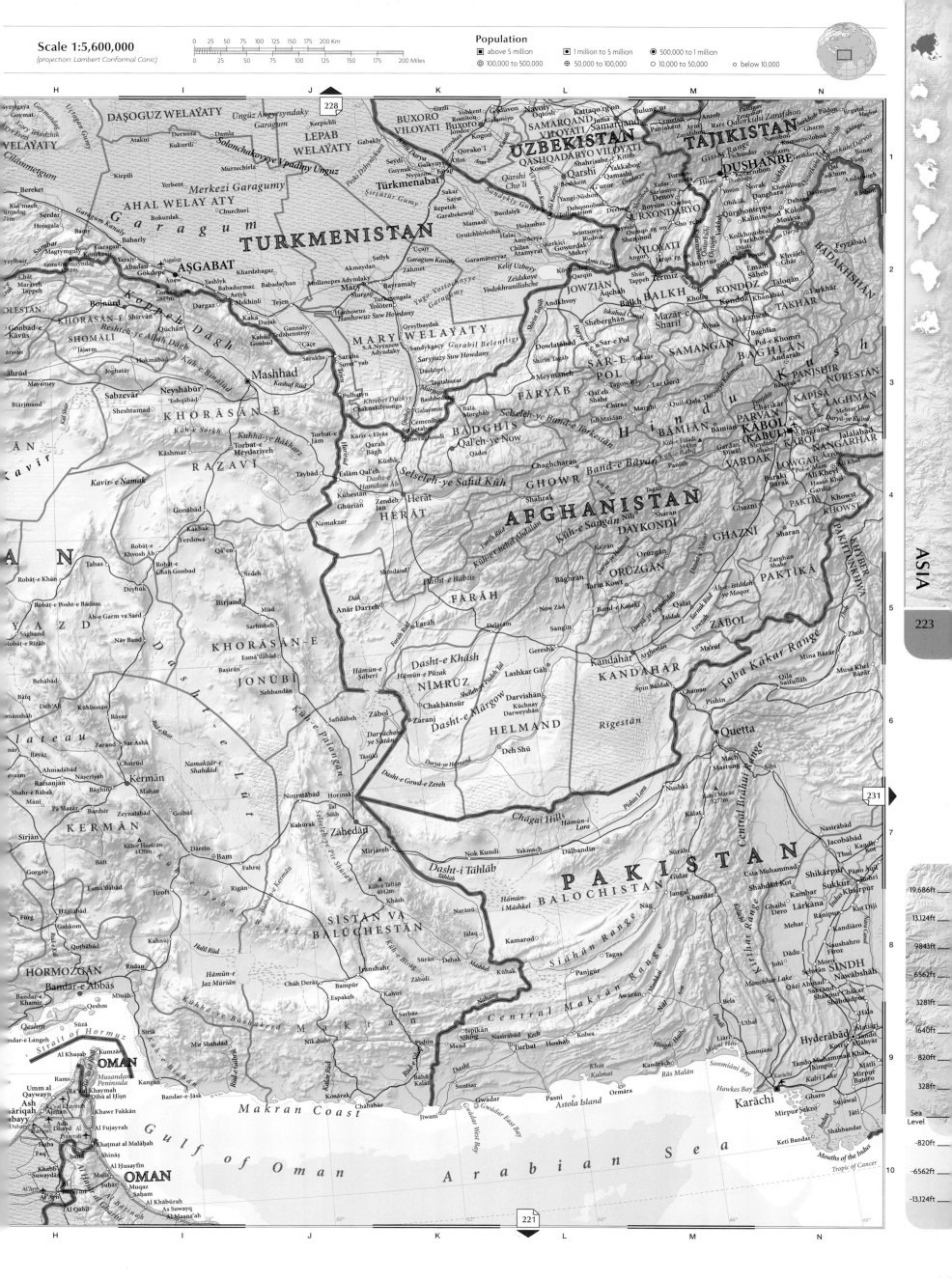

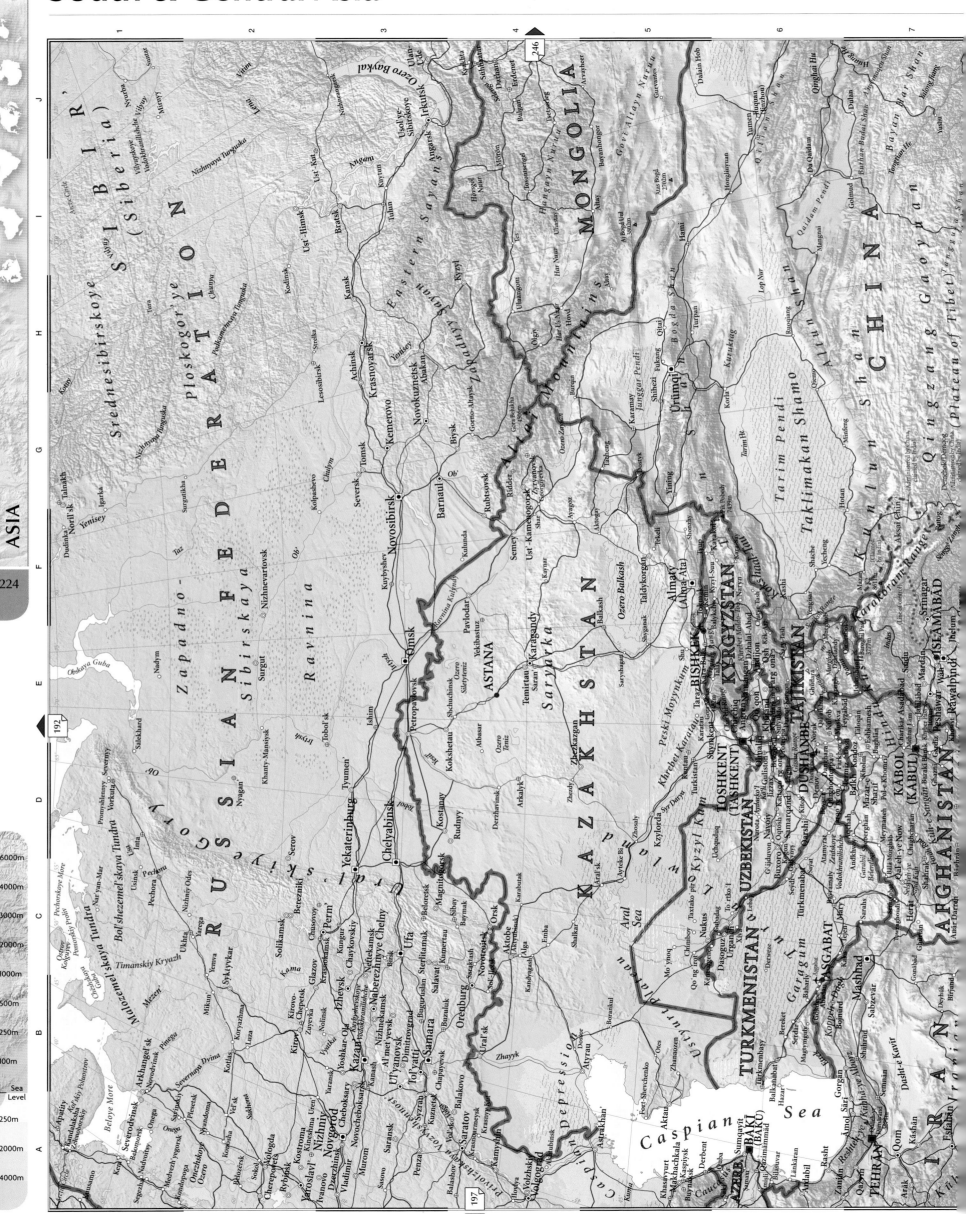

Kazakhstan

RUSSIAN

RESPUBLIKA MORDOVIYA
RESPUBLIKA TATARSTAN
RESPUBLIKA BASHKORTOSTAN
KURGANSKAYA OBLAST'

Ul'yanovsk
Saransk
Penza
PENZENSKAYA OBLAST'
Samara
Syzran'
Tol'yatti
Novokuybyshevsk
SAMARSKAYA OBLAST
Ufa
Chelyabinsk
Miass
Zlatoust
Magnitogorsk
Sterlitamak
Salavat
Orenburg
ORENBURGSKAYA OBLAST
Kostanay
Rudnyy
Troitsk
Saratov
Engel's
SARATOVSKAYA OBLAST'
Ural'sk
Aktobe (Aktyubinsk)
Orsk
Novotroitsk
Turgayskaya Stolovaya Strana
KOSTANAY
VOLGOGRADSKAYA OBLAST'
Volzhskiy
Akhtubinsk
ZAPADNYY KAZAKHSTAN
Derzhavinsk

Ryn-Peski
Atyrau
ATYRAU
Caspian Depression
AKTYUBINSK
Gory Mugodzhary
KA

RESPUBLIKA KALMYKIYA
Astrakhan
KAZAKHSTANSKAYA OBLAST'

RESPUBLIKA DAGESTAN
Makhachkala

Aral Sea
Ustyurt Plateau
Plato Mangystau
MANGYSTAU
Aktau
Zaliv Mangystau
Fort-Shevchenko

Sor Mertvyy Kultuk

Space Launching Centre
Baykonyr
KZYLORDA
Kyzylorda

Qoraqalpog'iston
QORAQALPOG'ISTON RESPUBLIKASI
Nukus
Lowland
NAVOIY VILOYATI
Kyzylkum
Navoiy

Caspian Sea

AZERBAIJAN
Sumqayıt
BAKI (BAKU)

Daşoguz
Urganch
XORAZM VILOYAT
Xiva
UZBEKISTAN
BUXORO VILOYATI
Buxoro
SAMARQAND VILOYATI
QASHQADARYO VILOYATI
Qarshi

BALKAN WELAÝATY
Krasnovodskoye Plato
Türkmenbaşy
Balkanabat
DAŞOGUZ WELAÝATY Garagum
LEBAP WELAÝATY
Türkmenabat
Merkezi Garagumy
AHAL WELAÝATY
Garagum
TURKMENISTAN
Aşgabat
MARY WELAÝATY
Mary

Köpetdag Gershi
IRAN

Ardabil
Rasht
Gorgan

Scale 1:6,250,000
(projection: Lambert Conformal Conic)

| 0 | 25 | 50 | 75 | 100 | 125 | 150 | 175 | 200 Km |
| 0 | 25 | 50 | 75 | 100 | 125 | 150 | 175 | 200 Miles |

Population
■ above 5 million
⊡ 1 million to 5 million
◉ 500,000 to 1 million
◎ 100,000 to 500,000
⊕ 50,000 to 100,000
⊙ 10,000 to 50,000
○ below 10,000

192

238

231

19,686ft
13,124ft
9843ft
6562ft
3281ft
1640ft
820ft
328ft
Sea Level
-820ft
-6562ft
-13,124ft

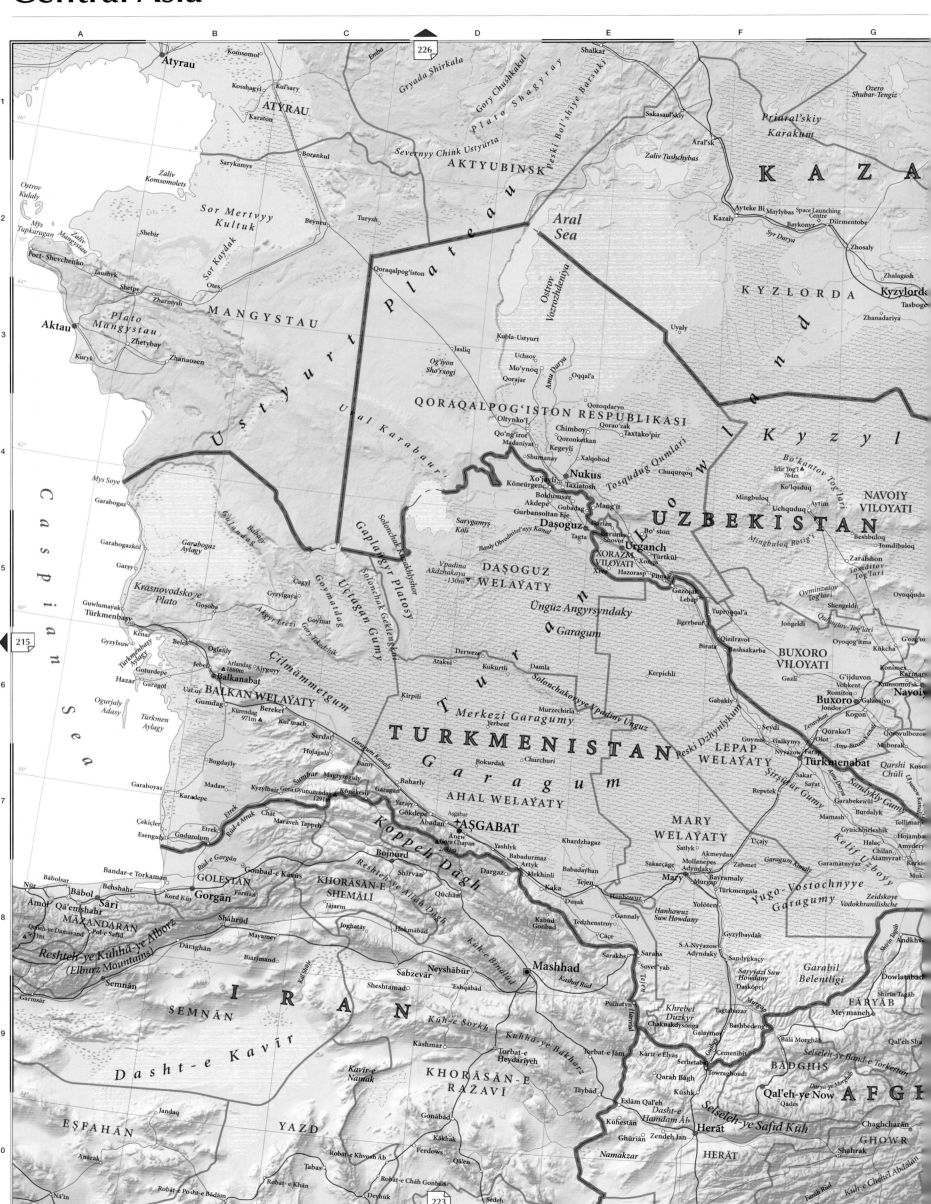

226

215

223

ASIA

228

Atyrau

Komsomol
Kul'sary
Kosshagyl
Karaton

ATYRAU

Sarykamys
Borankul

Ostrov
Kulaly

Mys
Tupkaragan

Zaliv
Komsomolets

Sor Mertvyy
Kultuk

Shebir

Beyneu
Turysh

Post-Shevchenko

Shetpe

MANGYSTAU

Zharmysh

Aktau

Plato
Mangystau

Zhetybay

Kuryk

Zhanaozen

Mys Soye

Garabogaz

Garabogazköl

Garabogaz
Aylagy

Garsy

Krasnovodskoye
Plato

Goshoba

Türkmenbaşy

Guwlumayak

Gyzylsuw

Kenar

Caspian Sea

Gryada Shirkala

Gory Chushkakul

Emba

Shalkar

Plato Shagyray

Peski Bol'shiye Barsuki

Severnyy Chink Ustyurta

Sakasaul'skiy

Aral'sk

AKTYUBINSK

Aral
Sea

Zaliv Tushchybas

KAZA

Ozero
Shubar-Tengiz

Priaral'skiy
Karakum

Ayteke Bi
Maylybas
Space Launching
Centre
Baykonyr
Diirmentobe

Kazaly
Qorao'zak
Syr Darya

Zhosaly

Zhalagash

KYZLORDA

Kyzylorda

Tasboge

Zhanadariya

Qoraqalpog'iston

Ostrov
Vozrozhdeniya

Kubla-Ustyurt

Uyaly

Jaslıq

Uchsoy

Og'iyon
Sho'rxogi

Mo'ynoq

Amu Darya

Qorajar

Oqqal'a

Qozoqdaryo

QORAQALPOG'ISTON RESPUBLIKASI

Chimboy
Qozonketkan
Taxtako'pir

Oltynko'l

Qo'ng'irot

Madaniyat

Xalqobod

Shumanay

Kegeyli

Nukus

Xo'jayli

Taxiatosh

Könergench

Bokdumsaz

Akdepe

Gubadag

Mang'it

Sarygamyş
Köli

Gurbansoltan Eje

Dashoguz

Gurlan

Berunıy

Shovot

Tagta

Bo' ston

Chuqurqog

Bo'kantov Tog'i
Idir Tog'i
764m

**NAVOIY
VILOYATI**

Beshbuloq

Mingbuloq

Uchquduq

Aytim

Tomditovul

Ko'lquduq

Zarafshon

Tomditov-
Tog'lari

UZBEKISTAN

Urganch

**XORAZM
VILOYATI**

Xiva
Hazarasp
Pitnak

Gazojak
Lebap

**DAŞOGUZ
WELAŸATY**

Vpadina
Akdzhakaya
-130m

 Üngüz Angyrsyndaky
Garagum

Jigerbent

Tuproqqal'a

Birata

Qizilravot

Bashsakarba

Oymınzatov
Tog'lari

Shiengeldi

Jongeldi

Oyoqog'itma

Quhujatov-Tog'lari

Oyoqog'itma

G'ozg'on

Kokcha

**BUXORO
VILOYATI**

Gazli

G'ijduvon

Vobkent
Romiton

Konimex

Karman

Buxoro

Galaosiyo

Navoiy

Derweze

Atakuy

Kükürtli

Damla

Kerpichli

Kirpili

Türkmenabat

Qorako'l

Qorovulbozor

Muborak

Qarshi
Chüli

Akyr Erezi

Goymat

Gory Takezhlik

Goymatdag

Uştagan Gumy

Goymatdag

Cagyl

Gyzylgaya

Madaw

Bugdayly

Garaboyaz

Ogurjaly
Adasy

Türkmen
Aylagy

BALKAN WELAŸATY

Balkanabat

Jebel

Garagöl

Hazar

Goturdepe

Uzil'up

Gumdag

Bereket

Küren dag
971m

Kul'mach

Serdar

Hojagala

Bamy

Baharly

TURKMENISTAN

Garagum

Merkezi Garagumy

Yerbent

Bokurdak

Churchuri

Murzechirla

AHAL WELAŸATY

Solonchakovyye Vpadiny Unguz

Gabakly

Seýdi

Galkynyş

Nyýazow

**LEPAP
WELAŸATY**

Peski Dzhynlykum

Olot

Amu-Buxoro

Tarap

Sakar

Saýat

Repetek

Garabekewül

Mamash

Burdalyk

Gyuichbirleshik

Chilan

Halaç

Atamyrat

Hojambo

Kerki

Şirşütür Gumy

Sandykly Gumy

Kelif Uzboýy

Üçajy

Şatlyk

Akmeydan

Zähmet

Garagum Kanaly

Garamätnyýaz

**MARY
WELAŸATY**

Mollanepes
Adyndaky

Bayramaly

Mary

Türkmengala

Murgap

Yolöten

Yugo-Vostochnyye
Garagumy

Vodokhranilishche

Zeidskoye
Vodokhranilishche

Cilmämmetgum

Arlandag
1880m
Ajyguyy

Koppeh Dagh

Gyzylbair Gora Gyunuzyndaky
1291m

Könekesir

Magtymguly

Gara ganl

Sumbar

Etrek

Maraveh Tappeh

Esenguly

Gudurolum

Çekiçler

Karadepe

Etrek

Rüd-e Atrak

Çât

Rüd-e Gorgân

Bandar-e Torkaman

Behshahr

GOLESTĀN

Gorgan

Fârsiân

Gonbad-e Kāvus

Yarajy

Gökdepe

Abadan

Anew

Gora Chapan
2889m

Aşgabat

Yashlyk

Babadurmaz

Artyk

Mekhinli

Dargaz

Kaka

**KHORĀSĀN-E
SHEMĀLİ**

Bojnürd

Reshteh-ye Allāh Dāgh

Shîrvân

Quchân

Babadayhan

Tejen

Dușak

Hanhowuz

Gannaly

Sarahs

S.A. Nyýazow
Adyndaky

Çäçe

Tedzhenstroy

Kabüd
Gonbad

Hokmābād

Joghatāy

Khardzhagaz

Sakarçäge

Mashhad

Sarakhs

Sandygkaçy

Sovet'yab

Gyzylbaydak

Sarýyazy Suw
Howdany

Garabil
Belentligi

Daşköpri

Nür

Bābolsar

Bābol

Qa'emshahr

Āmol

Sārī

Kord Küy

MĀZANDARĀN

Qaleh-ye Damāvand

Reshteh-ye Kuhhā-ye Alborz
(Elburz Mountains)

Semnān

SEMNĀN

Shāhrüd

Mayameh

Dārighān

Biārjmand

Pol-e Safid

Jājarm

Sabzevār

Sheshtamad

Neyshābür

Eshqābād

Kāshmar

**KHORĀSĀN-E
RAZAVĪ**

Torbat-e Jām

Kāriz-e Elyās

Kühestān

Herāt

Sețelheh

Cemenibit

Qarah Bāgh

Tăybād

Eslām Qal'eh

Dasht-e
Hamdam Ab

Zendeh Jan

Qal'eh-ye Now

Qādes

Selseleh-ye Safid Küh

HERĀT

Chaghcharān

Meymaneh

Bālā Morghāb

Shirin Tagāb

FĀRYĀB

Dowlatābād

Andkhvoy

Qal'eh-ye
Chehel Abdālān

Shahrak

GHOWR

AFC

Gonābād

Kākhak

Ferdows

Qā'en

Dasht-e Kavīr

Kavir-e
Namak

IRAN

Anārak

Na'in

Nür

Robāt-e Khvosh Āb

Ţabas

Robāt-e Po-sht-e Bādām

Robāt-e Khān

Robāt-e Chāh Gonbad

Deyhük

Sedeh

Jandaq

ESFAHĀN

YAZD

6000m
4000m
3000m
2000m
1000m
500m
250m
100m
Sea
Level
-250m
-2000m
-4000m

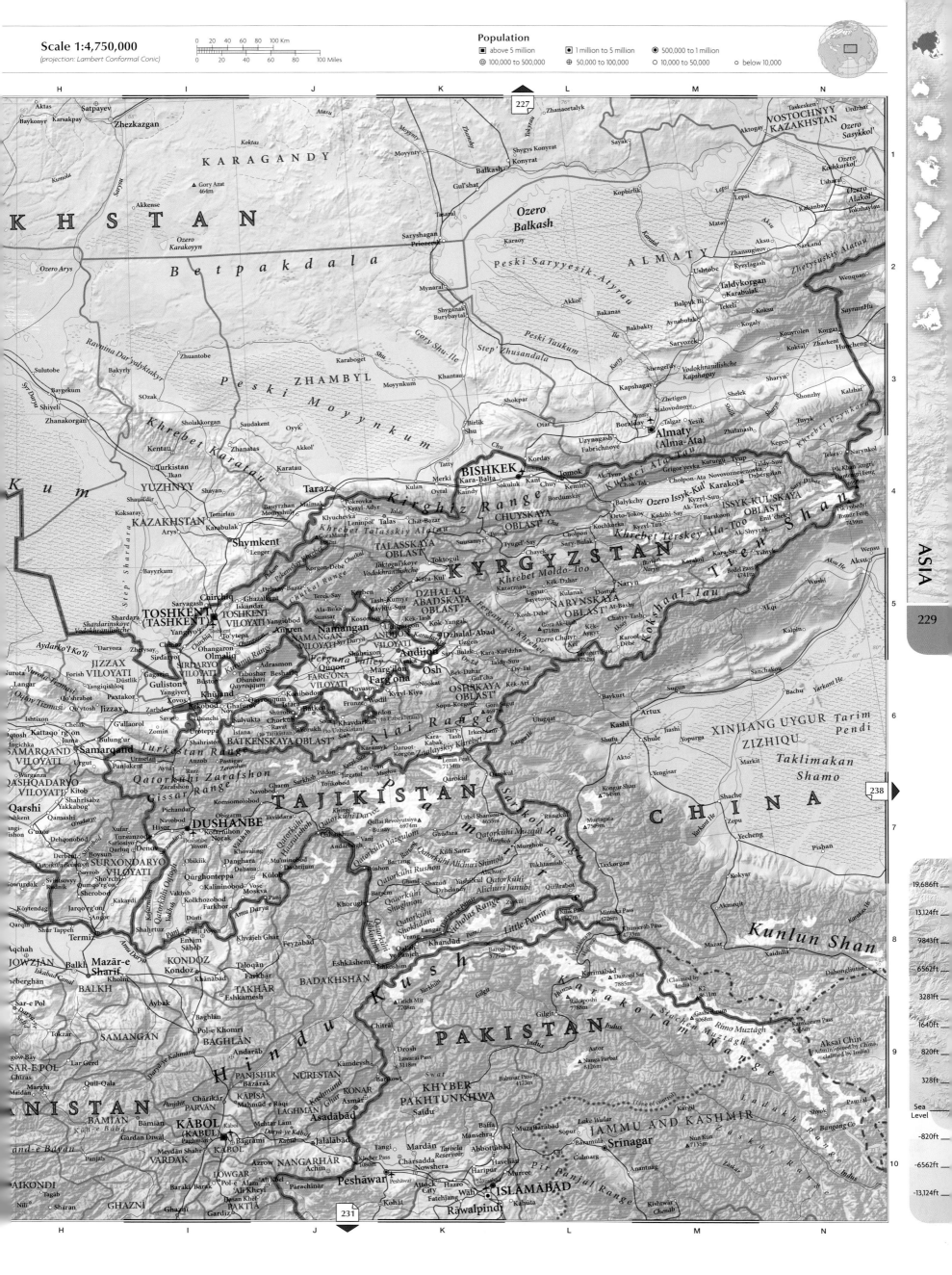

ASIA

230

223

Countries & Regions

TURKMENISTAN
UZBEKISTAN
DUSHANBE
AFGHANISTAN
IRAN
PAKISTAN
OMAN
U.A.E.
MASQAT (MUSCAT)

Provinces / Regions

GOLESTĀN · KHORĀSĀN-E SHEMĀLĪ · KHORĀSĀN-E RAZAVĪ · SEMNĀN · YAZD · KHORĀSĀN-E JANŪBĪ · KERMĀN · HORMOZGĀN · SĪSTĀN VA BALŪCHESTĀN · Iranian Plateau

MARY WELAYATY · AHAL WELAYATY · LEBAP WELAYATY

BĀDGHIS · HERĀT · GHOWR · FARĀH · NĪMRŪZ · HELMAND · KANDAHĀR · ZĀBOL · ORŪZGĀN · GHAZNĪ · PAKTĪKĀ · DAĪKONDĪ · BĀMĪĀN · PARVAN · VARDAK · BARAKĪ BARAK · FĀRYĀB · SAR-E POL · JOWZJĀN · BALKH · SAMANGAN · KONDOZ

BALOCHISTAN · SINDH · Central Brahui Range · Central Makran Range · Kirthar Range · Siahan Range · Toba Kakar Range · Chagai Hills

Cities & Towns

Aşgabat · Mashhad · Qal'eh-ye Now · Herāt · Kandahār · Lashkar Gāh · Zābol · Zaranj · Zāhedān · Kermān · Bam · Bandar-e 'Abbās · Quetta · Karāchi · Hyderābād · Sukkur · Larkāna · Shikārpur · Gwādar · Pasni · Ormāra · Turbat · Panjgūr · Chāh Bahār · Jīwani · MASQAT (MUSCAT)

Water Bodies

Gulf of Oman · Arabian Sea · Makran Coast · Strait of Hormuz · Dasht-e Kavīr · Dasht-e Lūt · Dasht-e Mārgow · Rigestān · Hāmūn-e Sāberī · Mouths of the Indus

Elevation scale

6000m · 4000m · 3000m · 2000m · 1000m · 500m · 250m · 100m · Sea Level · -250m · -2000m · -4000m

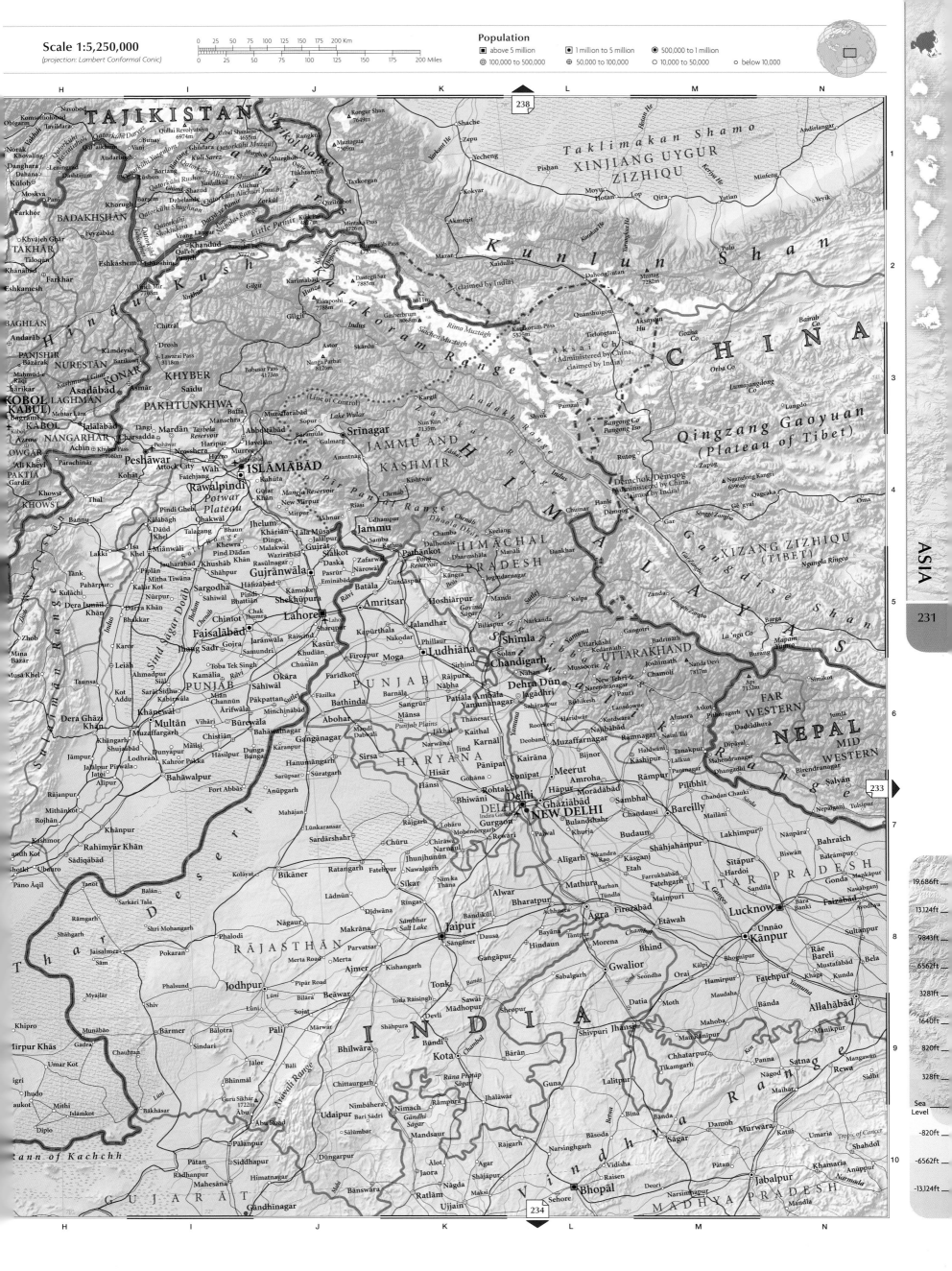

Northern India, Nepal & Bangladesh

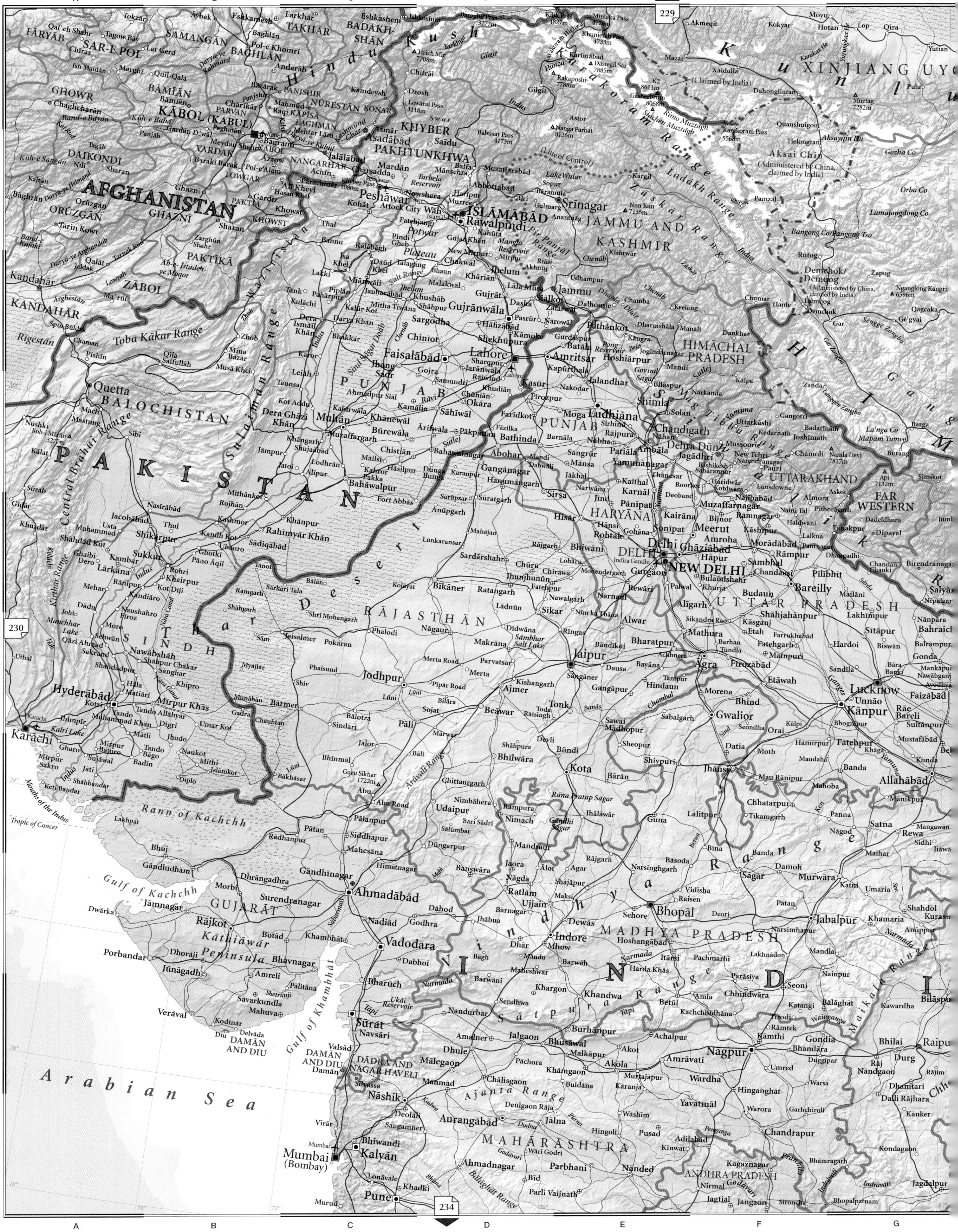

AFGHANISTAN

PAKISTAN

KANDAHAR

BALOCHISTAN

SINDH

PUNJAB

INDIA

RAJASTHAN

GUJARAT

MADHYA PRADESH

MAHARASHTRA

UTTAR PRADESH

HARYANA

HIMACHAL PRADESH

UTTARAKHAND

JAMMU AND KASHMIR

XINJIANG UYG.

ANDHRA PRADESH

Hindu Kush

Karakoram Range

Ladakh Range

Zaskar Range

Pir Panjal Range

Sulaiman Range

Central Brahui Range

Kirthar Range

Toba Kakar Range

Aravali Range

Satpura Range

Vindhya Range

Ajanta Range

Maikala Range

Thar Desert

Rann of Kachchh

Gulf of Kachchh

Gulf of Khambhat

Arabian Sea

Mouths of the Indus

Tropic of Cancer

KABOL (KABUL)

ISLAMABAD

Rawalpindi

Lahore

Peshawar

Srinagar

Jammu

Amritsar

Ludhiana

Chandigarh

Shimla

Dehra Dun

NEW DELHI

DELHI

Meerut

Jaipur

Agra

Gwalior

Lucknow

Kanpur

Allahabad

Jabalpur

Nagpur

Bhopal

Indore

Ahmadabad

Vadodara

Surat

Mumbai (Bombay)

Pune

Karachi

Hyderabad

Quetta

Jodhpur

Bikaner

Udaipur

Kota

Nashik

Aurangabad

Ganges

Indus

Narmada

Tapi

Sutlej

Chenab

Jhelum

Ravi

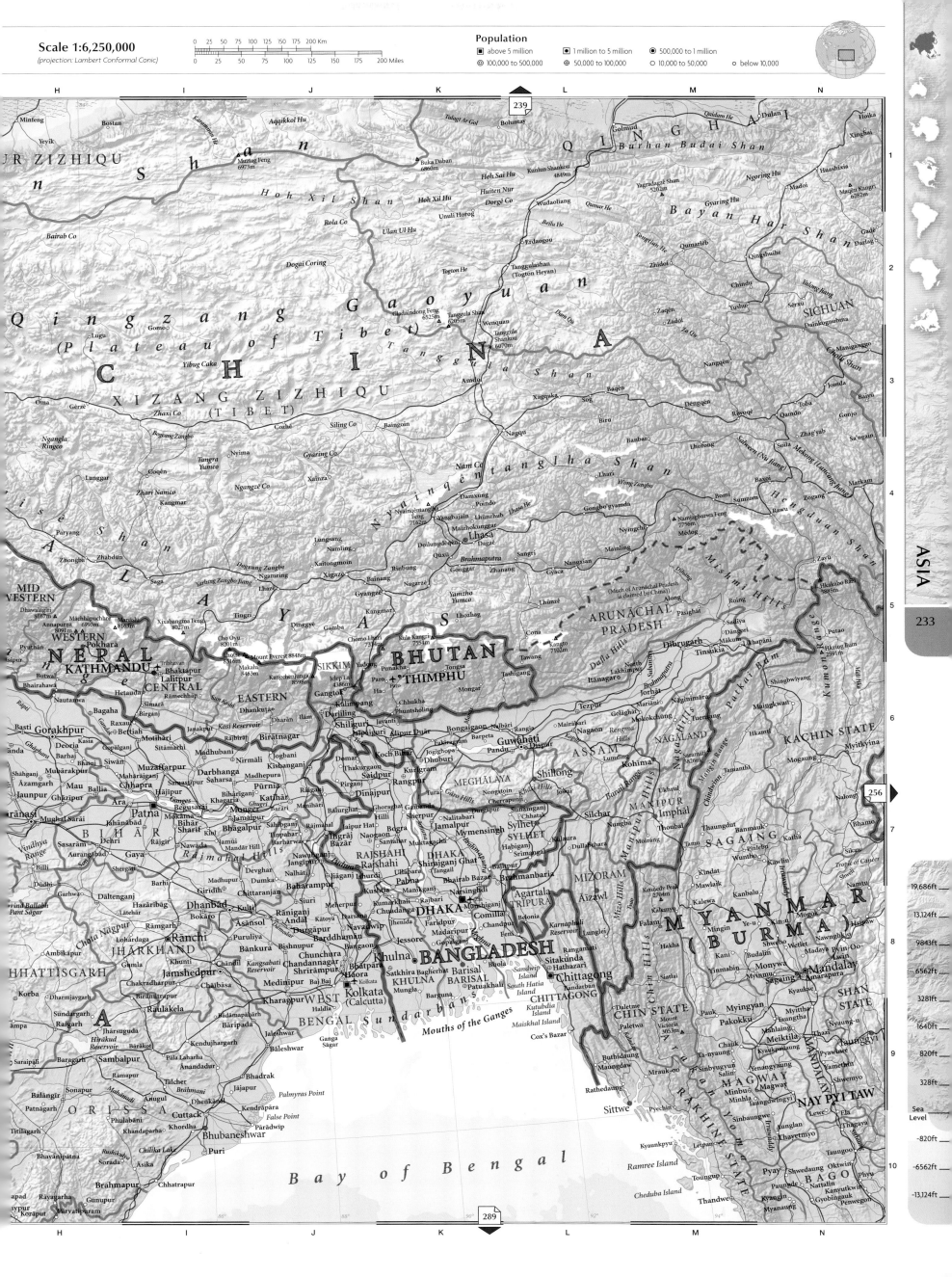

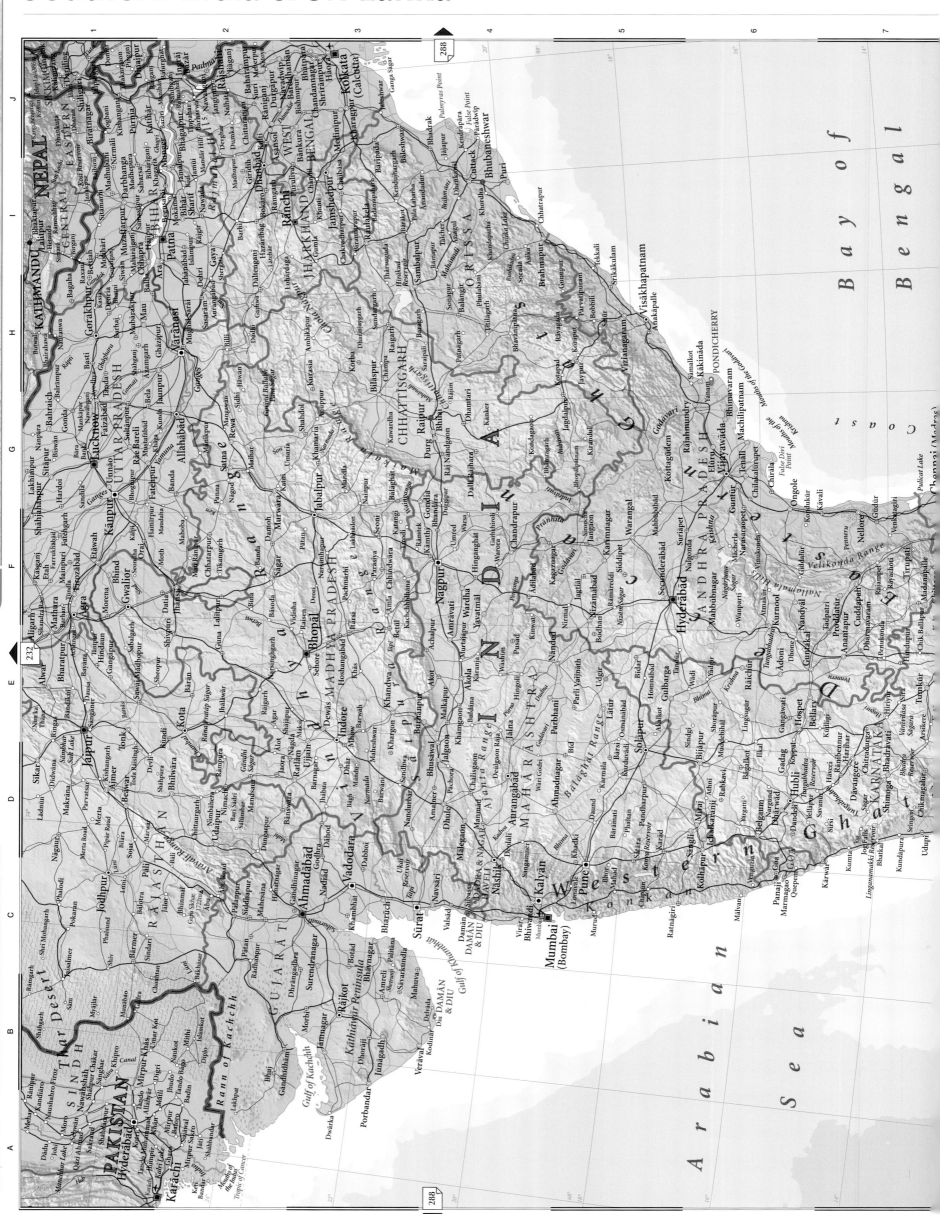

RUSSIAN

Omsk Irtysh Tomsk Achinsk Krasnoyarsk Kansk Ust'-Ilimsk Ust'-Kut
Kostanay Rudny Tatarsk Novosibirsk Yurga Bratsk
Kokshetau Shchuchinsk Berdsk Kemerovo Leninsk-Kuznetskiy Nizhneudinsk Angara Tayshet
Derzhavinsk Atbasar Karasuk Kiselevsk Novokuznetsk Abakan Minusinsk Zima Usol'ye-Sibirskoye Ozero Baykal
Arkalyk ASTANA Pavlodar Barnaul Novoaltaysk Mezhdurechensk Abaza Kyzyl Cheremkhovo Angarsk Irkutsk
Zhezkazgan Temirtau Karagandy Semey Ust'-Kamenogorsk Gorno-Altaysk Ak-Dovurak Selenginsk Ulan-Ude
Saryarka Shar Zyryanovsk Gora Belukha 4506m Erzin Kyakhta
KAZAKHSTAN Shar Georgiyevka Uvs Nuur Nogoonnuur Tsetserleg Sukhbaatar
Betpakdala Balkash Konyrat Ayagoz Aktogay Zaysan Burqin Altai Mountains Olgiy Ulaangom Hyargas Nuur Moron Erdenet Darhan
Ozero Balkash Saryshagan Ozero Zaysan Tacheng Tolbo Hovd Har Us Nuur Dzereg Uliastay Hangayn Nuruu Bulgan Ondorhaan
Buribaytal Ozero Akakol' Dostyk Karamay ULAANBAATAR (ULAN BATOR)
Saryozek Tekeli Shihezi Bayanhongor Arvayheer Mandalgovi
Shu Taldykorgan Yining Qitai MONGOLIA Choyr Ondorhaan
Taraz BISHKEK Almaty ÜRÜMQI Qijiaojing Hami Aj Bogd Uul 3802m Tsogt-Ovoo Saynshand
Shymkent Kapshagay Shonzhy Turpan Atas Bogd 2702m Dalandzadgad
KYRGYZSTAN Karakol Tien Shan Korla Kuruktag Govi Altayn Nuruu GOBI
Osh Naryn Kokshaal-Tau Tarim He Honglluyuan Dalain Hob Linhe Baotou
Kashi Tarim Pendi Anxi Yumen Qilian Shan Yabrai Shan Wuhai Ordos
XINJIANG UYGUR ZIZHIQU Lop Nur Jinchang Shandan Yinchuan
Taklimakan Shamo Ruoqiang Altun Shan Da Qaidam Qaidam Pendi Tengger Shamo NINGXIA Wuzhong
Shache Yecheng Qiemo Mangnai Golmud Delhi Qinghai Hu Xining GANSU Guyuan Suide
Hotan Kunlun Shan Burhan Budai Shan Dulan QINGHAI Lanzhou Tongchuan
Aksai Chin Qiang Bayan Har Shan Linxia Baoji Xianyang
Srinagar JAMMU AND KASHMIR Rutog C H I N A Yushu Anyemaqen Shan Tianshui Xi'an SHAANXI
Jammu Demchok Dogai Coring Amdo Tanggula Shan Markam Mianyang Hanzhong Ankang
Gujranwala Gar Qingzang Gaoyuan (Plateau of Tibet) Nyima Nagqu Luhuo Litang SICHUAN Chengdu Nanchong CHONGQING
Lahore HIMACHAL PRADESH Nam Co Damxung Qamdo Zhongdian Ya'an Sichuan Pendi Wanzhou Lichuan
Amritsar Shimla Nyainqentanglha Shan Lhasa Gongga Shan 7556m Leshan Chongqing
Ludhiana Chandigarh Xigaze Maizhokunggar Namjagbarwa Feng 7756m Zigong Neijiang Yibin
PUNJAB Dehra Dun Gyangze Mount Everest 8848m ARUNACHAL PRADESH Xichang Zunyi Huaihua
Delhi NEW DELHI UTTARAKHAND NEPAL Pokhara Itanagar Dibrugarh Panzhihua GUIZHOU Guiyang
Jaipur KATHMANDU Lalitpur Darjiling Gangtok THIMPHU ASSAM Dali Kunming Kaili Duyun
Agra Lucknow Gorakhpur Biratnagar BHUTAN Guwahati Qujing Anshun
Gwalior Kanpur Faizabad Koch Bihar Shillong Kohima YUNNAN Liuzhou
Jhansi Allahabad Varanasi Patna Rangpur MEGHALAYA Imphal Baoshan Kunming Guilin
BIHAR Bhagalpur Dinajpur Silchar MANIPUR Lincang GUANGXI ZHUANGZU ZIZHIQU
Sagar Gaya BANGLADESH Sylhet MIZORAM MYANMAR (BURMA) Gejiu Nanning Yulin
Bhopal Jabalpur JHARKHAND DHAKA Comilla Aizawl Lashio Red River Qinzhou
MADHYA PRADESH Asansol Pabna Agartala Falam Mandalay Keng Tung Beihai
Satpura Range Ranchi Bankura Khulna Barisal Chittagong Monywa Amarapura Shan Plateau HANOI Hainan
INDIA Jamshedpur Kolkata Howrah Kharagpur Chin Hills Pakokku Myingyan Jinghong HA NOI Haikou
Raulakela WEST BENGAL Mouths of the Ganges Arakan Yoma NAY PYI TAW Chiang Rai LAOS HAINAN
Nagpur Durg Bilaspur Sambalpur Mahanadi Baleshwar Minbu Thayetmyo Chiang Mai Louangphabang Hainan Dao Sanya
MAHARASHTRA Raipur CHHATTISGARH ORISSA Cuttack Bhubaneshwar Sittwe Pyay VIANGCHAN (VIENTIANE)
Chandrapur Gondia Jagdalpur Puri Brahmapur Ramree Island Cheduba Island Thandwe Pathein Bago Hinthada THAILAND
Hyderabad ANDHRA PRADESH Bay of Bengal Hinthada Yangon (Rangoon) Mawlamyine Nakhon Sawan Da Nang
Vijayawada Machilipatnam Mouths of the Irrawaddy Kyaikkami Tavoy Pakxe Champasak Quang Ngai

Western China

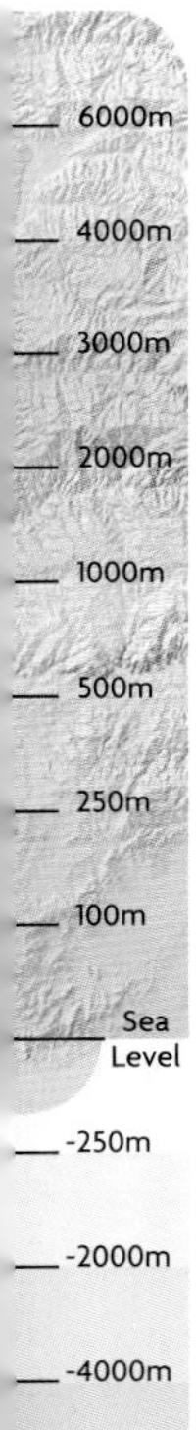

230

Scale legend:
- 6000m
- 4000m
- 3000m
- 2000m
- 1000m
- 500m
- 250m
- 100m
- Sea Level
- -250m
- -2000m
- -4000m

KAZAKHSTAN

RUSS FED.

KYRGYZSTAN

UZBEK.

TAJIKISTAN

AFGHANISTAN

PAKISTAN

INDIA

NEPAL

BHUTAN

CHINA

XINJIANG UYGUR ZIZHIQU

XIZANG ZIZHIQU (TIBET)

Taklimakan Shamo

Tarim Pendi

Kunlun Shan

Altun Shan

Junggar Pendi

Gurbantünggüt Shamo

Tien Shan

Qingzang (Plateau)

Bishkek

Almaty (Alma-Ata)

Toshkent (Tashkent)

Dushanbe

Ürümqi

Islāmābād

Srinagar

New Delhi

Kathmandu

Thimphu

Southeast China

QINGHAI

GANSU

NINGXIA

SHAANXI

SHANXI

XIZANG ZIZHIQU (TIBET)

SICHUAN

HUBEI

SHI CHINA

CHONGQING

INDIA

ARUNACHAL PRADESH
(Much of Arunachal Pradesh is claimed by China)

Qingzang Gaoyuan
(Plateau of Tibet)

YUNNAN

GUIZHOU

HUNAN

GUANGXI ZHUANGZU ZIZHIQU

KACHIN STATE

MYANMAR
(BURMA)

SHAN STATE

KAYAH STATE

KAYIN STATE

THAILAND

LAOS

VIETNAM

HAINAN

Hainan Dao

Gulf of Tongking

Lanzhou
Xining
Xianyang
Xi'an
Luoyang
Taiyuan
Chengdu
Chongqing
Kunming
Guiyang
Changsha
Hengyang
Liuzhou
Guilin
Nanning
HANOI
Hai Phong
Haikou
VIANGCHAN (VIENTIANE)
Chiang Mai
Taunggyi
Mawlamyine

Yangtze River Valley

SHAANXI
SICHUAN
Sichuan Pendi
CHONGQING
Chongqing
CHINA
HUBEI
HUNAN
GUIZHOU
Guiyang
YUNNAN
GUANGXI ZHUANGZU ZIZHIQU
VIETNAM
Chengdu
Mianyang
Guangyuan
Nanchong
Suining
Leshan
Zigong
Neijiang
Yibin
Luzhou
Dazhou
Wanzhou
Three Gorges Reservoir
Chang Jiang (Yangtze)
Yichang
Jingzhou
Xiangfan
Laohekou
Shiyan
Changde
Yiyang
Loudi
Xiangtan
Shaoyang
Hengyang
Huaihua
Zunyi
Anshun
Duyun
Kaili
Liuzhou
Guilin
Wuzhou
Nanning
Yulin
Qinzhou
Zhaotong
Qujing
Bose
Lao Cai
Ha Giang
Cao Bang
Lang Son
Yen Bai
Tuyen Quang
Thai Nguyen
Tropic of Cancer
6000m
4000m
3000m
2000m
1000m
500m
250m
100m
Sea Level
-250m
-2000m
-4000m
A
B
C
D
E
F
G
1
2
3
4
5
6
7
8
9
10
244
239
256

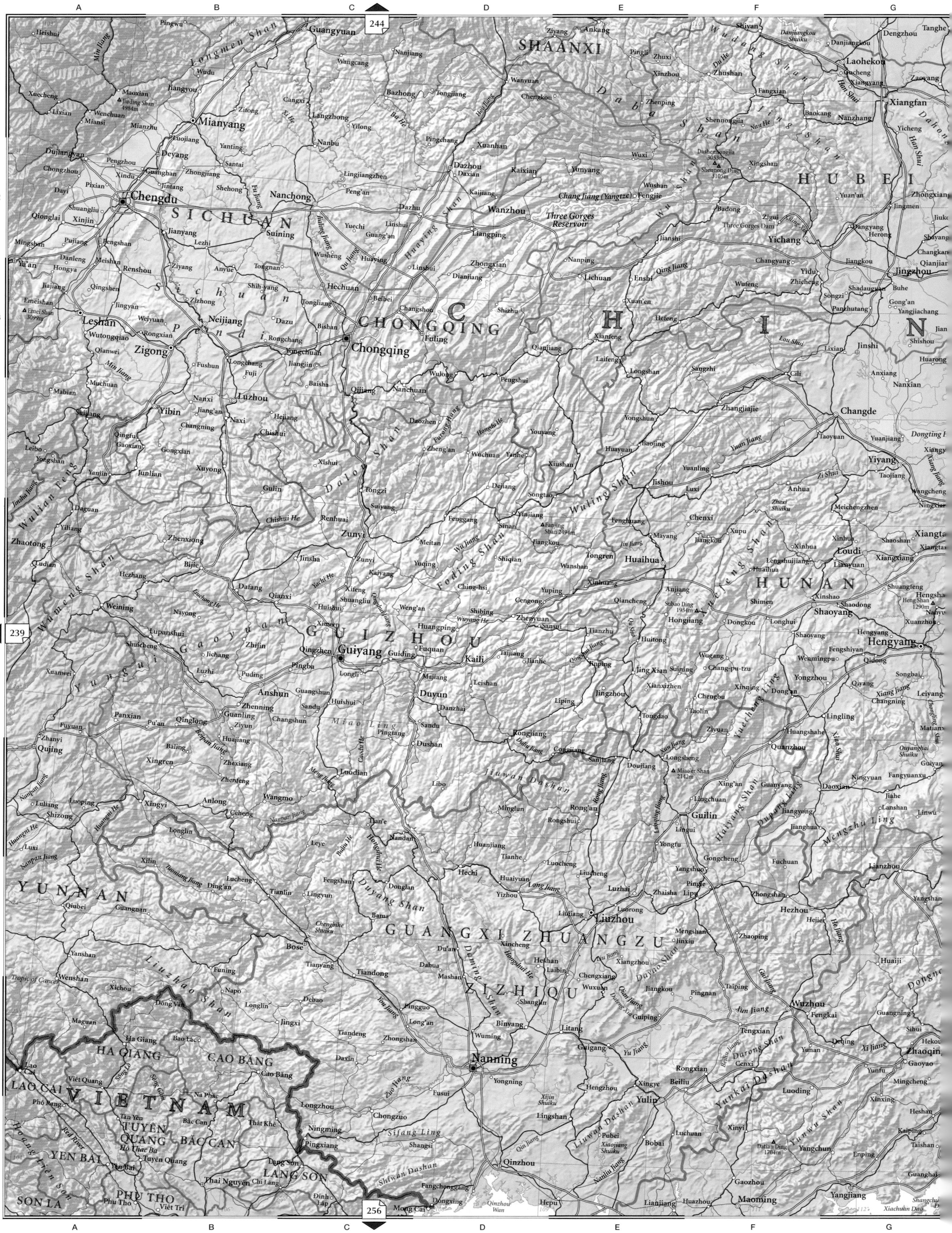

Scale 1:3,750,000

(projection: Lambert Conformal Conic)

0 20 40 60 80 100 Km
0   20   40   60   80 100 Miles

Population
▪ above 5 million   ▪ 1 million to 5 million   ◉ 500,000 to 1 million
◎ 100,000 to 500,000   ⊕ 50,000 to 100,000   ○ 10,000 to 50,000   ○ below 10,000

ASIA
243

(China and Taiwan claim
all of each other's territory)

19,686ft
13,124ft
9843ft
6562ft
3281ft
1640ft
820ft
328ft
Sea Level
-820ft
-6562ft
-13,124ft

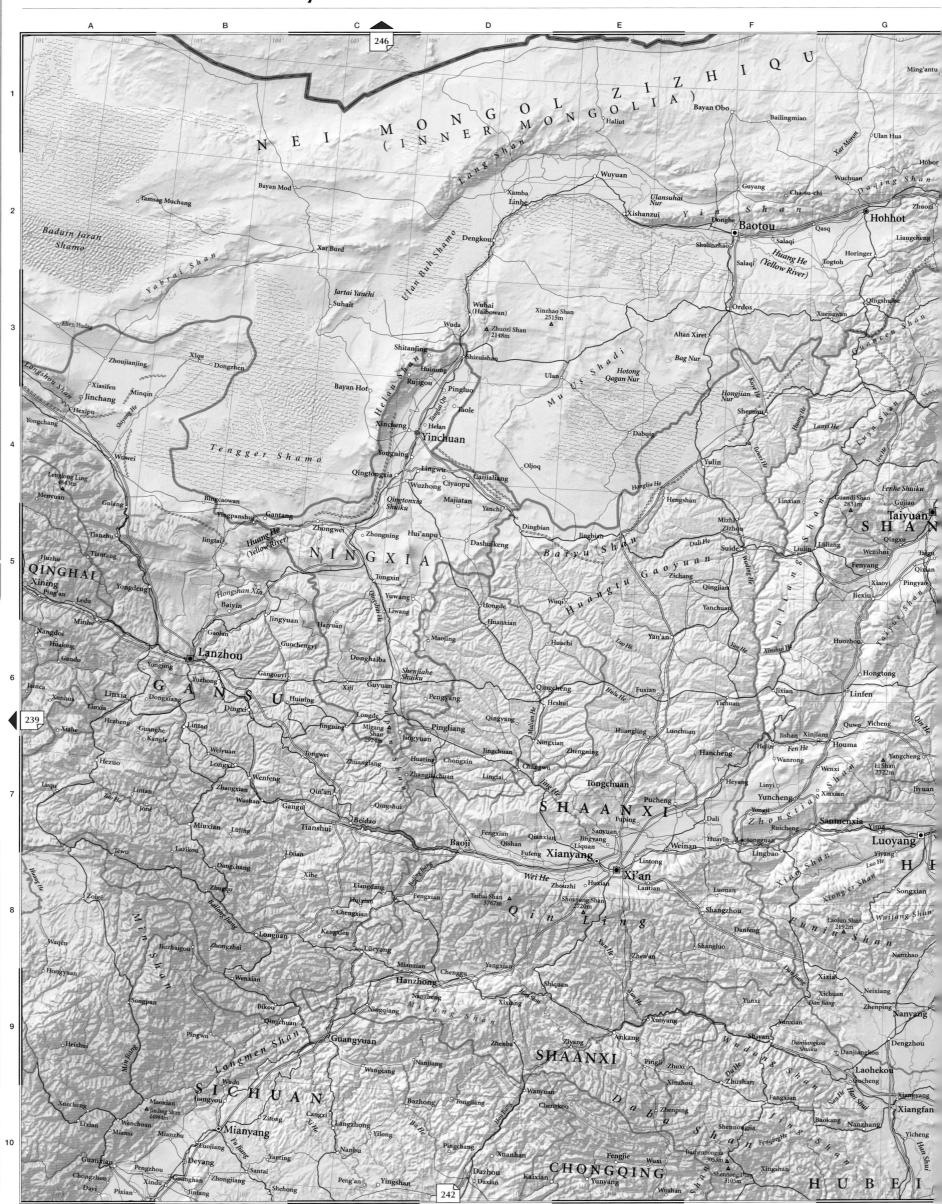

246

239

242

ASIA

244

6000m
4000m
3000m
2000m
1000m
500m
250m
100m
Sea
Level
−250m
−2000m
−4000m

Northeast China

193

239

240

RUSSIA

MONGOLIA

RESPUBLIKA ALTAY

RESPUBLIKA KHAKASIYA

KRASNOYARSKIY KRAY

RESPUBLIKA TYVA

IRKUTSKAYA OBLAST'

RESPUBLIKA BURYATIYA

HÖVSGÖL

UVS

BAYAN-ÖLGIY

HOVD

DZAVHAN

GOVI-ALTAY

ARHANGAY

BULGAN

SELENGE

ÖVÖRHANGAY

BAYANHONGOR

TÖV

HENTIY

DUNDGOVI

DORNOGOVI

ÖMNÖGOVI

XINJIANG UYGUR ZIZHIQU

NEI MONGOL

QINGHAI

GANSU

NINGXIA

SHAANXI

CHINA

Ulan-Ude

Irkutsk

ULAANBAATAR (ULAN BATOR)

Darhan

Erdenet

Baotou

Yinchuan

Lanzhou

Xining

Xian

Xianyang

Qinghai Hu

Ozero Baykal

Qingzang Gaoyuan (Plateau of Tibet)

Altai Mountains

Bogda Shan

Qaidam Pendi

Badain Jaran Shamo

Tengger Shamo

Huang He (Yellow River)

Sea Level

6000m
4000m
3000m
2000m
1000m
500m
250m
100m
Sea Level
-250m
-2000m
-4000m

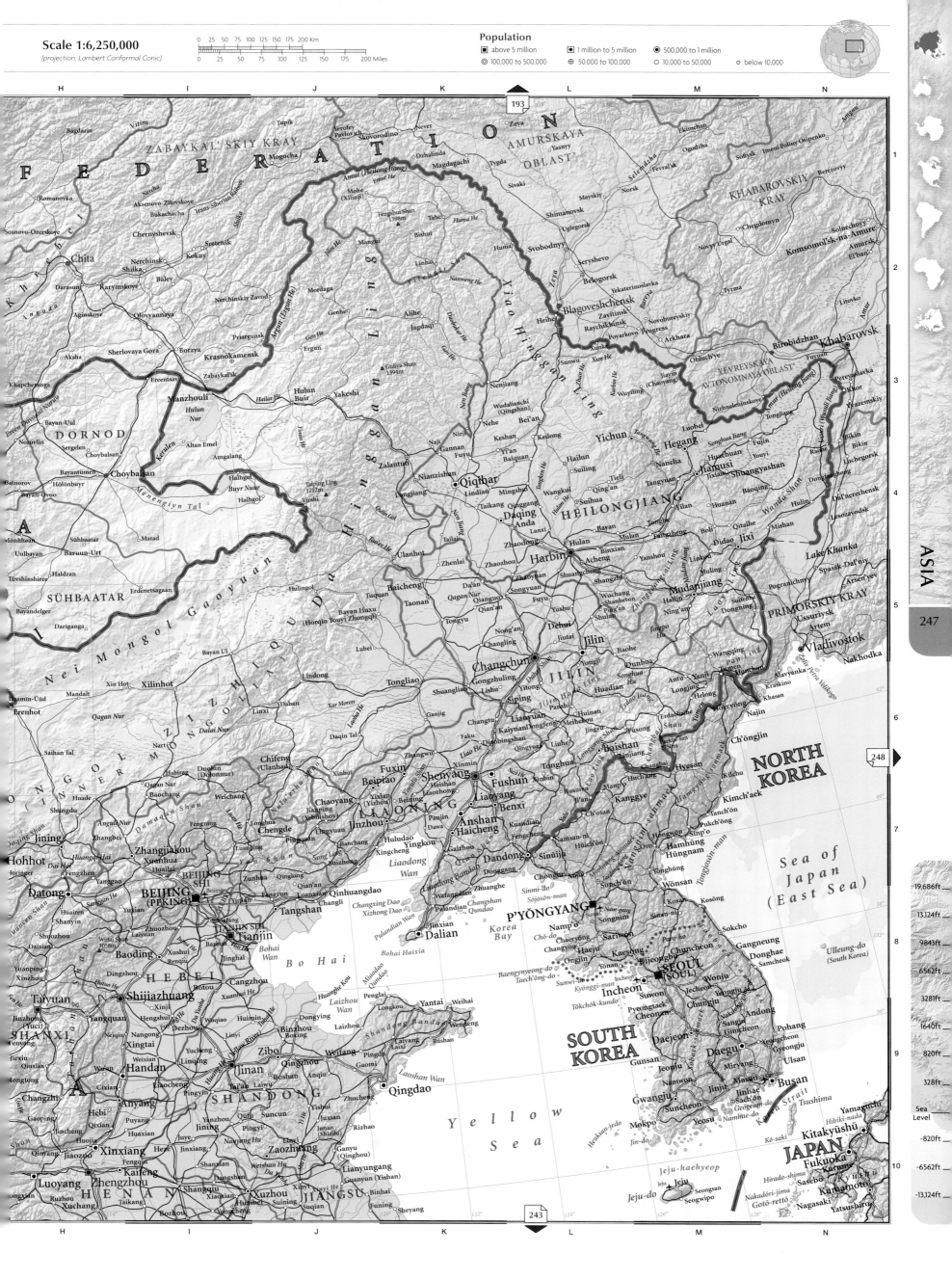

ASIA

248

245

247

286

Countries / Regions
NEI MONGOL ZIZHIQU (INNER MONGOLIA)

CHINA

LIAONING

JILIN

HEILONGJIANG

RUSSIAN FEDERATION

PRIMORSKIY KRAY

NORTH KOREA

SOUTH KOREA

JAPAN

Seas
Sea of Japan (East Sea)

Yellow Sea

East China Sea

Philippine Sea

Korea Bay

Liaodong Wan

Korea Strait

Selected place names

Laoha He, Tongliao, Shuangliao, Jiutai, Yushu, Shanhetun, Ping'an, Limkou, Didao, Jixi, Mishan, Türi Rog, Changchun, Jilin, Siping, Gongzhuling, Lishu, Yitong, Shulan, Jiaohe, Songhua Hu, Hailin, Muling, Muling, Mudanjiang, Lake Khanka, Suifenhe, Pogranichnyy, Spassk-Dal'niy, Daqin Tal, Fuxin, Zhangwu, Faku, Changtu, Yongji, Dunhua, Jingpo Hu, Wangqing, Anti, Yanji, Ning'an, Iesozavodsk, Dal'negorsk, Beipiao, Diaobingshan, Kaiyuan, Meihekou, Huadian, Panshi, Longjing, Tumen, Helong, Hunchun, Kraskino, Artem, Budnaya Pristan', Jinzhou, Yixian/Yizhou, Beining, Liaozhong, Xinmin, Tieling, Liuhe, Jingyu, Fusong, Erdaobaihe, Longjing, Hoeryong, Najin, Slavyanka, Zaliv Petra Velikogo, Nakhodka, Fushun, Shenyang, Anshan, Benxi, Dawa, Qingyuan, Huairen, Tonghua, Baishan, Xinjiang, Changbai, Hyesan, Ch'ŏngjin, Vladivostok, Ussuriysk, Haicheng, Yingkou, Gaizhou, Zhuanghe, Kuandian, Ji'an, Manp'o, Kanggye, Hongwŏn, Orong, Kilchu, Kimch'aek, Dandong, Sinŭiju, Namsan-ni, Ch'osan, Huich'ŏn, Myohyang-sanmaek, Kanggye, Hamgyŏng-sanmaek, Tanch'ŏn, Sinp'o, Pukch'ŏng, Dongou, Wafangdian, Changshan Qundao, Jinzhou, Palandian, Zhuanghe, Donggang, Sinmi-do, Sŏjosŏn-man, Chŏngju, Anju, Sunch'ŏn, Oro, Hamhŭng, Hŭngnam, P'YŎNGYANG, Namp'o, Ongnim, Yangdŏk, Wŏnsan, Yonghŭng, Tongjosŏn-man, Chŏngwon, Chaeryŏng, Sariwŏn, Kosan, Suan-ni, Baengnyeong-do, Daecheong-do, Ongjin, Haeju, Kaesŏng, Paro-ho, Kosŏng, Sunwi-do, Yonan, Uijeongbu, Chuncheon, Sokcho, Inch'ŏn, Incheon, SEOUL (SOUL), Suwon, Gyeonggi-man, Deokjeok-gundo, Pyeongtaek, Jecheon, Wonju, Gangneung, Donghae, Samcheok, Ulleung-do, Cheonan, Chungju, Yeongju, Daejeon, Andong, Gunsan, Jeonju, Gimcheon, Pohang, Gwangju, Naju, Namwon, Daegu, Yeongcheon, Gyeongju, Mokpo, Jinju, Miryang, Ulsan, Heuksan-jedo, Suncheon, Yeosu, Sacheon, Masan, Jinhae, Busan, Geogeum-do, Namhae-do, Jeju-haehyeop, Tsushima, Kami-Agata, Kami-Tsushima, Mitsushima, Izuhara, Kō-zaki, Jeju-do, Jeju, Seongsan, Seogwipo, Higashi-suidō, Iki, Genkai-nada, Uku-jima, Hirado, Fukue-jima, Gotō-rettō, Ōse-zaki, Fukue, Narao, Omura, Shimabara, Amakusa-nada, Ushibuka, Naga-shima, Akune, Koshikijima-rettō, Kusagaki-guntō, Kuro-shima, Kuchinoerabu-jima, Tokara-rettō, Suwanose-jima, Nakano-shima, Nishinoomote, Tanega-shima, Minamitane, Kamiyaku, Yaku-shima, Sata-misaki, Ōsumi-kaikyō, Ibusuki, Makurazaki, Noma-zaki, Kaseda, Kagoshima, Sendai, Ōkuchi, Hitoyoshi, Takanabe, Miyakonojō, Kanoya, Toi-misaki, Uchinoura, Kushima, Nichinan, Tarumizu, Miyazaki, Nobeoka, Hyūga, Tsuno, Saiki, Ōita, Beppu, Usuki, Saganoseki, Saga-noseki, Kumamoto, Yatsushiro, Isahaya, Nagasaki, Hondo, Shimo-shima, Nomo-zaki, Kuchinotsu, Arao, Ōmuta, Kurume, Kikuchi, Hita, Yamaga, Kuma, Shimonoseki, Kitakyūshū, Fukuoka, Karatsu, Kasuga, Onojō, Ogōri, Buzen, Usa, Nakatsu, Kunisaki, Shimonoseki, Ube, Hōfu, Yukuhashi, Takada, Moji, Saiki, Yamaguchi, Nagato, Hagi, Abu, Masuda, Hamada, Ōda, Susa, Kaike, Izumo, Hirata, Matsue, Yonago, Oki-shotō, Dōgo, Dōzen, Saigō, Nakano-shima, Oki-kaikyō, Shimane-hantō, Sakaiminato, Kurayoshi, Tottori, Iwami, Kyōga-misaki, Hamasaka, Kasumi, Aoya, Toyooka, Suzu-misaki, Wajima, Togi, Nanao, Himi, Uozu, Takaoka, Kanazawa, Hakui, Matto, Komatsu, Kaga, Mikuni, Fukui, Takefu, Echizen-misaki, Tsuruga, Obama, Maizuru, Miyazu, Fukuchiyama, Ayabe, Kameoka, Kyōto, Ōtsu, Ōtsu, Uji, Nara, Tenri, Kashihara, Wakayama, Gobō, Tanabe, Susami, Kushimoto, Shiono-misaki, Shingū, Kumano, Owase, Ō-shima, Nachikatsuura, Daiō-zaki, Toba, Ise, Tsu, Matsusaka, Iga, Nabari, Yokkaichi, Kuwana, Nagoya, Seto, Okazaki, Toyota, Anjō, Kariya, Gifu, Ōgaki, Ichinomiya, Gamagōri, Toyohashi, Hamamatsu, Enshū-nada, Kii-suidō, Muroto-zaki, Tokushima, Naruto, Takamatsu, Marugame, Kan'onji, Imabari, Matsuyama, Saijō, Niihama, Ōzu, Yawatahama, Uwajima, Sukumo, Nakamura, Tosa-wan, Kōchi, Kainan, Aki, Muroto, Akō, Himeji, Kakogawa, Akashi, Kōbe, Ōsaka, Sakai, Izumiōtsu, Kishiwada, Kansai, Awaji-shima, Sumoto, Hiroshima, Kure, Higashihiroshima, Mihara, Onomichi, Fukuyama, Kasaoka, Kurashiki, Okayama, Tsuyama, Chizu, Tsuyama, Ibara, Niimi, Shōbara, Miyoshi, Izumo, Ōtake, Iwakuni, Tokuyama, Shimonoseki, Yanai, Hikari, Kōriyama, Suō-nada, Iyo-nada, Hiuchi-nada, Bingo-nada, Bungo-suidō, Hyūga-nada, Suzuka, Chūgoku-sanchi, Shikoku-sanchi

Elevation scale
6000m
4000m
3000m
2000m
1000m
500m
250m
100m
Sea Level
-250m
-2000m
-4000m

**Sea of Japan
(East Sea)**

Liancourt Rocks

SOUTH KOREA

GANGWON-DO

GYEONGSANGBUK-DO

CHUNGCHEONGBUK-DO

Daejon

Daegu

DAEGU-SI

GYEONGSANGNAM-DO

JEOLLABUK-DO

Busan

ASIA

250

245

Korea Strait

Tsushima

Oki-shotō
Dōgo
Dōzen
Saigō
Nakano-shima
Chiburi-jima

Oki-kaikyō

Matsue
SHIMANE
TOTTORI
Tottori
OKAYAMA
HIROSHIMA
Hiroshima
Okayama
Kurashiki

Chūgoku-sanchi

Yamaguchi
YAMAGUCHI
Fukuyama

Kitakyūshū
Shimonoseki
Tokuyama
Iwakuni
Takamatsu
KAGAWA

Fukuoka
FUKUOKA
SAGA
Saga
Matsuyama
EHIME
TOKUSHIMA
Tokushima

Iki

Genkai-nada

Higashi-suidō

Gotō-rettō

NAGASAKI

Nagasaki

Suō-nada

Ōita
OITA
Beppu

KŌCHI
Kōchi
Shikoku

Iyo-nada

Kumamoto
KUMAMOTO

Kyūshū
Kyūshū-sanchi

Tosa-wan

East
China
Sea

MIYAZAKI

Miyazaki

KAGOSHIMA

Kagoshima

Philippine

Uji-guntō

Ōsumi-kaikyō

Kuro-shima

Iō-jima

Mage-shima

Tanega-shima

Nishinoomote

Kuchinoerabu-jima

Kamiyaku

Yaku-shima

Minamitane

Sea
Level

6000m
4000m
3000m
2000m
1000m
500m
250m
100m
Sea
Level
-250m
-2000m
-4000m

① East China Sea

Sakishima-shotō

Miyako-shotō

Yaeyama-shotō

OKINAWA

Yonaguni
Iriomote-jima
Ishigaki

Philippine
Sea

Scale 1:3,250,000

Haterung-jima

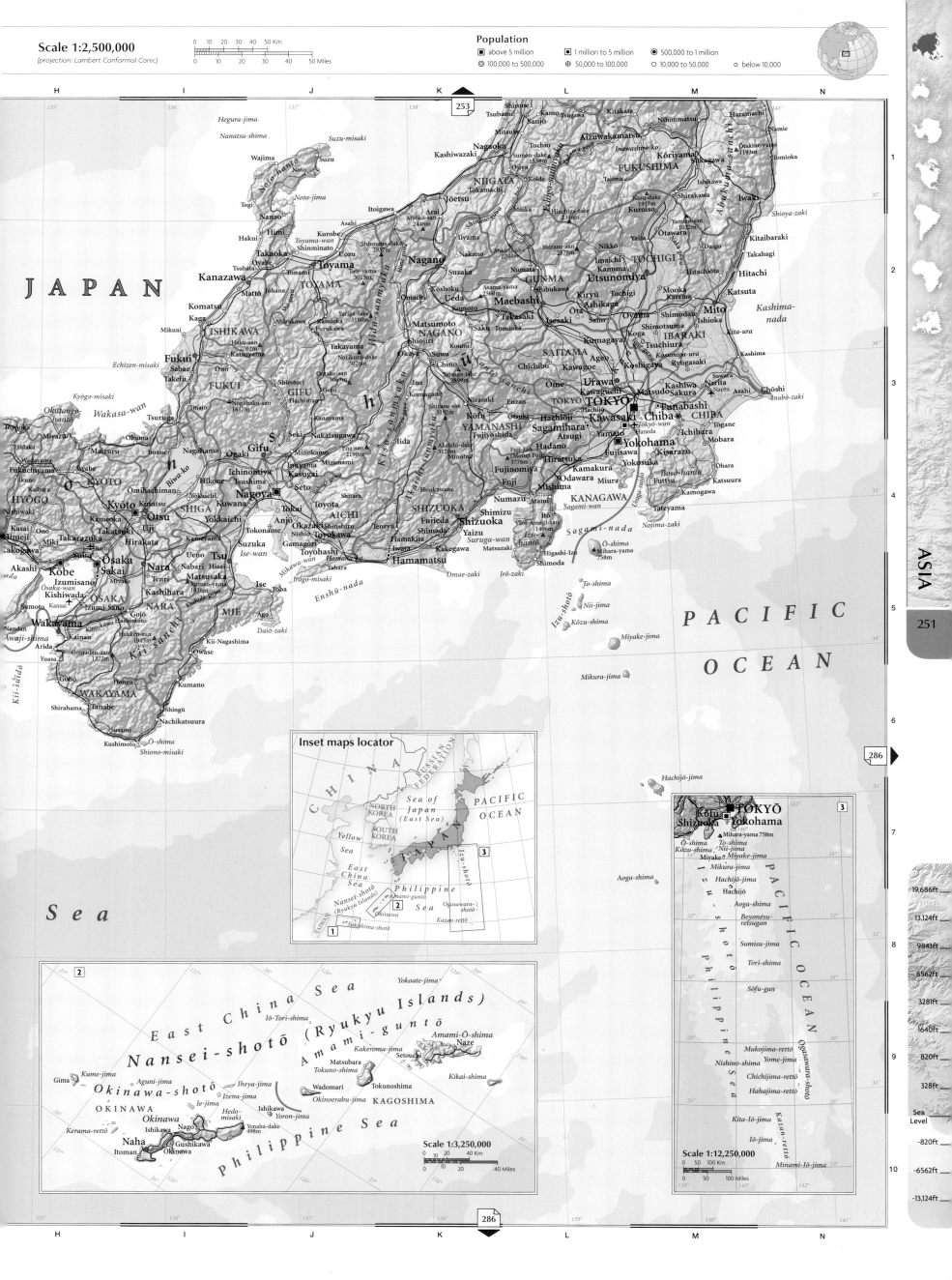

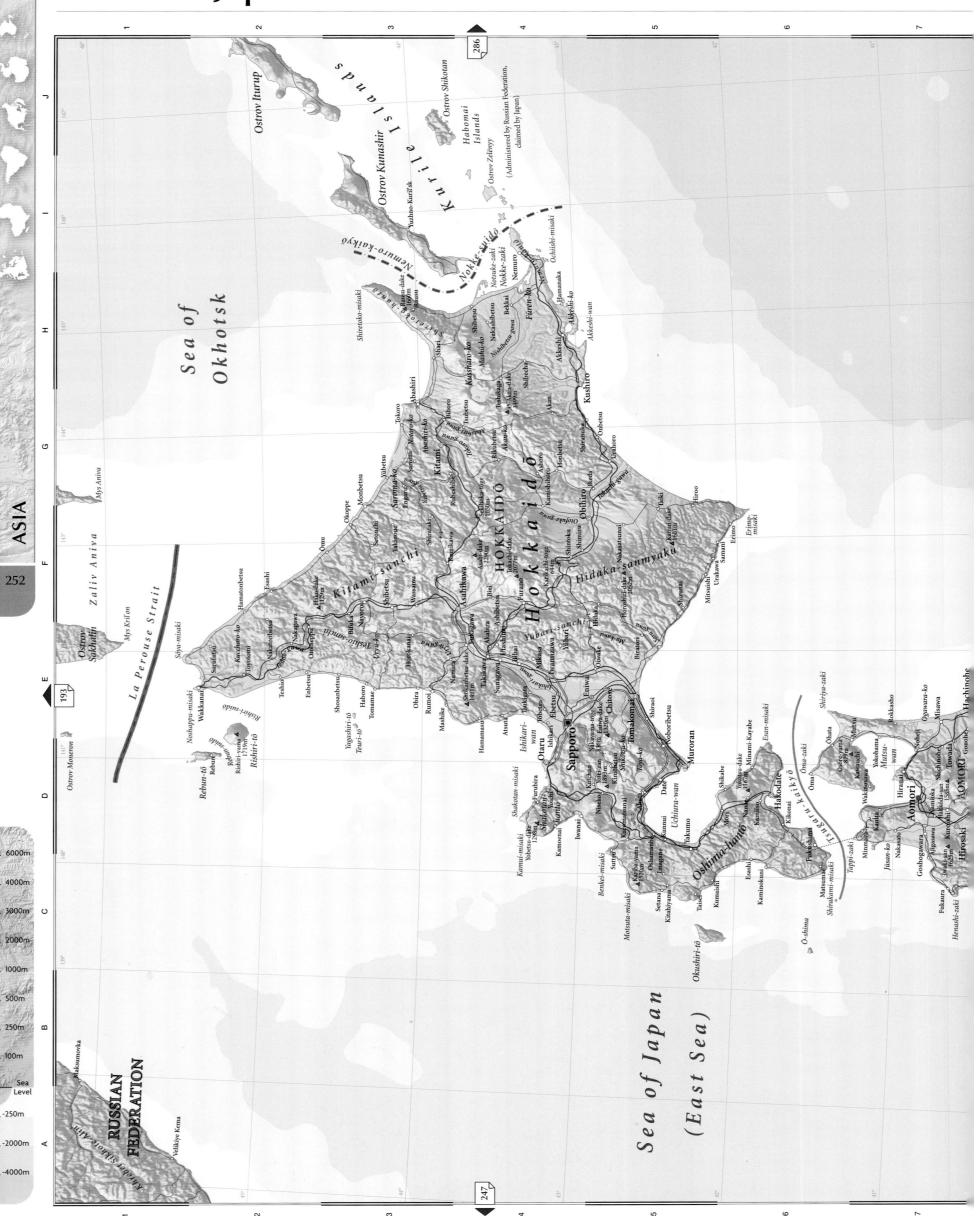

239

ASIA

234

Seas & Oceans

Bay of Bengal · Andaman Sea · Gulf of Thailand · Gulf of Mottama · Gulf of Tongking · South China Sea · Indian Ocean · Java Sea (Laut Jawa) · Flores Sea (Laut Flores) · Strait of Malacca · Makassar Strait (Selat Makassar)

Countries & Capitals

CHINA · INDIA · BANGLADESH · BHUTAN — THIMPHU · MYANMAR (BURMA) — NAY PYI TAW · LAOS — VIANGCHAN (VIENTIANE) · THAILAND — KRUNG THEP (BANGKOK) · VIETNAM — HA NOI · CAMBODIA — PHNUM PENH (PHNOM PENH) · MALAYSIA — KUALA LUMPUR / PUTRAJAYA · SINGAPORE — SINGAPORE · BRUNEI — BANDAR SERI BEGAWAN · INDONESIA — JAKARTA

Selected Cities

Lhasa · Dhaka · Kolkata · Chittagong · Mandalay · Yangon (Rangoon) · Chiang Mai · Kunming · Guiyang · Chongqing · Nanchang · Changsha · Fuzhou · Guangzhou · Hong Kong (Xianggang) · Kowloon · Macau (Aomen) · Nanning · Hai Phong · Da Nang · Ho Chi Minh · Phnum Penh · George Town · Ipoh · Medan · Palembang · Pontianak · Banjarmasin · Kuching · Kota Kinabalu · Surabaya · Bandung · Semarang · Denpasar · Makassar · Balikpapan

Physical Features

Himalayas · Mount Everest 8848m · Arakan Range · Shan Plateau · Korat Plateau · Annamite Mountains · Malay Peninsula · Borneo · Kalimantan · Sumatera (Sumatra) · Jawa (Java) · Bali · Nusa Tenggara · Greater Sunda Islands · Andaman Islands (to India) · Nicobar Islands (to India) · Paracel Islands (disputed) · Spratly Islands (disputed) · Mouths of the Ganges · Mouths of the Irrawaddy · Mouths of the Mekong · Tonlé Sap · Equator · Tropic of Cancer

Elevation scale

6000m · 4000m · 3000m · 2000m · 1000m · 500m · 250m · 100m · Sea Level · -250m · -2000m · -4000m

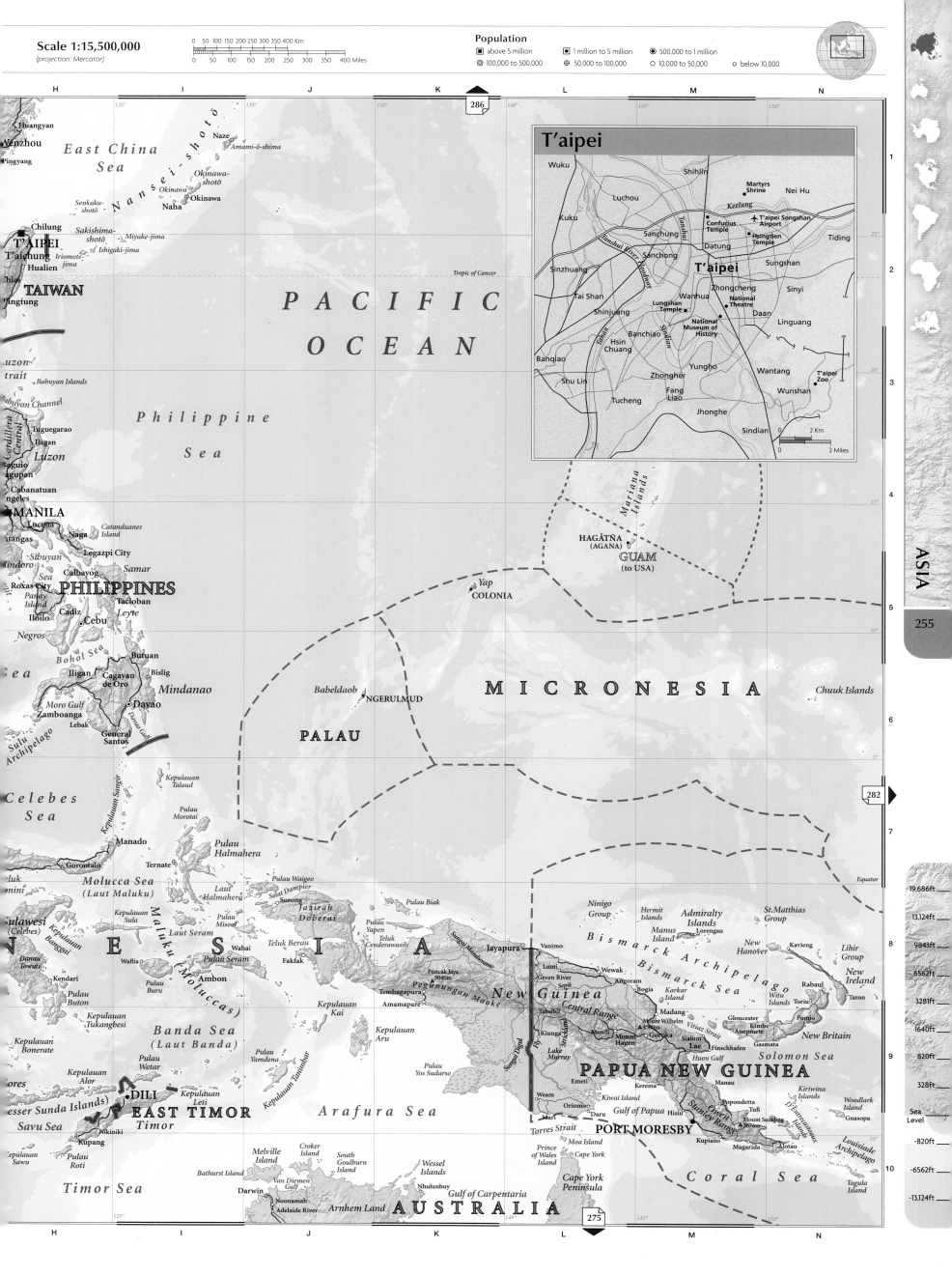

Singapore

Upper Peirce Reservoir
Central Catchment Nature Reserve
Ang Mo Kio
Buangkok
Tampines
Bukit Timah Nature Reserve
MacRitchie Reservoir
Kallang
Cola Keng
Toa Payoh
Tai Seng
Jurong East
Bukit Timah
K. G. Potong Pasir
Tan Tock Seng
Bedo
Raffles Park
Geylang Serai
Clementi
University of Singapore
Kandang Kerbau
National Stadium
National Museum
Cathedral
Queenstown
Raffles Hotel
City Hall
Pasir Panjang
Singapore
Singapore River
Marina South
Buona Vista
Telok Blangah
Cable Car
Pulau Brani
Keppel Harbour
South China Sea
Sentosa Island
Straits of Singapore
Palau Bukum
Palau Tembakul
Palau Sakijang Bendera
0   3 Km
0   3 Miles

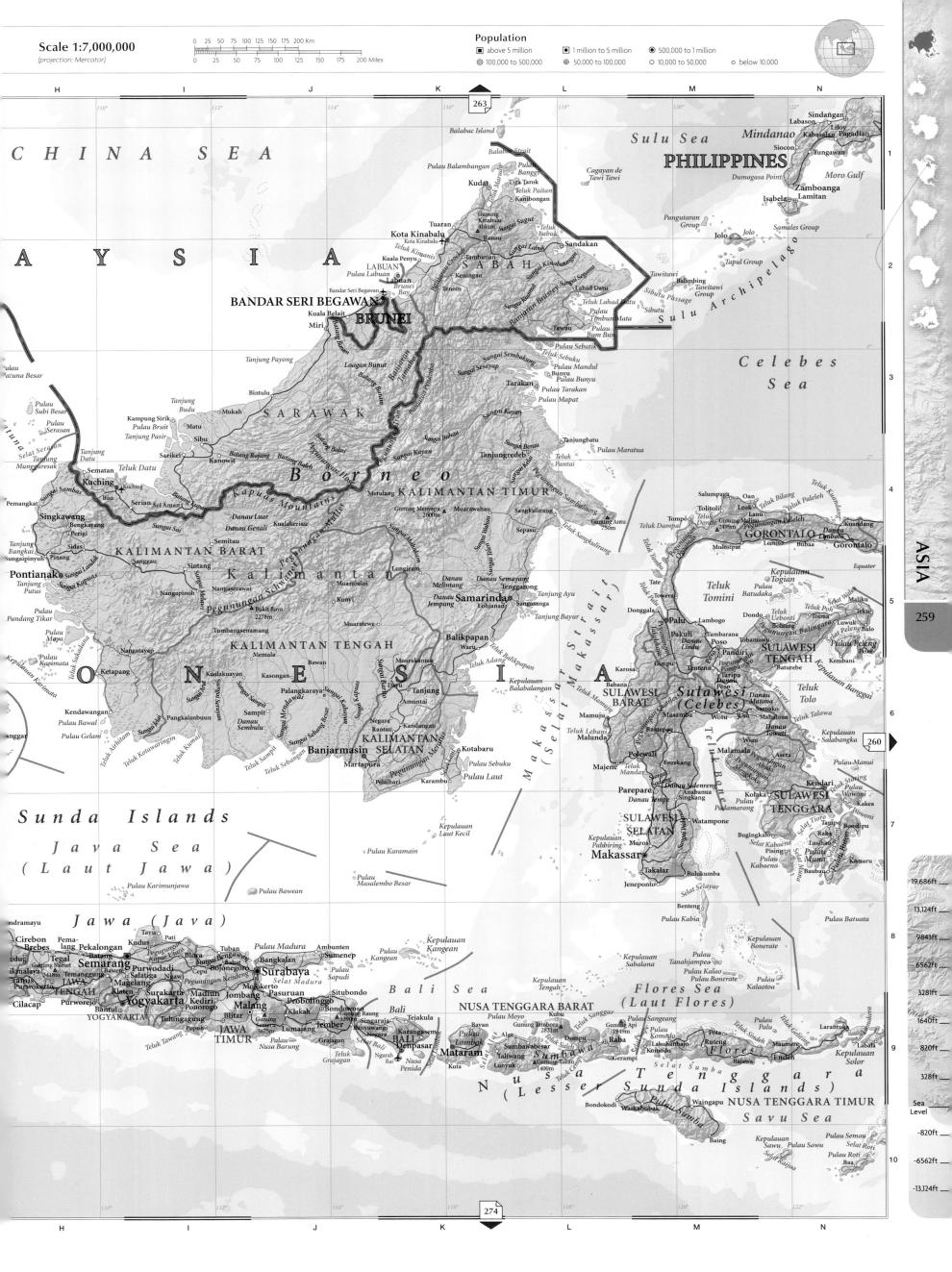

Eastern Maritime Southeast Asia

263

259

274

PHILIPPINES

Celebes Sea

*Molucca Sea
(Laut Maluku)*

Laut Halmaher

Laut Seram

MALUKU
UTARA

MALUKU

*Banda Sea
(Laut Banda)*

MALAYSIA

SABAH

LABUAN

SARAWAK

BRUNEI
BANDAR SERI
BEGAWAN

Borneo

KALIMANTAN
TIMUR

Kalimantan

KALIMANTAN
TENGAH

KALIMANTAN
SELATAN

Banjarmasin

*Makassar Strait
(Selat Makassar)*

SULAWESI
UTARA

GORONTALO

Manado

SULAWESI
TENGAH

SULAWESI
BARAT

*Sulawesi
(Celebes)*

SULAWESI
SELATAN

Makassar

SULAWESI
TENGGARA

Kendari

Ambon

*Teluk
Tomini*

*Teluk
Tolo*

*Teluk
Bone*

I N D O N E S

Laut Bali

NUSA TENGGARA BARAT

*Flores Sea
(Laut Flores)*

Savu Sea

NUSA TENGGARA TIMUR

Jawa (Java)

JAWA
TIMUR

BALI

Denpasar

Mataram

*N u s a   T e n g g a r a
(L e s s e r   S u n d a   I s l a n d s)*

Kupang

DILI
EAST TIMOR

I N D I A N

O C E A N

Timor Sea

6000m
4000m
3000m
2000m
1000m
500m
250m
100m
Sea
Level
-250m
-2000m
-4000m

Scale 1:7,000,000
(projection: Mercator)

0 25 50 75 100 125 150 175 200 Km

0 25 50 75 100 125 150 175 200 Miles

Population
■ above 5 million
■ 1 million to 5 million
◉ 500,000 to 1 million
◎ 100,000 to 500,000
⊕ 50,000 to 100,000
○ 10,000 to 50,000
∘ below 10,000

P A C I F I C   O C E A N

Equator

Kepulauan Asia
Kepulauan Mapia
Pulau Pegun
Pulau Bras
Kepulauan Ayu

Sedat Jailolo
Pulau Gebe
Kacepi
Kable Bet
Pulau Gag
Besir
Gam
Kobi
Lamlam
Urbinasopon
Pulau Waigeo
Warmandi
Koor
Gunung Kwoka
2425m
Sausapor
Sau Korem
Napido
Pulau Supiori
Sansundi
Pulau Bepondi
Pulau
Manim Soyek
Bosnabraidi
Sarwon
Kepulauan Raja Ampat
Pulau Boo
Todlo
Sorong
Makbon
Asbakin
Megamo
Mubrani
Andoi
Mandori
Pulau Biak
Biak
Kepulauan Pandaidori
Tanjung D'Urville
Teba
Apauwar
Wuvulu Island
Ningo Group
Aua Island
Atkri
Tip
Hebera
Pulau Kofiau
Saileen
Yellio
Kuwawin
Rawas
Gunung Mebo
2930m
Snabaio
Pulau Rumberpon
Pom
Ansas
Serui
Rori
Yaube
Wageseri
Matewar
Sarmi
Maffin
Kepulauan Podena
Kapocol
Pulau Misool
Gasim
Konda
Teminabuan
Timoforo
Baru
Mogoi
Barma
Inanwatan
Bintuni
Rasawi
Yomber
Pulau Maswaar
Kuran
Waren
Parador
Serami
Ansudi
Kaptiau
Nirahotong
Jayapura
Wutung
Vanimo
Yos Sudarso
Sissano
Aitape
Walis Island
Schouten Islands
IRIAN JAYA BARAT
Kepulauan Segaf
Teluk Warong
Teluk Berau
Sonar
Koagas
Andamata
Aredo
Sobiei
Pulau Roon
Teluk Cenderawasih
Kepulauan Moor
Asori
Pami
Van Rees
Peguanungan Van Rees
Gunung Dom
1430m
Rouffaer Reserves
Demta
Krau
Danau Sentani
SANDAUN
Imonda
Torricelli Mountains
Dreikikir
Green River
Senggi
Maprik
Kairiru Island
Muschu Island
Wewak
Wahai
Bemu
Kepulauan Pisang
Rumbati
Fakfak
Semenanjung Bomberai
Mamasiware
Wosimi
Maki
Biwe
Maniwori
Napanwainami
Van Daalen
Pisapa
Wunen
Woogi
Wosi
Naver
Patoasi
Amanab
Nuku
Juni
Amisibil
May River
Sepik
Ambunti
Chambri Lake
Angoram
Sepik
Kaup
Ilir
Nama
Kepulauan Gorong
Pulau Kasiui
Gulir
Manggawitu
Nusawulan
Modowi
Yapa Kopra
Umari
Uta
Kokenau
Peguanungan Tiya
Danau Paniai
Enarotali
Kobowre
Wandai
Banggelapa
Ilaga
Tiom
Puncak Jaya
5040m
Peguanungan Sudirman
Peguanungan Jayawijaya
New Guinea
Central Range
PAPUA
EAST SEPIK
Yaminbot
Kepulauan Banda
Pulau Manuk
Modowi
Aiduna
Wanapiri
Tembagapura
Sabang
Peguanungan Maoke
Oksibil
Kapella
3932m
Mount Aiyang
3325m
Telefomin
Ok Tedi
Lake Kopiago
Porgera
Laiagam
Wahgi
Wabag
Simbai
Bayer River
Maku Range
ENGA
Wapenamanda
Mount Hagen
Amamapare
Timika
Teluk Flamingo
Agats
Atsy
Karima
Sungai Baliem
Brazza
Kawentkim
Tarnbil
Ningerum
Kanggime
Ketu
Tari
Nipa
Mendi
Kompiam
WESTERN
GUINEA
Mabu
Wamip
Kiunga
Strickland
Konio
Poroma
NEW
Kagua
SOUTHERN HIGHLANDS
Mount Bosavi
2302m
Erave
Kikori
GULF
Pulau Warilau
Warilau
Pulau Lutur
Gumzai
Komfane
Biwarlaut
Sungai Digul
Sungai Kampung
Odammim
Mayu
Yar
Tanjung De Jongs
Oreyabo
Mapi
Bado
Keisak
Sobi
Tusirah
Abemaree
Lake Murray
Lake Murray
Fly
Tomu
Sirima
Tuma
Kikori
Motigio Island
Wair
Har
Remoon
Pulau Kur
Kepulauan Tayandu
Watmri
Pulau Kai Kecil
Weduar
Tanjung Weduar
Pulau Kai Besar
Dobo
Pulau Wokam
Namalau
Pulau Kobroor
Taberfane
Kepulauan Aru
Pulau Trangan
Baimun
Pulau Workai
Tanjung Ngabordamlu
Kepulauan Jin
Yomuka
Kaba
Pembre
Kofarau
Muting
Bupul
Kurik
Arak
Yodom
Solaka
Wamal
Alotip
Sungai Kumbe
Wowoi
Arama
Balimo
Daru
Kepulauan Kai
Manuwui
Yatoke
Pulau Babar
Amplawas
Eliase
Tanjung Aro Usu
Pulau Selaru
Pulau Larat
Larat
Pulau Yamdena
Pulau Wuliaru
Koreare
Amdassa
Saumlaki
Kepulauan Tanimbar
Kepulauan Babar
Pulau Yos Sudarso
Kladar
Wan
Mombun
Pulau Komoran
Tanjung Vals
Merauke
Sakiramke
Kondomirat
Weam
Morehead
Morehead
Emeti
Sibidiri
Oriomo
Mari
Wabuda Island
Purutu Island
Kiwai Island
Parama Island

A r a f u r a   S e a

Torres Strait
Badu Island
Moa Island
Prince of Wales Island
Cape York
Endeavour Strait

Coral Sea

Great Barrier Reef

Bathurst Island
Melville Island
Cobourg Peninsula
Croker Island
Marchinbar Island
Elcho Island
South Goulburn Island
Wessel Islands
Beagle Gulf
Van Diemen Gulf
Nhulunbuy
Cape York
Weipa
Cape York Peninsula

Darwin
A U S T R A L I A
Noonamah
Adelaide River
Daly River
Cooinda
Jabiru
Mount Evelyn
366m
A r n h e m   L a n d
Bulman

G u l f   o f   C a r p e n t a r i a

19,686ft
13,124ft
9843ft
6562ft
3281ft
1640ft
820ft
328ft
Sea Level
-820ft
-6562ft
-13,124ft

Scale 1:7,000,000
(projection: Mercator)

0 25 50 75 100 125 150 175 200 Km
0 25 50 75 100 125 150 175 200 Miles

Population

☐ above 5 million
⊡ 1 million to 5 million
◉ 500,000 to 1 million
⊚ 100,000 to 500,000
⊕ 50,000 to 100,000
○ 10,000 to 50,000
○ below 10,000

19,686ft
13,124ft
9843ft
6562ft
3281ft
1640ft
820ft
328ft
Sea Level
-820ft
-6562ft
-13,124ft

Tropic of Cancer

GUANGDONG
Kuangzhou
Foshan
Jiangmen
Zhongshan
Zhuhai
Macau (Aomen)
Shangchuan Dao
Huizhou
Dongguan
Shenzhen
Kowloon (Jiulong)
Hong Kong (Xianggang)
Chep Lap Kok
Honghai Wan
Haifeng
Lufeng
Puning
Chaoyang
Shantou
Nan'ao Dao

Chiat
Hsinying
Yuli
T'ainan
TAIWAN
P'ingtung
T'aitung
Kaohsiung
Kaohsiung Fangshan
Hengch'un
Lü Tao
Oluan Pi
Lan Yü

Bashi Channel

Batan Islands
Batan Island

Luzon Strait

Balintang Channel
Babuyan Island
Babuyan Islands
Babuyan Channel

Mayraira Point
Claveria
Escarpada Point
Laoag
Aparri
Mount Cagua 1133m
Cabugao
Dingras
Bangued
Tuao
Tuguegarao
Vigan
Tabuk
Candon
Bontoc
Ilagan
Bangar
Lal Trinidad
Cauayan
Lagawe
Echague
San Fernando
Bauang
Bayombong
Baguio
Cagayan
Bolinao
Dagupan
San Ildefonso Peninsula
Lingayen
San Carlos
San Jose City
Baler
Camiling
Tarlac
Palayan City
Masinloc
Iba
High Peak 2037m
Cabanatuan
Angeles
Mount Pinatubo 1485m
San Fernando
Olongapo
Malolos
Caloocan
Quezon City
Balanga
Pasig
MANILA
Imus
Ninoy Aquino
Laguna de Bay
Corregidor Island
Tagaytay
San Pablo
Nasugbu
Lipa
Lucena
Batangas

Luzon Sea
Philippine
Sierra Madre
Cordillera Central
Lingayen Gulf

Polillo Islands
Lamon Bay
Labo
Daet
Galauag
Caramoan
Catanduanes Island
Naga
Iriga
Virac
Tabaco
Mayon Volcano 2422m
Ligao
Legazpi City
Donsol
Sorsogon
Bulan
Catarman
Laoang

Lubang Island
Cape Calavite
Calapan
Boac
Catanauan
San Francisco
San Pascual
Mamburao
Mindoro
Pinamalayan
Marinduque
Burias Island
Sablayan
Mount Baco 2488m
Roxas
Tablas Island
Sibuyan Sea
Masbate
San Jose
Odiongan
Sibuyan Island
Cajidiocan
Calbayog
Samar
Dolores
Coron
Balud
Placer
Masbate
Borongan
Busuanga Island
Calamian Group
Jintotolo Channel
Biliran Island
Catbalogan

SPRATLY ISLANDS (disputed)
Northeast Cay
Southwest Cay
West York Island
Sandy Cay
Thitu Island
Nanshan Island
Flat Island
Loaita Island
Itu Aba Island
Sand Cay
Namyit Island
Lincoln Island

Culion Island
Linapacan Island
El Nido
Taytay
Cuyo West Pass
Cuyo East Pass
Ibajay
Kalibo
Roxas City
Culasi
Visayan Sea
Carigara
Ormoc
Tacloban
Leyte Gulf
Guiuan
Patnongon
Passi
Cadiz
Bogo
Baybay
Abuyog
San Jose de Buenavista
Iloilo
Silay
Bacolod
Cebu
Danao
Sagay
Sogod
Maasin
Dinagat Island
Miagao
San Carlos City
Bago
La Carlota
Toledo
Lapu-Lapu
Camotes Sea
Leyte
Himamaylan
Canlaon Volcano 2465m
Cebu
Panay Gulf
Negros
Argao
Bohol
Bais
Tagbilaran
Jagna
Surigao
Siargao Island
Sipalay
Bayawan
Dumaguete
Camiguin Island
Cabadbaran
Butuan
Tandag
Cagayan Islands
Siquijor Island
Siaton
Bohol Sea
Cagayan de Oro
Gingoog
Lianga
Siaton Point
Dipolog
Dapitan
Tagoloan
Prosperidad
Hinatuan
Oroquieta
Iligan
Malaybalay
Bislig
Mount Malindang 2425m
Iligan Bay
Ozamiz
Maramag
Monkayo
Sindangan
Tangub
Lake Lanao
Labason
Marawi
Nabunturan
Sulu Sea
Liloy
Tubod
Malabang
Tagum
Baganga
Kabasalan
Pagadian
Midsayap
Siocon
Karomatan
Cotabato
Mindanao
Davao
Manay
Tungawan
Sultan Kudarat
Nabunturan
Puerto Princesa
Quezon
Palawan
Kidapawan
Mount Apo 2954m
Davao Gulf
Lupon
Mati
Tacurong
Isulan
Lebak
Digos
Brooke's Point
Zamboanga
Isabela
Lamitan
Mount Busa 2083m
Kalamansig
Palimbang
Koronadal
Governor Generoso
Malita
Basilan
Surallah
Parker Volcano 1842m
Kiamba
General Santos
Cape San Agustin
Jolo
Jolo
Samales Group
Glan
Jose Abad Santos

Balabac Island
Balabac Strait
Pulau Balambangan
Pangutaran Group
Tinaca Point
Pulau Banggi
Cagayan de Tawi Tawi
Tawitawi
Balimbing
Tapul Group
Sarangani Islands
Kudat
Tiga Tarok
Teluk Paitan
Kanibongan
Sibutu Passage
Sulu Archipelago
Tawitawi Group
Celebes Sea
Kepulauan Nanusa

MALAYSIA
Tuaran
Gunung Kinabalu 4101m
Ranau
Sandakan
Kota Kinabalu
Keningau
Tambunan
Kinabatangan
Tenom
SABAH
Kuala Penyu
Pulau Labuan
Labuan
LABUAN
Miri
Kuala Belait
Seri Begawan
BRUNEI
BANDAR SERI BEGAWAN
SARAWAK
Teluk Lahad Datu
Tawau
Sebatik
Pulau Sebatik
Kepulauan Kawio
Pulau Karakelong
Kepulauan Talaud
Melanguane

PHILIPPINES
Philippine Sea
Moro Gulf
Dumagasa Point

243
260
286

ASIA

264

Baghdad

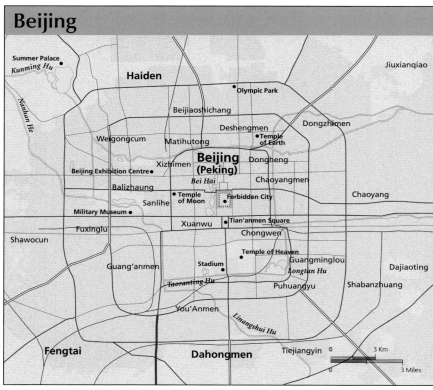

Tigris
Shaala
Quds
Zahrā
Tunis
Maghreb
Sadr City
Al'Azamiyah
Qanat Al Jaysh
Rusāfa
Khansā'
Arbataash
Shaikh
Aomar
Shaab
Stadium
Adel
Karkh
Gaiani
Baghdād
Iraqi National
Museum
Aalām
Liberation
Monument
Muthana
Amin
Khudra
International
Zone
(Green Zone)
Tishriyaa
Riyad
Wahda
Hamrā
Karradah
New Baghdād
Firdows
University
Diyālā
Jihād
Jizira
Amal Qadisiya
Tigris
Baghdād
Intl. Airport
Dōra

0 4 Km
0 4 Miles

Bangkok

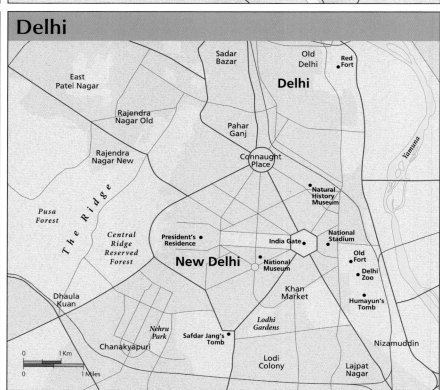

Bangkhen
Nonthaburi
Lad
Phrao
Chao Phraya
Bangsu
Bangsu
Chatuchak
Huay
Khwang
Bang Kapi
Dusit
Phaya
Thai
Chitralanda
Palace
Bangkok
Noi
National
Museum
Jim Thomson's
House
Wat Phra Kaeo & Grand Palace
Wat Arun
Khlong
Toey
Phasi
Charoen
Khlong
Krung Thep
(Bangkok)
Thonburi
Sathorn
Bang
Kholaem
Chao Phraya
Phra
Khanong
Chom
Thong
Yannawa
Phra
Pradaeng
Samut
Prakan
Ratburana

0 5 Km
0 5 Miles

Beijing

Summer Palace
Kunming Hu
Haiden
Jiuxianqiao
Olympic Park
Beijiaoshichang
Nanhan He
Deshengmen
Dongzhimen
Weigongcum
Matihutong
Temple
of Earth
Beijing Exhibition Centre
Xizhimen
Beijing
(Peking)
Dongheng
Balizhuang
Bei Hai
Chaoyangmen
Sanlihe
Temple
of Moon
Forbidden City
Chaoyang
Military Museum
Tian'anmen Square
Fuxinglu
Xuanwu
Chongwen
Shawocun
Temple of Heaven
Guang'anmen
Stadium
Guangminglou
Dajiaoting
Taoranting Hu
Longtun Hu
Shabanzhuang
Puhuangyu
You'Anmen
Linangshui Hu
Fengtai
Dahongmen
Tiejiangyin

0 3 Km
0 3 Miles

Delhi

Sadar
Bazar
Old
Delhi
Red
Fort
East
Patel Nagar
Delhi
Rajendra
Nagar Old
Pahar
Ganj
Rajendra
Nagar New
Connaught
Place
Yamuna
Natural
History
Museum
Pusa
Forest
President's
Residence
India Gate
National
Stadium
The Ridge
New Delhi
National
Museum
Old
Fort
Delhi
Zoo
Dhaula
Kuan
Khan
Market
Humayun's
Tomb
Central
Ridge
Reserved
Forest
Nehru
Park
Lodhi
Gardens
Nizamuddin
Chanakyapuri
Safdar Jang's
Tomb
Lodi
Colony
Lajpat
Nagar

0 1 Km
0 1 Miles

Dhaka

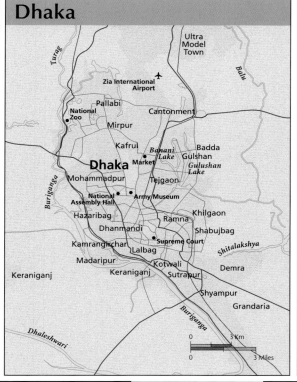

Ultra
Model
Town
Turag
Balu
Zia International
Airport
Pallabi
Cantonment
National
Zoo
Mirpur
Kafrul
Badda
Banani
Lake
Gulshan
Burignaga
Dhaka
Market
Gulushan
Lake
Mohammadpur
Tejgaon
National
Assembly Hall
Army Museum
Hazaribag
Ramna
Khilgaon
Dhanmandi
Shabujbag
Kamrangirchar
Supreme Court
Keraniganj
Lalbag
Shitalakshya
Madaripur
Kotwali
Demra
Keraniganj
Sutrapur
Shyampur
Grandaria
Buriganga
Dhaleshwari

0 3 Km
0 3 Miles

Kolkata

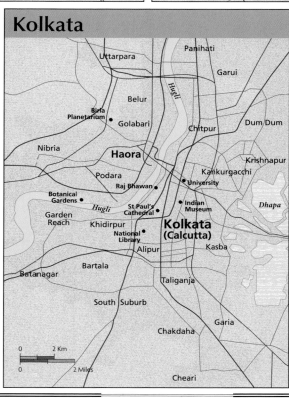

Panihati
Uttarpara
Garui
Hugli
Belur
Birla
Planetarium
Golabari
Chitpur
Dum Dum
Nibria
Krishnapur
Haora
Kankurgacchi
Podara
University
Raj Bhawan
Dhapa
Botanical
Gardens
St Paul's
Cathedral
Indian
Museum
Hugli
Garden
Reach
Khidirpur
Kolkata
(Calcutta)
National
Library
Alipur
Kasba
Batanagar
Bartala
Taliganja
Cheari
South Suburb
Chakdaha
Garia

0 2 Km
0 2 Miles

Kabul

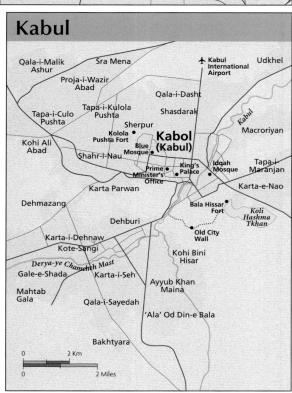

Qala-i-Malik
Ashur
Sra Mena
Kabul
International
Airport
Udkhel
Proja-i-Wazir
Abad
Qala-i-Dasht
Tapa-i-Culo
Pushta
Tapa-i-Kulola
Pushta
Shasdarak
Kabul
Kohi Ali
Abad
Sherpur
Kolola
Pushta Fort
Kabol
(Kabul)
Macroriyan
Blue
Mosque
Shahr-I-Nau
King's
Palace
Idgah
Mosque
Tapa-i-
Marānjan
Prime
Minister's
Office
Karta-e-Nao
Dehmazang
Karta Parwan
Bala Hissar
Fort
Koli
Hashma
Tkhan
Dehburi
Old City
Wall
Karta-i-Dehnaw
Kohi Bini
Hisar
Kote-Sangi
Derya-ye Chameneh Mast
Gale-e-Shada
Karta-i-Seh
Ayyub Khan
Maina
Mahtab
Gala
Qala-i-Sayedah
'Ala' Od Din-e Bala
Bakhtyara

0 2 Km
0 2 Miles

Hong Kong

Mong Kok
Kowloon City
Kowloon
Royal Observatory
Ho Man Tin
Hung Hom
Kowloon Bay
Hong Kong Coliseum
Tsim Sha Tsui
Space Museum & Planetarium
Star Ferry
Sai Ying Pun
Kennedy Town
North Point
Victoria Harbour
University of Hong Kong
Mid Levels
Sheung Wan
Convention Centre
Tun Lo Wan
Tai Tam
Government House
Hong Kong (Xianggang)
Wan Chai
Tai Hang
Victoria Peak 554m △
Hong Kong Island
Happy Valley
Tiger Balm Garden

0   1 Km
0   1 Miles

Istanbul

Alibey
Kemerburgaz
Istanbul Boğazı Bosporus
Beykoz
Ömerli
Hurriyet Abidesi
Kagithane
Tasdelen
Gaziosmanpasa
Şişli
Beşiktas
Esenler
Eyüp
Beyoglu
Galata Kulesi
Bagcilar
Fatih
Topkapi
Üsküdar
Ümraniye
Güngören
Kapati Çarsi
Ayasofya
Selimiye Kişlasi
Küçükçekmece
Bahçelievler
Blue Mosque
Zeytinburnu
Sultanbeyli
Bakirköy
Atatürk Intl. Airport
Marmara Sea
Maltepe
Kartal
Pendik
Adalar
Büyükada

0   5 Km
0   5 Miles

Kuala Lumpur

Lake Titiwangsa
Kepong
Sentul
National Art Gallery
Tunku
Baru
Ulu Kelang
Sungai Buloh
National Monument
Golden Triangle
Petronas Towers
Ampang
Damansara
National Mosque
Central Market
Lake gardens
Kuala Lumpur
Taman Meur
Bangsar
National Museum
Taman Mayang
Petaling Jaya
Salak Selatan
Pengkalan Udara Airport
Sungai Besi

0   1 Km
0   1 Miles

Ulan Bator

Gesper Temple
Government Palace
Gandan Monastery
Ulaanbaatar Museum
Ulaanbaatar (Ulan Bator)
Stadium
Winter Palace Museum of Bogd-Khan
Selbe
Selbe

0   1 Km
0   1 Miles

Islamabad

Faisal Mosque
Zoo
Parliament Building
Islamabad Museum
Supreme Court
Zone 1
Conference Centre
Islamabad Sports Complex
Islāmābād
Zone 4
Rawal Lake
Rawal Town
Zone 2
University
Zone 5
Margalea Railway Station
Islamabad Park
Rawalpindi
Islamabad International Airport

0   3 Km
0   3 Miles

Jakarta

Java Sea
Teluk Jakarta
Soekarno-Hatta International Airport
Penjaringan
Pademangan
Ancol
Tanjung Priok
Kalideres
Taman Sari
Jakarta Museum
Sunter
Koja
Merdeka Palace
Jakarta
National Monument
Cempaka Putih
Kembangan
Welcome Monument
Kebon Jeruk
Parliament House
Menteng
University Rawamangun
Pulo Gadung
Kebayoran Lama
Matraman
Jatinegara
Pancoran
Manggarai
Kebayoran Baru
Jakarta Halim Perdanakusuma Airport
Cilandak
Kramat Jati
Pasar Munggu
Ciracas
Jagakarsa

0   5 Km
0   5 Miles

Manila

Maypajo
Masambong
San Francisco de Monta
Quezon Memorial
Caloocan
Santa Mesa Heights
Quezon City
Cubao
Sampaloc
La Loma
New Manila
South China Sea
Tondo
University of Santo Thomas
Sampaloc
Manila
San Juan del Monte
Binondo
Quiapo
Ortigas
San Nicholas
San Miguel
Pasig
Fort Santiago
Malacañang Palace
Malacañang Park
Mandaluyong
Cathedral
Intramuros
Pandacan
Rizal Park
Paco
Santa Ana
National Library
Guadalupe
Ermita
Manila Bay
Malate
Metropolitan Museum
Rizal Stadium
Makati
Pasig

0   2 Km
0   2 Miles

H   I   J   K   L   M   N
1   2   3   4   5   6   7   8   9   10

Australasia and Oceania with a total land area of 3,285,048 sq miles (8,508,238 sq km), takes in 14 countries including the continent of Australia, New Zealand, Papua New Guinea, and many island groups scattered across the Pacific Ocean.

FACTFILE

N **Most Northerly Point:** Eastern Island, Midway Islands 28° 15′ N
S **Most Southerly Point:** Macquarie Island, Australia 54° 30′ S
E **Most Easterly Point:** Clipperton Island, 109° 12′ W
W **Most Westerly Point:** Cape Inscription, Australia 112° 57′ E

Largest Lakes:
1. Lake Eyre, Australia 3430 sq miles (8884 sq km)
2. Lake Torrens, Australia 2200 sq miles (5698 sq km)
3. Lake Gairdner, Australia 1679 sq miles (4349 sq km)
4. Lake Mackay, Australia 1349 sq miles (3494 sq km)
5. Lake Argyle, Australia 800 sq miles (2072 sq km)

Longest Rivers:
1. Murray-Darling, Australia 2330 miles (3750 km)
2. Cooper Creek, Australia 880 miles (1420 km)
3. Warburton-Georgina, Australia 870 miles (1400 km)
4. Sepik, Indonesia/Papua New Guinea 700 miles (1126 km)
5. Fly, Indonesia/Papua New Guinea 652 miles (1050 km)

Largest Islands:
1. New Guinea, 312,000 sq miles (808,000 sq km)
2. South Island, New Zealand 56,308 sq miles (145,836 sq km)
3. North Island, New Zealand 43,082 sq miles (111,583 sq km)
4. Tasmania, Australia 24,911 sq miles (64,519 sq km)
5. New Britain, Papua New Guinea 13,570 sq miles (35,145 sq km)

Highest Points:
1. Mount Wilhelm, Papua New Guinea 14,793 ft (4509 m)
2. Mount Giluwe, Papua New Guinea 14,331 ft (4368 m)
3. Mount Herbert, Papua New Guinea 13,999 ft (4267 m)
4. Mount Bangeta, Papua New Guinea 13,520 ft (4121 m)
5. Mount Victoria, Papua New Guinea 13,360 ft (4072 m)

Lowest Point:
▼ Lake Eyre, Australia -53 ft (-16 m) below sea level

Highest recorded temperature:
● Bourke, Australia 128°F (53°C)

Lowest recorded temperature:
⊖ Canberra, Australia -8°F (-22°C)

Wettest Place:
◉ Bellenden Ker, Australia 443 in (11,251 mm)

Driest Place:
⊖ Mulka Bore, Australia 4.05 in (102.8 mm)

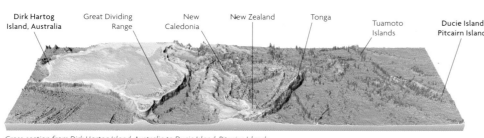

Cross-section from Dirk Hartog Island, Australia to Ducie Island, Pitcairn Islands

line of cross-section

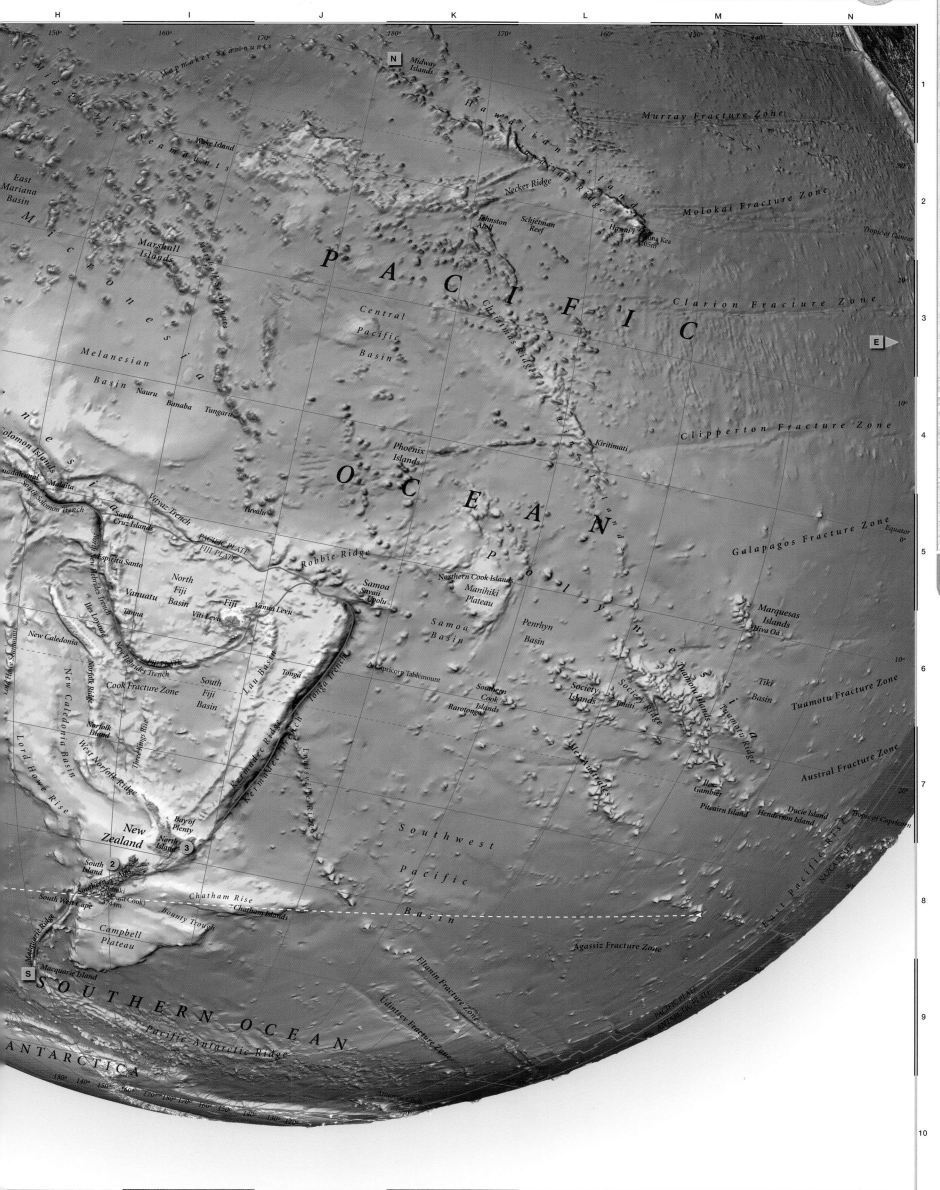

Political

Vast expanses of ocean separate this geographically fragmented realm, characterized more by each country's isolation than by any political unity. Australia's and New Zealand's traditional ties with the United Kingdom, as members of the Commonwealth, are now being called into question as Australasian and Oceanian nations are increasingly looking to forge new relationships with neighboring Asian countries like Japan. External influences have featured strongly in the politics of the Pacific Islands; the various territories of Micronesia were largely under US control until the late 1980s, and France, New Zealand, the USA and the UK still have territories under colonial rule in Polynesia. Nuclear weapons-testing by Western superpowers was widespread during the Cold War period, but has now been discontinued.

Population

- ■ above 5 million
- ▣ 1 million to 5 million
- ◉ 500,000 to 1 million
- ◎ 100,000 to 500,000
- ⊕ 50,000 to 100,000
- ⊙ 10,000 to 50,000
- ○ below 10,000
- ● Country capital
- ● State capital

Borders

- full international border
- indication of maritime country extent
- indication of maritime dependent territory extent
- state border

Communications

- major roads
- major railroads

Scale 1:32,000,000
(projection: Lambert Azimuthal Equal Area)

AUSTRALASIA & OCEANIA

AUSTRALASIA & OCEANIA

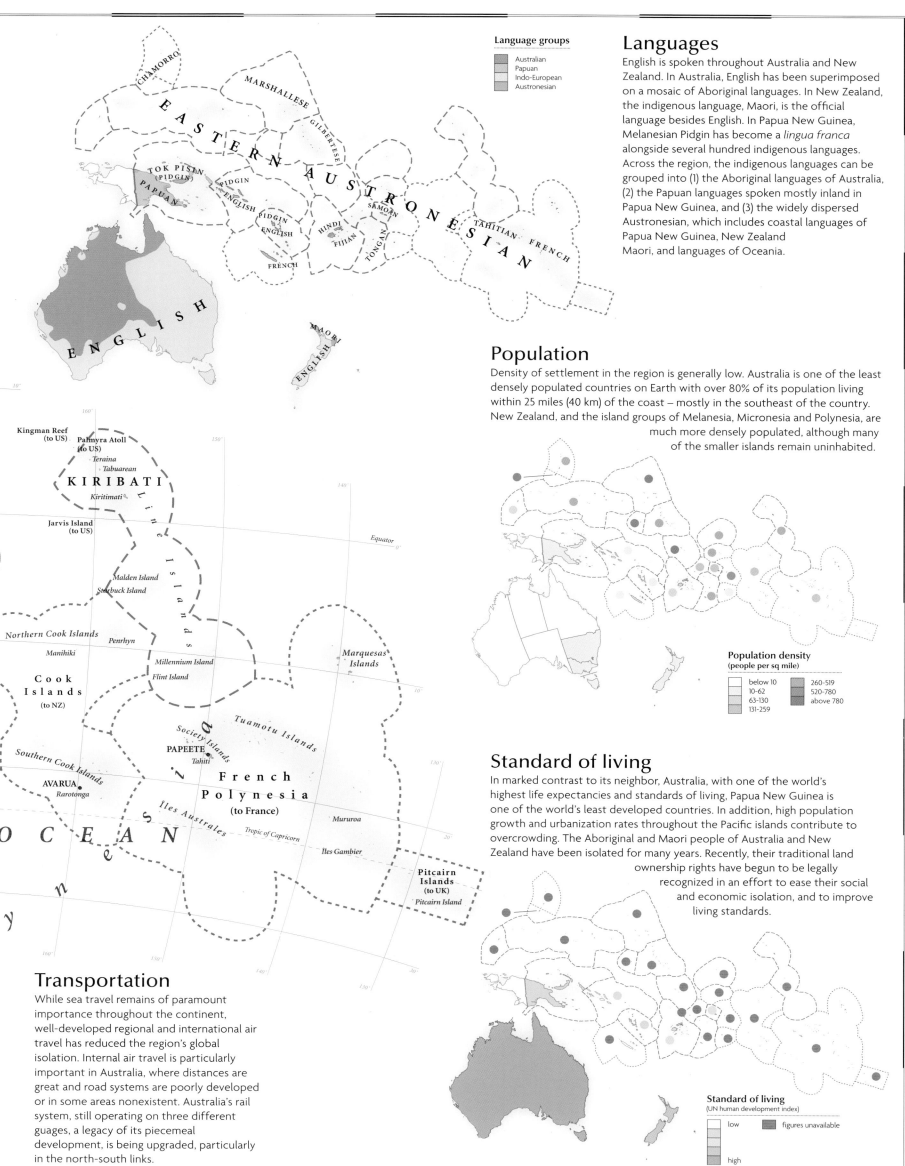

Languages

Language groups
- Australian
- Papuan
- Indo-European
- Austronesian

English is spoken throughout Australia and New Zealand. In Australia, English has been superimposed on a mosaic of Aboriginal languages. In New Zealand, the indigenous language, Maori, is the official language besides English. In Papua New Guinea, Melanesian Pidgin has become a *lingua franca* alongside several hundred indigenous languages. Across the region, the indigenous languages can be grouped into (1) the Aboriginal languages of Australia, (2) the Papuan languages spoken mostly inland in Papua New Guinea, and (3) the widely dispersed Austronesian, which includes coastal languages of Papua New Guinea, New Zealand Maori, and languages of Oceania.

Population

Density of settlement in the region is generally low. Australia is one of the least densely populated countries on Earth with over 80% of its population living within 25 miles (40 km) of the coast – mostly in the southeast of the country. New Zealand, and the island groups of Melanesia, Micronesia and Polynesia, are much more densely populated, although many of the smaller islands remain uninhabited.

Population density
(people per sq mile)
- below 10
- 10–62
- 63–130
- 131–259
- 260–519
- 520–780
- above 780

Standard of living

In marked contrast to its neighbor, Australia, with one of the world's highest life expectancies and standards of living, Papua New Guinea is one of the world's least developed countries. In addition, high population growth and urbanization rates throughout the Pacific islands contribute to overcrowding. The Aboriginal and Maori people of Australia and New Zealand have been isolated for many years. Recently, their traditional land ownership rights have begun to be legally recognized in an effort to ease their social and economic isolation, and to improve living standards.

Standard of living
(UN human development index)
- low
- high
- figures unavailable

Transportation

While sea travel remains of paramount importance throughout the continent, well-developed regional and international air travel has reduced the region's global isolation. Internal air travel is particularly important in Australia, where distances are great and road systems are poorly developed or in some areas nonexistent. Australia's rail system, still operating on three different guages, a legacy of its piecemeal development, is being upgraded, particularly in the north-south links.

269

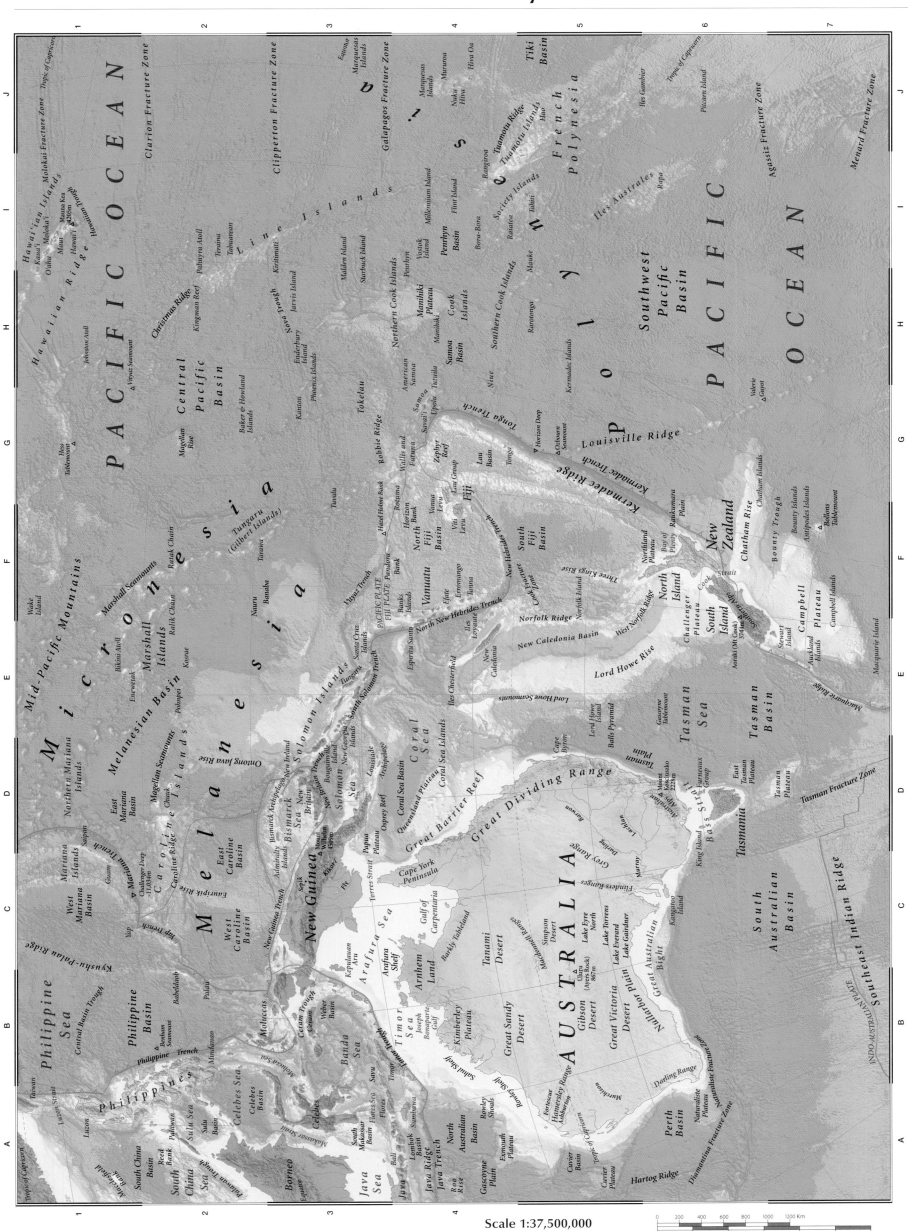

Scale 1:37,500,000
(projection: Lambert Azimuthal Equal Area)

0 200 400 600 800 1000 1200 Km
0 200 400 600 800 1000 1200 Miles

Climate

Surrounded by water, the climate of most areas is profoundly affected by the moderating effects of the oceans. Australia, however, is the exception. Its dry continental interior remains isolated from the ocean; temperatures soar during the day, and droughts are common. The coastal regions, where most people live, are cooler and wetter. The numerous islands scattered across the Pacific are generally hot and humid, subject to the different air circulation patterns and ocean currents that affect the area, including the El Niño ocean current anomaly, which produces extreme aridity.

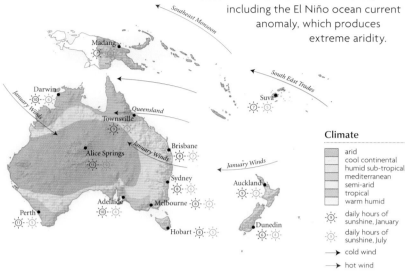

Climate

- arid
- cool continental
- humid sub-tropical
- mediterranean
- semi-arid
- tropical
- warm humid
- ☼ daily hours of sunshine, January
- ☼ daily hours of sunshine, July
- → cold wind
- → hot wind

Average Rainfall

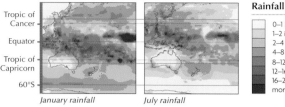

January rainfall   *July rainfall*

Rainfall

- 0–1 in (0–25 mm)
- 1–2 in (25–50 mm)
- 2–4 in (50–100 mm)
- 4–8 in (100–200 mm)
- 8–12 in (200–300 mm)
- 12–16 in (300–400 mm)
- 16–20 in (400–500 mm)
- more than 20 in (500 mm)

Average Temperature

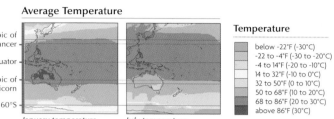

January temperature   *July temperature*

Temperature

- below -22°F (-30°C)
- -22 to -4°F (-30 to -20°C)
- -4 to 14°F (-20 to -10°C)
- 14 to 32°F (-10 to 0°C)
- 32 to 50°F (0 to 10°C)
- 50 to 68°F (10 to 20°C)
- 68 to 86°F (20 to 30°C)
- above 86°F (30°C)

Environmental issues

The prospect of rising sea levels poses a threat to many low-lying islands in the Pacific. Nuclear weapons-testing, once common throughout the region, was finally discontinued in 1996. Australia's ecological balance has been irreversibly altered by the introduction of alien species. Although it has the world's largest underground water reserve, the Great Artesian Basin, the availability of fresh water in Australia remains critical. Periodic droughts combined with over-grazing lead to desertification and increase the risk of devastating bush fires, and occasional flash floods.

☢ PACIFIC TEST SITES

Eniwetok Atoll, Marshall Islands
Bikini Atoll, Marshall Islands
Johnston Atoll
Mururoa Atoll, French Polynesia
Fangataua Atoll, French Polynesia
Christmas Island, Kiribati

Environmental issues

- national parks
- tropical forest
- forest destroyed
- desert
- desertification
- ∖ polluted rivers
- ☢ radioactive contamination
- marine pollution
- heavy marine pollution
- • poor urban air quality

Land use

Much of the region's industry is resource-based: sheep farming for wool and meat in Australia and New Zealand; mining in Australia and Papua New Guinea and fishing throughout the Pacific islands. Manufacturing is mainly limited to the large coastal cities in Australia and New Zealand, like Sydney, Adelaide, Melbourne, Brisbane, Perth, and Auckland, although small-scale enterprises operate in the Pacific islands, concentrating on processing of fish and foods. Tourism continues to provide revenue to the area—in Fiji it accounts for 15 percent of GNP.

Using the land and sea

- barren land
- cropland
- desert
- forest
- mountain region
- pasture
- sheep
- coconuts
- coffee
- fishing
- fruit
- shellfish
- sugar cane
- vineyards
- whaling
- wheat

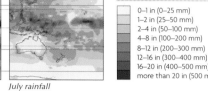

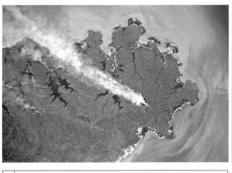

1 MELVILLE ISLAND, NORTHERN TERRITORY, AUSTRALIA
Lying off Australia's north coast, the island is sparsely populated consisting of sandy soils and mangrove swamps.

2 ANATAHAN, NORTHERN MARIANA ISLANDS
The volcano on Anatahan is one of 12 in the Mariana Islands and erupted on a large scale in April 2005.

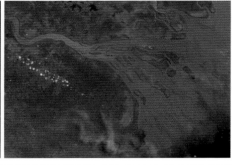

3 FLY RIVER, PAPUA NEW GUINEA
Flowing down from New Guinea's Central Range, the river carries a heavy load of sediment which it deposits in the Gulf of Papua, sometimes forming new islands.

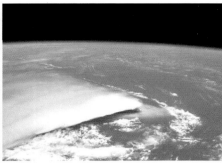

4 RABAUL VOLCANO, NEW BRITAIN, PAPUA NEW GUINEA
After erupting in 1994, this image shows how the highest particles blew west causing condensation of water vapor over a wide area.

9 ULURU/AYERS ROCK, NORTHERN TERRITORY, AUSTRALIA
This enormous sandstone rock occupies Australia's heart, both physically and emotionally.

10 JAMES RANGES, NORTHERN TERRITORY, AUSTRALIA
A series of low ridges, these hills lie at the geographical center of Australia.

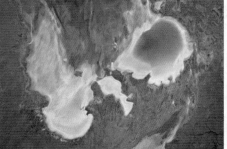

11 LAKE EYRE, SOUTH AUSTRALIA, AUSTRALIA
This great salt lake consists of north and south sections, joined by a narrow channel, Lake Eyre South being the smaller, elongated saltflat at the bottom of the image.

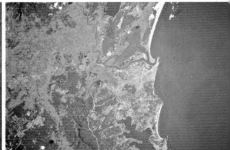

12 NEWCASTLE, NEW SOUTH WALES, AUSTRALIA
The industrial seaport of Newcastle lies on the south bank of Hunter river.

BIKINI ATOLL, MARSHALL ISLANDS 5
This atoll was the site of 23 atomic bomb tests in the 1940s and 1950s, involving the intentional sinking of at least 13 naval vessels in the shallow lagoon.

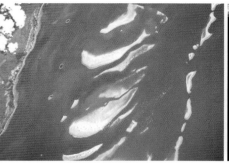

GREAT BARRIER REEF, QUEENSLAND, AUSTRALIA 6
The world's largest reef system is made up of 3000 individual reefs and 900 islands and stretches for 1600 miles (2600 km).

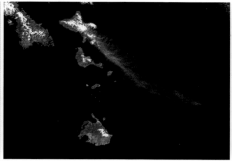

AMBRYM, VANUATU 7
Mount Marum, a 4166 ft (1270 m) volcano, erupted in April 2004 producing an extensive plume of ash.

KIRITIMATI, KIRIBATI 8
Kiritimati is the largest atoll in the Pacific Ocean, its interior lagoon filled in with coral growth.

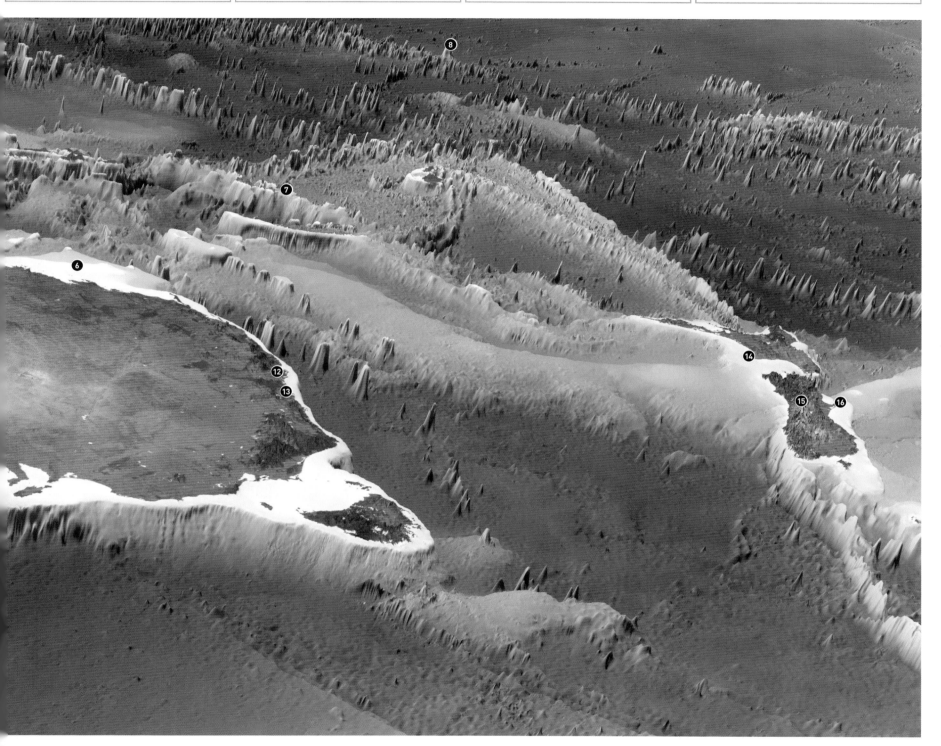

SYDNEY, NEW SOUTH WALES, AUSTRALIA 13
Expanding outward from the inlet of Port Jackson, Australia's largest city was founded in 1788.

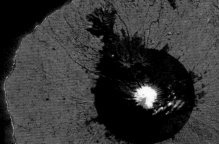

MOUNT TARANAKI, NORTH ISLAND, NEW ZEALAND 14
This dormant 2518 m (8261 ft) volcano is one of the most symmetrical in the world.

**AORAKI/MOUNT COOK,
SOUTH ISLAND, NEW ZEALAND** 15
New Zealand's highest peak rises 12,238 ft (3744 m) and is surrounded by permanent ice fields.

BANKS PENINSULA, SOUTH ISLAND, NEW ZEALAND 16
With a circular drainage pattern typical of eroded volcanoes, this is the only recognizably volcanic feature on New Zealand's South Island.

Australia

259

289

293

Grid references
A B C D E F G

Elevation scale
6000m
4000m
3000m
2000m
1000m
500m
250m
100m
Sea Level
-250m
-2000m
-4000m

Indonesia / Java region
Kepulauan Seribu
Serang
Soekarno-Hatta
Tangerang
JAKARTA
Java Sea
Pulau Madura
Semarang
Pekalongan
Surabaya
Bogor
Cianjur
Cirebon
Tegal
Brebes
Sukabumi
Bandung
Garut
Magelang
Purwodadi
Pasuruan
Probolinggo
Ciamis
Surakarta
Madiun
Kediri
Jombang
Malang
Jember
Cilacap
Yogyakarta
Denpasar
Jawa (Java)
Gunung Raung
Gunung Tjakan
Ngurah Rai
Mataram
Bali
Pulau Lombok
Bali Sea
Raba
Ruteng
Flores
Sumbawa
Kepulauan Kangean
Kepulauan Tengah
1152
Kepulauan Tengah
Larantuka
Labala
Rabi
Kalabahi
Manatuto
Tutuala
Laspalos
Kepulauan Alor
Selat Wetar
DILI
Mahina
EAST TIMOR
Suai
Kefamenanu
Soe
Yatoke
Amplawas
Eliase
Saumlaki
Kepulauan Tanimbar
Nusa Tenggara (Lesser Sunda Islands)
Savu Sea
Waingapu
Kupang
Baing
Baa
Pulau Roti
Pulau Sumba
Kepulauan Sawu
Nusa Tenggara
Timor Sea

INDONESIA

CHRISTMAS ISLAND
(to Australia)

Indian Ocean region
INDIAN
OCEAN
Tropic of Capricorn

Northern Australia coast
Croker Island
Melville Island
Gebin Peninsula
Bathurst Island
Van Diemen Gulf
Beagle Gulf
Darwin
Noonamah
Jabiru
AdelaideRiver
Cooinda
PineCreek
Mount Evelyn 465m
Katherine
Daly River
Mataranka
Cape Bougainville
Cape Londonderry
Joseph Bonaparte Gulf
Kalumburu
Larrima
Victoria River Roadhouse
DalyWater
Bonaparte Archipelago
Heywood Islands
Wyndham
Kununurra
Timber Creek
Top Springs Roadhouse
Adele Island
Collier Bay
Mount Hann 779m
Kimberley Plateau
Lake Argyle
Sturt Plain
Bigge Island
Durack Range
Turkey Creek
Victoria River
Kalkarindji
Lombadina
King Leopold Ranges
Kupingarri
Bungle Bungle
Mount Wells 970m
Kings
King Sound
Derby
HallsCreek
Tanami Desert
Broome
Fitzroy River
FitzroyCrossing
Rowley Shoals

Western Australia
Eighty Mile Beach
Great Sandy Desert
NORTHERN
AUSTRALIA
WESTERN AUSTRALIA
SOUTH
Dampier Archipelago
Port Hedland
De Grey River
Dampier
Wickham
Karratha
Roebourne
Whim Creek
MarbleBar
Percival Lakes
Tobin Lake
Lake Mackay
Yuendumu
Barrow Island
Fortescue River
Witteroom
Lake Dora
Lake Auld
Mount Liebig 1274m
Mount Zeil 1531m
Glen Helen
North West Cape
Onslow
Hamersley Range
Lake Disappointment
Gibson Desert
Hopkins Lake
Lake Neale
Hermannsburg
James Ranges
Exmouth
Learmonth
Tom Price
Paraburdoo
Newman
Lake Macdonald
Coral Bay
Kenneth Range
Mount Meharry 1251m
Little Sandy Desert
Lake Amadeus
Ashburton River
Kata Tjuta (Mount Olga) 1069m
Erldunda Roadhouse
Minilya
Barlee Range
Kumarina Roadhouse
Yulara
Uluru (Ayers Rock) 867m
Lake Macleod
Mount Augustus 1105m
Waldburg Range
Carnarvon Range
Lake Gregory
Lake Carnegie
Warburton
Tomkinson Ranges
Musgrave Ranges
Mount Morris 1288m
Bernier Island
Gascoyne River
Carnarvon
Gascoyne Junction
Robinson Range
Wiluna
Lake Way
Lake Wells
Everard Ranges
Dorre Island
Shark Bay
Murchison River
Meekatharra
Lake Carey
Dirk Hartog Island
Denham
Lake Annean
Lake Austin
Lake Throssell
LakeYeo
Great Victoria Desert
Lake Maurice
SteepPoint
Kalbarri
Yalgoo
Mount Magnet
Leonora
Lake Ballard
Lake Carey
Watson
Geraldton
Mongers Lake
Lake Barlee
Menzies
Lake Rebecca
Nullarbor Plain
Moora
Wubin
Lake Moore
Lake Cowan
Loongana
Reid
Pithara
Coolgardie
Kambalda
Lake Lefroy
Kalgoorlie
Kitchener
Rawlinna
Madura
Eucla
Bookal
The Pinnacles
Gingin
Merredin
Southern Cross
Balladonia
Caiguna
Cocklebiddy
Wanneroo
Northam
York
Perth
Fremantle
Rockingham
Brookton
Lake Johnston
Norseman
Lake Dundas
Tower Peak 594m
Esperance
Great Australian Bight
Mandurah
Kondinin
Lake Hope
Bunbury
Narrogin
Lake King
Ravensthorpe
Busselton
Collie
Wagin
Katanning
Margaret River
Bridgetown
Manjimup
Cape Leeuwin
Augusta
Pemberton
Mount Barker
Albany

Perth inset
Perth
Indian Ocean
Wembley Downs
Joondanna
Bayswater
Herdsman Lake
North Perth
City Beach
Lake Monger
Art Gallery of Western Australia
Jolimont
Subiaco
Swan River
Belmont Park
Alderbury Park
Kings Park
Perth
Redcliffe
Claremont
Zoo
South Perth
Carlisle
Dalkeith
Kensington
Cottesloe
Swan River
Applecross
Cannington
Mosman Park
Manning
Canning River
Fremantle
Myaree
Partwood
Piney Lakes Reserve
Bull Creek
Hilton
Murdoch
3 Km
3 Miles

Scale 1:13,000,000
(projection: Lambert Conformal Conic)

0 50 100 150 200 250 300 350 400 Km
0 50 100 150 200 250 300 350 400 Miles

Population
- ▣ above 5 million
- ▣ 1 million to 5 million
- ◉ 500,000 to 1 million
- ◎ 100,000 to 500,000
- ⊙ 50,000 to 100,000
- ⊙ 10,000 to 50,000
- ○ below 10,000

PAPUA NEW GUINEA

Arafura Sea

New Guinea

Gulf of Papua

PORT MORESBY

Torres Strait

Solomon Sea

Coral Sea

SOLOMON ISLANDS

HONIARA
Guadalcanal

Bougainville Island

CORAL SEA ISLANDS
(to Australia)

NEW CALEDONIA
(to France)

Gulf of Carpentaria

Arnhem Land

Cape York Peninsula

QUEENSLAND

Great Artesian Basin

Great Dividing Range

Great Barrier Reef

TERRITORY

Simpson Desert

Lake Eyre Basin

Sturt Stony Desert

Tennant Creek
Mount Isa
Cloncurry
Camooweal
Alice Springs

Macdonnell Ranges

AUSTRALIA

Townsville
Cairns
Mackay
Rockhampton
Gladstone
Bundaberg
Hervey Bay
Maryborough
Sunshine Coast
Brisbane
Ipswich
Gold Coast
Surfers Paradise

NEW SOUTH WALES

Tropic of Capricorn

PACIFIC OCEAN

Lord Howe Island
(to Australia)

Coffs Harbour
Grafton
Armidale
Tamworth
Dubbo
Newcastle
Sydney
Wollongong
CANBERRA
AUSTRALIAN CAPITAL TERRITORY
JERVIS BAY TERRITORY

Adelaide
Port Augusta
Port Pirie
Port Lincoln

Kangaroo Island

VICTORIA

Melbourne
Geelong
Ballarat
Bendigo
Portland

Bass Strait

King Island

TASMANIA

Hobart
Launceston
Devonport

Brisbane

Chermside
Everton Park
Toombul
Brisbane Airport
Wynnum
Lutwyche
Clayfield
The Gap
Red Hill
Newstead
Hawthorne
Manly
Tingalpa
Brisbane
Botanical Gardens
Queensland Art Gallery
Indooroopilly
Wolloongabba
Greenslopes
Carina Heights
Belmont
Corinda
Mount Gravatt
Burbank
Tingalpa Reservoir

3 Km
3 Miles

19,686ft
13,124ft
9843ft
6562ft
3281ft
1640ft
820ft
328ft
Sea Level
-820ft
-6562ft
-13,124ft

Southeast Australia

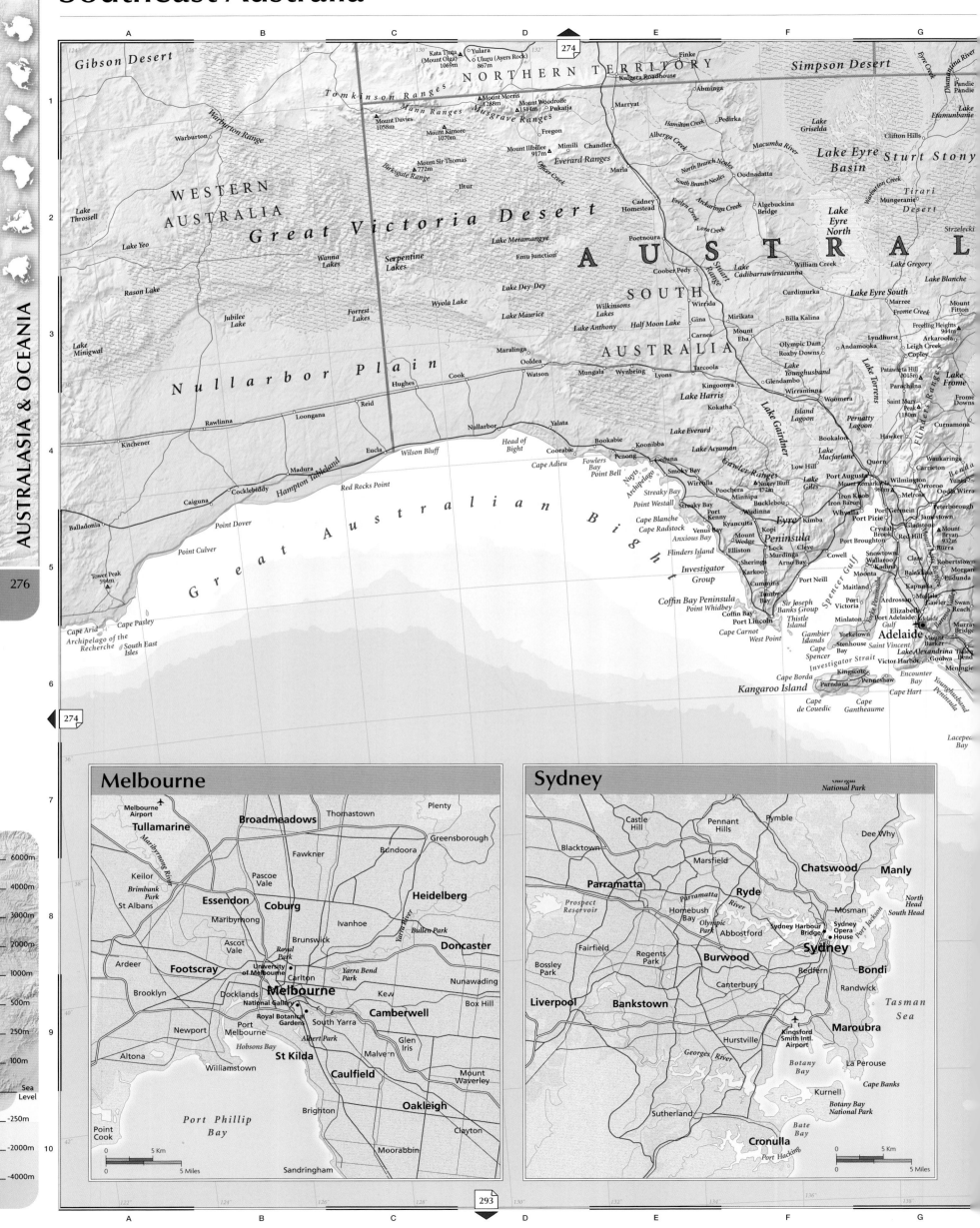

Scale 1:6,500,000
(projection: Lambert Conformal Conic)

0 25 50 75 100 125 150 175 200 Km
0 25 50 75 100 125 150 175 200 Miles

Population

☐ above 5 million   ☐ 1 million to 5 million   ◉ 500,000 to 1 million
◎ 100,000 to 500,000   ◉ 50,000 to 100,000   ○ 10,000 to 50,000   ○ below 10,000

19,686ft
13,124ft
9843ft
6562ft
3281ft
1640ft
820ft
328ft
Sea Level
-820ft
-6562ft
-13,124ft

QUEENSLAND

NEW SOUTH WALES

VICTORIA

AUSTRALIAN CAPITAL TERRITORY

JERVIS BAY TERRITORY

Great Dividing Range

Great Alps

TASMANIA

Tasmania

Bass Strait

Tasman Sea

Brisbane
Ipswich
Gold Coast
Sydney
Parramatta
Campbelltown
Wollongong
Newcastle
Canberra
Melbourne
Geelong
Hobart
Launceston

Fraser Island
King Island
Flinders Island

North Island

NEW ZEALAND

GISBORNE

HAWKE'S BAY

MANAWATU-WANGANUI

WELLINGTON

TARANAKI

WAIKATO

BAY OF PLENTY

NORTHLAND

AUCKLAND

NELSON

Bay of Plenty

Hawke Bay

Tasman Sea

Coromandel Peninsula

Coromandel Range

Ruahine Range

Kaweka Range

Kaimanawa Range

Raukumara Range

Ninety Mile Beach

Three Kings Islands

Cape Reinga

North Cape

Cape Maria van Diemen

Cape Karikari

Cape Brett

Bay of Islands

Great Exhibition Bay

Doubtless Bay

Parengarenga Harbour

Rangaunu Bay

Ahipara Bay

Hokianga Harbour

Kaipara Harbour

North Head

Manukau Harbour

Hauraki Gulf

Great Barrier Island

Little Barrier Island

Poor Knights Islands

Cavalli Islands

Hen and Chickens

Bream Head

Bream Bay

Cape Rodney

Mercury Islands

Great Mercury Island

The Aldermen Islands

Mayor Island

Motiti Island

Matakana Island

Mokohinau Islands

White Island

Cape Colville

Cape Runaway

East Cape

Hicks Bay

Te Araroa

Tolaga Bay

Tokomaru Bay

Mahia Peninsula

Portland Island

Cape Kidnappers

Cape Turnagain

Castlepoint

Flat Point

Mount Egmont (Mount Taranaki) 2518m

Mount Ruapehu 2797m

North Taranaki Bight

South Taranaki Bight

Cook Strait

Kapiti Island

Stephens Island

D'Urville Island

French Pass

Farewell Spit

Cape Farewell

Golden Bay

Tasman Bay

Separation Point

Cape Stephens

Whangarei

Dargaville

Kaikohe

Kerikeri

Russell

Kaitaia

Kawakawa

Maungaturoto

Helensville

Warkworth

Orewa

Takapuna

Auckland

Papakura

Pukekohe

Thames

Tauranga

Te Puke

Whakatane

Opotiki

Rotorua

Hamilton

Cambridge

Te Awamutu

Morrinsville

Matamata

Putaruru

Tokoroa

Taupo

Turangi

Waiouru

Raetihi

Taumarunui

Te Kuiti

Otorohanga

New Plymouth

Stratford

Eltham

Hawera

Patea

Wanganui

Palmerston North

Feilding

Marton

Bulls

Dannevirke

Woodville

Pahiatua

Masterton

Carterton

Greytown

Featherston

Upper Hutt

Lower Hutt

Porirua

Paraparaumu

Otaki

Levin

Shannon

Foxton

Napier

Hastings

Havelock North

Waipukurau

Waipawa

Wairoa

Gisborne

Nuhaka

Lake Taupo

Lake Rotorua

Lake Waikaremoana

Auckland (inset map)

Auckland

North Shore

Takapuna

Northcote

Devonport

Kauri Park

Point Chevalier

Te Atatu

Avondale

Green Bay

Blockhouse Bay

Glen Eden

Mount Roskill

Mount Eden

Royal Oak

Onehunga

Mount Wellington

Ellerslie

Remuera

Mission Bay

St. Johns Park

Glenn Innes

Grafton

Skytower

Auckland Zoo

Maritime Museum

Auckland Museum

Stardome & Auckland Observatory

One Tree Hill

Orewa

Karaka Bay

Browns Island

Motuihe Island

Motutapu Island

Rangitoto Island

Waitemata Harbour

Manukau Harbour

Lake Pupuke

Bucklands Beach

Highland Park

Pakuranga

Howick

Huntington Park

Clover Park

Otara

Manukau

Mangere

Ambury Park

Auckland Intl. Airport

Papatoetoe

Kohimarama Bay

Tamaki River

0 3 Km

0 3 Miles

Elevation scale

6000m
4000m
3000m
2000m
1000m
500m
250m
100m
Sea Level
-250m
-2000m
-4000m

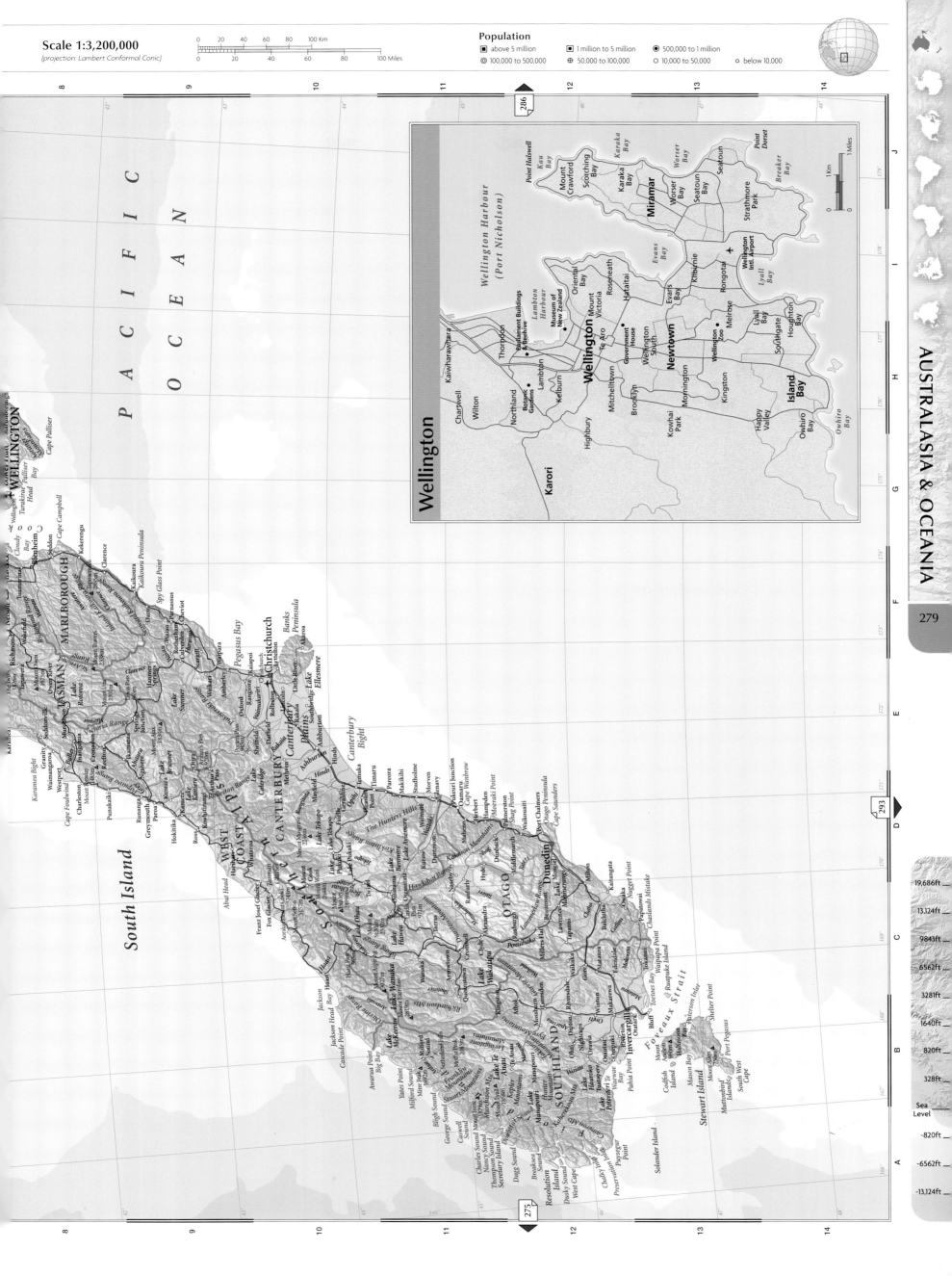

Papua New Guinea & Melanesia

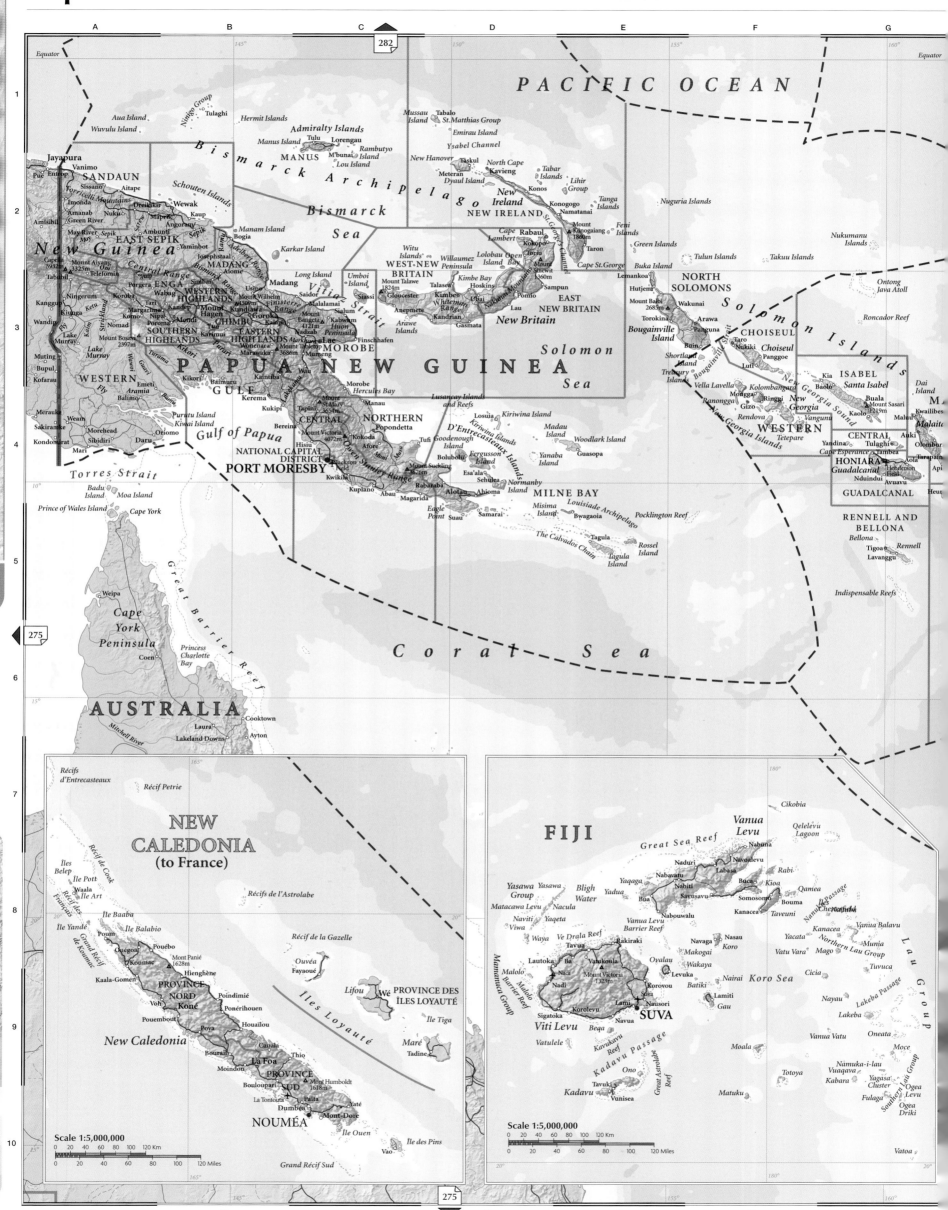

275

AUSTRALASIA & OCEANIA

PACIFIC OCEAN

Equator

Jayapura
Vanimo
Pue Entrop
Sissano
Aitape
SANDAUN
Imonda
Dreikikir
Wewak
Amanab
Nuku
Maprik
Angoram
Kaup
Green River
Amisibil
May River
Sepik
Ambunti
Yaminibot

New Guinea
Capella
3932m
Mount Aiyang
3325m
Om
Telefomin
Tabubil
Central Range
Ningerum
Porgera
Wabag
ENGA
Laiagam
Kandep
WESTERN HIGHLANDS
Kanggu
Kiunga
Koroba
Tari
Margarima
CHIMBU
Mount Hagen
Goroka
Kundiawa
Nomad
Komo
Nipa
Mendi
SOUTHERN HIGHLANDS
Poroma
Karimui
EASTERN HIGHLANDS
Mount Bosavi
2397m
Wandip
Lake Murray
Kaim
Ketu
Strickland
Muting
Lake Murray
Turama
Kikori
Baimuru
WESTERN
Bupul
Kofarau
Fly
Emeti
Aramia
Balimo
GULF
Kerema
Kukipi
Merauke
Weam
Morehead
Sakiramke
Sibidiri
Oriomo
Daru
Mari
Kondomirat
Kiwai Island
Purutu Island

Hermit Islands
Aua Island
Ningmo Group
Tulaghi
Wuvulu Island
Admiralty Islands
Manus Island
Tulu
Lorengau
MANUS
M'bunai
Rambutyo
Lou Island

Mussau Island
Tabalo
St. Matthias Group
Emirau Island
Ysabel Channel
Taskul
North Cape
Kavieng
Meteran
Dyaul Island
Konos
Bismarck Archipelago

Manam Island
Bogia
MADANG
Karkar Island
Adome
Mount Wilhelm
4509m
Simbai
Bundi
Finisterre Range
Madang
Saidor
Usino
Malalamai
Bismarck Sea
Long Island
Vitiaz Strait
Umboi Island
Stassi
Gloucester
Talasea
WEST NEW BRITAIN
Mount Talawe
1824m
Anepmete
Whiteman Range
Kandrian
Arawe Islands
New Britain
Gasmata

Tabar Islands
Lihir Group
Konogogo
Namatanai
Tanga Islands
NEW IRELAND
Cape Lambert
Rabaul
Kokopo
Open Bay
Lolobau Island
EAST NEW BRITAIN
Pomio
Sampun
Mount Sinewit
360m
Cape St. George

Bismarck Range
Gusap
Kaintiba
Lae
MOROBE
Finschhafen
Huon Peninsula
Bangeta
Nadzab
Wau
Bulolo
Mumeng
Morobe
Owen Stanley Range
Mount Victoria
4072m
Tapini
Afore
Kokoda
NORTHERN
Popondetta
CENTRAL
Bereina
Hisiu
NATIONAL CAPITAL DISTRICT
PORT MORESBY
Jackson Field
Kwikila
Abau
Kupiano
Magarida

Feni Islands
Green Islands
Nuguria Islands
Tulun Islands
Takuu Islands
Nukumanu Islands
Buka Island
NORTH SOLOMONS
Lemankoa
Hutjena
Mount Balbi
2685m
Wakunai
Torokina
Arawa
Panguna
Bougainville Island
Shortland Island
Buin
Treasury Islands
Solomon Islands
Ontong Java Atoll
Roncador Reef

Solomon Sea

Lusancay Islands and Reefs
Losuia
Kiriwina Island
Kiriwina Islands
Madau Island
Woodlark Island
D'Entrecasteaux Islands
Goodenough Island
Fergusson Island
Bolubolu
Guasopa
Esa'ala
Normanby Island
Schulea
Rabaraba
Alotau
MILNE BAY
Misima Island
Eagle Point
Ahioma
Bwagaoia
Pocklington Reef
Suau
Samarai
Louisiade Archipelago
Rossel Island
Tagula Island
The Calvados Chain

PAPUA NEW GUINEA

CHOISEUL
Taro
Nukiki
Lofung
Choiseul
Panggoe
Vella Lavella
Ranongga
Ringgi
Gizo
New Georgia
New Georgia Islands
New Georgia Sound
Rendova
Vangunu
Tetepare
WESTERN
ISABEL
Baolo
Buala
Mount Sasari
1219m
Santa Isabel
Dai Island
Maluu
CENTRAL
M
Kwailibes
Auki
Malaita
Olombur
Tulaghi
Tambea
HONIARA
Nduindui
Guadalcanal
Aola
Henderson
Avuavu
GUADALCANAL
Api
Heut

RENNELL AND BELLONA
Bellona
Tigoa
Lavanggu
Rennell

Indispensable Reefs

Australia

Badu Island
Moa Island
Torres Strait
Prince of Wales Island
Cape York
Weipa
Cape York Peninsula
Coen
Great Barrier Reef
Cooktown
Laura
Lakeland Downs
Ayton
Mitchell River
Princess Charlotte Bay

Coral Sea

NEW CALEDONIA
(to France)

Récifs d'Entrecasteaux
Récif Petrie
Îles Belep
Île Pott
Waala
Île Art
Île Baaba
Île Balabio
Poum
Pouébo
Quégoal
Koumac
Mont Panié
1628m
Kaala-Gomen
Hienghène
Grand Récif de Koumac
Voh
Poindimié
PROVINCE NORD
Koné
Ponérihouen
Pouembout
Houaïlou
Poya
Bourail
Canala
Moindou
La Foa
Thio
Boulouparis
PROVINCE SUD
Mont Humboldt
1618m
Paīta
La Tontouta
Yaté
Dumbéa
NOUMÉA
Mont-Dore
Île Ouen

Récif de l'Astrolabe
Récif de la Gazelle
Ouvéa
Fayaoué
Lifou
Wé
PROVINCE DES ÎLES LOYAUTÉ
Île Tiga
Maré
Tadine
Îles Loyauté
Vao
Île des Pins
Grand Récif Sud

New Caledonia

Scale 1:5,000,000
0 20 40 60 80 100 120 Km
0 20 40 60 80 100 120 Miles

FIJI

Cikobia
Vanua Levu
Naduri
Nabuna
Great Sea Reef
Navodevu
Qelelevu Lagoon
Nabavatu
Labasa
Rabi
Yaqaga
Yadua
Nabiti
Buca
Kioa
Yasawa Group
Yasawa
Nacula
Bligh Water
Savusavu
Somosomo
Bouma
Qamea
Matacawa Levu
Naviti
Yaqeta
Bua
Nabouwalu
Taveuni
Kanacea
Vanua Levu Barrier Reef
Viwa
Waya
Mananuca Group
Ve Drala Reef
Makogai
Koro
Yacata
Northern Lau Group
Mago
Vanua Balavu
Rakiraki
Tavua
Vatukoula
Ba
Nasau
Vatu Vara
Munia
Lautoka
Nadi
Malolo
Malolo Barrier Reef
Navaga
Nairai
Koro Sea
Cicia
Tuvuca
Nayau
Mamanuca Group
Levuka
Ovalau
Wakaya
Gau
Lakeba
Korovou
Mount Victoria
1323m
Batiki
Lamiti
Lakeba Passage
Sigatoka
Korolevu
Lami
SUVA
Navua
Nausori
Beqa
Viti Levu
Oneata
Vatulele
Kavukavu Reef
Moce
Vanua Vatu
Kadavu Passage
Totoya
Nāmuka-i-lau
Vuaqava
Kabara
Yagasa Cluster
Ono
Great Astrolabe Reef
Moala
Kadavu
Tavuki
Vunisea
Matuku
Fulaga
Ogea Levu
Ogea Driki
Vatoa
Southern Lau Group
Lau Group

Scale 1:5,000,000
0 20 40 60 80 100 120 Km
0 20 40 60 80 100 120 Miles

Scale 1:10,100,000
(projection: Mercator)

0 50 100 150 200 250 300 Km
0 50 100 150 200 250 300 Miles

Population
■ above 5 million   ◨ 1 million to 5 million   ◉ 500,000 to 1 million
◎ 100,000 to 500,000   ⊕ 50,000 to 100,000   ⊙ 10,000 to 50,000   ○ below 10,000

H   I   J   K   286   L   M   N

SOLOMON ISLANDS

1

CHOISEUL
Taro
Nukiki
Panggoe
Choiseul
Luti
Rob Roy
Kia

Roncador Reef

Hiu
Tegua
Loh
Toga
Torres Islands

Ureparapara

Mota Lava
Mota
Sola
Vanua Lava
Gaua
Banks Islands

Vella Lavella
Mongga
Kolombangara
Gizo
Gizo
Ringgi
Munda
Ranongga
Rendova
Vanguni
Nggatokae
Tetepare
Blanche Channel
New Georgia
New Georgia Islands
WESTERN
Vaghena
Manning Strait
Baolo
ISABEL
Santa Isabel
Buala
Mount Sasari 1219m
Kaolo
San Jorge
Dai Island

MALAITA

2

Mere Lava

Cape Cumberland
Nokuku
Big Bay
Port-Olry
Naone
Espiritu Santo
Mount Tabwemasana 1879m
Navonda
Ambae
Maéwo
Luganville
Malo
VANUATU

New Georgia Sound

Russell Islands
CENTRAL
Florida Islands
Tulaghi
Savo
Cape Esperance
Tambea
Yandina
HONIARA
Tangarare
Guadalcanal
Nduindui
Mount Popomanaseu 2330m
Aola
Avuavu
Henderson Field
Iron Bottom Sound
Maluu
Kwailibesi
Auki
Malaita
Olomburi
Baunani
Tarapaina
Maramasike
Apio

3

Bougainville Strait
Norsup
Unmet
Malekula
Lamap
Lamen Bay
Epi
Bwatnapne
Pentecost
Mount Marum 1270m
Toak
Paama
Ambrym
Lopevi

Indispensable Strait

GUADALCANAL

Ulawa Island
Three Sisters Islands
Heuru
Kirakira
San Cristobal
Hauraha

Tongoa
Emae
Shepherd Islands

4

RENNELL AND BELLONA
Bellona
Tigoa
Lavanggu
Rennell

MAKIRA-ULAWA

Nguna
Emao
Paonangisu
Bauer Field
Forari
PORT-VILA
Efate

LAITA
Sikaiana

SOLOMON ISLANDS

Maramasike
Ulawa Island
Three Sisters Islands
Kirakira
San Cristobal
Star Harbour
Hauraha
MAKIRA-ULAWA

Tikopia

Duff Islands
Reef Islands
Tinakula
Lata
Noka
Nendö
TEMOTU
Santa Cruz Islands
Utupua
Vanikolo

Scale 1:5,000,000
0 20 40 60 80 Km
0 20 40 60 80 Miles

Scale 1:5,000,000
0 20 40 60 80 100 120 Km
0 20 40 60 80 100 120 Miles

Unpongkor
Erromango
Ipota

Aniwa

Tanna
Isangel

5

Hiu
Torres Islands
Toga
Ureparapara
Vanua Lava
Sola
Banks Islands
Gaua

VANUATU

Aneityum

6

Cape Cumberland
Nokuku
Espiritu Santo
Mount Tabwemasana 1879m
Malo
Bougainville Strait
Norsup
Unmet
Malekula
Lamap
Lamen Bay
Port-Olry
Naone
Ambae
Navonda
Luganville
Maéwo
Bwatnapne
Pentecost
Mount Marum 1270m
Toak
Ambrym
Epi
Tongoa
Emae
Shepherd Islands
Nguna
Paonangisu
Bauer Field
Forari
PORT-VILA
Efate

Cikobia
Vanua Levu
Qelelevu Lagoon
Great Sea Reef
Nayolevu
Nabuna
Naduri
Labasa
Buca
Rabi
Nabayatu
Somosomo
Bouma
Yasawa Group
Bligh Water
Bua
Savusavu
Taveuni
Naitaba
Nabouwalu
Kanacea
Northern Lau Group
Vanua Balavu
Mago
Tavua
Rakiraki
Koro
Nasau
Lautoka
Ba
Mount Victoria 1323m
Ovalau
Levuka
Koro Sea
Cicia
Mamanuca Group
Nadi
Nausori
Korovou
Lamiti
Nayau
Viti Levu
Navua
Korolevu
SUVA
Gau
FIJI
Lakeba Passage
Lakeba
Vatulele
Beqa
Kadavu Passage
Oneata
Moce
Namuka-i-lau
Kabara
Vunisea
Moala
Ono
Totoya
Fulaga
Kadavu
Matuku
Vatoa

Lau Group
Southern Lau Group

284

Erromango
Unpongkor
Ipota
Tanna
Aniwa
Isangel
Futuna

Huon
Récifs d'Entrecasteaux
Récif Petrie
Grand Passage
Récif de Cook
Récifs des Français
Île Art
Waala
Île Balabio
Poum
Pouébo
Mont Panié 1628m
Koumac
Hienghène
Kaala-Gomen
PROVINCE NORD
Voh
Koné
Ponérihouen
Houailou
Poya
Bourail
Canala
New Caledonia
Thio
La Foa
PROVINCE SUD
La Tontouta
Dumbéa
NOUMÉA
Mont-Dore
Vao
Île des Pins
Grand Récif Sud

NEW CALEDONIA
(to France)

Ouvéa
Lifou
Fayaoué
Wé
Récifs de l'Astrolabe
PROVINCE DES ÎLES LOYAUTÉ
Îles Loyauté
Tadine
Maré

Aneityum

Récif Durand

Ono-i-lau

Île Walpole

8

Tropic of Capricorn

9

Tropic of Capricorn

PACIFIC OCEAN

10

278

H   I   J   K   L   M   N

AUSTRALASIA & OCEANIA

281

19,686ft
13,124ft
9843ft
6562ft
3281ft
1640ft
820ft
328ft
Sea Level
-820ft
-6562ft
-13,124ft

Micronesia

286

263

261

Tropic of Cancer

GUAM (to US)

Scale 1:825,000

- Ritidian Point
- Uruno Point
- Pati Point
- Andersen Air Force Base
- Yigo
- Mount Santa Rosa 252m
- Dededo
- Tumon Bay
- Tamuning
- Agana Bay
- Mongmong
- Asan Point
- Sinajana
- Asan
- Mount Tenjo
- Piti
- HAGÅTÑA (AGANA)
- Ordot
- Cabras Island
- Apra Harbor
- Barrigada
- Orote Peninsula
- 313m
- Chalan Pago
- Agat Bay
- Santa Rita
- Yona
- Apra Heights
- Pago Bay
- Agat
- Mount Lamlam 406m
- Talofofo
- Facpi Point
- Talofofo Bay
- Mount Bolanos
- 379m
- Cetti Bay
- Mount Sasalaguan
- Umatac Bay
- 337m
- Umatac
- Inarajan
- Merizo
- Aga Point
- Cocos Island

Philippine Sea

PACIFIC OCEAN

MICRONESIA

Scale 1:825,000

- Rumung
- Maap
- Munguuy Bay
- Yap
- Wanyaan
- Gagil Tamil
- Colonia
- Tamil Harbor
- Kanifaay

Philippine Sea

PACIFIC OCEAN

NORTHERN MARIANA ISLANDS (to US)

- Farallon de Pajaros
- Supply Reef
- Maug Islands
- Asuncion Island
- Agrihan
- Pagan
- Alamagan
- Guguan
- Zealandia Bank
- Sarigan
- Anatahan
- Farallon de Medinilla
- Susupe
- Saipan
- Tinian
- San Jose
- Aguijan
- Rota
- HAGÅTÑA (AGANA)
- Guam

Mariana Islands

PACIFI

GUAM (to US)

Philippine Sea

Caroline

- Ulithi Atoll
- Colonia
- Yap
- Fais
- Gaferut
- Ngulu Atoll
- Sorol
- Faraulep Atoll
- West Fayu Atoll
- Pikelot
- Magur Islands
- Namonuito Atoll
- Murilo Atoll
- Fayu
- Ngcheangel
- Ulul
- Hall Islands
- Nomo Atoll
- Olimarao Atoll
- Lamotrek Atoll
- Tarang Reef
- Pulap Atoll
- Weno
- Chuuk Islands
- Woleai Atoll
- Elato Atoll
- Satawal
- Puluwat Atoll
- Neoch
- Nama
- Oreor
- Babeldaob
- NGERULMUD
- Ifalik Atoll
- Manila Reef
- Losa
- Mecherchar
- Ngeruktabel
- Eauripik Atoll
- Pulusuk
- Atoll
- Ngeaur
- Beliliou
- Palau Islands
- CHUUK

PALAU

- Sonsorol Islands
- Pulo Anna
- Merir

MICRONESIA

PALAU
Scale 1:750,000

- Ngaregur
- Ollei
- Chol
- Aiwokako Passage
- Ngardmau Bay
- Ulimang
- Chelab
- Ngetbong
- Kgkeklau
- Babeldaob
- Imeong
- Ngermechau
- Ibobang
- Namai Bay
- NGERULMUD
- Melekeok
- Ngchemiangel
- Ngerkeai
- Komebail Lagoon
- Airai
- Arakabesan
- Ngetkip
- Oikurul
- Koror
- Airai
- Oreor

West Passage

Namelakl Passage

Philippine Sea

PACIFIC OCEAN

INDONESIA

- Pulau Waigeo
- Jazirah Doberai
- Pulau Misool
- Semenanjung Bomberai
- Pulau Seram (Ceram)
- Banda Sea
- Kepulauan Aru
- Pulau Kai Besar

Equator

MICRONESIA

Scale 1:1,500,000

PACIFIC OCEAN

- Piis Moen
- Lamoil
- Tora
- North Pass
- Tora Island Pass
- Falalu
- Northeast Island
- Chuuk Islands
- Ruo
- Falos
- Fono
- Quoi
- Falalig Pass
- Romanum
- Weno
- Weno
- Pata
- Eot
- Shiki Islands
- Piaanu Pass
- Tol
- Udot
- Dublon
- Lemotol Bay
- Fanapanges
- Parem
- Fanan
- Polle
- Totiw
- Fefan
- Etten
- Pisar
- Shichiyo Islands
- Tsis
- Uman
- Ollan
- Salat
- Salat Pass
- South Pass
- Otta Pass
- Uijec
- Otta
- Mesegon
- Feneppi
- Neoch
- Lauvergne Island
- Ipis

MICRONESIA

PAPUA NEW GUINEA

- New Ireland
- New Britain

Sea Level
- 6000m
- 4000m
- 3000m
- 2000m
- 1000m
- 500m
- 250m
- 100m
- Sea Level
- -250m
- -2000m
- -4000m

Scale 1:10,250,000
(projection: Mercator)

0 50 100 150 200 250 300 Km
0 50 100 150 200 250 300 Miles

Population
■ above 5 million   ■ 1 million to 5 million   ◉ 500,000 to 1 million
◉ 100,000 to 500,000   ⊕ 50,000 to 100,000   ○ 10,000 to 50,000   ○ below 10,000

NORTHERN MARIANA ISLANDS (to US)

Philippine Sea

Puntan Sabaneta
Punta Lagua Lichan
San Roque
Bird Island
Managaha
Tanapag
Kalabera
Puetton Tanapag
Capitol Hill
Garapan
Mount Tapochau
465m
Oleai
Saipan
San Vicente
Susupe
Kagman Point
Chalan Kanoa
Magicienne Bay
San Antonio
Saipan International

PACIFIC OCEAN

Saipan Channel
Puntan I Naftan

Scale 1:500,000
0 2 4 Km
0 2 4 Miles

MICRONESIA

PACIFIC OCEAN

Parem Island
Sokehs Island
Pohnpei
Kolonia
Takaieu Island
Nanuh
PALIKIR
Pohnpei
Pehleng
Nahnalaud
772m
Madolenihmw
Tomworoahlang
Kepirohi Falls
San Madol
Temwen Island
Ronkiti
Pwok
Rohi
Lohd

Scale 1:650,000
0 5 10 Km
0 5 10 Miles

WAKE ISLAND (to US)

Toki Point
Peale Island
Heel Point
Kuku Point
Flipper Point
Wilkes Island
Wake Lagoon
Settlement
Wake Island
Wake Island
Peacock Point

PACIFIC OCEAN

Scale 1:250,000
0 1 2 3 4 Km
0 1 2 3 4 Miles

Tropic of Cancer

PACIFIC OCEAN

c
r
o
n
e
s
i
a

Wake Island (to US)

MARSHALL ISLANDS

Sibylla Island
Bokaak Atoll

Bikar Atoll

Bikini Atoll
Rongelap Atoll
Enewetak Atoll
Rongrik Atoll
Utrik Atoll
Ailinginae Atoll
Taka Atoll
Ailuk Atoll
Mejit Island
Wotho Atoll
Jemo Island
Likiep Atoll
Wotje Atoll
Ujelang Atoll
Kwajalein Atoll
Erikub Atoll
Ujae Atoll
Maloelap Atoll
Lae Atoll
Lib
Aur Atoll
Namu Atoll
Jabwot
Ailinglaplap Atoll
Arno Atoll
Majuro Atoll
Jaluit Atoll
Mili Atoll
Namorik Atoll
Knox Atoll
Kili Island
Ratak Chain
Ralik Chain
Ebon Atoll

Minto Reef
Oroluk Atoll
Pakin Atoll
Kolonia
PALIKIR
Pohnpei
Mwokil Atoll
Ant Atoll
Namoluk Atoll
Pingelap Atoll
Lukunor Atoll
Ngetik Atoll
Satawan Atoll
Kosrae
Tofol
Mortlock Islands
POHNPEI
KOSRAE

Nukuoro Atoll

Makin
Butaritari
Tungaru (Gilbert Islands)
Abaiang
Marakei
Tarawa
BAIRIKI
Maiana
Kapingamarangi Atoll
Kuria
Abemama
Aranuka
Equator

Nauru
KIRIBATI
Banaba
Nonouti
NAURU
Tabiteuea
Beru

OCEAN

MICRONESIA

PACIFIC OCEAN

Tafunsak
Gabert
Mount Mutunte
593m
Okat Harbor
Lelu Island
Kosrae
Tofol
Lelu
Insiaf
Mount Finkol
629m
Malem
Utwe
Utwe Harbor

Scale 1:500,000
0 2 4 Km
0 2 4 Miles

NAURU

Anna Point
Baiti
Anabar
Nibok
Ijuw
Denig
Phosphate mineworks
Anibare
Nauru
Aiwo
Buada Lagoon
Anibare Bay
YAREN
Nauru International
Meneng Point

PACIFIC OCEAN

Scale 1:200,000
0 1 2 Km
0 1 2 Miles

MARSHALL ISLANDS

Rongrong
Iroj
Majuro Atoll
Laura
Kallalen
Enigu
Majuro Lagoon
Djarrit
Majuro
Dalap

PACIFIC OCEAN

Scale 1:1,000,000
0 5 10 Km
0 5 10 Miles

19,686ft
13,124ft
9843ft
6562ft
3281ft
1640ft
820ft
328ft
Sea Level
-820ft
-6562ft
-13,124ft

AUSTRALASIA & OCEANIA

284

Map Labels

MARSHALL ISLANDS
Erikub Atoll, Maloelap Atoll, Namu Atoll, Jabwot, Aur Atoll, Majuro Atoll, Arno Atoll, Jaluit Atoll, Mili Atoll, Knox Atoll, Kili Island, Ebon Atoll, Ralik Chain, Ratak Chain

Makin, Butaritari, Abaiang, Marakei, Tarawa, BAIRIKI, Maiana, Abemama, Kuria, Aranuka, Equator, Banaba, Nonouti, Beru, Nikunau, Tabiteuea, Onotoa, Tamana, Arorae, Tungaru (Gilbert Islands)

KIRIBATI
Howland Island (to US), Baker Island (to US), Phoenix Islands, McKean Island, Kanton, Enderbury Island, Birnie Island, Rawaki, Orona, Manra, Nikumaroro

PACIFIC
Jarvis Island (to US), Teraina, Tabuaeran, Palmyra Atoll (to US), Kingman Reef (to US)

TUVALU
Nanumea Atoll, Niutao, Nanumaga, Nui Atoll, Vaitupu, Nukufetau Atoll, Funafuti Atoll, FONGAFALE, Nukulaelae Atoll, Niulakita

TOKELAU (to NZ)
Atafu Atoll, Nukunonu Atoll, Fakaofo Atoll, Swans Island

WALLIS & FUTUNA (to France)
Îles Wallis, Île Futuna, Île Alofi

SAMOA — Savai'i, Sāmoa, 'Upolu
AMERICAN SAMOA (to US) — Manua Islands, Tutuila

COOK ISLANDS (to NZ)
Northern Cook Islands, Rakahanga, Manihiki, Pukapuka, Nassau, Suwarrow, Palmerston, Southern Cook Islands, Aitutaki, Manuae, Takute, AVARUA, Rarotonga

VANUATU
Mere Lava, Maéwo, Pentecost, Ambrym, Lopevi, Tongoa, Emao, PORT-VILA, Efate, Erromango, Ipota, Aniwa, Futuna, Isangel, Tanna, Aneityum, Maré, Île Walpole

FIJI
Vanua Levu, Nabuna, Rabi, Yasawa Group, Bua, Taveuni, Koro, Lautoka, Mamanuca Group, 'Ovalau, Viti Levu, SUVA, Gau, Cicia, Lakeba, Moala, Nayau, Totoya, Kadavu, Moala, Matuku, Vatoa, Lau Group

Niuatoputapu, Tafahi, Fonualei, Toku, Vava'u Group, Late, 'Uta Vava'u, Ha'ano, Ha'apai Group, Tofua, Kao, Lifuka, Otu Tolu Group, Kotu Group, Nomuka Group, Tonumea, NUKU'ALOFA, Tongatapu Group, Tongatapu, 'Eua

TONGA

NIUE (to NZ) — ALOFI, Niue

Tropic of Capricorn

Inset: KIRIBATI
PACIFIC OCEAN, Iku, Buariki, Taratai, Abaokoro, Marenanuka, Nabeina, Tabiteuea, Bikeman, Bikenebu, Bonriki, Betio, Eita, Banraeaba, BAIRIKI, Tarawa
Scale 1:1,000,000
0 5 10 km
0 5 10 Miles

Inset: TUVALU
Te Ava I Te Lape, Fualifeke, Amatuku, Tepuka, Fongafale, Fualopa, Funafuti, FONGAFALE, Fuafatu, Te Ava Fuagea, Funangongo, Vasafua, Te Ava Pua Pua, Fuagea, Tefala, Falefatu, Telele, Funafara, Teafuafou, Funafuti Atoll, PACIFIC OCEAN
Scale 1:500,000
0 2 4 Km
0 2 4 Miles

Inset: WALLIS & FUTUNA (to France)
PACIFIC OCEAN, Pointe Fatua, Pointe Matapu, Toloke, Mont Puke 524m, Île Futuna, Leava, Koliu, Pointe Vele, Mala'e, Alofitai, Mont Kolofau 417m, Pointe Matalesina, Pointe Sauma, Île Alofi
Scale 1:1,000,000
0 5 10 Km
0 5 10 Miles

Inset: WALLIS & FUTUNA (to France)
PACIFIC OCEAN, Nukuloa, Nukutapu, Hihifo, Île Luaniva, Îles Wallis, Baie de l'Ouest, Alele, Ahoa, Île Uvea, MATÁ'UTU, Baie de Matâ'utu, Mala'atoli, Île Nukuhifala, Tepa, Nukuâtea, Île Faioa, Île Fenuafo'o
Scale 1:1,000,000
0 5 10 Km
0 5 10 Miles

Inset: TONGA
Maniloa, Tau, Ata, Niu 'Aunofa, Atata, Poloa, Onevai, Motu Tupu, Nuku, Kolovai, Fafa, Kolonga, Fukave, 'Eua Iki, NUKU'ALOFA, Pangai, Piha Passage, Houma, Fanga 'Uta, Mu'a, Mui Hopohoponga, Vaina, Pea, Tongatapu, Fua'amotu, Tongatapu, Houma, Taloa, Houma, 'Eua, 'Ohonua, Kalau
Scale 1:1,000,000
0 5 10 Km
0 5 10 Miles

Inset: COOK ISLANDS (to NZ)
Te Aiti, Avatiu Harbour, Avarua Harbour, Nikao, AVARUA, Rarotonga, Ikurangi 485m, Arorangi, Maungaroa 509m, Matavera, Rarotonga, Te Manga 652m, Ngatangiia, Motutapu, Te Kou 564m, Oneroa, Muri, Titikaveka, Koromiri, Taakoka
Scale 1:325,000
0 2 4 Km
0 2 4 Miles

Elevation scale: 6000m, 4000m, 3000m, 2000m, 1000m, 500m, 250m, 100m, Sea Level, -250m, -2000m, -4000m

281
278

Scale 1:15,500,000
(projection: Mercator)

0 50 100 150 200 250 300 350 400 Km
0 50 100 150 200 250 300 350 400 Miles

Population
- ■ above 5 million
- ◉ 100,000 to 500,000
- ○ 10,000 to 50,000
- ◙ 1 million to 5 million
- ⊕ 50,000 to 100,000
- ○ below 10,000
- ◉ 500,000 to 1 million

SAMOA (inset)

Scale 1:3,000,000

0 20 40 Km
0 20 40 Miles

Savai'i
Falealupo, Sātaua, Fagamālo
Cape Puava, Mauga Silisili 1858m, Tuasivi
Fālelima, Sala'ilua, Satupa'iteau, Pu'apu'a, Salelologa
Cape Āsuisui, Iaga
Palauli Bay, Apolima Strait

'Upolu
ĀPIA, Felelolo, Fagaloa Bay
Matautu, Mauga Fito 1113m, Ti'avea
Lotofaga, Poutasi
Sāfata Bay, Salani

AMERICAN SAMOA (to US)
Manu'a Islands
Ofu, Olosega, Ta'ū
Luma
PAGO PAGO, Cape Matātula, 'Aunu'u Island
Cape Taputapu, Steps Point
Tutuila

PACIFIC OCEAN

KIRIBATI (inset)

Scale 1:1,175,000

0 5 10 Km
0 5 10 Miles

PACIFIC OCEAN
Northwest Point, Cape Manning
London, Banana, Northeast Point
Cook Island, Saint Stanislas, Manulu Lagoon
Paris, Bay
Poland
South West Point, Kiritimati (Christmas Island)
Vaskess Bay, Isles Lagoon, Joe's Hill 12m
Bay of Wrecks
Aeon Point
Azur Lagoon, Pelican Lagoon
South East Point

Equator

FRENCH POLYNESIA (to France) (inset — Tahiti)

Scale 1:1,000,000

0 5 10 Km
0 5 10 Miles

Îles du Vent
Baie d'Opunohu, Baie de Cook
Papetoai, Pointe Aroa
Mont Matotea 714m, Paopao, Baie de Matavai, Pointe Vénus, Papenoo
Moorea, Afareaitu, Mahina, Pirae, Tiarei
Haapiti, Mont Tohiea 1207m, PAPEETE, Faaa, Hitiaa
Pointe Nuupere, Punaauia, Mont Aorai 2066m
Pointe Nuuroa, Mont Orohena 2241m, Tahiti
Paea, Mont Tetufera 1799m, Faaone, Passe Tamotoe Baie de Taravao
Maraa, Taravao, Isthme de Taravao
Pointe Maraa, Papara, Afaahiti, Toahotu, Tautira
Récif Tepaee, Mataiea, Vairao, Presqu'île de Taiarapu
Teahupoo, Mont Rooniu 1332m

PACIFIC OCEAN

Main Map

PACIFIC OCEAN

Line Islands
Kiritimati (Christmas Island)
Malden Island
Starbuck Island
Penrhyn
Millennium Island
Vostok Island
Flint Island

Îles Marquises
Hatutu, Eiao
Nuku Hiva, Ua Huka
Taiohae, Ua Pu, Hiva Oa
Atuona, Tahuata, Motane
Fatu Hiva, Omoa

Îles Tuamotu
Îles du Roi Georges, Îles du Désappointement
Ahe, Manihi, Tepoto, Napuka
Mataiva, Tikehau, Takaroa, Tikei, Pukapuka
Rangiroa, Takapoto
Îles Palliser, Aratika
Îles Sous le Vent
Motu One, Toau, Kauehi
Maupiti, Tupai, Bora-Bora, Niau, Raraka, Takume, Fagatau, Fakahina
Manuae, Tahaa, Fare, Fakarava, Katiu, Makemo, Raroia
Maupihaa, Raiatea, Huahine, Faaite, Tahanea, Nihiru, Tehuata
Tetiaroa, Marutea, Tauere
Moorea, Anaa, Haraiki, Hikueru, Amanu, Tatakoto
PAPEETE, Tahiti, Mehetia, Reitoru, Marokau, Hao, Pukarua
Maiao, Îles du Vent, Ravahere, Negonego, Akiaki, Vahitahi, Reao
Archipel de la Société, Manuhagi, Paraoa, Vairaatea, Pinaki
Hereheretue, Ahunui
Îles du Duc de Gloucester
Mitiaro, Vanavana, Tureia, Groupe Actéon
Mauke, Tenararo, Marutea
FRENCH POLYNESIA (to France)
Maria, Tematagi, Moruroa, Maria
Rurutu, Fagataufa
Rangaia, Rimatara, Îles Gambier, Magareva, Temoe
Tubuai
Îles Australes
Raevavae
Rapa Iti
Maria, Marotiri

PACIFIC OCEAN

Tropic of Capricorn

PITCAIRN ISLANDS (to UK)

Oeno Island, Henderson Island
Ducie Island
Pitcairn Island

PITCAIRN ISLANDS (to UK) (inset)

Scale 1:125,000

0 0.5 1 Km
0 0.5 1 Miles

Young's Rock, Bounty Bay
ADAMSTOWN, Adam's Rock
Point Christian, Pitcairn Island
St Paul's Point

PACIFIC OCEAN

NIUE (to NZ) (inset)

Scale 1:1,000,000

0 5 10 Km
0 5 10 Miles

Hikutavake, Toi, Mutalau
Makefu, Tuapa
Makapu Point, Lakepa
Alofi Bay, **Niue**
ALOFI, Liku
Halagigie Point, Tamakautoga
Avatele, Hakupu
Tepa Point, Mata Point

PACIFIC OCEAN

PACIFIC OCEAN

Elevation scale

19,686ft
13,124ft
9843ft
6562ft
3281ft
1640ft
820ft
328ft
Sea Level
-820ft
-6562ft
-13,124ft

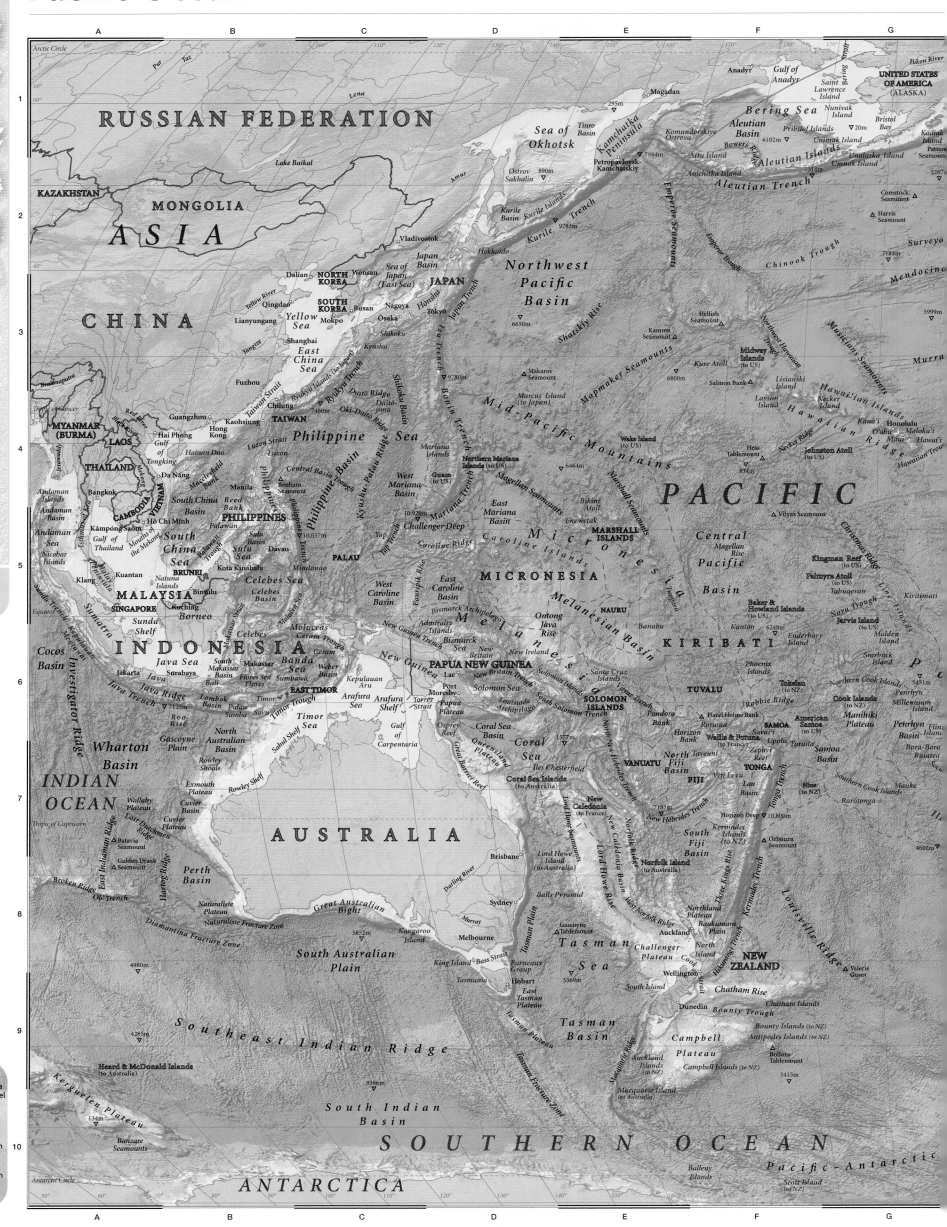

RUSSIAN FEDERATION

KAZAKHSTAN

MONGOLIA

ASIA

CHINA

Lake Baikal

Arctic Circle

Pur
Taz

Lena

Amur

Sea of
Okhotsk

Tinro
Basin

295m

Kamchatka Peninsula

Ostrov
Sakhalin

890m

Kurile
Basin

Kurile Islands

Kurile
Trench

9783m

Anadyr

Gulf of
Anadyr

Magadan

Komandorskiye
Ostrova

7864m

Petropavlovsk-
Kamchatskiy

Saint
Lawrence
Island

Bering Sea

Aleutian
Basin

Pribilof Islands

6102m

Bowers Ridge

Attu Island

Anchitka Island

Aleutian Islands

Aleutian Trench

931m

UNITED STATES
OF AMERICA
(ALASKA)

Nunivak
Island

20m

Bristol
Bay

Unimak Island

Kodiak
Island

Unalaska Island

Umnak Island

Patton
Seamount

5267m

Comstock
Seamount

Harris
Seamount

Surveyor

7184m

5999m

Northwest
Pacific
Basin

Emperor Seamounts

Emperor Trough

Chinook Trough

Mendocino

Murra

MYANMAR
(BURMA)

LAOS

THAILAND

Andaman
Islands

Andaman
Basin

Andaman
Sea

Nicobar
Islands

CAMBODIA

VIETNAM

Kuantan

Klang

SINGAPORE

MALAYSIA

BRUNEI

Bintulu

Kuching

Borneo

Natuna
Islands

Sunda
Shelf

INDONESIA

Jakarta

Java

Surabaya

Java Sea

Bali

Sunda Trench

Investigator Ridge

Cocos
Basin

Wharton
Basin

INDIAN
OCEAN

Broken Ridge

Naturaliste
Plateau

Naturaliste Fracture Zone

Diamantina Fracture Zone

4980m

Heard & McDonald Islands
(to Australia)

134m

Kerguelen Plateau

Banzare
Seamounts

Antarctic Circle

SOUTHEAST INDIAN RIDGE

4285m

5386m

South Indian
Basin

SOUTHERN OCEAN

ANTARCTICA

Sea
Level

-250m

-2000m

-4000m

Vladivostok

Dalian

NORTH
KOREA

Wonsan

SOUTH
KOREA

Mokpo

Qingdao

Yellow River

Lianyungang

Yellow
Sea

Shanghai

Yangtze

Fuzhou

East
China
Sea

Guangzhou

Hong Kong

Hai Phong

Gulf
of
Tongking

Hainan Dao

Da Nàng

Macclesfield
Bank

South China
Basin

Reed
Bank

Palawan

South
China
Sea

Manila

PHILIPPINES

Palawan
Trough

Davao

Celebes Sea

Kota Kinabalu

PALAU

Mindanao

Celebes
Basin

Molucca Strait

Celebes

Moluccas

Ceram Trough

Ceram

Banda
Sea

Makassar

Java Ridge

Lombok
Basin

Pulau

Sumbawa

Sumba

Flores Sea

Flores

Roo
Rise

7125m

Timor

Savu

Timor Trough

EAST TIMOR

North
Australian
Basin

Gascoyne
Plain

Rowley
Shoals

Exmouth
Plateau

Rowley Shelf

Wallaby
Plateau

Cuvier
Basin

Lost Dutchmen
Ridge

Batavia
Seamount

Gulden Draak
Seamount

Perth
Basin

Hokkaido

Kurile Trench

Sea of
Japan
(East Sea)

JAPAN

Nagoya

Honshu

Osaka

Tokyo

Shikoku

Kyushu

Izu Trench

Japan
Basin

Northwest
Pacific
Basin

6650m

Makarov
Seamount

Shatskiy Rise

Hellish
Seamount

Kammu
Seamount

6800m

Northwest Hawaiian Trough

Kure Atoll

Midway
Islands
(to US)

Musicians Seamounts

Salmon Bank

Lisianski
Island

Laysan
Island

Necker
Island

Hawaiian Islands

Kaua'i

O'ahu

Honolulu

Moloka'i

Maui

Hawaiian Ridge

Hawai'i

Hawaiian Trou

Dalian

Taiwan Strait

Chilung

TAIWAN

Kaohsiung

Luzon Strait

Luzon

Ryukyu Islands (to Japan)

Ryukyu Trench

460m

Daitō Ridge

Daitō-
jima

Oki-Daitō Ridge

Shikoku
Basin

Philippine
Sea

Central Basin
Fault

Benham
Seamount

Philippine Trough

10,057m

Sulu
Basin

Sulu
Sea

Kyushu-Palau Ridge

Central Basin Fault

West
Mariana
Basin

Mariana
Islands

Guam
(to US)

Northern Mariana
Islands (to US)

Mariana Trench

10,920m

Challenger Deep

Yap Trench

Yap

East
Mariana
Basin

West
Caroline
Basin

Caroline Ridge

East
Caroline
Basin

Eauripik Rise

MICRONESIA

MARSHALL
ISLANDS

Bikini
Atoll

Enewetak

6464m

Marshall Seamounts

Caroline Islands

Magellan Seamounts

Mid-Pacific Mountains

Wake Island
(to US)

Marcus Island
(to Japan)

Bonin Trench

Izu Trench

9780m

Mariana Trench

834m

Hess
Tablemount

Necker Ridge

Johnston Atoll
(to US)

PACIFIC

Central
Pacific
Basin

Micronesia

Central
Magellan
Rise

Vityaz Seamount

Kingman Reef
(to US)

Palmyra Atoll
(to US)

Christmas Ridge

Line Islands

Nova Trough

Jarvis Island
(to US)

Kiritimati

Baker &
Howland Islands
(to US)

Kanton

6249m

Enderbury
Island

Phoenix
Islands

Banaba

Ontong
Java
Rise

NAURU

KIRIBATI

Melanesian Basin

Starbuck
Island

Malden
Island

Penrhyn

Penrhyn
Basin

Millennium
Island

5451m

Flin
Island

Northern Cook Islands

Cook Islands
(to NZ)

Rarotonga

Southern Cook Islands

Manihiki
Plateau

Bora-Bora

Raiatea

Mauke

4602m

Broadmapura

Red River

Black River

Mekong

Tropic of Cancer

Equator

Gulf of
Thailand

Kâmpóng Saóm

Hô Chi Minh

Mouths of
the Mekong

Sumatra

Kalimantan

Mentawai

Makassar
Basin

Banda
Sea

Weber
Basin

Kepulauan
Aru

Arafura
Shelf

Arafura
Sea

Port
Moresby

Papua
Plateau

Torres
Strait

Gulf of
Carpentaria

Sahul Shelf Sea

Timor Sea

AUSTRALIA

Brisbane

Darling River

Murray

Sydney

Melbourne

Tropic of Capricorn

Cuvier
Plateau

5852m

Kangaroo
Island

South Australian
Plain

Great Australian
Bight

King Island

Bass Strait

Tasmania

Hobart

Furneaux
Group

East
Tasman
Plateau

New Guinea Trench

New Guinea

PAPUA NEW GUINEA

Lae

Admiralty
Islands

Bismarck
Sea

Bismarck Archipelago

New Britain

New Britain Trench

New
Ireland

Solomon Sea

Louisiade
Archipelago

Osprey
Reef

Coral
Sea

Queensland
Plateau

Great Barrier Reef

Coral Sea Islands
(to Australia)

Iles Chesterfield

Coral Sea Islands
(to Australia)

Melanesia

Solomon Islands

South Solomon Trench

SOLOMON
ISLANDS

Santa Cruz
Islands

Vitiaz Trench

Pandora
Bank

Horizon
Bank

Rotuma

Hazel Holme Bank

North New Hebrides Trench

New Hebrides Trench

VANUATU

New
Caledonia
(to France)

Coral Sea
Islands

1557m

North
Fiji
Basin

FIJI

Viti Levu

Lau
Basin

TUVALU

Robbie Ridge

Wallis & Futuna
(to France)

SAMOA

American
Samoa
(to US)

Upolu

Tutuila

Zephyr
Reef

Savai'i

Niue
(to NZ)

TONGA

Samoa
Basin

Tokelau
(to NZ)

Phoenix
Islands

7183m

Norfolk Island
(to Australia)

Lord Howe
Island
(to Australia)

Balls Pyramid

Lord Howe Seamounts

Lord Howe Rise

Norfolk Ridge

New Caledonia Basin

West Norfolk Ridge

Three Kings Rise

Horizon Deep

10,800m

Kermadec
Islands
(to NZ)

South
Fiji
Basin

Ozbourn
Seamount

Tonga Trench

Kermadec Trench

Louisville Ridge

Valerie
Guyot

Gascoyne
Tablemount

5369m

Tasman
Sea

Tasman Plain

Tasman Basin

Tasman Plateau

Macquarie Ridge

Macquarie Island
(to Australia)

Tasmantid Fracture Zone

Northland
Plateau

Raukumara
Plain

Auckland

North
Island

Wellington

Cook Strait

South Island

Dunedin

NEW
ZEALAND

Challenger
Plateau

Hikurangi Trench

Chatham Rise

Chatham Islands
(to NZ)

Bounty Trough

Bounty Islands (to NZ)

Antipodes Islands
(to NZ)

Campbell
Plateau

Auckland
Islands
(to NZ)

Campbell Islands (to NZ)

Bollons
Tablemount

5415m

Balleny
Islands

Scott Island
(to NZ)

Pacific-Antarctic

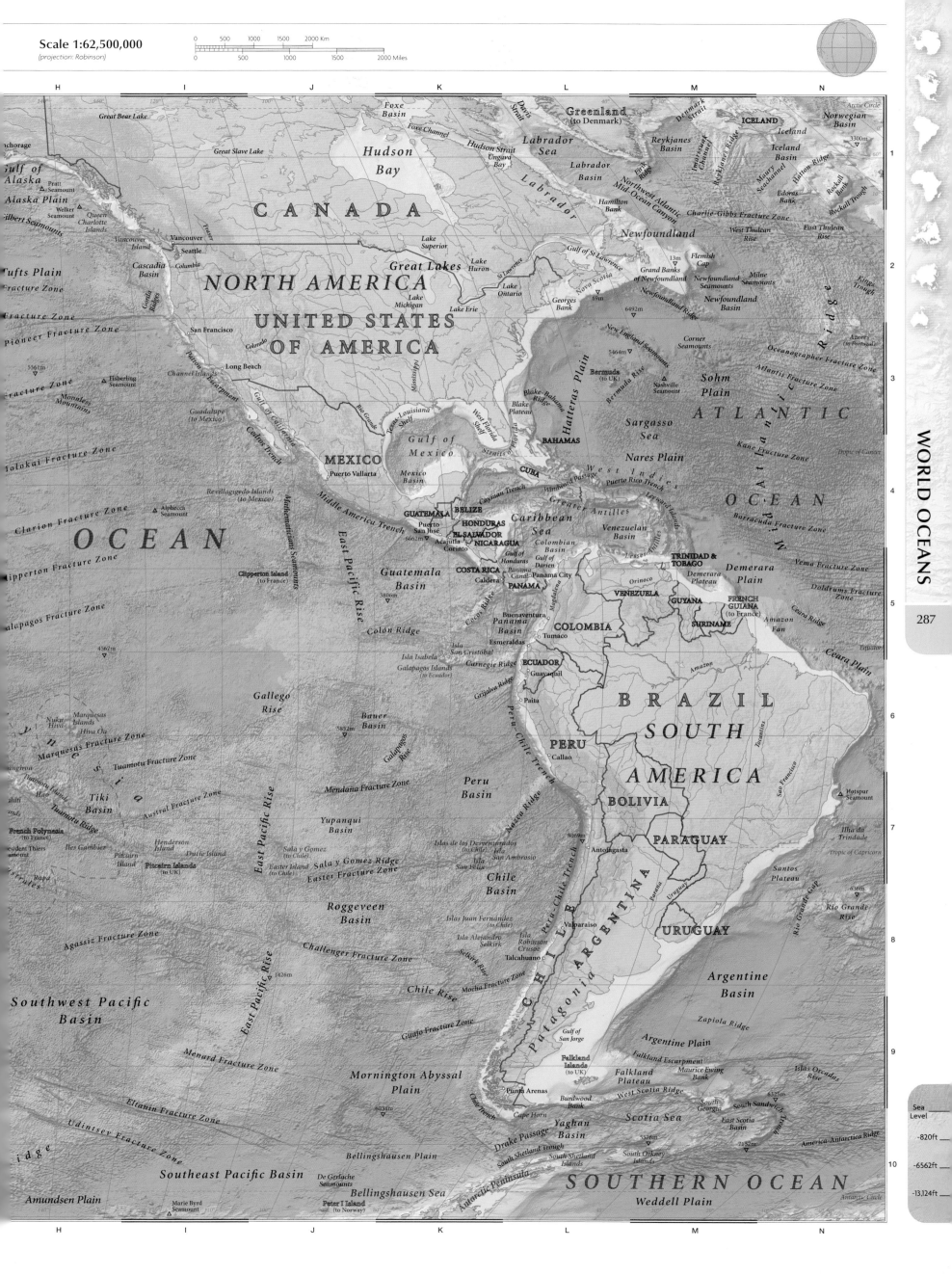

Indian Ocean

Scale 1:32,000,000
(projection: Robinson)

| 0 | 200 | 400 | 600 | 800 | 1000 | 1200 Km |
| 0 | 200 | 400 | 600 | 800 | 1000 | 1200 Miles |

Sea Level
-820ft
-6562ft
-13,124ft

INDONESIA
Banda Sea
EAST TIMOR
Timor Sea
Timor Trough
Savu Sea
Celebes
Java Sea
Sumbawa
Sumba
Pulau
Lombok Basin
Bali
Java
Sunda Shelf
Ashmore & Cartier Islands (to Australia)
Wyndham
Broome
Port Hedland
Rowley Shoals
North Australian Basin
Exmouth Plateau
Sahul Shelf

AUSTRALIA
Geraldton
Fremantle
Bunbury Albany
Great Australian Bight
5852m

SOUTHERN OCEAN
South Australian Basin
South Indian Basin
5386m

Java Ridge
7125m
Java Trench
Christmas Island (to Australia)
Roo Rise
Vening Meinesz Seamounts
Gascoyne Plain
Cuvier Basin
Perth Basin
Cocos Basin
Cocos Islands (to Australia)
Wharton Basin
5693m
Cuvier Plateau
Wallaby Plateau
Naturaliste Plateau
Naturaliste Fracture Zone

Investigator Ridge
5759m
416m
4023m
Lost Dutchmen Ridge
East Indiaman Ridge
Batavia Seamount
Golden Draak Seamount
Ob' Trench
Broken Ridge
Diamantina Fracture Zone
Southeast Indian Ridge
4980m
4285m

Ninetyeast Ridge
Osborn Plateau
5614m
Harriot Ridge

Mid-Indian Basin
Ceylon Plain
Amsterdam Fracture Zone
Amsterdam Island
St Paul Island

INDIAN OCEAN

Chagos Trench
Chagos-Laccadive Ridge
British Indian Ocean Territory (to UK)
Chagos Archipelago
Diego Garcia
Mid-Indian Ridge
3658m
Vema Fracture Zone
Egeria Fracture Zone
Marie Celeste Fracture Zone
Argo Fracture Zone
Rodrigues (to Mauritius)

Seguin Zone
Fracture Zone
Madingley Rise
Mahé
Seychelles Bank
Amirante Islands
Amirante Basin
SEYCHELLES
4880m
Amirante Ridge
Amirante Trench
Feed Seamount
Saya de Malha Bank
Nazareth Bank
Cargados Carajos Bank
MAURITIUS
702m
Réunion (to France)
Mascarene Plateau
Mascarene Plain
Mascarene Islands
Mascarene Basin
4936m

French Southern & Antarctic Territories (to France)
Kerguelen
Heard & McDonald Islands (to Australia)
Kerguelen Plateau
Banzare Seamounts
184m
686m
5386m

Crozet Basin
Crozet Islands
Crozet Plateau
Del Cano Rise
Prince Edward Islands (to South Africa)
935m
Lena Tablemount
Ob' Tablemount

Enderby Plain

Agalega Islands
Farquhar Group
Aldabra Group
Giraud Seamount
Mayotte (to France)
COMOROS
Comoro Basin
Mahajanga
Toamasina
1984m
4976m
MADAGASCAR
Madagascar Basin
Madagascar Plateau
Walters Shoal
Southwest Indian Ridge
Indomed Fracture Zone
Prince Edward Fracture Zone
Atlantic-Indian Basin

Mombasa
Pemba
Zanzibar
Dar es Salaam
Mafia
Cabo Delgado
Ravenna
Nacala
Lúrio
Quelimane
Beira
Davie Ridge
Bassas da India
Île Europa
Jaguar Seamount
Mozambique Channel
Mozambique Plateau
Mozambique Escarpment

Lake Kivu
BURUNDI
OF CONGO
TANZANIA
Lake Tanganyika
Lake Rukwa
Lake Nyasa
Lake Mweru
MALAWI
ZAMBIA
Lake Cabora Bassa
ZIMBABWE
Zambezi
Limpopo
MOZAMBIQUE
BOTSWANA
SWAZILAND
LESOTHO
SOUTH AFRICA
Maputo
Tugela
Natal Valley
69m
Durban
East London
Port Elizabeth
Mosselbaai
Cape Agulhas
Cape Town
Cape of Good Hope
Agulhas Bank
581m
Protea Seamount
African Seamount
Agulhas Plateau
Agulhas Basin
Natal Basin
Transkei Basin
Atlantic-Indian Ridge
Drakensberg
Orange River
Tropic of Capricorn
Antarctic Circle

SOUTHERN OCEAN

Sea Level
-250m
-2000m
-4000m

Grid columns: 1 2 3 4 5 6 7
Grid rows: J I H G F E D C B A

Land masses and regions

ARCTIC OCEAN

FINLAND
SWEDEN
NORWAY
Scandinavia
ESTONIA
LATVIA
LITHUANIA
BELARUS
RUS. FED.
POLAND
DENMARK
GERMANY
NETH.
BELGIUM
CZECH REPUBLIC
SLOVAKIA
AUSTRIA
SLOVENIA
CROATIA
HUNGARY
UKRAINE
ROMANIA
SERBIA
BOS. & HERZ.
MONTENEGRO
KOS.
MACEDONIA
ALBANIA
GREECE
ITALY
FRANCE
SWITZ.
SPAIN
PORTUGAL
UNITED KINGDOM
IRELAND
Ireland
Britain

EUROPE

LIBYA
TUNISIA
ALGERIA
MOROCCO
Western Sahara (occupied by Morocco)
MAURITANIA
MALI
NIGER
CHAD
Sahara
AFRICA
SENEGAL
GAMBIA
GUINEA-BISSAU
GUINEA
SIERRA LEONE
LIBERIA
IVORY COAST
GHANA
TOGO
BENIN
BURKINA
NIGERIA
CAMEROON
CENTRAL AFRICAN REPUBLIC
CONGO
EQUATORIAL
Gulf of Guinea

CANADA
NORTH AMERICA
UNITED STATES OF AMERICA
Greenland (to Denmark)
Ellesmere Island
Queen Elizabeth Islands
Victoria Island
Baffin Island
ICELAND
Reykjavik
Nuuk

MEXICO
GUATEMALA
BELIZE
HONDURAS
EL SALVADOR
NICARAGUA
COSTA RICA
PANAMA
CUBA
JAMAICA
HAITI
DOMINICAN REPUBLIC
BAHAMAS
BARBADOS
TRINIDAD & TOBAGO
COLOMBIA
VENEZUELA
GUYANA
SURINAME
FRENCH GUIANA (to France)

ATLANTIC OCEAN
Mid-Atlantic Ridge
Sargasso Sea
Mediterranean Sea
Barents Sea
Baltic Sea
Norwegian Sea
Greenland Sea
North Sea
Labrador Sea
Baffin Bay
Hudson Bay
Caribbean Sea
Gulf of Mexico
West Indies
Greater Antilles
Lesser Antilles

Sea floor features

Banks Rise
Barents Trough
Spitsbergen
Svalbard (to Norway)
Mohns Ridge
Jan Mayen (to Norway)
Jan Mayen Fracture Zone
Jan Mayen Ridge
Greenland Plain
Kolbeinsey Ridge
Iceland Plateau
Faeroe-Iceland Ridge
Faeroe Islands (to Denmark)
Shetland Islands
Great Fisher Bank
Iceland Basin
Norwegian Basin
Voring Plateau
Greenland-Iceland Rise
Denmark Strait
Greenland-Iceland Strait
Reykjanes Ridge
Reykjanes Basin
Hatton Ridge
Rockall
Rockall Trough
Porcupine Bank
Porcupine Plain
Goban Spur
Celtic Shelf
Biscay Plain
Bay of Biscay
Charcot Seamounts
Galicia Bank
Iberian Plain
Tagus Plain
Strait of Gibraltar
Madeira (to Portugal)
Madeira Plain
Canary Islands (to Spain)
Cape Verde Terrace
Cape Verde Plain
Cape Verde Basin
Gambia Plain
Sierra Leone Rise
Sierra Leone Basin
Guinea Basin
Canary Basin

Charlie-Gibbs Fracture Zone
Maury Seachannel
Maxwell Fracture Zone
Kurchatov Fracture Zone
Akademik Kurchatov Fracture Zone
East Azores Fracture Zone
Azores Fracture Zone
Azores (to Portugal)
Oceanographer Fracture Zone
Atlantis Fracture Zone
Kane Fracture Zone
Vema Fracture Zone
Barracuda Fracture Zone
Doldrums Fracture Zone
Four-North Fracture Zone
Saint Peter and Saint Paul Rock
Devil Fracture Zone
Pico Fracture Zone

Newfoundland Basin
Newfoundland Ridge
Flemish Cap
Grand Banks (of Newfoundland)
Northwest Atlantic Mid-Ocean Canyon
Milne Seamounts
New England Seamounts
Corner Seamounts
Nashville Seamount
Sohm Plain
Researcher Seamount
Bermuda (to UK)
Bermuda Rise
Nares Plain
Hatteras Plain
Blake Plateau
Blake-Bahama Ridge
Blake Basin
Bahama Basin
Great Bahama Bank
Puerto Rico Trench
Muertos Trough
Venezuelan Basin
Colombian Basin
Yucatan Channel
Yucatan Basin
Cayman Trench
West Florida Shelf
Florida Plain
Campeche Bank
Central Slope
Texas-Louisiana Shelf
Mexico Basin
Campeche Basin
Middle America Trench
Demerara Plain
Demerara Plateau
Ceara Ridge
Amazon Fan
Guatemala Basin
Cocos Ridge

Labrador Basin
Labrador Shelf
Hamilton Bank
Georges Bank
Scotia Shelf
Sable Island
Davis Strait
Cumberland Sound
Baffin Basin
Foxe Basin
Foxe Channel
Hudson Strait
Ungava Bay
Great Whale Bank
Great Lakes
Lake Superior
Lake Michigan
Lake Huron
Lake Erie
Lake Ontario

Depth soundings

567m
102m
5601m
2580m
3058m
57m
4139m
691m
623m
5550m
254m
4645m
4700m
5380m
457m
3883m
5356m
13m
5464m
6492m
5908m
5465m
457m
6662m
218m
69m

Cities

Montreal
New York
Boston
Baltimore
Halifax
Savannah
Jacksonville
Mobile
New Orleans
Houston
Corpus Christi
Tampico
Veracruz
Puerto San José
Belize City
Puerto Corinto
Corinto
Caldera
Limón
Colón
Panama City
Buenaventura
Cartagena
Barranquilla
Maracaibo
La Guaira
Georgetown
Paramaribo
Cayenne
Bordeaux
Nantes
Bilbao
Gijón
Lisbon
Leixões
Casablanca
Safi
Nouadhibou
Nouakchott
Dakar
Banjul
Bissau
Conakry
Freetown
Monrovia
Abidjan
Sekondi-Takoradi
Takoradi
Lomé
Porto-Novo
Lagos
Douala
Malabo
Port Harcourt
Belfast
Cork
Milford Haven
Southampton
Rotterdam
Reykjavik

Arctic Circle
Tropic of Cancer

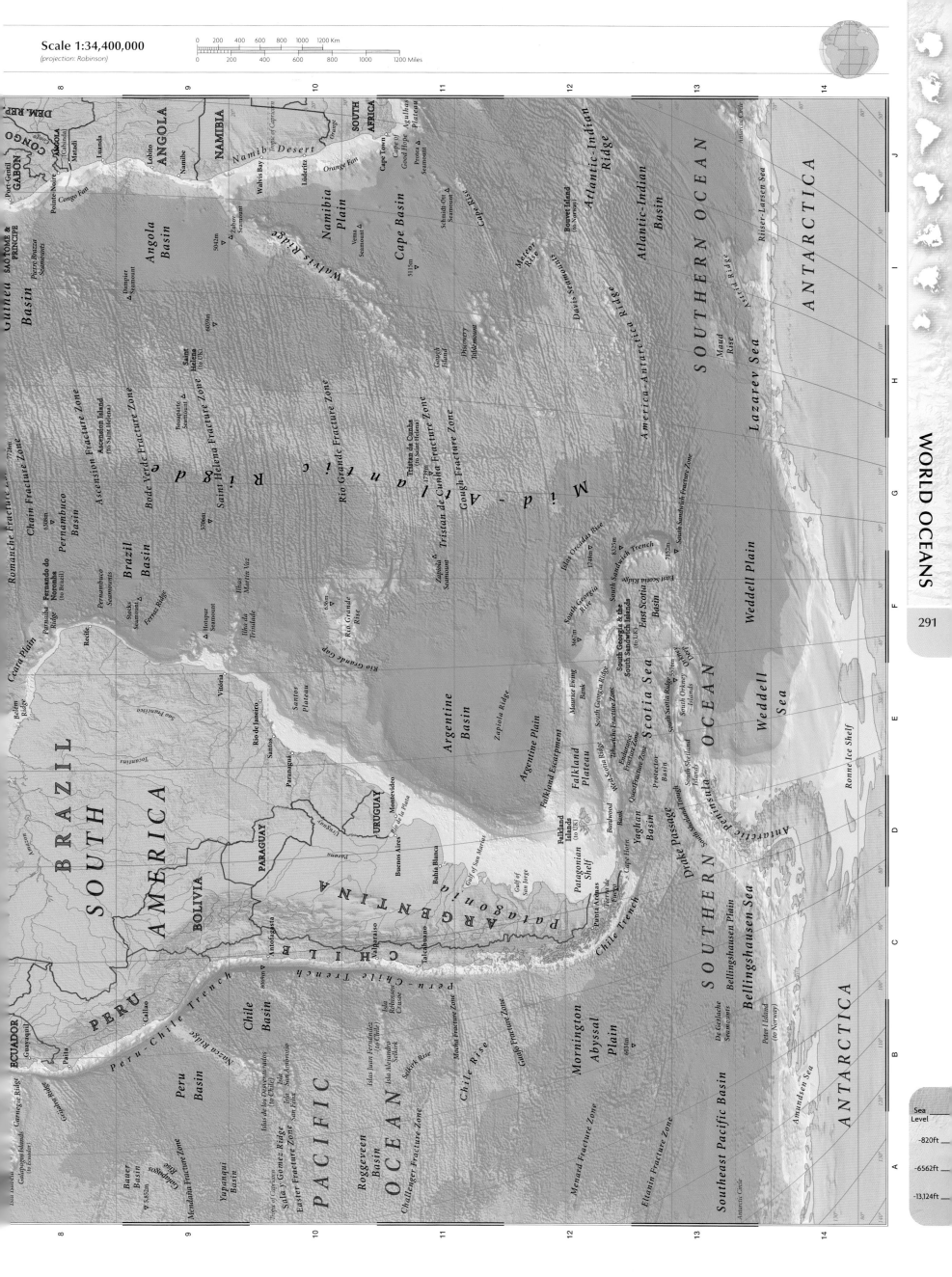

Scale 1:34,400,000
(projection: Robinson)

0 200 400 600 800 1000 1200 Km
0 200 400 600 800 1000 1200 Miles

Sea Level
-820ft
-6562ft
-13,124ft

Antarctica

ATLANTIC OCEAN

PACIFIC OCEAN

SOUTHERN OCEAN

Scotia Sea

Weddell Sea

Bellingshausen Sea

Amundsen Sea

Drake Passage

Punta Alta
Bahía Blanca
Río Colorado
Viedma
Golfo San Matías
Península Valdés
San Antonio Oeste
Puerto Lobos
Valcheta
Gaimán
Rawson
Río Negro
General Roca
Maquinchao
Golfo San Jorge
Comodoro Rivadavia
Puerto Deseado
Punta Pozos
Caleta Olivia
Jaramillo
Río Deseado
Puerto San Julián
Comandante Luis Peidra Buena
Bahía Grande
Río Gallegos
Cerro Tres Picos 2492m
San Carlos de Bariloche
Paso de Indios
Alto Río Senguer
Perito Moreno
Puerto Montt
San Valentín 4058m
Coihaique
Puerto Aisén
Cochrane
Calafate
Cerro Pirámide 3380m
Puerto Natales
Quellón
Ancud
Isla de Chiloé
Archipiélago de los Chonos
Península de Taitao
Golfo de Penas
Isla Wellington
CHILE
Punta Arenas
Porvenir
Ushuaia
Tierra del Fuego
Cabo de Hornos (Cape Horn)
Isla Santa Inés

FALKLAND ISLANDS (to UK)
Mount Adam 700m
West Falkland
STANLEY
East Falkland
Cape Meredith

South Orkney Islands
Laurie Island
Orcadas (Argentina)
Coronation Island
Signy (UK)

Clarence Island
Elephant Island
Joinville Island
Duddee Island
King George Island
General Bernardo O'Higgins (Chile)
Capitán Arturo Prat (Chile)
Esperanza (Argentina)
Marambio (Argentina)
Snowhill Island
James Ross Island
Robertson Island
Livingston Island
South Shetland Islands
Bransfield Strait
Davis Coast
Danco Coast
Graham Land
Brabant Island
Anvers Island
Palmer (US)
Vernadsky (Ukraine)
Churchill Peninsula
Larsen Ice Shelf
Cape Agassiz
Hearst Island
Ewing Island
Dolleman Island
Steele Island
Cape Bryant
Cape Knowles
Butler Island
Cape Mackintosh
Cape Deacon
Biscoe Islands
Lavoisier Island
Cape Mascart
Adelaide Island
Rothera (Argentina)
Marguerite Bay
Fallieres
San Martin
Mount Jackson 4190m
Cape Fiske
Fossil Bluff (UK)
George VI Sound
Douglas Range
Rothschild Island
Wilkins Ice Shelf
Alexander Island
English Coast
Charcot Island
Latady Island
Spaatz Island
Smyley Island
Case Island
Rydberg Peninsula
Sky-Blu (UK)
Zumberge Coast
Antarctic Peninsula
Palmer Land
Orville Coast
Ronne Ice Shelf
Ronne Entrance
Korff Ice Rise
Henry Ice Rise
Haag Nunataks
Rutford Ice Stream
Vinson Massif 4897m
Ellsworth Mountains
Ellsworth Land

Peter I Øy (to Norway)
Dendtler Island
Farwell Island
Dustin Island
Thurston Island
Noville Peninsula
Cape Flying Fish
King Peninsula
Burke Island
Bear Peninsula
Martin Peninsula
Wright Island
Carney Island
Siple Island
Mount Siple 3100m
Grant Island
Cape Burks
Newman Island
Abbot Ice Shelf
Eights Coast
Pine Island Glacier
Canisteo Peninsula
Sherman Island
Walgreen Coast
Bakutis Coast
Getz Ice Shelf
Hobbs Coast
Dean Island
Mount Sidley 4181m
Executive Committee Range
Mount Seelig 3022m
West Antarctica
Marie Byrd Land
Rockefeller Plateau
Saunders Coast
Ruppert Coast
Sulzberger Bay
Whitmore Mountains

Halley (UK)
Luitpold Coast
Belgrano II (Argentina)
Filchner Ice Shelf
Berkner Island
Black Coast
Bowman Coast
Foyn Coast

Limit of winter pack ice
Limit of summer pack ice
Antarctic Circle

Research stations on King George Island
Arctowski (to Poland)
Ártigas (to Uruguay)
Bellingshausen (to Russian Federation)
Comandante Ferraz (to Brazil)
Great Wall (to China)
Jubany (to Argentina)
King Sejong (to South Korea)
Teniente Rodolfo Marsh (to Chile)

TERRITORIAL CLAIMS

Argentinian claim
Brazilian zone of interest
British claim
Norwegian undefined limit
Chilean claim
Australian claim
French claim
Australian claim
New Zealand claim

6000m
4000m
3000m
2000m
1000m
500m
250m
100m
Sea Level
-250m
-2000m
-4000m

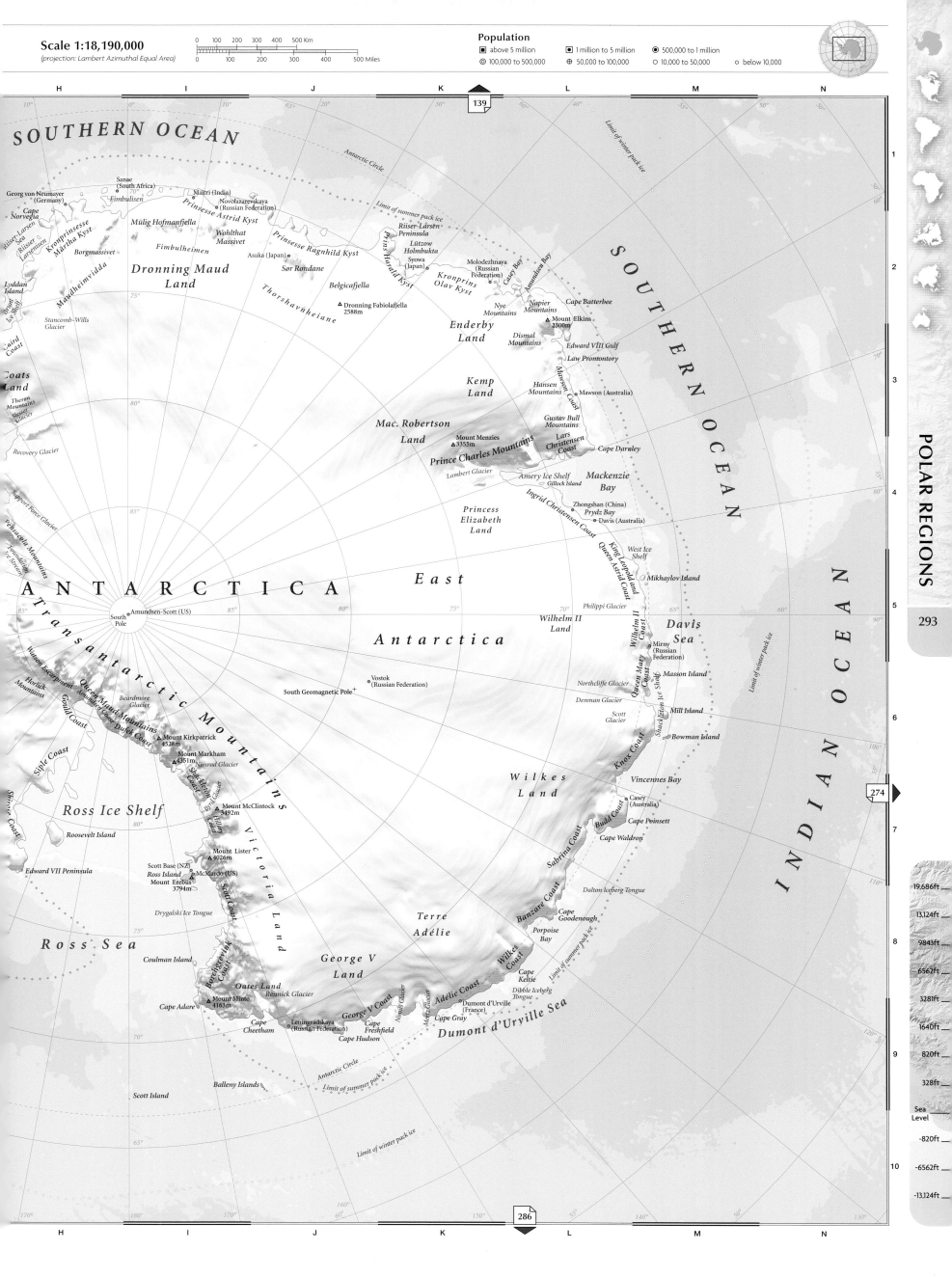

The Arctic

Geographical comparisons

Largest countries

Russian Federation	6,592,735 sq miles	(17,075,200 sq km)
Canada	3,855,171 sq miles	(9,984,670 sq km)
USA	3,717,792 sq miles	(9,629,091 sq km)
China	3,705,386 sq miles	(9,596,960 sq km)
Brazil	3,286,470 sq miles	(8,511,965 sq km)
Australia	2,967,893 sq miles	(7,686,850 sq km)
India	1,269,339 sq miles	(3,287,590 sq km)
Argentina	1,068,296 sq miles	(2,766,890 sq km)
Kazakhstan	1,049,150 sq miles	(2,717,300 sq km)
Algeria	919,590 sq miles	(2,318,740 sq km)

Smallest countries

Vatican City	0.17 sq miles	(0.44 sq km)
Monaco	0.75 sq miles	(1.95 sq km)
Nauru	8.1 sq miles	(21 sq km)
Tuvalu	10 sq miles	(26 sq km)
San Marino	24 sq miles	(61 sq km)
Liechtenstein	62 sq miles	(160 sq km)
Marshall Islands	70 sq miles	(181 sq km)
St. Kitts & Nevis	101 sq miles	(261 sq km)
Maldives	116 sq miles	(300 sq km)
Malta	122 sq miles	(316 sq km)

Largest islands

	To the nearest 1000 – or 100,000 for the largest	
Greenland	849,400 sq miles	(2,200,000 sq km)
New Guinea	312,000 sq miles	(808,000 sq km)
Borneo	292,222 sq miles	(757,050 sq km)
Madagascar	229,300 sq miles	(594,000 sq km)
Sumatra	202,300 sq miles	(524,000 sq km)
Baffin Island	183,800 sq miles	(476,000 sq km)
Honshu	88,800 sq miles	(230,000 sq km)
Britain	88,700 sq miles	(229,800 sq km)
Victoria Island	81,900 sq miles	(212,000 sq km)
Ellesmere Island	75,700 sq miles	(196,000 sq km)

Richest countries

	Annual (2010) GNI per capita, in US$
Monaco	197,460
Liechtenstein	135,540
Norway	85,380
Luxembourg	79,510
Switzerland	70,350
Denmark	59,980
Sweden	49,930
Netherlands	49,720
San Marino	50,670
Finland	47,170

Poorest countries

	Annual (2010) GNI per capita, in US$
Burundi	160
Congo, Dem. Rep.	180
Liberia	190
Malawi	330
Sierra Leone	340
Eritrea	340
Niger	360
Guinea	380
Ethiopia	380
Togo	440
Mozambique	440
Madagascar	440

Most populous countries

	2011
China	1,350,000,000
India	1,210,000,000
USA	318,000,000
Indonesia	232,000,000
Brazil	195,000,000
Pakistan	185,000,000
Bangladesh	164,000,000
Nigeria	158,000,000
Russian Federation	140,000,000
Japan	127,000,000

Least populous countries

	2011
Vatican City	832
Nauru	9322
Tuvalu	10,544
Palau	20,956
Monaco	30,539
San Marino	31,817
Liechtenstein	35,236
St Kitts & Nevis	50,314
Marshall Islands	67,182
Dominica	72,969
Andorra	84,825
Antigua & Barbuda	87,884

Most densely populated countries

	2011	
Monaco	40,719 people per sq mile	(15,661 per sq km)
Singapore	20,339 people per sq mile	(7869 per sq km)
Vatican City	4894 people per sq mile	(1891 per sq km)
Malta	3266 people per sq mile	(1250 per sq km)
Bangladesh	3180 people per sq mile	(1228 per sq km)
Bahrain	2930 people per sq mile	(1133 per sq km)
Maldives	2586 people per sq mile	(1000 per sq km)
Taiwan	1852 people per sq mile	(715 per sq km)
Mauritius	1811 people per sq mile	(699 per sq km)
Barbados	1807 people per sq mile	(698 per sq km)

Most sparsely populated countries

	2011	
Mongolia	4 people per sq mile	(2 per sq km)
Namibia	6 people per sq mile	(2 per sq km)
Australia	7 people per sq mile	(3 per sq km)
Botswana	8 people per sq mile	(3 per sq km)
Iceland	8 people per sq mile	(3 per sq km)
Mauritania	8 people per sq mile	(3 per sq km)
Surinam	8 people per sq mile	(3 per sq km)
Canada	9 people per sq mile	(4 per sq km)
Libya	9 people per sq mile	(4 per sq km)
Guyana	10 people per sq mile	(4 per sq km)

Most widely spoken languages

1. Chinese (Mandarin)	6. Arabic
2. English	7. Bengali
3. Hindi	8. Portuguese
4. Spanish	9. Malay-Indonesian
5. Russian	10. French

Largest conurbations

	Population
Tokyo	34,200,000
Mexico City	22,800,000
Seoul	22,300,000
New York	21,900,000
São Paulo	20,200,000
Mumbai	19,850,000
Delhi	19,700,000
Shanghai	18,150,000
Los Angeles	18,000,000
Osaka	16,800,000
Jakarta	16,550,000
Kolkata	15,650,000
Cairo	15,600,000
Manila	14,950,000
Karachi	14,300,000
Moscow	13,750,000
Buenos Aires	13,450,000
Dacca	13,250,000
Rio de Janeiro	12,150,000
Beijing	12,100,000
London	12,000,000
Tehran	11,850,000
Istanbul	11,500,000
Lagos	11,100,000
Shenzhen	10,700,000

Countries with the most land borders

14: China	(Afghanistan, Bhutan, India, Kazakhstan, Kyrgyzstan, Laos, Mongolia, Myanmar, Nepal, North Korea, Pakistan, Russian Federation, Tajikistan, Vietnam)
14: Russian Federation	(Azerbaijan, Belarus, China, Estonia, Finland, Georgia, Kazakhstan, Latvia, Lithuania, Mongolia, North Korea, Norway, Poland, Ukraine)
10: Brazil	(Argentina, Bolivia, Colombia, French Guiana, Guyana, Paraguay, Peru, Surinam, Uruguay, Venezuela)
9: Dem. Rep. Congo	(Angola, Burundi, Central African Republic, Congo, Rwanda, South Sudan, Tanzania, Uganda, Zambia)
9: Germany	(Austria, Belgium, Czech Republic, Denmark, France, Luxembourg, Netherlands, Poland, Switzerland)
8: Austria	(Czech Republic, Germany, Hungary, Italy, Liechtenstein, Slovakia, Slovenia, Switzerland)
8: France	(Andorra, Belgium, Germany, Italy, Luxembourg, Monaco, Spain, Switzerland)
8: Tanzania	(Burundi, Dem. Rep.Congo, Kenya, Malawi, Mozambique, Rwanda, Uganda, Zambia)
8: Turkey	(Armenia, Azerbaijan, Bulgaria, Georgia, Greece, Iran, Iraq, Syria)
8: Zambia	(Angola, Botswana, Dem. Rep. Congo, Malawi, Mozambique, Namibia, Tanzania, Zimbabwe)

Longest rivers

Nile (NE Africa)	4160 miles	(6695 km)
Amazon (South America)	4049 miles	(6516 km)
Yangtze (China)	3915 miles	(6299 km)
Mississippi/Missouri (USA)	3710 miles	(5969 km)
Ob'-Irtysh (Russian Federation)	3461 miles	(5570 km)
Yellow River (China)	3395 miles	(5464 km)
Congo (Central Africa)	2900 miles	(4667 km)
Mekong (Southeast Asia)	2749 miles	(4425 km)
Lena (Russian Federation)	2734 miles	(4400 km)
Mackenzie (Canada)	2640 miles	(4250 km)
Yenisey (Russian Federation)	2541 miles	(4090km)

Highest mountains

	Height above sea level	
Everest	29,029 ft	(8848 m)
K2	28,253 ft	(8611 m)
Kangchenjunga	28,210 ft	(8598 m)
Lhotse	27,940 ft	(8516 m)
Makalu	27,767 ft	(8463 m)
Cho Oyu	26,907 ft	(8201 m)
Dhaulagiri	26,796 ft	(8167 m)
Manaslu	26,783 ft	(8163 m)
Nanga Parbat	26,661 ft	(8126 m)
Annapurna	26,547 ft	(8091 m)

Largest bodies of inland water

	With area and depth	
Caspian Sea	143,243 sq miles (371,000 sq km)	3215 ft (980 m)
Lake Superior	31,151 sq miles (83,270 sq km)	1289 ft (393 m)
Lake Victoria	26,828 sq miles (69,484 sq km)	328 ft (100 m)
Lake Huron	23,436 sq miles (60,700 sq km)	751 ft (229 m)
Lake Michigan	22,402 sq miles (58,020 sq km)	922 ft (281 m)
Lake Tanganyika	12,703 sq miles (32,900 sq km)	4700 ft (1435 m)
Great Bear Lake	12,274 sq miles (31,790 sq km)	1047 ft (319 m)
Lake Baikal	11,776 sq miles (30,500 sq km)	5712 ft (1741 m)
Great Slave Lake	10,981 sq miles (28,440 sq km)	459 ft (140 m)
Lake Erie	9,915 sq miles (25,680 sq km)	197 ft (60 m)

Deepest ocean features

Challenger Deep, Mariana Trench (Pacific)	36,201 ft	(11,034 m)
Vityaz III Depth, Tonga Trench (Pacific)	35,704 ft	(10,882 m)
Vityaz Depth, Kurile-Kamchatka Trench (Pacific)	34,588 ft	(10,542 m)
Cape Johnson Deep, Philippine Trench (Pacific)	34,441 ft	(10,497 m)
Kermadec Trench (Pacific)	32,964 ft	(10,047 m)
Ramapo Deep, Japan Trench (Pacific)	32,758 ft	(9984 m)
Milwaukee Deep, Puerto Rico Trench (Atlantic)	30,185 ft	(9200 m)
Argo Deep, Torres Trench (Pacific)	30,070 ft	(9165 m)
Meteor Depth, South Sandwich Trench (Atlantic)	30,000 ft	(9144 m)
Planet Deep, New Britain Trench (Pacific)	29,988 ft	(9140 m)

Greatest waterfalls

	Mean flow of water	
Boyoma (Congo, Dem. Rep.)	600,400 cu. ft/sec	(17,000 cu.m/sec)
Khône (Laos/Cambodia)	410,000 cu. ft/sec	(11,600 cu.m/sec)
Niagara (USA/Canada)	195,000 cu. ft/sec	(5500 cu.m/sec)
Grande (Uruguay)	160,000 cu. ft/sec	(4500 cu.m/sec)
Paulo Afonso (Brazil)	100,000 cu. ft/sec	(2800 cu.m/sec)
Urubupunga (Brazil)	97,000 cu. ft/sec	(2750 cu.m/sec)
Iguaçu (Argentina/Brazil)	62,000 cu. ft/sec	(1700 cu.m/sec)
Maribondo (Brazil)	53,000 cu. ft/sec	(1500 cu.m/sec)
Victoria (Zimbabwe/Zambia)	39,000 cu. ft/sec	(1100 cu.m/sec)
Kabalega (Uganda)	42,000 cu. ft/sec	(1200 cu.m/sec)
Churchill (Canada)	35,000 cu. ft/sec	(1000 cu.m/sec)
Cauvery (India)	33,000 cu. ft/sec	(900 cu.m/sec)

Highest waterfalls

	* Indicates that the total height is a single leap	
Angel (Venezuela)	3212 ft	(979 m)
Tugela (South Africa)	3110 ft	(948 m)
Utigard (Norway)	2625 ft	(800 m)
Mongefossen (Norway)	2539 ft	(774 m)
Mtarazi (Zimbabwe)	2500 ft	(762 m)
Yosemite (USA)	2425 ft	(739 m)
Ostre Mardola Foss (Norway)	2156 ft	(657 m)
Tyssestrengane (Norway)	2119 ft	(646 m)
*Cuquenan (Venezuela)	2001 ft	(610 m)
Sutherland (New Zealand)	1903 ft	(580 m)
*Kjellfossen (Norway)	1841 ft	(561 m)

Largest deserts

	NB – Most of Antarctica is a polar desert, with only 50mm of precipitation annually	
Sahara	3,450,000 sq miles	(9,065,000 sq km)
Gobi	500,000 sq miles	(1,295,000 sq km)
Ar Rub al Khali	289,600 sq miles	(750,000 sq km)
Great Victorian	249,800 sq miles	(647,000 sq km)
Sonoran	120,000 sq miles	(311,000 sq km)
Kalahari	120,000 sq miles	(310,800 sq km)
Kara Kum	115,800 sq miles	(300,000 sq km)
Takla Makan	100,400 sq miles	(260,000 sq km)
Namib	52,100 sq miles	(135,000 sq km)
Thar	33,670 sq miles	(130,000 sq km)

Hottest inhabited places

Djibouti (Djibouti)	86° F	(30 °C)
Timbuktu (Mali)	84.7° F	(29.3 °C)
Tirunelveli (India)		
Tuticorin (India)		
Nellore (India)	84.5° F	(29.2 °C)
Santa Marta (Colombia)		
Aden (Yemen)	84° F	(28.9 °C)
Madurai (India)		
Niamey (Niger)		
Hodeida (Yemen)	83.8° F	(28.8 °C)
Ouagadougou (Burkina)		
Thanjavur (India)		
Tiruchchirappalli (India)		

Driest inhabited places

Aswan (Egypt)	0.02 in	(0.5 mm)
Luxor (Egypt)	0.03 in	(0.7 mm)
Arica (Chile)	0.04 in	(1.1 mm)
Ica (Peru)	0.1 in	(2.3 mm)
Antofagasta (Chile)	0.2 in	(4.9 mm)
Al Minya (Egypt)	0.2 in	(5.1 mm)
Asyut (Egypt)	0.2 in	(5.2 mm)
Callao (Peru)	0.5 in	(12.0 mm)
Trujillo (Peru)	0.55 in	(14.0 mm)
Al Fayyum (Egypt)	0.8 in	(19.0 mm)

Wettest inhabited places

Buenaventura (Colombia)	265 in	(6743 mm)
Monrovia (Liberia)	202 in	(5131 mm)
Pago Pago (American Samoa)	196 in	(4990 mm)
Mawlamyine (Myanmar)	191 in	(4852 mm)
Lae (Papua New Guinea)	183 in	(4645 mm)
Baguio (Luzon Island, Philippines)	180 in	(4573 mm)
Sylhet (Bangladesh)	176 in	(4457 mm)
Padang (Sumatra, Indonesia)	166 in	(4225 mm)
Bogor (Java, Indonesia)	166 in	(4225 mm)
Conakry (Guinea)	171 in	(4341 mm)

Countries of the World

There are currently 196 independent countries in the world – more than at any previous time – and almost 60 dependencies. Antarctica is the only land area on Earth that is not officially part of, and does not belong to, any single country.

In 1950, the world comprised 82 countries. In the decades following, many more states came into being as they achieved independence from their former colonial rulers. Most recent additions were caused by the breakup of the former Soviet Union in 1991, and the former Yugoslavia in 1992, which swelled the ranks of independent states. In July 2011, South Sudan became the latest country to be formed after declaring independence from Sudan.

Country factfile key

Formation Date of independence / date current borders were established

Population Total population / population density – based on total *land* area

Languages An asterisk (*) denotes the official language(s)

Calorie consumption Average number of calories consumed daily per person

AFGHANISTAN
Central Asia

Official name Islamic Republic of Afghanistan
Formation 1919 / 1919
Capital Kabul
Population 29.1 million / 116 people per sq mile (45 people per sq km)
Total area 250,000 sq. miles (647,500 sq. km)
Languages Pashtu*, Tajik, Dari*, Farsi, Uzbek, Turkmen
Religions Sunni Muslim 80%, Shi'a Muslim 19%, Other 1%
Ethnic mix Pashtun 38%, Tajik 25%, Hazara 19%, Uzbek and Turkmen 15%, Other 3%
Government Presidential system
Currency Afghani = 100 puls
Literacy rate 28%
Calorie consumption 1539 kilocalories

ALBANIA
Southeast Europe

Official name Republic of Albania
Formation 1912 / 1921
Capital Tirana
Population 3.2 million / 302 people per sq mile (117 people per sq km)
Total area 11,100 sq. miles (28,748 sq. km)
Languages Albanian*, Greek
Religions Sunni Muslim 70%, Albanian Orthodox 20%, Roman Catholic 10%
Ethnic mix Albanian 98%, Greek 1%, Other 1%
Government Parliamentary system
Currency Lek = 100 qindarka (qintars)
Literacy rate 96%
Calorie consumption 2904 kilocalories

ALGERIA
North Africa

Official name People's Democratic Republic of Algeria
Formation 1962 / 1962
Capital Algiers
Population 35.4 million / 38 people per sq mile (15 people per sq km)
Total area 919,590 sq. miles (2,381,740 sq. km)
Languages Arabic*, Tamazight (Kabyle, Shawia, Tamashek), French
Religions Sunni Muslim 99%, Christian & Jewish 1%
Ethnic mix Arab 75%, Berber 24%, European & Jewish 1%
Government Presidential system
Currency Algerian dinar = 100 centimes
Literacy rate 75%
Calorie consumption 3104 kilocalories

ANDORRA
Southwest Europe

Official name Principality of Andorra
Formation 1278 / 1278
Capital Andorra la Vella
Population 84,825 / 471 people per sq mile (182 people per sq km)
Total area 181 sq. miles (468 sq. km)
Languages Spanish, Catalan*, French, Portuguese
Religions Roman Catholic 94%, Other 6%
Ethnic mix Spanish 46%, Andorran 28%, Other 18%, French 8%
Government Parliamentary system
Currency Euro = 100 cents
Literacy rate 99%
Calorie consumption Not available

ANGOLA
Southern Africa

Official name Republic of Angola
Formation 1975 / 1975
Capital Luanda
Population 19 million / 39 people per sq mile (15 people per sq km)
Total area 481,351 sq. miles (1,246,700 sq. km)
Languages Portuguese*, Umbundu, Kimbundu, Kikongo
Religions Roman Catholic 68%, Protestant 20%, Indigenous beliefs 12%
Ethnic mix Ovimbundu 37%, Kimbundu 25%, Other 25%, Bakongo 13%
Government Presidential system
Currency Readjusted kwanza = 100 lwei
Literacy rate 70%
Calorie consumption 1949 kilocalories

ANTIGUA & BARBUDA
West Indies

Official name Antigua and Barbuda
Formation 1981 / 1981
Capital St. John's
Population 87,884 / 517 people per sq mile (200 people per sq km)
Total area 170 sq. miles (442 sq. km)
Languages English*, English patois
Religions Anglican 45%, Other Protestant 42%, Roman Catholic 10%, Other 3%
Religions Roman Catholic 90%, Other 6%, Protestant 2%, Jewish 2%
Ethnic mix Black African 95%, Other 5%
Government Parliamentary system
Currency East Caribbean dollar = 100 cents
Literacy rate 99%
Calorie consumption 2319 kilocalories

ARGENTINA
South America

Official name Republic of Argentina
Formation 1816 / 1816
Capital Buenos Aires
Population 40.7 million / 39 people per sq mile (15 people per sq km)
Total area 1,068,296 sq. miles (2,766,890 sq. km)
Languages Spanish*, Italian, Amerindian languages
Religions Roman Catholic 70%, Other 18%, Protestant 9%, Muslim 2%, Jewish 1%
Ethnic mix Indo-European 97%, Mestizo 2%, Amerindian 1%
Government Presidential system
Currency Argentine peso = 100 centavos
Literacy rate 98%
Calorie consumption 3001 kilocalories

ARMENIA
Southwest Asia

Official name Republic of Armenia
Formation 1991 / 1991
Capital Yerevan
Population 3.1 million / 269 people per sq mile (104 people per sq km)
Total area 11,506 sq. miles (29,800 sq. km)
Languages Armenian*, Azeri, Russian
Religions Armenian Apostolic Church (Orthodox) 88%, Other 6%, Armenian Catholic Church 6%
Ethnic mix Armenian 98%, Other 1%, Yezidi 1%
Government Parliamentary system
Currency Dram = 100 luma
Literacy rate 99%
Calorie consumption 2250 kilocalories

AUSTRALIA
Australasia & Oceania

Official name Commonwealth of Australia
Formation 1901 / 1901
Capital Canberra
Population 21.5 million / 7 people per sq mile (3 people per sq km)
Total area 2,967,893 sq. miles (7,686,850 sq. km)
Languages English*, Italian, Cantonese, Greek, Arabic, Vietnamese, Aboriginal languages
Religions Roman Catholic 26%, Nonreligious 19%, Anglican 19%, Other 17%, Other Christian 13%, United Church 6%
Ethnic mix European 90%, Asian 7%, Aboriginal 2%, Other 1%
Government Parliamentary system
Currency Australian dollar = 100 cents
Literacy rate 99%
Calorie consumption 3186 kilocalories

AUSTRIA
Central Europe

Official name Republic of Austria
Formation 1918 / 1919
Capital Vienna
Population 8.4 million / 263 people per sq mile (102 people per sq km)
Total area 32,378 sq. miles (83,858 sq. km)
Languages German*, Croatian, Slovenian, Hungarian (Magyar)
Religions Roman Catholic 78%, Nonreligious 9%, Other 8%, Protestant 5%
Ethnic mix Austrian 93%, Croat, Slovene, and Hungarian 6%, Other 1%
Government Parliamentary system
Currency Euro = 100 cents
Literacy rate 99%
Calorie consumption 3760 kilocalories

AZERBAIJAN
Southwest Asia

Official name Republic of Azerbaijan
Formation 1991 / 1991
Capital Baku
Population 8.9 million / 266 people per sq mile (103 people per sq km)
Total area 33,436 sq. miles (86,600 sq. km)
Languages Azeri*, Russian
Religions Shi'a Muslim 68%, Sunni Muslim 26%, Russian Orthodox 3%, Armenian Apostolic Church (Orthodox) 2%, Other 1%
Ethnic mix Azeri 91%, Other 3%, Armenian 2%, Russian 2%, Lazs 2%
Government Presidential system
Currency New manat = 100 gopik
Literacy rate 99%
Calorie consumption 2996 kilocalories

BAHAMAS
West Indies

Official name Commonwealth of the Bahamas
Formation 1973 / 1973
Capital Nassau
Population 300,000 / 78 people per sq mile (30 people per sq km)
Total area 5382 sq. miles (13,940 sq. km)
Languages English*, English Creole, French Creole
Religions Baptist 32%, Anglican 20%, Roman Catholic 19%, Other 17%, Methodist 6%, Church of God 6%
Ethnic mix Black African 85%, European 12%, Asian and Hispanic 3%
Government Parliamentary system
Currency Bahamian dollar = 100 cents
Literacy rate 96%
Calorie consumption 2701 kilocalories

BAHRAIN
Southwest Asia

Official name Kingdom of Bahrain
Formation 1971 / 1971
Capital Manama
Population 800,000 / 2930 people per sq mile (1133 people per sq km)
Total area 239 sq. miles (620 sq. km)
Languages Arabic
Religions Muslim (mainly Shi'a) 99%, Other 1%
Ethnic mix Bahraini 63%, Asian 19%, Other Arab 10%, Iranian 8%
Government Mixed monarchical–parliamentary system
Currency Bahraini dinar = 1000 fils
Literacy rate 91%
Calorie consumption Not available

BANGLADESH
South Asia

Official name People's Republic of Bangladesh
Formation 1971 / 1971
Capital Dhaka
Population 164 million / 3180 people per sq mile (1228 people per sq km)
Total area 55,598 sq. miles (144,000 sq. km)
Languages Bengali*, Urdu, Chakma, Marma (Magh), Garo, Khasi, Santhali, Tripuri, Mro
Religions Muslim (mainly Sunni) 88%, Hindu 11%, Other 1%
Ethnic mix Bengali 98%, Other 2%
Government Parliamentary system
Currency Taka = 100 poisha
Literacy rate 56%
Calorie consumption 2250 kilocalories

BARBADOS
West Indies

Official name Barbados
Formation 1966 / 1966
Capital Bridgetown
Population 300,000 / 1807 people per sq mile (698 people per sq km)
Total area 166 sq. miles (430 sq. km)
Languages Bajan (Barbadian English), English*
Religions Anglican 40%, Other 24%, Nonreligious 17%, Pentecostal 8%, Methodist 7%, Roman Catholic 4%
Ethnic mix Black African 92%, Other 3%, White 3%, Mixed race 2%
Government Parliamentary system
Currency Barbados dollar = 100 cents
Literacy rate 99%
Calorie consumption 3055 kilocalories

BELARUS
Eastern Europe

Official name Republic of Belarus
Formation 1991 / 1991
Capital Minsk
Population 9.6 million / 120 people per sq mile (46 people per sq km)
Total area 80,154 sq. miles (207,600 sq. km)
Languages Belarussian*, Russian*
Religions Orthodox Christian 80%, Roman Catholic 14%, Other 4%, Protestant 2%
Ethnic mix Belarussian 81%, Russian 11%, Polish 4%, Ukrainian 2%, Other 2%
Government Presidential system
Currency Belarussian rouble = 100 kopeks
Literacy rate 99%
Calorie consumption 3086 kilocalories

BELGIUM
Northwest Europe

Official name Kingdom of Belgium
Formation 1830 / 1919
Capital Brussels
Population 10.7 million / 844 people per sq mile (326 people per sq km)
Total area 11,780 sq. miles (30,510 sq. km)
Languages Dutch*, French*, German*
Religions Roman Catholic 88%, Other 10%, Muslim 2%
Ethnic mix Fleming 58%, Walloon 33%, Other 6%, Italian 2%, Moroccan 1%
Government Parliamentary system
Currency Euro = 100 cents
Literacy rate 99%
Calorie consumption 3690 kilocalories

BELIZE
Central America

Official name Belize
Formation 1981 / 1981
Capital Belmopan
Population 300,000 / 34 people per sq mile (13 people per sq km)
Total area 8867 sq. miles (22,966 sq. km)
Languages English Creole, Spanish, English*, Mayan, Garifuna (Carib)
Religions Roman Catholic 62%, Other 16%, Anglican 12%, Methodist 6%, Mennonite 4%
Ethnic mix Mestizo 49%, Creole 25%, Maya 11%, Garifuna 6%, Other 6%, Asian Indian 3%
Government Parliamentary system
Currency Belizean dollar = 100 cents
Literacy rate 75%
Calorie consumption 2719 kilocalories

BENIN
West Africa

Official name Republic of Benin
Formation 1960 / 1960
Capital Porto-Novo
Population 9.2 million / 215 people per sq mile (83 people per sq km)
Total area 43,483 sq. miles (112,620 sq. km)
Languages Fon, Bariba, Yoruba, Adja, Houeda, Somba, French*
Religions Indigenous beliefs and Voodoo 50%, Christian 30%, Muslim 20%
Ethnic mix Fon 41%, Other 21%, Adja 16%, Yoruba 12%, Bariba 10%
Government Presidential system
Currency CFA franc = 100 centimes
Literacy rate 42%
Calorie consumption 2512 kilocalories

BHUTAN
South Asia

Official name Kingdom of Bhutan
Formation 1656 / 1865
Capital Thimphu
Population 700,000 / 39 people per sq mile (15 people per sq km)
Total area 18,147 sq. miles (47,000 sq. km)
Languages Dzongkha*, Nepali, Assamese
Religions Mahayana Buddhist 75%, Hindu 25%
Ethnic mix Drukpa 50%, Nepalese 35%, Other 15%
Government Mixed monarchical–parliamentary system
Currency Ngultrum = 100 chetrum
Literacy rate 56%
Calorie consumption Not available

BOLIVIA
South America

Official name Plurinational State of Bolivia
Formation 1825 / 1938
Capital La Paz (administrative); Sucre (judicial)
Population 10 million / 24 people per sq mile (9 people per sq km)
Total area 424,162 sq. miles (1,098,580 sq. km)
Languages Aymara*, Quechua*, Spanish*
Religions Roman Catholic 93%, Other 7%
Ethnic mix Quechua 37%, Aymara 32%, Mixed race 13%, European 10%, Other 8%
Government Presidential system
Currency Boliviano = 100 centavos
Literacy rate 91%
Calorie consumption 2093 kilocalories

BOSNIA & HERZEGOVINA
Southeast Europe

Official name Bosnia and Herzegovina
Formation 1992 / 1992
Capital Sarajevo
Population 3.8 million / 192 people per sq mile (74 people per sq km)
Total area 19,741 sq. miles (51,129 sq. km)
Languages Bosnian*, Serbian*, Croatian*
Religions Muslim (mainly Sunni) 40%, Orthodox Christian 31%, Roman Catholic 15%, Other 14%
Ethnic mix Bosniak 48%, Serb 34%, Croat 16%, Other 2%
Government Parliamentary system
Currency Marka = 100 pfeninga
Literacy rate 98%
Calorie consumption 3084 kilocalories

BOTSWANA
Southern Africa

Official name Republic of Botswana
Formation 1966 / 1966
Capital Gaborone
Population 2 million / 9 people per sq mile (4 people per sq km)
Total area 231,803 sq. miles (600,370 sq. km)
Languages Setswana, English*, Shona, San, Khoikhoi, isiNdebele
Religions Christian (mainly Protestant) 70%, Nonreligious 20%, Traditional beliefs 6%, Other (including Muslim) 4%
Ethnic mix Tswana 79%, Kalanga 11%, Other 10%
Government Presidential system
Currency Pula = 100 thebe
Literacy rate 84%
Calorie consumption 2235 kilocalories

BRAZIL
South America

Official name Federative Republic of Brazil
Formation 1822 / 1828
Capital Brasília
Population 195 million / 60 people per sq mile (23 people per sq km)
Total area 3,286,470 sq. miles (8,511,965 sq. km)
Languages Portuguese*, German, Italian, Spanish, Polish, Japanese, Amerindian languages
Religions Roman Catholic 74%, Protestant 15%, Atheist 7%, Other 3%, Afro-American Spiritist 1%
Ethnic mix White 54%, Mixed race 38%, Black 6%, Other 2%
Government Presidential system
Currency Real = 100 centavos
Literacy rate 90%
Calorie consumption 3099 kilocalories

BRUNEI
Southeast Asia

Official name Sultanate of Brunei
Formation 1984 / 1984
Capital Bandar Seri Begawan
Population 400,000 / 197 people per sq mile (76 people per sq km)
Total area 2228 sq. miles (5770 sq. km)
Languages Malay*, English, Chinese
Religions Muslim (mainly Sunni) 66%, Buddhist 14%, Christian 10%, Other 10%
Ethnic mix Malay 67%, Chinese 16%, Other 11%, Indigenous 6%
Government Monarchy
Currency Brunei dollar = 100 cents
Literacy rate 95%
Calorie consumption 2987 kilocalories

BULGARIA
Southeast Europe

Official name Republic of Bulgaria
Formation 1908 / 1947
Capital Sofia
Population 7.5 million / 176 people per sq mile (68 people per sq km)
Total area 42,822 sq. miles (110,910 sq. km)
Languages Bulgarian*, Turkish, Romani
Religions Bulgarian Orthodox 83%, Muslim 12%, Other 4%, Roman Catholic 1%
Ethnic mix Bulgarian 84%, Turkish 9%, Roma 5%, Other 2%
Government Parliamentary system
Currency Lev = 100 stotinki
Literacy rate 98%
Calorie consumption 2761 kilocalories

BURKINA
West Africa

Official name Burkina Faso
Formation 1960 / 1960
Capital Ouagadougou
Population 16.3 million / 154 people per sq mile (60 people per sq km)
Total area 105,869 sq. miles (274,200 sq. km)
Languages Mossi, Fulani, French*, Tuareg, Dyula, Songhai
Religions Muslim 55%, Christian 25%, Traditional beliefs 20%
Ethnic mix Mossi 48%, Other 21%, Peul 10%, Lobi 7%, Bobo 7%, Mandé 7%
Government Presidential system
Currency CFA franc = 100 centimes
Literacy rate 29%
Calorie consumption 2669 kilocalories

BURUNDI
Central Africa

Official name Republic of Burundi
Formation 1962 / 1962
Capital Bujumbura
Population 8.5 million / 858 people per sq mile (331 people per sq km)
Total area 10,745 sq. miles (27,830 sq. km)
Languages Kirundi*, French*, Kiswahili
Religions Roman Catholic 62%, Traditional beliefs 23%, Muslim 10%, Protestant 5%
Ethnic mix Hutu 85%, Tutsi 14%, Twa 1%
Government Presidential system
Currency Burundian franc = 100 centimes
Literacy rate 67%
Calorie consumption 1680 kilocalories

CAMBODIA
Southeast Asia

Official name Kingdom of Cambodia
Formation 1953 / 1953
Capital Phnom Penh
Population 15.1 million / 222 people per sq mile (86 people per sq km)
Total area 69,900 sq. miles (181,040 sq. km)
Languages Khmer*, French, Chinese, Vietnamese, Cham
Religions Buddhist 93%, Muslim 6%, Christian 1%
Ethnic mix Khmer 90%, Vietnamese 5%, Other 4%, Chinese 1%
Government Parliamentary system
Currency Riel = 100 sen
Literacy rate 78%
Calorie consumption 2245 kilocalories

CAMEROON
Central Africa

Official name Republic of Cameroon
Formation 1960 / 1961
Capital Yaoundé
Population 20 million / 111 people per sq mile (43 people per sq km)
Total area 183,567 sq. miles (475,400 sq. km)
Languages Bamileke, Fang, Fulani, French*, English*
Religions Roman Catholic 35%, Traditional beliefs 25%, Muslim 22%, Protestant 18%
Ethnic mix Cameroon highlanders 31%, Other 21%, Equatorial Bantu 19%, Kirdi 11%, Fulani 10%, Northwestern Bantu 8%
Government Presidential system
Currency CFA franc = 100 centimes
Literacy rate 71%
Calorie consumption 2259 kilocalories

CANADA
North America

Official name Canada
Formation 1867 / 1949
Capital Ottawa
Population 33.9 million / 10 people per sq mile (4 people per sq km)
Total area 3,855,171 sq. miles (9,984,670 sq. km)
Languages English*, French*, Chinese, Italian, German, Ukrainian, Portuguese, Inuktitut, Cree
Religions Roman Catholic 44%, Protestant 29%, Other and nonreligious 27%
Ethnic mix European 87%, Asian 9%, Amerindian, Métis and Inuit 4%
Government Parliamentary system
Currency Canadian dollar = 100 cents
Literacy rate 99%
Calorie consumption 3530 kilocalories

CAPE VERDE
Atlantic Ocean

Official name Republic of Cape Verde
Formation 1975 / 1975
Capital Praia
Population 500,000 / 321 people per sq mile (124 people per sq km)
Total area 1557 sq. miles (4033 sq. km)
Languages Portuguese Creole, Portuguese*
Religions Roman Catholic 97%, Other 2%, Protestant (Church of the Nazarene) 1%
Ethnic mix Mestiço 71%, African 28%, European 1%
Government Mixed presidential–parliamentary system
Currency Escudo = 100 centavos
Literacy rate 85%
Calorie consumption 2549 kilocalories

CENTRAL AFRICAN REPUBLIC
Central Africa

Official name Central African Republic
Formation 1960 / 1960
Capital Bangui
Population 4.5 million / 19 people per sq mile (7 people per sq km)
Total area 240,534 sq. miles (622,984 sq. km)
Languages Sango, Banda, Gbaya, French*
Religions Traditional beliefs 35%, Roman Catholic 25%, Protestant 25%, Muslim 15%
Ethnic mix Baya 33%, Banda 27%, Other 17%, Mandjia 13%, Sara 10%
Government Presidential system
Currency CFA franc = 100 centimes
Literacy rate 55%
Calorie consumption 1956 kilocalories

CHAD
Central Africa

Official name Republic of Chad
Formation 1960 / 1960
Capital N'Djamena
Population 11.5 million / 24 people per sq mile (9 people per sq km)
Total area 495,752 sq. miles (1,284,000 sq. km)
Languages French*, Sara, Arabic*, Maba
Religions Muslim 51%, Christian 35%, Animist 7%, Traditional beliefs 7%
Ethnic mix Other 30%, Sara 28%, Mayo-Kebbi 12%, Arab 12%, Ouaddai 9%, Kanem-Bornou 9%
Government Presidential system
Currency CFA franc = 100 centimes
Literacy rate 34%
Calorie consumption 2040 kilocalories

CHILE
South America

Official name Republic of Chile
Formation 1818 / 1883
Capital Santiago
Population 17.1 million / 59 people per sq mile (23 people per sq km)
Total area 292,258 sq. miles (756,950 sq. km)
Languages Spanish*, Amerindian languages
Religions Roman Catholic 89%, Other and nonreligious 11%
Ethnic mix Mestizo and European 90%, Other Amerindian 9%, Mapuche 1%
Government Presidential system
Currency Chilean peso = 100 centavos
Literacy rate 99%
Calorie consumption 2957 kilocalories

CHINA
East Asia

Official name People's Republic of China
Formation 960 / 1999
Capital Beijing
Population 1.35 billion / 376 people per sq mile (145 people per sq km)
Total area 3,705,386 sq. miles (9,596,960 sq. km)
Languages Mandarin*, Wu, Cantonese, Hsiang, Min, Hakka, Kan
Religions Nonreligious 59%, Traditional beliefs 20%, Other 13%, Buddhist 6%, Muslim 2%
Ethnic mix Han 92%, Other 4%, Zhuang 1%, Hui 1%, Manchu 1%, Miao 1%
Government One-party state
Currency Renminbi (known as yuan) = 10 jiao = 100 fen
Literacy rate 94%
Calorie consumption 2974 kilocalories

COLOMBIA
South America

Official name Republic of Colombia
Formation 1819 / 1903
Capital Bogotá
Population 46.3 million / 115 people per sq mile (45 people per sq km)
Total area 439,733 sq. miles (1,138,910 sq. km)
Languages Spanish*, Wayuu, Páez, and other Amerindian languages
Religions Roman Catholic 95%, Other 5%
Ethnic mix Mestizo 58%, White 20%, European–African 14%, African 4%, frican–Amerindian 3%, Amerindian 1%
Government Presidential system
Currency Colombian peso = 100 centavos
Literacy rate 93%
Calorie consumption 2662 kilocalories

COMOROS
Indian Ocean

Official name Union of the Comoros
Formation 1975 / 1975
Capital Moroni
Population 700,000 / 813 people per sq mile (314 people per sq km)
Total area 838 sq. miles (2170 sq. km)
Languages Arabic*, Comoran*, French*
Religions Muslim (mainly Sunni) 98%, Other 1%, Roman Catholic 1%
Ethnic mix Comoran 97%, Other 3%
Government Presidential system
Currency Comoros franc = 100 centimes
Literacy rate 74%
Calorie consumption 1857 kilocalories

CONGO
Central Africa

Official name Republic of the Congo
Formation 1960 / 1960
Capital Brazzaville
Population 3.8 million / 29 people per sq mile (11 people per sq km)
Total area 132,046 sq. miles (342,000 sq. km)
Languages Kongo, Teke, Lingala, French*
Religions Traditional beliefs 50%, Roman Catholic 35%, Protestant 13%, Muslim 2%
Ethnic mix Bakongo 51%, Teke 17%, Other 16%, Mbochi 11%, Mbédé 5%
Government Presidential system
Currency CFA franc = 100 centimes
Literacy rate 87%
Calorie consumption 2513 kilocalories

CONGO, DEM. REP.
Central Africa

Official name Democratic Republic of the Congo
Formation 1960 / 1960
Capital Kinshasa
Population 67.8 million / 77 people per sq mile (30 people per sq km)
Total area 905,563 sq. miles (2,345,410 sq. km)
Languages Kiswahili, Tshiluba, Kikongo, Lingala, French*
Religions Roman Catholic 50%, Protestant 20%, Traditional beliefs and other 20%, Muslim 10%
Ethnic mix Other 55%, Mongo, Luba, Kongo, and Mangbetu-Azande 45%
Government Presidential system
Currency Congolese franc = 100 centimes
Literacy rate 67%
Calorie consumption 1585 kilocalories

COSTA RICA
Central America

Official name Republic of Costa Rica
Formation 1838 / 1838
Capital San José
Population 4.6 million / 233 people per sq mile (90 people per sq km)
Total area 19,730 sq. miles (51,100 sq. km)
Languages Spanish*, English Creole, Bribri, Cabecar
Religions Roman Catholic 71%, Evangelical 14%, Nonreligious 11%, Other 4%
Ethnic mix Mestizo and European 94%, Black 3%, Chinese 1%, Other 1%, Amerindian 1%
Government Presidential system
Currency Costa Rican colón = 100 céntimos
Literacy rate 96%
Calorie consumption 2813 kilocalories

CROATIA
Southeast Europe

Official name Republic of Croatia
Formation 1991 / 1991
Capital Zagreb
Population 4.4 million / 202 people per sq mile (78 people per sq km)
Total area 21,831 sq. miles (56,542 sq. km)
Languages Croatian*
Religions Roman Catholic 88%, Other 7%, Orthodox Christian 4%, Muslim 1%
Ethnic mix Croat 90%, Serb 5%, Other 5%
Government Parliamentary system
Currency Kuna = 100 lipa
Literacy rate 99%
Calorie consumption 2987 kilocalories

CUBA
West Indies

Official name Republic of Cuba
Formation 1902 / 1902
Capital Havana
Population 11.2 million / 262 people per sq mile (101 people per sq km)
Total area 42,803 sq. miles (110,860 sq. km)
Languages Spanish
Religions Nonreligious 49%, Roman Catholic 40%, Atheist 6%, Other 4%, Protestant 1%
Ethnic mix Mulatto (mixed race) 51%, White 37%, Black 11%, Chinese 1%
Government One-party state
Currency Cuban peso = 100 centavos
Literacy rate 99%
Calorie consumption 3295 kilocalories

CYPRUS
Northwest Asia

Official name Republic of Cyprus
Formation 1960 / 1960
Capital Nicosia
Population 900,000 / 252 people per sq mile (97 people per sq km)
Total area 3571 sq. miles (9250 sq. km)
Languages Greek*, Turkish*
Religions Orthodox Christian 78%, Muslim 18%, Other 4%
Ethnic mix Greek 81%, Turkish 11%, Other 8%
Government Presidential system
Currency Euro (new Turkish lira in TRNC) = 100 cents (euro); 100 kurus (Turkish lira)
Literacy rate 98%
Calorie consumption 3199 kilocalories

CZECH REPUBLIC
Central Europe

Official name Czech Republic
Formation 1993 / 1993
Capital Prague
Population 10.4 million / 342 people per sq mile (132 people per sq km)
Total area 30,450 sq. miles (78,866 sq. km)
Languages Czech*, Slovak, Hungarian (Magyar)
Religions Roman Catholic 39%, Atheist 38%, Other 18%, Protestant 3%, Hussite 2%
Ethnic mix Czech 90%, Moravian 4%, Other 4%, Slovak 2%
Government Parliamentary system
Currency Czech koruna = 100 haleru
Literacy rate 99%
Calorie consumption 3317 kilocalories

DENMARK
Northern Europe

Official name Kingdom of Denmark
Formation 950 / 1944
Capital Copenhagen
Population 5.5 million / 336 people per sq mile (130 people per sq km)
Total area 16,639 sq. miles (43,094 sq. km)
Languages Danish
Religions Evangelical Lutheran 95%, Roman Catholic 3%, Muslim 2%
Ethnic mix Danish 96%, Other (including Scandinavian and Turkish) 3%, Faeroese and Inuit 1%
Government Parliamentary system
Currency Danish krone = 100 øre
Literacy rate 99%
Calorie consumption 3397 kilocalories

DJIBOUTI
East Africa

Official name Republic of Djibouti
Formation 1977 / 1977
Capital Djibouti
Population 900,000 / 101 people per sq mile (39 people per sq km)
Total area 8494 sq. miles (22,000 sq. km)
Languages Somali, Afar, French*, Arabic*
Religions Muslim (mainly Sunni) 94%, Christian 6%
Ethnic mix Issa 60%, Afar 35%, Other 5%
Government Presidential system
Currency Djibouti franc = 100 centimes
Literacy rate 70%
Calorie consumption 2210 kilocalories

DOMINICA
West Indies

Official name Commonwealth of Dominica
Formation 1978 / 1978
Capital Roseau
Population 72,969 / 252 people per sq mile (97 people per sq km)
Total area 291 sq. miles (754 sq. km)
Languages French Creole, English*
Religions Roman Catholic 77%, Protestant 15%, Other 8%
Ethnic mix Black 87%, Mixed race 9%, Carib 3%, Other 1%
Government Parliamentary system
Currency East Caribbean dollar = 100 cents
Literacy rate 88%
Calorie consumption 3115 kilocalories

DOMINICAN REPUBLIC
West Indies

Official name Dominican Republic
Formation 1865 / 1865
Capital Santo Domingo
Population 10.2 million / 546 people per sq mile (211 people per sq km)
Total area 18,679 sq. miles (48,380 sq. km)
Languages Spanish*, French Creole
Religions Roman Catholic 95%, Other and nonreligious 5%
Ethnic mix Mixed race 73%, European 16%, Black African 11%
Government Presidential system
Currency Dominican Republic peso = 100 centavos
Literacy rate 88%
Calorie consumption 2263 kilocalories

EAST TIMOR
Southeast Asia

Official name Democratic Republic of Timor-Leste
Formation 2002 / 2002
Capital Dili
Population 1.2 million / 213 people per sq mile (82 people per sq km)
Total area 5756 sq. miles (14,874 sq. km)
Languages Tetum (Portuguese/Austronesian)*, Bahasa Indonesia, Portuguese
Religions Roman Catholic 95%, Other (including Muslim and Protestant) 5%
Ethnic mix Not available
Government Parliamentary system
Currency US dollar = 100 cents
Literacy rate 51%
Calorie consumption 2016 kilocalories

ECUADOR
South America

Official name Republic of Ecuador
Formation 1830 / 1942
Capital Quito
Population 13.8 million / 129 people per sq mile (50 people per sq km)
Total area 109,483 sq. miles (283,560 sq. km)
Languages Spanish*, Quechua, other Amerindian languages
Religions Roman Catholic 95%, Protestant, Jewish, and other 5%
Ethnic mix Mestizo 77%, White 11%, Amerindian 7%, Black African 5%
Government Presidential system
Currency US dollar = 100 cents
Literacy rate 84%
Calorie consumption 2304 kilocalories

EGYPT
North Africa

Official name Arab Republic of Egypt
Formation 1936 / 1982
Capital Cairo
Population 84.5 million / 220 people per sq mile (85 people per sq km)
Total area 386,660 sq. miles (1,001,450 sq. km)
Languages Arabic*, French, English, Berber
Religions Muslim (mainly Sunni) 90%, Coptic Christian and other 9%, Other Christian 1%
Ethnic mix Egyptian 99%, Nubian, Armenian, Greek, and Berber 1%
Government Transitional regime
Currency Egyptian pound = 100 piastres
Literacy rate 72%
Calorie consumption 3163 kilocalories

EL SALVADOR
Central America

Official name Republic of El Salvador
Formation 1841 / 1841
Capital San Salvador
Population 6.2 million / 775 people per sq mile (299 people per sq km)
Total area 8124 sq. miles (21,040 sq. km)
Languages Spanish
Religions Roman Catholic 80%, Evangelical 18%, Other 2%
Ethnic mix Mestizo 90%, White 9%, Amerindian 1%
Government Presidential system
Currency Salvadorean colón & US dollar = 100 centavos (colón); 100 cents (US dollar)
Literacy rate 84%
Calorie consumption 2585 kilocalories

EQUATORIAL GUINEA
Central Africa

Official name Republic of Equatorial Guinea
Formation 1968 / 1968
Capital Malabo
Population 700,000 / 65 people per sq mile (25 people per sq km)
Total area 10,830 sq. miles (28,051 sq. km)
Languages Spanish*, Fang, Bubi, French*
Religions Roman Catholic 90%, Other 10%
Ethnic mix Fang 85%, Other 11%, Bubi 4%
Government Presidential system
Currency CFA franc = 100 centimes
Literacy rate 93%
Calorie consumption Not available

ERITREA
East Africa

Official name State of Eritrea
Formation 1993 / 2002
Capital Asmara
Population 5.2 million / 115 people per sq mile (44 people per sq km)
Total area 46,842 sq. miles (121,320 sq. km)
Languages Tigrinya*, English*, Tigre, Afar, Arabic*, Saho, Bilen, Kunama, Nara, Hadareb
Religions Christian 50%, Muslim 48%, Other 2%
Ethnic mix Tigray 50%, Tigre 31%, Other 9%, Saho 5%, Afar 5%
Government Transitional regime
Currency Nakfa = 100 cents
Literacy rate 67%
Calorie consumption 1587 kilocalories

ESTONIA
Northeast Europe

Official name Republic of Estonia
Formation 1991 / 1991
Capital Tallinn
Population 1.3 million / 75 people per sq mile (29 people per sq km)
Total area 17,462 sq. miles (45,226 sq. km)
Languages Estonian*, Russian
Religions Evangelical Lutheran 56%, Orthodox Christian 25%, Other 19%
Ethnic mix Estonian 69%, Russian 25%, Other 4%, Ukrainian 2%
Government Parliamentary system
Currency Euro = 100 cents
Literacy rate 99%
Calorie consumption 3129 kilocalories

ETHIOPIA
East Africa

Official name Federal Democratic Republic of Ethiopia
Formation 1896 / 2002
Capital Addis Ababa
Population 85 million / 198 people per sq mile (77 people per sq km)
Total area 435,184 sq. miles (1,127,127 sq. km)
Languages Amharic*, Tigrinya, Galla, Sidamo, Somali, English, Arabic
Religions Orthodox Christian 40%, Muslim 40%, Traditional beliefs 15%, Other 5%
Ethnic mix Oromo 40%, Amhara 25%, Other 35%
Government Parliamentary system
Currency Birr = 100 cents
Literacy rate 36%
Calorie consumption 1952 kilocalories

FIJI
Australasia & Oceania

Official name Republic of the Fiji Islands
Formation 1970 / 1970
Capital Suva
Population 900,000 / 128 people per sq mile (49 people per sq km)
Total area 7054 sq. miles (18,270 sq. km)
Languages Fijian, English*, Hindi, Urdu, Tamil, Telugu
Religions Hindu 38%, Methodist 37%, Roman Catholic 9%, Muslim 8%, Other 8%
Ethnic mix Melanesian 51%, Indian 44%, Other 5%
Government Transitional regime
Currency Fiji dollar = 100 cents
Literacy rate 94%
Calorie consumption 3033 kilocalories

FINLAND
Northern Europe

Official name Republic of Finland
Formation 1917 / 1947
Capital Helsinki
Population 5.3 million / 45 people per sq mile (17 people per sq km)
Total area 130,127 sq. miles (337,030 sq. km)
Languages Finnish*, Swedish*, Sámi
Religions Evangelical Lutheran 83%, Other 15%, Roman Catholic 1%, Orthodox Christian 1%
Ethnic mix Finnish 93%, Other (including Sámi) 7%
Government Parliamentary system
Currency Euro = 100 cents
Literacy rate 99%
Calorie consumption 3215 kilocalories

FRANCE
Western Europe

Official name French Republic
Formation 987 / 1919
Capital Paris
Population 62.6 million / 295 people per sq mile (114 people per sq km)
Total area 211,208 sq. miles (547,030 sq. km)
Languages French*, Provençal, German, Breton, Catalan, Basque
Religions Roman Catholic 88%, Muslim 8%, Protestant 2%, Jewish 1%, Buddhist 1%
Ethnic mix French 90%, North African (mainly Algerian) 6%, German (Alsace) 2%, Other 2%
Government Mixed presidential–parliamentary system
Currency Euro = 100 cents
Literacy rate 99%
Calorie consumption 3553 kilocalories

GABON
Central Africa

Official name Gabonese Republic
Formation 1960 / 1960
Capital Libreville
Population 1.5 million / 15 people per sq mile (6 people per sq km)
Total area 103,346 sq. miles (267,667 sq. km)
Languages Fang, French*, Punu, Sira, Nzebi, Mpongwe
Religions Christian (mainly Roman Catholic) 55%, Traditional beliefs 40%, Other 4%, Muslim 1%
Ethnic mix Fang 26%, Shira-punu 24%, Other 16%, Foreign residents 15%, Nzabi-duma 11%, Mbédé-Teke 8%
Government Presidential system
Currency CFA franc = 100 centimes
Literacy rate 88%
Calorie consumption 2730 kilocalories

GAMBIA
West Africa

Official name Republic of the Gambia
Formation 1965 / 1965
Capital Banjul
Population 1.8 million / 466 people per sq mile (180 people per sq km)
Total area 4363 sq. miles (11,300 sq. km)
Languages Mandinka, Fulani, Wolof, Jola, Soninke, English*
Religions Sunni Muslim 90%, Christian 8%, Traditional beliefs 2%
Ethnic mix Mandinka 42%, Fulani 18%, Wolof 16%, Jola 10%, Serahuli 9%, Other 5%
Government Presidential system
Currency Dalasi = 100 butut
Literacy rate 46%
Calorie consumption 2345 kilocalories

GEORGIA
Southwest Asia

Official name Georgia
Formation 1991 / 1991
Capital Tbilisi
Population 4.2 million / 156 people per sq mile (60 people per sq km)
Total area 26,911 sq. miles (69,700 sq. km)
Languages Georgian*, Russian, Azeri, Armenian, Mingrelian, Ossetian, Abkhazian
Religions Georgian Orthodox 74%, Russian Orthodox 10%, Muslim 10%, Other 6%
Ethnic mix Georgian 84%, Armenian 6%, Azeri 6%, Russian 2%, Other 1%, Ossetian 1%
Government Presidential system
Currency Lari = 100 tetri
Literacy rate 99%
Calorie consumption 2813 kilocalories

GERMANY
Northern Europe

Official name Federal Republic of Germany
Formation 1871 / 1990
Capital Berlin
Population 82.1 million / 608 people per sq mile (235 people per sq km)
Total area 137,846 sq. miles (357,021 sq. km)
Languages German*, Turkish
Religions Protestant 34%, Roman Catholic 33%, Other 30%, Muslim 3%
Ethnic mix German 92%, Other 3%, Other European 3%, Turkish 2%
Government Parliamentary system
Currency Euro = 100 cents
Literacy rate 99%
Calorie consumption 3530 kilocalories

GHANA
West Africa

Official name Republic of Ghana
Formation 1957 / 1957
Capital Accra
Population 24.3 million / 274 people per sq mile (106 people per sq km)
Total area 92,100 sq. miles (238,540 sq. km)
Languages Twi, Fanti, Ewe, Ga, Adangbe, Gurma, Dagomba (Dagbani), English*
Religions Christian 69%, Muslim 16%, Traditional beliefs 9%, Other 6%
Ethnic mix Akan 49%, Mole-Dagbani 17%, Ewe 13%, Other 9%, Ga and Ga-Adangbe 8%, Guan 4%
Government Presidential system
Currency Cedi = 100 pesewas
Literacy rate 67%
Calorie consumption 2849 kilocalories

GREECE
Southeast Europe

Official name Hellenic Republic
Formation 1829 / 1947
Capital Athens
Population 11.2 million / 222 people per sq mile (86 people per sq km)
Total area 50,942 sq. miles (131,940 sq. km)
Languages Greek*, Turkish, Macedonian, Albanian
Religions Orthodox Christian 98%, Other 1%, Muslim 1%
Ethnic mix Greek 98%, Other 2%
Government Parliamentary system
Currency Euro = 100 cents
Literacy rate 97%
Calorie consumption 3700 kilocalories

GRENADA
West Indies

Official name Grenada
Formation 1974 / 1974
Capital St. George's
Population 108,419 / 828 people per sq mile (319 people per sq km)
Total area 131 sq. miles (340 sq. km)
Languages English*, English Creole
Religions Roman Catholic 68%, Anglican 17%, Other 15%
Ethnic mix Black African 82%, Mulatto (mixed race) 13%, East Indian 3%, Other 2%
Government Parliamentary system
Currency East Caribbean dollar = 100 cents
Literacy rate 96%
Calorie consumption 2320 kilocalories

GUATEMALA
Central America

Official name Republic of Guatemala
Formation 1838 / 1838
Capital Guatemala City
Population 14.4 million / 344 people per sq mile (133 people per sq km)
Total area 42,042 sq. miles (108,890 sq. km)
Languages Quiché, Mam, Cakchiquel, Kekchí, Spanish*
Religions Roman Catholic 65%, Protestant 33%, Other and nonreligious 2%
Ethnic mix Amerindian 60%, Mestizo 30%, Other 10%
Government Presidential system
Currency Quetzal = 100 centavos
Literacy rate 74%
Calorie consumption 2171 kilocalories

GUINEA
West Africa

Official name Republic of Guinea
Formation 1958 / 1958
Capital Conakry
Population 10.3 million / 109 people per sq mile (42 people per sq km)
Total area 94,925 sq. miles (245,857 sq. km)
Languages Pulaar, Malinké, Soussou, French*
Religions Muslim 85%, Christian 8%, Traditional beliefs 7%
Ethnic mix Peul 40%, Malinké 30%, Soussou 20%, Other 10%
Government Presidential system
Currency Guinea franc = 100 centimes
Literacy rate 40%
Calorie consumption 2529 kilocalories

GUINEA-BISSAU
West Africa

Official name Republic of Guinea-Bissau
Formation 1974 / 1974
Capital Bissau
Population 1.6 million / 147 people per sq mile (57 people per sq km)
Total area 13,946 sq. miles (36,120 sq. km)
Languages Portuguese Creole, Balante, Fulani, Malinké, Portuguese*
Religions Traditional beliefs 50%, Muslim 40%, Christian 10%
Ethnic mix Balante 30%, Fulani 20%, Other 16%, Mandyako 14%, Mandinka 13%, Papel 7%
Government Presidential system
Currency CFA franc = 100 centimes
Literacy rate 52%
Calorie consumption 2288 kilocalories

GUYANA
South America

Official name Cooperative Republic of Guyana
Formation 1966 / 1966
Capital Georgetown
Population 800,000 / 11 people per sq mile (4 people per sq km)
Total area 83,000 sq. miles (214,970 sq. km)
Languages English Creole, Hindi, Tamil, Amerindian languages, English*
Religions Christian 57%, Hindu 28%, Muslim 10%, Other 5%
Ethnic mix East Indian 43%, Black African 30%, Mixed race 17%, Amerindian 9%, Other 1%
Government Presidential system
Currency Guyanese dollar = 100 cents
Literacy rate 99%
Calorie consumption 2753 kilocalories

HAITI
West Indies

Official name Republic of Haiti
Formation 1804 / 1884
Capital Port-au-Prince
Population 10.2 million / 959 people per sq mile (370 people per sq km)
Total area 10,714 sq. miles (27,750 sq. km)
Languages French Creole*, French*
Religions Roman Catholic 55%, Protestant 28%, Other (including Voodoo) 16%, Nonreligious 1%
Ethnic mix Black African 95%, Mulatto (mixed race) and European 5%
Government Presidential system
Currency Gourde = 100 centimes
Literacy rate 62%
Calorie consumption 1848 kilocalories

HONDURAS
Central America

Official name Republic of Honduras
Formation 1838 / 1838
Capital Tegucigalpa
Population 7.6 million / 176 people per sq mile (68 people per sq km)
Total area 43,278 sq. miles (112,090 sq. km)
Languages Spanish*, Garífuna (Carib), English Creole
Religions Roman Catholic 97%, Protestant 3%
Ethnic mix Mestizo 90%, Black African 5%, Amerindian 4%, White 1%
Government Presidential system
Currency Lempira = 100 centavos
Literacy rate 84%
Calorie consumption 2601 kilocalories

HUNGARY
Central Europe

Official name Republic of Hungary
Formation 1918 / 1947
Capital Budapest
Population 10 million / 280 people per sq mile (108 people per sq km)
Total area 35,919 sq. miles (93,030 sq. km)
Languages Hungarian (Magyar)*
Religions Roman Catholic 52%, Calvinist 16%, Other 15%, Nonreligious 14%, Lutheran 3%
Ethnic mix Magyar 90%, Roma 4%, German 3%, Serb 2%, Other 1%
Government Parliamentary system
Currency Forint = 100 fillér
Literacy rate 99%
Calorie consumption 3438 kilocalories

ICELAND
Northwest Europe

Official name Republic of Iceland
Formation 1944 / 1944
Capital Reykjavík
Population 300,000 / 8 people per sq mile (3 people per sq km)
Total area 39,768 sq. miles (103,000 sq. km)
Languages Icelandic*
Religions Evangelical Lutheran 84%, Other (mostly Christian) 10%, Nonreligious 3%, Roman Catholic 3%
Ethnic mix Icelandic 94%, Other 5%, Danish 1%
Government Parliamentary system
Currency Icelandic króna = 100 aurar
Literacy rate 99%
Calorie consumption 3330 kilocalories

INDIA
South Asia

Official name Republic of India
Formation 1947 / 1947
Capital New Delhi
Population 1.21 billion / 1058 people per sq mile (409 people per sq km)
Total area 1,269,338 sq. miles (3,287,590 sq. km)
Languages Hindi*, English*, Urdu, Bengali, Marathi, Telugu, Tamil, Bihari, Gujarati, Kanarese
Religions Hindu 81%, Muslim 13%, Sikh 2%, Christian 2%, Buddhist 1%, Other 1%
Ethnic mix Indo-Aryan 72%, Dravidian 25%, Mongoloid and other 3%
Government Parliamentary system
Currency Indian rupee = 100 paise
Literacy rate 66%
Calorie consumption 2301 kilocalories

INDONESIA
Southeast Asia

Official name Republic of Indonesia
Formation 1949 / 1999
Capital Jakarta
Population 232 million / 335 people per sq mile (129 people per sq km)
Total area 741,096 sq. miles (1,919,440 sq. km)
Languages Javanese, Sundanese, Madurese, Bahasa Indonesia*, Dutch
Religions Sunni Muslim 86%, Protestant 6%, Roman Catholic 3%, Hindu 2%, Other 2%, Buddhist 1%
Ethnic mix Javanese 41%, Other 29%, Sundanese 15%, Coastal Malays 12%, Madurese 3%
Government Presidential system
Currency Rupiah = 100 sen
Literacy rate 92%
Calorie consumption 2535 kilocalories

IRAN
Southwest Asia

Official name Islamic Republic of Iran
Formation 1502 / 1990
Capital Tehran
Population 75.1 million / 119 people per sq mile (46 people per sq km)
Total area 636,293 sq. miles (1,648,000 sq. km)
Languages Farsi*, Azeri, Luri, Gilaki, Mazanderani, Kurdish, Turkmen, Arabic, Baluchi
Religions Shi'a Muslim 89%, Sunni Muslim 9%, Other 2%
Ethnic mix Persian 51%, Azari 24%, Other 10%, Lur and Bakhtiari 8%, Kurdish 7%
Government Islamic theocracy
Currency Iranian rial = 100 dinars
Literacy rate 85%
Calorie consumption 3042 kilocalories

IRAQ
Southwest Asia

Official name Republic of Iraq
Formation 1932 / 1990
Capital Baghdad
Population 31.5 million / 187 people per sq mile (72 people per sq km)
Total area 168,753 sq. miles (437,072 sq. km)
Languages Arabic*, Kurdish*, Turkic languages, Armenian, Assyrian
Religions Shi'a Muslim 60%, Sunni Muslim 35%, Other (including Christian) 5%
Ethnic mix Arab 80%, Kurdish 15%, Turkmen 3%, Other 2%
Government Parliamentary system
Currency New Iraqi dinar = 1000 fils
Literacy rate 78%
Calorie consumption 2197 kilocalories

IRELAND
Northwest Europe

Official name Ireland
Formation 1922 / 1922
Capital Dublin
Population 4.6 million / 173 people per sq mile (67 people per sq km)
Total area 27,135 sq. miles (70,280 sq. km)
Languages English*, Irish Gaelic*
Religions Roman Catholic 87%, Other and nonreligious 10%, Anglican 3%
Ethnic mix Irish 99%, Other 1%
Government Parliamentary system
Currency Euro = 100 cents
Literacy rate 99%
Calorie consumption 3532 kilocalories

ISRAEL
Southwest Asia

Official name State of Israel
Formation 1948 / 1994
Capital Jerusalem (not internationally recognized)
Population 7.3 million / 930 people per sq mile (359 people per sq km)
Total area 8019 sq. miles (20,770 sq. km)
Languages Hebrew*, Arabic*, Yiddish, German, Russian, Polish, Romanian, Persian
Religions Jewish 76%, Muslim (mainly Sunni) 16%, Other 4%, Druze 2%, Christian 2%
Ethnic mix Jewish 76%, Arab 20%, Other 4%
Government Parliamentary system
Currency Shekel = 100 agorot
Literacy rate 99%
Calorie consumption 3540 kilocalories

ITALY
Southern Europe

Official name Italian Republic
Formation 1861 / 1947
Capital Rome
Population 60.1 million / 529 people per sq mile (204 people per sq km)
Total area 116,305 sq. miles (301,230 sq. km)
Languages Italian*, German, French, Rhaeto-Romanic, Sardinian
Religions Roman Catholic 85%, Other and nonreligious 13%, Muslim 2%
Ethnic mix Italian 94%, Other 4%, Sardinian 2%
Government Parliamentary system
Currency Euro = 100 cents
Literacy rate 99%
Calorie consumption 3657 kilocalories

IVORY COAST
West Africa

Official name Republic of Côte d'Ivoire
Formation 1960 / 1960
Capital Yamoussoukro
Population 21.6 million / 176 people per sq mile (68 people per sq km)
Total area 124,502 sq. miles (322,460 sq. km)
Languages Akan, French*, Krou, Voltaique
Religions Muslim 38%, Roman Catholic 25%, Traditional beliefs 25%, Protestant 6%, Other 6%
Ethnic mix Akan 42%, Voltaique 18%, Mandé du Nord 17%, Krou 11%, Mandé du Sud 10%, Other 2%
Government Presidential system
Currency CFA franc = 100 centimes
Literacy rate 55%
Calorie consumption 2515 kilocalories

JAMAICA
West Indies

Official name Jamaica
Formation 1962 / 1962
Capital Kingston
Population 2.7 million / 646 people per sq mile (249 people per sq km)
Total area 4243 sq. miles (10,990 sq. km)
Languages English Creole, English*
Religions Other and nonreligious 45%, Other Protestant 20%, Church of God 18%, Baptist 10%, Anglican 7%
Ethnic mix Black African 91%, Mulatto (mixed race) 7%, European and Chinese 1%, East Indian 1%
Government Parliamentary system
Currency Jamaican dollar = 100 cents
Literacy rate 86%
Calorie consumption 2848 kilocalories

JAPAN
East Asia

Official name Japan
Formation 1590 / 1972
Capital Tokyo
Population 127 million / 874 people per sq mile (337 people per sq km)
Total area 145,882 sq. miles (377,835 sq. km)
Languages Japanese*, Korean, Chinese
Religions Shinto and Buddhist 76%, Buddhist 16%, Other (including Christian) 8%
Ethnic mix Japanese 99%, Other (mainly Korean) 1%
Government Parliamentary system
Currency Yen = 100 sen
Literacy rate 99%
Calorie consumption 2806 kilocalories

JORDAN
Southwest Asia

Official name Hashemite Kingdom of Jordan
Formation 1946 / 1967
Capital Amman
Population 6.5 million / 189 people per sq mile
(73 people per sq km)
Total area 35,637 sq. miles (92,300 sq. km)
Languages Arabic*
Religions Sunni Muslim 92%, Christian 6%,
Other 2%
Ethnic mix Arab 98%, Circassian 1%, Armenian 1%
Government Monarchy
Currency Jordanian dinar = 1000 fils
Literacy rate 92%
Calorie consumption 2977 kilocalories

KAZAKHSTAN
Central Asia

Official name Republic of Kazakhstan
Formation 1991 / 1991
Capital Astana
Population 15.8 million / 15 people per sq mile
(6 people per sq km)
Total area 1,049,150 sq. miles (2,717,300 sq. km)
Languages Kazakh*, Russian, Ukrainian, German,
Uzbek, Tatar, Uighur
Religions Muslim (mainly Sunni) 47%, Orthodox
Christian 44%, Other 7%, Protestant 2%
Ethnic mix Kazakh 57%, Russian 27%, Other 8%,
Ukrainian 3%, Uzbek 3%, German 2%
Government Presidential system
Currency Tenge = 100 tiyn
Literacy rate 99%
Calorie consumption 3359 kilocalories

KENYA
East Africa

Official name Republic of Kenya
Formation 1963 / 1963
Capital Nairobi
Population 40.9 million / 187 people per sq mile
(72 people per sq km)
Total area 224,961 sq. miles (582,650 sq. km)
Languages Kiswahili*, English*, Kikuyu, Luo,
Kalenjin, Kamba
Religions Christian 80%, Muslim 10%,
Traditional beliefs 9%, Other 1%
Ethnic mix Other 28%, Kikuyu 22%, Luo 14%,
Luhya 14%, Kamba 11%, Kalenjin 11%
Government Mixed Presidential–
Parliamentary system
Currency Kenya shilling = 100 cents
Literacy rate 87%
Calorie consumption 2060 kilocalories

KIRIBATI
Australasia & Oceania

Official name Republic of Kiribati
Formation 1979 / 1979
Capital Bairiki (Tarawa Atoll)
Population 100,743 / 368 people per sq mile
(142 people per sq km)
Total area 277 sq. miles (717 sq. km)
Languages English*, Kiribati
Religions Roman Catholic 55%, Kiribati Protestant
Church 36%, Other 9%
Ethnic mix Micronesian 99%, Other 1%
Government Elections involving
informal groupings
Currency Australian dollar = 100 cents
Literacy rate 99%
Calorie consumption 2854 kilocalories

KOSOVO (not yet fully recognized)
Southeast Europe

Official name Republic of Kosovo
Formation 2008 / 2008
Capital Pristina
Population 1.83 million / 433 people per sq mile
(167 people per sq km)
Total area 4212 sq. miles (10,908 sq. km)
Languages Albanian*, Serbian*, Bosniak, Gorani,
Roma, Turkish
Religions Muslim 92%, Orthodox Christian 4%,
Roman Catholic 4%
Ethnic mix Albanian 92%, Serb 4%, Bosniak and
Gorani 2%, Roma 1%, Turkish 1%
Government Parliamentary system
Currency Euro = 100 cents
Literacy rate 92%
Calorie consumption Not available

KUWAIT
Southwest Asia

Official name State of Kuwait
Formation 1961 / 1961
Capital Kuwait City
Population 3.1 million / 451 people per sq mile
(174 people per sq km)
Total area 6880 sq. miles (17,820 sq. km)
Languages Arabic*, English
Religions Sunni Muslim 45%, Shi'a Muslim 40%,
Christian, Hindu, and other 15%
Ethnic mix Kuwaiti 45%, Other Arab 35%,
South Asian 9%, Other 7%, Iranian 4%
Government Monarchy
Currency Kuwaiti dinar = 1000 fils
Literacy rate 94%
Calorie consumption 3038 kilocalories

KYRGYZSTAN
Central Asia

Official name Kyrgyz Republic
Formation 1991 / 1991
Capital Bishkek
Population 5.6 million / 73 people per sq mile
(28 people per sq km)
Total area 76,641 sq. miles (198,500 sq. km)
Languages Kyrgyz*, Russian*, Uzbek,
Tatar, Ukrainian
Religions Muslim (mainly Sunni) 70%,
Orthodox Christian 30%
Ethnic mix Kyrgyz 69%, Uzbek 14%, Russian 9%,
Other 6%, Uighur 1%, Dungan 1%
Government Transitional regime
Currency Som = 100 tyiyn
Literacy rate 99%
Calorie consumption 2672 kilocalories

LAOS
Southeast Asia

Official name Lao People's Democratic Republic
Formation 1953 / 1953
Capital Vientiane
Population 6.4 million / 72 people per sq mile
(28 people per sq km)
Total area 91,428 sq. miles (236,800 sq. km)
Languages Lao*, Mon-Khmer, Yao, Vietnamese,
Chinese, French
Religions Buddhist 65%, Other (including
animist) 34%, Christian 1%
Ethnic mix Lao Loum 66%, Lao Theung 30%,
Other 2%, Lao Soung 2%
Government One-party state
Currency New kip = 100 at
Literacy rate 73%
Calorie consumption 2227 kilocalories

LATVIA
Northeast Europe

Official name Republic of Latvia
Formation 1991 / 1991
Capital Riga
Population 2.2 million / 88 people per sq mile
(34 people per sq km)
Total area 24,938 sq. miles (64,589 sq. km)
Languages Latvian*, Russian
Religions Other 43%, Lutheran 24%, Roman
Catholic 18%, Orthodox Christian 15%
Ethnic mix Latvian 59%, Russian 28%,
Belarussian 4%, Other 4%, Ukrainian 3%,
Polish 2%
Government Parliamentary system
Currency Lats = 100 santimi
Literacy rate 99%
Calorie consumption 3019 kilocalories

LEBANON
Southwest Asia

Official name Republic of Lebanon
Formation 1941 / 1941
Capital Beirut
Population 4.3 million / 1089 people per sq mile
(420 people per sq km)
Total area 4015 sq. miles (10,400 sq. km)
Languages Arabic*, French, Armenian, Assyrian
Religions Muslim 60%, Christian 39%, Other 1%
Ethnic mix Arab 95%, Armenian 4%, Other 1%
Government Parliamentary system
Currency Lebanese pound = 100 piastres
Literacy rate 90%
Calorie consumption 3107 kilocalories

LESOTHO
Southern Africa

Official name Kingdom of Lesotho
Formation 1966 / 1966
Capital Maseru
Population 2.1 million / 179 people per sq mile
(69 people per sq km)
Total area 11,720 sq. miles (30,355 sq. km)
Languages English*, Sesotho*, isiZulu
Religions Christian 90%, Traditional beliefs 10%
Ethnic mix Sotho 99%, European and Asian 1%
Government Parliamentary system
Currency Loti & South African rand = 100 lisente
Literacy rate 90%
Calorie consumption 2468 kilocalories

LIBERIA
West Africa

Official name Republic of Liberia
Formation 1847 / 1847
Capital Monrovia
Population 4.1 million / 110 people per sq mile
(43 people per sq km)
Total area 43,000 sq. miles (111,370 sq. km)
Languages Kpelle, Vai, Bassa, Kru, Grebo, Kissi,
Gola, Loma, English*
Religions Traditional beliefs 40%, Christian 40%,
Muslim 20%
Ethnic mix Indigenous tribes (12 groups) 49%,
Kpellé 20%, Bassa 16%, Gio 8%, Krou 7%
Government Presidential system
Currency Liberian dollar = 100 cents
Literacy rate 59%
Calorie consumption 2163 kilocalories

LIBYA
North Africa

Official name Libyan Republic (post Gaddafi
regime)
Formation 1951 / 1951
Capital Tripoli
Population 6.5 million / 10 people per sq mile
(4 people per sq km)
Total area 679,358 sq. miles (1,759,540 sq. km)
Languages Arabic*, Tuareg
Religions Muslim (mainly Sunni) 97%, Other 3%
Ethnic mix Arab and Berber 97%, Other 3%
Government Transitional regime
Currency Libyan dinar = 1000 dirhams
Literacy rate 89%
Calorie consumption 3144 kilocalories

LIECHTENSTEIN
Central Europe

Official name Principality of Liechtenstein
Formation 1719 / 1719
Capital Vaduz
Population 35,236 / 568 people per sq mile
(220 people per sq km)
Total area 62 sq. miles (160 sq. km)
Languages German*, Alemannish dialect, Italian
Religions Roman Catholic 79%, Other 13%,
Protestant 8%
Ethnic mix Liechtensteiner 66%, Other 12%,
Swiss 10%, Austrian 6%, German 3%, Italian 3%
Government Parliamentary system
Currency Swiss franc = 100 rappen/centimes
Literacy rate 99%
Calorie consumption Not available

LITHUANIA
Northeast Europe

Official name Republic of Lithuania
Formation 1991 / 1991
Capital Vilnius
Population 3.3 million / 131 people per sq mile
(51 people per sq km)
Total area 25,174 sq. miles (65,200 sq. km)
Languages Lithuanian*, Russian
Religions Roman Catholic 79%, Other 15%,
Russian Orthodox 4%, Protestant 2%
Ethnic mix Lithuanian 85%, Polish 6%, Russian 5%,
Other 3%, Belarussian 1%
Government Parliamentary system
Currency Litas = 100 centu
Literacy rate 99%
Calorie consumption 3419 kilocalories

LUXEMBOURG
Northwest Europe

Official name Grand Duchy of Luxembourg
Formation 1867 / 1867
Capital Luxembourg-Ville
Population 500,000 / 501 people per sq mile
(193 people per sq km)
Total area 998 sq. miles (2586 sq. km)
Languages Luxembourgish*, German*, French*
Religions Roman Catholic 97%, Protestant,
Orthodox Christian, and Jewish 3%
Ethnic mix Luxembourger 62%,
Foreign residents 38%
Government Parliamentary system
Currency Euro = 100 cents
Literacy rate 99%
Calorie consumption 3685 kilocalories

MACEDONIA
Southeast Europe

Official name Republic of Macedonia
Formation 1991 / 1991
Capital Skopje
Population 2 million / 201 people per sq mile
(78 people per sq km)
Total area 9781 sq. miles (25,333 sq. km)
Languages Macedonian*, Albanian*, Turkish,
Romani, Serbian
Religions Orthodox Christian 65%, Muslim 29%,
Roman Catholic 4%, Other 2%
Ethnic mix Macedonian 64%, Albanian 25%,
Turkish 4%, Roma 3%, Other 2%, Serb 2%
Government Mixed presidential–parliamentary
system
Currency Macedonian denar = 100 deni
Literacy rate 97%
Calorie consumption 2983 kilocalories

MADAGASCAR
Indian Ocean

Official name Republic of Madagascar
Formation 1960 / 1960
Capital Antananarivo
Population 20.1 million / 90 people per sq mile
(35 people per sq km)
Total area 226,656 sq. miles (587,040 sq. km)
Languages Malagasy*, French*, English*
Religions Traditional beliefs 52%, Christian (mainly
Roman Catholic) 41%, Muslim 7%
Ethnic mix Other Malay 46%, Merina 26%,
Betsimisaraka 15%, Betsileo 12%, Other 1%
Government Transitional regime
Currency Ariary = 5 iraimbilanja
Literacy rate 64%
Calorie consumption 2133 kilocalories

MALAWI
Southern Africa

Official name Republic of Malawi
Formation 1964 / 1964
Capital Lilongwe
Population 15.7 million / 432 people per sq mile
(167 people per sq km)
Total area 45,745 sq. miles (118,480 sq. km)
Languages Chewa, Lomwe, Yao, Ngoni, English*
Religions Protestant 55%, Roman Catholic 20%,
Muslim 20%, Traditional beliefs 5%
Ethnic mix Bantu 99%, Other 1%
Government Presidential system
Currency Malawi kwacha = 100 tambala
Literacy rate 74%
Calorie consumption 2127 kilocalories

MALAYSIA
Southeast Asia

Official name Federation of Malaysia
Formation 1963 / 1965
Capital Kuala Lumpur; Putrajaya (administrative)
Population 27.9 million / 220 people per sq mile
(85 people per sq km)
Total area 127,316 sq. miles (329,750 sq. km)
Languages Bahasa Malaysia*, Malay, Chinese,
Tamil, English
Religions Muslim (mainly Sunni) 61%, Buddhist
19%, Christian 9%, Hindu 6%, Other 5%
Ethnic mix Malay 53%, Chinese 26%,
Indigenous tribes 12%, Indian 8%, Other 1%
Government Parliamentary system
Currency Ringgit = 100 sen
Literacy rate 92%
Calorie consumption 2908 kilocalories

MALDIVES
Indian Ocean

Official name Republic of Maldives
Formation 1965 / 1965
Capital Male'
Population 300,000 / 2586 people per sq mile
(1000 people per sq km)
Total area 116 sq. miles (300 sq. km)
Languages Dhivehi (Maldivian)*, Sinhala,
Tamil, Arabic
Religions Sunni Muslim 100%
Ethnic mix Arab–Sinhalese–Malay 100%
Government Presidential system
Currency Rufiyaa = 100 laari
Literacy rate 97%
Calorie consumption Not available

MALI
West Africa

Official name Republic of Mali
Formation 1960 / 1960
Capital Bamako
Population 13.3 million / 28 people per sq mile
(11 people per sq km)
Total area 478,764 sq. miles (1,240,000 sq. km)
Languages Bambara, Fulani, Senufo, Soninke,
French*
Religions Muslim (mainly Sunni) 90%,
Traditional beliefs 6%, Christian 4%
Ethnic mix Bambara 52%, Other 14%, Fulani 11%,
Saracolé 7%, Soninka 7%, Tuareg 5%, Mianka 4%
Government Presidential system
Currency CFA franc = 100 centimes
Literacy rate 23%
Calorie consumption 2579 kilocalories

MALTA
Southern Europe

Official name Republic of Malta
Formation 1964 / 1964
Capital Valletta
Population 400,000 / 3226 people per sq mile
(1250 people per sq km)
Total area 122 sq. miles (316 sq. km)
Languages Maltese*, English*
Religions Roman Catholic 98%,
Other and nonreligious 2%
Ethnic mix Maltese 96%, Other 4%
Government Parliamentary system
Currency Euro = 100 cents
Literacy rate 92%
Calorie consumption 3592 kilocalories

MARSHALL ISLANDS
Australasia & Oceania

Official name Republic of the Marshall Islands
Formation 1986 / 1986
Capital Majuro
Population 67,182 / 960 people per sq mile
(371 people per sq km)
Total area 70 sq. miles (181 sq. km)
Languages Marshallese*, English*,
Japanese, German
Religions Protestant 90%, Roman Catholic 8%,
Other 2%
Ethnic mix Micronesian 90%, Other 10%
Government Presidential system
Currency US dollar = 100 cents
Literacy rate 91%
Calorie consumption Not available

MAURITANIA
West Africa

Official name Islamic Republic of Mauritania
Formation 1960 / 1960
Capital Nouakchott
Population 3.4 million / 9 people per sq mile
(3 people per sq km)
Total area 397,953 sq. miles (1,030,700 sq. km)
Languages Hassaniyah Arabic*, Wolof, French
Religions Sunni Muslim 100%
Ethnic mix Maure 81%, Wolof 7%, Tukolor 5%,
Other 4%, Soninka 3%
Government Presidential system
Currency Ouguiya = 5 khoums
Literacy rate 58%
Calorie consumption 2823 kilocalories

MAURITIUS
Indian Ocean

Official name Republic of Mauritius
Formation 1968 / 1968
Capital Port Louis
Population 1.3 million / 1811 people per sq mile
(699 people per sq km)
Total area 718 sq. miles (1860 sq. km)
Languages French Creole, Hindi, Urdu, Tamil,
Chinese, English*, French
Religions Hindu 48%, Roman Catholic 24%,
Muslim 17%, Protestant 9%, Other 2%
Ethnic mix Indo-Mauritian 68%, Creole 27%,
Sino-Mauritian 3%, Franco-Mauritian 2%
Government Parliamentary system
Currency Mauritian rupee = 100 cents
Literacy rate 88%
Calorie consumption 2936 kilocalories

MEXICO
North America

Official name United Mexican States
Formation 1836 / 1848
Capital Mexico City
Population 111 million / 150 people per sq mile
(58 people per sq km)
Total area 761,602 sq. miles (1,972,550 sq. km)
Languages Spanish*, Nahuatl, Mayan, Zapotec,
Mixtec, Otomi, Totonac, Tzotzil, Tzeltal
Religions Roman Catholic 77%, Other 14%,
Protestant 6%, Nonreligious 3%
Ethnic mix Mestizo 60%, Amerindian 30%,
European 9%, Other 1%
Government Presidential system
Currency Mexican peso = 100 centavos
Literacy rate 93%
Calorie consumption 3245 kilocalories

MICRONESIA
Australasia & Oceania

Official name Federated States of Micronesia
Formation 1986 / 1986
Capital Palikir (Pohnpei Island)
Population 106,836 / 394 people per sq mile
(152 people per sq km)
Total area 271 sq. miles (702 sq. km)
Languages Trukese, Pohnpeian, Kosraean,
Yapese, English*
Religions Roman Catholic 50%,
Protestant 47%, Other 3%
Ethnic mix Chuukese 49%, Pohnpeian 24%,
Other 14%, Kosraean 6%, Yapese 5%, Asian 2%
Government Nonparty system
Currency US dollar = 100 cents
Literacy rate 81%
Calorie consumption Not available

MOLDOVA
Southeast Europe

Official name Republic of Moldova
Formation 1991 / 1991
Capital Chisinau
Population 3.6 million / 277 people per sq mile
(107 people per sq km)
Total area 13,067 sq. miles (33,843 sq. km)
Languages Moldovan*, Ukrainian, Russian
Religions Orthodox Christian 93%,
Other 6%, Baptist 1%
Ethnic mix Moldovan 84%, Ukrainian 7%,
Gagauz 5%, Russian 2%, Bulgarian 1%, Other 1%
Government Parliamentary system
Currency Moldovan leu = 100 bani
Literacy rate 99%
Calorie consumption 2907 kilocalories

MONACO
Southern Europe

Official name Principality of Monaco
Formation 1861 / 1861
Capital Monaco-Ville
Population 30,539 / 40,719 people per sq mile
(15,661 people per sq km)
Total area 0.75 sq. miles (1.95 sq. km)
Languages French*, Italian, Monégasque, English
Religions Roman Catholic 89%,
Protestant 6%, Other 5%
Ethnic mix French 47%, Other 21%,
Italian 16%, Monégasque 16%
Government Mixed monarchical–
parliamentary system
Currency Euro = 100 cents
Literacy rate 99%
Calorie consumption Not available

MONGOLIA
East Asia

Official name Mongolia
Formation 1924 / 1924
Capital Ulan Bator
Population 2.7 million / 4 people per sq mile (2 people per sq km)
Total area 604,247 sq. miles (1,565,000 sq. km)
Languages Khalkha Mongolian*, Kazakh, Chinese, Russian
Religions Tibetan Buddhist 50%, Nonreligious 40%, Shamanist and Christian 6%, Muslim 4%
Ethnic mix Khalkh 95%, Kazakh 4%, Other 1%
Government Mixed presidential–parliamentary system
Currency Tugrik (tögrög) = 100 möngö
Literacy rate 98%
Calorie consumption 2254 kilocalories

MONTENEGRO
Southeast Europe

Official name Montenegro
Formation 2006 / 2006
Capital Podgorica
Population 600,000 / 113 people per sq mile (43 people per sq km)
Total area 5332 sq. miles (13,812 sq. km)
Languages Montenegrin*, Serbian, Albanian, Bosniak, Croatian
Religions Orthodox Christian 74%, Muslim 18%, Other 4%, Roman Catholic 4%
Ethnic mix Montenegrin 43%, Serb 32%, Other 12%, Bosniak 8%, Albanian 5%
Government Parliamentary system
Currency Euro = 100 cents
Literacy rate 98%
Calorie consumption 2445 kilocalories

MOROCCO
North Africa

Official name Kingdom of Morocco
Formation 1956 / 1969
Capital Rabat
Population 32.4 million / 188 people per sq mile (73 people per sq km)
Total area 172,316 sq. miles (446,300 sq. km)
Languages Arabic*, Tamazight (Berber), French, Spanish
Religions Muslim (mainly Sunni) 99%, Other (mostly Christian) 1%
Ethnic mix Arab 70%, Berber 29%, European 1%
Government Mixed monarchical–parliamentary system
Currency Moroccan dirham = 100 centimes
Literacy rate 56%
Calorie consumption 3230 kilocalories

MOZAMBIQUE
Southern Africa

Official name Republic of Mozambique
Formation 1975 / 1975
Capital Maputo
Population 23.4 million / 77 people per sq mile (30 people per sq km)
Total area 309,494 sq. miles (801,590 sq. km)
Languages Makua, Xitsonga, Sena, Lomwe, Portuguese*
Religions Traditional beliefs 56%, Christian 30%, Muslim 14%
Ethnic mix Makua Lomwe 47%, Tsonga 23%, Malawi 12%, Shona 11%, Yao 4%, Other 3%
Government Presidential system
Currency New metical = 100 centavos
Literacy rate 55%
Calorie consumption 2071 kilocalories

MYANMAR (BURMA)
Southeast Asia

Official name Union of Myanmar
Formation 1948 / 1948
Capital Nay Pyi Taw
Population 50.5 million / 199 people per sq mile (77 people per sq km)
Total area 261,969 sq. miles (678,500 sq. km)
Languages Burmese*, Shan, Karen, Rakhine, Chin, Yangbye, Kachin, Mon
Religions Buddhist 89%, Christian 4%, Muslim 4%, Other 2%, Animist 1%
Ethnic mix Burman (Bamah) 68%, Other 12%, Shan 9%, Karen 7%, Rakhine 4%
Government Presidential system
Currency Kyat = 100 pyas
Literacy rate 92%
Calorie consumption 2438 kilocalories

NAMIBIA
Southern Africa

Official name Republic of Namibia
Formation 1990 / 1994
Capital Windhoek
Population 2.2 million / 7 people per sq mile (3 people per sq km)
Total area 318,694 sq. miles (825,418 sq. km)
Languages Ovambo, Kavango, English*, Bergdama, German, Afrikaans
Religions Christian 90%, Traditional beliefs 10%
Ethnic mix Ovambo 50%, Other tribes 22%, Kavango 9%, Herero 7%, Damara 7%, Other 5%
Government Presidential system
Currency Namibian dollar & South African rand = 100 cents
Literacy rate 88%
Calorie consumption 2349 kilocalories

NAURU
Australasia & Oceania

Official name Republic of Nauru
Formation 1968 / 1968
Capital None
Population 9322 / 1151 people per sq mile (444 people per sq km)
Total area 8.1 sq. miles (21 sq. km)
Languages Nauruan*, Kiribati, Chinese, Tuvaluan, English
Religions Nauruan Congregational Church 60%, Roman Catholic 35%, Other 5%
Ethnic mix Nauruan 93%, Chinese 5%, Other Pacific islanders 1%, European 1%
Government Nonparty system
Currency Australian dollar = 100 cents
Literacy rate 95%
Calorie consumption Not available

NEPAL
South Asia

Official name Federal Democratic Republic of Nepal
Formation 1769 / 1769
Capital Kathmandu
Population 29.9 million / 566 people per sq mile (219 people per sq km)
Total area 54,363 sq. miles (140,800 sq. km)
Languages Nepali*, Maithili, Bhojpuri
Religions Hindu 81%, Buddhist 11%, Muslim 4%, Other (including Christian) 4%
Ethnic mix Other 52%, Chhetri 16%, Hill Brahman 13%, Magar 7%, Tharu 7%, Tamang 5%
Government Transitional regime
Currency Nepalese rupee = 100 paisa
Literacy rate 59%
Calorie consumption 2349 kilocalories

NETHERLANDS
Northwest Europe

Official name Kingdom of the Netherlands
Formation 1648 / 1839
Capital Amsterdam; The Hague (administrative)
Population 16.7 million / 1275 people per sq mile (492 people per sq km)
Total area 16,033 sq. miles (41,526 sq. km)
Languages Dutch*, Frisian
Religions Roman Catholic 36%, Other 34%, Protestant 27%, Muslim 3%
Ethnic mix Dutch 82%, Other 12%, Surinamese 2%, Turkish 2%, Moroccan 2%
Government Parliamentary system
Currency Euro = 100 cents
Literacy rate 99%
Calorie consumption 3243 kilocalories

NEW ZEALAND
Australasia & Oceania

Official name New Zealand
Formation 1947 / 1947
Capital Wellington
Population 4.3 million / 41 people per sq mile (16 people per sq km)
Total area 103,737 sq. miles (268,680 sq. km)
Languages English*, Maori*
Religions Anglican 24%, Other 22%, Presbyterian 18%, Nonreligious 16%, Roman Catholic 15%, Methodist 5%
Ethnic mix European 75%, Maori 15%, Other 7%, Samoan 3%
Government Parliamentary system
Currency New Zealand dollar = 100 cents
Literacy rate 99%
Calorie consumption 3150 kilocalories

NICARAGUA
Central America

Official name Republic of Nicaragua
Formation 1838 / 1838
Capital Managua
Population 5.8 million / 127 people per sq mile (49 people per sq km)
Total area 49,998 sq. miles (129,494 sq. km)
Languages Spanish*, English Creole, Miskito
Religions Roman Catholic 80%, Protestant Evangelical 17%, Other 3%
Ethnic mix Mestizo 69%, White 17%, Black 9%, Amerindian 5%
Government Presidential system
Currency Córdoba oro = 100 centavos
Literacy rate 80%
Calorie consumption 2400 kilocalories

NIGER
West Africa

Official name Republic of Niger
Formation 1960 / 1960
Capital Niamey
Population 15.9 million / 33 people per sq mile (13 people per sq km)
Total area 489,188 sq. miles (1,267,000 sq. km)
Languages Hausa, Djerma, Fulani, Tuareg, Teda, French*
Religions Muslim 99%, Other (including Christian) 1%
Ethnic mix Hausa 53%, Djerma and Songhai 21%, Tuareg 11%, Fulani 7%, Kanuri 6%, Other 2%
Government Presidential system
Currency CFA franc = 100 centimes
Literacy rate 30%
Calorie consumption 2306 kilocalories

NIGERIA
West Africa

Official name Federal Republic of Nigeria
Formation 1960 / 1961
Capital Abuja
Population 158 million / 450 people per sq mile (174 people per sq km)
Total area 356,667 sq. miles (923,768 sq. km)
Languages Hausa, English*, Yoruba, Ibo
Religions Muslim 50%, Christian 40%, Traditional beliefs 10%
Ethnic mix Other 29%, Hausa 21%, Yoruba 21%, Ibo 18%, Fulani 11%
Government Presidential system
Currency Naira = 100 kobo
Literacy rate 61%
Calorie consumption 2708 kilocalories

NORTH KOREA
East Asia

Official name Democratic People's Republic of Korea
Formation 1948 / 1953
Capital Pyongyang
Population 24 million / 516 people per sq mile (199 people per sq km)
Total area 46,540 sq. miles (120,540 sq. km)
Languages Korean*
Religions Atheist 100%
Ethnic mix Korean 100%
Government One-party state
Currency North Korean won = 100 chon
Literacy rate 99%
Calorie consumption 2146 kilocalories

NORWAY
Northern Europe

Official name Kingdom of Norway
Formation 1905 / 1905
Capital Oslo
Population 4.9 million / 41 people per sq mile (16 people per sq km)
Total area 125,181 sq. miles (324,220 sq. km)
Languages Norwegian* (Bokmål "book language" and Nynorsk "new Norsk"), Sámi
Religions Evangelical Lutheran 88%, Other and nonreligious 8%, Muslim 2%, Roman Catholic 1%, Pentecostal 1%
Ethnic mix Norwegian 93%, Other 6%, Sámi 1%
Government Parliamentary system
Currency Norwegian krone = 100 øre
Literacy rate 99%
Calorie consumption 3455 kilocalories

OMAN
Southwest Asia

Official name Sultanate of Oman
Formation 1951 / 1951
Capital Muscat
Population 2.9 million / 35 people per sq mile (14 people per sq km)
Total area 82,031 sq. miles (212,460 sq. km)
Languages Arabic*, Baluchi, Farsi, Hindi, Punjabi
Religions Ibadi Muslim 75%, Other Muslim and Hindu 25%
Ethnic mix Arab 88%, Baluchi 4%, Indian and Pakistani 3%, Persian 3%, African 2%
Government Monarchy
Currency Omani rial = 1000 baisa
Literacy rate 87%
Calorie consumption Not available

PAKISTAN
South Asia

Official name Islamic Republic of Pakistan
Formation 1947 / 1971
Capital Islamabad
Population 185 million / 621 people per sq mile (240 people per sq km)
Total area 310,401 sq. miles (803,940 sq. km)
Languages Punjabi, Sindhi, Pashtu, Urdu*, Baluchi, Brahui
Religions Sunni Muslim 77%, Shi'a Muslim 20%, Hindu 2%, Christian 1%
Ethnic mix Punjabi 56%, Pathan (Pashtun) 15%, Sindhi 14%, Mohajir 7%, Other 4%, Baluchi 4%
Government Presidential system
Currency Pakistani rupee = 100 paisa
Literacy rate 56%
Calorie consumption 2251 kilocalories

PALAU
Australasia & Oceania

Official name Republic of Palau
Formation 1994 / 1994
Capital Ngerulmud
Population 20,956 / 107 people per sq mile (41 people per sq km)
Total area 177 sq. miles (458 sq. km)
Languages Palauan*, English, Japanese, Angaur, Tobi, Sonsorolese
Religions Christian 66%, Modekngei 34%
Ethnic mix Palauan 74%, Filipino 16%, Other 6%, Chinese and other Asian 4%
Government Nonparty system
Currency US dollar = 100 cents
Literacy rate 98%
Calorie consumption Not available

PANAMA
Central America

Official name Republic of Panama
Formation 1903 / 1903
Capital Panama City
Population 3.5 million / 119 people per sq mile (46 people per sq km)
Total area 30,193 sq. miles (78,200 sq. km)
Languages English Creole, Spanish*, Amerindian languages, Chibchan languages
Religions Roman Catholic 84%, Protestant 15%, Other 1%
Ethnic mix Mestizo 70%, Black 14%, White 10%, Amerindian 6%
Government Presidential system
Currency Balboa & US dollar = 100 centésimos
Literacy rate 94%
Calorie consumption 2451 kilocalories

PAPUA NEW GUINEA
Australasia & Oceania

Official name Independent State of Papua New Guinea
Formation 1975 / 1975
Capital Port Moresby
Population 6.9 million / 39 people per sq mile (15 people per sq km)
Total area 178,703 sq. miles (462,840 sq. km)
Languages Pidgin English, Papuan, English*, Motu, 800 (est.) native languages
Religions Protestant 60%, Roman Catholic 37%, Other 3%
Ethnic mix Melanesian and mixed race 100%
Government Parliamentary system
Currency Kina = 100 toea
Literacy rate 60%
Calorie consumption 2193 kilocalories

PARAGUAY
South America

Official name Republic of Paraguay
Formation 1811 / 1938
Capital Asunción
Population 6.5 million / 42 people per sq mile (16 people per sq km)
Total area 157,046 sq. miles (406,750 sq. km)
Languages Guaraní, Spanish*, German
Religions Roman Catholic 90%, Protestant (including Mennonite) 10%
Ethnic mix Mestizo 91%, Other 7%, Amerindian 2%
Government Presidential system
Currency Guaraní = 100 céntimos
Literacy rate 95%
Calorie consumption 2622 kilocalories

PERU
South America

Official name Republic of Peru
Formation 1824 / 1941
Capital Lima
Population 29.5 million / 60 people per sq mile (23 people per sq km)
Total area 496,223 sq. miles (1,285,200 sq. km)
Languages Spanish*, Quechua, Aymara
Religions Roman Catholic 81%, Other 19%
Ethnic mix Amerindian 45%, Mestizo 37%, White 15%, Other 3%
Government Presidential system
Currency New sol = 100 céntimos
Literacy rate 90%
Calorie consumption 2426 kilocalories

PHILIPPINES
Southeast Asia

Official name Republic of the Philippines
Formation 1946 / 1946
Capital Manila
Population 93.6 million / 813 people per sq mile (314 people per sq km)
Total area 115,830 sq. miles (300,000 sq. km)
Languages Filipino, English*, Tagalog*, Cebuano, Ilocano, Hiligaynon, many other local languages
Religions Roman Catholic 81%, Protestant 9%, Muslim 5%, Other (including Buddhist) 5%
Ethnic mix Other 34%, Tagalog 28%, Cebuano 13%, Ilocano 9%, Hiligaynon 8%, Bisaya 8%
Government Presidential system
Currency Philippine peso = 100 centavos
Literacy rate 95%
Calorie consumption 2518 kilocalories

POLAND
Northern Europe

Official name Republic of Poland
Formation 1918 / 1945
Capital Warsaw
Population 38 million / 323 people per sq mile (125 people per sq km)
Total area 120,728 sq. miles (312,685 sq. km)
Languages Polish*
Religions Roman Catholic 93%, Other and nonreligious 5%, Orthodox Christian 2%
Ethnic mix Polish 98%, Other 2%
Government Parliamentary system
Currency Zloty = 100 groszy
Literacy rate 99%
Calorie consumption 3397 kilocalories

PORTUGAL
Southwest Europe

Official name Republic of Portugal
Formation 1139 / 1640
Capital Lisbon
Population 10.7 million / 301 people per sq mile (116 people per sq km)
Total area 35,672 sq. miles (92,391 sq. km)
Languages Portuguese*
Religions Roman Catholic 92%, Protestant 4%, Nonreligious 3%, Other 1%
Ethnic mix Portuguese 98%, African and other 2%
Government Parliamentary system
Currency Euro = 100 cents
Literacy rate 95%
Calorie consumption 3583 kilocalories

QATAR
Southwest Asia

Official name State of Qatar
Formation 1971 / 1971
Capital Doha
Population 1.5 million / 353 people per sq mile (136 people per sq km)
Total area 4416 sq. miles (11,437 sq. km)
Languages Arabic*
Religions Muslim (mainly Sunni) 95%, Other 5%
Ethnic mix Qatari 20%, Other Arab 20%, Indian 20%, Nepalese 13%, Filipino 10%, Other 10%, Pakistani 7%
Government Monarchy
Currency Qatar riyal = 100 dirhams
Literacy rate 95%
Calorie consumption Not available

ROMANIA
Southeast Europe

Official name Romania
Formation 1878 / 1947
Capital Bucharest
Population 21.2 million / 238 people per sq mile (92 people per sq km)
Total area 91,699 sq. miles (237,500 sq. km)
Languages Romanian*, Hungarian (Magyar), Romani, German
Religions Romanian Orthodox 87%, Protestant 5%, Roman Catholic 5%, Other 3%
Ethnic mix Romanian 89%, Magyar 7%, Roma 3%, Other 1%
Government Presidential system
Currency New Romanian leu = 100 bani
Literacy rate 98%
Calorie consumption 3510 kilocalories

RUSSIAN FEDERATION
Europe / Asia

Official name Russian Federation
Formation 1480 / 1991
Capital Moscow
Population 140 million / 21 people per sq mile (8 people per sq km)
Total area 6,592,735 sq. miles (17,075,200 sq. km)
Languages Russian*, Tatar, Ukrainian, Chavash, various other national languages
Religions Orthodox Christian 75%, Muslim 14%, Other 11%
Ethnic mix Russian 80%, Other 12%, Tatar 4%, Ukrainian 2%, Chavash 1%, Bashkir 1%
Government Mixed Presidential–Parliamentary system
Currency Russian rouble = 100 kopeks
Literacy rate 99%
Calorie consumption 3272 kilocalories

RWANDA
Central Africa

Official name Republic of Rwanda
Formation 1962 / 1962
Capital Kigali
Population 10.3 million / 1069 people per sq mile (413 people per sq km)
Total area 10,169 sq. miles (26,338 sq. km)
Languages Kinyarwanda*, French, Kiswahili, English
Religions Christian 94%, Muslim 5%, Traditional beliefs 1%
Ethnic mix Hutu 85%, Tutsi 14%, Other (including Twa) 1%
Government Presidential system
Currency Rwanda franc = 100 centimes
Literacy rate 71%
Calorie consumption 2054 kilocalories

ST KITTS & NEVIS
West Indies

Official name Federation of Saint Christopher and Nevis
Formation 1983 / 1983
Capital Basseterre
Population 50,314 / 362 people per sq mile (140 people per sq km)
Total area 101 sq. miles (261 sq. km)
Languages English*, English Creole
Religions Anglican 33%, Methodist 29%, Other 22%, Moravian 9%, Roman Catholic 7%
Ethnic mix Black 95%, Mixed race 3%, White 1%, Other and Amerindian 1%
Government Parliamentary system
Currency East Caribbean dollar = 100 cents
Literacy rate 98%
Calorie consumption 2452 kilocalories

ST LUCIA
West Indies

Official name Saint Lucia
Formation 1979 / 1979
Capital Castries
Population 161,557 / 685 people per sq mile (265 people per sq km)
Total area 239 sq. miles (620 sq. km)
Languages English*, French Creole
Religions Roman Catholic 90%, Other 10%
Ethnic mix Black 83%, Mulatto (mixed race) 13%, Asian 3%, Other 1%
Government Parliamentary system
Currency East Caribbean dollar = 100 cents
Literacy rate 95%
Calorie consumption 2744 kilocalories

ST VINCENT & THE GRENADINES
West Indies

Official name Saint Vincent and the Grenadines
Formation 1979 / 1979
Capital Kingstown
Population 103,869 / 793 people per sq mile (305 people per sq km)
Total area 150 sq. miles (389 sq. km)
Languages English*, English Creole
Religions Anglican 46%, Methodist 28%, Roman Catholic 13%, Other 12%
Ethnic mix Black 66%, Mulatto (mixed race) 19%, Other 12%, Carib 2%
Government Parliamentary system
Currency East Caribbean dollar = 100 cents
Literacy rate 88%
Calorie consumption 2806 kilocalories

SAMOA
Australasia & Oceania

Official name Independent State of Samoa
Formation 1962 / 1962
Capital Apia
Population 200.000 / 183 people per sq mile (71 people per sq km)
Total area 1104 sq. miles (2860 sq. km)
Languages Samoan*, English*
Religions Christian 99%, Other 1%
Ethnic mix Polynesian 91%, Euronesian 7%, Other 2%
Government Parliamentary system
Currency Tala = 100 sene
Literacy rate 99%
Calorie consumption 2878 kilocalories

SAN MARINO
Southern Europe

Official name Republic of San Marino
Formation 1631 / 1631
Capital San Marino
Population 31,817 / 1326 people per sq mile (522 people per sq km)
Total area 23.6 sq. miles (61 sq. km)
Languages Italian*
Religions Roman Catholic 93%, Other and nonreligious 7%
Ethnic mix Sammarinese 88%, Italian 10%, Other 2%
Government Parliamentary system
Currency Euro = 100 cents
Literacy rate 99%
Calorie consumption Not available

SÃO TOMÉ & PRÍNCIPE
West Africa

Official name Democratic Republic of São Tomé and Príncipe
Formation 1975 / 1975
Capital São Tomé
Population 179,506 / 484 people per sq mile (187 people per sq km)
Total area 386 sq. miles (1001 sq. km)
Languages Portuguese Creole, Portuguese*
Religions Roman Catholic 84%, Other 16%
Ethnic mix Black 90%, Portuguese and Creole 10%
Government Presidential system
Currency Dobra = 100 céntimos
Literacy rate 89%
Calorie consumption 2662 kilocalories

SAUDI ARABIA
Southwest Asia

Official name Kingdom of Saudi Arabia
Formation 1932 / 1932
Capital Riyadh
Population 26.2 million / 32 people per sq mile (12 people per sq km)
Total area 756,981 sq. miles (1,960,582 sq. km)
Languages Arabic*
Religions Sunni Muslim 85%, Shi'a Muslim 15%
Ethnic mix Arab 72%, Foreign residents (mostly south and southeast Asian) 20%, Afro-Asian 8%
Government Monarchy
Currency Saudi riyal = 100 halalat
Literacy rate 86%
Calorie consumption 3133 kilocalories

SENEGAL
West Africa

Official name Republic of Senegal
Formation 1960 / 1960
Capital Dakar
Population 12.9 million / 174 people per sq mile (67 people per sq km)
Total area 75,749 sq. miles (196,190 sq. km)
Languages Wolof, Pulaar, Serer, Diola, Mandinka, Malinké, Soninké, French*
Religions Sunni Muslim 95%, Christian (mainly Roman Catholic) 4%, Traditional beliefs 1%
Ethnic mix Wolof 43%, Serer 15%, Peul 14%, Other 14%, Toucouleur 9%, Diola 5%
Government Presidential system
Currency CFA franc = 100 centimes
Literacy rate 50%
Calorie consumption 2318 kilocalories

SERBIA
Southeast Europe

Official name Republic of Serbia
Formation 2006 / 2008
Capital Belgrade
Population 9.9 million / 331 people per sq mile (128 people per sq km)
Total area 29,905 sq. miles (77,453 sq. km)
Languages Serbian*, Hungarian (Magyar)
Religions Orthodox Christian 85%, Roman Catholic 6%, Other 6%, Muslim 3%
Ethnic mix Serb 83%, Other 10%, Magyar 4%, Bosniak 2%, Roma 1%
Government Parliamentary system
Currency Serbian dinar = 100 para
Literacy rate 98%
Calorie consumption 2729 kilocalories

SEYCHELLES
Indian Ocean

Official name Republic of Seychelles
Formation 1976 / 1976
Capital Victoria
Population 89,188 / 858 people per sq mile (330 people per sq km)
Total area 176 sq. miles (455 sq. km)
Languages French Creole*, English*, French*
Religions Roman Catholic 82%, Anglican 6%, Other (including Muslim) 6%, Other Christian 3%, Hindu 2%, Seventh-day Adventist 1%
Ethnic mix Creole 89%, Indian 5%, Other 4%, Chinese 2%
Government Presidential system
Currency Seychelles rupee = 100 cents
Literacy rate 92%
Calorie consumption 2426 kilocalories

SIERRA LEONE
West Africa

Official name Republic of Sierra Leone
Formation 1961 / 1961
Capital Freetown
Population 5.8 million / 210 people per sq mile (81 people per sq km)
Total area 27,698 sq. miles (71,740 sq. km)
Languages Mende*, Temne, Krio, English
Religions Muslim 60%, Christian 30%, Traditional beliefs 10%
Ethnic mix Mende 35%, Temne 32%, Other 21%, Limba 8%, Kuranko 4%
Government Presidential system
Currency Leone = 100 cents
Literacy rate 41%
Calorie consumption 2128 kilocalories

SINGAPORE
Southeast Asia

Official name Republic of Singapore
Formation 1965 / 1965
Capital Singapore
Population 4.8 million / 20,339 people per sq mile (7869 people per sq km)
Total area 250 sq. miles (648 sq. km)
Languages Mandarin*, Malay*, Tami*l, English*
Religions Buddhist 55%, Taoist 22%, Muslim 16%, Hindu, Christian, and Sikh 7%
Ethnic mix Chinese 74%, Malay 14%, Indian 9%, Other 3%
Government Parliamentary system
Currency Singapore dollar = 100 cents
Literacy rate 95%
Calorie consumption Not available

SLOVAKIA
Central Europe

Official name Slovak Republic
Formation 1993 / 1993
Capital Bratislava
Population 5.4 million / 285 people per sq mile (110 people per sq km)
Total area 18,859 sq. miles (48,845 sq. km)
Languages Slovak*, Hungarian (Magyar), Czech
Religions Roman Catholic 69%, Other 13%, Nonreligious 13%, Greek Catholic (Uniate) 4%, Orthodox Christian 1%
Ethnic mix Slovak 86%, Magyar 10%, Roma 2%, Other 1%, Czech 1%
Government Parliamentary system
Currency Euro = 100 cents
Literacy rate 99%
Calorie consumption 2885 kilocalories

SLOVENIA
Central Europe

Official name Republic of Slovenia
Formation 1991 / 1991
Capital Ljubljana
Population 2 million / 256 people per sq mile (99 people per sq km)
Total area 7820 sq. miles (20,253 sq. km)
Languages Slovenian*
Religions Roman Catholic 58%, Other 28%, Atheist 10%, Muslim 2%, Orthodox Christian 2%
Ethnic mix Slovene 83%, Other 12%, Serb 2%, Croat 2%, Bosniak 1%
Government Parliamentary system
Currency Euro = 100 cents
Literacy rate 99%
Calorie consumption 3220 kilocalories

SOLOMON ISLANDS
Australasia & Oceania

Official name Solomon Islands
Formation 1978 / 1978
Capital Honiara
Population 500,000 / 46 people per sq mile (18 people per sq km)
Total area 10,985 sq. miles (28,450 sq. km)
Languages English*, Pidgin English, Melanesian Pidgin, around 120 others
Religions Church of Melanesia (Anglican) 34%, Roman Catholic 19%, South Seas Evangelical Church 17%, Methodist 11%, Other 19%
Ethnic mix Melanesian 93%, Polynesian 4%, Other 3%
Government Parliamentary system
Currency Solomon Islands dollar = 100 cents
Literacy rate 77%
Calorie consumption 2434 kilocalories

SOMALIA
East Africa

Official name Somalia
Formation 1960 / 1960
Capital Mogadishu
Population 9.4 million / 39 people per sq mile (15 people per sq km)
Total area 246,199 sq. miles (637,657 sq. km)
Languages Somali*, Arabic*, English, Italian
Religions Sunni Muslim 99%, Christian 1%
Ethnic mix Somali 85%, Other 15%
Government Transitional regime
Currency Somali shilin = 100 senti
Literacy rate 24%
Calorie consumption 1762 kilocalories

SOUTH AFRICA
Southern Africa

Official name Republic of South Africa
Formation 1934 / 1994
Capital Pretoria (Tshwane); Cape Town; Bloemfontein
Population 50.5 million / 107 people per sq mile (41 people per sq km)
Total area 471,008 sq. miles (1,219,912 sq. km)
Languages English, isiZulu, isiXhosa, Afrikaans, Sepedi, Setswana, Sesotho, Xitsonga, siSwati, Tshivenda, isiNdebele
Religions Christian 68%, Traditional beliefs and animist 29%, Muslim 2%, Hindu 1%
Ethnic mix Black 80%, White 9%, Colored 9%, Asian 2%
Government Presidential system
Currency Rand = 100 cents
Literacy rate 89%
Calorie consumption 2986 kilocalories

SOUTH KOREA
East Asia

Official name Republic of Korea
Formation 1948 / 1953
Capital Seoul
Population 48.5 million / 1272 people per sq mile (491 people per sq km)
Total area 38,023 sq. miles (98,480 sq. km)
Languages Korean*
Religions Mahayana Buddhist 47%, Protestant 38%, Roman Catholic 11%, Confucianist 3%, Other 1%
Ethnic mix Korean 100%
Government Presidential system
Currency South Korean won = 100 chon
Literacy rate 99%
Calorie consumption 3074 kilocalories

SOUTH SUDAN
East Africa

Official name Republic of South Sudan
Formation 2011 / 2011
Capital Juba
Population 8.3 million / 33 people per sq mile (13 people per sq km)
Total area 248,777 sq. miles (644,329 sq. km)
Languages Arabic, Dinka, Nuer, Zande, Bari, Shilluk, Lotuko
Religions Not available
Ethnic mix Dinka 40%, Nuer 15%, Shilluk/Anwak 10%, Azande 10%, Arab 10%, Bari 10%, Other 5%
Government Presidential system
Currency South Sudan Pound = 100 piastres
Literacy rate 37%
Calorie consumption Not available

SPAIN
Southwest Europe

Official name Kingdom of Spain
Formation 1492 / 1713
Capital Madrid
Population 45.3 million / 235 people per sq mile (91 people per sq km)
Total area 194,896 sq. miles (504,782 sq. km)
Languages Spanish*, Catalan*, Galician*, Basque*
Religions Roman Catholic 96%, Other 4%
Ethnic mix Castilian Spanish 72%, Catalan 17%, Galician 6%, Basque 2%, Other 2%, Roma 1%
Government Parliamentary system
Currency Euro = 100 cents
Literacy rate 98%
Calorie consumption 3271 kilocalories

SRI LANKA
South Asia

Official name Democratic Socialist Republic of Sri Lanka
Formation 1948 / 1948
Capital Colombo / Sri Jayewardenepura Kotte
Population 20.4 million / 816 people per sq mile (315 people per sq km)
Total area 25,332 sq. miles (65,610 sq. km)
Languages Sinhala*, Tamil*, Sinhala-Tamil, English
Religions Buddhist 69%, Hindu 15%, Muslim 8%, Christian 8%
Ethnic mix Sinhalese 74%, Tamil 18%, Moor 7%, Other 1%
Government Mixed presidential–parliamentary system
Currency Sri Lanka rupee = 100 cents
Literacy rate 91%
Calorie consumption 2392 kilocalories

SUDAN
East Africa

Official name Republic of the Sudan
Formation 1956 / 2011
Capital Khartoum
Population 34 million / 47 people per sq mile (18 people per sq km)
Total area 718,722 sq. miles (1,861,481 sq. km)
Languages Arabic, Nubian, Beja, Fur
Religions Almost 100% Muslim (mainly Sunni)
Ethnic mix Arab 60%, Other 18%, Nubian 10%, Beja 8%, Fur 3%, Zaghawa 1%
Government Presidential system
Currency New Sudanese pound = 100 piastres
Literacy rate 70%
Calorie consumption 2266 kilocalories

SURINAME
South America

Official name Republic of Suriname
Formation 1975 / 1975
Capital Paramaribo
Population 500,000 / 8 people per sq mile (3 people per sq km)
Total area 63,039 sq. miles (163,270 sq. km)
Languages Sranan (creole), Dutch*, Javanese, Sarnami Hindi, Saramaccan, Chinese, Carib
Religions Hindu 27%, Protestant 25%, Roman Catholic 23%, Muslim 20%, Traditional beliefs 5%
Ethnic mix East Indian 27%, Creole 18%, Black 15%, Javanese 15%, Mixed race 13%, Other 12%
Government Parliamentary system
Currency Surinamese dollar = 100 cents
Literacy rate 95%
Calorie consumption 2468 kilocalories

SWAZILAND
Southern Africa

Official name Kingdom of Swaziland
Formation 1968 / 1968
Capital Mbabane
Population 1.2 million / 181 people per sq mile (70 people per sq km)
Total area 6704 sq. miles (17,363 sq. km)
Languages English*, siSwati*, isiZulu, Xitsonga
Religions Traditional beliefs 40%, Other 30%, Roman Catholic 20%, Muslim 10%
Ethnic mix Swazi 97%, Other 3%
Government Monarchy
Currency Lilangeni = 100 cents
Literacy rate 87%
Calorie consumption 2307 kilocalories

SWEDEN
Northern Europe

Official name Kingdom of Sweden
Formation 1523 / 1921
Capital Stockholm
Population 9.3 million / 59 people per sq mile (23 people per sq km)
Total area 173,731 sq. miles (449,964 sq. km)
Languages Swedish*, Finnish, Sámi
Religions Evangelical Lutheran 75%, Other 13%, Muslim 5%, Other Protestant 5%, Roman Catholic 2%
Ethnic mix Swedish 86%, Foreign-born or first-generation immigrant 12%, Finnish & Sámi 2%
Government Parliamentary system
Currency Swedish krona = 100 öre
Literacy rate 99%
Calorie consumption 3116 kilocalories

SWITZERLAND
Central Europe

Official name Swiss Confederation
Formation 1291 / 1857
Capital Bern
Population 7.6 million / 495 people per sq mile (191 people per sq km)
Total area 15,942 sq. miles (41,290 sq. km)
Languages German*, Swiss-German, French*, Italian*, Romansch
Religions Roman Catholic 42%, Protestant 35%, Other and nonreligious 19%, Muslim 4%
Ethnic mix German 64%, French 20%, Other 9.5%, Italian 6%, Romansch 0.5%
Government Parliamentary system
Currency Swiss franc = 100 rappen/centimes
Literacy rate 99%
Calorie consumption 3421 kilocalories

SYRIA
Southwest Asia

Official name Syrian Arab Republic
Formation 1941 / 1967
Capital Damascus
Population 22.5 million / 317 people per sq mile (122 people per sq km)
Total area 71,498 sq. miles (184,180 sq. km)
Languages Arabic*, French, Kurdish, Armenian, Circassian, Turkic languages, Assyrian, Aramaic
Religions Sunni Muslim 74%, Alawi 12%, Christian 10%, Druze 3%, Other 1%
Ethnic mix Arab 90%, Kurdish 9%, Armenian, Turkmen, and Circassian 1%
Government One-party state
Currency Syrian pound = 100 piastres
Literacy rate 84%
Calorie consumption 3049 kilocalories

TAIWAN
East Asia

Official name Republic of China (ROC)
Formation 1949 / 1949
Capital Taipei
Population 23.1 million / 1852 people per sq mile (715 people per sq km)
Total area 13,892 sq. miles (35,980 sq. km)
Languages Amoy Chinese, Mandarin Chinese*, Hakka Chinese
Religions Buddhist, Confucianist, and Taoist 93%, Christian 5%, Other 2%
Ethnic mix Han (pre-20th-century migration) 84%, Han (20th-century migration) 14%, Aboriginal 2%
Government Presidential system
Currency Taiwan dollar = 100 cents
Literacy rate 98%
Calorie consumption Not available

TAJIKISTAN
Central Asia

Official name Republic of Tajikistan
Formation 1991 / 1991
Capital Dushanbe
Population 7.1 million / 129 people per sq mile (50 people per sq km)
Total area 55,251 sq. miles (143,100 sq. km)
Languages Tajik*, Uzbek, Russian
Religions Sunni Muslim 95%, Shi'a Muslim 3%, Other 2%
Ethnic mix Tajik 80%, Uzbek 15%, Other 3%, Russian 1%, Kyrgyz 1%
Government Presidential system
Currency Somoni = 100 diram
Literacy rate 99%
Calorie consumption 2127 kilocalories

TANZANIA
East Africa

Official name United Republic of Tanzania
Formation 1964 / 1964
Capital Dodoma
Population 45 million / 132 people per sq mile (51 people per sq km)
Total area 364,898 sq. miles (945,087 sq. km)
Languages Kiswahili*, Sukuma, Chagga, Nyamwezi, Hehe, Makonde, Yao, Sandawe, English*
Religions Christian 63%, Muslim 35%, Other 2%
Ethnic mix Native African (over 120 tribes) 99%, European, Asian, and Arab 1%
Government Presidential system
Currency Tanzanian shilling = 100 cents
Literacy rate 73%
Calorie consumption 2017 kilocalories

THAILAND
Southeast Asia

Official name Kingdom of Thailand
Formation 1238 / 1907
Capital Bangkok
Population 68.1 million / 345 people per sq mile (133 people per sq km)
Total area 198,455 sq. miles (514,000 sq. km)
Languages Thai*, Chinese, Malay, Khmer, Mon, Karen, Miao
Religions Buddhist 95%, Muslim 4%, Other (including Christian) 1%
Ethnic mix Thai 83%, Chinese 12%, Malay 3%, Khmer and Other 2%
Government Parliamentary system
Currency Baht = 100 satang
Literacy rate 94%
Calorie consumption 2529 kilocalories

TOGO
West Africa

Official name Republic of Togo
Formation 1960
Capital Lomé
Population 6.8 million / 324 people per sq mile (125 people per sq km)
Total area 21,924 sq. miles (56,785 sq. km)
Languages Ewe, Kabye, Gurma, French*
Religions Christian 47%, Traditional beliefs 33%, Muslim 14%, Other 6%
Ethnic mix Ewe 46%, Other African 41%, Kabye 12%, European 1%
Government Presidential system
Currency CFA franc = 100 centimes
Literacy rate 57%
Calorie consumption 2146 kilocalories

TONGA
Australasia & Oceania

Official name Kingdom of Tonga
Formation 1970 / 1970
Capital Nuku'alofa
Population 105,916 / 381 people per sq mile (147 people per sq km)
Total area 289 sq. miles (748 sq. km)
Languages English*, Tongan*
Religions Free Wesleyan 41%, Other 17%, Roman Catholic 16%, Church of Jesus Christ of Latter-day Saints 14%, Free Church of Tonga 12%
Ethnic mix Tongan 98%, Other 2%
Government Monarchy
Currency Pa'anga (Tongan dollar) = 100 seniti
Literacy rate 99%
Calorie consumption Not available

TRINIDAD & TOBAGO
West Indies

Official name Republic of Trinidad and Tobago
Formation 1962 / 1962
Capital Port-of-Spain
Population 1.3 million / 656 people per sq mile (253 people per sq km)
Total area 1980 sq. miles (5128 sq. km)
Languages English Creole, English*, Hindi, French, Spanish
Religions Other 30%, Roman Catholic 26%, Hindu 23%, Anglican 8%, Baptist 7%, Muslim 6%
Ethnic mix East Indian 40%, Black 38%, Mixed race 20%, White & Chinese 1%, Other 1%
Government Parliamentary system
Currency Trinidad and Tobago dollar = 100 cents
Literacy rate 99%
Calorie consumption 2713 kilocalories

TUNISIA
North Africa

Official name Republic of Tunisia
Formation 1956 / 1956
Capital Tunis
Population 10.4 million / 173 people per sq mile (67 people per sq km)
Total area 63,169 sq. miles (163,610 sq. km)
Languages Arabic*, French
Religions Muslim (mainly Sunni) 98%, Christian 1%, Jewish 1%
Ethnic mix Arab and Berber 98%, European 1%, Jewish 1%
Government Transitional regime
Currency Tunisian dinar = 1000 millimes
Literacy rate 78%
Calorie consumption 3312 kilocalories

TURKEY
Asia / Europe

Official name Republic of Turkey
Formation 1923 / 1939
Capital Ankara
Population 75.7 million / 255 people per sq mile (98 people per sq km)
Total area 301,382 sq. miles (780,580 sq. km)
Languages Turkish*, Kurdish, Arabic, Circassian, Armenian, Greek, Georgian, Ladino
Religions Muslim (mainly Sunni) 99%, Other 1%
Ethnic mix Turkish 70%, Kurdish 20%, Other 8%, Arab 2%
Government Parliamentary system
Currency Turkish lira = 100 kurus
Literacy rate 91%
Calorie consumption 3482 kilocalories

TURKMENISTAN
Central Asia

Official name Turkmenistan
Formation 1991 / 1991
Capital Ashgabat
Population 5.2 million / 28 people per sq mile (11 people per sq km)
Total area 188,455 sq. miles (488,100 sq. km)
Languages Turkmen*, Uzbek, Russian, Kazakh, Tatar
Religions Sunni Muslim 89%, Orthodox Christian 9%, Other 2%
Ethnic mix Turkmen 85%, Other 6%, Uzbek 5%, Russian 4%
Government One-party state
Currency New manat = 100 tenge
Literacy rate 99%
Calorie consumption 2754 kilocalories

TUVALU
Australasia & Oceania

Official name Tuvalu
Formation 1978 / 1978
Capital Fongafale (Funafuti Atoll)
Population 10,544 / 1054 people per sq mile (406 people per sq km)
Total area 10 sq. miles (26 sq. km)
Languages Tuvaluan, Kiribati, English*
Religions Church of Tuvalu 97%, Other 1%, Baha'i 1%, Seventh-day Adventist 1%
Ethnic mix Polynesian 96%, Micronesian 4%
Government Nonparty system
Currency Australian dollar and Tuvaluan dollar = 100 cents
Literacy rate 98%
Calorie consumption Not available

UGANDA
East Africa

Official name Republic of Uganda
Formation 1962 / 1962
Capital Kampala
Population 33.8 million / 439 people per sq mile (169 people per sq km)
Total area 91,135 sq. miles (236,040 sq. km)
Languages Luganda, Nkole, Chiga, Lango, Acholi, Teso, Lugbara, English*
Religions Christian 85%, Muslim (mainly Sunni) 12%, Other 3%
Ethnic mix Other 50%, Baganda 17%, Banyakole 10%, Basoga 9%, Bakiga 7%, Iteso 7%
Government Presidential system
Currency New Uganda shilling = 100 cents
Literacy rate 74%
Calorie consumption 2247 kilocalories

UKRAINE
Eastern Europe

Official name Ukraine
Formation 1991 / 1991
Capital Kiev
Population 45.4 million / 195 people per sq mile (75 people per sq km)
Total area 223,089 sq. miles (603,700 sq. km)
Languages Ukrainian*, Russian, Tatar
Religions Christian (mainly Orthodox) 95%, Other 5%
Ethnic mix Ukrainian 78%, Russian 17%, Other 5%
Government Presidential system
Currency Hryvna = 100 kopiykas
Literacy rate 99%
Calorie consumption 3230 kilocalories

UNITED ARAB EMIRATES
Southwest Asia

Official name United Arab Emirates
Formation 1971 / 1972
Capital Abu Dhabi
Population 4.7 million / 146 people per sq mile (56 people per sq km)
Total area 32,000 sq. miles (82,880 sq. km)
Languages Arabic*, Farsi, Indian and Pakistani languages, English
Religions Muslim (mainly Sunni) 96%, Christian, Hindu, and other 4%
Ethnic mix Asian 60%, Emirian 25%, Other Arab 12%, European 3%
Government Monarchy
Currency UAE dirham = 100 fils
Literacy rate 90%
Calorie consumption 3138 kilocalories

UNITED KINGDOM
Northwest Europe

Official name United Kingdom of Great Britain and Northern Ireland
Formation 1707 / 1922
Capital London
Population 61.9 million / 664 people per sq mile (256 people per sq km)
Total area 94,525 sq. miles (244,820 sq. km)
Languages English*, Welsh* (in Wales), Gaelic
Religions Anglican 45%, Other & non-religious 39%, Roman Catholic 9%, Presbyterian 4%, Muslim 3%
Ethnic mix English 80%, Scottish 9%, West Indian, Asian, & other 5%, Welsh 3%, Northern Irish 3%
Government Parliamentary system
Currency Pound sterling = 100 pence
Literacy rate 99%
Calorie consumption 3442 kilocalories

UNITED STATES
North America

Official name United States of America
Formation 1776 / 1959
Capital Washington D.C.
Population 318 million / 90 people per sq mile (35 people per sq km)
Total area 3,717,792 sq. miles (9,626,091 sq. km)
Languages English*, Spanish, Chinese, French, German, Tagalog, Vietnamese, Italian, Korean, Russian, Polish
Religions Protestant 52%, Roman Catholic 25%, Other & nonreligious 20%, Jewish 2%, Muslim 1%
Ethnic mix White 62%, Hispanic 13%, Black American/African 13%, Other 8%, Asian 4%
Government Presidential system
Currency US dollar = 100 cents
Literacy rate 99%
Calorie consumption 3770 kilocalories

URUGUAY
South America

Official name Eastern Republic of Uruguay
Formation 1828 / 1828
Capital Montevideo
Population 3.4 million / 50 people per sq mile (19 people per sq km)
Total area 68,039 sq. miles (176,220 sq. km)
Languages Spanish*
Religions Roman Catholic 66%, Other and nonreligious 30%, Jewish 2%, Protestant 2%
Ethnic mix White 90%, Mestizo 6%, Black 4%
Government Presidential system
Currency Uruguayan peso = 100 centésimos
Literacy rate 98%
Calorie consumption 2818 kilocalories

UZBEKISTAN
Central Asia

Official name Republic of Uzbekistan
Formation 1991 / 1991
Capital Tashkent
Population 27.8 million / 161 people per sq mile (62 people per sq km)
Total area 172,741 sq. miles (447,400 sq. km)
Languages Uzbek*, Russian, Tajik, Kazakh
Religions Sunni Muslim 88%, Orthodox Christian 9%, Other 3%
Ethnic mix Uzbek 80%, Other 6%, Russian 6%, Tajik 5%, Kazakh 3%
Government Presidential system
Currency Som = 100 tiyin
Literacy rate 99%
Calorie consumption 2525 kilocalories

VANUATU
Australasia & Oceania

Official name Republic of Vanuatu
Formation 1980 / 1980
Capital Port Vila
Population 200,000 / 42 people per sq mile (16 people per sq km)
Total area 4710 sq. miles (12,200 sq. km)
Languages Bislama* (Melanesian pidgin), English*, French*, other indigenous languages
Religions Presbyterian 37%, Other 19%, Roman Catholic 15%, Anglican 15%, Traditional beliefs 8%, Seventh-day Adventist 6%
Ethnic mix ni-Vanuatu 94%, European 4%, Other 2%
Government Parliamentary system
Currency Vatu = 100 centimes
Literacy rate 82%
Calorie consumption 2722 kilocalories

VATICAN CITY
Southern Europe

Official name State of the Vatican City
Formation 1929 / 1929
Capital Vatican City
Population 832 / 4894 people per sq mile (1891 people per sq km)
Total area 0.17 sq. miles (0.44 sq. km)
Languages Italian*, Latin*
Religions Roman Catholic 100%
Ethnic mix Not avaialable
Government Papal state
Currency Euro = 100 cents
Literacy rate 99%
Calorie consumption Not available

VENEZUELA
South America

Official name Bolivarian Republic of Venezuela
Formation 1830 / 1830
Capital Caracas
Population 29 million / 85 people per sq mile (33 people per sq km)
Total area 352,143 sq. miles (912,050 sq. km)
Languages Spanish*, Amerindian languages
Religions Roman Catholic 96%, Protestant 2%, Other 2%
Ethnic mix Mestizo 69%, White 20%, Black 9%, Amerindian 2%
Government Presidential system
Currency Bolívar fuerte = 100 céntimos
Literacy rate 95%
Calorie consumption 2582 kilocalories

VIETNAM
Southeast Asia

Official name Socialist Republic of Vietnam
Formation 1976 / 1976
Capital Hanoi
Population 89 million / 708 people per sq mile (274 people per sq km)
Total area 127,243 sq. miles (329,560 sq. km)
Languages Vietnamese*, Chinese, Thai, Khmer, Muong, Nung, Miao, Yao, Jarai
Religions Other 74%, Buddhist 14%, Roman Catholic 7%, Cao Dai 3%, Protestant 2%
Ethnic mix Vietnamese 86%, Other 8%, Thai 2%, Muong 2%, Tay 2%
Government One-party state
Currency Dông = 10 hao = 100 xu
Literacy rate 93%
Calorie consumption 2769 kilocalories

YEMEN
Southwest Asia

Official name Republic of Yemen
Formation 1990 / 1990
Capital Sana
Population 24.3 million / 112 people per sq mile (43 people per sq km)
Total area 203,849 sq. miles (527,970 sq. km)
Languages Arabic*
Religions Sunni Muslim 55%, Shi'a Muslim 42%, Christian, Hindu, and Jewish 3%
Ethnic mix Arab 99%, Afro-Arab, Indian, Somali, and European 1%
Government Presidential system
Currency Yemeni rial = 100 fils
Literacy rate 62%
Calorie consumption 2032 kilocalories

ZAMBIA
Southern Africa

Official name Republic of Zambia
Formation 1964 / 1964
Capital Lusaka
Population 13.3 million / 47 people per sq mile (18 people per sq km)
Total area 290,584 sq. miles (752,614 sq. km)
Languages Bemba, Tonga, Nyanja, Lozi, Lala-Bisa, Nsenga, English*
Religions Christian 63%, Traditional beliefs 36%, Muslim and Hindu 1%
Ethnic mix Bemba 34%, Other African 26%, Tonga 16%, Nyanja 14%, Lozi 9%, European 1%
Government Presidential system
Currency Zambian kwacha = 100 ngwee
Literacy rate 71%
Calorie consumption 1885 kilocalories

ZIMBABWE
Southern Africa

Official name Republic of Zimbabwe
Formation 1980 / 1980
Capital Harare
Population 12.6 million / 84 people per sq mile (33 people per sq km)
Total area 150,803 sq. miles (390,580 sq. km)
Languages Shona, isiNdebele, English*
Religions Syncretic (Christian/traditional beliefs) 50%, Christian 25%, Traditional beliefs 24%, Other (including Muslim) 1%
Ethnic mix Shona 71%, Ndebele 16%, Other African 11%, White 1%, Asian 1%,
Government Presidential system
Currency Zimbabwe dollar suspended in 2009
Literacy rate 92%
Calorie consumption 2207 kilocalories

Geographical names

The following glossary lists geographical terms occurring on the maps and in main-entry names in the Index-Gazetteer. These terms may precede, follow or be run together with the proper element of the name; where they precede it the term is reversed for indexing purposes - thus Poluostrov Yamal is indexed as Yamal, Poluostrov.

Key

Geographical term
Language, Term

A

Å *Danish, Norwegian*, River
Āb *Persian*, River
Adrar *Berber*, Mountains
Agía, Ágios *Greek*, Saint
Air *Indonesian*, River
Ákra *Greek*, Cape, point
Alpen *German*, Alps
Alt- *German*, Old
Altiplanicie *Spanish*, Plateau
Älve, -älven *Swedish*, River
-ån *Swedish*, River
Anse *French*, Bay
'Aqabat *Arabic*, Pass
Archipiélago *Spanish*, Archipelago
Arcipelago *Italian*, Archipelago
Arquipélago *Portuguese*, Archipelago
Arrecife(s) *Spanish*, Reef(s)
Aru *Tamil*, River
Augstiene *Latvian*, Upland
Aukštuma *Lithuanian*, Upland
Aust- *Norwegian*, Eastern
Avtonomnyy Okrug *Russian*, Autonomous district
Āw *Kurdish*, River
'Ayn *Arabic*, Spring, well
'Ayoûn *Arabic*, Wells

B

Baelt *Danish*, Strait
Bahía *Spanish*, Bay
Baḩr *Arabic*, River
Baía *Portuguese*, Bay
Baie *French*, Bay
Bañado *Spanish*, Marshy land
Bandao *Chinese*, Peninsula
Banjaran *Malay*, Mountain range
Barajı *Turkish*, Dam
Barragem *Portuguese*, Reservoir
Bassin *French*, Basin
Batang *Malay*, Stream
Beinn, Ben *Gaelic*, Mountain
-berg *Afrikaans, Norwegian*, Mountain
Besar *Indonesian, Malay*, Big
Birkat, Birket *Arabic*, Lake, well, cistern
Boğazı *Turkish*, Lake
Boka *Serbo-Croatian*, Bay
Bol'sh-aya, -iye, -oy, -oye *Russian*, Big
Botigh(i) *Uzbek*, Depression basin
-bre(en) *Norwegian*, Glacier
Bredning *Danish*, Bay
Bucht *German*, Bay
Bugt(en) *Danish*, Bay
Buḩayrat *Arabic*, Lake, reservoir
Buḩeiret *Arabic*, Lake
Bukit *Malay*, Mountain
-bukta *Norwegian*, Bay
bukten *Swedish*, Bay
Bulag *Mongolian*, Spring
Bulak *Uighur*, Spring
Burnu *Turkish*, Cape, point
Buuraha *Somali*, Mountains

C

Cabo *Portuguese*, Cape
Caka *Tibetan*, Salt lake
Canal *Spanish*, Channel
Cap *French*, Cape
Capo *Italian*, Cape, headland
Cascada *Portuguese*, Waterfall
Cayo(s) *Spanish*, Islet(s), rock(s)
Cerro *Spanish*, Hill
Chaîne *French*, Mountain range
Chapada *Portuguese*, Hills, upland
Chau *Cantonese*, Island
Chāy *Turkish*, River
Chhâk *Cambodian*, Bay
Chhu *Tibetan*, River
-chŏsuji *Korean*, Reservoir
Chott *Arabic*, Depression, salt lake
Chŭli *Uzbek*, Grassland, steppe
Ch'ün-tao *Chinese*, Island group
Chuŏr Phnum *Cambodian*, Mountains
Ciudad *Spanish*, City, town
Co *Tibetan*, Lake
Colline(s) *French*, Hill(s)
Cordillera *Spanish*, Mountain range
Costa *Spanish*, Coast
Côte *French*, Coast
Coxilha *Portuguese*, Mountains
Cuchilla *Spanish*, Mountains

D

Daban *Mongolian, Uighur*, Pass
Dağı *Azerbaijani, Turkish*, Mountain
Dağları *Azerbaijani, Turkish*, Mountains
-dake *Japanese*, Peak
-dal(en) *Norwegian*, Valley
Danau *Indonesian*, Lake
Dao *Chinese*, Island
Đao *Vietnamese*, Island
Daryā *Persian*, River
Daryācheh *Persian*, Lake
Dasht *Persian*, Desert, plain
Dawḩat *Arabic*, Bay
Denizi *Turkish*, Sea
Dere *Turkish*, Stream
Desierto *Spanish*, Desert
Dili *Azerbaijani*, Spit
-do *Korean*, Island
Dooxo *Somali*, Valley
Düzü *Azerbaijani*, Steppe
-dwīp *Bengali*, Island

E

-eilanden *Dutch*, Islands
Embalse *Spanish*, Reservoir
Ensenada *Spanish*, Bay
Erg *Arabic*, Dunes
Estany *Catalan*, Lake
Estero *Spanish*, Inlet
Estrecho *Spanish*, Strait
Étang *French*, Lagoon, lake
-ey *Icelandic*, Island
Ezero *Bulgarian, Macedonian*, Lake
Ezers *Latvian*, Lake

F

Feng *Chinese*, Peak
Fjord *Danish*, Fjord
-fjord(en) *Danish, Norwegian, Swedish*, fjord
-fjördhur *Icelandic*, Fjord
Fleuve *French*, River
Fliegu *Maltese*, Channel
-fljór *Icelandic*, River
-flói *Icelandic*, Bay
Forêt *French*, Forest

G

-gan *Japanese*, Rock
-gang *Korean*, River
Ganga *Hindi, Nepali, Sinhala*, River
Gaoyuan *Chinese*, Plateau
Garagumy *Turkmen*, Sands
-gawa *Japanese*, River
Gebel *Arabic*, Mountain
-gebirge *German*, Mountain range
Ghadīr *Arabic*, Well
Ghubbat *Arabic*, Bay
Gjiri *Albanian*, Bay
Gol *Mongolian*, River
Golfe *French*, Gulf
Golfo *Italian, Spanish*, Gulf
Göl(ü) *Turkish*, Lake
Golyam, -a *Bulgarian*, Big
Gora *Russian, Serbo-Croatian*, Mountain
Góra *Polish*, mountain
Gory *Russian*, Mountain
Gryada *Russian*, ridge
Guba *Russian*, Bay
-gundo *Korean*, island group
Gunung *Malay*, Mountain

H

Ḩadd *Arabic*, Spit
-haehyŏp *Korean*, Strait
Haff *German*, Lagoon
Hai *Chinese*, Bay, lake, sea
Haixia *Chinese*, Strait
Hamada *Arabic*, Plateau
Ḩammādat *Arabic*, Plateau
Hāmūn *Persian*, Lake
-hantō *Japanese*, Peninsula
Har, Haré *Hebrew*, Mountain
Ḩarrat *Arabic*, Lava-field
Hav(et) *Danish*, Swedish, Sea
Hawr *Arabic*, Lake
Hāyk' *Amharic*, Lake
He *Chinese*, River
-hegység *Hungarian*, Mountain range
Heide *German*, Heath, moorland
Helodrano *Malagasy*, Bay
Higashi- *Japanese*, East(ern)
Ḩiṣā' *Arabic*, Well
Hka *Burmese*, River
-ho *Korean*, Lake
Holot *Hebrew*, Dunes
Hora *Belarussian, Czech*, Mountain
Hrada *Belarussian*, Mountain, ridge
Hsi *Chinese*, River
Hu *Chinese*, Lake
Huk *Danish*, Point

I

Île(s) *French*, Island(s)
Ilha(s) *Portuguese*, Island(s)
Ilhéu(s) *Portuguese*, Islet(s)
Imeni *Russian*, In the name of
Inish- *Gaelic*, Island
Insel(n) *German*, Island(s)
Irmağı, Irmak *Turkish*, River
Isla(s) *Spanish*, Island(s)
Isola (Isole) *Italian*, Island(s)

J

Jabal *Arabic*, Mountain
Jāl *Arabic*, Ridge
-järv *Estonian*, Lake
-järvi *Finnish*, Lake
Jazā'ir *Arabic*, Islands
Jazīrat *Arabic*, Island
Jazīreh *Persian*, Island
Jebel *Arabic*, Mountain
Jezero *Serbo-Croatian*, Lake
Jezioro *Polish*, Lake
Jiang *Chinese*, River
-jima *Japanese*, Island
Jižní *Czech*, Southern
-jõgi *Estonian*, River
-joki *Finnish*, River
-jökull *Icelandic*, Glacier
Jūn *Arabic*, Bay
Juzur *Arabic*, Islands

K

Kaikyō *Japanese*, Strait
-kaise *Lappish*, Mountain
Kali *Nepali*, River
Kalnas *Lithuanian*, Mountain
Kalns *Latvian*, Mountain
Kang *Chinese*, Harbor
Kangri *Tibetan*, Mountain(s)
Kaôh *Cambodian*, Island
Kapp *Norwegian*, Cape
Káto *Greek*, Lower
Kavīr *Persian*, Desert
K'edi *Georgian*, Mountain range
Kediet *Arabic*, Mountain
Kepi *Albanian*, Cape, point
Kepulauan *Indonesian, Malay*, Island group
Khalig, Khalīj *Arabic*, Gulf
Khawr *Arabic*, Inlet
Khola *Nepali*, River
Khrebet *Russian*, Mountain range
Ko *Thai*, Island
-ko *Japanese*, Inlet, lake
Kólpos *Greek*, Bay
-kopf *German*, Peak
Körfäzi *Azerbaijani*, Bay
Körfezi *Turkish*, Bay
Kõrgustik *Estonian*, Upland
Kosa *Russian, Ukrainian*, Spit
Koshi *Nepali*, River
Kou *Chinese*, River-mouth
Kowtal *Persian*, Pass
Kray *Russian*, Region, territory
Kryazh *Russian*, Ridge
Kuduk *Uighur*, Well
Kūh(hā) *Persian*, Mountain(s)
-kul' *Russian*, Lake
Kŭl(i) *Tajik, Uzbek*, Lake
-kundo *Korean*, Island group
-kysten *Norwegian*, Coast
Kyun *Burmese*, Island

L

Laaq *Somali*, Watercourse
Lac *French*, Lake
Lacul *Romanian*, Lake
Lagh *Somali*, Stream
Lago *Italian, Portuguese, Spanish*, Lake
Lagoa *Portuguese*, Lagoon
Laguna *Italian, Spanish*, Lagoon, lake
Laht *Estonian*, Bay
Laut *Indonesian*, Bay
Lembalemba *Malagasy*, Plateau
Lerr *Armenian*, Mountain
Lerrnashght'a *Armenian*, Mountain range
Les *Czech*, Forest
Lich *Armenian*, Lake
Liehtao *Chinese*, Island group
Liqeni *Albanian*, Lake
Límni *Greek*, Lake
Ling *Chinese*, Mountain range
Llano *Spanish*, Plain, prairie
Lumi *Albanian*, River
Lyman *Ukrainian*, Estuary

M

Madīnat *Arabic*, City, town
Mae Nam *Thai*, River
-mägi *Estonian*, Hill
Maja *Albanian*, Mountain
Mal *Albanian*, Mountains
Mal-aya, -oye, -yy, *Russian*, Small
-man *Korean*, Bay
Mar *Spanish*, Sea
Marios *Lithuanian*, Lake
Massif *French*, Mountains
Meer *German*, Lake
-meer *Dutch*, Lake
Melkosopochnik *Russian*, Plain
-meri *Estonian*, Sea
Mifraz *Hebrew*, Bay
Minami- *Japanese*, South(ern)
-misaki *Japanese*, Cape, point
Monkhafad *Arabic*, Depression
Montagne(s) *French*, Mountain(s)
Montañas *Spanish*, Mountains
Mont(s) *French*, Mountain(s)
Monte *Italian, Portuguese*, Mountain
More *Russian*, Sea
Mörön *Mongolian*, River
Mys *Russian*, Cape, point

N

-nada *Japanese*, Open stretch of water
Nagor'ye *Russian*, Upland
Naḩal *Hebrew*, River
Nahr *Arabic*, River
Nam *Laotian*, River
Namakzār *Persian*, Salt desert
Né-a, -on, -os *Greek*, New
Nedre- *Norwegian*, Lower
-neem *Estonian*, Cape, point
Nehri *Turkish*, River
-nes *Norwegian*, Cape, point
Nevado *Spanish*, Snow-capped mountain
Nieder- *German*, Lower
Nishi- *Japanese*, West(ern)
-nísi *Greek*, Island
Nisoi *Greek*, Islands
Nizhn-eye, -iy, -iye, -yaya *Russian*, Lower
Nizmennost' *Russian*, Lowland, plain
Nord *Danish, French, German*, North
Norte *Portuguese, Spanish*, North
Nos *Bulgarian*, Point, spit
Nosy *Malagasy*, Island
Nov-a, -i, *Bulgarian, Serbo-Croatian*, New
Nov-aya, -o, -oye, -yy, -yye *Russian*, New
Now-a, -e, -y *Polish*, New
Nur *Mongolian*, Lake
Nuruu *Mongolian*, Mountains
Nuur *Mongolian*, Lake
Nyzovyna *Ukrainian*, Lowland, plain

O

-ø *Danish*, Island
Ober- *German*, Upper
Oblast' *Russian*, Province
Órmos *Greek*, Bay
Orol(i) *Uzbek*, Island
Øster- *Norwegian*, Eastern
Ostrov(a) *Russian*, Island(s)
Otok *Serbo-Croatian*, Island
Oued *Arabic*, Watercourse
-oy *Faeroese*, Island
-øy(a) *Norwegian*, Island
Oya *Sinhala*, River
Ozero *Russian, Ukrainian*, Lake

P

Passo *Italian*, Pass
Pegunungan *Indonesian, Malay*, Mountain range
Pélagos *Greek*, Sea
Pendi *Chinese*, Basin
Penisola *Italian*, Peninsula
Pertuis *French*, Strait
Peski *Russian*, Sands
Phanom *Thai*, Mountain
Phou *Laotian*, Mountain
Pi *Chinese*, Point
Pic *Catalan, French*, Peak
Pico *Portuguese, Spanish*, Peak
-piggen *Danish*, Peak
Pik *Russian*, Peak
Pivostriv *Ukrainian*, Peninsula
Planalto *Portuguese*, Plateau
Planina, Planini *Bulgarian, Macedonian, Serbo-Croatian*, Mountain range
Plato *Russian*, Plateau
Ploskogor'ye *Russian*, Upland
Poluostrov *Russian*, Peninsula
Ponta *Portuguese*, Point
Porthmós *Greek*, Strait
Pótamos *Greek*, River
Presa *Spanish*, Dam
Prokhod *Bulgarian*, Pass
Proliv *Russian*, Strait
Pulau *Indonesian, Malay*, Island
Pulu *Malay*, Island
Punta *Spanish*, Point
Pushcha *Belorussian*, Forest
Puszcza *Polish*, Forest

Q

Qā' *Arabic*, Depression
Qalamat *Arabic*, Well
Qatorkŭh(i) *Tajik*, Mountain
Qiuling *Chinese*, Hills
Qolleh *Persian*, Mountain
Qu *Tibetan*, Stream
Quan *Chinese*, Well
Qulla(i) *Tajik*, Peak
Qundao *Chinese*, Island group

R

Raas *Somali*, Cape
-rags *Latvian*, Cape
Ramlat *Arabic*, Sands
Ra's *Arabic*, Cape, headland, point
Ravnina *Bulgarian, Russian*, Plain
Récif *French*, Reef
Recife *Portuguese*, Reef
Reka *Bulgarian*, River
Represa (Rep.) *Portuguese, Spanish*, Reservoir
Reshteh *Persian*, Mountain range
Respublika *Russian*, Republic, first-order administrative division
Respublika(si) *Uzbek*, Republic, first-order administrative division
-retsugan *Japanese*, Chain of rocks
-rettō *Japanese*, Island chain
Riacho *Spanish*, Stream
Riban' *Malagasy*, Mountains
Rio *Portuguese*, River
Río *Spanish*, River
Riu *Catalan*, River
Rivier *Dutch*, River
Rivière *French*, River
Rowd *Pashtu*, River
Rt *Serbo-Croatian*, Point
Rūd *Persian*, River
Rūdkhāneh *Persian*, River
Rudohorie *Slovak*, Mountains
Ruisseau *French*, Stream

S

-saar *Estonian*, Island
-saari *Finnish*, Island
Sabkhat *Arabic*, Salt marsh
Sāgar(a) *Hindi*, Lake, reservoir
Şaḩrā' *Arabic*, Desert
Saint, Sainte *French*, Saint
Salar *Spanish*, Salt-pan
Salto *Portuguese, Spanish*, Waterfall
Samudra *Sinhala*, Reservoir
-san *Japanese, Korean*, Mountain
-sanchi *Japanese*, Mountains
-sandur *Icelandic*, Beach
Sankt *German, Swedish*, Saint
-sanmaek *Korean*, Mountain range
-sanmyaku *Japanese*, Mountain range
San, Santa, Santo *Italian, Portuguese, Spanish*, Saint
São *Portuguese*, Saint
Sarīr *Arabic*, Desert
Sebkha, Sebkhet *Arabic*, Depression, salt marsh
Sedlo *Czech*, Pass
See *German*, Lake
Selat *Indonesian*, Strait
Selatan *Indonesian*, Southern
-selkä *Finnish*, Lake, ridge
Selseleh *Persian*, Mountain range
Serra *Portuguese*, Mountain
Serranía *Spanish*, Mountain
-seto *Japanese*, Channel, strait
Sever-naya, -noye, -nyy, -o *Russian*, Northern
Sha'ib *Arabic*, Watercourse
Shākh *Kurdish*, Mountain
Shamo *Chinese*, Desert
Shan *Chinese*, Mountain(s)
Shankou *Chinese*, Pass
Shanmo *Chinese*, Mountain range
Shaṭṭ *Arabic*, Distributary
Shet' *Amharic*, River
Shi *Chinese*, Municipality
-shima *Japanese*, Island
Shiqqat *Arabic*, Depression
-shotō *Japanese*, Group of islands
Shuiku *Chinese*, Reservoir
Shūrkhog(i) *Uzbek*, Salt marsh
Sierra *Spanish*, Mountains
Sint *Dutch*, Saint
-sjø(en) *Norwegian*, Lake
-sjön *Swedish*, Lake
Solonchak *Russian*, Salt lake
Solonchakovyye Vpadiny *Russian*, Salt basin, wetlands
Sơn *Vietnamese*, Mountain
Sông *Vietnamese*, River
Sør- *Norwegian*, Southern
-spitze *German*, Peak
Star-á, -é *Czech*, Old
Star-aya, -oye, -yy, -yye *Russian*, Old
Stenó *Greek*, Strait
Step' *Russian*, Steppe
Štít *Slovak*, Peak
Stœng *Cambodian*, River
Stolovaya Strana *Russian*, Plateau
Stredné *Slovak*, Middle
Střední *Czech*, Middle
Stretto *Italian*, Strait
Su Anbarı *Azerbaijani*, Reservoir
-suidō *Japanese*, Channel, strait
Sund *Swedish*, Sound, strait
Sungai *Indonesian, Malay*, River
Suu *Turkish*, River

T

Tal *Mongolian*, Plain
Tandavan' *Malagasy*, Mountain range
Tangorombohitr' *Malagasy*, Mountain massif
Tanjung *Indonesian, Malay*, Cape, point
Tao *Chinese*, Island
Ţaraq *Arabic*, Hills
Tassili *Berber*, Mountain, plateau
Tau *Russian*, Mountain(s)
Taungdan *Burmese*, Mountain range
Techníti Límni *Greek*, Reservoir
Tekojärvi *Finnish*, Reservoir
Teluk *Indonesian, Malay*, Bay
Tengah *Indonesian*, Middle
Terara *Amharic*, Mountain
Timur *Indonesian*, Eastern
-tind(an) *Norwegian*, Peak
Tizma(si) *Uzbek*, Mountain range, ridge
-tō *Japanese*, island
Tog *Somali*, Valley
-tōge *Japanese*, pass
Togh(i) *Uzbek*, mountain
Tônlé *Cambodian*, Lake
Top *Dutch*, Peak
-tunturi *Finnish*, Mountain
Ţuraq *Arabic*, hills
Tur'at *Arabic*, Channel

U

Udde(n) *Swedish*, Cape, point
'Uqlat *Arabic*, Well
Utara *Indonesian*, Northern
Uul *Mongolian*, Mountains

V

Väin *Estonian*, Strait
Vallée *French*, Valley
Varful *Romanian*, Peak
-vatn *Icelandic*, Lake
-vatnet *Norwegian*, Lake
Velayat *Turkmen*, Province
-vesi *Finnish*, Lake
Vestre- *Norwegian*, Western
-vidda *Norwegian*, Plateau
-vík *Icelandic*, Bay
-viken *Swedish*, Bay, inlet
Vinh *Vietnamese*, Bay
Víztárloló *Hungarian*, Reservoir
Vodaskhovishcha *Belarussian*, Reservoir
Vodokhranilishche (Vdkhr.) *Russian*, Reservoir
Vodoskhovyshche (Vdskh.) *Ukrainian*, Reservoir
Volcán *Spanish*, Volcano
Vostochn-o, yy *Russian*, Eastern
Vozvyshennost' *Russian*, Upland, plateau
Vozyera *Belarussian*, Lake
Vpadina *Russian*, Depression
Vrchovina *Czech*, Mountains
Vrh *Croat, Slovene*, Peak
Vychodné *Slovak*, Eastern
Vysochyna *Ukrainian*, Upland
Vysočina *Czech*, Upland

W

Waadi *Somali*, Watercourse
Wādī *Arabic* Watercourse
Wāḩat, Wâhat *Arabic*, Oasis
Wald *German*, Forest
Wan *Chinese*, Bay
Way *Indonesian*, River
Webi *Somali*, River
Wenz *Amharic*, River
Wiloyat(i) *Uzbek*, Province
Wyżyna *Polish*, Upland
Wzgórza *Polish*, Upland
Wzvyshsha *Belarussian*, Upland

X

Xé *Laotian*, River
Xi *Chinese*, Stream

Y

-yama *Japanese*, Mountain
Yanchi *Chinese*, Salt lake
Yanhu *Chinese*, Salt lake
Yarımadası *Azerbaijani, Turkish*, Peninsula
Yaylası *Turkish*, Plateau
Yazovir *Bulgarian*, Reservoir
Yoma *Burmese*, Mountains
Ytre- *Norwegian*, Outer
Yü *Chinese*, Island
Yunhe *Chinese*, Canal
Yuzhn-o, -yy *Russian*, Southern

Z

-zaki *Japanese*, Cape, point
Zaliv *Bulgarian, Russian*, Bay
-zan *Japanese*, Mountain
Zangbo *Tibetan*, River
Zapadn-aya, -o, -yy *Russian*, Western
Západné *Slovak*, Western
Západní *Czech*, Western
Zatoka *Polish, Ukrainian*, Bay
-zee *Dutch*, Sea
Zemlya *Russian*, Earth, land
Zizhiqu *Chinese*, Autonomous region

100 Mile House - Aceh

INDEX

THIS INDEX LISTS all the placenames and features shown on the regional and continental maps in this Atlas. Placenames are referenced to the largest scale map on which they appear. The policy followed throughout the Atlas is to use the local spelling or local name at regional level; commonly-used English language names may occasionally be added (in parentheses) where this is an aid to identification e.g. Firenze (Florence). English names, where they exist, have been used for all international features e.g. oceans and country names; they are also used on the continental maps and in the introductory World section; these are then fully cross-referenced to the local names found on the regional maps. The index also contains commonly-found alternative names and variant spellings, which are also fully cross-referenced.

All main entry names are those of settlements unless otherwise indicated by the use of italicized definitions or representative symbols, which are keyed at the foot of each page.

GLOSSARY OF ABBREVIATIONS

This glossary provides a comprehensive guide to the abbreviations used in this Atlas, and in the Index.

A
abbrev. abbreviated
AD Anno Domini
Afr. Afrikaans
Alb. Albanian
Amh. Amharic
anc. ancient
approx. approximately
Ar. Arabic
Arm. Armenian
ASEAN Association of South East Asian Nations
ASSR Autonomous Soviet Socialist Republic
Aust. Australian
Az. Azerbaijani
Azerb. Azerbaijan

B
Basq. Basque
BC before Christ
Bel. Belarussian
Ben. Bengali
Ber. Berber
B-H Bosnia-Herzegovina
bn billion (one thousand million)
BP British Petroleum
Bret. Breton
Brit. British
Bul. Bulgarian
Bur. Burmese

C
C central
C. Cape
°C degrees Centigrade
CACM Central America Common Market
Cam. Cambodian
Cant. Cantonese
CAR Central African Republic
Cast. Castilian
Cat. Catalan
CEEAC Central America Common Market
Chin. Chinese
CIS Commonwealth of Independent States
cm centimetre(s)
Cro. Croat
Cz. Czech
Czech Rep. Czech Republic

D
Dan. Danish
Div. Divehi
Dom. Rep. Dominican Republic
Dut. Dutch

E
E east
EC see EU
EEC see EU
ECOWAS Economic Community of West African States
ECU European Currency Unit
EMS European Monetary System
Eng. English
est estimated
Est. Estonian
EU European Union (previously European Community [EC], European Economic Community [EEC])

F
°F degrees Fahrenheit
Faer. Faeroese
Fij. Fijian
Fin. Finnish
Fr. French
Fris. Frisian
ft foot/feet
FYROM Former Yugoslav Republic of Macedonia

G
g gram(s)
Gael. Gaelic
Gal. Galician
GDP Gross Domestic Product (the total value of goods and services produced by a country excluding income from foreign countries)
Geor. Georgian
Ger. German
Gk Greek
GNP Gross National Product (the total value of goods and services produced by a country)

H
Heb. Hebrew
HEP hydro-electric power
Hind. Hindi
hist. historical
Hung. Hungarian

I
I. Island
Icel. Icelandic
in inch(es)
In. Inuit (Eskimo)
Ind. Indonesian
Intl International
Ir. Irish
Is Islands
It. Italian

J
Jap. Japanese

K
Kaz. Kazakh
kg kilogram(s)
Kir. Kirghiz
km kilometre(s)
km² square kilometre (singular)
Kor. Korean
Kurd. Kurdish

L
L. Lake
LAIA Latin American Integration Association
Lao. Laotian
Lapp. Lappish
Lat. Latin
Latv. Latvian
Liech. Liechtenstein
Lith. Lithuanian
Lux. Luxembourg

M
m million/metre(s)
Mac. Macedonian
Maced. Macedonia
Mal. Malay
Malg. Malagasy
Malt. Maltese
mi. mile(s)
Mong. Mongolian
Mt. Mountain
Mts Mountains

N
N north
NAFTA North American Free Trade Agreement
Nep. Nepali
Neth. Netherlands
Nic. Nicaraguan
Nor. Norwegian
NZ New Zealand

P
Pash. Pashtu
PNG Papua New Guinea
Pol. Polish
Poly. Polynesian
Port. Portuguese
prev. previously

R
Rep. Republic
Res. Reservoir
Rmsch Romansch
Rom. Romanian
Rus. Russian
Russ. Fed. Russian Federation

S
S south
SADC Southern Africa Development Community
SCr. Serbo-Croatian
Sinh. Sinhala
Slvk Slovak
Slvn. Slovene
Som. Somali
Sp. Spanish
St., St Saint
Strs Straits
Swa. Swahili
Swe. Swedish
Switz. Switzerland

T
Taj. Tajik
Th. Thai
Thai. Thailand
Tib. Tibetan
Turk. Turkish
Turkm. Turkmenistan

U
UAE United Arab Emirates
Uigh. Uighur
UK United Kingdom
Ukr. Ukrainian
UN United Nations
Urd. Urdu
US/USA United States of America
USSR Union of Soviet Socialist Republics
Uzb. Uzbek

V
var. variant
Vdkhr. Vodokhranilishche (Russian for reservoir)
Vdskh. Vodoskhovyshche (Ukrainian for reservoir)
Vtn. Vietnamese

W
W west
Wel. Welsh

Y
Yugo. Yugoslavia

1

56 *E6* **100 Mile House** *var.* Hundred Mile House. British Columbia, SW Canada *51°39′N 121°19′W*
115 *H9* **25 de Agosto** Florida, Uruguay *34°25′S 56°24′W*
25 de Mayo *see* Veinticinco de Mayo, Buenos Aires
25 de Mayo *see* Veinticinco de Mayo, La Pampa
215 *N5* **26 Bakı Komissarı** *Rus.* Imeni 26 Bakinskikh Komissarov. SE Azerbaijan *39°18′N 49°13′E*
26 Baku Komissarlary Adyndaky *see* Uzboý

A

Aa *see* Gauja
155 *D13* **Aabenraa** *var.* Åbenrå, *Ger.* Apenrade. Sønderjylland, SW Denmark *55°03′N 09°26′E*
155 *D10* **Aabybro** *var.* Åbybro. Nordjylland, N Denmark *57°09′N 09°32′E*
181 *A10* **Aachen** *Dut.* Aken, *Fr.* Aix-la-Chapelle; *anc.* Aquae Grani, Aquisgranum. Nordrhein-Westfalen, W Germany *50°47′N 06°06′E*
218 *F4* **Aadchît** Lebanon *33°20′N 35°25′E*
218 *F4* **Aaïtaït** Lebanon *33°33′N 35°40′E*
Aaiún *see* Laâyoune
178 *J3* **Aakirkeby** *var.* Åkirkeby. Bornholm, E Denmark *55°04′N 14°56′E*
218 *G1* **Aakkâr el Aatîga** Lebanon
155 *D11* **Aalborg** *var.* Ålborg, Ålborg-Nørresundby; *anc.* Alburgum. Nordjylland, N Denmark *57°03′N 09°56′E*
Aalborg Bugt *see* Ålborg Bugt
179 *E12* **Aalen** Baden-Württemberg, S Germany *48°50′N 10°06′E*
155 *D11* **Aalestrup** *var.* Ålestrup. Viborg, NW Denmark *56°42′N 09°31′E*
218 *F3* **Aaley** Lebanon *33°48′N 35°35′E*
162 *E6* **Aalsmeer** Noord-Holland, C Netherlands *52°17′N 04°43′E*
163 *D10* **Aalst** Oost-Vlaanderen, C Belgium *50°57′N 04°03′E*
162 *F7* **Aalst** *Fr.* Alost. Noord-Brabant, S Netherlands *51°23′N 05°29′E*
162 *I7* **Aalten** Gelderland, E Netherlands *51°56′N 06°35′E*
163 *C9* **Aalter** Oost-Vlaanderen, NW Belgium *51°05′N 03°28′E*
Aanaar *see* Inari
Aanaarjävri *see* Inarijärvi
141 *H5* **Aandster** North West, South Africa *27°25′S 25°10′E*
153 *H8* **Äänekoski** Länsi-Suomi, W Finland *62°34′N 25°45′E*
218 *G3* **Aanjar** *var.* ʻAnjar. C Lebanon *33°45′N 35°56′E*
218 *G3* **Aanjar** Lebanon *33°43′N 35°55′E*
138 *E7* **Aansluit** Northern Cape, N South Africa *26°41′S 22°24′E*
218 *G2* **Aaqoûra** Lebanon
218 *G2* **Aaqoûra** Lebanon *34°07′N 35°54′E*
Aar *see* Aare
176 *D4* **Aarau** Aargau, N Switzerland *47°22′N 08°00′E*
176 *C4* **Aarberg** Bern, W Switzerland *47°19′N 07°54′E*
163 *C9* **Aardenburg** Zeeland, SW Netherlands *51°16′N 03°27′E*
174 *B3* **Aare** *var.* Aar. River W Switzerland
174 *B2* **Aargau** *Fr.* Argovie. ◆ *canton* N Switzerland
Aarhus *see* Århus
Aarlen *see* Arlon
155 *D11* **Aars** *var.* Års. Nordjylland, N Denmark *56°49′N 09°32′E*
163 *E10* **Aarschot** Vlaams Brabant, C Belgium *50°59′N 04°50′E*
Aassi, Nahr el *see* Orontes
Aat *see* Ath
218 *F3* **Aayoûn es Sîmâne** Lebanon *34°00′N 35°49′E*
239 *K7* **Aba** *prev.* Ngawa. Sichuan, C China *32°51′N 101°46′E*
134 *J6* **Aba** Orientale, NE Dem. Rep. Congo *03°52′N 30°14′E*
133 *K8* **Aba** Abia, S Nigeria *05°06′N 07°22′E*
220 *D3* **Abā al Qazāz, Bi'r** *well* NW Saudi Arabia
Abā as Suʻūd *see* Najrān
107 *H4* **Abacaxis, Rio** River NW Brazil
Abaco Island *see* Great Abaco/Little Abaco
Abaco Island *see* Great Abaco, N Bahamas
222 *D6* **Ābādān** Khūzestān, SW Iran *30°24′N 48°18′E*
228 *D7* **Abadan** *prev.* Bezmein, Büzmeýin, *Rus.* Byuzmeyin. Ahal Welaýaty, C Turkmenistan *38°08′N 57°53′E*
222 *F6* **Ābādeh** Fārs, C Iran *31°06′N 52°40′E*
130 *G4* **Abadla** W Algeria *31°04′N 02°39′W*
110 *E1* **Abaeté** Minas Gerais, SE Brazil *19°10′S 45°24′W*
113 *H5* **Abaí** Caazapá, S Paraguay *25°58′S 55°54′W*
Abai *see* Blue Nile
284 *B2* **Abaiang** *var.* Apia; *prev.* Charlotte Island. *atoll* Tungaru, W Kiribati
Abaj *see* Abay
133 *K7* **Abaji** Federal Capital District, C Nigeria *08°35′N 06°54′E*
79 *J5* **Abajo Peak** ▲ Utah, W USA *37°51′N 109°28′W*
133 *K8* **Abakaliki** Ebonyi, SE Nigeria *06°18′N 08°07′E*
192 *G8* **Abakan** Respublika Khakasiya, S Russian Federation *53°43′N 91°25′E*
227 *N1* **Abakan** River S Russian Federation
133 *I4* **Abala** Tillabéri, SW Niger *14°55′N 03°27′E*
133 *J4* **Abalak** Tahoua, C Niger *15°28′N 06°18′E*
191 *H8* **Abalyanka** *Rus.* Obolyanka. River N Belarus
192 *G7* **Aban** Krasnoyarskiy Kray, S Russian Federation *56°41′N 96°04′E*
222 *G6* **Āb Anbār-e Kān Sorkh** Yazd, C Iran *31°22′N 53°38′E*
105 *F8* **Abancay** Apurímac, SE Peru *13°37′S 72°52′W*
173 *K6* **Abanilla** Murcia, Spain *38°12′N 1°03′W*
284 *D1* **Abaokoro** *atoll* Tungaru, W Kiribati
Abariringa *see* Kanton
222 *G6* **Abarkūh** Yazd, C Iran *31°07′N 53°17′E*
252 *G3* **Abashiri** *var.* Abasiri. Hokkaidō, NE Japan *44°N 144°15′E*
252 *G3* **Abashiri-gawa** River Hokkaidō, NE Japan
252 *G3* **Abashiri-ko** Lake Hokkaidō, NE Japan
Abasiri *see* Abashiri
87 *K8* **Abasolo** Chiapas, Mexico *16°48′N 92°10′W*
85 *K5* **Abasolo** Guanajuato, Mexico
85 *M7* **Abasolo** Tamaulipas, C Mexico *24°02′N 98°18′W*
87 *H8* **Abasolo del Valle** Veracruz-Llave, Mexico *17°46′N 95°30′W*
280 *C4* **Abau** Central, S Papua New Guinea *10°04′S 148°34′E*
227 *I4* **Abay** *var.* Abaj. Karaganda, C Kazakhstan *49°38′N 72°50′E*
136 *D5* **Ābaya Hāyk'** *Eng.* Lake Margherita, *It.* Abbaia. Lake SW Ethiopia
Ābay Wenz *see* Blue Nile
192 *G8* **Abaza** Respublika Khakasiya, S Russian Federation *52°40′N 89°58′E*
Abbaia *see* Ābaya Hāyk'
222 *G8* **Āb Bārīk** Fārs, S Iran
175 *B10* **Abbasanta** Sardegna, Italy, C Mediterranean Sea *40°08′N 08°49′E*
Abbatis Villa *see* Abbeville
72 *D4* **Abbaye, Point** *headland* Michigan, N USA *46°58′N 88°08′W*
Abbazia *see* Opatija
Abbé, Lake *see* Abhe, Lake
165 *H2* **Abbeville** *anc.* Abbatis Villa. Somme, N France *50°06′N 01°50′E*
69 *I3* **Abbeville** Alabama, S USA *31°35′N 85°16′W*
69 *K2* **Abbeville** Georgia, SE USA *31°58′N 83°18′W*
68 *C4* **Abbeville** Louisiana, S USA *29°58′N 92°08′W*
67 *H8* **Abbeville** South Carolina, SE USA *34°10′N 82°23′W*
157 *B10* **Abbeyfeale** *Ir.* Mainistir na Féile. SW Ireland *52°24′N 09°21′W*
160 *A2* **Abbeyleix** Laois, Ireland *52°54′N 7°21′W*
176 *E7* **Abbiategrasso** Lombardia, NW Italy *45°24′N 08°55′E*
154 *J1* **Abborrträsk** Norrbotten, N Sweden *65°24′N 19°33′E*
292 *F5* **Abbot Ice Shelf** *ice shelf* Antarctica
160 *G8* **Abbotsbury** United Kingdom *50°40′N 2°36′W*
140 *D9* **Abbotsdale** Western Cape, South Africa *33°29′S 18°40′E*
76 *C2* **Abbotsford** British Columbia, SW Canada *49°02′N 122°18′W*
72 *C5* **Abbotsford** Wisconsin, N USA *44°57′N 90°19′W*
231 *I4* **Abbottābād** Khyber Pakhtunkhwa, NW Pakistan *34°12′N 73°15′E*
191 *H9* **Abchuha** *Rus.* Obchuga. Minskaya Voblasts', NW Belarus *54°30′N 29°22′E*
162 *F6* **Abcoude** Utrecht, C Netherlands *52°17′N 04°59′E*
216 *F2* **ʻAbd al ʻAzīz, Jabal** ▲▲ NE Syria
221 *I9* **ʻAbd al Kūrī** *island* SE Yemen
197 *K3* **Abdulino** Orenburgskaya Oblast', W Russian Federation *53°37′N 53°39′E*
134 *F2* **Abéché** *var.* Abécher, Abeshr. Ouaddaï, SE Chad *13°49′N 20°49′E*
Abécher *see* Abéché
223 *I5* **Āb-e Garm va Sard** Yazd, E Iran
133 *I2* **Abeïbara** Kidal, NE Mali *19°07′N 01°52′E*
171 *H3* **Abejar** Castilla-León, N Spain *41°48′N 02°47′W*
102 *B5* **Abejorral** Antioquia, W Colombia *05°48′N 75°28′W*
Abela *see* Ávila
141 *K3* **Abel Erasmuspas** *pass* Limpopo, South Africa
Abellinum *see* Avellino
152 *C5* **Abeløya** *island* Kong Karls Land, E Svalbard
136 *D4* **Ābeltī** Oromīya, C Ethiopia *08°09′N 37°31′E*
284 *B3* **Abemama** *var.* Apamama; *prev.* Roger Simpson Island. *atoll* Tungaru, W Kiribati
261 *L7* **Abemaree** *var.* Abermarre. Papua, E Indonesia *07°03′S 140°10′E*
181 *J13* **Abenberg** Bayern, Germany *49°15′N 10°58′E*
132 *G8* **Abengourou** E Ivory Coast *06°42′N 03°27′W*
172 *G5* **Abenójar** Castilla-La Manacha, Spain *38°53′N 4°21′W*
Åbenrå *see* Aabenraa
179 *G12* **Abens** River SE Germany
133 *I7* **Abeokuta** Ogun, SW Nigeria *07°07′N 03°21′E*
160 *E4* **Aberaeron** SW Wales, United Kingdom *52°15′N 04°15′W*
Aberbrothock *see* Arbroath
Abercorn *see* Mbala
74 *E3* **Abercrombie** North Dakota, N USA *46°25′N 96°42′W*
160 *F6* **Aberdare** United Kingdom *51°43′N 3°27′W*
160 *D3* **Aberdaron** United Kingdom *52°49′N 4°42′W*
277 *L4* **Aberdeen** New South Wales, SE Australia *32°09′S 150°55′E*
57 *M6* **Aberdeen** Saskatchewan, S Canada *52°15′N 106°19′W*
138 *F9* **Aberdeen** Eastern Cape, S South Africa *32°30′S 24°00′E*
156 *G5* **Aberdeen** *anc.* Devana. NE Scotland, United Kingdom *57°10′N 02°04′W*
64 *E9* **Aberdeen** Maryland, NE USA *39°28′N 76°09′W*
66 *C8* **Aberdeen** Mississippi, S USA *33°49′N 88°32′W*
67 *J7* **Aberdeen** North Carolina, SE USA *35°07′N 79°25′W*
74 *D4* **Aberdeen** South Dakota, N USA *45°27′N 98°29′W*
76 *B4* **Aberdeen** Washington, NW USA *46°57′N 123°48′W*
140 *G8* **Aberdeen Kendrew** Eastern Cape, South Africa *32°33′S 24°33′E*
55 *I3* **Aberdeen Lake** Lake Nunavut, NE Canada
140 *G9* **Aberdeen Road** Eastern Cape, South Africa *32°45′S 24°19′E*
160 *E3* **Aberdyfi** United Kingdom *52°33′N 4°02′W*
159 *H1* **Aberfeldy** C Scotland, United Kingdom *56°38′N 03°49′W*
160 *E2* **Aberffraw** United Kingdom *53°11′N 4°27′W*
158 *G2* **Aberfoyle** United Kingdom *56°11′N 4°23′W*
160 *G5* **Abergavenny** *anc.* Gobannium. SE Wales, United Kingdom *51°50′N 03°W*
160 *E5* **Abergorlech** United Kingdom *51°59′N 4°04′W*
Abergwaun *see* Fishguard
159 *I3* **Aberlady** United Kingdom *56°00′N 2°51′W*
Abermarre *see* Abemaree
70 *D3* **Abernathy** Texas, SW USA *33°49′N 101°50′W*
159 *I2* **Abernethy** C Scotland, United Kingdom
160 *E4* **Aberporth** United Kingdom *52°08′N 4°33′W*
Abersee *see* Wolfgangsee
160 *E3* **Abersoch** United Kingdom *52°49′N 4°30′W*
Abertawe *see* Swansea
Aberteifi *see* Cardigan
160 *G6* **Abertillery** United Kingdom *51°44′N 3°08′W*
76 *D8* **Abert, Lake** Lake Oregon, NW USA
160 *E4* **Aberystwyth** W Wales, United Kingdom *52°25′N 04°05′W*
Abeshr *see* Abéché
Ábeskovvu *see* Abisko
176 *G9* **Abetone** Toscana, C Italy *44°09′N 10°42′E*
195 *L4* **Abez'** Respublika Komi, NW Russian Federation *66°32′N 61°41′E*
222 *E3* **Āb Garm** Qazvin, N Iran
220 *F7* **Abhā** ʻAsīr, SW Saudi Arabia *18°16′N 42°32′E*
222 *E3* **Abhar** Zanjān, NW Iran *36°05′N 49°18′E*
Abhé Bad/Ābhē Bid Hāyk' *see* Abhe, Lake
136 *F3* **Abhe, Lake** *var.* Lake Abbé, *Amh.* Ābhē Bid Hāyk', *Som.* Abhé Bad. Lake Djibouti/Ethiopia
133 *J7* **Abia** ◆ *state* SE Nigeria
217 *K6* **ʻAbīd ʻAlī** Wāsiţ, E Iraq *32°20′N 45°58′E*
191 *I10* **Abidavichy** *Rus.* Obidovichi. Mahilyowskaya Voblasts', E Belarus *53°20′N 30°25′E*
187 *J3* **Abide** Çanakkale, NW Turkey *40°04′N 26°13′E*
132 *F8* **Abidjan** S Ivory Coast *05°19′N 04°01′W*
140 *E5* **Abierkwasputs** *salt lake* Northern Cape, South Africa
Āb-i-Istāda *see* Īstādeh-ye Moqor, Āb-e-
218 *F6* **Abila** Jordan
75 *E9* **Abilene** Kansas, C USA *38°55′N 97°14′W*
70 *F4* **Abilene** Texas, SW USA *32°27′N 99°44′W*
Abindonia *see* Abingdon
161 *I6* **Abingdon** *anc.* Abindonia. S England, United Kingdom *51°41′N 01°17′W*
73 *B10* **Abingdon** Illinois, N USA *40°48′N 90°24′W*
67 *H5* **Abingdon** Virginia, NE USA *36°42′N 81°59′W*
Abingdon *see* Pinta, Isla
65 *M3* **Abington** Massachusetts, USA *42°06′N 70°57′W*
64 *F7* **Abington** Pennsylvania, NE USA *40°06′N 75°05′W*
196 *F8* **Abinsk** Krasnodarskiy Kray, SW Russian Federation *44°51′N 38°12′E*
79 *L6* **Abiquiu Reservoir** Reservoir New Mexico, SW USA
Āb-i-safed *see* Sefīd, Darya-ye
152 *F5* **Abisko** *Lapp.* Ábeskovvu. Norrbotten, N Sweden *68°21′N 18°50′E*
51 *J8* **Abitibi** River Ontario, S Canada
58 *F7* **Abitibi, Lac** Lake Ontario/Québec, S Canada
136 *E2* **Ābīy Ādī** Tigray, N Ethiopia *13°40′N 38°57′E*
190 *E5* **Abja-Paluoja** Viljandimaa, S Estonia *58°08′N 25°20′E*
Abkhazia *see* Ap'khazet'i
173 *I8* **Abla** Andalucía, Spain *37°08′N 2°47′W*
276 *E1* **Abminga** South Australia *26°07′S 134°49′E*
129 *I4* **Abnūb** *var.* Abnûb. C Egypt *27°18′N 31°09′E*
Abnûb *see* Abnūb
Åbo *see* Turku
232 *D4* **Abohar** Punjab, N India *30°11′N 74°14′E*
132 *G8* **Aboisso** SE Ivory Coast *05°26′N 03°13′W*
133 *N1* **Abo, Massif d'** ▲▲ NW Chad
133 *I7* **Abomey** S Benin *07°14′N 02°00′E*
167 *M10* **Abondance** Rhône-Alpes, France *46°17′N 6°44′E*
134 *C6* **Abong Mbang** Est, SE Cameroon *03°58′N 13°10′E*
183 *G12* **Abony** Pest, C Hungary *47°10′N 20°00′E*
134 *E3* **Abou-Déïa** Salamat, SE Chad *11°30′N 19°18′E*
Aboudouhour *see* Abū aḑ Ḑuhūr
Abou Kémal *see* Abū Kamāl
Abou Simbel *see* Abū Sunbul
215 *K5* **Abovyan** C Armenia *40°16′N 44°33′E*
263 *K4* **Abra** River Luzon, N Philippines
129 *N9* **Abrād, Wādī** *seasonal river* W Yemen
Abraham Bay *see* The Carlton
118 *C6* **Abranquil** Maule, Chile *35°45′S 71°33′W*
172 *C4* **Abrantes** *var.* Abrántes. Santarém, C Portugal *39°28′N 08°12′W*
112 *D3* **Abra Pampa** Jujuy, N Argentina *22°47′S 65°41′W*
Abrashlare *see* Brezovo
111 *J3* **Abre Campo** Minas Gerais, Brazil *20°18′S 42°29′W*
102 *C4* **Abrego** Norte de Santander, N Colombia *08°08′N 73°14′W*
Abrene *see* Pytalovo
84 *C6* **Abreojos, Punta** *headland* NW Mexico *26°43′N 113°36′W*
169 *M3* **Abriés** Provence-Alpes-Côte d'Azur, France *44°47′N 6°56′E*
115 *J4* **Abrojal** Rivera, Uruguay *31°45′S 55°01′W*
98 *G5* **Abrolhos Bank** *undersea feature* W Atlantic Ocean *18°30′S 38°45′W*
191 *E11* **Abrova** *Rus.* Obrovo. Brestskaya Voblasts', SW Belarus *52°30′N 25°34′E*
188 *C7* **Abrud** *Ger.* Gross-Schlatten, *Hung.* Abrudbánya. Alba, SW Romania *46°16′N 23°05′E*
Abrudbánya *see* Abrud
190 *C5* **Abruka** *island* SW Estonia
175 *F8* **Abruzzese, Appennino** ▲▲ C Italy
175 *G8* **Abruzzo** ◆ *region* C Italy
220 *F8* **ʻAbs** *var.* Sūq ʻAbs. W Yemen *16°42′N 42°55′E*
77 *J6* **Absaroka Range** ▲▲ Montana/Wyoming, NW USA
64 *G9* **Absecon** New Jersey, USA *39°26′N 74°30′W*
215 *N4* **Abşeron Yarımadası** *Rus.* Apsheronskiy Poluostrov. *peninsula* E Azerbaijan
222 *F4* **Āb Shīrīn** Eşfahān, C Iran *34°17′N 51°17′E*
217 *L7* **Abtān** Maysān, SE Iraq *31°37′N 47°06′E*
177 *I3* **Abtenau** Salzburg, NW Austria *47°33′N 13°21′E*
232 *C7* **Ābu** Rājasthān, N India *24°41′N 72°50′E*
250 *D5* **Abu** Yamaguchi, Honshū, SW Japan *34°30′N 131°26′E*
216 *D3* **Abū aḑ Ḑuhūr** *Fr.* Aboudouhour. Idlib, NW Syria *35°30′N 37°00′E*
221 *J4* **Abū al Abyaḑ** *island* C United Arab Emirates
218 *H3* **Abū al ʻAţā, Jabal** ▲▲ Syria
216 *E6* **Abū al Ḩuşayn, Khabrat** Lake N Jordan
217 *I5* **Abū al Jīr** Al Anbār, C Iraq *33°16′N 42°55′E*
217 *M8* **Abū al Khaşīb** *var.* Abul Khasib. Al Başrah, SE Iraq *30°26′N 48°00′E*
217 *K8* **Abū at Tubrah, Thaqb** *well* S Iraq
219 *B11* **Abu Aweigila** Egypt *30°50′N 34°07′E*
Abu Balâs *see* Abu Ballās
129 *H5* **Abu Ballās** *var.* Abu Balâs. ▲ SW Egypt *24°28′N 27°36′E*
Abu Dhabi *see* Abū Z̧abī
217 *I5* **Abū Farūkh** Al Anbār, C Iraq *33°06′N 43°18′E*
134 *H3* **Abu Gabra** Southern Darfur, W Sudan *11°02′N 26°50′E*
217 *H6* **Abū Ghār, Shaʻīb** *dry watercourse* S Iraq
129 *J8* **Abu Hamed** River Nile, N Sudan *19°32′N 33°20′E*
216 *G4* **Abū Ḩardān** *var.* Hajîne. Dayr az Zawr, E Syria *34°45′N 40°49′E*
217 *J5* **Abū Ḩasāwīyah** Diyālá, E Iraq *33°52′N 44°47′E*
216 *E6* **Abū Ḩifnah, Wādī** *dry watercourse* N Jordan
133 *K7* **Abuja** ● (Nigeria) Federal Capital District, C Nigeria *09°04′N 07°28′E*
217 *I6* **Abū Jahaf, Wādī** *dry watercourse* C Iraq
104 *E5* **Abujao, Río** River E Peru
217 *J8* **Abū Jasrah** Al Muthanná, S Iraq *30°43′N 44°50′E*
219 *F12* **Abū Jurdhān** Jordan
216 *G4* **Abū Kamāl** *Fr.* Abou Kémal. Dayr az Zawr, E Syria *34°29′N 40°56′E*
260 *D5* **Abuki, Pegunungan** ▲▲ Sulawesi, C Indonesia
253 *D11* **Abukuma-gawa** River Honshū, C Japan
253 *D11* **Abukuma-sanchi** ▲▲ Honshū, C Japan
Abula *see* Ávila
Abul Khasib *see* Abū al Khaşīb
134 *F6* **Abumombazi** *var.* Abumonbazi. Equateur, N Dem. Rep. Congo *03°43′N 22°06′E*
Abumonbazi *see* Abumombazi
106 *E6* **Abunā** Rondônia, W Brazil *09°41′S 65°20′W*
106 *D7* **Abunā, Rio** *var.* Río Abuná. River Bolivia/Brazil
219 *G8* **Abū Nuşayr** *var.* Abu Nuseir. ʻAmmān, W Jordan *32°03′N 35°58′E*
219 *G8* **Abū Nuşayr** Jordan *32°05′N 35°52′E*
Abu Nuseir *see* Abū Nuşayr
217 *J8* **Abū Qabr** Al Muthanná, S Iraq *31°03′N 44°34′E*
218 *I2* **Abu Raḩbah** Syria *34°26′N 37°12′E*
216 *E4* **Abū Raḩbah, Jabal** ▲▲ C Syria
217 *I4* **Abū Rajāsh** Şalāḩ ad Dīn, N Iraq *34°47′N 43°36′E*
217 *K8* **Abū Raqrāq, Ghadīr** *well* S Iraq
232 *C7* **Ābu Road** Rājasthān, N India *24°29′N 72°47′E*
136 *E1* **Abu Shagara, Ras** *headland* NE Sudan *18°04′N 38°31′E*
129 *I6* **Abu Simbel** *var.* Abu Sūnbul. *headland* Egypt
Abu Simbel *see* Abū Sunbul
217 *K8* **Abū Sudayrah** Al Muthanná, S Iraq *30°55′N 44°58′E*
217 *J7* **Abū Şukhayr** Al Qādisīyah, S Iraq *31°54′N 44°27′E*
Abū Sunbul *see* Abū Sunbul
Abu Sūnbul *see* Abu Simbel
252 *D5* **Abuta** Hokkaidō, NE Japan *42°34′N 140°44′E*
219 *G12* **Abū Ţarafah, Wādī** *dry watercourse* Jordan
279 *C9* **Abut Head** *headland* South Island, New Zealand *43°06′S 170°16′E*
136 *A1* **Abu ʻUrug** Northern Kordofan, C Sudan *15°52′N 30°25′E*
136 *E4* **Ābuyē Mēda** ▲ C Ethiopia *10°28′N 39°44′E*
263 *M7* **Abuyog** Leyte, C Philippines *10°45′N 124°58′E*
134 *J2* **Abu Zabad** Western Kordofan, C Sudan *12°21′N 29°16′E*
221 *J4* **Abū Z̧abī** *var.* Abū Z̧abī, *Eng.* Abu Dhabi. ● (United Arab Emirates) Abū Z̧aby, C United Arab Emirates *24°30′N 54°20′E*
Abū Z̧abī *see* Abū Z̧abī
129 *J3* **Abu Zenîma** E Egypt *29°01′N 33°08′E*
155 *H9* **Åby** Östergötland, S Sweden *58°40′N 16°10′E*
Abyaḑ, Al Baḩr al *see* White Nile
Åbybro *see* Aabybro
134 *I3* **Abyei** Western Kordofan, S Sudan *09°35′N 28°28′E*
Abyla *see* Ávila
Abymes *see* les Abymes
Abyssinia *see* Ethiopia
Açâba *see* Assaba
102 *C6* **Acacias** Meta, C Colombia *03°59′N 73°46′W*
55 *L3* **Acadia, Cape** *headland* Nunavut, C Canada
111 *I3* **Acaiaca** Minas Gerais, Brazil *20°21′S 43°09′W*
108 *C4* **Açailândia** Maranhão, E Brazil *04°51′S 47°26′W*
Acaill *see* Achill Island
88 *C5* **Acajutla** Sonsonate, W El Salvador *13°34′N 89°50′W*
172 *E7* **Acalá del Río** Andalucía, Spain *37°31′N 5°59′W*
134 *A7* **Acalayong** SW Equatorial Guinea *01°05′N 09°34′E*
86 *E6* **Acámbaro** Guanajuato, C Mexico *20°01′N 100°42′W*
86 *E6* **Acambay** México, Mexico *19°57′N 99°51′W*
102 *A4* **Acandí** Chocó, NW Colombia *08°32′N 77°20′W*
170 *C3* **A Cañiza** *var.* La Cañiza. Galicia, NW Spain *42°13′N 08°16′W*
86 *B3* **Acaponeta** Nayarit, C Mexico *22°30′N 105°21′W*
85 *I8* **Acaponeta, Río de** River C Mexico
86 *E8* **Acapulco** *var.* Acapulco de Juárez. Guerrero, S Mexico *16°51′N 99°53′W*
Acapulco de Juárez *see* Acapulco
103 *J7* **Acarai Mountains** *Sp.* Serra Acaraí. ▲▲ Brazil/Guyana
Acaraí, Serra *see* Acarai Mountains
108 *G3* **Acaraú** Ceará, NE Brazil *04°35′S 37°37′W*
102 *E3* **Acarigua** Portuguesa, N Venezuela *09°35′N 69°12′W*
170 *D1* **A Carreira** Galicia, NW Spain *43°21′N 08°12′W*
86 *F7* **Acatepec** Puebla, Mexico *19°02′N 98°17′W*
86 *F5* **Acatepec** Puebla, Mexico
85 *M7* **Acatlán** Jalisco, W Mexico *23°58′N 99°08′W*
87 *H7* **Acatlán** Oaxaca, Mexico *18°32′N 96°37′W*
86 *F7* **Acatlán** *var.* Acatlán de Osorio. Puebla, S Mexico *18°12′N 98°02′W*
86 *C5* **Acatlán de Juárez** Jalisco, Mexico *20°25′N 103°35′W*
Acatlán de Osorio *see* Acatlán
87 *I7* **Acayucan** *var.* Acayucán. Veracruz-Llave, E Mexico *17°59′N 94°58′W*
Accho *see* Akko
67 *M4* **Accomac** Virginia, NE USA *37°43′N 75°41′N*
168 *D6* **Accous** Aquitaine, France *42°59′N 0°36′W*
133 *H8* **Accra** ● (Ghana)SE Ghana *05°33′N 00°15′W*
159 *J9* **Accrington** NW England, United Kingdom *53°46′N 02°21′W*
114 *B7* **Acebal** Santa Fe, C Argentina *33°14′S 60°50′W*
115 *K4* **Aceguá** Rio Grande du Sol, S Brazil *31°52′S 54°12′W*
115 *K4* **Acegua** Cerro Largo, Uruguay *31°48′S 54°18′W*
258 *C3* **Aceh** *off.* Daerah Istimewa Aceh, *var.* Acheen, Achin, Atchin, Atjeh. ◆ *autonomous district* NW Indonesia

◆ Country
● Country Capital
◇ Dependent Territory
○ Dependent Territory Capital
◆ Administrative Regions
✈ International Airport
▲ Mountain
▲▲ Mountain Range
Volcano
River
Lake
Reservoir

INDEX

◆ Country   ◇ Dependent Territory   ✕ Administrative Regions   ▲ Mountain   ✦ Volcano   ◎ Lake
● Country Capital   ○ Dependent Territory Capital   ✈ International Airport   ▲ Mountain Range   ♒ River   ◙ Reservoir

◆ Country   ◇ Dependent Territory   ◆ Administrative Regions   ▲ Mountain   ⊙ Volcano   ⊜ Lake
● Country Capital   ○ Dependent Territory Capital   ✕ International Airport   ▲ Mountain Range   ✆ River   ◻ Reservoir

Altsohl – Angles-sur-l'Anglin
INDEX
310

Altsohl *see* Zvolen
Álttesjávri *see* Altevatnet
88 E1 **Altun Ha** *ruins* Belize, N Belize
Altun Kupri *see* Altin Köprü
239 H5 **Altun Shan** ▲ C China 39°19´N 93°37´E
236 C5 **Altun Shan** *var.* Altyn Tagh. ▲▲ NW China
78 C1 **Alturas** California, W USA 41°28´N 120°32´W
75 C13 **Altus** Oklahoma, C USA 34°39´N 99°21´W
75 C13 **Altus Lake** ⊠ Oklahoma, C USA
Altvater *see* Praděd
Altyn Tagh *see* Altun Shan
Alu *see* Shortland Island
al-'Ubaila *see* Al 'Ubaylah
216 G4 **Al 'Ubaydī** Al Anbār, W Iraq 34°22´N 41°15´E
221 I5 **Al 'Ubaylah** *var.* al-'Ubaila. Ash Sharqīyah, E Saudi Arabia 22°02´N 50°57´E
221 I5 **Al 'Ubaylah** *spring/well* E Saudi Arabia 22°02´N 50°56´E
Al Ubayyiḍ *see* El Obeid
221 I4 **Al 'Udayd** *var.* Al Odaid. Abū Ẓaby, W United Arab Emirates 24°34´N 51°27´E
190 F6 **Alūksne** *Ger.* Marienburg. Alūksne, NE Latvia 57°26´N 27°02´E
220 D3 **Al 'Ulā** Al Madīnah, NW Saudi Arabia 26°39´N 37°55´E
288 D6 **Alula-Fartak Trench** *var.* Illaue Fartak Trench. *undersea feature* W Indian Ocean 14°04´N 51°47´E
219 I9 **Al 'Umarī** 'Ammān, E Jordan 37°30´N 31°30´E
219 I9 **Al Umarī** Jordan 31°32´N 37°04´E
73 I10 **Alum Creek Lake** ⊠ Ohio, N USA
116 C6 **Aluminé** Neuquén, C Argentina 39°15´S 71°00´W
118 D10 **Alumine, Lago** ⊛ Neuquén, Argentina
154 I7 **Alunda** Uppsala, C Sweden 60°04´N 18°04´E
189 J10 **Alupka** Avtonomna Respublika Krym, S Ukraine 44°24´N 34°01´E
128 D3 **Al 'Uqaylah** N Libya 30°13´N 19°12´E
Al Uqşur *see* Luxor
Al Urdunn *see* Jordan
258 D4 **Alur Panal** *bay* Sumatera, W Indonesia
Alur Setar *see* Alor Setar
221 J6 **Al 'Urūq al Mu'tariḍah** *salt lake* SE Saudi Arabia
217 H4 **Ālūs** Al Anbār, C Iraq 34°05´N 42°27´E
189 K9 **Alushta** Avtonomna Respublika Krym, S Ukraine 44°41´N 34°24´E
128 B5 **Al 'Uwaynāt** *var.* Al Awaynāt. SW Libya 25°47´N 10°34´E
217 J4 **Al 'Uẓaym** *var.* Adhaim. Diyālá, E Iraq 34°12´N 44°31´E
75 D11 **Alva** Oklahoma, C USA 36°48´N 98°40´W
170 D5 **Alva** ≈ N Portugal
155 F10 **Älvängen** Västra Götaland, S Sweden 57°56´N 12°09´E
62 C4 **Alvanley** Ontario, S Canada 44°33´N 81°05´W
87 H7 **Alvarado** Veracruz-Llave, E Mexico 18°47´N 95°45´W
71 H5 **Alvarado** Texas, SW USA 32°24´N 97°12´W
87 H7 **Alvarado, Laguna** *inlet* E Mexico
106 E3 **Alvarães** Amazonas, NW Brazil 03°13´S 64°53´W
114 B7 **Álvarez** Santa Fe, Argentina 33°08´S 60°48´W
85 H4 **Álvaro Obregón** Chihuahua, Mexico 28°45´N 106°52´W
87 J7 **Álvaro Obregón** Tabasco, Mexico 18°35´N 92°39´W
84 F5 **Álvaro Obregón, Presa** ⊠ W Mexico
154 E5 **Alvdal** Hedmark, S Norway 62°07´N 10°39´E
154 G6 **Älvdalen** Dalarna, C Sweden 61°13´N 14°04´E
113 H7 **Alvear** Corrientes, NE Argentina 29°05´S 56°35´W
161 H4 **Alvechurch** United Kingdom 52°20´N 1°57´W
172 B5 **Alverca do Ribatejo** Lisboa, C Portugal 38°56´N 09°01´W
180 G7 **Alverdissen** Nordrhein-Westfalen, Germany 52°02´E 9°08´N
155 G11 **Alvesta** Kronoberg, S Sweden 56°52´N 14°34´E
161 I4 **Alveston** United Kingdom 52°12´N 1°39´W
172 B4 **Alviela, Rio** ≈ Santarém, Portugal
71 I7 **Alvin** Texas, SW USA 29°25´N 95°14´W
111 I3 **Alvinópolis** Minas Gerais, Brazil 20°06´S 43°03´W
154 I6 **Älvkarleby** Uppsala, C Sweden 60°34´N 17°30´E
70 G4 **Alvord** Texas, SW USA 33°22´N 97°39´W
154 G5 **Älvros** Jämtland, C Sweden 62°04´N 14°30´E
152 G6 **Älvsbyn** Norrbotten, N Sweden 65°41´N 21°00´E
217 M10 **Al Wafrā'** SE Kuwait 28°38´N 47°57´E
220 D3 **Al Wajh** Tabūk, NW Saudi Arabia 26°16´N 36°30´E
221 I4 **Al Wakrah** *var.* Wakra. C Qatar 25°09´N 51°36´E
216 F5 **al Walaj, Sha'īb** *dry watercourse* W Iraq
232 E6 **Alwar** Rājasthān, N India 27°32´N 76°35´E
220 G3 **Al Warī'ah** Ash Sharqīyah, N Saudi Arabia 27°54´N 47°23´E
235 D9 **Alwaye** *var.* Aluva. Kerala, SW India 10°06´N 76°23´E *see also* Aluva
160 F2 **Alwen, Llyn** ⊛ United Kingdom
Alxa Zuoqi *see* Bayan Hot
Alx Youqi *see* Ehen Hudag
Al Yaman *see* Yemen
218 F6 **Al Yarmūk** Irbid, N Jordan 32°41´N 35°55´E
Alyat/Alyaty-Pristan' *see* Älät
187 I3 **Alykí** *var.* Aliki. Thásos, N Greece 40°36´N 24°45´E
159 I1 **Alyth** United Kingdom 56°37´N 3°13´W
191 D9 **Alytus** *Pol.* Olita. Alytus, S Lithuania 54°24´N 24°02´E
191 D9 **Alytus** ⬖ *province* S Lithuania
179 H13 **Alz** ≈ SE Germany
86 C6 **Alzada** Colima, Mexico 19°15´N 103°31´W
77 M6 **Alzada** Montana, NW USA 45°00´N 104°24´W
193 H7 **Alzamay** Irkutskaya Oblast', S Russian Federation 55°33´N 98°36´E
181 G11 **Alzenau** Bayern, Germany 50°05´E 9°04´N
163 H14 **Alzette** ≈ S Luxembourg
181 E12 **Alzey** Rheinland-Pfalz, Germany 49°45´E 8°07´N
171 I6 **Alzira** *var.* Alcira ; *anc.* Saetabicula, Suero. País Valenciano, E Spain 39°10´N 00°27´W
169 I5 **Alzon** Languedoc-Roussillon, France 43°58´N 3°26´E
168 G6 **Alzonne** Languedoc-Roussillon, France 43°16´N 2°11´E
Al Zubair *see* Az Zubayr
274 G5 **Amadeus, Lake** *seasonal lake* Northern Territory, C Australia
136 A5 **Amadi** Western Equatoria, S South Sudan 05°32´N 30°20´E
55 M1 **Amadjuak Lake** ⊛ Baffin Island, Nunavut, N Canada
80 D3 **Amador City** California, USA 38°25´N 120°49´W
155 F12 **Amager** *island* E Denmark
250 C6 **Amagi** *var.* Asakura. Fukuoka, Kyūshū, SW Japan 33°28´N 130°37´E
251 L4 **Amagi-san** ▲ Honshū, S Japan 34°51´N 138°57´E
260 G5 **Amahai** *var.* Masohi. Palau Seram, E Indonesia 03°19´S 128°56´E
82 G9 **Amak Island** *island* Alaska, USA
250 C7 **Amakusa-nada** *gulf* SW Japan
155 F8 **Åmål** Västra Götaland, S Sweden 59°04´N 12°41´E
102 C4 **Amalfi** Antioquia, N Colombia 06°54´N 75°04´W
175 G9 **Amalfi** Campania, S Italy 40°37´N 14°35´E
141 H5 **Amalia** North-West, South Africa 27°15´S 25°03´E
186 F6 **Amaliáda** *var.* Amaliás. Dytikí Elláda, S Greece 37°48´N 21°21´E
Amaliás *see* Amaliáda
234 D4 **Amalner** Mahārāshtra, C India 21°03´N 75°04´E
261 K6 **Amamapare** Papua, E Indonesia 04°51´S 136°44´E
113 H3 **Amambaí, Serra de** *var.* Cordillera de Amambay, Serra de Amambay. ▲ Brazil/Paraguay *see also* Amambay, Cordillera de
113 H3 **Amambay** *off.* Departamento del Amambay. ⬖ *department* E Paraguay
113 H3 **Amambay, Cordillera de** *var.* Serra de Amambaí, Serra de Amambay. ▲ Brazil/Paraguay *see also* Amambaí, Serra de
Amambay, Departamento del *see* Amambay
Amambay, Serra de *see* Amambaí, Serra de/Amambay, Cordillera de
251 J9 **Amami-guntō** *island group* SW Japan
251 K9 **Amami-Ō-shima** *island* S Japan
280 A2 **Amanab** Sandaun, NW Papua New Guinea 03°38´S 141°16´E
167 L7 **Amance** Franche-Comté, France 47°48´N 6°04´E
167 L9 **Amancey** Franche-Comté, France 47°02´N 6°05´E
177 J10 **Amandola** Marche, C Italy 42°58´N 13°22´E
175 H11 **Amantea** Calabria, SW Italy 39°06´N 16°05´E
285 K7 **Amanu** *island* Îles Tuamotu, C French Polynesia
141 K7 **Amanzimtoti** Kwazulu Natal, South Africa 30°03´S 30°53´E
Amanzimtoti *see* eManzimtoti
108 A1 **Amapá** Amapá, NE Brazil 02°00´N 50°50´W
108 A1 **Amapá** *off.* Estado de Amapá; *prev.* Território de Amapá. ⬖ *state* NE Brazil
Amapá, Estado de *see* Amapá
88 E5 **Amapala** Valle, S Honduras 13°16´N 87°39´W
Amapá, Território de *see* Amapá
136 E3 **Āmara** *var.* Amhara. ⬖ N Ethiopia
Amara *see* Al 'Amārah
172 C1 **Amarante** Porto, N Portugal 41°16´N 08°05´W
256 C4 **Amarapura** Mandalay, C Myanmar (Burma) 21°54´N 96°01´E
Amardalay *see* Delgertsogt
172 D6 **Amareleja** Beja, S Portugal 38°12´N 07°13´W
81 H8 **Amargosa Desert** *plain* Nevada, USA
81 H8 **Amargosa Range** ▲▲ California, W USA
80 H7 **Amargosa Valley** Nevada, USA 36°39´N 116°24´W
70 E2 **Amarillo** Texas, SW USA 35°13´N 101°50´W
Amarinthos *see* Amárynthos
175 F8 **Amaro, Monte** ▲ C Italy 42°03´N 14°06´E
187 H6 **Amárynthos** *var.* Amarinthos. Évvoia, C Greece 38°24´N 23°53´E
219 E9 **'Amasa** Israel
Amasia *see* Amasya
214 F5 **Amasya** *anc.* Amasia. Amasya, N Turkey 40°37´N 35°50´E
214 F5 **Amasya** ⬖ *province* N Turkey
87 K9 **Amatenango** Chiapas, Mexico 15°26´N 92°07´W
88 D3 **Amatique, Bahía de** *bay* Gulf of Honduras, W Caribbean Sea
86 C5 **Amatitàn** Jalisco, Mexico 20°50´N 103°43´W
88 C4 **Amatitlán, Lago de** ⊛ S Guatemala
86 B5 **Amatlàn de Cañas** Nayarit, Mexico 20°48´N 104°24´W
174 F7 **Amatrice** Lazio, C Italy 42°38´N 13°19´E
284 F1 **Amatuku** *atoll* C Tuvalu
163 F11 **Amay** Liège, E Belgium 50°33´N 05°19´E
98 C3 **Amazon** *Sp.* Amazonas. ≈ Brazil/Peru
106 D4 **Amazonas** *off.* Estado do Amazonas. ⬖ *state* N Brazil
102 D9 **Amazonas** *off.* Comisaria del Amazonas. ⬖ *province* SE Colombia
104 C4 **Amazonas** *off.* Departamento de Amazonas. ⬖ *department* N Peru
102 G6 **Amazonas** *off.* Territorio Amazonas. ⬖ *federal territory* S Venezuela
Amazonas *see* Amazon
Amazonas, Comisaria del *see* Amazonas
Amazonas, Departamento de *see* Amazonas
Amazonas, Estado do *see* Amazonas
Amazonas, Territorio *see* Amazonas
98 D3 **Amazon Basin** *basin* N South America
95 L3 **Amazon Fan** *undersea feature* W Atlantic Ocean 05°00´N 47°30´W
108 C1 **Amazon, Mouths of the** *delta* NE Brazil
281 M2 **Ambae** *var.* Aoba, Omba. *island* C Vanuatu
232 E4 **Ambāla** Haryāna, NW India 30°19´N 76°49´E
235 G11 **Ambalangoda** Southern Province, SW Sri Lanka 06°14´N 80°03´E
235 G11 **Ambalantota** Southern Province, S Sri Lanka 06°07´N 81°01´E
139 L8 **Ambalavao** Fianarantsoa, C Madagascar 21°50´S 46°56´E
102 C5 **Ambalema** Tolima, C Colombia 04°49´N 74°48´W
134 B6 **Ambam** Sud, S Cameroon 02°23´N 11°17´E
139 M5 **Ambanja** Antsirañana, N Madagascar 13°40´S 48°27´E
193 L3 **Ambarchik** Respublika Sakha (Yakutiya), NE Russian Federation 69°33´N 162°08´E
116 E1 **Ambargasta, Salinas de** *salt lake* C Argentina
194 E4 **Ambarnyy** Respublika Kareliya, NW Russian Federation 65°53´N 33°44´E
104 C2 **Ambato** Tungurahua, C Ecuador 01°18´S 78°39´W
139 L8 **Ambato Finandrahana** Fianarantsoa, SE Madagascar
139 M7 **Ambatolampy** Antananarivo, C Madagascar 19°21´S 47°27´E
139 L6 **Ambatomainty** Mahajanga, W Madagascar 17°40´S 45°39´E
139 M6 **Ambatondrazaka** Toamasina, C Madagascar 17°49´S 48°28´E
168 F1 **Ambazac** Limousin, France 45°57´N 1°24´E
260 G6 **Ambelau, Pulau** *island* E Indonesia
179 G11 **Amberg** *var.* Amberg in der Oberpfalz. Bayern, SE Germany 49°26´N 11°52´E
Amberg in der Oberpfalz *see* Amberg
88 E1 **Ambergris Cay** *island* NE Belize
165 J6 **Ambérieu-en-Bugey** Ain, E France 45°57´N 05°21´E
279 E9 **Amberley** Canterbury, South Island, New Zealand 43°09´S 172°43´E
165 I6 **Ambert** Puy-de-Dôme, C France 45°33´N 03°45´E
Ambianum *see* Amiens
132 C4 **Ambidédi** Kayes, SW Mali 14°37´N 11°49´W
234 H3 **Ambikāpur** Chhattīsgarh, C India 23°09´N 83°12´E
139 M4 **Ambilobe** Antsirañana, N Madagascar 13°10´S 49°03´E
159 K5 **Amble** United Kingdom 55°20´N 1°35´W
83 H4 **Ambler** Alaska, USA 67°05´N 157°51´W
64 F7 **Ambler** Pennsylvania, USA 40°09´N 75°13´W
159 I7 **Ambleside** United Kingdom 54°25´N 2°58´W
Amblève *see* Amel
Ambo *see* Hāgere Hiywet
139 L10 **Amboasary** Toliara, S Madagascar 25°01´S 46°23´E
139 N6 **Ambodifotatra** *var.* Ambodifototra. Toamasina, E Madagascar 16°59´S 49°51´E
Amboenten *see* Ambunten
139 M7 **Ambohidratrimo** Antananarivo, C Madagascar 18°48´S 47°26´E
139 M8 **Ambohimahasoa** Fianarantsoa, SE Madagascar 21°07´S 47°13´E
139 N5 **Ambohitralanana** Antsirañana, NE Madagascar 15°13´S 50°28´E
261 K5 **Amboi, Kepulauan** *island group* E Indonesia
Amboina *see* Ambon
164 G4 **Amboise** Indre-et-Loire, C France 47°25´N 01°00´E
260 G5 **Ambon** *prev.* Amboina, Amboyna. Pulau Ambon, E Indonesia 03°41´S 128°10´E
260 G5 **Ambon, Pulau** *island* E Indonesia
137 D9 **Amboseli, Lake** ⊛ Kenya/Tanzania
139 M8 **Ambositra** Fianarantsoa, SE Madagascar 20°31´S 47°15´E
139 L10 **Ambovombe** Toliara, S Madagascar 25°10´S 46°06´E
81 H11 **Amboy** California, W USA 34°33´N 115°44´W
73 C9 **Amboy** Illinois, N USA 41°42´N 89°19´W
Amboyna *see* Ambon
Ambracia *see* Árta
Ambre, Cap d' *see* Bobaomby, Tanjona
62 C8 **Ambridge** Pennsylvania, NE USA 40°33´N 80°11´W
Ambrim *see* Ambrym
135 C10 **Ambriz** Bengo, NW Angola 07°55´S 13°11´E
Ambrizete *see* N'Zeto
114 A1 **Ambrosetti** Santa Fe, C Argentina 30°01´S 61°33´W
281 M3 **Ambrym** *var.* Ambrim. *island* C Vanuatu
259 J8 **Ambunten** *prev.* Amboenten. Pulau Madura, E Indonesia 06°55´S 113°45´E
261 N6 **Ambunti** East Sepik, NW Papua New Guinea 04°12´S 142°49´E
235 F8 **Āmbūr** Tamil Nādu, SE India 12°48´N 78°44´E
218 F2 **Amchit** Lebanon
218 F2 **Amchit** Lebanon 34°09´N 35°39´E
82 B10 **Amchitka Island** *island* Aleutian Islands, Alaska, USA
82 C10 **Amchitka Pass** *strait* Aleutian Islands, Alaska, USA
221 H8 **'Amd** C Yemen 15°10´N 47°58´E
134 F2 **Am Dam** Ouaddaï, E Chad 12°46´N 20°29´E
261 I7 **Amdassa** Pulau Yamdena, E Indonesia 07°40´S 131°24´E
195 K1 **Amderma** Nenetskiy Avtonomnyy Okrug, NW Russian Federation 69°45´N 61°36´E
239 H8 **Amdo** Xizang Zizhiqu, W China 32°15´N 91°43´E
86 E6 **Amealco** Hidalgo, Mexico 20°14´N 99°33´W
86 E6 **Amealco** Querétaro de Arteaga, Mexico 20°11´N 100°09´W
86 B5 **Ameca** Jalisco, SW Mexico 20°34´N 104°03´W
86 F6 **Amecameca** *var.* Amecameca de Juárez. México, C Mexico 19°08´N 98°48´W
Amecameca de Juárez *see* Amecameca
112 E10 **Ameghino** Buenos Aires, E Argentina 34°51´S 62°28´W
163 H11 **Amel** *Fr.* Amblève. Liège, E Belgium 50°20´N 06°13´E
162 G3 **Ameland** *Fris.* It Amelân. *island* Waddeneilanden, N Netherlands
Amelân, It *see* Ameland
174 E7 **Amelia** Umbria, C Italy 42°33´N 12°26´E
67 K4 **Amelia Court House** Virginia, NE USA 37°20´N 77°59´W
69 L4 **Amelia Island** *island* Florida, SE USA
169 H8 **Amélie-les-Bains-Palalda** Languedoc-Roussillon, France 42°28´N 2°40´E
65 I3 **Amenia** New York, NE USA 41°51´N 73°31´W
America *see* United States of America
291 H13 **America-Antarctica Ridge** *undersea feature* S Atlantic Ocean
America in Miniature *see* Maryland
110 C8 **Americana** São Paulo, S Brazil 22°44´S 47°19´W
80 B2 **American Canyon** California, USA 38°11´N 122°16´W
77 H8 **American Falls** Idaho, NW USA 42°47´N 112°51´W
77 H8 **American Falls Reservoir** ⊠ Idaho, NW USA
79 H2 **American Fork** Utah, W USA 40°24´N 111°47´W
286 G6 **American Samoa** ◇ *US unincorporated territory* W Polynesia
110 B6 **Américo Brasiliense** São Paulo, Brazil 21°43´S 48°07´W
69 J2 **Americus** Georgia, SE USA 32°04´N 84°13´W
162 G7 **Amerongen** Utrecht, C Netherlands 52°00´N 05°30´E
162 G6 **Amersfoort** Utrecht, C Netherlands 52°09´N 05°23´E
161 J6 **Amersham** SE England, United Kingdom 51°40´N 00°37´W
72 A5 **Amery** Wisconsin, N USA 45°18´N 92°20´W
293 L4 **Amery Ice Shelf** *ice shelf* Antarctica
74 G7 **Ames** Iowa, C USA 42°01´N 93°37´W
65 M1 **Amesbury** Massachusetts, NE USA 42°51´N 70°55´W
Amestratus *see* Mistretta
186 G5 **Amfíkleia** *var.* Amfíklia. Stereá Elláda, C Greece 38°38´N 22°35´E
Amfíklia *see* Amfíkleia
186 F5 **Amfilochía** *var.* Amfilokhía. Dytikí Elláda, C Greece 38°52´N 21°09´E
Amfilokhía *see* Amfilochía
187 H2 **Amfípoli** *anc.* Amphipolis. *site of ancient city* Kentrikí Makedonía, NE Greece
186 G5 **Ámfissa** Stereá Elláda, C Greece 38°32´N 22°22´E
193 K6 **Amga** Respublika Sakha (Yakutiya), NE Russian Federation 60°55´N 131°45´E
193 K6 **Amga** ≈ NE Russian Federation
247 I4 **Amgalang** *var.* Xin Barag Zuoqi. Nei Mongol Zizhiqu, N China 48°12´N 118°15´E
193 M3 **Amguema** ≈ NE Russian Federation
193 L7 **Amgun'** ≈ SE Russian Federation
Amhara *see* Āmara
63 N2 **Amherst** Nova Scotia, SE Canada 45°50´N 64°14´W
65 J2 **Amherst** Massachusetts, NE USA 42°22´N 72°31´W
64 A1 **Amherst** New York, NE USA 42°57´N 78°47´W
70 D3 **Amherst** Texas, SW USA 33°59´N 102°24´W
67 K4 **Amherst** Virginia, NE USA 37°35´N 79°04´W
Amherst *see* Kyaikkami
62 A6 **Amherstburg** Ontario, S Canada 42°05´N 83°06´W
67 H4 **Amherstdale** West Virginia, NE USA 37°46´N 81°46´W
62 F4 **Amherst Island** *island* Ontario, SE Canada
Amida *see* Diyarbakır
74 A3 **Amidon** North Dakota, N USA 46°29´N 103°19´W
172 C3 **Amieira** Castelo Branco, Portugal 39°59´N 7°55´W
172 B3 **Amieira** Coimbra, Portugal 40°05´N 8°46´W
165 H2 **Amiens** *anc.* Ambianum, Samarobriva. Somme, N France 49°54´N 02°18´E
216 G5 **'Āmij, Wādī** *var.* Wadi 'Amīq. *dry watercourse* W Iraq
214 G8 **Amik Ovasī** ⊛ S Turkey
132 B9 **Amilcar Cabral** ✈ Sal, NE Cape Verde
Amilḩayt, Wādī *see* Umm al Ḩayt, Wādī
167 H7 **Amilly** Centre, France 47°59´N 2°46´E
Amíndaion/Amindeo *see* Amýntaio
235 C8 **Amīndīvi Islands** *island group* Lakshadweep, India, N Indian Ocean
217 K4 **Amīn Ḩabīb** Diyālá, E Iraq 34°17´N 45°10´E
138 D6 **Aminuis** Omaheke, E Namibia 23°43´S 19°21´E
218 F2 **Amioun** N Lebanon
218 F2 **Amioun** Lebanon 34°18´N 35°48´E
'Amīq, Wadi *see* 'Āmij, Wādī
222 D5 **Amīrābād** Īlām, NW Iran 33°20´N 46°16´E
Amirante Bank *see* Amirante Ridge
289 C8 **Amirante Basin** *undersea feature* W Indian Ocean 07°00´S 54°00´E
289 C8 **Amirante Islands** *var.* Amirantes Group. *island group* C Seychelles
289 D8 **Amirante Ridge** *var.* Amirante Bank. *undersea feature* W Indian Ocean 06°00´S 53°10´E
Amirantes Group *see* Amirante Islands
289 D8 **Amirante Trench** *undersea feature* W Indian Ocean 08°00´S 52°30´E
261 M6 **Amisibil** Papua, E Indonesia 03°59´S 140°35´E
55 H8 **Amisk Lake** ⊛ Saskatchewan, C Canada
Amistad, Presa de la *see* Amistad Reservoir
70 E7 **Amistad Reservoir** *var.* Presa de la Amistad. ⊠ Mexico/USA
Amisus *see* Samsun
68 E4 **Amite** *var.* Amite City. Louisiana, S USA 30°40´N 90°30´W
Amite City *see* Amite
75 H13 **Amity** Arkansas, C USA 34°15´N 93°27´W
232 F9 **Amla** *prev.* Amulla. Madhya Pradesh, C India 21°53´N 78°10´E
82 D10 **Amlia Island** *island* Aleutian Islands, Alaska, USA
160 E1 **Amlwch** NW Wales, United Kingdom 53°25´N 04°23´W
Ammaia *see* Portalegre
219 G8 **'Ammān** *var.* Amman; *anc.* Philadelphia, *Bibl.* Rabbah Ammon, Rabbath Ammon. ● (Jordan) 'Ammān, NW Jordan 31°57´N 35°56´E
219 G8 **'Ammān** *off.* Muḩāfazat 'Ammān; *prev.* Al 'Aşimah. ⬖ *governorate* NW Jordan
160 E5 **Ammanford** United Kingdom 51°48´N 3°59´W
'Ammān, Muḩāfazat *see* 'Ammān
152 I7 **Ämmänsaari** Oulu, E Finland 64°51´N 28°58´E
152 E6 **Ammarnäs** Västerbotten, N Sweden 65°58´N 16°10´E
295 L7 **Ammassalik** *var.* Angmagssalik. Tunu, S Greenland 65°51´N 37°30´W
180 C6 **Ammeloe** Nordrhein-Westfalen, Germany 52°04´E 6°47´N
179 F13 **Ammer** ≈ SE Germany
181 I9 **Ammern** Thüringen, Germany 51°14´E 10°27´N
179 F13 **Ammersee** ⊛ SE Germany
163 F8 **Ammerzoden** Gelderland, C Netherlands 51°46´N 05°07´E
Ammóchostos *see* Gazimağusa
Ammóchostos, Kólpos *see* Gazimağusa Körfezi
Amnok-kang *see* Yalu
Amoea *see* Portalegre
Amoentai *see* Amuntai
Amoerang *see* Amurang
222 F3 **Āmol** *var.* Amul. Māzandarān, N Iran 36°31´N 52°24´E
181 F10 **Amoneburg** Hessen, Germany 50°48´E 8°54´N
172 B3 **Amor** Leiria, Portugal 39°48´N 8°52´W
187 J8 **Amorgós** Amorgós, Kykládes, Greece, Aegean Sea 36°49´N 25°54´E
187 J8 **Amorgós** *island* Kykládes, Greece, Aegean Sea
66 C8 **Amory** Mississippi, S USA 33°58´N 88°29´W
58 F7 **Amos** Québec, SE Canada 48°34´N 78°08´W
154 D7 **Åmot** Buskerud, S Norway 59°52´N 09°55´E
155 C8 **Åmot** Telemark, S Norway 59°34´N 07°59´E
154 F7 **Åmotfors** Värmland, C Sweden 59°46´N 12°24´E
132 E3 **Amourj** Hodh ech Chargui, SE Mauritania 16°04´N 07°12´W
Amoy *see* Xiamen
139 L10 **Ampanihy** Toliara, SW Madagascar 24°40´S 44°45´E
235 G10 **Ampara** *var.* Amparai. Eastern Province, E Sri Lanka 07°17´N 81°41´E
139 M6 **Amparafaravola** Toamasina, E Madagascar 17°33´S 48°13´E
Amparai *see* Ampara
110 D8 **Amparo** São Paulo, S Brazil 22°40´S 46°49´W
111 I4 **Amparo da Serra** Minas Gerais, Brazil 20°31´S 42°49´W
139 M7 **Ampasimanolotra** Toamasina, E Madagascar 18°49´S 49°04´E
105 G9 **Ampato, Nevado** ▲ S Peru 15°52´S 71°51´W
179 G12 **Amper** ≈ SE Germany
Amphipolis *see* Amfípoli
262 G4 **Amphitrite Group** *island group* N Paracel Islands
261 H8 **Amplawas** *var.* Emplawas. Pulau Babar, E Indonesia 08°01´S 129°42´E
169 J1 **Amplepuis** Rhône-Alpes, France 45°59´N 4°20´E
171 J4 **Amposta** Cataluña, NE Spain 40°43´N 00°34´E
59 I7 **Amqui** Québec, SE Canada 48°28´N 67°27´W
220 F8 **'Amrān** W Yemen 15°39´N 43°59´E
Amraoti *see* Amrāvati
234 E4 **Amrāvati** *prev.* Amraoti. Mahārāshtra, C India 20°56´N 77°45´E
219 E14 **'Amrāwah** Jordan
219 E14 **Amrāwah** Jordan 32°41´N 35°56´E
232 B9 **Amreli** Gujarāt, W India 21°36´N 71°20´E
176 E3 **Amriswil** Thurgau, NE Switzerland 47°33´N 09°18´E
216 C4 **'Amrīt** *ruins* Ţarţūs, W Syria
232 D3 **Amritsar** Punjab, N India 31°38´N 74°55´E
232 F5 **Amroha** Uttar Pradesh, N India 28°54´N 78°29´E
178 C3 **Amrum** *island* NW Germany
154 J2 **Åmsele** Västerbotten, N Sweden 64°31´N 19°24´E
162 F6 **Amstelveen** Noord-Holland, C Netherlands 52°18´N 04°50´E
162 F6 **Amsterdam** ● (Netherlands) Noord-Holland, C Netherlands 52°22´N 04°54´E
141 K4 **Amsterdam** Mpumalanga, South Africa 26°37´S 30°40´E
65 H1 **Amsterdam** New York, NE USA 42°56´N 74°11´W
289 F11 **Amsterdam Fracture Zone** *tectonic feature* S Indian Ocean
289 F11 **Amsterdam Island** *island* NE French Southern and Antarctic Territories
177 K2 **Amstetten** Niederösterreich, N Austria 48°08´N 14°52´E
134 F3 **Am Timan** Salamat, SE Chad 11°02´N 20°17´E
228 G7 **Amu-Buxoro Kanali** *var.* Aral-Bukhorskiy Kanal. *canal* C Uzbekistan
216 G1 **'Āmūdah** *var.* Amude. Al Ḩasakah, N Syria 37°06´N 40°56´E
230 G2 **Amu Darya** *Rus.* Amudar'ya, *Taj.* Dar''yoi Amu, *Turkm.* Amyderya, *Uzb.* Amudaryo; *anc.* Oxus. ≈ C Asia
Amu-Dar'ya *see* Amyderýa
Amudar'ya/Amudaryo/Amu, Dar''yoi *see* Amu Darya
Amude *see* 'Āmūdah
220 E1 **'Amūd, Jabal al** ▲ NW Saudi Arabia 30°59´N 39°17´E
82 E10 **Amukta Island** *island* Aleutian Islands, Alaska, USA
82 D10 **Amukta Pass** *strait* Aleutian Islands, Alaska, USA
Amul *see* Āmol
Amulla *see* Amla
159 H2 **Amulree** United Kingdom 56°30´N 3°47´W
53 H3 **Amund Ringnes Island** *Island* Nunavut, N Canada
Amundsen Basin *see* Fram Basin
293 L2 **Amundsen Bay** *bay* Antarctica
293 H6 **Amundsen Coast** *physical region* Antarctica
52 D6 **Amundsen Gulf** *gulf* Northwest Territories, N Canada
287 H10 **Amundsen Plain** *undersea feature* S Pacific Ocean
293 I5 **Amundsen-Scott** *US research station* Antarctica 89°59´S 10°00´E
292 F7 **Amundsen Sea** *sea* S Pacific Ocean
154 G6 **Amungen** ⊛ C Sweden
259 K6 **Amuntai** *prev.* Amoentai. Borneo, C Indonesia 02°24´S 115°14´E
205 M4 **Amur** *Chin.* Heilong Jiang. ≈ China/Russian Federation
260 E3 **Amurang** *prev.* Amoerang. Sulawesi, C Indonesia 01°12´N 124°37´E
260 E3 **Amurang, Teluk** *bay* Sulawesi, C Indonesia
170 G2 **Amurrio** País Vasco, N Spain 43°03´N 03°00´W
193 L8 **Amursk** Khabarovskiy Kray, SE Russian Federation 50°13´N 136°34´E
193 J7 **Amurskaya Oblast'** ⬖ *province* SE Russian Federation
129 J8 **'Amur, Wadi** ≈ NE Sudan
186 F5 **Amvrakikós Kólpos** *gulf* W Greece
Amvrosiyevka *see* Amvrosiyivka
189 M6 **Amvrosiyivka** *Rus.* Amvrosiyevka. Donets'ka Oblast', SE Ukraine 47°46´N 38°30´E
228 G7 **Amyderýa** *Rus.* Amu-Dar'ya. Lebap Welaýaty, NE Turkmenistan 37°58´N 65°14´E
Amyderya *see* Amu Darya
186 F3 **Amýntaio** *var.* Amindeo; *prev.* Amíndaion. Dytikí Makedonía, N Greece 40°42´N 21°42´E
72 G2 **Amyot** Ontario, S Canada 48°28´N 84°58´W
285 J7 **Anaa** *atoll* Îles Tuamotu, C French Polynesia
Anabanoea *see* Anabanua
260 C6 **Anabanua** *prev.* Anabanoea. Sulawesi, C Indonesia 03°58´S 120°07´E
283 J9 **Anabar** NE Nauru 0°30´S 166°56´E
193 I4 **Anabar** ≈ NE Russian Federation
An Abhainn Mhór *see* Blackwater
103 H3 **Anaco** Anzoátegui, NE Venezuela 09°30´N 64°28´W
77 H5 **Anaconda** Montana, NW USA 46°09´N 112°56´W
76 C3 **Anacortes** Washington, NW USA 48°30´N 122°36´W
75 D12 **Anadarko** Oklahoma, C USA 35°04´N 98°16´W
172 B2 **Anadia** Aveiro, N Portugal 40°26´N 08°27´W
Anadolu Dağları *see* Doğu Karadeniz Dağları
193 N3 **Anadyr'** Chukotskiy Avtonomnyy Okrug, NE Russian Federation 64°41´N 177°22´E
193 M3 **Anadyr'** ≈ NE Russian Federation
Anadyr, Gulf of *see* Anadyrskiy Zaliv
193 N3 **Anadyrskiy Zaliv** *Eng.* Gulf of Anadyr. *gulf* NE Russian Federation
187 J8 **Anáfi** *anc.* Anaphe. *island* Kykládes, Greece, Aegean Sea
175 F8 **Anagni** Lazio, C Italy 41°43´N 13°12´E
'Ānah *see* 'Annah
78 D8 **Anaheim** California, W USA 33°50´N 117°54´W
56 C5 **Anahim Lake** British Columbia, SW Canada 52°26´N 125°13´W
85 L5 **Anáhuac** Nuevo León, NE Mexico 27°13´N 100°09´W
71 I7 **Anahuac** Texas, SW USA 29°44´N 94°41´W
235 E9 **Anai Mudi** ▲ S India 10°16´N 77°08´E
Anaiza *see* 'Unayzah
234 H5 **Anakāpalle** Andhra Pradesh, E India 17°42´N 83°06´E
118 B1 **Anakena, Playa de** *beach* Easter Island, Chile, E Pacific Ocean
83 I3 **Anaktuvuk Pass** Alaska, USA 68°08´N 151°44´W
83 I3 **Anaktuvuk River** ≈ Alaska, USA
139 M5 **Analalava** Mahajanga, NW Madagascar 14°38´S 47°46´E
90 D4 **Ana Maria, Golfo de** *gulf* N Caribbean Sea
Anambas Islands *see* Anambas, Kepulauan
258 F3 **Anambas, Kepulauan** *var.* Anambas Islands. *island group* W Indonesia
133 K8 **Anambra** ⬖ *state* SE Nigeria
74 C2 **Anamoose** North Dakota, N USA 47°50´N 100°14´W
74 I7 **Anamosa** Iowa, C USA 42°06´N 91°17´W
214 E8 **Anamur** İçel, S Turkey 36°06´N 32°49´E
214 E8 **Anamur Burnu** *headland* S Turkey 36°03´N 32°49´E
250 G6 **Anan** Tokushima, Shikoku, SW Japan 33°54´N 134°40´E
234 I4 **Ānandadur** Orissa, E India 21°14´N 86°10´E
234 E7 **Anantapur** Andhra Pradesh, S India 14°41´N 77°36´E
232 E2 **Anantnāg** *var.* Islamabad. Jammu and Kashmir, NW India 33°44´N 75°11´E
Ananyev *see* Anan'yiv
188 G6 **Anan'yiv** *Rus.* Ananyev. Odes'ka Oblast', SW Ukraine 47°43´N 29°51´E
196 F8 **Anapa** Krasnodarskiy Kray, SW Russian Federation 44°55´N 37°20´E
Anaphe *see* Anáfi
109 B10 **Anápolis** Goiás, C Brazil 16°19´S 48°58´W
223 H6 **Anār** Kermān, C Iran 30°49´N 55°18´E
Anár *see* Inari
222 G5 **Anārak** Eşfahān, C Iran 33°21´N 53°43´E
Anar Dara *see* Anār Darreh
230 D4 **Anār Darreh** *var.* Anar Dara. Farāh, W Afghanistan 32°45´N 61°38´E
Anárjohka *see* Inarijoki
69 M4 **Anastasia Island** *island* Florida, SE USA
282 E3 **Anatahan** *island* C Northern Mariana Islands
204 G4 **Anatolia** *plateau* C Turkey
148 E8 **Anatolian Plate** *tectonic feature* Asia/Europe
187 I2 **Anatolikí Makedonía kai Thráki** *Eng.* Macedonia East and Thrace. ⬖ *region* NE Greece
Anatom *see* Aneityum
116 F1 **Añatuya** Santiago del Estero, N Argentina 28°28´S 62°52´W
An Baile Meánach *see* Ballymena
An Bhearú *see* Barrow
An Bhóinn *see* Boyne
An Blascaod Mór *see* Great Blasket Island
Anbu *see* Chao'an
An Cabhán *see* Cavan
An Caisleán Nua *see* Newcastle
An Caisleán Riabhach *see* Castlerea, Ireland
An Caisleán Riabhach *see* Castlereagh
104 C6 **Ancash** *off.* Departamento de Ancash. ⬖ *department* W Peru
Ancash, Departamento de *see* Ancash
An Cathair *see* Caher
164 F4 **Ancenis** Loire-Atlantique, NW France 47°23´N 01°10´W
167 K6 **Ancerville** Lorraine, France 48°38´N 5°02´E
An Chanáil Ríoga *see* Royal Canal
An Cheacha *see* Caha Mountains
111 M4 **Anchieta** Espírito Santo, Brazil 20°48´S 40°39´W
83 I6 **Anchorage** Alaska, USA 61°13´N 149°52´W
83 I6 **Anchorage** ✈ Alaska, USA 61°08´N 150°00´W
83 I7 **Anchor Point** Alaska, USA 59°46´N 151°49´W
An Chorr Chríochach *see* Cookstown
132 E10 **Anchorstock Point** *headland* W Tristan da Cunha 37°07´S 12°21´W
172 G4 **Anchuras** Castilla-La Manacha, Spain 39°29´N 4°50´W
An Clochán *see* Clifden
An Clochán Liath *see* Dunglow
69 K6 **Anclote Keys** *island group* Florida, SE USA
An Cóbh *see* Cobh
105 H9 **Ancohuma, Nevado de** ▲ W Bolivia 15°51´S 68°33´W
An Comar *see* Comber
104 D7 **Ancón** Lima, W Peru 11°45´S 77°08´W
177 J9 **Ancona** Marche, C Italy 43°38´N 13°30´E
159 J4 **Ancroft** United Kingdom 55°42´N 2°00´W
Ancuabe *see* Ancuabi
137 E13 **Ancuabi** *var.* Ancuabe. Cabo Delgado, NE Mozambique 13°00´S 39°50´E
117 B8 **Ancud** *prev.* San Carlos de Ancud. Los Lagos, S Chile 41°53´S 73°50´W
117 B8 **Ancud, Golfo de** *gulf* S Chile
Ancyra *see* Ankara
193 K9 **Anda** Heilongjiang, NE China 46°25´N 125°20´E
118 D8 **Andacollo** Neuquén, Argentina 37°11´S 70°41´W
105 F8 **Andahuaylas** Apurímac, S Peru 13°39´S 73°24´W
An Daingean *see* Dingle
233 J8 **Andāl** West Bengal, NE India 23°35´N 87°14´E
154 C4 **Åndalsnes** Møre og Romsdal, S Norway 62°33´N 07°42´E
170 F7 **Andalucía** *Eng.* Andalusia. ⬖ *autonomous community* S Spain
130 G1 **Andalucía** *cultural region* S Spain
69 H3 **Andalusia** Alabama, S USA 31°18´N 86°29´W
Andalusia *see* Andalucía
257 A10 **Andaman and Nicobar Islands** *var.* Andamans and Nicobars. ⬖ *union territory* India, NE Indian Ocean
288 H6 **Andaman Basin** *undersea feature* NE Indian Ocean 10°00´N 94°00´E
257 B9 **Andaman Islands** *island group* India, NE Indian Ocean
Andamans and Nicobars *see* Andaman and Nicobar Islands
288 H6 **Andaman Sea** *sea* NE Indian Ocean
112 C1 **Andamarca** Oruro, C Bolivia 18°46´S 67°31´W
261 I5 **Andamata** Papua, E Indonesia 02°40´S 132°30´E
276 F3 **Andamooka** South Australia 30°26´S 137°12´E
221 K5 **'Andām, Wādī** *seasonal river* NE Oman
139 N5 **Andapa** Antsirañana, NE Madagascar 14°39´S 49°40´E
231 H3 **Andarāb** *var.* Banow. Baghlān, NE Afghanistan 35°36´N 69°18´E
Andarbag *see* Andarbogh
229 J7 **Andarbogh** *Rus.* Andarbag, Anderbak. S Tajikistan 37°51´N 71°45´E
176 E5 **Andeer** Graubünden, S Switzerland 46°36´N 09°24´E
167 K6 **Andelot** Champagne-Ardenne, France 48°15´N 5°18´E
152 E4 **Andenes** Nordland, C Norway 69°18´N 16°10´E
163 F11 **Andenne** Namur, SE Belgium 50°29´N 05°06´E
133 I4 **Andéramboukane** Gao, E Mali 15°24´N 03°03´E
Anderbak *see* Andarbogh
163 D10 **Anderlecht** Brussels, C Belgium 50°50´N 04°18´E
163 D11 **Anderlues** Hainaut, S Belgium 50°24´N 04°16´E
176 E5 **Andermatt** Uri, C Switzerland 46°39´N 08°36´E
181 D11 **Andernach** *anc.* Antunnacum. Rheinland-Pfalz, SW Germany 50°26´N 07°24´E
168 C3 **Andernos-les-Bains** Aquitaine, France 44°44´N 1°06´W
282 B1 **Andersen Air Force Base** *air base* NE Guam 13°34´N 144°55´E
83 I5 **Anderson** Alaska, USA 64°20´N 149°11´W
78 B2 **Anderson** California, W USA 40°26´N 122°21´W
73 F10 **Anderson** Indiana, N USA 40°06´N 85°40´W
75 G11 **Anderson** Missouri, C USA 36°39´N 94°26´W
67 H7 **Anderson** South Carolina, SE USA 34°30´N 82°39´W
71 H6 **Anderson** Texas, SW USA 30°29´N 96°00´W
52 C6 **Anderson** ≈ Northwest Territories, NW Canada
155 F10 **Anderstorp** Jönköping, S Sweden 57°17´N 13°38´E
102 B5 **Andes** Antioquia, W Colombia 05°40´N 75°56´W
95 I5 **Andes** ▲▲ W South America
74 D6 **Andes, Lake** ⊛ South Dakota, N USA
152 E4 **Andfjorden** *fjord* E Norwegian Sea
234 F6 **Andhra Pradesh** ⬖ *state* E India
162 F5 **Andijk** Noord-Holland, NW Netherlands 52°38´N 05°00´E
229 K5 **Andijon** *Rus.* Andizhan. Andijon Viloyati, E Uzbekistan 40°46´N 72°19´E
229 K5 **Andijon Viloyati** *Rus.* Andizhanskaya Oblast'. ⬖ *province* E Uzbekistan
Andikíthira *see* Antikýthira
139 M6 **Andilamena** Toamasina, C Madagascar 17°00´S 48°35´E
222 E5 **Andīmeshk** *var.* Andimishk; *prev.* Salehābād. Khūzestān, SW Iran 32°30´N 48°26´E
Andimishk *see* Andīmeshk
243 H4 **Anding** Hunan, E China 28°35´N 113°40´E
114 B6 **Andino** Santa Fe, Argentina 32°40´S 60°53´W
Andipáros *see* Antíparos
Andipaxi *see* Antípaxoi
Andípsara *see* Antípsara
214 G7 **Andırın** Kahramanmaraş, S Turkey 37°33´N 36°18´E
238 E6 **Andirlangar** Xinjiang Uygur Zizhiqu, NW China 37°38´N 83°40´E
Andírrion *see* Antírrio
Ándissa *see* Ántissa
Andizhan *see* Andijon
Andizhanskaya Oblast' *see* Andijon Viloyati
230 F2 **Andkhvoy** Fāryāb, N Afghanistan 36°56´N 65°08´E
171 H2 **Andoain** País Vasco, N Spain 43°13´N 02°02´W
261 J4 **Andoi** Papua, E Indonesia 0°53´S 133°59´E
248 C6 **Andong** *Jap.* Antō. E South Korea 36°34´N 128°44´E
250 B2 **Andong-ho** *prev.* Andong Lake. ⊛
Andong Lake *see* Andong-ho
245 L7 **Andongwei** Jiangsu, E China 34°54´N 119°06´E
177 I2 **Andorf** Oberösterreich, N Austria 48°22´N 13°33´E
171 I4 **Andorra** Aragón, NE Spain 40°59´N 00°27´W
171 J2 **Andorra** *off.* Principality of Andorra, *Cat.* Valls d'Andorra, *Fr.* Vallée d'Andorre. ◆ *monarchy* SW Europe
Andorra *see* Andorra la Vella
171 K2 **Andorra la Vella** *var.* Andorra, *Fr.* Andorre la Vielle, *Sp.* Andorra la Vieja. ● (Andorra) C Andorra 42°30´N 01°30´E
Andorra la Vieja *see* Andorra la Vella
Andorra, Principality of *see* Andorra
Andorra, Valls d'/Andorra, Vallée d' *see* Andorra
Andorre la Vielle *see* Andorra la Vella
161 I7 **Andover** S England, United Kingdom 51°13´N 01°28´W
75 E10 **Andover** Kansas, C USA 37°42´N 97°08´W
65 L2 **Andover** Massachusetts, USA 42°40´N 71°08´W
64 C3 **Andover** New York, USA 42°09´N 77°48´W
152 E4 **Andøya** *island* C Norway
113 J2 **Andradina** São Paulo, S Brazil 20°54´S 51°19´W
171 L6 **Andratx** Mallorca, Spain, W Mediterranean Sea 39°35´N 02°25´E
82 G5 **Andreafsky River** ≈ Alaska, USA
82 D10 **Andreanof Islands** *island group* Aleutian Islands, Alaska, USA
194 D10 **Andreapol'** Tverskaya Oblast', W Russian Federation 56°38´N 32°17´E
Andreas, Cape *see* Zafer Burnu
Andreevka *see* Kabanbay
110 G6 **Andrelândia** Minas Gerais, Brazil 21°44´S 44°18´W
114 G7 **Andresito** Flores, Uruguay 33°08´S 57°09´W
66 G7 **Andrews** North Carolina, SE USA 35°19´N 84°01´W
67 J9 **Andrews** South Carolina, SE USA 33°27´N 79°33´W
70 D5 **Andrews** Texas, SW USA 32°19´N 102°34´W
288 C7 **Andrew Seamount** N Indian Ocean
288 C7 **Andrew Tablemount** *var.* Gora Andryu. *undersea feature* W Indian Ocean 06°45´N 50°30´E
Andreyevka *see* Kabanbay
169 J2 **Andrézieux** Rhône-Alpes, France 45°32´N 4°16´E
175 H9 **Andria** Puglia, SE Italy 41°13´N 16°17´E
140 E4 **Andriesvale** Northern Cape, South Africa 26°56´S 20°39´E
184 F6 **Andrijevica** E Montenegro 42°45´N 19°45´E
186 F7 **Andrítsaina** Pelopónnisos, S Greece 37°29´N 21°52´E
Andropov *see* Rybinsk
187 I6 **Ándros** Ándros, Kykládes, Greece, Aegean Sea 37°49´N 24°54´E
187 J6 **Ándros** *island* Kykládes, Greece, Aegean Sea
63 J4 **Androscoggin River** ≈ Maine/New Hampshire, NE USA
61 M10 **Andros Island** *island* NW Bahamas
197 J3 **Androsovka** Samarskaya Oblast', W Russian Federation 52°41´N 49°34´E
61 M10 **Andros Town** Andros Island, NW Bahamas 24°40´N 77°47´W
235 C9 **Āndrott Island** *island* Lakshadweep, India, N Indian Ocean
188 G3 **Andrushivka** Zhytomyrs'ka Oblast', N Ukraine 50°01´N 29°02´E
183 G8 **Andrychów** Małopolskie, S Poland 49°51´N 19°18´E
Andryu, Gora *see* Andrew Tablemount
195 M8 **Andryushkino** Sverdlovskaya Oblasť, Russian Federation
152 F4 **Andselv** Troms, N Norway 69°05´N 18°30´E
134 I6 **Andudu** Orientale, NE Dem. Rep. Congo 02°26´N 28°39´E
170 F7 **Andújar** *anc.* Illiturgis. Andalucía, SW Spain 38°02´N 04°03´W
135 D12 **Andulo** Bié, W Angola 11°29´S 16°43´E
165 I8 **Anduze** Gard, S France 44°03´N 03°59´E
An Earagail *see* Errigal Mountain
155 G10 **Aneby** Jönköping, S Sweden 57°50´N 14°45´E
Anécho *see* Aného
133 H3 **Anéfis** Kidal, NE Mali 18°05´N 00°38´E
91 K5 **Anegada** *island* NE British Virgin Islands
116 G7 **Anegada, Bahía** *bay* E Argentina
91 L5 **Anegada Passage** *passage* Anguilla/British Virgin Islands
133 I8 **Aného** *var.* Anécho; *prev.* Petit-Popo. S Togo 06°14´N 01°36´E
281 N6 **Aneityum** *var.* Anatom; *prev.* Kéamu. *island* S Vanuatu
118 F10 **Añelo** Neuquén, Argentina 38°21´S 68°47´W
188 G7 **Anenii Noi** *Rus.* Novyye Aneny. C Moldova 46°52´N 29°10´E
280 C3 **Anepmete** New Britain, E Papua New Guinea 05°47´S 148°37´E
168 E7 **Aneto** ▲ NE Spain 42°36´N 00°37´E
228 D7 **Änew** *Rus.* Annau. Ahal Welaýaty, C Turkmenistan 37°51´N 58°22´E
Änewetak *see* Enewetak Atoll
133 M2 **Aney** Agadez, NE Niger 19°22´N 13°00´E
245 L9 **Anfeng** Jiangsu, W China 33°05´N 120°06´E
An Fheoir *see* Nore
243 I5 **Anfu** Jiangxi, China 27°14´N 114°22´E
86 D6 **Angahuàn** Michoacán, Mexico 19°33´N 102°11´W
250 B3 **An'gang** 35°58´N 129°14´E
250 B3 **An-gang** *prev.* An'gang. Kyŏngsang-bukto, South Korea 36°00´N 129°14´E
An'gang *see* An-gang
193 H8 **Angara** ≈ C Russian Federation
193 H8 **Angarsk** Irkutskaya Oblast', S Russian Federation 52°31´N 103°55´E
110 A9 **Angatuba** São Paulo, Brazil 23°29´S 48°25´W
Angaur *see* Ngeaur
154 H4 **Ånge** Västernorrland, C Sweden 62°31´N 15°40´E
Angel *see* Úhlava
84 D3 **Ángel de la Guarda, Isla** *island* NW Mexico
263 K5 **Angeles** *off.* Angeles City. Luzon, N Philippines 15°16´N 120°37´E
Angeles City *see* Angeles
Angel Falls *see* Ángel, Salto
155 F11 **Ängelholm** Skåne, S Sweden 56°14´N 12°52´E
114 A4 **Angélica** Santa Fe, C Argentina 31°33´S 61°33´W
71 I5 **Angelina River** ≈ Texas, SW USA
103 I5 **Ángel, Salto** *Eng.* Angel Falls. *waterfall* E Venezuela
154 H7 **Ängelsberg** Västmanland, C Sweden 59°57´N 16°01´E
80 D3 **Angels Camp** California, W USA 38°03´N 120°31´W
177 L3 **Anger** Steiermark, SE Austria 47°16´N 15°41´E
Angerapp *see* Ozersk
Angerburg *see* Węgorzewo
154 H2 **Ångermanälven** ≈ N Sweden
178 I6 **Angermünde** Brandenburg, NE Germany 53°02´N 13°59´E
164 F4 **Angers** *anc.* Juliomagus. Maine-et-Loire, NW France 47°30´N 00°33´W
166 G6 **Angervilliers** Essonne, N France 48°35´N 02°03´E
153 G8 **Ängesön** *island* N Sweden
53 M8 **Angijak Island** *Island* Nunavut, NE Canada
55 I4 **Angikuni Lake** ⊛ Nunavut, C Canada
Angistro *see* Ágkistro
187 H2 **Angítis** ≈ NE Greece
257 H9 **Ângk Tasaôm** *prev.* Angtassom. Takêv, S Cambodia
278 B13 **Anglem, Mount** ▲ Stewart Island, Southland, SW New Zealand 46°44´S 167°56´E
169 H8 **Anglès** Cataluña, Spain 41°57´N 2°39´E
157 F9 **Anglesey** *cultural region* NW Wales, United Kingdom
160 E2 **Anglesey** *island* NW Wales, United Kingdom
166 F9 **Angles-sur-l'Anglin** Poitou-Charentes, France 46°42´N 0°52´E

◆ Country
● Country Capital
◇ Dependent Territory
○ Dependent Territory Capital
⬖ Administrative Regions
✈ International Airport
▲ Mountain
▲▲ Mountain Range
Volcano
≈ River
⊛ Lake
⊠ Reservoir

◆ Country	▲ Administrative Regions	▲ Volcano
● Country Capital	✕ International Airport	≈ River
◇ Dependent Territory	▲ Mountain	☒ Lake
○ Dependent Territory Capital	▲ Mountain Range	☒ Reservoir

◆ Country   ◇ Dependent Territory   ◆ Administrative Regions   ▲ Mountain   ✕ Volcano   ⊚ Lake
● Country Capital   ○ Dependent Territory Capital   ✈ International Airport   ▲ Mountain Range   ↔ River   ⊞ Reservoir

◆ Country	◇ Dependent Territory	◆ Administrative Regions	▲ Mountain	✕ Volcano	⊗ Lake
● Country Capital	○ Dependent Territory Capital	✕ International Airport	▲ Mountain Range	⊗ River	⊠ Reservoir

◆ Country   ◇ Dependent Territory   ◈ Administrative Regions   ▲ Mountain   ▲ Volcano   ◎ Lake
● Country Capital   ○ Dependent Territory Capital   ✈ International Airport   ▲ Mountain Range   ↔ River   ◙ Reservoir

◆ Country   ◇ Dependent Territory   ◈ Administrative Regions   ▲ Mountain   ⊠ Volcano   ⊡ Lake
● Country Capital   ◉ Dependent Territory Capital   ✈ International Airport   ▲▲ Mountain Range   ♦ River   ⊠ Reservoir

Bonavista - Brandenburg
INDEX
321

59 M6 **Bonavista** Newfoundland, Newfoundland and Labrador, SE Canada 48°38′N 53°08′W
59 M6 **Bonavista Bay** *inlet* NW Atlantic Ocean
158 F2 **Bonawe** W Scotland, United Kingdom
131 L1 **Bon, Cap** *headland* N Tunisia 37°05′N 11°04′E
160 D5 **Boncath** United Kingdom 52°00′N 4°37′W
159 I4 **Bonchester Bridge** United Kingdom 55°24′N 2°39′W
135 B8 **Bonda** Ogooué-Lolo, C Gabon 0°50′S 12°28′E
197 H3 **Bondari** Tambovskaya Oblast', W Russian Federation 52°58′N 42°02′E
176 G7 **Bondeno** Emilia-Romagna, C Italy 44°53′N 11°24′E
72 D4 **Bond Falls Flowage** ◎ Michigan, N USA
134 G6 **Bondo** Orientale, N Dem. Rep. Congo 03°52′N 23°41′E
260 C8 **Bondokodi** Pulau Sumba, S Indonesia 09°36′S 119°01′E
132 G7 **Bondoukou** E Ivory Coast 08°03′N 02°45′W
Bondoukui/Bondoukuy *see* Boundoukui
259 J9 **Bondowoso** Jawa, C Indonesia 07°54′S 113°50′E
77 J7 **Bondurant** Wyoming, C USA 43°14′N 110°26′W
Bône *see* Annaba, Algeria
Bone *see* Watampone, Indonesia
140 E8 **Bonekraal** Northern Cape, South Africa 31°48′S 20°35′E
72 A5 **Bone Lake** ◎ Wisconsin, N USA
260 E6 **Bonelipu** Pulau Buton, C Indonesia 04°42′S 123°09′E
181 D8 **Bonen** Nordrhein-Westfalen, Germany 51°36′E 7°46′N
260 D7 **Bonerate, Kepulauan** *var.* Macan. *island group* C Indonesia
260 D7 **Bonerate, Pulau** *island* Kepulauan Bonerate, C Indonesia
159 H3 **Bo'ness** United Kingdom 56°01′N 3°37′W
74 D6 **Bonesteel** South Dakota, N USA 43°01′N 98°55′W
173 K5 **Bonete** Castilla-La Manacha, Spain 38°53′N 1°21′W
116 C1 **Bonete, Cerro** ▲ N Argentina 27°58′S 68°22′W
260 D5 **Bone, Teluk** *bay* Sulawesi, C Indonesia
176 C3 **Bonfol** Jura, NW Switzerland 47°28′N 07°08′E
233 K6 **Bongaigaon** Assam, NE India 26°30′N 90°31′E
134 F7 **Bongandanga** Equateur, NW Dem. Rep. Congo 01°28′N 21°03′E
134 G4 **Bongo, Massif des** *var.* Chaîne des Mongos. ▲▲ NE Central African Republic
134 D3 **Bongor** Mayo-Kébbi, SW Chad 10°18′N 15°20′E
132 F8 **Bongouanou** E Ivory Coast 06°39′N 04°12′W
256 J7 **Bông Sơn** *var.* Hoai Nhơn. Binh Đinh, C Vietnam 14°28′N 109°00′E
71 H4 **Bonham** Texas, SW USA 33°36′N 96°12′W
Bonhard *see* Bonyhád
167 M6 **Bonhomme, Col du** *pass* NE France
175 B8 **Bonifacio** Corse, France, C Mediterranean Sea 41°24′N 09°09′E
Bonifacio, Bocche de/Bonifacio, Bouches de *see* Bonifacio, Strait of
175 C8 **Bonifacio, Strait of** *Fr.* Bouches de Bonifacio, *It.* Bocche di Bonifacio. *strait* C Mediterranean Sea
69 I4 **Bonifay** Florida, SE USA 30°49′N 85°42′W
Bonin Islands *see* Ogasawara-shotō
286 D4 **Bonin Trench** *undersea feature* NW Pacific Ocean
69 L8 **Bonita Springs** Florida, SE USA 26°19′N 81°48′W
88 G3 **Bonito, Pico** ▲ N Honduras 15°33′N 86°55′W
181 C10 **Bonn** Nordrhein-Westfalen, W Germany 50°44′N 07°06′E
152 E5 **Bonnåsjøen** Nordland, C Norway 67°35′N 15°39′E
62 E3 **Bonnechere** Ontario, SE Canada 45°39′N 77°36′W
62 E3 **Bonnechere** ≈ Ontario, SE Canada
76 F3 **Bonners Ferry** Idaho, NW USA 48°41′N 116°19′W
166 G9 **Bonnet** Centre, France 46°42′N 1°51′E
164 G4 **Bonnétable** Sarthe, NW France 48°09′N 00°24′E
66 A3 **Bonne Terre** Missouri, C USA 37°55′N 90°33′W
54 C2 **Bonnet Plume** ≈ Yukon Territory, NW Canada
165 H4 **Bonneval** Eure-et-Loir, C France 48°12′N 01°23′E
167 M10 **Bonneville** Haute-Savoie, E France 46°05′N 06°25′E
78 G2 **Bonneville Salt Flats** *salt flat* Utah, W USA
166 G5 **Bonniéres-sur-Seine** Yvelines, N France 49°02′N 01°35′E
169 K5 **Bonnieux** Provence-Alpes-Côte d'Azur, France 43°49′N 5°18′E
133 K9 **Bonny** Rivers, S Nigeria 04°25′N 07°13′E
Bonny, Bight of *see* Biafra, Bight of
79 N3 **Bonny Reservoir** ⊠ Colorado, C USA
159 I3 **Bonnyrigg** United Kingdom 55°52′N 3°06′W
57 K4 **Bonnyville** Alberta, SW Canada 54°16′N 110°46′W
175 B9 **Bono** Sardegna, Italy, C Mediterranean Sea 40°24′N 09°01′E
261 K5 **Bonoi** Papua, E Indonesia 01°46′S 137°45′E
Bononia *see* Vidin, Bulgaria
Bononia *see* Boulogne-sur-Mer, France
175 B9 **Bonorva** Sardegna, Italy, C Mediterranean Sea 40°27′N 08°46′E
73 D12 **Bonpas Creek** ≈ Illinois, N USA
284 D2 **Bonriki** Tarawa, W Kiribati 01°23′N 173°09′E
81 E12 **Bonsall** California, USA 33°17′N 117°14′W
277 L3 **Bonshaw** New South Wales, SE Australia 29°06′S 151°15′E
132 C7 **Bonthe** SW Sierra Leone 07°32′N 12°30′W
263 K4 **Bontoc** Luzon, N Philippines 17°04′N 120°58′E
160 F6 **Bonvilston** S Wales, United Kingdom 51°28′N 3°20′W
71 J6 **Bon Wier** Texas, SW USA 30°43′N 93°40′W
183 F13 **Bonyhád** *Ger.* Bonhard. Tolna, S Hungary 46°20′N 18°31′E
276 E4 **Bookabie** South Australia 31°49′S 132°41′E
276 F4 **Bookaloo** South Australia 31°56′S 137°21′E
79 J3 **Book Cliffs** *cliff* Colorado/Utah, W USA
261 H4 **Boo, Kepulauan** *island group* E Indonesia
70 E1 **Booker** Texas, SW USA 36°27′N 100°32′W
132 E7 **Boola** SE Guinea 08°22′N 08°41′W
277 J5 **Booligal** New South Wales, SE Australia 33°56′S 144°54′E
163 E9 **Boom** Antwerpen, N Belgium 51°05′N 04°24′E
89 H4 **Boom** *var.* Boon. Región Autónoma Atlántico Norte, NE Nicaragua 14°52′N 83°36′W
277 L2 **Boomi** New South Wales, SE Australia 28°43′S 149°35′E
Boon *see* Boom
239 I2 **Bööncagaan Nuur** ◎ S Mongolia
74 G7 **Boone** Iowa, C USA 42°04′N 93°52′W
67 I6 **Boone** North Carolina, SE USA 36°13′N 81°41′W
75 G12 **Booneville** Arkansas, C USA 35°09′N 93°57′W
66 G4 **Booneville** Kentucky, S USA 37°26′N 83°45′W
66 C7 **Booneville** Mississippi, S USA 34°39′N 88°34′W
64 C8 **Boonsboro** Maryland, NE USA 39°30′N 77°39′W
65 H6 **Boonton** New Jersey, USA 40°54′N 74°24′W
78 A3 **Boonville** California, W USA 38°58′N 123°21′W
73 E12 **Boonville** Indiana, N USA 38°03′N 87°16′W
75 H9 **Boonville** Missouri, C USA 38°58′N 92°43′W
62 G5 **Boonville** New York, NE USA 43°28′N 75°17′W
136 G4 **Boorama** Awdal, NW Somalia 09°58′N 43°15′E
277 J3 **Booroondarra, Mount** *hill* New South Wales, SE Australia
277 I5 **Booroorban** New South Wales, SE Australia 34°55′S 144°45′E
277 K5 **Boorowa** New South Wales, SE Australia 34°26′S 148°42′E
163 E10 **Boortmeerbeek** Vlaams Brabant, C Belgium 50°58′N 04°27′E
166 F4 **Boos** Haute-Normandie, France 49°23′N 1°12′E
136 I3 **Boosaaso** *var.* Bandar Kassim, Bender Qaasim, Bosaso, *It.* Bender Cassim. Bari, N Somalia 11°26′N 49°37′E
180 H1 **Boostedt** Schleswig-Holstein, Germany 54°01′E 10°02′N
63 K5 **Boothbay Harbor** Maine, NE USA 43°52′N 69°35′W
Boothia Felix *see* Boothia Peninsula
53 H7 **Boothia, Gulf of** *gulf* Nunavut, NE Canada
53 H7 **Boothia Peninsula** *prev.* Boothia Felix. *peninsula* Nunavut, NE Canada
159 I10 **Bootle** United Kingdom 53°28′N 3°01′W
134 B7 **Booué** Ogooué-Ivindo, NE Gabon 0°03′S 11°58′E
179 E12 **Bopfingen** Baden-Württemberg, S Germany 48°51′N 10°21′E
245 J6 **Boping** Shandong, E China 36°35′N 116°07′E
243 K8 **Boping Ling** ▲▲ Fujan, China
181 D11 **Boppard** Rheinland-Pfalz, W Germany 50°13′N 07°36′E
115 N3 **Boqueirão** Rio Grande do Sul, Brazil 31°17′S 52°05′W
112 F3 **Boquerón** *off.* Departamento de Boquerón. ◐ *department* W Paraguay
Boquerón, Departamento de *see* Boquerón
89 I9 **Boquete** *var.* Bajo Boquete. Chiriquí, W Panama 08°45′N 82°26′W
85 H5 **Boquilla, Presa de la** ⊠ N Mexico
85 J4 **Boquillas** *var.* Boquillas del Carmen. Coahuila, NE Mexico 29°10′N 102°55′W
Boquillas del Carmen *see* Boquillas
192 G6 **Bor** Krasnoyarskiy Kray, C Russian Federation 61°28′N 90°09′E
185 H4 **Bor** Serbia, E Serbia 44°05′N 22°07′E
136 B5 **Bor** Jonglei, C South Sudan 06°12′N 31°33′E
155 G10 **Bor** Jönköping, S Sweden 57°04′N 14°10′E
214 F7 **Bor** Niğde, S Turkey 37°49′N 35°00′E
285 I6 **Bora-Bora** *island* Îles Sous le Vent, W French Polynesia
256 G7 **Borabu** Maha Sarakham, E Thailand 16°01′N 103°06′E
110 A7 **Boracéia** São Paulo, Brazil 22°10′S 48°45′W
137 J14 **Boraha, Nosy** *island* E Madagascar
77 H6 **Borah Peak** ▲ Idaho, NW USA 44°21′N 113°53′W
227 K7 **Boralday** *prev.* Burunday. Almaty, SE Kazakhstan 43°21′N 76°48′E
227 M4 **Boran** *prev.* Buran. Vostochnyy Kazakhstan, E Kazakhstan 48°00′N 85°09′E
226 C6 **Borankul** *prev.* Opornyy. Mangistau, SW Kazakhstan 46°09′N 54°32′E
155 F10 **Borås** Västra Götaland, S Sweden 57°44′N 12°55′E
222 F7 **Borāzjān** *var.* Borazjān. Būshehr, S Iran 29°19′N 51°12′E
Borazjān *see* Borāzjān
107 H4 **Borba** Amazonas, N Brazil 04°39′S 59°35′W
172 C5 **Borba** Évora, S Portugal 38°48′N 07°28′W
Borbetomagus *see* Worms
103 H4 **Borbón** Bolívar, E Venezuela 07°55′N 64°03′W
108 I5 **Borborema, Planalto da** *plateau* NE Brazil
188 F10 **Borcea, Braţul** ≈ S Romania
Borchalo *see* Marneuli
293 I8 **Borchgrevink Coast** *physical region* Antarctica
215 I4 **Borçka** Artvin, NE Turkey 41°24′N 41°38′E
162 I6 **Borculo** Gelderland, E Netherlands 52°07′N 06°31′E
276 F6 **Borda, Cape** *headland* South Australia 35°45′S 136°34′E
110 D7 **Borda da Matta** Minas Gerais, Brazil 22°16′S 46°10′W
164 F7 **Bordeaux** *anc.* Burdigala. Gironde, SW France 44°49′N 00°33′W
57 M6 **Borden** Saskatchewan, S Canada 52°23′N 107°10′W
52 F3 **Borden Island** *Island* Northwest Territories/ Nunavut, N Canada
72 H3 **Borden Lake** ◎ Ontario, S Canada
53 I6 **Borden Peninsula** *peninsula* Baffin Island, Nunavut, NE Canada
159 I5 **Borders** *cultural region* S Scotland, United Kingdom
277 H6 **Bordertown** South Australia 36°21′S 140°48′E
152 B2 **Bordheyri** Vestfirdhir, NW Iceland 65°12′N 21°09′W
154 B1 **Bordhoy** *Dan.* Bordø. *island* NE Faeroe Islands
176 D9 **Bordighera** Liguria, NW Italy 43°48′N 07°40′E
173 N9 **Bordj Abou El Hassen** Algeria 36°27′N 01°18′E
131 I2 **Bordj-Bou-Arreridj** *var.* Bordj Bou Arreridj, Bordj Bou Arréridj. N Algeria 36°02′N 04°49′E
171 K10 **Bordj Bounaama** Algeria
131 I1 **Bordj El Bahri, Cap de** *headland* N Algeria 36°52′N 03°13′E
171 M9 **Bordj Menaiel** Algeria
131 J5 **Bordj Omar Driss** E Algeria 28°09′N 06°52′E
171 N9 **Bordj Zemoura** Algeria
222 F8 **Bord Khūn** Hormozgān, S Iran
Bordø *see* Bordhoy
161 J7 **Bordon** S England, United Kingdom 51°05′N 00°56′W
229 L4 **Bordunskiy** Chuyskaya Oblast', N Kyrgyzstan 42°37′N 75°31′E
159 I5 **Boreland** United Kingdom 55°12′N 3°19′W
155 H9 **Borensberg** Östergötland, S Sweden 58°33′N 15°15′E
Borgå *see* Porvoo
152 E2 **Borgarfjördhur** Austurland, NE Iceland 65°32′N 13°46′W
152 B2 **Borgarnes** Vesturland, W Iceland 64°33′N 21°55′W
154 F1 **Børgefjell** ▲▲ C Norway
181 G8 **Borgentreich** Nordrhein-Westfalen, Germany 51°34′E 9°15′N
162 I4 **Borger** Drenthe, NE Netherlands 52°54′N 06°48′E
70 E2 **Borger** Texas, SW USA 35°40′N 101°24′W
155 I11 **Borgholm** Kalmar, S Sweden 56°50′N 16°41′E
180 D6 **Borghorst** Nordrhein-Westfalen, Germany 52°08′E 7°25′N
175 H11 **Borgia** Calabria, SW Italy 38°48′N 16°28′E
163 F10 **Borgloon** Limburg, NE Belgium 50°48′N 05°21′E
Borg Massif *see* Borgmassivet
293 H2 **Borgmassivet** *Eng.* Borg Massif. ▲▲ Antarctica
68 E4 **Borgne, Lake** ◎ Louisiana, S USA
169 N2 **Borgofranco d'Ivrea** Piemonte, NW Italy 45°30′N 07°51′E
176 E6 **Borgomanero** Piemonte, NE Italy 45°42′N 08°33′E
174 D5 **Borgo Panigale** ✈ (Bologna) Emilia-Romagna, N Italy 44°33′N 11°16′E
175 F8 **Borgorose** Lazio, C Italy 42°10′N 13°15′E
176 C8 **Borgo San Dalmazzo** Piemonte, N Italy 44°19′N 07°29′E
176 G9 **Borgo San Lorenzo** Toscana, C Italy 43°58′N 11°22′E
176 D6 **Borgosesia** Piemonte, NE Italy 45°41′N 08°21′E
176 F8 **Borgo Val di Taro** Emilia-Romagna, C Italy 44°29′N 09°48′E
176 G6 **Borgo Valsugana** Trentino-Alto Adige, N Italy 46°04′N 11°31′E
158 G6 **Borgue** United Kingdom 54°48′N 4°08′W
Borhoyn Tal *see* Dzamïn-Üüd
256 G6 **Borikhan** *var.* Borikhane. Bolikhamxai, C Laos 18°36′N 103°43′E
Borikhane *see* Borikhan
226 C3 **Borili** *prev.* Burlin. Zapadnyy Kazakhstan, NW Kazakhstan 51°25′N 52°42′E
Borislav *see* Boryslav
197 H4 **Borisoglebsk** Voronezhskaya Oblast', W Russian Federation 51°23′N 42°00′E
Borisov *see* Barysaw
Borisovgrad *see* Pŭrvomay
Borispol' *see* Boryspil'
139 M5 **Boriziny** *prev./Fr.* Port-Bergé. Mahajanga, NW Madagascar 15°31′S 47°40′E
171 H3 **Borja** Aragón, NE Spain 41°50′N 01°32′W
Borjas Blancas *see* Les Borges Blanques
215 J4 **Borjomi** *Rus.* Borzhomi. C Georgia 41°50′N 43°24′E
190 G7 **Borkavichy** *Rus.* Borkovichi. Vitsyebskaya Voblasts', N Belarus 55°40′N 28°20′E
181 G9 **Borken** Hessen, C Germany 51°01′N 09°16′E
180 C7 **Borken** Nordrhein-Westfalen, W Germany 51°51′N 06°51′E
152 E4 **Borkenes** Troms, N Norway 68°46′N 16°10′E
133 N2 **Borkou-Ennedi-Tibesti** *off.* Préfecture du Borkou-Ennedi-Tibesti. ◐ *prefecture* N Chad
Borkou-Ennedi-Tibesti, Préfecture du *see* Borkou-Ennedi-Tibesti
Borkovichi *see* Borkavichy
180 C2 **Borkum** *island* NW Germany
136 F7 **Bor, Lagh** *var.* Lak Bor. *dry watercourse* NE Kenya
Bor, Lak *see* Bor, Lagh
154 H7 **Borlänge** Dalarna, C Sweden 60°29′N 15°25′E
187 M5 **Borlu** Manisa, Turkey 38°46′N 28°29′E
169 L6 **Bormes-les-Mimosas** Provence-Alpes-Côte d'Azur, France 43°09′N 6°20′E
176 D8 **Bormida** ≈ NW Italy
176 F5 **Bormio** Lombardia, N Italy 46°27′N 10°24′E
179 H8 **Borna** Sachsen, E Germany 51°07′N 12°30′E
162 I6 **Borne** Overijssel, E Netherlands 52°18′N 06°45′E
163 D9 **Bornem** Antwerpen, N Belgium 51°06′N 04°14′E
259 J4 **Borneo** *island* Brunei/Indonesia/Malaysia
181 C10 **Bornheim** Nordrhein-Westfalen, W Germany 50°46′N 06°58′E
178 J2 **Bornholm** ◐ *county* E Denmark
178 I2 **Bornholm** *island* E Denmark
133 M5 **Borno** ◐ *state* NE Nigeria
170 E8 **Bornos** Andalucía, S Spain 36°50′N 05°42′W
187 K5 **Bornova** İzmir, Turkey 38°28′N 27°13′E
239 K1 **Bornuur** Töv, C Mongolia 48°28′N 106°15′E
64 E1 **Borodino** New York, USA 42°52′N 76°20′W
190 G1 **Borodinskoye** Leningradskaya Oblast', Russian Federation
188 G3 **Borodyanka** Kyyivs'ka Oblast', N Ukraine 50°40′N 29°54′E
193 K6 **Borogontsy** Respublika Sakha (Yakutiya), NE Russian Federation 62°42′N 131°01′E
238 E3 **Borohoro Shan** ▲▲ NW China
190 J3 **Borok** Novgorodskaya Oblast', Russian Federation
132 G5 **Boromo** SW Burkina 11°47′N 02°54′W
81 F9 **Boron** California, W USA 35°00′N 117°42′W
263 M7 **Borongan** Samar, C Philippines 11°26′N 125°30′E
Borongo *see* Black Volta
Boron'ki *see* Baron'ki
Borosjenő *see* Ineu
Borossebes *see* Sebiş
132 E7 **Borotou** NW Ivory Coast 08°46′N 07°30′W
159 K8 **Boroughbridge** United Kingdom 54°05′N 1°24′W
189 M4 **Borova** Kharkivs'ka Oblast', E Ukraine 49°22′N 37°39′E
185 I5 **Borovan** Vratsa, NW Bulgaria 43°25′N 23°45′E
194 E9 **Borovichi** Novgorodskaya Oblast', W Russian Federation 58°24′N 33°56′E
190 H5 **Borovichi** Pskovskaya Oblast', Russian Federation
Borovlje *see* Ferlach
184 E3 **Borovo** Vukovar-Srijem, NE Croatia 45°22′N 18°57′E
Borovoye *see* Burabay
196 F2 **Borovsk** Kaluzhskaya Oblast', W Russian Federation 55°12′N 36°22′E
195 N9 **Borovskiy** Tyumenskaya Oblast', C Russian Federation 57°04′N 65°37′E
226 G2 **Borovskoye** Kostanay, N Kazakhstan 53°48′N 64°17′E
155 G12 **Borrby** Skåne, S Sweden 55°27′N 14°10′E
81 F12 **Borrego Springs** California, USA 33°15′N 116°23′W
160 A3 **Borris** Carlow, Ireland 52°36′N 6°55′W
275 H3 **Borroloola** Northern Territory, N Australia 16°09′S 136°18′E
188 B6 **Borş** Bihor, NW Romania 47°07′N 21°49′E
188 D6 **Borşa** *Hung.* Borsa. Maramureş, N Romania 47°40′N 24°37′E
188 D7 **Borsec** *Ger.* Bad Borseck, *Hung.* Borszék. Harghita, C Romania 46°58′N 25°32′E
152 H3 **Børselv** *Lapp.* Bissojohka. Finnmark, N Norway 70°18′N 25°35′E
184 F10 **Borsh** *var.* Borshi. Vlorë, S Albania 40°04′N 19°51′E
Borshchev *see* Borshchiv
188 E5 **Borshchiv** *Pol.* Borszczów, *Rus.* Borshchev. Ternopil's'ka Oblast', W Ukraine 48°48′N 26°00′E
Borshi *see* Borsh
183 I10 **Borsod-Abaúj-Zemplén** *off.* Borsod-Abaúj-Zemplén Megye. ◐ *county* NE Hungary
Borsod-Abaúj-Zemplén Megye *see* Borsod-Abaúj-Zemplén
163 C8 **Borssele** Zeeland, SW Netherlands 51°26′N 03°45′E
180 I6 **Börssum** Niedersachsen, Germany 52°04′E 10°35′N
Borszczów *see* Borshchiv
Borszék *see* Borsec
Bortala *see* Bole
160 E4 **Borth** United Kingdom 52°29′N 4°03′W
165 H6 **Bort-les-Orgues** Corrèze, C France 45°28′N 02°31′E
Bor u České Lípy *see* Nový Bor
Bor-Üdzüür *see* Altay
222 F6 **Borūjen** Chahār Maḩall va Bakhtīārī, C Iran 32°N 51°09′E
222 E4 **Borūjerd** *var.* Burujird. Lorestān, W Iran 33°55′N 48°46′E
188 C4 **Boryslav** *Pol.* Borysław, *Rus.* Borislav. L'vivs'ka Oblast', NW Ukraine 49°18′N 23°28′E
Borysław *see* Boryslav
189 H3 **Boryspil'** *Rus.* Borispol'. Kyyivs'ka Oblast', N Ukraine 50°21′N 30°59′E
189 H3 **Boryspil'** *Rus.* Borispol'. ✈ (Kyyiv) Kyyivs'ka Oblast', N Ukraine 50°21′N 30°46′E
Borzhomi *see* Borjomi
189 I2 **Borzna** Chernihivs'ka Oblast', NE Ukraine 51°15′N 32°25′E
193 J8 **Borzya** Zabaykalskiy Kray, S Russian Federation 50°18′N 116°24′E
175 B9 **Bosa** Sardegna, Italy, C Mediterranean Sea 40°18′N 08°28′E
184 C3 **Bosanska Dubica** *var.* Kozarska Dubica. ◐ Republika Srpska, NW Bosnia and Herzegovina
184 D3 **Bosanska Gradiška** *var.* Gradiška. ◐ Republika Srpska, N Bosnia and Herzegovina
184 C3 **Bosanska Kostajnica** *var.* Srpska Kostajnica. ◐ Republika Srpska, NW Bosnia and Herzegovina
184 C3 **Bosanska Krupa** *var.* Krupa, Krupa na Uni. ◐ Federacija Bosna I Hercegovina, NW Bosnia and Herzegovina
184 D3 **Bosanski Brod** *var.* Srpski Brod. ◐ Republika Srpska, N Bosnia and Herzegovina
184 C4 **Bosanski Petrovac** *var.* Petrovac. Federacija Bosna I Hercegovina, NW Bosnia and Herzegovina 44°34′N 16°21′E
184 E3 **Bosanski Šamac** *var.* Šamac. Republika Srpska, N Bosnia and Herzegovina 45°03′N 18°27′E
184 C4 **Bosansko Grahovo** *var.* Grahovo, Hrvatsko Grahovi. Federacija Bosna I Hercegovina, W Bosnia and Herzegovina 44°10′N 16°22′E
Bosaso *see* Boosaaso
180 I1 **Bosau** Schleswig-Holstein, Germany 54°07′E 10°26′N
280 A3 **Bosavi, Mount** ⛰ W Papua New Guinea 06°33′S 142°50′E
160 D8 **Boscastle** United Kingdom 50°41′N 4°41′W
242 C8 **Bose** Guangxi Zhuangzu Zizhiqu, S China 23°55′N 106°32′E
245 K6 **Boshan** Shandong, E China 36°32′N 117°47′E
160 D6 **Bosherston** United Kingdom 51°37′N 4°56′W
141 H6 **Boshof** Free State, South Africa 28°33′S 25°14′E
185 H6 **Bosilegrad** *prev.* Bosiljgrad. Serbia, SE Serbia 42°30′N 22°30′E
Bosiljgrad *see* Bosilegrad
Bösing *see* Pezinok
180 G6 **Bösingfeld** Nordrhein-Westfalen, Germany 52°04′E 9°07′N
162 E7 **Boskoop** Zuid-Holland, C Netherlands 52°04′N 04°40′E
183 D9 **Boskovice** *Ger.* Boskowitz. Jihomoravský Kraj, SE Czech Republic 49°30′N 16°39′E
Boskowitz *see* Boskovice
141 H5 **Boskuil** North West, South Africa 27°24′S 25°52′E
184 E3 **Bosna** ≈ N Bosnia and Herzegovina
261 K4 **Bosnabraidi** Papua, E Indonesia 0°49′S 136°00′E
184 D5 **Bosna I Hercegovina, Federacija** ◐ *republic* Bosnia and Herzegovina
184 D4 **Bosnia and Herzegovina** *off.* Republic of Bosnia and Herzegovina. ◆ *republic* SE Europe
Bosnia and Herzegovina, Republic of *see* Bosnia and Herzegovina
134 F6 **Bosobolo** Equateur, NW Dem. Rep. Congo 04°11′N 19°55′E
253 C14 **Bōsō-hantō** *peninsula* Honshū, S Japan
Bosora *see* Buşrá ash Shām
Bosphorus/Bosporus *see* İstanbul Boğazı
141 H4 **Bospoort** North-West, South Africa 26°37′S 26°12′E
Bosporus Cimmerius *see* Kerch Strait
Bosporus Thracius *see* İstanbul Boğazı
Bosra *see* Buşrá ash Shām
134 D5 **Bossangoa** Ouham, C Central African Republic 06°32′N 17°25′E
Bossé Bangou *see* Bossey Bangou
134 E5 **Bossembélé** Ombella-Mpoko, C Central African Republic 05°13′N 17°39′E
134 D5 **Bossentélé** Ouham-Pendé, W Central African Republic 05°36′N 16°37′E
133 H5 **Bossey Bangou** *var.* Bossé Bangou. Tillabéri, SW Niger 13°22′N 01°18′E
140 E6 **Bossiekom** Northern Cape, South Africa 29°17′S 20°22′E
68 B1 **Bossier City** Louisiana, S USA 32°31′N 93°43′W
140 C3 **Bossiesvlei** Hardap, S Namibia 25°02′S 16°48′E
133 M4 **Bosso** Diffa, SE Niger 13°42′N 13°18′E
116 J1 **Bossoroca** Rio Grande do Sul, S Brazil 28°45′S 54°54′W
113 H6 **Bossoroca** Rio Grande do Sul, S Brazil 28°45′S 54°54′W
238 E6 **Bostan** Xinjiang Uygur Zizhiqu, W China 41°20′N 83°15′E
222 D2 **Bostānābād** Āžarbāyjān-e Sharqī, N Iran 37°52′N 46°51′E
238 F4 **Bosten Hu** *var.* Bagrax Hu. ◎ NW China
161 K2 **Boston** *prev.* St.Botolph's Town. E England, United Kingdom 52°59′N 00°01′W
63 J6 **Boston** *state capital* Massachusetts, NE USA 42°22′N 71°04′W
228 E5 **Bo'ston** *Rus.* Bustan. Qoraqalpog'iston Respublikasi, W Uzbekistan 41°49′N 60°51′E
56 E8 **Boston Bar** British Columbia, SW Canada 49°54′N 121°22′W
75 G12 **Boston Mountains** ▲▲ Arkansas, C USA
Bostyn' *see* Bastyn'
184 E3 **Bosut** ≈ E Croatia
232 C8 **Botād** Gujarāt, W India 22°12′N 71°44′E
227 J4 **Botakara** *Kas.* Botaqara; *prev.* Ul'yanovskiy. Karaganda, C Kazakhstan 50°05′N 73°45′E
277 L5 **Botany Bay** *inlet* New South Wales, SE Australia
Botaqara *see* Botakara
141 L5 **Boteler Point** *point* KwaZulu-Natal, South Africa
110 D6 **Botelhos** Minas Gerais, Brazil 21°39′S 46°24′W
138 E4 **Boteti** *var.* Botletle. ≈ N Botswana
185 J6 **Botev** ▲ C Bulgaria 42°45′N 24°57′E
185 I6 **Botevgrad** *prev.* Orkhaniye. Sofiya, W Bulgaria 42°55′N 23°47′E
141 K5 **Bothaspas** *pass* South Africa
159 I6 **Bothel** Cumbria, NW England, United Kingdom 54°44′N 3°16′E
154 J4 **Bothnia, Gulf of** *Fin.* Pohjanlahti, *Swe.* Bottniska Viken. *gulf* N Baltic Sea
277 J10 **Bothwell** Tasmania, SE Australia 42°24′S 147°01′E
170 D3 **Boticas** Vila Real, N Portugal 41°41′N 07°40′W
103 L6 **Boti-Pasi** Sipaliwini, C Suriname 04°15′N 55°27′W
Botletle *see* Boteti
197 I9 **Botlikh** Chechenskaya Respublika, SW Russian Federation 42°39′N 46°12′E
188 G7 **Botna** ≈ E Moldova
188 E6 **Botoşani** *Hung.* Botosány. Botoşani, NE Romania 47°44′N 26°41′E
188 E6 **Botoşani** ◐ *county* NE Romania
Botosány *see* Botoşani
245 J4 **Botou** *prev.* Bozhen. Hebei, E China 38°09′N 116°37′E
163 H11 **Botrange** ▲ E Belgium 50°30′N 06°03′E
175 I11 **Botricello** Calabria, SW Italy 38°56′N 16°51′E
138 G8 **Botshabelo** Free State, C South Africa 29°15′S 26°51′E
154 J2 **Botsmark** Västerbotten, N Sweden 64°15′N 20°15′E
140 G1 **Botswana** *off.* Republic of Botswana. ◆ *republic* S Africa
Botswana, Republic of *see* Botswana
140 D8 **Botterkloof Pass** Northern Cape, South Africa
74 C1 **Bottineau** North Dakota, N USA 48°50′N 100°28′W
Bottniska Viken *see* Bothnia, Gulf of
181 C8 **Bottrop** Nordrhein-Westfalen, Germany 51°31′E 6°55′N
110 A8 **Botucatu** São Paulo, S Brazil 22°52′S 48°30′W
132 F7 **Bouaflé** C Ivory Coast 06°59′N 05°45′W
132 F7 **Bouaké** *var.* Bwake. C Ivory Coast 07°42′N 05°00′W
134 D5 **Bouar** Nana-Mambéré, W Central African Republic 05°58′N 15°38′E
175 B13 **Bou Arada** Tunisia
130 G3 **Bouarfa** NE Morocco 32°33′N 01°54′W
166 C8 **Bouaye** Pays de la Loire, France 47°09′N 1°42′W
183 B9 **Boubín** ▲ SW Czech Republic 49°00′N 13°51′E
134 E5 **Bouca** Ouham, W Central African Republic 06°57′N 18°18′E
168 C5 **Boucau** Aquitaine, France 43°32′N 1°30′W
165 J8 **Bouches-du-Rhône** ◐ *department* SE France
167 H4 **Bouchoir** Picardie, France 49°45′N 2°41′E
169 J5 **Boucoiran-et-Noziéres** Languedoc-Roussillon, France 43°59′N 4°11′E
130 C5 **Bou Craa** *var.* Bu Craa. NW Western Sahara 26°32′N 12°52′W
63 N1 **Bouctouche** New Brunswick, SE Canada 46°28′N 64°43′W
132 G2 **Boû Djébéha** *oasis* C Mali
176 C4 **Boudry** Neuchâtel, W Switzerland 46°57′N 06°46′E
135 C9 **Bouenza** ◐ *province* S Congo
274 F2 **Bougainville, Cape** *cape* Western Australia
117 I10 **Bougainville, Cape** *headland* East Falkland, Falkland Islands 51°18′S 58°28′W
Bougainville, Détroit de *see* Bougainville Strait
280 E3 **Bougainville Island** *island* NE Papua New Guinea
280 F3 **Bougainville Strait** *strait* N Solomon Islands
281 M3 **Bougainville Strait** *Fr.* Détroit de Bougainville. *strait* C Vanuatu
261 H4 **Bouganville, Selat** *strait* Papua, E Indonesia
131 J1 **Bougaroun, Cap** *headland* NE Algeria 37°07′N 06°18′E
171 N9 **Bougga** Algeria
133 I2 **Boughessa** Kidal, NE Mali 20°05′N 02°13′E
Bougie *see* Béjaïa
132 E5 **Bougouni** Sikasso, SW Mali 11°25′N 07°28′W
171 J10 **Bouguirat** Algeria
175 C14 **Bou Hadjila** Tunisia
171 J10 **Bou Hanifla El Hamamat** Algeria
163 F13 **Bouillon** Luxembourg, SE Belgium 49°47′N 05°04′E
131 I1 **Bouira** *var.* Bouïra. N Algeria 36°22′N 03°55′E
130 E4 **Bou-Izakarn** SW Morocco 29°12′N 09°43′W
130 C6 **Boujdour** *var.* Bojador. W Western Sahara 26°06′N 14°29′W
171 K9 **Bou Kadir** Algeria
130 F2 **Boukhalef** ✈ (Tanger) N Morocco 35°45′N 05°53′W
Boukombé *see* Boukoumbé
133 H6 **Boukoumbé** *var.* Boukombé. C Benin 10°13′N 01°09′E
132 B1 **Boû Lanouâr** Dakhlet Nouâdhibou, W Mauritania 21°17′N 16°29′W
167 L4 **Boulay - Moselle** Lorraine, France 49°11′N 6°30′E
79 L3 **Boulder** Colorado, C USA 40°02′N 105°18′W
77 I5 **Boulder** Montana, NW USA 46°14′N 112°07′W
81 J9 **Boulder City** Nevada, W USA 35°58′N 114°49′W
80 B4 **Boulder Creek** California, USA 37°08′N 122°07′W
81 F13 **Boulevard** California, USA 32°40′N 116°16′W
275 I5 **Boulia** Queensland, C Australia 23°02′S 139°58′E
62 G1 **Boullé** ≈ Québec, SE Canada
164 F5 **Boulogne** ≈ NW France
Boulogne *see* Boulogne-sur-Mer
167 H5 **Boulogne-Billancourt** Île-de-France, N France Europe 48°50′N 02°14′E
168 E6 **Boulogne-sur-Geese** Midi-Pyrénées, France 43°18′N 0°39′E
171 J1 **Boulogne-sur-Gesse** Haute-Garonne, S France 43°18′N 00°38′E
157 J12 **Boulogne-sur-Mer** *var.* Boulogne; *anc.* Bononia, Gesoriacum, Gessoriacum. Pas-de-Calais, N France 50°43′N 01°36′E
166 F7 **Bouloire** Pays de la Loire, France 47°58′N 0°33′E
280 B10 **Bouloupari** Province Sud, S New Caledonia 21°54′S 166°04′E
133 H5 **Boulsa** C Burkina 12°41′N 00°29′W
133 L4 **Boultoum** Zinder, C Niger 14°43′N 10°22′E
280 F8 **Bouma** Taveuni, N Fiji 16°49′S 179°50′W
134 C6 **Boumba** ≈ SE Cameroon
132 D3 **Boûmdeïd** *var.* Boumdeït. Assaba, S Mauritania 17°26′N 11°21′W
Boumdeït *see* Boûmdeïd
171 M8 **Boumerdes** Algeria
186 F5 **Boumistós** ▲ W Greece 38°48′N 20°59′E
132 G6 **Bouna** NE Ivory Coast 09°16′N 03°00′W
63 J3 **Boundary Bald Mountain** ▲ Maine, NE USA 45°45′N 70°10′W
80 G5 **Boundary Peak** ▲ Nevada, W USA 37°50′N 118°21′W
132 E6 **Boundiali** N Ivory Coast 09°30′N 06°31′W
135 D8 **Boundji** Cuvette, C Congo 01°05′S 15°18′E
132 F5 **Boundoukui** *var.* Bondoukui, Bondoukuy. W Burkina 11°51′N 03°47′W
79 H2 **Bountiful** Utah, W USA 40°53′N 111°52′W
Bounty Basin *see* Bounty Trough
285 N9 **Bounty Bay** *bay* Pitcairn Island, C Pacific Ocean
286 F9 **Bounty Islands** *island group* S New Zealand
267 I8 **Bounty Trough** *var.* Bounty Basin. *undersea feature* S Pacific Ocean
167 H3 **Bouquemaison** Picardie, France 50°13′N 2°20′E
280 B9 **Bourail** Province Sud, C New Caledonia 21°35′S 165°29′E
75 I10 **Bourbeuse River** ≈ Missouri, C USA
165 I5 **Bourbon-Lancy** Saône-et-Loire, C France 46°39′N 03°48′E
167 H9 **Bourbon-l'Archambault** Auvergne, France 46°35′N 3°03′E
73 D9 **Bourbonnais** Illinois, N USA 41°08′N 87°52′W
165 I5 **Bourbonnais** *cultural region* C France
165 J4 **Bourbonne-les-Bains** Haute-Marne, N France 48°00′N 05°43′E
Bourbon Vendée *see* la Roche-sur-Yon
166 G1 **Bourbourg** Nord-Pas-de-Calais, France 50°57′N 2°12′E
166 A6 **Bourbriac** Bretagne, France 48°29′N 3°11′W
169 K4 **Bourdeaux** Rhône-Alpes, France 44°35′N 5°08′E
168 D6 **Bourdettes** Aquitaine, France 43°12′N 0°16′W
131 K4 **Bourdj Messaouda** E Algeria 30°18′N 09°19′E
133 H3 **Bourem** Gao, C Mali 16°56′N 00°21′W
Bourg *see* Bourg-en-Bresse
166 F4 **Bourg-Achard** Haute-Normandie, France 49°21′N 0°49′E
165 H6 **Bourganeuf** Creuse, C France 45°57′N 01°47′E
Bourgas *see* Burgas
169 K3 **Bourg-de-Péage** Rhône-Alpes, France 45°02′N 5°03′E
Bourge-en-Bresse *see* Bourg-en-Bresse
165 J6 **Bourg-en-Bresse** *var.* Bourg, Bourge-en-Bresse. Ain, E France 46°12′N 05°13′E
165 H5 **Bourges** *anc.* Avaricum. Cher, C France 47°06′N 02°24′E
165 J6 **Bourget, Lac du** ◎ E France
169 H2 **Bourg-Lastic** Auvergne, France 45°39′N 2°34′E
168 G8 **Bourg-Madame** Languedoc-Roussillon, France 42°26′N 1°56′E
166 C8 **Bourgneuf-en-Retz** Pays de la Loire, France 47°03′N 1°57′W
165 I4 **Bourgogne** *Eng.* Burgundy. ◐ *region* E France
165 J6 **Bourgoin-Jallieu** Isère, E France 45°34′N 05°16′E
165 J7 **Bourg-St-Andéol** Ardèche, E France 44°24′N 04°36′E
165 K6 **Bourg-St-Maurice** Savoie, E France 45°37′N 06°49′E
176 C6 **Bourg St. Pierre** Valais, SW Switzerland 45°54′N 07°10′E
166 F4 **Bourgthéroulde** Haute-Normandie, France 49°18′N 0°52′E
166 E8 **Bourgueil** Centre, France 47°17′N 0°10′E
132 B2 **Boû Rjeimât** *well* W Mauritania
277 J3 **Bourke** New South Wales, SE Australia 30°08′S 145°57′E
53 H2 **Bourne, Cape** *headland* Nunavut, N Canada
161 I8 **Bournemouth** S England, United Kingdom 50°43′N 01°54′W
163 H13 **Bourscheid** Diekirch, NE Luxembourg 49°55′N 06°04′E
161 I5 **Bourton-on-the-Water** C England, United Kingdom 51°52′N 01°49′W
131 I2 **Bou Saâda** *var.* Bou Saada. N Algeria 35°10′N 04°09′E
175 B13 **Bou Salem** Tunisia
81 I13 **Bouse Wash** ≈ Arizona, SW USA
173 L10 **Bou Sfer** Algeria 35°42′N 00°48′W
165 H6 **Boussac** Creuse, C France 46°20′N 02°12′E
168 F6 **Boussens** Haute-Garonne, S France 43°11′N 00°58′E
134 D3 **Bousso** *prev.* Fort-Bretonnet. Chari-Baguirmi, S Chad 10°32′N 16°45′E
171 L9 **Boutarik** Algeria
132 B3 **Boutilimit** Trarza, SW Mauritania 17°33′N 14°42′W
171 I10 **Bou Tliélis** Algeria
290 I12 **Bouvet Island** ◇ *Norwegian dependency* S Atlantic Ocean
166 C8 **Bouvron** Pays de la Loire, France 47°25′N 1°51′W
167 M5 **Bouxwiller** Alsace, France 48°49′N 7°29′E
133 J4 **Bouza** Tahoua, SW Niger 14°25′N 06°09′E
167 L4 **Bouzanville** Lorraine, France 49°18′N 6°32′E
171 K9 **Bouzghaïa** Algeria
177 J5 **Bovec** *Ger.* Flitsch, *It.* Plezzo. NW Slovenia 46°21′N 13°33′E
181 H8 **Bovenden** Niedersachsen, Germany 51°35′E 9°56′N
162 F5 **Bovenkarspel** Noord-Holland, NW Netherlands 52°33′N 05°03′E
74 G3 **Bovey** Minnesota, N USA 47°18′N 93°25′W
76 F4 **Bovill** Idaho, NW USA 46°50′N 116°24′W
70 D3 **Bovina** Texas, SW USA 34°30′N 102°52′W
175 G9 **Bovino** Puglia, SE Italy 41°14′N 15°19′E
114 D4 **Bovril** Entre Ríos, E Argentina 31°24′S 59°25′W
74 B1 **Bowbells** North Dakota, N USA 48°48′N 102°15′W
57 J8 **Bow City** Alberta, SW Canada 50°27′N 112°16′W
74 D4 **Bowdle** South Dakota, N USA 45°27′N 99°39′W
275 K4 **Bowen** Queensland, NE Australia 20°S 148°10′E
286 F1 **Bowers Ridge** *undersea feature* S Bering Sea 50°00′N 180°00′W
159 J7 **Bowes** United Kingdom 54°30′N 2°00′W
52 G8 **Bowes Point** *headland* Nunavut, N Canada 67°46′N 101°51′W
64 D10 **Bowie** Maryland, USA 39°0′N 76°47′W
70 G4 **Bowie** Texas, SW USA 33°33′N 97°51′W
57 K8 **Bow Island** Alberta, SW Canada 49°53′N 111°24′W
Bowkān *see* Būkān
159 J8 **Bowland, Forest of** *forest* N England, United Kingdom
66 E5 **Bowling Green** Kentucky, S USA 37°00′N 86°29′W
75 I9 **Bowling Green** Missouri, C USA 39°21′N 91°11′W
73 H9 **Bowling Green** Ohio, N USA 41°22′N 83°40′W
67 L3 **Bowling Green** Virginia, NE USA 38°02′N 77°22′W
80 D2 **Bowman** California, USA 38°57′N 121°03′W
74 A3 **Bowman** North Dakota, N USA 46°11′N 103°26′W
55 M1 **Bowman Bay** *bay* NW Atlantic Ocean
292 E3 **Bowman Coast** *physical region* Antarctica
74 A4 **Bowman-Haley Lake** ⊠ North Dakota, N USA
293 M6 **Bowman Island** *island* Antarctica
158 E4 **Bowmore** United Kingdom 55°45′N 6°17′W
159 I7 **Bowness on Windermere** United Kingdom 54°22′N 2°55′W
Bowo *see* Bomi
277 L5 **Bowral** New South Wales, SE Australia 34°28′S 150°52′E
138 F3 **Bowwood** Southern, S Zambia 17°09′S 26°16′E
161 H6 **Box** United Kingdom 51°25′N 2°15′W
181 H13 **Boxberg** Baden-Württemberg, Germany 49°29′E 9°38′N
74 B6 **Box Butte Reservoir** ⊠ Nebraska, C USA
74 A5 **Box Elder** South Dakota, N USA 44°06′N 103°04′W
155 G9 **Boxholm** Östergötland, S Sweden 58°12′N 15°05′E
Bo Xian/Boxian *see* Bozhou
245 K5 **Boxing** Shandong, E China 37°06′N 118°05′E
163 H8 **Boxmeer** Noord-Brabant, SE Netherlands 51°39′N 05°57′E
163 F8 **Boxtel** Noord-Brabant, S Netherlands 51°36′N 05°20′E
214 F4 **Boyabat** Sinop, N Turkey 41°27′N 34°45′E
102 D5 **Boyacá** *off.* Departamento de Boyacá. ◐ *province* C Colombia
Boyacá, Departamento de *see* Boyacá
189 H3 **Boyarka** Kyyivs'ka Oblast', N Ukraine 50°19′N 30°20′E
68 C3 **Boyce** Louisiana, S USA 31°23′N 92°40′W
77 J5 **Boyd** Montana, NW USA 45°27′N 109°03′W
70 G4 **Boyd** Texas, SW USA 33°01′N 97°33′W
67 K5 **Boydton** Virginia, NE USA 36°40′N 78°26′W
Boyer Ahmadī va Kohkīlūyeh *see* Kohgīlūyeh va Bowyer Aḩmad
74 F7 **Boyer River** ≈ Iowa, C USA
64 F7 **Boyertown** Pennsylvania, NE USA 40°20′N 75°38′W
118 C5 **Boyeruca** Maule, Chile 34°41′S 72°03′W
80 B2 **Boyes Hot Springs** California, USA 38°19′N 122°29′W
67 L5 **Boykins** Virginia, NE USA 36°35′N 77°11′W
57 J4 **Boyle** Alberta, SW Canada 54°38′N 112°45′W
158 B8 **Boyle** *Ir.* Mainistirna Búille. C Ireland 53°58′N 08°18′W
158 D9 **Boyne** ≈ Ireland
157 D9 **Boyne** *Ir.* An Bhóinn. ≈ E Ireland
72 G5 **Boyne City** Michigan, N USA 45°13′N 85°00′W
69 N8 **Boynton Beach** Florida, SE USA 26°31′N 80°04′W
229 H7 **Boysun** *Rus.* Baysun. Surkhondaryo Viloyati, S Uzbekistan 38°14′N 67°08′E
160 E8 **Boyton** United Kingdom 50°42′N 4°23′W
Bozau *see* Întorsura Buzăului
187 J4 **Bozcaada** *Island* Çanakkale, NW Turkey
214 B6 **Boz Dağları** ▲▲ W Turkey
187 M6 **Bozdoğan** Aydın, Turkey 37°40′N 28°19′E
77 I5 **Bozeman** Montana, NW USA 45°40′N 111°02′W
Bozen *see* Bolzano
134 E6 **Bozene** Equateur, NW Dem. Rep. Congo 02°56′N 19°15′E
Bozhen *see* Botou
245 J8 **Bozhou** *var.* Boxian, Bo Xian. Anhui, E China 33°46′N 115°44′E
214 D7 **Bozkır** Konya, S Turkey 37°10′N 32°15′E
214 F5 **Bozok Yaylasī** *plateau* C Turkey
169 H4 **Bozouls** Midi-Pyrénées, France 44°28′N 2°43′E
134 D5 **Bozoum** Ouham-Pendé, W Central African Republic 06°17′N 16°26′E
215 H7 **Bozova** Sanlıurfa, S Turkey 37°23′N 38°33′E
Bozrah *see* Buşrá ash Shām
214 C5 **Bozüyük** Bilecik, NW Turkey 39°55′N 30°02′E
218 F2 **Bqâa Kafra** Lebanon 34°14′N 36°00′E
176 D8 **Bra** Piemonte, NW Italy 44°42′N 07°51′E
292 EE3 **Brabant Island** *island* Antarctica
163 E11 **Brabant Walloon** ◐ *province* C Belgium
184 C5 **Brač** *var.* Brach, *It.* Brazza; *anc.* Brattia. *island* S Croatia
Bracara Augusta *see* Braga
175 E8 **Bracciano** Lazio, C Italy 42°04′N 12°12′E
175 E8 **Bracciano, Lago di** ◎ C Italy
62 D3 **Bracebridge** Ontario, S Canada 45°02′N 79°19′W
Brach *see* Brač
154 G4 **Bräcke** Jämtland, C Sweden 62°43′N 15°30′E
180 H3 **Brackel** Niedersachsen, Germany 53°18′E 10°02′N
181 G14 **Brackenheim** Baden-Württemberg, Germany 49°05′E 9°04′N
70 E7 **Brackettville** Texas, SW USA 29°19′N 100°27′W
158 C10 **Bracknagh** Offaly, Ireland 53°13′N 7°06′W
161 J6 **Bracknell** S England, United Kingdom 51°26′N 00°46′W
159 H2 **Braco** United Kingdom 56°15′N 3°53′W
113 K6 **Braço do Norte** Santa Catarina, S Brazil 28°16′S 49°11′W
188 B7 **Brad** *Hung.* Brád. Hunedoara, SW Romania 45°52′N 23°00′E
175 H9 **Bradano** ≈ S Italy
65 C9 **Braddock Heights** Maryland, NE USA 39°25′N 77°30′W
69 L7 **Bradenton** Florida, SE USA 27°30′N 82°34′W
91 M6 **Brades O** (Montserrat) SW Montserrat 16°44′N 62°14′W
62 D4 **Bradford** Ontario, S Canada 44°09′N 79°34′W
159 K9 **Bradford** N England, United Kingdom 53°48′N 01°45′W
75 I12 **Bradford** Arkansas, C USA 35°25′N 91°27′W
64 A3 **Bradford** Pennsylvania, NE USA 41°57′N 78°38′W
75 H14 **Bradley** Arkansas, C USA 33°06′N 93°39′W
80 B6 **Bradley** California, USA 35°52′N 120°48′W
70 F5 **Bradshaw** Texas, SW USA 32°06′N 99°52′W
70 F6 **Brady** Texas, SW USA 31°08′N 99°22′W
70 F6 **Brady Creek** ≈ Texas, SW USA
155 D12 **Brædstrup** Vejle, C Denmark 55°58′N 09°38′E
156 F5 **Braemar** NE Scotland, United Kingdom 57°12′N 02°52′W
183 G8 **Braesko** Tarnów, SE Poland 49°59′N 20°28′E
188 E6 **Brăeşti** Botoşani, NW Romania 47°50′N 26°26′E
170 C3 **Braga** *anc.* Bracara Augusta. Braga, NW Portugal 41°32′N 08°26′W
170 D3 **Braga** ◐ *district* N Portugal
185 K5 **Bragadiru** Teleorman, S Romania 43°43′N 25°32′E
114 B10 **Bragado** Buenos Aires, E Argentina 35°10′S 60°29′W
170 E3 **Bragança** *Eng.* Braganza; *anc.* Julio Briga. Bragança, NE Portugal 41°47′N 06°46′W
170 D3 **Bragança** ◐ *district* N Portugal
110 D8 **Bragança Paulista** São Paulo, S Brazil 22°55′S 46°30′W
Braganza *see* Bragança
Bragin *see* Brahin
74 H4 **Braham** Minnesota, N USA 45°43′N 93°10′W
Brahe *see* Brda
Brahestad *see* Raahe
191 H12 **Brahin** *Rus.* Bragin. Homyel'skaya Voblasts', SE Belarus 51°47′N 30°16′E
233 K7 **Brahmanbaria** Chittagong, E Bangladesh 23°58′N 91°04′E
234 I4 **Brāhmani** ≈ E India
234 I4 **Brahmapur** Orissa, E India 19°21′N 84°51′E
205 J6 **Brahmaputra** *var.* Padma, Tsangpo, *Ben.* Jamuna, *Chin.* Yarlung Zangbo Jiang, *Ind.* Bramaputra, Dihang, Siang. ≈ S Asia
160 D3 **Braich y Pwll** *headland* NW Wales, United Kingdom 52°47′N 04°46′W
277 K6 **Braidwood** New South Wales, SE Australia 35°26′S 149°48′E
73 D9 **Braidwood** Illinois, N USA 41°16′N 88°12′W
188 F9 **Brăila** Brăila, E Romania 45°17′N 27°57′E
188 F9 **Brăila** ◐ *county* SE Romania
163 E10 **Braine-l'Alleud** Brabant Walloon, C Belgium 50°41′N 04°22′E
163 D11 **Braine-le-Comte** Hainaut, SW Belgium 50°37′N 04°08′E
74 G3 **Brainerd** Minnesota, N USA 46°22′N 94°10′W
161 L5 **Braintree** United Kingdom 51°53′N 0°34′E
65 M3 **Braintree** Massachusetts, USA 42°13′N 71°00′W
159 I7 **Braithwaite** United Kingdom 54°35′N 3°11′W
163 F11 **Braives** Liège, E Belgium 50°37′N 05°09′E
141 K1 **Brak** ≈ Limpopo, South Africa
138 F8 **Brak** ≈ C South Africa
Brak *see* Birāk
180 F3 **Brake** Niedersachsen, Germany 53°20′E 8°29′N
163 C10 **Brakel** Oost-Vlaanderen, SW Belgium 50°50′N 03°48′E
180 G7 **Brakel** Nordrhein-Westfalen, Germany 51°43′E 9°11′N
162 F7 **Brakel** Gelderland, C Netherlands 51°49′N 05°05′E
132 C3 **Brakna** ◐ *region* S Mauritania
140 F8 **Brakpoort** Northern Cape, South Africa 31°15′S 22°58′E
140 D6 **Brakrivier** ≈ Northern Cape, South Africa
141 I4 **Brakspruit** North West, South Africa 26°35′S 26°37′E
155 F9 **Brålanda** Västra Götaland, S Sweden 58°32′N 12°18′E
Bramaputra *see* Brahmaputra
155 C12 **Bramming** Ribe, W Denmark 55°28′N 08°42′E
62 D5 **Brampton** Ontario, S Canada 43°42′N 79°46′W
159 I6 **Brampton** United Kingdom 54°57′N 2°44′W
180 E6 **Bramsche** Niedersachsen, NW Germany 52°25′N 07°58′E
161 I7 **Bramshaw** United Kingdom 50°56′N 1°37′W
188 D8 **Bran** *Ger.* Törzburg, *Hung.* Törcsvár. Braşov, S Romania 45°31′N 25°23′E
74 H4 **Branch** Minnesota, N USA 45°29′N 92°57′W
67 I9 **Branchville** South Carolina, SE USA 33°15′N 80°49′W
95 N4 **Branco, Cabo** *headland* E Brazil 07°08′S 34°45′W
103 I8 **Branco, Rio** ≈ N Brazil
138 B5 **Brandberg** ▲ NW Namibia 21°20′S 14°22′E
154 D7 **Brandbu** Oppland, S Norway 60°24′N 10°30′E
141 K3 **Branddraai** Mpumalanga, South Africa 24°38′S 30°37′E
155 C12 **Brande** Ringkøbing, W Denmark 55°57′N 09°08′E
Brandebourg *see* Brandenburg
178 H7 **Brandenburg** *var.* Brandenburg an der Havel. Brandenburg, NE Germany 52°25′N 12°34′E

◆ Country
● Country Capital
◇ Dependent Territory
○ Dependent Territory Capital
◐ Administrative Regions
✈ International Airport
▲ Mountain
▲▲ Mountain Range
⛰ Volcano
≈ River
◎ Lake
⊠ Reservoir

| ◆ Country | ◇ Dependent Territory | ✦ Administrative Regions | ▲ Mountain | ✕ Volcano | ⬤ Lake |
| ● Country Capital | ○ Dependent Territory Capital | ✕ International Airport | ▲ Mountain Range | ⌇ River | ◆ Reservoir |

◆ Country	◇ Dependent Territory	◇ Administrative Regions	▲ Mountain	▲ Volcano	◎ Lake
● Country Capital	○ Dependent Territory Capital	✈ International Airport	▲ Mountain Range	≈ River	⊞ Reservoir

Chaghcharān - Chenyang
INDEX
327

230 F3 **Chaghcharān** *var.* Chakhcharan, Cheghcheran, Qala Āhangarān. Ghowr, C Afghanistan 34°28′N 65°18′E
165 J5 **Chagny** Saône-et-Loire, C France 46°54′N 04°45′E
289 F8 **Chagos Archipelago** *var.* Oil Islands. *island group* British Indian Ocean Territory
205 H9 **Chagos Bank** *undersea feature* C Indian Ocean 06°15′S 72°00′E
205 H8 **Chagos-Laccadive Plateau** *undersea feature* N Indian Ocean 03°00′S 73°00′E
289 E8 **Chagos Trench** *undersea feature* N Indian Ocean 07°00′S 73°30′E
89 K8 **Chagres, Río** ≈ C Panama
91 L8 **Chaguanas** Trinidad, Trinidad and Tobago 10°31′N 61°25′W
102 G3 **Chaguaramas** Guárico, N Venezuela 09°23′N 66°18′W
Chagyl *see* Çagyl
Chahār Maḩāll and Bakhtiyāri *see* Chahār Maḩāl va Bakhtīārī
Chahār Maḩall va Bakhtīārī, Ostān-e *see* Chahār Maḩāl va Bakhtīārī
222 F6 **Chahār Maḩāl va Bakhtīārī** *off.* Ostān-e Chahār Maḩall va Bakhtīārī, *var.* Chahār Maḩāll and Bakhtiyāri. ◈ *province* SW Iran
Chāh Bahār/Chahbar *see* Chābahār
223 J8 **Chāh Derāz** Sīstān va Balūchestān, SE Iran 27°07′N 60°01′E
Chāh Gay *see* Chāgai Hills
87 I9 **Chahuites** Oaxaca, Mexico 16°18′N 94°11′W
256 F7 **Chai Badan** Lop Buri, C Thailand 15°08′N 101°03′E
233 I8 **Chāībāsa** Jhārkhand, N India 22°31′N 85°50′E
166 D6 **Chailland** Pays de la Loire, France 48°14′N 0°52′W
166 D10 **Chaillé-les-Marais** Pays de la Loire, France 46°23′N 1°01′W
135 B8 **Chaillu, Massif du** ▲▲ C Gabon
256 E7 **Chai Nat** *var.* Chainat, Jainat, Jayanath. Chai Nat, C Thailand 15°10′N 100°10′E
Chainat *see* Chai Nat
291 G8 **Chain Fracture Zone** *tectonic feature* E Atlantic Ocean
288 D7 **Chain Ridge** *undersea feature* W Indian Ocean 06°00′N 54°00′E
Chairn, Ceann an *see* Carnsore Point
238 F3 **Chaiwopu** Xinjiang Uygur Zizhiqu, W China 43°32′N 87°55′E
256 F7 **Chaiyaphum** *var.* Jayabum. Chaiyaphum, C Thailand 15°46′N 101°55′E
114 F2 **Chajarí** Entre Ríos, E Argentina 30°45′S 57°57′W
245 L9 **Chajian** Anhui, E China 32°40′N 118°46′E
88 C3 **Chajul** Quiché, W Guatemala 15°28′N 91°02′W
139 H3 **Chakari** Mashonaland West, N Zimbabwe 18°05′S 29°51′E
137 E10 **Chake Chake** Pemba South, E Tanzania 05°12′S 39°44′E
230 D5 **Chakhānsūr** Nīmrūz, SW Afghanistan 31°11′N 62°06′E
Chakhānsūr *see* Nīmrūz
Chakhcharan *see* Chaghcharān
231 J5 **Chak Jhumra** *var.* Jhumra. Punjab, E Pakistan 31°33′N 73°14′E
228 E9 **Chaknakdysonga** Ahal Welaýaty, S Turkmenistan 35°39′N 61°24′E
233 I8 **Chakradharpur** Jhāarkhand, N India 22°42′N 85°38′E
231 I4 **Chakwāl** Punjab, NE Pakistan 32°56′N 72°53′E
105 E9 **Chala** Arequipa, SW Peru 15°52′S 74°13′W
164 G7 **Chalais** Charente, W France 45°16′N 00°02′E
176 D5 **Chalais** Valais, SW Switzerland 46°18′N 07°37′E
187 I7 **Chalándri** *var.* Halandri; *prev.* Khalándrion. *prehistoric site* Sýros, Kykládes, Greece, Aegean Sea
283 H2 **Chalan Kanoa** Saipan, S Northern Mariana Islands 15°08′S 145°43′E
282 B2 **Chalan Pago** C Guam
Chalap Dalam/Chalap Dalan *see* Chehel Abdālān, Kūh-e
88 D4 **Chalatenango** Chalatenango, N El Salvador 14°04′N 88°53′W
88 D4 **Chalatenango** ◈ *department* NW El Salvador
139 K2 **Chalaua** Nampula, NE Mozambique 16°04′S 39°08′E
136 D7 **Chalbi Desert** *desert* N Kenya
86 G8 **Chalcatongo** Oaxaca, Mexico 17°02′N 97°35′W
85 J8 **Chalchihuites** Zacatecas, Mexico 23°29′N 103°53′W
87 I8 **Chalchijapan** Veracruz-Llave, Mexico 17°27′N 94°51′W
88 D4 **Chalchuapa** Santa Ana, W El Salvador 13°59′N 89°41′W
Chalcidice *see* Chalkidikí
Chalcis *see* Chalkída
Chālderān *see* Sīāh Chashmeh
161 I8 **Chale** United Kingdom 50°35′N 1°19′W
165 I4 **Châlette-sur-Loing** Loiret, C France 48°01′N 02°45′E
59 J7 **Chaleur Bay** *Fr.* Baie des Chaleurs. *bay* New Brunswick/Québec, E Canada
Chaleurs, Baie des *see* Chaleur Bay
105 F8 **Chalhuanca** Apurímac, S Peru 14°17′S 73°15′W
167 K7 **Chalindrey** Champagne-Ardenne, France 47°48′N 5°26′E
243 H6 **Chaling** Hunan, China 26°29′N 113°19′E
118 D1 **Chalinguita** Coquimbo, Chile 31°45′S 70°58′W
234 D4 **Chālisgaon** Mahārāshtra, C India 20°29′N 75°10′E
187 L8 **Chálki** *island* Dodekánisa, Greece, Aegean Sea
186 G4 **Chalkiádes** Thessalía, C Greece 39°24′N 22°25′E
187 H6 **Chalkída** *var.* Halkida, *prev.* Khalkís; *anc.* Chalcis. Evvoia, E Greece 38°27′N 23°38′E
187 H3 **Chalkidikí** *var.* Khalkidhikí; *anc.* Chalcidice. *peninsula* NE Greece
278 A12 **Chalky Inlet** *inlet* South Island, New Zealand
83 J4 **Chalkyitsik** Alaska, USA 66°39′N 143°43′W
164 F5 **Challans** Vendée, NW France 46°51′N 01°52′W
112 C1 **Challapata** Oruro, SW Bolivia 18°50′S 66°45′W
80 E1 **Challenge** California, USA 39°29′N 121°13′W
286 D5 **Challenger Deep** *undersea feature* W Pacific Ocean 11°20′N 142°12′E
Challenger Deep *see* Mariana Trench
287 J8 **Challenger Fracture Zone** *tectonic feature* SE Pacific Ocean
286 E8 **Challenger Plateau** *undersea feature* E Tasman Sea
76 G6 **Challis** Idaho, NW USA 44°31′N 114°14′W
158 G6 **Challoch** United Kingdom 54°58′N 4°32′W
68 E4 **Chalmette** Louisiana, S USA 29°56′N 89°57′W
194 E7 **Chalna** Respublika Kareliya, NW Russian Federation 61°53′N 33°59′E
166 D8 **Chalonnes-sur-Loire** Pays de la Loire, France 47°21′N 0°46′W
165 J3 **Châlons-en-Champagne** *prev.* Châlons-sur-Marne, *hist.* Arcae Remorum; *anc.* Carolopois. Marne, NE France 48°58′N 04°22′E
Châlons-sur-Marne *see* Châlons-en-Champagne
165 J5 **Chalon-sur-Saône** *anc.* Cabillonum. Saône-et-Loire, C France 46°47′N 04°51′E
Chaltel, Cerro *see* Fitzroy, Monte
164 G6 **Châlus** Haute-Vienne, C France 45°38′N 01°00′E
222 F3 **Chālūs** Māzandarān, N Iran 36°40′N 51°25′E
179 H11 **Cham** Bayern, SE Germany 49°13′N 12°40′E
79 L5 **Chama** New Mexico, SW USA 36°54′N 106°34′W
Cha Mai *see* Thung Song
140 B5 **Chamais Bay** Karas, Namibia
140 C5 **Chamaites** Karas, S Namibia 27°15′S 17°52′E
169 H1 **Chamaliéres** Auvergne, France 45°47′N 3°04′E
230 F6 **Chaman** Baluchistān, SW Pakistan 30°55′N 66°27′E
79 L6 **Chama, Rio** ≈ New Mexico, SW USA
232 E3 **Chamba** Himāchal Pradesh, N India 32°33′N 76°10′E
137 D12 **Chamba** Ruvuma, S Tanzania 11°33′S 37°01′E
232 E6 **Chambal** ≈ C India
57 N7 **Chamberlain** Saskatchewan, S Canada 50°49′N 105°29′W
115 H6 **Chamberlain** Uruguay 32°37′S 56°29′W
74 D5 **Chamberlain** South Dakota, N USA 43°48′N 99°19′W
63 K2 **Chamberlain Lake** ◎ Maine, NE USA
83 J2 **Chamberlin, Mount** ▲ Alaska, USA 69°16′N 144°54′W
79 J7 **Chambers** Arizona, SW USA 35°11′N 109°25′W
64 C8 **Chambersburg** Pennsylvania, NE USA 39°54′N 77°39′W
72 E5 **Chambers Island** *island* Wisconsin, N USA
165 K6 **Chambéry** *anc.* Camberia. Savoie, E France 45°34′N 05°56′E
137 B12 **Chambeshi** Northern, NE Zambia 10°55′S 31°07′E
137 A12 **Chambeshi** ≈ NE Zambia
131 K2 **Chambi, Jebel** *var.* Jabal ash Sha'nabī. ▲ W Tunisia 35°16′N 08°39′E
81 H11 **Chambless** California, USA 34°34′N 115°33′W
167 L5 **Chambley-Bussiéres** Lorraine, France 49°03′N 5°54′E
167 H10 **Chambon-sur-Voueize** Limousin, France 46°11′N 2°25′E
166 G8 **Chambord** Centre, France 47°37′N 1°31′E
166 F8 **Chambray** Centre, France 47°20′N 0°43′E
261 N6 **Chambri Lake** ◎ W Papua New Guinea
217 K7 **Chamcham** Al Muthanná, S Iraq 31°17′N 45°05′E
217 J3 **Chamchamāļ** At Ta'mīn, N Iraq 35°32′N 44°50′E
86 B6 **Chamela** Jalisco, SW Mexico 19°31′N 105°02′W
88 E3 **Chamelecón, Río** ≈ NW Honduras
112 D7 **Chamical** La Rioja, C Argentina 30°21′S 66°19′W
187 K9 **Chamilí** *island* Kykládes, Greece, Aegean Sea
115 H9 **Chamizo** Lavalleja, Uruguay 34°15′S 55°56′W
257 G9 **Châmnar** Kaôh Kông, SW Cambodia 11°45′N 103°32′E
232 F4 **Chamoli** Uttarakhand, N India 30°22′N 79°19′E
169 M1 **Chamonix-Mont-Blanc** Haute-Savoie, E France 45°55′N 06°52′E
234 H3 **Chāmpa** Chhattīsgarh, C India 22°02′N 82°42′E
168 E2 **Champagnac-de-Bélair** Aquitaine, France 45°24′N 0°42′E
54 B3 **Champagne** Yukon Territory, W Canada 60°48′N 136°22′W
165 J3 **Champagne** *cultural region* N France
Champagne *see* Campania
165 J3 **Champagne-Ardenne** ◈ *region* N France
168 E1 **Champagne-Mouton** Poitou-Charentes, France 45°59′N 0°25′E
165 K5 **Champagnole** Jura, E France 46°44′N 05°55′E
167 J8 **Champagny** Bourgogne, France 47°28′N 4°46′E
73 D10 **Champaign** Illinois, N USA 40°07′N 88°15′W
256 H7 **Champasak** Champasak, S Laos 14°50′N 105°51′E
167 M6 **Champ de Feu** ▲ NE France 48°24′N 07°15′E
166 D10 **Champdeniers** Poitou-Charentes, France 46°29′N 0°24′W
59 I4 **Champdoré, Lac** ◎ Québec, NE Canada
169 H2 **Champeix** Auvergne, France 45°35′N 3°08′E
88 B4 **Champerico** Retalhuleu, SW Guatemala 14°18′N 91°54′W
176 C5 **Champéry** Valais, SW Switzerland 46°12′N 06°52′E
167 I6 **Champigny** Bourgogne, France 48°19′N 3°08′E
63 H3 **Champlain** New York, NE USA 44°58′N 73°25′W
63 H5 **Champlain Canal** *canal* New York, NE USA
63 H3 **Champlain, Lac** ◎ Québec, Canada/USA *see also* Champlain, Lake
63 H4 **Champlain, Lake** ◎ Canada/USA *see also* Champlain, Lac
165 J4 **Champlitte** Haute-Saône, E France 47°36′N 05°31′E
167 K7 **Champlitte-la-Ville** Franche-Comté, France 47°37′N 5°32′E
169 N1 **Champoluc** Valle D'Aosta, NW Italy 45°49′N 07°43′E
87 L6 **Champotón** Campeche, SE Mexico 19°18′N 90°43′W
235 E8 **Chāmrājnagar** *var.* Chamrajnagar. Karnātaka, S India 12°00′N 77°18′E
Chamrajnagar *see* Chāmrājnagar
169 L2 **Chamrousse** Rhône-Alpes, France 45°08′N 5°54′E
172 B4 **Chamusca** Santarém, C Portugal 39°21′N 08°29′W
191 I12 **Chamyarysy** *Rus.* Chemerisy. Homyel'skaya Voblasts', SE Belarus 51°42′N 30°27′E
197 I3 **Chamzinka** Respublika Mordoviya, W Russian Federation 54°22′N 45°22′E
169 I4 **Chanac** Languedoc-Roussillon, France 44°28′N 3°20′E
Chanáil Mhór, An *see* Grand Canal
Chanak *see* Çanakkale
112 B5 **Chañaral** Atacama, N Chile 26°19′S 70°34′W
170 D7 **Chança, Rio** *var.* Chanza. ≈ Portugal/Spain
114 A10 **Chancay** Buenos Aires, Argentina 35°03′S 61°15′W
104 D7 **Chancay** Lima, W Peru 11°36′S 77°14′W
Chan-chiang/Chanchiang *see* Zhanjiang
116 B5 **Chanco** Maule, C Chile 35°43′S 72°35′W
83 I3 **Chandalar** Alaska, USA 67°30′N 148°29′W
83 I4 **Chandalar River** ≈ Alaska, USA
232 G5 **Chandan Chauki** Uttar Pradesh, N India 28°32′N 80°43′E
233 J8 **Chandannagar** *prev.* Chandernagore. West Bengal, E India 22°52′N 88°21′E
232 F5 **Chandausi** Uttar Pradesh, N India 28°27′N 78°43′E
68 F5 **Chandeleur Islands** *island group* Louisiana, S USA
68 F4 **Chandeleur Sound** *sound* N Gulf of Mexico
Chandernagore *see* Chandannagar
232 E4 **Chandīgarh** *state capital* Punjab, N India 30°41′N 76°51′E
233 I8 **Chāndil** Jhārkhand, NE India 22°58′N 86°04′E
276 E1 **Chandler** South Australia 26°59′S 133°22′E
59 J7 **Chandler** Québec, SE Canada 48°21′N 64°41′W
75 E12 **Chandler** Oklahoma, C USA 35°43′N 96°54′W
71 I5 **Chandler** Texas, SW USA 32°18′N 95°28′W
83 I3 **Chandler River** ≈ Alaska, USA
104 G7 **Chandles, Río** ≈ E Peru
239 I2 **Chandmanī** *var.* Talshand. Govī-Altayī, C Mongolia 45°21′N 98°00′E
239 H2 **Chandmanī** *var.* Urdgol. Hovd, W Mongolia 47°39′N 92°46′E
62 E4 **Chandos Lake** ◎ Ontario, SE Canada
233 K8 **Chandpur** Chittagong, C Bangladesh 23°13′N 90°43′E
234 F4 **Chandrapur** Mahārāshtra, C India 19°58′N 79°21′E
138 G2 **Changa** Southern, S Zambia 16°24′S 28°27′E
250 B4 **Chang-an** 35°18′N 129°14′E
Chang'an *see* Rong'an, Guangxi Zhuangzu Zizhiqu, S China
Changan *see* Xi'an, Shaanxi, C China
235 E9 **Changanācheri** *var.* Changannassery. Kerala, SW India 09°26′N 76°31′E *see also* Changannassery
139 I5 **Changane** ≈ S Mozambique
139 I2 **Changara** Tete, NW Mozambique 16°54′S 33°15′E
248 D3 **Changbai** *var.* Changbai Chaoxianzu Zizhixian. Jilin, NE China 41°25′N 128°08′E
Changbai Chaoxianzu Zizhixian *see* Changbai
248 D2 **Changbai Shan** ▲▲ NE China
237 J4 **Changchun** *var.* Ch'angch'un, Ch'ang-ch'un; *prev.* Hsinking. *province capital* Jilin, NE China 43°53′N 125°18′E
Ch'angch'un/Ch'ang-ch'un *see* Changchun
242 G4 **Changde** Hunan, S China 29°04′N 111°42′E
243 J1 **Changfeng** Anhui, China 32°17′N 117°05′E
245 H8 **Changge** Henan, China 34°07′N 113°28′E
245 N3 **Changhai** Liaoning, China 39°10′N 122°20′E
243 M8 **Changhua** *Jap.* Shōka. C Taiwan 24°06′N 120°31′E
258 F4 **Changi** ✈ (Singapore) E Singapore 01°22′N 103°58′E
238 F3 **Changji** Xinjiang Uygur Zizhiqu, NW China 44°02′N 87°12′E
240 F10 **Changjiang** *var.* Changjiang Lizu Zizhixian, Shiliu. Hainan, S China 19°16′N 109°09′E
243 H3 **Chang Jiang** *var.* Yangtze Kiang, *Eng.* Yangtze. ≈ C China
242 E2 **Chang Jiang** *Eng.* Yangtze. ≈ SW China
243 N1 **Changjiang Kou** *delta* E China
Changjiang Lizu Zizhixian *see* Changjiang
242 G2 **Changkang** Hubei, C China 30°36′N 112°53′E
Changkiakow *see* Zhangjiakou
257 F9 **Chang, Ko** *island* S Thailand
243 L6 **Changle** Fujan, China 25°35′N 119°19′E
243 H4 **Changle** Hunan, E China 28°51′N 113°17′E
245 K5 **Changle** Shandong, E China 36°42′N 118°50′E
243 M1 **Changlezhen** Jiangsu, E China 31°56′N 121°14′E
245 K3 **Changli** Hebei, E China 39°44′N 119°13′E
247 K5 **Changling** Jilin, NE China 44°15′N 124°03′E
242 G6 **Changning** Hunan, China 26°14′N 112°14′E
242 B4 **Changning** Sichuan, C China 28°35′N 104°57′E
Changning *see* Xunwu
250 B3 **Changnyeong** *prev.* Ch'angnyŏng. 35°32′N 128°30′E
Ch'angnyŏng *see* Changnyeong
245 J3 **Changping** Beijing Shi, N China 40°08′N 116°08′E
242 F6 **Chang-pu-tzu** Hunan, SE China 26°38′N 110°24′E
245 J6 **Changqing** Shandong, China 36°20′N 116°25′E
243 H5 **Changsha** *var.* Ch'angsha, Ch'ang-sha. *province capital* Hunan, S China 28°10′N 113°E
Ch'angsha/Ch'ang-sha *see* Changsha
243 L4 **Changshan** Zhejiang, SE China 28°54′N 118°30′E
245 N3 **Changshan Qundao** *island group* NE China
242 C3 **Changshou** Chongqing Shi, C China 29°31′N 107°01′E
243 H4 **Changshou** Hunan, E China 28°43′N 113°56′E
243 M1 **Changshu** *var.* Ch'ang-shu. Jiangsu, E China 31°39′N 120°45′E
Ch'ang-shu *see* Changshu
242 C6 **Changshun** Guizhou, S China 25°59′N 106°25′E
Changsu *see* Jangsu
243 K8 **Changtai** Fujan, China 24°22′N 117°28′E
243 J7 **Changting** Fujan, China 25°31′N 116°13′E
248 B1 **Changtu** Liaoning, NE China 42°50′N 123°59′E
89 I8 **Changuinola** Bocas del Toro, NW Panama 09°28′N 82°31′W
239 H5 **Changweiliang** Qinghai, W China 38°24′N 92°08′E
250 B4 **Ch'Ang Won** 35°14′N 128°39′E
244 D7 **Changwu** *var.* Zhaoren. Shaanxi, C China 35°12′N 107°46′E
243 L2 **Changxing** Zhejiang, China 31°01′N 119°33′E
245 M3 **Changxing Dao** *island* N China
167 J10 **Changy** Rhône-Alpes, France 46°09′N 3°54′E
242 F3 **Changyang** *var.* Longzhouping. Hubei, C China 30°45′N 111°13′E
245 L5 **Changyi** Shandong, E China 36°51′N 119°23′E
248 B4 **Changyŏn** SW North Korea 38°19′N 125°15′E
245 H6 **Changzhi** Shanxi, C China 36°10′N 113°02′E
245 H6 **Changzhi** Shanxi, China 36°01′N 113°01′E
243 L1 **Changzhou** Jiangsu, E China 31°45′N 119°58′E
187 H9 **Chaniá** *var.* Hania, Khaniá, *Eng.* Canea; *anc.* Cydonia. Kríti, Greece, E Mediterranean Sea 35°31′N 24°00′E
112 D4 **Chañi, Nevado de** ▲ NW Argentina 24°09′S 65°44′W
187 H9 **Chanión, Kólpos** *gulf* Kríti, Greece, E Mediterranean Sea
Chankiri *see* Çankırı
73 D9 **Channahon** Illinois, N USA 41°25′N 88°13′W
235 E8 **Channapatna** Karnātaka, E India 12°43′N 77°14′E
166 B4 **Channel Islands** *Fr.* Iles Normandes. *island group* S English Channel
81 B11 **Channel Islands** *island group* California, W USA
59 K7 **Channel-Port aux Basques** Newfoundland and Labrador, SE Canada 47°35′N 59°02′W
Channel, The *see* English Channel
161 N7 **Channel Tunnel** *tunnel* France/United Kingdom
70 D2 **Channing** Texas, SW USA 35°41′N 102°21′W
Chantabun/Chantaburi *see* Chanthaburi
170 D2 **Chantada** Galicia, NW Spain 42°36′N 07°46′W
167 I10 **Chantelle** Auvergne, France 46°14′N 3°09′E
86 F9 **Chantengo, Laguna de** *bay* Guerrero, S Mexico Central America
257 F8 **Chanthaburi** *var.* Chantabun, Chantaburi. Chantaburi, S Thailand 12°35′N 102°08′E
165 H3 **Chantilly** Oise, N France 49°12′N 02°28′E
166 D9 **Chantonnay** Pays de la Loire, France 46°41′N 1°03′W
53 H8 **Chantrey Inlet** *inlet* Nunavut, N Canada
217 K8 **Chanūn as Sa'ūdī** Dhī Qār, S Iraq 31°04′N 46°00′E
75 F10 **Chanute** Kansas, C USA 37°40′N 95°27′W
227 J1 **Chany, Ozero** ◎ C Russian Federation
Chanza *see* Chança, Rio
243 J9 **Chao'an** *var.* Anbu. Guangdong, SE China 23°27′N 116°41′E
Ch'ao-an/Chaochow *see* Chaozhou
243 K1 **Chaohu** Anhui, China 31°22′N 117°31′E
243 K2 **Chaohu** Anhui, E China 31°36′N 117°55′E
243 K2 **Chao Hu** ◎ E China
245 M6 **Chaolian Dao** *island* Shandong, China
262 B5 **Chao Phraya, Mae Nam** ≈ C Thailand
Chaor He *see* Qulin Gol
Chaouèn *see* Chefchaouen
167 J7 **Chaource** Champagne-Ardenne, France 48°04′N 4°08′E
243 J9 **Chaoyang** Guangdong, S China 23°17′N 116°33′E
243 J9 **Chaoyang** Guangdong, China 23°10′N 116°22′E
245 L1 **Chaoyang** Liaoning, NE China 41°34′N 120°29′E
Chaoyang *see* Jiayin, Heilongjiang, China
Chaoyang *see* Jiayan
Chaoyang *see* Huinan, Jilin China
243 J9 **Chaozhou** *var.* Chaoan, Chao'an, Ch'ao-an; *prev.* Chaochow. Guangdong, SE China 23°42′N 116°36′E
108 E4 **Chapadinha** Maranhão, E Brazil 03°45′S 43°23′W
58 G7 **Chapais** Québec, SE Canada 49°47′N 74°54′W
84 C3 **Chapala** Baja California Norte, NW Mexico 29°24′N 114°21′W
86 C5 **Chapala** Jalisco, SW Mexico 20°20′N 103°10′W
86 C5 **Chapala, Lago de** ◎ C Mexico
85 I10 **Chapalilla** Nayarit, Mexico
223 I2 **Chapan, Gora** ▲ C Turkmenistan 37°48′N 58°03′E
106 E10 **Chapare, Río** ≈ C Bolivia
102 B6 **Chaparral** Tolima, C Colombia 03°45′N 75°30′W
226 C3 **Chapayev** Zapadnyy Kazakhstan, NW Kazakhstan 50°12′N 51°09′E
193 I6 **Chapayevo** Respublika Sakha (Yakutiya), NE Russian Federation 60°03′N 117°19′E
197 J3 **Chapayevsk** Samarskaya Oblast', W Russian Federation 52°57′N 49°42′E
113 I6 **Chapecó** Santa Catarina, S Brazil 27°14′S 52°41′W
113 J5 **Chapecó, Rio** ≈ S Brazil
159 K10 **Chapel en le Frith** United Kingdom 53°19′N 1°54′W
66 D6 **Chapel Hill** Tennessee, S USA 35°38′N 86°40′W
90 F8 **Chapelton** C Jamaica 18°05′N 77°16′W
114 F4 **Chapicuy** Paysandú, Uruguay 31°40′S 57°55′W
58 E7 **Chapleau** Ontario, SE Canada 47°50′N 83°24′W
57 M7 **Chaplin** Saskatchewan, S Canada 50°27′N 106°37′W
196 G3 **Chaplygin** Lipetskaya Oblast', W Russian Federation 53°13′N 39°58′E
189 J7 **Chaplynka** Khersons'ka Oblast', S Ukraine 46°20′N 33°34′E
53 I8 **Chapman, Cape** *headland* Nunavut, NE Canada 69°15′N 89°09′W
70 G9 **Chapman Ranch** Texas, SW USA 27°32′N 97°25′W
Chapman's *see* Okwa
67 H4 **Chapmanville** West Virginia, NE USA 37°58′N 82°01′W
74 B7 **Chappell** Nebraska, C USA 41°05′N 102°28′W
Chapra *see* Chhapra
104 D3 **Chapuli, Río** ≈ N Peru
114 A8 **Chapuy** Santa Fe, Argentina 33°48′S 61°45′W
218 F5 **Chaqra** Lebanon 33°11′N 35°28′E
132 C1 **Châr** *well* N Mauritania
193 J7 **Chara** Zabaykalskiy Kray, S Russian Federation 56°57′N 118°05′E
193 J7 **Chara** ≈ C Russian Federation
102 C5 **Charala** Santander, C Colombia 06°17′N 73°09′W
85 L8 **Charcas** San Luis Potosí, C Mexico 23°09′N 101°10′W
70 G8 **Charco** Texas, SW USA 28°42′N 97°35′E
85 I4 **Charco de Peña** Chihuahua, Mexico 28°31′N 104°59′W
85 J6 **Charcos de Risa** Coahuila, Mexico 26°12′N 103°06′W
292 E4 **Charcot Island** *island* Antarctica
290 H4 **Charcot Seamounts** *undersea feature* E Atlantic Ocean 11°30′W 45°00′N
160 G8 **Chard** United Kingdom 50°52′N 2°58′W
Chardara *see* Shardara
Chardarinskoye Vodokhranilishche *see* Shardarinskoye Vodokhranilishche
73 J9 **Chardon** Ohio, N USA 41°34′N 81°12′W
90 G6 **Chardonnières** SW Haiti 18°16′N 74°10′W
Chardzhev *see* Türkmenabat
Chardzhevskaya Oblast *see* Lebap Welaýaty
Chardzhou/Chardzhui *see* Türkmenabat
164 G6 **Charente** ◈ *department* W France
164 F6 **Charente** ≈ W France
164 F6 **Charente-Maritime** ◈ *department* W France
167 H9 **Charenton-du-Cher** Centre, France 46°44′N 2°39′E
215 K5 **Ch'arents'avan** C Armenia 40°23′N 44°41′E
133 N6 **Chari** *var.* Shari. ≈ Central African Republic/Chad
133 L6 **Chari-Baguirmi** *off.* Préfecture du Chari-Baguirmi. ◈ *prefecture* SW Chad
Chari-Baguirmi, Préfecture du *see* Chari-Baguirmi
231 H3 **Chārīkār** Parvān, NE Afghanistan 35°01′N 69°11′E
161 L7 **Charing** United Kingdom 51°12′N 0°48′E
75 H8 **Chariton** Iowa, C USA 41°00′N 93°18′W
75 H9 **Chariton River** ≈ Missouri, C USA
103 K4 **Charity** NW Guyana 07°22′N 58°34′W
72 H7 **Charity Island** *island* Michigan, N USA
Chärjew *see* Türkmenabat
Chärjew Oblasty *see* Lebap Welaýaty
Charkhlik/Charkhliq *see* Ruoqiang
141 J4 **Charl Cilliers** Mpumalanga, South Africa 26°40′S 29°11′E
163 E11 **Charleroi** Hainaut, S Belgium 50°25′N 04°27′E
55 I7 **Charles** Manitoba, C Canada 55°27′N 100°58′W
63 I1 **Charlesbourg** Québec, SE Canada 46°50′N 71°15′W
67 M4 **Charles, Cape** *headland* Virginia, NE USA 37°09′N 75°57′W
74 H6 **Charles City** Iowa, C USA 43°04′N 92°40′W
67 L4 **Charles City** Virginia, NE USA 37°21′N 77°05′W
167 H5 **Charles de Gaulle** ✈ (Paris) Seine-et-Marne, N France 49°04′N 02°36′E
55 N2 **Charles Island** *island* Nunavut, NE Canada
Charles Island *see* Santa María, Isla
74 H5 **Charles-Lindbergh** ✈ (Minneapolis/Saint Paul) Minnesota, N USA 44°47′N 93°12′W
73 B8 **Charles Mound** *hill* Illinois, N USA
278 A11 **Charles Sound** *sound* South Island, New Zealand
279 D8 **Charleston** West Coast, South Island, New Zealand 41°54′S 171°25′E
71 J2 **Charleston** Arkansas, C USA 35°19′N 94°02′W
73 D11 **Charleston** Illinois, N USA 39°30′N 88°10′W
66 B8 **Charleston** Mississippi, S USA 34°00′N 90°03′W
66 B5 **Charleston** Missouri, C USA 36°54′N 89°22′W
67 J9 **Charleston** South Carolina, SE USA 32°48′N 79°57′W
67 I3 **Charleston** *state capital* West Virginia, NE USA 38°21′N 81°38′W
62 F4 **Charleston Lake** ◎ Ontario, SE Canada
81 I8 **Charleston Peak** ▲ Nevada, W USA 36°16′N 115°40′W
91 L6 **Charlestown** Nevis, Saint Kitts and Nevis 17°08′N 62°37′W
73 F12 **Charlestown** Indiana, N USA 38°27′N 85°40′W
63 I5 **Charlestown** New Hampshire, NE USA 43°14′N 72°23′W
64 B9 **Charles Town** West Virginia, NE USA 39°18′N 77°54′W
277 J1 **Charleville** Queensland, E Australia 26°25′S 146°18′E
165 J2 **Charleville-Mézières** Ardennes, N France 49°45′N 04°43′E
72 F5 **Charlevoix** Michigan, N USA 45°19′N 85°15′W
72 G5 **Charlevoix, Lake** ◎ Michigan, N USA
83 J4 **Charley River** ≈ Alaska, USA
290 F3 **Charlie-Gibbs Fracture Zone** *tectonic feature* N Atlantic Ocean
165 I6 **Charlieu** Loire, E France 46°11′N 04°10′E
73 G8 **Charlotte** Michigan, N USA 42°33′N 84°50′W
67 I7 **Charlotte** North Carolina, SE USA 35°14′N 80°51′W
66 D6 **Charlotte** Tennessee, S USA 36°11′N 87°18′W
70 F8 **Charlotte** Texas, SW USA 28°51′N 98°42′W
67 I7 **Charlotte** ✈ North Carolina, SE USA 35°12′N 80°54′W
91 K6 **Charlotte Amalie** *prev.* Saint Thomas. ○ (Virgin Islands (US)) Saint Thomas, N Virgin Islands (US) 18°22′N 64°56′W
67 K5 **Charlotte Court House** Virginia, NE USA 37°04′N 78°37′W
69 L8 **Charlotte Harbor** *inlet* Florida, SE USA
Charlotte Island *see* Abaiang
154 F7 **Charlottenberg** Värmland, C Sweden 59°53′N 12°17′E
Charlottenhof *see* Aegviidu
67 K4 **Charlottesville** Virginia, NE USA 38°02′N 78°29′W
59 J8 **Charlottetown** *province capital* Prince Edward Island, Prince Edward Island, SE Canada 46°14′N 63°09′W
Charlotte Town *see* Roseau, Dominica
Charlotte Town *see* Gouyave, Grenada
103 J2 **Charlotteville** Tobago, Trinidad and Tobago 11°16′N 60°33′W
277 I6 **Charlton** Victoria, SE Australia 36°18′S 143°19′E
58 F6 **Charlton Island** *island* Northwest Territories, C Canada
167 I5 **Charly-sur-Marne** Picardie, France 48°58′N 3°17′E
165 K3 **Charmes** Vosges, NE France 48°19′N 06°19′E
191 D11 **Charnawchytsy** *Rus.* Chernavchitsy. Brestskaya Voblasts', SW Belarus 52°13′N 23°44′E
167 K10 **Charnay-lès-Mâcon** Bourgogne, France 46°18′N 4°47′E
63 J2 **Charny** Québec, SE Canada 46°43′N 71°15′W
167 I7 **Charny** Bourgogne, France 47°53′N 3°06′E
167 K4 **Charny-sur-Meuse** Lorraine, France 49°12′N 5°22′E
167 J10 **Charolles** Bourgogne, France 46°26′N 4°17′E
166 G9 **Chârost** Centre, France 46°59′N 2°08′E
110 B7 **Charqueada** São Paulo, Brazil 22°30′S 47°46′W
115 N1 **Charqueadas** Rio Grande do Sul, Brazil 29°58′S 51°38′W
166 E10 **Charroux** Poitou-Charentes, France 46°09′N 0°24′E
231 I4 **Chārsadda** Khyber Pakhtunkhwa, NW Pakistan 34°12′N 71°46′E
Charshanga/Charshangngy/Charshangy *see* Köýtendag
Charsk *see* Shar
275 J4 **Charters Towers** Queensland, NE Australia 20°02′S 146°20′E
63 J3 **Chartierville** Québec, SE Canada 45°19′N 71°13′W
165 H3 **Chartres** *anc.* Autricum, Civitas Carnutum. Eure-et-Loir, C France 48°27′N 01°27′E
Charyn *see* Sharyn
Charyn *see* Sharyn
116 H4 **Chascomús** Buenos Aires, E Argentina 35°34′S 58°01′W
56 F7 **Chase** British Columbia, SW Canada 50°49′N 119°41′W
67 K5 **Chase City** Virginia, NE USA 36°48′N 78°27′W
63 K2 **Chase, Mount** ▲ Maine, NE USA 46°06′N 68°30′W
191 H8 **Chashniki** Vitsyebskaya Voblasts', N Belarus 54°52′N 29°10′E
186 F4 **Chásia** ▲▲ C Greece
74 G5 **Chaska** Minnesota, N USA 44°47′N 93°36′W
278 C13 **Chaslands Mistake** *headland* South Island, New Zealand 46°37′S 169°21′E
195 I7 **Chasovo** Respublika Komi, NW Russian Federation 61°58′N 50°34′E
Chasovo *see* Vazhgort
168 E1 **Chasseneuil** Poitou-Charentes, France 45°49′N 0°27′E
194 D9 **Chastova** Novgorodskaya Oblast', NW Russian Federation 58°37′N 32°05′E
223 H2 **Chāt** Golestān, N Iran 37°52′N 55°27′E
Chatak *see* Chhatak
Chatang *see* Zhanang
83 J4 **Chatanika** Alaska, USA 65°06′N 147°28′W
83 J4 **Chatanika River** ≈ Alaska, USA
229 K4 **Chat-Bazar** Talasskaya Oblast', NW Kyrgyzstan 42°29′N 72°37′E
91 M3 **Chateaubelair** Saint Vincent, W Saint Vincent and the Grenadines 13°15′N 61°05′W
166 C6 **Châteaubourg** Bretagne, France 48°07′N 1°24′W
114 A8 **Chateaubriand** Santa Fe, Argentina 33°38′S 61°52′W
164 F4 **Châteaubriant** Loire-Atlantique, NW France 47°43′N 01°22′W
165 I5 **Château-Chinon** Nièvre, C France 47°04′N 03°50′E
176 C5 **Château d'Oex** Vaud, W Switzerland 46°28′N 07°09′E
164 G4 **Château-du-Loir** Sarthe, NW France 47°40′N 00°25′E
165 H4 **Châteaudun** Eure-et-Loir, C France 48°04′N 01°20′E
166 C7 **Châteaugiron** Bretagne, France 48°03′N 1°30′W
164 F4 **Château-Gontier** Mayenne, NW France 47°49′N 00°42′W
63 H3 **Châteauguay** Québec, SE Canada 45°22′N 73°44′W
166 E8 **Château-la-Valliére** Centre, France 47°33′N 0°19′E
168 E2 **Château-l'Évèque** Aquitaine, France 45°15′N 0°40′E
164 D4 **Châteaulin** Finistère, NW France 48°12′N 04°07′W
165 H5 **Châteaumeillant** Cher, C France 46°33′N 02°10′E
169 I3 **Châteauneuf-de-Randon** Languedoc-Roussillon, France 44°39′N 3°40′E
166 A6 **Châteauneuf-du-Faou** Bretagne, France 48°11′N 3°49′W
166 F6 **Châteauneuf-en-Thymerais** Centre, France 48°35′N 1°15′E
168 D2 **Châteauneuf-sur-Charente** Charente, W France 45°34′N 00°33′W
167 H7 **Châteauneuf-sur-Loire** Centre, France 47°52′N 2°14′E
166 D7 **Châteauneuf-sur-Sarthe** Pays de la Loire, France 47°41′N 0°29′W
167 I8 **Châteauneuf-Val-de-Bargis** Bourgogne, France 47°17′N 3°14′E
166 F10 **Châteauponsac** Limousin, France 46°08′N 1°17′E
167 J4 **Château-Porcien** Champagne-Ardenne, France 49°32′N 4°15′E
169 J5 **Châteaurenard** Provence-Alpes-Côte d'Azur, France 43°49′N 4°50′E
166 F8 **Château-Renault** Indre-et-Loire, C France 47°34′N 00°52′E
165 H5 **Châteauroux** *prev.* Indreville. Indre, C France 46°50′N 01°43′E
165 K3 **Château-Salins** Moselle, NE France 48°50′N 06°29′E
165 I3 **Château-Thierry** Aisne, N France 49°03′N 03°24′E
167 K7 **Châteauvillain** Champagne-Ardenne, France 48°02′N 4°55′E
169 I1 **Châteldon** Auvergne, France 45°58′N 3°31′E
163 E11 **Châtelet** Hainaut, S Belgium 50°24′N 04°32′E
Châtelherault *see* Châtellerault
164 G5 **Châtellerault** *var.* Châtelherault. Vienne, W France 46°49′N 00°33′E
74 H5 **Chatfield** Minnesota, N USA 43°51′N 92°11′W
63 M1 **Chatham** New Brunswick, SE Canada 47°02′N 65°30′W
62 B6 **Chatham** Ontario, S Canada 42°24′N 82°11′W
161 L6 **Chatham** SE England, United Kingdom 51°23′N 00°31′E
73 C11 **Chatham** Illinois, N USA 39°40′N 89°42′W
67 J5 **Chatham** Virginia, NE USA 36°49′N 79°26′W
117 B12 **Chatham, Isla** *island* S Chile
Chatham Island *see* San Cristóbal, Isla
Chatham Island Rise *see* Chatham Rise
286 F9 **Chatham Islands** *island group* New Zealand, SW Pacific Ocean
267 I8 **Chatham Rise** *var.* Chatham Island Rise. *undersea feature* S Pacific Ocean
83 M7 **Chatham Strait** *strait* Alaska, USA
Chathóir, Rinn *see* Cahore Point
167 H7 **Châtillon-Coligny** Centre, France 47°50′N 2°51′E
167 I9 **Châtillon-en-Bazois** Bourgogne, France 47°03′N 3°40′E
169 K3 **Châtillon-en-Diois** Rhône-Alpes, France 44°41′N 5°28′E
167 K10 **Châtillon-sur-Chalaronne** Rhône-Alpes, France 46°07′N 4°58′E
165 H5 **Châtillon-sur-Indre** Indre, C France 46°58′N 01°10′E
167 I5 **Châtillon-sur-Marne** Champagne-Ardenne, France 49°06′N 3°45′E
165 J4 **Châtillon-sur-Seine** Côte d'Or, C France 47°51′N 04°30′E
229 J5 **Chatkal** *Uzb.* Chotqol. ≈ Kyrgyzstan/Uzbekistan
229 J5 **Chatkal Range** *Rus.* Chatkal'skiy Khrebet. ▲▲ Kyrgyzstan/Uzbekistan
Chatkal'skiy Khrebet *see* Chatkal Range
68 F3 **Chatom** Alabama, S USA 31°28′N 88°15′W
Chatrapur *see* Chhatrapur
223 H6 **Chatrūd** Kermān, C Iran 30°39′N 56°57′E
66 F7 **Chatsworth** Georgia, SE USA 34°46′N 84°46′W
Chāttagām *see* Chittagong
69 I4 **Chattahoochee** Florida, SE USA 30°40′N 84°51′W
69 I3 **Chattahoochee River** ≈ SE USA
66 F7 **Chattanooga** Tennessee, S USA 35°05′N 85°16′W
161 K4 **Chatteris** United Kingdom 52°27′N 0°03′E
229 L5 **Chatyr-Kël', Ozero** ◎ C Kyrgyzstan
229 M5 **Chatyr-Tash** Narynskaya Oblast', C Kyrgyzstan 40°54′N 76°22′E
63 J3 **Chaudière** ≈ Québec, SE Canada
257 H9 **Châu Đôc** *var.* Chauphu, Chau Phu. An Giang, S Vietnam 10°53′N 105°07′E
167 J10 **Chauffailles** Bourgogne, France 46°12′N 4°20′E
232 C6 **Chauhtan** *prev.* Chohtan. Rājasthān, NW India 25°27′N 71°08′E
256 C5 **Chauk** Magway, W Myanmar (Burma) 20°52′N 94°50′E
167 H3 **Chaulnes** Picardie, France 49°49′N 2°48′E
167 K7 **Chaumant** Champagne-Ardenne, France 48°07′N 5°08′E
167 K9 **Chaumergy** Franche-Comté, France 46°51′N 5°29′E
165 J4 **Chaumont** *prev.* Chaumont-en-Bassigny. Haute-Marne, N France 48°07′N 05°08′E
Chaumont-en-Bassigny *see* Chaumont
166 G4 **Chaumont-en-Vexin** Picardie, France 49°16′N 1°53′E
167 K5 **Chaumont-sur-Aire** Lorraine, France 48°56′N 5°15′E
166 F8 **Chaumont-sur-Loire** Centre, France 47°29′N 1°11′E
193 L3 **Chaunskaya Guba** *bay* NE Russian Federation
165 I2 **Chauny** Aisne, N France 49°37′N 03°13′E
256 I7 **Châu Ô** *var.* Binh Sơn. Quang Ngai, C Vietnam 15°18′N 108°45′E
Chau Phu *see* Châu Đôc
164 F3 **Chausey, Îles** *island group* N France
167 K9 **Chaussin** Franche-Comté, France 46°58′N 5°25′E
Chausy *see* Chavusy
62 D6 **Chautauqua Lake** ◎ New York, NE USA
ChâuThanh *see* Ba Ria
166 F9 **Chauvigny** Vienne, W France 46°35′N 00°37′E
194 F4 **Chavan'ga** Murmanskaya Oblast', NW Russian Federation 66°07′N 37°44′E
62 E1 **Chavannes, Lac** ◎ Québec, SE Canada
Chavantes, Represa de *see* Xavantes, Represa de
112 G7 **Chavarría** Corrientes, NE Argentina 28°57′S 58°35′W
Chavash Respubliki *see* Chuvashskaya Respublika
170 D3 **Chaves** *anc.* Aquae Flaviae. Vila Real, N Portugal 41°44′N 07°28′W
Chávez, Isla *see* Santa Cruz, Isla
167 I4 **Chavignon** Picardie, France 49°29′N 3°31′E
138 E1 **Chavuma** North Western, NW Zambia 13°04′S 22°43′E
191 I9 **Chavusy** *Rus.* Chausy. Mahilyowskaya Voblasts', E Belarus 53°48′N 30°58′E
Chayan *see* Shayan
243 J8 **Chayang** Guangdong, SE China 24°31′N 116°40′E
229 L5 **Chayek** Narynskaya Oblast', C Kyrgyzstan 41°54′N 74°28′E
217 J4 **Chāy Khānah** Diyālá, E Iraq 34°19′N 44°33′E
195 K10 **Chaykovskiy** Permskaya Oblast', NW Russian Federation 56°45′N 54°09′E
86 G9 **Chayuco** Oaxaca, Mexico 16°24′N 97°49′W
169 J2 **Chazelles-sur-Lyon** Rhône-Alpes, France 45°38′N 4°23′E
257 I8 **Chbar** Môndól Kiri, E Cambodia 12°46′N 107°10′E
161 H2 **Cheadle** United Kingdom 52°59′N 1°59′W
66 E9 **Cheaha Mountain** ▲ Alabama, S USA 33°29′N 85°48′W
Cheatharlach *see* Carlow
67 J2 **Cheat River** ≈ NE USA
183 A8 **Cheb** *Ger.* Eger. Karlovarský Kraj, W Czech Republic 50°05′N 12°23′E
218 F4 **Chebaâ** Lebanon 33°21′N 35°44′E
197 I2 **Cheboksary** Chuvashskaya Respublika, W Russian Federation 56°06′N 47°15′E
72 G5 **Cheboygan** Michigan, N USA 45°40′N 84°28′W
Chechaouèn *see* Chefchaouen
Chechenia *see* Chechenskaya Respublika
197 I9 **Chechenskaya Respublika** *Eng.* Chechenia, Chechnia, *Rus.* Chechnya. ◈ *autonomous republic* SW Russian Federation
121 H2 **Chech, Erg** *desert* Algeria/Mali
Chechevichi *see* Chachevichy
Che-chiang *see* Zhejiang
Chechnia/Chechnya *see* Chechenskaya Respublika
Chech'ŏn *see* Jecheon
182 G7 **Chęciny** Świętokrzyskie, S Poland 50°51′N 20°31′E
75 F12 **Checotah** Oklahoma, C USA 35°28′N 95°31′W
59 K8 **Chedabucto Bay** *inlet* Nova Scotia, E Canada
160 G7 **Cheddar** United Kingdom 51°17′N 2°47′W
256 B5 **Cheduba Island** *island* W Myanmar (Burma)
64 A1 **Cheektowaga** New York, USA 42°54′N 78°45′W
277 J1 **Cheepie** Queensland, Australia
79 L3 **Cheesman Lake** ▣ Colorado, C USA
293 J9 **Cheetham, Cape** *headland* Antarctica 70°26′S 162°40′E
166 E10 **Chef-Boutonne** Poitou-Charentes, France 46°06′N 0°03′W
130 F2 **Chefchaouen** *var.* Chaouèn, Chechaouèn, *Sp.* Xauen. N Morocco 35°10′N 05°16′W
Chefoo *see* Yantai
82 G7 **Chefornak** Alaska, USA 60°09′N 164°09′W
193 K8 **Chegdomyn** Khabarovskiy Kray, SE Russian Federation 51°09′N 132°58′E
130 F6 **Chegga** Tiris Zemmour, NE Mauritania 25°27′N 05°49′W
Cheghcheran *see* Chaghcharān
76 C4 **Chehalis** Washington, NW USA 46°39′N 122°57′W
76 B4 **Chehalis River** ≈ Washington, NW USA
230 E4 **Chehel Abdālān, Kūh-e** *var.* Chalap Dalam, *Pash.* Chalap Dalan. ▲▲ C Afghanistan
186 F3 **Cheimadítis, Límni** *var.* Límni Cheimadítis. ◎ N Greece
Cheimadítis, Límni *see* Cheimadítis, Límni
169 M5 **Cheiron, Mont** ▲ SE France 43°49′N 07°00′E
241 L2 **Cheju** ✈ S South Korea 33°31′N 126°29′E
Cheju *see* Jeju
Cheju-do *see* Jeju-do
237 J6 **Cheju-haehyeop** *Eng.* Cheju Strait. *strait* S South Korea
Cheju Strait *see* Cheju-haehyeop
Chekiang *see* Zhejiang
Chekichler/Chekishlyar *see* Çekiçler
218 F2 **Chekka** Lebanon
218 F2 **Chekka** Lebanon 34°20′N 35°44′E
87 L7 **Chekubul** Campeche, Mexico
282 C9 **Chelab** Babeldaob, N Palau
229 H6 **Chelak** *Rus.* Chelek. Samarqand Viloyati, C Uzbekistan 39°55′N 66°45′E
76 D3 **Chelan, Lake** ▣ Washington, NW USA
Chelek *see* Chelak
Cheleken *see* Hazar
172 D6 **Cheles** Extremadura, Spain 38°31′N 7°17′W
Chélif/Chéliff *see* Chelif, Oued
131 H2 **Chelif, Oued** *var.* Chélif, Chéliff, Chellif, Shellif. ≈ N Algeria
Chelkar *see* Shalkar
Chelkar Ozero *see* Shalkar, Ozero
171 M10 **Chellal** Algeria
118 D1 **Chellepín** Coquimbo, Chile 31°53′S 70°46′W
Chellif *see* Chelif, Oued
182 J7 **Chełm** *Rus.* Kholm. Lubelskie, SE Poland 51°08′N 23°29′E
182 F4 **Chełmno** *Ger.* Culm, Kulm. Kujawski-pomorskie, C Poland 53°21′N 18°27′E
186 G6 **Chelmós** *var.* Ároania. ▲▲ S Greece
62 C2 **Chelmsford** Ontario, S Canada 46°33′N 81°16′W
161 L5 **Chelmsford** E England, United Kingdom 51°44′N 00°28′E
65 L2 **Chelmsford** Massachusetts, USA 42°36′N 71°22′W
182 F5 **Chełmża** *Ger.* Culmsee, Kulmsee. Kujawski-pomorskie, C Poland 53°11′N 18°34′E
65 L2 **Chelsea** Massachusetts, USA 42°24′N 71°02′W
75 F11 **Chelsea** Oklahoma, C USA 36°32′N 95°25′W
63 I5 **Chelsea** Vermont, NE USA 43°58′N 72°29′W
161 H5 **Cheltenham** C England, United Kingdom 51°54′N 02°04′W
171 I5 **Chelva** País Valenciano, E Spain 39°45′N 01°00′W
197 N1 **Chelyabinsk** Chelyabinskaya Oblast', C Russian Federation 55°12′N 61°25′E
197 M2 **Chelyabinskaya Oblast'** ◈ *province* C Russian Federation
193 H3 **Chelyuskin, Mys** *headland* N Russian Federation 77°42′N 104°13′E
192 F8 **Chemal** Altayskiy Kray, S Russian Federation 51°22′N 85°08′E
87 N5 **Chemax** Yucatán, SE Mexico 20°41′N 87°54′W
139 J3 **Chemba** Sofala, C Mozambique 17°11′S 34°53′E
137 A12 **Chembe** Luapula, NE Zambia 11°58′S 28°45′E
Chemenibit *see* Çemenibit
Chemerisy *see* Chamyarysy
188 E5 **Chemerivtsi** Khmel'nyts'ka Oblast', W Ukraine 49°00′N 26°21′E
164 F5 **Chemillé** Maine-et-Loire, NW France 47°15′N 00°42′W
167 K9 **Chemin** Franche-Comté, France 46°59′N 5°19′E
137 G11 **Chemin Grenier** S Mauritius 20°29′S 57°28′E
179 H9 **Chemnitz** *prev.* Karl-Marx-Stadt. Sachsen, E Germany 50°50′N 12°55′E
Chemulpo *see* Incheon
76 C7 **Chemult** Oregon, NW USA 43°14′N 121°48′W
64 D3 **Chemung River** ≈ New York/Pennsylvania, NE USA
231 I5 **Chenāb** ≈ India/Pakistan
83 J4 **Chena Hot Springs** Alaska, USA 65°06′N 146°02′W
64 F2 **Chenango River** ≈ New York, NE USA
87 L6 **Chencoh** Campeche, Mexico 19°26′N 89°49′W
87 L6 **Chencoyí** Campeche, Mexico 19°48′N 90°14′W
258 D2 **Chenderoh, Tasik** ◎ Peninsular Malaysia
166 G10 **Chénérailles** Limousin, France 46°07′N 2°10′E
63 I2 **Chêne, Rivière du** ≈ Québec, SE Canada
76 F4 **Cheney** Washington, NW USA 47°29′N 117°34′W
75 D10 **Cheney Reservoir** ▣ Kansas, C USA
245 I6 **Cheng'an** Hebei, China 36°16′N 114°25′E
242 C8 **Chengbihe Shuiku** ▣ Guangxi, China
242 F6 **Chengbu** Hunan, SE China 26°22′N 110°19′E
Chengchiatun *see* Liaoyuan
Ch'eng-chou/Chengchow *see* Zhengzhou
245 K2 **Chengde** *var.* Jehol. Hebei, E China 41°N 117°57′E
245 K2 **Chengde** Hebei, China 40°28′N 118°05′E
243 J1 **Chengdong Hu** ◎ Anhui, China
242 A2 **Chengdu** *var.* Chengtu, Ch'eng-tu. *province capital* Sichuan, C China 30°41′N 104°03′E
243 N9 **Chenggong** S Taiwan 23°06′N 121°22′E
244 D9 **Chenggu** Shaanxi, China 33°05′N 107°12′E
243 J9 **Chenghai** Guangdong, S China 23°30′N 116°42′E
Chenghsien *see* Zhengzhou
Chengjiang *see* Taihe
242 E1 **Chengkou** Chongqing Shi, C China 31°35′N 108°24′E
240 F9 **Chengmai** *var.* Jinjiang. Hainan, S China 19°45′N 109°56′E
245 N5 **Chengshan** Shandong, E China 37°22′N 122°33′E
245 N5 **Chengshan Jiao** *cape* NE China
Chengshou *see* Yangshan
Chengtu/Ch'eng-tu *see* Chengdu
Chengwen *see* Chindu
244 C8 **Chengxian** *var.* Cheng Xiang. Gansu, C China 33°42′N 105°45′E
242 E9 **Chengxiang** Guang Zhuangzu Zizhiqu, S China 23°42′N 109°17′E
Cheng Xiang *see* Chengxian
Chengyang *see* Juxian
Chengzhong *see* Ningming
245 N3 **Chengzitan** Liaoning, NE China 39°30′N 122°30′E
Chenkiang *see* Zhenjiang
234 G7 **Chennai** *prev.* Madras. *state capital* Tamil Nādu, S India 13°05′N 80°18′E
234 G7 **Chennai** ✈ Tamil Nādu, S India 13°07′N 80°13′E
166 F8 **Chenonceaux** Centre, France 47°20′N 1°04′E
165 J5 **Chenôve** Côte d'Or, C France 47°16′N 05°00′E
Chenstokhov *see* Częstochowa
242 F5 **Chenxi** *var.* Chenyang. Hunan, S China 28°02′N 110°15′E
Chen Xian/Chenxian/Chen Xiang *see* Chenzhou
245 N1 **Chenxiangtun** Liaoning, China 41°20′N 123°18′E
Chenyang *see* Chenxi

◆ Country
● Country Capital
◇ Dependent Territory
○ Dependent Territory Capital
◈ Administrative Regions
✈ International Airport
▲ Mountain
▲▲ Mountain Range
⛰ Volcano
≈ River
◎ Lake
▣ Reservoir

INDEX

328

◆ Country
● Country Capital
◇ Dependent Territory
○ Dependent Territory Capital
◆ Administrative Regions
✈ International Airport
▲ Mountain
▲ Mountain Range
▲ Volcano
⁊ River
⊙ Lake
⊟ Reservoir

◆ Country ◇ Dependent Territory ◆ Administrative Regions ▲ Mountain ☫ Volcano ☺ Lake
● Country Capital ○ Dependent Territory Capital ✈ International Airport ▲ Mountain Range ⟂ River ☒ Reservoir

◆ Country
● Country Capital
◊ Dependent Territory
○ Dependent Territory Capital
◇ Administrative Regions
✕ International Airport
▲ Mountain
▲ Mountain Range
℞ Volcano
℞ River
⊕ Lake
⊞ Reservoir

Crossgar - Damoûr
INDEX
332

158 E7 **Crossgar** United Kingdom 54°24′N 5°42′W
158 G5 **Crosshill** United Kingdom 55°19′N 4°38′W
67 H8 **Cross Hill** South Carolina, SE USA 34°18′N 81°58′W
63 L4 **Cross Island** *island* Maine, NE USA
55 J7 **Cross Lake** Manitoba, C Canada 54°38′N 97°35′W
68 B1 **Cross Lake** ⊠ Louisiana, S USA
158 D8 **Crossmaglen** United Kingdom 54°05′N 6°36′W
81 J12 **Crossman Peak** ▲ Arizona, SW USA 34°33′N 114°09′W
70 F5 **Cross Plains** Texas, SW USA 32°07′N 99°10′W
133 K8 **Cross River** ◈ *state* SE Nigeria
66 F6 **Crossville** Tennessee, S USA 35°57′N 85°02′W
159 I9 **Croston** United Kingdom 53°39′N 2°46′W
72 I7 **Croswell** Michigan, N USA 43°16′N 82°37′W
62 F4 **Crotch Lake** ◎ Ontario, SE Canada
Croton/Crotona *see* Crotone
175 I11 **Crotone** *var.* Cotrone; *anc.* Croton, Crotona. Calabria, SW Italy 39°05′N 17°07′E
65 H5 **Croton-on-Hudson** New York, USA 41°13′N 73°53′W
161 L6 **Crouch** ≈ United Kingdom
77 K5 **Crow Agency** Montana, NW USA 45°35′N 107°28′W
161 L7 **Crowborough** United Kingdom 51°03′N 0°09′E
277 M4 **Crowdy Head** *headland* New South Wales, SE Australia 31°52′S 152°45′E
70 F3 **Crowell** Texas, SW USA 33°59′N 99°45′W
277 J4 **Crowl Creek** *seasonal river* New South Wales, SE Australia
68 C4 **Crowley** Louisiana, S USA 30°11′N 92°21′W
80 F5 **Crowley, Lake** ⊠ California, W USA
75 J12 **Crowleys Ridge** *hill range* Arkansas, C USA
73 E9 **Crown Point** Indiana, N USA 41°25′N 87°22′W
79 K6 **Crownpoint** New Mexico, SW USA 35°40′N 108°09′W
53 I7 **Crown Prince Frederick Island** *Island* Nunavut, NE Canada
77 I5 **Crow Peak** ▲ Montana, NW USA 46°17′N 111°54′W
80 C4 **Crows Landing** California, USA 37°24′N 121°04′W
57 I8 **Crowsnest Pass** *pass* Alberta/British Columbia, SW Canada
161 J6 **Crowthorne** United Kingdom 51°22′N 0°49′W
74 G3 **Crow Wing River** ≈ Minnesota, N USA
161 K6 **Croydon** SE England, United Kingdom 51°21′N 00°06′W
Crozer, Mount *see* Finkol, Mount
289 D11 **Crozet Basin** *undersea feature* S Indian Ocean 39°00′S 60°00′E
289 D12 **Crozet Islands** *island group* French Southern and Antarctic Territories
289 D12 **Crozet Plateau** *var.* Crozet Plateaus. *undersea feature* SW Indian Ocean 46°00′S 51°00′E
Crozet Plateaus *see* Crozet Plateau
52 E4 **Crozier Channel** *Sea waterway* Northwest Territories, NW Canada
164 D3 **Crozon** Finistère, NW France 48°14′N 04°31′W
Cruacha Dubha, Na *see* Macgillycuddy's Reeks
158 F2 **Cruachan, Ben** ▲ United Kingdom 56°25′N 5°08′W
Cruach Phádraig *see* Croagh Patrick
188 F9 **Crucea** Constanţa, SE Romania 44°30′N 28°18′E
90 D4 **Cruces** Cienfuegos, C Cuba 22°20′N 80°17′W
84 G4 **Cruces** Chihuahua, Mexico 29°26′N 107°24′W
175 I11 **Crucoli Torretta** Calabria, SW Italy 39°26′N 17°03′E
85 M7 **Cruillas** Tamaulipas, C Mexico 24°43′N 98°26′W
290 G5 **Cruiser Tablemount** *undersea feature* E Atlantic Ocean 32°00′N 28°00′W
158 E6 **Crumlin** United Kingdom 54°37′N 6°14′W
159 I7 **Crummock Water** ◎ United Kingdom
167 L10 **Cruseilles** Rhône-Alpes, France 46°02′N 6°07′E
114 A7 **Cruz Alta** Córdoba, Argentina 33°0′S 61°49′W
113 I6 **Cruz Alta** Rio Grande do Sul, S Brazil 28°38′S 53°38′W
90 E5 **Cruz, Cabo** *headland* S Cuba 19°50′N 77°43′W
115 H9 **Cruz de los Caminos** Canelones, Uruguay 34°38′S 55°58′W
115 K5 **Cruz de Piedra** Cerro Largo, Uruguay 32°02′S 54°11′W
110 F7 **Cruzeiro** São Paulo, S Brazil 22°33′S 44°59′W
110 D1 **Cruzeiro da Fortaleza** Minas Gerais, Brazil 18°58′S 46°40′W
113 I4 **Cruzeiro do Oeste** Paraná, S Brazil 23°45′S 53°03′W
106 A5 **Cruzeiro do Sul** Acre, W Brazil 07°40′S 72°39′W
86 F8 **Cruz Grande** Guerrero, Mexico 16°44′N 99°08′W
160 D5 **Crymych** United Kingdom 51°58′N 4°39′W
80 F2 **Crystal Bay** Nevada, USA 39°14′N 120°0′W
69 K6 **Crystal Bay** *bay* Florida, SE USA NE Gulf of Mexico Atlantic Ocean
64 A1 **Crystal Beach** New York, NE USA 42°48′N 77°15′W
276 G5 **Crystal Brook** South Australia 33°24′S 138°10′E
55 I10 **Crystal City** Manitoba, S Canada 49°07′N 98°54′W
75 J10 **Crystal City** Missouri, C USA 38°13′N 90°22′W
70 F8 **Crystal City** Texas, SW USA 28°43′N 99°51′W
72 D4 **Crystal Falls** Michigan, N USA 46°06′N 88°20′W
69 I4 **Crystal Lake** Florida, SE USA 30°26′N 85°41′W
72 F6 **Crystal Lake** ◎ Michigan, N USA
69 L6 **Crystal River** Florida, SE USA 28°54′N 82°35′W
79 K3 **Crystal River** ≈ Colorado, C USA
68 E2 **Crystal Springs** Mississippi, S USA 31°59′N 90°21′W
Csaca *see* Čadca
Csakathurn/Csáktornya *see* Čakovec
Csap *see* Chop
Csepén *see* Čepin
Cserépalja *see* Crepaja
Csermő *see* Cermei
Csíkszereda *see* Miercurea-Ciuc
183 G12 **Csongrád** Csongrád, SE Hungary 46°42′N 20°09′E
183 G12 **Csongrád** *off.* Csongrád Megye. ◈ *county* SE Hungary
Csongrád Megye *see* Csongrád
183 E11 **Csorna** Győr-Moson-Sopron, NW Hungary 47°37′N 17°14′E
Csucsa *see* Ciucea
183 E13 **Csurgó** Somogy, SW Hungary 46°16′N 17°09′E
Csurog *see* Čurug
102 G3 **Cúa** Miranda, N Venezuela 10°14′N 66°58′W
86 F9 **Cuajinicuilapa** Guerrero, S Mexico 16°28′N 98°25′W
135 D10 **Cuale** Malanje, NW Angola 08°22′S 16°10′E
121 K7 **Cuando** *var.* Kwando. ≈ S Africa
135 E14 **Cuando Cubango** *var.* Kuando-Kubango. ◈ *province* SE Angola
135 E14 **Cuangar** Cuando Cubango, S Angola 17°34′S 18°39′E
135 E11 **Cuango** Lunda Norte, NE Angola 09°10′S 17°59′E
135 D10 **Cuango** Uíge, NW Angola 06°20′S 16°42′E
135 D10 **Cuango** *var.* Kwango. ≈ Angola/Dem. Rep. Congo *see also* Kwango
Cuan, Loch *see* Strangford Lough
135 C11 **Cuanza** *var.* Kwanza. ≈ C Angola
135 D11 **Cuanza Norte** *var.* Kuanza Norte. ◈ *province* NE Angola
135 C12 **Cuanza Sul** *var.* Kuanza Sul. ◈ *province* NE Angola
115 H2 **Cuareim, Río** *var.* Río Quaraí. ≈ Brazil/Uruguay *see also* Quaraí, Rio
Cuareim, Río *see* Quaraí, Rio
114 G2 **Cuaró** Artigas, Uruguay 30°37′S 56°54′W
85 K6 **Cuates de Australia** Coahuila, Mexico 26°19′N 102°17′W
135 E13 **Cuatir** ≈ S Angola
85 K5 **Cuatro Ciénegas** *var.* Cuatro Ciénegas de Carranza. Coahuila, NE Mexico 27°00′N 102°03′W
Cuatro Ciénegas de Carranza *see* Cuatro Ciénegas
85 H4 **Cuauhtémoc** Chihuahua, N Mexico 28°22′N 106°52′W
85 J7 **Cuauhtémoc** Durango, Mexico 24°17′N 103°49′W
85 N9 **Cuauhtemoc** Tamaulipas, Mexico 22°32′N 98°09′W
87 I8 **Cuauhtémoc** Veracruz-Llave, Mexico 17°18′N 94°43′W
85 N10 **Cuautepec** Puebla, Mexico
86 B6 **Cuautitlán** Jalisco, Mexico 19°26′N 104°23′W
86 B5 **Cuautla** Jalisco, Mexico 20°11′N 104°21′W
86 F7 **Cuautla** Morelos, S Mexico 18°48′N 98°56′W
172 C6 **Cuba** Beja, S Portugal 38°10′N 07°54′W
75 I10 **Cuba** Missouri, C USA 38°03′N 91°24′W
79 L6 **Cuba** New Mexico, SW USA 36°01′N 106°57′W
64 B3 **Cuba** New York, USA 42°13′N 78°17′W
90 D4 **Cuba** *off.* Republic of Cuba. ◆ *republic* W West Indies
95 I1 **Cuba** *island* W West Indies
135 C12 **Cubal** Benguela, W Angola 12°58′S 14°16′E
135 D13 **Cubango** *var.* Kuvango, *Port.* Vila Artur de Paiva, Vila da Ponte. Huíla, SW Angola 14°27′S 16°18′E
135 F14 **Cubango** *var.* Kavango, Kavengo, Kubango, Okavango, Okavanggo. ≈ S Africa *see also* Okavango
Cubango *see* Okavango
102 D4 **Cubará** Boyacá, N Colombia 07°01′N 72°07′W
Cuba, Republic of *see* Cuba
110 D10 **Cubatão** São Paulo, Brazil 23°53′S 46°25′W
214 E5 **Çubuk** Ankara, N Turkey 40°13′N 33°02′E
114 B9 **Cucha Cucha** Buenos Aires, Argentina 34°36′S 60°24′W
135 D13 **Cuchi** Cuando Cubango, C Angola 14°40′S 16°58′E
115 J5 **Cuchilla Caraguatá** Uruguay 32°14′S 54°59′W
114 G7 **Cuchilla del Perdido** Uruguay 33°35′S 57°18′W
115 H5 **Cuchilla de Peralta** Uruguay 32°26′S 56°21′W
114 D7 **Cuchilla Redonda** Entre Ríos, Argentina 33°05′S 59°07′W
85 I3 **Cuchillo Parado** Chihuahua, Mexico 29°27′N 104°53′W
88 B3 **Cuchumatanes, Sierra de los** ▲▲ W Guatemala
161 K7 **Cuckfield** United Kingdom 51°01′N 0°08′W
Cuculaya, Rio *see* Kukalaya, Rio
135 E11 **Cucumbi** *prev.* Trás-os-Montes. Lunda Sul, NE Angola 10°13′S 19°04′E
84 E3 **Cucurpé** Sonora, Mexico 30°20′N 110°43′W
102 D4 **Cúcuta** *var.* San José de Cúcuta. Norte de Santander, N Colombia 07°55′N 72°31′W
73 D8 **Cudahy** Wisconsin, N USA 42°54′N 87°51′W
235 F8 **Cuddalore** Tamil Nādu, SE India 11°43′N 79°46′E
234 F7 **Cuddapah** Andhra Pradesh, S India 14°30′N 78°50′E
159 K9 **Cudworth** United Kingdom 53°34′N 1°25′W
170 F4 **Cuéllar** Castilla-León, N Spain 41°24′N 04°19′W
135 E12 **Cuemba** *var.* Coemba. Bié, C Angola 12°09′S 18°07′E
104 C3 **Cuenca** Azuay, S Ecuador 02°54′S 79°W
171 H5 **Cuenca** *anc.* Conca. Castilla-La Mancha, C Spain 40°04′N 02°07′W
171 H5 **Cuenca** ◈ *province* Castilla-La Mancha, C Spain
85 J7 **Cuencamé** *var.* Cuencamé de Ceniceros. Durango, C Mexico 24°53′N 103°41′W
Cuencamé de Ceniceros *see* Cuencamé
173 J3 **Cuenca, Serrania de** ▲▲ Castilla-La Manacha, Spain
171 H5 **Cuenca, Serrania de** ▲▲ C Spain
Cuera *see* Chur
86 D5 **Cuerámaro** Guanajuato, Mexico 20°37′N 101°43′W
170 G3 **Cuerda del Pozo, Embalse de la** ⊠ N Spain
86 F7 **Cuernavaca** Morelos, S Mexico 18°57′N 99°15′W
71 H7 **Cuero** Texas, SW USA 29°06′N 97°19′W
118 G2 **Cuero, Alto del** ▲ Mendoza, Argentina 32°36′S 67°48′W
169 L6 **Cuers** Provence-Alpes-Côte d'Azur, France 43°14′N 6°04′E
90 F5 **Cueto** Holguín, E Cuba 20°43′N 75°54′W
86 G6 **Cuetzalán** *var.* Cuetzalán del Progreso. Puebla, S Mexico 20°00′N 97°27′W
Cuetzalán del Progreso *see* Cuetzalán
173 J8 **Cuevas de Almanzora** Andalucía, S Spain 37°19′N 01°52′W
172 F8 **Cuevas del Becerro** Andalucía, Spain 36°52′N 5°02′W
Cuevas de Vinromá *see* Les Coves de Vinromà
114 G8 **Cufré** Uruguay 34°12′S 57°06′W
188 C8 **Cugir** *Hung.* Kudzsir. Alba, SW Romania 45°48′N 23°25′E
107 I9 **Cuiabá** *prev.* Cuyabá. *state capital* Mato Grosso, SW Brazil 15°32′S 56°05′W
107 I10 **Cuiabá, Rio** ≈ SW Brazil
86 G8 **Cuicatlán** *var.* San Juan Bautista Cuicatlán. Oaxaca, SE Mexico 17°49′N 96°59′W
118 B2 **Cuidado, Punta** *headland* Easter Island, Chile, E Pacific Ocean 27°08′S 109°18′W
Cúige *see* Connaught
Cúige Laighean *see* Leinster
Cúige Mumhan *see* Munster
Cuihua *see* Daguan
162 G7 **Cuijck** Noord-Brabant, SE Netherlands 51°41′N 05°56′E
Cúil an tSúdaire *see* Portarlington
88 C4 **Cuilapa** Santa Rosa, S Guatemala 14°16′N 90°18′W
88 B3 **Cuilco, Río** ≈ W Guatemala
Cúil Mhuine *see* Collooney
Cúil Raithin *see* Coleraine
135 D12 **Cuima** Huambo, C Angola 13°16′S 15°39′E
167 K10 **Cuiseaux** Bourgogne, France 46°30′N 5°24′E
167 K10 **Cuisiat** Rhône-Alpes, France 46°18′N 5°23′E
135 E14 **Cuito** *var.* Kwito. ≈ SE Angola
135 E13 **Cuíto Cuanavale** Cuando Cubango, E Angola 15°01′S 19°07′E
86 D6 **Cuitzeo, Lago de** ◎ C Mexico
75 I9 **Cuivre River** ≈ Missouri, C USA
Çuka *see* Çukë
258 E3 **Cukai** *var.* Chukai, Kemaman. Terengganu, Peninsular Malaysia 04°15′N 103°25′E
184 F10 **Çukë** *var.* Çuka. Vlorë, S Albania 39°50′N 20°01′E
187 N3 **Çukurhisar** Eskişehir, Turkey 39°50′N 30°19′E
167 H10 **Culan** Centre, France 46°33′N 2°21′E
Cularo *see* Grenoble
263 L7 **Culasi** Panay Island, C Philippines 11°21′N 122°05′E
77 M3 **Culbertson** Montana, NW USA 48°09′N 104°30′W
75 C8 **Culbertson** Nebraska, C USA 40°13′N 100°50′W
277 J6 **Culcairn** New South Wales, SE Australia 35°41′S 147°01′E
158 C5 **Culdaff** Donegal, Ireland 55°17′N 7°10′W
91 J8 **Culebra** *var.* Dewey. E Puerto Rico 18°19′N 65°17′W
91 J8 **Culebra, Isla de** *island* E Puerto Rico
79 M5 **Culebra Peak** ▲ Colorado, C USA 37°07′N 105°11′W
170 E3 **Culebra, Sierra de la** ▲▲ NW Spain
162 F7 **Culemborg** Gelderland, C Netherlands 51°57′N 05°17′E
118 C6 **Culenar** Maule, Chile 35°27′S 71°42′W
215 L6 **Culfa** *Rus.* Dzhul'fa. SW Azerbaijan 38°58′N 45°37′E
159 J6 **Culgaith** United Kingdom 54°39′N 2°36′W
277 J3 **Culgoa River** ≈ New South Wales/Queensland, SE Australia
84 G7 **Culiacán** *var.* Culiacán Rosales, Culiacán-Rosales. Sinaloa, C Mexico 24°48′N 107°25′W
Culiacán-Rosales/Culiacán Rosales *see* Culiacán
263 K7 **Culion Island** *island* Calamian Group, W Philippines
171 H8 **Cúllar-Baza** Andalucía, S Spain 37°35′N 02°34′W
171 I6 **Cullera** País Valenciano, E Spain 39°10′N 00°15′W
66 D8 **Cullman** Alabama, S USA 34°10′N 86°50′W
160 F8 **Cullompton** United Kingdom 50°52′N 3°24′W
176 C5 **Cully** Vaud, W Switzerland 46°58′N 06°46′E
Culm *see* Chełmno
Culmsee *see* Chełmża
67 K3 **Culpeper** Virginia, NE USA 38°28′N 78°00′W
159 H3 **Culross** United Kingdom 56°03′N 3°37′W
159 H4 **Culter Fell** ▲ United Kingdom 55°32′N 3°30′W
279 E9 **Culverden** Canterbury, South Island, New Zealand 42°46′S 172°51′E
276 A5 **Culver, Point** *headland* Western Australia, S Australia 32°54′S 124°43′E
161 I4 **Culworth** United Kingdom 52°06′N 1°12′W
138 F4 **Cum** *var.* Xhumo. Central, C Botswana 21°13′S 24°38′E
103 H2 **Cumaná** Sucre, NE Venezuela 10°29′N 64°12′W
103 H3 **Cumanacoa** Sucre, NE Venezuela 10°17′N 63°58′W
102 A8 **Cumbal, Nevado de** *elevation* S Colombia
66 G5 **Cumberland** Kentucky, S USA 36°55′N 83°00′W
64 A8 **Cumberland** Maryland, NE USA 39°40′N 78°47′W
67 K4 **Cumberland** Virginia, NE USA 37°31′N 78°16′W
281 L2 **Cumberland, Cape** *var.* Cape Nahoi. *headland* Espiritu Santo, N Vanuatu 14°39′S 166°35′E
55 H8 **Cumberland House** Saskatchewan, C Canada 53°57′N 102°21′W
69 L3 **Cumberland Island** *island* Georgia, SE USA
66 F5 **Cumberland, Lake** ⊠ Kentucky, S USA
53 L7 **Cumberland Peninsula** *peninsula* Baffin Island, Nunavut, NE Canada
46 E6 **Cumberland Plateau** *plateau* E USA
72 C3 **Cumberland Point** *headland* Michigan, N USA 47°51′N 89°14′W
66 G5 **Cumberland River** ≈ Kentucky/Tennessee, S USA
53 M8 **Cumberland Sound** *inlet* Baffin Island, Nunavut, NE Canada
159 H3 **Cumbernauld** S Scotland, United Kingdom 55°57′N 04°W
172 D6 **Cumbres Mayores** Andalucía, Spain 38°04′N 6°38′W
159 I4 **Cumbria** *cultural region* NW England, United Kingdom
157 F8 **Cumbrian Mountains** ▲▲ NW England, United Kingdom
159 H6 **Cummertrees** United Kingdom 54°59′N 3°21′W
66 F8 **Cumming** Georgia, SE USA 34°12′N 84°08′W
Cummin in Pommern *see* Kamień Pomorski
276 F5 **Cummins** South Australia 34°17′S 135°43′E
158 G4 **Cumnock** W Scotland, United Kingdom 55°32′N 04°28′W
84 F3 **Cumpas** Sonora, NW Mexico 30°N 109°48′W
214 E7 **Çumra** Konya, C Turkey 37°34′N 32°38′E
159 I6 **Cumrew** United Kingdom 54°50′N 2°42′W
84 F5 **Cumuripa** Sonora, Mexico 28°09′N 109°55′W
116 B6 **Cunco** Araucanía, C Chile 38°55′S 72°02′W
118 D1 **Cuncumén** Coquimbo, Chile 31°54′S 70°37′W
118 C4 **Cuncumén** Valparaíso, Chile 33°44′S 71°25′W
102 C5 **Cundinamarca** *off.* Departamento de Cundinamarca. ◈ *province* C Colombia
Cundinamarca, Departamento de *see* Cundinamarca
87 J7 **Cunduacán** Tabasco, SE Mexico 18°00′N 93°07′W
135 D14 **Cunene** ◈ *province* S Angola
135 B14 **Cunene** *var.* Kunene. ≈ Angola/Namibia *see also* Kunene
176 D8 **Cuneo** *Fr.* Coni. Piemonte, NW Italy 44°23′N 07°32′E
110 F8 **Cunha** São Paulo, Brazil 23°05′S 44°58′W
135 F13 **Cunjamba** Cuando Cubango, E Angola 15°22′S 20°07′E
118 D1 **Cunlagua** Coquimbo, Chile 31°44′S 70°55′W
169 I2 **Cunlhat** Auvergne, France 45°38′N 3°35′E
277 J2 **Cunnamulla** Queensland, E Australia 28°09′S 145°44′E
81 J13 **Cunningham Pass** *pass* Nevada, USA
243 I4 **Cunqian** Jiangxi, E China 28°28′N 115°09′E
Čunusavvon *see* Junosuando
Cuokkarašša *see* Čohkarášša
176 D7 **Cuorgne** Piemonte, NE Italy 45°23′N 07°34′E
243 K1 **Cuozhen** Anhui, E China 31°49′N 117°28′E
159 I2 **Cupar** E Scotland, United Kingdom 56°19′N 03°01′W
188 F6 **Cupcina** *Rus.* Kupchino; *prev.* Calinisc, Kalinisk. N Moldova 48°07′N 27°22′E
80 B3 **Cupertino** California, USA 37°19′N 122°02′W
102 A4 **Cupica** Chocó, W Colombia 06°43′N 77°31′W
102 A5 **Cupica, Golfo de** *gulf* W Colombia
184 G4 **Ćuprija** Serbia, E Serbia 43°57′N 21°21′E
84 E7 **Cupula, Pico** ▲ Baja California Sur, NW Mexico
86 C5 **Cuquío** Jalisco, Mexico 20°55′N 103°02′W
Cura *see* Villa de Cura
102 E1 **Curaçao** *island* Netherlands Antilles
104 G6 **Curanja, Río** ≈ E Peru
104 E3 **Curaray, Rio** ≈ Ecuador/Peru
118 C3 **Curaumilla, Punta** *point* Valparaíso, Chile
188 E10 **Curcani** Călăraşi, SE Romania 44°11′N 26°39′E
276 F3 **Curdimurka** South Australia 29°27′S 136°56′E
165 I4 **Cure** ≈ C France
137 G10 **Curepipe** C Mauritius 20°19′S 57°31′E
103 I3 **Curiapo** Delta Amacuro, NE Venezuela 10°03′N 63°05′W
Curia Rhaetorum *see* Chur
116 B4 **Curicó** Maule, C Chile 35°00′S 71°15′W
Curieta *see* Krk
137 J8 **Curieuse** *island* Inner Islands, NE Seychelles
106 C7 **Curitiba** Acre, W Brazil 10°08′S 69°00′W
113 K5 **Curitiba** *prev.* Curytiba. *state capital* Paraná, S Brazil 25°25′S 49°25′W
113 J6 **Curitibanos** Santa Catarina, S Brazil 27°18′S 50°35′W
277 L4 **Curlewis** New South Wales, SE Australia 31°09′S 150°18′E
276 G4 **Curnamona** South Australia 31°39′S 139°35′E
135 B14 **Curoca** ≈ SW Angola
277 L4 **Currabubula** New South Wales, SE Australia 31°17′S 150°43′E
158 C10 **Curragh, The** *physical region* E Ireland
108 I5 **Currais Novos** Rio Grande do Norte, E Brazil 06°12′S 36°30′W
78 F4 **Currant** Nevada, W USA 38°43′N 115°27′W
78 F4 **Currant Mountain** ▲ Nevada, W USA 38°56′N 115°19′W
61 M9 **Current** Eleuthera Island, C Bahamas 25°24′N 76°44′W
75 I11 **Current River** ≈ Arkansas/Missouri, C USA
277 I8 **Currie** Tasmania, SE Australia 39°59′S 143°51′E
159 I3 **Currie** United Kingdom 55°54′N 3°18′W
67 M5 **Currituck** North Carolina, SE USA 36°29′N 76°02′W
67 M5 **Currituck Sound** *sound* North Carolina, SE USA
83 I6 **Curry** Alaska, USA 62°36′N 150°00′W
Curtbunar *see* Tervel
188 D9 **Curtea de Argeş** *var.* Curtea-de-Arges. Argeş, S Romania 45°06′N 24°40′E
Curtea-de-Arges *see* Curtea de Argeş
188 A7 **Curtici** *Ger.* Kurtitsch, *Hung.* Kürtös. Arad, W Romania 46°21′N 21°17′E
118 C6 **Curtiduría** Maule, Chile 35°28′S 71°56′W
115 H5 **Curtina** Uruguay 32°09′S 56°07′W
170 D2 **Curtis** Galicia, NW Spain 43°09′N 08°10′W
277 J8 **Curtis Group** *island group* Tasmania, SE Australia
275 L5 **Curtis Island** *island* Queensland, SE Australia
53 I8 **Curtis River** ≈ Nunavut, NE Canada
108 B1 **Curuá, Ilha do** *island* NE Brazil
95 K4 **Curuá, Rio** ≈ N Brazil
106 A4 **Curuçá, Rio** ≈ NW Brazil
184 F2 **Čurug** *Hung.* Csurog. Vojvodina, N Serbia 45°30′N 20°02′E
114 A2 **Curupayti** Santa Fe, Argentina 30°24′S 61°40′W
114 E1 **Curuzú Cuatiá** Corrientes, NE Argentina 29°50′S 58°05′W
110 G1 **Curvelo** Minas Gerais, SE Brazil 18°45′S 44°27′W
64 A5 **Curwensville** Pennsylvania, NE USA 40°57′N 78°29′W
72 D4 **Curwood, Mount** ▲ Michigan, N USA 46°42′N 88°14′W
Curytiba *see* Curitiba
Curzola *see* Korčula
88 D5 **Cuscatlán** ◈ *department* C El Salvador
105 F8 **Cusco** *var.* Cuzco. Cusco, C Peru 13°35′S 72°02′W
105 F8 **Cusco** *off.* Departamento de Cusco, *var.* Cuzco. ◈ *department* C Peru
Cusco, Departamento de *see* Cusco
158 E5 **Cushendall** United Kingdom 55°05′N 6°03′W
158 E5 **Cushendun** United Kingdom 55°08′N 6°02′W
75 E12 **Cushing** Oklahoma, C USA 36°01′N 96°46′W
71 I5 **Cushing** Texas, SW USA 31°48′N 94°50′W
85 H4 **Cusihuiriachic** Chihuahua, N Mexico 28°16′N 106°46′W
165 I6 **Cusset** Allier, C France 46°08′N 03°27′E
69 I2 **Cusseta** Georgia, SE USA 32°18′N 84°46′W
74 A5 **Custer** South Dakota, N USA 43°46′N 103°36′W
Cüstrin *see* Kostrzyn
77 H3 **Cut Bank** Montana, NW USA 48°38′N 112°20′W
Cutch, Gulf of *see* Kachchh, Gulf of
69 I2 **Cuthbert** Georgia, SE USA 31°46′N 84°47′W
57 L5 **Cut Knife** Saskatchewan, S Canada 52°40′N 108°54′W
80 E6 **Cutler** California, USA 36°31′N 119°17′W
69 N9 **Cutler Ridge** Florida, SE USA 25°34′N 80°21′W
68 E5 **Cut Off** Louisiana, S USA 29°32′N 90°20′W
118 F10 **Cutral-Có** Neuquén, C Argentina 38°56′S 69°13′W
158 A10 **Cutra, Lough** ◎ Galway, Ireland
175 I11 **Cutro** Calabria, SW Italy 39°01′N 16°59′E
234 I4 **Cuttack** Orissa, E India 20°28′N 85°53′E
86 E7 **Cutzamalá de Pinzón** Guerrero, Mexico 18°28′N 100°34′W
135 D13 **Cuvelai** Cunene, SW Angola 15°40′S 15°48′E
134 C7 **Cuvette** *var.* Région de la Cuvette. ◈ *province* C Congo
134 C7 **Cuvette-Ouest** ◈ *province* C Congo
Cuvette, Région de la *see* Cuvette
289 I10 **Cuvier Basin** *undersea feature* E Indian Ocean
289 I10 **Cuvier Plateau** *undersea feature* E Indian Ocean
167 H4 **Cuvilly** Picardie, France 49°33′N 2°42′E
135 C12 **Cuvo** ≈ W Angola
180 F2 **Cuxhaven** Niedersachsen, NW Germany 53°51′N 08°43′E
Cuyabá *see* Cuiabá
81 C8 **Cuyama** California, USA 34°56′N 119°37′W
263 K7 **Cuyo East Pass** *passage* C Philippines
263 K7 **Cuyo West Pass** *passage* C Philippines
Cuyuni, Río *see* Cuyuni River
103 J4 **Cuyuni River** *var.* Río Cuyuni. ≈ Guyana/Venezuela
86 B6 **Cuyutlán** Jalisco, SW Mexico 18°55′N 104°04′W
86 C5 **Cuyutlán** Jalisco, W Mexico 21°03′N 103°33′W
Cuzco *see* Cusco
160 G6 **Cwmbran** *Wel.* Cwmbrân. SW Wales, United Kingdom 51°39′N 03°W
Cwmbrân *see* Cwmbran
74 B7 **C. W. McConaughy, Lake** ⊠ Nebraska, C USA
137 A9 **Cyangugu** SW Rwanda 02°27′S 29°00′E
182 C6 **Cybinka** *Ger.* Ziebingen. Lubuskie, W Poland 52°11′N 14°46′E
Cyclades *see* Kykládes
Cydonia *see* Chaniá
159 H10 **Cyffylliog** United Kingdom 53°06′N 3°25′W
Cymru *see* Wales
66 F3 **Cynthiana** Kentucky, S USA 38°22′N 84°18′W
160 F2 **Cynwyd** United Kingdom 52°57′N 3°25′W
57 L8 **Cypress Hills** ▲▲ Alberta/Saskatchewan, SW Canada
Cypro-Syrian Basin *see* Cyprus Basin
218 C2 **Cyprus** *off.* Republic of Cyprus, *Gk.* Kypros, *Turk.* Kıbrıs, Kıbrıs Cumhuriyeti. ◆ *republic* E Mediterranean Sea
144 G9 **Cyprus** *Gk.* Kypros, *Turk.* Kıbrıs. *island* E Mediterranean Sea
148 F9 **Cyprus Basin** *var.* Cypro-Syrian Basin. *undersea feature* E Mediterranean Sea 34°00′N 34°00′E
Cyprus, Republic of *see* Cyprus
128 F2 **Cyrenaica** ◈ *cultural region* NE Libya
Cythera *see* Kýthira
Cythnos *see* Kýthnos
182 D4 **Czaplinek** *Ger.* Tempelburg. Zachodnio-pomorskie, NW Poland 53°33′N 16°14′E
Czarna Woda *see* Wda
182 E4 **Czarne** Pomorskie, N Poland 53°40′N 17°00′E
182 D5 **Czarnków** Wielkopolskie, C Poland 52°53′N 16°32′E
183 C9 **Czech Republic** *Cz.* Česká Republika. ◆ *republic* C Europe
Czegléd *see* Cegléd
Czenstochau *see* Częstochowa
Czerkow *see* Čerchov
Czernowitz *see* Chernivtsi
182 E4 **Czersk** Pomorskie, N Poland 53°48′N 17°58′E
182 F7 **Częstochowa** *Ger.* Czenstochau, Tschenstochau, *Rus.* Chenstokhov. Śląskie, S Poland 50°49′N 19°07′E
182 D5 **Człopa** *Ger.* Schloppe. Zachodnio-pomorskie, NW Poland 53°05′N 16°05′E
182 E4 **Człuchów** *Ger.* Schlochau. Pomorskie, NW Poland 53°41′N 17°20′E

D

181 E10 **Daaden** Rheinland-Pfalz, Germany 50°44′E 7°58′N
247 K5 **Da'an** *var.* Dalai. Jilin, NE China 45°28′N 124°18′E
63 J2 **Daaquam** Québec, SE Canada 46°36′N 70°03′W
Daawo, Webi *see* Dawa Wenz
102 E2 **Dabajuro** Falcón, NW Venezuela 11°00′N 70°41′W
132 F7 **Dabakala** NE Ivory Coast 08°19′N 04°24′W
247 J6 **Daban** *var.* Bairin Youqi. Nei Mongol Zizhiqu, N China 43°33′N 118°40′E
183 G12 **Dabas** Pest, C Hungary 47°36′N 18°22′E
242 E1 **Daba Shan** ▲▲ C China
Dabba *see* Daocheng
220 D3 **Dabbāgh, Jabal** ▲ NW Saudi Arabia 27°52′N 35°48′E
102 B4 **Dabeiba** Antioquia, NW Colombia 07°01′N 76°18′W
140 D6 **Dabenoris** Northern Cape, South Africa 28°55′S 18°39′E
232 C8 **Dabhoi** Gujarāt, W India 22°08′N 73°28′E
243 I2 **Dabie Shan** ▲▲ C China
219 H9 **Dabi, Wādī** Jordan
167 M5 **Dabo** Lorraine, France 48°39′N 7°14′E
132 D6 **Dabola** C Guinea 10°48′N 11°02′W
132 F8 **Dabou** S Ivory Coast 05°20′N 04°23′W
244 E4 **Dabqig** *prev.* Uxin Qi. Nei Mongol Zizhiqu, N China 38°29′N 108°48′E
182 I4 **Dąbrowa Białostocka** Podlaskie, NE Poland 53°38′N 23°18′E
183 H8 **Dąbrowa Tarnowska** Małopolskie, S Poland 50°10′N 21°E
191 H12 **Dabryn'** *Rus.* Dobryn'. Homyel'skaya Voblasts', SE Belarus 51°46′N 29°12′E
239 I6 **Dabsan Hu** ◎ C China
243 J8 **Dabu** *var.* Huliao. Guangdong, S China 24°19′N 116°07′E
188 C10 **Dăbuleni** Dolj, SW Romania 43°48′N 24°05′E
Dacca *see* Dhaka
179 F12 **Dachau** Bayern, SE Germany 48°15′N 11°26′E
245 L2 **Dachengzi** Liaoning, China 41°05′N 119°26′E
Dachuan *see* Dazhou
Dacia Bank *see* Dacia Seamount
290 H5 **Dacia Seamount** *var.* Dacia Bank. *undersea feature* E Atlantic Ocean 31°10′N 13°42′W
79 M3 **Dacono** Colorado, C USA 40°04′N 104°56′W
159 I6 **Dacre** United Kingdom 54°37′N 2°50′W
Đắc Tô *see* Đăk Tô
Dacura *see* Dákura
69 L6 **Dade City** Florida, SE USA 28°21′N 82°12′W
232 G5 **Ḍaḍeldhurā** *var.* Dandeldhura. Far Western, W Nepal 29°12′N 80°31′E
69 I1 **Dadeville** Alabama, S USA 32°49′N 85°45′W
245 L6 **Dadian** Shandong, E China 36°10′N 119°07′E
Dadong *see* Donggang
165 H8 **Dadou** ≈ S France
234 C4 **Dādra and Nagar Haveli** ◈ *union territory* W India
230 G8 **Dādu** Sind, SE Pakistan 26°42′N 67°48′E
240 C4 **Dadu He** ≈ C China
248 B5 **Daecheong-do** *prev.* Taechŏng-do. *island* NW South Korea
250 A2 **Daecheong Lake** *prev.* Taech'ŏng Lake. ◎
248 C6 **Daegu** *off.* Taegu-gwangyŏksi, *Jap.* Taikyū; *prev.* Taegu. SE South Korea 35°55′N 128°33′E
250 B3 **Daegu-si** *prev.* Taegu City. ◈
248 C6 **Daejeon** *off.* Taejŏn-gwangyŏksi, *Jap.* Taiden; *prev.* Taejŏn. C South Korea 36°20′N 127°28′E
Daerah Istimewa Aceh *see* Aceh
Daerah Khusus Ibukota Jakarta *see* Jakarta Raya
263 L5 **Daet** Luzon, N Philippines 14°06′N 122°57′E
242 B5 **Dafang** Guizhou, S China 27°07′N 105°40′E
243 H6 **Dafen** Jiangxi, SE China 26°16′N 114°12′E
245 M8 **Dafeng** Jiangsu, China 33°07′N 120°17′E
Dafeng *see* Shanglin
233 L5 **Dafla Hills** ▲▲ NE India
57 N6 **Dafoe** Saskatchewan, S Canada 51°46′N 104°11′W
132 B3 **Dagana** N Senegal 16°28′N 15°35′W
Dagana *see* Massakory, Chad
Dagana *see* Dahana, Tajikistan
243 L4 **Dagangtou** Zhejiang, E China 28°18′N 119°45′E
187 M4 **Dağardı** Kütahya, Turkey 39°26′N 29°00′E
Dagcagoin *see* Zoigê
190 F7 **Dagda** Krāslava, SE Latvia 56°06′N 27°36′E
Dagden *see* Hiiumaa
Dagden-Sund *see* Soela Väin
161 K6 **Dagenham** United Kingdom 51°33′N 0°10′E
197 I9 **Dagestan, Respublika** *prev.* Dagestanskaya ASSR, *Eng.* Daghestan. ◈ *autonomous republic* SW Russian Federation
Dagestanskaya ASSR *see* Dagestan, Respublika
197 J10 **Dagestanskiye Ogni** Respublika Dagestan, SW Russian Federation 42°09′N 48°08′E
Dagezhen *see* Fengning
81 F10 **Daggett** California, USA 34°52′N 116°53′W
278 A12 **Dagg Sound** *sound* South Island, New Zealand
Daghestan *see* Dagestan, Respublika
221 L4 **Daghmar** NE Oman 23°09′N 59°01′E
Dağliq Quarabağ *see* Nagorno-Karabakh
Dagö *see* Hiiumaa
102 B6 **Dagua** Valle del Cauca, W Colombia 03°39′N 76°40′W
242 A5 **Daguan** *var.* Cuihua. Yunnan, SW China 27°42′N 103°51′E
263 K4 **Dagupan** *off.* Dagupan City. Luzon, N Philippines 16°05′N 120°21′E
Dagupan City *see* Dagupan
238 G9 **Dagzê** *var.* Dêqên. Xizang Zizhiqu, W China 29°38′N 91°15′E
229 J7 **Dahana** *Rus.* Dagana, Dakhana. SW Tajikistan 38°03′N 69°51′E
248 C1 **Dahei Shan** ▲▲ N China
237 I2 **Da Hinggan Ling** *Eng.* Great Khingan Range. ▲▲ NE China
Dahlac Archipelago *see* Dahlak Archipelago
136 F1 **Dahlak Archipelago** *var.* Dahlac Archipelago. *island group* E Eritrea
181 B11 **Dahlem** Nordrhein-Westfalen, Germany 50°23′E 6°33′N
66 G7 **Dahlonega** Georgia, SE USA 34°31′N 83°59′W
175 B14 **Dahmani** Tunisia
178 H7 **Dahme** Brandenburg, E Germany 52°10′N 13°47′E
180 J1 **Dahme** Schleswig-Holstein, Germany 54°13′E 11°05′N
178 I7 **Dahme** ≈ E Germany
171 K10 **Dahmouni** Algeria
136 H1 **Dahm, Ramlat** *desert* NW Yemen
181 D14 **Dahn** Rheinland-Pfalz, Germany 49°09′E 7°47′N
232 D8 **Dāhod** *prev.* Dohad. Gujarāt, W India 22°48′N 74°18′E
Dahomey *see* Benin
238 D6 **Dahongliutan** Xinjiang Uygur Zizhiqu, NW China 35°59′N 79°12′E
242 G2 **Dahong Shan** ▲▲ Hubei, China
Dahra *see* Dara
171 k9 **Dahra, Massif** ▲▲ Algeria
180 J5 **Dähre** Sachsen-Anhalt, Germany 52°48′E 10°54′N
218 F4 **Dahr el Ahmar** Lebanon 33°31′N 35°50′E
243 H4 **Dahu** Jiangxi, E China 28°25′N 113°56′E
243 N3 **Dahu** Zhejiang, E China 29°14′N 121°42′E
242 D8 **Dahua** Guangxi, China 23°26′N 107°35′E
Dahuaishu *see* Hongtong
217 I1 **Dahūk** *var.* Dohuk, *Kurd.* Dihōk. Dahūk, N Iraq 36°52′N 43°01′E
245 N1 **Dahuofang Shuiku** ⊠ Liaoning, China
245 M1 **Dahushan** Liaoning, NE China 41°37′N 122°09′E
188 E10 **Daia** Giurgiu, S Romania 44°00′N 25°59′E
245 J4 **Daicheng** Hebei, E China 38°42′N 116°38′E
253 D12 **Daigo** Ibaraki, Honshū, S Japan 36°43′N 140°22′E
245 H2 **Dai Hai** ◎ N China
Daihoku *see* T'aipei
281 J2 **Dai Island** *island* N Solomon Islands
256 D6 **Daik-u** Bago, SW Myanmar (Burma) 17°46′N 96°40′E
218 G6 **Dā'il** Dar'ā, S Syria 32°45′N 36°08′E
218 G6 **Dāīl** Syria 32°45′N 36°08′E
257 J8 **Đai Lanh** Khanh Hoa, S Vietnam 12°49′N 109°20′E
158 G5 **Dailly** United Kingdom 55°16′N 4°43′W
243 K7 **Daimao Shan** ▲▲ SE China
170 G6 **Daimiel** Castilla-La Mancha, C Spain 39°04′N 03°37′W
186 G8 **Daimoniá** Pelopónnisos, S Greece 36°38′N 22°54′E
Dainan *see* T'ainan
158 C10 **Daingean** Offaly, Ireland 53°18′N 7°17′W
71 I4 **Daingerfield** Texas, SW USA 33°03′N 94°42′W
Daingin, Bá an *see* Dingle Bay
239 J8 **Dainkognubma** Xizang Zizhiqu, W China 32°26′N 97°58′E
251 J5 **Daiō-zaki** *headland* Honshū, SW Japan 34°15′N 136°50′E
Dairbhre *see* Valencia Island
116 F5 **Daireaux** Buenos Aires, E Argentina 36°34′S 61°40′W
Dairen *see* Dalian
Dairût *see* Dayrūţ
250 F4 **Dai-sen** ▲ Kyūshū, SW Japan 35°22′N 133°33′E
71 I7 **Daisetta** Texas, SW USA 30°06′N 94°38′W
243 N2 **Daishan** Zhejiang, E China 30°17′N 122°07′E
286 C4 **Daitō-jima** *island group* SW Japan
286 C4 **Daitō Ridge** *undersea feature* N Philippine Sea 25°30′N 133°00′E
243 L7 **Daitou** Fujian, SE China 25°16′N 119°14′E
245 H4 **Daixian** *var.* Dai Xian, Shangguan. Shanxi, C China 39°10′N 112°57′E
Dai Xian *see* Daixian
Daiyue *see* Shanyin
243 K7 **Daiyun Shan** ▲▲ SE China
91 H5 **Dajabón** NW Dominican Republic 19°35′N 71°41′W
239 K8 **Dajin Chuan** ≈ C China
243 M4 **Dajing** Zhejiang, E China 28°25′N 121°09′E
243 I8 **Dajishan** Fujian, SE China 24°35′N 114°23′E
230 D4 **Dak** ◎ W Afghanistan
132 A4 **Dakar** ● (Senegal) W Senegal 14°44′N 17°27′W
132 A4 **Dakar** ✈ W Senegal 14°42′N 17°27′W
Đak Glây *see* Đak Glei
256 I7 **Đak Glei** *prev.* Đak Glây. Kon Tum, C Vietnam 15°05′N 107°42′E
Dakhana *see* Dahana
Dakhla *see* Ad Dakhla
132 B1 **Dakhlet Nouâdhibou** ◈ *region* NW Mauritania
Đak Lap *see* Kiên Đưc
Đak Nông *see* Gia Nghia
133 K4 **Dakoro** Maradi, S Niger 14°29′N 06°45′E
74 G6 **Dakota City** Iowa, C USA 42°42′N 94°13′W
74 F7 **Dakota City** Nebraska, C USA 42°25′N 96°25′W
Đakovica *see* Gjakovë
184 E3 **Đakovo** *var.* Djakovo, *Hung.* Diakovár. Osijek-Baranja, E Croatia 45°18′N 18°24′E
Dakshin *see* Deccan
256 I7 **Đăk Tô** *var.* Đăc Tô. Kon Tum, C Vietnam 14°35′N 107°55′E
89 H4 **Dákura** *var.* Dacura. Región Autónoma Atlántico Norte, NE Nicaragua 14°22′N 83°13′W
154 E7 **Dal** Akershus, S Norway 60°19′N 11°16′E
135 F12 **Dala** Lunda Sul, E Angola 11°04′S 20°15′E
132 C6 **Dalaba** W Guinea 10°47′N 12°12′W
Dalai *see* Da'an
239 J4 **Dalain Hob** *var.* Ejin Qi. Nei Mongol Zizhiqu, N China 41°59′N 101°04′E
Dalai Nor *see* Hulun Nur
239 N2 **Dalai Nur** *salt lake* N China
Dala-Jarna *see* Järna
154 H7 **Dalälven** ≈ C Sweden
214 B7 **Dalaman** Muğla, SW Turkey 36°47′N 28°47′E
214 B8 **Dalaman** ✈ Muğla, SW Turkey 36°37′N 28°51′E
214 C7 **Dalaman Çayı** ≈ SW Turkey
236 F4 **Dalandzadgad** Ömnögovĭ, S Mongolia 43°35′N 104°23′E
155 B9 **Dalane** *physical region* S Norway
283 N10 **Dalap-Uliga-Djarrit** *var.* Delap-Uliga-Darrit, D-U-D. *island group* Ratak Chain, SE Marshall Islands
154 G7 **Dalarna** *prev.* Kopparberg. ◈ *county* C Sweden
154 G6 **Dalarna** *prev. Eng.* Dalecarlia. *cultural region* C Sweden
155 J8 **Dalarö** Stockholm, C Sweden 59°07′N 18°25′E
257 I9 **Đa Lat** Lâm Đông, S Vietnam 11°56′N 108°25′E
Dalay *see* Bayandalay
230 E7 **Dālbandīn** *var.* Dāl Bandin. Baluchistān, SW Pakistan 28°48′N 64°08′E
155 F9 **Dalbosjön** *lake bay* S Sweden
277 L2 **Dalby** Queensland, E Australia 27°11′S 151°12′E
154 B6 **Dale** Hordaland, S Norway 60°35′N 05°48′E
154 A5 **Dale** Sogn Og Fjordane, S Norway 61°22′N 05°24′E
76 E6 **Dale** Oregon, NW USA 44°58′N 118°56′W
70 G7 **Dale** Texas, SW USA 29°56′N 97°34′W
Dalecarlia *see* Dalarna
64 C10 **Dale City** Virginia, NE USA 38°38′N 77°18′W
66 F5 **Dale Hollow Lake** ⊠ Kentucky/Tennessee, S USA
162 I5 **Dalen** Drenthe, NE Netherlands 52°42′N 06°45′E
155 C8 **Dalen** Telemark, S Norway 59°25′N 07°58′E
256 B4 **Daletme** Chin State, W Myanmar (Burma) 21°44′N 92°48′E
69 I3 **Daleville** Alabama, S USA 31°18′N 85°42′W
162 H5 **Dalfsen** Overijssel, E Netherlands 52°31′N 06°16′E
70 D1 **Dalhart** Texas, SW USA 36°05′N 102°31′W
181 G8 **Dalhausen** Nordrhein-Westfalen, Germany 51°37′E 9°17′N
59 I7 **Dalhousie** New Brunswick, SE Canada 48°03′N 66°22′W
232 E3 **Dalhousie** Himāchal Pradesh, N India 32°32′N 76°01′E
52 C6 **Dalhousie, Cape** *headland* Northwest Territories, NW Canada
244 F7 **Dali** Shaanxi, China 34°28′N 109°34′E
240 B6 **Dali** *var.* Xiaguan. Yunnan, SW China 25°34′N 100°11′E
Dali *see* Idálion
245 M3 **Dalian** *var.* Dairen, Dalien, Jay Dairen, Lüda, Talien, *Rus.* Dalny. Liaoning, NE China 38°53′N 121°37′E
243 H9 **Daliang** Guangdong, SE China 22°50′N 113°15′E
245 M4 **Dalian Wan** *bay* Liaoning, China
170 G9 **Dalías** Andalucía, S Spain 36°49′N 02°50′W
Dalien *see* Dalian
244 F5 **Dali He** ≈ Shaanxi, China
Dalijan *see* Delījān
218 E6 **Daliyat el Karmel** Israel 32°41′N 35°02′E
218 E6 **Daliyya** Israel 32°35′N 35°04′E
184 E2 **Dalj** *Hung.* Dalja. Osijek-Baranja, E Croatia 45°29′N 19°00′E
Dalja *see* Dalj
159 I3 **Dalkeith** United Kingdom 55°52′N 3°04′W
76 B6 **Dallas** Oregon, NW USA 44°56′N 123°20′W
64 E5 **Dallas** Pennsylvania, USA 41°20′N 75°58′W
71 H4 **Dallas** Texas, SW USA 32°47′N 96°48′W
71 H4 **Dallas-Fort Worth** ✈ Texas, SW USA 32°37′N 97°16′W
234 G4 **Dalli Rājhara** *var.* Dhalli Rajhara. Chhattīsgarh, C India 20°32′N 81°10′E
83 M8 **Dall Island** *island* Alexander Archipelago, Alaska, USA
82 G7 **Dall Lake** ◎ Alaska, USA
Dállogilli *see* Korpilombolo
133 I5 **Dallol Bosso** *seasonal river* W Niger
221 I4 **Dalmā** *island* W United Arab Emirates
184 C5 **Dalmacija** *Eng.* Dalmatia, *Ger.* Dalmatien, *It.* Dalmazia. *cultural region* S Croatia
158 F2 **Dalmally** United Kingdom 56°24′N 4°58′W
141 K4 **Dalmanutha** Mpumalanga, South Africa 30°54′S 26°29′E
Dalmatia/Dalmatien/Dalmazia *see* Dalmacija
195 M10 **Dalmatovo** Kurganskaya Oblast, Russian Federation
158 G5 **Dalmellington** United Kingdom 55°19′N 4°23′W
141 J2 **Dalmeny** Limpopo, South Africa 23°11′S 29°13′E
193 L9 **Dal'negorsk** Primorskiy Kray, SE Russian Federation 44°27′N 135°30′E
237 K3 **Dal'nerechensk** Primorskiy Kray, SE Russian Federation 45°57′N 133°42′E
Dalny *see* Dalian
132 E7 **Daloa** C Ivory Coast 06°56′N 06°28′W
242 C4 **Dalou Shan** ▲▲ S China
158 G4 **Dalry** United Kingdom 55°41′N 4°43′W
158 G4 **Dalrymple** United Kingdom 55°23′N 4°35′W
275 K4 **Dalrymple Lake** ◎ Queensland, E Australia
62 D4 **Dalrymple Lake** ◎ Ontario, S Canada
275 K4 **Dalrymple, Mount** ▲ Queensland, E Australia 21°01′S 148°34′E
153 G10 **Dalsbruk** *Fin.* Taalintehdas. Länsi-Suomi, W Finland 60°02′N 22°31′E
155 F10 **Dalsjöfors** Västra Götaland, S Sweden 57°43′N 13°05′E
155 F8 **Dals Långed** *var.* Långed. Västra Götaland, S Sweden 58°54′N 12°20′E
159 I6 **Dalston** United Kingdom 54°50′N 2°59′W
233 H8 **Dāltenganj** *prev.* Daltonganj. Jhārkhand, N India 24°02′N 84°07′E
159 H5 **Dalton** United Kingdom 55°03′N 3°23′W
66 F7 **Dalton** Georgia, SE USA 34°46′N 84°58′W
65 I2 **Dalton** Massachusetts, USA 42°28′N 73°10′W
Daltonganj *see* Dāltenganj
293 L8 **Dalton Iceberg Tongue** *ice feature* Antarctica
159 I8 **Dalton in Furness** United Kingdom 54°09′N 3°10′W
243 H5 **Daluli** Jiangxi, SE China 27°32′N 113°40′E
152 C1 **Dalvík** Nordhurland Eystra, N Iceland 65°58′N 18°31′W
Dálvvadis *see* Jokkmokk
160 G8 **Dalwood** United Kingdom 50°48′N 3°04′W
55 K3 **Daly Bay** *coastal sea feature* Nunavut, C Canada
80 B3 **Daly City** California, W USA 37°44′N 122°27′W
274 G2 **Daly River** ≈ Northern Territory, N Australia
274 G3 **Daly Waters** Northern Territory, N Australia 16°21′S 133°22′E
191 D12 **Damachava** *var.* Damachova, *Pol.* Domaczewo, *Rus.* Domachëvo. Brestskaya Voblasts', SW Belarus 51°45′N 23°36′E
Damachova *see* Damachava
133 L4 **Damagaram Takaya** Zinder, S Niger 14°02′N 09°28′E
234 C4 **Damān** Damān and Diu, W India 20°25′N 72°58′E
232 B9 **Damān and Diu** ◈ *union territory* W India
129 I3 **Damanhūr** *anc.* Hermopolis Parva. N Egypt 31°03′N 30°28′E
245 I2 **Damaqun Shan** ▲▲ E China
134 E5 **Damara** Ombella-Mpoko, S Central African Republic 05°00′N 18°45′E
138 C5 **Damaraland** *physical region* C Namibia
260 G7 **Damar, Kepulauan** *var.* Baraf Daja Islands, Kepulauan Barat Daya. *island group* C Indonesia
258 D3 **Damar Laut** Perak, Peninsular Malaysia 04°13′N 100°36′E
260 G4 **Damar, Pulau** *island* Maluku, E Indonesia
Damas *see* Dimashq
133 M5 **Damasak** Borno, NE Nigeria 13°10′N 12°40′E
Damasco *see* Dimashq
64 C9 **Damascus** Maryland, USA 39°17′N 77°12′W
67 H5 **Damascus** Virginia, NE USA 36°37′N 81°46′W
Damascus *see* Dimashq
133 M5 **Damaturu** Yobe, NE Nigeria 11°44′N 11°58′E
260 F2 **Damau** Pulau Kaburuang, N Indonesia 03°46′N 126°49′E
222 F3 **Damāvand, Qolleh-ye** ▲ N Iran 35°56′N 52°08′E
168 E4 **Damazan** Aquitaine, France 44°17′N 0°16′E
135 C10 **Damba** Uíge, NW Angola 06°44′S 15°20′E
188 D9 **Dâmboviţa** *prev.* Dîmboviţa. ◈ *county* SE Romania
188 D9 **Dâmboviţa** *prev.* Dîmboviţa. ≈ S Romania
137 G10 **D'Ambre, Île** *island* NE Mauritius
235 G10 **Dambulla** Central Province, C Sri Lanka 07°51′N 80°40′E
167 L6 **Dameleviéres** Lorraine, France 48°33′N 6°23′E
90 G6 **Dame-Marie** SW Haiti 18°36′N 74°26′W
90 F6 **Dame Marie, Cap** *headland* SW Haiti 18°37′N 74°24′W
222 G3 **Dāmghān** Semnān, N Iran 36°13′N 54°22′E
85 M9 **Damían Carmona** San Luis Potosí, Mexico 22°05′N 99°18′W
Damietta *see* Dumyāt
245 I6 **Daming** Hebei, China 36°10′N 115°05′E
242 D8 **Daming Shan** ▲▲ Guangxi, China
218 F7 **Dāmiyā** Jordan 32°06′N 35°33′E
218 F7 **Dāmiyā** Al Balqā', NW Jordan 32°07′N 35°33′E
228 D6 **Damla** Daşoguz Welaýaty, N Turkmenistan 40°05′N 59°15′E
Dammām *see* Ad Dammān
180 E5 **Damme** Niedersachsen, NW Germany 52°31′N 08°12′E
233 J8 **Dāmodar** ≈ NE India
232 F8 **Damoh** Madhya Pradesh, C India 23°50′N 79°30′N
132 G7 **Damongo** NW Ghana 09°05′N 01°49′W
218 E3 **Damoûr** *var.* Ad Dāmūr. W Lebanon 33°36′N 35°30′E

◆ Country
● Country Capital
◇ Dependent Territory
○ Dependent Territory Capital
◈ Administrative Regions
✈ International Airport
▲ Mountain
▲▲ Mountain Range
Volcano
≈ River
◎ Lake
⊠ Reservoir

◆ Country   ◇ Dependent Territory   ◈ Administrative Regions   ▲ Mountain   🌋 Volcano   ◎ Lake
● Country Capital   ○ Dependent Territory Capital   ✕ International Airport   ▲ Mountain Range   ♦ River   ◉ Reservoir

197 H7 **Divnoye** Stavropol'skiy Kray, SW Russian Federation 45°54′N 43°18′E
132 F8 **Divo** S Ivory Coast 05°50′N 05°22′W
191 I8 **Divo** Smolenskaya Oblast', Russian Federation
Divodurum Mediomatricum see Metz
215 H6 **Divriği** Sivas, C Turkey 39°23′N 38°06′E
Diwaniyah see Ad Dīwānīyah
80 H2 **Dixie Valley** Nevada, USA 39°41′N 118°05′W
62 E1 **Dix Milles, Lac** ◎ Québec, SE Canada
Dixmude/Dixmuide see Diksmuide
80 C2 **Dixon** California, W USA 38°19′N 121°49′W
73 C9 **Dixon** Illinois, N USA 41°51′N 89°26′W
66 D4 **Dixon** Kentucky, S USA 37°30′N 87°39′W
75 I10 **Dixon** Missouri, C USA 37°59′N 92°05′W
79 L6 **Dixon** New Mexico, SW USA 36°10′N 105°49′W
54 A6 **Dixon Entrance** strait Canada/USA
64 A6 **Dixonville** Pennsylvania, NE USA 40°43′N 79°01′W
215 K6 **Diyadin** Ağrı, E Turkey 39°33′N 43°41′E
Diyālá, Nahr see Sīrvān, Rūdkhāneh-ye
217 K4 **Diyālá, Sirwan Nahr** var. Rudkhaneh-ye Sīrvān, Sīrwān. ≈ Iran/Iraq see also Sīrvān, Rudkhaneh-ye
215 I7 **Diyarbakır** var. Diarbekr; anc. Amida. Diyarbakır, SE Turkey 37°55′N 40°14′E
215 I7 **Diyarbakır** var. Diarbekr. ◈ province SE Turkey
Dizful see Dezfūl
134 C6 **Dja** ≈ SE Cameroon
Djadié see Zadié
133 L1 **Djado** Agadez, NE Niger 21°00′N 12°11′E
133 M1 **Djado, Plateau du** ▲▲ NE Niger
Djailolo see Halmahera, Pulau
Djajapura see Jayapura
Djakarta see Jakarta
Djakarta Raya see Jakarta Raya
Djakovo see Đakovo
135 C8 **Djambala** Plateaux, C Congo 02°32′S 14°43′E
Djambi see Jambi
Djambi see Hari, Batang
131 K6 **Djanet** prev. Fort Charlet. SE Algeria 24°34′N 09°33′E
131 K5 **Djanet** E Algeria 28°43′N 08°57′E
Djaul see Dyaul Island
Djawa see Jawa
Djéblé see Jablah
134 E2 **Djédaa** Batha, C Chad 13°31′N 18°34′E
131 I2 **Djelfa** var. El Djelfa. N Algeria 34°43′N 03°14′E
134 H5 **Djéma** Haut-Mbomou, E Central African Republic 06°04′N 25°20′E
Djember see Jember
Djeneponto see Jeneponto
132 F4 **Djenné** var. Jenné. Mopti, C Mali 13°55′N 04°31′W
Djérablous see Jarābulus
Djerba see Jerba, Île de
134 C5 **Djérem** ≈ C Cameroon
Djevdjelija see Gevgelija
132 G4 **Djibo** N Burkina 14°09′N 01°38′W
136 G3 **Djibouti** var. Jibuti. ● (Djibouti) E Djibouti 11°33′N 42°55′E
136 G3 **Djibouti** off. Republic of Djibouti, var. Jibuti; prev. French Somaliland, French Territory of the Afars and Issas, Fr. Côte Française des Somalis, Territoire Français des Afars et des Issas. ◆ republic E Africa
136 G3 **Djibouti** ✈ C Djibouti 11°29′N 42°54′E
Djibouti, Republic of see Djibouti
Djidjel/Djidjelli see Jijel
Djidji see Dilo
171 J10 **Djillali Ben Amar** Algeria
103 L6 **Djoemoe** Sipaliwini, C Suriname 04°00′N 55°27′W
Djokjakarta see Yogyakarta
135 F9 **Djoku-Punda** Kasai-Occidental, S Dem. Rep. Congo 05°27′S 20°58′E
134 G7 **Djolu** Equateur, N Dem. Rep. Congo 0°35′N 22°30′E
Djombang see Jombang
Ďjorče Petrov see Đorče Petrov
134 C7 **Djoua** ≈ Congo/Gabon
133 I6 **Djougou** W Benin 09°42′N 01°38′E
134 B6 **Djoum** Sud, S Cameroon 02°38′N 12°51′E
134 E1 **Djourab, Erg du** desert N Chad
134 J6 **Djugu** Orientale, NE Dem. Rep. Congo 01°55′N 30°31′E
Djumbir see Ďumbier
152 D2 **Djúpivogur** Austurland, SE Iceland 64°40′N 14°18′W
154 G6 **Djura** Dalarna, C Sweden 60°37′N 15°00′E
Djurdjevac see Đurđevac
D'Kar see Dekar
294 F3 **Dmitriya Lapteva, Proliv** strait N Russian Federation
196 E4 **Dmitriyev-L'govskiy** Kurskaya Oblast', W Russian Federation 52°08′N 35°09′E
Dmitriyevsk see Makiyivka
196 F1 **Dmitrov** Moskovskaya Oblast', W Russian Federation 56°23′N 37°30′E
Dmitrovichi see Dzmitravichy
196 E4 **Dmitrovsk-Orlovskiy** Orlovskaya Oblast', W Russian Federation 52°28′N 35°01′E
189 I2 **Dmytrivka** Chernihivs'ka Oblast', N Ukraine 50°56′N 32°57′E
Dnepr see Dnieper
Dneprodzerzhinsk see Romaniv
Dneprodzerzhinskoye Vodokhranilishche see Dniprodzerzhyns'ke Vodoskhovyshche
Dnepropetrovsk see Dnipropetrovs'k
Dnepropetrovskaya Oblast' see Dnipropetrovs'ka Oblast'
Dneprorudnoye see Dniprorudne
Dneprovskiy Liman see Dniprovs'kyy Lyman
Dneprovsko-Bugskiy Kanal see Dnyaprowska-Buhski Kanal
Dnestr see Dniester
Dnestrovskiy Liman see Dnistrovs'kyy Lyman
148 E6 **Dnieper** Bel. Dnyapro, Rus. Dnepr, Ukr. Dnipro. ≈ E Europe
189 H3 **Dnieper Lowland** Bel. Prydnyaprowskaya Nizina, Ukr. Prydniprovs'ka Nyzovyna. lowlands Belarus/Ukraine
188 D5 **Dniester** Rom. Nistru, Rus. Dnestr, Ukr. Dnister; anc. Tyras. ≈ Moldova/Ukraine
Dnipro see Dnieper
Dniprodzerzhyns'k see Romaniv
189 J5 **Dniprodzerzhyns'ke Vodoskhovyshche** Rus. Dneprodzerzhinskoye Vodokhranilishche. ⊠ C Ukraine
189 K5 **Dnipropetrovs'k** Rus. Dnepropetrovsk; prev. Yekaterinoslav. Dnipropetrovs'ka Oblast', E Ukraine 48°28′N 35°E
189 K5 **Dnipropetrovs'k** ✈ Dnipropetrovs'ka Oblast', S Ukraine 48°20′N 35°04′E
Dnipropetrovs'k see Dnipropetrovs'ka Oblast'
189 K5 **Dnipropetrovs'ka Oblast'** var. Dnipropetrovs'k, Rus. Dnepropetrovskaya Oblast'. ◈ province E Ukraine
189 K6 **Dniprorudne** Rus. Dneprorudnoye. Zaporiz'ka Oblast', SE Ukraine 47°21′N 35°00′E
189 H8 **Dniprovs'kyy Lyman** Rus. Dneprovskiy Liman. bay S Ukraine
Dnister see Dniester
189 H8 **Dnistrovs'kyy Lyman** Rus. Dnestrovskiy Liman. inlet S Ukraine
194 D9 **Dno** Pskovskaya Oblast', W Russian Federation 57°48′N 29°58′E
Dnyapro see Dnieper
191 E12 **Dnyaprowska-Buhski Kanal** Rus. Dneprovsko-Bugskiy Kanal. canal SW Belarus
63 M1 **Doaktown** New Brunswick, SE Canada 46°34′N 66°06′W
134 D4 **Doba** Logone-Oriental, S Chad 08°40′N 16°50′E
190 C6 **Dobele** Ger. Doblen. Dobele, W Latvia 56°36′N 23°14′E
179 H8 **Döbeln** Sachsen, E Germany 51°07′N 13°07′E
261 I4 **Doberai, Jazirah** Dut. Vogelkop. peninsula Papua, E Indonesia
182 D5 **Dobiegniew** Ger. Lubuskie, Woldenberg Neumark. Lubuskie, W Poland 52°58′N 15°43′E
Doblen see Dobele
137 F8 **Dobli** spring/well SW Somalia 0°24′N 41°18′E
261 J7 **Dobo** Pulau Wamar, E Indonesia 05°45′S 134°12′E
184 D3 **Doboj** Republiks Srpska, N Bosnia and Herzegovina 44°45′N 18°03′E
223 H8 **Doborjī** var. Fūrg. Fārs, S Iran 28°16′N 55°13′E
185 H2 **Dobra** Hunedoara, W Romania
110 A6 **Dobrado** São Paulo, Brazil 21°31′S 48°23′W
182 G4 **Dobre Miasto** Ger. Guttstadt. Warmińsko-mazurskie, NE Poland 53°59′N 20°25′E
185 M5 **Dobrich** Rom. Bazargic; prev. Tolbukhin. Dobrich, NE Bulgaria 43°35′N 27°49′E
185 M4 **Dobrich** ◈ province NE Bulgaria
196 G4 **Dobrinka** Lipetskaya Oblast', W Russian Federation 52°10′N 40°30′E
197 H5 **Dobrinka** Volgogradskaya Oblast', SW Russian Federation 50°52′N 41°48′E
Dobrla Vas see Eberndorf
182 F7 **Dobrodzień** Ger. Guttentag. Opolskie, S Poland 50°43′N 18°24′E
Dobrogea see Dobruja
189 L5 **Dobropillya** Rus. Dobropol'ye. Donets'ka Oblast', SE Ukraine 48°25′N 37°02′E
Dobropol'ye see Dobropillya
189 H5 **Dobrovelychkivka** Kirovohrads'ka Oblast', C Ukraine 48°22′N 31°12′E
190 G3 **Dobruchi** Pskovskaya Oblast', Russian Federation
Dobrudja/Dobrudzha see Dobruja
188 F10 **Dobruja** var. Dobrudja, Bul. Dobrudzha, Rom. Dobrogea. physical region Bulgaria/Romania
191 I11 **Dobrush** Homyel'skaya Voblasts', SE Belarus 52°25′N 31°19′E
195 K9 **Dobryanka** Permskaya Oblast', NW Russian Federation 58°28′N 56°27′E
189 H1 **Dobryanka** Chernihivs'ka Oblast', N Ukraine 52°03′N 31°09′E
Dobryn' see Dabryn'
67 I5 **Dobson** North Carolina, SE USA 36°25′N 80°45′W
111 N2 **Doce, Rio** ≈ Esperíto Santo, Brazil
111 K1 **Doce, Rio** ≈ SE Brazil
161 L2 **Docking** United Kingdom 52°54′N 0°37′E
154 I3 **Docksta** Västernorrland, C Sweden 63°06′N 18°22′E
85 L8 **Doctor Arroyo** Nuevo León, NE Mexico 23°40′N 100°09′W
85 M6 **Doctor Coss** Nuevo León, Mexico 25°55′N 99°11′W
85 L6 **Doctor González** Nuevo León, Mexico
86 E5 **Doctor Mora** Guanajuato, Mexico 21°09′N 100°19′W
112 E3 **Doctor Pedro P. Peña** Boquerón, W Paraguay 22°22′S 62°23′W
260 G3 **Dodaga** Pulau Halmahera, E Indonesia 01°06′N 128°10′E
235 E8 **Dodda Betta** ▲ S India 11°28′N 76°44′E
Dodecanese see Dodekánisa
187 K7 **Dodekánisa** var. Nóties Sporádes, Eng. Dodecanese; prev. Dhodhekánisos, Dodekanisos. island group SE Greece
Dodekanisos see Dodekánisa
181 F9 **Dodenau** Hessen, Germany 51°01′E 8°35′N
75 C10 **Dodge City** Kansas, C USA 37°45′N 100°01′W
72 C7 **Dodgeville** Wisconsin, N USA 42°57′N 90°08′W
160 D9 **Dodman Point** headland SW England, United Kingdom 50°13′N 04°47′W
136 E5 **Dodola** Oromīya, C Ethiopia 07°00′N 39°15′E
137 D10 **Dodoma** ● (Tanzania) Dodoma, C Tanzania 06°11′S 35°45′E
137 D10 **Dodoma** ◈ region C Tanzania
186 F4 **Dodóni** var. Dhodhóni. site of ancient city Ípeiros, W Greece
77 K3 **Dodson** Montana, NW USA 48°25′N 108°18′W
70 F2 **Dodson** Texas, SW USA 34°46′N 100°01′W
162 H7 **Doesburg** Gelderland, E Netherlands 52°01′N 06°08′E
162 H7 **Doetinchem** Gelderland, E Netherlands 51°58′N 06°17′E
238 G7 **Dogai Coring** var. Lake Montcalm. ◎ W China
214 G7 **Doğanşehir** Malatya, C Turkey 38°07′N 37°54′E
144 C6 **Dogger Bank** undersea feature C North Sea 55°00′N 03°00′E
69 J5 **Dog Island** island Florida, SE USA
72 G2 **Dog Lake** ◎ Ontario, S Canada
176 D8 **Dogliani** Piemonte, NE Italy 44°33′N 07°55′E
250 F2 **Dōgo** island Oki-shotō, SW Japan
222 F7 **Do Gonbadān** var. Dow Gonbadān, Gonbadān. Kohkīlūyeh va Būyer AḨmad, SW Iran 30°12′N 50°48′E
133 I5 **Dogondoutchi** Dosso, SW Niger 13°36′N 04°03′E
Dōgo-san see Dōgo-yama
250 F4 **Dōgo-yama** var. Dōgo-san. ▲ Kyūshū, SW Japan 35°03′N 133°12′E
Dogrular see Pravda
215 K6 **Doğubayazıt** Ağrı, E Turkey 39°33′N 44°07′E
215 I5 **Doğu Karadeniz Dağları** var. Anadolu Dağları. ▲▲ NE Turkey
238 F9 **Dogxung Zangbo** ≈ W China
250 B1 **Dogye** prev. Togye. 37°13′N 129°02′E
Doha see Ad Dawḩah
Dohad see Dāhod
Dohuk see Dahūk
238 G9 **Doilungdêqên** var. Namka. Xizang Zizhiqu, W China 29°41′N 90°58′E
186 G2 **Doïráni, Límni** var. Limni Doïranis, Bul. Ezero Doyransko. ◎ N Greece
Doire see Londonderry
163 E12 **Doische** Namur, S Belgium 50°09′N 04°43′E
109 H8 **Dois de Julho** ✈ (Salvador) Bahia, NE Brazil 12°04′S 38°58′W
113 I5 **Dois Vizinhos** Paraná, S Brazil 25°47′S 53°03′W
136 D2 **Doka** Gedaref, E Sudan 13°30′N 35°47′E
Doka see Kéita, Bahr
217 J2 **Dokan** var. Dūkān. As Sulaymānīyah, E Iraq 35°55′N 44°58′E
Dokdo see Liancourt Rocks
154 D6 **Dokka** Oppland, S Norway 60°49′N 10°04′E
162 H3 **Dokkum** Friesland, N Netherlands 53°20′N 06°E
162 G3 **Dokkumer Ee** ≈ N Netherlands
132 D5 **Doko** NE Guinea 11°46′N 08°58′W
Dokshitsy see Dokshytsy
191 G8 **Dokshytsy** Rus. Dokshitsy. Vitsyebskaya Voblasts', N Belarus 54°54′N 27°46′E
189 M6 **Dokuchayevs'k** var. Dokuchayevsk. Donets'ka Oblast', SE Ukraine 47°43′N 37°41′E
Dokuchayevsk see Dokuchayevs'k
Dolak, Pulau see Yos Sudarso, Pulau
74 E5 **Doland** South Dakota, N USA 44°51′N 98°06′W
81 J10 **Dolan Springs** Nevada, USA 35°36′N 114°15′W
117 E8 **Dolavón** Chaco, S Argentina 43°16′S 65°44′W
59 H7 **Dolbeau** Québec, SE Canada 48°52′N 72°15′W
164 F3 **Dol-de-Bretagne** Ille-et-Vilaine, NW France 48°33′N 01°45′W
290 F7 **Doldrums Fracture Zone** tectonic feature W Atlantic Ocean
165 J5 **Dôle** Jura, E France 47°05′N 05°30′E
160 F3 **Dolgellau** NW Wales, United Kingdom 52°45′N 03°54′W
Dolginovo see Dawhinava
Dolgi, Ostrov see Dolgiy, Ostrov
195 K2 **Dolgiy, Ostrov** var. Ostrov Dolgi. island NW Russian Federation
239 K2 **Dölgöön** Övörhangay, C Mongolia 45°57′N 103°14′E
175 B10 **Dolianova** Sardegna, Italy, C Mediterranean Sea 39°23′N 09°08′E
Dolina see Dolyna
193 M8 **Dolinsk** Ostrov Sakhalin, Sakhalinskaya Oblast', SE Russian Federation 47°20′N 142°52′E
Dolinskaya see Dolyns'ka
135 B9 **Dolisie** prev. Loubomo. Niari, S Congo 04°12′S 12°41′E
188 C10 **Dolj** ◈ county SW Romania
159 H2 **Dollar** United Kingdom 56°09′N 3°40′W
162 J3 **Dollard** bay NW Germany
180 H6 **Dollbergen** Niedersachsen, Germany 52°24′E 10°11′N
292 F3 **Dolleman Island** island Antarctica
185 J5 **Dolni Dŭbnik** Pleven, N Bulgaria 43°24′N 24°25′E
185 I5 **Dolni Lom** Vidin, NW Bulgaria 43°31′N 22°46′E
Dolnja Lendava see Lendava
185 K6 **Dolno Panicherevo** var. Panicherevo. Sliven, C Bulgaria 42°36′N 25°51′E
182 D7 **Dolnośląskie** ◈ province SW Poland
183 F9 **Dolný Kubín** Hung. Alsókubin. Žilinský Kraj, N Slovakia 49°12′N 19°17′E
177 H7 **Dolo** Veneto, NE Italy 45°25′N 12°06′E
Dolomites/Dolomiti see Dolomitiche, Alpi
177 H5 **Dolomitiche, Alpi** var. Dolomiti, Eng. Dolomites. ▲▲ NE Italy
Dolonnur see Duolun
Doloon see Tsogt-Ovoo
116 H5 **Dolores** Buenos Aires, E Argentina 36°21′S 57°39′W
88 D2 **Dolores** Petén, N Guatemala 16°33′N 89°26′W
263 M6 **Dolores** Samar, C Philippines 12°01′N 125°27′E
171 I7 **Dolores** País Valenciano, E Spain 38°09′N 00°45′W
114 E7 **Dolores** Soriano, SW Uruguay 33°34′S 58°15′W
86 E5 **Dolores Hidalgo** var. Ciudad de Dolores Hidalgo. Guanajuato, C Mexico 21°10′N 100°55′W
52 E7 **Dolphin and Union Strait** strait Northwest Territories/Nunavut, N Canada
117 I10 **Dolphin, Cape** headland East Falkland, Falkland Islands 51°15′S 58°57′W
90 D7 **Dolphin Head** hill W Jamaica
140 A4 **Dolphin Head** var. Cape Dernberg. headland SW Namibia 25°33′S 14°36′E
182 E6 **Dolsk** Ger. Dolzig. Weilkopolskie, C Poland 51°59′N 17°03′E
160 E8 **Dolton** United Kingdom 50°53′N 4°02′W
256 H5 **Đô Lương** Nghê An, N Vietnam 18°51′N 105°19′E
160 F2 **Dolwyddelan** United Kingdom 53°03′N 3°53′W
188 D4 **Dolyna** Rus. Dolina. Ivano-Frankivs'ka Oblast', W Ukraine 48°58′N 24°01′E
189 I6 **Dolyns'ka** Rus. Dolinskaya. Kirovohrads'ka Oblast', S Ukraine 48°06′N 32°46′E
Dolzig see Dolsk
Domachëvo/Domaczewo see Damachava
189 H6 **Domanivka** Mykolayivs'ka Oblast', S Ukraine 47°40′N 30°56′E
233 J6 **Domar** Rajshahi, N Bangladesh 26°08′N 88°57′E
176 F4 **Domat/Ems** Graubünden, SE Switzerland 46°50′N 09°28′E
183 A9 **Domažlice** Ger. Taus. Plzeňský Kraj, W Czech Republic 49°26′N 12°54′E
197 M4 **Dombarovskiy** Orenburgskaya Oblast', W Russian Federation 50°53′N 59°18′E
154 D5 **Dombås** Oppland, S Norway 62°04′N 09°07′E
167 L5 **Dombasle-sur-Meurthe** Lorraine, France 48°38′N 6°21′E
139 I4 **Dombe** Manica, C Mozambique 19°59′S 33°24′E
135 C12 **Dombe Grande** Benguela, C Angola 12°57′S 13°07′E
165 J6 **Dombes** physical region E France
261 K5 **Dombo** Papua, E Indonesia 01°52′S 137°09′E
183 F13 **Dombóvár** Tolna, S Hungary 46°24′N 18°09′E
163 C8 **Domburg** Zeeland, SW Netherlands 51°34′N 03°30′E
111 J2 **Dom Cavàti** Minas Gerais, Brazil 19°23′S 42°06′W
107 M3 **Dom Eliseu** Pará, NE Brazil 04°02′S 47°31′W
Domel Island see Letsôk-aw Kyun
169 L2 **Doméne** Rhône-Alpes, France 45°12′N 5°50′E
169 H1 **Dôme, Puy de** ▲ C France 45°46′N 03°00′E
81 I13 **Dome Rock Mountains** ▲▲ Arizona, SW USA
Domesnes, Cape see Kolkasrags
167 L5 **Domévre-en-Haye** Lorraine, France 48°49′N 5°55′E
112 B7 **Domeyko** Atacama, N Chile 28°58′S 70°54′W
112 B4 **Domeyko, Cordillera** ▲▲ N Chile
115 N2 **Dom Feliciano** Rio Grande do Sul, Brazil 30°42′S 52°07′W
164 F3 **Domfront** Orne, N France 48°35′N 00°39′W
261 K5 **Dom, Gunung** ▲ Papua, E Indonesia 02°41′S 137°00′E
111 M3 **Domingos Martins** Espírito Santo, Brazil 20°22′S 40°40′W
114 D5 **Domínguez** Entre Ríos, Argentina 31°59′S 58°58′W
91 L1 **Dominica** off. Commonwealth of Dominica. ◆ republic E West Indies
95 K2 **Dominica** island Dominica
Dominica Channel see Martinique Passage
Dominica, Commonwealth of see Dominica
89 H9 **Dominical** Puntarenas, SE Costa Rica 09°16′N 83°52′W
91 I5 **Dominican Republic** ◆ republic C West Indies
91 L1 **Dominica Passage** passage E Caribbean Sea
53 K9 **Dominion, Cape** headland Nunavut, N Canada
111 I1 **Dom Joaquim** Minas Gerais, Brazil 18°57′S 43°16′W
168 F3 **Domme** Aquitaine, France 44°48′N 1°13′E
163 G8 **Dommel** ≈ S Netherlands
136 H5 **Domo** Sumalē, E Ethiopia 07°53′N 46°55′E
196 F2 **Domodedovo** ✈ (Moskva) Moskovskaya Oblast', W Russian Federation 55°19′N 37°55′E
176 D5 **Domodossola** Piemonte, NE Italy 46°07′N 08°20′E
186 G5 **Domokós** var. Dhomokós. Stereá Elláda, C Greece 39°07′N 22°18′E
139 I9 **Domoni** Anjouan, SE Comoros 12°15′S 44°39′E
190 J2 **Domozhirovo** Leningradskaya Oblast', Russian Federation
167 L6 **Dompaire** Lorraine, France 48°13′N 6°13′E
115 J3 **Dom Pedrito** Rio Grande do Sul, S Brazil 31°00′S 54°40′W
167 I10 **Dompierre-sur-Besbre** Auvergne, France 46°31′N 3°41′E
Dompoe see Dompu
260 C8 **Dompu** prev. Dompoe. Sumbawa, C Indonesia 08°30′S 118°28′E
167 K6 **Domrémy-la-Pucelle** Lorraine, France 48°27′N 5°41′E
Domschale see Domžale
111 I3 **Dom Silvério** Minas Gerais, Brazil 20°09′S 42°58′W
118 D7 **Domuyo, Volcán** ⋀ W Argentina 36°36′S 70°22′W
110 F7 **Dom Viçoso** Minas Gerais, Brazil 22°13′S 45°09′W
177 K5 **Domžale** Ger. Domschale. C Slovenia 46°09′N 14°33′E
196 G4 **Don** var. Duna, Tanais. ≈ SW Russian Federation
159 L9 **Don** ≈ United Kingdom
156 G5 **Don** ≈ NE Scotland, United Kingdom
111 I5 **Dona Eusébia** Minas Gerais, Brazil 21°18′S 42°48′W
158 F6 **Donaghadee** E Northern Ireland, United Kingdom 54°39′N 05°31′W
277 I6 **Donald** Victoria, SE Australia 36°27′S 143°03′E
68 D4 **Donaldsonville** Louisiana, S USA 30°06′N 90°59′W
69 I3 **Donalsonville** Georgia, SE USA 31°02′N 84°52′W
172 G7 **Doña Mencía** Andalucía, Spain 37°33′N 4°21′W
158 E8 **Donard, Slieve** ▲ United Kingdom 54°11′N 5°55′W
Donau see Danube
179 C13 **Donaueschingen** Baden-Württemberg, SW Germany 47°57′N 08°30′E
179 F12 **Donaumoos** wetland S Germany
179 F12 **Donauwörth** Bayern, S Germany 48°43′N 10°46′E
177 K3 **Donawitz** Steiermark, SE Austria 47°23′N 15°00′E
189 M5 **Donbass** industrial region Russian Federation/Ukraine
170 E6 **Don Benito** Extremadura, W Spain 38°57′N 05°52′W
159 L9 **Doncaster** anc. Danum. N England, United Kingdom 53°32′N 01°07′W
90 F7 **Don Christophers Point** headland C Jamaica 18°19′N 76°48′W
114 C5 **Don Cristóbal** Entre Ríos, Argentina 32°04′S 60°00′W
103 L5 **Donderkamp** Sipaliwini, NW Suriname 05°18′N 56°22′W
135 C11 **Dondo** Cuanza Norte, NW Angola 09°40′S 14°24′E
260 D4 **Dondo** Sulawesi, N Indonesia 0°54′S 121°33′E
139 J4 **Dondo** Sofala, C Mozambique 19°41′S 34°45′E
260 C3 **Dondo, Teluk** bay Sulawesi, N Indonesia
235 G11 **Dondra Head** headland S Sri Lanka 05°57′N 80°33′E
Dondușani see Dondușeni
188 F5 **Dondușeni** var. Dondușani, Rus. Dondyushany. N Moldova 48°13′N 27°38′E
Dondyushany see Dondușeni
158 B6 **Donegal** Ir. Dún na nGall. Donegal, NW Ireland 54°39′N 08°06′W
158 B6 **Donegal** Ir. Dún na nGall. cultural region NW Ireland
158 A7 **Donegal Bay** Ir. Bá Dhún na nGall. bay NW Ireland
144 F6 **Donets** ≈ Russian Federation/Ukraine
189 M5 **Donets'k** Rus. Donetsk; prev. Stalino. Donets'ka Oblast', E Ukraine 47°58′N 37°50′E
189 M5 **Donets'k** ✈ Donets'ka Oblast', E Ukraine 48°03′N 37°44′E
Donets'k see Donets'ka Oblast'
189 M6 **Donets'ka Oblast'** var. Donets'k, Rus. Donetskaya Oblast'; prev. Rus. Stalins'kaya Oblast'. ◈ province SE Ukraine
Donetskaya Oblast' see Donets'ka Oblast'
121 I5 **Donga** ≈ Cameroon/Nigeria
242 F6 **Dong'an** Hunan, SE China 26°24′N 111°17′E
243 L2 **Dongba** Jiangsu, E China 31°18′N 119°03′E
243 J5 **Dongbei** Jiangxi, SE China 27°13′N 116°07′E
240 D6 **Dongchuan** Yunnan, SW China 26°09′N 103°10′E
Dongcun see Haiyang
245 J6 **Dong'e** var. Tongcheng. Shandong, E China 36°20′N 116°14′E
163 F8 **Dongen** Noord-Brabant, S Netherlands 51°38′N 04°56′E
240 F10 **Dongfang** var. Basuo. Hainan, S China 19°05′N 108°40′E
247 N4 **Dongfanghong** Heilongjiang, NE China 46°13′N 133°13′E
248 C2 **Dongfeng** Jilin, NE China 42°39′N 125°33′E
260 C4 **Donggala** Sulawesi, C Indonesia 0°40′S 119°44′E
248 B3 **Donggang** var. Dadong; prev. Donggou. Liaoning, NE China 39°52′N 124°08′E
245 L7 **Donggang** Shandong, E China 35°25′N 119°30′E
245 L8 **Donggou** Jiangsu, E China 33°36′N 119°39′E
Donggou see Donggang
243 H9 **Dongguan** Guangdong, S China 23°03′N 113°43′E
245 J5 **Dongguang** Hebei, E China 37°53′N 116°32′E
256 I6 **Đông Ha** Quang Tri, C Vietnam 16°45′N 107°10′E
248 D5 **Donghae** prev. Tonghae. NE South Korea 37°26′N 129°09′E
245 L7 **Donghai** Jiangsu, China 34°19′N 118°27′E
Dong Hai see East China Sea
244 C6 **Donghaiba** Ningxia, China 36°11′N 105°25′E
240 G9 **Donghai Dao** island S China
244 F2 **Donghe** Nei Mongol Zizhiqu, N China 40°40′N 110°02′E
246 D7 **Dong He** Mong. Narin Gol. ≈ N China
Donghe see Wangcang
243 N9 **Dongho** S Taiwan 22°58′N 121°18′E
256 H6 **Đông Hơi** Quang Binh, C Vietnam 17°32′N 106°35′E
243 H3 **Dong Hu** ≈ Hubei, China
Donghua see Huating
Donghuang see Xishui
Dongkan see Binhai
242 F6 **Dongkou** Hunan, S China 27°06′N 110°35′E
242 C8 **Donglan** Guangxi, China 24°19′N 107°13′E
256 H6 **Đông Lê** Quang Binh, C Vietnam 17°52′N 105°49′E
Dongliao see Liaoyuan
245 N1 **Dongling** Liaoning, NE China 41°49′N 123°35′E
243 J3 **Dongliu** Anhui, E China 30°13′N 116°55′E
243 J7 **Dongliu** Fujian, SE China 25°09′N 115°59′E
245 I7 **Dongming** Shandong, China 35°11′N 115°04′E
Dong-nai see Đông Nai, Sông
257 I9 **Đông Nai, Sông** var. Dong-nai, Dong Noi, Donnai. ≈ S Vietnam
243 H8 **Dongnan Qiuling** plateau SE China
248 E1 **Dongning** Heilongjiang, NE China 44°01′N 131°03′E
Dong Noi see Đông Nai, Sông
135 D13 **Dongo** Huíla, C Angola 14°35′S 15°51′E
129 I8 **Dongola** var. Donqola, Dunqulah. Northern, N Sudan 19°10′N 30°27′E
134 E6 **Dongou** Likouala, NE Congo 02°05′N 18°E
Đông Phu see Đông Xoai
245 J6 **Dongping** Shandong, E China 35°56′N 116°28′E
Dongping see Anhua
Dong Rak, Phanom see Dângrêk, Chuŏr Phnum
243 K9 **Dongshan** Fujan, China 23°25′N 117°14′E
243 K9 **Dongshan Dao** island SE China
Dongsha Qundao see Tungsha Tao
Dongsheng see Ordos
241 J3 **Dongtai** Jiangsu, E China 32°50′N 120°22′E
242 G4 **Dongting Hu** var. Tung-t'ing Hu. ◎ S China
242 B9 **Đông Văn** Nam Ha, Vietnam 23°16′N 105°22′E
244 B6 **Dongxiang** Gansu, C China 35°44′N 103°19′E
243 J4 **Dongxiang** var. Xiaogang. Jiangxi, S China 28°16′N 116°32′E
242 D10 **Dongxing** Guangxi, China 21°20′N 107°35′E
257 I9 **Đông Xoai** var. Đông Phu. Sông Be, S Vietnam 11°31′N 106°55′E
243 M3 **Dongyang** Zhejiang, China 29°10′N 120°08′E
245 K5 **Dongying** Shandong, E China 37°17′N 118°50′E
245 K5 **Dongying** Shandong, E China 37°27′N 118°01′E
243 L5 **Dongyou** Shandong, E China 27°10′N 118°38′E
244 B3 **Dongzhen** Gansu, China 38°34′N 103°25′E
243 J3 **Dongzhi** Anhui, China 30°04′N 117°00′E
161 K2 **Donington** United Kingdom 52°54′N 0°12′W
75 I11 **Doniphan** Missouri, C USA 36°39′N 90°51′W
Donja Łužica see Niederlausitz
54 A3 **Donjek** ≈ Yukon Territory, W Canada
184 C4 **Donji Lapac** Lika-Senj, W Croatia 44°33′N 15°58′E
184 E2 **Donji Miholjac** Osijek-Baranja, NE Croatia 45°45′N 18°10′E
185 H4 **Donji Milanovac** Serbia, E Serbia 44°27′N 22°06′E
184 D4 **Donji Vakuf** var. Srbobran. ◈ Federacija Bosna I Hercegovina, C Bosnia and Herzegovina
162 H4 **Donkerbroek** Friesland, N Netherlands 52°58′N 05°15′E
141 H7 **Donkerpoort** Free State, South Africa 25°47′S 28°30′E
85 L5 **Don Martín** Coahuila, Mexico 27°32′N 100°37′W
257 E8 **Don Muang** ✈ (Krung Thep) Nonthaburi, C Thailand 13°51′N 100°40′E
70 G10 **Donna** Texas, SW USA 26°10′N 98°03′W
63 I2 **Donnacona** Québec, SE Canada 46°41′N 71°46′W
Donnai see Đông Nai, Sông
75 I8 **Donnellson** Iowa, C USA 40°38′N 91°33′W
57 H3 **Donnelly** Alberta, W Canada 55°42′N 117°06′W
167 I6 **Donnemarie-en-Montois** Île-de-France, France 48°29′N 3°08′E
179 C10 **Donnersberg** ▲ W Germany 49°37′N 07°54′E
161 H5 **Donnington** United Kingdom 52°00′N 2°25′W
141 K7 **Donnybrook** KwaZulu-Natal, South Africa 29°56′S 29°52′E
Donoso see Miguel de la Borda
171 H1 **Donostia-San Sebastián** País Vasco, N Spain 43°19′N 01°59′W
187 J7 **Donoúsa** var. Donoússa. island Kykládes, Greece, Aegean Sea
Donoússa see Donoúsa
80 D4 **Don Pedro Reservoir** ⊠ California, W USA
Donqola see Dongola
196 G3 **Donskoy** Tul'skaya Oblast', W Russian Federation 54°02′N 38°27′E
263 L6 **Donsol** Luzon, N Philippines 12°56′N 123°34′E
168 F2 **Donzenac** Limousin, France 45°14′N 1°32′E
169 J4 **Donzére** Rhône-Alpes, France 44°27′N 4°43′E
167 I8 **Donzy** Bourgogne, France 47°22′N 3°08′E
136 F6 **Doolow** Sumalē, E Ethiopia 04°10′N 42°05′E
83 I3 **Doonerak, Mount** ▲ Alaska, USA 67°54′N 150°33′W
158 G5 **Doon, Loch** ◎ United Kingdom
162 F7 **Doorn** Utrecht, C Netherlands 52°02′N 05°21′E
141 J3 **Doornfontein** South Africa 25°38′S 28°18′E
Doornik see Tournai
72 E6 **Door Peninsula** peninsula Wisconsin, N USA
136 I4 **Dooxo Nugaaleed** var. Nogal Valley. valley E Somalia
Do Qu see Da Qu
176 D6 **Dora Baltea** anc. Duria Major. ≈ NW Italy
274 E4 **Dora, Lake** salt lake Western Australia
176 C7 **Dora Riparia** anc. Duria Minor. ≈ NW Italy
Dorbiljin see Emin
Dorbod/Dorbod Mongolzu Zizhixian see Taikang
Dorbod Mongolzu Zizhixian see Taikang
184 G7 **Đorče Petrov** var. Ďjorče Petrov, Gorče Petrov. N Macedonia 42°01′N 21°21′E
62 C5 **Dorchester** Ontario, S Canada 43°00′N 81°04′W
161 H8 **Dorchester** anc. Durnovaria. S England, United Kingdom 50°43′N 02°26′W
55 L1 **Dorchester, Cape** headland Baffin Island, Nunavut, NE Canada 65°25′N 77°25′W
140 C1 **Dordabis** Khomas, C Namibia 22°57′S 17°39′E
167 H7 **Dordives** Centre, France 48°09′N 2°46′E
164 G7 **Dordogne** ◈ department SW France
165 H7 **Dordogne** ≈ W France
162 E7 **Dordrecht** var. Dordt, Dort. Zuid-Holland, SW Netherlands 51°48′N 04°40′E
Dordt see Dordrecht
57 L4 **Doré Lake** Saskatchewan, C Canada 54°37′N 107°36′W
165 I6 **Dore, Monts** ▲▲ C France
111 H5 **Dores de Campos** Minas Gerais, Brazil 21°06′S 44°02′W
111 I1 **Dores de Guanhães** Minas Gerais, Brazil 19°03′S 42°57′W
111 K4 **Dores do Rio Preto** Espírito Santo, Brazil 20°42′S 41°50′W
111 I5 **Dores do Turvo** Minas Gerais, Brazil 20°58′S 43°11′W
179 G12 **Dorfen** Bayern, SE Germany 48°16′N 12°06′E
175 C9 **Dorgali** Sardegna, Italy, C Mediterranean Sea 40°18′N 09°34′E
239 H7 **Dorgê Co** var. Elsen Nur. ◎ C China
239 H1 **Dörgön** var. Seer. Hovd, W Mongolia 48°18′N 92°37′E
133 H4 **Dori** N Burkina 14°03′N 00°02′W
138 D9 **Doring** ≈ S South Africa
140 D8 **Doringboes** Western Cape, South Africa 31°58′S 19°13′E
74 J1 **Dorion** Ontario, S Canada 48°47′N 88°32′W
161 K7 **Dorking** United Kingdom 51°13′N 0°20′W
181 E9 **Dorlar** Nordrhein-Westfalen, Germany 51°13′E 8°14′N
181 C9 **Dormagen** Nordrhein-Westfalen, W Germany 51°06′N 06°49′E
165 I3 **Dormans** Marne, N France 49°03′N 03°44′E
167 N8 **Dornach** Solothurn, NW Switzerland 47°29′N 07°37′E
Dorna Watra see Vatra Dornei
176 F3 **Dornbirn** Vorarlberg, W Austria 47°25′N 09°46′E
167 I9 **Dornes** Bourgogne, France 46°43′N 3°21′E
156 F4 **Dornoch** N Scotland, United Kingdom 57°52′N 04°01′W
156 F4 **Dornoch Firth** inlet N Scotland, United Kingdom
239 N1 **Dornod** ◈ province E Mongolia
239 L2 **Dornogovĭ** ◈ province SE Mongolia
133 H4 **Doro** Tombouctou, S Mali 16°07′N 00°57′W
188 E10 **Dorobanțu** Călărași, S Romania 44°15′N 26°55′E
183 F11 **Dorog** Komárom-Esztergom, N Hungary 47°43′N 18°42′E
196 E2 **Dorogobuzh** Smolenskaya Oblast', W Russian Federation 54°56′N 33°16′E
188 E6 **Dorohoi** Botoșani, NE Romania 47°57′N 26°24′E
154 H2 **Dorotea** Västerbotten, N Sweden 64°17′N 16°30′E
Dorpat see Tartu
181 D12 **Dörrebach** Rheinland-Pfalz, Germany 49°57′E 7°43′N
274 C6 **Dorre Island** island Western Australia
277 M3 **Dorrigo** New South Wales, SE Australia 30°22′S 152°43′E
80 E3 **Dorrington** California, USA 38°18′N 120°17′W
78 B1 **Dorris** California, W USA 41°58′N 121°54′W
62 D3 **Dorset** Ontario, SE Canada 45°12′N 78°52′W
166 B1 **Dorset** cultural region S England, United Kingdom
180 H7 **Dorste** Niedersachsen, Germany 51°42′E 10°09′N
180 C7 **Dorsten** Nordrhein-Westfalen, W Germany 51°38′N 06°58′E
160 G5 **Dorstone** United Kingdom 52°04′N 3°00′W
Dort see Dordrecht
167 L10 **Dortan** Rhône-Alpes, France 46°19′N 5°40′E
181 D8 **Dortmund** Nordrhein-Westfalen, W Germany 51°31′N 07°28′E
180 D6 **Dortmund-Ems-Kanal** canal W Germany
214 G8 **Dörtyol** Hatay, S Turkey 36°51′N 36°11′E
Do Rūd see Dow Rūd
180 F2 **Dorum** Niedersachsen, Germany 53°41′E 8°34′N
134 I5 **Doruma** Orientale, N Dem. Rep. Congo 04°35′N 27°43′E
63 H3 **Dorval** ✈ (Montréal) Québec, SE Canada 45°27′N 73°46′W
180 G4 **Dörverden** Niedersachsen, Germany 52°51′E 9°14′N
239 H1 **Dörvöljin** var. Buga. Dzavhan, W Mongolia 47°42′N 94°53′E
91 I8 **Dos Bocas, Lago** ◎ C Puerto Rico
170 E8 **Dos Hermanas** Andalucía, S Spain 37°16′N 05°55′W
Dospad Dagh see Rhodope Mountains
80 C5 **Dos Palos** California, W USA 37°00′N 120°39′W
185 J7 **Dospat** Smolyan, S Bulgaria 41°39′N 24°10′E
185 J7 **Dospat, Yazovir** ⊠ SW Bulgaria
178 G6 **Dosse** ≈ NE Germany
133 I5 **Dosso** Dosso, SW Niger 13°03′N 03°10′E
133 I5 **Dosso** ◈ department SW Niger
226 C5 **Dossor** Atyrau, SW Kazakhstan 47°31′N 53°01′E
229 I6 **Do'stlik** Jizzax Viloyati, C Uzbekistan 40°37′N 67°59′E
229 L5 **Dostuk** Narynskaya Oblast', C Kyrgyzstan 41°19′N 75°40′E
227 M6 **Dostyk** prev. Druzhba. Almaty, SE Kazakhstan 45°15′N 82°29′E
69 I3 **Dothan** Alabama, S USA 31°13′N 85°23′W
83 J5 **Dot Lake** Alaska, USA 63°39′N 144°10′W
180 E4 **Dötlingen** Niedersachsen, Germany 52°56′E 8°23′N
191 D8 **Dotnuva** Kaunas, C Lithuania 55°23′N 23°53′E
163 B10 **Dottignies** Hainaut, W Belgium 50°43′N 03°16′E
165 I1 **Douai** prev. Douay; anc. Duacum. Nord, N France 50°22′N 03°04′E
62 F1 **Douaire, Lac** ◎ Québec, SE Canada
134 A6 **Douala** var. Duala. Littoral, W Cameroon 04°04′N 09°43′E
134 A6 **Douala** ✈ Littoral, W Cameroon 03°57′N 09°48′E
164 D4 **Douarnenez** Finistère, NW France 48°05′N 04°20′W
164 D3 **Douarnenez, Baie de** bay NW France
Douay see Douai
70 E4 **Double Mountain Fork Brazos River** ≈ Texas, SW USA
66 D8 **Double Springs** Alabama, S USA 34°09′N 87°24′W
165 J5 **Doubs** ◈ department E France
174 A2 **Doubs** ≈ France/Switzerland
278 A12 **Doubtful Sound** sound South Island, New Zealand
278 F2 **Doubtless Bay** bay North Island, New Zealand
71 I6 **Doucette** Texas, SW USA 30°48′N 94°25′W
166 F4 **Doudeville** Haute-Normandie, France 49°43′N 0°48′E
245 I3 **Doudian** Beijing Shi, N China 39°41′N 116°02′E
164 G5 **Doué-la-Fontaine** Maine-et-Loire, NW France 47°12′N 00°16′W
132 G4 **Douentza** Mopti, S Mali 14°59′N 02°57′W
158 G8 **Douglas** ○ (Isle of Man) E Isle of Man 54°09′N 04°28′W
140 G6 **Douglas** Northern Cape, C South Africa 29°04′S 23°47′E
83 M7 **Douglas** Alexander Archipelago, Alaska, USA 58°12′N 134°18′W
79 J10 **Douglas** Arizona, SW USA 31°20′N 109°32′W
69 K3 **Douglas** Georgia, SE USA 31°30′N 82°51′W
77 M8 **Douglas** Wyoming, C USA 42°48′N 105°23′W
72 G5 **Douglas Lake** ◎ Michigan, N USA
66 G6 **Douglas Lake** ⊠ Tennessee, S USA
83 I7 **Douglas, Mount** ▲ Alaska, USA 58°51′N 153°31′W
292 E4 **Douglas Range** ▲▲ Alexander Island, Antarctica
64 E7 **Douglassville** Pennsylvania, NE USA 40°15′N 75°43′W
242 E7 **Doujiang** Guang Zhuangzu Zizhiqu, S China 25°46′N 109°41′E
186 E5 **Doukáto, Ákra** headland Lefkáda, W Greece 38°35′N 20°33′E
167 K6 **Doulaincourt** Champagne-Ardenne, France 48°19′N 5°12′E
165 H2 **Doullens** Somme, N France 50°09′N 02°21′E
218 F2 **Douma** Lebanon
218 F2 **Douma** Lebanon 34°12′N 35°50′E
Douma see Dūmā
134 C6 **Doumé** Est, E Cameroon 04°14′N 13°27′E
159 H2 **Doune** United Kingdom 56°12′N 4°05′W
163 C11 **Dour** Hainaut , S Belgium 50°24′N 03°47′E
109 B9 **Dourada, Serra** ▲▲ S Brazil
110 A7 **Dourado** São Paulo, Brazil 22°07′S 48°18′W
113 H3 **Dourados** Mato Grosso do Sul, S Brazil 22°09′S 54°52′W
165 H3 **Dourdan** Essonne, N France 48°33′N 01°58′E
168 G6 **Dourgne** Midi-Pyrénées, France 43°29′N 2°09′E
172 B1 **Douro** Sp. Duero. ≈ Portugal/Spain see also Duero
Douro see Duero
170 C4 **Douro Litoral** former province N Portugal
243 I7 **Doushui Shuiku** ⊠ Jiangxi, China
167 L10 **Douvaine** Rhône-Alpes, France 46°19′N 6°18′E
Douvres see Dover
171 I1 **Douze** ≈ SW France
277 J10 **Dover** Tasmania, SE Australia 43°19′S 147°01′E
161 M7 **Dover** Fr. Douvres, Lat. Dubris Portus. SE England, United Kingdom 51°08′N 03°E
64 F9 **Dover** state capital Delaware, NE USA 39°09′N 75°31′W
63 J5 **Dover** New Hampshire, NE USA 43°10′N 70°50′W
64 G6 **Dover** New Jersey, NE USA 40°51′N 74°33′W
73 J10 **Dover** Ohio, N USA 40°31′N 81°28′W
66 D5 **Dover** Tennessee, S USA 36°30′N 87°50′W
65 I4 **Dover Plains** New York, USA 41°44′N 73°35′W
276 B5 **Dover, Point** headland Western Australia, S Australia 32°32′S 125°32′E
165 H1 **Dover, Strait of** var. Straits of Dover, Fr. Pas de Calais. strait England, United Kingdom/France
Dover, Straits of see Dover, Strait of
218 E5 **Dovév** Israel 33°03′N 35°24′E
Dovlen see Devin
154 D5 **Dovre** Oppland, S Norway 61°59′N 09°16′E
154 C4 **Dovrefjell** plateau S Norway
Dovsk see Dowsk
137 C13 **Dowa** Central, C Malawi 13°40′S 33°55′E
73 F9 **Dowagiac** Michigan, N USA 41°58′N 86°06′W
Dow Gonbadān see Do Gonbadān
230 F2 **Dowlatābād** Fāryāb, N Afghanistan 36°30′N 64°51′E
77 I8 **Downey** Idaho, NW USA 42°25′N 112°06′W
161 L3 **Downham Market** E England, United Kingdom 52°35′N 00°23′E
80 E1 **Downieville** California, W USA 39°34′N 120°49′W
64 F7 **Downingtown** Pennsylvania, USA 40°0′N 75°42′W
158 E7 **Downpatrick** Ir. Dún Pádraig. SE Northern Ireland, United Kingdom 54°20′N 05°43′W
75 D9 **Downs** Kansas, C USA 39°30′N 98°33′W
64 G3 **Downsville** New York, NE USA 42°03′N 74°59′W
161 I7 **Downton** United Kingdom 51°00′N 1°44′W
158 B7 **Dowra** Cavan, Ireland 54°11′N 8°01′W
222 E5 **Dow Rūd** var. Do Rūd, Durud. Lorestān, W Iran 33°28′N 49°04′E
74 G6 **Dows** Iowa, C USA 42°39′N 93°30′W
191 I10 **Dowsk** Rus. Dovsk. Homyel'skaya Voblasts', SE Belarus 53°09′N 30°28′E
78 C3 **Doyle** California, W USA 40°00′N 120°06′W
64 F7 **Doylestown** Pennsylvania, NE USA 40°18′N 75°08′W
Doyransko, Ezero see Doïráni, Límni
185 J5 **Doyrentsi** Lovech, N Bulgaria 43°13′N 24°46′E
250 F3 **Dōzen** island Oki-shotō, SW Japan
62 E1 **Dozois, Réservoir** ⊠ Québec, SE Canada
130 E5 **Drâa** seasonal river S Morocco
171 M9 **Draa El Mizan** Algeria
Drâa, Hammada du see Dra, Hamada du
Drabble see José Enrique Rodó
189 I4 **Drabiv** Cherkas'ka Oblast', C Ukraine 49°57′N 32°10′E
Drable see José Enrique Rodó
176 B7 **Drac** ≈ E France
Drač/Draç see Durrës
113 J3 **Dracena** São Paulo, S Brazil 21°27′S 51°30′W
162 H4 **Drachten** Friesland, N Netherlands 53°07′N 06°06′E
152 E5 **Drag** Lapp. Ájluokta. Nordland, C Norway 68°02′N 16°E
188 F10 **Dragalina** Călărași, SE Romania 44°26′N 27°19′E
188 D10 **Drăgănești-Vlașca** Teleorman, S Romania 44°05′N 25°39′E
188 C9 **Drăgășani** Vâlcea, SW Romania 44°40′N 24°16′E
185 I6 **Dragoman** Sofiya, W Bulgaria 42°32′N 22°56′E
187 K10 **Dragonáda** island SE Greece
Dragonera, Isla see Sa Dragonera
91 K8 **Dragon's Mouths, The** strait Trinidad and Tobago/Venezuela
155 F12 **Dragør** København, E Denmark 55°36′N 12°42′E
185 H7 **Dragovishtitsa** Kysutendil, W Bulgaria 42°22′N 22°39′E
165 K8 **Draguignan** Var, SE France 43°31′N 06°31′E
130 F4 **Dra, Hamada du** var. Hammada du Drâa, Haut Plateau du Dra. plateau W Algeria
Dra, Haut Plateau du see Dra, Hamada du
191 E11 **Drahichyn** Pol. Drohiczyn Poleski, Rus. Drogichin. Brestskaya Voblasts', SW Belarus 52°11′N 25°10′E
74 C2 **Drake** North Dakota, N USA 47°54′N 100°23′W
141 K6 **Drakensberg** ▲▲ Lesotho/South Africa
141 J6 **Drakensberg** ▲▲ South Africa
292 D2 **Drake Passage** passage Atlantic Ocean/Pacific Ocean
185 L5 **Dralfa** Tŭrgovishte, N Bulgaria 43°17′N 26°25′E
187 I2 **Dráma** var. Dhráma. Anatolikí Makedonía kai Thráki, NE Greece 41°09′N 24°10′E
Dramburg see Drawsko Pomorskie
154 D7 **Drammen** Buskerud, S Norway 59°44′N 10°12′E
152 B1 **Drangajökull** ▲ NW Iceland 66°13′N 22°18′W
155 C8 **Drangedal** Telemark, S Norway 59°05′N 09°05′E
152 B2 **Drangsnes** Vestfirdhir, NW Iceland 65°42′N 21°27′W
180 F2 **Drangstedt** Niedersachsen, Germany 53°37′E 8°46′N
Drann see Dravinja
181 H8 **Dransfeld** Niedersachsen, Germany 51°30′E 9°46′N
158 D6 **Draperstown** United Kingdom 54°48′N 6°46′W
177 K5 **Drau** var. Drava, Eng. Drave, Hung. Dráva. ≈ C Europe see also Drava
Drau see Drava
144 E7 **Drava** var. Drau, Eng. Drave, Hung. Dráva. ≈ C Europe see also Drau
Dráva/Drave see Drau/Drava
177 L5 **Dravinja** Ger. Drann. ≈ NE Slovenia
177 K5 **Dravograd** Ger. Unterdrauburg; prev. Spodnji Dravograd. N Slovenia 46°36′N 15°00′E
182 D5 **Drawa** ≈ NW Poland
182 D5 **Drawno** Zachodnio-pomorskie, NW Poland 53°12′N 15°44′E
182 D4 **Drawsko Pomorskie** Ger. Dramburg. Zachodnio-pomorskie, NW Poland 53°32′N 15°48′E
74 E2 **Drayton** North Dakota, N USA 48°34′N 97°10′W
57 I5 **Drayton Valley** Alberta, SW Canada 53°15′N 115°00′W
175 A13 **Dréan** Tunisia
180 D6 **Dreierwalde** Nordrhein-Westfalen, Germany 52°20′E 7°31′N
181 F10 **Dreihausen** Hessen, Germany 50°43′E 8°52′N
280 A2 **Dreikikir** East Sepik, NW Papua New Guinea 03°42′S 142°46′E
Dreikirchen see Teiuș
181 C12 **Dreis** Rheinland-Pfalz, Germany 49°56′E 6°49′N
159 I3 **Drem** United Kingdom 56°00′N 2°47′W
141 H8 **Drennan** Eastern Cape, South Africa 32°26′S 25°44′E
180 D7 **Drensteinfurt** Nordrhein-Westfalen, Germany 51°48′E 7°45′N
162 I5 **Drenthe** ◈ province NE Netherlands
187 I4 **Drépano, Akrotírio** var. Akrotírio Dhrepanon. headland N Greece 39°56′N 23°57′E
Drepanum see Trapani
62 B6 **Dresden** Ontario, S Canada 42°34′N 82°09′W
179 I8 **Dresden** Sachsen, E Germany 51°03′N 13°43′E
66 C5 **Dresden** Tennessee, S USA 36°17′N 88°42′W
190 H7 **Dretun'** Vitsyebskaya Voblasts', N Belarus 55°41′N 29°13′E
165 H3 **Dreux** anc. Drocae, Durocasses. Eure-et-Loir, C France 48°44′N 01°23′E
154 E5 **Drevsjø** Hedmark, S Norway 61°52′N 12°01′E
66 A8 **Drew** Mississippi, S USA 33°48′N 90°31′W

◆ Country
● Country Capital
◇ Dependent Territory
○ Dependent Territory Capital
◈ Administrative Regions
✈ International Airport
▲ Mountain
▲▲ Mountain Range
⋀ Volcano
≈ River
◎ Lake
⊠ Reservoir

Drezdenko – Eagle River

182 D5 **Drezdenko** Ger. Driesen. Lubuskie, W Poland 52°51′N 15°50′E
162 F7 **Driebergen** var. Driebergen-Rijsenburg. Utrecht, C Netherlands 52°03′N 05°17′E
Driebergen-Rijsenburg see Driebergen
Driesen see Drezdenko
159 M8 **Driffield** E England, United Kingdom 54°00′N 00°28′W
72 I1 **Driftwood** Ontario, S Canada 49°07′N 81°23′W
159 H7 **Drigg** United Kingdom 54°22′N 3°26′W
77 I7 **Driggs** Idaho, NW USA 43°44′N 111°06′W
158 E1 **Drimnin** United Kingdom 56°36′N 6°00′W
Drin see Drinit, Lumi i
184 E5 **Drina** ≈ Bosnia and Herzegovina/Serbia
180 G7 **Dringenberg** Nordrhein-Westfalen, Germany 51°40′E 9°03′N
Drin, Gulf of see Drinit, Gjiri i
184 G6 **Drini i Bardh{194}** Serb. Beli Drim. ≈ Albania/Serbia
184 E7 **Drinit, Gjiri i** var. Pellg i Drinit, Eng. Gulf of Drin. gulf NW Albania
184 F7 **Drinit, Lumi i** var. Drin. ≈ NW Albania
Drinit, Pellg i see Drinit, Gjiri i
Drinit të Zi, Lumi i see Black Drin
184 F9 **Dríno** var. Drino, Drínos Pótamos, Alb. Lumi i Drinos. ≈ Albania/Greece
Drinos, Lumi i/Drínos Pótamos see Dríno
70 G6 **Dripping Springs** Texas, SW USA 30°11′N 98°04′W
70 G9 **Driscoll** Texas, SW USA 27°40′N 97°45′W
68 C2 **Driskill Mountain** ▲ Louisiana, S USA 32°25′N 92°54′W
Drissa see Drysa
184 C5 **Drniš** It. Šibenik-Knin. Šibenik-Knin, S Croatia 43°51′N 16°10′E
155 E8 **Drøbak** Akershus, S Norway 59°40′N 10°40′E
188 B9 **Drobeta-Turnu Severin** prev. Turnu Severin. Mehedinţi, SW Romania 44°39′N 22°40′E
Drocae see Dreux
188 F6 **Drochia** Rus. Drokiya. N Moldova 48°02′N 27°46′E
180 G2 **Drochtersen** Niedersachsen, Germany 53°42′E 9°23′N
140 F8 **Droerivier** Western Cape, South Africa 32°25′S 22°31′E
158 D9 **Drogheda** Ir. Droichead Átha. NE Ireland 53°43′N 06°21′W
Drogichin see Drahichyn
Drogobych see Drohobych
Drohiczyn Poleski see Drahichyn
188 C4 **Drohobych** Pol. Drohobycz, Rus. Drogobych. L'vivs'ka Oblast', NW Ukraine 49°22′N 23°33′E
Drohobycz see Drohobych
Droichead Átha see Drogheda
Droicheadna Bandan see Bandon
Droichead na Banna see Banbridge
157 C9 **Droichead Nua** E Ireland 52°12′N 06°40′W
Droim Mór see Dromore
161 H4 **Droitwich** United Kingdom 52°16′N 2°09′W
Drokiya see Drochia
158 B7 **Dromahair** Leitrim, Ireland 54°14′N 8°18′W
158 E7 **Dromara** United Kingdom 54°22′N 6°01′W
165 J7 **Drôme** ◈ department E France
165 J7 **Drôme** ≈ E France
158 B8 **Dromod** Leitrim, Ireland 53°52′N 7°55′W
158 E7 **Dromore** Ir. Droim Mór. SE Northern Ireland, United Kingdom 54°25′N 06°09′W
158 A7 **Dromore West** Sligo, Ireland 54°15′N 8°54′W
176 C8 **Dronero** Piemonte, NE Italy 44°28′N 07°25′E
159 K10 **Dronfield** United Kingdom 53°18′N 1°28′W
164 G7 **Dronne** ≈ SW France
293 J2 **Dronning Fabiolafjella** var. Mount Victor. ▲ Antarctica 72°49′S 33°01′E
293 I2 **Dronning Maud Land** physical region Antarctica
162 G3 **Dronrijp** Fris. Dronryp. Friesland, N Netherlands 53°12′N 05°37′E
Dronryp see Dronrijp
162 G5 **Dronten** Flevoland, C Netherlands 52°31′N 05°41′E
Drontheim see Trondheim
164 G7 **Dropt** ≈ SW France
231 I3 **Drosh** Khyber Pakhtunkhwa, NW Pakistan 35°33′N 71°48′E
Drossen see Ośno Lubuskie
166 F7 **Droué** Centre, France 48°02′N 1°05′E
Drug see Durg
Drujba see Pitnak
191 F8 **Drūkšiai** ◎ NE Lithuania
Druk-yul see Bhutan
158 A7 **Drumcliff** Sligo, Ireland 54°20′N 8°30′W
158 G4 **Drumclog** C Scotland, United Kingdom
158 C5 **Drumfree** Donegal, Ireland 55°12′N 7°24′W
57 J7 **Drumheller** Alberta, SW Canada 51°28′N 112°42′W
158 B8 **Drumkeeran** Leitrim, Ireland 54°10′N 8°09′W
158 B8 **Drumlish** Longford, Ireland 53°49′N 7°46′W
77 H4 **Drummond** Montana, NW USA 46°39′N 113°12′W
62 A2 **Drummond Island** island Michigan, N USA
Drummond Island see Tabiteuea
67 M5 **Drummond, Lake** ◎ Virginia, NE USA
63 I2 **Drummondville** Québec, SE Canada 45°52′N 72°28′W
158 F6 **Drummore** United Kingdom 54°40′N 4°54′W
83 J6 **Drum, Mount** ▲ Alaska, USA 62°11′N 144°37′W
158 C6 **Drumquin** United Kingdom 54°37′N 7°30′W
71 H1 **Drumright** Oklahoma, C USA 35°59′N 96°36′W
158 B8 **Drumshanbo** Leitrim, Ireland 54°03′N 8°02′W
163 F8 **Drunen** Noord-Brabant, S Netherlands 51°41′N 05°08′E
159 K5 **Druridge Bay** bay United Kingdom
Druskienniki see Druskininkai
191 D9 **Druskininkai** Pol. Druskienniki. Alytus, S Lithuania 54°00′N 24°00′E
162 G7 **Druten** Gelderland, SE Netherlands 51°53′N 05°37′E
190 F7 **Druya** Vitsyebskaya Voblasts', NW Belarus 55°47′N 27°27′E
189 J1 **Druzhba** Sums'ka Oblast', NE Ukraine 52°01′N 33°56′E
Druzhba see Dostyk, Kazakhstan
Druzhba see Pitnak, Uzbekistan
193 K4 **Druzhina** Respublika Sakha (Yakutiya), NE Russian Federation 68°01′N 144°58′E
189 L5 **Druzhkivka** Donets'ka Oblast', E Ukraine 48°38′N 37°31′E
184 C4 **Drvar** Federacija Bosna I Hercegovina, W Bosnia and Herzegovina 44°21′N 16°24′E
184 D5 **Drvenik** Split-Dalmacija, SE Croatia 43°10′N 17°13′E
185 K6 **Dryanovo** Gabrovo, N Bulgaria 42°58′N 25°28′E
75 A11 **Dry Cimarron River** ≈ Kansas/Oklahoma, C USA
58 B6 **Dryden** Ontario, C Canada 49°48′N 92°48′W
70 D7 **Dryden** Texas, SW USA 30°01′N 102°06′W
293 I8 **Drygalski Ice Tongue** ice feature Antarctica
141 H4 **Dry Harts** ≈ North-West, South Africa
190 G7 **Drysa** Rus. Drissa. ≈ N Belarus
69 K10 **Dry Tortugas** island Florida, SE USA
134 A5 **Dschang** Ouest, W Cameroon 05°28′N 10°02′E
102 E3 **Duaca** Lara, N Venezuela 10°22′N 69°08′W
Duacum see Douai
Duala see Douala
242 D8 **Du'an** Guangxi, China 23°34′N 108°03′E
91 H5 **Duarte, Pico** ▲ C Dominican Republic 19°02′N 70°57′W
111 J6 **Duas Barras** Rio de Janeiro, Brazil 22°02′S 42°32′W
220 C3 **Ḍubā** Tabūk, NW Saudi Arabia 27°26′N 35°42′E
Dubai see Dubayy
188 G6 **Dubăsari** Rus. Dubossary. NE Moldova 47°16′N 29°07′E
188 G6 **Dubăsari Reservoir** ⊞ NE Moldova
55 I4 **Dubawnt Lake** ◎ Northwest Territories/Nunavut, N Canada
72 C6 **Du Bay, Lake** ⊞ Wisconsin, N USA
221 J4 **Dubayy** Eng. Dubai. Dubayy, NE United Arab Emirates 25°11′N 55°18′E
221 J4 **Dubayy** Eng. Dubai. ✈ Dubayy, NE United Arab Emirates 25°15′N 55°22′E
277 K4 **Dubbo** New South Wales, SE Australia 32°16′S 148°41′E
176 E3 **Dübendorf** Zürich, NW Switzerland 47°23′N 08°37′E
84 G3 **Dublán** Chihuahua, Mexico 30°26′N 107°56′W
158 D10 **Dublin** Ir. Baile Átha Cliath; anc. Eblana. ● (Ireland) Dublin, E Ireland 53°20′N 06°15′W
69 K2 **Dublin** Georgia, SE USA 32°32′N 82°54′W
70 G5 **Dublin** Texas, SW USA 32°05′N 98°20′W
160 B1 **Dublin** Ir. Baile Átha Cliath; anc. Eblana. cultural region E Ireland
157 D9 **Dublin Airport** ✈ Dublin, E Ireland 53°25′N 06°18′W
158 E10 **Dublin Bay** bay Dublin, Ireland
282 F9 **Dublon** var. Tonoas. island Chuuk Islands, C Micronesia
196 F1 **Dubna** Moskovskaya Oblast', W Russian Federation 56°45′N 37°09′E
183 E10 **Dubňany** Ger. Dubnian. Jihomoravský Kraj, SE Czech Republic 48°54′N 17°00′E
Dubnian see Dubňany
183 F10 **Dubnica nad Váhom** Hung. Máriatölgyes; prev. Dubnicz. Trenčiansky Kraj, W Slovakia 48°58′N 18°10′E
Dubnicz see Dubnica nad Váhom
188 E3 **Dubno** Rivnens'ka Oblast', NW Ukraine 50°28′N 25°40′E
77 H7 **Dubois** Idaho, NW USA 44°10′N 112°13′W
64 A5 **Du Bois** Pennsylvania, NE USA 41°07′N 78°45′W
77 J7 **Dubois** Wyoming, C USA 43°31′N 109°37′W
Dubossary see Dubăsari
191 J9 **Dubovitsy** Smolenskaya Oblast', Russian Federation
197 I6 **Dubovka** Volgogradskaya Oblast', SW Russian Federation 49°10′N 48°49′E
132 C6 **Dubréka** SW Guinea 09°48′N 13°31′W
72 G2 **Dubreuilville** Ontario, S Canada 48°21′N 84°31′W
Dubris Portus see Dover
191 G12 **Dubrova** Homyel'skaya Voblasts', SE Belarus 51°47′N 28°13′E
Dubrovačko-Neretvanska Županija see Dubrovnik-Neretva
196 E3 **Dubrovka** Bryanskaya Oblast', W Russian Federation 53°44′N 33°27′E
190 H5 **Dubrovka** Pskovskaya Oblast', Russian Federation
184 D6 **Dubrovnik** It. Ragusa. Dubrovnik-Neretva, SE Croatia 42°40′N 18°06′E
184 E6 **Dubrovnik** ✈ Dubrovnik-Neretva, SE Croatia 42°34′N 18°17′E
184 D6 **Dubrovnik-Neretva** off. Dubrovačko-Neretvanska Županija. ◈ province SE Croatia
Dubrovno see Dubrowna
188 E2 **Dubrovytsya** Rivnens'ka Oblast', NW Ukraine 51°34′N 26°37′E
191 I9 **Dubrowna** Rus. Dubrovno. Vitsyebskaya Voblasts', N Belarus 54°35′N 30°41′E
74 I6 **Dubuque** Iowa, C USA 42°30′N 90°40′W
191 C8 **Dubysa** ≈ C Lithuania
Đưc Cơ see Chư Ty
285 J7 **Duc de Gloucester, Îles du** Eng. Duke of Gloucester Islands. island group C French Polynesia
166 C6 **Ducey** Basse-Normandie, France 48°37′N 1°18′W
243 J4 **Duchang** Jiangxi, China 29°10′N 116°07′E
183 B8 **Duchcov** Ger. Dux. Ústecký Kraj, NW Czech Republic 50°37′N 13°45′E
79 I3 **Duchesne** Utah, W USA 40°09′N 110°24′W
285 N8 **Ducie Island** atoll E Pitcairn Islands
55 I9 **Duck Bay** Manitoba, S Canada 52°11′N 100°08′W
69 M10 **Duck Key** island Florida Keys, Florida, SE USA
57 M5 **Duck Lake** Saskatchewan, S Canada 52°52′N 106°12′W
55 I9 **Duck Mountain** ▲▲ Manitoba, S Canada
66 D6 **Duck River** ≈ Tennessee, S USA
66 F7 **Ducktown** Tennessee, S USA 35°01′N 84°24′W
80 D7 **Ducor** California, USA 35°54′N 119°03′W
256 J7 **Đưc Phô** Quang Ngai, C Vietnam 14°56′N 108°55′E
Đưc Trong see Liên Nghia
D-U-D see Dalap-Uliga-Djarrit
159 J4 **Duddo** United Kingdom 55°40′N 2°06′W
159 I7 **Duddon** ≈ United Kingdom
163 H14 **Dudelange** var. Forge du Sud, Ger. Dudelingen. Luxembourg, S Luxembourg 49°28′N 06°05′E
181 B12 **Dudeldorf** Rheinland-Pfalz, Germany 49°59′E 6°38′N
Dudelingen see Dudelange
181 I8 **Duderstadt** Niedersachsen, C Germany 51°31′N 10°16′E
233 H8 **Dūdhi** Uttar Pradesh, N India 24°09′N 83°16′E
192 G4 **Dudinka** Krasnoyarskiy Kray, N Russian Federation 69°27′N 86°13′E
161 H4 **Dudley** C England, United Kingdom 52°30′N 02°05′W
234 E4 **Dudna** ≈ C India
132 E8 **Duékoué** W Ivory Coast 05°50′N 05°22′W
170 F3 **Dueñas** Castilla-León, N Spain 41°52′N 04°33′W
170 E2 **Duerna** ≈ NW Spain
170 D4 **Duero** Port. Douro. ≈ Portugal/Spain see also Douro
Duero see Douro
Duesseldorf see Düsseldorf
67 H8 **Due West** South Carolina, SE USA 34°19′N 82°23′W
293 I6 **Dufek Coast** physical region Antarctica
163 E9 **Duffel** Antwerpen, C Belgium 51°06′N 04°30′E
58 F2 **Dufferin, Cape** headland Québec, NE Canada
78 D1 **Duffer Peak** ▲ Nevada, W USA 41°40′N 118°45′W
281 I4 **Duff Islands** island group E Solomon Islands
Dufour, Pizzo/Dufour, Punta see Dufour Spitze
174 B4 **Dufour Spitze** It. Pizzo Dufour, Punta Dufour. ▲ Italy/Switzerland 45°54′N 07°50′E
184 B2 **Duga Resa** Karlovac, C Croatia 45°25′N 15°30′E
68 C2 **Dugdemona River** ≈ Louisiana, S USA
114 D9 **Duggan** Buenos Aires, Argentina 34°13′S 59°38′W
234 G4 **Duggīpar** Mahārāshtra, C India 21°06′N 80°10′E
184 B4 **Dugi Otok** var. Isola Grossa, It. Isola Lunga. island W Croatia
184 C5 **Dugopolje** Split-Dalmacija, S Croatia 43°35′N 16°35 E
242 F1 **Du He** ≈ C China
102 G6 **Duida, Cerro** ▲ S Venezuela 03°21′N 65°45′W
Duinekerke see Dunkerque
181 C8 **Duisburg** prev. Duisburg-Hamborn. Nordrhein-Westfalen, W Germany 51°25′N 06°47′E
Duisburg-Hamborn see Duisburg
163 D8 **Duiveland** island SW Netherlands
141 L2 **Duivelskloof** Limpopo, South Africa 23°42′S 30°08′E
162 H7 **Duiven** Gelderland, E Netherlands 51°57′N 06°02′E
217 L6 **Dujaylah, Hawr ad** ◎ S Iraq
245 I6 **Dujiangyan** var. Guankou; prev. Guanxian. Shandong, China 36°17′N 115°16′E
242 A2 **Dujiangyan** var. Guanxian, Guan Xian. Sichuan, C China 31°01′N 103°40′E
136 G7 **Dujuuma** Shabeellaha Hoose, S Somalia 01°04′N 42°37′E
Dūkān see Dokan
83 N8 **Duke Island** island Alexander Archipelago, Alaska, USA
Dukelský Priesmy/Dukelský Průsmyk see Dukla Pass
Duke of Gloucester Islands see Duc de Gloucester, Îles du
136 B5 **Duk Faiwil** Jonglei, C South Sudan 07°30′N 31°27′E
221 I4 **Dukhān** C Qatar 25°29′N 50°48′E
Dukhan Heights see Dukhān, Jabal
222 F10 **Dukhān, Jabal** var. Dukhan Heights. hill range S Qatar
197 J4 **Dukhovnitskoye** Saratovskaya Oblast', W Russian Federation 52°31′N 48°32′E
196 E2 **Dukhovshchina** Smolenskaya Oblast', W Russian Federation 55°15′N 32°22′E
Dukielska, Przełęcz see Dukla Pass
183 H9 **Dukla** Podkarpackie, SE Poland 49°33′N 21°40′E
Duklai Hág see Dukla Pass
183 H9 **Dukla Pass** Cz. Dukelský Průsmyk, Ger. Dukla-Pass, Hung. Duklai Hág, Pol. Przełęcz Dukielska, Slvk. Dukelský Priesmy. pass Poland/Slovakia
Dukla-Pass see Dukla Pass
Dukou see Panzhihua
191 F8 **Dūkštas** Utena, E Lithuania 55°32′N 26°21′E
Dulaan see Herlenbayan-Ulaan
277 L1 **Dulacca** Queensland, Australia
239 I6 **Dulan** var. Qagan Us. Qinghai, C China 36°11′N 97°51′E
79 L5 **Dulce** New Mexico, SW USA 36°55′N 107°00′W
89 H9 **Dulce, Golfo** gulf S Costa Rica
Dulce, Golfo see Izabal, Lago de
88 G4 **Dulce Nombre de Culmí** Olancho, C Honduras 15°09′N 85°37′W
116 F2 **Dulce, Río** ≈ C Argentina
193 J5 **Dulgalakh** ≈ NE Russian Federation
185 M5 **Dŭlgopol** Varna, E Bulgaria 43°05′N 27°24′E
242 D7 **Duliu Jiang** ≈ Guizhou, China
233 L7 **Dullabchara** Assam, NE India 24°25′N 92°22′E
64 C10 **Dulles** ✈ (Washington DC)Virginia, NE USA 39°00′N 77°27′W
141 K3 **Dullstroom** Mpumalanga, South Africa 25°25′S 30°07′E
180 D7 **Dülmen** Nordrhein-Westfalen, W Germany 51°51′N 07°17′E
190 G5 **Dulovka** Pskovskaya Oblast', Russian Federation
185 L4 **Dulovo** Silistra, NE Bulgaria 43°51′N 27°10′E
74 H3 **Duluth** Minnesota, N USA 46°47′N 92°06′W
160 F7 **Dulverton** United Kingdom 51°02′N 3°33′W
81 E13 **Dulzura** California, USA 32°39′N 116°47′W
218 H4 **Dūmā** Fr. Douma. Dimashq, SW Syria 33°33′N 36°24′E
263 K9 **Dumagasa Point** headland Mindanao, S Philippines 07°01′N 121°54′E
263 L8 **Dumaguete** var. Dumaguete City. Negros, C Philippines 09°16′N 123°17′E
Dumaguete City see Dumaguete
258 D4 **Dumai** Sumatera, W Indonesia 01°39′N 101°28′E
277 L2 **Dumaresq River** ≈ New South Wales/Queensland, SE Australia
75 I13 **Dumas** Arkansas, C USA 33°53′N 91°29′W
70 D1 **Dumas** Texas, SW USA 35°51′N 101°57′W
218 H4 **Ḍumayr** Dimashq, W Syria 33°36′N 36°28′E
158 G3 **Dumbarton** W Scotland, United Kingdom 55°57′N 04°35′W
156 E6 **Dumbarton** cultural region C Scotland, United Kingdom
280 C10 **Dumbéa** Province Sud, S New Caledonia 22°11′S 166°27′E
183 G10 **Ďumbier** Ger. Djumbir, Hung. Gyömbér. ▲ C Slovakia 48°54′N 19°36′E
188 D7 **Dumbrăveni** Ger. Elisabethstedt, Hung. Erzsébetváros; prev. Ebesfalva, Eppeschdorf, Ibaşfalău. Sibiu, C Romania 46°14′N 24°34′E
188 E8 **Dumbrăveni** Vrancea, E Romania 45°31′N 27°09′E
159 H5 **Dumfries** S Scotland, United Kingdom 55°04′N 03°37′W
156 F7 **Dumfries and Galloway** cultural region SW Scotland, United Kingdom
233 J7 **Dumka** Jhārkhand, NE India 24°17′N 87°15′E
218 G4 **Dummar** Syria 33°32′N 36°14′E
Dümmer see Dümmersee
180 E5 **Dümmersee** var. Dümmer. ◎ NW Germany
219 E8 **Dūmō** West Bank 31°59′N 35°12′E
62 E2 **Dumoine** ≈ Québec, SE Canada
62 E1 **Dumoine, Lac** ◎ Québec, SE Canada
110 B5 **Dumont** São Paulo, Brazil 21°09′S 47°58′W
293 K9 **Dumont d'Urville** French research station Antarctica 66°24′S 139°38′E
293 L9 **Dumont d'Urville Sea** sea S Pacific Ocean
62 F2 **Dumont, Lac** ◎ Québec, SE Canada
129 I2 **Dumyāt** var. Dumyât, Eng. Damietta. N Egypt 31°26′N 31°48′E
Duna see Danube, C Europe
Düna see Western Dvina
Duna see Don, Russian Federation
Dünaburg see Daugavpils
183 F12 **Dunaföldvár** Tolna, C Hungary 46°48′N 18°55′E
Dunaj see Wien, Austria
Dunaj see Danube, C Europe
183 H8 **Dunajec** ≈ S Poland
183 E11 **Dunajská Streda** Hung. Dunaszerdahely. Trnavský Kraj, W Slovakia 48°N 17°28′E
158 E8 **Dunany Point** headland Louth, Ireland 53°52′N 6°14′W
Dunapentele see Dunaújváros
Dunărea see Danube
188 F9 **Dunărea Veche, Braţul** ≈ SE Romania
188 G9 **Dunării, Delta** delta SE Romania
Dunaszerdahely see Dunajská Streda
183 F12 **Dunaújváros** prev. Dunapentele, Sztálinváros. Fejér, C Hungary 47°N 18°55′E
Dunav see Danube
185 K5 **Dunavska Ravnina** Eng. Danubian Plain. lowlands N Bulgaria
185 I4 **Dunavtsi** Vidin, NW Bulgaria 43°54′N 22°49′E
Dunayevtsy see Dunayivtsi
188 E5 **Dunayivtsi** Rus. Dunayevtsy. Khmel'nyts'ka Oblast', NW Ukraine 48°56′N 26°50′E
278 D11 **Dunback** Otago, South Island, New Zealand 45°22′S 170°37′E
159 J3 **Dunbar** SE Scotland, United Kingdom
159 H2 **Dunblane** United Kingdom 56°12′N 3°58′W
158 D10 **Dunboyne** Ireland 53°24′N 6°28′W
56 D9 **Duncan** Vancouver Island, British Columbia, SW Canada 48°46′N 123°10′W
79 J9 **Duncan** Arizona, SW USA 32°43′N 109°06′W
75 D13 **Duncan** Oklahoma, C USA 34°30′N 97°57′W
Duncan Island see Pinzón, Isla
160 A4 **Duncannon** Wexford, Ireland 52°13′N 6°55′W
257 A9 **Duncan Passage** strait Andaman Sea/Bay of Bengal
156 G3 **Duncansby Head** headland N Scotland, United Kingdom 58°37′N 03°01′W
62 D3 **Dunchurch** Ontario, S Canada 45°36′N 79°54′W
160 B4 **Duncormick** Wexford, Ireland 52°14′N 6°39′W
190 C5 **Dundaga** Talsi, NW Latvia 57°29′N 22°19′E
62 C4 **Dundalk** Ontario, S Canada 44°11′N 80°22′W
158 D8 **Dundalk** Ir. Dún Dealgan. Louth, NE Ireland 54°01′N 06°25′W
64 D9 **Dundalk** Maryland, NE USA 39°15′N 76°31′W
158 E8 **Dundalk Bay** Ir. Cuan Dhún Dealgan. bay NE Ireland
62 C5 **Dundas** Ontario, S Canada 43°16′N 79°55′W
274 E7 **Dundas, Lake** salt lake Western Australia
52 F5 **Dundas Peninsula** Peninsula Northwest Territories, NW Canada
Dundbürd see Batnorov
Dún Dealgan see Dundalk
62 G3 **Dundee** Québec, SE Canada 45°01′N 74°27′W
139 H7 **Dundee** KwaZulu/Natal, E South Africa 28°09′S 30°12′E
141 K5 **Dundee** KwaZulu-Natal, South Africa 28°10′S 30°14′E
159 I2 **Dundee** E Scotland, United Kingdom 56°28′N 03°W
73 H9 **Dundee** Michigan, N USA 41°57′N 83°39′W
70 F3 **Dundee** Texas, SW USA 33°43′N 98°52′W
292 E2 **Dundee Island** island Antarctica
239 K2 **Dundgovĭ** ◈ province C Mongolia
245 I1 **Dund Hot** Inner Mongolia, China 42°08′N 116°00′E
158 G4 **Dundonald** United Kingdom 55°34′N 4°35′W
159 H6 **Dundrennan** United Kingdom 54°49′N 3°57′W
158 E7 **Dundrum** United Kingdom 54°15′N 5°51′W
158 E8 **Dundrum Bay** Ir. Cuan Dhún Droma. inlet NW Irish Sea
261 L5 **Dundu** ≈ Papua, E Indonesia
57 M6 **Dundurn** Saskatchewan, S Canada 51°43′N 106°27′W
Dund-Us see Hovd
Dund-Us see Hovd
278 D12 **Dunedin** Otago, South Island, New Zealand 45°52′S 170°31′E
277 K4 **Dunedoo** New South Wales, SE Australia 32°04′S 149°23′E
158 B5 **Dunfanaghy** Ir. Dún Fionnachaidh. NW Ireland 55°11′N 07°59′W
159 H3 **Dunfermline** C Scotland, United Kingdom 56°04′N 03°29′W
Dún Fionnachaidh see Dunfanaghy
231 J6 **Dunga Bunga** Punjab, E Pakistan 29°51′N 73°19′E
158 D7 **Dungannon** Ir. Dún Geanainn. C Northern Ireland, United Kingdom 54°31′N 06°46′W
Dun Garbháin see Dungarvan
232 D7 **Dūngarpur** Rājasthān, N India 23°50′N 73°43′E
157 C11 **Dungarvan** Ir. Dun Garbháin. Waterford, S Ireland 52°05′N 07°37′W
179 H12 **Dungau** cultural region SE Germany
Dún Geanainn see Dungannon
161 M7 **Dungeness** headland SE England, United Kingdom 50°55′N 00°58′E
117 D13 **Dungeness, Punta** headland S Argentina 52°25′S 68°25′W
158 D6 **Dungiven** United Kingdom 54°56′N 6°55′W
Dungloe see Dunglow
158 B5 **Dunglow** var. Dungloe, Ir. An Clochán Liath. Donegal, NW Ireland 54°57′N 08°22′W
277 L4 **Dungog** New South Wales, SE Australia 32°24′S 151°45′E
134 I6 **Dungu** Orientale, NE Dem. Rep. Congo 03°40′N 28°32′E
258 E2 **Dungun** var. Kuala Dungun. Terengganu, Peninsular Malaysia 04°47′N 103°26′E
129 K7 **Dungûnab** Red Sea, NE Sudan 21°10′N 37°09′E
63 H3 **Dunham** Québec, SE Canada 45°08′N 72°48′W
Dunheved see Launceston
Dunholme see Durham
237 J4 **Dunhua** Jilin, NE China 43°22′N 128°12′E
239 H5 **Dunhuang** Gansu, N China 40°10′N 94°40′E
277 H7 **Dunkeld** Victoria, SE Australia 37°41′S 142°19′E
159 H1 **Dunkeld** United Kingdom 56°34′N 3°35′W
165 H1 **Dunkerque** Eng. Dunkirk, Flem. Duinekerke; prev. Dunquerque. Nord, N France 51°06′N 02°34′E
157 F12 **Dunkery Beacon** ▲ SW England, United Kingdom 51°10′N 03°36′W
62 D6 **Dunkirk** New York, NE USA 42°28′N 79°19′W
Dunkirk see Dunkerque
132 G8 **Dunkwa** SW Ghana 05°59′N 01°45′W
157 D9 **Dún Laoghaire** Eng. Dunleary; prev. Kingstown. E Ireland 53°17′N 06°08′W
80 E6 **Dunlap** California, USA 36°44′N 119°07′W
74 F7 **Dunlap** Iowa, C USA 41°51′N 95°36′W
66 E6 **Dunlap** Tennessee, S USA 35°22′N 85°23′W
Dunleary see Dún Laoghaire
158 D8 **Dunleer** Louth, Ireland 53°50′N 6°24′W
166 G10 **Dun-le-Palestel** Limousin, France 46°18′N 1°40′E
158 G4 **Dunlop** United Kingdom 55°42′N 4°32′W
Dún Mánmhaí see Dunmanway
157 B11 **Dunmanway** Ir. Dún Mánmhaí. Cork, SW Ireland 51°43′N 09°07′W
158 A9 **Dunmore** Galway, Ireland 53°37′N 8°44′W
64 F4 **Dunmore** Pennsylvania, NE USA 41°25′N 75°37′W
160 A4 **Dunmore East** Waterford, Ireland 52°09′N 6°59′W
80 F7 **Dunmovin** California, USA 36°05′N 117°58′W
158 E7 **Dunmurry** United Kingdom 54°33′N 6°01′W
67 K6 **Dunn** North Carolina, SE USA 35°18′N 78°36′W
158 C6 **Dunnamanagh** United Kingdom 54°52′N 7°18′W
Dún na nGall see Donegal
69 L5 **Dunnellon** Florida, SE USA 29°03′N 82°27′W
156 F3 **Dunnet Head** headland N Scotland, United Kingdom 58°40′N 03°27′W
80 C1 **Dunnigan** California, USA 38°53′N 121°58′W
159 H2 **Dunning** United Kingdom 56°18′N 3°35′W
74 C7 **Dunning** Nebraska, C USA 41°49′N 100°04′W
62 D6 **Dunnville** Ontario, S Canada 42°54′N 79°36′W
158 F3 **Dunoon** United Kingdom 55°57′N 4°57′W
Dún Pádraig see Downpatrick
Dunquerque see Dunkerque
Dunqulah see Dongola
159 J3 **Duns** SE Scotland, United Kingdom 55°46′N 02°13′W
161 K3 **Dunsby** United Kingdom 52°49′N 0°21′W
159 H5 **Dunscore** SW Scotland, United Kingdom 55°08′N 3°47′W
74 C1 **Dunseith** North Dakota, N USA 48°48′N 100°03′W
160 F8 **Dunsford** United Kingdom 50°41′N 3°41′W
158 D9 **Dunshaughlin** Meath, Ireland 53°31′N 6°32′W
78 B1 **Dunsmuir** California, W USA 41°12′N 122°19′W
161 J5 **Dunstable** Lat. Durocobrivae. E England, United Kingdom 51°53′N 00°32′W
278 C11 **Dunstan Mountains** ▲▲ South Island, New Zealand
53 I3 **Dunsterville, Cape** headland Nunavut, N Canada
165 H5 **Dun-sur-Auron** Cher, C France 46°52′N 02°40′E
167 K4 **Dun-sur-Meuse** Lorraine, France 49°23′N 5°11′E
278 D11 **Duntroon** Canterbury, South Island, New Zealand 44°52′S 170°40′E
158 G4 **Dunure** United Kingdom 55°24′N 4°45′W
231 I6 **Dunyāpur** Punjab, E Pakistan 29°48′N 71°48′E
247 K3 **Duobukur He** ≈ NE China
245 J1 **Duolun** var. Dolonnur. Nei Mongol Zizhiqu, N China 42°11′N 116°30′E
257 G10 **Dương Đông** Kiên Giang, S Vietnam 10°15′N 103°58′E
242 F7 **Dupang Ling** ▲▲ Guangxi, China
242 F7 **Dupang Ling** ▲▲ Hunan, China
141 H7 **Dupleston** Free State, South Africa 30°20′S 26°12′E
185 I7 **Dupnitsa** prev. Marek, Stanke Dimitrov. Kyustendil, W Bulgaria 42°16′N 23°07′E
181 B13 **Düppenweiler** Saarland, Germany 49°25′E 6°46′N
74 B4 **Dupree** South Dakota, N USA 45°03′N 101°36′W
77 H3 **Dupuyer** Montana, NW USA 48°13′N 112°34′W
221 K6 **Duqm** var. Daqm. E Oman 19°42′N 57°40′E
117 A12 **Duque de York, Isla** island S Chile
219 E9 **Dūrā** West Bank 31°30′N 35°02′E
274 F3 **Durack Range** ▲▲ Western Australia
214 F4 **Durağan** Sinop, N Turkey 41°26′N 35°03′E
165 K7 **Durance** ≈ SE France
73 G8 **Durand** Michigan, N USA 42°54′N 83°58′W
72 A6 **Durand** Wisconsin, N USA 44°37′N 91°56′W
280 D9 **Durand, Récif** reef SE New Caledonia
85 I8 **Durango** var. Victoria de Durango. Durango, W Mexico 24°03′N 104°38′W
171 H2 **Durango** País Vasco, N Spain 43°10′N 02°38′W
79 K5 **Durango** Colorado, C USA 37°13′N 107°51′W
85 I7 **Durango** ◈ state C Mexico
185 M5 **Durankulak** Rom. Răcari; prev. Blatnitsa, Duranulac. Dobrich, NE Bulgaria 43°41′N 28°31′E
66 B9 **Durant** Mississippi, S USA 33°04′N 89°51′W
75 F13 **Durant** Oklahoma, C USA 33°59′N 96°24′W
Duranulac see Durankulak
170 G4 **Duratón** ≈ N Spain
114 D5 **Durazno** Entre Ríos, Argentina 31°59′S 59°17′W
115 H7 **Durazno** var. San Pedro de Durazno. Durazno, C Uruguay 33°22′S 56°31′W
115 H6 **Durazno** ◈ department C Uruguay
Durazzo see Durrës
139 H8 **Durban** var. Port Natal. KwaZulu/Natal, E South Africa 29°51′S 31°E
141 K7 **Durban** KwaZulu-Natal, South Africa 29°51′S 31°01′E
139 H8 **Durban** ✈ KwaZulu/Natal, E South Africa 29°55′S 31°01′E
190 B6 **Durbe** Ger. Durben. Liepāja, W Latvia 56°34′N 21°22′E
Durben see Durbe
163 G11 **Durbuy** Luxembourg, SE Belgium 50°21′N 05°27′E
170 G8 **Dúrcal** Andalucía, S Spain 37°00′N 03°24′W
184 D2 **Đurđevac** Ger. Sankt Georgen, Hung. Szentgyörgy; prev. Djurdjevac, Gjurgjevac. Koprivnica-Kri»zevci, N Croatia 46°02′N 17°03′E
184 F6 **Đurđevica Tara** N Montenegro 43°09′N 19°18′E
157 G12 **Durdle Door** natural arch S England, United Kingdom
238 G2 **Düre** Xinjiang Uygur Zizhiqu, W China 46°30′N 88°26′E
181 B10 **Düren** anc. Marcodurum. Nordrhein-Westfalen, W Germany 50°48′N 06°30′E
234 G4 **Durg** prev. Drug. Chhattīsgarh, C India 21°12′N 81°20′E
233 K7 **Durgapur** Dhaka, N Bangladesh 25°10′N 90°41′E
233 J8 **Durgāpur** West Bengal, NE India 23°30′N 87°20′E
62 C4 **Durham** Ontario, S Canada 44°10′N 80°48′W
159 K6 **Durham** hist. Dunholme. N England, United Kingdom 54°47′N 01°34′W
67 K6 **Durham** North Carolina, SE USA 36°N 78°54′W
159 K6 **Durham** cultural region N England, United Kingdom
258 D4 **Duri** Sumatera, W Indonesia 01°13′N 101°13′E
Duria Major see Dora Baltea
Duria Minor see Dora Riparia
Durlas see Thurles
220 G4 **Ḍurmā** Ar Riyāḍ, C Saudi Arabia 24°37′N 46°06′E
181 E14 **Durmersheim** Baden-Württemberg, Germany 48°56′E 8°16′N
184 E5 **Durmitor** ▲ N Montenegro
156 E3 **Durness** N Scotland, United Kingdom 58°34′N 04°46′W
177 M2 **Dürnkrut** Niederösterreich, E Austria 48°28′N 16°50′E
Durnovaria see Dorchester
Durobrivae see Rochester
Durocasses see Dreux
Durocobrivae see Dunstable
Durocortorum see Reims
Durostorum see Silistra
Durovernum see Canterbury
184 F8 **Durrës** var. Durrësi, Dursi, It. Durazzo, SCr. Drač, Turk. Draç. Durrës, W Albania 41°20′N 19°26′E
184 F8 **Durrës** ◈ district W Albania
Durrësi see Durrës
161 I7 **Durrington** United Kingdom 51°11′N 1°46′W
160 A3 **Durrow** Laois, Ireland 52°51′N 7°24′W
157 A11 **Dursey Island** Ir. Oileán Baoi. island SW Ireland
Dursi see Durrës
161 H6 **Dursley** United Kingdom 51°41′N 2°21′W
187 M4 **Dursunbey** Balıkesir, Turkey 39°35′N 28°38′E
Duru see Wuchuan
Durud see Dow Rūd
187 M2 **Durusu Gölü** ◎ NW Turkey
278 F7 **D'Urville Island** island C New Zealand
261 K4 **D'Urville, Tanjung** headland Papua, E Indonesia 01°26′S 137°52′E
228 E8 **Duşak** Rus. Dushak. Ahal Welaýaty, S Turkmenistan 37°15′N 59°57′E
Dusa Mareb/Dusa Marreb see Dhuusa Marreeb
190 E7 **Dusetos** Utena, NE Lithuania 55°44′N 25°49′E
Dushak see Duşak
242 C7 **Dushan** Guizhou, S China 25°50′N 107°36′E
229 I7 **Dushanbe** var. Dyushambe; prev. Stalinabad, Taj. Stalinobod. ● (Tajikistan) W Tajikistan 38°35′N 68°44′E
229 I7 **Dushanbe** ✈ W Tajikistan 38°31′N 68°49′E
215 K4 **Dushet'i** E Georgia 42°07′N 44°44′E
64 D4 **Dushore** Pennsylvania, NE USA 41°30′N 76°23′W
278 A12 **Dusky Sound** sound South Island, New Zealand
181 C9 **Düsseldorf** var. Duesseldorf. Nordrhein-Westfalen, W Germany 51°14′N 06°49′E
229 I8 **Dŭstí** Rus. Dusti. SW Tajikistan 37°22′N 68°41′E
292 F5 **Dustin Island** island Antarctica
Dutch East Indies see Indonesia
Dutch Guiana see Suriname
82 F9 **Dutch Harbor** Unalaska Island, Alaska, USA 53°51′N 166°33′W
78 G3 **Dutch Mount** ▲ Utah, W USA 40°16′N 113°56′W
Dutch New Guinea see Papua
Dutch West Indies see Netherlands Antilles
140 G2 **Dutlwe** Kweneng, S Botswana 23°58′S 23°56′E
121 M10 **Du Toit Fracture Zone** tectonic feature SW Indian Ocean
195 K6 **Dutovo** Respublika Komi, NW Russian Federation 63°45′N 56°38′E
133 K6 **Dutsan Wai** var. Dutsen Wai. Kaduna, C Nigeria 10°49′N 08°15′E
133 L5 **Dutse** Jigawa, N Nigeria 11°43′N 09°25′E
Dutsen Wai see Dutsan Wai
Duttia see Datia
62 B6 **Dutton** Ontario, S Canada 42°40′N 81°28′W
79 H5 **Dutton, Mount** ▲ Utah, W USA 38°00′N 112°10′W
139 G9 **Dutywa** prev. Idutywa. Eastern Cape, SE South Africa 32°06′S 28°20′E see also Idutywa
238 G2 **Duut** Hovd, W Mongolia 47°28′N 91°52′E
62 F2 **Duval, Lac** ◎ Québec, SE Canada
197 M1 **Duvan** Respublika Bashkortostan, W Russian Federation 55°42′N 57°56′E
187 M4 **Düvertepe** Balıkesir, Turkey 39°14′N 28°26′E
216 E6 **Duwaykhilat Satīḩ ar Ruwayshid** seasonal river SE Jordan
Dux see Duchcov
65 M3 **Duxbury** Massachusetts, USA 42°03′N 70°40′W
243 K8 **Duxun** Fujian, SE China 23°57′N 117°36′E
242 C7 **Duyang Shan** ▲▲ S China
257 H10 **Duyên Hai** Tra Vinh, S Vietnam 09°39′N 106°28′E
242 C6 **Duyun** Guizhou, S China 26°16′N 107°29′E
187 N5 **Düzagaç** Afyonkarahisar, Turkey 38°48′N 30°10′E
214 D4 **Düzce** Düzce, NW Turkey 40°51′N 31°09′E
214 D4 **Düzce** ◈ province NW Turkey
Duzdab see Zāhedān
Duzenkyr, Khrebet see Duzkyr, Khrebet
228 F9 **Duzkyr, Khrebet** prev. Khrebet Duzenkyr. ▲▲ S Turkmenistan
Dvina Bay see Chëshskaya Guba
Dvinsk see Daugavpils
194 F5 **Dvinskaya Guba** bay NW Russian Federation
184 C3 **Dvor** Sisak-Moslavina, C Croatia 45°05′N 16°22′E
189 M3 **Dvorichna** Kharkivs'ka Oblast', E Ukraine 49°52′N 37°43′E
183 D8 **Dvůr Králové nad Labem** Ger. Königinhof an der Elbe. Královéhradecký Kraj, N Czech Republic 50°27′N 15°50′E
140 G7 **Dwaal** Northern Cape, South Africa 31°01′S 24°42′E
141 I3 **Dwaalboom** Limpopo, South Africa 24°43′S 26°49′E
232 A8 **Dwārka** Gujarāt, W India 22°14′N 68°58′E
140 E10 **Dwarskloof** pass Western Cape, South Africa
73 D9 **Dwight** Illinois, N USA 41°05′N 88°25′W
162 H4 **Dwingeloo** Drenthe, NE Netherlands 52°49′N 06°20′E
76 F4 **Dworshak Reservoir** ⊞ Idaho, NW USA
140 F9 **Dwyka** ≈ Western Cape, South Africa
Dyal see Dyaul Island
Dyanev see Galkynyş
Dyatlovo see Dzyatlava
280 D2 **Dyaul Island** var. Djaul, Dyal. island NE Papua New Guinea
80 G5 **Dyer** Nevada, USA 37°40′N 118°04′W
66 C6 **Dyer** Tennessee, S USA 36°04′N 88°59′W
52 E4 **Dyer Bay** coastal sea feature Northwest Territories, NW Canada
53 M7 **Dyer, Cape** headland Baffin Island, Nunavut, NE Canada 66°37′N 61°13′W
66 B6 **Dyersburg** Tennessee, S USA 36°02′N 89°21′W
73 B8 **Dyersville** Iowa, C USA 42°29′N 91°07′W
157 F11 **Dyfed** cultural region SW Wales, United Kingdom
160 E3 **Dyffryn** United Kingdom 52°47′N 4°06′W
160 F3 **Dyfi** ≈ United Kingdom
Dyhernfurth see Brzeg Dolny
183 C10 **Dyje** var. Thaya. ≈ Austria/Czech Republic see also Thaya
Dyje see Thaya
189 J4 **Dykan'ka** Poltavs'ka Oblast', C Ukraine 49°48′N 34°33′E
197 H9 **Dykhtau** ▲ SW Russian Federation 43°01′N 42°56′E
183 A8 **Dyleń** Ger. Tillenberg. ▲ NW Czech Republic 49°58′N 12°31′E
182 G4 **Dylewska Góra** ▲ N Poland 53°33′N 19°57′E
161 M7 **Dymchurch** United Kingdom 51°01′N 1°00′E
189 H3 **Dymer** Kyyivs'ka Oblast', N Ukraine 50°50′N 30°20′E
189 L5 **Dymytrov** Rus. Dimitrov. Donets'ka Oblast', SE Ukraine 48°18′N 37°19′E
183 I8 **Dynów** Podkarpackie, SE Poland 49°49′N 22°14′E
159 I3 **Dysart** United Kingdom 56°08′N 3°07′W
73 A8 **Dysart** Iowa, C USA 42°10′N 92°18′W
Dysna see Dzisna
187 I6 **Dýstos, Límni** var. Límni Dístos. ◎ Évvoia, C Greece
186 F5 **Dytikí Elláda** Eng. Greece West, var. Dytikí Ellás. ◈ region C Greece
Dytikí Ellás see Dytikí Elláda
186 F4 **Dytikí Makedonía** Eng. Macedonia West. ◈ region N Greece
Dyurment'yube see Diirmentobe
197 L2 **Dyurtyuli** Respublika Bashkortostan, W Russian Federation 55°31′N 54°49′E
Dyushambe see Dushanbe
239 K1 **Dzaamar** var. Bat-Öldziyt. Töv, C Mongolia 48°10′N 104°49′E
Dzaanhushuu see Ihtamir
Dza Chu see Mekong
Dzadgay see Bömbögör
239 I2 **Dzag** Bayanhongor, C Mongolia 46°54′N 99°11′E
Dzalaa see Shinejinst
239 M2 **Dzamïn-Üüd** var. Borhoyn Tal. Dornogovĭ, SE Mongolia 43°43′N 111°53′E
139 J10 **Dzaoudzi** E Mayotte 12°48′S 45°18′E
Dzaudzhikau see Vladikavkaz
239 I1 **Dzavhan** ◈ province NW Mongolia
239 H2 **Dzavhan Gol** ≈ NW Mongolia
239 H1 **Dzavhanmandal** var. Nuga. Dzavhan, W Mongolia 48°17′N 95°07′E
Dzegstey see Ögiynuur
239 H2 **Dzereg** var. Altanteel. Hovd, W Mongolia 47°05′N 92°57′E
197 H1 **Dzerzhinsk** Nizhegorodskaya Oblast', W Russian Federation 56°20′N 43°22′E
Dzerzhinsk see Dzyarzhynsk Belarus
Dzerzhinsk see Romaniv
Dzerzhinskiy see Nar'yan-Mar
Dzerzhinskoye see Tokzhaylau
Dzerzhyns'k see Romaniv
Džetygara see Zhitikara
Dzhailgan see Jayilgan
Dzhalagash see Zhalagash
229 K5 **Dzhalal-Abad** Kir. Jalal-Abad. Dzhalal-Abadskaya Oblast', W Kyrgyzstan 40°56′N 73°00′E
229 K5 **Dzhalal-Abadskaya Oblast'** Kir. Jalal-Abad Oblasty. ◈ province W Kyrgyzstan
Dzhalilabad see Cälilabad
193 J8 **Dzhalinda** Amurskaya Oblast', SE Russian Federation 53°29′N 123°53′E
226 C3 **Dzhambeyty** Zapadnyy Kazakhstan, W Kazakhstan 50°16′N 52°35′E
Dzhambeyty see Zhympity
Dzhambul see Taraz
Dzhambulskaya Oblast' see Zhambyl
215 J3 **Dzhangitau** ▲ SW Russian Federation 43°01′N 43°03′E
226 A3 **Dzhanibek** prev. Dzhanybek, Kaz. Zhänibek. Zapadnyy Kazakhstan, W Kazakhstan 49°27′N 46°51′E
Dzhankel'dy see Jongeldi
189 K8 **Dzhankoy** Avtonomna Respublika Krym, S Ukraine 45°40′N 34°20′E
Dzhansugurov see Zhansugirov
229 J5 **Dzhany-Bazar** var. Yangibazar. Dzhalal-Abadskaya Oblast', W Kyrgyzstan 41°40′N 70°49′E
Dzhanybek see Dzhanibek
193 J5 **Dzhardzhan** Respublika Sakha (Yakutiya), NE Russian Federation 68°47′N 123°51′E
Dzharkurgan see Jarqo'rg'on
189 J8 **Dzharylhats'ka Zatoka** gulf S Ukraine
Dzhayilgan see Jayilgan
Dzhebel see Jebel
229 K8 **Dzhelandy** SE Tajikistan 37°34′N 72°35′E
229 N4 **Dzhergalan** Kir. Jyrgalan. Issyk-Kul'skaya Oblast', NE Kyrgyzstan 42°37′N 78°56′E
Dzhezkazgan see Zhezkazgan
Dzhigirbent see Jigerbent
Dzhirgatal' see Jirgatol
Dzhizak see Jizzax
Dzhizakskaya Oblast' see Jizzax Viloyati
193 K7 **Dzhugdzhur, Khrebet** ▲▲ E Russian Federation
Dzhul'fa see Culfa
Dzhuma see Juma
Dzhungarskiy Alatau see Zhetysuskiy Alatau
Dzhusaly see Zhosaly
228 F6 **Dzhynlykum, Peski** desert E Turkmenistan
182 G5 **Działdowo** Warmińsko-Mazurskie, C Poland 53°13′N 20°12′E
183 G8 **Działoszyce** Świętokrzyskie, C Poland 50°21′N 20°19′E
87 L5 **Dzibalché** Campeche, Mexico 20°19′N 90°03′W
87 L6 **Dzibalchén** Campeche, Mexico 19°31′N 89°45′W
87 M4 **Dzidzantún** Yucatán, E Mexico
183 D8 **Dzierżoniów** Ger. Reichenbach. Dolnośląskie, SW Poland 50°43′N 16°40′E
87 M4 **Dzilam de Bravo** Yucatán, E Mexico 21°24′N 88°52′W
191 G8 **Dzisna** Rus. Disna. Vitsyebskaya Voblasts', N Belarus 55°33′N 28°13′E
191 G8 **Dzisna** Lith. Dysna, Rus. Disna. ≈ Belarus/Lithuania
87 M5 **Dzitás** Yucatán, Mexico 20°51′N 88°31′W
191 D12 **Dzivin** Rus. Divin. Brestskaya Voblasts', SW Belarus 51°58′N 24°33′E
191 H9 **Dzmitravichy** Rus. Dmitrovichi. Minskaya Voblasts', C Belarus 53°58′N 29°14′E
Dzogsool see Bayantsagaan
205 K4 **Dzungaria** var. Sungaria, Zungaria. physical region W China
Dzungarian Basin see Junggar Pendi
Dzür see Tes
239 J2 **Dzüünbayan-Ulaan** var. Bayan-Ulaan. Övörhangay, C Mongolia 46°38′N 102°30′E
Dzüünbulag see Matad, Dornod, Mongolia
Dzüünbulag see Uulbayan, Sühbaatar, Mongolia
239 K1 **Dzuunmod** Töv, C Mongolia 47°45′N 107°00′E
Dzuunmod see Ider
Dzüün Soyonï Nuruu see Eastern Sayans
Dzüyl see Tonhil
Dzvina see Western Dvina
191 F10 **Dzyarzhynsk Belarus** Rus. Dzerzhinsk; prev. Kaydanovo. Minskaya Voblasts', C Belarus 53°41′N 27°09′E
191 E10 **Dzyatlava** Pol. Zdzięciół, Rus. Dyatlovo. Hrodzyenskaya Voblasts', W Belarus 53°27′N 25°23′E

E

E see Hubei
Éadan Doire see Edenderry
257 I8 **Ea Drăng** var. Ea H'leo. Đăc Lăc, S Vietnam 13°09′N 108°14′E
79 N4 **Eads** Colorado, C USA 38°28′N 102°46′W
79 J8 **Eagar** Arizona, SW USA 34°05′N 109°17′W
83 K4 **Eagle** Alaska, USA 64°47′N 141°12′W
59 K5 **Eagle** ≈ Newfoundland and Labrador, E Canada
50 D4 **Eagle** ≈ Yukon Territory, NW Canada
74 F4 **Eagle Bend** Minnesota, N USA 46°10′N 95°02′W
74 C4 **Eagle Butte** South Dakota, N USA 44°58′N 101°13′W
63 K1 **Eagle Lake** Maine, NE USA 47°01′N 68°35′W
71 H7 **Eagle Lake** Texas, SW USA 29°35′N 96°19′W
58 B6 **Eagle Lake** ◎ Ontario, S Canada
80 E2 **Eagle Lake** ◎ California, W USA
63 K2 **Eagle Lake** ◎ Maine, NE USA
81 H12 **Eagle Mountain** California, USA 33°51′N 115°29′W
74 I2 **Eagle Mountain** ▲ Minnesota, N USA 47°54′N 90°33′W
70 G4 **Eagle Mountain Lake** ⊞ Texas, SW USA
79 M6 **Eagle Nest Lake** ⊞ New Mexico, SW USA
70 E8 **Eagle Pass** Texas, SW USA 28°44′N 100°31′W
117 H11 **Eagle Passage** passage SW Atlantic Ocean
78 C2 **Eagle Peak** ▲ California, W USA 41°16′N 120°12′W
80 F4 **Eagle Peak** ▲ California, W USA 38°11′N 119°22′W
79 J8 **Eagle Peak** ▲ New Mexico, SW USA 33°39′N 109°36′W
52 A7 **Eagle Plain** Yukon Territory, NW Canada 66°23′N 136°42′W
76 B8 **Eagle Point** Oregon, NW USA 42°28′N 122°48′W
280 D5 **Eagle Point** headland SE Papua New Guinea 10°31′S 149°53′E
83 I6 **Eagle River** Alaska, USA 61°18′N 149°38′W
72 D3 **Eagle River** Michigan, N USA 47°24′N 88°18′W
72 C5 **Eagle River** Wisconsin, N USA 45°56′N 89°15′W

◆ Country
● Country Capital
◇ Dependent Territory
○ Dependent Territory Capital
◈ Administrative Regions
✈ International Airport
▲ Mountain
▲▲ Mountain Range
Volcano
≈ River
◎ Lake
⊞ Reservoir

INDEX

Eagle Rock – Eleven Point River
INDEX
337

67 *J4* **Eagle Rock** Virginia, NE USA 37°40′N 79°46′W
158 *G4* **Eaglesham** United Kingdom 55°44′N 4°16′W
78 *G9* **Eagletail Mountains** ▲▲ Arizona, SW USA
Ea H'leo *see* Ea Drăng
257 *I8* **Ea Kar** Đăc Lăc, S Vietnam 12°47′N 108°26′E
161 *K6* **Ealing** United Kingdom 51°30′N 0°19′W
Eanjum *see* Anjum
Eanodat *see* Enontekiö
159 *J8* **Earby** United Kingdom 53°55′N 2°07′W
58 *B6* **Ear Falls** Ontario, C Canada 50°38′N 93°13′W
75 *J12* **Earle** Arkansas, C USA 35°16′N 90°28′W
80 *D7* **Earlimart** California, W USA 35°52′N 119°17′W
66 *D4* **Earlington** Kentucky, S USA 37°16′N 87°30′W
159 *I4* **Earlston** United Kingdom 55°38′N 2°40′W
64 *F1* **Earlville** New York, NE USA 42°44′N 75°32′W
74 *F7* **Early** Iowa, C USA 42°27′N 95°09′W
159 *I2* **Earn** 〰 United Kingdom
158 *G2* **Earn, Loch** ◎ C Scotland, United Kingdom
278 *B11* **Earnslaw, Mount** ▲ South Island, New Zealand 44°34′S 168°26′E
81 *I12* **Earp** California, USA 34°10′N 114°18′W
70 *D3* **Earth** Texas, SW USA 34°13′N 102°24′W
159 *M9* **Easington** N England, United Kingdom 54°47′N 01°21′W
159 *L8* **Easingwold** United Kingdom 54°07′N 1°12′W
67 *H7* **Easley** South Carolina, SE USA 34°49′N 82°36′W
East *see* Est
East Açores Fracture Zone *see* East Azores Fracture Zone
159 *J6* **East Allen** 〰 United Kingdom
157 *I10* **East Anglia** *physical region* E England, United Kingdom
63 *I3* **East Angus** Québec, SE Canada 45°29′N 71°39′W
293 *K5* **East Antarctica** *prev.* Greater Antarctica. *physical region* Antarctica
64 *F4* **East Ararat** Pennsylvania, NE USA 41°47′N 75°29′W
64 *A1* **East Aurora** New York, NE USA 42°44′N 78°36′W
East Australian Basin *see* Tasman Basin
East Azerbaijan *see* Āžarbāyjān-e Sharqī
290 *G4* **East Azores Fracture Zone** *var.* East Açores Fracture Zone. *tectonic feature* E Atlantic Ocean
68 *F5* **East Bay** *bay* Louisiana, S USA
71 *H7* **East Bernard** Texas, SW USA 29°32′N 96°04′W
74 *H4* **East Bethel** Minnesota, N USA 45°24′N 93°14′W
East Borneo *see* Kalimantan Timur
161 *L8* **Eastbourne** SE England, United Kingdom 50°46′N 00°16′E
161 *J2* **East Bridgford** United Kingdom 52°58′N 0°57′W
64 *K3* **East Brooklyn** Connecticut, NE USA 41°47′N 71°53′W
63 *J2* **East-Broughton** Québec, SE Canada 46°14′N 71°05′W
91 *H4* **East Caicos** *island* E Turks and Caicos Islands
65 *I3* **East Canaan** Connecticut, USA 42°01′N 73°17′W
278 *J4* **East Cape** *headland* North Island, New Zealand 37°40′S 178°31′E
266 *G3* **East Caroline Basin** *undersea feature* SW Pacific Ocean 04°00′N 146°45′E
286 *C3* **East China Sea** *Chin.* Dong Hai. *sea* W Pacific Ocean
161 *L3* **East Dereham** E England, United Kingdom 52°41′N 00°55′E
73 *B8* **East Dubuque** Illinois, N USA 42°29′N 90°38′W
57 *L8* **Eastend** Saskatchewan, S Canada 49°29′N 108°48′W
287 *J7* **Easter Fracture Zone** *tectonic feature* E Pacific Ocean
136 *E7* **Eastern** ◐ *province* Kenya
233 *J6* **Eastern** ◐ *zone* E Nepal
235 *G10* **Eastern** ◐ *province* E Sri Lanka
139 *I1* **Eastern** ◐ *province* E Zambia
138 *F9* **Eastern Cape** *off.* Eastern Cape Province, *Afr.* Oos-Kaap. ◐ *province* SE South Africa
Eastern Cape Province *see* Eastern Cape
Eastern Desert *see* Sahara el Sharqîya
136 *C6* **Eastern Equatoria** ◐ *state* SE South Sudan
Eastern Euphrates *see* Murat Nehri
234 *G5* **Eastern Ghats** ▲▲ SE India
280 *B3* **Eastern Highlands** ◐ *province* C Papua New Guinea
Eastern Region *see* Ash Sharqīyah
193 *H8* **Eastern Sayans** *Mong.* Dzüün Soyonï Nuruu, *Rus.* Vostochnyy Sayan. ▲▲ Mongolia/Russian Federation
Eastern Scheldt *see* Oosterschelde
Eastern Sierra Madre *see* Madre Oriental, Sierra
Eastern Transvaal *see* Mpumalanga
55 *I8* **Easterville** Manitoba, C Canada 53°06′N 99°53′W
Easterwâlde *see* Oosterwolde
117 *G13* **East Falkland** *var.* Isla Soledad. *island* E Falkland Islands
65 *M4* **East Falmouth** Massachusetts, NE USA 41°34′N 70°31′W
East Fayu *see* Fayu
East Flanders *see* Oost-Vlaanderen
64 *K3* **Eastford** Connecticut, NE USA 41°54′N 72°04′W
83 *J3* **East Fork Chandalar River** 〰 Alaska, USA
74 *G6* **East Fork Des Moines River** 〰 Iowa/Minnesota, C USA
East Frisian Islands *see* Ostfriesische Inseln
159 *J6* **Eastgate** United Kingdom 54°44′N 2°04′W
65 *H1* **East Glenville** New York, NE USA 42°53′N 73°55′W
74 *E2* **East Grand Forks** Minnesota, N USA 47°54′N 97°59′W
65 *L4* **East Greenwich** Rhode Island, USA 41°40′N 71°27′W
161 *K7* **East Grinstead** SE England, United Kingdom 51°08′N 00°00′W
65 *J3* **Easthampton** Massachusetts, USA 42°16′N 72°40′W
65 *K5* **East Hampton** New York, USA 40°58′N 72°11′W
65 *J4* **East Hartford** Connecticut, NE USA 41°45′N 72°36′W
65 *J5* **East Haven** Connecticut, NE USA 41°16′N 72°52′W
161 *I6* **East Ilsley** United Kingdom 51°32′N 1°17′W
289 *H10* **East Indiaman Ridge** *undersea feature* E Indian Ocean
205 *L10* **East Indies** *island group* SE Asia
161 *H5* **Eastington** United Kingdom 51°45′N 2°20′W
East Java *see* Jawa Timur
72 *G5* **East Jordan** Michigan, N USA 45°09′N 85°07′W
East Kalimantan *see* Kalimantan Timur
East Kazakhstan *see* Vostochnyy Kazakhstan
158 *G4* **East Kilbride** S Scotland, United Kingdom 55°46′N 04°10′W
70 *F5* **Eastland** Texas, SW USA 32°23′N 98°50′W
73 *G8* **East Lansing** Michigan, N USA 42°44′N 84°28′W
81 *J9* **East Las Vegas** Nevada, W USA 36°05′N 115°02′W
161 *I7* **Eastleigh** S England, United Kingdom 50°58′N 01°22′W
159 *I3* **East Linton** United Kingdom 55°59′N 2°39′W
67 *I1* **East Liverpool** Ohio, N USA 40°37′N 80°34′W
141 *I9* **East London** *Afr.* Oos-Londen; *prev.* Emonti, Port Rex. Eastern Cape, S South Africa 33°S 27°54′E
81 *D10* **East Los Angeles** California, USA 34°01′N 118°10′W
58 *F5* **Eastmain** Québec, E Canada 52°11′N 78°27′W
58 *G6* **Eastmain** 〰 Québec, C Canada
63 *I3* **Eastman** Québec, SE Canada 45°19′N 72°18′W
69 *K2* **Eastman** Georgia, SE USA 32°12′N 83°10′W
267 *H2* **East Mariana Basin** *undersea feature* W Pacific Ocean
64 *I6* **East Meadow** New York, NE USA 40°42′N 73°33′W
73 *B9* **East Moline** Illinois, N USA 41°30′N 90°26′W
280 *D3* **East New Britain** ◐ *province* E Papua New Guinea
74 *G7* **East Nishnabotna River** 〰 Iowa, C USA
65 *I6* **East Northport** New York, USA 40°53′N 73°19′W
295 *I2* **East Novaya Zemlya Trough** *var.* Novaya Zemlya Trough. *undersea feature* W Kara Sea
East Nusa Tenggara *see* Nusa Tenggara Timur
161 *H9* **Easton** United Kingdom 50°32′N 2°27′W
80 *D6* **Easton** California, USA 36°39′N 119°47′W
64 *E10* **Easton** Maryland, NE USA 38°46′N 76°04′W
64 *F6* **Easton** Pennsylvania, NE USA 40°41′N 75°13′W
65 *H6* **East Orange** New Jersey, USA 40°46′N 74°12′W
287 *J5* **East Pacific Rise** *undersea feature* E Pacific Ocean 20°00′S 115°00′W
East Pakistan *see* Bangladesh
67 *I1* **East Palestine** Ohio, N USA 40°49′N 80°32′W
73 *C10* **East Peoria** Illinois, N USA 40°40′N 89°34′W
66 *F8* **East Point** Georgia, SE USA 33°40′N 84°26′W
141 *H9* **Eastpoort** Eastern Cape, South Africa 32°40′S 25°53′E
63 *M3* **Eastport** Maine, NE USA 44°54′N 66°59′W
66 *B5* **East Prairie** Missouri, C USA 36°46′N 89°23′W
65 *L3* **East Providence** Rhode Island, NE USA 41°48′N 71°20′W
64 *J6* **East Quogue** New York, NE USA 40°50′N 72°34′W
80 *I1* **East Range** ▲▲ Nevada, USA
66 *F7* **East Ridge** Tennessee, S USA 35°00′N 85°15′W
64 *C1* **East Rochester** New York, NE USA 43°06′N 77°29′W
161 *M7* **Eastry** United Kingdom 51°14′N 1°18′E
73 *B12* **East Saint Louis** Illinois, N USA 38°35′N 90°07′W
159 *I3* **East Saltoun** United Kingdom 55°54′N 2°50′W
291 *F13* **East Scotia Basin** *undersea feature* SE Scotia Sea
291 *F12* **East Scotia Ridge** S Atlantic Ocean
205 *N5* **East Sea** *var.* Sea of Japan, *Rus.* Yapanskoye More. *Sea* NW Pacific Ocean *see also* Japan, Sea of
280 *A2* **East Sepik** ◐ *province* NW Papua New Guinea
288 *C6* **East Sheba Ridge** *undersea feature* W Arabian Sea 14°30′N 56°15′E
East Siberian Sea *see* Vostochno-Sibirskoye More
64 *G1* **East Springfield** New York, USA 42°50′N 74°49′W
64 *F5* **East Stroudsburg** Pennsylvania, NE USA 41°00′N 75°10′W
161 *L7* **East Sussex** *cultural region* SE England, United Kingdom
East Tasmanian Rise/East Tasmania Plateau/East Tasmania Rise *see* East Tasman Plateau
286 *D9* **East Tasman Plateau** *var.* East Tasmanian Rise, East Tasmania Plateau, East Tasmania Rise. *undersea feature* SW Tasman Sea
290 *G3* **East Thulean Rise** *undersea feature* N Atlantic Ocean
260 *F8* **East Timor** *var.* Loro Sae; *prev.* Portuguese Timor, Timor Timur. ◆ *country* S Indonesia
159 *M10* **Eastville** United Kingdom 53°05′N 0°06′E
67 *M4* **Eastville** Virginia, NE USA 37°22′N 75°58′W
80 *G3* **East Walker River** 〰 California/Nevada, W USA
161 *I2* **Eastwood** United Kingdom 53°00′N 1°18′W
79 *M2* **Eaton** Colorado, C USA 40°31′N 104°42′W
63 *I3* **Eaton** 〰 Québec, SE Canada
57 *L7* **Eatonia** Saskatchewan, S Canada 51°13′N 109°22′W
73 *G8* **Eaton Rapids** Michigan, N USA 42°30′N 84°39′W
66 *G9* **Eatonton** Georgia, SE USA 33°19′N 83°23′W
76 *C4* **Eatonville** Washington, NW USA 46°51′N 122°19′W
72 *B5* **Eau Claire** Wisconsin, N USA 44°50′N 91°30′W
58 *G4* **Eau Claire, Lac à l'** ◎ Québec, SE Canada
Eau Claire, Lac à L' *see* St. Clair, Lake
72 *C5* **Eau Claire River** 〰 Wisconsin, N USA
282 *E6* **Eauripik Atoll** *atoll* Caroline Islands, C Micronesia
286 *C5* **Eauripik Rise** *undersea feature* W Pacific Ocean 03°00′N 142°00′E
164 *G8* **Eauze** Gers, S France 43°52′N 00°06′E
85 *N9* **Ébano** San Luis Potosí, C Mexico 22°16′N 98°26′W
160 *G5* **Ebbw Vale** SE Wales, United Kingdom 51°48′N 03°13′W
134 *B6* **Ebebiyin** NE Equatorial Guinea 02°08′N 11°15′E
181 *I12* **Ebelsbach** Bayern, Germany 49°59′E 10°41′N
155 *E12* **Ebeltoft** Århus, C Denmark 56°11′N 10°42′E
177 *L2* **Ebenfurth** Niederösterreich, E Austria 47°53′N 16°22′E
64 *A6* **Ebensburg** Pennsylvania, NE USA 40°28′N 78°44′W
177 *J3* **Ebensee** Oberösterreich, N Austria 47°48′N 13°46′E
181 *J11* **Ebensfeld** Bayern, Germany 50°04′E 10°57′N
181 *F13* **Eberbach** Baden-Württemberg, SW Germany 49°28′N 08°58′E
214 *D6* **Eber Gölü** *salt lake* C Turkey
181 *J11* **Ebern** Saarland, Germany 50°05′E 10°48′N
177 *K5* **Eberndorf** *Slvn.* Dobrla Vas. Kärnten, S Austria 46°33′N 14°35′E
178 *I6* **Eberswalde-Finow** Brandenburg, E Germany 52°50′N 13°48′E
Ebesfalva *see* Dumbrăveni
252 *E4* **Ebetsu** *var.* Ebetu. Hokkaidō, NE Japan 43°08′N 141°37′E
Ebetu *see* Ebetsu
Ebinayon *see* Evinayong
238 *E3* **Ebinur Hu** ◎ NW China
216 *D3* **Ebla** *Ar.* Tell Mardīkh. *site of ancient city* Idlib, NW Syria
Eblana *see* Dublin
176 *E4* **Ebnat** Sankt Gallen, NE Switzerland 47°16′N 09°07′E
175 *G9* **Eboli** Campania, S Italy 40°37′N 15°03′E
134 *B6* **Ebolowa** Sud, S Cameroon 02°56′N 11°11′E
135 *H9* **Ebombo** Kasai-Oriental, C Dem. Rep. Congo 05°42′S 26°07′E
283 *L7* **Ebon Atoll** *var.* Epoon. *atoll* Ralik Chain, S Marshall Islands
140 *A1* **Ebony** Erongo, Namibia 22°05′S 15°15′E
133 *K8* **Ebonyi** ◐ *state* SE Nigeria
Ebora *see* Évora
Eboracum *see* York
Eborodunum *see* Yverdon
181 *I12* **Ebrach** Bayern, C Germany 49°49′N 10°30′E
177 *L2* **Ebreichsdorf** Niederösterreich, E Austria 47°58′N 16°24′E
167 *I10* **Ébreuil** Auvergne, France 46°07′N 3°05′E
171 *H3* **Ebro** 〰 NE Spain
170 *F2* **Ebro, Embalse del** ⊠ N Spain
180 *I4* **Ebsdorf** Niedersachsen, Germany 53°02′E 10°25′N
Eburacum *see* York
Ebusus *see* Ibiza
Ebusus *see* Eivissa
87 *H9* **Ecatepec** Durango, Mexico 16°17′N 95°53′W
163 *D11* **Écaussinnes-d'Enghien** Hainaut, SW Belgium 50°34′N 04°10′E
Ecbatana *see* Hamadān
141 *I9* **Ecca Pass** *pass* Eastern Cape, South Africa
159 *I5* **Ecclefechan** United Kingdom 55°03′N 3°16′W
67 *I4* **Eccles** West Virginia, NE USA 37°46′N 81°16′W
161 *H3* **Eccleshall** United Kingdom 52°51′N 2°15′W
263 *L4* **Echague** Luzon, N Philippines 16°42′N 121°37′E
Ech Cheliff/Ech Chleff *see* Chlef
245 *J6* **Echeng** Shandong, E China 36°09′N 116°02′E
Echeng *see* Ezhou
253 *B11* **Echigo-sanmyaku** ▲▲ Honshū, C Japan
186 *F6* **Echinádes** *island group* W Greece
187 *I2* **Echínos** *var.* Ehinos, Ekhínos. Anatolikí Makedonía kai Thráki, NE Greece 41°16′N 25°00′E
Echizen *see* Takefu
251 *I3* **Echizen-misaki** *headland* Honshū, SW Japan 35°59′N 135°57′E
Echmiadzin *see* Vagharshapat
83 *N2* **Echo Bay** Northwest Territories, NW Canada 66°04′N 118°W
78 *G6* **Echo Bay** Nevada, W USA 36°19′N 114°27′W
79 *J6* **Echo Cliffs** *cliff* Arizona, SW USA
62 *A1* **Echo Lake** ◎ Ontario, S Canada
80 *E2* **Echo Summit** ▲ California, W USA 38°47′N 120°06′W
163 *G9* **Echt** Limburg, SE Netherlands 51°07′N 05°52′E
180 *H7* **Echte** Niedersachsen, Germany 51°47′E 10°04′N
179 *D12* **Echterdingen** ✈ (Stuttgart) Baden-Württemberg, SW Germany 48°40′N 09°13′E
163 *I13* **Echternach** Grevenmacher, E Luxembourg 49°49′N 06°25′E
277 *I6* **Echuca** Victoria, SE Australia 36°10′S 144°20′E
181 *F11* **Echzell** Hessen, Germany 50°24′E 8°54′N
170 *F8* **Ecija** *anc.* Astigi. Andalucía, SW Spain 37°33′N 05°04′W
114 *G9* **Ecilda Paullier** San Jose, Uruguay 34°24′S 57°06′W
Eckengraf *see* Viesīte
178 *E4* **Eckernförde** Schleswig-Holstein, N Germany 54°28′N 09°49′E
178 *E3* **Eckernförder Bucht** *inlet* N Germany
159 *K10* **Eckington** United Kingdom 53°18′N 1°22′W
166 *E7* **Ecommay** Pays de la Loire, France 47°50′N 0°16′E
62 *F1* **Écorce, Lac de l'** ◎ Québec, SE Canada
104 *D2* **Ecuador** *off.* Republic of Ecuador. ◆ *republic* NW South America
Ecuador, Republic of *see* Ecuador
166 *F9* **Écueillé** Centre, France 47°05′N 1°21′E
155 *E8* **Ed** Västra Götaland, S Sweden 58°55′N 11°55′E
Ed *see* 'Īdi
162 *F5* **Edam** Noord-Holland, C Netherlands 52°30′N 05°02′E
141 *J6* **Edashi** KwaZulu-Natal, South Africa 29°06′S 29°40′E
156 *G3* **Eday** *island* NE Scotland, United Kingdom
70 *G10* **Edcouch** Texas, SW USA 26°17′N 97°57′W
134 *H3* **Ed Da'ein** Southern Darfur, W Sudan 11°25′N 26°08′E
136 *C3* **Ed Damazin** *var.* Ad Damazīn. Blue Nile, E Sudan 11°45′N 34°20′E
136 *C1* **Ed Damer** *var.* Ad Dāmir, Ad Damar. River Nile, NE Sudan 17°37′N 33°59′E
136 *B1* **Ed Debba** Northern, N Sudan 18°02′N 30°56′E
180 *G2* **Eddelak** Schleswig-Holstein, Germany 53°57′E 9°09′N
159 *I4* **Eddleston** United Kingdom 55°43′N 3°13′W
218 *F4* **Ed Dnaïbé** Lebanon 33°28′N 35°44′E
218 *F4* **Ed Douaïr** Lebanon 33°23′N 35°25′E
136 *B2* **Ed Dueim** *var.* Ad Duwaym, Ad Duwēm. White Nile, C Sudan 13°38′N 32°36′E
277 *K9* **Eddystone Point** *headland* Tasmania, SE Australia 41°01′S 148°18′E
157 *F13* **Eddystone Rocks** *rocks* SW England, United Kingdom
75 *H8* **Eddyville** Iowa, C USA 41°09′N 92°37′W
66 *C5* **Eddyville** Kentucky, S USA 37°03′N 88°02′W
162 *G7* **Ede** Gelderland, C Netherlands 52°03′N 05°40′E
133 *J7* **Ede** Osun, SW Nigeria 07°40′N 04°21′E
134 *A6* **Edéa** Littoral, SW Cameroon 03°47′N 10°08′E
55 *I5* **Edehon Lake** ◎ Nunavut, C Canada
183 *H10* **Edelény** Borsod-Abaúj-Zemplén, NE Hungary 48°18′N 20°40′E
180 *I6* **Edemissen** Niedersachsen, Germany 52°23′E 10°16′N
277 *K7* **Eden** New South Wales, SE Australia 37°04′S 149°51′E
67 *J5* **Eden** North Carolina, SE USA 36°29′N 79°46′W
70 *F6* **Eden** Texas, SW USA 31°13′N 99°51′W
159 *I6* **Eden** 〰 NW England, United Kingdom
141 *H6* **Edenburg** Free State, C South Africa 29°45′S 25°57′E
278 *C12* **Edendale** Southland, South Island, New Zealand 46°18′S 168°48′E
158 *C10* **Edenderry** *Ir.* Éadan Doire. Offaly, C Ireland 53°21′N 07°03′W
277 *H7* **Edenhope** Victoria, SE Australia 37°04′S 141°15′E
159 *K10* **Edensor** United Kingdom 53°13′N 1°38′W
67 *M6* **Edenton** North Carolina, SE USA 36°04′N 76°39′W
141 *I5* **Edenville** Free State, South Africa 27°33′S 27°40′E
181 *G9* **Eder** 〰 NW Germany
261 *L7* **Ederah** 〰 Papua, E Indonesia
158 *C7* **Ederny** United Kingdom 54°33′N 7°40′W
181 *F9* **Edersee** ◎ W Germany
186 *G3* **Édessa** *var.* Édhessa. Kentrikí Makedonía, N Greece 40°48′N 22°03′E
Edessa *see* Şanlıurfa
Edfu *see* Idfū
75 *E8* **Edgar** Nebraska, C USA 40°22′N 97°58′W
65 *M4* **Edgartown** Martha's Vineyard, Massachusetts, NE USA 41°23′N 70°30′W
83 *L7* **Edgecumbe, Mount** ▲ Baranof Island, Alaska, USA 57°03′N 135°45′W
67 *H8* **Edgefield** South Carolina, SE USA 33°50′N 81°57′W
74 *D3* **Edgeley** North Dakota, N USA 46°19′N 98°42′W
59 *I1* **Edgell Island** *Island* Nunavut, NE Canada
64 *D9* **Edgemere** Maryland, USA 39°15′N 76°27′W
74 *A6* **Edgemont** South Dakota, N USA 43°18′N 103°49′W
152 *B5* **Edgeøya** *island* S Svalbard
75 *G9* **Edgerton** Kansas, C USA 38°45′N 95°00′W
74 *F5* **Edgerton** Minnesota, N USA 43°52′N 96°07′W
64 *G7* **Edgewater Park** New Jersey, USA 40°04′N 74°54′W
64 *E9* **Edgewood** Maryland, NE USA 39°20′N 76°21′W
71 *H4* **Edgewood** Texas, SW USA 32°42′N 95°53′W
158 *C9* **Edgeworthstown** Longford, Ireland 53°42′N 7°37′W
161 *H3* **Edgmond** United Kingdom 52°46′N 2°25′W
159 *J9* **Edgworth** United Kingdom 53°38′N 2°23′W
Édhessa *see* Édessa
75 *H8* **Edina** Missouri, C USA 40°10′N 92°10′W
70 *G10* **Edinburg** Texas, SW USA 26°18′N 98°10′W
132 *E10* **Edinburgh** *var.* Settlement of Edinburgh. ○ (Tristan da Cunha) NW Tristan da Cunha 37°03′S 12°18′W
159 *I3* **Edinburgh** ◐ S Scotland, United Kingdom 55°57′N 03°13′W
73 *F11* **Edinburgh** Indiana, N USA 39°19′N 86°00′W
156 *F6* **Edinburgh** ✈ S Scotland, United Kingdom 55°57′N 03°22′W
188 *F5* **Edineţ** *var.* Edineţi, *Rus.* Yedintsy. NW Moldova 48°10′N 27°18′E
Edineţi *see* Edineţ
Edingen *see* Enghien
214 *B4* **Edirne** *Eng.* Adrianople; *anc.* Adrianopolis, Hadrianopolis. Edirne, NW Turkey 41°40′N 26°34′E
214 *B4* **Edirne** ◐ *province* NW Turkey
81 *D8* **Edison** California, USA 35°21′N 118°52′W
64 *G6* **Edison** New Jersey, NE USA 40°31′N 74°24′W
67 *J10* **Edisto Island** South Carolina, SE USA 32°34′N 80°17′W
67 *I9* **Edisto River** 〰 South Carolina, SE USA
77 *I5* **Edith, Mount** ▲ Montana, NW USA 46°25′N 111°10′W
75 *E12* **Edmond** Oklahoma, C USA 35°40′N 97°30′W
76 *C3* **Edmonds** Washington, NW USA 47°48′N 122°22′W
57 *I5* **Edmonton** *province capital* Alberta, SW Canada 53°34′N 113°25′W
161 *K6* **Edmonton** United Kingdom 51°36′N 0°04′W
66 *E5* **Edmonton** Kentucky, S USA 36°59′N 85°39′W
57 *I5* **Edmonton** ✈ Alberta, SW Canada 53°22′N 113°43′W
74 *D2* **Edmore** North Dakota, N USA 48°22′N 98°26′W
63 *K1* **Edmundston** New Brunswick, SE Canada 47°22′N 68°20′W
71 *H8* **Edna** Texas, SW USA 29°00′N 96°41′W
83 *M8* **Edna Bay** Kosciusko Island, Alaska, USA 55°54′N 133°40′W
133 *J8* **Edo** ◐ *state* S Nigeria
176 *F5* **Edolo** Lombardia, N Italy 46°13′N 10°20′E
290 *G3* **Edoras Bank** *undersea feature* C Atlantic Ocean
63 *I1* **Édouard, Lac** Québec, SE Canada 47°39′N 72°16′W
156 *E4* **Edrachillis Bay** *bay* NW Scotland, United Kingdom
214 *B5* **Edremit** Balıkesir, NW Turkey 39°34′N 27°01′E
214 *A5* **Edremit Körfezi** *gulf* NW Turkey
218 *F3* **Ed Saaloûk** Lebanon 33°43′N 35°45′E
154 *J7* **Edsbro** Stockholm, C Sweden 59°54′N 18°30′E
155 *H9* **Edsbruk** Kalmar, S Sweden 58°01′N 16°30′E
154 *H6* **Edsbyn** Gävleborg, C Sweden 61°22′N 15°45′E
57 *H5* **Edson** Alberta, SW Canada 53°36′N 116°28′W
112 *E10* **Eduardo Castex** La Pampa, C Argentina 35°55′S 64°18′W
106 *G3* **Eduardo Gomes** ✈ (Manaus) Amazonas, NW Brazil 05°55′S 35°15′W
Edwardesabad *see* Bannu
121 *L6* **Edward, Lake** *var.* Albert Edward Nyanza, Edward Nyanza, Lac Idi Amin, Lake Rutanzige. ◎ Uganda/Dem. Rep. Congo
Edward Nyanza *see* Edward, Lake
81 *E9* **Edwards** California, USA 34°56′N 117°56′W
68 *E2* **Edwards** Mississippi, S USA 32°19′N 90°36′W
70 *E6* **Edwards Plateau** *plain* Texas, SW USA
73 *B9* **Edwards River** 〰 Illinois, N USA
73 *B12* **Edwardsville** Illinois, N USA 38°48′N 89°57′W
293 *L3* **Edward VIII Gulf** *bay* Antarctica
293 *H7* **Edward VII Peninsula** *peninsula* Antarctica
159 *I1* **Edzell** United Kingdom 56°48′N 2°39′W
54 *B5* **Edziza, Mount** ▲ British Columbia, W Canada 57°43′N 130°39′W
54 *F4* **Edzo** *prev.* Rae-Edzo. Northwest Territories, NW Canada 62°44′N 115°55′W
82 *G7* **Eek** Alaska, USA 60°13′N 162°01′W
163 *C9* **Eeklo** *var.* Eekloo. Oost-Vlaanderen, NW Belgium 51°11′N 03°34′E
Eekloo *see* Eeklo
82 *G7* **Eek River** 〰 Alaska, USA
162 *I4* **Eelde** Drenthe, NE Netherlands 53°07′N 06°30′E
78 *A3* **Eel River** 〰 California, W USA
73 *F10* **Eel River** 〰 Indiana, N USA
Eems *see* Ems
162 *I3* **Eemshaven** Groningen, NE Netherlands 53°28′N 06°50′E
162 *I3* **Eems Kanaal** *canal* NE Netherlands
162 *H6* **Eerbeek** Gelderland, E Netherlands 52°07′N 06°04′E
163 *B9* **Eernegem** West-Vlaanderen, W Belgium 51°08′N 03°03′E
163 *F9* **Eersel** Noord-Brabant, S Netherlands 51°22′N 05°19′E
Eesti Vabariik *see* Estonia
281 *M4* **Efate** *var.* Efate, *Fr.* Vaté; *prev.* Sandwich Island. *island* C Vanuatu
Efate *see* Efate
177 *J2* **Eferding** Oberösterreich, N Austria 48°18′N 14°00′E
181 *J11* **Effelder** Thüringen, Germany 50°23′E 11°05′N
181 *J12* **Effeltrich** Bayern, Germany 49°40′E 11°06′N
73 *D11* **Effingham** Illinois, N USA 39°07′N 88°32′W
188 *G10* **Eforie-Nord** Constanţa, SE Romania 44°04′N 28°37′E
188 *G10* **Eforie-Sud** Constanţa, E Romania 44°00′N 28°38′E
Efyrnwy, Afon *see* Vyrnwy
160 *F3* **Efyrnwy, Llyn** ◎ N Wales, United Kingdom
Eg *see* Hentiy
168 *B7* **Ega** 〰 Navarra, Spain
175 *D12* **Egadi, Isole** *island group* S Italy
78 *F4* **Egan Range** ▲▲ Nevada, W USA
62 *F3* **Eganville** Ontario, SE Canada 45°33′N 77°03′W
Ege Denizi *see* Aegean Sea
83 *H8* **Egegik** Alaska, USA 58°13′N 157°22′W
183 *G11* **Eger** *Ger.* Erlau. Heves, NE Hungary 47°54′N 20°22′E
Eger *see* Cheb, Czech Republic
Eger *see* Ohre, Czech Republic/Germany
289 *E9* **Egeria Fracture Zone** *tectonic feature* W Indian Ocean
155 *A9* **Egersund** Rogaland, S Norway 58°27′N 06°01′E
181 *F8* **Egge-gebirge** ▲▲ C Germany
177 *I2* **Eggelsberg** Oberösterreich, N Austria 48°04′N 13°00′E
177 *L1* **Eggenburg** Niederösterreich, NE Austria 48°29′N 15°49′E
179 *H12* **Eggenfelden** Bayern, SE Germany 48°24′N 12°45′E
64 *G8* **Egg Harbor City** New Jersey, NE USA 39°31′N 74°39′W
132 *F10* **Egg Island** *island* W Saint Helena
277 *I8* **Egg Lagoon** Tasmania, SE Australia 39°42′S 143°57′E
161 *J6* **Egham** United Kingdom 51°25′N 0°34′W
163 *F11* **Éghezèe** Namur, C Belgium 50°36′N 04°55′E
152 *D2* **Egilsstadhir** Austurland, E Iceland 65°14′N 14°21′W
Egina *see* Aígina
Egindibulaq *see* Yegindybulak
Egio *see* Aígio
168 *G2* **Égletons** Corrèze, C France 45°24′N 02°01′E
158 *C5* **Eglinton** United Kingdom 55°01′N 7°11′W
52 *E4* **Eglinton Island** *Island* Northwest Territories, NW Canada
160 *E8* **Egloskerry** United Kingdom 50°39′N 4°27′W
162 *E5* **Egmond aan Zee** Noord-Holland, NW Netherlands 52°37′N 04°37′E
Egmont *see* Taranaki, Mount
278 *F6* **Egmont, Cape** *headland* North Island, New Zealand 39°18′S 173°44′E
Egoli *see* Johannesburg
159 *H7* **Egremont** United Kingdom 54°28′N 3°31′W
214 *C6* **Eğridir Gölü** ◎ W Turkey
Eğri Palanka *see* Kriva Palanka
159 *L7* **Egton** United Kingdom 54°26′N 0°45′W
155 *D12* **Egtved** Vejle, C Denmark 55°34′N 09°18′E
114 *A3* **Egusquiza** Santa Fe, Argentina 31°06′S 61°39′W
166 *G10* **Éguzon** Centre, France 46°27′N 1°35′E
129 *H4* **Egypt** *off.* Arab Republic of Egypt, *Ar.* Jumhūrīyah Mişr al 'Arabīyah, *prev.* United Arab Republic; *anc.* Aegyptus. ◆ *republic* NE Africa
73 *C13* **Egypt, Lake Of** ⊠ Illinois, N USA
218 *G2* **Ehden** Lebanon 34°17′N 35°57′E
246 *D8* **Ehen Hudag** *var.* Alx Youqi. Nei Mongol Zizhiqu, N China 39°12′N 101°40′E
250 *F6* **Ehime** *off.* Ehime-ken. ◐ *prefecture* Shikoku, SW Japan
Ehime-ken *see* Ehime
179 *E12* **Ehingen** Baden-Württemberg, S Germany 48°16′N 09°43′E
Ehinos *see* Echínos
81 *I13* **Ehrenberg** Nevada, USA 33°36′N 114°32′W
180 *F5* **Ehrenburg** Niedersachsen, Germany 52°45′E 8°42′N
67 *I9* **Ehrhardt** South Carolina, SE USA 33°06′N 81°00′W
181 *E10* **Ehringshausen** Hessen, Germany 50°36′E 8°23′N
176 *G4* **Ehrwald** Tirol, W Austria 47°24′N 10°52′E
285 *K4* **Eiao** *island* Îles Marquises, NE French Polynesia
171 *H2* **Eibar** País Vasco, N Spain 43°11′N 02°28′W
181 *E10* **Eibelshausen** Hessen, Germany 50°49′E 8°21′N
162 *I6* **Eibergen** Gelderland, E Netherlands 52°06′N 06°39′E
177 *K4* **Eibiswald** Steiermark, SE Austria 46°40′N 15°15′E
181 *E12* **Eich** Rheinland-Pfalz, Germany 49°45′E 8°24′N
181 *G11* **Eichelsdorf** Hessen, Germany 50°27′E 9°03′N
181 *H10* **Eichenzell** Hessen, Germany 50°29′E 9°42′N
179 *H14* **Eichham** ▲ SW Austria 47°04′N 12°24′E
181 *I8* **Eichsfeld** *hill range* C Germany
181 *J14* **Eichstätt** Bayern, SE Germany 48°53′N 11°11′E
180 *H5* **Eicklingen** Niedersachsen, Germany 52°33′E 10°11′N
180 *G1* **Eider** 〰 N Germany
154 *B7* **Eidfjord** Hordaland, S Norway 60°26′N 07°05′E
154 *C4* **Eidsvåg** Møre og Romsdal, S Norway 62°46′N 08°00′E
154 *E7* **Eidsvoll** Akershus, S Norway 60°19′N 11°14′E
152 *A5* **Eidsvollfjellet** ▲ NW Svalbard 79°13′N 13°23′E
Eier-Berg *see* Suur Munamägi
181 *C11* **Eifel** *plateau* W Germany
174 *B3* **Eiger** ▲ C Switzerland 46°33′N 08°02′E
158 *E1* **Eigg** *island* W Scotland, United Kingdom
225 *E12* **Eight Degree Channel** *channel* India/Maldives
90 *E1* **Eight Mile Rock** Grand Bahama Island, N Bahamas 26°28′N 78°43′W
292 *F5* **Eights Coast** *physical region* Antarctica
274 *E4* **Eighty Mile Beach** *beach* Western Australia
163 *G10* **Eijsden** Limburg, SE Netherlands 50°47′N 05°41′E
155 *D8* **Eikeren** ◎ S Norway
Eil *see* Eyl
Eilat *see* Elat
277 *J7* **Eildon** Victoria, SE Australia 37°17′S 145°57′E
277 *J7* **Eildon, Lake** ◎ Victoria, SE Australia
136 *B1* **Eilei** Northern Kordofan, C Sudan 16°33′N 30°54′E
179 *H8* **Eilenburg** Sachsen, E Germany 51°28′N 12°37′E
Eil Malk *see* Mecherchar
219 *D14* **Eilot** Israel 29°34′N 34°58′E
180 *G5* **Eilvese** Niedersachsen, Germany 52°32′E 9°25′N
180 *I4* **Eimke** Niedersachsen, Germany 52°58′E 10°19′N
154 *E6* **Eina** Oppland, S Norway 60°37′N 10°37′E
219 *C11* **Ein Avdat** *prev.* En 'Avedat. *well* S Israel
180 *H7* **Einbeck** Niedersachsen, C Germany 51°49′N 09°52′E
163 *G8* **Eindhoven** Noord-Brabant, S Netherlands 51°26′N 05°30′E
Ein Gedi *see* En Gedi
176 *E4* **Einsiedeln** Schwyz, NE Switzerland 47°07′N 08°45′E
172 *D2* **Eirado** Guarda, Portugal 40°46′N 7°29′W
Éire *see* Ireland
Éireann, Muir *see* Irish Sea
Eirik Outer Ridge *see* Eirik Ridge
290 *E3* **Eirik Ridge** *var.* Eirik Outer Ridge. *undersea feature* E Labrador Sea
152 *B2* **Eiríksjökull** ▲ C Iceland 64°47′N 20°23′W
106 *C5* **Eirunepé** Amazonas, N Brazil 06°38′S 69°53′W
163 *G10* **Eisden** Limburg, NE Belgium 51°05′N 05°42′E
180 *H7* **Eisdorf** Niedersachsen, Germany 51°46′E 10°10′N
138 *D4* **Eiseb** 〰 Botswana/Namibia
Eisen *see* Yeongcheon
181 *I9* **Eisenach** Thüringen, C Germany 50°59′N 10°19′E
Eisenburg *see* Vasvár
177 *K3* **Eisenerz** Steiermark, SE Austria 47°33′N 14°53′E
178 *I7* **Eisenhüttenstadt** Brandenburg, E Germany 52°09′N 14°36′E
177 *K5* **Eisenkappel** *Slvn.* Železna Kapela. Kärnten, S Austria 46°27′N 14°33′E
Eisenmarkt *see* Hunedoara
177 *L3* **Eisenstadt** Burgenland, E Austria 47°50′N 16°32′E
181 *E10* **Eiserfeld** Nordrhein-Westfalen, Germany 50°50′E 7°59′N
Eishū *see* Yeongju
191 *E9* **Eišiškes** Vilnius, SE Lithuania 54°10′N 24°59′E
179 *G8* **Eisleben** Sachsen-Anhalt, C Germany 51°32′N 11°33′E
284 *B2* **Eita** Tarawa, W Kiribati 01°21′N 173°05′E
Eitape *see* Aitape
181 *D10* **Eitorf** Nordrhein-Westfalen, Germany 50°46′E 7°27′N
180 *G4* **Eitze** Niedersachsen, Germany 52°54′E 9°17′N
171 *K6* **Eivissa** *var.* Iviza, *Cast.* Ibiza; *anc.* Ebusus. Ibiza, Spain, W Mediterranean Sea 38°54′N 01°26′E
Eivissa *see* Ibiza
171 *I3* **Ejea de los Caballeros** Aragón, NE Spain 42°07′N 01°09′W
84 *C1* **Ejido Durango** Baja California Norte, NW Mexico
84 *E7* **Ejido Insurgentes** Baja California Sur, NW Mexico 25°18′N 111°51′W
Ejin Qi *see* Dalain Hob
Ejmiadzin/Ejmiatsin *see* Vagharshapat
173 *L2* **Ejulve** Aragón, Spain 40°46′N 0°33′W
132 *G7* **Ejura** C Ghana 07°23′N 01°22′W
86 *B6* **Ejutla** Jalisco, Mexico 19°57′N 104°04′W
86 *G9* **Ejutla** *var.* Ejutla de Crespo. Oaxaca, SE Mexico 16°33′N 96°40′W
Ejutla de Crespo *see* Ejutla
77 *M5* **Ekalaka** Montana, NW USA 45°52′N 104°32′W
Ekapa *see* Cape Town
Ekaterinodar *see* Krasnodar
153 *H10* **Ekenäs** *Fin.* Tammisaari. Etelä-Suomi, SW Finland 60°00′N 23°30′E
228 *B7* **Ekerem** *Rus.* Okarem. Balkan Welaýaty, W Turkmenistan 38°06′N 53°52′E
278 *H7* **Eketahuna** Manawatu-Wanganui, North Island, New Zealand 40°41′S 175°40′E
Ekhínos *see* Echínos
Ekiatapskiy Khrebet *see* Ekvyvatapskiy Khrebet
Ekibastuz *see* Yekibastuz
193 *K7* **Ekimchan** Amurskaya Oblast', SE Russian Federation 53°04′N 132°56′E
133 *J7* **Ekiti** ◐ *state* S Nigeria
154 *I7* **Ekoln** ◎ C Sweden
129 *K8* **Ekowit** Red Sea, NE Sudan 18°46′N 37°07′E
155 *G10* **Eksjö** Jönköping, S Sweden 57°40′N 15°00′E
140 *C6* **Eksteenfontein** Northern Cape, South Africa 28°50′S 17°15′E
154 *J2* **Ekträsk** Västerbotten, N Sweden 64°28′N 19°49′E
83 *H7* **Ekuk** Alaska, USA 58°48′N 158°25′W
141 *I8* **Ekuphumleni** Eastern Cape, South Africa 32°04′S 26°47′E
193 *M2* **Ekvyvatapskiy Khrebet** *prev.* Ekiatapskiy Khrebet. ▲▲ NE Russian Federation
58 *E5* **Ekwan** 〰 Ontario, C Canada
58 *E5* **Ekwan Point** *headland* Onatario, S Canada
83 *H7* **Ekwok** Alaska, USA 59°21′N 157°28′W
256 *C5* **Ela** Mandalay, C Myanmar (Burma) 19°37′N 96°15′E
218 *G1* **El Aabboûdîyé** Lebanon 34°38′N 36°07′E
218 *G1* **El Aabdé** Lebanon 34°31′N 35°58′E
El Aaiun *see* El Ayoun
El-Aanata *see* Al'Ānāt
218 *G1* **El Aarîda** Lebanon 34°38′N 35°59′E
136 *H5* **Ēl Ābrēd** Sumalē, E Ethiopia 05°33′N 45°12′E
171 *L9* **El Affroun** Algeria
187 *H8* **Elafónisos** *island* S Greece
187 *H9* **Elafonísou, Porthmós** *strait* S Greece
El-Aïoun *see* El Ayoun
El 'Alamein *see* Al 'Alamayn
85 *L6* **El Álamo** Nuevo León, Mexico 26°29′N 99°46′W
84 *G4* **El Álamo** Sonora, N Mexico
86 *G5* **El Alazán** Veracruz-Llave, C Mexico 21°06′N 97°43′W
106 *C10* **El Alto** *var.* La Paz. ✈ (La Paz) La Paz, W Bolivia 16°31′S 68°07′W
Elam *see* Īlām
171 *I10* **El Amiria** Algeria
El Amparo *see* El Amparo de Apure
102 *E4* **El Amparo de Apure** *var.* El Amparo. Apure, C Venezuela 07°07′N 70°47′W
141 *J3* **Elands** 〰 Mpumalanga, South Africa
171 *N8* **El Aouana** Algeria
175 *A14* **El Aouinet** Tunisia
260 *G6* **Elara** Pulau Ambelau, E Indonesia 03°49′S 127°10′E
El Araïch/El Araïche *see* Larache
84 *D4* **El Arco** Baja California Norte, NW Mexico 28°03′N 113°25′W
El 'Arîsh *see* Al 'Arīsh
118 *D3* **El Arrayán** Región Metropolitana, Chile 33°21′S 70°28′W
187 *K10* **Elása** *island* SE Greece
El Asnam *see* Chlef
Elassón *see* Elassóna
186 *G4* **Elassóna** *prev.* Elassón. Thessalía, C Greece 39°53′N 22°10′E
170 *G1* **El Astillero** Cantabria, N Spain 43°23′N 03°45′W
219 *D14* **Elat** *var.* Eilat, Elath. Southern, S Israel 29°33′N 34°57′E
Elat, Gulf of *see* Aqaba, Gulf of
Elath *see* Elat, Israel
Elath *see* Al 'Aqabah, Jordan
186 *E5* **Eláti** ▲ Lefkáda, Iónia Nisiá, Greece, C Mediterranean Sea 38°43′N 20°38′E
282 *E6* **Elato Atoll** *atoll* Caroline Islands, C Micronesia
128 *G8* **El'Atrun** Northern Darfur, NW Sudan 18°11′N 26°40′E
171 *K9* **El Attaf** Algeria
130 *G2* **El Ayoun** *var.* El Aaiun, El-Aïoun, La Youne. NE Morocco 34°39′N 02°29′W
215 *H6* **Elâzığ** *var.* Elâzig, Elâziz. Elâzığ, E Turkey 38°41′N 39°14′E
215 *H6* **Elâzığ** *var.* Elâzig, Elâziz. ◐ *province* C Turkey
Elâzig/Elâziz *see* Elâzığ
69 *H3* **Elba** Alabama, S USA 31°24′N 86°04′W
174 *C7* **Elba, Isola d'** *island* Archipelago Toscano, C Italy
193 *L8* **El'ban** Khabarovskiy Kray, E Russian Federation 50°03′N 136°34′E
102 *C3* **El Banco** Magdalena, N Colombia 09°00′N 74°01′W
El Barco *see* O Barco
170 *E5* **El Barco de Ávila** Castilla-León, N Spain 40°21′N 05°31′W
El Barco de Valdeorras *see* O Barco
218 *F4* **El Barouk, Jabal** ▲▲ C Lebanon
184 *F8* **Elbasan** *var.* Elbasani. Elbasan, C Albania 41°07′N 20°04′E
184 *F8* **Elbasan** ◐ *district* C Albania
Elbasani *see* Elbasan
102 *F3* **El Baúl** Cojedes, C Venezuela 08°59′N 68°16′W
148 *C6* **Elbe** *Cz.* Labe. 〰 Czech Republic/Germany
178 *G7* **Elbe-Havel-Kanal** *canal* E Germany
180 *I3* **Elbe-Lübeck-Kanal** *canal* N Germany
El Beni *see* Beni
218 *G3* **El Beqaa** *var.* Al Biqā', Bekaa Valley. *valley* E Lebanon
70 *F4* **Elbert** Texas, SW USA 33°15′N 98°58′W
79 *L3* **Elbert, Mount** ▲ Colorado, C USA 39°07′N 106°26′W
67 *H8* **Elberton** Georgia, SE USA 34°06′N 82°52′W
180 *I4* **Elbe-Seiten-Kanal** *canal* N Germany
164 *G3* **Elbeuf** Seine-Maritime, N France 49°16′N 01°01′E
Elbing *see* Elbląg
218 *G1* **El Bîré** Lebanon 34°35′N 36°14′E
214 *G7* **Elbistan** Kahramanmaraş, S Turkey 38°14′N 37°11′E
218 *E5* **El Bîyâda** Lebanon 33°10′N 35°11′E
182 *F4* **Elbląg** *var.* Elblag, *Ger.* Elbing. Warmińsko-Mazurskie, NE Poland 54°10′N 19°25′E
89 *H6* **El Bluff** Región Autónoma Atlántico Sur, SE Nicaragua 12°00′N 83°40′W
172 *E2* **El Bodón** Castilla y León, Spain 40°29′N 6°34′W
118 *D6* **El Bolsico** Maule, Chile 35°15′S 71°11′W
117 *B8* **El Bolsón** Río Negro, W Argentina 41°59′S 71°35′W
171 *H6* **El Bonillo** Castilla-La Mancha, C Spain 38°57′N 02°32′W
118 *F2* **El Borbollón** Mendoza, Argentina 32°48′S 68°45′W
171 *J10* **El Bordj** Algeria
El Bordo *see* Patía
El Boulaida/El Boulaïda *see* Blida
57 *M7* **Elbow** Saskatchewan, S Canada 51°07′N 106°30′W
74 *F4* **Elbow Lake** Minnesota, N USA 45°59′N 95°58′W
114 *E5* **El Brillante** Entre Ríos, Argentina 32°11′S 58°13′W
197 *H9* **El'brus** *var.* Gora El'brus. ▲ SW Russian Federation 42°29′E 43°21′N
El'brus, Gora *see* El'brus
197 *H9* **El'brusskiy** Karachayevo-Cherkesskaya Respublika, SW Russian Federation 43°36′N 42°06′E
136 *A5* **El Buhayrat** *var.* Lakes State. ◐ *state* C South Sudan
El Bur *see* Ceel Buur
162 *G6* **Elburg** Gelderland, E Netherlands 52°27′N 05°46′E
170 *G3* **El Burgo de Osma** Castilla-León, C Spain 41°36′N 03°04′W
Elburz Mountains *see* Alborz, Reshteh-ye Kūhhā-ye
84 *E8* **El Cajete** Baja California Sur, NW Mexico 24°15′N 110°37′W
85 *I7* **El Cajete** Durango, W Mexico 24°53′N 105°8′W
81 *E13* **El Cajon** California, W USA 32°46′N 116°52′W
117 *C12* **El Calafate** *var.* Calafate. Santa Cruz, S Argentina 50°20′S 72°13′W
103 *I4* **El Callao** Bolívar, E Venezuela 07°18′N 61°48′W
71 *H7* **El Campo** Texas, SW USA 29°12′N 96°16′W
102 *D4* **El Cantón** Barinas, W Venezuela 07°23′N 71°10′W
80 *E4* **El Capitan** ▲ California, W USA 37°46′N 119°39′W
102 *D3* **El Carmelo** Zulia, NW Venezuela 10°20′N 71°48′W
112 *D4* **El Carmen** Jujuy, NW Argentina 24°24′S 65°16′W
86 *C5* **El Carmen** Jalisco, Mexico 20°24′N 102°25′W
85 *M7* **El Carmen** Nuevo León, Mexico 24°59′N 99°26′W
102 *C3* **El Carmen de Bolívar** Bolívar, NW Colombia 09°43′N 75°07′W
172 *G3* **El Carpio de Tajo** Castilla-La Manacha, Spain 39°53′N 4°27′W
86 *E8* **El Carrizal** Guerrero, Mexico 16°58′N 100°08′W
84 *F4* **El Carrizal** Guerrero, S Mexico 28°55′N 109°38′W
85 *H3* **El Carrizo** Chihuahua, Mexico 30°14′N 106°38′W
103 *H5* **El Casabe** Bolívar, SE Venezuela 06°26′N 63°35′W
89 *H7* **El Castillo de La Concepción** Río San Juan, SE Nicaragua 11°01′N 84°24′W
172 *E7* **El Castillo de las Guardas** Andalucía, Spain 37°41′N 6°18′W
El Cayo *see* San Ignacio
81 *G14* **El Centro** California, W USA 32°47′N 115°33′W
81 *E11* **El Cerrito** California, USA 33°50′N 117°31′W
80 *B2* **El Cerrito** California, USA 37°55′N 122°19′W
85 *J10* **El Cérró** Oaxaca, Mexico
114 *E8* **El Cerro** Colonia, Uruguay 33°57′S 58°14′W
102 *G3* **El Chaparro** Anzoátegui, NE Venezuela 09°12′N 65°03′W
85 *H4* **El Charco** Chihuahua, Mexico 28°25′N 106°10′W
131 *H1* **Elche** *Cat.* Elx; *anc.* Ilici, *Lat.* Illicis. País Valenciano, E Spain 38°16′N 00°41′W
171 *H7* **Elche de la Sierra** Castilla-La Mancha, C Spain 38°27′N 02°03′W
87 *J8* **El Chichónal, Volcán** ⛰ SE Mexico 17°20′N 93°12′W
84 *C2* **El Chinero** Baja California Norte, NW Mexico
275 *H2* **Elcho Island** *island* Wessel Islands, Northern Territory, N Australia
118 *D8* **El Cholar** Neuquén, Argentina 37°25′S 70°39′W
84 *B3* **El Consuelo** Baja California Norte, NW Mexico 30°09′N 115°47′W
85 *K4* **El Consuelo** Coahuila, NW Mexico
117 *C8* **El Corcovado** Chubut, SW Argentina 43°31′S 71°30′W
87 *K7* **El Corozal** Campeche, Mexico 18°17′N 91°08′W
172 *E1* **El Cubo de Don Sancho** Castilla y León, Spain 40°53′N 6°18′W
172 *F1* **El Cubo de Tierra del Vino** Castilla y León, Spain 41°15′N 5°42′W
87 *N4* **El Cuyo** Yucatán, Mexico 21°31′N 87°41′W
171 *I7* **Elda** País Valenciano, E Spain 38°29′N 00°47′W
84 *D3* **El Dátil** Sonora, Mexico 30°07′N 112°15′W
178 *G5* **Elde** 〰 NE Germany
162 *G7* **Elden** Gelderland, E Netherlands 51°57′N 05°53′E
136 *E6* **El Der** *spring/well* S Ethiopia 03°55′N 39°48′E
El Dere *see* Ceel Dheere
64 *D9* **Eldersburg** Maryland, USA 39°24′N 76°57′W
84 *B1* **El Descanso** Baja California Norte, NW Mexico 32°08′N 116°51′W
84 *D3* **El Desemboque** Sonora, NW Mexico 30°33′N 112°59′W
102 *C3* **El Difícil** *var.* Ariguaní. Magdalena, N Colombia 09°55′N 74°12′W
193 *K6* **El'dikan** Respublika Sakha (Yakutiya), NE Russian Federation 60°46′N 135°04′E
El Djazaïr *see* Alger
El Djelfa *see* Djelfa
75 *H8* **Eldon** Iowa, C USA 40°55′N 92°13′W
75 *H10* **Eldon** Missouri, C USA 38°21′N 92°34′W
102 *B7* **El Doncello** Caquetá, S Colombia 01°43′N 75°17′W
74 *H7* **Eldora** Iowa, C USA 42°21′N 93°06′W
113 *I5* **Eldorado** Misiones, NE Argentina 26°24′S 54°38′W
84 *G8* **El Dorado** Sinaloa, C Mexico 24°19′N 107°23′W
75 *H14* **El Dorado** Arkansas, C USA 33°12′N 92°40′W
73 *D13* **Eldorado** Illinois, N USA 37°48′N 88°26′W
75 *E10* **El Dorado** Kansas, C USA 37°51′N 96°52′W
75 *C13* **Eldorado** Oklahoma, C USA 34°28′N 99°39′W
70 *E6* **Eldorado** Texas, SW USA 30°53′N 100°37′W
103 *I4* **El Dorado** Bolívar, E Venezuela 06°45′N 61°37′W
102 *C6* **El Dorado** ✈ (Bogotá) Cundinamarca, C Colombia 01°15′N 71°52′W
El Dorado *see* California
75 *E10* **El Dorado Lake** ⊠ Kansas, C USA
75 *G10* **El Dorado Springs** Missouri, C USA 37°53′N 94°01′W
136 *C7* **Eldoret** Rift Valley, W Kenya 0°31′N 35°17′E
74 *I7* **Eldridge** Iowa, C USA 41°39′N 90°34′W
155 *F11* **Eldsberga** Halland, S Sweden 56°36′N 13°00′E
70 *F3* **Electra** Texas, SW USA 34°01′N 98°55′W
79 *K5* **Electra Lake** ⊠ Colorado, C USA
82 *B1* **'Ele'ele** *var.* Eleele. Kaua'i, Hawaii, USA, C Pacific Ocean 21°54′N 159°35′W
Eleele *see* 'Ele'ele
141 *L2* **Elefantes** 〰 Gaza, Mozambique
Elefantes *see* Lepelle
187 *H6* **Elefsína** *prev.* Elevsís. Attikí, C Greece 38°02′N 23°33′E
187 *H6* **Eléftheres** *anc.* Eleutherae. *site of ancient city* Attikí/Stereá Elláda, C Greece
187 *I2* **Eleftheroúpoli** *prev.* Elevtheroúpolis. Anatolikí Makedonía kai Thráki, NE Greece 40°55′N 24°15′E
130 *G5* **El Eglab** ▲▲ SW Algeria
190 *D7* **Eleja** Jelgava, C Latvia 56°24′N 23°41′E
173 *I9* **El Ejido** Andalucía, Spain 36°47′N 2°49′W
Elek *see* Yelek
191 *D8* **Elektrėnai** Vilnius, SE Lithuania 54°47′N 24°35′E
196 *G2* **Elektrostal'** Moskovskaya Oblast', W Russian Federation 55°47′N 38°24′E
136 *D6* **Elemi Triangle** *disputed region* Kenya/Sudan
102 *C9* **El Encanto** Amazonas, S Colombia 01°45′S 73°12′W
79 *L9* **Elephant Butte Reservoir** ⊠ New Mexico, SW USA
Éléphant, Chaîne de l' *see* Dâmrei, Chuŏr Phmun
292 *D2* **Elephant Island** *island* South Shetland Islands, Antarctica
Elephant River *see* Olifants
El Escorial *see* San Lorenzo de El Escorial
Élesd *see* Aleşd
185 *I7* **Eleshnitsa** 〰 W Bulgaria
215 *J6* **Eleşkirt** Ağrı, E Turkey 39°22′N 42°48′E
86 *G6* **El Espinal** Veracruz-Llave, Mexico 20°16′N 97°24′W
88 *D3* **El Estor** Izabal, E Guatemala 15°37′N 89°22′W
85 *M9* **El Estribo** San Luis Potosí, Mexico
171 *N9* **El Eulma** Algeria
Eleutherae *see* Eléftheres
61 *M9* **Eleuthera Island** *island* N Bahamas
79 *L4* **Elevenmile Canyon Reservoir** ⊠ Colorado, C USA
75 *I11* **Eleven Point River** 〰 Arkansas/Missouri, C USA

◆ Country
● Country Capital
◇ Dependent Territory
○ Dependent Territory Capital
◐ Administrative Regions
✈ International Airport
▲ Mountain
▲▲ Mountain Range
⛰ Volcano
〰 River
◎ Lake
⊠ Reservoir

Elevsís - Eppelborn
INDEX
338

Elevsís *see* Elefsína
Elevtheroúpolis *see* Eleftheroúpoli
175 C13 **El Fahs** Tunisia
El Faiyûm *see* Al Fayyūm
134 H2 **El Fasher** *var.* Al Fāshir. Northern Darfur, W Sudan 13°37′N 25°22′E
El Fashn *see* Al Fashn
El Ferrol/El Ferrol del Caudillo *see* Ferrol
83 L7 **Elfin Cove** Chichagof Island, Alaska, USA 58°09′N 136°16′W
171 L3 **El Fluvià** ≈ NE Spain
218 G3 **El Fourzol** Lebanon 33°52′N 35°57′E
84 G6 **El Fuerte** Sinaloa, W Mexico 26°28′N 108°35′W
134 I3 **El Fula** Western Kordofan, C Sudan 11°44′N 28°20′E
El Gedaref *see* Gedaref
134 G2 **El Geneina** *var.* Ajjinena, Al-Genain, Al Junaynah. Western Darfur, W Sudan 13°27′N 22°30′E
114 F9 **El General** Colonia, SW Uruguay 34°24′S 57°49′W
171 J10 **El Ghomri** Algeria
156 F4 **Elgin** NE Scotland, United Kingdom 57°39′N 03°20′W
73 D8 **Elgin** Illinois, N USA 42°02′N 88°16′W
74 D7 **Elgin** Nebraska, C USA 41°58′N 98°04′W
78 G5 **Elgin** Nevada, W USA 37°19′N 114°30′W
74 B3 **Elgin** North Dakota, N USA 46°24′N 101°51′W
75 D13 **Elgin** Oklahoma, C USA 34°46′N 98°17′W
70 G6 **Elgin** Texas, SW USA 30°21′N 97°22′W
193 K5 **El'ginskiy** Respublika Sakha (Yakutiya), NE Russian Federation 64°27′N 141°57′E
El Gîza *see* Giza
168 A6 **Elgóibar** Pais Vasco, Spain 43°13′N 2°24′W
131 I4 **El Goléa** *var.* Al Golea. C Algeria 30°35′N 02°59′E
84 C2 **El Golfo de Santa Clara** Sonora, NW Mexico 31°48′N 114°40′W
136 C7 **Elgon, Mount** ▲ E Uganda 01°07′N 34°29′E
154 E5 **Elgpiggen** ▲ S Norway 62°13′N 11°18′E
171 J3 **El Grado** Aragón, NE Spain 42°09′N 00°13′E
86 F6 **El Grand** Hidalgo, C Mexico 20°20′N 98°52′W
85 J4 **El Guaje** Coahuila, Mexico 28°05′N 103°17′W
85 J4 **El Guaje, Laguna** ⊠ NE Mexico
102 D3 **El Guayabo** Zulia, W Venezuela 08°37′N 72°20′W
132 G1 **El Guețțâra** *oasis* N Mali
130 D7 **El Ḩammâmi** *desert* N Mauritania
130 E7 **El Ḩank** *cliff* N Mauritania
175 B14 **El Haouareb** Tunisia
El Haseke *see* Al Ḩasakah
136 C2 **El Hawata** Gedaref, E Sudan 13°25′N 34°42′E
El Higo *see* Higos
171 J10 **El H'Manda** Algeria
118 D9 **El Huecú** Neuquén, Argentina 37°37′S 70°36′W
261 H8 **Eliase** Pulau Selaru, E Indonesia 08°16′S 130°49′E
110 C8 **Elias Fausto** São Paulo, Brazil 23°02′S 47°23′W
Elías Piña *see* Comendador
70 G4 **Eliasville** Texas, SW USA 32°55′N 98°46′W
Elichpur *see* Achalpur
79 N8 **Elida** New Mexico, SW USA 33°57′N 103°39′W
86 G5 **El Idolo, Isla** *island* Veracruz-Llave, Mexico
159 I2 **Elie** United Kingdom 56°12′N 2°49′W
186 G6 **Elikónas** ▲▲ C Greece
121 K6 **Elila** ≈ W Dem. Rep. Congo
140 E10 **Elim** Western Cape, South Africa 34°35′S 19°45′E
82 G5 **Elim** Alaska, USA 64°37′N 162°15′W
Elimberrum *see* Auch
85 K4 **El Infante** Coahuila, Mexico 28°44′N 101°55′W
Eliocroca *see* Lorca
114 A3 **Elisa** Santa Fe, C Argentina 30°42′S 61°04′W
Elisabethstedt *see* Dumbrăveni
Élisabethville *see* Lubumbashi
197 H7 **Elista** Respublika Kalmykiya, SW Russian Federation 46°18′N 44°09′E
276 G5 **Elizabeth** South Australia 34°44′S 138°39′E
65 H6 **Elizabeth** New Jersey, USA 40°40′N 74°13′W
67 I2 **Elizabeth** West Virginia, NE USA 39°04′N 81°24′W
63 J5 **Elizabeth, Cape** *headland* Maine, NE USA 43°34′N 70°12′W
67 M5 **Elizabeth City** North Carolina, SE USA 36°18′N 76°16′W
67 H5 **Elizabethton** Tennessee, S USA 36°22′N 82°15′W
73 D13 **Elizabethtown** Illinois, N USA 37°24′N 88°21′W
66 E4 **Elizabethtown** Kentucky, S USA 37°41′N 85°51′W
63 H4 **Elizabethtown** New York, NE USA 44°13′N 73°38′W
67 K7 **Elizabethtown** North Carolina, SE USA 34°36′N 78°36′W
64 D7 **Elizabethtown** Pennsylvania, NE USA 40°08′N 76°36′W
168 C6 **Elizondo** Navarra, Spain 43°09′N 1°31′W
130 E3 **El-Jadida** *prev.* Mazagan. W Morocco 33°15′N 08°27′W
El Jafr *see* Jafr, Qā' al
85 J6 **El Jaralito** Durango, Mexico 26°08′N 104°05′W
136 B3 **El Jebelein** White Nile, E Sudan 12°38′N 32°51′E
182 I4 **Ełk** *Ger.* Lyck. Warmińsko-mazurskie, NE Poland 53°51′N 22°20′E
80 E6 **Elk** California, USA 36°45′N 119°30′W
182 I4 **Ełk** ≈ NE Poland
74 I6 **Elkader** Iowa, C USA 42°51′N 91°24′W
175 A13 **El Kala** Tunisia
136 B2 **El Kamlin** Gezira, C Sudan 15°03′N 33°11′E
171 N10 **El Kantara** Algeria
76 G5 **Elk City** Idaho, NW USA 45°50′N 115°28′W
75 C12 **Elk City** Oklahoma, C USA 35°24′N 99°24′W
78 B3 **Elk Creek** California, W USA 39°34′N 122°34′W
74 B5 **Elk Creek** ≈ South Dakota, N USA
131 K1 **El Kef** *var.* Al Kāf, Le Kef. NW Tunisia 36°13′N 08°44′E
130 E3 **El Kelâa Srarhna** *var.* Kal al Sraghna. C Morocco 32°05′N 07°20′W
181 D10 **Elkenroth** Rheinland-Pfalz, Germany 50°44′E 7°53′N
El Kerak *see* Al Karak
57 I8 **Elkford** British Columbia, SW Canada 49°58′N 114°57′W
80 C2 **Elk Grove** California, USA 38°25′N 121°22′W
El Khalil *see* Hebron
129 I8 **El Khandaq** Northern, N Sudan 18°34′N 30°34′E
El Khârga *see* Al Khārijah
73 F9 **Elkhart** Indiana, N USA 41°40′N 85°58′W
75 B11 **Elkhart** Kansas, C USA 37°00′N 101°51′W
71 I5 **Elkhart** Texas, SW USA 31°37′N 95°34′W
72 D7 **Elkhart Lake** ◎ Wisconsin, N USA
El Khartûm *see* Khartoum
219 B10 **El Kharûba** Egypt 31°11′N 33°57′E
79 K2 **Elkhead Mountains** ▲▲ Colorado, C USA
64 F4 **Elk Hill** ▲ Pennsylvania, NE USA 41°42′N 75°33′W
218 F4 **El Khiyam** *var.* Al Khiyām, Khiam. S Lebanon 33°12′N 35°42′E
73 D8 **Elkhorn** Wisconsin, N USA 42°40′N 88°34′W
74 E7 **Elkhorn River** ≈ Nebraska, C USA
197 H9 **El'khotovo** Respublika Severnaya Osetiya, SW Russian Federation 43°18′N 44°17′E
185 L7 **Elkhovo** *prev.* Kizilagach. Yambol, E Bulgaria 42°10′N 26°34′E
67 I6 **Elkin** North Carolina, SE USA 36°14′N 80°51′W
67 J3 **Elkins** West Virginia, NE USA 38°56′N 79°53′W
293 L2 **Elkins, Mount** ▲ Antarctica 66°25′S 53°54′E
72 J3 **Elk Lake** Ontario, S Canada 47°44′N 80°19′W
72 F6 **Elk Lake** ◎ Michigan, N USA
64 C3 **Elkland** Pennsylvania, NE USA 41°59′N 77°16′W
78 F2 **Elko** Nevada, W USA 40°48′N 115°46′W
57 K4 **Elk Point** Alberta, SW Canada 53°52′N 110°49′W
74 E6 **Elk Point** South Dakota, N USA 42°42′N 96°37′W
64 D9 **Elkridge** Maryland, USA 39°13′N 76°43′W
74 G4 **Elk River** Minnesota, N USA 45°18′N 93°34′W
66 D7 **Elk River** ≈ Alabama/Tennessee, S USA
67 I3 **Elk River** ≈ West Virginia, NE USA
171 N8 **El Kseur** Algeria
175 B14 **El Ksour** Tunisia
66 D5 **Elkton** Kentucky, S USA 36°49′N 87°11′W
64 E8 **Elkton** Maryland, NE USA 39°37′N 75°50′W
74 F5 **Elkton** South Dakota, N USA 44°14′N 96°28′W
66 D7 **Elkton** Tennessee, S USA 35°01′N 86°51′W
67 K3 **Elkton** Virginia, NE USA 38°22′N 78°35′W
El Kuneitra *see* Al Qunayṭirah
219 D13 **El Kuntilla** Egypt 30°00′N 34°41′E
136 F5 **El Kure** Somali, E Ethiopia 05°37′N 42°05′E
134 I3 **El Lagowa** Western Kordofan, C Sudan 11°23′N 29°10′E
83 J6 **Ellamar** Alaska, USA 60°54′N 146°37′W
159 K9 **Elland** United Kingdom 53°41′N 1°50′W
218 G2 **El Laqlouq** Lebanon
218 G2 **El Laqlouq** Lebanon 34°09′N 35°53′E
158 E3 **Ellary** United Kingdom 55°55′N 5°37′W
Ellás *see* Greece
161 H2 **Ellastone** United Kingdom 52°58′N 1°49′W
69 J2 **Ellaville** Georgia, SE USA 32°14′N 84°18′W
295 J7 **Ellef Ringnes Island** *island* Nunavut, N Canada
181 I14 **Ellenberg** Baden-Württemberg, Germany 49°01′E 10°13′N
74 H5 **Ellendale** Minnesota, N USA 43°53′N 93°19′W
74 D4 **Ellendale** North Dakota, N USA 45°57′N 98°33′W
79 I4 **Ellen, Mount** ▲ Utah, W USA 38°06′N 110°48′W
76 D4 **Ellensburg** Washington, NW USA 47°00′N 124°34′W
65 H4 **Ellenville** New York, NE USA 41°43′N 74°24′W
Ellep *see* Lib
67 J7 **Ellerbe** North Carolina, SE USA 35°04′N 79°45′W
160 G2 **Ellesmere** W England, United Kingdom
53 H4 **Ellesmere Island** *island* Queen Elizabeth Islands, Nunavut, N Canada
278 E10 **Ellesmere, Lake** ◎ South Island, New Zealand
159 I10 **Ellesmere Port** C England, United Kingdom 53°17′N 02°54′W
73 E11 **Ellettsville** Indiana, N USA 39°13′N 86°37′W
163 C10 **Ellezelles** Hainaut, SW Belgium 50°44′N 03°40′E
52 F9 **Ellice** ≈ Nunavut, NE Canada
Ellice Islands *see* Tuvalu
Ellichpur *see* Achalpur
64 D9 **Ellicott City** Maryland, NE USA 39°16′N 76°48′W
66 F7 **Ellijay** Georgia, SE USA 34°42′N 84°28′W
86 B6 **El Limón** Jalisco, Mexico 19°49′N 104°11′W
181 J14 **Ellingen** Bayern, Germany 49°04′E 10°58′N
159 K4 **Ellingham** United Kingdom 55°31′N 1°43′W
75 I11 **Ellington** Missouri, C USA 37°14′N 90°58′W
75 D10 **Ellinwood** Kansas, C USA 38°21′N 98°34′W
141 I8 **Elliot** Eastern Cape, SE South Africa 31°20′S 27°51′E
141 J8 **Elliotdale** Eastern Cape, South Africa 31°58′S 28°41′E
62 B2 **Elliot Lake** Ontario, S Canada 46°24′N 82°38′W
275 K4 **Elliot, Mount** ▲ Queensland, E Australia 19°36′S 147°02′E
67 J3 **Elliott Knob** ▲ Virginia, NE USA 38°10′N 79°18′W
75 C9 **Ellis** Kansas, C USA 38°56′N 99°33′W
141 I2 **Ellisras** Limpopo, South Africa 23°40′S 27°44′E
276 F5 **Elliston** South Australia 33°40′S 134°56′E
68 F3 **Ellisville** Mississippi, S USA 31°36′N 89°12′W
171 K3 **El Llobregat** ≈ NE Spain
156 G5 **Ellon** NE Scotland, United Kingdom 57°22′N 02°06′W
Ellore *see* Elūru
67 J9 **Elloree** South Carolina, SE USA 33°34′N 80°37′W
75 D9 **Ellsworth** Kansas, C USA 38°45′N 98°15′W
63 L4 **Ellsworth** Maine, NE USA 44°32′N 68°25′W
72 A6 **Ellsworth** Wisconsin, N USA 44°44′N 92°29′W
75 D13 **Ellsworth, Lake** ⊠ Oklahoma, C USA
292 F5 **Ellsworth Land** *physical region* Antarctica
292 G5 **Ellsworth Mountains** ▲▲ Antarctica
181 H14 **Ellwangen** Baden-Württemberg, S Germany 48°58′N 10°07′E
62 C8 **Ellwood City** Pennsylvania, NE USA 40°49′N 80°15′W
180 G3 **Elm** Niedersachsen, Germany 53°31′E 9°12′N
176 E4 **Elm** Glarus, NE Switzerland 46°55′N 09°09′E
76 B4 **Elma** Washington, NW USA 47°00′N 123°24′W
218 F3 **El Machnaqa** Lebanon 34°05′N 35°46′E
130 E5 **El Mahbas** *var.* Mahbés. SW Western Sahara 27°26′N 09°09′W
117 C8 **El Maitén** Chubut, W Argentina 42°03′S 71°10′W
214 C8 **Elmalı** Antalya, SW Turkey 36°43′N 29°19′E
136 B2 **El Manaqil** Gezira, C Sudan 14°12′N 33°01′E
102 G7 **El Mango** Amazonas, S Venezuela 01°55′N 66°35′W
87 J9 **El Manguito** Chiapas, Mexico 15°46′N 93°32′W
El Manṣûra *see* Al Manṣūrah
103 I4 **El Manteco** Bolívar, E Venezuela 07°27′N 62°32′W
118 E4 **El Manzanito** Región Metropolitana, Chile 33°46′S 70°10′W
218 G3 **El Masnaa** Lebanon 33°42′N 35°54′E
85 I5 **El Mayor** Baja California Sur, NW Mexico
219 A10 **El Mazâr** Egypt 31°02′N 33°22′E
75 D8 **Elm Creek** Nebraska, C USA 40°43′N 99°22′W
84 E7 **El Médano** Baja California Sur, NW Mexico 24°33′N 111°30′W
El Mediyya *see* Médéa
133 K3 **Elméki** Agadez, C Niger 17°52′N 08°07′E
118 D2 **El Melón** Valparaíso, Chile 32°42′S 71°13′W
118 C5 **El Membrillo** Libertador General Bernardo O'Higgins, Chile 34°48′S 71°39′W
176 G4 **Elmen** Tirol, W Austria 47°22′N 10°34′E
64 F8 **Elmer** New Jersey, NE USA 39°34′N 75°09′W
141 I2 **Elmeston** Limpopo, South Africa 23°53′S 27°39′E
218 F2 **El Mina** *var.* Al Mīnā'. N Lebanon 34°28′N 35°49′E
218 F2 **El Mîna** Lebanon 34°20′N 35°43′E
El Minya *see* Al Minyā
62 C5 **Elmira** Ontario, S Canada 43°35′N 80°34′W
64 D3 **Elmira** New York, NE USA 42°06′N 76°50′W
79 H8 **El Mirage** Arizona, SW USA 33°36′N 112°19′W
74 D4 **Elm Lake** ⊠ South Dakota, N USA
218 G2 **El Mogheïri** Lebanon 34°06′N 35°52′E
El Moján *see* San Rafael
170 G4 **El Molar** Madrid, C Spain 40°43′N 03°35′W
172 G4 **El Molinillo** Castilla-La Manacha, Spain 39°28′N 4°13′W
65 I6 **Elmont** New York, USA 40°42′N 73°43′W
118 C6 **El Morro** Maule, Chile 35°27′S 71°54′W
132 E1 **El Mrâyer** *well* C Mauritania
130 E7 **El Mreiti** *well* N Mauritania
132 E2 **El Mreyyé** *desert* E Mauritania
74 D4 **Elm River** ≈ North Dakota/South Dakota, N USA
180 H2 **Elmshorn** Schleswig-Holstein, N Germany 53°45′N 09°39′E
181 E13 **Elmstein** Rheinland-Pfalz, Germany 49°22′E 7°56′N
134 I3 **El Muglad** Western Kordofan, C Sudan 11°02′N 27°44′E
El Muwaqqar *see* Al Muwaqqar
62 C4 **Elmvale** Ontario, S Canada 44°34′N 79°53′W
73 C10 **Elmwood** Illinois, N USA 40°46′N 89°58′W
75 C11 **Elmwood** Oklahoma, C USA 36°37′N 100°31′W
165 I9 **Elne** *anc.* Illiberis. Pyrénées-Orientales, S France 42°36′N 02°58′E
102 C6 **El Nevado, Cerro** *elevation* C Colombia
263 K7 **El Nido** Palawan, W Philippines 11°10′N 119°25′E
118 F5 **El Nihuil** Mendoza, W Argentina 34°58′S 68°40′W
129 H3 **El Nouzha** ✈ (Alexandria) N Egypt 31°06′N 29°58′E
84 F4 **El Novillo** Sonora, Mexico 28°58′N 109°39′W
84 C1 **El Oasis** Sonora, Mexico
136 A2 **El Obeid** *var.* Al Obayyid, Al Ubayyiḍ. Northern Kordofan, C Sudan 13°11′N 30°10′E
110 E6 **Elói Mendes** Minas Gerais, Brazil 21°37′S 45°34′W
114 D2 **El Ombú** Entre Ríos, Argentina 30°28′S 59°15′W
114 F6 **El Ombu** Rio Negro, Uruguay 32°48′S 57°24′W
86 E6 **El Oro** México, S Mexico 19°51′N 100°07′W
104 B3 **El Oro** ◈ *province* SW Ecuador
114 A8 **Elortondo** Santa Fe, C Argentina 33°42′S 61°37′W
102 E4 **Elorza** Apure, C Venezuela 07°02′N 69°30′W
El Ouâdi *see* El Oued
131 J3 **El Oued** *var.* Al Oued, El Ouâdi, El Wad. NE Algeria 33°20′N 06°53′E
86 F5 **Eloxochitlàn** Hidalgo, Mexico 20°45′N 98°48′W
79 I9 **Eloy** Arizona, SW USA 32°47′N 111°33′W
167 M6 **Éloyes** Lorraine, France 48°06′N 6°37′E
87 L9 **El Palmar** Quezaltenango, Guatemala
103 I4 **El Palmar** Bolívar, E Venezuela 08°01′N 61°53′W
85 I6 **El Palmito** Durango, W Mexico 25°40′N 104°59′W
103 I4 **El Pao** Bolívar, E Venezuela 08°03′N 62°40′W
102 F3 **El Pao** Cojedes, N Venezuela 09°40′N 68°08′W
84 D2 **El Papalote** Sonora, Mexico
114 C7 **El Paraíso** Buenos Aires, Argentina 33°34′S 59°59′W
88 G5 **El Paraíso** El Paraíso, S Honduras 13°51′N 86°31′W
86 E8 **El Paraíso** Guerrero, Mexico 17°21′N 100°43′W
88 G4 **El Paraíso** ◈ *department* SE Honduras
173 H2 **El Pardo** Madrid, Spain 40°32′N 3°46′W
73 C10 **El Paso** Illinois, N USA 40°44′N 89°01′W
70 A5 **El Paso** Texas, SW USA 31°45′N 106°30′W
70 A5 **El Paso** ✈ Texas, SW USA 31°48′N 106°24′W
85 I4 **El Pastor** Chihuahua, Mexico
173 I4 **El Pedernoso** Castilla-La Manacha, Spain 39°29′N 2°45′W
172 F7 **El Pedroso** Andalucía, Spain 37°51′N 5°46′W
85 L7 **El Peñuelo** Nuevo León, Mexico 24°34′N 100°46′W
85 L7 **El Pequeño** Nuevo León, Mexico 24°04′N 100°16′W
171 J4 **El Perelló** Cataluña, NE Spain 40°53′N 00°43′E
158 B8 **Elphin** Roscommon, C Ireland 53°51′N 08°55′W
103 H2 **El Pilar** Sucre, NE Venezuela 10°31′N 63°12′W
114 C4 **El Pingo** Entre Rios, Argentina 31°36′S 59°48′W
88 D4 **El Pital, Cerro** ▲ El Salvador/Honduras 14°19′N 89°06′W
80 E4 **El Portal** California, W USA 37°40′N 119°46′W
85 H2 **El Porvenir** Chihuahua, N Mexico 31°15′N 105°48′W
89 L8 **El Porvenir** Kuna Yala, N Panama 09°33′N 78°56′W
85 L7 **El Potosí** Nuevo León, Mexico 24°51′N 100°19′W
86 D8 **El Potosí, Bahía** *bay* Guerrero, S Mexico Central America
118 C4 **El Prado** Región Metropolitana, Chile 33°55′S 71°30′W
171 K4 **El Prat de Llobregat** Cataluña, NE Spain 41°20′N 02°05′E
88 E3 **El Progreso** Yoro, NW Honduras 15°25′N 87°49′W
84 E4 **El Progreso** Baja California Norte, NW Mexico
88 C4 **El Progreso** *off.* Departamento de El Progreso. ◈ *department* C Guatemala
El Progreso *see* Guastatoya
El Progreso, Departamento de *see* El Progreso
170 F5 **El Puente del Arzobispo** Castilla-La Mancha, C Spain 39°48′N 05°10′W
170 E9 **El Puerto de Santa María** Andalucía, S Spain 36°36′N 06°13′W
112 C6 **El Puesto** Catamarca, NW Argentina 27°57′S 67°37′W
El Qâhira *see* Cairo
218 F4 **El Qaraaoun** Lebanon 33°33′N 35°43′E
El Qaṣr *see* Al Qaṣr
El Qatrani *see* Al Qaṭrānah
85 H8 **El Quelite** Sinaloa, C Mexico 23°37′N 106°26′W
116 B2 **Elqui, Río** ≈ N Chile
El Q'unayṭirah *see* Al Qunayṭirah
El Quneitra *see* Al Qunayṭirah
219 C11 **El Quṣeima** Egypt 30°40′N 34°22′E
El Quseir *see* Al Quṣayr
El Quweira *see* Al Quwayrah
220 F8 **El-Rahaba** ✈ (Şan'ā') W Yemen 15°28′N 44°12′E
89 H6 **El Rama** Región Autónoma Atlántico Sur, SE Nicaragua 12°09′N 84°15′W
89 M9 **El Real** *var.* El Real de Santa María. Darién, SE Panama 08°06′N 77°42′W
El Real de Santa María *see* El Real
85 I8 **El Refugio** Durango, Mexico 23°34′N 104°20′W
86 E5 **El Refugio** Guanajuato, Mexico 21°13′N 100°18′W
85 K4 **El Remolino** Coahuila, Mexico 28°45′N 101°05′W
75 D12 **El Reno** Oklahoma, C USA 35°32′N 95°57′W
85 L8 **El Retorno** San Luis Potosí, Mexico
85 I7 **El Rodeo** Durango, C Mexico 25°12′N 104°35′W
170 E8 **El Ronquillo** Andalucía, S Spain 37°43′N 06°09′W
84 B3 **El Rosario** ≈ Baja California Norte, NW Mexico
57 L7 **Elrose** Saskatchewan, S Canada 51°07′N 107°59′W
72 B7 **Elroy** Wisconsin, N USA 43°43′N 90°16′W
172 F8 **El Rubio** Andalucía, Spain 37°21′N 4°59′W
54 B2 **Elsa** Yukon Territory, NW Canada
70 G10 **Elsa** Texas, SW USA 26°17′N 97°59′W
El Şaff *see* Aş Şaff
85 L7 **El Salado** San Luis Potosí, Mexico 24°18′N 100°52′W
85 H7 **El Salado** Sinaloa, Mexico 24°31′N 107°09′W
85 M8 **El Salado** Tamaulipas, W Mexico
85 I8 **El Salto** Durango, C Mexico 23°47′N 105°22′W
88 C5 **El Salvador** *off.* Republica de El Salvador. ◆ *republic* Central America
El Salvador, Republica de *see* El Salvador
102 F4 **El Samán de Apure** Apure, C Venezuela 07°54′N 68°44′W
72 H2 **Elsas** Ontario, S Canada 48°31′N 82°53′W
84 E2 **El Sásabe** *var.* Aduana del Sásabe. Sonora, NW Mexico 31°27′N 111°31′W
Elsass *see* Alsace
172 F8 **El Saucejo** Andalucía, Spain 37°04′N 5°06′W
85 L4 **El Saucito** Coahuila, Mexico 28°30′N 100°29′W
84 F5 **El Saucito** Sonora, NE Mexico
85 H4 **El Sáuz** Chihuahua, N Mexico 29°03′N 106°15′W
85 K5 **El Sauz** Coahuila, Mexico 27°38′N 101°11′W
84 F5 **El Sauz** Sonora, NE Mexico
75 I9 **Elsberry** Missouri, C USA 39°10′N 90°46′W
159 J5 **Elsdon** United Kingdom 55°13′N 2°06′W
91 I6 **El Seibo** *var.* Santa Cruz de El Seibo, Santa Cruz del Seibo. E Dominican Republic 18°45′N 69°04′W
88 B4 **El Semillero Barra Nahualate** Escuintla, SW Guatemala 14°01′N 91°28′W
Elsene *see* Ixelles
181 G12 **Elsenfeld** Bayern, Germany 49°51′E 9°10′N
Elsen Nur *see* Dorgê Co
79 H4 **Elsinore** Utah, W USA 38°40′N 112°09′W
Elsinore *see* Helsingør
163 G10 **Elsloo** Limburg, SE Netherlands 50°57′N 05°46′E
64 F8 **Elsmere** Delaware, USA 39°44′N 75°36′W
113 I6 **El Soberbio** Misiones, NE Argentina 27°15′S 54°05′W
114 B8 **El Socorro** Buenos Aires, Argentina 33°40′S 60°42′W
84 B3 **El Socorro** Baja California Norte, NW Mexico 30°19′N 115°49′W
85 L9 **El Socorro** San Luis Potosí, NW Mexico
102 G3 **El Socorro** Guárico, C Venezuela 09°00′N 65°42′W
102 F3 **El Sombrero** Guárico, N Venezuela 09°25′N 67°06′W
118 E5 **El Sosneado** Mendoza, Argentina 35°04′S 69°34′W
181 E9 **Elspe** Nordrhein-Westfalen, Germany 51°09′E 8°03′N
162 G6 **Elspeet** Gelderland, E Netherlands 52°19′N 05°47′E
159 H4 **Elsrickle** United Kingdom 55°40′N 3°29′W
162 G7 **Elst** Gelderland, E Netherlands 51°55′N 05°51′E
179 H8 **Elsterwerda** Brandenburg, E Germany 51°27′N 13°32′E
85 H3 **El Sueco** Chihuahua, N Mexico 29°53′N 106°24′W
El Suweida *see* As Suwaydā'
El Suweis *see* Suez
161 K4 **Elsworth** United Kingdom 52°15′N 0°04′W
84 F3 **El Tajo** Sonora, Mexico 30°31′N 109°39′W
114 G7 **El Tala** Flores, Uruguay 33°15′S 57°20′W
87 J9 **El Talismán** Chiapas, SE Mexico 15°42′N 92°42′W
87 J9 **El Talisman** ≈ Chiapas, Mexico
102 B7 **El Tambo** Cauca, SW Colombia 02°25′N 76°50′W
267 K9 **Eltanin Fracture Zone** *tectonic feature* SE Pacific Ocean
175 A13 **El Tarf** Tunisia
114 B10 **El Tejar** Buenos Aires, Argentina 35°13′S 61°03′W
180 B7 **Elten** Nordrhein-Westfalen, Germany 51°52′E 6°09′N
171 L3 **El Ter** ≈ NE Spain
278 G6 **Eltham** Taranaki, North Island, New Zealand 39°26′S 174°25′E
219 C14 **El Thamad** Egypt 29°41′N 34°17′E
103 H3 **El Tigre** Anzoátegui, NE Venezuela 08°55′N 64°15′W
El Tigrito *see* San José de Guanipa
102 E3 **El Tocuyo** Lara, N Venezuela 09°48′N 69°51′W
86 E8 **El Tomatal** Baja California Sur, NW Mexico
197 I6 **El'ton** Volgogradskaya Oblast', SW Russian Federation 49°07′N 46°50′E
161 K3 **Elton** United Kingdom 52°32′N 0°23′W
85 I10 **El Tonino** Nayarit, Mexico 21°02′N 105°11′W
76 E5 **Eltopia** Washington, NW USA 46°33′N 118°59′W
118 D3 **El Toro** Región Metropolitana, Chile 33°20′S 71°10′W
El Toro *see* Mare de Déu del Toro
114 A5 **El Trébol** Santa Fe, C Argentina 32°12′S 61°40′W
70 A6 **El Trece** Chihuahua, Mexico
114 A10 **El Triunfo** Buenos Aires, Argentina 35°06′S 61°31′W
84 F8 **El Triunto** Baja California Sur, NW Mexico 23°47′N 110°08′W
86 A5 **El Tuito** Jalisco, SW Mexico 20°19′N 105°22′W
85 H5 **El Tule** Chihuahua, Mexico 27°03′N 106°16′W
86 A5 **El Tule** Jalisco, Mexico 20°01′N 105°14′W
85 K4 **El Tuli** Coahuila, Mexico 28°30′N 101°29′W
El Ţûr *see* Aţ Ţūr
118 C3 **El Turco** Región Metropolitana, Chile 33°33′S 71°29′W
181 E12 **Eltville** Hessen, Germany 50°02′E 8°07′N
243 N10 **Eluanbi** *Eng.* Cape Olwanpi. *headland* S Taiwan 21°57′N 120°48′E
234 G6 **Elūru** *prev.* Ellore. Andhra Pradesh, E India 16°45′N 81°10′E
190 F5 **Elva** *Ger.* Elwa. Tartumaa, SE Estonia 58°13′N 26°25′E
79 L6 **El Vado Reservoir** ⊠ New Mexico, SW USA
89 K9 **El Valle** Coclé, C Panama 08°39′N 80°08′W
159 H4 **Elvanfoot** United Kingdom 55°26′N 3°39′W
172 D5 **Elvas** Portalegre, C Portugal 38°53′N 07°10′W
166 B7 **Elven** Bretagne, France 47°44′N 2°35′W
85 K5 **El Venado** Coahuila, Mexico 26°47′N 101°56′W
102 F4 **El Venado** Apure, C Venezuela 07°25′N 68°46′W
171 K4 **El Vendrell** Cataluña, NE Spain 41°13′N 01°32′E
85 H6 **El Vergel** Chihuahua, Mexico 26°28′N 106°22′W
85 J9 **El Vergel** Zacatecas, N Mexico
154 E6 **Elverum** Hedmark, S Norway 60°54′N 11°33′E
88 E6 **El Viejo** Chinandega, NW Nicaragua 12°39′N 87°11′W
102 D4 **El Viejo, Cerro** ▲ C Colombia 07°31′N 72°56′W
102 D3 **El Vigía** Mérida, NW Venezuela 08°38′N 71°39′W
171 H3 **El Villar de Arnedo** La Rioja, N Spain 42°19′N 02°05′W
114 D10 **Elvira** Buenos Aires, Argentina 35°14′S 59°29′W
106 A5 **Elvira** Amazonas, W Brazil 07°12′S 69°56′W
Elwa *see* Elva
El Wad *see* El Oued
136 F7 **El Wak** North Eastern, NE Kenya 02°46′N 40°57′E
77 I3 **Elwell, Lake** ⊠ Montana, NW USA
73 F10 **Elwood** Indiana, N USA 40°16′N 85°50′W
75 G9 **Elwood** Kansas, C USA 39°43′N 94°52′W
75 C8 **Elwood** Nebraska, C USA 40°35′N 99°51′W
Elx *see* Elche
181 J9 **Elxleben** Thüringen, Germany 51°03′E 10°57′N
161 K4 **Ely** E England, United Kingdom 52°24′N 00°15′E
74 H2 **Ely** Minnesota, N USA 47°54′N 91°52′W
78 G3 **Ely** Nevada, W USA 39°15′N 114°53′W
160 F6 **Ely** ≈ United Kingdom
El Yopal *see* Yopal
73 I9 **Elyria** Ohio, N USA 41°22′N 82°06′W
91 J8 **El Yunque** ▲ E Puerto Rico 18°15′N 65°46′W
179 C13 **Elz** ≈ SW Germany
85 H6 **El Zape** Durango, Mexico
281 M4 **Emae** *island* Shepherd Islands, C Vanuatu
190 E4 **Emajõgi** *Ger.* Embach. ≈ SE Estonia
Emāmrūd *see* Shāhrūd
230 G2 **Emām Şāḩeb** *var.* Emam Saheb, Hazarat Imam. Kunduz, NE Afghanistan 37°11′N 68°55′E
Emam Saheb *see* Emām Şāḩeb
Emāmshahr *see* Shāhrūd
155 H10 **Emån** ≈ S Sweden
141 K4 **eManzana** *prev.* Badplaas. Mpumalanga, South Africa 25°57′S 30°34′E *see also* Badplaas
141 K7 **eManzimtoti** *prev.* Amanzimtoti. Kwazulu Natal, South Africa 30°03′S 30°53′E *see also* Amanzimtoti
281 M4 **Emao** *island* C Vanuatu
226 E4 **Emba** *Kaz.* Embi. Aktyubinsk, W Kazakhstan 48°50′N 58°10′E
Emba *see* Zhem
Embach *see* Emajõgi
141 J4 **Embalenhle** Mpumalanga, South Africa 26°32′S 29°04′E
116 C6 **Embalse Cerros Colorados** *lakes* Neuquén, Argentina
173 J6 **Embalse de El Cenajo** ⊠ Spain
112 D4 **Embarcación** Salta, N Argentina 23°15′S 64°05′W
54 F6 **Embarras Portage** Alberta, C Canada
73 D12 **Embarras River** ≈ Illinois, N USA
88 M9 **Emberá-Wounaan** *var.* Cemaco. ◈ *special territory* E Panama
Embi *see* Emba
173 J1 **Embid** Castilla-La Manacha, Spain 40°58′N 1°43′W
159 K4 **Embleton** United Kingdom 55°29′N 1°37′W
169 L3 **Embrun** Provence-Alpes-Côte d'Azur, France 44°34′N 6°30′E
137 D8 **Embu** Eastern, C Kenya 0°32′N 37°28′E
180 C3 **Emden** Niedersachsen, NW Germany 53°22′N 07°12′E
242 A3 **Emeishan** Sichuan, China 29°22′N 103°17′E
240 D4 **Emei Shan** ▲ Sichuan, C China 29°32′N 103°21′E
Emek Khula *see* Émeq Ḩula
219 D8 **'Émeq Ayyalon** Israel
218 E7 **Émeq Dotan** ▲▲ West Bank
218 F5 **Émeq Ḩula** *var.* Emek Khula. ▲▲ Israel
74 E2 **Emerado** North Dakota, N USA 47°55′N 97°21′W
275 K5 **Emerald** Queensland, E Australia 23°33′S 148°11′E
52 F4 **Emerald Isle** *Island* Northwest Territories, NW Canada
Emerald Isle *see* Montserrat
106 D8 **Emero, Río** ≈ W Bolivia
55 J10 **Emerson** Manitoba, S Canada 49°01′N 97°07′W
75 F8 **Emerson** Iowa, C USA 41°00′N 95°22′W
74 E7 **Emerson** Nebraska, C USA 42°16′N 96°43′W
80 F5 **Emerson Lake** ◎ California, USA
79 I4 **Emery** Utah, W USA 38°54′N 111°16′W
Emesa *see* Ḩimş
214 C6 **Emet** Kütahya, W Turkey 39°22′N 29°15′E
280 A4 **Emeti** Western, SW Papua New Guinea 07°54′S 143°18′E
80 E1 **Emigrant Gap** California, USA 39°18′N 120°40′W
78 F2 **Emigrant Pass** *pass* Nevada, W USA
80 G5 **Emigrant Peak** ▲ Nevada, USA 37°58′N 117°54′W
128 D7 **Emi Koussi** ▲ N Chad 19°52′N 18°34′E
114 B3 **Emilia** Santa Fe, Argentina 31°06′S 60°42′W
Emilia *see* Emilia-Romagna
87 K7 **Emiliano Zapata** Chiapas, SE Mexico 17°42′N 91°46′W
85 J7 **Emiliano Zapata** Coahuila, Mexico 25°29′N 102°56′W
84 E5 **Emiliano Zapata** Sonora, NE Mexico
174 E5 **Emilia-Romagna** *prev.* Emilia; *anc.* Æmilia. ◈ *region* N Italy
114 C9 **Emilio Ayarza** Buenos Aires, Argentina 34°45′S 60°03′W
238 E2 **Emin** *var.* Dorbiljin. Xinjiang Uygur Zizhiqu, NW China 46°30′N 83°42′E
231 J5 **Eminābād** Punjab, E Pakistan 32°02′N 73°51′E
66 F3 **Eminence** Kentucky, S USA 38°22′N 85°10′W
75 I11 **Eminence** Missouri, C USA 37°09′N 91°22′W
185 M6 **Emine, Nos** *headland* E Bulgaria 42°43′N 27°53′E
238 E2 **Emin He** ≈ NW China
280 D1 **Emirau Island** *island* N Papua New Guinea
214 D6 **Emirdağ** Afyon, W Turkey 39°01′N 31°09′E
141 L3 **Emjejane** *prev.* Hectorspruit. Mpumalanga, South Africa 25°26′S 31°41′E *see also* Hectorspruit
141 K4 **Emjindini** Mpumalanga, South Africa 25°47′S 31°03′E
180 H1 **Emkendorf** Schleswig-Holstein, Germany 54°16′E 9°51′N
141 K7 **eMkhomazi** *prev.* Umkomaas. KwaZulu-Natal, South Africa 30°12′S 30°48′E *see also* Umkomaas
141 K4 **eMkhondo** *prev.* Piet Retief. Mpumalanga, E South Africa 27°00′S 30°49′E *see also* Piet Retief
155 H11 **Emmaboda** Kalmar, S Sweden 56°36′N 15°30′E
190 C4 **Emmaste** Hiiumaa, W Estonia 58°43′N 22°36′E
64 F6 **Emmaus** Pennsylvania, NE USA 40°32′N 75°28′W
277 L3 **Emmaville** New South Wales, SE Australia 29°26′S 151°38′E
176 D4 **Emme** ≈ W Switzerland
162 G5 **Emmeloord** Flevoland, N Netherlands 52°43′N 05°46′E
181 D11 **Emmelshausen** Rheinland-Pfalz, Germany 50°09′E 7°34′N
162 I5 **Emmen** Drenthe, NE Netherlands 52°48′N 06°57′E
176 D4 **Emmen** Luzern, C Switzerland 47°03′N 08°14′E
179 C13 **Emmendingen** Baden-Württemberg, SW Germany 48°07′N 07°51′E
162 J4 **Emmer-Compascuum** Drenthe, NE Netherlands 52°47′N 07°03′E
180 B7 **Emmerich** Nordrhein-Westfalen, W Germany 51°49′N 06°16′E
180 H6 **Emmern** Niedersachsen, Germany 52°03′E 9°23′N
76 F7 **Emmett** Idaho, NW USA 43°52′N 116°30′W
65 C8 **Emmitsburg** Maryland, NE USA 39°42′N 77°19′W
82 G5 **Emmonak** Alaska, USA 62°46′N 164°31′W
160 A2 **Emo** Laois, Ireland 53°06′N 7°13′W
Emona *see* Ljubljana
Emonti *see* East London
70 D7 **Emory Peak** ▲ Texas, SW USA 29°15′N 103°18′W
84 E5 **Empalme** Sonora, NW Mexico 27°57′N 110°49′W
114 B7 **Empalme Constitución** Santa Fe, Argentina 33°16′S 60°23′W
139 H8 **Empangeni** KwaZulu/Natal, E South Africa 28°45′S 31°54′E
116 H1 **Empedrado** Corrientes, NE Argentina 27°59′S 58°47′W
286 E2 **Emperor Seamounts** *undersea feature* NW Pacific Ocean 42°00′N 170°00′E
286 F2 **Emperor Trough** *undersea feature* N Pacific Ocean
78 D2 **Empire** Nevada, W USA 40°26′N 119°21′W
Empire State of the South *see* Georgia
Empire State, The *see* New York
Emplawas *see* Amplawas
176 G9 **Empoli** Toscana, C Italy 43°43′N 10°57′E
75 F10 **Emporia** Kansas, C USA 38°24′N 96°10′W
67 L5 **Emporia** Virginia, NE USA 36°42′N 77°33′W
64 B4 **Emporium** Pennsylvania, NE USA 41°31′N 78°14′W
Empty Quarter *see* Ar Rub' al Khālī
180 D4 **Ems** *Dut.* Eems. ≈ NW Germany
180 D6 **Emsbüren** Niedersachsen, Germany 52°24′E 7°18′N
180 D6 **Emsdetten** Nordrhein-Westfalen, NW Germany 52°11′N 07°32′E
Ems-Hunte Canal *see* Küstenkanal
180 D3 **Ems-Jade-Kanal** *canal* NW Germany
181 J13 **Emskirchen** Bayern, Germany 49°33′E 10°43′N
180 D4 **Emsland** *cultural region* NW Germany
181 G9 **Emstal** Hessen, Germany 51°13′E 9°16′N
161 J8 **Emsworth** United Kingdom 50°51′N 0°56′W
276 D2 **Emu Junction** South Australia 28°39′S 132°13′E
247 K1 **Emur He** ≈ NE China
141 J4 **Emzinoi** Mpumalanga, South Africa 26°35′S 29°32′E
103 J5 **Enachu Landing** NW Guyana 06°09′N 60°02′W
154 F3 **Enafors** Jämtland, C Sweden 63°17′N 12°24′E
154 H5 **Enånger** Gävleborg, C Sweden 61°30′N 17°10′E
156 E4 **Enard Bay** *bay* NW Scotland, United Kingdom
Enareträsk *see* Inarijärvi
261 K6 **Enarotali** Papua, E Indonesia 03°55′S 136°21′E
251 J4 **Ena-san** ▲ Honshū, S Japan 35°27′N 137°36′E
En 'Avedat *see* Ein Avdat
252 E2 **Enbetsu** Hokkaidō, NE Japan 44°44′N 141°47′E
115 M3 **Encantadas, Serra das** ▲▲ S Brazil
60 C9 **Encantado, Cerro** ▲ NW Mexico 26°46′N 112°33′W
113 H6 **Encarnación** Itapúa, S Paraguay 27°20′S 55°50′W
86 D4 **Encarnación de Díaz** Jalisco, SW Mexico 21°33′N 102°13′W
245 J5 **Encheng** Shandong, E China 37°09′N 116°16′E
132 G8 **Enchi** SW Ghana 05°53′N 02°48′W
70 F8 **Encinal** Texas, SW USA 28°02′N 99°21′W
81 E12 **Encinitas** California, W USA 33°02′N 117°17′W
70 G9 **Encino** Texas, SW USA 26°58′N 98°06′W
168 B8 **Enciso** La Rioja, Spain 42°09′N 2°16′W
118 G2 **Encón** San Juan, Argentina 32°12′S 67°47′W
102 D3 **Encontrados** Zulia, NW Venezuela 09°04′N 72°16′W
276 G6 **Encounter Bay** *inlet* South Australia
113 H7 **Encruzilhada** Rio Grande do Sul, S Brazil 28°58′S 55°31′W
115 M2 **Encruzilhada do Sul** Rio Grande do Sul, S Brazil 30°30′S 52°32′W
183 H10 **Encs** Borsod-Abaúj-Zemplén, NE Hungary 48°21′N 21°09′E
275 J1 **Endeavour Strait** *strait* Queensland, NE Australia
260 D8 **Endeh** Flores, S Indonesia 08°48′S 121°37′E
155 D12 **Endelave** *island* C Denmark
284 E3 **Enderbury Island** *atoll* Phoenix Islands, C Kiribati
56 F7 **Enderby** British Columbia, SW Canada 50°34′N 119°09′W
293 K3 **Enderby Land** *physical region* Antarctica
289 C13 **Enderby Plain** *undersea feature* S Indian Ocean
74 E3 **Enderlin** North Dakota, N USA 46°37′N 97°36′W
Endersdorf *see* Jędrzejów
75 B8 **Enders Reservoir** ⊠ Nebraska, C USA
64 E3 **Endicott** New York, NE USA 42°06′N 76°03′W
83 H3 **Endicott Mountains** ▲▲ Alaska, USA
159 J10 **Endon** United Kingdom 53°05′N 2°07′W
181 E8 **Endorf** Nordrhein-Westfalen, Germany 51°17′E 8°02′N
291 D13 **Endurance Fracture Zone** *tectonic feature* N Scotia Sea Atlantic Ocean
64 E3 **Endwell** New York, USA 42°07′N 76°01′W
189 K6 **Enerhodar** Zaporiz'ka Oblast', SE Ukraine 47°30′N 34°40′E
104 E7 **Ene, Río** ≈ C Peru
283 J5 **Enewetak Atoll** *var.* Ānewetak, Eniwetok. *atoll* Ralik Chain, W Marshall Islands
187 J3 **Enez** Edirne, NW Turkey 40°44′N 26°05′E
218 F2 **Enfé.** Lebanon
218 F2 **Enfé** Lebanon 34°21′N 35°44′E
175 C14 **Enfida** Tunisia
161 K6 **Enfield** United Kingdom 51°40′N 0°04′W
65 J3 **Enfield** Connecticut, USA 41°59′N 72°36′W
67 L5 **Enfield** North Carolina, SE USA 36°10′N 77°40′W
280 A3 **Enga** ◈ *province* W Papua New Guinea
91 J6 **Engaño, Cabo** *headland* E Dominican Republic 18°36′N 68°19′W
252 G3 **Engaru** Hokkaidō, NE Japan 44°06′N 143°30′E
141 I8 **Engcobo** Eastern Cape, South Africa 31°40′S 28°00′E
219 E9 **En Gedi** *var.* Ein Gedi. Southern, S Israel 31°27′N 35°23′E
176 D4 **Engelberg** Unterwalden, C Switzerland 46°51′N 08°25′E
67 M6 **Engelhard** North Carolina, SE USA 35°30′N 76°00′W
197 I4 **Engel's** Saratovskaya Oblast', W Russian Federation 51°27′N 46°09′E
179 D13 **Engen** Baden-Württemberg, SW Germany 47°52′N 08°46′E
111 H7 **Engenheiro Paulo de Frontin** Rio de Janeiro, Brazil 22°33′S 43°41′W
180 F6 **Enger** Nordrhein-Westfalen, Germany 52°08′E 8°34′N
Engeten *see* Aiud
218 F6 **'En Gev** Israel 32°46′N 35°38′E
258 E7 **Enggano, Pulau** *island* W Indonesia
136 E1 **Enghershatu** ▲ N Eritrea 16°41′N 38°21′E
163 D10 **Enghien** *Dut.* Edingen. Hainaut, SW Belgium 50°42′N 04°03′E
75 I13 **England** Arkansas, C USA 34°32′N 91°58′W
157 H10 **England** *Lat.* Anglia. ◈ *national region* England, United Kingdom
53 I7 **Englefield, Cape** *headland* Nunavut, NE Canada 69°51′N 85°31′W
58 F7 **Englehart** Ontario, S Canada 47°50′N 79°52′W
79 M3 **Englewood** Colorado, C USA 39°39′N 104°59′W
73 E12 **English** Indiana, N USA 38°20′N 86°28′W
83 I7 **English Bay** Alaska, USA 59°21′N 151°55′W
English Bazar *see* Ingrāj Bāzār
166 E3 **English Channel** *var.* The Channel, *Fr.* la Manche. *channel* NW Europe
292 F4 **English Coast** *physical region* Antarctica
171 I6 **Enguera** País Valenciano, E Spain 38°58′N 00°42′W
190 C6 **Engure** Tukums, W Latvia 57°09′N 23°13′E
190 C6 **Engures Ezers** ◎ NW Latvia
215 J3 **Enguri** *Rus.* Inguri. ≈ NW Georgia
Engyum *see* Gangi
75 D11 **Enid** Oklahoma, C USA 36°25′N 97°53′W
66 B8 **Enid Lake** ⊠ Mississippi, S USA
283 N10 **Enigu** *island* Ratak Chain, SE Marshall Islands
Enikale Strait *see* Kerch Strait
229 N4 **Enil'chek** Issyk-Kul'skaya Oblast', E Kyrgyzstan 42°04′N 79°01′E
186 G5 **Enipéfs** ≈ C Greece
252 E5 **Eniwa** Hokkaidō, NE Japan 42°53′N 141°14′E
252 E5 **Eniwa-dake** ⛰ Hokkaidō, NE Japan 42°48′N 141°15′E
Eniwetok *see* Enewetak Atoll
Enjiang *see* Yongfeng
Enkeldoorn *see* Chivhu
181 D13 **Enkenbach** Rheinland-Pfalz, Germany 49°29′E 7°53′N
193 L6 **Enken, Mys** *prev.* Mys Enkan. *headland* NE Russian Federation 58°29′N 141°27′E
Enken, Mys *see* Enken, Mys
162 F5 **Enkhuizen** Noord-Holland, NW Netherlands 52°34′N 05°03′E
181 C12 **Enkirch** Rheinland-Pfalz, Germany 49°59′E 7°07′N
177 I2 **Enknach** ≈ N Austria
154 I7 **Enköping** Uppsala, C Sweden 59°38′N 17°05′E
175 F12 **Enna** *var.* Castrogiovanni, Henna. Sicilia, Italy, C Mediterranean Sea 37°34′N 14°16′E
55 I5 **Ennadai Lake** ◎ Nunavut, C Canada
134 I2 **En Nahud** Western Kordofan, C Sudan 12°41′N 28°28′E
218 E5 **En Nâqoûra** *var.* An Nāqūrah. SW Lebanon 33°06′N 33°30′E
218 E5 **En Nâqoûra** Lebanon 33°07′N 35°08′E
En Nazira *see* Natzrat
128 F8 **Ennedi** *plateau* E Chad
158 C9 **Ennell, Lough** ◎ Ireland
181 D8 **Ennepetal** Nordrhein-Westfalen, W Germany 51°18′N 07°23′E
159 I7 **Ennerdale Water** ◎ United Kingdom
169 H1 **Ennezat** Auvergne, France 45°54′N 3°13′E
277 J3 **Enngonia** New South Wales, SE Australia 29°19′S 145°52′E
180 E7 **Enniger** Nordrhein-Westfalen, Germany 51°50′E 7°57′N
180 E7 **Ennigerloh** Nordrhein-Westfalen, Germany 51°50′E 8°01′N
157 B10 **Ennis** *Ir.* Inis. Clare, W Ireland 52°50′N 08°59′W
77 I6 **Ennis** Montana, NW USA 45°21′N 111°45′W
71 H5 **Ennis** Texas, SW USA 32°19′N 96°37′W
160 B3 **Enniscorthy** *Ir.* Inis Córthaidh. SE Ireland 52°30′N 06°34′W
160 B2 **Enniskerry** Wicklow, Ireland 53°12′N 6°10′W
158 C7 **Enniskillen** *var.* Inniskilling, *Ir.* Inis Ceithleann. SW Northern Ireland, United Kingdom 54°21′N 07°38′W
157 B10 **Ennistimon** *Ir.* Inis Díomáin. Clare, W Ireland 52°57′N 09°17′W
177 J2 **Enns** Oberösterreich, N Austria 48°13′N 14°28′E
177 J2 **Enns** ≈ C Austria
153 J8 **Eno** Itä-Suomi, SE Finland 62°45′N 30°15′E
70 D3 **Enochs** Texas, SW USA 33°51′N 102°46′W
153 I8 **Enonkoski** Itä-Suomi, E Finland 62°04′N 28°53′E
152 G4 **Enontekiö** *Lapp.* Eanodat. Lappi, N Finland 68°25′N 23°40′E
67 H7 **Enoree** South Carolina, SE USA 34°39′N 81°58′W
67 H7 **Enoree River** ≈ South Carolina, SE USA
63 H4 **Enosburg Falls** Vermont, NE USA 44°54′N 72°50′W
242 G10 **Enping** Guangdong, China 22°07′N 112°11′E
260 C5 **Enrekang** Sulawesi, C Indonesia 03°33′S 119°46′E
114 D7 **Enrique Carbo** Entre Ríos, E Argentina
91 H6 **Enriquillo** SW Dominican Republic 17°57′N 71°13′W
91 H6 **Enriquillo, Lago** ◎ SW Dominican Republic
162 G5 **Ens** Flevoland, N Netherlands 52°39′N 05°49′E
162 I6 **Enschede** Overijssel, E Netherlands 52°13′N 06°55′E
114 F10 **Ensenada** Buenos Aires, Argentina 34°53′S 57°53′W
84 B1 **Ensenada** Baja California Norte, NW Mexico 31°52′N 116°32′W
84 C2 **Ensenada Blanca** Baja California Norte Sur, Mexico
84 F8 **Ensenada Los Muertos** Baja California Sur, NW Mexico 24°00′N 109°50′W
181 C14 **Ensheim** ✈ (Saarbrücken) Saarland, W Germany 49°13′N 07°09′E
242 E3 **Enshi** Hubei, C China 30°16′N 109°26′E
251 J5 **Enshū-nada** *gulf* SW Japan
167 M7 **Ensisheim** Alsace, France 47°52′N 7°21′E
68 G4 **Ensley** Florida, SE USA 30°31′N 87°16′W
Enso *see* Svetogorsk
161 I5 **Enstone** United Kingdom 51°55′N 1°27′W
137 B8 **Entebbe** S Uganda 0°07′N 32°30′E
137 B8 **Entebbe** ✈ C Uganda 0°04′N 32°29′E
179 G10 **Entenbühl** ▲ Czech Republic/Germany 50°09′N 12°10′E
162 I6 **Enter** Overijssel, E Netherlands 52°19′N 06°34′E
69 I3 **Enterprise** Alabama, S USA 31°19′N 85°50′W
80 D2 **Enterprise** California, USA 38°32′N 120°51′W
76 F5 **Enterprise** Oregon, NW USA 45°25′N 117°18′W
78 G5 **Enterprise** Utah, W USA 37°33′N 113°42′W
76 D3 **Entiat** Washington, NW USA 47°39′N 120°15′W
173 J9 **Entinas, Punta de las** *headland* S Spain 36°40′N 02°44′W
176 D4 **Entlebuch** Luzern, W Switzerland 47°02′N 08°04′E
176 D4 **Entlebuch** *valley* C Switzerland
169 N4 **Entracque** Piemonte, NW Italy 44°14′N 07°23′E
117 D12 **Entrada, Punta** *headland* S Argentina
172 C7 **Entradas** Beja, Portugal 37°47′N 8°01′W
165 H7 **Entraygues-sur-Truyère** Aveyron, S France 44°39′N 02°36′E
281 H7 **Entrecasteaux, Récifs d'** *reef* N New Caledonia
111 J2 **Entre Félhas** Minas Gerais, Brazil 19°37′S 42°14′W
114 D4 **Entre Ríos** *off.* Provincia de Entre Ríos. ◈ *province* NE Argentina
88 G4 **Entre Ríos, Cordillera** ▲▲ Honduras/Nicaragua
Entre Ríos, Provincia de *see* Entre Ríos
169 M5 **Entrevaux** Provence-Alpes-Côte d'Azur, France 43°57′N 6°49′E
172 B4 **Entroncamento** Santarém, C Portugal 39°28′N 08°28′W
261 M5 **Entrop** Papua, E Indonesia 02°37′S 140°43′E
141 K6 **Entumeni** KwaZulu-Natal, South Africa 28°51′S 31°19′E
133 K8 **Enugu** Enugu, S Nigeria 06°24′N 07°24′E
133 K8 **Enugu** ◈ *state* SE Nigeria
82 E3 **Enurmino** Chukotskiy Avtonomnyy Okrug, Russian Federation 66°54′N 171°54′E
102 B5 **Envigado** Antioquia, W Colombia 06°09′N 75°38′W
106 B5 **Envira** Amazonas, W Brazil 07°12′S 69°59′W
Enyélé *see* Enyellé
134 E6 **Enyellé** *var.* Enyélé. Likouala, NE Congo 02°49′N 18°02′E
181 F14 **Enz** ≈ SW Germany
253 B13 **Enzan** *var.* Kōshū. Yamanashi, Honshū, S Japan 35°44′N 138°43′E
170 D1 **Eo** ≈ NW Spain
Eochaill *see* Youghal
Eochaille, Cuan *see* Youghal Bay
175 G11 **Eolie, Isole** *var.* Isole Lipari, *Eng.* Aeolian Islands, Lipari Islands. *island group* S Italy
282 E9 **Eot** *island* Chuuk, C Micronesia
186 G3 **Epanomí** Kentrikí Makedonía, N Greece 40°25′N 22°57′E
162 H6 **Epe** Gelderland, E Netherlands 52°21′N 05°59′E
133 I8 **Epe** Lagos, S Nigeria 06°37′N 04°01′E
134 D7 **Epéna** Likouala, NE Congo 01°28′N 17°29′E
Eperies/Eperjes *see* Prešov
165 I3 **Épernay** *anc.* Sparnacum. Marne, N France 49°02′N 03°58′E
166 G6 **Épernon** Centre, France 48°37′N 1°41′E
79 I3 **Ephraim** Utah, W USA 39°21′N 111°35′W
64 E7 **Ephrata** Pennsylvania, NE USA 40°09′N 76°08′W
76 D4 **Ephrata** Washington, NW USA 47°19′N 119°33′W
281 M3 **Epi** *var.* Épi. *island* C Vanuatu
Épi *see* Epi
171 I3 **Épila** Aragón, NE Spain 41°34′N 01°19′W
167 J9 **Épinac-les-Mines** Bourgogne, France 46°59′N 4°31′E
167 L6 **Épinal** Vosges, NE France 48°10′N 06°28′E
Epiphania *see* Ḩamāh
Epirus *see* Ípeiros
218 B2 **Episkopí** SW Cyprus 34°37′N 32°53′E
Episkopi Bay *see* Episkopí, Kólpos
218 B2 **Episkopí, Kólpos** *var.* Episkopi Bay. *bay* SE Cyprus
Epitoli *see* Tshwane
Epoon *see* Ebon Atoll
Eporedia *see* Ivrea
181 C13 **Eppelborn** Saarland, Germany 49°24′E 6°58′N

◆ Country
● Country Capital
◇ Dependent Territory
○ Dependent Territory Capital
◈ Administrative Regions
✈ International Airport
▲ Mountain
▲▲ Mountain Range
⛰ Volcano
≈ River
◎ Lake
⊠ Reservoir

◆ Country   ◇ Dependent Territory   ◆ Administrative Regions   ▲ Mountain   ℞ Volcano   ◎ Lake
● Country Capital   ○ Dependent Territory Capital   × International Airport   ▲ Mountain Range   ⚡ River   ◎ Reservoir

◆ Country   ◇ Dependent Territory   ◇ Administrative Regions   ▲ Mountain   🌋 Volcano   ◎ Lake
● Country Capital   ○ Dependent Territory Capital   ✈ International Airport   ▲ Mountain Range   ✍ River   🌊 Reservoir

Gamleby – Gerlachovský štít
INDEX
343

155 *H10* **Gamleby** Kalmar, S Sweden *57°54′N 16°25′E*
Gammelstad *see* Gammelstaden
152 *G6* **Gammelstaden** ***var.*** Gammelstad. Norrbotten, N Sweden *65°38′N 22°05′E*
Gammouda *see* Sidi Bouzid
140 *D7* **Gamoep** Northern Cape, South Africa *29°54′S 18°25′E*
235 *G10* **Gampola** Central Province, C Sri Lanka *07°10′N 80°34′E*
261 *H4* **Gam, Pulau** *island* E Indonesia
262 *D1* **Gâm, Sông** ≈ N Vietnam
159 *L10* **Gamston** United Kingdom *53°16′N 0°56′W*
152 *H3* **Gamvik** Finnmark, N Norway *71°04′N 28°08′E*
235 *B14* **Gan** Addu Atoll, C Maldives
Gan *see* Gansu, China
Gan *see* Jiangxi, China
Ganaane *see* Juba
79 *J7* **Ganado** Arizona, SW USA *35°42′N 109°31′W*
71 *H8* **Ganado** Texas, SW USA *29°02′N 96°30′W*
141 *J4* **Ga-Nala** ***prev.*** Kriel. Mpumalanga, South Africa *26°16′S 29°14′E* ***see also*** Kriel
62 *F4* **Gananoque** Ontario, SE Canada *44°21′N 76°11′W*
Ganāveh *see* Bandar-e Gonāveh
215 *L5* **Gäncä** ***Rus.*** Gyandzha; ***prev.*** Kirovabad, Yelisavetpol. W Azerbaijan *40°42′N 46°23′E*
Ganchi *see* Ghonchí
Gand *see* Gent
135 *C12* **Ganda** ***var.*** Mariano Machado, ***Port.*** Vila Mariano Machado. Benguela, W Angola *13°02′S 14°40′E*
135 *G10* **Gandajika** Kasai-Oriental, S Dem. Rep. Congo *06°42′S 24°01′E*
233 *H6* **Gandak** ***Nep.*** Nārāyāni. ≈ India/Nepal
59 *M6* **Gander** Newfoundland and Labrador, SE Canada *48°56′N 54°33′W*
59 *M6* **Gander** ✈ Newfoundland and Labrador, E Canada *49°03′N 54°49′W*
180 *F4* **Ganderkesee** Niedersachsen, NW Germany *53°01′N 08°33′E*
171 *J4* **Gandesa** Cataluña, NE Spain *41°03′N 00°26′E*
232 *B8* **Gāndhīdhām** Gujarāt, W India *23°08′N 70°05′E*
232 *C8* **Gāndhīnagar** *state capital* Gujarāt, W India *23°12′N 72°37′E*
232 *D7* **Gāndhi Sāgar** ◎ C India
171 *J6* **Gandia** ***prev.*** Gandía. País Valenciano, E Spain *38°59′N 00°11′W*
Gandía *see* Gandia
244 *A6* **Gando** Qinghai, C China *35°53′N 102°19′E*
239 *H6* **Gang** Qinghai, W China
232 *D4* **Gangānagar** Rājasthān, NW India *29°54′N 73°56′E*
232 *E6* **Gangāpur** Rājasthān, N India *26°30′N 76°49′E*
233 *J9* **Ganga Sāgar** West Bengal, NE India *21°39′N 88°05′E*
Gangavathi *see* Gangāwati
234 *E6* **Gangāwati** ***var.*** Gangavathi. Karnātaka, C India *15°26′N 76°35′E*
239 *J6* **Gangca** ***var.*** Shaliuhe. Qinghai, C China *37°21′N 100°09′E*
233 *H4* **Gangdisê Shan** ***Eng.*** Kailas Range. ▲▲ W China
165 *I8* **Ganges** Hérault, S France *43°57′N 03°42′E*
232 *G6* **Ganges** ***Ben.*** Padma. ≈ Bangladesh/India ***see also*** Padma
Ganges *see* Padma
Ganges Cone *see* Ganges Fan
288 *G6* **Ganges Fan** ***var.*** Ganges Cone. *undersea feature* N Bay of Bengal *12°00′N 87°00′E*
233 *K9* **Ganges, Mouths of the** *delta* Bangladesh/India
175 *F12* **Gangi** ***anc.*** Engyum. Sicilia, Italy, C Mediterranean Sea *37°48′N 14°13′E*
64 *C3* **Gang Mills** New York, NE USA *42°08′N 77°06′W*
248 *C5* **Gangneung** ***Jap.*** Kōryō; ***prev.*** Kangnŭng. NE South Korea *37°47′N 128°51′E*
232 *F4* **Gangotri** Uttarakhand, N India *30°56′N 79°02′E*
244 *B6* **Gangouyi** Gansu, China *35°35′N 105°01′E*
Gangra *see* Çankırı
243 *M9* **Gangshan** C Taiwan *22°47′N 120°16′E*
233 *J6* **Gangtok** *state capital* Sikkim, N India *27°20′N 88°39′E*
244 *C7* **Gangu** ***var.*** Daxiangshan. Gansu, C China *34°38′N 105°18′E*
250 *B1* **Gangwon-do** ***prev.*** Kangwŏn-do. ◈
247 *K3* **Gan He** ≈ NE China
260 *G4* **Gani** Pulau Halmahera, E Indonesia *0°45′S 128°13′E*
243 *I6* **Gan Jiang** ≈ S China
248 *B1* **Ganjig** ***var.*** Horqin Zuoyi Houqi. Nei Mongol Zizhiqu, N China *42°53′N 122°22′E*
190 *J2* **Gan'kovo** Leningradskaya Oblast', Russian Federation
228 *E8* **Gannaly** Ahal Welaýaty, S Turkmenistan *37°02′N 60°43′E*
247 *K4* **Gannan** Heilongjiang, NE China *47°58′N 123°36′E*
165 *I6* **Gannat** Allier, C France *46°06′N 03°12′E*
77 *J7* **Gannett Peak** ▲ Wyoming, C USA *43°10′N 109°39′W*
74 *D5* **Gannvalley** South Dakota, N USA *44°01′N 98°59′W*
239 *H6* **Ganq** Qinghai Sheng, China *37°23′N 92°23′E*
Ganqu *see* Lhünzhub
177 *L2* **Gänserndorf** Niederösterreich, NE Austria *48°21′N 16°43′E*
Gansos, Lago dos *see* Goose Lake
244 *A4* **Gansu** ***var.*** Gan, Gansu Sheng, Kansu. ◈ *province* N China
Gansu Sheng *see* Gansu
132 *D7* **Ganta** ***var.*** Gahnpa. NE Liberia *07°15′N 08°59′W*
244 *B5* **Gantang** Ningxia, China *37°17′N 104°20′E*
276 *G6* **Gantheaume, Cape** *headland* South Australia *36°04′S 137°28′E*
Gantsevichi *see* Hantsavichy
243 *I7* **Ganxian** Jiangxi, China *25°31′N 115°01′E*
219 *D8* **Gan Yavné** Israel *31°47′N 34°43′E*
140 *G4* **Ganyesa** North-West, South Africa *26°36′S 24°11′E*
245 *L7* **Ganyu** ***var.*** Qingkou. Jiangsu, E China *34°52′N 119°11′E*
226 *B5* **Ganyushkino** Atyrau, SW Kazakhstan *46°38′N 49°12′E*
243 *I7* **Ganzhou** Jiangxi, S China *25°51′N 114°59′E*
Ganzhou *see* Zhangye
133 *H3* **Gao** Gao, E Mali *16°16′N 00°03′E*
133 *I3* **Gao** ◈ *region* SE Mali
243 *I4* **Gao'an** Jiangxi, S China *28°24′N 115°27′E*
245 *I3* **Gaobeidian** Hebei, China *39°12′N 115°31′E*
245 *I4* **Gaocheng** Hebei, China *38°01′N 114°30′E*
Gaocheng *see* Litang
245 *L8* **Gaogou** Jiangsu, E China *34°01′N 119°11′E*
Gaohe *see* Huaining
Gaohebu *see* Huaining
244 *B6* **Gaolan** Gansu, China *36°12′N 103°35′E*
Gaoleshan *see* Xianfeng
245 *L6* **Gaomi** Shandong, C China *36°23′N 119°45′E*
245 *H6* **Gaoping** Shanxi, C China *35°51′N 112°55′E*
243 *K6* **Gaoqiao** Fujian, SE China *26°34′N 117°47′E*
239 *J5* **Gaotai** Gansu, N China *39°22′N 99°44′E*
245 *J5* **Gaotang** Shandong, E China *36°52′N 116°14′E*
Gaoth Dobhair *see* Gweedore
132 *G6* **Gaoua** SW Burkina *10°18′N 03°12′W*
132 *C5* **Gaoual** N Guinea *11°44′N 13°14′W*
242 *A4* **Gaoxian** Sichuan, China *28°.2′N 104°33′E*
Gaoxiong *see* Kaohsiung
242 *G9* **Gaoyao** Guangdong, China *23°02′N 112°26′E*
241 *J3* **Gaoyou** ***var.*** Dayishan. Jiangsu, E China *32°48′N 119°26′E*
241 *I3* **Gaoyou Hu** ◎ E China
242 *F10* **Gaozhou** Guangdong, S China *21°56′N 110°49′E*
165 *K7* **Gap** ***anc.*** Vapincum. Hautes-Alpes, SE France *44°33′N 06°05′E*
228 *C5* **Gaplaňgyr Platosy** ***Rus.*** Plato Kaplangky. *ridge* Turkmenistan/Uzbekistan
238 **Gar** ***var.*** Shiquanhe. Xizang Zizhiqu, W China *32°31′N 80°04′E*
Gar *see* Gar Xincun
Garabekevyul *see* Garabekewül
228 *G7* **Garabekewül** ***Rus.*** Garabekevyul, Karabekaul. Lebap Welaýaty, E Turkmenistan *38°31′N 64°04′E*
228 *G9* **Garabil Belentligi** ***Rus.*** Vozvyshennost' Karabil'. ▲▲ S Turkmenistan
228 *A4* **Garabogaz** ***Rus.*** Bekdash. Balkan Welaýaty, NW Turkmenistan *41°33′N 52°33′E*
228 *B5* **Garabogaz Aylagy** ***Rus.*** Zaliv Kara-Bogaz-Gol. *bay* NW Turkmenistan
228 *A5* **Garabogazköl** ***Rus.*** Kara-Bogaz-Gol. Balkan Welaýaty, NW Turkmenistan *41°03′N 52°52′E*
89 *L9* **Garachiné** Darién, SE Panama *08°03′N 78°22′W*
89 *L9* **Garachiné, Punta** *headland* SE Panama *08°05′N 78°23′W*
228 *C7* **Garagan** ***Rus.*** Karagan. Ahal Welaýaty, C Turkmenistan *38°16′N 57°34′E*
102 *C5* **Garagoa** Boyacá, C Colombia *05°05′N 73°20′W*
228 *A6* **Garagöl'** ***Rus.*** Karagel'. Balkan Welaýaty, W Turkmenistan *39°24′N 53°13′E*
228 *D7* **Garagum** ***var.*** Garagumy, Qara Qum, ***Eng.*** Black Sand Desert, Kara Kum; ***prev.*** Peski Karakumy. *desert* C Turkmenistan
228 *C7* **Garagum Kanaly** ***var.*** Kara Kum Canal, ***Rus.*** Karagumskiy Kanal, Karakumskiy Kanal. *canal* C Turkmenistan
Garagumy *see* Garagum
277 *L3* **Garah** New South Wales, SE Australia *29°07′S 149°37′E*
170 *A10* **Garajonay** ▲ Gomera, Islas Canarias, NE Atlantic Ocean *28°07′N 17°14′W*
185 *L5* **Gara Khitrino** Shumen, NE Bulgaria *43°26′N 26°55′E*
132 *E6* **Garalo** Sikasso, SW Mali *10°58′N 07°26′W*
158 *B8* **Gara, Lough** ◎ Ireland
Garam *see* Hron, Slovakia
228 *G8* **Garamätnyýaz** ***Rus.*** Karamet-Niyaz. Lebap Welaýaty, E Turkmenistan *37°45′N 64°28′E*
Garamszentkereszt *see* Žiar nad Hronom
133 *H5* **Garango** S Burkina *11°45′N 00°30′W*
108 *I6* **Garanhuns** Pernambuco, E Brazil *08°53′S 36°28′W*
141 *I3* **Ga-Rankuwa** North West, South Africa *25°37′S 27°59′E*
283 *H1* **Garapan** Saipan, S Northern Mariana Islands *15°12′S 145°43′E*
Gárasavvon *see* Karesuando
Gárassavon *see* Kaaresuvanto
134 *F4* **Garba** Bamingui-Bangoran, N Central African Republic *09°09′N 20°24′E*
Garba *see* Jiulong
136 *F6* **Garbahaarrey** ***It.*** Garba Harre. Gedo, SW Somalia *03°14′N 42°18′E*
Garba Harre *see* Garbahaarrey
136 *E7* **Garba Tula** Eastern, C Kenya *0°31′N 38°35′E*
75 *E11* **Garber** Oklahoma, C USA *36°26′N 97°35′W*
78 *A2* **Garberville** California, W USA *40°07′N 123°48′W*
Garbo *see* Lhozhag
161 *L4* **Garboldisham** United Kingdom *52°23′N 0°57′E*
180 *G6* **Garbsen** Niedersachsen, N Germany *52°25′N 09°36′E*
113 *K3* **Garça** São Paulo, S Brazil *22°14′S 49°36′W*
85 *J10* **García de la Cadena** Zacatecas, Mexico
170 *F6* **García de Solá, Embalse de** ⊠ C Spain
165 *I8* **Gard** ◈ *department* S France
165 *I8* **Gard** ≈ S France
174 *D4* **Garda, Lago di** ***var.*** Benaco, ***Eng.*** Lake Garda, ***Ger.*** Gardasee. ◎ NE Italy
Garda, Lake *see* Garda, Lago di
Gardan Divāl *see* Gardan Dīwāl
230 *G3* **Gardan Dīwāl** ***var.*** Gardan Divāl. Vardak, C Afghanistan *34°30′N 68°15′E*
165 *J8* **Gardanne** Bouches-du-Rhône, SE France *43°27′N 05°28′E*
Gardasee *see* Garda, Lago di
180 *J5* **Gardelegen** Sachsen-Anhalt, C Germany *52°31′N 11°25′E*
62 *A1* **Garden** ≈ Ontario, S Canada
69 *M2* **Garden City** Georgia, SE USA *32°06′N 81°09′W*
75 *B10* **Garden City** Kansas, C USA *37°57′N 100°54′W*
75 *G10* **Garden City** Missouri, C USA *38°34′N 94°12′W*
70 *E5* **Garden City** Texas, SW USA *31°51′N 101°30′W*
66 *D8* **Gardendale** Alabama, S USA *33°39′N 86°48′W*
81 *D11* **Garden Grove** California, USA *33°46′N 117°56′W*
72 *F5* **Garden Island** *island* Michigan, N USA
68 *F5* **Garden Island Bay** *bay* Louisiana, S USA
72 *F5* **Garden Peninsula** *peninsula* Michigan, N USA
Garden State, The *see* New Jersey
154 *E7* **Gardermoen** Akershus, S Norway *60°10′N 11°04′E*
154 *E7* **Gardermoen** ✈ (Oslo) Akershus, S Norway *60°12′N 11°05′E*
Gardeyz/Gardez *see* Gardīz
154 *G1* **Gardiken** ◎ N Sweden
63 *K4* **Gardiner** Maine, NE USA *44°13′N 69°46′W*
77 *I6* **Gardiner** Montana, NW USA *45°02′N 110°42′W*
65 *K5* **Gardiners Island** *island* New York, NE USA
231 *H4* **Gardīz** ***var.*** Gardeyz, Gardez, Gordiaz. Paktīā, E Afghanistan *33°35′N 69°14′E*
65 *K2* **Gardner** Massachusetts, USA *42°35′N 72°00′W*
54 *B7* **Gardner Canal** *Sea waterway* British Columbia, SW Canada
Gardner Island *see* Nikumaroro
63 *L3* **Gardner Lake** ◎ Maine, NE USA
80 *F2* **Gardnerville** Nevada, W USA *38°55′N 119°44′W*
Gardo *see* Qardho
176 *F6* **Gardone Val Trompia** Lombardia, N Italy *45°40′N 10°11′E*
Garegegasnjárga *see* Karigasniemi
168 *D4* **Garein** Aquitaine, France *44°03′N 0°39′W*
158 *F3* **Garelochhead** United Kingdom *56°05′N 4°51′W*
82 *C10* **Gareloi Island** *island* Aleutian Islands, Alaska, USA
Gares *see* Puente la Reina
176 *D8* **Garessio** Piemonte, NE Italy *44°14′N 08°01′E*
76 *F4* **Garfield** Washington, NW USA *47°00′N 117°07′W*
73 *I9* **Garfield Heights** Ohio, N USA *41°25′N 81°36′W*
159 *K9* **Garforth** United Kingdom *53°47′N 1°23′W*
Gargaliani *see* Gargaliánoi
186 *F7* **Gargaliánoi** ***var.*** Gargaliani. Pelopónnisos, S Greece *37°04′N 21°38′E*
175 *H8* **Gargàno, Promontorio del** *headland* SE Italy *41°51′N 16°11′E*
176 *F4* **Gargellen** Graubünden, W Switzerland *46°57′N 09°55′E*
166 *G10* **Gargilesse-Dampierre** Centre, France *46°31′N 1°36′E*
154 *I1* **Gargnäs** Västerbotten, N Sweden *65°19′N 18°00′E*
190 *B7* **Gargždai** Klaipėda, W Lithuania *55°42′N 21°24′E*
234 *F4* **Garhchiroli** Mahārāshtra, C India *20°14′N 79°58′E*
233 *H8* **Garhwa** Jhārkhand, N India *24°07′N 83°52′E*
195 *M8* **Gari** Sverdlovskaya Oblasť, Russian Federation
261 *J6* **Gariau** Papua, E Indonesia *03°43′S 134°54′E*
141 *H7* **Gariep Dam** Free State, South Africa *30°35′S 25°30′E*
140 *D7* **Garies** Northern Cape, W South Africa *30°30′S 18°00′E*
175 *F9* **Garigliano** ≈ C Italy
114 *E9* **Garín** Buenos Aires, Argentina *34°25′S 58°46′W*
137 *E8* **Garissa** Coast, E Kenya *0°27′S 39°39′E*
67 *K7* **Garland** North Carolina, SE USA *34°45′N 78°25′W*
71 *H4* **Garland** Texas, SW USA *32°50′N 96°37′W*
79 *H1* **Garland** Utah, W USA *41°43′N 112°07′W*
176 *E7* **Garlasco** Lombardia, N Italy *45°12′N 08°59′E*
191 *D8* **Garliava** Kaunas, S Lithuania *54°49′N 23°52′E*
158 *G6* **Garlieston** United Kingdom *54°47′N 4°22′W*
Garm *see* Gharm
222 *E6* **Garm, Āb-e** ***var.*** Rūd-e Khersān. ≈ SW Iran
179 *F14* **Garmisch-Partenkirchen** Bayern, S Germany *47°30′N 11°05′E*
222 *F4* **Garmsār** ***prev.*** Qishlaq. Semnān, N Iran *35°18′N 52°22′E*
Garmser *see* Darvīshān
74 *G6* **Garner** Iowa, C USA *43°06′N 93°36′W*
67 *K6* **Garner** North Carolina, SE USA *35°42′N 78°36′W*
75 *F10* **Garnett** Kansas, C USA *38°16′N 95°15′W*
163 *H13* **Garnich** Luxembourg, SW Luxembourg *49°37′N 05°57′E*
277 *I5* **Garnpung, Lake** *salt lake* New South Wales, SE Australia
Garoe *see* Garoowe
Garoet *see* Garut
233 *K7* **Gāro Hills** *hill range* NE India
165 *H8* **Garonne** ***anc.*** Garumna. ≈ S France
136 *I4* **Garoowe** ***var.*** Garoe. Nugaal, N Somalia *08°24′N 48°29′E*
134 *C4* **Garoua** ***var.*** Garua. Nord, N Cameroon *09°17′N 13°22′E*
134 *C5* **Garoua Boulaï** Est, E Cameroon *05°54′N 14°33′E*
132 *G3* **Garou, Lac** ◎ C Mali
155 *G8* **Garphyttan** Örebro, C Sweden *59°18′N 14°54′E*
74 *F6* **Garretson** South Dakota, N USA *43°43′N 96°30′W*
73 *F9* **Garrett** Indiana, N USA *41°21′N 85°08′W*
158 *B7* **Garrison** United Kingdom *54°25′N 8°05′W*
77 *H5* **Garrison** Montana, NW USA *46°32′N 112°46′W*
74 *C2* **Garrison** North Dakota, N USA *47°36′N 101°25′W*
71 *I5* **Garrison** Texas, SW USA *31°49′N 94°29′W*
74 *B2* **Garrison Dam** *dam* North Dakota, N USA
158 *E5* **Garron Point** *headland* United Kingdom *55°03′N 5°55′W*
170 *E5* **Garrovillas** Extremadura, W Spain *39°43′N 06°33′W*
173 *J8* **Garrucha** Andalucía, Spain *37°11′N 1°49′W*
159 *H1* **Garry** ≈ C Scotland, United Kingdom
Garrygala *see* Magtymguly
55 *I2* **Garry Lake** ◎ Nunavut, N Canada
Gars *see* Gars am Kamp
177 *K1* **Gars am Kamp** ***var.*** Gars. Niederösterreich, NE Austria *48°35′N 15°40′E*
180 *H5* **Garssen** Niedersachsen, Germany *52°40′E 10°08′N*
137 *F9* **Garsen** Coast, S Kenya *02°16′S 40°07′E*
Garshy *see* Garşy
62 *C2* **Garson** Ontario, S Canada *46°33′N 80°51′W*
159 *I8* **Garstang** United Kingdom *53°54′N 2°46′W*
177 *J2* **Garsten** Oberösterreich, N Austria *48°00′N 14°24′E*
228 *A5* **Garşy** ***var.*** Garshy, ***Rus.*** Karshi. Balkan Welaýaty, NW Turkmenistan *40°45′N 52°50′E*
Gartar *see* Qianning
165 *H6* **Gartempe** ≈ C France
160 *F4* **Garth** United Kingdom *52°08′N 3°31′W*
Gartog *see* Markam
159 *L8* **Garton on the Wolds** United Kingdom *54°01′N 0°30′W*
Garua *see* Garoua
140 *B4* **Garub** Karas, SW Namibia *26°33′S 16°00′E*
Garumna *see* Garonne
258 *G8* **Garut** ***prev.*** Garoet. Jawa, C Indonesia *07°15′S 107°55′E*
158 *D6* **Garvagh** United Kingdom *54°59′N 6°40′W*
159 *I3* **Garvald** United Kingdom *55°55′N 2°39′W*
158 *E3* **Garvard** W Scotland, United Kingdom
158 *E2* **Garvellachs** *island group* W Scotland, United Kingdom
278 *C12* **Garvie Mountains** ▲▲ South Island, New Zealand
182 *H6* **Garwolin** Mazowieckie, E Poland *51°54′N 21°36′E*
71 *H7* **Garwood** Texas, SW USA *29°25′N 96°26′W*
238 *D8* **Gar Xincun** ***prev.*** Gar. Xizang Zizhiqu, W China *32°04′N 80°01′E*
73 *E9* **Gary** Indiana, N USA *41°36′N 87°21′W*
71 *J5* **Gary** Texas, SW USA *32°00′N 94°21′W*
250 *E5* **Garyū-san** ▲ Kyūshū, SW Japan *34°40′N 132°12′E*
238 *D8* **Gar Zangbo** ≈ W China
85 *M7* **Garza Valdés** Tamaulipas, Mexico *24°31′N 99°23′W*
240 *C3* **Garzê** Sichuan, C China *31°40′N 99°58′E*
102 *B7* **Garzón** Huila, S Colombia *02°14′N 75°37′W*
Gasan-Kuli *see* Esenguly
73 *F10* **Gas City** Indiana, N USA *40°29′N 85°36′W*
164 *F8* **Gascogne** ***Eng.*** Gascony. *cultural region* S France
75 *I10* **Gasconade River** ≈ Missouri, C USA
Gascony *see* Gascogne
274 *D5* **Gascoyne Junction** Western Australia *25°06′S 115°10′E*
289 *I9* **Gascoyne Plain** *undersea feature* E Indian Ocean
274 *C5* **Gascoyne River** ≈ Western Australia
286 *E8* **Gascoyne Tablemount** *undersea feature* N Tasman Sea *36°30′S 156°30′E*
121 *L4* **Gash** ***var.*** Nahr al Qāsh. ≈ W Sudan
231 *K2* **Gasherbrum** ▲ NE Pakistan *35°39′N 76°34′E*
Gas Hu *see* Gas Hure Hu
133 *L5* **Gashua** Yobe, NE Nigeria *12°55′N 11°10′E*
238 *G6* **Gas Hure Hu** ***var.*** Gas Hu. ◎ C China
261 *I4* **Gasim** Papua, E Indonesia *01°21′S 131°27′E*
Gásluokta *see* Kjøpsvik
255 *N9* **Gasmata** New Britain, E Papua New Guinea *06°12′S 150°25′E*
69 *L8* **Gasparilla Island** *island* Florida, SE USA
258 *G6* **Gaspar, Selat** *strait* W Indonesia
59 *J7* **Gaspé** Québec, SE Canada *48°50′N 64°33′W*
59 *J7* **Gaspé, Péninsule de** ***var.*** Péninsule de la Gaspésie. *peninsula* Québec, SE Canada
Gaspésie, Péninsule de la *see* Gaspé, Péninsule de
253 *C10* **Gas-san** ▲ Honshū, C Japan *38°33′N 140°02′E*
133 *L7* **Gassol** Taraba, E Nigeria *08°28′N 10°24′E*
Gastein *see* Badgastein
67 *I7* **Gastonia** North Carolina, SE USA *35°14′N 81°12′W*
67 *L5* **Gaston, Lake** ⊠ North Carolina/Virginia, SE USA
186 *F6* **Gastoúni** Dytikí Elláda, S Greece *37°51′N 21°15′E*
117 *C8* **Gastre** Chubut, S Argentina *42°20′S 69°10′W*
Gat *see* Ghāt
173 *J9* **Gata, Cabo de** *cape* S Spain
Gata, Cape *see* Gátas, Akrotíri
171 *J6* **Gata de Gorgos** País Valenciano, E Spain *38°45′N 00°06′E*
188 *A8* **Gătaia** ***Ger.*** Gataja, ***Hung.*** Gátalja; ***prev.*** Gáttája. Timiş, W Romania *45°24′N 21°26′E*
Gataja/Gátalja *see* Gătaia
218 *B3* **Gátas, Akrotíri** ***var.*** Cape Gata. *headland* S Cyprus *34°34′N 33°03′E*
170 *D5* **Gata, Sierra de** ▲▲ W Spain
172 *E3* **Gata, Sierra de** ▲▲ Spain
194 *D8* **Gatchina** Leningradskaya Oblast', NW Russian Federation *59°34′N 30°06′E*
67 *H5* **Gate City** Virginia, NE USA *36°38′N 82°37′W*
158 *G6* **Gatehouse of Fleet** SW Scotland, United Kingdom *54°54′N 04°12′W*
65 *I1* **Gates** New York, USA *43°05′N 73°38′W*
159 *K6* **Gateshead** NE England, United Kingdom *54°57′N 01°37′W*
52 *G7* **Gateshead Island** *island* Nunavut, N Canada
67 *L5* **Gatesville** North Carolina, SE USA *36°24′N 76°46′W*
70 *G5* **Gatesville** Texas, SW USA *31°26′N 97°46′W*
62 *F3* **Gatineau** Québec, SE Canada *45°29′N 75°40′W*
62 *F2* **Gatineau** ≈ Ontario/Québec, SE Canada
66 *G6* **Gatlinburg** Tennessee, S USA *35°42′N 83°30′W*
Gatooma *see* Kadoma
Gáttája *see* Gătaia
89 *K9* **Gatún, Lago** ⊠ C Panama
108 *F5* **Gaturiano** Piauí, NE Brazil *06°53′S 41°45′W*
157 *I12* **Gatwick** ✈ (London) SE England, United Kingdom *51°10′N 00°12′W*
280 *F9* **Gau** ***prev.*** Ngau. *island* C Fiji
281 *M2* **Gaua** ***var.*** Santa Maria. *Island* Banks Island, N Vanuatu
170 *E9* **Gaucín** Andalucía, S Spain *36°31′N 05°19′W*
Gauhāti *see* Guwāhāti
190 *E5* **Gauja** ***Ger.*** Aa. ≈ Estonia/Latvia
190 *F5* **Gaujiena** Alūksne, NE Latvia *57°31′N 26°24′E*
67 *I3* **Gauley River** ≈ West Virginia, NE USA
Gaul/Gaule *see* France
181 *E12* **Gau-Odernheim** Rheinland-Pfalz, Germany *49°47′E 8°12′N*
163 *C11* **Gaurain-Ramecroix** Hainaut, SW Belgium *50°35′N 03°31′E*
154 *C7* **Gaustatoppen** ▲ S Norway *59°50′N 08°39′E*
138 *G6* **Gauteng** ***off.*** Gauteng Province; ***prev.*** Pretoria-Witwatersrand-Vereeniging. ◈ *province* NE South Africa
Gauteng *see* Germiston, South Africa
Gauteng *see* Johannesburg, South Africa
Gauteng Province *see* Gauteng
261 *L5* **Gauttier, Pegunungan** ▲▲ Papua, E Indonesia
110 *A6* **Gavão Peixoto** São Paulo, Brazil *21°50′S 48°30′W*
215 *K5* **Gavarr** ***prev.*** Kamo. C Armenia *40°21′N 45°07′E*
222 *G8* **Gāvbandī** Hormozgān, S Iran *27°07′N 53°21′E*
187 *H10* **Gavdopoúla** *island* SE Greece
187 *H10* **Gávdos** *island* SE Greece
168 *D6* **Gave d'Oleron** SW France
164 *F8* **Gave d'Oloron** ≈ SW France
163 *C10* **Gavere** Oost-Vlaanderen, NW Belgium *50°56′N 03°41′E*
172 *B4* **Gaviao** Santarém, Portugal *39°16′N 8°18′W*
81 *B8* **Gaviota** California, USA *34°28′N 120°13′W*
154 *I6* **Gävle** ***var.*** Gäfle; ***prev.*** Gefle. Gävleborg, C Sweden *60°41′N 17°09′E*
154 *H5* **Gävleborg** ***var.*** Gäfleborg, Gefleborg. ◈ *county* C Sweden
154 *I6* **Gävlebukten** *bay* C Sweden
166 *C5* **Gavray** Basse-Normandie, France *48°55′N 1°21′W*
194 *G10* **Gavrilov-Yam** Yaroslavskaya Oblast', W Russian Federation *57°19′N 39°52′E*
190 *G5* **Gavry** Pskovskaya Oblast', Russian Federation
187 *M8* **Gâvurağılı** Muğla, Turkey *36°20′N 29°12′E*
276 *G5* **Gawler** South Australia *34°38′S 138°44′E*
276 *F4* **Gawler Ranges** *hill range* South Australia
Gawso *see* Goaso
239 *J4* **Gaxun Nur** ◎ N China
233 *I7* **Gaya** Bihār, N India *24°48′N 85°E*
133 *I5* **Gaya** Dosso, SW Niger *11°52′N 03°28′E*
Gaya *see* Kyjov
72 *G6* **Gaylord** Michigan, N USA *45°01′N 84°40′W*
74 *G5* **Gaylord** Minnesota, N USA *44°33′N 94°13′W*
277 *M1* **Gayndah** Queensland, E Australia *25°37′S 151°31′E*
195 *K8* **Gayny** Permskaya Kray, NW Russian Federation *60°19′N 54°15′E*
Gaysin *see* Haysyn
Gayvorno *see* Hayvoron
219 *C9* **Gaza** ***Ar.*** Ghazzah, ***Heb.*** 'Azza. NE Gaza Strip *31°30′N 34°E*
139 *I5* **Gaza** ***off.*** Província de Gaza. ◈ *province* SW Mozambique
Gaz-Achak *see* Gazojak
229 *I5* **G'azalkent** ***Rus.*** Gazalkent. Toshkent Viloyati, E Uzbekistan *41°30′N 69°46′E*
Gazalkent *see* G'azalkent
Gazandzhyk/Gazanjyk *see* Bereket
133 *K5* **Gazaoua** Maradi, S Niger *13°28′N 07°54′E*
Gaza, Província de *see* Gaza
219 *C9* **Gaza Strip** ***Ar.*** Qita Ghazzah. *disputed region* SW Asia
280 *B8* **Gazelle, Récif de la** *reef* C New Caledonia
214 *G8* **Gaziantep** ***var.*** Gazi Antep; ***prev.*** Aintab, Antep. Gaziantep, S Turkey *37°04′N 37°21′E*
214 *G7* **Gaziantep** ***var.*** Gazi Antep. ◈ *province* S Turkey
Gazi Antep *see* Gaziantep
218 *D2* **Gazimağusa** ***var.*** Famagusta, ***Gk.*** Ammóchostos. E Cyprus *35°07′N 33°57′E*
218 *D2* **Gazimağusa Körfezi** ***var.*** Famagusta Bay, ***Gk.*** Kólpos Ammóchostos. *bay* E Cyprus
228 *F6* **Gazli** Buxoro Viloyati, C Uzbekistan *40°09′N 63°28′E*
228 *E5* **Gazojak** ***Rus.*** Gaz-Achak. Lebap Welaýaty, NE Turkmenistan *41°12′N 61°24′E*
134 *F6* **Gbadolite** Equateur, NW Dem. Rep. Congo *04°14′N 20°59′E*
132 *D7* **Gbanga** ***var.*** Gbarnga. N Liberia *07°02′N 09°30′W*
Gbarnga *see* Gbanga
133 *I6* **Gbéroubouè** ***var.*** Béroubouay. N Benin *10°35′N 02°47′E*
133 *K7* **Gboko** Benue, S Nigeria *07°21′N 08°57′E*
Gcuwa *see* Butterworth
182 *F3* **Gdańsk** ***Fr.*** Dantzig, ***Ger.*** Danzig. Pomorskie, N Poland *54°22′N 18°35′E*
Gdan'skaya Bukhta/Gdańsk, Gulf of *see* Danzig, Gulf of
Gdańska, Zakota *see* Danzig, Gulf of
Gdingen *see* Gdynia
194 *C8* **Gdov** Pskovskaya Oblast', W Russian Federation *58°43′N 27°51′E*
182 *F3* **Gdynia** ***Ger.*** Gdingen. Pomorskie, N Poland *54°31′N 18°30′E*
75 *D12* **Geary** Oklahoma, C USA *35°37′N 98°19′W*
140 *G6* **Geaspan** Northern Cape, South Africa *29°19′S 24°26′E*
168 *D5* **Geaune** Aquitaine, France *43°39′N 0°23′W*
Geavvú *see* Kevo
132 *B5* **Gêba, Rio** ≈ C Guinea-Bissau
219 *A11* **Gebel Maghâra** ▲ Egypt
219 *A12* **Gebel Yi'allaq** ▲ Egypt
261 *H4* **Gebe, Pulau** *island* E Indonesia
181 *D10* **Gebhardshain** Rheinland-Pfalz, Germany *50°45′E 7°49′N*
214 *C4* **Gebze** Kocaeli, NW Turkey *40°48′N 29°26′E*
218 *C2* **Geçitkale** ***var.*** Lefkonico, ***Gk.*** Lefkónikon. NE Cyprus *35°16′N 33°44′E*
136 *C2* **Gedaref** ***var.*** Al Qaḑārif, El Gedaref. Gedaref, E Sudan *14°03′N 35°24′E*
136 *C2* **Gedaref** ◈ *state* E Sudan
219 *D8* **Gedera** Israel *31°49′N 34°46′E*
181 *G11* **Gedern** Hessen, Germany *50°26′E 9°12′N*
134 *H2* **Gedid Ras el Fil** Southern Darfur, W Sudan *12°45′N 25°45′E*
163 *F12* **Gedinne** Namur, SE Belgium *49°57′N 04°55′E*
214 *C6* **Gediz** Kütahya, W Turkey *39°04′N 29°25′E*
214 *C6* **Gediz Nehri** ≈ W Turkey
136 *H5* **Gedlegubē** Sumalē, E Ethiopia *06°53′N 45°08′E*
161 *K2* **Gedney Drove End** E England, United Kingdom *52°51′N 00°06′E*
136 *F7* **Gedo** ***off.*** Gobolka Gedo. ◈ *region* SW Somalia
Gedo, Gobolka *see* Gedo
155 *E13* **Gedser** Storstrøm, SE Denmark *54°34′N 11°57′E*
163 *F9* **Geel** ***var.*** Gheel. Antwerpen, N Belgium *51°10′N 04°59′E*
277 *I7* **Geelong** Victoria, SE Australia *38°10′S 144°21′E*
Ge'e'mu *see* Golmud
163 *F8* **Geertruidenberg** Noord-Brabant, S Netherlands *51°43′N 04°52′E*
180 *D5* **Geeste** Niedersachsen, Germany *52°36′E 7°16′N*
180 *F3* **Geeste** ≈ NW Germany
180 *I3* **Geesthacht** Schleswig-Holstein, N Germany *53°25′N 10°22′E*
158 *B8* **Geevagh** Sligo, Ireland *54°06′N 8°15′W*
277 *J10* **Geeveston** Tasmania, SE Australia *43°12′S 146°54′E*
Gefle *see* Gävle
Gefleborg *see* Gävleborg
238 *D8* **Gê'gyai** Xizang Zizhiqu, W China *32°29′N 81°04′E*
180 *D4* **Gehlenberg** Niedersachsen, Germany *52°59′E 7°45′N*
180 *G6* **Gehrden** Niedersachsen, Germany *52°19′E 9°36′N*
133 *M5* **Geidam** Yobe, NE Nigeria *12°52′N 11°55′E*
57 *M1* **Geikie** ≈ Saskatchewan, C Canada
181 *A9* **Geilenkirchen** Nordrhein-Westfalen, Germany *50°58′E 6°07′N*
154 *C7* **Geilo** Buskerud, S Norway *60°32′N 08°13′E*
181 *E13* **Geinsheim** Rheinland-Pfalz, Germany *49°18′E 8°15′N*
154 *C5* **Geiranger** Møre og Romsdal, S Norway *62°07′N 07°12′E*
181 *H10* **Geisa** Thüringen, Germany *50°43′E 9°58′N*
179 *E12* **Geislingen** ***var.*** Geislingen an der Steige. Baden-Württemberg, SW Germany *48°37′N 09°50′E*
Geislingen an der Steige *see* Geislingen
64 *A7* **Geistown** Pennsylvania, USA *40°17′N 78°52′W*
137 *B9* **Geita** Mwanza, NW Tanzania *02°52′S 32°12′E*
154 *D7* **Geithus** Buskerud, S Norway *59°56′N 09°58′E*
240 *C7* **Gejiu** ***var.*** Kochiu. Yunnan, S China *23°22′N 103°07′E*
Gëkdepe *see* Gökdepe
228 *C5* **Geklengkui, Solonchak** ***var.*** Solonchak Goklenkuy. *salt marsh* NW Turkmenistan
136 *A5* **Gel** ≈ C South Sudan
175 *F13* **Gela** ***prev.*** Terranova di Sicilia. Sicilia, Italy, C Mediterranean Sea *37°05′N 14°15′E*
136 *H5* **Geladī** SE Ethiopia *06°58′N 46°24′E*
259 *H6* **Gelam, Pulau** ***var.*** Pulau Galam. *island* N Indonesia
Gelaozu Miaozu Zhizhixian *see* Wuchuan
162 *H7* **Gelderland** ***prev. Eng.*** Guelders. ◈ *province* E Netherlands
162 *F7* **Geldermalsen** Gelderland, C Netherlands *51°53′N 05°17′E*
181 *B8* **Geldern** Nordrhein-Westfalen, W Germany *51°31′N 06°19′E*
163 *G8* **Geldrop** Noord-Brabant, SE Netherlands *51°25′N 05°34′E*
163 *G10* **Geleen** Limburg, SE Netherlands *50°57′N 05°49′E*
196 *F8* **Gelendzhik** Krasnodarskiy Kray, SW Russian Federation *44°34′N 38°06′E*
Gelib *see* Jilib
214 *B5* **Gelibolu** ***Eng.*** Gallipoli. Çanakkale, NW Turkey *40°25′N 26°41′E*
187 *K3* **Gelibolu Yarımadası** ***Eng.*** Gallipoli Peninsula. *peninsula* NW Turkey
260 *D8* **Geliting, Teluk** *bay* Nusa Tenggara, S Indonesia
160 *F6* **Gelligaer** United Kingdom *51°40′N 3°15′W*
136 *H5* **Gellinsor** Mudug, C Somalia *06°25′N 46°44′E*
181 *G11* **Gelnhausen** Hessen, C Germany *50°12′N 09°12′E*
181 *C8* **Gelsenkirchen** Nordrhein-Westfalen, W Germany *51°30′N 07°05′E*
159 *H6* **Gelston** United Kingdom *54°54′N 3°54′W*
140 *B3* **Geluk** Hardap, SW Namibia *24°35′S 15°48′E*
140 *E5* **Geluksspruit** Northern Cape, South Africa *28°06′S 20°57′E*
141 *K5* **Gelukstadt** KwaZulu-Natal, South Africa *27°58′S 31°02′E*
163 *E11* **Gembloux** Namur, Belgium *50°34′N 04°42′E*
167 *K8* **Gemeaux** Bourgogne, France *47°29′N 5°08′E*
134 *E6* **Gemena** Equateur, NW Dem. Rep. Congo *03°13′N 19°49′E*
169 *K6* **Gémenos** Provence-Alpes-Côte d'Azur, France *43°18′N 5°38′E*
181 *E14* **Gemersheim** Rheinland-Pfalz, Germany *49°13′E 8°22′N*
163 *G8* **Gemert** Noord-Brabant, SE Netherlands *51°33′N 05°41′E*
214 *C5* **Gemlik** Bursa, NW Turkey *40°26′N 29°10′E*
Gem of the Mountains *see* Idaho
177 *I5* **Gemona del Friuli** Friuli-Venezia Giulia, NE Italy *46°18′N 13°12′E*
168 *D2* **Gémozac** Poitou-Charentes, France *45°34′N 0°40′W*
140 *E3* **Gemsbok National Park** *national park* S Botswana
140 *G4* **Gemsbokvlakte** North-West, South Africa *25°54′S 24°30′E*
Gem State *see* Idaho
181 *H12* **Gemünden** Bayern, Germany *50°03′E 9°42′N*
181 *F9* **Gemünden** Hessen, Germany *50°58′E 8°58′N*
181 *D12* **Gemünden** Rheinland-Pfalz, Germany *49°54′E 7°28′N*
Genalē Wenz *see* Juba
258 *I4* **Genali, Danau** ◎ Borneo, N Indonesia
163 *E11* **Genappe** Walloon Brabant, C Belgium *50°39′N 04°27′E*
215 *I6* **Genç** Bingöl, E Turkey *38°44′N 40°35′E*
166 *E10* **Gençay** Poitou-Charentes, France *46°23′N 0°24′E*
Genck *see* Genk
162 *H5* **Genemuiden** Overijssel, E Netherlands *52°38′N 06°03′E*
116 *E5* **General Acha** La Pampa, C Argentina *37°25′S 64°38′W*
114 *E6* **General Almada** Entre Ríos, Argentina *32°50′S 58°48′W*
116 *G5* **General Alvear** Buenos Aires, E Argentina *36°03′S 60°01′W*
118 *G5* **General Alvear** Mendoza, W Argentina *34°59′S 67°40′W*
114 *A9* **General Arenales** Buenos Aires, E Argentina *34°21′S 61°20′W*
85 *I7* **General Arnulfo R. Gómez** Durango, Mexico *24°43′N 104°53′W*
116 *H5* **General Belgrano** Buenos Aires, E Argentina *35°47′S 58°30′W*
292 *E2* **General Bernardo O'Higgins** *Chilean research station* Antarctica *63°09′S 57°13′W*
85 *M6* **General Bravo** Nuevo León, NE Mexico *25°47′N 99°04′W*
115 *N1* **General Câmara** Rio Grande do Sul, Brazil *29°54′S 51°46′W*
114 *E4* **General Campos** Entre Rios, Argentina *31°30′S 58°24′W*
112 *F6* **General Capdevila** Chaco, N Argentina *27°25′S 61°30′W*
General Carrera, Lago *see* Buenos Aires, Lago
85 *K7* **General Cepeda** Coahuila, NE Mexico *25°18′N 101°24′W*
116 *E7* **General Conesa** Río Negro, E Argentina *40°06′S 64°26′W*
115 *K7* **General Enrique Martínez** Treinta y Tres, E Uruguay *33°13′S 53°47′W*
85 *I7* **General Escobedo** Durango, Mexico *25°30′N 105°15′W*
112 *E2* **General Eugenio A. Garay** ***var.*** Fortín General Eugenio Garay; ***prev.*** Yrendagüé. Nueva Asunción, NW Paraguay *20°30′S 61°56′W*
114 *D6* **General Galarza** Entre Ríos, E Argentina *32°43′S 59°24′W*
114 *B8* **General Gelly** Santa Fe, Argentina *33°36′S 60°36′W*
116 *H5* **General Guido** Buenos Aires, E Argentina *36°36′S 57°45′W*
General José F.Uriburu *see* Zárate
116 *H5* **General Juan Madariaga** Buenos Aires, E Argentina *37°00′S 57°09′W*
86 *E8* **General Juan N Alvarez** ✈ (Acapulco) Guerrero, S Mexico *16°47′N 99°47′W*
114 *B7* **General Lagos** Santa Fe, Argentina *33°06′S 60°34′W*
116 *G5* **General La Madrid** Buenos Aires, E Argentina *37°17′S 61°20′W*
114 *D10* **General Las Heras** Buenos Aires, Argentina *34°54′S 58°54′W*
116 *H5* **General Lavalle** Buenos Aires, E Argentina *36°25′S 56°56′W*
118 *C10* **General López** Araucanía, Chile *38°41′S 72°22′W*
General Machado *see* Camacupa
116 *D1* **General Manuel Belgrano, Cerro** ▲ W Argentina *29°05′S 67°05′W*
85 *L6* **General Mariano Escobero** ✈ (Monterrey) Nuevo León, NE Mexico *25°47′N 100°00′W*
116 *G4* **General O'Brien** Buenos Aires, Argentina *35°00′S 61°00′W*
114 *B10* **General O'Brien** Buenos Aires, E Argentina *34°54′S 60°45′W*
85 *K9* **General Pánfilo Natera** Zacatecas, Mexico *22°40′N 102°07′W*
116 *F4* **General Pico** La Pampa, C Argentina *35°43′S 63°45′W*
112 *F6* **General Pinedo** Chaco, N Argentina *27°17′S 61°20′W*
114 *A10* **General Pinto** Buenos Aires, E Argentina *34°45′S 61°50′W*
116 *H5* **General Pirán** Buenos Aires, E Argentina *37°16′S 57°46′W*
114 *C5* **General Ramirez** Entre Rios, Argentina *32°12′S 60°18′W*
89 *H9* **General, Río** ≈ S Costa Rica
116 *D6* **General Roca** Río Negro, C Argentina *39°00′S 67°35′W*
114 *D9* **General Rodríguez** Buenos Aires, Argentina *34°37′S 58°57′W*
114 *C7* **General Rojo** Buenos Aires, Argentina *33°28′S 60°17′W*
263 *M9* **General Santos** ***off.*** General Santos City. Mindanao, S Philippines *06°10′N 125°10′E*
General Santos City *see* General Santos
85 *M6* **General Terán** Nuevo León, NE Mexico *25°18′N 99°40′W*
185 *M5* **General Toshevo** ***Rom.*** I.G.Duca; ***prev.*** Casim, Kasimköj. Dobrich, NE Bulgaria *43°43′N 28°04′E*
114 *B10* **General Viamonte** Buenos Aires, E Argentina *35°01′S 61°00′W*
116 *F4* **General Villegas** Buenos Aires, E Argentina *35°02′S 63°01′W*
Gênes *see* Genova
64 *B2* **Genesee River** ≈ New York/Pennsylvania, NE USA
73 *B9* **Geneseo** Illinois, N USA *41°27′N 90°08′W*
64 *C1* **Geneseo** New York, NE USA *42°48′N 77°46′W*
106 *D7* **Geneshuaya, Río** ≈ N Bolivia
69 *I3* **Geneva** Alabama, S USA *31°01′N 85°51′W*
73 *D9* **Geneva** Illinois, N USA *41°53′N 88°18′W*
75 *E8* **Geneva** Nebraska, C USA *40°31′N 97°36′W*
64 *D1* **Geneva** New York, NE USA *42°52′N 76°58′W*
73 *J9* **Geneva** Ohio, NE USA *41°48′N 80°53′W*
Geneva *see* Genève
176 *B5* **Geneva, Lake** ***Fr.*** Lac de Genève, Lac Léman, le Léman, ***Ger.*** Genfer See. ◎ France/Switzerland
176 *B5* **Genève** ***Eng.*** Geneva, ***Ger.*** Genf, ***It.*** Ginevra. Genève, SW Switzerland *46°13′N 06°09′E*
176 *B5* **Genève** ***Eng.*** Geneva, ***Ger.*** Genf, ***It.*** Ginevra. ◈ *canton* SW Switzerland
174 *A3* **Genève** ***var.*** Geneva. ✈ Vaud, SW Switzerland *46°13′N 06°06′E*
Genève, Lac de *see* Geneva, Lake
Genf *see* Genève
Genfer See *see* Geneva, Lake
193 *J8* **Genhe** ***prev.*** Ergun Zuoqi. Nei Mongol Zizhiqu, N China *50°48′N 121°30′E*
247 *J3* **Gen He** ≈ NE China
Genichesk *see* Heniches'k
172 *F7* **Genil** ≈ S Spain
163 *G10* **Genk** ***var.*** Genck. Limburg, NE Belgium *50°58′N 05°30′E*
250 *C6* **Genkai-nada** *gulf* Kyūshū, SW Japan
167 *K8* **Genlis** Bourgogne, France *47°14′N 5°13′E*
175 *B10* **Gennargentu, Monti del** ▲▲ Sardegna, Italy, C Mediterranean Sea
163 *H8* **Gennep** Limburg, SE Netherlands *51°43′N 05°58′E*
166 *E8* **Gennes** Pays de la Loire, France *47°20′N 0°14′W*
73 *D8* **Genoa** Illinois, N USA *42°06′N 88°41′W*
74 *E7* **Genoa** Nebraska, C USA *41°27′N 97°43′W*
Genoa *see* Genova
Genoa, Gulf of *see* Genova, Golfo di
169 *N3* **Genola** Piemonte, NW Italy *44°35′N 07°39′E*
176 *E8* **Genova** ***Eng.*** Genoa; ***anc.*** Genua, ***Fr.*** Gênes. Liguria, NW Italy *44°28′N 09°E*
174 *C6* **Genova, Golfo di** ***Eng.*** Gulf of Genoa. *gulf* NW Italy
105 *B9* **Genovesa, Isla** ***var.*** Tower Island. *island* Galapagos Islands, Ecuador, E Pacific Ocean
Genshū *see* Wonju
181 *E12* **Gensingen** Rheinland-Pfalz, Germany *49°54′E 7°56′N*
163 *C9* **Gent** ***Eng.*** Ghent, ***Fr.*** Gand. Oost-Vlaanderen, NW Belgium *51°02′N 03°42′E*
258 *G8* **Genteng** Jawa, C Indonesia *07°21′S 106°20′E*
178 *G7* **Genthin** Sachsen-Anhalt, E Germany *52°24′N 12°10′E*
75 *G11* **Gentry** Arkansas, C USA *36°16′N 94°28′W*
Genua *see* Genova
175 *E8* **Genzano di Roma** Lazio, C Italy *41°42′N 12°42′E*
248 *B7* **Geogeum-do** ***prev.*** Kōgŭm-do. *island* S South Korea
248 *C7* **Geogeum-do** ***Jap.*** Kyōsai-tō; ***prev.*** Kōje-do. *island* S South Korea
250 *B4* **Geoje** ***prev.*** Kōje. *34°53′N 128°37′E*
Geokchay *see* Göyçay
Geok-Tepe *see* Gökdepe
192 *F1* **Georga, Zemlya** ***Eng.*** George Land. *island* Zemlya Frantsa-Iosifa, N Russian Federation
138 *E10* **George** Western Cape, S South Africa *33°57′S 22°28′E*
59 *I3* **George** ≈ Newfoundland and Labrador/Québec, E Canada
160 *E7* **Georgeham** United Kingdom *51°08′N 4°12′W*
117 *H11* **George Island** *island* S Falkland Islands
277 *K6* **George, Lake** ◎ New South Wales, SE Australia
137 *A8* **George, Lake** ◎ SW Uganda
69 *L5* **George, Lake** ◎ Florida, SE USA
63 *H5* **George, Lake** ⊠ New York, NE USA
George Land *see* Georga, Zemlya
Georgenburg *see* Jurbarkas
George River *see* Kangiqsualujjuaq
290 *C4* **Georges Bank** *undersea feature* W Atlantic Ocean *41°15′N 67°30′W*
278 *A11* **George Sound** *sound* South Island, New Zealand
132 *C9* **Georgetown** ○ (Ascension Island) NW Ascension Island *17°56′S 14°25′W*
275 *J3* **Georgetown** Queensland, NE Australia *18°17′S 143°37′E*
277 *J9* **George Town** Tasmania, SE Australia *41°04′S 146°48′E*
61 *M10* **George Town** Great Exuma Island, C Bahamas *23°28′N 75°47′W*
90 *C5* **George Town** ***var.*** Georgetown. ○ (Cayman Islands) Grand Cayman, SW Cayman Islands *19°16′N 81°23′W*
132 *B4* **Georgetown** E Gambia *13°33′N 14°49′W*
103 *K4* **Georgetown** ● (Guyana) N Guyana *06°46′N 58°10′W*
258 *D2* **George Town** ***var.*** Penang, Pinang. Pinang, Peninsular Malaysia *05°28′N 100°20′E*
91 *M3* **Georgetown** Saint Vincent, Saint Vincent and the Grenadines *13°19′N 61°09′W*
80 *E2* **Georgetown** California, USA *38°54′N 120°50′W*
64 *F10* **Georgetown** Delaware, NE USA *38°39′N 75°22′W*
69 *I2* **Georgetown** Georgia, SE USA *31°52′N 85°04′W*
66 *F3* **Georgetown** Kentucky, S USA *38°13′N 84°30′W*
67 *K9* **Georgetown** South Carolina, SE USA *33°23′N 79°18′W*
70 *G6* **Georgetown** Texas, SW USA *30°39′N 97°42′W*
103 *K4* **Georgetown** ✈ N Guyana *06°46′N 58°10′W*
Georgetown *see* George Town
293 *J9* **George V Coast** *physical region* Antarctica
292 *F4* **George VI Ice Shelf** *ice shelf* Antarctica
292 *F4* **George VI Sound** *sound* Antarctica
293 *J8* **George V Land** *physical region* Antarctica
70 *G8* **George West** Texas, SW USA *28°21′N 98°08′W*
215 *J3* **Georgia** ***off.*** Republic of Georgia, ***Geor.*** Sak'art'velo, ***Rus.*** Gruzinskaya SSR, Gruziya. ◆ *republic* SW Asia
69 *K1* **Georgia** ***off.*** State of Georgia, ***also known as*** Empire State of the South, Peach State. ◈ *state* SE USA
62 *C3* **Georgian Bay** *lake bay* Ontario, S Canada
Georgia, Republic of *see* Georgia
56 *C8* **Georgia, Strait of** *strait* British Columbia, W Canada
Georgi Dimitrov *see* Kostenets
Georgi Dimitrov, Yazovir *see* Koprinka, Yazovir
Georgiu-Dezh *see* Liski
227 *L4* **Georgiyevka** Vostochnyy Kazakhstan, E Kazakhstan *49°19′N 81°35′E*
Georgiyevka *see* Korday
197 *H8* **Georgiyevsk** Stavropol'skiy Kray, SW Russian Federation *44°07′N 43°22′E*
180 *D3* **Georgsheil** Niedersachsen, Germany *53°28′E 7°19′N*
180 *E6* **Georgsmarienhütte** Niedersachsen, NW Germany *52°13′N 08°02′E*
293 *H1* **Georg von Neumayer** *German research station* Antarctica *70°41′S 08°18′W*
179 *G9* **Gera** Thüringen, E Germany *50°51′N 12°13′E*
181 *J10* **Gera** ≈ C Germany
163 *D10* **Geraardsbergen** Oost-Vlaanderen, SW Belgium *50°47′N 03°53′E*
181 *H14* **Gerabronn** Baden-Württemberg, Germany *49°15′E 9°55′N*
186 *G7* **Geráki** Pelopónnisos, S Greece *36°56′N 22°46′E*
75 *I10* **Gerald** Missouri, C USA *38°24′N 91°20′W*
95 *L5* **Geral de Goiás, Serra** ▲▲ E Brazil
278 *D10* **Geraldine** Canterbury, South Island, New Zealand *44°06′S 171°14′E*
274 *D6* **Geraldton** Western Australia *28°48′S 114°40′E*
58 *D6* **Geraldton** Ontario, S Canada *49°44′N 86°59′W*
113 *J5* **Geral, Serra** ▲▲ S Brazil
260 *C8* **Gerampi** Sumbawa, S Indonesia *08°47′S 118°51′E*
165 *K4* **Gérardmer** Vosges, NE France *48°05′N 06°54′E*
Gerasa *see* Jarash
Gerdauen *see* Zheleznodorozhnyy
83 *I6* **Gerdine, Mount** ▲ Alaska, USA *61°40′N 152°21′W*
214 *D5* **Gerede** Bolu, N Turkey *40°48′N 32°13′E*
214 *E5* **Gerede Çayı** ≈ N Turkey
230 *E5* **Gereshk** Helmand, SW Afghanistan *31°50′N 64°32′E*
179 *G13* **Geretsried** Bayern, S Germany *47°51′N 11°28′E*
171 *H8* **Gérgal** Andalucía, S Spain *37°07′N 02°34′W*
74 *A7* **Gering** Nebraska, C USA *41°49′N 103°39′W*
78 *D2* **Gerlach** Nevada, W USA *40°38′N 119°21′W*
Gerlachfalvi Csúcs/Gerlachovka *see* Gerlachovský štít
183 *G9* **Gerlachovský štít** ***var.*** Gerlachovka, ***Ger.*** Gerlsdorfer Spitze, ***Hung.*** Gerlachfalvi Csúcs; ***prev.*** Stalinov Štít, ***Ger.*** Franz-Josef Spitze, ***Hung.*** Ferencz-Jósef Csúcs. ▲ N Slovakia *49°12′N 20°09′E*

◆ Country
● Country Capital
◇ Dependent Territory
○ Dependent Territory Capital
◈ Administrative Regions
✈ International Airport
▲ Mountain
▲▲ Mountain Range
Ѫ Volcano
≈ River
◎ Lake
⊠ Reservoir

167 N8 **Gerlafingen** Solothurn, NW Switzerland 47°10′N 07°35′E
Gerlsdorfer Spitze see Gerlachovský štít
217 K2 **Germak** As Sulaymānīyah, E Iraq 35°49′N 46°09′E
German East Africa see Tanzania
Germanicopolis see Çankırı
Germanicum, Mare/German Ocean see North Sea
Germanovichi see Hyermanavichy
German Southwest Africa see Namibia
66 B7 **Germantown** Tennessee, S USA 35°06′N 89°51′W
181 I8 **Germany** off. Federal Republic of Germany, Bundesrepublik Deutschland, *Ger.* Deutschland. ◆ federal republic N Europe
Germany, Federal Republic of see Germany
179 F13 **Germering** Bayern, SE Germany 48°07′N 11°22′E
138 G6 **Germiston** *var.* Gauteng. Gauteng, NE South Africa 26°15′S 28°10′E
Gernika see Gernika-Lumo
171 H1 **Gernika-Lumo** *var.* Guernica, Guernica, Guernica y Lumo. País Vasco, N Spain 43°19′N 02°40′W
251 J3 **Gero** Gifu, Honshū, SW Japan 35°48′N 137°15′E
186 G8 **Geroliménas** Pelopónnisos, S Greece 36°28′N 22°25′E
Gerona see Girona
163 E11 **Gerpinnes** Hainaut, S Belgium 50°20′N 04°38′E
Gers ◆ *department* S France
154 G8 **Gers** ◆ *department* S France
181 G4 **Gersheim** Saarland, W Germany 49°09′E 7°12′N
180 D5 **Gersten** Niedersachsen, Germany 52°33′E 7°31′N
181 H9 **Gerstungen** Thüringen, Germany 50°58′E 10°04′N
Gerunda see Girona
169 H1 **Gerzat** Auvergne, France 45°50′N 3°09′E
238 E7 **Gêrzê** *var.* Luring. Xizang Zizhiqu, W China 32°19′N 84°05′E
214 F4 **Gerze** Sinop, N Turkey 41°48′N 35°13′E
180 F7 **Gescher** Nordrhein-Westfalen, Germany 51°39′E 8°31′N
218 F6 **Gesher** Israel 32°37′N 35°33′E
Gesher HaZiv see Gesher HaZiv
218 E5 **Gesher HaZiv** *var.* Gesher HaZiv. Northern, N Israel 33°02′N 9°08′E
Gesoriacum see Boulogne-sur-Mer
114 A5 **Gessler** Santa Fe, Argentina 31°53′S 61°08′W
169 N4 **Gesso** ✕ W Italy
Gessoriacum see Boulogne-sur-Mer
163 F11 **Gesves** Namur, SE Belgium 50°24′N 05°04′E
154 J7 **Geta** Åland, SW Finland 60°22′N 19°49′E
153 G8 **Getafe** Madrid, C Spain 40°18′N 03°44′W
155 F11 **Getinge** Halland, S Sweden 56°66′N 12°42′E
64 C8 **Gettysburg** Pennsylvania, NE USA 39°49′N 77°13′W
74 C4 **Gettysburg** South Dakota, N USA 45°00′N 99°57′W
292 F7 **Getz Ice Shelf** *ice shelf* Antarctica
250 A4 **Geumo-do** *prev.* Kŭmo-do.
250 B4 **Geunpo** *prev.* Kŭnp'o. South Korea 34°43′N 128°35′E
218 D6 **Geva Karmel** Israel 32°39′N 34°57′E
215 J7 **Gevaş** Van, SE Turkey 38°16′N 43°05′E
218 E6 **Gevat** Israel 32°40′N 35°12′E
181 D8 **Gevelsberg** Nordrhein-Westfalen, Germany 51°19′E 7°20′N
Gevgeli see Gevgelija
185 M8 **Gevgelija** *var.* Đevđelija, Djevdjelija, *Turk.* Gevgeli. SE Macedonia 41°09′N 22°30′E
167 K9 **Gevrey** Franche-Comté, France 47°02′N 5°27′E
165 K5 **Gex** Ain, E France 46°21′N 06°02′E
141 H4 **Geysdorp** North-West, South Africa 26°32′S 25°18′E
80 B1 **Geyserville** California, USA 38°42′N 122°54′W
152 B3 **Geysir** *physical region* SW Iceland
214 C2 **Geyve** Sakarya, NW Turkey 40°30′N 30°18′E
136 C2 **Gezira** ◆ *state* E Sudan
140 G3 **Ghaap Plateau** *Afr.* Ghaapplato. *plateau* C South Africa
Ghaapplato see Ghaap Plateau
Ghaba see Al Ghābah
219 H4 **Ghabiya, Wādi el** Egypt
216 D5 **Ghāb, Tall al** SE Syria 35°09′N 37°48′E
217 H6 **Ghadaf, Wādi al** *dry watercourse* C Iraq
219 D7 **Ghadaf, Wādi al** *dry watercourse* Jordan
128 D3 **Ghadāmis** *var.* Ghadamès, Rhadames. W Libya 30°08′N 09°30′E
221 K6 **Ghadan** E Oman 20°20′N 57°58′E
128 C4 **Ghadūwah** C Libya 26°36′N 14°26′E
216 E4 **Ghafurov** *Rus.* Gafurov; *prev.* Sovetabad. NW Tajikistan 40°13′N 69°43′E
233 H6 **Ghāghara** ✑ S Asia
239 G10 **Ghaibi Dero** Sind, SE Pakistan 27°35′N 67°42′E
221 L5 **Ghalat** E Oman 21°06′N 58°51′E
132 C7 **Ghamūkah, Hawr** ◎ S Iraq
132 D4 **Ghana** off. Republic of Ghana. ◆ *republic* W Africa
221 K6 **Ghanah** *springwell* S Oman 18°53′N 56°34′E
Ghanongga see Ranongga
138 C5 **Ghanzi** *var.* Khanzi. Ghanzi, W Botswana 21°39′S 21°38′E
138 E5 **Ghanzi** *var.* Ghansi, Ghansiland, Khanzi. ◆ *district* C Botswana
121 K8 **Ghanzi** *var.* Kanzi. ✕ Botswana/South Africa
Ghap'an see Kapan
219 H4 **Gharandal** Al Aqabah, SW Jordan 30°12′N 35°18′E
217 K9 **Gharbiyah, Shaʿib al** ◎ Iraq
Gharbt, Jabal al see Liban, Jebel
131 J3 **Ghardaïa** N Algeria 32°30′N 03°44′E
175 A13 **Ghardimaou** Tunisia
218 G5 **Ghārīyat ash Sharqīyah** Syria 32°40′N 36°16′E
229 J7 **Gharm** *Rus.* Garm. C Tajikistan 39°03′N 70°25′E
230 G10 **Gharo** Sind, SE Pakistan 24°44′N 67°35′E
217 L7 **Gharrāf, Shaṭṭ al** ✑ S Iraq
Gharvān see Gharyān
128 C2 **Gharyān** *var.* Gharvān. NW Libya 32°10′N 13°01′E
128 A5 **Ghāt** *var.* Gat. SW Libya 24°58′N 10°11′E
Ghawdex see Gozo
221 I4 **Ghayathi** Abū Ẓaby, W United Arab Emirates 23°51′N 53°01′E
Ghazal, Baḥr al see Ghazal, Bahr
133 A4 **Ghazal, Bahr al** *var.* Soro. *seasonal river* C Chad
136 A3 **Ghazal, Baḥr el** *var.* Ghazal, Bahr al Ghazāl. ◆ N South Sudan
229 I7 **Ghazalkent** Toshkent Viloyati, E Uzbekistan 41°30′N 69°46′E
130 G2 **Ghazaouet** NW Algeria 35°08′N 01°50′W
232 E3 **Ghāziābād** Uttar Pradesh, N India 28°42′N 77°28′E
233 F7 **Ghāzīpur** Uttar Pradesh, N India 25°36′N 83°36′E
230 F4 **Ghazni** *var.* Ghazni, Ghazni. E Afghanistan 33°31′N 68°24′E
230 G4 **Ghazni** ◆ *province* SE Afghanistan
Ghazzah see Gaza
218 F4 **Ghazzé** Lebanon 33°40′N 35°49′E
Gheel see Geel
219 A13 **Gheita, Wādi** Egypt
Ghelizâne see Relizane
Ghent see Gent
Gheorghe Brațul see Sfântu Gheorghe, Brațul
Gheorghe Gheorghiu-Dej see Onești
188 D7 **Gheorgheni** *prev.* Gheorghieni, Sîn-Miclăuș, *Ger.* Niklasmarkt, *Hung.* Gyergyószentmiklós. Harghita, C Romania 46°43′N 25°36′E
Gheorghieni see Gheorgheni
188 D7 **Gherla** *Ger.* Neuschliss, *Hung.* Szamosújvár; *prev.* Armenierstadt. Cluj, NW Romania 47°02′N 23°55′E
Ghevault see Ghuwayfāt
228 G8 **Ghijduwon** Buxoro Viloyati, C Uzbekistan 40°06′N 64°39′E
Ghilan see Gīlān
175 B10 **Ghilarza** Sardegna, Italy, C Mediterranean Sea 40°09′N 08°50′E
Ghilizane see Relizane
Ghirīş *prev.* Câmpia Turzii
175 G8 **Ghisonaccia** Corse, France, C Mediterranean Sea 42°00′N 09°25′E
Ghizo see Gizo
159 H1 **Ghlo, Beinn a'** ▲ United Kingdom 56°50′N 3°43′W
229 J6 **Ghonchi** *Rus.* Ganchi. NW Tajikistan 39°57′N 69°10′E
Ghor see Ghowr
67 K2 **Ghoraghat** Rajshahi, NW Bangladesh 25°18′N 89°20′E
231 H7 **Ghotki** Sind, SE Pakistan 28°00′N 69°21′E
230 E7 **Ghowr** *var.* Ghor. ◆ *province* C Afghanistan
171 J10 **Ghriss** Algeria
229 J7 **Ghūdara** *var.* Gudara, *Rus.* Kudara. SE Tajikistan 38°28′N 72°39′E
233 J7 **Ghugri** ✑ N India
Ghund *Rus.* Gunt. ✑ SE Tajikistan
Ghurābīyah, Shaʿib al see Gharbīyah, Shaʿib al
Ghurdaqah see Hurghada
230 D3 **Ghūriān** Herāt, W Afghanistan 34°20′N 61°26′E
221 I4 **Ghuwayfāt** *var.* Ghuwaifat. Abū Ẓaby, W United Arab Emirates 24°06′N 51°49′E
140 G9 **Ghwarriespoort** *pas* Eastern Cape, South Africa 33°00′N 22°05′E
257 J9 **Gia Nghia** *var.* Đắc Nông. Đắc Lắc, S Vietnam 11°59′N 107°42′E
186 G3 **Giannitsá** *var.* Yiannitsá. Kentrikí Makedonía, N Greece 40°49′N 22°24′E
175 **Giannutri, Isola di** *island* Archipelago Toscano, C Italy
158 D1 **Giant's Causeway** *Ir.* Clochán an Aifir. *lava flow* N Ireland, United Kingdom
257 H10 **Giá Rai** Minh Hai, S Vietnam 09°15′N 105°28′E

175 G12 **Giarre** Sicilia, Italy, C Mediterranean Sea 37°44′N 15°12′E
169 H1 **Giat** Auvergne, France 45°48′N 2°29′E
169 M3 **Giaveno** Piemonte, NW Italy 45°02′N 07°21′E
90 F4 **Gibara** Holguín, E Cuba 21°09′N 76°11′W
95 D8 **Gibbon** Nebraska, C USA 40°45′N 98°50′W
78 F3 **Gibbon** Oregon, NW USA 45°40′N 118°22′W
67 H5 **Gibbsboro** New Jersey, USA 39°50′N 74°58′W
67 M10 **Gibbs Hill** *hill* S Bermuda
140 C3 **Gibeon** Hardap, Namibia 25°08′S 17°46′E
152 F4 **Gibostad** Troms, N Norway 69°21′N 18°01′E
170 D8 **Gibraleón** Andalucía, S Spain 37°23′N 06°58′W
170 E9 **Gibraltar** ○ (Gibraltar) S Gibraltar 36°08′N 05°21′W
130 G2 **Gibraltar** ◇ *UK dependent territory* SW Europe
170 E9 **Gibraltar, Détroit de/Gibraltar, Estrecho de** see Gibraltar, Strait of
170 E9 **Gibraltar, Strait of** *Fr.* Détroit de Gibraltar, *Sp.* Estrecho de Gibraltar. *strait* Atlantic Ocean/ Mediterranean Sea
73 H9 **Gibsonburg** Ohio, N USA 41°22′N 83°19′W
73 D10 **Gibson City** Illinois, N USA 40°27′N 88°22′W
274 F4 **Gibson Desert** *desert* Western Australia
56 D8 **Gibsons** British Columbia, SW Canada 49°24′N 123°32′W
230 F7 **Gidār** Baluchistān, SW Pakistan 28°16′N 66°00′E
234 F6 **Giddalūr** Andhra Pradesh, E India 15°24′N 78°54′E
71 H7 **Giddings** Texas, SW USA 30°12′N 96°59′W
80 E3 **Gideon** Missouri, C USA 36°27′N 89°55′W
219 A13 **Gidi, Wādi Abu** Egypt
136 D3 **Gidolē** Southern Nationalities, S Ethiopia 05°31′N 37°26′E
218 E6 **Gidona** Israel 32°32′N 35°21′E
H13 **Giebelstadt** Bayern, Germany 49°39′E 9°57′N
Giebnegáisi see Kebnekaise
181 I8 **Giebolshausen** Niedersachsen, Germany 51°37′E 10°13′N
191 E8 **Giedraičiai** Utena, E Lithuania 55°05′N 25°16′E
165 H4 **Gien** Loiret, C France 47°40′N 02°37′E
169 L6 **Giens** Provence-Alpes-Côte d'Azur, France 43°02′N 6°08′E
140 G7 **Giesenskraal** Northern Cape, South Africa 30°32′S 23°18′E
181 F10 **Giessen** Hessen, W Germany 50°35′N 08°41′E
181 J10 **Giessübel** Thüringen, Germany 50°32′E 10°55′N
162 I4 **Gieten** Drenthe, NE Netherlands 53°00′N 06°43′E
158 G3 **Giffnock** United Kingdom 55°48′N 4°17′W
69 V7 **Gifford** Florida, SE USA 27°40′N 80°40′W
57 H3 **Gifford** Baffin Island, Nunavut, NE Canada
181 I5 **Gifhorn** Niedersachsen, Germany 52°28′N 10°33′E
57 H8 **Gift Lake** Alberta, W Canada 55°49′N 115°57′W
251 J3 **Gifu** *var.* Gifu-ken, *var.* Gihu. ◆ *prefecture* Honshū, SW Japan
251 J3 **Gifu** Gifu, Honshū, SW Japan 35°24′N 136°46′E
Gifu-ken see Gifu
196 G7 **Gigant** Rostovskaya Oblast', SW Russian Federation 46°29′N 41°18′E
102 B3 **Gigante, Sierra de la** ▲ NW Mexico
105 B5 **Gigante** Huila, S Colombia 02°24′N 75°34′W
Gigiga see Jijiga
159 I8 **Giggleswick** United Kingdom 54°03′N 2°16′W
158 G4 **Gigha Island** *island* SW Scotland, United Kingdom
158 A4 **Gigha, Sound of** *strait* W Scotland, United Kingdom
175 D8 **Giglio, Isola del** *island* Archipelago Toscano, C Italy
Gihu see Gifu
250 B4 **Gijang** *prev.* Kijang. 35°14′N 129°12′E
228 G4 **G'ijduvon** *Rus.* Gizhduvon. Buxoro Viloyati, C Uzbekistan 40°06′N 64°38′E
170 G1 **Gijón** Asturias, NW Spain 43°32′N 05°40′W
139 A7 **Gikongoro** SW Rwanda 02°30′S 29°32′E
79 H9 **Gila Bend** Arizona, SW USA 32°57′N 112°43′W
79 H9 **Gila Bend Mountains** ▲ Arizona, USA
79 G8 **Gila Mountains** ▲ Arizona, SW USA
222 E2 **Gīlān** *var.* Gilān, *var.* Ghilan, Guilan. ◆ *province* NW Iran
79 K9 **Gila River** ✑ Arizona, SW USA
114 D6 **Gila** Entre Ríos, Argentina 32°32′S 58°56′W
74 F3 **Gilbert** Minnesota, N USA 47°29′N 92°27′W
56 D7 **Gilbert, Mount** ▲ British Columbia, SW Canada 50°49′N 124°01′W
275 J3 **Gilbert River** ✑ Queensland, NE Australia
42 M **Gilbert Seamounts** *undersea feature* NE Pacific Ocean 52°50′N 150°00′W
180 C6 **Gildehaus** Niedersachsen, Germany 52°18′E 7°07′N
77 I3 **Gildford** Montana, NW USA 48°34′N 110°21′W
139 K2 **Gilé** Zambézia, NE Mozambique 16°10′S 28°17′E
141 J2 **Gilead** Limpopo, South Africa 23°39′S 28°52′E
72 C4 **Gile Flowage** ◎ Wisconsin, N USA
74 F4 **Giles, Lake** *salt lake* South Australia
218 D7 **Gilf Kebir Plateau** see Haqbat al Jilf al Kabir
158 D7 **Gilford** United Kingdom 54°22′N 6°20′W
277 K4 **Gilgandra** New South Wales, SE Australia 31°43′S 148°39′E
Gilgâu see Gâlgău
183 G9 **Gilgil** Rift Valley, SW Kenya 0°29′S 36°19′E
231 L2 **Gilgit** Jammu and Kashmir, NE India 35°54′N 74°09′E
231 I2 **Gilgit** ✑ N Pakistan
55 I7 **Gillam** Manitoba, C Canada 56°25′N 94°45′W
155 F12 **Gilleleje** Frederiksborg, E Denmark 56°05′N 12°17′E
181 C11 **Gillenfeld** Rheinland-Pfalz, Germany 50°07′E 6°54′N
73 C11 **Gillespie** Illinois, N USA 39°07′N 89°49′W
77 V3 **Gillette** Wyoming, C USA 44°17′N 105°30′W
53 K7 **Gillian, Lake** ◎ Nunavut, NE Canada
161 L6 **Gillingham** SE England, United Kingdom 51°24′N 00°33′E
158 I4 **Gill, Lough** ◎ Ireland
291 A4 **Gillock Island** *island* Antarctica
213 H7 **Gillot** ✕ (St-Denis) N Réunion 20°53′S 55°31′E
113 G10 **Gill Point** *headland* N Saint Helena 15°59′S 05°38′W
73 D10 **Gilman** Illinois, N USA 40°44′N 87°58′W
71 H4 **Gilmer** Texas, SW USA 32°44′N 94°58′W
159 H2 **Gilmerton** United Kingdom 56°23′N 3°48′W
55 H4 **Gilmour Island** *island* Nunavut, C Canada
Gilolo see Halmahera, Pulau
80 C5 **Gilo Wenz** ✑ SW Ethiopia
84 D4 **Gilroy** California, W USA 37°00′N 121°34′W
261 N7 **Giluwe, Mount** ▲ W Papua New Guinea 06°03′S 143°52′E
193 I7 **Gilyuy** ✑ SE Russian Federation
163 F8 **Gilze** Noord-Brabant, S Netherlands 51°33′N 04°56′E
251 H4 **Gimbi** *var.* Kume-jima, SW Japan
136 D4 **Gimbi** *It.* Ghimbi. Oromiya, C Ethiopia 09°13′N 35°39′E
248 C7 **Gimcheon** *prev.* Kimch'ŏn. C South Korea 36°10′N 128°07′E
248 C7 **Gimhae** *var.* Kim Hae. ✕ (Busan) SE South Korea 35°10′N 128°57′E
91 J3 **Gimie, Mount** ▲ C Saint Lucia 13°51′N 61°00′W
55 I9 **Gimli** Manitoba, S Canada 50°39′N 97°00′W
Gimma see Jima
154 I9 **Gimo** Uppsala, C Sweden 60°11′N 18°12′E
171 J3 **Gimone** ✑ S France
168 F8 **Gimont** Midi-Pyrénées, France 43°38′N 0°52′E
Gimpoe see Gimpu
260 C4 **Gimpu** *prev.* Gimpoe. Sulawesi, C Indonesia 01°38′S 120°00′E
276 B3 **Gina** South Australia 29°58′S 134°33′E
Ginevra see Genève
163 F10 **Gingelom** Limburg, NE Belgium 50°46′N 05°09′E
274 D4 **Gingin** Western Australia 31°22′S 115°51′E
141 L5 **Gingindlovu** KwaZulu-Natal, South Africa 29°01′S 31°35′E
Gingindlovu see KwaGingindlovu
263 M8 **Gingoog** Mindanao, S Philippines 08°47′N 125°05′E
136 D5 **Ginir** Oromiya, C Ethiopia 07°12′N 40°43′E
219 A13 **Girāfi, Wādi** Egypt
73 C11 **Girard** Illinois, N USA 39°27′N 89°46′W
75 G9 **Girard** Kansas, C USA 37°30′N 94°50′W
73 I4 **Girard** Ohio, N USA 41°08′N 80°42′W
104 B2 **Girardot** Cundinamarca, C Colombia 04°19′N 74°47′W
289 C9 **Giraud Seamount** *undersea feature* SW Indian Ocean 07°57′S 46°55′E
135 B13 **Giraul** ✑ SW Angola
159 G **Girdle Ness** *headland* NE Scotland, United Kingdom 57°09′N 02°04′W
215 H5 **Giresun** *var.* Kerasunt; *anc.* Cerasus, Pharnacia. Giresun, NE Turkey 40°55′N 38°35′E
215 H5 **Giresun** ◆ *province* NE Turkey
215 H5 **Giresun Dağları** ▲ N Turkey
Girga see Jirjā
Girgeh see Jirjā

Girgenti see Agrigento
233 I8 **Giridīh** Jhārkhand, NE India 24°10′N 86°20′E
277 J4 **Girilambone** New South Wales, SE Australia 31°19′S 146°57′E
218 C2 **Girne** *Gk.* Keryneia, Kyrenia. N Cyprus 35°19′N 33°19′E
167 M7 **Giromagny** Franche-Comté, France 47°45′N 6°50′E
171 L3 **Girona** *var.* Gerona; *anc.* Gerunda. Cataluña, NE Spain 41°59′N 02°49′E
171 L3 **Girona** *var.* Gerona. ◆ *province* Cataluña, NE Spain
164 F7 **Gironde** ◆ *department* SW France
171 I3 **Gironella** Cataluña, NE Spain 42°02′N 01°53′E
H8 **Girou** ✑ S France
158 F5 **Girvan** W Scotland, United Kingdom 55°14′N 04°53′W
278 D6 **Girvas** Texas, SW USA 31°05′N 102°24′W
278 J5 **Gisborne** Gisborne, North Island, New Zealand 38°41′S 178°01′E
274 G5 **Gisborne** ◆ *unitary authority* North Island, New Zealand
278 J5 **Gisborne District** see Gisborne
159 I8 **Giseiburn** United Kingdom 53°56′N 2°16′W
Giseifu see Uijeongbu
Gisenye see Gisenyi
137 A8 **Gisenyi** *var.* Gisenye. NW Rwanda 01°42′S 29°18′E
155 F10 **Gislaved** Jönköping, S Sweden 57°19′N 13°30′E
165 H3 **Gisors** Eure, N France 49°18′N 01°46′E
Gissar see Hisor
229 I7 **Gissar Range** *Rus.* Gissarskiy Khrebet. ▲ Tajikistan/Uzbekistan
Gissarskiy Khrebet see Gissar Range
163 B9 **Gistel** West-Vlaanderen, W Belgium 51°07′N 02°58′E
137 A8 **Giswil** Unterwalden, C Switzerland 46°49′N 08°11′E
186 E4 **Gitana** *ancient monument* Ípeiros, W Greece
A9 **Gitarama** ▲ 02°05′S 29°45′E
137 A9 **Gitega** C Burundi 03°26′S 29°56′E
Githio see Gytheio
180 I7 **Gittelde** Niedersachsen, Germany 51°48′E 10°12′N
174 C3 **Giubiasco** Ticino, S Switzerland 46°11′N 09°01′E
174 F7 **Giulianova** Abruzzi, C Italy 42°46′N 13°58′E
Giulie, Alpi see Julian Alps
Giumri see Gyumri
188 F7 **Giurgeni** Ialomița, SE Romania 44°45′N 27°48′E
188 E10 **Giurgiu** Giurgiu, S Romania 43°53′N 25°58′E
188 E10 **Giurgiu** ◆ *county* SE Romania
218 D7 **Giv'at Ḥayyim** *var.* Giv'at Khaim. Central, C Israel 32°23′N 34°56′E
Giv'at Khaim see Giv'at Ḥayyim
155 C12 **Give** Vejle, C Denmark 55°51′N 09°15′E
166 G5 **Giverny** Haute-Normandie, France 49°04′N 1°32′E
167 J3 **Givet** Ardennes, N France 50°08′N 04°50′E
165 K5 **Givry-en-Argonne** Champagne-Ardenne, France 48°57′N 4°53′E
141 K2 **Giyani** Limpopo, NE South Africa 23°20′S 30°37′E
136 C4 **Giyon** Oromiya, C Ethiopia 08°31′N 37°58′E
129 I3 **Giza** *var.* Al Jīzah, El Giza, Egypt 30°01′N 31°13′E
129 I2 **Giza, Pyramids of** *ancient monument* N Egypt
Gizhduvon see G'ijduvon
193 M5 **Gizhiginskaya Guba** *bay* E Russian Federation
281 H2 **Gizo** Gizo, NW Solomon Islands 08°03′S 156°49′E
281 H2 **Gizo** *var.* Ghizo. *island* W Solomon Islands
182 I4 **Giżycko** *Ger.* Lötzen. Warmińsko-Mazurskie, NE Poland 54°03′N 21°48′E
Gyzmałów see Hrymayliv
184 F7 **Gjakovë** *Serb.* Đakovica. ▲ S Serbia 42°23′N 20°30′E
184 D5 **Gjende** ◎ S Norway
184 F6 **Gjeravicë** *Serb.* Đeravica. ▲ S Serbia 42°33′N 20°08′E
154 C8 **Gjerstad** Aust-Agder, S Norway 58°54′N 09°03′E
184 G5 **Gjilan** *Serb.* Gnjilane. E Kosovo 42°27′N 21°28′E
184 E9 **Gjinokastër** *var.* Gjinokastra; *prev.* Gjinokastër, *Gk.* Argyrokastron, *It.* Argirocastro. Gjirokastër, S Albania 40°04′N 20°08′E
184 F9 **Gjinokastër** ◆ *district* S Albania
Gjirokastra see Gjirokastër
53 H6 **Gjoa Haven** *var.* Uqsuqtuuq. King William Island, Nunavut, NW Canada 68°38′N 95°57′W
154 D6 **Gjøvik** Oppland, S Norway 60°47′N 10°40′E
184 E9 **Gjuhëzës, Kepi i** *headland* SW Albania 40°25′N 19°19′E
Gjurgjevac see Đurđevac
186 D5 **Gkióna** *var.* Giona. ▲ C Greece
218 C2 **Gkréko, Akrotíri** *var.* Cape Greco, Pidálion. *cape* E Cyprus 34°56′N 34°04′E
163 F10 **Glabbeek-Zuurbemde** Vlaams Brabant, C Belgium 50°54′N 04°58′E
59 K8 **Glace Bay** Cape Breton Island, Nova Scotia, SE Canada 46°12′N 59°57′W
56 C4 **Glacier Bay** *inlet* Alaska, USA 58°40′N 137°30′W
76 D3 **Glacier Peak** ▲ Washington, NW USA 48°06′N 121°06′W
79 I11 **Glouster** Ohio, N USA 39°30′N 82°04′W
88 G7 **Glovers Reef** *reef* E Belize
65 H1 **Gloversville** New York, NE USA 43°03′N 74°20′W
182 E4 **Głowno** Łódź, C Poland 51°58′N 19°43′E
183 G8 **Głubczyce** *Ger.* Leobschütz. Opolskie, S Poland 50°13′N 17°50′E
196 G3 **Glubokiy** Rostovskaya Oblast', SW Russian Federation 48°34′N 40°16′E
227 L3 **Glubokoye** Vostochnyy Kazakhstan, E Kazakhstan 50°08′N 82°16′E
Glubokoye see Hlybokaye
183 G8 **Głuchołazy** *Ger.* Ziegenhals. Opolskie, S Poland 50°20′N 17°23′E
180 I2 **Glückstadt** Schleswig-Holstein, N Germany 53°47′N 09°26′E
Glukhov see Hlukhiv
159 I2 **Glusburn** United Kingdom 53°54′N 2°00′W
Glusk/Glussk see Hlusk
Glybokaya see Hlyboka
161 J8 **Glynbwch** United Kingdom 52°56′N 3°01′W
160 F2 **Glyn-Ceiriog** United Kingdom 52°56′N 3°11′W
160 F2 **Glyn-Dyfrdwy** United Kingdom 52°58′N 3°25′W
155 C11 **Glyngøre** Viborg, NW Denmark 56°45′N 08°52′E
197 I3 **Gmelinka** Volgogradskaya Oblast', SW Russian Federation 50°45′N 46°52′E
177 I4 **Gmünd** Kärnten, S Austria 46°56′N 13°32′E
177 K1 **Gmünd** Niederösterreich, N Austria 48°47′N 14°59′E
Gmünd see Schwäbisch Gmünd
177 J3 **Gmunden** Oberösterreich, N Austria 47°56′N 13°48′E
Gmundner See see Traunsee
155 G9 **Gnarp** Gävleborg, C Sweden 62°03′N 17°16′E
155 I2 **Gnas** Steiermark, SE Austria 46°53′N 15°48′E
Gnaviyani see Fuammulah
Gnesen see Gniezno
155 I8 **Gnesta** Södermanland, C Sweden 59°05′N 17°20′E
182 E4 **Gniezno** *Ger.* Gnesen. Weilkopolskie, C Poland 52°32′N 17°32′E
Gnjilane see Gjilan
160 F2 **Gnosall** United Kingdom 52°47′N 2°15′W
155 G10 **Gnosjö** Jönköping, S Sweden 57°22′N 13°44′E
234 C5 **Goa** *var.* Old Goa, *state* W India
234 C5 **Goa** *prev.* Old Goa, Vela Goa, Velha Goa. Goa, W India 15°31′N 73°56′E
Goabus see Kābdalis
234 C5 **Goa** ◆ *state* W India
87 N10 **Goascorán, Río** ✑ El Salvador/Honduras
132 G4 **Goaso** *var.* Gawso. W Ghana 06°49′N 02°27′W
158 F1 **Goatfell** ▲ United Kingdom 55°37′N 5°11′W
136 E5 **Goba** *It.* Ghinda. Hararī, C Ethiopia 07°02′N 39°58′E
140 B4 **Gobabeb** Erongo, W Namibia 23°32′S 15°03′E
138 C3 **Gobabis** Omaheke, E Namibia 22°25′S 18°58′E
Gobannium see Abergavenny
290 H3 **Goban Spur** *undersea feature* NW Atlantic Ocean
118 G9 **Gobernador Ayala** Mendoza, Argentina
114 B4 **Gobernador Candioti** Santa Fe, Argentina 31°14′S 60°41′W
116 C3 **Gobernador Civit** Mendoza, Argentina 33°39′S 59°53′W
117 C12 **Gobernador Crespo** Santa Fe, Argentina 30°18′S 60°24′W
117 C12 **Gobernador Gregores** Santa Cruz, S Argentina 48°43′S 70°11′W
113 H4 **Gobernador Ingeniero Virasoro** Corrientes, NE Argentina 28°04′S 56°08′W
114 C6 **Gobernador Udaondo** Buenos Aires, Argentina 35°13′S 58°56′W
251 H6 **Gobō** Wakayama, Honshū, SW Japan 33°52′N 135°09′E
Gobolka Awdal see Awdal
Gobolka Sahil see Sool
180 D2 **Goch** Nordrhein-Westfalen, W Germany 51°41′N 06°10′E
138 C3 **Gochas** Hardap, S Namibia 24°54′S 18°45′E
181 H12 **Gochsheim** Bayern, Germany 50°01′E 10°17′N
160 G3 **Godalming** United Kingdom 51°10′N 0°37′W
234 G5 **Godāvari** *var.* Godavari. ✑ C India
234 **Godāvari** see Godāvari

234 H6 **Godāvari, Mouths of the** *delta* E India
59 I2 **Godbout** Québec, SE Canada 49°19′N 67°37′W
75 D9 **Goddard** Kansas, C USA 37°39′N 97°34′W
181 F9 **Goddelsheim** Hessen, Germany 51°12′E 8°49′N
62 B5 **Goderich** Ontario, S Canada 43°45′N 81°43′W
166 G4 **Goderville** Haute-Normandie, France 49°39′N 0°22′E
Godhavn see Qeqertarsuaq
232 G4 **Godhra** Gujarāt, W India 22°49′N 73°40′E
183 G11 **Gödöllő** Pest, N Hungary 47°36′N 19°20′E
118 G3 **Godoy Cruz** Mendoza, W Argentina 32°59′S 68°49′W
55 K6 **Gods** ✑ Manitoba, C Canada
55 J5 **Gods Lake** ◎ Manitoba, C Canada
55 J5 **Gods Lake Narrows** Manitoba, C Canada 54°29′N 94°21′W
55 K3 **Gods Mercy, Bay of** *coastal sea feature* Nunavut, C Canada
Godthaab/Godthåb see Nuuk
Godwin Austen, Mount see K2
Goede Hoop, Kaap de see Good Hope, Cape of
Goedgepunt see Nhlangano
Goeie Hoop, Kaap die see Good Hope, Cape of
59 I4 **Goëlands, Lac aux** ◎ Québec, SE Canada
162 B7 **Goeree** *island* SW Netherlands
163 D8 **Goes** Zeeland, SW Netherlands 51°30′N 03°55′E
250 A1 **Goesan** *var.* Koesan. Ch'ungch'ŏng-bukto, South Korea 36°49′N 127°54′E
Goëse-center see Göttingen
81 I11 **Goffs** California, USA 34°55′N 115°04′W
63 I5 **Goffstown** New Hampshire, NE USA 43°01′N 71°34′W
62 E3 **Gogama** Ontario, S Canada 47°42′N 81°44′W
250 E4 **Go-gawa** ✑ Honshū, SW Japan
72 G2 **Gogebic, Lake** ◎ Michigan, N USA
72 C4 **Gogebic Range** *hill range* Michigan/Wisconsin, N USA
Gogi Lerr see Gogi, Mount
215 L5 **Gogi, Mount** *Arm.* Gogi Lerr, *Az.* Küküdağ. ▲ Armenia/Azerbaijan 39°33′N 45°35′E
194 G3 **Gogland, Ostrov** *island* NW Russian Federation
183 E8 **Gogolin** Opolskie, S Poland 50°28′N 18°04′E
Gogonnou see Gogonou
133 I5 **Gogounou** *var.* Gogonou. N Benin 10°50′N 02°50′E
232 E5 **Gohāna** Haryāna, N India 29°06′N 76°43′E
111 L1 **Goiabeira** Minas Gerais, Brazil 19°00′S 41°18′W
111 I5 **Goianá** Minas Gerais, Brazil 21°32′S 43°12′W
109 B10 **Goiânia** Goiás, C Brazil 16°43′S 49°18′W
109 B10 **Goianésia** Goiás, C Brazil 15°21′S 49°08′W
109 C9 **Goiás** off. Estado de Goiás; *prev.* Goiaz, Goyaz. ◆ *state* C Brazil
109 C9 **Goiás** *var.* Goyaz. C Brazil 15°57′S 49°18′W
Goiás, Estado de see Goiás
Goiaz see Goiás
158 A4 **Goil, Loch** *inlet* United Kingdom
113 J4 **Goio-Erê** Paraná, SW Brazil 24°08′S 53°02′W
163 E8 **Goirle** Noord-Brabant, S Netherlands 51°31′N 05°04′E
172 C5 **Góis** Coimbra, N Portugal 40°10′N 08°06′W
251 I5 **Gojō** *var.* Gozyô. Nara, Honshū, SW Japan 34°21′N 135°42′E
231 H6 **Gojra** Punjab, E Pakistan 31°10′N 72°43′E
250 D7 **Gokase-gawa** ✑ Kyūshū, SW Japan
214 A3 **Gökçeada** *var.* Imroz Adası, *Gk.* Imbros. *island* NW Turkey
Gökçeada see Imroz
228 G3 **Gökdepe** *Rus.* Gökdepe, Geok-Tepe. Ahal Welaýaty, C Turkmenistan 38°09′N 58°10′E
214 C4 **Gökırmak** ✑ N Turkey
215 J7 **Göksu** ▲ S Turkey
215 I3 **Göksun** Kahramanmaraş, C Turkey 38°03′N 36°30′E
214 G6 **Göksu Nehri** ✑ S Turkey
138 G3 **Gokwe** Midlands, NW Zimbabwe 18°13′S 28°55′E
154 D6 **Gol** Buskerud, S Norway 60°42′N 08°57′E
233 J7 **Golāghāt** Assam, NE India 26°31′N 93°54′E
158 A5 **Gola Island** *island* Donegal, Ireland
182 F5 **Gołańcz** Wielkopolskie, C Poland 52°57′N 17°17′E
216 D2 **Golan Heights** ▲ Syria
216 E3 **Golan Heights** *Ar.* Al Jawlān, *Heb.* HaGolan. ▲ SW Syria
Golārā see Ārān-va-Bīdgol
Golaya Pristan' see Hola Prystan'
223 J4 **Golbāf** Kermān, E Iran 35°44′E
214 C4 **Gölbaşı** Adıyaman, S Turkey 37°46′N 37°40′E
179 H14 **Gölbner** ▲ SW Austria 46°51′N 13°37′E
80 J1 **Golconda** Nevada, W USA 40°56′N 117°22′W
73 C11 **Golconda** Illinois, N USA 40°55′N 112°27′W
235 F4 **Golconda Fort** ▲
230 F5 **Gölcük** Kocaeli, NW Turkey 40°42′N 29°50′E
182 I3 **Gołdap** *Ger.* Goldap. Warmińsko-Mazurskie, NE Poland 54°18′N 22°19′E
182 I3 **Gołdap** ✑ NE Poland
76 B7 **Gold Beach** Oregon, NW USA 42°24′N 124°27′W
277 M2 **Gold Coast** *cultural region* Queensland, E Australia
132 D5 **Gold Coast** *coastal region* S Ghana
83 I5 **Gold Creek** Alaska, USA 62°48′N 149°40′W
77 I7 **Golden** British Columbia, SW Canada
79 I5 **Golden** Colorado, C USA 39°40′N 105°12′W
278 F7 **Golden Bay** *bay* South Island, New Zealand
75 I5 **Golden City** Missouri, C USA 37°23′N 94°05′W
76 D5 **Goldendale** Washington, NW USA 45°49′N 120°49′W
Goldener Tisch see Zlatý Stôl
90 A4 **Golden Grove** E Jamaica 17°56′N 76°17′W
62 E3 **Golden Lake** ◎ Ontario, SE Canada
68 E2 **Golden Meadow** Louisiana, S USA 29°22′N 90°15′W
Golden State, The see California
139 I3 **Golden Valley** Mashonaland West, N Zimbabwe 18°11′S 29°50′E
114 B4 **Goldey** Buenos Aires, Argentina 32°37′S 59°18′W
80 H6 **Goldfield** Nevada, USA 37°42′N 117°15′W
Goldingen see Kuldīga
80 F4 **Gold Point** Nevada, USA 37°21′N 117°22′W
56 D5 **Gold River** Vancouver Island, British Columbia, SW Canada 49°41′N 126°05′W
81 A13 **Gold Run** California, USA 39°11′N 120°51′W
67 K6 **Goldsboro** North Carolina, SE USA 35°23′N 77°59′W
75 D13 **Goldsmith** Texas, SW USA 31°58′N 102°36′W
70 F4 **Goldthwaite** Texas, SW USA 31°28′N 98°35′W
215 H6 **Göle** *prev.* Merdenik. 40°47′N 42°36′E
185 G8 **Golema Ada** ▲ N Bulgaria
185 I7 **Golema Planina** ▲ N Bulgaria
185 G8 **Golemi Vrŭkh** ▲ W Bulgaria 42°41′N 22°38′E
214 C4 **Göleniów** *var.* Gollnow.
182 C3 **Goleniów** *Ger.* Gollnow. Zachodnio-pomorskie, NW Poland 53°34′N 14°50′E
81 C11 **Goleta** California, USA 34°26′N 119°50′W
88 G15 **Golfito** Puntarenas, SE Costa Rica 08°42′N 83°10′W
187 N7 **Gölhisar** Burdur, Turkey 37°09′N 29°42′E
70 D4 **Goliad** Texas, SW USA 28°40′N 97°26′W
184 F3 **Golija** ▲ W Serbia
184 E3 **Golija** ▲ SE Serbia
214 E5 **Gölköy** Ordu, N Turkey 40°39′N 37°37′E
Gollel see Lavumisa
177 L2 **Göllersbach** ✑ NE Austria
181 I9 **Göllingen** Thüringen, Germany 51°21′E 11°01′N
Gollnow see Goleniów
214 C6 **Gölmarmara** Manisa, Turkey 38°43′N 27°55′E
161 I6 **Golmud** *var.* Ge'e'mu, Golmo, *Chin.* Ko-erh-mu. Qinghai, C China 36°22′N 94°55′E
174 C4 **Golo** ✑ Corse, France, C Mediterranean Sea
Golovanevsk see Holovanivs'k
Golovchin see Halowchyn
223 I2 **Golpāyegān** *var.* Gulpaigan. Eṣfahān, W Iran 33°24′N 50°18′E
Gol'shany see Hal'shany
155 F4 **Golspie** United Kingdom 57°59′N 3°59′W
156 G10 **Golubac** Serbia, NE Serbia 44°38′N 21°36′E
231 C11 **Golub-Dobrzyń** Kujawski-pomorskie, C Poland
135 C11 **Golungo Alto** Cuanza Norte, NW Angola 09°10′S 14°45′E
185 L5 **Golyama Kamchiya** ✑ E Bulgaria
185 L5 **Golyam Beglik** ◎ SW Bulgaria
185 L5 **Golyama Syutkya** ▲ S Bulgaria 41°55′N 24°03′E
185 I7 **Golyam Perelik** ▲ S Bulgaria 41°50′N 24°33′E
191 I11 **Golynki** Smolenskaya Oblast', Russian Federation
185 M5 **Goma** Nord-Kivu, NE Dem. Rep. Congo
251 L6 **Goman-zan** ▲ Honshū, SW Japan 34°05′N 135°34′E
168 B9 **Gómara** Castilla y León, Spain 41°37′N 2°13′W
133 I6 **Gombe** Gombe, E Nigeria 10°19′N 11°02′E
137 B8 **Gombe** Antalya, Turkey
121 L6 **Gombe** ✑ E Tanzania

Legend row:
◆ Country
○ Country Capital
◇ Dependent Territory
○ Dependent Territory Capital
✕ International Airport
◆ Administrative Regions
▲ Mountain
▲ Mountain Range
▲ Volcano
✑ River
◎ Lake
◎ Reservoir

Great Artesian Basin - Guarujá
INDEX
346

275 J5 **Great Artesian Basin** lowlands Queensland, C Australia
280 E9 **Great Astrolabe Reef** reef Kadavu, SW Fiji
276 C4 **Great Australian Bight** bight S Australia
159 L7 **Great Ayton** N England, United Kingdom 54°28′N 01°09′W
290 B6 **Great Bahama Bank** undersea feature E Gulf of Mexico 23°15′N 78°00′W
278 H3 **Great Barrier Island** island N New Zealand
275 K3 **Great Barrier Reef** reef Queensland, NE Australia
65 I3 **Great Barrington** Massachusetts, NE USA 42°11′N 73°20′W
42 D6 **Great Basin** basin W USA
52 C8 **Great Bear Lake** Fr. Grand Lac de l'Ours. ◎ Northwest Territories, NW Canada
54 D2 **Great Bear River** ≈ Northwest Territories, NW Canada
161 I6 **Great Bedwyn** United Kingdom 51°22′N 1°36′W
Great Belt see Storebælt
75 D10 **Great Bend** Kansas, C USA 38°22′N 98°47′W
Great Bermuda see Bermuda
157 A11 **Great Blasket Island** Ir. An Blascaod Mór. island SW Ireland
Great Britain see Britain
159 M10 **Great Carlton** United Kingdom 53°20′N 0°07′E
257 B11 **Great Channel** channel Andaman Sea/Indian Ocean
257 B8 **Great Coco Island** island SW Myanmar (Burma)
Great Crosby see Crosby
67 M5 **Great Dismal Swamp** wetland North Carolina/Virginia, SE USA
77 K8 **Great Divide Basin** basin Wyoming, C USA
275 K5 **Great Dividing Range** ▲▲ NE Australia
62 B3 **Great Duck Island** island Ontario, S Canada
161 L5 **Great Dunmow** SE England, United Kingdom 51°51′N 00°21′E
Great Elder Reservoir see Waconda Lake
90 E5 **Greater Antilles** island group West Indies
141 L5 **Greater St Lucia Wetland Park** Kwazulu Natal, South Africa
205 L9 **Greater Sunda Islands** var. Sunda Islands. island group Indonesia
161 J4 **Great Everdon** United Kingdom 52°12′N 1°08′W
278 F1 **Great Exhibition Bay** inlet North Island, New Zealand
61 M10 **Great Exuma Island** island C Bahamas
77 I4 **Great Falls** Montana, NW USA 47°30′N 111°18′W
67 I7 **Great Falls** South Carolina, SE USA 34°34′N 80°54′W
141 I9 **Great Fish** ≈ Eastern Cape, South Africa
144 C5 **Great Fisher Bank** undersea feature C North Sea 57°00′N 04°00′E
141 I9 **Great Fish Point** point Eastern Cape, South Africa
Great Glen see Mor, Glen
161 K4 **Great Gransden** United Kingdom 52°11′N 0°08′W
Great Grimsby see Grimsby
90 F3 **Great Guana Cay** island C Bahamas
159 J9 **Great Harwood** United Kingdom 53°47′N 2°25′W
290 E2 **Great Hellefiske Bank** undersea feature N Atlantic Ocean
183 G12 **Great Hungarian Plain** var. Great Alfold, Plain of Hungary, Hung. Alföld. plain SE Europe
90 G4 **Great Inagua** var. Inagua Islands. island S Bahamas
Great Indian Desert see Thar Desert
138 E9 **Great Karoo** var. Great Karroo, High Veld, Afr. Groot Karoo, Hoë Karoo. plateau region S South Africa
Great Karroo see Great Karoo
Great Kei see Nciba
Great Khingan Range see Da Hinggan Ling
62 B2 **Great La Cloche Island** island Ontario, S Canada
277 J9 **Great Lake** ◎ Tasmania, SE Australia
Great Lake see Tônlé Sap
61 J3 **Great Lakes** lakes Ontario, Canada/USA
Great Lakes State see Michigan
161 H5 **Great Malvern** W England, United Kingdom 52°07′N 02°19′W
278 H3 **Great Mercury Island** island N New Zealand
Great Meteor Seamount see Great Meteor Tablemount
290 F5 **Great Meteor Tablemount** var. Great Meteor Seamount. undersea feature E Atlantic Ocean 30°00′N 28°30′W
73 G11 **Great Miami River** ≈ Ohio, N USA
257 A11 **Great Nicobar** island Nicobar Islands, India, NE Indian Ocean
161 M5 **Great Oakley** United Kingdom 51°54′N 1°12′E
220 B3 **Great Oasis, The** var. Khārga Oasis. oasis S Egypt
159 H10 **Great Ormes Head** headland N Wales, United Kingdom
159 I6 **Great Orton** United Kingdom 54°52′N 3°03′W
161 L3 **Great Ouse** var. Ouse. ≈ E England, United Kingdom
277 K10 **Great Oyster Bay** bay Tasmania, SE Australia
90 E8 **Great Pedro Bluff** headland W Jamaica 17°51′N 77°44′W
67 J8 **Great Pee Dee River** ≈ North Carolina/South Carolina, SE USA
205 M6 **Great Plain of China** plain E China
42 E6 **Great Plains** var. High Plains. plains Canada/USA
79 N4 **Great Plains Reservoirs** ⊠ Colorado, C USA
65 N4 **Great Point** headland Nantucket Island, Massachusetts, NE USA 41°23′N 70°03′W
124 F6 **Great Rift Valley** var. Rift Valley. depression Asia/Africa
137 C10 **Great Ruaha** ≈ S Tanzania
161 L3 **Great Ryburgh** United Kingdom 52°49′N 0°55′E
65 H1 **Great Sacandaga Lake** ⊠ New York, NE USA
174 A4 **Great Saint Bernard Pass** Fr. Col du Grand-Saint-Bernard, It. Passo del Gran San Bernardo. pass Italy/Switzerland
90 E1 **Great Sale Cay** island N Bahamas
Great Salt Desert see Kavīr, Dasht-e
79 H3 **Great Salt Lake** salt lake Utah, W USA
78 G2 **Great Salt Lake Desert** plain Utah, W USA
75 D11 **Great Salt Plains Lake** ⊠ Oklahoma, C USA
128 G4 **Great Sand Sea** desert Egypt/Libya
274 F4 **Great Sandy Desert** desert Western Australia
Great Sandy Desert see Ar Rub' al Khālī
Great Sandy Island see Fraser Island
280 E8 **Great Sea Reef** reef Vanua Levu, N Fiji
82 D9 **Great Sitkin Island** island Aleutian Islands, Alaska, USA
54 F4 **Great Slave Lake** Fr. Grand Lac des Esclaves. ◎ Northwest Territories, NW Canada
66 G6 **Great Smoky Mountains** ▲▲ North Carolina/Tennessee, SE USA
56 D1 **Great Snow Mountain** ▲ British Columbia, W Canada 57°22′N 124°08′W
Great Socialist People's Libyan Arab Jamahiriya see Libya
67 M10 **Great Sound** sound Bermuda, NW Atlantic Ocean
160 E8 **Great Torrington** United Kingdom 50°57′N 4°09′W
276 D2 **Great Victoria Desert** desert South Australia/Western Australia
292 D2 **Great Wall** Chinese research station South Shetland Islands, Antarctica 61°57′S 58°23′W
63 M4 **Great Wass Island** island Maine, NE USA
288 J4 **Great Yangtze Bank** N Indian Ocean
161 N3 **Great Yarmouth** var. Yarmouth. E England, United Kingdom 52°37′N 01°44′E
161 L5 **Great Yeldham** SE England, United Kingdom 52°01′N 00°33′E
217 I2 **Great Zab** Ar. Az Zāb al Kabīr, Kurd. Zē-i Bādinān, Turk. Büyükzap Suyu. ≈ Iraq/Turkey
155 E9 **Grebbestad** Västra Götaland, S Sweden 58°42′N 11°15′E
Grebenka see Hrebinka
181 G8 **Grebenstein** Hessen, Germany 51°27′E 9°25′N
89 H8 **Grecia** Alajuela, C Costa Rica 10°04′N 84°19′W
114 G6 **Greco** Río Negro, W Uruguay 32°49′S 57°03′W
Greco, Cape see Gkréko, Akrotíri
170 F5 **Gredos, Sierra de** ▲▲ W Spain
172 F3 **Gredos, Sierra de** ▲▲ Spain
62 E5 **Greece** New York, NE USA 43°12′N 77°41′W
187 H4 **Greece** off. Hellenic Republic, Gk. Ellás; anc. Hellas. ◆ republic SE Europe
Greece Central see Stereá Elláda
Greece West see Dytikí Elláda
79 M2 **Greeley** Colorado, C USA 40°21′N 104°41′W
74 D7 **Greeley** Nebraska, C USA 41°33′N 98°31′W
64 G4 **Greeley** Pennsylvania, USA 41°25′N 75°00′W
53 I2 **Greely Fiord** coastal sea feature Nunavut, N Canada
192 G1 **Greem-Bell, Ostrov** Eng. Graham Bell Island. island Zemlya Frantsa-Iosifa, N Russian Federation
81 D8 **Greenacres** California, USA 35°23′N 119°07′W
72 D6 **Green Bay** Wisconsin, N USA 44°32′N 88°W
72 D6 **Green Bay** lake bay Michigan/Wisconsin, N USA
67 J3 **Greenbrier River** ≈ West Virginia, NE USA
74 F2 **Greenbush** Minnesota, N USA 48°42′N 96°10′W
277 L7 **Green Cape** headland New South Wales, SE Australia 37°15′S 150°03′E
158 E8 **Greencastle** United Kingdom 54°02′N 6°06′W
73 E11 **Greencastle** Indiana, N USA 39°38′N 86°51′W
64 B8 **Greencastle** Pennsylvania, NE USA 39°47′N 77°43′W
75 H8 **Green City** Missouri, C USA 40°16′N 92°57′W
64 E2 **Greene** New York, USA 42°20′N 75°46′W
67 H6 **Greeneville** Tennessee, S USA 36°10′N 82°50′W
80 B5 **Greenfield** California, W USA 36°19′N 121°15′W
81 D8 **Greenfield** California, USA 35°16′N 119°0′W
73 F11 **Greenfield** Indiana, N USA 39°47′N 85°46′W
65 J2 **Greenfield** Massachusetts, NE USA 42°33′N 72°34′W
75 G11 **Greenfield** Missouri, C USA 37°25′N 93°50′W
73 H11 **Greenfield** Ohio, N USA 39°21′N 83°22′W
66 C6 **Greenfield** Tennessee, S USA 36°09′N 88°48′W
73 D8 **Greenfield** Wisconsin, N USA 42°55′N 87°59′W
75 H11 **Green Forest** Arkansas, C USA 36°19′N 93°24′W
64 D9 **Green Haven** Maryland, USA 39°08′N 76°33′W
159 J6 **Greenhead** United Kingdom 54°58′N 2°31′W
79 M4 **Greenhorn Mountain** ▲ Colorado, C USA 37°50′N 104°59′W
Green Island see Lü Tao
280 E2 **Green Islands** var. Nissan Islands. island group NE Papua New Guinea
57 L4 **Green Lake** Saskatchewan, C Canada 54°15′N 107°51′W
72 D7 **Green Lake** ◎ Wisconsin, N USA
295 K7 **Greenland** Dan. Grønland, Inuit Kalaallit Nunaat. ◇ Danish external territory NE North America
144 A2 **Greenland** island NE North America
295 K5 **Greenland Plain** undersea feature N Greenland Sea
295 K5 **Greenland Sea** sea Arctic Ocean
159 J4 **Greenlaw** United Kingdom 55°42′N 2°28′W
159 H2 **Greenloaning** United Kingdom 56°14′N 3°53′W
159 H5 **Green Lowther** hill United Kingdom
79 L3 **Green Mountain Reservoir** ⊠ Colorado, C USA
63 I5 **Green Mountains** ▲▲ Vermont, NE USA
Green Mountain State see Vermont
158 G3 **Greenock** W Scotland, United Kingdom 55°57′N 04°45′W
160 B4 **Greenore Point** headland Wexford, Ireland 52°14′N 6°18′W
83 J2 **Greenough, Mount** ▲ Alaska, USA 69°15′N 141°37′W
64 K5 **Greenport** New York, NE USA 41°06′N 72°21′W
280 A2 **Green River** Sandaun, NW Papua New Guinea 03°54′S 141°08′E
79 I4 **Green River** Utah, W USA 39°00′N 110°07′W
77 J9 **Green River** Wyoming, C USA 41°33′N 109°27′W
79 J4 **Green River** ≈ W USA
73 C9 **Green River** ≈ Illinois, N USA
66 E5 **Green River** ≈ Kentucky, C USA
74 B3 **Green River** ≈ North Dakota, N USA
79 I4 **Green River** ≈ Utah, W USA
56 D10 **Green River** ≈ Washington, NW USA
77 J7 **Green River** ≈ Wyoming, C USA
66 F4 **Green River Lake** ⊠ Kentucky, S USA
68 G1 **Greensboro** Alabama, S USA 32°42′N 87°36′W
66 G8 **Greensboro** Georgia, SE USA 33°34′N 83°10′W
67 J6 **Greensboro** North Carolina, SE USA 36°04′N 79°48′W
73 F11 **Greensburg** Indiana, N USA 39°20′N 85°28′W
75 D10 **Greensburg** Kansas, C USA 37°36′N 99°17′W
66 E4 **Greensburg** Kentucky, S USA 37°14′N 85°30′W
62 C8 **Greensburg** Pennsylvania, NE USA 40°18′N 79°32′W
79 J8 **Greens Peak** ▲ Arizona, SW USA 34°06′N 109°34′W
67 K8 **Green Swamp** wetland North Carolina, SE USA
64 F5 **Greentown** Pennsylvania, USA 41°19′N 75°18′W
67 H3 **Greenup** Kentucky, S USA 38°34′N 82°49′W
79 I10 **Green Valley** Arizona, SW USA 31°49′N 111°00′W
64 D8 **Green Valley** Maryland, USA 39°36′N 76°29′W
132 D8 **Greenville** var. Sino, Sinoe. SE Liberia 05°01′N 09°03′W
69 H2 **Greenville** Alabama, S USA 31°49′N 86°37′W
69 K4 **Greenville** Florida, SE USA 30°28′N 83°37′W
66 F9 **Greenville** Georgia, SE USA 33°03′N 84°42′W
73 C12 **Greenville** Illinois, N USA 38°53′N 89°24′W
66 D4 **Greenville** Kentucky, S USA 37°11′N 87°11′W
63 K3 **Greenville** Maine, NE USA 45°26′N 69°36′W
72 F7 **Greenville** Michigan, N USA 43°10′N 85°15′W
66 A8 **Greenville** Mississippi, S USA 33°24′N 91°03′W
67 L6 **Greenville** North Carolina, SE USA 35°36′N 77°23′W
73 G10 **Greenville** Ohio, N USA 40°06′N 84°37′W
65 L3 **Greenville** Rhode Island, NE USA 41°52′N 71°33′W
67 H7 **Greenville** South Carolina, SE USA 34°51′N 82°24′W
71 H4 **Greenville** Texas, SW USA 33°09′N 96°07′W
161 K6 **Greenwich** United Kingdom 51°28′N 0°0′E
65 I5 **Greenwich** Connecticut, USA 41°02′N 73°38′W
73 I10 **Greenwich** Ohio, N USA 41°01′N 82°31′W
75 G12 **Greenwood** Arkansas, C USA 35°13′N 94°15′W
80 D2 **Greenwood** California, USA 38°54′N 120°55′W
73 F11 **Greenwood** Indiana, N USA 39°38′N 86°06′W
66 A8 **Greenwood** Mississippi, S USA 33°30′N 90°11′W
67 H8 **Greenwood** South Carolina, SE USA 34°11′N 82°10′W
67 H8 **Greenwood, Lake** ⊠ South Carolina, SE USA
67 H7 **Greer** South Carolina, SE USA 34°56′N 82°13′W
75 H12 **Greers Ferry Lake** ⊠ Arkansas, C USA
75 G13 **Greeson, Lake** ⊠ Arkansas, C USA
161 J3 **Greetham** United Kingdom 52°42′N 0°37′W
180 C3 **Greetsiel** Niedersachsen, Germany 53°30′E 7°06′N
181 B9 **Grefrath** Nordrhein-Westfalen, Germany 51°10′E 6°38′N
115 I9 **Gregorio Aznàrez** Maldonado, Uruguay 34°43′S 55°25′W
91 H5 **Gregorio Luperón** ✕ N Dominican Republic 19°43′N 70°43′W
141 J1 **Gregory** Limpopo, South Africa 22°38′S 28°55′E
74 D6 **Gregory** South Dakota, N USA 43°11′N 99°26′W
276 G2 **Gregory, Lake** salt lake South Australia
274 E5 **Gregory Lake** ◎ Western Australia
275 J4 **Gregory Range** ▲▲ Queensland, E Australia
Greifenberg/Greifenberg in Pommern see Gryfice
Greifenhagen see Gryfino
178 H4 **Greifswald** Mecklenburg-Vorpommern, NE Germany 54°04′N 13°24′E
178 I4 **Greifswalder Bodden** bay NE Germany
177 K2 **Grein** Oberösterreich, N Austria 48°14′N 14°50′E
179 G9 **Greiz** Thüringen, C Germany 50°40′N 12°11′E
180 J1 **Gremersdorf** Schleswig-Holstein, Germany 54°20′E 10°56′N
195 L9 **Gremyachinsk** Permskaya Oblast', NW Russian Federation 58°33′N 57°52′E
Grenå see Grenaa
155 E11 **Grenaa** var. Grenå. Århus, C Denmark 56°25′N 10°53′E
66 B8 **Grenada** Mississippi, S USA 33°46′N 89°48′W
91 N3 **Grenada** ◆ commonwealth republic SE West Indies
95 K2 **Grenada** island Grenada
95 J2 **Grenada Basin** undersea feature W Atlantic Ocean 13°30′N 62°00′W
66 B8 **Grenada Lake** ⊠ Mississippi, S USA
168 F5 **Grenade-sur-Garonne** Midi-Pyrénées, France 43°46′N 1°17′E
168 D5 **Grenade-sur-l'Adour** Aquitaine, France 43°47′N 0°25′W
103 I1 **Grenadines, The** island group Grenada/St Vincent and the Grenadines
176 C4 **Grenchen** Fr. Granges. Solothurn, NW Switzerland 47°13′N 07°24′E
277 K5 **Grenfell** New South Wales, SE Australia 33°54′S 148°09′E
55 H9 **Grenfell** Saskatchewan, S Canada 50°24′N 102°56′W
152 C1 **Grenivík** Nordhurland Eystra, N Iceland 65°57′N 18°10′W
165 J7 **Grenoble** anc. Cularo, Gratianopolis. Isère, E France 45°11′N 05°42′E
74 A1 **Grenora** North Dakota, N USA 48°36′N 103°57′W
159 K9 **Grenoside** United Kingdom 53°26′N 1°29′W
152 I3 **Grense-Jakobselv** Finnmark, N Norway 69°46′N 30°39′E
91 N3 **Grenville** E Grenada 12°07′N 61°37′W
169 L5 **Gréoux-les-Bains** Provence-Alpes-Côte d'Azur, France 43°45′N 5°53′E
160 G2 **Gresford** United Kingdom 53°05′N 2°58′W
76 C5 **Gresham** Oregon, NW USA 45°30′N 122°25′W
Gresk see Hresk
176 D6 **Gressoney-St-Jean** Valle d'Aosta, NW Italy 45°48′N 07°49′E
169 L2 **Grésy-sur-Isére** Rhône-Alpes, France 45°36′N 6°15′E
159 I6 **Gretna** United Kingdom 54°59′N 3°04′W
68 E4 **Gretna** Louisiana, S USA 29°54′N 90°03′W
67 J5 **Gretna** Virginia, NE USA 36°57′N 79°21′W
159 I5 **Gretna Green** United Kingdom 54°59′N 3°04′W
162 E7 **Grevelingen** inlet S North Sea
180 I3 **Greven** Mecklenburg-Vorpommern, Germany 53°29′E 10°48′N
180 D6 **Greven** Nordrhein-Westfalen, NW Germany 52°07′N 07°38′E
186 F3 **Grevená** Dytikí Makedonía, N Greece 40°05′N 21°26′E
181 B9 **Grevenbroich** Nordrhein-Westfalen, W Germany 51°06′N 06°34′E
163 I13 **Grevenmacher** Grevenmacher, E Luxembourg 49°41′N 06°27′E
163 H13 **Grevenmacher** ◐ district E Luxembourg
180 J2 **Grevesmühlen** Mecklenburg-Vorpommern, N Germany 53°52′N 11°12′E
279 D9 **Grey** ≈ South Island, New Zealand
158 E7 **Greyabbey** United Kingdom 54°32′N 5°34′W
77 K6 **Greybull** Wyoming, C USA 44°29′N 108°03′W
77 K6 **Greybull River** ≈ Wyoming, C USA
117 G11 **Grey Channel** sound Falkland Islands
Greyerzer See see Gruyère, Lac de la
59 L6 **Grey Islands** island group Newfoundland and Labrador, E Canada
65 I2 **Greylock, Mount** ▲ Massachusetts, NE USA 42°38′N 73°09′W
279 D9 **Greymouth** West Coast, South Island, New Zealand 42°29′S 171°14′E
277 I2 **Grey Range** ▲▲ New South Wales/Queensland, E Australia
141 H9 **Greystone** Eastern Cape, South Africa 31°54′S 26°02′E
160 B2 **Greystones** Ir. Na Clocha Liatha. E Ireland 53°08′N 06°05′W
278 G7 **Greytown** Wellington, North Island, New Zealand 41°04′S 175°29′E
139 H8 **Greytown** KwaZulu/Natal, E South Africa 29°04′S 30°35′E
Greytown see San Juan del Norte
163 E10 **Grez-Doiceau** Dut. Graven. Walloon Brabant, C Belgium 50°43′N 04°41′E
166 D7 **Grez-en-Bouére** Pays de la Loire, France 47°53′N 0°31′W
168 G4 **Grézes** Midi-Pyrénées, France 44°37′N 1°49′E
187 I6 **Griá, Akrotírio** headland Ándros, Kykládes, Greece, Aegean Sea 37°54′N 24°57′E
197 H4 **Gribanovskiy** Voronezhskaya Oblast', W Russian Federation 51°27′N 41°53′E
134 E4 **Gribingui** ≈ N Central African Republic
80 D1 **Gridley** California, W USA 39°21′N 121°41′W
140 G6 **Griekwastad** var. Griquatown. Northern Cape, C South Africa 28°50′S 23°16′E
181 F12 **Griesheim** Hessen, Germany 49°52′E 8°35′N
66 F9 **Griffin** Georgia, SE USA 33°15′N 84°17′W
277 J5 **Griffith** New South Wales, SE Australia 34°18′S 146°04′E
62 C3 **Griffith Island** island Ontario, S Canada
181 G9 **Grifte** Hessen, Germany 51°13′E 9°27′N
67 L6 **Grifton** North Carolina, SE USA 35°22′N 77°26′W
Grigioni see Graubünden
191 E9 **Grigiškes** Vilnius, SE Lithuania 54°42′N 25°00′E
169 K4 **Grignan** Rhône-Alpes, France 44°25′N 4°54′E
168 D4 **Grignols** Aquitaine, France 44°23′N 0°02′W
188 G7 **Grigoriopol** C Moldova 47°09′N 29°18′E
229 M4 **Grigor'yevka** Issyk-Kul'skaya Oblast', E Kyrgyzstan 42°43′N 77°27′E
287 K6 **Grijalva Ridge** undersea feature E Pacific Ocean
87 J8 **Grijalva, Río** var. Tabasco. ≈ Guatemala/Mexico
87 J7 **Grijalva, Río** ≈ Mexico
172 B1 **Grijó** Porto, Portugal 41°02′N 8°35′W
162 H3 **Grijpskerk** Groningen, NE Netherlands 53°15′N 06°18′E
140 B5 **Grillenthal** Karas, SW Namibia 26°55′S 15°24′E
134 F5 **Grimari** Ouaka, C Central African Republic 05°44′N 20°02′E
169 M6 **Grimaud** Provence-Alpes-Côte d'Azur, France 43°16′N 6°31′E
Grimaylov see Hrymayliv
163 E10 **Grimbergen** Vlaams Brabant, C Belgium 50°56′N 04°22′E
277 I9 **Grim, Cape** headland Tasmania, SE Australia 40°42′S 144°42′E
80 C1 **Grimes** California, USA 39°04′N 121°54′W
178 H4 **Grimmen** Mecklenburg-Vorpommern, NE Germany 54°06′N 13°03′E
62 D5 **Grimsby** Ontario, S Canada 43°12′N 79°35′W
159 M9 **Grimsby** prev. Great Grimsby. E England, United Kingdom 53°35′N 00°05′W
152 C1 **Grímsey** var. Grimsey. island N Iceland
Grimsey see Grímsey
56 G2 **Grimshaw** Alberta, W Canada 56°11′N 117°37′W
155 C9 **Grimstad** Aust-Agder, S Norway 58°20′N 08°35′E
152 B3 **Grindavík** Reykjanes, W Iceland 65°57′N 18°10′W
176 D5 **Grindelwald** Bern, S Switzerland 46°37′N 08°04′E
159 J8 **Grindleton** United Kingdom 53°54′N 2°22′W
155 C12 **Grindsted** Ribe, W Denmark 55°46′N 08°56′E
74 H7 **Grinnell** Iowa, C USA 41°44′N 92°43′W
53 H4 **Grinnell Peninsula** peninsula Northwest Territories, Devon Island, N Canada
174 G4 **Grintovec** ▲ N Slovenia 46°21′N 14°31′E
Griquatown see Griekwastad
53 I4 **Grise Fjord** var Aujuittuq. Northwest Territories, Ellesmere Island, N Canada 76°10′N 83°15′W
276 F1 **Griselda, Lake** salt lake South Australia
166 G1 **Gris-Nez, Cap** cape N France
Grisons see Graubünden
154 J7 **Grisslehamn** Stockholm, C Sweden 60°04′N 18°50′E
159 I7 **Grizebeck** United Kingdom 54°15′N 3°10′W
165 H1 **Griz Nez, Cap** headland N France 50°51′N 01°34′E
80 E2 **Grizzly Flat** California, USA 38°38′N 120°32′W
185 H5 **Grljan** Serbia, E Serbia 43°52′N 22°18′E
184 C3 **Grmeč** ▲▲ NW Bosnia and Herzegovina
163 E9 **Grobbendonk** Antwerpen, N Belgium 51°12′N 04°41′E
Grobin see Grobiņa
190 B6 **Grobiņa** Ger. Grobin. Liepāja, W Latvia 56°32′N 21°12′E
141 J3 **Groblersdal** Mpumalanga, NE South Africa 25°15′S 29°25′E
140 F6 **Groblershoop** Northern Cape, W South Africa 28°51′S 22°01′E
Gródek Jagielloński see Horodok
177 I3 **Grödig** Salzburg, W Austria 47°42′N 13°06′E
183 E8 **Grodków** Opolskie, S Poland 50°42′N 17°23′E
Grodnenskaya Oblast' see Hrodzyenskaya Voblasts'
Grodno see Hrodna
182 H6 **Grodzisk Mazowiecki** Mazowieckie, C Poland 52°09′N 20°38′E
182 D6 **Grodzisk Wielkopolski** Wielkopolskie, C Poland 52°13′N 16°21′E
Grodzyanka see Hradzyanka
140 C7 **Groen** ≈ Northern Cape, South Africa
140 G7 **Groen** ≈ Northern Cape, South Africa
162 I7 **Groenlo** Gelderland, E Netherlands 52°02′N 06°36′E
140 D5 **Groenrivier** Karas, SE Namibia 27°27′S 18°52′E
71 H5 **Groesbeck** Texas, SW USA 31°31′N 96°35′W
162 H7 **Groesbeek** Gelderland, SE Netherlands 51°47′N 05°56′E
141 J2 **Groesbeek** Limpopo, South Africa 23°52′S 28°26′E
166 A7 **Groix, Île de** island Bretagne, France
164 E4 **Groix, Îles de** island group NW France
182 H6 **Grójec** Mazowieckie, C Poland 51°51′N 20°52′E
175 C13 **Grombalia** Tunisia
180 C6 **Gronau** var. Gronau in Westfalen. Nordrhein-Westfalen, NW Germany 52°13′N 07°02′E
Gronau in Westfalen see Gronau
154 F2 **Grong** Nord-Trøndelag, C Norway 64°29′N 12°19′E
155 H11 **Grönhögen** Kalmar, S Sweden 56°16′N 16°09′E
181 H14 **Gröningen** Baden-Württemberg, Germany 49°11′E 10°04′N
180 J7 **Gröningen** Sachsen-Anhalt, Germany 51°56′E 11°13′N
162 I3 **Groningen** Groningen, NE Netherlands 53°13′N 06°35′E
103 L5 **Groningen** Saramacca, N Suriname 05°45′N 55°31′W
162 I3 **Groningen** ◐ province NE Netherlands
Grønland see Greenland
176 E5 **Grono** Graubünden, S Switzerland 46°15′N 09°07′E
155 H10 **Grönskåra** Kalmar, S Sweden 57°04′N 15°45′E
70 E2 **Groom** Texas, SW USA 35°12′N 101°06′W
80 J7 **Groom Lake** ◎ Nevada, W USA
140 G9 **Groot** ≈ Eastern Cape, South Africa
138 F10 **Groot** ≈ S South Africa
140 F10 **Groot** ≈ Western Cape, South Africa
141 H8 **Groot Brak** ≈ Eastern Cape, South Africa
140 D8 **Grootdrif** Western Cape, South Africa 31°27′S 18°57′E
140 F5 **Grootdrink** Northern Cape, South Africa 26°29′S 22°14′E
275 H2 **Groote Eylandt** island Northern Territory, N Australia
162 H3 **Grootegast** Groningen, NE Netherlands 53°11′N 06°12′E
138 C4 **Grootfontein** Otjozondjupa, N Namibia 19°32′S 18°05′E
140 D5 **Groot Karasberge** ▲▲ S Namibia
Groot Karoo see Great Karoo
141 J9 **Groot Kei** ≈ Eastern Cape, South Africa
Groot-Kei see Nciba
141 I3 **Groot-Marico** North-West, South Africa 25°36′S 26°25′E
140 C6 **Grootmis** Northern Cape, South Africa 29°39′S 17°05′E
141 I4 **Grootpan** North West, South Africa 26°01′S 26°25′E
140 G9 **Grootrivierberge** ▲▲ Eastern Cape, South Africa
140 E7 **Grootvloer** salt lake Northern Cape, South Africa
91 J3 **Gros Islet** N Saint Lucia 14°04′N 60°57′W
90 G5 **Gros-Morne** NW Haiti 19°45′N 72°46′W
59 L6 **Gros Morne** ▲ Newfoundland, Newfoundland and Labrador, E Canada 49°38′N 57°45′W
165 J5 **Grosne** ≈ C France
91 J3 **Gros Piton** ▲ SW Saint Lucia 13°48′N 61°04′W
Grossa, Isola see Dugi Otok
181 F11 **Grossauheim** Hessen, Germany 50°06′E 8°57′N
Grossbetschkerek see Zrenjanin
181 I8 **Grossbodungen** Thüringen, Germany 51°28′E 10°30′N
180 D3 **Grossefehn** Niedersachsen, Germany 53°24′E 7°33′N
Grosse Isper see Grosse Ysper
Grosse Kokel see Târnava Mare
179 G12 **Grosse Laaber** var. Grosse Laber. ≈ SE Germany
Grosse Laber see Grosse Laaber
Grosse Morava see Velika Morava
181 J8 **Grossenehrich** Thüringen, Germany 51°15′E 10°50′N
179 I8 **Grossenhain** Sachsen, E Germany 51°18′N 13°31′E
180 E4 **Grossenkneten** Niedersachsen, Germany 52°57′E 8°16′N
180 I2 **Grossensee** Schleswig-Holstein, Germany 53°37′E 10°21′N
177 L2 **Grossenzersdorf** Niederösterreich, NE Austria 48°12′N 16°33′E
179 H11 **Grosser Arber** ▲ SE Germany 49°07′N 13°10′E
181 J10 **Grosser Beerberg** ▲ C Germany 50°39′N 10°45′E
181 F11 **Grosser Feldberg** ▲ W Germany 50°13′N 08°28′E
181 G14 **Grosserlach** Baden-Württemberg, Germany 49°03′E 9°31′N
174 E3 **Grosser Löffler** It. Monte Lovello. ▲ Austria/Italy 47°02′N 11°56′E
174 E3 **Grosser Möseler** var. Mesule. ▲ Austria/Italy 47°01′N 11°52′E
180 I1 **Grosser Plöner See** ◎ N Germany
179 H11 **Grosser Rachel** ▲ SE Germany 48°59′N 13°23′E
Grosser Sund see Suur Väin
179 H14 **Grosses Wiesbachhorn** var. Wiesbachhorn. ▲ W Austria 47°09′N 12°44′E
174 D7 **Grosseto** Toscana, C Italy 42°45′N 11°07′E
179 G12 **Grosse Vils** ≈ SE Germany
177 K2 **Grosse Ysper** var. Grosse Isper. ≈ N Austria
181 F12 **Gross-Gerau** Hessen, W Germany 49°55′N 08°28′E
177 K2 **Gross Gerungs** Niederösterreich, N Austria 48°33′N 14°58′E
179 H14 **Grossglockner** ▲ W Austria 47°05′N 12°39′E
180 H5 **Gross Hehlen** Niedersachsen, Germany 52°39′E 10°03′N
180 C5 **Gross Hesepe** Niedersachsen, Germany 52°37′E 7°14′N
181 G12 **Grossheubach** Bayern, Germany 49°44′E 9°14′N
64 G4 **Grossinger** New York, NE USA 41°47′N 74°43′W
Grosskanizsa see Nagykanizsa
Gross-Karol see Carei
Grosskikinda see Kikinda
177 K4 **Grossklein** Steiermark, SE Austria 46°43′N 15°24′E
Grosskoppe see Velká Deštná
Grossmeseritsch see Velké Meziříčí
Grossmichel see Michalovce
181 G12 **Grossostheim** Bayern, C Germany 49°54′N 09°03′E
177 L3 **Grosspetersdorf** Burgenland, SE Austria 47°15′N 16°19′E
177 J3 **Grossraming** Oberösterreich, C Austria 47°54′N 14°34′E
179 I8 **Grossräschen** Brandenburg, E Germany 51°34′N 14°00′E
Grossrauschenbach see Revúca
180 H7 **Gross Rhüden** Niedersachsen, Germany 51°57′E 10°07′N
181 H13 **Grossrinderfeld** Baden-Württemberg, Germany 49°39′E 9°45′N
Gross-Sankt-Johannis see Suure-Jaani
Gross-Schlatten see Abrud
Gross-Skaisgirren see Bol'shakovo
Gross-Steffelsdorf see Rimavská Sobota
Gross Strehlitz see Strzelce Opolskie
180 J6 **Gross Twülpstedt** Niedersachsen, Germany 52°22′E 10°55′N
181 F12 **Gross-Umstadt** Hessen, Germany 49°52′E 8°56′N
179 G14 **Grossvenediger** ▲ W Austria 47°07′N 12°19′E
Grosswardein see Oradea
Gross Wartenberg see Syców
167 M5 **Grostenquin** Lorraine, France 48°59′N 6°44′E
177 K6 **Grosuplje** C Slovenia 46°00′N 14°36′E
163 E9 **Grote Nete** ≈ N Belgium
154 C5 **Grotli** Oppland, S Norway 62°02′N 07°36′E
65 K4 **Groton** Connecticut, NE USA 41°20′N 72°03′W
74 E4 **Groton** South Dakota, N USA 45°27′N 98°06′W
175 I10 **Grottaglie** Puglia, SE Italy 40°32′N 17°26′E
175 G9 **Grottaminarda** Campania, S Italy 41°04′N 15°02′E
177 J10 **Grottammare** Marche, C Italy 43°00′N 13°52′E
67 K3 **Grottoes** Virginia, NE USA 38°16′N 78°49′W
Grou see Grouw
59 I6 **Groulx, Monts** ▲▲ Québec, E Canada
58 E7 **Groundhog** ≈ Ontario, S Canada
78 G1 **Grouse Creek** Utah, W USA 41°41′N 113°52′W
78 G1 **Grouse Creek Mountains** ▲▲ Utah, W USA
162 G4 **Grouw** Fris. Grou. Friesland, N Netherlands 53°07′N 05°51′E
75 G11 **Grove** Oklahoma, C USA 36°35′N 94°46′W
73 H11 **Grove City** Ohio, N USA 39°52′N 83°05′W
62 C7 **Grove City** Pennsylvania, NE USA 41°09′N 80°02′W
68 G2 **Grove Hill** Alabama, S USA 31°42′N 87°46′W
80 D4 **Groveland** California, USA 37°50′N 120°14′W
77 I8 **Grover** Wyoming, C USA 42°48′N 110°57′W
80 B7 **Grover Beach** California, USA 35°07′N 120°37′W
78 C7 **Grover City** California, W USA 35°08′N 120°37′W
71 J7 **Groves** Texas, SW USA 29°57′N 93°55′W
63 I4 **Groveton** New Hampshire, NE USA 44°35′N 71°28′W
71 I6 **Groveton** Texas, SW USA 31°04′N 95°08′W
79 H9 **Growler Mountains** ▲▲ Arizona, SW USA
Grozdovo see Bratya Daskalovi
197 I9 **Groznyy** Chechenskaya Respublika, SW Russian Federation 43°20′N 45°43′E
Grubeshov see Hrubieszów
184 D2 **Grubišno Polje** Bjelovar-Bilogora, NE Croatia 45°42′N 17°09′E
Grudovo see Sredets
182 F4 **Grudziądz** Ger. Graudenz. Kujawsko-pomorskie, C Poland 53°29′N 18°45′E
169 H6 **Gruissan** Languedoc-Roussillon, France 43°06′N 3°05′E
70 G10 **Grulla** var. La Grulla. Texas, SW USA 26°15′N 98°37′W
86 B6 **Grullo** Jalisco, SW Mexico 19°45′N 104°15′W
121 L6 **Grumeti** ≈ N Tanzania
155 F8 **Grums** Värmland, C Sweden 59°22′N 13°11′E
140 D5 **Grünau** Karas, Namibia 27°44′S 18°22′E
177 J3 **Grünau im Almtal** Oberösterreich, N Austria 47°51′N 13°56′E
181 F10 **Grünberg** Hessen, W Germany 50°36′N 08°57′E
Grünberg/Grünberg in Schlesien see Zielona Góra
152 A2 **Grundarfjördhur** Vestfirdhir, W Iceland 64°55′N 23°15′W
181 H14 **Gründelhardt** Baden-Württemberg, Germany 49°05′E 9°59′N
67 H4 **Grundy** Virginia, NE USA 37°17′N 82°06′W
74 H7 **Grundy Center** Iowa, C USA 42°21′N 92°46′W
Grüneberg see Zielona Góra
180 G3 **Grünendeich** Niedersachsen, Germany 53°34′E 9°36′N
181 H13 **Grünsfeld** Baden-Württemberg, Germany 49°37′E 9°45′N
181 E13 **Grünstadt** Rheinland-Pfalz, Germany 49°34′E 8°10′N
114 A4 **Gruttly** Santa Fe, Argentina 31°16′S 61°03′W
70 E1 **Gruver** Texas, SW USA 36°16′N 101°24′W
174 A3 **Gruyère, Lac de la** Ger. Greyerzer See. ◎ SW Switzerland
176 C5 **Gruyères** Fribourg, W Switzerland 46°34′N 07°04′E
190 C7 **Gruzdžiai** Šiauliai, N Lithuania 56°06′N 23°15′E
Gruzinskaya SSR/Gruziya see Georgia
Gryada Akkyr see Akgyr Erezi
190 I7 **Gryadtsy** Tverskaya Oblast', Russian Federation
190 I3 **Gryady** Novgorodskaya Oblast', Russian Federation
196 G4 **Gryazi** Lipetskaya Oblast', W Russian Federation 52°27′N 39°56′E
194 G9 **Gryazovets** Vologodskaya Oblast', NW Russian Federation 58°52′N 40°12′E
183 H9 **Grybów** Małopolskie, SE Poland 49°35′N 20°54′E
154 H6 **Grycksbo** Dalarna, C Sweden 60°40′N 15°30′E
182 C4 **Gryfice** Ger. Greifenberg, Greifenberg in Pommern. Zachodnio-pomorskie, NW Poland 53°55′N 15°11′E
182 C5 **Gryfino** Ger. Greifenhagen. Zachodnio-pomorskie, NW Poland 53°15′N 14°30′E
152 E4 **Gryllefjord** Troms, N Norway 69°21′N 17°07′E
154 G7 **Grythyttan** Örebro, C Sweden 59°52′N 14°31′E
181 H14 **Gschwend** Baden-Württemberg, Germany 48°56′E 9°44′N
176 C5 **Gstaad** Bern, W Switzerland 46°30′N 07°16′E
89 I8 **Guabito** Bocas del Toro, NW Panama 09°30′N 82°35′W
90 E5 **Guacanayabo, Golfo de** gulf S Cuba
85 H6 **Guachochi** Chihuahua, N Mexico
85 H5 **Guachochic** Chihuahua, Mexico
111 K4 **Guaçuí** Espírito Santo, Brazil 20°46′S 41°41′W
173 H7 **Guadahortuna** Andalucía, Spain 37°34′N 3°24′W
172 E5 **Guadajira** ≈ SW Spain
172 G7 **Guadajoz** ≈ S Spain
86 C5 **Guadalajara** Jalisco, C Mexico 20°43′N 103°24′W
170 G4 **Guadalajara** Ar. Wad Al-Hajarah; anc. Arriaca. Castilla-La Mancha, C Spain 40°37′N 03°10′W
171 H4 **Guadalajara** ◐ province Castilla-La Mancha, C Spain
170 E7 **Guadalcanal** Andalucía, S Spain 38°06′N 05°49′W
281 J3 **Guadalcanal** off. Guadalcanal Province. ◐ province C Solomon Islands
281 J3 **Guadalcanal** island C Solomon Islands
Guadalcanal Province see Guadalcanal
173 I6 **Guadalén** ≈ Andalucía, Spain
170 G7 **Guadalén** ≈ S Spain
173 K7 **Guadalentín** ≈ SE Spain
170 E9 **Guadalete** ≈ SW Spain
172 G9 **Guadalhorce** ≈ Spain
170 G7 **Guadalimar** ≈ S Spain
173 I5 **Guadalmena** ≈ S Spain
170 F7 **Guadalmez** ≈ W Spain
171 I4 **Guadalope** ≈ E Spain
172 E8 **Guadalquivir** ≈ W Spain
170 E8 **Guadalquivir, Marismas del** var. Las Marismas. wetland SW Spain
172 E8 **Guadalquivir, Marismas del** marsh Spain
85 K6 **Guadalupe** Coahuila, Mexico 26°08′N 101°17′W
84 E3 **Guadalupe** San Luis Potosí, C Mexico 29°58′N 110°35′W
85 K9 **Guadalupe** Zacatecas, C Mexico 22°47′N 102°30′W
105 D8 **Guadalupe** Ica, W Peru 13°59′S 75°49′W
170 F6 **Guadalupe** Extremadura, W Spain 39°26′N 05°18′W
79 H9 **Guadalupe** Arizona, SW USA 33°20′N 111°57′W
81 B8 **Guadalupe** California, W USA 34°55′N 120°34′W
287 I3 **Guadalupe** island NW Mexico
Guadalupe see Canelones
85 I7 **Guadalupe Aguilera** Durango, C Mexico 24°27′N 104°42′W
85 H2 **Guadalupe Bravos** Chihuahua, N Mexico 31°22′N 106°04′W
84 D5 **Guadalupe de los Reyes** Baja California Sur, NW Mexico 27°19′N 113°21′W
86 F8 **Guadalupe de Ramírez** Oaxaca, Mexico 17°45′N 98°09′W
84 A3 **Guadalupe, Isla** island NW Mexico
79 M9 **Guadalupe Mountains** ▲▲ New Mexico/Texas, SW USA
70 B5 **Guadalupe Peak** ▲ Texas, SW USA 31°53′N 104°51′W
70 G7 **Guadalupe River** ≈ SW USA
170 F6 **Guadalupe, Sierra de** ▲▲ W Spain
85 J7 **Guadalupe Victoria** Durango, C Mexico 24°30′N 104°08′W
85 H6 **Guadalupe y Calvo** Chihuahua, N Mexico 26°04′N 106°58′W
170 G4 **Guadarrama** Madrid, C Spain 40°40′N 04°06′W
170 G5 **Guadarrama** ≈ C Spain
170 F4 **Guadarrama, Puerto de** pass C Spain
170 G4 **Guadarrama, Sierra de** ▲▲ C Spain
173 J3 **Guadazaón** ≈ Castilla-La Manacha, Spain
171 H5 **Guadazaón** ≈ C Spain
91 J1 **Guadeloupe** ◇ French overseas department E West Indies
95 K2 **Guadeloupe** island group E West Indies
91 J1 **Guadeloupe Passage** passage E Caribbean Sea
170 D7 **Guadiana** ≈ Portugal/Spain
170 G8 **Guadiana Menor** ≈ S Spain
173 I7 **Guadiana Menor** ≈ Spain
171 H4 **Guadiela** ≈ C Spain
170 G8 **Guadix** Andalucía, S Spain 37°19′N 03°08′W
Guad-i-Zirreh see Gowd-e Zereh, Dasht-e
287 K9 **Guafo Fracture Zone** tectonic feature SE Pacific Ocean
117 A9 **Guafo, Isla** island S Chile
88 G4 **Guaimaca** Francisco Morazán, C Honduras 14°34′N 86°49′W
102 F7 **Guainía** off. Comisaría del Guainía. ◐ province E Colombia
Guainía, Comisaría del see Guainía
102 F7 **Guainía, Río** ≈ Colombia/Venezuela
103 H5 **Guaiquinima, Cerro** elevation SE Venezuela
113 I4 **Guaíra** Paraná, S Brazil 24°05′S 54°15′W
110 A3 **Guaíra** São Paulo, S Brazil 20°17′S 48°21′W
113 H5 **Guairá** off. Departamento del Guairá. ◐ department S Paraguay
Guairá, Departamento del see Guairá
Guaire see Gorey
117 B9 **Guaiteca, Isla** island S Chile
90 E4 **Guajaba, Cayo** headland C Cuba 21°50′N 77°33′W
106 E7 **Guajará-Mirim** Rondônia, W Brazil 10°50′S 65°21′W
Guajira see La Guajira
Guajira, Departamento de La see La Guajira
102 D2 **Guajira, Península de la** peninsula N Colombia
88 G4 **Gualaco** Olancho, C Honduras 15°00′N 86°03′W
78 A3 **Gualala** California, W USA 38°45′N 123°33′W
88 D3 **Gualán** Zacapa, C Guatemala 15°06′N 89°22′W
114 D7 **Gualeguay** Entre Ríos, E Argentina 33°09′S 59°20′W
114 E6 **Gualeguaychú** Entre Ríos, E Argentina 33°03′S 58°31′W
114 D6 **Gualeguay, Río** ≈ E Argentina
116 E7 **Gualicho, Salina del** salt lake E Argentina
118 D10 **Gualletue, Laguna** ◎ Araucanía, Chile
118 B8 **Gualpen, Punta** point Bío-Bío, Chile
282 A1 **Guam** ◇ US unincorporated territory W Pacific Ocean
117 A9 **Guamblin, Isla** island Archipiélago de los Chonos, S Chile
116 F5 **Guaminí** Buenos Aires, E Argentina 37°01′S 62°28′W
84 G7 **Guamúchil** Sinaloa, C Mexico 25°23′N 108°01′W
102 D2 **Guana** var. Misión de Guana. Zulia, NW Venezuela 11°07′N 72°17′W
90 C3 **Guanabacoa** La Habana, W Cuba 23°02′N 82°12′W
88 G8 **Guanacaste** off. Provincia de Guanacaste. ◐ province NW Costa Rica
88 G7 **Guanacaste, Cordillera de** ▲▲ NW Costa Rica
Guanacaste, Provincia de see Guanacaste
85 H6 **Guanaceví** Durango, C Mexico 25°55′N 105°51′W
90 A3 **Guanahacabibes, Golfo de** gulf W Cuba
88 G2 **Guanaja, Isla de** island Islas de la Bahía, N Honduras
90 C3 **Guanajay** La Habana, W Cuba 22°56′N 82°42′W
86 D5 **Guanajuato** Guanajuato, C Mexico 21°N 101°19′W
86 D5 **Guanajuato** ◐ state C Mexico
102 E3 **Guanare** Portuguesa, N Venezuela 09°04′N 69°45′W
102 F4 **Guanare, Río** ≈ W Venezuela
102 E3 **Guanarito** Portuguesa, NW Venezuela 08°43′N 69°12′W
244 G3 **Guancen Shan** ▲▲ C China
112 C7 **Guandacol** La Rioja, W Argentina 29°32′S 68°37′W
244 G4 **Guandi Shan** ▲ Shanxi, China 37°32′N 111°17′E
243 H8 **Guandu** Guangdong, SE China 24°17′N 113°53′E
243 H4 **Guandu** Hunan, SE China 28°21′N 113°53′E
90 B3 **Guane** Pinar del Río, W Cuba 22°12′N 84°05′W
242 C2 **Guang'an** Sichuan, C China 30°18′N 106°22′E
243 J6 **Guangchang** Jiangxi, SE China 26°57′N 116°25′E
243 L2 **Guangde** Anhui, China 30°32′N 119°14′E
243 H9 **Guangdong** var. Guangdong Sheng, Kuang-tung, Kwangtung, Yue. ◐ province S China
Guangdong Sheng see Guangdong
243 K4 **Guangfeng** Jiangxi, China 28°16′N 118°07′E
242 G10 **Guanghai** Guangdong, China 21°57′N 112°47′E
242 A2 **Guanghan** Sichuan, China 30°35′N 104°09′E
244 A6 **Guanghe** Gansu, China 35°17′N 103°20′E
Guanghua see Laohekou
Guangju see Gwangju
243 K3 **Guangming Ding** ▲ Anhui, China 30°06′N 118°04′E
242 B8 **Guangnan** var. Liancheng. Yunnan, SW China 24°07′N 104°54′E
242 G9 **Guangning** Guangdong, China 23°23′N 112°15′E
245 K5 **Guangrao** Shandong, E China 37°08′N 118°29′E
243 H2 **Guangshui** Hubei, E China 31°37′N 113°49′E
243 H2 **Guangshui** prev. Yinshan. Hubei, C China 31°41′N 113°53′E
242 C6 **Guangshun** Guizhou, S China 26°11′N 106°22′E
118 C1 **Guanguali** Coquimbo, Chile 32°08′S 71°23′W
Guangxi see Guangxi Zhuangzu Zizhiqu
242 D8 **Guangxi Zhuangzu Zizhiqu** var. Guangxi, Gui, Kuang-hsi, Kwangsi, Eng. Kwangsi Chuang Autonomous Region. ◐ autonomous region S China
242 C1 **Guangyuan** var. Kuang-yuan, Kwangyuan. Sichuan, C China 32°27′N 105°49′E
243 K5 **Guangze** Fujan, China 27°19′N 117°13′E
243 H9 **Guangzhou** var. Kuang-chou, Kwangchow, Eng. Canton. province capital Guangdong, S China 23°11′N 113°19′E
111 I1 **Guanhães** Minas Gerais, SE Brazil 18°46′S 42°58′W
243 M3 **Guanhaiwei** Zhejiang, E China 30°11′N 121°24′E
Guankou see Dujiangyan
242 B6 **Guanling** var. Guanling Bouyeizu Miaozu Zizhixian. Guizhou, S China 26°00′N 105°40′E
Guanling Bouyeizu Miaozu Zizhixian see Guanling
243 L7 **Guanqiao** Fujian, SE China 24°48′N 118°26′E
103 H3 **Guanta** Anzoátegui, NE Venezuela 10°15′N 64°38′W
90 F5 **Guantánamo** Guantánamo, SE Cuba 20°06′N 75°16′W
90 F5 **Guantánamo, Bahia de** Eng. Guantanamo Bay. US military base SE Cuba 20°06′N 75°16′W
Guantanamo Bay see Guantánamo, Bahia de
245 I6 **Guantao** Hebei, China 36°30′N 115°24′E
245 I3 **Guanting Shuiku** ⊠ Hebei, China
Guanxian see Dujiangyan
Guanxian/Guan Xian see Dujiangyan
242 F7 **Guanyang** Guangxi, China 25°17′N 111°05′E
245 L8 **Guanyun** var. Yishan. Jiangsu, E China 34°18′N 119°14′E
110 E4 **Guapé** Minas Gerais, Brazil 20°47′S 45°55′W
102 A7 **Guapí** Cauca, SW Colombia 02°36′N 77°54′W
89 H8 **Guápiles** Limón, NE Costa Rica 10°15′N 83°46′W
111 I7 **Guapimirim** Rio de Janeiro, Brazil 22°32′S 42°59′W
113 J7 **Guaporé** Rio Grande do Sul, S Brazil 28°55′S 51°53′W
95 K5 **Guaporé, Rio** var. Río Iténez. ≈ Bolivia/Brazil see also Río Iténez
Guaporé, Rio see Iténez, Río
110 B4 **Guará** São Paulo, Brazil 20°26′S 47°50′W
111 I4 **Guaraciaba** Minas Gerais, Brazil 20°34′S 43°00′W
104 C2 **Guaranda** Bolívar, C Ecuador 01°35′S 78°59′W
110 C5 **Guaranésia** Minas Gerais, Brazil 21°18′S 46°48′W
113 I4 **Guaraniaçu** Paraná, S Brazil 25°05′S 52°52′W
110 B6 **Guaraparà** São Paulo, Brazil 21°30′S 48°02′W
111 M4 **Guarapari** Espírito Santo, SE Brazil 20°39′S 40°31′W
113 J5 **Guarapuava** Paraná, S Brazil 25°22′S 51°28′W
111 I6 **Guararà** Minas Gerais, Brazil 21°43′S 43°02′W
113 J3 **Guararapes** São Paulo, S Brazil 21°16′S 50°37′W
110 E9 **Guararema** São Paulo, Brazil 23°25′S 46°02′W
171 I3 **Guara, Sierra de** ▲▲ NE Spain
110 F8 **Guaratinguetá** São Paulo, S Brazil 22°44′S 45°16′W
172 D2 **Guarda** Guarda, N Portugal 40°32′N 07°17′W
172 D2 **Guarda** ◐ district N Portugal
Guardak see Magdanly
173 L6 **Guardamar del Segura** Valenciana, Spain 38°06′N 0°39′W
114 D5 **Guardamonte** Entre Ríos, Argentina 32°05′S 59°18′W
170 F2 **Guardo** Castilla-León, N Spain 42°48′N 04°50′W
110 B9 **Guarei** São Paulo, Brazil 23°22′S 48°10′W
170 E6 **Guareña** Extremadura, W Spain 38°51′N 06°06′W
110 A5 **Guariba** São Paulo, Brazil 21°21′S 48°14′W
113 K5 **Guaricana, Pico** ▲ S Brazil 25°13′S 48°50′W
102 F3 **Guárico** off. Estado Guárico. ◐ state N Venezuela
Guárico, Estado see Guárico
90 G5 **Guarico, Punta** headland E Cuba 20°36′N 74°43′W
102 F4 **Guárico, Río** ≈ C Venezuela
173 H6 **Guarromàn** Andalucía, Spain 38°11′N 3°41′W
110 D10 **Guarujá** São Paulo, SE Brazil 23°50′S 46°27′W

◆ Country
● Country Capital
◇ Dependent Territory
○ Dependent Territory Capital
◐ Administrative Regions
✕ International Airport
▲ Mountain
▲▲ Mountain Range
Volcano
≈ River
◎ Lake
⊠ Reservoir

◆ Country   ● Country Capital   ◇ Dependent Territory   ○ Dependent Territory Capital   ◈ Administrative Regions   ✕ International Airport   ▲ Mountain   ▲ Mountain Range   ▼ Volcano   ⚓ River   ◎ Lake   ◎ Reservoir

◆ Country   ◇ Dependent Territory   ◈ Administrative Regions   ▲ Mountain   ⊕ Volcano   ◎ Lake
● Country Capital   ○ Dependent Territory Capital   ✕ International Airport   ▲ Mountain Range   ◢ River   ▣ Reservoir

◆ Country   ◇ Dependent Territory   ▲ Administrative Regions   ▲ Mountain   ▲ Volcano   ⊚ Lake
● Country Capital   ○ Dependent Territory Capital   ✕ International Airport   ▲ Mountain Range   ⚟ River   ◆ Reservoir

Humbe - Imuris

135 C14 **Humbe** Cunene, SW Angola 16°37′S 14°52′E
157 I9 **Humber** *estuary* E England, United Kingdom
159 M9 **Humberston** United Kingdom 53°32′N 0°02′W
Humberto *see* Umberto
71 I7 **Humble** Texas, SW USA 29°58′N 95°15′W
114 A4 **Humboldt** Santa Fe, Argentina 31°25′S 61°05′W
74 G6 **Humboldt** Iowa, C USA 42°42′N 94°13′W
75 F10 **Humboldt** Kansas, C USA 37°48′N 95°26′W
75 F8 **Humboldt** Nebraska, C USA 40°09′N 95°56′W
80 I1 **Humboldt** Nevada, W USA 40°36′N 118°15′W
66 C6 **Humboldt** Tennessee, S USA 35°49′N 88°55′W
78 A2 **Humboldt Bay** *bay* California, W USA
80 H2 **Humboldt Lake** ◎ Nevada, W USA
280 C9 **Humboldt, Mont** ▲ S New Caledonia 21°57′S 166°24′E
80 I1 **Humboldt Range** ▲▲ Nevada, USA
80 J1 **Humboldt River** ≈ Nevada, W USA
80 I2 **Humboldt Salt Marsh** *wetland* Nevada, W USA
80 E6 **Hume** California, USA 36°47′N 118°55′W
277 J6 **Hume, Lake** ◎ New South Wales/Victoria, SE Australia
183 I9 **Humenné** *Ger.* Homenau, *Hung.* Homonna. Prešovský Kraj, E Slovakia 48°57′N 21°54′E
75 G8 **Humeston** Iowa, C USA 40°51′N 93°30′W
181 G8 **Hümme** Hessen, Germany 51°32′E 9°24′N
102 E3 **Humocaro Bajo** Lara, N Venezuela 09°41′N 70°00′W
74 E7 **Humphrey** Nebraska, C USA 41°38′N 97°29′W
80 F5 **Humphreys, Mount** ▲ California, W USA 37°11′N 118°39′W
79 I7 **Humphreys Peak** ▲ Arizona, SW USA 35°18′N 111°40′W
183 C9 **Humpolec** *Ger.* Gumpolds, Humpoletz. Vysočina, C Czech Republic 49°33′N 15°23′E
Humpoletz *see* Humpolec
153 H9 **Humppila** Etelä-Suomi, S Finland 60°54′N 23°21′E
76 B4 **Humptulips** Washington, NW USA 47°13′N 123°57′W
128 D3 **Hūn** N Libya 29°06′N 15°56′E
152 B1 **Húnaflói** *bay* NW Iceland
242 G4 **Hunan** *var.* Hunan Sheng, Xiang. ◈ *province* S China
Hunan Sheng *see* Hunan
248 E2 **Hunchun** Jilin, NE China 42°51′N 130°21′E
155 E12 **Hundested** Frederiksborg, E Denmark 55°58′N 11°53′E
Hundred Mile House *see* 100 Mile House
188 C8 **Hunedoara** *Ger.* Eisenmarkt, *Hung.* Vajdahunyad. Hunedoara, SW Romania 45°45′N 22°54′E
188 C8 **Hunedoara** ◈ *county* W Romania
181 H10 **Hünfeld** Hessen, C Germany 50°41′N 09°46′E
Hungarian People's Republic *see* Hungary
183 F12 **Hungary** *off.* Republic of Hungary, *Ger.* Ungarn, *Hung.* Magyarország, *Rom.* Ungaria, *SCr.* Mađarska, *Ukr.* Uhorshchyna; *prev.* Hungarian People's Republic. ◆ *republic* C Europe
Hungary, Plain of *see* Great Hungarian Plain
Hungary, Republic of *see* Hungary
181 F10 **Hungen** Hessen, Germany 50°28′E 8°54′N
277 I2 **Hungerford** Queensland, Australia
Hŭnghae *see* Heunghae
Hungiy *see* Urgamal
248 C4 **Hŭngnam** E North Korea 39°50′N 127°36′E
77 H3 **Hungry Horse Reservoir** ⊞ Montana, NW USA
Hungt'ou *see* Lan Yü
Hung-tse Hu *see* Hongze Hu
256 H5 **Hưng Yên** Hai Hưng, N Vietnam 20°38′N 106°05′E
245 N1 **Hun He** ≈ Liaoning, China
Hunjiang *see* Baishan
155 E9 **Hunnebostrand** Västra Götaland, S Sweden 58°26′N 11°19′E
181 C12 **Hunsrück** ▲▲ W Germany
161 L2 **Hunstanton** E England, United Kingdom 52°57′N 00°27′E
235 D8 **Hunsūr** Karnātaka, E India 12°18′N 76°15′E
Hunt *see* Hangay
180 E6 **Hunte** ≈ NW Germany
114 B9 **Hunter** Buenos Aires, Argentina 34°14′S 60°35′W
74 E3 **Hunter** North Dakota, N USA 47°10′N 97°11′W
70 G7 **Hunter** Texas, SW USA 29°47′N 98°01′W
278 C10 **Hunter** ≈ South Island, New Zealand
53 K6 **Hunter, Cape** *headland* Nunavut, NE Canada
277 I8 **Hunter Island** *island* Tasmania, SE Australia
65 H3 **Hunter Mountain** ▲ New York, NE USA 42°10′N 74°13′W
278 B12 **Hunter Mountains** ▲▲ South Island, New Zealand
277 L4 **Hunter River** ≈ New South Wales, SE Australia
76 E3 **Hunters** Washington, NW USA 48°07′N 118°13′W
278 D11 **Hunters Hills, The** *hill range* South Island, New Zealand
278 H6 **Hunterville** Manawatu-Wanganui, North Island, New Zealand 39°55′S 175°34′E
73 E12 **Huntingburg** Indiana, N USA 38°18′N 86°57′W
161 K4 **Huntingdon** E England, United Kingdom 52°20′N 00°12′W
64 B6 **Huntingdon** Pennsylvania, NE USA 40°28′N 78°00′W
66 C6 **Huntingdon** Tennessee, S USA 36°00′N 88°25′W
73 F10 **Huntington** Indiana, N USA 40°52′N 85°30′W
76 F6 **Huntington** Oregon, NW USA 44°22′N 117°18′W
71 I6 **Huntington** Texas, SW USA 31°16′N 94°34′W
79 I3 **Huntington** Utah, W USA 39°19′N 110°57′W
67 H3 **Huntington** West Virginia, NE USA 38°25′N 82°27′W
81 D11 **Huntington Beach** California, W USA 33°39′N 118°00′W
78 F3 **Huntington Creek** ≈ Nevada, W USA
141 K1 **Huntleigh** Limpopo, South Africa 22°41′S 29°48′E
161 H5 **Huntley** United Kingdom 51°52′N 2°24′W
278 G4 **Huntly** Waikato, North Island, New Zealand 37°34′S 175°09′E
156 G5 **Huntly** NE Scotland, United Kingdom 57°25′N 02°48′W
54 C4 **Hunt, Mount** ▲ Yukon Territory, NW Canada 61°29′N 129°10′W
62 D3 **Huntsville** Ontario, S Canada 45°20′N 79°14′W
66 D7 **Huntsville** Alabama, S USA 34°44′N 86°35′W
75 G12 **Huntsville** Arkansas, C USA 36°04′N 93°46′W
75 H9 **Huntsville** Missouri, C USA 39°27′N 92°31′W
66 F5 **Huntsville** Tennessee, S USA 36°25′N 84°30′W
71 I6 **Huntsville** Texas, SW USA 30°43′N 95°34′W
79 H2 **Huntsville** Utah, W USA 41°16′N 111°47′W
87 L5 **Hunucmá** Yucatán, SE Mexico 20°59′N 89°55′W
245 H3 **Hunyuan** Shanxi, China 39°25′N 113°25′E
231 J2 **Hunza** ≈ NE Pakistan
Hunza *see* Karīmābād
Hunze *see* Oostermoers Vaart
238 D3 **Huocheng** *var.* Shuiding. Xinjiang Uygur Zizhiqu, NW China 44°03′N 80°49′E
245 H7 **Huojia** Henan, C China 35°14′N 113°38′E
Huolin Gol *see* Hulingol
281 H7 **Huon** *reef* N New Caledonia
255 M9 **Huon Gulf** *gulf* E Papua New Guinea
280 C3 **Huon Peninsula** *headland* C Papua New Guinea 06°24′S 147°50′E
243 J1 **Huoqiu** Anhui, China 32°11′N 116°10′E
243 J2 **Huoshan** Anhui, E China 31°25′N 116°20′E
Huoshao Dao *see* Lü Tao
Huoshao Tao *see* Lan Yü
244 G6 **Huozhou** Shanxi, China 36°20′N 111°25′E
Hupeh/Hupei *see* Hubei
181 I8 **Hüpstedt** Thüringen, Germany 51°20′E 10°27′N
218 F6 **Ḩuqoq** *var.* Khukok. Northern, N Israel 32°52′N 35°29′E
Hurama *see* Hongyuan
Hurano *see* Furano
154 E7 **Hurdalsjøen** *prev.* Hurdalssjøen. ◎ S Norway
Hurdalssjøen *see* Hurdalsjøen
62 B3 **Hurd, Cape** *headland* Ontario, S Canada 45°12′N 81°43′W
Hurdegaryp *see* Hardegarijp
74 C3 **Hurdsfield** North Dakota, N USA 47°24′N 99°55′W
Hüremt *see* Sayhan, Bulgan, Mongolia
Hüremt *see* Taragt, Övörhangay, Mongolia
129 J4 **Hurghada** *var.* Al Ghurdaqah, Ghurdaqah. E Egypt 27°17′N 33°47′E
121 L5 **Huri Hills** ▲▲ NW Kenya
79 K9 **Hurley** New Mexico, SW USA 32°42′N 108°07′W
72 C4 **Hurley** Wisconsin, N USA 46°25′N 90°15′W
158 G4 **Hurlford** United Kingdom 55°35′N 4°27′W
64 E10 **Hurlock** Maryland, NE USA 38°37′N 75°51′W
239 K3 **Hürmen** *var.* Tsoohor. Ömnögovĭ, S Mongolia 43°15′N 104°04′E
161 I8 **Hurn** United Kingdom 50°46′N 1°49′W
80 C6 **Huron** California, USA 36°12′N 120°06′W
74 D5 **Huron** South Dakota, N USA 44°19′N 98°13′W
72 H6 **Huron, Lake** ◎ Canada/USA
72 D4 **Huron Mountains** *hill range* Michigan, N USA
78 G5 **Hurricane** Utah, W USA 37°10′N 113°18′W
67 H3 **Hurricane** West Virginia, NE USA 38°25′N 82°01′W
79 H6 **Hurricane Cliffs** *cliff* Arizona, SW USA
69 K3 **Hurricane Creek** ≈ Georgia, SE USA
154 C5 **Hurrungane** ▲ S Norway 61°25′N 07°48′E
161 I7 **Hursley** United Kingdom 51°01′N 1°24′W
181 C9 **Hürth** Nordrhein-Westfalen, W Germany 50°52′N 06°49′E
Hurukawa *see* Furukawa
279 F9 **Hurunui** ≈ South Island, New Zealand
155 C11 **Hurup** Viborg, NW Denmark 56°46′N 08°26′E
159 K7 **Hurworth** United Kingdom 54°29′N 1°31′W
189 K9 **Hurzuf** Avtonomna Respublika Krym, S Ukraine 44°33′N 34°18′E
Huş *see* Huşi
154 B2 **Húsavík** *Dan.* Husevig. Sandoy, C Faeroe Islands 65°24′N 06°38′W
152 C1 **Húsavík** Nordhurland Eystra, NE Iceland 66°03′N 17°20′W
Husevig *see* Húsavík
Hushi *see* Xiuyu
245 N1 **Hushitai** Liaoning, NE China 41°56′N 123°31′E
188 F7 **Huşi** *var.* Huş. Vaslui, E Romania 46°40′N 28°05′E
155 G10 **Huskvarna** Jönköping, S Sweden 57°47′N 14°15′E
83 H4 **Huslia** Alaska, USA 65°42′N 156°24′W
Husn *see* Al Ḩuşn
154 A7 **Husnes** Hordaland, S Norway 59°52′N 05°46′E
Husté *see* Khust
178 D4 **Husum** Schleswig-Holstein, N Germany 54°29′N 09°04′E
154 J3 **Husum** Västernorrland, C Sweden 63°21′N 19°12′E
188 E4 **Husyatyn** Ternopil's'ka Oblast', W Ukraine 49°04′N 26°10′E
Huszt *see* Khust
Hutag *see* Hutag-Öndör
239 J1 **Hutag-Öndör** *var.* Hutag. Bulgan, N Mongolia 49°22′N 102°50′E
140 G8 **Hutchinson** Northern Cape, South Africa 31°30′S 23°11′E
75 D10 **Hutchinson** Kansas, C USA 38°03′N 97°56′W
74 G5 **Hutchinson** Minnesota, N USA 44°53′N 94°22′W
69 N7 **Hutchinson Island** *island* Florida, SE USA
79 I7 **Hutch Mountain** ▲ Arizona, SW USA 34°49′N 111°22′W
220 F8 **Ḩūth** NW Yemen 16°14′N 44°E
280 E3 **Hutjena** Buka Island, NE Papua New Guinea 05°19′S 154°40′E
243 K7 **Hutou** Fujian, SE China 25°14′N 118°02′E
177 J4 **Hüttenberg** Kärnten, S Austria 46°58′N 14°33′E
70 G6 **Hutto** Texas, SW USA 30°32′N 97°33′W
159 N10 **Huttoft** United Kingdom 53°15′N 0°16′E
159 M8 **Hutton** United Kingdom 53°58′N 0°26′W
277 K1 **Hutton, Mount** ▲ Queensland, Australia 25°51′S 148°20′E
Huttu *see* Futtsu
176 D4 **Huttwil** Bern, W Switzerland 47°06′N 07°48′E
238 F3 **Hutubi** Xinjiang Uygur Zizhiqu, NW China 44°10′N 86°51′E
245 H4 **Hutuo He** ≈ C China
Hutyû *see* Fuchū
244 E8 **Huxian** Shaanxi, China 34°04′N 108°22′E
278 C10 **Huxley, Mount** ▲ South Island, New Zealand 44°02′S 169°42′E
163 F11 **Huy** *Dut.* Hoei, Hoey. Liège, E Belgium 50°32′N 05°14′E
243 L7 **Huyang** Fujian, SE China 25°24′N 118°25′E
243 L2 **Huzhou** *var.* Wuxing. Zhejiang, SE China 30°54′N 120°05′E
244 A5 **Huzhu** *var.* Weiyuan. Qinghai, China 36°51′N 102°03′E
Huzi *see* Fuji
Huzieda *see* Fujieda
Huzinomiya *see* Fujinomiya
Huzisawa *see* Fujisawa
Huziyosida *see* Fujiyoshida
152 B2 **Hvammstangi** Nordhurland Vestra, N Iceland 65°22′N 20°54′W
152 D3 **Hvannadalshnúkur** ⛰ S Iceland 64°01′N 16°39′W
184 C5 **Hvar** *It.* Lesina. Split-Dalmacija, S Croatia 43°10′N 16°27′E
184 C5 **Hvar** *It.* Lesina; *anc.* Pharus. *island* S Croatia
189 J9 **Hvardiys'ke** *Rus.* Gvardeyskoye. Avtonomna Respublika Krym, S Ukraine 45°08′N 34°01′E
152 B3 **Hveragerdhi** Sudhurland, SW Iceland 64°00′N 21°13′W
155 C12 **Hvide Sande** Ringkøbing, W Denmark 56°00′N 08°08′E
152 B3 **Hvitá** ≈ C Iceland
155 D8 **Hvittingfoss** Buskerud, S Norway 59°28′N 10°00′E
152 B3 **Hvolsvöllur** Sudhurland, SW Iceland 63°44′N 20°12′W
Hwach'ŏn-chŏsuji *see* Paro-ho
Hwainan *see* Huainan
Hwalien *see* Hualien
138 F3 **Hwange** *prev.* Wankie. Matabeleland North, W Zimbabwe 18°18′S 26°31′E
Hwang-Hae *see* Yellow Sea
Hwangshih *see* Huangshi
139 H3 **Hwedza** Mashonaland East, E Zimbabwe 18°35′S 31°35′E
117 B10 **Hyades, Cerro** ▲ S Chile 46°57′S 73°09′W
246 E3 **Hyalganat** *var.* Selenge. Bulgan, N Mongolia 49°34′N 104°18′E
65 N4 **Hyannis** Massachusetts, NE USA 41°38′N 70°15′W
74 B7 **Hyannis** Nebraska, C USA 42°00′N 101°45′W
239 H1 **Hyargas Nuur** ◎ NW Mongolia
Hybla/Hybla Major *see* Paternò
83 M8 **Hydaburg** Prince of Wales Island, Alaska, USA 55°10′N 132°44′W
278 D11 **Hyde** Otago, South Island, New Zealand 45°17′S 170°17′E
159 J10 **Hyde** United Kingdom 53°27′N 2°05′W
66 G5 **Hyden** Kentucky, S USA 37°08′N 83°23′W
65 H4 **Hyde Park** New York, NE USA 41°46′N 73°52′W
83 N7 **Hyder** Alaska, USA 55°55′N 130°01′W
81 J14 **Hyder** Nevada, USA 33°01′N 113°21′W
234 F5 **Hyderābād** *var.* Haidarabad. *state capital* Andhra Pradesh, C India 17°22′N 78°26′E
230 G9 **Hyderābād** *var.* Haidarabad. Sind, SE Pakistan 25°26′N 68°22′E
165 K9 **Hyères** Var, SE France 43°07′N 06°08′E
165 K9 **Hyères, Îles d'** *island group* S France
191 F8 **Hyermanavichy** *Rus.* Germanovichi. Vitsyebskaya Voblasts', N Belarus 55°24′N 27°48′E
248 D3 **Hyesan** NE North Korea 41°18′N 128°13′E
54 C4 **Hyland** ≈ Yukon Territory, NW Canada
155 F11 **Hyltebruk** Halland, S Sweden 57°N 13°14′E
159 H4 **Hyndfordbridge-end** United Kingdom 55°40′N 3°44′W
64 A8 **Hyndman** Pennsylvania, NE USA 39°49′N 78°42′W
76 G7 **Hyndman Peak** ▲ Idaho, NW USA 43°45′N 114°07′W
158 D2 **Hynish** United Kingdom 56°26′N 6°53′W
251 H4 **Hyōgo** *off.* Hyōgo-ken. ◈ *prefecture* Honshū, SW Japan
Hyōgo-ken *see* Hyōgo
250 G4 **Hyōno-sen** ▲ Kyūshū, SW Japan 35°21′N 134°30′E
Hypanis *see* Kuban'
Hypsas *see* Belice
Hyrcania *see* Gorgān
79 H1 **Hyrum** Utah, W USA 41°37′N 111°51′W
152 I7 **Hyrynsalmi** Oulu, C Finland 64°41′N 28°30′E
77 K5 **Hysham** Montana, NW USA 46°16′N 107°14′W
56 F3 **Hythe** Alberta, W Canada 55°18′N 119°44′W
161 M7 **Hythe** SE England, United Kingdom 51°05′N 01°04′E
250 D7 **Hyūga** Miyazaki, Kyūshū, SW Japan 32°25′N 131°38′E
Hyvinge *see* Hyvinkää
153 H10 **Hyvinkää** *Swe.* Hyvinge. Etelä-Suomi, S Finland 60°37′N 24°50′E

I

218 G3 **Iaat** Lebanon
218 G3 **Iaat** Lebanon 34°02′N 36°10′E
188 D6 **Iacobeni** *Ger.* Jakobeny. Suceava, NE Romania 47°24′N 25°20′E
Iader *see* Zadar
139 L9 **Iakora** Fianarantsoa, SE Madagascar 23°04′S 46°40′E
261 N7 **Ialibu** Southern Highlands, W Papua New Guinea 06°18′S 144°00′E
188 E9 **Ialomiţa** *var.* Jalomitsa. ◈ *county* SE Romania
188 D9 **Ialomiţa** ≈ SE Romania
188 G7 **Ialoveni** *Rus.* Yaloveny. C Moldova 46°57′N 28°47′E
188 F8 **Ialpug** *var.* Ialpugul Mare, *Rus.* Yalpug. ≈ Moldova/Ukraine
Ialpugul Mare *see* Ialpug
69 J4 **Iamonia, Lake** ◎ Florida, SE USA
188 F9 **Ianca** Brăila, SE Romania 45°06′N 27°29′E
111 J2 **Iapu** Minas Gerais, Brazil 19°26′S 42°13′W
188 F7 **Iaşi** *Ger.* Jassy. Iaşi, NE Romania 47°08′N 27°38′E
188 F7 **Iaşi** *Ger.* Jassy, Yassy. ◈ *county* NE Romania
187 I2 **Íasmos** Anatolikí Makedonía kai Thráki, NE Greece 41°07′N 25°12′E
68 C2 **Iatt, Lake** ⊞ Louisiana, S USA
102 E8 **Iauretê** Amazonas, NW Brazil 0°37′N 69°10′W
263 K5 **Iba** Luzon, N Philippines 15°25′N 119°55′E
133 J7 **Ibadan** Oyo, SW Nigeria 07°22′N 04°01′E
102 B6 **Ibagué** Tolima, C Colombia 04°27′N 75°14′W
113 K4 **Ibaiti** Paraná, S Brazil 23°49′S 50°15′W
263 L7 **Ibajay** Panay Island, C Philippines 11°42′N 122°17′E
78 G3 **Ibapah Peak** ▲ Utah, W USA 39°51′N 113°55′W
Ibar *see* Ibër
250 F5 **Ibara** Okayama, Honshū, SW Japan 34°35′N 133°25′E
253 C13 **Ibaraki** *off.* Ibaraki-ken. ◈ *prefecture* Honshū, S Japan
Ibaraki-ken *see* Ibaraki
104 C1 **Ibarra** *var.* San Miguel de Ibarra. Imbabura, N Ecuador 0°23′S 78°08′W
Ibaşfalău *see* Dumbrăveni
110 B6 **Ibaté** São Paulo, Brazil 21°57′S 48°00′W
111 K3 **Ibatiba** Espírito Santo, Brazil 20°14′S 41°31′W
220 F9 **Ibb** W Yemen 13°55′N 44°10′E
180 D6 **Ibbenbüren** Nordrhein-Westfalen, NW Germany 52°17′N 07°43′E
134 D6 **Ibenga** ≈ N Congo
184 G6 **Ibër** *Serb.* Ibar. ≈ C Serbia
104 H7 **Iberia** Madre de Dios, E Peru 11°21′S 69°36′W
Iberia *see* Spain
Iberian Mountains *see* Ibérico, Sistema
148 A8 **Iberian Peninsula** *physical region* Portugal/Spain
290 H4 **Iberian Plain** *undersea feature* E Atlantic Ocean 13°30′W 43°45′N
Ibérica, Cordillera *see* Ibérico, Sistema
171 H4 **Ibérico, Sistema** *var.* Cordillera Ibérica, *Eng.* Iberian Mountains. ▲▲ NE Spain
111 H5 **Ibertioga** Minas Gerais, Brazil 21°25′S 43°58′W
59 H4 **Iberville Lac d'** ◎ Québec, NE Canada
133 J6 **Ibeto** Niger, W Nigeria 10°30′N 05°07′E
81 H9 **Ibex Hills** ▲▲ California, USA
133 L7 **Ibi** Taraba, C Nigeria 08°13′N 09°46′E
171 I7 **Ibi** País Valenciano, E Spain 38°38′N 00°35′W
109 D11 **Ibiá** Minas Gerais, SE Brazil 19°30′S 46°31′W
115 J1 **Ibicuí, Rio** ≈ S Brazil
114 D8 **Ibicuy** Entre Ríos, E Argentina 33°44′S 59°10′W
110 C4 **Ibiraci** Minas Gerais, Brazil 20°28′S 47°08′W
115 I1 **Ibirapuitã** ≈ S Brazil
111 H3 **Ibirité** Minas Gerais, Brazil 20°02′S 44°04′W
110 A6 **Ibitinga** São Paulo, Brazil 21°45′S 48°49′W
110 D6 **Ibitiúra** Minas Gerais, Brazil 22°04′S 46°26′W
110 G5 **Ibituruna** Minas Gerais, Brazil 21°09′S 44°45′W
110 C9 **Ibiúna** São Paulo, Brazil 23°39′S 47°13′W
171 K6 **Ibiza** *var.* Iviza, *Cast.* Eivissa; *anc.* Ebusus. *island* Islas Baleares, Spain, W Mediterranean Sea
Ibiza *see* Eivissa
216 D3 **Ibn Wardān, Qaşr** *ruins* Ḩamāh, C Syria
Ibo *see* Sassandra
282 C9 **Ibobang** Babeldaob, N Palau
261 I5 **Ibonma** Papua, E Indonesia 03°27′S 133°30′E
109 E8 **Ibotirama** Bahia, E Brazil 12°13′S 43°12′W
221 K5 **Ibrā** NE Oman 22°45′N 58°30′E
197 I2 **Ibresi** Chuvashskaya Respublika, W Russian Federation 55°22′N 47°04′E
221 K5 **'Ibrī** NW Oman 23°12′N 56°28′E
187 K3 **Ibrikbaba** , Turkey 40°36′N 26°32′E
161 I8 **Ibsley** United Kingdom 50°53′N 1°47′W
161 I3 **Ibstock** United Kingdom 52°40′N 1°24′W
250 C9 **Ibusuki** Kagoshima, Kyūshū, SW Japan 31°15′N 130°40′E
105 E8 **Ica** Ica, SW Peru 14°02′S 75°48′W
105 E8 **Ica** *off.* Departamento de Ica. ◈ *department* SW Peru
Ica, Departamento de *see* Ica
118 D10 **Icalma, Laguna de** ◎ Araucanía, Chile
102 F8 **Içana** Amazonas, NW Brazil 0°22′N 67°25′W
Icaria *see* Ikaría
106 C3 **Içá, Rio** *var.* Río Putumayo. ≈ NW South America *see also* Putumayo, Río
Içá, Rio *see* Putumayo, Río
214 E8 **İçel** *prev.* Ichili; *prev.* Mersin. ◈ *province* S Turkey
İçel *see* Mersin
152 C2 **Iceland** *off.* Republic of Iceland, *Dan.* Island, *Icel.* Ísland. ◆ *republic* N Atlantic Ocean
148 A4 **Iceland** *island* N Atlantic Ocean
290 G2 **Iceland Basin** *undersea feature* N Atlantic Ocean 61°00′N 19°00′W
Icelandic Plateau *see* Iceland Plateau
295 L5 **Iceland Plateau** *var.* Icelandic Plateau. *undersea feature* S Greenland Sea 12°00′W 69°30′N
Iceland, Republic of *see* Iceland
234 D6 **Ichalkaranji** Mahārāshtra, W India 16°42′N 74°28′E
250 D8 **Ichifusa-yama** ▲ Kyūshū, SW Japan 32°18′N 131°05′E
253 C13 **Ichihara** *var.* Itihara. Chiba, Honshū, S Japan 35°32′N 140°04′E
Ichiki-Kushikino *see* Kushikino
Ichili *see* İçel
251 J4 **Ichinomiya** *var.* Itinomiya. Aichi, Honshū, SW Japan 35°18′N 136°48′E
253 D9 **Ichinoseki** *var.* Itinoseki. Iwate, Honshū, C Japan 38°56′N 141°08′E
189 I2 **Ichnya** Chernihivs'ka Oblast', NE Ukraine 50°52′N 32°24′E
106 D10 **Ichoa, Río** ≈ C Bolivia
181 J9 **Ichtershausen** Thüringen, Germany 50°53′E 10°58′N
111 L4 **Iconha** Espírito Santo, Brazil 20°48′S 40°48′W
Iconium *see* Konya
Iculisma *see* Angoulême
83 K6 **Icy Bay** *inlet* Alaska, USA
82 G2 **Icy Cape** *headland* Alaska, USA 70°19′N 161°52′W
83 M7 **Icy Strait** *strait* Alaska, USA
75 G13 **Idabel** Oklahoma, C USA 33°54′N 94°50′W
74 F7 **Ida Grove** Iowa, C USA 42°21′N 95°28′W
133 K7 **Idah** Kogi, S Nigeria 07°06′N 06°45′E
76 G7 **Idaho** *off.* State of Idaho, *also known as* Gem of the Mountains, Gem State. ◈ *state* NW USA
76 F7 **Idaho City** Idaho, NW USA 43°48′N 115°51′W
77 I7 **Idaho Falls** Idaho, NW USA 43°28′N 112°01′W
218 C2 **Idálion** *var.* Dali, Dhali. C Cyprus 35°00′N 33°25′E
70 E3 **Idalou** Texas, SW USA 33°40′N 101°40′W
172 D3 **Idanha-a-Nova** Castelo Branco, C Portugal 39°55′N 07°15′W
181 C12 **Idar-Oberstein** Rheinland-Pfalz, SW Germany 49°43′N 07°19′E
190 F3 **Ida-Virumaa** *var.* Ida-Viru Maakond. ◈ *province* NE Estonia
Ida-Viru Maakond *see* Ida-Virumaa
160 F8 **Ideford** United Kingdom 50°35′N 3°34′W
194 E5 **Idel'** Respublika Kareliya, NW Russian Federation 64°08′N 34°12′E
134 A6 **Idenao** Sud-Ouest, SW Cameroon 04°04′N 09°01′E
Idenburg-rivier *see* Taritatu, Sungai
Idensalmi *see* Iisalmi
239 I1 **Ider** *var.* Dzuunmod. Hövsgöl, C Mongolia 48°09′N 97°22′E
Ider *see* Galt
129 J5 **Idfū** *var.* Edfu. SE Egypt 24°55′N 32°52′E
Ídhi Óros *see* Ídi
Ídhra *see* Ýdra
136 F2 **'Īdi** *var.* Ed. SE Eritrea 13°54′N 41°39′E
258 C2 **Idi** Sumatera, W Indonesia 05°00′N 98°00′E
187 I10 **Ídi** *var.* Ídhi Óros. ▲▲ Kríti, Greece, E Mediterranean Sea
Idi Amin, Lac *see* Edward, Lake
174 D6 **Idice** ≈ N Italy
132 B3 **Idîni** Trarza, W Mauritania 17°58′N 15°40′W
135 E9 **Idiofa** Bandundu, SW Dem. Rep. Congo 05°00′S 19°38′E
83 H6 **Iditarod River** ≈ Alaska, USA
Idjavuotna *see* Ifjord
154 G7 **Idkerberget** Dalarna, C Sweden 60°22′N 15°15′E
216 D2 **Idlib** Idlib, NW Syria 35°57′N 36°38′E
216 D2 **Idlib** *off.* Muḩāfaẓat Idlib. ◈ *governorate* NW Syria
Idlib, Muḩāfaẓat *see* Idlib
161 I7 **Idmiston** United Kingdom 51°08′N 1°43′W
Idra *see* Ýdra
154 F5 **Idre** Dalarna, C Sweden 61°52′N 12°45′E
80 C5 **Idria** California, USA 36°25′N 120°40′W
Idria *see* Idrija
177 J6 **Idrija** *It.* Idria. W Slovenia 46°00′N 14°59′E
181 E11 **Idstein** Hessen, W Germany 50°10′N 08°16′E
138 G9 **Idutywa** Eastern Cape, SE South Africa 32°06′S 28°20′E
Idutywa *see* Dutywa
81 F12 **Idyllwild** California, USA 33°44′N 116°43′W
Idzhevan *see* Ijevan
190 D6 **Iecava** Bauska, S Latvia 56°36′N 24°10′E
251 I9 **Ie-jima** *var.* Ii-shima. *island* Nansei-shotō, SW Japan
163 B10 **Ieper** *Fr.* Ypres. West-Vlaanderen, W Belgium 50°51′N 02°53′E
187 J10 **Ierápetra** Kríti, Greece, E Mediterranean Sea 35°00′N 25°45′E
187 H8 **Iérax, Akrotírio** *headland* S Greece 36°45′N 23°06′E
Ierisós *see* Ierissós
187 H3 **Ierissós** *var.* Ierisós. Kentrikí Makedonía, N Greece 40°24′N 23°53′E
188 D7 **Iernut** *Hung.* Radnót. Mureş, C Romania 46°27′N 24°15′E
177 I9 **Iesi** *var.* Jesi. Marche, C Italy 43°33′N 13°16′E
152 G4 **Iešjavri** ◎ N Norway
Iesolo *see* Jesolo
282 E6 **Ifalik Atoll** *atoll* Caroline Islands, C Micronesia
139 M8 **Ifanadiana** Fianarantsoa, SE Madagascar 21°19′S 47°39′E
133 J7 **Ife** Osun, SW Nigeria 07°25′N 04°31′E
133 K2 **Iferouâne** Agadez, N Niger 19°05′N 08°24′E
Iferten *see* Yverdon
152 H3 **Ifjord** *Lapp.* Idjavuotna. Finnmark, N Norway 70°27′N 27°06′E
133 I2 **Ifôghas, Adrar des** *var.* Adrar des Iforas. ▲▲ NE Mali
Iforas, Adrar des *see* Ifôghas, Adrar des
130 F3 **Ifrane** C Morocco 33°31′N 05°09′W
260 G3 **Iga** Pulau Halmahera, E Indonesia 01°23′N 128°17′E
136 C7 **Iganga** SE Uganda 0°34′N 33°27′E
110 B3 **Igarapava** São Paulo, S Brazil 20°01′S 47°46′W
110 G3 **Igarapé** Minas Gerais, Brazil 20°04′S 44°18′W
110 A7 **Igarassú** São Paulo, Brazil 22°31′S 48°34′W
110 E8 **Igaratà** São Paulo, Brazil 23°12′S 46°07′W
110 G3 **Igaratinga** Minas Gerais, Brazil 19°56′S 44°42′W
192 G5 **Igarka** Krasnoyarskiy Kray, N Russian Federation 67°31′N 86°33′E
Igaunija *see* Estonia
215 K5 **Iğdir** Iğdir, Turkey 39°55′N 44°02′E
215 K5 **Iğdir** ◈ *province* NE Turkey
I.G.Duca *see* General Toshevo
Igel *see* Jihlava
154 I5 **Iggesund** Gävleborg, C Sweden 61°38′N 17°04′E
160 G2 **Ightfield** United Kingdom 52°56′N 2°37′W
83 H3 **Igikpak, Mount** ▲ Alaska, USA 67°28′N 154°55′W
83 H7 **Igiugig** Alaska, USA 59°19′N 155°53′W
Iglau/Iglawa/Igława *see* Jihlava
175 B10 **Iglesias** Sardegna, Italy, C Mediterranean Sea 39°20′N 08°34′E
197 L2 **Iglino** Respublika Bashkortostan, W Russian Federation 54°51′N 56°29′E
Igló *see* Spišská Nová Ves
53 J7 **Igloolik** Nunavut, N Canada 69°24′N 81°55′W
58 C6 **Ignace** Ontario, S Canada 49°26′N 91°40′W
85 J7 **Ignacio Allende** Durango, Mexico 24°28′N 104°00′W
87 H7 **Ignacio de la Llave** Veracruz-Llave, Mexico 18°43′N 95°59′W
85 M8 **Ignacio Zaragoza** Tamaulipas, Mexico 23°11′N 98°47′W
191 E8 **Ignalina** Utena, E Lithuania 55°20′N 26°10′E
197 I3 **Ignatovka** Ul'yanovskaya Oblast', W Russian Federation 53°56′N 47°40′E
194 F8 **Ignatovo** Vologodskaya Oblast', NW Russian Federation 60°47′N 37°51′E
187 L1 **İğneada** Kırklareli, NW Turkey 41°54′N 27°58′E
214 C4 **İğneada Burnu** *headland* NW Turkey 41°54′N 28°03′E
Igombe *see* Gombe
186 E4 **Igoumenítsa** Ípeiros, W Greece 39°30′N 20°16′E
195 J9 **Igra** Udmurtskaya Respublika, NW Russian Federation 57°30′N 53°01′E
195 M5 **Igrim** Khanty-Mansiyskiy Avtonomnyy Okrug-Yugra, N Russian Federation 63°09′N 64°33′E
113 I5 **Iguaçu, Rio** *Sp.* Río Iguazú. ≈ Argentina/Brazil *see also* Iguazú, Río
Iguaçu, Rio *see* Iguazú, Río
113 I5 **Iguaçu, Salto do** *Sp.* Cataratas del Iguazú; *prev.* Victoria Falls. *waterfall* Argentina/Brazil *see also* Iguazú, Cataratas del
Iguaçu, Salto do *see* Iguazú, Cataratas del
111 J8 **Iguaha Grande** Rio de Janeiro, Brazil 22°48′S 42°18′W
86 E7 **Iguala** *var.* Iguala de la Independencia. Guerrero, S Mexico 18°21′N 99°31′W
171 K3 **Igualada** Cataluña, NE Spain 41°35′N 01°37′E
Iguala de la Independencia *see* Iguala
110 E3 **Iguatama** Minas Gerais, Brazil 20°10′S 45°42′W
113 I5 **Iguazú, Cataratas del** *Port.* Salto do Iguaçu; *prev.* Victoria Falls. *waterfall* Argentina/Brazil *see also* Iguaçu, Salto do
Iguazú, Cataratas del *see* Iguaçu, Salto do
113 I5 **Iguazú, Río** *var.* Río Iguaçu. ≈ Argentina/Brazil *see also* Iguaçu, Rio
Iguazú, Río *see* Iguaçu, Rio
Iguéla *see* Ntchongorove
Iguid, Erg *see* Iguîdi, 'Erg
120 G3 **Iguîdi, 'Erg** *var.* Erg Iguid. *desert* Algeria/Mauritania
139 N4 **Iharaña** *prev.* Vohémar. Antsiranana, NE Madagascar 13°22′S 50°00′E
235 B10 **Ihavandhippolhu Atoll** *var.* Ihavandiffulu Atoll. *atoll* N Maldives
Ihavandiffulu Atoll *see* Ihavandhippolhu Atoll
Ih Bulag *see* Hanbogd
251 I9 **Iheya-jima** *island* Nansei-shotō, SW Japan
Ihhayrhan *see* Bayan-Önjüül
239 L1 **Ihhet** *var.* Bayan. Dornogovĭ, SE Mongolia 46°15′N 110°16′E
180 F2 **Ihlienworth** Niedersachsen, Germany 53°44′E 8°55′N
139 L9 **Ihosy** Fianarantsoa, S Madagascar 22°23′S 46°09′E
Ihsüüj *see* Bayanchandmanĭ
239 J1 **Ihtamir** *var.* Dzaanhushuu. Arhangay, C Mongolia 47°36′N 101°06′E
239 I1 **Ih-Uul** *var.* Bayan-Uhaa. Dzavhan, C Mongolia 48°41′N 98°46′E
239 J1 **Ih-Uul** *var.* Selenge. Hövsgöl, N Mongolia 49°25′N 101°30′E
152 H6 **Ii** Oulu, C Finland 65°18′N 25°23′E
251 K4 **Iida** Nagano, Honshū, S Japan 35°32′N 137°48′E
253 C11 **Iide-san** ▲ Honshū, C Japan 38°03′N 139°39′E
152 I6 **Iijoki** ≈ C Finland
Iinnasuolu *see* Hinnøya
190 F4 **Iisaku** *Ger.* Isaak. Ida-Virumaa, NE Estonia 59°06′N 27°19′E
194 C6 **Iisalmi** *var.* Idensalmi. Itä-Suomi, C Finland 63°32′N 27°10′E
Ii-shima *see* Ie-jima
251 K2 **Iiyama** Nagano, Honshū, S Japan 36°52′N 138°22′E
250 D6 **Iizuka** Fukuoka, Kyūshū, SW Japan 33°38′N 130°40′E
110 F5 **Ijaci** Minas Gerais, Brazil 21°10′S 44°56′W
133 I7 **Ijebu-Ode** Ogun, SW Nigeria 06°46′N 03°57′E
215 K4 **Ijevan** *Rus.* Idzhevan. N Armenia 40°53′N 45°07′E
162 E5 **IJmuiden** Noord-Holland, W Netherlands 52°28′N 04°38′E
162 H6 **IJssel** *var.* Yssel. ≈ Netherlands
162 G5 **IJsselmeer** *prev.* Zuider Zee. ◎ N Netherlands
162 H5 **IJsselmuiden** Overijssel, E Netherlands 52°34′N 05°55′E
162 F7 **IJsselstein** Utrecht, C Netherlands 52°01′N 05°02′E
113 I6 **Ijuí** Rio Grande do Sul, S Brazil 28°23′S 53°55′W
113 H6 **Ijuí, Rio** ≈ S Brazil
283 J9 **Ijuw** NE Nauru 0°30′S 166°57′E
163 C9 **IJzendijke** Zeeland, SW Netherlands 51°20′N 03°36′E
163 B9 **Ijzer** ≈ W Belgium
Ikaahuk *see* Sachs Harbour
153 G9 **Ikaalinen** Länsi-Suomi, W Finland 61°46′N 23°05′E
139 L8 **Ikalamavony** Fianarantsoa, SE Madagascar 21°10′S 46°35′E
Ikaluktutiak *see* Cambridge Bay
279 E8 **Ikamatua** West Coast, South Island, New Zealand 42°16′S 171°42′E
227 H7 **Ikan** *prev.* Staroikan. Yuzhnyy Kazakhstan, S Kazakhstan 43°09′N 68°34′E
133 J7 **Ikare** Ondo, SW Nigeria 07°36′N 05°52′E
187 J7 **Ikaría** *var.* Kariot, Nicaria, Nikaria; *anc.* Icaria. *island* Dodekánisa, Greece, Aegean Sea
155 C12 **Ikast** Ringkøbing, W Denmark 56°09′N 09°10′E
278 I5 **Ikawhenua Range** ▲▲ North Island, New Zealand
252 G5 **Ikeda** Hokkaidō, NE Japan 42°54′N 143°25′E
250 G5 **Ikeda** Tokushima, Shikoku, SW Japan 34°00′N 133°47′E
133 I8 **Ikeja** Lagos, SW Nigeria 06°36′N 03°16′E
135 G8 **Ikela** Equateur, C Dem. Rep. Congo 01°11′S 23°16′E
185 I6 **Ikhtiman** Sofiya, W Bulgaria 42°26′N 23°49′E
250 C6 **Iki** *island* SW Japan
197 I8 **Iki Burul** Respublika Kalmykiya, SW Russian Federation 45°48′N 44°44′E
250 C6 **Iki-suidō** *strait* SW Japan
250 B6 **Ikitsuki-shima** *island* SW Japan
215 I5 **İkizdere** Rize, NE Turkey 40°47′N 40°34′E
83 H8 **Ikolik, Cape** *headland* Kodiak Island, Alaska, USA 57°12′N 154°46′W
133 K8 **Ikom** Cross River, SE Nigeria 05°57′N 08°43′E
139 M8 **Ikongo** *prev.* Fort-Carnot. Fianarantsoa, SE Madagascar 21°52′S 47°27′E
83 H2 **Ikpikpuk River** ≈ Alaska, USA
284 C1 **Iku** *prev.* Lone Tree Islet. *atoll* Tungaru, W Kiribati
251 H4 **Ikuno** Hyōgo, Honshū, SW Japan 35°13′N 134°48′E
284 G10 **Ikurangi** ▲ Rarotonga, S Cook Islands 21°12′S 159°45′W
261 K6 **Ilaga** Papua, E Indonesia 03°54′S 137°30′E
263 L4 **Ilagan** Luzon, N Philippines 17°08′N 121°54′E
222 D4 **Īlām** *var.* Elam. Īlām, W Iran 33°37′N 46°27′E
233 J6 **Ilām** Eastern, E Nepal 26°52′N 87°58′E
222 D5 **Īlām** *off.* Ostān-e Īlām. ◈ *province* W Iran
Īlām, Ostān-e *see* Īlām
243 N7 **Ilan** *Jap.* Giran. N Taiwan 24°45′N 121°44′E
228 D5 **Ilanly Obvodnitel'nyy Kanal** *canal* N Turkmenistan
176 E4 **Ilanz** Graubünden, S Switzerland 46°46′N 09°10′E
133 I7 **Ilaro** Ogun, SW Nigeria 06°52′N 03°01′E
105 H9 **Ilave** Puno, S Peru 16°07′S 69°40′W
182 G4 **Iława** *Ger.* Deutsch-Eylau. Warmińsko-Mazurskie, NE Poland 53°36′N 19°35′E
175 J14 **Il-Bajja ta' Marsaxlokk** *var.* Marsaxlokk Bay. *bay* SE Malta
193 J6 **Ilbenge** Respublika Sakha (Yakutiya), NE Russian Federation 62°52′N 124°13′E
160 G7 **Ilchester** United Kingdom 51°0′N 2°41′W
205 J4 **Ile** *var.* Ili, *Chin.* Ili He, *Rus.* Reka Ili. ≈ China/Kazakhstan *see also* Ili He
Ile *see* Ili He
57 L3 **Île-à-la-Crosse** Saskatchewan, C Canada 55°29′N 108°00′W
135 F9 **Ilebo** *prev.* Port-Francqui. Kasai-Occidental, W Dem. Rep. Congo 04°19′S 20°32′E
165 I3 **Île-de-France** ◈ *region* N France
Ilek *see* Yelek
Ilerda *see* Lleida
133 J7 **Ilesha** Osun, SW Nigeria 07°35′N 04°49′E
280 C9 **Îles Loyauté, Province des** ◈ *province* E New Caledonia
55 J7 **Ilford** Manitoba, C Canada 56°02′N 95°48′W
185 K3 **Ilfov** ◈ *county* S Romania
160 E7 **Ilfracombe** SW England, United Kingdom 51°12′N 04°10′W
214 E4 **Ilgaz Dağları** ▲▲ N Turkey
214 D6 **Ilgın** Konya, W Turkey 38°16′N 31°57′E
113 J2 **Ilha Solteira** São Paulo, S Brazil 20°28′S 51°19′W
170 C4 **Ílhavo** Aveiro, N Portugal 40°36′N 08°40′W
140 A2 **Ilhea Point** *headland* Erongo, Namibia
109 H9 **Ilhéus** Bahia, E Brazil 14°50′S 39°06′W
Ili *see* Ile/Ili He
188 B8 **Ilia** *Hung.* Marosillye. Hunedoara, SW Romania 45°57′N 22°40′E
83 H7 **Iliamna** Alaska, USA 59°42′N 154°49′W
83 H7 **Iliamna Lake** ◎ Alaska, USA
215 H6 **İliç** Erzincan, C Turkey 39°27′N 38°34′E
187 L4 **Ilıca** Balıkesir, Turkey 39°53′N 27°47′E
Il'ichevsk *see* Şărur, Azerbaijan
Il'ichevsk *see* Illichivs'k, Ukraine
Ilici *see* Elche
110 E4 **Ilicinea** Minas Gerais, Brazil 20°56′S 45°50′W
79 N2 **Iliff** Colorado, C USA 40°46′N 103°04′W
263 M8 **Iligan** *off.* Iligan City. Mindanao, S Philippines 08°12′N 124°16′E
263 M8 **Iligan Bay** *bay* S Philippines
Iligan City *see* Iligan
238 E3 **Ili He** *var.* Ili, *Kaz.* Ile, *Rus.* Reka Ili. ≈ China/Kazakhstan *see also* Ile
Ili He *see* Ile
104 C2 **Iliniza** ▲ N Ecuador 0°37′S 78°41′W
190 I7 **Il'ino** Tverskaya Oblast', Russian Federation
Ilinski *see* Il'inskiy
195 K9 **Il'inskiy** *var.* Ilinski. Permskaya Oblast', NW Russian Federation 58°33′N 55°31′E
190 I1 **Il'inskiy** Respublika Kareliya, Russian Federation
64 G1 **Ilion** New York, NE USA 43°01′N 75°02′W
177 J6 **Ilirska Bistrica** *prev.* Bistrica, *Ger.* Feistritz, Illyrisch-Feistritz, *It.* Villa del Nevoso. SW Slovenia 45°34′N 14°12′E
215 I7 **Ilısu Barajı** ⊞ SE Turkey
234 E6 **Ilkal** Karnātaka, C India 15°59′N 76°08′E
161 I2 **Ilkeston** C England, United Kingdom 52°59′N 01°18′W
159 K8 **Ilkley** United Kingdom 53°55′N 1°49′W
175 I14 **Il-Kullana** *headland* SW Malta 35°49′N 14°26′E
176 F4 **Ill** ≈ W Austria
165 K4 **Ill** ≈ NE France
116 B3 **Illapel** Coquimbo, C Chile 31°40′S 71°13′W
118 D1 **Illapel, Río** ≈ Coquimbo, Chile
Illaue Fartak Trench *see* Alula-Fartak Trench
276 D1 **Illbillee, Mount** ▲ South Australia 27°01′S 132°13′E
164 F4 **Ille-et-Vilaine** ◈ *department* NW France
133 J4 **Illéla** Tahoua, SW Niger 14°25′N 05°10′E
179 E13 **Iller** ≈ S Germany
179 E12 **Illertissen** Bayern, S Germany 48°13′N 10°08′E
171 M5 **Illes Baleares** ◈ *autonomous community* E Spain
170 G5 **Illescas** Castilla-La Mancha, C Spain 40°08′N 03°51′W
115 I7 **Illescas** Florida, Uruguay 33°36′S 55°20′W
Ille-sur-la-Têt *see* Ille-sur-Têt
169 H7 **Ille-sur-Têt** *var.* Ille-sur-la-Têt. Pyrénées-Orientales, S France 42°40′N 02°37′E
Illiberis *see* Elne
189 H8 **Illichivs'k** *Rus.* Il'ichevsk. Odes'ka Oblast', SW Ukraine 46°18′N 30°36′E
Illicis *see* Elche
166 F6 **Illiers** Centre, France 48°18′N 1°15′E
165 H4 **Illiers-Combray** Eure-et-Loir, C France 48°18′N 01°15′E
73 C10 **Illinois** *off.* State of Illinois, *also known as* Prairie State, Sucker State. ◈ *state* C USA
61 H6 **Illinois River** ≈ Illinois, N USA
188 G4 **Illintsi** Vinnyts'ka Oblast', C Ukraine 49°07′N 29°13′E
Illiturgis *see* Andújar
131 K6 **Illizi** SE Algeria 26°30′N 08°28′E
75 J11 **Illmo** Missouri, C USA 37°13′N 89°30′W
Illurco *see* Lorca
Illuro *see* Mataró
Illyrisch-Feistritz *see* Ilirska Bistrica
181 J10 **Ilm** ≈ C Germany
181 J10 **Ilmenau** Thüringen, C Germany 50°40′N 10°55′E
194 D9 **Il'men', Ozero** ◎ NW Russian Federation
105 G10 **Ilo** Moquegua, SW Peru 17°42′S 71°20′W
263 L7 **Iloilo** *off.* Iloilo City. Panay Island, C Philippines 10°42′N 122°34′E
Iloilo City *see* Iloilo
184 F3 **Ilok** *Hung.* Újlak. Vojvodina, NW Serbia 45°12′N 19°22′E
153 J8 **Ilomantsi** Itä-Suomi, SE Finland 62°40′N 30°55′E
88 D5 **Ilopango, Lago de** *volcanic lake* C El Salvador
133 J7 **Ilorin** Kwara, W Nigeria 08°32′N 04°35′E
189 M5 **Ilovays'k** *Rus.* Ilovaysk. Donets'ka Oblast', SE Ukraine 47°55′N 38°14′E
Ilovaysk *see* Ilovays'k
197 H6 **Ilovlya** Volgogradskaya Oblast', SW Russian Federation 49°45′N 44°19′E
175 I13 **Il-Ponta ta' San Dimitri** *var.* Ras San Dimitri, San Dimitri Point. *headland* Gozo, NW Malta 36°04′N 14°12′E
193 M5 **Il'pyrskoye** Kamchatskaya Oblast, E Russian Federation 60°00′N 164°16′E
180 H6 **Ilsede** Niedersachsen, Germany 52°16′E 10°12′N
181 H14 **Ilshofen** Baden-Württemberg, Germany 49°10′E 9°55′N
196 F8 **Il'skiy** Krasnodarskiy Kray, SW Russian Federation 44°52′N 38°26′E
276 D2 **Iltur** South Australia 27°33′S 130°31′E
261 L5 **Ilugwa** Papua, E Indonesia 03°42′S 139°09′E
İluh *see* Batman
190 F7 **Ilūkste** Daugvapils, SE Latvia 55°58′N 26°21′E
261 I6 **Ilur** Pulau Gorong, E Indonesia 04°00′S 131°25′E
76 B4 **Ilwaco** Washington, NW USA 46°19′N 124°03′W
Il'yaly *see* Gurbansoltan Eje
İlyasbaba Burnu *see* Tekke Burnu
195 K6 **Ilych** ≈ NW Russian Federation
179 H12 **Ilz** ≈ SE Germany
182 H7 **Iłża** Radom, SE Poland 51°09′N 21°15′E
250 F5 **Imabari** *var.* Imaharu. Ehime, Shikoku, SW Japan 34°04′N 132°59′E
252 C5 **Imagane** Hokkaidō, NE Japan 42°26′N 140°00′E
Imaharu *see* Imabari
253 C12 **Imaichi** *var.* Imaiti. Tochigi, Honshū, S Japan 36°43′N 139°41′E
Imaiti *see* Imaichi
251 I3 **Imajō** Fukui, Honshū, SW Japan 35°45′N 136°10′E
217 I6 **Imām Ibn Hāshim** Karbalā', C Iraq 32°46′N 43°21′E
217 J7 **Imān 'Abd Allāh** Al Qādisīyah, S Iraq 31°36′N 44°34′E
250 F7 **Imano-yama** ▲ Shikoku, SW Japan 32°51′N 132°48′E
250 C6 **Imari** Saga, Kyūshū, SW Japan 33°18′N 129°51′E
290 F3 **Imarssuak Channel** N Atlantic Ocean
287 M1 **Imarssuak Channel** N Pacific Ocean
Imarssuak Mid-Ocean Seachannel *see* Imarssuak Seachannel
290 F2 **Imarssuak Seachannel** *var.* Imarssuak Mid-Ocean Seachannel. *channel* N Atlantic Ocean
153 I9 **Imatra** Etelä-Suomi, SE Finland 61°14′N 28°50′E
251 I4 **Imazu** Shiga, Honshū, SW Japan 35°25′N 136°00′E
104 C1 **Imbabura** ◈ *province* N Ecuador
103 J5 **Imbaimadai** W Guyana 05°44′N 60°23′W
111 I7 **Imbariê** Rio de Janeiro, Brazil 22°38′S 43°12′W
111 K2 **Imbé** Minas Gerais, Brazil 19°36′S 41°58′W
113 K6 **Imbituba** Santa Catarina, S Brazil 28°15′S 48°44′W
75 I11 **Imboden** Arkansas, C USA 36°12′N 91°10′W
Imbros *see* Gökçeada
Imeni 26 Bakinskikh Komissarov *see* 26 Bakı Komissarı
Imeni 26 Bakinskikh Komissarov *see* Uzboý
194 G8 **Imeni Babushkina** Vologodskaya Oblast', NW Russian Federation 59°40′N 43°04′E
196 F4 **Imeni Karla Libknekhta** Kurskaya Oblast', W Russian Federation 51°36′N 35°28′E
Imeni Mollanepesa *see* Mollanepes Adyndaky
193 L7 **Imeni Poliny Osipenko** Khabarovskiy Kray, SE Russian Federation 52°21′N 136°17′E
Imeni S. A. Niyazova *see* S. A.Nyýazow Adyndaky
Imeni Sverdlova Rudnik *see* Sverdlovs'k
282 C9 **Imeong** Babeldaob, N Palau
181 B10 **Imgenbroich** Nordrhein-Westfalen, Germany 50°34′E 6°16′N
136 F5 **Īmī** Sumalē, E Ethiopia 06°27′N 42°10′E
187 K7 **Imia** *Turk.* Kardak. *island* Dodekánisa, Greece, Aegean Sea
Imishli *see* İmişli
215 M5 **İmişli** *Rus.* Imishli. C Azerbaijan 39°54′N 48°04′E
248 C4 **Imjin-gang** ≈ North Korea/South Korea
80 I1 **Imlay** Nevada, W USA 40°39′N 118°10′W
73 H8 **Imlay City** Michigan, N USA 43°01′N 83°04′W
218 E7 **Immātīn** West Bank 32°11′N 35°09′E
180 H6 **Immensen** Niedersachsen, Germany 52°24′E 10°04′N
69 M8 **Immokalee** Florida, SE USA 26°24′N 81°25′W
133 K8 **Imo** ◈ *state* SE Nigeria
177 H8 **Imola** Emilia-Romagna, N Italy 44°22′N 11°43′E
280 A2 **Imonda** Sandaun, NW Papua New Guinea 03°21′S 141°10′E
Imoschi *see* Imotski
184 D5 **Imotski** *It.* Imoschi. Split-Dalmacija, SE Croatia 43°28′N 17°13′E
108 C4 **Imperatriz** Maranhão, NE Brazil 05°32′S 47°28′W
176 D9 **Imperia** Liguria, NW Italy 43°53′N 08°03′E
105 D8 **Imperial** Lima, W Peru 13°04′S 76°21′W
81 G13 **Imperial** California, W USA 32°51′N 115°34′W
75 B8 **Imperial** Nebraska, C USA 40°30′N 101°37′W
70 D5 **Imperial** Texas, SW USA 31°15′N 102°40′W
81 D13 **Imperial Beach** California, USA 32°35′N 117°07′W
78 G9 **Imperial Dam** *dam* California, W USA
81 H14 **Imperial Reservoir** ⊞ Nevada, USA
118 B10 **Imperial, Río** ≈ Araucanía, Chile
134 E7 **Impfondo** Likouala, NE Congo 01°37′N 18°04′E
233 M7 **Imphāl** *state capital* Manipur, NE India 24°47′N 93°55′E
165 I5 **Imphy** Nièvre, C France 46°55′N 03°16′E
141 J8 **Impisi** Eastern Cape, South Africa 31°05′S 29°53′E
176 G9 **Impruneta** Toscana, C Italy 43°42′N 11°16′E
214 A5 **İmroz** *var.* Gökçeada. Çanakkale, NW Turkey 40°06′N 25°50′E
Imroz Adası *see* Gökçeada
176 G4 **Imst** Tirol, W Austria 47°14′N 10°45′E
218 I7 **Imtān** Syria 32°24′N 36°49′E
84 E2 **Imuris** Sonora, NW Mexico 30°48′N 110°52′W

◆ Country
● Country Capital
◇ Dependent Territory
○ Dependent Territory Capital
◈ Administrative Regions
✈ International Airport
▲ Mountain
▲▲ Mountain Range
⛰ Volcano
≈ River
◎ Lake
⊞ Reservoir

INDEX

● Country   ◇ Dependent Territory   ◈ Administrative Regions   ▲ Mountain   ✖ Volcano   ◉ Lake
● Country Capital   ○ Dependent Territory Capital   ✈ International Airport   ▲ Mountain Range   ♐ River   ◻ Reservoir

K

◆ Country	◇ Dependent Territory	◈ Administrative Regions	▲ Mountain	☒ Volcano	⊚ Lake
◆ Country Capital	○ Dependent Territory Capital	✕ International Airport	▲ Mountain Range	♒ River	⊚ Reservoir

◆ Country   ◇ Dependent Territory   ⬥ Administrative Regions   ▲ Mountain   🌋 Volcano   ⊜ Lake
● Country Capital   ○ Dependent Territory Capital   ✕ International Airport   ▲ Mountain Range   ♣ River   ⊟ Reservoir

◆ Country   ◇ Dependent Territory   ◆ Administrative Regions   ▲ Mountain   ▲ Volcano   ◙ Lake
● Country Capital   ○ Dependent Territory Capital   ✕ International Airport   ▲ Mountain Range   ❧ River   ◙ Reservoir

Kloten - Koror

174 C2 **Kloten** Zürich, N Switzerland *47°27′N 08°35′E*
174 C2 **Kloten** ✈ (Zürich) Zürich, N Switzerland *47°25′N 08°36′E*
181 C11 **Klotten** Rheinland-Pfalz, Germany *50°10′E 7°12′N*
180 J5 **Klötze** Sachsen-Anhalt, C Germany *52°37′N 11°09′E*
58 G2 **Klotz, Lac** ◎ Québec, NE Canada
179 I8 **Klotzsche** ✈ (Dresden) Sachsen, E Germany *51°06′N 13°44′E*
54 A3 **Kluane Lake** ◎ Yukon Territory, W Canada
Kluang *see* Keluang
182 F7 **Kluczbork** ***Ger.*** Kreuzburg, Kreuzburg in Oberschlesien. Opolskie, S Poland *50°59′N 18°13′E*
83 L6 **Klukwan** Alaska, USA *59°24′N 135°49′W*
181 C12 **Klüsserath** Rheinland-Pfalz, Germany *49°50′E 6°51′N*
180 J2 **Klütz** Mecklenburg-Vorpommern, Germany *53°58′E 11°10′N*
Klyastitsy *see* Klyastsitsy
190 G7 **Klyastsitsy** ***Rus.*** Klyastitsy. Vitsyebskaya Voblasts', N Belarus *55°53′N 28°36′E*
197 K2 **Klyavlino** Samarskaya Oblast', W Russian Federation *54°21′N 52°12′E*
144 F6 **Klyaz'in** ≈ W Russian Federation
197 H1 **Klyaz'ma** ≈ W Russian Federation
191 F10 **Klyetsk** ***Pol.*** Kleck, ***Rus.*** Kletsk. Minskaya Voblasts', SW Belarus *53°04′N 26°38′E*
229 J4 **Klyuchevka** Talasskaya Oblast', NW Kyrgyzstan *42°34′N 71°45′E*
193 M6 **Klyuchevskaya Sopka, Vulkan** 🌋 E Russian Federation *56°03′N 160°38′E*
193 M5 **Klyuchi** Kamchatskiy Oblast', E Russian Federation *56°18′N 160°44′E*
155 B9 **Knaben** Vest-Agder, S Norway *58°46′N 07°04′E*
155 F11 **Knäred** Halland, S Sweden *56°30′N 13°21′E*
159 K8 **Knaresborough** N England, United Kingdom *54°01′N 01°35′W*
159 J6 **Knarsdale** United Kingdom *54°52′N 2°30′W*
180 I5 **Knesebeck** Niedersachsen, Germany *52°41′E 10°42′N*
185 J5 **Knezha** Vratsa, NW Bulgaria *43°29′N 24°04′E*
70 E5 **Knickerbocker** Texas, SW USA *31°18′N 100°35′W*
74 B3 **Knife River** ≈ North Dakota, N USA
56 C7 **Knight Inlet** *inlet* British Columbia, W Canada
83 J6 **Knight Island** *island* Alaska, USA
160 G4 **Knighton** E Wales, United Kingdom *52°20′N 03°01′W*
80 D3 **Knights Ferry** California, USA *37°49′N 120°40′W*
78 B4 **Knights Landing** California, W USA *38°47′N 121°43′W*
184 C4 **Knin** Šibenik-Knin, S Croatia *44°03′N 16°12′E*
290 G7 **Knipovich Seamount** C Atlantic Ocean
70 F7 **Knippal** Texas, SW USA
177 K4 **Knittelfeld** Steiermark, C Austria *47°14′N 14°50′E*
161 I2 **Kniveton** United Kingdom *53°02′N 1°42′W*
154 I7 **Knivsta** Uppsala, C Sweden *59°43′N 17°49′E*
185 H5 **Knjaževac** Serbia, E Serbia *43°34′N 22°16′E*
75 G9 **Knob Noster** Missouri, C USA *38°47′N 93°33′W*
158 B9 **Knockcroghery** Roscommon, Ireland *53°34′N 8°06′W*
158 F4 **Knockenkelly** W Scotland, United Kingdom
160 A4 **Knocktopher** Kilkenny, Ireland *52°29′N 7°13′W*
163 B9 **Knokke-Heist** West-Vlaanderen, NW Belgium *51°21′N 03°19′E*
155 D10 **Knøsen** *hill* N Denmark
Knosós *see* Knossos
187 J10 **Knossos** ***Gk.*** Knosós. *prehistoric site* Kríti, Greece, E Mediterranean Sea
70 E5 **Knott** Texas, SW USA *32°21′N 101°35′W*
159 K9 **Knottingley** United Kingdom *53°42′N 1°14′W*
161 I4 **Knowle** United Kingdom *52°23′N 1°44′W*
292 F3 **Knowles, Cape** *headland* Antarctica *71°45′S 60°20′W*
73 E9 **Knox** Indiana, N USA *41°17′N 86°37′W*
74 D2 **Knox** North Dakota, N USA *48°19′N 99°43′W*
62 D7 **Knox** Pennsylvania, NE USA *41°13′N 79°33′W*
283 M6 **Knox Atoll** ***var.*** Ņadikdik, Narikrik. *atoll* Ratak Chain, SE Marshall Islands
54 A6 **Knox, Cape** *headland* Graham Island, British Columbia, SW Canada *54°05′N 133°02′W*
70 F4 **Knox City** Texas, SW USA *33°25′N 99°49′W*
293 M6 **Knox Coast** *physical region* Antarctica
73 I10 **Knox Lake** ⊠ Ohio, N USA
69 J1 **Knoxville** Georgia, SE USA *32°44′N 83°58′W*
73 B9 **Knoxville** Illinois, N USA *40°54′N 90°16′W*
66 G6 **Knoxville** Tennessee, S USA *35°58′N 83°55′W*
295 J7 **Knud Rasmussen Land** *physical region* N Greenland
Knüll *see* Knüllgebirge
181 G9 **Knüllgebirge** ***var.*** Knüll. ▲▲ C Germany
159 J10 **Knutsford** United Kingdom *53°18′N 2°22′W*
190 G7 **Knyazevo** Pskovskaya Oblast', Russian Federation
194 E4 **Knyazhegubskoye Vodokhranilishche** ◎ NW Russian Federation
Knyazhevo *see* Sredishte
Knyazhitsy *see* Knyazhytsy
191 H9 **Knyazhytsy** ***Rus.*** Knyazhitsy. Mahilyowskaya Voblasts', E Belarus *54°10′N 30°28′E*
138 E10 **Knysna** Western Cape, SW South Africa *34°03′S 23°03′E*
261 I5 **Koagas** Papua, E Indonesia *02°40′S 132°16′E*
137 E10 **Koani** Zanzibar South, E Tanzania *06°08′S 39°18′E*
Koartac *see* Quaqtaq
258 G6 **Koba** Pulau Bangka, W Indonesia *02°30′S 106°26′E*
250 D8 **Kobayashi** ***var.*** Kobayasi. Miyazaki, Kyūshū, SW Japan *32°00′N 130°58′E*
Kobayasi *see* Kobayashi
226 D4 **Kobda** ***prev.*** Khobda, Novoalekseyevka. Aktyubinsk, W Kazakhstan *50°09′N 55°39′E*
226 D3 **Kobda** ***Kaz.*** Ülkenqobda; ***prev.*** Bol'shaya Khobda. ≈ Kazakhstan/Russian Federation
Kobdo *see* Hovd
251 H5 **Kōbe** Hyōgo, Honshū, SW Japan *34°40′N 135°10′E*
Kobelyaki *see* Kobelyaky
189 J4 **Kobelyaky** ***Rus.*** Kobelyaki. Poltavs'ka Oblast', NE Ukraine *49°10′N 34°13′E*
155 F12 **København** ***Eng.*** Copenhagen; ***anc.*** Hafnia. ● (Denmark) Sjælland, København, E Denmark *55°43′N 12°34′E*
155 F12 **København** ***off.*** Københavns Amt. ◈ *county* E Denmark
Københavns Amt *see* København
132 D3 **Kobenni** Hodh el Gharbi, S Mauritania *15°58′N 09°24′W*
261 H5 **Kobi** Pulau Seram, E Indonesia *02°56′S 129°53′E*
181 D11 **Koblenz** ***prev.*** Coblenz, ***Fr.*** Coblence; ***anc.*** Confluentes. Rheinland-Pfalz, W Germany *50°21′N 07°36′E*
176 D3 **Koblenz** Aargau, N Switzerland *47°34′N 08°16′E*
261 J6 **Kobowre, Pegunungan** ▲▲ Papua, E Indonesia
Kobrin *see* Kobryn
261 J7 **Kobroor, Pulau** *island* Kepulauan Aru, E Indonesia
191 D11 **Kobryn** ***Rus.*** Kobrin. Brestskaya Voblasts', SW Belarus *52°13′N 24°21′E*
83 H4 **Kobuk** Alaska, USA *66°54′N 156°52′W*
83 H4 **Kobuk River** ≈ Alaska, USA
215 I4 **K'obulet'i** W Georgia *41°47′N 41°47′E*
193 J6 **Kobyay** Respublika Sakha (Yakutiya), NE Russian Federation *63°36′N 126°33′E*
187 K3 **Kocacesme** Çanakkale, Turkey *40°40′N 26°48′E*
214 C4 **Kocaeli** ◈ *province* NW Turkey
185 H7 **Kočani** NE FYR Macedonia *41°55′N 22°25′E*
187 L6 **Koçarlı** Aydın, Turkey *37°46′N 27°42′E*
184 F4 **Koceljevo** Serbia, W Serbia *44°28′N 19°49′E*
177 K6 **Kočevje** ***Ger.*** Gottschee. S Slovenia *45°41′N 14°48′E*
233 K6 **Koch Bihār** West Bengal, NE India *26°19′N 89°26′E*
Kochchi *see* Cochin/Kochi
193 H5 **Kochechum** ≈ N Russian Federation
181 G13 **Kocher** ≈ SW Germany
195 K8 **Kochevo** Permskaya Kray, NW Russian Federation *59°37′N 54°16′E*
250 F6 **Kōchi** ***var.*** Kôti. Kōchi, Shikoku, SW Japan *33°31′N 133°30′E*
250 F6 **Kōchi** ***off.*** Kōchi-ken, ***var.*** Kôti. ◈ *prefecture* Shikoku, SW Japan
Kōchi-ken *see* Kōchi
53 J7 **Koch Island** *Island* Nunavut, NE Canada
Kochiu *see* Gejiu
Kochkor *see* Kochkorka
229 L4 **Kochkorka** ***Kir.*** Kochkor. Narynskaya Oblast', C Kyrgyzstan *42°09′N 75°42′E*
195 L4 **Kochmes** Respublika Komi, NW Russian Federation *66°10′N 60°46′E*
197 I8 **Kochubey** Respublika Dagestan, SW Russian Federation *44°25′N 46°33′E*
187 I5 **Kochýlas** ▲ Skýros, Vóreies Sporádes, Greece, Aegean Sea *38°50′N 24°35′E*
182 I6 **Kock** Lubelskie, E Poland *51°39′N 22°26′E*
137 E8 **Kodacho** *spring/well* S Kenya *01°52′S 39°22′E*
235 G10 **Koddiyar Bay** *bay* NE Sri Lanka
83 I8 **Kodiak** Kodiak Island, Alaska, USA *57°47′N 152°24′W*
83 I8 **Kodiak Island** *island* Alaska, USA
232 B9 **Kodīnār** Gujarāt, W India *20°44′N 70°46′E*
194 G6 **Kodino** Arkhangel'skaya Oblast', NW Russian Federation *63°36′N 39°54′E*
193 H7 **Kodinsk** Krasnoyarskiy Kray, C Russian Federation *58°37′N 99°18′E*
136 B4 **Kodok** Upper Nile, NE South Sudan *09°51′N 32°07′E*
188 G6 **Kodyma** Odes'ka Oblast', SW Ukraine *48°05′N 29°09′E*
Koedoes *see* Kudus
140 F6 **Koegasbrug** Northern Cape, South Africa *29°18′S 22°21′E*
140 E6 **Koegrabie** Northern Cape, South Africa *29°04′S 21°47′E*
163 B9 **Koekelare** West-Vlaanderen, W Belgium *51°07′N 02°58′E*
Koeln *see* Köln
Koepang *see* Kupang
Ko-erh-mu *see* Golmud
163 F9 **Koersel** Limburg, NE Belgium *51°04′N 05°17′E*
140 D4 **Koës** Karas, SE Namibia *25°59′S 19°08′E*
Koesan *see* Goesan
Koetai *see* Mahakam, Sungai
Koetaradja *see* Banda Aceh
81 I13 **Kofa Mountains** ▲▲ Arizona, SW USA
261 M7 **Kofarau** Papua, E Indonesia *07°29′S 140°28′E*
229 I7 **Kofarnihon** ***Rus.*** Kofarnikhon; ***prev.*** Ordzhonikidzeabad, ***Taj.*** Orjonikidzeobod, Yangi-Bazar. W Tajikistan *38°32′N 68°56′E*
229 I8 **Kofarnihon** ***Rus.*** Kafirnigan. ≈ SW Tajikistan
Kofarnikhon *see* Kofarnihon
141 H6 **Koffiefontein** Free State, South Africa *29°24′S 25°01′E*
261 H4 **Kofiau, Pulau** ***var.*** Kafiau. *island* Kepulauan Raja Ampat, E Indonesia
187 I10 **Kófinas** ▲ Kríti, Greece, E Mediterranean Sea *34°58′N 25°03′E*
218 C2 **Kofínou** ***var.*** Kophinou. S Cyprus *34°49′N 33°24′E*
177 K4 **Köflach** Steiermark, SE Austria *47°04′N 15°04′E*
133 H8 **Koforidua** SE Ghana *06°01′N 00°12′W*
250 F4 **Kōfu** Tottori, Honshū, SW Japan *35°16′N 133°31′E*
253 B13 **Kōfu** ***var.*** Kôhu. Yamanashi, Honshū, S Japan *35°41′N 138°33′E*
253 C13 **Koga** Ibaraki, Honshū, S Japan *36°12′N 139°42′E*
137 B10 **Koga** Tabora, C Tanzania *06°08′S 32°20′E*
Kogălniceanu *see* Mihail Kogălniceanu
59 J3 **Kogaluk** ≈ Newfoundland and Labrador, E Canada
58 G2 **Kogaluk, Riviére** ≈ Québec, NE Canada
227 L6 **Kogaly** ***Kaz.*** Qoghaly; ***prev.*** Kugaly. Almaty, SE Kazakhstan *44°30′N 78°40′E*
192 F6 **Kogalym** Khanty-Mansiyskiy Avtonomnyy Okrug-Yugra, C Russian Federation *62°13′N 74°34′E*
155 F12 **Køge** Roskilde, E Denmark *55°28′N 12°12′E*
178 G2 **Køge Bugt** *bay* E Denmark
133 J7 **Kogi** ◈ *state* C Nigeria
228 G6 **Kogon** ***Rus.*** Kagan. Buxoro Viloyati, C Uzbekistan *39°47′N 64°29′E*
Kŏgŭm-do *see* Geogeum-do
Kőhalom *see* Rupea
250 B1 **Kohan** Kangwŏn-do, South Korea *37°12′N 128°51′E*
231 I4 **Kohāt** Khyber Pakhtunkhwa, NW Pakistan *33°37′N 71°30′E*
222 F6 **Kohgīlūyeh va Bowyer Aḩmad** ***off.*** Ostān-e Kohkīlūyeh va Būyer Aḩmadī, ***var.*** Boyer Ahmadī va Kohkīlūyeh. ◈ *province* SW Iran
190 E4 **Kohila** ***Ger.*** Koil. Raplamaa, NW Estonia *59°09′N 24°45′E*
233 M6 **Kohīma** *state capital* Nāgāland, E India *25°40′N 94°08′E*
Koh I Noh *see* Büyükağrı Dağı
Kohkīlūyeh va Būyer Aḩmadī, Ostān-e *see* Kohgīlūyeh va Bowyer Aḩmad
Kohsān *see* Kūhestān
190 F3 **Kohtla-Järve** Ida-Virumaa, NE Estonia *59°22′N 27°21′E*
Kôhu *see* Kōfu
87 M7 **Kohunlich** Quintana Roo, Mexico *18°25′N 88°48′W*
Kohyl'nyk *see* Cogîlnic
253 B11 **Koide** Niigata, Honshū, C Japan *37°13′N 138°58′E*
54 A2 **Koidern** Yukon Territory, W Canada *61°55′N 140°22′W*
132 D7 **Koidu** E Sierra Leone *08°40′N 11°01′W*
190 E4 **Koigi** Järvamaa, C Estonia *58°51′N 25°45′E*
Koil *see* Kohila
139 I9 **Koimbani** Grande Comore, NW Comoros *11°37′S 43°23′E*
140 C7 **Koingnaas** Northern Cape, South Africa *30°12′S 17°17′E*
217 J2 **Koi Sanjaq** ***var.*** Koysanjaq, Kūysanjaq. Arbīl, N Iraq *36°05′N 44°38′E*
Koivisto *see* Primorsk
Kōje *see* Geoje
Kōje-do *see* Geogeum-do
136 E4 **K'ok'a Hāyk'** ◎ C Ethiopia
Kokand *see* Qo'qon
276 F4 **Kokatha** South Australia *31°17′S 135°16′E*
228 G6 **Ko'kcha** ***Rus.*** Kokcha. Buxoro Viloyati, C Uzbekistan *40°30′N 64°58′E*
Kokcha *see* Ko'kcha
Kokchetav *see* Kokshetau
153 G9 **Kokemäenjoki** ≈ SW Finland
261 K6 **Kokenau** ***var.*** Kokonau. Papua, E Indonesia *04°38′S 136°24′E*
140 D5 **Kokerboom** Karas, SE Namibia *28°11′S 19°25′E*
191 H9 **Kokhanava** ***Rus.*** Kokhanovo. Vitsyebskaya Voblasts', NE Belarus *54°28′N 29°59′E*
Kokhanovichi *see* Kakhanavichy
Kokhanovo *see* Kokhanava
Kök-Janggak *see* Kok-Yangak
152 G7 **Kokkola** ***Swe.*** Karleby; ***prev. Swe.*** Gamlakarleby. Länsi-Suomi, W Finland *63°50′N 23°10′E*
238 F2 **Kok Kuduk** *spring/well* N China *46°03′N 87°34′E*
190 E6 **Koknese** Aizkraukle, C Latvia *56°38′N 25°27′E*
133 J6 **Koko** Kebbi, W Nigeria *11°25′N 04°33′E*
280 C4 **Kokoda** Northern, S Papua New Guinea *08°52′S 147°44′E*
132 D5 **Kokofata** Kayes, W Mali *12°48′N 09°56′W*
82 G3 **Kokolik River** ≈ Alaska, USA
73 F10 **Kokomo** Indiana, N USA *40°29′N 86°07′W*
Kokonau *see* Kokenau
140 G2 **Kokong** Southern, Botswana *24°20′S 22°58′E*
Koko Nor *see* Qinghai Hu, China
Koko Nor *see* Qinghai, China
280 D2 **Kokopo** ***var.*** Kopopo; ***prev.*** Herbertshöhe. New Britain, E Papua New Guinea *04°18′S 152°17′E*
Kokpekti *see* Kokpekty
Kokpekti *see* Kokpekty
227 L4 **Kokpekty** ***prev.*** Kokpekti. Vostochnyy Kazakhstan, E Kazakhstan *48°47′N 82°28′E*
227 L4 **Kokpekty** ***prev.*** Kokpekti. ≈ E Kazakhstan
83 H5 **Kokrines** Alaska, USA *64°58′N 154°42′W*
83 H4 **Kokrines Hills** ▲▲ Alaska, USA
227 H8 **Koksaray** Yuzhnyy Kazakhstan, S Kazakhstan *42°34′N 68°06′E*
229 M5 **Kokshaal-Tau** ***Rus.*** Khrebet Kakshaal-Too. ▲▲ China/Kyrgyzstan
227 H2 **Kokshetau** ***Kaz.*** Kökshetaū; ***prev.*** Kokchetav. Kokshetau, N Kazakhstan *53°18′N 69°25′E*
Kökshetaū *see* Kokshetau
163 A9 **Koksijde** West-Vlaanderen, W Belgium *51°07′N 02°40′E*
51 J6 **Koksoak** ≈ Québec, E Canada
139 H8 **Kokstad** KwaZulu/Natal, E South Africa *30°23′S 29°23′E*
227 L6 **Koksu** ***Kaz.*** Rūdnīchnyy. Almaty, SE Kazakhstan *44°39′N 78°57′E*
227 L7 **Koktal** ***Kaz.*** Köktal. Almaty, SE Kazakhstan *44°05′N 79°44′E*
227 H5 **Koktas** ≈ C Kazakhstan
Kök-Tash *see* Këk-Tash
Koktokay *see* Fuyun
250 C8 **Kokubu** ***var.*** Kirishima. Kagoshima, Kyūshū, SW Japan *31°45′N 130°45′E*
193 J8 **Kokuy** Zabaykalskiy Kray, S Russian Federation *52°13′N 117°18′E*
229 K5 **Kok-Yangak** ***Kir.*** Kök-Janggak. Dzhalal-Abadskaya Oblast', W Kyrgyzstan *41°02′N 73°11′E*
238 C6 **Kokyar** Xinjiang Uygur Zizhiqu, W China *37°41′N 77°15′E*
230 F8 **Kolāchi** ***var.*** Kulachi. ≈ SW Pakistan
132 D7 **Kolahun** N Liberia *08°24′N 10°02′W*
260 D6 **Kolaka** Sulawesi, C Indonesia *04°04′S 121°38′E*
K'o-la-ma-i *see* Karamay
Kola Peninsula *see* Kol'skiy Poluostrov
234 F7 **Kolār** Karnātaka, E India *13°10′N 78°10′E*
235 F8 **Kolār Gold Fields** Karnātaka, E India *12°56′N 78°16′E*
152 G5 **Kolari** Lappi, NW Finland *67°20′N 23°51′E*
183 E11 **Kolárovo** ***Ger.*** Gutta; ***prev.*** Guta, ***Hung.*** Gúta. Nitriansky Kraj, SW Slovakia *47°54′N 18°01′E*
232 C5 **Kolāyat** Rājasthān, NW India *27°56′N 73°02′E*
155 H8 **Kolbäck** Västmanland, C Sweden *59°33′N 16°15′E*
Kolbcha *see* Kowbcha
295 L6 **Kolbeinsey Ridge** *undersea feature* Denmark Strait/Norwegian Sea *69°00′N 17°30′W*
Kolberg *see* Kołobrzeg
154 E7 **Kolbotn** Akershus, S Norway *62°15′N 10°24′E*
183 H8 **Kolbuszowa** Podkarpackie, SE Poland *50°12′N 22°07′E*
190 I2 **Kolchanovo** Leningradskaya Oblast', Russian Federation
196 G1 **Kol'chugino** Vladimirskaya Oblast', W Russian Federation *56°19′N 39°24′E*
132 B5 **Kolda** S Senegal *12°58′N 14°58′W*
155 D12 **Kolding** Vejle, C Denmark *55°29′N 09°30′E*
135 G9 **Kole** Kasai-Oriental, SW Dem. Rep. Congo *03°30′S 22°28′E*
134 H6 **Kole** Orientale, N Dem. Rep. Congo *02°08′N 25°25′E*
Kōle *see* Kili Island
171 L9 **Koléa** Algeria
144 D4 **Kölen** ***Nor.*** Kjølen. ▲▲ Norway/Sweden
Kolepom, Pulau *see* Yos Sudarso, Pulau
190 E3 **Kolga Laht** ***Ger.*** Kolko-Wiek. *bay* N Estonia
195 I2 **Kolguyev, Ostrov** *island* NW Russian Federation
234 D6 **Kolhāpur** Mahārāshtra, SW India *16°42′N 74°13′E*
235 C13 **Kolhumadulu** ***var.*** Thaa Atoll. *atoll* S Maldives
153 J8 **Koli** ***var.*** Kolinkylä. Itä-Suomi, E Finland *63°06′N 29°46′E*
83 H7 **Koliganek** Alaska, USA *59°43′N 157°16′W*
183 C8 **Kolín** ***Ger.*** Kolin. Střední Čechy, C Czech Republic *50°02′N 15°10′E*
Kolinkylä *see* Koli
284 A10 **Koliu** Île Futuna, W Wallis and Futuna
194 B9 **Kolka** Latvia
190 C5 **Kolka** Talsi, NW Latvia *57°44′N 22°34′E*
190 C5 **Kolkasrags** ***prev. Eng.*** Cape Domesnes. *headland* NW Latvia *57°45′N 22°35′E*
225 H9 **Kolkata** ***prev.*** Calcutta. *state capital* West Bengal, NE India *22°30′N 88°20′E*
Kolkhozabad *see* Kolkhozobod
229 I8 **Kolkhozobod** ***Rus.*** Kolkhozabad; ***prev.*** Kaganovichabad, Tugalan. SW Tajikistan *37°33′N 68°34′E*
Kolki/Kołki *see* Kolky
Kolko-Wiek *see* Kolga Laht
188 E2 **Kolky** ***Pol.*** Kołki, ***Rus.*** Kolki. Volyns'ka Oblast', NW Ukraine *51°05′N 25°40′E*
235 E8 **Kollegāl** Karnātaka, W India *12°08′N 77°06′E*
162 H3 **Kollum** Friesland, N Netherlands *53°17′N 06°09′E*
Kolmar *see* Colmar
181 C9 **Köln** ***var.*** Koeln, ***Eng./Fr.*** Cologne, ***prev.*** Cöln; ***anc.*** Colonia Agrippina, Oppidum Ubiorum. Nordrhein-Westfalen, W Germany *50°57′N 06°57′E*
182 H4 **Kolno** Podlaskie, NE Poland *53°24′N 21°57′E*
182 F6 **Koło** Wielkopolskie, C Poland *52°11′N 18°39′E*
82 B1 **Kōloa** ***var.*** Koloa. Kaua'i, Hawaii, USA, C Pacific Ocean *21°54′N 159°28′W*
Koloa *see* Kōloa
182 D4 **Kołobrzeg** ***Ger.*** Kolberg. Zachodnio-pomorskie, NW Poland *54°11′N 15°34′E*
284 A10 **Kolofau, Mont** 🌋 Île Alofi, S Wallis and Futuna *14°21′S 178°02′W*
195 H9 **Kologriv** Kostromskaya Oblast', NW Russian Federation *58°49′N 44°22′E*
132 E5 **Kolokani** Koulikoro, W Mali *13°35′N 08°01′W*
132 F6 **Koloko** W Burkina *11°06′N 05°18′W*
281 H2 **Kolombangara** ***var.*** Kilimbangara, Nduke. *island* New Georgia Islands, NW Solomon Islands
Kolomea *see* Kolomyya
196 G2 **Kolomna** Moskovskaya Oblast', W Russian Federation *55°03′N 38°52′E*
188 D5 **Kolomyya** ***Ger.*** Kolomea. Ivano-Frankivs'ka Oblast', W Ukraine *48°31′N 25°00′E*
132 E6 **Kolondiéba** Sikasso, SW Mali *11°04′N 06°55′W*
284 E9 **Kolonga** Tongatapu, S Tonga *21°07′S 175°05′W*
283 J1 **Kolonia** ***var.*** Colonia. Pohnpei, E Micronesia *06°57′N 158°12′E*
Kolonja *see* Kolonjë
184 F9 **Kolonjë** ***var.*** Kolonja. Fier, C Albania *40°49′N 19°37′E*
Kolonjë *see* Ersekë
Kolosjoki *see* Nikel'
Kolotambu *see* Avuavu
284 D9 **Kolovai** Tongatapu, S Tonga *21°05′S 175°20′W*
260 E6 **Kolowanawatobo, Teluk** *bay* Pulau Buton, C Indonesia
Kolozsvár *see* Cluj-Napoca
177 K6 **Kolpa** ***Ger.*** Kulpa, ***SCr.*** Kupa. ≈ Croatia/Slovenia
192 F7 **Kolpashevo** Tomskaya Oblast', C Russian Federation *58°21′N 82°44′E*
194 D8 **Kolpino** Leningradskaya Oblast', NW Russian Federation *59°44′N 30°39′E*
178 H5 **Kölpinsee** ◎ NE Germany
Kólpos Mórfu *see* Güzelyurt
228 F4 **Ko'lquduq** ***Rus.*** Kulkuduk. Navoiy Viloyati, N Uzbekistan *42°36′N 63°24′E*
194 F4 **Kol'skiy Poluostrov** ***Eng.*** Kola Peninsula. *peninsula* NW Russian Federation
197 K3 **Koltubanovskiy** Orenburgskaya Oblast', W Russian Federation *53°00′N 52°00′E*
184 F4 **Kolubara** ≈ C Serbia
Kolupchii *see* Gurkovo
182 G6 **Koluszki** Łódźskie, C Poland *51°44′N 19°50′E*
195 K4 **Kolva** ≈ NW Russian Federation
154 E1 **Kolvereid** Nord-Trøndelag, W Norway *64°47′N 11°22′E*
135 H11 **Kolwezi** Katanga, S Dem. Rep. Congo *10°43′S 25°29′E*
193 L4 **Kolyma** ≈ NE Russian Federation
Kolyma Lowland *see* Kolymskaya Nizmennost'
Kolyma Range/Kolymskiy, Khrebet *see* Kolymskoye Nagor'ye
193 L4 **Kolymskaya Nizmennost'** ***Eng.*** Kolyma Lowland. *lowlands* NE Russian Federation
193 L3 **Kolymskoye** Respublika Sakha (Yakutiya), NE Russian Federation *68°42′N 158°46′E*
193 M4 **Kolymskoye Nagor'ye** ***var.*** Khrebet Kolymskiy, ***Eng.*** Kolyma Range. ▲▲ E Russian Federation
193 M2 **Kolyuchinskaya Guba** *bay* NE Russian Federation
Kol'zhat *see* Kalzhat
185 I5 **Kom** ▲ NW Bulgaria *43°10′N 23°02′E*
136 D4 **Koma** Oromīya, C Ethiopia *08°19′N 36°48′E*
133 L5 **Komadugu Gana** ≈ NE Nigeria
251 K3 **Komagane** Nagano, Honshū, S Japan *35°44′N 137°54′E*
140 C7 **Komaggas** Northern Cape, South Africa *29°48′S 17°30′E*
134 J7 **Komanda** Orientale, NE Dem. Rep. Congo *01°25′N 29°43′E*
294 C5 **Komandorskaya Basin** ***var.*** Kamchatka Basin. *undersea feature* SW Bering Sea *57°00′N 168°00′E*
193 N5 **Komandorskiye Ostrova** ***Eng.*** Commander Islands. *island group* E Russian Federation
Komárfalva *see* Comănești
183 F11 **Komárno** ***Ger.*** Komorn, ***Hung.*** Komárom. Nitriansky Kraj, SW Slovakia *47°46′N 18°07′E*
183 F11 **Komárom** Komárom-Esztergom, NW Hungary *47°43′N 18°06′E*
Komárom *see* Komárno
183 F11 **Komárom-Esztergom** ***off.*** Komárom-Esztergom Megye. ◈ *county* N Hungary
Komárom-Esztergom Megye *see* Komárom-Esztergom
141 L3 **Komatipoort** Mpumalanga, South Africa *25°26′S 31°56′E*
141 K4 **Komatirivier** ≈ Mpumalanga, South Africa
251 I2 **Komatsu** ***var.*** Komatu. Ishikawa, Honshū, SW Japan *36°25′N 136°27′E*
250 G5 **Komatsushima** Tokushima, Shikoku, SW Japan *34°00′N 134°36′E*
Komatu *see* Komatsu
138 C4 **Kombat** Otjozondjupa, N Namibia *19°42′S 17°45′E*
Kombissiguiri *see* Kombissiri
132 G5 **Kombissiri** ***var.*** Kombissiguiri. C Burkina *12°01′N 01°27′W*
282 C10 **Komebail Lagoon** *lagoon* N Palau
137 B9 **Kome Island** *island* N Tanzania
Komeyo *see* Wandai
261 J6 **Komfane** Pulau Wokam, E Indonesia *05°36′S 134°42′E*
141 I9 **Komga** Eastern Cape, South Africa *32°35′S 27°54′E*
189 H7 **Kominternivs'ke** Odes'ka Oblast', SW Ukraine *46°52′N 30°56′E*
195 J5 **Komi, Respublika** ◈ *autonomous republic* NW Russian Federation
140 D8 **Komkans** Western Cape, South Africa *31°13′S 18°03′E*
183 F13 **Komló** Baranya, SW Hungary *46°11′N 18°15′E*
140 F9 **Kommandokraal** Western Cape, South Africa *33°08′S 25°05′E*
141 I6 **Kommissiepoort** Free State, South Africa *29°19′S 27°17′E*
Kommunarsk *see* Alchevs'k
Kommunizm, Qullai *see* Ismoili Somoní, Qullai
280 A3 **Komo** Southern Highlands, W Papua New Guinea *06°06′S 142°52′E*
260 C8 **Komodo** Pulau Komodo, S Indonesia *08°35′S 119°27′E*
260 C8 **Komodo, Pulau** *island* Nusa Tenggara, S Indonesia
132 F6 **Komoé** ***var.*** Komoé Fleuve. ≈ E Ivory Coast
Komoé Fleuve *see* Komoé
129 J5 **Kom Ombo** ***var.*** Kôm Ombo, Kawm Umbū. SE Egypt *24°26′N 32°57′E*
135 C9 **Komono** Lékoumou, SW Congo *03°15′S 13°14′E*
261 L8 **Komoran** Papua, E Indonesia *08°14′S 138°51′E*
261 L8 **Komoran, Pulau** *island* E Indonesia
Komorn *see* Komárno
Komornok *see* Comorâște
251 K2 **Komoro** Nagano, Honshū, S Japan *36°20′N 138°26′E*
Komosolabad *see* Komsomolobod
Komotau *see* Chomutov
187 J2 **Komotiní** ***var.*** Gümüljina, ***Turk.*** Gümülcine. Anatolikí Makedonía kai Thráki, NE Greece *41°07′N 25°27′E*
184 F6 **Komovi** ▲▲ E Montenegro
189 I5 **Kompaniyivka** Kirovohrads'ka Oblast', C Ukraine *48°16′N 32°12′E*
261 N6 **Kompiam** Enga, W Papua New Guinea *05°23′S 143°08′E*
Kompong *see* Kâmpóng Chhnăng
Kompong Cham *see* Kâmpóng Cham
Kompong Kleang *see* Kâmpóng Khleăng
Kompong Som *see* Sihanoukville
Kompong Speu *see* Kâmpóng Spoe
Komrat *see* Comrat
140 E9 **Komsberg** ▲ Northern Cape, South Africa *32°40′S 20°49′E*
226 C5 **Komsomol** ***prev.*** Komsomol'skiy. Atyrau, W Kazakhstan *47°18′N 53°37′E*
195 L3 **Komsomol** ***prev.*** Komsomol'skiy. Respublika Komi, NW Russian Federation *67°33′N 64°00′E*
193 H2 **Komsomolets, Ostrov** *island* Severnaya Zemlya, N Russian Federation
226 B6 **Komsomolets, Zaliv** *lake gulf* SW Kazakhstan
Komsomol/Komsomolets *see* Karabalyk, Kostanay, Kazakhstan
229 J7 **Komsomolobod** ***Rus.*** Komosolabad. C Tajikistan *38°51′N 69°54′E*
194 G10 **Komsomol'sk** Ivanovskaya Oblast', W Russian Federation *56°58′N 40°15′E*
189 J4 **Komsomol's'k** Poltavs'ka Oblast', C Ukraine *49°01′N 33°37′E*
228 G6 **Komsomol'sk** Navoiy Viloyati, N Uzbekistan *40°14′N 65°10′E*
Komsomol'skiy *see* Komsomol
193 L8 **Komsomol'sk-na-Amure** Khabarovskiy Kray, SE Russian Federation *50°32′N 136°59′E*
Komsomol'sk-na-Ustyurte *see* Kubla-Ustyurt
226 F4 **Komsomol'skoye** Aktyubinsk, NW Kazakhstan
197 I5 **Komsomol'skoye** Saratovskaya Oblast', W Russian Federation *50°45′N 47°00′E*
227 H4 **Kon** ≈ C Kazakhstan
Kona *see* Kailua-Kona
194 F10 **Konakovo** Tverskaya Oblast', W Russian Federation *56°42′N 36°44′E*
231 H3 **Konar** ***Per.*** Konarhā, ***Pash.*** Kunar. ◈ *province* E Afghanistan
223 J9 **Konārak** Sīstān va Balūchestān, SE Iran *25°26′N 60°23′E*
Konarhā *see* Konar
75 E13 **Konawa** Oklahoma, C USA *34°57′N 96°45′W*
261 I4 **Konda** Papua, E Indonesia *01°34′S 131°58′E*
195 N7 **Konda** ≈ C Russian Federation
234 G4 **Kondagaon** Chhattīsgarh, C India *19°38′N 81°41′E*
62 F1 **Kondiaronk, Lac** ◎ Québec, SE Canada
274 D7 **Kondinin** Western Australia *32°31′S 118°15′E*
195 N7 **Kondinskoye** Khanty-Mansiyskiy Avtonomnyy Okrug-Yugra, Russian Federation
137 D10 **Kondoa** Dodoma, C Tanzania *04°54′S 35°46′E*
197 I3 **Kondol'** Penzenskaya Oblast', W Russian Federation *52°49′N 45°03′E*
185 M7 **Kondolovo** Burgas, E Bulgaria *42°07′N 27°43′E*
261 M8 **Kondomirat** Papua, E Indonesia *08°57′S 140°55′E*
194 E7 **Kondopoga** Respublika Kareliya, NW Russian Federation *62°13′N 34°17′E*
230 G2 **Kondoz** ***var.*** Kondūz, Qondūz, ***Pash.*** Kunduz, Kundūz. Kunduz, NE Afghanistan *36°49′N 68°50′E*
230 G2 **Kondoz** ***Pash.*** Kunduz. ◈ *province* NE Afghanistan
234 F6 **Kondukūr** ***var.*** Kandukur. Andhra Pradesh, E India *15°17′N 79°49′E*
Kondūz *see* Kondoz
280 B9 **Koné** Province Nord, W New Caledonia *21°04′S 164°51′E*
Konechnaya *see* Kurchatov
228 C7 **Könekesir** Balkan Welaýaty, W Turkmenistan *38°16′N 56°51′E*
228 E4 **Köneürgenç** ***var.*** Köneürgench, ***Rus.*** Kёneurgench; ***prev.*** Kunya-Urgench. Daşoguz Welaýaty, N Turkmenistan *42°21′N 59°09′E*
132 F6 **Kong** N Ivory Coast *09°10′N 04°33′W*
83 J2 **Kongakut River** ≈ Alaska, USA
243 J2 **Kongcheng** Anhui, E China *31°02′N 117°05′E*
243 L7 **Kongcheng** Fujian, SE China *25°49′N 119°32′E*
295 L7 **Kong Christian IX Land** ***Eng.*** King Christian IX Land. *physical region* SE Greenland
295 K6 **Kong Christian X Land** ***Eng.*** King Christian X Land. *physical region* E Greenland
295 K8 **Kong Frederik IX Land** *physical region* SW Greenland
295 J6 **Kong Frederik VIII Land** ***Eng.*** King Frederik VIII Land. *physical region* NE Greenland
295 L8 **Kong Frederik VI Kyst** ***Eng.*** King Frederik VI Coast. *physical region* SE Greenland
257 F9 **Kŏng, Kaôh** ***prev.*** Kas Kong. *island* SW Cambodia
152 C5 **Kong Karls Land** ***Eng.*** King Charles Islands. *island group* SE Svalbard
136 C5 **Kong Kong** ≈ E South Sudan
243 J3 **Konglong** Hubei, E China *29°53′N 115°54′E*
Kongo *see* Congo (river)
138 E3 **Kongola** Caprivi, NE Namibia *17°47′S 23°24′E*
135 I9 **Kongolo** Katanga, E Dem. Rep. Congo *05°20′S 26°58′E*
136 B5 **Kongor** Jonglei, C South Sudan *07°09′N 31°44′E*
295 L6 **Kong Oscar Fjord** *fjord* E Greenland
132 G5 **Kongoussi** N Burkina *13°19′N 01°31′W*
155 D8 **Kongsberg** Buskerud, S Norway *59°39′N 09°38′E*
152 C5 **Kongsøya** *island* Kong Karls Land, E Svalbard
154 E7 **Kongsvinger** Hedmark, S Norway *60°10′N 12°00′E*
Kongtong *see* Pingliang
257 H8 **Kông, Tônlé** ***var.*** Xê Kong. ≈ Cambodia/Laos
238 C5 **Kongur Shan** ▲ NW China *38°39′N 75°21′E*
137 D10 **Kongwa** Dodoma, C Tanzania *06°13′S 36°28′E*
Kong, Xê *see* Kông, Tônlé
Konia *see* Konya
229 J6 **Konibodom** ***Rus.*** Kanibadam. N Tajikistan *40°16′N 70°20′E*
182 G7 **Koniecpol nad Pilicą** Śląskie, S Poland *50°47′N 19°45′E*
Konieh *see* Konya
181 J8 **Königerode** Sachsen-Anhalt, Germany *51°36′E 11°13′N*
Königgrätz *see* Hradec Králové
Königinhof an der Elbe *see* Dvůr Králové nad Labem
181 I11 **Königsberg** Bayern, Germany *50°05′E 10°35′N*
179 F12 **Königsbrunn** Bayern, S Germany *48°16′N 10°52′E*
181 J10 **Königsee** Thüringen, Germany *50°40′E 11°06′N*
179 H13 **Königssee** ◎ SE Germany
181 H13 **Konigshofen** Baden-Wurttemburg, Germany *49°32′N 09°43′E*
180 I7 **Königshütte** Sachsen-Anhalt, Germany *51°45′E 10°45′N*
Königshütte *see* Chorzów
180 J6 **Königslutter** Niedersachsen, Germany *52°15′E 10°49′N*
181 E11 **Königstein** Hessen, Germany *50°11′E 8°28′N*
179 I14 **Königstuhl** ▲ S Austria *46°57′N 13°47′E*
177 K2 **Königswiesen** Oberösterreich, N Austria *48°25′N 14°48′E*
181 C10 **Königswinter** Nordrhein-Westfalen, W Germany *50°40′N 07°12′E*
228 G6 **Konimex** ***Rus.*** Kenimekh. Navoiy Viloyati, N Uzbekistan *40°14′N 65°10′E*
182 F6 **Konin** ***Ger.*** Kuhnau. Weilkopolskie, C Poland *52°13′N 18°17′E*
Koninkrijk der Nederlanden *see* Netherlands
186 E4 **Konispol** ***var.*** Konispoli. Vlorë, S Albania *39°40′N 20°10′E*
Konispoli *see* Konispol
186 E3 **Kónitsa** Ípeiros, W Greece *40°04′N 20°48′E*
Konitz *see* Chojnice
176 D4 **Köniz** Bern, W Switzerland *46°56′N 07°25′E*
184 D5 **Konjic** ◈ Federacija Bosna I Hercegovina, S Bosnia and Herzegovina
152 F4 **Könkämäälven** ≈ Finland/Sweden
234 C5 **Konkan** *plain* W India
140 C5 **Konkiep** ≈ S Namibia
132 C6 **Konkouré** ≈ W Guinea
132 F4 **Konna** Mopti, S Mali *14°58′N 03°49′W*
280 E2 **Konogaiang, Mount** ▲ New Ireland, NE Papua New Guinea *04°05′S 152°43′E*
280 D2 **Konogogo** New Ireland, NE Papua New Guinea *03°25′S 152°09′E*
176 D4 **Konolfingen** Bern, W Switzerland *46°53′N 07°36′E*
132 G8 **Konongo** C Ghana *06°39′N 01°06′W*
280 D2 **Konos** New Ireland, NE Papua New Guinea *03°09′S 151°47′E*
194 G8 **Konosha** Arkhangel'skaya Oblast', NW Russian Federation *60°58′N 40°09′E*
189 J2 **Konotop** Sums'ka Oblast', NE Ukraine *51°15′N 33°14′E*
182 G7 **Końskie** Šiętokrzyskie, C Poland *51°12′N 20°23′E*
Konstantinovka *see* Kostyantynivka
196 G6 **Konstantinovsk** Rostovskaya Oblast', SW Russian Federation *47°37′N 41°07′E*
176 E3 **Konstanz** ***var.*** Constanz, ***Eng.*** Constance, ***hist.*** Kostnitz; ***anc.*** Constantia. Baden-Württemberg, S Germany *47°40′N 09°10′E*
Konstanza *see* Constanța
133 J6 **Kontagora** Niger, W Nigeria *10°25′N 05°29′E*
134 B4 **Kontcha** Nord, N Cameroon *08°00′N 12°13′E*
163 E9 **Kontich** Antwerpen, N Belgium *51°08′N 04°27′E*
153 J8 **Kontiolahti** Itä-Suomi, SE Finland *62°46′N 29°51′E*
152 I7 **Kontiomäki** Oulu, C Finland *64°20′N 28°09′E*
256 I7 **Kon Tum** ***var.*** Kontum. Kon Tum, C Vietnam *14°23′N 108°00′E*
Kontum *see* Kon Tum
Konur *see* Sulakyurt
214 E7 **Konya** ***var.*** Konieh, ***prev.*** Konia; ***anc.*** Iconium. Konya, C Turkey *37°51′N 32°30′E*
214 D7 **Konya** ***var.*** Konia, Konieh. ◈ *province* C Turkey
235 C5 **Konya Reservoir** ***prev.*** Shivāji Sāgar. ⊠ W India
227 J5 **Konyrat** ***var.*** Kounradskiy, ***Kaz.*** Qongyrat. Karaganda, SE Kazakhstan *46°57′N 75°01′E*
227 L7 **Konyrolen** Almaty, SE Kazakhstan *44°16′N 79°18′E*
137 D8 **Konza** Eastern, S Kenya *01°44′S 37°07′E*
162 E5 **Koog aan den Zaan** Noord-Holland, C Netherlands *52°28′N 04°49′E*
276 E4 **Koonibba** South Australia *31°55′S 133°23′E*
73 E9 **Koontz Lake** Indiana, N USA *41°25′N 86°24′W*
140 E5 **Koopan-Suid** Northern Cape, South Africa *27°17′S 20°21′E*
261 I4 **Koor** Papua, E Indonesia *0°21′S 132°28′E*
277 K5 **Koorawatha** New South Wales, SE Australia *34°03′S 148°33′E*
190 F4 **Koosa** Tartumaa, E Estonia *58°31′N 27°06′E*
76 G3 **Kootenai** ***var.*** Kootenay. ≈ Canada/USA ***see also*** Kootenay
Kootenai *see* Kootenay
57 H8 **Kootenay** ***var.*** Kootenai. ≈ Canada/USA ***see also*** Kootenai
Kootenay *see* Kootenai
76 F2 **Kootenay Arrow Lake** ◎ British Columbia, SW Canada
138 D9 **Kootjieskolk** Northern Cape, W South Africa *31°16′S 20°21′E*
140 E8 **Kootjieskolk** *marsh* Northern Cape, South Africa
Kopal *see* Koppal
184 G6 **Kopaonik** ▲▲ S Serbia
Kopar *see* Koper
152 D1 **Kópasker** Nordhurland Eystra, N Iceland *66°15′N 16°23′W*
152 B3 **Kópavogur** Reykjanes, W Iceland *64°06′N 21°47′W*
227 K6 **Kopbirlik** ***prev.*** Kīrov, Kirova. Almaty, SE Kazakhstan *46°24′N 77°16′E*
177 J6 **Koper** ***It.*** Capodistria; ***prev.*** Kopar. SW Slovenia *45°32′N 13°43′E*
141 J1 **Kopersspruit** Limpopo, South Africa *22°34′S 28°30′E*
155 A8 **Kopervik** Rogaland, S Norway *59°17′N 05°20′E*
213 J2 **Köpetdag Gershi** ▲▲ Iran/Turkmenistan
Köpetdag Gershi/Kopetdag, Khrebet *see* Koppeh Dāgh
197 N1 **Kopeysk** Kurganskaya Oblast', C Russian Federation *55°06′N 61°31′E*
Kophinou *see* Kofínou
276 F5 **Kopi** South Australia *33°24′S 135°40′E*
Kopiago *see* Lake Copiago
233 L6 **Kopili** ≈ NE India
155 H8 **Köping** Västmanland, C Sweden *59°31′N 16°00′E*
184 F7 **Koplik** ***var.*** Kopliku. Shkodër, NW Albania *42°12′N 19°26′E*
Kopliku *see* Koplik
Kopopo *see* Kokopo
190 G3 **Kopor'ye** Leningradskaya Oblast', Russian Federation
234 E6 **Koppal** ***var.*** Kopal. Karnātaka, S India *15°21′N 76°09′E*
154 E5 **Koppang** Hedmark, S Norway *61°34′N 11°04′E*
154 G7 **Kopparberg** Örebro, C Sweden *59°52′N 15°02′E*
Kopparberg *see* Dalarna
223 I3 **Koppeh Dāgh** ***Rus.*** Khrebet Kopetdag, ***Turkm.*** Köpetdag Gershi. ▲▲ Iran/Turkmenistan
Koppename *see* Coppename Rivier
141 I5 **Koppies** Free State, South Africa *27°14′S 27°35′E*
141 I5 **Koppiesdam** ⊠ Free State, South Africa
154 F7 **Koppom** Värmland, C Sweden *59°42′N 12°07′E*
Kopreinitz *see* Koprivnica
185 K6 **Koprinka, Yazovir** ***prev.*** Yazovir Georgi Dimitrov. ⊠ C Bulgaria
184 C1 **Koprivnica** ***Ger.*** Kopreinitz, ***Hung.*** Kaproncza. Koprivnica-Križevci, N Croatia *46°10′N 16°49′E*
184 C2 **Koprivnica-Križevci** ***off.*** Koprivničko-Križevačka Županija. ◈ *province* N Croatia
183 F9 **Kopřivnice** ***Ger.*** Nesselsdorf. Moravskoslezský Kraj, E Czech Republic *49°36′N 18°09′E*
Koprivničko-Križevačka Županija *see* Koprivnica-Križevci
Köprülü *see* Veles
Koptsevichi *see* Kaptsevichy
Kopyl' *see* Kapyl'
191 H9 **Kopys'** Vitsyebskaya Voblasts', NE Belarus *54°19′N 30°18′E*
184 G7 **Korab** ▲ Albania/FYR Macedonia *41°48′N 20°33′E*
Korabavur Pastligi *see* Karabaur', Uval
194 G4 **Korabel'noye** Murmanskaya Oblast', NW Russian Federation *67°00′N 41°10′E*
136 G5 **K'orahē** Sumalē, E Ethiopia *06°36′N 44°21′E*
187 J4 **Kórakas, Akrotírio** *cape* Lésvos, E Greece
184 B3 **Korana** ≈ C Croatia
140 F5 **Korannaberg** ▲▲ Northern Cape, South Africa
234 H5 **Korāput** Orissa, E India *18°48′N 82°41′E*
Korat *see* Nakhon Ratchasima
256 G7 **Korat Plateau** *plateau* E Thailand
217 J1 **Kōrāwa, Sar-i** ▲ NE Iraq *37°08′N 44°39′E*
234 H3 **Korba** Chhattīsgarh, C India *22°25′N 82°43′E*
175 C13 **Korba** Tunisia
181 F8 **Korbach** Hessen, C Germany *51°16′N 08°52′E*
181 E8 **Körbecke** Nordrhein-Westfalen, Germany *51°30′E 8°07′N*
Korça *see* Korçë
184 G9 **Korçë** ***var.*** Korça, ***Gk.*** Korytsa, ***It.*** Corriza; ***prev.*** Koritsa. Korçë, SE Albania *40°38′N 20°47′E*
184 G9 **Korçë** ◈ *district* SE Albania
184 D6 **Korčula** ***It.*** Curzola. Dubrovnik-Neretva, S Croatia *42°57′N 17°08′E*
184 C6 **Korčula** ***It.*** Curzola; ***anc.*** Corcyra Nigra. *island* S Croatia
184 C6 **Korčulanski Kanal** *channel* S Croatia
227 J7 **Korday** ***prev.*** Georgiyevka. Zhambyl, SE Kazakhstan *43°03′N 74°43′E*
181 B12 **Kordel** Rheinland-Pfalz, Germany *49°50′E 6°38′N*
222 D3 **Kordestān** ***off.*** Ostān-e Kordestān, ***var.*** Kurdestan. ◈ *province* W Iran
Kordestān, Ostān-e *see* Kordestān
222 G3 **Kord Kūy** ***var.*** Kurd Kui. Golestán, N Iran *36°49′N 54°05′E*
245 N4 **Korea Bay** *bay* China/North Korea
Korea, Democratic People's Republic of *see* North Korea
261 H7 **Koreare** Pulau Yamdena, E Indonesia *07°33′S 131°13′E*
Korea, Republic of *see* South Korea
250 B4 **Korea Strait** ***Jap.*** Chōsen-kaikyō, ***Kor.*** Taehan-haehyŏp. *channel* Japan/South Korea
Korelichi/Korelicze *see* Karelichy
136 E3 **Korem** Tigrai, N Ethiopia *12°32′N 39°29′E*
133 J4 **Korén Adoua** ≈ C Niger
196 E4 **Korenevo** Kurskaya Oblast', W Russian Federation *51°21′N 34°53′E*
196 G8 **Korenovsk** Krasnodarskiy Kray, SW Russian Federation *45°28′N 39°25′E*
188 F3 **Korets'** ***Pol.*** Korzec, ***Rus.*** Korets. Rivnens'ka Oblast', NW Ukraine *50°38′N 27°12′E*
Korets *see* Korets'
193 M4 **Korf** Kamchatskaya Oblast, E Russian Federation *60°20′N 165°37′E*
292 G4 **Korff Ice Rise** *ice cap* Antarctica
227 H4 **Korgalzhyn** ***var.*** Kurgal'dzhino, Kurgal'dzhinsky, ***Kaz.*** Qorghalzhyn. Akmola, C Kazakhstan *50°33′N 69°58′E*
227 L7 **Korgas** ; ***prev.*** Khorgos. Almaty, SE Kazakhstan *44°13′N 80°22′E*
152 D6 **Korgen** Troms, N Norway *66°04′N 13°51′E*
229 J5 **Korgon-Dëbë** Dzhalal-Abadskaya Oblast', W Kyrgyzstan *41°51′N 70°52′E*
132 F6 **Korhogo** N Ivory Coast *09°29′N 05°39′W*
140 E9 **Koringplass** Western Cape, South Africa *29°38′S 17°45′E*
186 G6 **Korinthiakós Kólpos** ***Eng.*** Gulf of Corinth; ***anc.*** Corinthiacus Sinus. *gulf* C Greece
186 G6 **Kórinthos** ***anc.*** Corinthus ***Eng.*** Corinth. Pelopónnisos, S Greece *37°56′N 22°55′E*
184 G7 **Koritnik** ▲ S Serbia *42°06′N 20°34′E*
Koritsa *see* Korçë
253 D11 **Kōriyama** Fukushima, Honshū, C Japan *37°25′N 140°20′E*
214 C7 **Korkuteli** Antalya, SW Turkey *37°07′N 30°11′E*
238 F4 **Korla** ***Chin.*** K'u-erh-lo. Xinjiang Uygur Zizhiqu, NW China *41°48′N 86°10′E*
181 G9 **Körle** Hessen, Germany *51°10′E 9°31′N*
192 F6 **Korliki** Khanty-Mansiyskiy Avtonomnyy Okrug-Yugra, C Russian Federation *61°28′N 82°12′E*
Körlin an der Persante *see* Karlino
Korma *see* Karma
72 H3 **Kormak** Ontario, S Canada *47°38′N 83°00′W*
Kormakíti, Akrotíri/Kormakiti, Cape/Kormakítis *see* Koruçam Burnu
183 D12 **Körmend** Vas, W Hungary *47°02′N 16°35′E*
217 J3 **Kōrmōr** Şalāḩ ad Dīn, E Iraq *35°06′N 44°47′E*
184 B4 **Kornat** ***It.*** Incoronata. *island* W Croatia
Korneshty *see* Cornești
177 L2 **Korneuburg** Niederösterreich, NE Austria *48°22′N 16°20′E*
227 H2 **Korneyevka** Severnyy Kazakhstan, N Kazakhstan *54°01′N 68°30′E*
155 E8 **Kornsjø** Østfold, S Norway *58°55′N 11°40′E*
132 G4 **Koro** Mopti, S Mali *14°05′N 03°06′W*
280 F8 **Koro** *island* C Fiji
280 A3 **Koroba** Southern Highlands, W Papua New Guinea *05°46′S 142°48′E*
196 F5 **Korocha** Belgorodskaya Oblast', W Russian Federation *50°49′N 37°08′E*
214 E5 **Köroğlu Dağları** ▲▲ C Turkey
277 M4 **Korogoro Point** *headland* New South Wales, SE Australia *31°03′S 153°04′E*
137 E10 **Korogwe** Tanga, E Tanzania *05°10′S 38°30′E*
277 I7 **Koroit** Victoria, SE Australia *38°17′S 142°22′E*
280 E9 **Korolevu** Viti Levu, W Fiji *18°12′S 177°44′E*
284 G10 **Koromiri** *island* S Cook Islands
263 M9 **Koronadal** Mindanao, S Philippines *06°23′N 124°54′E*
187 H3 **Koróneia, Límni** ***var.*** Límni Korónia. ◎ N Greece
186 F8 **Koróni** Pelopónnisos, S Greece *36°47′N 21°57′E*
Korónia, Límni *see* Koróneia, Límni
182 E5 **Koronowo** ***Ger.*** Krone an der Brahe. Kujawski-pomorskie, C Poland *53°18′N 17°56′E*
189 I2 **Korop** Chernihivs'ka Oblast', N Ukraine *51°35′N 32°57′E*
187 H6 **Koropí** Attikí, C Greece *37°54′N 23°52′E*
282 C10 **Koror** Oreor, N Palau *07°21′N 134°28′E*

◆ Country
● Country Capital
◇ Dependent Territory
○ Dependent Territory Capital
◈ Administrative Regions
✈ International Airport
▲ Mountain
▲▲ Mountain Range
🌋 Volcano
≈ River
◎ Lake
⊠ Reservoir

INDEX

◆ Country   ◇ Dependent Territory   ◆ Administrative Regions   ▲ Mountain   ℞ Volcano   ◎ Lake
● Country Capital   ○ Dependent Territory Capital   ✕ International Airport   ▲▲ Mountain Range   ♒ River   ☒ Reservoir

◆ Country
● Country Capital
◇ Dependent Territory
○ Dependent Territory Capital
◈ Administrative Regions
✈ International Airport
▲ Mountain
▲▲ Mountain Range
✕ Volcano
✓ River
◎ Lake
⊟ Reservoir

◆ Country ◇ Dependent Territory ◆ Administrative Regions ▲ Mountain ☒ Volcano ◎ Lake
● Country Capital ○ Dependent Territory Capital ✕ International Airport ▲ Mountain Range ☰ River ⊜ Reservoir

Lipari Islands/Lipari, Isole - Longhorsley
INDEX
368

Lipari Islands/Lipari, Isole see Eolie, Isole
175 G12 **Lipari, Isola** *island* Isole Eolie, S Italy
188 E5 **Lipcani** *Rus.* Lipkany. N Moldova 48°16′N 26°47′E
153 I8 **Liperi** Itä-Suomi, SE Finland 62°33′N 29°29′E
196 G4 **Lipetsk** Lipetskaya Oblast', W Russian Federation 52°37′N 39°38′E
196 G4 **Lipetskaya Oblast'** ◈ *province* W Russian Federation
112 C3 **Lipez, Cordillera de** ▲▲ SW Bolivia
161 J7 **Liphook** United Kingdom 51°04′N 0°48′W
182 C5 **Lipiany** *Ger.* Lippehne. Zachodnio-pomorskie, W Poland 53°00′N 14°58′E
184 D3 **Lipik** Požega-Slavonija, NE Croatia 45°24′N 17°08′E
118 C5 **Lipimávida** Maule, Chile 34°51′S 72°09′W
194 F8 **Lipin Bor** Vologodskaya Oblast', NW Russian Federation 60°12′N 38°04′E
242 E6 **Liping** *var.* Defeng. Guizhou, S China 26°16′N 109°08′E
Lipkany see Lipcani
191 E9 **Lipnishki** Hrodzyenskaya Voblasts', W Belarus 54°00′N 25°37′E
182 F5 **Lipno** Kujawsko-pomorskie, C Poland 52°52′N 19°11′E
188 B7 **Lipova** *Hung.* Lippa. Arad, W Romania 46°05′N 21°42′E
Lipovets see Lypovets'
Lippa see Lipova
180 F7 **Lippe** ≈ W Germany
Lippehne see Lipiany
180 E7 **Lippstadt** Nordrhein-Westfalen, W Germany 51°41′N 08°20′E
70 F1 **Lipscomb** Texas, SW USA 36°14′N 100°16′W
Lipsia/Lipsk see Leipzig
Liptau-Sankt-Nikolaus/Liptószentmiklós see Liptovský Mikuláš
183 G9 **Liptovský Mikuláš** *Ger.* Liptau-Sankt-Nikolaus, *Hung.* Liptószentmiklós. Žilinský Kraj, N Slovakia 49°06′N 19°36′E
277 J8 **Liptrap, Cape** *headland* Victoria, SE Australia 38°55′S 145°58′E
242 F8 **Lipu** *var.* Licheng. Guangxi Zhuangzu Zizhiqu, S China 24°25′N 110°15′E
243 N4 **Lipu** Zhejiang, SE China 28°58′N 121°37′E
244 E7 **Liquan** Shaanxi, China 34°17′N 108°16′E
136 B7 **Lira** N Uganda 02°15′N 32°55′E
105 E8 **Lircay** Huancavelica, C Peru 12°59′S 74°44′W
118 C6 **Lircay, Río** ≈ Maule, Chile
175 F8 **Liri** ≈ C Italy
226 F2 **Lisakovsk** Kostanay, NW Kazakhstan 52°32′N 62°32′E
134 F6 **Lisala** Equateur, N Dem. Rep. Congo 02°10′N 21°29′E
158 C7 **Lisbellaw** United Kingdom 54°19′N 7°32′W
170 C6 **Lisboa** *Eng.* Lisbon; *anc.* Felicitas Julia, Olisipo. ● (Portugal) Lisboa, W Portugal 38°44′N 09°08′W
170 B6 **Lisboa** *Eng.* Lisbon. ◈ *district* C Portugal
63 I4 **Lisbon** New Hampshire, NE USA 44°11′N 71°52′W
74 E3 **Lisbon** North Dakota, N USA 46°27′N 97°42′W
Lisbon see Lisboa
63 J4 **Lisbon Falls** Maine, NE USA 44°00′N 70°03′W
158 E7 **Lisburn** *Ir.* Lios na gCearrbhach. E Northern Ireland, United Kingdom 54°31′N 06°03′W
82 F3 **Lisburne, Cape** *headland* Alaska, USA 68°52′N 166°13′W
157 B10 **Liscannor Bay** *Ir.* Bá Lios Ceannúir. *inlet* W Ireland
185 H7 **Lisec** ▲ E FYR Macedonia 41°46′N 22°30′E
244 G7 **Li Shan** ▲ Shanxi, China 35°15′N 111°35′E
240 C7 **Lishe Jiang** ≈ SW China
Lishi see Lüliang
243 L1 **Lishu** Jiangsu, E China 31°38′N 119°02′E
248 B1 **Lishu** Jilin, NE China 43°25′N 124°19′E
243 L4 **Lishui** Zhejiang, SE China 28°27′N 119°25′E
286 F3 **Lisianski Island** *island* Hawaiian Islands, Hawai'i, USA
Lisichansk see Lysychans'k
164 G3 **Lisieux** *anc.* Noviomagus. Calvados, N France 49°09′N 00°13′E
160 E9 **Liskeard** SW England, United Kingdom
196 G4 **Liski** *prev.* Georgiu-Dezh. Voronezhskaya Oblast', W Russian Federation 51°00′N 39°36′E
64 E2 **Lisle** New York, NE USA 42°21′N 76°00′W
165 H3 **l'Isle-Adam** Val-d'Oise, N France 49°07′N 02°13′E
166 E8 **L'Isle-Bouchard** Centre, France 47°07′N 0°25′E
168 F6 **L'Isle-en-Dodon** Midi-Pyrénées, France 43°23′N 0°51′E
168 F6 **l'Isle-Jourdain** Midi-Pyrénées, France 43°37′N 01°05′E
Lisle/l'Isle see Lille
165 J8 **l'Isle-sur-la-Sorgue** Vaucluse, SE France 43°55′N 05°03′E
167 M8 **L'Isle-sur-le-Doubs** Franche-Comté, France 47°27′N 6°35′E
168 G5 **Lisle-sur-Tarn** Midi-Pyrénées, France 43°51′N 1°48′E
63 J1 **L'Islet** Québec, SE Canada 47°07′N 70°18′W
277 I7 **Lismore** Victoria, SE Australia 37°59′S 143°18′E
157 C11 **Lismore** *Ir.* Lios Mór. S Ireland 52°10′N 07°10′W
158 F2 **Lismore** *island* United Kingdom
158 C7 **Lisnaskea** United Kingdom 54°15′N 7°27′W
161 J7 **Liss** United Kingdom 51°02′N 0°54′W
Lissa see Vis, Croatia
Lissa see Leszno, Poland
162 E6 **Lisse** Zuid-Holland, W Netherlands 52°15′N 04°33′E
185 K8 **Líssos** *var.* Filiouri. ≈ NE Greece
155 B9 **Lista** *peninsula* S Norway
155 B9 **Listafjorden** *fjord* S Norway
293 I7 **Lister, Mount** ▲ Antarctica 78°12′S 161°46′E
197 H4 **Listopadovka** Voronezhskaya Oblast', W Russian Federation 51°54′N 41°08′E
62 C5 **Listowel** Ontario, S Canada 43°44′N 80°57′W
157 B10 **Listowel** *Ir.* Lios Tuathail. Kerry, SW Ireland 52°27′N 09°29′W
242 E9 **Litang** Guangxi Zhuangzu Zizhiqu, S China 23°09′N 109°08′E
240 C4 **Litang** *var.* Gaocheng. Sichuan, C China 30°03′N 100°12′E
240 C5 **Litang Qu** ≈ C China
103 M6 **Litani** *var.* Itany. ≈ French Guiana/Suriname
218 E4 **Lītani, Nahr el** *var.* Nahr al Litant. ≈ C Lebanon
Litant, Nahr al see Lītani, Nahr el
Litauen see Lithuania
161 L3 **Litcham** United Kingdom 52°43′N 0°48′E
73 C11 **Litchfield** Illinois, N USA 39°17′N 89°52′W
74 G4 **Litchfield** Minnesota, N USA 45°09′N 94°31′W
79 H8 **Litchfield Park** Arizona, SW USA 33°29′N 112°21′W
159 I9 **Litherland** United Kingdom 53°28′N 3°00′W
277 L5 **Lithgow** New South Wales, SE Australia 33°30′S 150°09′E
187 I10 **Líthino, Akrotírio** *headland* Kríti, Greece, E Mediterranean Sea 34°55′N 24°43′E
191 D8 **Lithuania** *off.* Republic of Lithuania, *Ger.* Litauen, *Lith.* Lietuva, *Pol.* Litwa, *Rus.* Litva; *prev.* Lithuanian SSR, *Rus.* Litovskaya SSR. ◆ *republic* NE Europe
Lithuanian SSR see Lithuania
Lithuania, Republic of see Lithuania
177 K5 **Litija** *Ger.* Littai. C Slovenia 46°03′N 14°50′E
64 E7 **Lititz** Pennsylvania, NE USA 40°09′N 76°18′W
186 G3 **Litóchoro** *var.* Litohoro, Litókhoron. Kentrikí Makedonía, N Greece 40°06′N 22°30′E
Litohoro/Litókhoron see Litóchoro
183 B8 **Litoměřice** *Ger.* Leitmeritz. Ústecký Kraj, NW Czech Republic 50°33′N 14°10′E
183 D8 **Litomyšl** *Ger.* Leitomischl. Pardubický Kraj, C Czech Republic 49°54′N 16°18′E
183 E9 **Litovel** *Ger.* Littau. Olomoucký Kraj, E Czech Republic 49°42′N 17°05′E
193 L8 **Litovko** Khabarovskiy Kray, SE Russian Federation 49°22′N 135°10′E
Litovskaya SSR see Lithuania
Littai see Litija
Littau see Litovel
61 M9 **Little Abaco** *var.* Abaco Island. *island* N Bahamas
183 F11 **Little Alföld** *Ger.* Kleines Ungarisches Tiefland, *Hung.* Kisalföld, *Slvk.* Podunajská Rovina. *plain* Hungary/Slovakia
257 A9 **Little Andaman** *island* Andaman Islands, India, NE Indian Ocean
75 E10 **Little Arkansas River** ≈ Kansas, C USA
278 G3 **Little Barrier Island** *island* N New Zealand
Little Belt see Lillebælt
83 J4 **Little Black River** ≈ Alaska, USA
75 D8 **Little Blue River** ≈ Kansas/Nebraska, C USA
159 J9 **Littleborough** United Kingdom 53°38′N 2°06′W
54 F5 **Little Buffalo River** ≈ Northwest Territories/Alberta. NW Canada
90 D5 **Little Cayman** *island* E Cayman Islands
55 J6 **Little Churchill** ≈ Manitoba, C Canada
257 B8 **Little Coco Island** *island* SW Myanmar (Burma)
79 I6 **Little Colorado River** ≈ Arizona, SW USA
62 B2 **Little Current** Manitoulin Island, Ontario, S Canada 45°57′N 81°56′W
58 D6 **Little Current** ≈ Ontario, S Canada
82 F4 **Little Diomede Island** *island* Alaska, USA
90 F3 **Little Exuma** *island* C Bahamas
74 G4 **Little Falls** Minnesota, N USA 45°59′N 94°21′W
64 G1 **Little Falls** New York, NE USA 43°02′N 74°51′W
70 D3 **Littlefield** Texas, SW USA 33°56′N 102°20′W
141 H9 **Little Fish** ≈ Eastern Cape, South Africa
74 G2 **Littlefork** Minnesota, N USA 48°24′N 93°33′W
74 G2 **Little Fork River** ≈ Minnesota, N USA
56 F7 **Little Fort** British Columbia, SW Canada 51°27′N 120°15′W
55 J8 **Little Grand Rapids** Manitoba, C Canada 52°06′N 95°29′W
161 J8 **Littlehampton** SE England, United Kingdom 50°48′N 00°33′W
78 E2 **Little Humboldt River** ≈ Nevada, W USA
61 N10 **Little Inagua** *var.* Inagua Islands. *island* S Bahamas
67 I3 **Little Kanawha River** ≈ West Virginia, NE USA
138 E10 **Little Karoo** *plateau* S South Africa
140 E9 **Little Karroo** ▲▲ Western Cape, South Africa
83 H9 **Little Koniuji Island** *island* Shumagin Islands, Alaska, USA
81 F8 **Little Lake** California, USA 35°56′N 117°54′W
90 D8 **Little London** W Jamaica 18°15′N 78°13′W
54 F3 **Little Marten Lake** ◎ Northwest Territories, NW Canada
59 K5 **Little Mecatina** *Fr.* Rivière du Petit Mécatina. ≈ Newfoundland and Labrador/Québec, E Canada
156 D4 **Little Minch, The** *strait* NW Scotland, United Kingdom
75 H13 **Little Missouri River** ≈ Arkansas, USA
77 M6 **Little Missouri River** ≈ NW USA
74 A2 **Little Muddy River** ≈ North Dakota, N USA
257 B11 **Little Nicobar** *island* Nicobar Islands, India, NE Indian Ocean
75 G10 **Little Osage River** ≈ Missouri, C USA
161 L3 **Little Ouse** ≈ United Kingdom
157 I10 **Little Ouse** ≈ E England, United Kingdom
231 J2 **Little Pamir** *Pash.* Pāmīr-e Khord, *Rus.* Malyy Pamir. ▲▲ Afghanistan/Tajikistan
67 J8 **Little Pee Dee River** ≈ North Carolina/South Carolina, SE USA
161 L3 **Littleport** United Kingdom 52°27′N 0°18′E
75 I12 **Little Red River** ≈ Arkansas, C USA
Little Rhody see Rhode Island
278 F10 **Little River** Canterbury, South Island, New Zealand 43°45′S 172°49′E
67 K8 **Little River** South Carolina, SE USA 33°52′N 78°36′W
75 J12 **Little River** ≈ Arkansas/Missouri, C USA
75 G13 **Little River** ≈ Arkansas/Oklahoma, USA
69 J3 **Little River** ≈ Georgia, SE USA
68 C2 **Little River** ≈ Louisiana, S USA
71 H6 **Little River** ≈ Texas, SW USA
75 I13 **Little Rock** *state capital* Arkansas, C USA 34°45′N 92°17′W
81 E10 **Littlerock** California, USA 34°31′N 117°59′W
72 E7 **Little Sable Point** *headland* Michigan, N USA 43°38′N 86°32′W
169 M1 **Little Saint Bernard Pass** *Fr.* Col du Petit St-Bernard, *It.* Colle del Piccolo San Bernardo. *pass* France/Italy
79 H5 **Little Salt Lake** ◎ Utah, W USA
274 E5 **Little Sandy Desert** *desert* Western Australia
65 H7 **Little Silver** New Jersey, USA 40°20′N 74°03′W
74 F7 **Little Sioux River** ≈ Iowa, C USA
82 B9 **Little Sitkin Island** *island* Aleutian Islands, Alaska, USA
57 H4 **Little Smoky** Alberta, W Canada 54°35′N 117°06′W
56 G4 **Little Smoky** ≈ Alberta, W Canada
79 K2 **Little Snake River** ≈ Colorado, C USA
67 M10 **Little Sound** *bay* Bermuda, NW Atlantic Ocean
79 M3 **Littleton** Colorado, C USA 39°36′N 105°01′W
63 I4 **Littleton** New Hampshire, NE USA 44°18′N 71°46′W
64 A2 **Little Valley** New York, NE USA 42°15′N 78°47′W
73 D12 **Little Wabash River** ≈ Illinois, N USA
161 L2 **Little Walsingham** United Kingdom 52°53′N 0°52′E
62 A2 **Little White River** ≈ Ontario, S Canada
74 C6 **Little White River** ≈ South Dakota, N USA
75 D14 **Little Wichita River** ≈ Texas, SW USA
217 K2 **Little Zab** *Ar.* Nahraz Zāb aş Şaghīr, *Kurd.* Zē-i Kōya, *Per.* Rūdkhāneh-ye Zāb-e Kūchek. ≈ Iran/Iraq
134 A5 **Littoral** ◈ *province* W Cameroon
Littoria see Latina
Litva/Litwa see Lithuania
183 B8 **Litvínov** *Ger.* Leutensdorf. Ústecký Kraj, NW Czech Republic 50°38′N 13°30′E
188 F4 **Lityn** Vinnyts'ka Oblast', C Ukraine 49°19′N 28°06′E
243 J8 **Liuche** Jiangxi, SE China 24°36′N 115°35′E
242 E8 **Liucheng** Guangxi, China 24°24′N 109°09′E
243 L4 **Liucheng** Zhejiang, SE China 28°37′N 119°36′E
243 H1 **Liuchia-ho** Hubei, E China 32°05′N 113°37′E
242 B5 **Liuchong He** ≈ Guizhou, China
Liu-chou/Liuchow see Liuzhou
118 D10 **Liucura** Araucanía, Chile 38°39′S 71°05′W
118 B8 **Liucura** Bío-Bío, Chile 36°52′S 72°23′W
245 M5 **Liugezhuang** Shandong, E China 36°47′N 121°19′E
245 L2 **Liugu He** ≈ Liaoning, China
248 C2 **Liuhe** Jilin, NE China 42°15′N 125°49′E
243 K2 **Liujiadun** Anhui, E China 31°03′N 117°27′E
242 E8 **Liujiang** Guangxi, China 24°09′N 109°12′E
242 E8 **Liu Jiang** ▲▲ Guangxi, China
Liujiaxia see Yongjing
Liukang Tenggaya, Kepulauan see Sabalana, Kepulauan
244 F5 **Liulin** Shanxi, China 37°16′N 110°31′E
Liulin see Jonê
244 C7 **Liupan Shan** ▲▲ Ningxia, China
Liupanshui see Lupanshui
139 L2 **Liúpo** Nampula, NE Mozambique 15°36′S 39°57′E
242 E10 **Liuwan Dashan** ▲▲ Guangxi, China
138 E1 **Liuwa Plain** *plain* W Zambia
243 H5 **Liuyang** Hunan, China 28°05′N 113°22′E
242 B9 **Liuzhao Shan** ▲▲ Guangxi, China
242 E8 **Liuzhou** *var.* Liu-chou, Liuchow. Guangxi Zhuangzu Zizhiqu, S China 24°09′N 108°55′E
188 C6 **Livada** *Hung.* Sárköz. Satu Mare, NW Romania 47°52′N 23°04′E
187 J7 **Liváda, Akrotírio** *headland* Tínos, Kykládes, Greece, Aegean Sea 37°36′N 25°15′E
186 G6 **Livádeia** *prev.* Levádia. Stereá Elláda, C Greece 38°24′N 22°51′E
Livádi see Liádi
Livanátai see Livanátes
187 H5 **Livanátes** *prev.* Livanátai. Stereá Elláda, C Greece 38°43′N 23°03′E
190 E7 **Līvāni** *Ger.* Lievenhof. Preiļi, SE Latvia 56°22′N 26°12′E
166 E5 **Livarot** Basse-Normandie, France 49°01′N 0°09′E
117 I11 **Lively Island** *island* SE Falkland Islands
117 I11 **Lively Sound** *sound* SE Falkland Islands
83 I4 **Livengood** Alaska, USA 65°31′N 148°32′W
177 I6 **Livenza** ≈ NE Italy
80 D1 **Live Oak** California, W USA 39°17′N 121°41′W
80 B4 **Live Oak** California, USA 36°59′N 121°59′W
69 K4 **Live Oak** Florida, SE USA 30°18′N 82°59′W
81 F13 **Live Oak Springs** California, USA 32°41′N 116°20′W
80 B3 **Livermore** California, W USA 37°40′N 121°46′W
66 D4 **Livermore** Kentucky, S USA 37°31′N 87°08′W
63 J4 **Livermore Falls** Maine, NE USA 44°30′N 70°09′W
70 C6 **Livermore, Mount** ▲ Texas, SW USA 30°37′N 104°10′W
168 G3 **Livernon** Midi-Pyrénées, France 44°39′N 1°51′E
63 N4 **Liverpool** Nova Scotia, SE Canada 44°03′N 64°43′W
159 I10 **Liverpool** NW England, United Kingdom 53°25′N 02°55′W
52 C6 **Liverpool Bay** *coastal sea feature* Northwest Territories
159 I9 **Liverpool Bay** *bay* United Kingdom
277 L4 **Liverpool Range** ▲▲ New South Wales, SE Australia
88 D3 **Lívingston** Izabal, E Guatemala 15°50′N 88°44′W
159 H3 **Livingston** C Scotland, United Kingdom 55°51′N 03°31′W
68 G2 **Livingston** Alabama, S USA 32°35′N 88°12′W
80 C4 **Livingston** California, W USA 37°22′N 120°45′W
68 D4 **Livingston** Louisiana, S USA 30°30′N 90°45′W
77 I5 **Livingston** Montana, NW USA 45°40′N 110°33′W
66 F5 **Livingston** Tennessee, S USA 36°22′N 85°20′W
71 I6 **Livingston** Texas, SW USA 30°42′N 94°58′W
138 F3 **Livingstone** *var.* Maramba. Southern, S Zambia 17°51′S 25°48′E
278 B11 **Livingstone Mountains** ▲▲ South Island, New Zealand
137 C12 **Livingstone Mountains** ▲▲ S Tanzania
137 C12 **Livingstonia** Northern, N Malawi 10°29′S 34°06′E
292 D3 **Livingston Island** *island* Antarctica
71 I6 **Livingston, Lake** ▣ Texas, SW USA
64 G3 **Livingston Manor** New York, USA 41°54′N 74°50′W
184 D5 **Livno** ◈ Federicija Bosna I Hercegovina, SW Bosnia and Herzegovina
196 F4 **Livny** Orlovskaya Oblast', W Russian Federation 52°25′N 37°42′E
152 H6 **Livojoki** ≈ C Finland
73 H8 **Livonia** Michigan, N USA 42°22′N 83°22′W
176 F10 **Livorno** *Eng.* Leghorn. Toscana, C Italy 43°32′N 10°18′E
169 N2 **Livorno Ferraris** Piemonte, NW Italy 45°16′N 08°04′E
Livramento see Santana do Livramento
221 J5 **Līwā** *var.* Al Liwā'. *oasis region* S United Arab Emirates
137 E12 **Liwale** Lindi, SE Tanzania 09°46′S 37°56′E
244 C5 **Liwang** Ningxia, N China 36°42′N 106°05′E
137 C14 **Liwonde** Southern, S Malawi 15°01′S 35°15′E
181 E10 **Lixfeld** Hessen, Germany 50°48′E 8°24′N
244 B8 **Lixian** *var.* Li Xian. Gansu, C China 34°15′N 105°07′E
242 G3 **Lixian** Hunan, China 29°23′N 111°28′E
242 A1 **Lixian** *var.* Li Xian, Zagunao. Sichuan, C China 31°27′N 103°06′E
Li Xian see Lixian
Lixian Jiang see Black River
245 J9 **Lixin** Anhui, China 33°04′N 116°07′E
186 E6 **Lixoúri** *prev.* Lixoúrion. Kefallinía, Iónia Nisiá, Greece, C Mediterranean Sea 38°14′N 20°24′E
Lixoúrion see Lixoúri
Lixus see Larache
243 L2 **Liyang** Jiangsu, China 31°16′N 119°17′E
160 D10 **Lizard** SW England, United Kingdom 49°58′N 05°14′W
77 J8 **Lizard Head Peak** ▲ Wyoming, C USA 42°47′N 109°12′W
157 E13 **Lizard Point** *headland* SW England, United Kingdom 49°57′N 05°12′W
Lizarra see Estella
188 A9 **Ljig** Serbia, C Serbia 44°14′N 20°16′E
Ljouwert see Leeuwarden
Ljubelj see Loibl Pass
177 J5 **Ljubljana** *Ger.* Laibach, *It.* Lubiana; *anc.* Aemona, Emona. ● (Slovenia) C Slovenia 46°03′N 14°29′E
174 G4 **Ljubljana** ✈ C Slovenia 46°14′N 14°26′E
184 G7 **Ljuboten** *Alb.* Luboten. ▲ S Serbia 42°12′N 21°06′E
155 J10 **Ljugarn** Gotland, SE Sweden 57°23′N 18°45′E
144 D4 **Ljungan** ≈ N Sweden
154 F4 **Ljungan** ≈ C Sweden
155 G11 **Ljungby** Kronoberg, S Sweden 56°49′N 13°55′E
155 H9 **Ljungsbro** Östergötland, S Sweden 58°31′N 15°30′E
155 E9 **Ljungskile** Västra Götaland, S Sweden 58°14′N 11°55′E
154 H5 **Ljusdal** Gävleborg, C Sweden 61°50′N 16°10′E
154 H5 **Ljusnan** ≈ C Sweden
154 I6 **Ljusne** Gävleborg, C Sweden 61°11′N 17°07′E
155 J8 **Ljusterö** Stockholm, C Sweden 59°31′N 18°40′E
177 L5 **Ljutomer** *Ger.* Luttenberg. NE Slovenia 46°31′N 16°12′E
169 H9 **Llagostera** Cataluña, Spain 41°49′N 2°54′E
116 B6 **Llaima, Volcán** ⋀ S Chile 39°01′S 71°38′W
114 B3 **Llambí Campbell** Santa Fe, Argentina 31°11′S 60°45′W
160 E3 **Llanaber** United Kingdom 52°44′N 4°05′W
160 E2 **Llanaelhaearn** NW Wales, United Kingdom 52°59′N 04°24′W
160 E2 **Llanaelhaiarn** United Kingdom 52°58′N 4°24′W
160 F3 **Llanarmon Dyffryn Ceiriog** NE Wales, United Kingdom 52°52′N 03°21′W
160 E3 **Llanbedr** United Kingdom 52°49′N 4°06′W
160 E3 **Llanbedrog** United Kingdom 52°51′N 4°29′W
160 E2 **Llanberis** United Kingdom 53°07′N 4°09′W
160 F4 **Llanbister** United Kingdom 52°21′N 3°18′W
160 F3 **Llanbrynmair** United Kingdom 52°35′N 3°39′W
171 L2 **Llançà** *var.* Llansá. Cataluña, NE Spain 42°23′N 03°08′E
118 F6 **Llancanelo, Laguna** ◎ Mendoza, Argentina
160 E5 **Llandeilo** United Kingdom 51°53′N 4°00′W
160 F4 **Llandinam** United Kingdom 52°29′N 3°26′W
160 F5 **Llandovery** C Wales, United Kingdom 52°01′N 03°47′W
160 F2 **Llandrillo** United Kingdom 52°55′N 3°27′W
160 F4 **Llandrindod Wells** E Wales, United Kingdom 52°15′N 03°23′W
160 F1 **Llandudno** N Wales, United Kingdom 53°19′N 03°49′W
160 G3 **Llandyssil** United Kingdom 52°33′N 3°11′W
160 E5 **Llandyssul** United Kingdom 52°02′N 4°18′W
160 E3 **Llanegryn** United Kingdom 52°37′N 4°04′W
160 F2 **Llanelidan** United Kingdom 53°02′N 3°20′W
160 E6 **Llanelli** *prev.* Llanelly. SW Wales, United Kingdom 51°41′N 04°12′W
Llanelly see Llanelli
170 F1 **Llanes** Asturias, N Spain 43°25′N 04°46′W
160 E1 **Llanfachreth** United Kingdom 53°19′N 4°32′W
160 E2 **Llanfaelog** United Kingdom 53°14′N 4°28′W
160 E1 **Llanfaethlu** United Kingdom 53°21′N 4°32′W
160 F3 **Llanfair Caereinion** United Kingdom 52°40′N 3°19′W
160 E4 **Llanfair Clydogau** United Kingdom 52°08′N 4°01′W
160 F2 **Llanfair Talhaiarn** United Kingdom 53°13′N 3°36′W
160 G3 **Llanfechain** United Kingdom 52°46′N 3°12′W
160 F5 **Llanfrynach** United Kingdom 51°55′N 3°21′W
160 F3 **Llanfyllin** United Kingdom 52°45′N 3°15′W
160 D5 **Llanfyrnach** United Kingdom 51°57′N 4°35′W
160 F3 **Llangadfan** C Wales, United Kingdom 52°41′N 3°28′W
160 E2 **Llangefni** NW Wales, United Kingdom 53°15′N 04°17′W
160 E1 **Llangoed** NW Wales, United Kingdom
160 G2 **Llangollen** NE Wales, United Kingdom 52°58′N 03°10′W
160 F3 **Llangower** NW Wales, United Kingdom
160 E4 **Llangranog** W Wales, United Kingdom 52°09′N 4°29′W
170 E1 **Llangréu** *var.* Langreo, Sama de Langreo. Asturias, N Spain 43°18′N 05°40′W
160 G4 **Llangunllo** United Kingdom 52°20′N 3°10′W
160 F4 **Llangurig** United Kingdom 52°24′N 3°36′W
160 F2 **Llangwm** United Kingdom 52°59′N 3°32′W
160 E4 **Llangybi** United Kingdom 52°09′N 4°03′W
160 F5 **Llangynidr** United Kingdom 51°52′N 3°13′W
160 F4 **Llanidloes** United Kingdom 52°28′N 3°32′W
160 E4 **Llanilar** United Kingdom 52°21′N 4°01′W
160 E2 **Llanllyfni** United Kingdom 53°02′N 4°17′W
160 E6 **Llanmadog** United Kingdom 51°37′N 4°15′W
160 E4 **Llannon** United Kingdom 52°17′N 4°11′W
84 G5 **Llano** Sonora, Mexico
70 G6 **Llano** Texas, SW USA 30°49′N 98°42′W
86 G5 **Llano Enmedio** Veracruz-Llave, Mexico 20°49′N 98°01′W
85 I9 **Llano Grande** Durango, Mexico 22°58′N 104°24′W
70 F6 **Llano River** ≈ Texas, SW USA
102 E4 **Llanos** *physical region* Colombia/Venezuela
116 B7 **Llanquihue, Lago** ◎ S Chile
160 F2 **Llanrhaiadr** United Kingdom 53°09′N 3°23′W
160 E6 **Llanrhidian** United Kingdom 51°36′N 4°10′W
160 E4 **Llanrhystyd** United Kingdom 52°18′N 4°09′W
160 D5 **Llanrian** United Kingdom 51°56′N 5°10′W
160 F2 **Llanrwst** United Kingdom 53°09′N 3°48′W
Llansá see Llançà
160 F2 **Llansannan** United Kingdom 53°10′N 3°36′W
160 E5 **Llansawel** United Kingdom 52°00′N 4°01′W
160 G3 **Llansilin** United Kingdom 52°50′N 3°11′W
160 F6 **Llantwit Major** United Kingdom 51°24′N 3°29′W
160 F3 **Llanuwchllyn** United Kingdom 52°52′N 3°40′W
160 F3 **Llanwddyn** United Kingdom 52°45′N 3°26′W
160 E5 **Llanwenog** United Kingdom 52°05′N 4°12′W
160 F5 **Llanwrda** United Kingdom 51°58′N 3°52′W
160 F3 **Llanwrin** United Kingdom 52°37′N 3°48′W
160 F4 **Llanwrthwl** United Kingdom 52°16′N 3°30′W
160 F5 **Llanwrtyd Wells** United Kingdom 52°06′N 3°38′W
160 D5 **Llanycefn** United Kingdom 51°53′N 4°46′W
168 F7 **Llavorsí** Cataluña, Spain 42°29′N 1°13′E
171 J3 **Lleida** *Cast.* Lérida; *anc.* Ilerda. Cataluña, NE Spain 41°38′N 00°35′E
118 C6 **Llepo** Maule, Chile 35°55′S 71°31′W
85 M8 **Llera de Canales** Tamaulipas, Mexico 23°19′N 99°01′W
170 E7 **Llerena** Extremadura, W Spain 38°13′N 06°00′W
118 B9 **Lleulleu, Lago** ◎ Bío-Bío, Chile
160 E2 **Llewelyn, Carnedd** ▲ United Kingdom 53°10′N 3°57′W
160 E2 **Lleyn Peninsula** *peninsula* NW Wales, United Kingdom
118 A8 **Llico** Bío-Bío, Chile 37°12′S 73°34′W
118 D1 **Llimpo** Coquimbo, Chile 31°48′S 70°52′W
173 L4 **Llíria** País Valenciano, E Spain 39°38′N 00°36′W
160 E2 **Llithfaen** United Kingdom 52°57′N 4°27′W
171 K2 **Llívia** Cataluña, NE Spain 42°27′N 02°00′E
Llodio see Laudio
171 L3 **Lloret de Mar** Cataluña, NE Spain 41°42′N 02°51′E
Llorri see Toretta de l'Orrí
54 C5 **Lloyd George, Mount** ▲ British Columbia, W Canada 57°46′N 124°57′W
57 K5 **Lloydminster** Alberta/Saskatchewan, SW Canada 53°18′N 110°00′W
170 E1 **Lluanco** *var.* Luanco. Asturias, N Spain 43°36′N 05°48′W
171 L6 **Llucmajor** Mallorca, Spain, W Mediterranean Sea 39°29′N 02°53′E
114 G3 **Lluveras** Salto, Uruguay 31°10′S 57°05′W
160 E3 **Llwyngwril** United Kingdom 52°40′N 4°05′W
160 F4 **Llyn Brianne Reservoir** ▣ E Wales, United Kingdom
160 F5 **Llyswen** United Kingdom 52°02′N 3°16′W
79 I4 **Loa** Utah, W USA 38°24′N 111°38′W
259 J3 **Loagan Bunut** ◎ East Malaysia
263 H7 **Loaita Island** *island* W Spratly Islands
82 D3 **Loa, Mauna** ▲ Hawai'i, USA 19°28′N 155°39′W
118 B6 **Loanco, Río** ≈ Maule, Chile
Loanda see Luanda
135 E10 **Loange** ≈ S Dem. Rep. Congo
135 B9 **Loango** Kouilou, S Congo 04°38′S 11°50′E
176 D9 **Loano** Liguria, NW Italy 44°07′N 08°15′E
112 B3 **Loa, Río** ≈ N Chile
168 D8 **Loarre** Aragón, Spain 42°19′N 0°37′W
85 J9 **Lobatos** Zacatecas, Mexico
141 H3 **Lobatse** *var.* Lobatsi. Kgatleng, SE Botswana 25°11′S 25°40′E
Lobatsi see Lobatse
179 J8 **Löbau** Sachsen, E Germany 51°07′N 14°40′E
134 D6 **Lobaye** ◈ *prefecture* SW Central African Republic
134 D5 **Lobaye** ≈ SW Central African Republic
163 D11 **Lobbes** Hainaut, S Belgium 50°21′N 04°16′E
118 C1 **Lobera, Punta** *point* Coquimbo, Chile
116 H6 **Lobería** Buenos Aires, E Argentina 38°08′S 58°48′W
118 B7 **Loberia, Punta** *point* Bío-Bío, Chile
182 D4 **Łobez** *Ger.* Labes. Zacodnio-pomorskie, NW Poland 53°38′N 15°39′E
135 C12 **Lobito** Benguela, W Angola 12°20′S 13°34′E
Lobkovichi see Labkovichy
Lob Nor see Lop Nur
261 J5 **Lobo** Papua, E Indonesia 03°41′S 134°06′E
170 D6 **Lobón** Extremadura, W Spain 38°51′N 06°38′W
114 D10 **Lobos** Buenos Aires, E Argentina 35°11′S 59°08′W
84 D3 **Lobos, Cabo** *headland* NW Mexico 29°53′N 112°43′W
87 N7 **Lobos, Cayo** *island* Quintana Roo, Mexico
84 E5 **Lobos, Isla** *island* NW Mexico
Lobositz see Lovosice
Lobsens see Łobżenica
Loburi see Lop Buri
195 L8 **Lobva** Sverdlovskaya Oblast', Russian Federation 59°11′N 60°30′E
182 E5 **Łobżenica** *Ger.* Lobsens. Wielkopolskie, C Poland 53°19′N 17°11′E
176 E5 **Locarno** *Ger.* Luggarus. Ticino, S Switzerland 46°11′N 08°48′E
118 D4 **Lo Chacón** Región Metropolitana, Chile 33°42′S 71°02′W
158 E1 **Lochailort** United Kingdom 56°53′N 5°40′W
158 E1 **Lochaline** United Kingdom 56°32′N 5°47′W
159 H5 **Locharbriggs** United Kingdom 55°06′N 3°35′W
156 D5 **Lochboisdale** NW Scotland, United Kingdom 57°08′N 07°17′W
158 E2 **Lochbuie** United Kingdom 56°21′N 5°51′W
158 E2 **Lochdon** United Kingdom 56°26′N 5°41′W
158 G2 **Lochearnhead** United Kingdom 56°23′N 4°17′W
162 H6 **Lochem** Gelderland, E Netherlands 52°10′N 06°25′E
164 G5 **Loches** Indre-et-Loire, C France 47°08′N 01°00′E
Loch Garman see Wexford
159 I3 **Lochgelly** United Kingdom 56°08′N 3°19′W
158 F3 **Lochgilphead** W Scotland, United Kingdom 56°02′N 05°27′W
158 F2 **Lochgoilhead** United Kingdom 56°10′N 4°54′W
141 K4 **Lochiel** Mpumalanga, South Africa 26°09′S 30°47′E
156 E4 **Lochinver** N Scotland, United Kingdom 58°10′N 05°15′W
159 I2 **Loch Leven** ◎ United Kingdom
80 B1 **Loch Lomond** California, USA 38°52′N 122°43′W
158 G2 **Loch Lubnaig** ◎ United Kingdom
158 G2 **Loch Lyon** ◎ United Kingdom
159 H5 **Lochmaben** United Kingdom 55°07′N 3°27′W
156 D4 **Lochmaddy** NW Scotland, United Kingdom 57°35′N 07°10′W
156 F5 **Lochnagar** ▲ C Scotland, United Kingdom 56°58′N 03°09′W
158 F4 **Lochranza** United Kingdom 55°42′N 5°12′W
163 D9 **Lochristi** Oost-Vlaanderen, NW Belgium 51°07′N 03°49′E
156 E5 **Lochy, Loch** ◎ N Scotland, United Kingdom
276 F5 **Lock** South Australia 33°37′S 135°45′E
80 D3 **Lockeford** California, USA 38°10′N 121°09′W
159 H5 **Lockerbie** S Scotland, United Kingdom 55°11′N 03°27′W
75 G13 **Lockesburg** Arkansas, C USA 33°58′N 94°10′W
277 J6 **Lockhart** New South Wales, SE Australia 35°15′S 146°43′E
70 G7 **Lockhart** Texas, SW USA 29°54′N 97°41′W
54 F3 **Lockhart Lake** ◎ Northwest Territories, NW Canada
64 C5 **Lock Haven** Pennsylvania, NE USA 41°08′N 77°27′W
70 E3 **Lockney** Texas, SW USA 34°06′N 101°27′W
178 I6 **Löcknitz** ≈ NE Germany
62 D5 **Lockport** New York, NE USA 43°09′N 78°40′W
80 B6 **Lockwood** California, USA 35°57′N 121°05′W
166 B7 **Locmariaquer** Bretagne, France 47°34′N 2°57′W
166 B7 **Locminé** Bretagne, France 47°53′N 2°50′W
257 H9 **Lôc Ninh** Sông Be, S Vietnam 11°51′N 106°35′E
175 H12 **Locri** Calabria, SW Italy 38°16′N 16°16′E
Locse see Levoča
75 H8 **Locust Creek** ≈ Missouri, C USA
66 D8 **Locust Fork** ≈ Alabama, S USA
75 F12 **Locust Grove** Oklahoma, C USA 36°12′N 95°10′W
219 D8 **Lod** Israel 31°57′N 34°53′E
154 B5 **Lodalskåpa** ▲ S Norway 61°47′N 07°10′E
161 M3 **Loddon** United Kingdom 52°32′N 1°29′E
Lodensee see Klooga
165 I8 **Lodève** *anc.* Luteva. Hérault, S France 43°44′N 03°19′E
194 E8 **Lodeynoye Pole** Leningradskaya Oblast', NW Russian Federation 60°41′N 33°29′E
77 K5 **Lodge Grass** Montana, NW USA 45°19′N 107°20′W
74 A7 **Lodgepole Creek** ≈ Nebraska/Wyoming, C USA
231 I6 **Lodhrān** Punjab, E Pakistan 29°32′N 71°40′E
176 F7 **Lodi** Lombardia, NW Italy 45°19′N 09°30′E
80 C3 **Lodi** California, W USA 38°07′N 121°17′W
73 I9 **Lodi** Ohio, N USA 41°00′N 82°01′W
152 E4 **Lødingen** *Lapp.* Lådik. Nordland, C Norway 68°25′N 16°00′E
135 G9 **Lodja** Kasai-Oriental, C Dem. Rep. Congo 03°29′S 23°25′E
77 K10 **Lodore, Canyon of** *canyon* Colorado, C USA
171 H2 **Lodosa** Navarra, N Spain 42°26′N 02°05′W
136 D6 **Lodwar** Rift Valley, NW Kenya 03°06′N 35°38′E
182 G6 **Łódź** *Rus.* Lodz. Łódź, C Poland 51°51′N 19°26′E
182 G6 **Łódzskie** ◈ *province* C Poland
256 F6 **Loei** *var.* Loey, Muang Loei. Loei, C Thailand 17°32′N 101°40′E
162 F6 **Loenen** Utrecht, C Netherlands 52°13′N 05°01′E
256 G7 **Loeng Nok Tha** Yasothon, E Thailand 16°12′N 104°31′E
141 H10 **Loerie** Eastern Cape, South Africa 33°52′S 25°02′E
140 D7 **Loeriesfontein** Northern Cape, W South Africa 30°59′S 19°29′E
Loewoek see Luwuk
Loey see Loei
132 D7 **Lofa** ≈ N Liberia
177 I3 **Lofer** Salzburg, C Austria 47°37′N 12°42′E
152 D5 **Lofoten** *var.* Lofoten Islands. *island group* C Norway
Lofoten Islands see Lofoten
155 I9 **Loftahammar** Kalmar, S Sweden 57°55′N 16°45′E
141 H7 **Lofter** Free State, South Africa 30°09′S 25°44′E
159 L7 **Loftus** United Kingdom 54°33′N 0°53′W
197 H5 **Log** Volgogradskaya Oblast', SW Russian Federation 49°32′N 43°52′E
133 I5 **Loga** Dosso, SW Niger 13°40′N 03°15′E
141 H4 **Logageng** North-West, South Africa 25°56′S 24°43′E
74 F7 **Logan** Iowa, C USA 41°38′N 95°47′W
75 C9 **Logan** Kansas, C USA 39°39′N 99°34′W
73 I11 **Logan** Ohio, N USA 39°32′N 82°24′W
79 H1 **Logan** Utah, W USA 41°45′N 111°50′W
67 H4 **Logan** West Virginia, NE USA 37°52′N 82°00′W
78 G6 **Logandale** Nevada, W USA 36°36′N 114°28′W
65 M2 **Logan International** ✈ (Boston) Massachusetts, NE USA 42°22′N 71°00′W
56 F8 **Logan Lake** British Columbia, SW Canada 50°28′N 120°42′W
66 E9 **Logan Martin Lake** ▣ Alabama, S USA
54 A3 **Logan, Mount** ▲ Yukon Territory, W Canada 60°32′N 140°34′W
76 D3 **Logan, Mount** ▲ Washington, NW USA 48°32′N 120°57′W
77 H3 **Logan Pass** *pass* Montana, NW USA
73 E10 **Logansport** Indiana, N USA 40°44′N 86°25′W
68 B2 **Logansport** Louisiana, S USA 31°58′N 94°00′W
Logar see Lowgar
121 J7 **Loge** ≈ NW Angola
Logishin see Lahishyn
Log na Coille see Lugnaquillia Mountain
134 C3 **Logone** *var.* Lagone. ≈ Cameroon/Chad
134 D4 **Logone-Occidental** *off.* Préfecture du Logone-Occidental. ◈ *prefecture* SW Chad
134 D4 **Logone Occidental** ≈ SW Chad
Logone-Occidental, Préfecture du see Logone-Occidental
134 D4 **Logone-Oriental** *off.* Préfecture du Logone-Oriental. ◈ *prefecture* SW Chad
134 D4 **Logone Oriental** ≈ SW Chad
Logone Oriental see Pendé
Logone-Oriental, Préfecture du see Logone-Oriental
L'Ogooué-Ivindo see Ogooué-Ivindo
L'Ogooué-Lolo see Ogooué-Lolo
L'Ogooué-Maritime see Ogooué-Maritime
Logoysk see Lahoysk
171 H2 **Logroño** *anc.* Vareia, *Lat.* Juliobriga. La Rioja, N Spain 42°28′N 02°26′W
170 E6 **Logrosán** Extremadura, W Spain 39°21′N 05°29′W
155 D11 **Løgstør** Nordjylland, N Denmark 56°57′N 09°19′E
155 D11 **Løgten** Århus, C Denmark 56°17′N 10°20′E
155 C13 **Løgumkloster** Sønderjylland, SW Denmark 55°04′N 08°58′E
Lögurinn see Lagarfljót
281 L1 **Loh** *island* Torres Islands, N Vanuatu
233 I8 **Lohārdaga** Jhārkhand, N India 23°27′N 84°42′E
232 E5 **Lohāru** Haryāna, N India 28°28′N 75°50′E
140 F5 **Lohatlha** Northern Cape, South Africa 28°03′S 23°03′E
181 C8 **Lohausen** ✈ (Düsseldorf) Nordrhein-Westfalen, W Germany 51°18′N 06°51′E
283 K2 **Lohd** Pohnpei, E Micronesia
152 H5 **Lohiniva** Lappi, N Finland 67°09′N 25°04′E
Lohiszyn see Lahishyn
153 H10 **Lohja** *var.* Lojo. Etelä-Suomi, S Finland 60°14′N 24°07′E
259 L5 **Lohjanan** Borneo, C Indonesia
70 F6 **Lohn** Texas, SW USA 31°15′N 99°22′W
181 E10 **Löhnberg** Hessen, Germany 50°31′E 8°16′N
180 C5 **Löhne** Niedersachsen, NW Germany 52°40′N 08°13′E
Lohr see Lohr am Main
181 F10 **Lohra** Hessen, Germany 50°44′E 8°38′N
181 G12 **Lohr am Main** *var.* Lohr. Bayern, C Germany 50°00′N 09°30′E
183 B12 **Loibl Pass** *Ger.* Loiblpass, *Slvn.* Ljubelj. *pass* Austria/Slovenia
Loiblpass see Loibl Pass
256 D5 **Loikaw** Kayah State, C Myanmar (Burma) 19°40′N 97°17′E
153 G9 **Loimaa** Länsi-Suomi, SW Finland 60°51′N 23°03′E
165 H4 **Loing** ≈ C France
256 G5 **Loi, Phou** ▲ N Laos 20°18′N 103°14′E
164 G4 **Loir** ≈ C France
165 I6 **Loire** ◈ *department* E France
165 I7 **Loire** *var.* Liger. ≈ C France
164 F4 **Loire-Atlantique** ◈ *department* NW France
165 H4 **Loiret** ◈ *department* C France
165 H4 **Loir-et-Cher** ◈ *department* C France
166 D7 **Loiron** Pays de la Loire, France 48°04′N 0°56′W
179 F13 **Loisach** ≈ SE Germany
104 C3 **Loja** Loja, S Ecuador 03°59′S 79°16′W
170 F8 **Loja** Andalucía, S Spain 37°10′N 04°09′W
104 B3 **Loja** ◈ *province* S Ecuador
Lojo see Lohja
188 D3 **Lokachi** Volyns'ka Oblast', NW Ukraine 50°44′N 24°39′E
135 H8 **Lokandu** Maniema, C Dem. Rep. Congo 02°34′S 25°44′E
152 I5 **Lokan Tekojärvi** ◎ NE Finland
215 N5 **Lökbatan** *Rus.* Lokbatan. E Azerbaijan 40°21′N 49°43′E
Lokbatan see Lökbatan
163 D9 **Lokeren** Oost-Vlaanderen, NW Belgium 51°06′N 03°59′E
Lokhvitsa see Lokhvytsya
189 J3 **Lokhvytsya** *Rus.* Lokhvitsa. Poltavs'ka Oblast', NE Ukraine 50°22′N 33°16′E
136 D7 **Lokichar** Rift Valley, NW Kenya 02°23′N 35°40′E
136 C6 **Lokichokio** Rift Valley, NW Kenya 04°16′N 34°22′E
136 D6 **Lokitaung** Rift Valley, NW Kenya 04°15′N 35°45′E
152 H5 **Lokka** Lappi, N Finland 67°48′N 27°41′E
154 D3 **Løkken Verk** Sør-Trøndelag, S Norway 63°06′N 09°43′E
194 D10 **Loknya** Pskovskaya Oblast', W Russian Federation 56°48′N 30°08′E
133 K7 **Loko** Nassarawa, C Nigeria 08°00′N 07°48′E
133 K7 **Lokoja** Kogi, C Nigeria 07°48′N 06°45′E
136 D7 **Lokori** Rift Valley, W Kenya 01°56′N 36°03′E
133 I8 **Lokossa** S Benin 06°38′N 01°43′E
190 E3 **Loksa** *Ger.* Loxa. Harjumaa, NW Estonia 59°32′N 25°42′E
59 I1 **Loks Land** *island* Nunavut, NE Canada
134 I4 **Lol** ≈ NW South Sudan
132 E7 **Lola** SE Guinea 07°52′N 08°29′W
80 F1 **Lola, Mount** ▲ California, W USA 39°27′N 120°20′W
137 D9 **Loliondo** Arusha, NE Tanzania 02°03′S 35°46′E
155 E13 **Lolland** *prev.* Laaland. *island* S Denmark
280 D3 **Lolobau Island** *island* E Papua New Guinea
260 G2 **Loloda Utara, Kepulauan** *island group* E Indonesia
134 B6 **Lolodorf** Sud, SW Cameroon 03°17′N 10°50′E
86 F5 **Lolotla** Hidalgo, C Mexico 20°51′N 98°43′W
140 G4 **Lolwane** North West, South Africa 26°58′S 23°57′E
185 I5 **Lom** *prev.* Lom-Palanka. Montana, NW Bulgaria 43°49′N 23°16′E
185 I5 **Lom** ≈ NW Bulgaria
135 H8 **Lomami** ≈ C Dem. Rep. Congo
105 E9 **Lomas** Arequipa, SW Peru 15°29′S 74°54′W
117 D13 **Lomas, Bahía** *bay* S Chile
86 G4 **Lomas del Real** Tamaulipas, Mexico 22°30′N 97°54′W
114 E9 **Lomas de Zamora** Buenos Aires, E Argentina 34°53′S 58°26′W
114 E10 **Loma Verde** Buenos Aires, E Argentina 35°16′S 58°24′W
274 E3 **Lombadina** Western Australia 16°39′S 122°54′E
174 C4 **Lombardia** *Eng.* Lombardy. ◈ *region* N Italy
Lombardy see Lombardia
164 G8 **Lombez** Gers, S France 43°29′N 00°54′E
260 E8 **Lomblen, Pulau** *island* Nusa Tenggara, S Indonesia
289 I8 **Lombok Basin** *undersea feature* E Indian Ocean 09°50′S 116°00′E
260 B8 **Lombok, Pulau** *island* Nusa Tenggara, C Indonesia
259 K9 **Lombok, Selat** *strait* S Indonesia
133 H8 **Lomé** ● (Togo) S Togo 06°08′N 01°13′E
133 H8 **Lomé** ✈ S Togo 06°08′N 01°13′E
135 G8 **Lomela** Kasai-Oriental, C Dem. Rep. Congo 02°19′S 23°15′E
70 G6 **Lometa** Texas, SW USA 31°13′N 98°23′W
134 C6 **Lomié** Est, SE Cameroon 03°09′N 13°35′E
72 D7 **Lomira** Wisconsin, N USA 43°36′N 88°26′W
155 F12 **Lomma** Skåne, S Sweden 55°41′N 13°05′E
163 F9 **Lommel** Limburg, N Belgium 51°14′N 05°19′E
181 C10 **Lommersum** Nordrhein-Westfalen, Germany 50°43′E 6°48′N
80 D1 **Lomo** California, USA 39°13′N 121°39′W
158 G3 **Lomond, Loch** ◎ C Scotland, United Kingdom
295 H5 **Lomonosov Ridge** *var.* Harris Ridge, *Rus.* Khrebet Homonsova. *undersea feature* Arctic Ocean 88°00′N 140°00′E
Lomonsova, Khrebet see Lomonosov Ridge
Lom-Palanka see Lom
Lomphat see Lumphăt
81 B8 **Lompoc** California, W USA 34°39′N 120°29′W
256 F6 **Lom Sak** *var.* Muang Lom Sak. Phetchabun, C Thailand 16°45′N 101°12′E
182 H5 **Łomża** *Rus.* Lomzha. Podlaskie, NE Poland 53°11′N 22°04′E
Lomzha see Łomża
Lonaula see Lonāvale
234 C5 **Lonāvale** *prev.* Lonaula. Mahārāshtra, W India 18°45′N 73°27′E
116 B6 **Loncoche** Araucanía, C Chile 39°22′S 72°34′W
118 C9 **Loncopangue** Bío-Bío, Chile 37°46′S 71°47′W
118 D9 **Loncopue** Neuquén, W Argentina 38°04′S 70°43′W
163 D10 **Londerzeel** Vlaams Brabant, C Belgium 51°00′N 04°19′E
166 G3 **Londiniéres** Haute-Normandie, France 49°50′N 1°24′E
Londinium see London
62 B5 **London** Ontario, S Canada 42°59′N 81°13′W
285 M1 **London** Kiritimati, E Kiribati 02°00′N 157°28′W
161 K6 **London** *anc.* Augusta, *Lat.* Londinium. ● (United Kingdom) SE England, United Kingdom 51°30′N 00°10′W
66 G5 **London** Kentucky, S USA 37°07′N 84°05′W
73 H11 **London** Ohio, NE USA 39°52′N 83°27′W
70 F6 **London** Texas, SW USA 30°40′N 99°33′W
157 I11 **London City** ✈ SE England, United Kingdom 51°31′N 00°07′E
158 C5 **Londonderry** *var.* Derry, *Ir.* Doire. NW Northern Ireland, United Kingdom 55°N 07°19′W
274 F2 **Londonderry, Cape** *cape* Western Australia
117 C14 **Londonderry, Isla** *island* S Chile
89 I4 **Londres, Cayos** *reef* NE Nicaragua
113 J4 **Londrina** Paraná, S Brazil 23°18′S 51°13′W
75 E13 **Lone Grove** Oklahoma, C USA 34°11′N 97°15′W
62 C3 **Lonely Island** *island* Ontario, S Canada
80 H5 **Lone Mountain** ▲ Nevada, W USA 38°01′N 117°28′W
71 H4 **Lone Oak** Texas, SW USA 33°02′N 95°58′W
80 F7 **Lone Pine** California, W USA 36°36′N 118°04′W
Lone Star State see Texas
Lone Tree Islet see Iku
135 E13 **Longa** Cuando Cubango, C Angola 14°44′S 18°36′E
135 C11 **Longa** ≈ W Angola
135 E13 **Longa** ≈ SE Angola
242 C9 **Long'an** Guangxi, China 23°06′N 107°25′E
Long'an see Pingwu
248 C2 **Longang Shan** ▲▲ NE China
294 E6 **Longa, Proliv** *Eng.* Long Strait. *strait* NE Russian Federation
118 C6 **Longavi, Río** ≈ Maule, Chile
80 E3 **Long Barn** California, USA 38°06′N 120°08′W
90 E8 **Long Bay** *bay* W Jamaica
67 K9 **Long Bay** *bay* North Carolina/South Carolina, E USA
81 D11 **Long Beach** California, W USA 33°46′N 118°11′W
68 F4 **Long Beach** Mississippi, S USA 30°21′N 89°09′W
65 I6 **Long Beach** Long Island, New York, NE USA 40°34′N 73°38′W
76 B4 **Long Beach** Washington, NW USA 46°21′N 124°03′W
65 H8 **Long Beach Island** *island* New Jersey, NE USA
132 E10 **Longbluff** *headland* SW Tristan da Cunha
69 L7 **Longboat Key** *island* Florida, SE USA
65 H7 **Long Branch** New Jersey, NE USA 40°18′N 73°59′W
161 H4 **Longbridge** United Kingdom 52°24′N 1°59′W
161 H7 **Longbridge Deverill** United Kingdom 51°10′N 2°11′W
90 F4 **Long Cay** *island* SE Bahamas
242 B3 **Longchang** Chongqing Shi, C China 29°21′N 105°18′E
Longcheng see Xiaoxian
243 I8 **Longchuan** *var.* Laolong. Guangdong, S China 24°07′N 115°10′E
Longchuan see Nanhua
Longchuan Jiang see Shweli
76 E6 **Long Creek** Oregon, NW USA 44°40′N 119°07′W
244 C6 **Longde** Ningxia, N China 35°37′N 106°07′E
161 I2 **Long Eaton** United Kingdom 52°54′N 1°16′W
167 K7 **Longeau** Champagne-Ardenne, France 47°46′N 5°18′E
277 J9 **Longford** Tasmania, SE Australia 41°41′S 147°03′E
158 B9 **Longford** *Ir.* An Longfort. Longford, C Ireland 53°45′N 07°50′W
159 K5 **Longframlington** United Kingdom 55°17′N 1°47′W
Longgang see Dazu
245 J7 **Longgu** Jiangsu, E China 34°54′N 116°48′E
243 J5 **Longgudu** Jiangxi, SE China 27°43′N 116°15′E
243 K8 **Longhai** Fujan, China 24°16′N 117°29′E
243 H6 **Longhai** Hunan, SE China 26°28′N 113°17′E
141 H9 **Long Hope** Eastern Cape, South Africa 32°51′S 25°48′E
159 K5 **Longhorsley** United Kingdom 55°14′N 1°46′W

◆ Country
● Country Capital
◇ Dependent Territory
○ Dependent Territory Capital
◈ Administrative Regions
✈ International Airport
▲ Mountain
▲▲ Mountain Range
⋀ Volcano
≈ River
◎ Lake
▣ Reservoir

M

76 *C6* **Madras** Oregon, NW USA *44°39′N 121°08′W*
Madras *see* Chennai
Madras *see* Tamil Nādu
110 *G5* **Madre de Deus de Minas** Minas Gerais, Brazil *21°29′S 44°20′W*
104 *G7* **Madre de Dios** *off.* Departamento de Madre de Dios. ⬖ *department* E Peru
Madre de Dios, Departamento de *see* Madre de Dios
117 *A12* **Madre de Dios, Isla** *island* S Chile
106 *C8* **Madre de Dios, Río** 〰 Bolivia/Peru
42 *E9* **Madre del Sur, Sierra** ▲▲ S Mexico
85 *N6* **Madre, Laguna** *lagoon* NE Mexico
70 *G10* **Madre, Laguna** *lagoon* Texas, SW USA
79 *K8* **Madre Mount** ▲ New Mexico, SW USA *34°18′N 107°54′W*
42 *D8* **Madre Occidental, Sierra** *var.* Western Sierra Madre. ▲▲ C Mexico
42 *E8* **Madre Oriental, Sierra** *var.* Eastern Sierra Madre. ▲▲ C Mexico
87 *J9* **Madre, Sierra** *var.* Sierra de Soconusco. ▲▲ Guatemala/Mexico
263 *L4* **Madre, Sierra** ▲▲ Luzon, N Philippines
79 *K2* **Madre, Sierra** ▲▲ Colorado/Wyoming, C USA
170 *G5* **Madrid** ● (Spain) Madrid, C Spain *40°25′N 03°43′W*
74 *G7* **Madrid** Iowa, C USA *41°52′N 93°49′W*
170 *G4* **Madrid** ⬖ *autonomous community* C Spain
170 *G6* **Madridejos** Castilla-La Mancha, C Spain *39°29′N 03°32′W*
170 *F4* **Madrigal de las Altas Torres** Castilla-León, N Spain *41°05′N 05°00′W*
170 *E6* **Madrigalejo** Extremadura, W Spain *39°08′N 05°36′W*
78 *A2* **Mad River** 〰 California, W USA
88 *G5* **Madriz** ⬖ *department* NW Nicaragua
173 *H1* **Madrona** Castilla y León, Spain *40°54′N 4°10′W*
170 *E6* **Madroñera** Extremadura, W Spain *39°25′N 05°46′W*
276 *B4* **Madura** Western Australia *31°52′S 127°01′E*
Madura *see* Madurai
235 *E9* **Madurai** *prev.* Madura, Mathurai. Tamil Nādu, S India *09°55′N 78°07′E*
259 *J8* **Madura, Pulau** *prev.* Madoera. *island* C Indonesia
259 *J8* **Madura, Selat** *strait* C Indonesia
197 *J10* **Madzhalis** Respublika Dagestan, SW Russian Federation *42°12′N 47°46′E*
185 *K7* **Madzharovo** Khaskovo, S Bulgaria *41°36′N 25°52′E*
139 *I1* **Madzimoyo** Eastern, E Zambia *13°42′S 32°34′E*
253 *B12* **Maebashi** *var.* Maebasi, Mayebashi. Gunma, Honshū, S Japan *36°24′N 139°02′E*
Maebasi *see* Maebashi
256 *E5* **Mae Chan** Chiang Rai, NW Thailand *20°13′N 99°52′E*
256 *D5* **Mae Hong Son** *var.* Maehongson, Muai To. Mae Hong Son, NW Thailand *19°16′N 97°56′E*
Maehongson *see* Mae Hong Son
166 *A6* **Maël-Carhaix** Bretagne, France *48°17′N 3°25′W*
168 *E10* **Maella** Aragón, Spain *41°08′N 0°09′E*
Mae Nam Khong *see* Mekong
256 *E5* **Mae Nam Nan** 〰 NW Thailand
256 *E7* **Mae Nam Tha Chin** 〰 W Thailand
256 *E5* **Mae Nam Yom** 〰 W Thailand
160 *E2* **Maentwrog** United Kingdom *52°56′N 3°59′W*
250 *B1* **Maepo** *prev.* Maep'o. *37°02′N 128°17′E*
Maep'o *see* Maepo
256 *D6* **Mae Sariang** Mae Hong Son, NW Thailand *18°08′N 97°57′E*
79 *J2* **Maeser** Utah, W USA *40°28′N 109°35′W*
Maeseyck *see* Maaseik
256 *D6* **Mae Sot** *var.* Ban Mae Sot. Tak, W Thailand *16°44′N 98°32′E*
160 *F6* **Maesteg** United Kingdom *51°36′N 3°39′W*
90 *E5* **Maestra, Sierra** ▲▲ E Cuba
Maestricht *see* Maastricht
256 *E5* **Mae Suai** *var.* Ban Mae Suai. Chiang Rai, NW Thailand *19°43′N 99°30′E*
256 *E5* **Mae Tho, Doi** ▲ NW Thailand *18°56′N 99°20′E*
139 *L6* **Maevatanana** Mahajanga, C Madagascar *16°57′S 46°50′E*
281 *M2* **Maéwo** *prev.* Aurora. *island* C Vanuatu
260 *G4* **Mafa** Pulau Halmahera, E Indonesia *0°01′N 127°50′E*
141 *I6* **Mafeteng** W Lesotho *29°48′S 27°15′E*
163 *F11* **Maffe** Namur, SE Belgium *50°21′N 05°19′E*
261 *L5* **Maffin** Papua, E Indonesia *01°57′S 138°48′E*
277 *J7* **Maffra** Victoria, SE Australia *37°59′S 147°03′E*
137 *F11* **Mafia** *island* E Tanzania
137 *E11* **Mafia Channel** *sea waterway* E Tanzania
141 *H4* **Mafikeng** North-West, N South Africa *25°53′S 25°39′E*
113 *K5* **Mafra** Santa Catarina, S Brazil *26°08′S 49°47′W*
172 *A5* **Mafra** Lisboa, C Portugal *38°57′N 09°19′W*
221 *J4* **Mafraq** Abū Ẕaby, C United Arab Emirates *24°21′N 54°33′E*
Mafraq/Muḩāfaẓat al Mafraq *see* Al Mafraq
141 *J7* **Mafube** Eastern Cape, South Africa *30°10′S 28°43′E*
193 *L5* **Magadan** Magadanskaya Oblast', E Russian Federation *59°38′N 150°50′E*
193 *L5* **Magadanskaya Oblast'** ⬖ *province* E Russian Federation
176 *E5* **Magadino** Ticino, S Switzerland *46°09′N 08°50′E*
117 *C13* **Magallanes** *var.* Región de Magallanes y de la Antártica Chilena. ⬖ *region* S Chile
Magallanes *see* Punta Arenas
Magallanes, Estrecho de *see* Magellan, Strait of
Magallanes y de la Antártica Chilena, Región de *see* Magallanes
62 *E2* **Maganasipi, Lac** ◎ Québec, SE Canada
102 *C3* **Magangué** Bolívar, N Colombia *09°14′N 74°46′W*
285 *L8* **Magareva** *var.* Mangareva. *island* Îles Tuamotu, SE French Polynesia
133 *K5* **Magaria** Zinder, S Niger *13°00′N 08°55′E*
280 *C4* **Magarida** Central, SW Papua New Guinea *10°10′S 149°21′E*
263 *L4* **Magat** 〰 Luzon, N Philippines
75 *H12* **Magazine Mountain** ▲ Arkansas, C USA *35°10′N 93°38′W*
132 *C7* **Magburaka** C Sierra Leone *08°44′N 11°57′W*
193 *J8* **Magdagachi** Amurskaya Oblast', SE Russian Federation *53°25′N 125°41′E*
114 *F10* **Magdalena** Buenos Aires, E Argentina *35°05′S 57°30′W*
106 *E8* **Magdalena** Beni, N Bolivia *13°22′S 64°07′W*
85 *H3* **Magdalena** Jalisco, W Mexico *30°33′N 106°31′W*
84 *E3* **Magdalena** Sonora, NW Mexico *30°38′N 110°59′W*
79 *L8* **Magdalena** New Mexico, SW USA *34°07′N 107°14′W*
102 *C3* **Magdalena** *off.* Departamento del Magdalena. ⬖ *province* N Colombia
84 *D7* **Magdalena, Bahía** *bay* W Mexico
Magdalena, Departamento del *see* Magdalena
117 *B9* **Magdalena, Isla** *island* Archipiélago de los Chonos, S Chile
84 *D7* **Magdalena, Isla** *island* NW Mexico
95 *I3* **Magdalena, Río** 〰 C Colombia
84 *E3* **Magdalena, Río** 〰 NW Mexico
Magdalen Islands *see* Madeleine, Îles de la
229 *H8* **Magdanly** *Rus.* Govurdak; *prev.* gowurdak, Guardak. Lebap Welaýaty, E Turkmenistan *37°50′N 66°06′E*
178 *G7* **Magdeburg** Sachsen-Anhalt, C Germany *52°08′N 11°39′E*
68 *E2* **Magee** Mississippi, S USA *31°52′N 89°43′W*
158 *E6* **Magee, Island** *island* United Kingdom
259 *H8* **Magelang** Jawa, C Indonesia *07°28′S 110°11′E*
286 *F5* **Magellan Rise** *undersea feature* C Pacific Ocean
286 *D4* **Magellan Seamounts** *undersea feature* W Pacific Ocean
117 *C13* **Magellan, Strait of** *Sp.* Estrecho de Magallanes. *strait* Argentina/Chile
219 *C9* **Magen** Israel *31°17′N 34°25′E*
176 *E7* **Magenta** Lombardia, NW Italy *45°28′N 08°52′E*
Magerøy *see* Magerøya
152 *G3* **Magerøya** *var.* Magerøy, *Lapp.* Máhkarávju. *island* N Norway
250 *C10* **Mage-shima** *island* Nansei-shotō, SW Japan
176 *E5* **Maggia** Ticino, S Switzerland *46°15′N 08°42′E*
176 *E5* **Maggia** 〰 SW Switzerland
Maggiore, Lago *see* Maggiore, Lake
174 *C4* **Maggiore, Lake** *It.* Lago Maggiore. ◎ Italy/Switzerland
90 *E8* **Maggotty** W Jamaica *18°09′N 77°46′W*
132 *C4* **Maghama** Gorgol, S Mauritania *15°31′N 12°50′W*
219 *H10* **Maghār, Wādī** *dry watercourse* Jordan
218 *G7* **Maghayyir as Sarḩān** Jordan *32°28′N 36°12′W*
158 *D6* **Maghera** *Ir.* Machaire Rátha. C Northern Ireland, United Kingdom *54°51′N 06°40′W*
158 *D6* **Magherafelt** *Ir.* Machaire Fíolta. C Northern Ireland, United Kingdom *54°45′N 06°36′W*
158 *D7* **Magheralin** United Kingdom *54°28′N 6°16′W*
283 *H2* **Magicienne Bay** *bay* Saipan, S Northern Mariana Islands
170 *G8* **Magina** ▲ S Spain *37°43′N 03°24′W*
137 *C12* **Magingo** Ruvuma, S Tanzania *09°57′S 35°23′E*
184 *D4* **Maglaj** ⬖ Federacija Bosna I Hercegovina, N Bosnia and Herzegovina
175 *J10* **Maglie** Puglia, SE Italy *40°07′N 18°18′E*
79 *H2* **Magna** Utah, W USA *40°42′N 112°06′W*
166 *F10* **Magnac-Laval** Limousin, France *46°13′N 1°10′E*
Magnesia *see* Manisa
62 *C3* **Magnetawan** 〰 Ontario, S Canada
197 *M3* **Magnitogorsk** Chelyabinskaya Oblast', C Russian Federation *53°28′N 59°06′E*
75 *H14* **Magnolia** Arkansas, C USA *33°17′N 93°16′W*
68 *E3* **Magnolia** Mississippi, S USA *31°08′N 90°27′W*
71 *I6* **Magnolia** Texas, SW USA *30°12′N 95°46′W*
Magnolia State *see* Mississippi
154 *F7* **Magnor** Hedmark, S Norway *59°57′N 12°14′E*
166 *G5* **Magny-en-Vexin** Val-d'Oise, France *49°09′N 1°47′E*
280 *G8* **Mago** *prev.* Mango. *island* Lau Group, E Fiji
139 *H2* **Màgoé** Tete, NW Mozambique *15°50′S 31°42′E*
63 *I3* **Magog** Québec, SE Canada *45°16′N 72°09′W*
141 *K2* **Magoro** Limpopo, South Africa *23°18′S 30°19′E*
138 *G2* **Magoye** Southern, S Zambia *16°00′S 27°34′E*
86 *G4* **Magozal** Veracruz-Llave, C Mexico *21°33′N 97°57′W*
59 *J6* **Magpie** Québec, E Canada
171 *N10* **Magra** Algeria
57 *J9* **Magrath** Alberta, SW Canada *49°27′N 112°52′W*
171 *I6* **Magre** 〰 E Spain
173 *N9* **Magroua, Cap** *cape* Algeria
80 *G6* **Magruder Mountain** ▲ Nevada, USA *37°25′N 117°33′W*
132 *C3* **Magta' Laḩjar** *var.* Magta Lahjar, Magta' Lahjar, Magtá Lahjar. Brakna, SW Mauritania *17°27′N 13°07′W*
228 *C7* **Magtymguly** *prev.* Garrygala, *Rus.* Kara-Kala. Balkan Welaýaty, W Turkmenistan *38°27′N 56°15′E*
242 *A9* **Maguan** Yunnan, China *23°00′N 104°14′E*
139 *I6* **Magude** Maputo, S Mozambique *25°02′S 32°40′E*
141 *L5* **Magudu** KwaZulu-Natal, South Africa *27°32′S 31°39′E*
158 *C7* **Maguires Bridge** United Kingdom *54°18′N 7°28′W*
133 *M5* **Magumeri** Borno, NE Nigeria *12°07′N 12°48′E*
282 *F6* **Magur Islands** *island group* Caroline Islands, C Micronesia
55 *J4* **Maguse Lake** ◎ Nunavut, E Canada
256 *C5* **Magway** *var.* Magwe. Magway, W Myanmar (Burma) *20°08′N 94°55′E*
256 *C5* **Magway** *var.* Magwe. ⬖ *division* C Myanmar (Burma)
Magwe *see* Magway
Magyar-Becse *see* Bečej
Magyarkanizsa *see* Kanjiža
Magyarország *see* Hungary
Magyarzsombor *see* Zimbor
222 *D3* **Mahābād** *var.* Mehabad; *prev.* Sāūjbulāgh. Āžarbāyjān-e Gharbī, NW Iran *36°44′N 45°44′E*
288 *E7* **Mahabiss Fracture Zone** *tectonic feature* N Indian Ocean
139 *L8* **Mahabo** Toliara, W Madagascar *20°22′S 44°39′E*
Maha Chai *see* Samut Sakhon
234 *C5* **Mahād** Mahārāshtra, W India *18°04′N 73°21′E*
136 *H7* **Mahadday Weyne** Shabeellaha Dhexe, C Somalia *02°55′N 45°30′E*
134 *J6* **Mahagi** Orientale, NE Dem. Rep. Congo *02°16′N 30°59′E*
Mahāil *see* Muhāyil
139 *M6* **Mahajamba** *seasonal river* NW Madagascar
232 *D5* **Mahājan** Rājasthān, NW India *28°47′N 73°50′E*
139 *L5* **Mahajanga** *var.* Majunga. Mahajanga, NW Madagascar *15°40′S 46°20′E*
139 *M5* **Mahajanga** ⬖ *province* W Madagascar
139 *L5* **Mahajanga** ✈ Mahajanga, NW Madagascar *15°40′S 46°20′E*
259 *K4* **Mahakam, Sungai** *var.* Koetai, Kutai. 〰 Borneo, C Indonesia
141 *I2* **Mahalapye** *var.* Mahalatswe. Central, SE Botswana *23°02′S 26°53′E*
Mahalatswe *see* Mahalapye
260 *D5* **Mahalona** Sulawesi, C Indonesia *02°37′S 121°26′E*
Mahameru *see* Semeru, Gunung
223 *I7* **Māhān** Kermān, E Iran *30°00′N 57°00′E*
234 *G3* **Mahānadi** 〰 Chhattīsgarh, India
139 *M7* **Mahanoro** Toamasina, E Madagascar *19°53′S 48°48′E*
64 *E6* **Mahanoy City** Pennsylvania, USA *40°49′N 76°09′W*
233 *H6* **Mahārājganj** Bihār, N India *26°07′N 84°31′E*
234 *D4* **Mahārāshtra** ⬖ *state* W India
139 *L6* **Mahavavy** *seasonal river* N Madagascar
235 *G10* **Mahaweli Ganga** 〰 C Sri Lanka
Mahbés *see* El Mahbas
234 *F5* **Mahbūbābād** Andhra Pradesh, E India *17°35′N 80°00′E*
234 *E6* **Mahbūbnagar** Andhra Pradesh, C India *16°46′N 78°01′E*
220 *E4* **Mahd adh Dhahab** Al Madīnah, W Saudi Arabia *23°33′N 40°56′E*
103 *J5* **Mahdia** C Guyana *05°16′N 59°08′W*
131 *L2* **Mahdia** *var.* Al Mahdīyah, Mehdia. NE Tunisia *35°14′N 11°06′E*
235 *D8* **Mahe** *Fr.* Mahé; *prev.* Mayyali. Pondicherry, SW India *11°41′N 75°31′E*
137 *I9* **Mahé** ✈ Mahé, NE Seychelles *04°37′S 55°27′E*
137 *I9* **Mahé** *island* Inner Islands, NE Seychelles
Mahé *see* Mahe
137 *G11* **Mahebourg** SE Mauritius *20°24′S 57°42′E*
231 *M6* **Mahendranagar** Far Western, W Nepal *28°58′N 80°13′E*
137 *D11* **Mahenge** Morogoro, SE Tanzania *08°41′S 36°41′E*
278 *D11* **Maheno** Otago, South Island, New Zealand *45°10′S 170°51′E*
232 *C8* **Mahesāna** Gujarāt, W India *23°37′N 72°28′E*
232 *D8* **Maheshwar** Madhya Pradesh, C India *22°11′N 75°40′E*
233 *L9* **Maheskhali Island** *var.* Maiskhal Island. *island* SE Bangladesh
232 *D8* **Mahi** 〰 N India
278 *J6* **Mahia Peninsula** *peninsula* North Island, New Zealand
191 *H9* **Mahilyow** *Rus.* Mogilëv. Mahilyowskaya Voblasts', E Belarus *53°55′N 30°23′E*
191 *I9* **Mahilyowskaya Voblasts'** *prev. Rus.* Mogilëvskaya Oblast'. ⬖ *province* E Belarus
285 *M3* **Mahina** Tahiti, W French Polynesia *17°29′S 149°27′W*
278 *C12* **Mahinerangi, Lake** ◎ South Island, New Zealand
Máhkarávju *see* Magerøya
139 *H7* **Mahlabatini** KwaZulu/Natal, E South Africa *28°15′S 31°28′E*
256 *C4* **Mahlaing** Mandalay, C Myanmar (Burma) *21°03′N 95°44′E*
177 *L4* **Mahldorf** Steiermark, SE Austria *46°54′N 15°55′E*
Mahmūd-e 'Erāqī *see* Maḩmūd-e Rāqī
231 *H3* **Maḩmūd-e Rāqī** *var.* Mahmūd-e 'Erāqī. Kāpīsā, NE Afghanistan *35°01′N 69°20′E*
Mahmudiya *see* Al Maḩmūdīyah
187 *M2* **Mahmutbey** İstanbul, NW Turkey *41°03′N 28°50′E*
74 *F3* **Mahnomen** Minnesota, N USA *47°19′N 95°58′W*
232 *F7* **Mahoba** Uttar Pradesh, N India *25°18′N 79°53′E*
171 *M5* **Mahón** *Cat.* Maó, *Eng.* Port Mahon; *anc.* Portus Magonis. Menorca, Spain, W Mediterranean Sea *39°54′N 04°15′E*
137 *E10* **Mahonda** Zanzibar North, E Tanzania *6°00′S 39°14′E*
62 *D8* **Mahoning Creek Lake** ▣ Pennsylvania, NE USA
54 *D2* **Mahony Lake** ◎ Northwest Territories, NW Canada
171 *H6* **Mahora** Castilla-La Mancha, C Spain *39°13′N 01°44′W*
Mähren *see* Moravia
Mährisch-Budwitz *see* Moravské Budějovice
Mährisch-Kromau *see* Moravský Krumlov
Mährisch-Neustadt *see* Uničov
Mährisch-Schönberg *see* Šumperk
Mährisch-Trübau *see* Moravská Třebová
Mährisch-Weisskirchen *see* Hranice
Māh-Shahr *see* Bandar-e Māhshahr
135 *I8* **Mahulu** Maniema, E Dem. Rep. Congo *01°04′S 27°10′E*
232 *C9* **Mahuva** Gujarāt, W India *21°06′N 71°46′E*
141 *J2* **Mahwelereng** Limpopo, South Africa *24°09′S 28°59′E*
187 *L1* **Mahya Dağı** ▲ NW Turkey *41°47′N 27°34′E*
171 *J4* **Maials** *var.* Mayals. Cataluña, NE Spain *41°22′N 00°30′E*
284 *B2* **Maiana** *prev.* Hall Island. *atoll* Tungaru, W Kiribati
285 *I7* **Maiao** *var.* Tapuaemanu, Tubuai-Manu. *island* Îles du Vent, W French Polynesia
102 *D2* **Maicao** La Guajira, N Colombia *11°23′N 72°16′W*
Mai Ceu/Mai Chio *see* Maych'ew
165 *K5* **Maîche** Doubs, E France *47°15′N 06°43′E*
161 *H7* **Maiden Bradley** United Kingdom *51°09′N 2°17′W*
161 *J6* **Maidenhead** S England, United Kingdom *51°32′N 00°44′W*
158 *F5* **Maidens** United Kingdom *55°20′N 4°49′W*
57 *L5* **Maidstone** Saskatchewan, S Canada *53°06′N 109°21′W*
161 *L7* **Maidstone** SE England, United Kingdom *51°17′N 00°31′E*
133 *M5* **Maiduguri** Borno, NE Nigeria *11°51′N 13°10′E*
176 *F4* **Maienfeld** Sankt Gallen, NE Switzerland *47°01′N 09°30′E*
188 *D8* **Măieruş** *Hung.* Szászmagyarós. Braşov, C Romania *45°55′N 25°30′E*
Maigh Chromtha *see* Macroom
Maigh Eo *see* Mayo
167 *H4* **Maignelay** Picardie, France *49°33′N 2°31′E*
102 *G5* **Maigualida, Sierra** ▲▲ S Venezuela
232 *G7* **Maihar** Madhya Pradesh, C India *24°18′N 80°46′E*
232 *G9* **Maikala Range** ▲▲ C India
121 *K6* **Maiko** 〰 W Dem. Rep. Congo
Mailand *see* Milano
232 *G5* **Mailāni** Uttar Pradesh, N India *28°17′N 80°20′E*
167 *K10* **Maillat** Rhône-Alpes, France *46°08′N 5°33′E*
167 *J6* **Mailly-le-Camp** Champagne-Ardenne, France *48°40′N 4°13′E*
231 *I6* **Māilsi** Punjab, E Pakistan *29°46′N 72°15′E*
227 *I8* **Maimak** Talasskaya Oblast', NW Kyrgyzstan *42°40′N 71°12′E*
Maimāna *see* Meymaneh
261 *J5* **Maimawa** Papua, E Indonesia *03°21′S 133°36′E*
Maimuna *see* Al Maymūnah
219 *G8* **Māīn** Jordan *31°40′N 35°44′E*
181 *E12* **Main** 〰 C Germany
186 *G8* **Maïna** *ancient monument* Pelopónnisos, S Greece
186 *F7* **Maínalo** ▲▲ S Greece
179 *G12* **Mainburg** Bayern, SE Germany *48°40′N 11°48′E*
Main Camp *see* Banana
62 *B3* **Main Channel** *lake channel* Ontario, S Canada
135 *E8* **Mai-Ndombe, Lac** *prev.* Lac Léopold II. ◎ W Dem. Rep. Congo
181 *J13* **Main-Donau-Kanal** *canal* SE Germany
63 *K2* **Maine** *off.* State of Maine, *also known as* Lumber State, Pine Tree State. ⬖ *state* NE USA
164 *G4* **Maine** *cultural region* NW France
164 *G4* **Maine-et-Loire** ⬖ *department* NW France
63 *K5* **Maine, Gulf of** *gulf* NE USA
133 *M5* **Maïné-Soroa** Diffa, SE Niger *13°14′N 12°00′E*
256 *D2* **Maingkwan** *var.* Mungkawn. Kachin State, N Myanmar (Burma) *26°20′N 96°37′E*
181 *G14* **Mainhardt** Baden-Württemberg, Germany *49°05′E 9°33′N*
Main Island *see* Bermuda
Mainistir Fhear Maí *see* Fermoy
Mainistirna Búille *see* Boyle
Mainistir na Corann *see* Midleton
Mainistir na Féile *see* Abbeyfeale
156 *F3* **Mainland** *island* Orkney, NE Scotland, United Kingdom
156 *G1* **Mainland** *island* Shetland, NE Scotland, United Kingdom
239 *H9* **Mainling** *var.* Tungdor. Xizang Zizhiqu, W China *29°12′N 94°06′E*
232 *F6* **Mainpuri** Uttar Pradesh, N India *27°14′N 79°01′E*
165 *H3* **Maintenon** Eure-et-Loir, C France *48°35′N 01°34′E*
139 *K7* **Maintirano** Mahajanga, W Madagascar *18°01′S 44°03′E*
152 *I7* **Mainua** Oulu, C Finland *64°05′N 27°28′E*
181 *E12* **Mainz** *Fr.* Mayence. Rheinland-Pfalz, SW Germany *50°00′N 08°16′E*
132 *B10* **Maio** *var.* Vila do Maio. Maio, S Cape Verde *15°07′N 23°12′W*
132 *B10* **Maio** *var.* Mayo. *island* Ilhas de Sotavento, SE Cape Verde
118 *E4* **Maipo, Volcán** ⛰ Chile *34°09′S 69°51′W*
116 *H5* **Maipú** Buenos Aires, E Argentina *36°52′S 57°52′W*
118 *F3* **Maipú** Mendoza, E Argentina *33°00′S 68°46′W*
116 *B4* **Maipú** Santiago, C Chile *33°30′S 70°52′W*
176 *C8* **Maira** 〰 NW Italy
176 *F5* **Maira** *It.* Mera. 〰 Italy/Switzerland
233 *L6* **Mairābari** Assam, NE India *26°28′N 92°22′E*
172 *F8* **Mairena del Alcor** Andalucía, Spain *37°22′N 5°45′W*
90 *G5* **Maisí** Guantánamo, E Cuba *20°13′N 74°08′W*
191 *E8* **Maišiagala** Vilnius, SE Lithuania *54°52′N 25°03′E*
Maiskhal Island *see* Maheskhali Island
257 *E9* **Mai Sombun** Chumphon, SW Thailand *10°49′N 99°13′E*
Mai Son *see* Hat Lot
167 *H6* **Maisse** Île-de-France, France *48°23′N 02°22′E*
Maisur *see* Karnātaka, India
Maisur *see* Mysore, India
118 *C6* **Maitenes** Maule, Chile *35°37′S 71°23′W*
277 *L5* **Maitland** New South Wales, SE Australia *32°33′S 151°33′E*
276 *G5* **Maitland** South Australia *34°21′S 137°42′E*
62 *C4* **Maitland** 〰 Ontario, S Canada
293 *I1* **Maitri** *Indian research station* Antarctica *70°03′S 08°59′E*
243 *H3* **Maiwang** Hubei, C China *30°31′N 113°36′E*
239 *H9* **Maizhokunggar** Xizang Zizhiqu, W China *29°50′N 91°40′E*
89 *I6* **Maíz, Islas del** *var.* Corn Islands. *island group* SE Nicaragua
251 *H3* **Maizuru** Kyōto, Honshū, SW Japan *35°30′N 135°20′E*
102 *C3* **Majagual** Sucre, N Colombia *08°36′N 74°39′W*
87 *N6* **Majahual** Quintana Roo, E Mexico *18°43′N 87°43′W*
Majardah, Wādī *see* Medjerda, Oued/Mejerda
218 *E7* **Majdal Banī Fāḑel** West Bank *32°04′N 35°21′E*
218 *E5* **Majd el-Kurūm** Israel *32°55′N 35°16′E*
111 *I7* **Majé** Rio de Janeiro, Brazil *22°39′S 43°01′W*
Mājeej *see* Mejit Island
260 *C5* **Majene** *prev.* Madjene. Sulawesi, C Indonesia *03°33′S 118°59′E*
89 *L9* **Majé, Serranía de** ▲▲ E Panama
184 *E4* **Majevica** ▲▲ NE Bosnia and Herzegovina
136 *D5* **Majī** Southern Nationalities, S Ethiopia *06°11′N 35°32′E*
242 *D6* **Majiang** Guizhou, China *26°17′N 107°22′E*
244 *D5* **Majiatan** Ningxia, China *37°28′N 106°29′E*
Majiazhou *see* Mashi
221 *K4* **Majīs** NW Oman *24°25′N 56°34′E*
Majorca *see* Mallorca
Mājro *see* Majuro Atoll
Majunga *see* Mahajanga
283 *N10* **Majuro** ✈ Majuro Atoll, SE Marshall Islands *07°05′N 171°08′E*
283 *N10* **Majuro Atoll** *var.* Mājro. *atoll* Ratak Chain, SE Marshall Islands
283 *M10* **Majuro Lagoon** *lagoon* Majuro Atoll, SE Marshall Islands
132 *B4* **Maka** C Senegal *13°40′N 14°12′W*
135 *B9* **Makabana** Niari, SW Congo *03°28′S 12°36′E*
82 *B2* **Makahū'ena Point** *var.* Makahuena Point. *headland* Kaua'i, Hawai'i, USA *21°52′N 159°28′W*
82 *B2* **Makakilo City** O'ahu, Hawaii, USA, C Pacific Ocean *21°21′N 158°05′W*
138 *E4* **Makalamabedi** Central, C Botswana *20°19′S 23°51′E*
Makale *see* Mek'elē
233 *J6* **Makalu** *Chin.* Makaru Shan. ▲ China/Nepal *27°53′N 87°09′E*
137 *C11* **Makampi** Mbeya, S Tanzania *08°00′S 33°17′E*
Makanchi *see* Makanshy
227 *L5* **Makanshy** *prev.* Makanchi. Vostochnyy Kazakhstan, E Kazakhstan *46°47′N 82°00′E*
89 *H5* **Makantaka** Región Autónoma Atlántico Norte, NE Nicaragua *13°13′N 84°04′W*
285 *H10* **Makapu Point** *headland* W Niue *18°59′S 169°56′E*
278 *B12* **Makarewa** Southland, South Island, New Zealand *46°17′S 168°16′E*
188 *G3* **Makariv** Kyyivs'ka Oblast', N Ukraine *50°28′N 29°49′E*
278 *C10* **Makarora** 〰 South Island, New Zealand
193 *M8* **Makarov** Ostrov Sakhalin, Sakhalinskaya Oblast', SE Russian Federation *48°24′N 142°37′E*
295 *H5* **Makarov Basin** *undersea feature* Arctic Ocean
286 *D3* **Makarov Seamount** *undersea feature* W Pacific Ocean *29°30′N 153°30′E*
184 *C5* **Makarska** *It.* Macarsca. Split-Dalmacija, SE Croatia *43°18′N 17°00′E*
Makaru Shan *see* Makalu
195 *H9* **Makar'yev** Kostromskaya Oblast', NW Russian Federation *57°52′N 43°46′E*
137 *B11* **Makasa** Northern, NE Zambia *09°42′S 31°54′E*
Makasar *see* Makassar
Makasar, Selat *see* Makassar Strait
260 *C6* **Makassar** *var.* Macassar, Makasar; *prev.* Ujungpandang. Sulawesi, C Indonesia *05°09′S 119°28′E*
286 *B6* **Makassar Strait** *Ind.* Makasar Selat. *strait* C Indonesia
226 *C5* **Makat** *Kaz.* Maqat. Atyrau, SW Kazakhstan *47°40′N 53°28′E*
285 *J6* **Makatea** *island* Îles Tuamotu, C French Polynesia
217 *K4* **Makātū** Diyālá, E Iraq *33°55′N 45°25′E*
139 *L8* **Makay** *var.* Massif du Makay. ▲▲ SW Madagascar
Makay, Massif du *see* Makay
187 *J2* **Makaza** *pass* Bulgaria/Greece
261 *I4* **Makbon** Papua, E Indonesia *0°43′S 131°30′E*
Makedonija *see* Macedonia, FYR
285 *H9* **Makefu** W Niue *18°59′S 169°55′W*
285 *K6* **Makemo** *atoll* Îles Tuamotu, C French Polynesia
132 *C6* **Makeni** C Sierra Leone *08°57′N 12°02′W*
Makenzen *see* Orlyak
Makeyevka *see* Makiyivka
197 *J9* **Makhachkala** *prev.* Petrovsk-Port. Respublika Dagestan, SW Russian Federation *42°58′N 47°30′E*
139 *H5* **Makhado** *prev.* Louis Trichardt. Northern, NE South Africa *23°01′S 29°43′E*
226 *C5* **Makhambet** Atyrau, W Kazakhstan *47°35′N 51°35′E*
Makharadze *see* Ozurget'i
217 *L9* **Makhfar al Buşayyah** Al Muthanná, S Iraq *30°09′N 46°09′E*
217 *I3* **Makhmūr** Arbīl, N Iraq *35°47′N 43°32′E*
195 *M8* **Makhnevo** Sverdlovskaya Oblast', Russian Federation
190 *H5* **Makhnovka** Pskovskaya Oblast', Russian Federation
219 *I10* **Makhrūq, Wadi al** *dry watercourse* E Jordan
219 *D11* **Makhtésh Ramon** ▲▲ Israel
217 *I3* **Makḩūl, Jabal** ▲▲ C Iraq
136 *I1* **Makhyah, Wādī** *dry watercourse* N Yemen
261 *J5* **Maki** Papua, E Indonesia *03°00′S 134°10′E*
260 *F3* **Makian, Pulau** *island* Maluku, E Indonesia
278 *D11* **Makikihi** Canterbury, South Island, New Zealand *44°36′S 171°09′E*
284 *B2* **Makin** *prev.* Pitt Island. *atoll* Tungaru, W Kiribati
137 *E9* **Makindu** Eastern, S Kenya *02°15′S 37°49′E*
227 *I2* **Makinsk** Akmola, N Kazakhstan *52°40′N 70°28′E*
Makira *see* Makira-Ulawa
Makira *see* San Cristobal
281 *K4* **Makira-Ulawa** *prev.* Makira. ⬖ *province* SE Solomon Islands
189 *M5* **Makiyivka** *Rus.* Makeyevka; *prev.* Dmitriyevsk. Donets'ka Oblast', E Ukraine *47°57′N 37°47′E*
220 *E5* **Makkah** *Eng.* Mecca. Makkah, W Saudi Arabia *21°28′N 39°50′E*
220 *E5* **Makkah** *var.* Minţaqat Makkah. ⬖ *province* W Saudi Arabia
Makkah, Minţaqat *see* Makkah
59 *K4* **Makkovik** Newfoundland and Labrador, NE Canada *55°06′N 59°07′W*
162 *G4* **Makkum** Friesland, N Netherlands *53°03′N 05°25′E*
183 *H13* **Makó** *Rom.* Macău. Csongrád, SE Hungary *46°14′N 20°28′E*
Mako *see* Makung
62 *C1* **Makobe Lake** ◎ Ontario, S Canada
280 *E8* **Makogai** *island* C Fiji
134 *B7* **Makokou** Ogooué-Ivindo, NE Gabon *0°38′N 12°47′E*
137 *C11* **Makongolosi** Mbeya, S Tanzania *08°24′S 33°09′E*
58 *C4* **Makoop Lake** ◎ Ontario, SE Canada
140 *F3* **Makopong** Kgalagadi, Botswana *25°20′S 22°59′E*
137 *A8* **Makota** SW Uganda *0°37′S 30°12′E*
134 *D7* **Makoua** Cuvette, C Congo *0°01′S 15°40′E*
171 *M8* **Makouda** Algeria
182 *H5* **Maków Mazowiecki** Mazowieckie, C Poland *52°51′N 21°06′E*
183 *G9* **Maków Podhalański** Małopolskie, S Poland *49°43′N 19°40′E*
223 *J9* **Makran** *cultural region* Iran/Pakistan
232 *D6* **Makrāna** Rājasthān, N India *27°02′N 74°44′E*
223 *J10* **Makran Coast** *coastal region* SE Iran
191 *D12* **Makrany** *Rus.* Mokrany. Brestskaya Voblasts', SW Belarus *51°50′N 24°15′E*
Makrinoros *see* Makrynóros
187 *H6* **Makrónisosi** *island* Kykládes, Greece, Aegean Sea
186 *F5* **Makrynóros** *var.* Makrinoros. ▲▲ C Greece
187 *H6* **Makryplági** ▲ C Greece *38°00′N 23°06′E*
Maksamaa *see* Maxmo
Maksatha *see* Maksatikha
Maksaticha *see* Maksatikha
194 *E9* **Maksatikha** *var.* Maksatha, Maksaticha. Tverskaya Oblast', W Russian Federation *57°49′N 35°46′E*
218 *G3* **Maksé** Lebanon *33°49′N 35°50′E*
232 *E8* **Maksi** Madhya Pradesh, C India *23°20′N 76°36′E*
252 *B1* **Maksumovka** Primorskiy Kray, SE Russian Federation *46°05′N 137°54′E*
175 *B14* **Maktar** Tunisia
222 *C1* **Mākū** Āžarbāyjān-e Gharbī, NW Iran *39°20′N 44°50′E*
256 *C2* **Mākum** Assam, NE India *27°28′N 95°28′E*
Makun *see* Makung
243 *M9* **Makung** *prev.* Mako, Makun. W Taiwan *23°35′N 119°35′E*
250 *C9* **Makurazaki** Kagoshima, Kyūshū, SW Japan *31°16′N 130°18′E*
133 *K7* **Makurdi** Benue, C Nigeria *07°42′N 08°36′E*
227 *H1* **Makushino** Kurganskaya Oblast', C Russian Federation *55°11′N 67°16′E*
82 *F9* **Makushin Volcano** ▲ Unalaska Island, Alaska, USA *53°53′N 166°55′W*
141 *H5* **Makwassie** North West, South Africa *27°19′S 25°59′E*
139 *H3* **Makwiro** Mashonaland West, N Zimbabwe *17°58′S 30°25′E*
105 *D8* **Mala** Lima, W Peru *12°40′S 76°36′W*
154 *I1* **Malå** Västerbotten, N Sweden *65°12′N 18°45′E*
Mala *see* Mallow, Ireland
Mala *see* Malaita, Solomon Islands
263 *M9* **Malabang** Mindanao, S Philippines
235 *D8* **Malabār Coast** *coast* SW India
134 *A6* **Malabo** *prev.* Santa Isabel. ● (Equatorial Guinea) Isla de Bioco, NW Equatorial Guinea *03°43′N 08°52′E*
134 *A6* **Malabo** ✈ Isla de Bioco, N Equatorial Guinea *03°44′N 08°51′E*
114 *G8* **Mal Abrigo** Uruguay *34°09′S 56°57′W*
Malaca *see* Málaga
Malacca *see* Melaka
258 *C2* **Malacca, Strait of** *Ind.* Selat Malaka. *strait* Indonesia/Malaysia
Malacka *see* Malacky
183 *E10* **Malacky** *Hung.* Malacka. Bratislavský Kraj, W Slovakia *48°26′N 17°01′E*
77 *I8* **Malad City** Idaho, NW USA *42°10′N 112°16′W*
189 *I3* **Mala Divytsya** Chernihivs'ka Oblast', N Ukraine *50°40′N 32°13′E*
191 *F9* **Maladzyechna** *Pol.* Molodeczno, *Rus.* Molodechno. Minskaya Voblasts', C Belarus *54°19′N 26°51′E*
284 *C10* **Mala'etoli** Île Uvea, E Wallis and Futuna
102 *D4* **Málaga** Santander, C Colombia *06°44′N 72°45′W*
170 *F9* **Málaga** *anc.* Malaca. Andalucía, S Spain *36°43′N 04°25′W*
80 *D6* **Malaga** California, USA *36°41′N 119°44′W*
79 *N9* **Malaga** New Mexico, SW USA *32°10′N 104°04′W*
170 *F8* **Málaga** ⬖ *province* Andalucía, S Spain
170 *F9* **Málaga** ✈ Andalucía, S Spain *36°38′N 04°36′W*
Malagasy Republic *see* Madagascar
170 *G6* **Malagón** Castilla-La Mancha, C Spain *39°10′N 03°51′W*
158 *E10* **Malahide** *Ir.* Mullach Íde. Dublin, E Ireland *53°27′N 06°09′W*
281 *K2* **Malaita** *off.* Malaita Province. ⬖ *province* N Solomon Islands
281 *J2* **Malaita** *var.* Mala. *island* N Solomon Islands
Malaita Province *see* Malaita
136 *B4* **Malakal** Upper Nile, NE South Sudan *09°31′N 31°40′E*
184 *B3* **Mala Kapela** ▲▲ NW Croatia
71 *H5* **Malakoff** Texas, SW USA *32°10′N 96°00′W*
Malakula *see* Malekula
231 *J5* **Malakwāl** *var.* Mālikwāla. Punjab, E Pakistan *32°32′N 73°18′E*
280 *C3* **Malalamai** Madang, W Papua New Guinea *05°49′S 146°44′E*
275 *K1* **Malalaua** Gulf, S Papua New Guinea *08°05′S 146°09′E*
260 *D5* **Malamala** Sulawesi, C Indonesia *03°21′S 120°58′E*
259 *J9* **Malang** Jawa, C Indonesia *07°59′S 112°45′E*
137 *D13* **Malanga** Niassa, N Mozambique *13°27′S 36°05′E*
Malange *see* Malanje
152 *F4* **Malangen** *sound* N Norway
135 *D11* **Malanje** *var.* Malange. Malanje, NW Angola *09°34′S 16°25′E*
135 *D11* **Malanje** *var.* Malange. ⬖ *province* N Angola
230 *E9* **Malān, Rās** *cape* SW Pakistan
133 *I5* **Malanville** NE Benin *11°50′N 03°23′E*
Malapane *see* Ozimek
235 *D8* **Malappuram** Kerala, SW India *11°00′N 76°02′E*
89 *K10* **Mala, Punta** *headland* S Panama *07°28′N 79°58′W*
230 *E9* **Malar** Baluchistān, SW Pakistan *26°19′N 64°55′E*
155 *H8* **Mälaren** ◎ C Sweden
112 *B10* **Malargüe** Mendoza, W Argentina *35°32′S 69°35′W*
58 *F7* **Malartic** Québec, SE Canada *48°09′N 78°09′W*
191 *D12* **Malaryta** *Pol.* Maloryta, *Rus.* Malorita. Brestskaya Voblasts', SW Belarus *51°47′N 24°05′E*
117 *D9* **Malaspina** Chubut, SE Argentina *44°56′S 66°52′W*
83 *K6* **Malaspina Glacier** *glacier* Yukon Territory, W Canada
83 *K6* **Malaspina Glacier** *glacier* Alaska, USA
215 *H7* **Malatya** *anc.* Melitene. Malatya, SE Turkey *38°22′N 38°18′E*
215 *H6* **Malatya** ⬖ *province* C Turkey
169 *K4* **Malaucéne** Provence-Alpes-Côte d'Azur, France *44°10′N 5°08′E*
Malavate *see* Pédima
189 *I5* **Mala Vyska** *Rus.* Malaya Viska. Kirovohrads'ka Oblast', S Ukraine *48°37′N 31°36′E*
137 *C13* **Malawi** *off.* Republic of Malaŵi; *prev.* Nyasaland, Nyasaland Protectorate. ◆ *republic* S Africa
Malawi, Lake *see* Nyasa, Lake
Malaŵi, Republic of *see* Malawi
153 *G8* **Malax** *Fin.* Maalahti. Länsi-Suomi, W Finland *62°55′N 21°30′E*
194 *D9* **Malaya Vishera** Novgorodskaya Oblast', W Russian Federation *58°52′N 32°12′E*
Malaya Viska *see* Mala Vyska
263 *M8* **Malaybalay** Mindanao, S Philippines *08°10′N 125°08′E*
222 *E4* **Malāyer** *prev.* Daulatabad. Hamadān, W Iran *34°20′N 48°47′E*
258 *D2* **Malay Peninsula** *peninsula* Malaysia/Thailand
258 *F2* **Malaysia** *off.* Malaysia, *var.* Federation of Malaysia; *prev.* the separate territories of Federation of Malaya, Sarawak and Sabah (North Borneo) and Singapore. ◆ *monarchy* SE Asia
Malaysia, Federation of *see* Malaysia
215 *J6* **Malazgirt** Muş, E Turkey *39°09′N 42°30′E*
133 *J4* **Malbaza** Tahoua, S Niger *13°57′N 05°32′E*
182 *F4* **Malbork** *Ger.* Marienburg, Marienburg in Westpreussen. Pomorskie, N Poland *54°01′N 19°03′E*
181 *C12* **Malborn** Rheinland-Pfalz, Germany *49°43′E 6°59′N*
160 *F9* **Malborough** United Kingdom *50°14′N 3°49′W*
178 *H5* **Malchin** Mecklenburg-Vorpommern, N Germany *53°43′N 12°46′E*
178 *H5* **Malchiner See** ◎ NE Germany
163 *C9* **Maldegem** Oost-Vlaanderen, NW Belgium *51°12′N 03°27′E*
162 *G7* **Malden** Gelderland, SE Netherlands *51°47′N 05°51′E*
65 *L2* **Malden** Massachusetts, NE USA *42°25′N 71°04′W*
75 *J11* **Malden** Missouri, C USA *36°33′N 89°58′W*
285 *H4* **Malden Island** *prev.* Independence Island. *atoll* E Kiribati
225 *E13* **Maldive Islands** *island group* Maldive Islands, NW Maldives
288 *F7* **Maldives** *off.* Maldivian Divehi, Republic of Maldives. ◆ *republic* N Indian Ocean
Maldives, Republic of *see* Maldives
Maldivian Divehi *see* Maldives
161 *L5* **Maldon** E England, United Kingdom *51°44′N 00°40′E*
115 *J10* **Maldonado** Maldonado, S Uruguay *34°57′S 54°59′W*
115 *J9* **Maldonado** ⬖ *department* S Uruguay
86 *F9* **Maldonado, Punta** *headland* S Mexico *16°18′N 98°31′W*
176 *G5* **Malè** Trentino-Alto Adige, N Italy *46°21′N 10°51′E*
235 *C12* **Male'** *Div.* Maale. ● (Maldives) Male' Atoll, C Maldives *04°10′N 73°29′E*
132 *D5* **Maléa** *var.* Maléya. NE Guinea *11°46′N 09°43′W*
Maléas, Ákra *see* Agriliá, Akrotírio
187 *H8* **Maléas, Akrotírio** *headland* S Greece *36°25′N 23°11′E*
235 *C12* **Male' Atoll** *var.* Kaafu Atoll. *atoll* C Maldives
Malebo, Pool *see* Stanley Pool
234 *D4* **Mālegaon** Mahārāshtra, W India *20°33′N 74°32′E*
136 *B5* **Malek** Jonglei, C South Sudan *06°04′N 31°36′E*
281 *M3* **Malekula** *var.* Malakula; *prev.* Mallicolo. *island* W Vanuatu
283 *I10* **Malem** Kosrae, E Micronesia *05°16′N 163°01′E*
139 *K2* **Malema** Nampula, N Mozambique *14°57′S 37°28′E*
135 *H10* **Malemba-Nkulu** Katanga, SE Dem. Rep. Congo *08°01′S 26°48′E*
194 *F6* **Malen'ga** Respublika Kareliya, NW Russian Federation *63°50′N 36°21′E*
180 *I1* **Malente** Schleswig-Holstein, Germany *54°11′E 10°34′N*
155 *H11* **Målerås** Kalmar, S Sweden *56°55′N 15°34′E*
165 *H4* **Malesherbes** Loiret, C France *48°18′N 02°25′E*
187 *H5* **Malesína** Stereá Elláda, E Greece *38°37′N 23°15′E*
166 *B7* **Malestroit** Bretagne, France *47°49′N 2°23′W*
Maléya *see* Maléa
197 *I9* **Malgobek** Respublika Ingushetiya, SW Russian Federation *43°34′N 44°34′E*
171 *L3* **Malgrat de Mar** Cataluña, NE Spain *41°39′N 02°45′E*
134 *H1* **Malha** Northern Darfur, W Sudan *15°07′N 26°00′E*
217 *I4* **Malḩah** *var.* Malḩāt. Şalāḩ ad Dīn, C Iraq *34°44′N 42°41′E*
159 *J8* **Malham** United Kingdom *54°03′N 2°09′W*
Malḩāt *see* Malḩah
76 *E7* **Malheur Lake** ◎ Oregon, NW USA
76 *E7* **Malheur River** 〰 Oregon, NW USA
132 *C5* **Mali** NW Guinea *12°08′N 12°29′W*
132 *G3* **Mali** *off.* Republic of Mali, *Fr.* République du Mali; *prev.* French Sudan, Sudanese Republic. ◆ *republic* W Africa
260 *F8* **Maliana** W East Timor *08°57′S 125°25′E*
244 *D6* **Malian He** 〰 Gansu, China
81 *C10* **Malibu** California, USA *34°0′N 118°49′W*
166 *E7* **Malicorne-sur-Sarthe** Pays de la Loire, France *47°49′N 0°05′W*
218 *H6* **Māliḩah** Syria *32°44′N 36°12′E*
256 *D2* **Mali Hka** 〰 N Myanmar (Burma)
Mali Idjoš *see* Mali Iđoš
184 *F2* **Mali Iđoš** *var.* Mali Idjoš, *Hung.* Kishegyes; *prev.* Krivaja. Vojvodina, N Serbia *45°43′N 19°40′E*
184 *G7* **Mali i Sharrit** *Serb.* Šar Planina. ▲▲ FYR Macedonia/Serbia
Mali i Zi *see* Crna Gora
184 *F2* **Mali Kanal** *canal* N Serbia
260 *E4* **Maliku** Sulawesi, N Indonesia *0°36′S 123°13′E*
Malik, Wadi al *see* Milk, Wadi el
Mālikwāla *see* Malakwāl
257 *D8* **Mali Kyun** *var.* Tavoy Island. *island* Mergui Archipelago, S Myanmar (Burma)
155 *H10* **Målilla** Kalmar, S Sweden *57°24′N 15°49′E*
184 *A4* **Mali Lošinj** *It.* Lussinpiccolo. Primorje-Gorski Kotar, W Croatia *44°31′N 14°28′E*
158 *C5* **Malin** Donegal, Ireland *55°18′N 7°16′W*
Malin *see* Malyn
86 *E7* **Malinalco** México, Mexico *18°57′N 99°30′W*
263 *L8* **Malindang, Mount** ▲ Mindanao, S Philippines *08°12′N 123°37′E*
137 *F9* **Malindi** Coast, SE Kenya *03°14′S 40°05′E*
Malines *see* Mechelen
156 *C7* **Malin Head** *Ir.* Cionn Mhálanna. *headland* NW Ireland *55°37′N 07°37′W*
158 *A6* **Malin More** Donegal, Ireland *54°42′N 8°46′W*
260 *D3* **Malino, Gunung** ▲ Sulawesi, N Indonesia *0°44′N 120°45′E*
184 *G9* **Maliq** *var.* Maliqi. Korçë, SE Albania *40°45′N 20°45′E*
Maliqi *see* Maliq
Mali, Republic of *see* Mali
Mali, République du *see* Mali
263 *M9* **Malita** Mindanao, S Philippines *06°13′N 125°39′E*
234 *E4* **Malkāpur** Mahārāshtra, C India *20°52′N 76°18′E*
214 *B4* **Malkara** Tekirdağ, NW Turkey *40°54′N 26°54′E*
191 *F11* **Mal'kavichy** *Rus.* Mal'kovichi. Brestskaya Voblasts', SW Belarus *52°31′N 26°36′E*
Malkiye *see* Al Mālikīyah
218 *F5* **Malkiyya** Israel *33°06′N 35°31′E*
187 *K1* **Malko Sharkovo, Yazovir** ▣ SE Bulgaria
185 *M7* **Malko Tŭrnovo** Burgas, E Bulgaria *42°00′N 27°33′E*
Mal'kovichi *see* Mal'kavichy
277 *K7* **Mallacoota** Victoria, SE Australia *37°34′S 149°45′E*
218 *I6* **Mallāḩ** Syria *32°30′N 36°51′E*
156 *E5* **Mallaig** N Scotland, United Kingdom *57°04′N 05°48′W*
276 *G5* **Mallala** South Australia *34°29′S 138°30′E*
129 *I4* **Mallawī** *var.* Mallawi. C Egypt *27°44′N 30°50′E*
Mallawi *see* Mallawī
118 *B9* **Malleco, Río** 〰 Araucanía, Chile
171 *I3* **Mallén** Aragón, NE Spain *41°53′N 01°25′W*
176 *G5* **Malles Venosta** *Ger.* Mals im Vinschgau. Trentino-Alto Adige, N Italy *46°40′N 10°37′E*
Mallicolo *see* Malekula
180 *J3* **Malliss** Mecklenburg-Vorpommern, Germany *53°13′E 11°19′N*
177 *I4* **Mallnitz** Salzburg, S Austria *46°58′N 13°09′E*
171 *L5* **Mallorca** *Eng.* Majorca; *anc.* Baleares Major. *island* Islas Baleares, Spain, W Mediterranean Sea
157 *B10* **Mallow** *Ir.* Mala. SW Ireland *52°08′N 08°39′W*
160 *F3* **Mallwyd** United Kingdom *52°41′N 3°41′W*
154 *E2* **Malm** Nord-Trøndelag, C Norway *64°04′N 11°12′E*
155 *G10* **Malmbäck** Jönköping, S Sweden *57°34′N 14°30′E*
152 *F5* **Malmberget** *Lapp.* Malmivaara. Norrbotten, N Sweden *67°09′N 20°39′E*
163 *H11* **Malmédy** Liège, E Belgium *50°26′N 06°02′E*
138 *D10* **Malmesbury** Western Cape, SW South Africa *33°28′S 18°43′E*
Malmivaara *see* Malmberget
155 *H8* **Malmköping** Södermanland, C Sweden *59°08′N 16°49′E*
155 *F12* **Malmö** Skåne, S Sweden *55°36′N 13°E*
155 *F12* **Malmo** ✈ Skåne, S Sweden *55°33′N 13°23′E*
102 *F2* **Malmok** *headland* Bonaire, S Netherlands Antilles *12°16′N 68°21′W*
155 *H9* **Malmslätt** Östergötland, S Sweden *58°25′N 15°30′E*
195 *J10* **Malmyzh** Kirovskaya Oblast', NW Russian Federation *56°30′N 50°37′E*
104 *B4* **Mal Nomre, Punta** *headland* NW Peru *06°03′S 81°08′W*
281 *L3* **Malo** *island* W Vanuatu
196 *F4* **Maloarkhangel'sk** Orlovskaya Oblast', W Russian Federation *52°25′N 36°37′E*
Maloelap *see* Maloelap Atoll
283 *M6* **Maloelap Atoll** *var.* Maloelap. *atoll* E Marshall Islands
Maloenda *see* Malunda
176 *F5* **Maloja** Graubünden, S Switzerland *46°25′N 09°42′E*
137 *B12* **Malole** Northern, NE Zambia *10°05′S 31°37′E*
167 *H1* **Malo-les-Bains** Nord-Pas-de-Calais, France *51°03′N 2°24′E*
280 *D9* **Malolo** *island* Mamanuca Group, W Fiji
280 *D9* **Malolo Barrier Reef** *var.* Ro Ro Reef. *reef* W Fiji
263 *K5* **Malolos** Luzon, N Philippines *14°51′N 120°49′E*
62 *G4* **Malone** New York, NE USA *44°51′N 74°18′W*
135 *G11* **Malonga** Katanga, S Dem. Rep. Congo *10°26′S 23°10′E*
183 *G8* **Małopolska** *plateau* S Poland
183 *G8* **Małopolskie** ⬖ *province* SE Poland
Malorita/Maloryta *see* Malaryta
194 *F6* **Maloshuyka** Arkhangel'skaya Oblast', NW Russian Federation *63°43′N 37°20′E*
185 *I7* **Mal'ovitsa** ▲ W Bulgaria *42°12′N 23°19′E*
227 *K7* **Malovodnoye** Almaty, SE Kazakhstan *43°31′N 77°42′E*
154 *A5* **Måløy** Sogn Og Fjordane, S Norway *61°57′N 05°06′E*
196 *F2* **Maloyaroslavets** Kaluzhskaya Oblast', W Russian Federation *55°03′N 36°31′E*
195 *I3* **Malozemel'skaya Tundra** *physical region* NW Russian Federation
170 *E6* **Malpartida de Cáceres** Extremadura, W Spain *39°26′N 06°30′W*
170 *E5* **Malpartida de Plasencia** Extremadura, W Spain *39°59′N 06°03′W*
160 *G2* **Malpas** United Kingdom *53°01′N 2°46′W*
85 *K9* **Malpaso** Zacatecas, Mexico *22°37′N 102°46′W*
174 *C4* **Malpensa** ✈ (Milano) Lombardia, N Italy *45°41′N 08°40′E*
130 *D7* **Malqṭeïr** *desert* N Mauritania
181 *E14* **Malsch** Baden-Württemberg, Germany *48°53′E 8°20′N*
181 *G9* **Malsfeld** Hessen, Germany *51°05′E 9°32′N*
Mals im Vinschgau *see* Malles Venosta
190 *F7* **Malta** Rēzekne, SE Latvia *56°19′N 27°11′E*
172 *D2* **Malta** Guarda, Portugal *40°44′N 7°06′W*
77 *K3* **Malta** Montana, NW USA *48°21′N 107°52′W*
175 *J13* **Malta** *off.* Republic of Malta. ◆ *republic* C Mediterranean Sea
177 *I4* **Malta** *var.* Maltabach. 〰 S Austria
175 *J13* **Malta** *island* Malta, C Mediterranean Sea
Maltabach *see* Malta
Malta, Canale di *see* Malta Channel
175 *G13* **Malta Channel** *It.* Canale di Malta. *strait* Italy/Malta
140 *C3* **Maltahöhe** Hardap, SW Namibia *24°50′S 17°00′E*
Malta, Republic of *see* Malta
159 *L10* **Maltby** United Kingdom *53°25′N 1°12′W*
159 *M10* **Maltby le Marsh** United Kingdom *53°18′N 0°12′E*
187 *M2* **Maltepe** İstanbul, NW Turkey *40°56′N 29°09′E*
159 *L8* **Malton** N England, United Kingdom *54°07′N 00°50′W*

◆ Country
● Country Capital
◇ Dependent Territory
○ Dependent Territory Capital
⬖ Administrative Regions
✈ International Airport
▲ Mountain
▲▲ Mountain Range
⛰ Volcano
〰 River
◎ Lake
▣ Reservoir

◆ Country
● Country Capital
◇ Dependent Territory
○ Dependent Territory Capital
✕ Administrative Regions
✕ International Airport
▲ Mountain
▲ Mountain Range
★ Volcano
≈ River
⊗ Lake
⊠ Reservoir

◆ Country
◇ Dependent Territory
♦ Country Capital
◇ Dependent Territory Capital
◈ Administrative Regions
▲ Mountain
▲ Mountain Range
✕ International Airport
🌋 Volcano
◈ River
◎ Lake
◈ Reservoir

Mmathethe - Monticello

141 H3 **Mmathethe** Southern, Botswana *25°19′S 25°16′E*
141 J8 **Mncwasa Point** *point* Eastern Cape, South Africa
90 F5 **Moa** Holguín, E Cuba *20°42′N 74°57′W*
132 D7 **Moa** ⛐ Guinea/Sierra Leone
79 J4 **Moab** Utah, W USA *38°35′N 109°34′W*
275 J1 **Moa Island** *island* Queensland, NE Australia
280 F9 **Moala** *island* S Fiji
139 I6 **Moamba** Maputo, SW Mozambique *25°35′S 32°13′E*
135 C8 **Moanda** *var.* Mouanda. Haut-Ogooué, SE Gabon *01°31′S 13°07′E*
260 G8 **Moa, Pulau** *island* Kepulauan Leti, E Indonesia
139 I2 **Moatize** Tete, NW Mozambique *16°04′S 33°43′E*
135 J10 **Moba** Katanga, E Dem. Rep. Congo *07°03′S 29°52′E*
253 C13 **Mobara** Chiba, Honshū, S Japan *35°26′N 140°20′E*
Mobagor *see* Montego Bay
134 F6 **Mobaye** Basse-Kotto, S Central African Republic *04°19′N 21°17′E*
134 F6 **Mobayi-Mbongo** Equateur, NW Dem. Rep. Congo *04°21′N 21°10′E*
70 E2 **Mobeetie** Texas, SW USA *35°33′N 100°25′W*
75 H9 **Moberly** Missouri, C USA *39°25′N 92°26′W*
68 G4 **Mobile** Alabama, S USA *30°42′N 88°03′W*
68 G4 **Mobile Bay** *bay* Alabama, S USA
68 G4 **Mobile River** ⛐ Alabama, S USA
74 C4 **Mobridge** South Dakota, N USA *45°32′N 100°25′W*
Mobutu Sese Seko, Lac *see* Albert, Lake
91 H5 **Moca** N Dominican Republic *19°26′N 70°33′W*
Moçâmedes *see* Namibe
80 D4 **Moccasin** California, USA *37°49′N 120°18′W*
256 G5 **Mộc Châu** Sơn La, N Vietnam *20°49′N 104°38′E*
280 G9 **Moce** *island* Lau Group, E Fiji
173 H3 **Mocejón** Castilla-La Mancha, Spain *39°55′N 3°54′W*
Mocha *see* Al Mukhā
287 L8 **Mocha Fracture Zone** *tectonic feature* SE Pacific Ocean
116 A6 **Mocha, Isla** *island* C Chile
104 C5 **Moche, Río** ⛐ W Peru
257 H9 **Mộc Hoa** Long An, S Vietnam *10°46′N 105°56′E*
136 G6 **Mochrum** United Kingdom *54°47′N 4°34′W*
141 H2 **Mochudi** Kgatleng, SE Botswana *24°25′S 26°07′E*
137 F12 **Mocímboa da Praia** *var.* Vila de Mocímboa da Praia. Cabo Delgado, N Mozambique *11°17′S 40°21′E*
154 G7 **Mockfjärd** Dalarna, C Sweden *60°30′N 14°57′E*
67 I6 **Mocksville** North Carolina, SE USA *35°53′N 80°33′W*
76 B4 **Moclips** Washington, NW USA *47°11′N 124°13′W*
135 C12 **Môco** *var.* Morro de Môco. ▲ W Angola *12°36′S 15°09′E*
102 B7 **Mocoa** Putumayo, SW Colombia *01°07′N 76°38′W*
110 C5 **Mococa** São Paulo, S Brazil *21°30′S 47°00′W*
Môco, Morro de *see* Môco
114 F2 **Mocoretá** Corrientes, Argentina *30°38′S 57°58′W*
84 G7 **Mocorito** Sinaloa, C Mexico *25°24′N 107°55′W*
84 H3 **Moctezuma** Chihuahua, N Mexico *30°10′N 106°28′W*
85 L9 **Moctezuma** San Luis Potosí, C Mexico *22°46′N 101°06′W*
84 F3 **Moctezuma** Sonora, NW Mexico *29°50′N 109°40′W*
85 K8 **Moctezuma, Río** ⛐ C Mexico
Mó, Cuan *see* Clew Bay
139 J2 **Mocuba** Zambézia, NE Mozambique *16°50′S 37°02′E*
169 M2 **Modane** Savoie, E France *45°14′N 06°41′E*
141 H6 **Modder** ⛐ Northern Cape, South Africa
176 G8 **Modena** *anc.* Mutina. Emilia-Romagna, N Italy *44°39′N 10°55′E*
78 G5 **Modena** Utah, W USA *37°46′N 113°54′W*
80 C4 **Modesto** California, W USA *37°38′N 121°02′W*
175 G13 **Modica** *anc.* Motyca. Sicilia, Italy, C Mediterranean Sea *36°52′N 14°45′E*
141 J3 **Modimolle** Limpopo, South Africa *24°41′S 28°24′E*
141 J3 **Modimolle** *prev.* Nylstroom. Limpopo, NE South Africa *24°39′N 28°23′E*
134 F6 **Modjamboli** Equateur, N Dem. Rep. Congo *02°27′N 22°03′E*
Modjokerto *see* Mojokerto
177 L2 **Mödling** Niederösterreich, NE Austria *48°06′N 16°18′E*
Modohn *see* Madona
Modot *see* Tsenhermandal
261 J6 **Modowi** Papua, E Indonesia *04°05′S 134°39′E*
184 E3 **Modračko Jezero** ⊠ NE Bosnia and Herzegovina
184 E3 **Modriča** Republika Srpska, N Bosnia and Herzegovina *44°57′N 18°17′E*
277 J6 **Moe** Victoria, SE Australia *38°11′S 146°18′E*
Moearatewe *see* Muaratewe
111 H3 **Moeda** Minas Gerais, Brazil *20°20′S 44°03′W*
Moei, Mae Nam *see* Thaungyin
160 E1 **Moelfre** United Kingdom *53°21′N 4°14′W*
156 E6 **Moelv** Hedmark, S Norway *60°55′N 10°47′E*
110 F3 **Moema** Minas Gerais, Brazil *19°50′S 45°24′W*
152 F4 **Moen** Troms, N Norway *69°08′N 18°35′E*
Möen *see* Møn, Denmark
Moen *see* Weno, Micronesia
Moena *see* Muna, Pulau
79 I6 **Moenkopi Wash** ⛐ Arizona, SW USA
278 D11 **Moeraki Point** *headland* South Island, New Zealand *45°23′S 170°52′E*
163 D9 **Moerbeke** Oost-Vlaanderen, NW Belgium *51°11′N 03°57′E*
163 E8 **Moerdijk** Noord-Brabant, S Netherlands *51°42′N 04°37′E*
Moero, Lac *see* Mweru, Lake
181 B8 **Moers** *var.* Mörs. Nordrhein-Westfalen, W Germany *51°27′N 06°36′E*
Moesi *see* Musi, Air
Moeskroen *see* Mouscron
140 F5 **Moeswal** Northern Cape, South Africa *27°50′S 22°33′E*
159 H5 **Moffat** S Scotland, United Kingdom *55°29′N 03°36′W*
278 B11 **Moffat Peak** ▲ South Island, New Zealand *44°57′S 168°10′E*
135 I8 **Moga** Sud-Kivu, E Dem. Rep. Congo *02°16′S 26°54′E*
232 E4 **Moga** Punjab, N India *30°49′N 75°13′E*
Mogadiscio/Mogadishu *see* Muqdisho
Mogador *see* Essaouira
172 E1 **Mogadouro** Bragança, N Portugal *41°20′N 06°43′W*
172 D1 **Mogadouro, Serra do** ▲ Bragança, Portugal
141 J1 **Mogalakwena** ⛐ Limpopo, South Africa
141 J2 **Mogalakwenastroom** Limpopo, South Africa *23°46′S 28°37′E*
141 J2 **Mogalak-wenastroom** Limpopo, South Africa *23°46′S 28°43′E*
253 C9 **Mogami-gawa** ⛐ Honshū, C Japan
256 D3 **Mogaung** Kachin State, N Myanmar (Burma) *25°20′N 96°54′E*
182 H6 **Mogielnica** Mazowieckie, C Poland *51°40′N 20°42′E*
Mogilëv *see* Mahilyow
Mogilev-Podol'skiy *see* Mohyliv-Podil's'kyy
Mogilëvskaya Oblast' *see* Mahilyowskaya Voblasts'
182 E5 **Mogilno** Kujawsko-pomorskie, C Poland *52°39′N 17°58′E*
139 L2 **Mogincual** Nampula, NE Mozambique *15°33′S 40°28′E*
186 G2 **Moglenítsas** ⛐ N Greece
177 H6 **Mogliano Veneto** Veneto, NE Italy *45°34′N 12°14′E*
184 F9 **Mogliçë** Korçë, SE Albania *40°43′N 20°22′E*
193 J8 **Mogocha** Zabaykalskiy Kray, S Russian Federation *53°39′N 119°47′E*
192 F7 **Mogochin** Tomskaya Oblast', C Russian Federation *57°42′N 83°24′E*
136 B4 **Mogogh** Jonglei, NE South Sudan *08°26′N 31°19′E*
261 I5 **Mogoi** Papua, E Indonesia *01°44′S 133°13′E*
256 D4 **Mogok** Mandalay, C Myanmar (Burma) *22°55′N 96°29′E*
141 I2 **Mogol** ⛐ Limpopo, South Africa
79 K9 **Mogollon Mountains** ▲ New Mexico, SW USA
79 I8 **Mogollon Rim** *cliff* Arizona, SW USA
116 H6 **Mogotes, Punta** *headland* E Argentina *38°03′S 57°31′W*
88 G5 **Mogotón** ▲ NW Nicaragua *13°45′N 86°22′W*
170 D8 **Moguer** Andalucía, S Spain *37°15′N 06°52′W*
141 I2 **Mogwadi** *prev.* Dendron. Limpopo, South Africa *23°23′S 29°20′E see also* Dendron
141 J3 **Mogwase** North-West, South Africa *25°11′S 27°16′E*
183 F13 **Mohács** Baranya, SW Hungary *46°N 18°40′E*
278 H6 **Mohaka** ⛐ North Island, New Zealand
141 I7 **Mohale's Hoek** Lesotho *30°09′S 27°29′E*
74 C1 **Mohall** North Dakota, N USA *48°45′N 101°30′W*
Moḥammadābād *see* Dargaz
223 J7 **Moḥammadābād-e Rigān** Kermān, SE Iran *28°39′N 59°01′E*
171 J10 **Mohammadia** Algeria
130 F2 **Mohammedia** *prev.* Fédala. NW Morocco *33°46′N 07°16′W*
130 E3 **Mohammed V** ✈ (Casablanca) W Morocco *33°07′N 08°28′W*
Mohammerah *see* Khorramshahr
81 J10 **Mohave, Lake** ⊠ Arizona/Nevada, W USA
81 J12 **Mohave Mountains** ▲ Arizona, SW USA
81 J12 **Mohave Peak** ▲ Nevada, USA *35°37′N 114°30′W*
64 G1 **Mohawk** New York, NE USA *43°00′N 75°00′W*
78 G9 **Mohawk Mountains** ▲ Arizona, SW USA
64 G1 **Mohawk River** ⛐ New York, NE USA
247 J1 **Mohe** *var.* Xilinji. Heilongjiang, NE China *53°01′N 122°26′E*
155 G11 **Moheda** Kronoberg, S Sweden *57°00′N 14°34′E*
Mohéli *see* Mwali
232 E5 **Mohendergarh** Haryāna, N India *28°17′N 76°14′E*
82 F7 **Mohican, Cape** *headland* Nunivak Island, Alaska, USA *60°12′N 167°25′W*
158 B8 **Mohill** Leitrim, Ireland *53°55′N 7°52′W*
Mohn *see* Muhu
181 E8 **Möhne** ⛐ W Germany
181 E8 **Möhne-Stausee** ⊠ W Germany
152 C5 **Mohn, Kapp** *headland* NW Svalbard *79°26′N 25°44′E*
295 L4 **Mohns Ridge** *undersea feature* Greenland Sea/ Norwegian Sea *72°30′N 05°00′E*
105 H9 **Moho** Puno, SE Peru *15°21′S 69°32′W*
Mohokare *see* Caledon
155 G9 **Moholm** Västra Götaland, S Sweden *58°37′N 14°04′E*
79 H7 **Mohon Peak** ▲ Arizona, SW USA *34°55′N 113°07′W*
137 E11 **Mohoro** Pwani, E Tanzania *08°09′S 39°10′E*
Mohra *see* Moravice
Mohrungen *see* Morąg
188 F5 **Mohyliv-Podil's'kyy** *Rus.* Mogilev-Podol'skiy. Vinnyts'ka Oblast', C Ukraine *48°29′N 27°49′E*
155 B9 **Moi** Rogaland, S Norway *58°27′N 06°32′E*
168 G9 **Moia** Cataluña, Spain *41°49′N 2°06′E*
Moili *see* Mwali
280 B9 **Moindou** Province Sud, C New Caledonia *21°42′S 165°40′E*
188 E7 **Moinești** *Hung.* Mojnest. Bacău, E Romania *46°27′N 26°31′E*
Móinteach Mílic *see* Mountmellick
158 D7 **Moira** United Kingdom *54°30′N 6°17′W*
62 E4 **Moira** ⛐ Ontario, SE Canada
152 E6 **Mo i Rana** Nordland, C Norway *66°19′N 14°10′E*
233 M7 **Moirāng** Manipur, NE India *24°29′N 93°45′E*
167 L10 **Moirans-en-Montagne** Franche-Comté, France *46°26′N 5°44′E*
187 I10 **Moíres** Kríti, Greece, E Mediterranean Sea *35°03′N 24°51′E*
190 E5 **Mõisaküla** *Ger.* Moiseküll. Viljandimaa, S Estonia *58°05′N 25°12′E*
166 C7 **Moisdon-la-Rivière** Pays de la Loire, France *47°37′N 1°22′W*
Moiseküll *see* Mõisaküla
114 A3 **Moisés Ville** Santa Fe, Argentina *30°43′S 61°29′W*
59 I6 **Moisie** Québec, E Canada *50°12′N 66°06′W*
59 I6 **Moisie** ⛐ Québec, SE Canada
164 G8 **Moissac** Tarn-et-Garonne, S France *44°07′N 01°05′E*
134 E4 **Moïssala** Moyen-Chari, S Chad *08°21′N 17°46′E*
103 H4 **Moitaco** Bolívar, E Venezuela *08°00′N 64°22′W*
155 H8 **Möja** Stockholm, C Sweden *59°25′N 18°55′E*
171 H8 **Mojácar** Andalucía, S Spain *37°09′N 01°50′W*
172 G1 **Mojados** Castilla y León, Spain *41°26′N 4°39′W*
81 E9 **Mojave** California, W USA *35°03′N 118°10′W*
81 G10 **Mojave Desert** *plain* California, W USA
81 G10 **Mojave River** ⛐ California, W USA
110 D9 **Moji das Cruzes** São Paulo, Brazil *23°31′S 46°11′W*
110 G7 **Moji-Guaçu** São Paulo, Brazil *22°22′S 46°57′W*
110 C7 **Moji-Mirim** *var.* Moji-Mirim. São Paulo, S Brazil *22°26′S 46°55′W*
Moji-Mirim *see* Moji-Mirim
184 F6 **Mojkovac** E Montenegro *42°57′N 19°34′E*
Mojnest *see* Moinești
259 J8 **Mojokerto** *prev.* Modjokerto. Jawa, C Indonesia *07°25′S 112°31′E*
114 D4 **Mojones Norte** Entre Ríos, Argentina *31°29′S 59°13′W*
Mōka *see* Mooka
233 I7 **Mokāma** *prev.* Mokameh, Mukama. Bihār, N India *25°24′N 85°55′E*
135 I12 **Mokambo** Katanga, SE Dem. Rep. Congo *12°23′S 28°21′E*
Mokameh *see* Mokāma
278 G5 **Mokau** Waikato, North Island, New Zealand *38°42′S 174°37′E*
278 G5 **Mokau** ⛐ North Island, New Zealand
80 E3 **Mokelumne River** ⛐ California, W USA
140 G5 **Mokgareng** North-West, South Africa *27°31′S 24°43′E*
141 H3 **Mokgora** North West, South Africa *25°23′S 26°05′E*
141 I6 **Mokhotlong** NE Lesotho *29°19′S 29°06′E*
Mokil Atoll *see* Mwokil Atoll
154 H7 **Möklinta** Västmanland, C Sweden *60°04′N 16°34′E*
Mokna *see* Mokra Gora
175 C14 **Moknine** Tunisia
278 H3 **Mokohinau Islands** *island group* N New Zealand
233 M6 **Mokokchūng** Nāgāland, NE India *26°20′N 94°30′E*
134 C3 **Mokolo** Extrême-Nord, N Cameroon *10°49′N 13°54′E*
141 J2 **Mokopane** Limpopo, South Africa *24°10′S 29°00′E*
138 G6 **Mokopane** *prev.* Potgietersrus. Limpopo, NE South Africa *24°09′S 28°58′E*
278 C12 **Mokoreta** ⛐ South Island, New Zealand
248 B7 **Mokpo** *Jap.* Moppo; *prev.* Mokp'o. SW South Korea *34°50′N 126°26′E*
Mokp'o *see* Mokpo
184 F6 **Mokra Gora** *Alb.* Mokna. ▲ S Serbia
Mokrany *see* Makrany
197 H2 **Moksha** ⛐ W Russian Federation
223 K8 **Mok Sukhteh-ye Pāyīn** Sīstān va Balūchestān, SE Iran
Moktama *see* Mottama
133 I6 **Mokwa** Niger, W Nigeria *09°19′N 05°01′E*
163 F9 **Mol** *prev.* Moll. Antwerpen, N Belgium *51°11′N 05°07′E*
175 I9 **Mola di Bari** Puglia, SE Italy *41°03′N 17°05′E*
Molai *see* Moláoi
86 F5 **Molango** Hidalgo, C Mexico *20°48′N 98°44′W*
186 G8 **Moláoi** *var.* Molai. Pelopónnisos, S Greece *36°48′N 22°51′E*
87 N5 **Molas** Quintana Roo, Mexico *20°36′N 86°44′W*
87 N5 **Molas del Norte, Punta** *var.* Punta Molas. *headland* SE Mexico *20°34′N 86°43′W*
Molas, Punta *see* Molas del Norte, Punta
173 K5 **Molatón** ▲ Castilla-La Manacha, Spain *38°59′N 1°24′W*
171 I6 **Molatón** ▲ C Spain *38°58′N 01°19′W*
180 E4 **Molbergen** Niedersachsen, Germany *52°52′E 7°56′N*
160 G2 **Mold** NE Wales, United Kingdom *53°10′N 03°08′W*
Moldau *see* Vltava, Czech Republic
Moldau *see* Moldova
Moldavia *see* Moldova
Moldavian SSR/Moldavskaya SSR *see* Moldova
154 C4 **Molde** Møre og Romsdal, S Norway *62°44′N 07°08′E*
Moldotau, Khrebet *see* Moldo-Too, Khrebet
229 L5 **Moldo-Too, Khrebet** *prev.* Khrebet Moldotau. ▲ C Kyrgyzstan
188 G6 **Moldova** *off.* Republic of Moldova, *var.* Moldavia; *prev.* Moldavian SSR, *Rus.* Moldavskaya SSR. ◆ *republic* SE Europe
188 E6 **Moldova** *Eng.* Moldavia, *Ger.* Moldau. *former province* NE Romania
188 E6 **Moldova** ⛐ N Romania
188 C9 **Moldova Nouă** *Ger.* Neumoldowa, *Hung.* Újmoldova. Caraş-Severin, SW Romania *44°45′N 21°39′E*
Moldova, Republic of *see* Moldova
188 B9 **Moldova Veche** *Ger.* Altmoldowa, *Hung.* Ómoldova. Caraş-Severin, SW Romania *44°45′N 21°13′E*
188 D8 **Moldoveanul, Vârful** *var.* Moldoveanu; *prev.* Vîrful Moldoveanu. ▲ C Romania *45°35′N 24°48′E*
Moldoveanul *see* Vârful Moldoveanu
161 K7 **Mole** ⛐ United Kingdom
141 J5 **Molen** ⛐ Free State, South Africa
141 H2 **Molepolole** Kweneng, SE Botswana *24°25′S 25°30′E*
90 G5 **Môle-St-Nicolas** NW Haiti *19°46′N 73°19′W*
191 E8 **Molėtai** Utena, E Lithuania *55°14′N 25°25′E*
175 H9 **Molfetta** Puglia, SE Italy *41°12′N 16°35′E*
260 E3 **Molibagu** Sulawesi, N Indonesia *0°25′N 123°57′E*
164 F8 **Molières** Midi-Pyrénées, France *44°11′N 1°22′E*
116 B5 **Molina** Maule, C Chile *35°06′S 71°18′W*
171 H4 **Molina de Aragón** Castilla-La Mancha, C Spain *40°50′N 01°54′W*
171 I7 **Molina de Segura** Murcia, SE Spain *38°03′N 01°11′W*
113 D10 **Molina, Río** ⛐ Región Metropolitana, Chile
73 B9 **Moline** Illinois, N USA *41°30′N 90°31′W*
75 F11 **Moline** Kansas, C USA *37°21′N 96°18′W*
116 C5 **Molineros** Libertador General Bernardo O'Higgins, Chile *34°31′S 71°36′W*
243 L1 **Molingguan** Jiangsu, E China *31°50′N 118°50′E*
185 B5 **Molino Doll** Entre Ríos, Argentina *32°20′S 60°25′W*
135 J10 **Moliro** Katanga, SE Dem. Rep. Congo *08°11′S 30°31′E*
175 G8 **Molise** ◆ *region* S Italy
168 G7 **Molitg** Languedoc-Roussillon, France *42°39′N 2°23′E*
155 G8 **Molkom** Värmland, C Sweden *59°36′N 13°43′E*
177 I4 **Möll** ⛐ S Austria
Moll *see* Mol
160 F7 **Molland** United Kingdom *51°02′N 3°42′W*
228 F8 **Mollanepes Adyndaky** *Rus.* Imeni Mollanepesa. Mary Welaýaty, S Turkmenistan *37°36′N 61°54′E*
155 F11 **Mölle** Skåne, S Sweden *56°15′N 12°19′E*
105 F10 **Mollendo** Arequipa, SW Peru *17°02′S 72°01′W*
169 F9 **Mollerusa** Cataluña, Spain *41°38′N 0°54′E*
171 J3 **Mollerussa** Cataluña, NE Spain *41°37′N 00°53′E*
118 C2 **Molles, Punta** *point* Valparaíso, Chile
180 I2 **Mölln** Schleswig-Holstein, Germany *53°38′E 10°41′N*
155 E10 **Mölndal** Västra Götaland, S Sweden *57°39′N 12°05′E*
155 F10 **Mölnlycke** Västra Götaland, S Sweden *57°39′N 12°09′E*
189 K6 **Molochans'k** *Rus.* Molochansk. Zaporiz'ka Oblast', SE Ukraine *47°10′N 35°38′E*
189 K7 **Molochna** *Rus.* Molochnaya. ⛐ S Ukraine
Molochnaya *see* Molochna
189 K7 **Molochnyy Lyman** *bay* N Black Sea
Molodechno/Molodecžno *see* Maladzyechna
293 K2 **Molodezhnaya** *Russian research station* Antarctica *67°33′S 46°12′E*
194 E9 **Mologa** ⛐ NW Russian Federation
82 C2 **Moloka'i** *var.* Molokai. *island* Hawaiian Islands, Hawai'i, USA
267 M2 **Molokai Fracture Zone** *tectonic feature* NE Pacific Ocean
194 F9 **Molokovo** Tverskaya Oblast', W Russian Federation *58°10′N 36°43′E*
195 I9 **Moloma** ⛐ NW Russian Federation
277 K5 **Molong** New South Wales, SE Australia *33°07′S 148°52′E*
140 F4 **Molopo** *seasonal river* Botswana/South Africa
140 G3 **Molopoivier** North-West, South Africa *25°44′S 24°17′E*
186 G5 **Mólos** Stereá Elláda, C Greece *38°48′N 22°39′E*
260 D3 **Molosipat** Sulawesi, N Indonesia *0°28′N 121°08′E*
190 G3 **Moloskovitsy** Leningradskaya Oblast', Russian Federation
Molotov *see* Severodvinsk, Arkhangel'skaya Oblast', Russian Federation
Molotov *see* Perm', Permskaya Oblast', Russian Federation
134 C6 **Moloundou** Est, SE Cameroon *02°03′N 15°14′E*
165 K3 **Molsheim** Bas-Rhin, NE France *48°33′N 07°30′E*
55 I8 **Molson Lake** ◎ Manitoba, C Canada
140 F8 **Molteno Pass** *pass* Western Cape, South Africa
Moluccas *see* Maluku
260 E4 **Molucca Sea** *Ind.* Laut Maluku. *sea* E Indonesia
Molukken *see* Maluku
139 J2 **Molumbo** Zambézia, N Mozambique *15°33′S 36°19′E*
261 I7 **Molu, Pulau** *island* Maluku, E Indonesia
194 I5 **Molvotitsy** Novgorodskaya Oblast', Russian Federation
139 K2 **Moma** Nampula, NE Mozambique *16°42′S 39°12′E*
193 K5 **Moma** ⛐ NE Russian Federation
261 K6 **Momats** ⛐ Papua, E Indonesia
85 J9 **Momax** Zacatecas, Mexico *21°56′N 103°19′W*
88 G6 **Mombacho, Volcán** ⛰ SW Nicaragua *11°49′N 85°58′W*
137 E9 **Mombasa** Coast, SE Kenya *04°04′N 39°40′E*
137 E9 **Mombasa** ✈ Coast, SE Kenya *04°01′S 39°31′E*
172 F3 **Mombeltrán** Castilla y León, Spain *40°16′N 5°01′W*
Mombetsu *see* Monbetsu
181 G11 **Mömbris** Bayern, Germany *50°04′E 9°10′N*
261 L8 **Mombum** Papua, E Indonesia *08°16′S 138°51′E*
185 K8 **Momchilgrad** *prev.* Mastanli. Kŭrdzhali, S Bulgaria *41°33′N 25°25′E*
163 D12 **Momignies** Hainaut, S Belgium *50°02′N 04°10′E*
102 B3 **Momil** Córdoba, NW Colombia *09°15′N 75°40′W*
181 G12 **Mömlingen** Bayern, Germany *49°52′E 9°05′N*
88 G6 **Momotombo, Volcán** ⛰ W Nicaragua *12°25′N 86°33′W*
104 B1 **Mompiche, Ensenada de** *bay* NW Ecuador
134 F7 **Mompono** Equateur, NW Dem. Rep. Congo *0°11′N 21°31′E*
102 C3 **Mompós** Bolívar, NW Colombia *09°15′N 74°29′W*
155 F13 **Møn** *prev.* Möen. *island* SE Denmark
79 H3 **Mona** Utah, W USA *39°49′N 111°52′W*
Mona, Canal de la *see* Mona Passage
156 C5 **Monach Islands** *island group* NW Scotland, United Kingdom
165 L8 **Monaco** *var.* Monaco-Ville; *anc.* Monoecus. ● (Monaco) S Monaco *43°46′N 07°23′E*
165 L8 **Monaco** *off.* Principality of Monaco. ◆ *monarchy* W Europe
Monaco *see* München
Monaco Basin *see* Canary Basin
Monaco, Principality of *see* Monaco
Monaco-Ville *see* Monaco
156 F5 **Monadhliath Mountains** ▲ N Scotland, United Kingdom
103 H3 **Monagas** *off.* Estado Monagas. ◆ *state* NE Venezuela
Monagas, Estado *see* Monagas
158 C7 **Monaghan** *Ir.* Muineachán. Monaghan, N Ireland *54°15′N 06°58′W*
158 C8 **Monaghan** *Ir.* Muineachán. *cultural region* N Ireland
89 K10 **Monagrillo** Herrera, S Panama *08°00′N 80°28′W*
70 D5 **Monahans** Texas, SW USA *31°35′N 102°54′W*
91 J6 **Mona, Isla** *island* W Puerto Rico
91 I6 **Mona Passage** *Sp.* Canal de la Mona. *channel* Dominican Republic/Puerto Rico
89 I8 **Mona, Punta** *headland* E Costa Rica *09°44′N 82°48′W*
235 G11 **Monaragala** Uva Province, SE Sri Lanka *06°52′N 81°22′E*
77 I4 **Monarch** Montana, NW USA *47°04′N 110°51′W*
56 D6 **Monarch Mountain** ▲ British Columbia, SW Canada *51°59′N 125°56′W*
Monasterio *see* Monesterio
Monasterzyska *see* Monastyrys'ka
175 C14 **Monastir** NE Tunisia Africa *35°46′N 10°49′E*
Monastir *see* Bitola
Monastyriska *see* Monastyrys'ka
191 I9 **Monastyrshchina** Smolenskaya Oblast', Russian Federation
188 G5 **Monastyryshche** Cherkas'ka Oblast', C Ukraine *48°59′N 29°47′E*
188 D4 **Monastyrys'ka** *Pol.* Monasterzyska, *Rus.* Monastyriska. Ternopil's'ka Oblast', W Ukraine *49°05′N 25°10′E*
134 B6 **Monatélé** Centre, SW Cameroon *04°16′N 11°12′E*
252 F3 **Monbetsu** *var.* Mombetsu, Monbetu. Hokkaidō, NE Japan *44°23′N 143°22′E*
Monbetu *see* Monbetsu
176 D7 **Moncalieri** Piemonte, NW Italy *45°N 07°41′E*
170 C3 **Monção** Viana do Castelo, N Portugal *42°03′N 08°29′W*
172 G2 **Moncayo** ▲ N Spain *41°43′N 01°51′W*
171 H3 **Moncayo, Sierra del** ▲ N Spain
168 B9 **Moncayo, Sierra del** ▲ Spain
167 L5 **Moncel-sur-Seille** Lorraine, France *48°46′N 6°25′E*
194 E3 **Monchegorsk** Murmanskaya Oblast', NW Russian Federation *67°56′N 32°47′E*
181 B9 **Mönchengladbach** *prev.* München-Gladbach. Nordrhein-Westfalen, W Germany *51°12′N 06°35′E*
172 B7 **Monchique** Faro, S Portugal *37°19′N 08°33′W*
170 C8 **Monchique, Serra de** ▲ S Portugal
172 B8 **Monchique, Serra de** ▲ Faro, Portugal
67 J9 **Moncks Corner** South Carolina, SE USA *33°12′N 80°00′W*
168 F5 **Monclar-de-Quercy** Midi-Pyrénées, France *43°58′N 1°35′E*
85 K5 **Monclova** Coahuila, NE Mexico *26°55′N 101°25′W*
166 B6 **Moncontour** Bretagne, France *48°21′N 2°39′W*
166 D9 **Moncontour** Poitou-Charentes, France *46°53′N 0°01′W*
Moncorvo *see* Torre de Moncorvo
166 D9 **Moncoutant** Poitou-Charentes, France *46°43′N 0°35′W*
63 N2 **Moncton** New Brunswick, SE Canada *46°04′N 64°50′W*
170 C5 **Mondego, Cabo** *headland* N Portugal *40°10′N 08°58′W*
172 B3 **Mondego, Rio** ⛐ N Portugal
141 K5 **Mondlo** Kwazulu Natal, South Africa *27°59′S 30°43′E*
170 D1 **Mondoñedo** Galicia, NW Spain *43°25′N 07°22′W*
163 H14 **Mondorf-les-Bains** Grevenmacher, SE Luxembourg *49°30′N 06°16′E*
164 G4 **Mondoubleau** Loir-et-Cher, C France *48°00′N 00°49′E*
176 D8 **Mondovì** Piemonte, NW Italy *44°23′N 07°56′E*
72 A6 **Mondovi** Wisconsin, N USA *44°34′N 91°40′W*
169 J4 **Mondragon** Provence-Alpes-Côte d'Azur, France *44°14′N 4°43′E*
168 A6 **Mondragón** País Vasco, Spain *43°04′N 2°29′W*
Mondragón *see* Arrasate
175 F9 **Mondragone** Campania, S Italy *41°07′N 13°53′E*
174 F2 **Mondsee** ◎ N Austria
193 H8 **Mondy** Respublika Buryatiya, S Russian Federation *51°41′N 101°03′E*
168 D6 **Monein** Aquitaine, France *43°20′N 0°35′W*
186 H7 **Monemvasiá** *var.* Monemvasía. Pelopónnisos, S Greece *36°22′N 23°03′E*
252 E1 **Moneron, Ostrov** *island* SE Russian Federation
169 N4 **Monesiglio** Piemonte, NW Italy *44°27′N 08°07′E*
62 C9 **Monessen** Pennsylvania, NE USA *40°07′N 79°51′W*
170 E7 **Monesterio** *var.* Monasterio. Extremadura, W Spain *38°05′N 06°16′W*
169 K3 **Monestier-de-Clermont** Rhône-Alpes, France *44°54′N 5°38′E*
168 G5 **Monestiés** Midi-Pyrénées, France *44°04′N 2°06′E*
75 G11 **Monett** Missouri, C USA *36°55′N 93°55′W*
66 A6 **Monette** Arkansas, C USA *35°53′N 90°20′W*
62 C2 **Monetville** Ontario, S Canada *46°08′N 80°24′W*
162 B6 **Moneymore** United Kingdom *54°42′N 6°41′W*
177 J6 **Monfalcone** Friuli-Venezia Giulia, NE Italy *45°49′N 13°32′E*
172 D5 **Monforte** Portalegre, C Portugal *39°03′N 07°26′W*
170 D2 **Monforte de Lemos** Galicia, NW Spain *42°32′N 07°30′W*
134 G6 **Monga** Orientale, N Dem. Rep. Congo *04°12′N 22°49′E*
137 E11 **Monga** Lindi, SE Tanzania *09°05′S 37°51′E*
110 D10 **Mongaguá** São Paulo, Brazil *24°06′S 46°37′W*
136 B6 **Mongalla** Central Equatoria, S South Sudan *05°12′N 31°42′E*
233 K6 **Mongar** E Bhutan *27°16′N 91°07′E*
256 I4 **Mong Cai** *var.* Hai Ninh. Quang Ninh, N Vietnam *21°33′N 107°56′E*
274 D6 **Mongers Lake** *salt lake* Western Australia
281 H1 **Mongga** Kolombangara, NW Solomon Islands *07°51′S 157°00′E*
256 E5 **Möng Hpayak** Shan State, E Myanmar (Burma) *20°56′N 100°00′E*
Monghyr *see* Munger
174 B5 **Mongioie** ▲ NW Italy *44°13′N 07°46′E*
256 D8 **Möng Küng** Shan State, E Myanmar (Burma) *21°39′N 97°31′E*
233 K8 **Mongla** *var.* Mungla. Khulna, S Bangladesh *22°18′N 89°34′E*
282 B2 **Mongmong** C Guam
256 D5 **Möng Nai** Shan State, E Myanmar (Burma) *20°28′N 97°51′E*
134 E2 **Mongo** Guéra, C Chad *12°12′N 18°40′E*
132 C6 **Mongo** ⛐ N Sierra Leone
236 F3 **Mongolia** *Mong.* Mongol Uls. ◆ *republic* E Asia
205 L5 **Mongolia, Plateau of** *plateau* E Mongolia
Mongolküre *see* Zhaosu
Mongol Uls *see* Mongolia
134 B7 **Mongomo** E Equatorial Guinea *01°39′N 11°18′E*
246 G4 **Mönggönmorit** *var.* Bulag. Töv, C Mongolia *48°09′N 108°33′E*
133 M5 **Mongonu** *var.* Monguno. Borno, NE Nigeria *12°42′N 13°37′E*
Mongora *see* Saidu
134 G2 **Mongororo** Ouaddaï, SE Chad *12°03′N 22°26′E*
Mongos, Chaîne des *see* Bongo, Massif des
134 E6 **Mongoumba** Lobaye, SW Central African Republic *03°39′N 18°30′E*
Mongrove, Punta *see* Cayacal, Punta
138 E2 **Mongu** Western, W Zambia *15°13′S 23°09′E*
132 C3 **Mônguel** Gorgol, SW Mauritania *16°25′N 13°08′W*
Monguno *see* Mongonu
256 E4 **Möng Yai** Shan State, E Myanmar (Burma) *22°25′N 98°02′E*
256 E4 **Möng Yang** Shan State, E Myanmar (Burma) *21°52′N 99°31′E*
256 D3 **Möng Yu** Shan State, E Myanmar (Burma) *24°00′N 97°57′E*
Mönhbulag *see* Yösöndzüyl
181 C9 **Monheim** Nordrhein-Westfalen, Germany *51°05′E 6°53′N*
239 M1 **Mönhhaan** *var.* Bayasgalant. Sühbaatar, E Mongolia *46°55′N 112°11′E*
239 H2 **Mönhhayrhan** *var.* Tsenher. Hovd, W Mongolia *47°07′N 92°04′E*
280 C4 **Moni** ⛐ S Papau New Guinea
159 H5 **Moniaive** United Kingdom *55°11′N 3°55′W*
159 I2 **Monifieth** United Kingdom *56°29′N 2°49′W*
114 A2 **Monigotes** Santa Fe, Argentina *30°30′S 61°39′W*
159 I1 **Monikie** United Kingdom *56°32′N 2°49′W*
187 I3 **Moní Megístis Lávras** *monastery* Kentrikí Makedonía, N Greece
102 C5 **Moniquirá** Boyacá, C Colombia *05°54′N 73°35′W*
165 I7 **Monistrol-sur-Loire** Haute-Loire, C France *45°19′N 04°12′E*
80 J4 **Monitor Range** ▲ Nevada, W USA
187 I3 **Moní Vatopedíou** *monastery* Kentrikí Makedonía, N Greece
114 B5 **Monje** Santa Fe, Argentina *32°24′S 60°54′W*
263 N9 **Monkayo** Mindanao, S Philippines *07°45′N 125°58′E*
Monkchester *see* Newcastle upon Tyne
137 C13 **Monkey Bay** Southern, SE Malawi *14°09′S 34°53′E*
89 H7 **Monkey Point** *var.* Punta Mico, Punte Mono, Punto Mico. *headland* SE Nicaragua *11°37′N 83°39′W*
Monkey River *see* Monkey River Town
88 E2 **Monkey River Town** *var.* Monkey River. Toledo, SE Belize *16°22′N 88°29′W*
62 G3 **Monkland** Ontario, SE Canada *45°11′N 74°51′W*
135 F8 **Monkoto** Equateur, NW Dem. Rep. Congo *01°39′S 20°41′E*
160 G5 **Monmouth** *Wel.* Trefynwy. SE Wales, United Kingdom *51°50′N 02°43′W*
73 B9 **Monmouth** Illinois, N USA *40°54′N 90°39′W*
76 B6 **Monmouth** Oregon, NW USA *44°51′N 123°13′W*
157 G11 **Monmouth** *cultural region* SE Wales, United Kingdom
166 F8 **Monnaie** Centre, France *47°30′N 0°46′E*
165 H3 **Monnerville** Essonne, N France *48°20′N 02°03′E*
162 F5 **Monnickendam** Noord-Holland, C Netherlands *52°28′N 05°02′E*
133 H7 **Mono** ⛐ C Togo
Monoecus *see* Monaco
80 F5 **Mono Hot Springs** California, USA *37°20′N 119°01′W*
80 F4 **Mono Lake** ◎ California, W USA
81 E9 **Monolith** California, USA *35°07′N 118°22′W*
187 L8 **Monólithos** Ródos, Dodekánisa, Greece, Aegean Sea *36°08′N 27°45′E*
65 N4 **Monomoy Island** *island* Massachusetts, NE USA
73 E10 **Monon** Indiana, N USA *40°52′N 86°54′W*
72 B7 **Monona** Iowa, C USA *43°03′N 91°23′W*
72 C8 **Monona** Wisconsin, N USA *43°03′N 89°18′W*
72 C9 **Monongahela** Pennsylvania, NE USA *40°10′N 79°54′W*
62 C9 **Monongahela River** ⛐ NE USA
175 I9 **Monopoli** Puglia, SE Italy *40°57′N 17°18′E*
Mono, Punte *see* Monkey Point
183 G11 **Monor** Pest, C Hungary *47°21′N 19°27′E*
Monostor *see* Beli Manastir
134 F1 **Monou** Borkou-Ennedi-Tibesti, NE Chad *16°22′N 22°15′E*
131 H1 **Monóvar** *Cat.* Monòver. País Valenciano, E Spain *38°26′N 00°50′W*
Monòver *see* Monóvar
168 F3 **Monpazier** Aquitaine, France *44°41′N 0°54′E*
171 I4 **Monreal del Campo** Aragón, NE Spain *40°47′N 01°20′W*
175 F12 **Monreale** Sicilia, Italy, C Mediterranean Sea *38°05′N 13°17′E*
158 G6 **Monreith** United Kingdom *54°44′N 4°33′W*
66 G8 **Monroe** Georgia, SE USA *33°47′N 83°42′W*
74 H7 **Monroe** Iowa, C USA *41°31′N 93°06′W*
68 C2 **Monroe** Louisiana, S USA *32°32′N 92°06′W*
73 H9 **Monroe** Michigan, N USA *41°55′N 83°24′W*
65 H5 **Monroe** New York, NE USA *41°18′N 74°09′W*
67 I7 **Monroe** North Carolina, SE USA *35°00′N 80°35′W*
79 H4 **Monroe** Utah, W USA *38°37′N 112°07′W*
76 C3 **Monroe** Washington, NW USA *47°51′N 121°58′W*
73 C8 **Monroe** Wisconsin, N USA *42°35′N 89°39′W*
75 I9 **Monroe City** Missouri, C USA *39°39′N 91°43′W*
73 E11 **Monroe Lake** ⊠ Indiana, N USA
68 G3 **Monroeville** Alabama, S USA *31°31′N 87°19′W*
62 C8 **Monroeville** Pennsylvania, NE USA *40°24′N 79°44′W*
132 D8 **Monrovia** ● (Liberia) W Liberia *06°18′N 10°48′W*
132 D8 **Monrovia** ✈ W Liberia *06°22′N 10°50′W*
171 I4 **Monroyo** Aragón, NE Spain *40°47′N 00°03′W*
163 D11 **Mons** *Dut.* Bergen. Hainaut, S Belgium *50°28′N 03°58′E*
172 D3 **Monsanto** Castelo Branco, C Portugal *40°02′N 07°07′W*
177 H7 **Monselice** Veneto, NE Italy *45°15′N 11°47′E*
110 F6 **Monsenhor Paulo** Minas Gerais, Brazil *21°46′S 45°33′W*
84 E6 **Monserrat, Isla** *island* Baja California Sur, NW Mexico
65 H5 **Monsey** New York, USA *41°07′N 74°04′W*
167 J10 **Monsols** Rhône-Alpes, France *46°13′N 4°31′E*
64 K3 **Monson** Massachusetts, NE USA *42°06′N 72°19′W*
256 D7 **Mon State** ◆ *state* S Myanmar (Burma)
162 D7 **Monster** Zuid-Holland, W Netherlands *52°01′N 04°10′E*
155 H10 **Mönsterås** Kalmar, S Sweden *57°03′N 16°27′E*
181 D10 **Montabaur** Rheinland-Pfalz, W Germany *50°25′N 07°48′E*
169 I6 **Montagnac** Languedoc-Roussillon, France *43°29′N 3°29′E*
177 H7 **Montagnana** Veneto, NE Italy *45°14′N 11°31′E*
169 I4 **Montagne de l'Aigoual** ▲ Languedoc-Roussillon, France *44°07′N 3°35′E*
84 C1 **Montagne, Isla** *island* Baja California Norte, NW Mexico
140 E9 **Montagu** Western Cape, South Africa *33°47′S 20°07′E*
78 B1 **Montague** California, W USA *41°43′N 122°31′W*
70 G3 **Montague** Texas, SW USA *33°40′N 97°44′W*
275 K8 **Montague Island** *island* New South Wales, SE Australia
83 J7 **Montague Island** *island* Alaska, USA
83 J7 **Montague Strait** *strait* N Gulf of Alaska
140 F10 **Montagu Pass** *pass* Western Cape, South Africa
164 F5 **Montaigu** Vendée, NW France *46°58′N 01°18′W*
Montaigu *see* Scherpenheuvel
171 I4 **Montalbán** Aragón, NE Spain *40°49′N 00°48′W*
173 I3 **Montalbo** Castilla-La Manacha, Spain *39°52′N 2°41′W*
177 H10 **Montalcino** Toscana, C Italy *43°01′N 11°34′E*
170 D3 **Montalegre** Vila Real, N Portugal *41°49′N 07°48′W*
168 C2 **Montalivet-les-Bains** Aquitaine, France *45°23′N 1°09′W*
172 C7 **Montalvo** Beja, Portugal *37°46′N 7°32′W*
172 B6 **Montalvo** Setúbal, Portugal *38°24′N 8°38′W*
185 I5 **Montana** *prev.* Ferdinand, Mikhaylovgrad. Montana, NW Bulgaria *43°25′N 23°14′E*
176 D5 **Montana** Valais, SW Switzerland *46°23′N 07°29′E*
83 I6 **Montana** Alaska, USA *62°06′N 150°03′W*
185 I5 **Montana** ◆ *province* NW Bulgaria
77 M4 **Montana** *off.* State of Montana, *also known as* Mountain State, Treasure State. ◆ *state* NW USA
170 E6 **Montánchez** Extremadura, W Spain *39°15′N 06°07′W*
Montaña *see* La Montaña
172 C4 **Montargil** Portalegre, C Portugal *39°05′N 08°10′W*
170 C6 **Montargil, Barragem de** ⊠ C Portugal
165 I4 **Montargis** Loiret, C France *48°N 02°44′E*
168 F5 **Montastruc-la-Conseillère** Midi-Pyrénées, France *43°43′N 1°36′E*
165 H3 **Montataire** Oise, N France *49°16′N 02°24′E*
165 H8 **Montauban** Tarn-et-Garonne, S France *44°01′N 01°20′E*
166 C6 **Montauban-de-Bretagne** Bretagne, France *48°12′N 2°03′W*
65 K5 **Montauk** Long Island, New York, NE USA *41°01′N 71°58′W*
65 L5 **Montauk Point** *headland* Long Island, New York, NE USA *41°04′N 71°51′W*
165 J4 **Montbard** Côte d'Or, C France *47°35′N 04°25′E*
168 G4 **Montbazens** Midi-Pyrénées, France *44°29′N 2°14′E*
165 K4 **Montbéliard** Doubs, E France *47°31′N 06°49′E*
71 I7 **Mont Belvieu** Texas, SW USA *29°51′N 94°53′W*
167 L9 **Montbenoît** Franche-Comté, France *46°59′N 6°28′E*
171 J4 **Montblanc** *prev.* Montblanch. Cataluña, NE Spain *41°23′N 01°10′E*
168 F10 **Montblanch** Cataluña, Spain *41°22′N 1°10′E*
Montblanch *see* Montblanc
167 L8 **Montbozon** Franche-Comté, France *47°28′N 6°16′E*
169 I2 **Montbrison** Loire, E France *45°37′N 04°04′E*
168 E2 **Montbron** Poitou-Charentes, France *45°40′N 0°30′E*
Montcalm, Lake *see* Dogai Coring
165 I5 **Montceau-les-Mines** Saône-et-Loire, C France *46°40′N 04°19′E*
169 M2 **Mont Cenis, Col du** *pass* E France
167 I9 **Montchanin** Bourgogne, France *46°45′N 4°27′E*
167 J9 **Montcornet** Picardie, France *49°41′N 4°01′E*
168 F4 **Montcuq** Midi-Pyrénées, France *44°20′N 1°13′E*
169 M3 **Mont-Dauphin** Provence-Alpes-Côte d'Azur, France *44°40′N 6°37′E*
164 F8 **Mont-de-Marsan** Landes, SW France *43°54′N 00°30′W*
165 H2 **Montdidier** Somme, N France *49°39′N 02°35′E*
280 C10 **Mont-Dore** Province Sud, S New Caledonia *22°18′S 166°34′E*
66 E7 **Monteagle** Tennessee, S USA *35°15′N 85°47′W*
112 D2 **Monteagudo** Chuquisaca, S Bolivia *19°48′S 63°57′W*
168 B8 **Monteagudo** Navarra, Spain *41°58′N 1°41′W*
168 B9 **Monteagudo de las Vicarías** Castilla y León, Spain *41°22′N 2°10′W*
86 G8 **Monte Albán** *ruins* Oaxaca, S Mexico
171 H6 **Montealegre del Castillo** Castilla-La Mancha, C Spain *38°48′N 01°18′W*
110 A5 **Monte Alto** São Paulo, Brazil *21°17′S 48°29′W*
109 F9 **Monte Azul** Minas Gerais, SE Brazil *15°13′S 42°53′W*
63 G3 **Montebello** Québec, SE Canada *45°40′N 74°56′W*
177 H6 **Montebelluna** Veneto, NE Italy *45°46′N 12°03′E*
110 D5 **Monte Belo** Minas Gerais, Brazil *21°20′S 46°23′W*
166 C4 **Montebourg** Basse-Normandie, France *49°29′N 1°23′W*
113 H5 **Montecarlo** Misiones, NE Argentina *26°38′S 54°45′W*
110 B1 **Monte Carmelo** Minas Gerais, Brazil *18°43′S 47°29′W*
114 F2 **Monte Caseros** Corrientes, NE Argentina *30°15′S 57°39′W*
113 J5 **Monte Castelo** Santa Catarina, S Brazil *26°34′S 50°12′W*
176 G9 **Montecatini Terme** Toscana, C Italy *43°53′N 10°46′E*
141 I2 **Monte Christo** Limpopo, South Africa *23°52′S 29°55′E*
88 E4 **Montecillos, Cordillera de** ▲ W Honduras
118 G5 **Monte Comén** Mendoza, W Argentina *34°35′S 67°53′W*
91 H5 **Monte Cristi** *var.* San Fernando de Monte Cristi. NW Dominican Republic *19°52′N 71°39′W*
106 C3 **Monte Cristo** Amazonas, W Brazil *03°14′S 68°00′W*
175 D8 **Montecristo, Isola di** *island* Archipelago Toscano, C Italy
80 H5 **Monte Cristo Range** ▲ Nevada, USA
Monte Croce Carnico, Passo di *see* Plöcken Pass
107 K2 **Monte Dourado** Pará, NE Brazil *0°48′S 52°32′W*
85 J9 **Monte Escobedo** Zacatecas, C Mexico *22°19′N 103°30′W*
177 I10 **Montefalco** Umbria, C Italy *42°54′N 12°40′E*
175 E8 **Montefiascone** Lazio, C Italy *42°33′N 12°01′E*
170 F8 **Montefrío** Andalucía, S Spain *37°19′N 04°00′W*
90 E7 **Montego Bay** *var.* Mobay. W Jamaica *18°28′N 77°55′W*
Montego Bay *see* Sangster
170 E5 **Montehermoso** Extremadura, W Spain *40°05′N 06°20′W*
110 E8 **Monteiro Lobato** São Paulo, Brazil *22°58′S 45°50′W*
170 C6 **Montejunto, Serra de** ▲ C Portugal *39°10′N 09°01′W*
Monteleone di Calabria *see* Vibo Valentia
102 B4 **Montelíbano** Córdoba, NW Colombia *08°02′N 75°29′W*
165 J7 **Montélimar** *anc.* Acunum Acusio, Montilium Adhemari. Drôme, E France *44°33′N 04°45′E*
170 E8 **Montellano** Andalucía, S Spain *37°00′N 05°34′W*
78 G2 **Montello** Nevada, W USA *41°18′N 114°10′W*
72 C7 **Montello** Wisconsin, N USA *43°47′N 89°20′W*
117 E9 **Montemayor, Meseta de** *plain* SE Argentina
110 C8 **Monte Mor** São Paulo, Brazil *22°57′S 47°20′W*
85 L7 **Montemorelos** Nuevo León, NE Mexico *25°10′N 99°52′W*
172 C5 **Montemor-o-Novo** Évora, S Portugal *38°38′N 08°13′W*
172 B3 **Montemor-o-Velho** *var.* Montemor-o-Vélho. Coimbra, N Portugal *40°11′N 08°41′W*
Montemor-o-Vélho *see* Montemor-o-Velho
170 D4 **Montemuro, Serra de** ▲ N Portugal *40°59′N 07°59′W*
164 G7 **Montendre** Charente-Maritime, W France *45°17′N 00°24′W*
113 I7 **Montenegro** Rio Grande do Sul, S Brazil *29°40′S 51°32′W*
184 E7 **Montenegro** *Serb.* Crna Gora. ◆ *republic* SW Europe
116 B2 **Monte Patria** Coquimbo, N Chile *30°40′S 71°00′W*
91 I6 **Monte Plata** E Dominican Republic *18°50′N 69°47′W*
137 E13 **Montepuez** Cabo Delgado, N Mozambique *13°09′S 39°00′E*
137 E13 **Montepuez** ⛐ N Mozambique
177 H10 **Montepulciano** Toscana, C Italy *43°02′N 11°51′E*
112 E5 **Monte Quemado** Santiago del Estero, N Argentina *25°48′S 62°52′W*
165 I3 **Montereau-Faut-Yonne** *anc.* Condate. Seine-St-Denis, N France *48°23′N 02°57′E*
172 B3 **Monte Redondo** Leiria, Portugal *39°54′N 8°50′W*
80 A4 **Monterey** California, W USA *36°36′N 121°53′W*
66 E6 **Monterey** Tennessee, S USA *36°09′N 85°16′W*
67 J3 **Monterey** Virginia, NE USA *38°24′N 79°36′W*
Monterey *see* Monterrey
80 A4 **Monterey Bay** *bay* California, W USA
102 B3 **Montería** Córdoba, NW Colombia *08°45′N 75°54′W*
106 F10 **Montero** Santa Cruz, C Bolivia *17°20′S 63°15′W*
112 D6 **Monteros** Tucumán, C Argentina *27°12′S 65°30′W*
170 D3 **Monterrei** Galicia, NW Spain *41°56′N 07°27′W*
85 L6 **Monterrey** *var.* Monterey. Nuevo León, NE Mexico *25°41′N 100°16′W*
172 B4 **Montes** Leiria, Portugal *39°37′N 8°57′W*
115 I9 **Montes** Canelones, Uruguay *34°24′S 55°30′W*
76 B4 **Montesano** Washington, NW USA *46°58′N 123°37′W*
175 H10 **Montesano sulla Marcellana** Campania, S Italy *40°15′N 15°41′E*
175 H8 **Monte Sant' Angelo** Puglia, SE Italy *41°43′N 15°58′E*
108 G7 **Monte Santo** Bahia, E Brazil *10°25′S 39°18′W*
175 C10 **Monte Santu, Capo di** *headland* Sardegna, Italy, C Mediterranean Sea *40°05′N 09°43′E*
109 E10 **Montes Claros** Minas Gerais, SE Brazil *16°45′S 43°52′W*
114 A6 **Montes de Oca** Santa Fe, Argentina *32°35′S 61°46′W*
110 D7 **Monte Sião** Minas Gerais, Brazil *22°26′S 46°34′W*
184 A6 **Montesilvano Marina** Abruzzo, C Italy *42°28′N 14°07′E*
168 F6 **Montesquieu-Volvestre** Midi-Pyrénées, France *43°13′N 1°14′E*
168 E5 **Montestruc-sur-Gers** Midi-Pyrénées, France *43°48′N 0°37′E*
66 D9 **Montevallo** Alabama, S USA *33°06′N 86°51′W*
177 H10 **Montevarchi** Toscana, C Italy *43°32′N 11°34′E*
114 B4 **Monte Vera** Santa Fe, Argentina *31°31′S 60°40′W*
115 H10 **Montevideo** ● (Uruguay) Montevideo, S Uruguay *34°55′S 56°10′W*
74 F5 **Montevideo** Minnesota, N USA *44°56′N 95°43′W*
79 L5 **Monte Vista** Colorado, C USA *37°33′N 106°08′W*
69 J2 **Montezuma** Georgia, SE USA *32°18′N 84°01′W*
74 H7 **Montezuma** Iowa, C USA *41°35′N 92°31′W*
75 C10 **Montezuma** Kansas, C USA *37°33′N 100°25′W*
80 H5 **Montezuma Peak** ▲ Nevada, USA *37°42′N 117°22′W*
169 J2 **Montfaucon** Auvergne, France *45°10′N 4°18′E*
167 K4 **Montfaucon-d'Argonne** Lorraine, France *49°17′N 5°08′E*
168 C5 **Montfort-en-Chalosse** Aquitaine, France *43°43′N 0°50′W*
166 G5 **Montfort-l'Amaury** Yvelines, N France *48°46′N 01°48′E*
166 C6 **Montfort-sur-Meu** Bretagne, France *48°08′N 1°58′W*
169 M3 **Montgenèvre** Provence-Alpes-Côte d'Azur, France *44°56′N 6°43′E*
169 M3 **Montgenèvre, Col de** *pass* France/Italy
167 H5 **Montgeron** Île-de-France, France *48°42′N 02°27′E*
168 F6 **Montgiscard** Midi-Pyrénées, France *43°27′N 1°35′E*
160 G3 **Montgomery** E Wales, United Kingdom *52°38′N 03°05′W*
69 H2 **Montgomery** *state capital* Alabama, S USA *32°22′N 86°18′W*
74 G5 **Montgomery** Minnesota, N USA *44°26′N 93°34′W*
64 D5 **Montgomery** Pennsylvania, NE USA *41°08′N 76°52′W*
67 I3 **Montgomery** West Virginia, NE USA *38°07′N 81°19′W*
157 F10 **Montgomery** *cultural region* E Wales, United Kingdom
Montgomery *see* Sāhīwāl
75 I9 **Montgomery City** Missouri, C USA *38°57′N 91°27′W*
80 G5 **Montgomery Pass** *pass* Nevada, W USA
164 G7 **Montguyon** Charente-Maritime, W France *45°12′N 00°13′W*
167 J3 **Monthermé** Champagne-Ardenne, France *49°53′N 4°44′E*
176 C5 **Monthey** Valais, SW Switzerland *46°15′N 06°56′E*
167 J4 **Monthois** Champagne-Ardenne, France *49°19′N 4°43′E*
75 I14 **Monticello** Arkansas, C USA *33°38′N 91°49′W*
69 J4 **Monticello** Florida, SE USA *30°33′N 83°52′W*
66 G9 **Monticello** Georgia, SE USA *33°18′N 83°40′W*
73 D10 **Monticello** Illinois, N USA *40°01′N 88°34′W*
73 E10 **Monticello** Indiana, N USA *40°45′N 86°46′W*
74 I7 **Monticello** Iowa, C USA *42°14′N 91°11′W*
66 F5 **Monticello** Kentucky, S USA *36°50′N 84°50′W*
74 G4 **Monticello** Minnesota, N USA *45°19′N 93°45′W*
68 E3 **Monticello** Mississippi, S USA *31°33′N 90°06′W*

◆ Country
● Country Capital
◇ Dependent Territory
○ Dependent Territory Capital
◆ Administrative Regions
✈ International Airport
▲ Mountain
▲ Mountain Range
⛰ Volcano
⛐ River
◎ Lake
⊠ Reservoir

INDEX

◆ Country	◇ Dependent Territory	◈ Administrative Regions	▲ Mountain	◭ Volcano	◉ Lake
● Country Capital	○ Dependent Territory Capital	✕ International Airport	▲ Mountain Range	◀ River	▤ Reservoir

◆ Country
◆ Country Capital
○ Dependent Territory
○ Dependent Territory Capital
✕ Administrative Regions
✕ International Airport
▲ Mountain
▲ Mountain Range
▲ Volcano
✍ River
☺ Lake
☐ Reservoir

Narasaraopet - Neuenburg an der Elbe
INDEX
381

234 F6 **Narasaraopet** Andhra Pradesh, E India 16°16′N 80°06′E
238 E3 **Narat** Xinjiang Uygur Zizhiqu, W China 43°20′N 84°02′E
257 F11 **Narathiwat** *var.* Naradhivas. Narathiwat, SW Thailand 06°25′N 101°48′E
79 N6 **Nara Visa** New Mexico, SW USA 35°35′N 103°06′W
Nārāyāni *see* Gandak
Narbada *see* Narmada
Narbo Martius *see* Narbonne
165 I9 **Narbonne** *anc.* Narbo Martius. Aude, S France 43°11′N 03°E
169 H6 **Narbonne-Plage** Languedoc-Roussillon, France 43°10′N 3°10′E
161 I3 **Narborough** United Kingdom 52°34′N 1°12′W
Narborough Island *see* Fernandina, Isla
170 E1 **Narcea** ≈ NW Spain
114 B3 **Naré** Santa Fe, Argentina 30°58′S 60°28′W
232 F4 **Narendranagar** Uttarakhand, N India 30°10′N 78°21′E
Nares Abyssal Plain *see* Nares Plain
290 D6 **Nares Plain** *var.* Nares Abyssal Plain. *undersea feature* NW Atlantic Ocean 23°30′N 63°00′W
Nares Stræde *see* Nares Strait
295 I7 **Nares Strait** *Dan.* Nares Stræde. *strait* Canada/Greenland
182 I5 **Narew** ≈ E Poland
234 D6 **Nargund** Karnātaka, W India 15°43′N 75°23′E
140 C2 **Narib** Hardap, S Namibia 24°11′S 17°46′E
140 C7 **Nariep** Northern Cape, South Africa 30°46′S 17°44′E
Narikrik *see* Knox Atoll
158 B6 **Narin** Donegal, Ireland 54°50′N 8°28′W
Narin Gol *see* Dong He
102 A7 **Nariño** *off.* Departamento de Narino. ⬖ *province* SW Colombia
253 C13 **Narita** Chiba, Honshū, S Japan 35°46′N 140°20′E
253 C13 **Narita** ✈ (Tōkyō) Chiba, Honshū, S Japan 35°45′N 140°23′E
Narıya *see* An Nu'ayrīyah
246 C2 **Nariyn Gol** ≈ Mongolia/Russian Federation
239 J2 **Nariynteel** *var.* Tsagaan-Ovoo. Övörhangay, C Mongolia 45°57′N 101°25′E
232 F4 **Nārkanda** Himāchal Pradesh, NW India 31°14′N 77°27′E
152 H6 **Narkaus** Lappi, NW Finland 66°13′N 26°09′E
232 G8 **Narmada** *var.* Narbada. ≈ C India
232 E5 **Narnaul** *var.* Nārnaul. Haryāna, N India 28°04′N 76°10′E
175 F13 **Naro** Sicilia, Italy, C Mediterranean Sea 37°18′N 13°48′E
Narodichi *see* Narodychi
195 L5 **Narodnaya, Gora** ▲ NW Russian Federation 65°04′N 60°12′E
188 G2 **Narodychi** *Rus.* Narodichi. Zhytomyrs'ka Oblast', N Ukraine 51°11′N 29°01′E
196 F2 **Naro-Fominsk** Moskovskaya Oblast', W Russian Federation 55°25′N 36°41′E
137 D8 **Narok** Rift Valley, SW Kenya 01°04′S 35°54′E
170 D1 **Narón** Galicia, NW Spain 43°31′N 08°08′W
277 L6 **Narooma** New South Wales, SE Australia 36°16′S 150°08′E
Narova *see* Narva
Narovlya *see* Narowlya
231 J5 **Nārowāl** Punjab, E Pakistan 32°04′N 74°54′E
191 H12 **Narowlya** *Rus.* Narovlya. Homyel'skaya Voblasts', SE Belarus 51°48′N 29°30′E
153 G8 **Närpes** *Fin.* Närpiö. Länsi-Suomi, W Finland 62°28′N 21°19′E
Närpiö *see* Närpes
277 L3 **Narrabri** New South Wales, SE Australia 30°21′S 149°48′E
65 L4 **Narragansett Pier** Rhode Island, USA 41°26′N 71°27′W
277 J5 **Narrandera** New South Wales, SE Australia 34°46′S 146°32′E
277 K3 **Narran Lake** ◎ New South Wales, SE Australia
274 D7 **Narrogin** Western Australia 32°53′S 117°17′E
277 K4 **Narromine** New South Wales, SE Australia 32°16′S 148°15′E
67 I4 **Narrows** Virginia, NE USA 37°19′N 80°48′W
64 G4 **Narrowsburg** New York, USA 41°37′N 75°04′W
295 M8 **Narsarsuaq** ✈ Kitaa, S Greenland 61°07′N 45°03′W
232 F8 **Narsimhapur** Madhya Pradesh, C India 22°58′N 79°15′E
233 K7 **Narsingdi** *var.* Narsinghdi. Dhaka, C Bangladesh 23°56′N 90°40′E
Narsinghdi *see* Narsingdi
232 E8 **Narsinghgarh** Madhya Pradesh, C India 23°42′N 77°08′E
239 N2 **Nart** Nei Mongol Zizhiqu, N China 42°54′N 115°55′E
Nartës, Gjol i/Nartës, Laguna e *see* Nartës, Liqeni i
184 E9 **Nartës, Liqeni i** *var.* Gjol i Nartës, Laguna e Nartës. ◎ SW Albania
186 G5 **Nartháki** ▲ C Greece 39°12′N 22°24′E
197 H9 **Nartkala** Kabardino-Balkarskaya Respublika, SW Russian Federation 43°34′N 43°55′E
140 D4 **Narubis** Karas, Namibia 26°58′S 18°36′E
250 G5 **Naruto** Tokushima, Shikoku, SW Japan 34°11′N 134°37′E
194 C8 **Narva** Ida-Virumaa, NE Estonia 59°23′N 28°12′E
190 F4 **Narva** *prev.* Narova. ≈ Estonia/Russian Federation
190 F3 **Narva Bay** *Est.* Narva Laht, *Ger.* Narwa-Bucht, *Rus.* Narvskiy Zaliv. *bay* Estonia/Russian Federation
Narva Laht *see* Narva Bay
194 C8 **Narva Reservoir** *Est.* Narva Veehoidla, *Rus.* Narvskoye Vodokhranilishche. ⊠ Estonia/Russian Federation
Narva Veehoidla *see* Narva Reservoir
152 F4 **Narvik** Nordland, C Norway 68°26′N 17°24′E
Narvskiy Zaliv *see* Narva Bay
Narvskoye Vodokhranilishche *see* Narva Reservoir
Narwa-Bucht *see* Narva Bay
232 E4 **Narwāna** Haryāna, NW India 29°36′N 76°11′E
195 J3 **Nar'yan-Mar** *prev.* Beloshchel'ye, Dzerzhinskiy. Nenetskiy Avtonomnyy Okrug, NW Russian Federation 67°38′N 53°E
192 F6 **Narym** Tomskaya Oblast', C Russian Federation 58°59′N 81°20′E
Narymskiy Khrebet *see* Khrebet Naryn
229 L5 **Naryn** Narynskaya Oblast', C Kyrgyzstan 41°24′N 76°E
229 K5 **Naryn** ≈ Kyrgyzstan/Uzbekistan
238 D3 **Narynkol** *Kaz.* Narynqol. Almaty, SE Kazakhstan 42°45′N 80°12′E
Naryn Oblasty *see* Narynskaya Oblast'
Narynqol *see* Narynkol
229 L5 **Narynskaya Oblast'** *Kir.* Naryn Oblasty. ⬖ *province* C Kyrgyzstan
Naryn Zhotasy *see* Khrebet Naryn
196 F3 **Naryshkino** Orlovskaya Oblast', W Russian Federation 53°00′N 35°41′E
169 N3 **Narzole** Piemonte, NW Italy 44°35′N 07°52′E
154 G7 **Nås** Dalarna, C Sweden 60°28′N 14°30′E
56 B2 **Nass** ≈ British Columbia, SW Canada
152 E6 **Nasafjellet** *Lapp.* Násávárre. ▲ C Norway 66°29′N 15°23′E
154 H3 **Näsåker** Västernorrland, C Sweden 63°27′N 16°55′E
61 M9 **Nassau** ● (Bahamas) New Providence, N Bahamas 25°03′N 77°21′W
280 F8 **Nasau** Koro, C Fiji 17°20′S 179°26′E
181 D11 **Nassau** Rheinland-Pfalz, Germany 50°19′E 7°48′N
284 F5 **Nassau** *island* N Cook Islands
188 D6 **Năsăud** *Ger.* Nussdorf, *Hung.* Naszód. Bistriţa-Năsăud, N Romania 47°16′N 24°24′E
Násávárre *see* Nasafjellet
169 H3 **Nasbinals** Lozère, S France 44°40′N 03°03′E
Na Sceirí *see* Skerries
Nase *see* Naze
278 D11 **Naseby** Otago, South Island, New Zealand 45°02′S 170°09′E
161 J4 **Naseby** United Kingdom 52°23′N 0°59′W
223 H7 **Nāşerīyeh** Kermān, C Iran
75 G14 **Nash** Texas, SW USA 33°26′N 94°04′W
234 C4 **Nāshik** *prev.* Nāsik. Mahārāshtra, W India 20°05′N 73°48′E
104 E2 **Nashiño, Río** ≈ Ecuador/Peru
72 A7 **Nashua** Iowa, C USA 42°57′N 92°32′W
77 L3 **Nashua** Montana, NW USA 48°06′N 106°16′W
65 L1 **Nashua** New Hampshire, NE USA 42°45′N 71°26′W
75 G13 **Nashville** Arkansas, C USA 33°57′N 93°50′W
69 K3 **Nashville** Georgia, SE USA 31°12′N 83°15′W
73 C12 **Nashville** Illinois, N USA 38°20′N 89°22′W
73 F11 **Nashville** Indiana, N USA 39°13′N 86°15′W
67 L6 **Nashville** North Carolina, SE USA 35°58′N 78°00′W
66 D6 **Nashville** *state capital* Tennessee, S USA 36°11′N 86°48′W
66 D6 **Nashville** ✈ Tennessee, S USA 36°06′N 86°44′W
290 D5 **Nashville Seamount** *undersea feature* NW Atlantic Ocean 30°00′N 57°20′W
184 E2 **Našice** Osijek-Baranja, E Croatia 45°29′N 18°05′E
182 H5 **Nasielsk** Mazowieckie, C Poland 52°33′N 20°46′E
153 H9 **Näsijärvi** ◎ SW Finland
Nāsik *see* Nāshik
136 B4 **Nasir** Upper Nile, NE South Sudan 08°37′N 33°06′E
230 G7 **Nasīrābād** Baluchistān, SW Pakistan 28°25′N 68°29′E
230 D9 **Nasirābād** Baluchistān, SW Pakistan 26°15′N 62°32′E
Nasir, Buhayrat/Nâşir, Buḩeiret *see* Nasser, Lake
Nāsiri *see* Ahvāz
Nasiriya *see* An Nāşirīyah
Nás na Ríogh *see* Naas
175 G12 **Naso** Sicilia, Italy, C Mediterranean Sea 38°07′N 14°46′E
Nasratabad *see* Zābol
133 K7 **Nassarawa** Nassarawa, C Nigeria 08°33′N 07°42′E
69 L4 **Nassau Sound** *sound* Florida, SE USA
176 G4 **Nassereith** Tirol, W Austria 47°19′N 10°51′E
129 J6 **Nasser, Lake** *var.* Buhayrat Nasir, Buḩayrat Nāşir, Buḩeiret Nâşir. ◎ Egypt/Sudan
155 G10 **Nässjö** Jönköping, S Sweden 57°39′N 14°40′E
163 F12 **Nassogne** Luxembourg, SE Belgium 50°08′N 05°19′E
58 G3 **Nastapoka Islands** *island group* Northwest Territories, C Canada
181 D11 **Nastätten** Rheinland-Pfalz, Germany 50°12′E 7°52′N
153 H9 **Nastola** Etelä-Suomi, S Finland 60°57′N 25°56′E
253 C11 **Nasu-dake** ▲ Honshū, S Japan 37°07′N 139°57′E
263 K5 **Nasugbu** Luzon, N Philippines 14°03′N 120°39′E
190 H5 **Nasva** Pskovskaya Oblast', Russian Federation
154 H5 **Näsviken** Gävleborg, C Sweden 61°46′N 16°55′E
Naszód *see* Năsăud
138 F4 **Nata** Central, NE Botswana 20°11′S 26°10′E
102 C6 **Natagaima** Tolima, C Colombia 03°38′N 75°07′W
108 J5 **Natal** *state capital* Rio Grande do Norte, E Brazil 05°46′S 35°15′W
258 C5 **Natal** Sumatera, N Indonesia 0°32′N 99°07′E
Natal *see* KwaZulu/Natal
289 B10 **Natal Basin** *var.* Mozambique Basin. *undersea feature* W Indian Ocean 30°00′S 40°00′E
70 F7 **Natalia** Texas, SW USA 29°11′N 98°51′W
195 L10 **Natal'insk** Sverdlovskaya Oblast', Russian Federation
54 C7 **Natalkuz Lake** ◎ British Columbia, SW Canada
121 M9 **Natal Valley** *undersea feature* SW Indian Ocean 31°00′S 33°15′E
Natanya *see* Netanya
222 F5 **Naţanz** Eşfahān, C Iran 33°31′N 51°55′E
59 K6 **Natashquan** Québec, E Canada 50°10′N 61°50′W
59 K6 **Natashquan** ≈ Newfoundland and Labrador/Québec, E Canada
68 D3 **Natchez** Mississippi, S USA 31°34′N 91°24′W
68 B2 **Natchitoches** Louisiana, S USA 31°45′N 93°05′W
110 E7 **Natércia** Minas Gerais, Brazil 22°07′S 45°30′W
167 N10 **Naters** Valais, S Switzerland 46°22′N 08°00′E
Nathanya *see* Netanya
152 B5 **Nathorst Land** *physical region* W Svalbard
Nathula *see* Nacula
280 B4 **National Capital District** ⬖ *province* S Papua New Guinea
81 E13 **National City** California, W USA 32°40′N 117°06′W
278 G6 **National Park** Manawatu-Wanganui, North Island, New Zealand 39°11′S 175°22′E
54 D6 **Nation River** ≈ British Columbia, SW Canada
133 H6 **Natitingou** NW Benin 10°21′N 01°26′E
55 L3 **Native Bay** *coastal sea feature* Nunavut, NE Canada
111 K5 **Natividade** Rio de Janeiro, Brazil 21°03′S 41°59′W
110 F9 **Natividade** São Paulo, Brazil 23°24′S 45°26′W
84 B5 **Natividad, Isla** *island* NW Mexico
219 G9 **Natl** Jordan 31°39′N 35°52′E
159 I7 **Natland** United Kingdom 54°17′N 2°44′W
84 G4 **Nàtora** Sonora, Mexico 28°56′N 108°39′W
253 D10 **Natori** Miyagi, Honshū, C Japan 38°12′N 140°51′E
62 C8 **Natrona Heights** Pennsylvania, NE USA 40°37′N 79°42′W
137 D9 **Natron, Lake** ◎ Kenya/Tanzania
Natsrat *see* Natzrat
256 C6 **Nattalin** Bago, C Myanmar (Burma) 18°25′N 95°34′E
152 G6 **Nattavaara** *Lapp.* Nahtavárr. Norrbotten, N Sweden 66°45′N 20°58′E
177 J2 **Natternbach** Oberösterreich, N Austria 48°26′N 13°44′E
155 H11 **Nättraby** Blekinge, S Sweden 56°12′N 15°30′E
258 G3 **Natuna Besar, Pulau** *island* Kepulauan Natuna, W Indonesia
Natuna Islands *see* Natuna, Kepulauan
258 G3 **Natuna, Kepulauan** *var.* Natuna Islands. *island group* W Indonesia
258 G4 **Natuna, Laut** *Eng.* Natuna Sea. *sea* W Indonesia
Natuna Sea *see* Natuna, Laut
66 G4 **Natural Bridge** *tourist site* Kentucky, C USA
289 I11 **Naturaliste Fracture Zone** *tectonic feature* E Indian Ocean
266 E6 **Naturaliste Plateau** *undersea feature* E Indian Ocean
218 E6 **Natzrat** *var.* Natsrat, *Ar.* En Nazira, *Eng.* Nazareth; *prev.* Nazerat. Northern, N Israel 32°42′N 35°18′E
Nau *see* Nov
165 H8 **Naucelle** Aveyron, S France 44°10′N 02°19′E
140 B2 **Nauchas** Hardap, C Namibia 23°40′S 16°19′E
176 G4 **Nauders** Tirol, W Austria 46°52′N 10°31′E
140 G8 **Naudesbergpas** *pass* Eastern Cape, South Africa
141 I7 **Naudesnek** *pass* Eastern Cape, South Africa
Naugard *see* Nowogard
65 J4 **Naugatuck** Connecticut, USA 41°29′N 73°03′W
190 D7 **Naujamiestis** Panevėžys, C Lithuania 55°42′N 24°10′E
190 C7 **Naujoji Akmenė** Šiaulai, NW Lithuania 56°20′N 22°57′E
231 H9 **Naukot** *var.* Naokot. Sind, SE Pakistan 24°52′N 69°27′E
181 G8 **Naumburg** Hessen, Germany 51°15′E 9°10′N
179 G8 **Naumburg** *var.* Naumburg an der Saale. Sachsen-Anhalt, C Germany 51°09′N 11°48′E
Naumburg am Queis *see* Nowogrodziec
Naumburg an der Saale *see* Naumburg
118 B1 **Naunau** *ancient monument* Easter Island, Chile, E Pacific Ocean
118 E9 **Naunauco** Neuquén, Argentina 37°37′S 70°11′W
219 F8 **Nā'ūr** 'Ammān, W Jordan 31°52′N 35°50′E
219 F8 **Nāūr** Jordan 31°53′N 35°50′E
181 E11 **Naurod** Hessen, Germany 50°08′E 8°18′N
283 J10 **Nauru** *off.* Republic of Nauru; *prev.* Pleasant Island. ◆ *republic* W Pacific Ocean
267 I4 **Nauru** *island* W Pacific Ocean
283 J10 **Nauru International** ✈ S Nauru
Nauru, Republic of *see* Nauru
Nausari *see* Navsāri
65 N4 **Nauset Beach** *beach* Massachusetts, NE USA
Naushahra *see* Nowshera
230 G8 **Naushahro Fīroz** Sind, SE Pakistan 26°51′N 68°11′E
Naushara *see* Nowshera
280 E9 **Nausori** Viti Levu, W Fiji 18°01′S 178°31′E
104 F4 **Nauta** Loreto, N Peru 04°31′S 73°36′W
233 H6 **Nautanwa** Uttar Pradesh, N India 27°26′N 83°25′E
86 G6 **Nautla** Veracruz-Llave, E Mexico 20°15′N 96°45′W
Nauzad *see* Now Zād
85 L4 **Nava** Coahuila, NE Mexico 28°28′N 100°45′W
Navabad *see* Navobod
172 F2 **Navacepeda de Tormes** Castilla y León, Spain 40°22′N 5°15′W
170 F4 **Nava del Rey** Castilla-León, N Spain 41°19′N 05°04′W
233 J8 **Navadwīp** *prev.* Nabadwip. West Bengal, NE India 23°24′N 88°23′E
280 F8 **Navaga** Koro, W Fiji 17°21′S 179°22′E
170 F5 **Navahermosa** Castilla-La Mancha, C Spain 39°39′N 04°25′W
191 E10 **Navahrudak** *Pol.* Nowogródek, *Rus.* Novogrudok. Hrodzyenskaya Voblasts', W Belarus 53°36′N 25°50′E
191 E10 **Navahrudskaye Wzvyshsha** ▲▲ W Belarus
79 I5 **Navajo Mount** ▲ Utah, W USA 37°00′N 110°52′W
79 K5 **Navajo Reservoir** ⊠ New Mexico, SW USA
263 M7 **Naval** Biliran Island, C Philippines 11°32′N 124°26′E
172 G1 **Navalmanzano** Castilla y León, Spain 41°13′N 4°15′W
170 E5 **Navalmoral de la Mata** Extremadura, W Spain 39°54′N 05°33′W
172 G2 **Navalperal de Pinares** Castilla y León, Spain 40°35′N 4°24′W
172 F5 **Navalvillar de Pela** Extremadura, Spain 39°06′N 5°28′W
170 E6 **Navalvillar de Pelea** Extremadura, W Spain 39°05′N 05°27′W
158 D9 **Navan** *Ir.* An Uaimh. E Ireland 53°39′N 06°41′W
Navanagar *see* Jāmnagar
191 G8 **Navapolatsk** *Rus.* Novopolotsk. Vitsyebskaya Voblasts', N Belarus 55°34′N 28°35′E
230 G4 **Nāvar, Dasht-e** *Pash.* Dasht-i-Nawar. *desert* C Afghanistan
193 N3 **Navarin, Mys** *headland* NE Russian Federation 62°18′N 179°06′E
117 D14 **Navarino, Isla** *island* S Chile
171 H2 **Navarra** *Eng./Fr.* Navarre. ⬖ *autonomous community* N Spain
Navarre *see* Navarra
168 D6 **Navarrenx** Aquitaine, France 43°20′N 0°45′W
171 H2 **Navarrete** La Rioja, N Spain 42°26′N 02°34′W
114 D10 **Navarro** Buenos Aires, E Argentina 35°00′S 59°15′W
168 C7 **Navascués** Navarra, Spain 42°43′N 1°07′W
172 D4 **Navas del Madroño** Extremadura, Spain 39°37′N 6°39′W
172 G1 **Navas de Oro** Castilla y León, Spain 41°12′N 4°26′W
170 G7 **Navas de San Juan** Andalucía, S Spain 38°11′N 03°19′W
172 D3 **Navasfrías** Castilla y León, Spain 40°18′N 6°49′W
71 H6 **Navasota** Texas, SW USA 30°23′N 96°05′W
71 H6 **Navasota River** ≈ Texas, SW USA
90 F6 **Navassa Island** ◇ *US unincorporated territory* C West Indies
191 G11 **Navasyolki** *Rus.* Novosëlki. Homyel'skaya Voblasts', SE Belarus 52°24′N 28°33′E
191 E10 **Navayel'nya** *Pol.* Nowojelnia, *Rus.* Novoyel'nya. Hrodzyenskaya Voblasts', W Belarus 53°28′N 25°35′E
172 D2 **Nave** Guarda, Portugal 40°24′N 6°58′W
159 M10 **Navenby** United Kingdom 53°06′N 0°31′W
261 L5 **Naver** Papua, E Indonesia 03°27′S 139°45′E
190 E4 **Navesti** ≈ C Estonia
170 E1 **Navia** Asturias, N Spain 43°33′N 06°43′W
170 E1 **Navia** ≈ NW Spain
113 I3 **Naviraí** Mato Grosso do Sul, SW Brazil 23°01′S 54°09′W
280 D8 **Naviti** *island* Yasawa Group, NW Fiji
196 E3 **Navlya** Bryanskaya Oblast', W Russian Federation 52°47′N 34°28′E
280 F8 **Navoalevu** Vanua Levu, N Fiji 16°22′S 179°28′E
229 J7 **Navobod** *Rus.* Navabad, Novabad. C Tajikistan 39°00′N 70°06′E
Navoi *see* Navoiy
228 G6 **Navoiy** *Rus.* Navoi. Navoiy Viloyati, C Uzbekistan 40°05′N 65°23′E
Navoiyskaya Oblast' *see* Navoiy Viloyati
228 G4 **Navoiy Viloyati** *Rus.* Navoiyskaya Oblast'. ⬖ *province* N Uzbekistan
84 F5 **Navojoa** Sonora, NW Mexico 27°04′N 109°28′W
Navolat *see* Navolato
84 G7 **Navolato** *var.* Navolat. Sinaloa, C Mexico 24°46′N 107°42′W
281 M2 **Navonda** Ambae, C Vanuatu 15°21′S 167°58′E
Návpaktos *see* Náfpaktos
Návplion *see* Náfplio
133 H6 **Navrongo** N Ghana 10°51′N 01°03′W
232 C9 **Navsāri** *var.* Nausari. Gujarāt, W India 20°55′N 72°55′E
280 E9 **Navua** Viti Levu, W Fiji 18°15′S 178°10′E
53 I5 **Navy Board Inlet** *coastal sea feature* Nunavut, NE Canada
218 G5 **Nawá** Dar'ā, S Syria 32°53′N 36°03′E
218 G5 **Nawá** Syria 32°53′N 36°03′E
Nawabashah *see* Nawābshāh
233 J7 **Nawabganj** Rajshahi, NW Bangladesh 24°35′N 88°21′E
232 G6 **Nawābganj** Uttar Pradesh, N India 26°52′N 82°09′E
230 G9 **Nawābshāh** *var.* Nawabashah. Sind, S Pakistan 26°15′N 68°26′E
233 I7 **Nawāda** Bihār, N India 24°54′N 85°33′E
232 D5 **Nawalgarh** Rājasthān, N India 27°48′N 75°21′E
Nawar, Dasht-i- *see* Nāvar, Dasht-e
256 D4 **Nawnghkio** *var.* Nawngkio. Shan State, C Myanmar (Burma) 22°17′N 96°50′E
Nawngkio *see* Nawnghkio
215 L6 **Naxçıvan** *Rus.* Nakhichevan'. SW Azerbaijan 39°14′N 45°24′E
242 B4 **Naxi** Sichuan, C China 28°50′N 105°20′E
187 J7 **Náxos** *var.* Naxos. Náxos, Kykládes, Greece, Aegean Sea 36°07′N 25°24′E
187 J7 **Náxos** *island* Kykládes, Greece, Aegean Sea
168 D6 **Nay** Aquitaine, France 43°11′N 0°16′W
85 I9 **Nayar** Nayarit, Mexico 22°16′N 104°28′W
85 I9 **Nayarit** ⬖ *state* C Mexico
280 G9 **Nayau** *island* Lau Group, E Fiji
223 I5 **Nāy Band** Yazd, E Iran 32°26′N 57°30′E
161 L5 **Nayland** E England, United Kingdom 51°58′N 00°46′E
242 B6 **Nayong** Guizhou, China 26°16′N 105°13′E
252 F3 **Nayoro** Hokkaidō, NE Japan 44°22′N 142°27′E
254 C3 **Nay Pyi Taw** ● Mandalay, C Myanmar (Burma) 19°44′N 96°16′E
172 B4 **Nazaré** *var.* Nazare. Leiria, C Portugal 39°36′N 09°04′W
Nazare *see* Nazaré
85 J7 **Nazareno** Durango, Mexico 25°23′N 103°25′W
64 F6 **Nazareth** Pennsylvania, USA 40°44′N 75°19′W
70 D3 **Nazareth** Texas, SW USA 34°32′N 102°06′W
Nazareth *see* Natzrat
289 D9 **Nazareth Bank** *undersea feature* W Indian Ocean
85 J7 **Nazas** Durango, C Mexico 25°15′N 104°06′W
85 I7 **Nazas, Río** ≈ Durango, Mexico
105 E9 **Nazca** Ica, S Peru 14°53′S 74°54′W
42 G10 **Nazca Plate** *tectonic feature*
287 L7 **Nazca Ridge** *undersea feature* E Pacific Ocean 22°00′S 82°00′W
251 K9 **Naze** *var.* Nase. Kagoshima, Amami-ōshima, SW Japan 28°21′N 129°30′E
218 E6 **Nazerat** Israel 32°42′N 35°17′E
Nazerat *see* Natzrat
215 J6 **Nazik Gölü** ◎ E Turkey
214 B7 **Nazilli** Aydın, SW Turkey 37°55′N 28°20′E
215 I6 **Nazımiye** Tunceli, E Turkey 39°12′N 39°51′E
192 F6 **Nazino** Tomskaya Oblast', C Russian Federation 60°02′N 78°51′E
Nazinon *see* Red Volta
190 I3 **Naziya** Leningradskaya Oblast', Russian Federation
56 D5 **Nazko** British Columbia, SW Canada 52°57′N 123°44′W
218 E7 **Nazlat Isā** West Bank 32°24′N 35°03′E
218 E7 **Nazlat Israelā** West Bank 32°24′N 35°03′E
197 I9 **Nazran'** Respublika Ingushetiya, SW Russian Federation 43°14′N 44°47′E
136 E4 **Nazrēt** *var.* Adama, Hadama. Oromīya, C Ethiopia 08°31′N 39°20′E
Nazwāh *see* Nizwa
192 E7 **Nazyvayevsk** Omskaya Oblast', C Russian Federation 55°35′N 71°13′E
138 G1 **Nchanga** Copperbelt, C Zambia 12°30′S 27°53′E
135 I11 **Nchelenge** Luapula, N Zambia 09°20′S 28°50′E
Ncheu *see* Ntcheu
141 I8 **Nciba** *prev.* Swart Kei. ≈ Eastern Cape, South Africa *see also* Swart Kei
138 G9 **Nciba** *Eng.* Great Kei; *prev.* Groot-Kei. ≈ S South Africa
Ndaghamcha, Sebkra de *see* Te-n-Dghâmcha, Sebkhet
137 C10 **Ndala** Tabora, C Tanzania 04°45′S 33°15′E
135 C11 **N'Dalatando** *Port.* Salazar, Vila Salazar. Cuanza Norte, NW Angola 09°19′S 14°48′E
141 K7 **Ndaleni** Kwazulu Natal, South Africa 29°55′S 30°19′E
133 I6 **Ndali** C Benin 09°50′N 02°46′E
137 A8 **Ndeke** SW Uganda 0°11′S 30°04′E
134 F4 **Ndélé** Bamingui-Bangoran, N Central African Republic 08°24′N 20°41′E
135 B8 **Ndendé** Ngounié, S Gabon 02°21′S 11°20′E
135 B9 **Ndindi** Nyanga, S Gabon 03°47′S 11°06′E
134 C2 **Ndjamena** *var.* N'Djamena; *prev.* Fort-Lamy. ● (Chad) Chari-Baguirmi, W Chad 12°08′N 15°02′E
134 C2 **Ndjamena** ✈ Chari-Baguirmi, W Chad 12°09′N 15°00′E
N'Djamena *see* Ndjamena
134 B7 **Ndjolé** Moyen-Ogooué, W Gabon 0°07′S 10°45′E
138 G1 **Ndola** Copperbelt, C Zambia 12°59′S 28°35′E
Ndrhamcha, Sebkha de *see* Te-n-Dghâmcha, Sebkhet
134 G5 **Ndu** Orientale, N Dem. Rep. Congo 04°36′N 22°49′E
137 C9 **Nduguti** Singida, C Tanzania 04°19′S 34°40′E
281 J3 **Nduindui** Guadalcanal, C Solomon Islands 09°46′S 159°54′E
Nduke *see* Kolombangara
141 L5 **Ndumo** KwaZulu-Natal, South Africa 26°55′S 32°15′E
141 L6 **Ndundula** KwaZulu-Natal, South Africa 28°41′S 31°31′E
141 K6 **Ndwedwe** KwaZulu-Natal, South Africa 29°30′S 30°56′E
Ndzouani *see* Nzwani
186 G4 **Néa Anchiálos** *var.* Nea Anhialos, Néa Ankhíalos. Thessalía, C Greece 39°16′N 22°49′E
Nea Anhialos/Néa Ankhíalos *see* Néa Anchiálos
187 H5 **Néa Artáki** Évvoia, C Greece 38°31′N 23°39′E
158 D6 **Neagh, Lough** ◎ E Northern Ireland, United Kingdom
76 B3 **Neah Bay** Washington, NW USA 48°21′N 124°39′W
187 J8 **Nea Kaméni** *island* Kykládes, Greece, Aegean Sea
274 G5 **Neale, Lake** ◎ Northern Territory, C Australia
187 H3 **Néa Moudanía** *var.* Néa Moudhaniá. Kentrikí Makedonía, N Greece 40°14′N 23°17′E
Néa Moudhaniá *see* Néa Moudanía
188 E7 **Neamţ** ⬖ *county* NE Romania
Neapel *see* Napoli
186 F3 **Neápoli** *prev.* Neápolis. Dytikí Makedonía, N Greece 40°19′N 21°23′E
187 J10 **Neápoli** Kríti, Greece, E Mediterranean Sea 35°15′N 25°37′E
187 H8 **Neápoli** Pelopónnisos, S Greece 36°29′N 23°05′E
Neápolis *see* Neápoli, Greece
Neapolis *see* Napoli, Italy
Neapolis *see* Nablus, West Bank
82 A9 **Near Islands** *island group* Aleutian Islands, Alaska, USA
160 F6 **Neath** S Wales, United Kingdom 51°40′N 03°48′W
187 H2 **Néa Zíchni** *var.* Néa Zíkhni; *prev.* Néa Zíkhna. Kentrikí Makedonía, NE Greece 41°02′N 23°50′E
Néa Zíkhna/Néa Zíkhni *see* Néa Zíchni
88 C3 **Nebaj** Quiché, W Guatemala 15°25′N 91°05′W
132 G6 **Nebbou** S Burkina 11°22′N 01°49′W
277 J2 **Nebine Creek** ≈ Queensland, SE Australia
Nebitdag *see* Balkanabat
102 G8 **Neblina, Pico da** ▲ NW Brazil 0°49′N 66°31′W
194 E8 **Nebolchi** Novgorodskaya Oblast', W Russian Federation 59°08′N 33°19′E
79 H3 **Nebo, Mount** ▲ Utah, W USA 39°47′N 111°46′W
74 C7 **Nebraska** *off.* State of Nebraska, *also known as* Blackwater State, Cornhusker State, Tree Planters State. ⬖ *state* C USA
75 F8 **Nebraska City** Nebraska, C USA 40°38′N 95°52′W
175 G12 **Nebrodi, Monti** *var.* Monti Caronie. ▲▲ Sicilia, Italy, C Mediterranean Sea
56 D4 **Nechako** ≈ British Columbia, SW Canada
74 E1 **Neche** North Dakota, N USA 48°57′N 97°33′W
71 I5 **Neches** Texas, SW USA 31°51′N 95°28′W
71 I5 **Neches River** ≈ Texas, SW USA
181 G14 **Neckar** ≈ SW Germany
181 F13 **Neckargemünd** Baden-Württemberg, Germany 49°24′E 8°48′N
181 G13 **Neckargerach** Baden-Württemberg, Germany 49°24′E 9°04′N
181 G14 **Neckarsulm** Baden-Württemberg, SW Germany 49°12′N 09°13′E
286 G3 **Necker Island** *island* C British Virgin Islands
267 L2 **Necker Ridge** *undersea feature* N Pacific Ocean
116 H6 **Necochea** Buenos Aires, E Argentina 38°34′S 58°42′W
161 L3 **Necton** United Kingdom 52°39′N 0°46′E
170 D1 **Neda** Galicia, NW Spain 43°29′N 08°09′W
186 F7 **Néda** *var.* Nédas. ≈ S Greece
Nédas *see* Néda
71 J7 **Nederland** Texas, SW USA 29°58′N 93°59′W
Nederland *see* Netherlands
162 G7 **Neder Rijn** *Eng.* Lower Rhine. ≈ C Netherlands
163 G9 **Nederweert** Limburg, SE Netherlands 51°17′N 05°45′E
155 D8 **Nedre Tokke** ◎ S Norway
Nedrigaylov *see* Nedryhayliv
189 J2 **Nedryhayliv** *Rus.* Nedrigaylov. Sums'ka Oblast', NE Ukraine 50°51′N 33°54′E
162 I6 **Neede** Gelderland, E Netherlands 52°08′N 06°36′E
65 L2 **Needham** Massachusetts, USA 42°17′N 71°14′W
77 J7 **Needle Mountain** ▲ Wyoming, C USA 44°03′N 109°33′W
81 I11 **Needles** California, W USA 34°50′N 114°37′W
161 I8 **Needles Point** *headland* United Kingdom 50°40′N 1°35′W
157 H12 **Needles, The** *rocks* S England, United Kingdom
112 G5 **Ñeembucú** *off.* Departamento de Ñeembucú. ⬖ *department* SW Paraguay
Ñeembucú, Departamento de *see* Ñeembucú
72 D6 **Neenah** Wisconsin, N USA 44°09′N 88°26′W
55 I9 **Neepawa** Manitoba, S Canada 50°14′N 99°29′W
53 J7 **Neergaard Lake** ◎ Nunavut, NE Canada
180 D3 **Neermoor** Niedersachsen, Germany 53°18′E 7°26′N
163 G9 **Neerpelt** Limburg, NE Belgium 51°13′N 05°26′E
180 I3 **Neetze** Niedersachsen, Germany 53°16′E 10°38′N
131 K2 **Nefta** ✈ W Tunisia 34°03′N 08°05′E
196 G8 **Neftegorsk** Krasnodarskiy Kray, SW Russian Federation 44°21′N 39°40′E
197 K1 **Neftekamsk** Respublika Bashkortostan, W Russian Federation 56°07′N 54°13′E
197 I8 **Neftekumsk** Stavropol'skiy Kray, SW Russian Federation 44°45′N 45°00′E
192 F6 **Nefteyugansk** Khanty-Mansiyskiy Avtonomnyy Okrug-Yugra, C Russian Federation 61°07′N 72°18′E
Neftezavodsk *see* Seýdi
175 B13 **Nefza** Tunisia
135 D10 **Negage** *var.* N'Gage. Uíge, NW Angola 07°47′S 15°27′E
Negapatam/Negapattinam *see* Nāgappattinam
259 J9 **Negara** Bali, Indonesia 08°21′S 114°35′E
259 K6 **Negara** Borneo, C Indonesia 02°40′S 115°05′E
Negara Brunei Darussalam *see* Brunei
72 E4 **Negaunee** Michigan, N USA 46°30′N 87°36′W
219 D9 **Negba** Israel 31°40′N 34°41′E
136 E6 **Negēlē** *var.* Negelli, *It.* Neghelli. Oromīya, C Ethiopia 05°13′N 39°43′E
Negelli *see* Negēlē
Negeri Pahang Darul Makmur *see* Pahang
Negeri Selangor Darul Ehsan *see* Selangor
258 E3 **Negeri Sembilan** *var.* Negri Sembilan. ⬖ *state* Peninsular Malaysia
152 B6 **Negerpynten** *headland* S Svalbard 77°15′N 22°40′E
Negev *see* HaNegev
Neghelli *see* Negēlē
188 D8 **Negoiu** *var.* Negoiul. ▲ S Romania 45°34′N 24°34′E
Negoiul *see* Negoiu
137 E12 **Negomane** *var.* Negomano. Cabo Delgado, N Mozambique 11°22′S 38°32′E
Negomano *see* Negomane
235 F10 **Negombo** Western Province, SW Sri Lanka 07°13′N 79°51′E
285 K7 **Negonego** *prev.* Nengonengo. *atoll* Îles Tuamotu, C French Polynesia
Negoreloye *see* Nyeharelaye
185 H4 **Negotin** Serbia, E Serbia 44°14′N 22°31′E
185 H8 **Negotino** C Macedonia 41°29′N 22°04′E
Negra, Punto *headland* NW Peru 06°03′S 81°08′W
170 C2 **Negreira** Galicia, NW Spain 42°54′N 08°46′W
168 F5 **Nègrepelisse** Midi-Pyrénées, France 44°04′N 1°31′E
188 F7 **Negreşti** Vaslui, E Romania 46°50′N 27°28′E
Negreşti *see* Negreşti-Oaş
188 C6 **Negreşti-Oaş** *Hung.* Avasfelsőfalu; *prev.* Negreşti. Satu Mare, NE Romania 47°56′N 23°22′E
90 D7 **Negril** W Jamaica 18°16′N 78°21′W
Negri Sembilan *see* Negeri Sembilan
118 C1 **Negro, Ensenada del** *bay* Coquimbo, Chile
116 E6 **Negro, Río** ≈ E Argentina
112 F5 **Negro, Río** ≈ NE Argentina
106 F9 **Negro, Río** ≈ E Bolivia
98 D3 **Negro, Rio** ≈ N South America
115 J5 **Negro, Río** ≈ Brazil/Uruguay
118 E4 **Negro, Río** ≈ Región Metropolitana, Chile
112 G4 **Negro, Río** ≈ C Paraguay
Negro, Río *see* Chixoy, Río, Guatemala/Mexico
Negro, Río *see* Sico Tinto, Río, Honduras
263 L8 **Negros** *island* C Philippines
188 F10 **Negru Vodă** Constanţa, SE Romania 43°49′N 28°12′E
63 N1 **Neguac** New Brunswick, SE Canada 47°16′N 65°04′W
72 G2 **Negwazu, Lake** ◎ Ontario, S Canada
Négyfalu *see* Săcele
76 B5 **Nehalem** Oregon, NW USA 45°42′N 123°55′W
76 B5 **Nehalem River** ≈ Oregon, NW USA
Nehavend *see* Nahāvand
223 J6 **Nehbandān** Khorāsān, E Iran 31°00′N 60°00′E
247 K3 **Nehe** Heilongjiang, NE China 48°28′N 124°52′E
91 H6 **Neiba** *var.* Neyba. SW Dominican Republic 18°31′N 71°25′W
Néid, Carn Uí *see* Mizen Head
152 I3 **Neiden** Finnmark, N Norway 69°41′N 29°23′E
Neidín *see* Kenmare
Néifinn *see* Nephin
167 L10 **Neige, Crêt de la** ▲ E France 46°18′N 05°58′E
137 I10 **Neiges, Piton des** ▲ C Réunion 21°05′S 55°28′E
63 J1 **Neiges, Rivière des** ≈ Québec, SE Canada
242 B3 **Neijiang** Sichuan, C China 29°32′N 105°03′E
140 E6 **Neilersdrif** Northern Cape, South Africa 28°45′S 20°59′E
72 B6 **Neillsville** Wisconsin, N USA 44°34′N 90°36′W
Nei Monggol Zizhiqu/Nei Mongol *see* Nei Mongol Zizhiqu
247 I5 **Nei Mongol Gaoyuan** *plateau* NE China
244 F1 **Nei Mongol Zizhiqu** *var.* Nei Mongol, *Eng.* Inner Mongolia, Inner Mongolian Autonomous Region; *prev.* Nei Monggol Zizhiqu. ⬖ *autonomous region* N China
245 I5 **Neiqiu** Hebei, E China 37°22′N 114°34′E
Neiriz *see* Neyrīz
179 J8 **Neisse** *Pol.* Nisa *Cz.* Lužická Nisa, *Ger.* Lausitzer Neisse, Nysa Łużycka. ≈ C Europe
Neisse *see* Nysa
102 B6 **Neiva** Huila, S Colombia 02°58′N 75°15′W
244 G9 **Neixiang** Henan, China 33°03′N 111°50′E
239 N7 **Neixiang** Henan, C China 33°08′N 111°50′E
Nejafabad *see* Najafābād
55 I5 **Nejanilini Lake** ◎ Manitoba, C Canada
87 H9 **Nejapa** Oaxaca, Mexico 16°37′N 95°59′W
Nejd *see* Najd
136 D4 **Nek'emtē** *var.* Lakemti, Nakamti. Oromīya, C Ethiopia 09°06′N 36°31′E
197 H5 **Nekhayevskaya** Volgogradskaya Oblast', SW Russian Federation 50°25′N 41°44′E
72 C6 **Nekoosa** Wisconsin, N USA 44°19′N 89°54′W
Neksø Bornholm *see* Nexø
172 C2 **Nelas** Viseu, N Portugal 40°32′N 07°52′W
194 D10 **Nelidovo** Tverskaya Oblast', W Russian Federation 56°13′N 32°45′E
74 E7 **Neligh** Nebraska, C USA 42°07′N 98°01′W
193 K6 **Nel'kan** Khabarovskiy Kray, E Russian Federation 57°44′N 136°09′E
152 H4 **Nellim** *var.* Nellimö, *Lapp.* Njellim. Lappi, N Finland 68°49′N 28°18′E
Nellimö *see* Nellim
234 F7 **Nellore** Andhra Pradesh, E India 14°29′N 80°E
141 K4 **Nelsbergpas** *pass* Mpumalanga, South Africa
114 B4 **Nelson** Santa Fe, C Argentina 31°16′S 60°45′W
56 G9 **Nelson** British Columbia, SW Canada 49°29′N 117°17′W
279 F8 **Nelson** Nelson, South Island, New Zealand 41°17′S 173°17′E
159 J8 **Nelson** NW England, United Kingdom 53°51′N 02°13′W
75 D8 **Nelson** Nebraska, C USA 40°12′N 98°04′W
81 J10 **Nelson** Nevada, USA 35°42′N 114°49′W
278 E7 **Nelson** ⬖ *unitary authority* South Island, New Zealand
55 J7 **Nelson** ≈ Manitoba, C Canada
277 M5 **Nelson Bay** New South Wales, SE Australia 32°48′S 152°10′E
277 H7 **Nelson, Cape** *headland* Victoria, SE Australia 38°25′S 141°33′E
117 B12 **Nelson, Estrecho** *strait* SE Pacific Ocean
55 I7 **Nelson House** Manitoba, C Canada 55°49′N 98°51′W
72 B4 **Nelson Lake** ◎ Wisconsin, N USA
80 G7 **Nelson Range** *ridge* California, USA
73 I11 **Nelsonville** Ohio, N USA 39°27′N 82°13′W
75 G8 **Nelsoon River** ≈ Iowa/Missouri, C USA
140 F8 **Nelspoort** Western Cape, South Africa 32°07′S 23°00′E
141 K3 **Nelspruit** Mpumalanga, NE South Africa 25°28′S 30°58′E
Nelspruit *see* Mbombela
132 E3 **Néma** Hodh ech Chargui, SE Mauritania 16°32′N 07°12′W
191 C8 **Neman** *Ger.* Ragnit. Kaliningradskaya Oblast', W Russian Federation 55°01′N 22°00′E
144 E5 **Neman** *Bel.* Nyoman, *Ger.* Memel, *Lith.* Nemunas, *Pol.* Niemen. ≈ NE Europe
Nemausus *see* Nîmes
186 G6 **Neméa** Pelopónnisos, S Greece 37°49′N 22°40′E
Německý Brod *see* Havlíčkův Brod
58 E7 **Nemegosenda** ≈ Ontario, S Canada
191 E8 **Nemencinė** Vilnius, SE Lithuania 54°50′N 25°29′E
Nemetocenna *see* Arras
Nemirov *see* Nemyriv
165 H4 **Nemours** Seine-et-Marne, N France 48°16′N 02°41′E
Nemunas *see* Neman
252 I4 **Nemuro** Hokkaidō, NE Japan 43°20′N 145°35′E
252 I4 **Nemuro-hantō** *peninsula* Hokkaidō, NE Japan
252 I3 **Nemuro-kaikyō** *strait* Japan/Russian Federation
252 H4 **Nemuro-wan** *bay* N Japan
188 C3 **Nemyriv** *Rus.* Nemirov. L'vivs'ka Oblast', NW Ukraine 50°08′N 23°28′E
188 G5 **Nemyriv** *Rus.* Nemirov. Vinnyts'ka Oblast', C Ukraine 48°58′N 28°50′E
157 C10 **Nenagh** *Ir.* An tAonach. Tipperary, C Ireland 52°52′N 08°12′W
83 I5 **Nenana** Alaska, USA 64°33′N 149°05′W
83 I5 **Nenana River** ≈ Alaska, USA
281 I5 **Nendö** *var.* Swallow Island. *island* Santa Cruz Islands, E Solomon Islands
180 F5 **Nendorf** Niedersachsen, Germany 52°30′E 8°59′N
161 K3 **Nene** ≈ E England, United Kingdom
195 K3 **Nenetskiy Avtonomnyy Okrug** ⬖ *autonomous district* Arkhangel'skaya Oblast', NW Russian Federation
Nengonengo *see* Negonego
193 K8 **Nenjiang** Heilongjiang, NE China 49°11′N 125°18′E
247 K3 **Nen Jiang** *var.* Nonni. ≈ NE China
181 E11 **Nentershausen** Rheinland-Pfalz, Germany 50°25′E 7°56′N
159 J6 **Nenthead** United Kingdom 54°46′N 2°20′W
282 F10 **Neoch** *atoll* Caroline Islands, C Micronesia
186 F6 **Neochóri** Dytikí Elláda, C Greece 38°23′N 21°14′E
75 F11 **Neodesha** Kansas, C USA 37°25′N 95°40′W
74 F7 **Neola** Iowa, C USA 41°27′N 95°40′W
186 G5 **Néo Monastíri** *var.* Néon Monastiri. Thessalía, C Greece 39°22′N 21°55′E
Néon Karlovasi/Néon Karlovásion *see* Karlovási
Néon Monastiri *see* Néo Monastíri
75 G11 **Neosho** Missouri, C USA 36°53′N 94°24′W
75 F10 **Neosho River** ≈ Kansas/Oklahoma, C USA
219 E10 **Ne'ot HaKikkar** Israel 30°57′N 35°22′E
219 E13 **Ne'ot Smadar** Israel
193 H7 **Nepa** ≈ C Russian Federation
233 I5 **Nepal** *off.* Nepal. ◆ *monarchy* S Asia
Nepal *see* Nepal
232 G5 **Nepālganj** Mid Western, SW Nepal 28°04′N 81°37′E
62 F3 **Nepean** Ontario, SE Canada 45°19′N 75°54′W
79 H3 **Nephi** Utah, W USA 39°43′N 111°50′W
157 B8 **Nephin** *Ir.* Néifinn. ▲ W Ireland 54°00′N 09°21′W
63 M1 **Nepisiguit** ≈ New Brunswick, SE Canada
121 K5 **Nepoko** ≈ NE Dem. Rep. Congo
110 F5 **Nepomuceno** Minas Gerais, Brazil 21°14′S 45°15′W
65 H7 **Neptune** New Jersey, NE USA 40°10′N 74°03′W
174 F7 **Nera** *anc.* Nar. ≈ C Italy
164 G8 **Nérac** Lot-et-Garonne, SW France 44°08′N 00°21′E
277 M2 **Nerang** Queensland, Australia
183 C8 **Neratovice** *Ger.* Neratowitz. Středocesky Kraj, C Czech Republic 50°16′N 14°31′E
Neratowitz *see* Neratovice
193 J8 **Nercha** ≈ S Russian Federation
193 J8 **Nerchinsk** Zabaykalskiy Kray, S Russian Federation 52°01′N 116°25′E
194 G10 **Nerekhta** Kostromskaya Oblast', NW Russian Federation 57°27′N 40°33′E
190 E7 **Nereta** Aizkraukle, S Latvia 56°12′N 25°18′E
174 F7 **Nereto** Abruzzo, C Italy 42°49′N 13°50′E
184 D5 **Neretva** ≈ Bosnia and Herzegovina/Croatia
186 E5 **Nerikós** *ruins* Lefkáda, Iónia Nísiá, Greece, C Mediterranean Sea
135 F13 **Neriquinha** Cuando Cubango, SE Angola 15°44′S 21°34′E
191 D8 **Neris** *Bel.* Viliya, *Pol.* Wilia; *prev. Pol.* Wilja. ≈ Belarus/Lithuania
Neris *see* Viliya
167 H10 **Néris-les-Bains** Auvergne, France 46°17′N 2°40′E
170 G9 **Nerja** Andalucía, S Spain 36°45′N 03°35′W
194 F10 **Nerl'** ≈ W Russian Federation
195 L6 **Nerokhi** Khanty-Mansiyskiy Avtonomnyy Okrug-Yugra, Russian Federation
169 J1 **Néronde** Rhône-Alpes, France 45°50′N 4°14′E
261 I6 **Nerong, Selat** *strait* Kepulauan Kai, E Indonesia
171 H7 **Nerpio** Castilla-La Mancha, C Spain 38°08′N 02°18′W
118 C5 **Nerquihue** Libertador General Bernardo O'Higgins, Chile 34°40′S 71°34′W
170 E8 **Nerva** Andalucía, S Spain 37°40′N 06°31′W
193 J7 **Neryungri** Respublika Sakha (Yakutiya), NE Russian Federation 56°38′N 124°19′E
162 G3 **Nes** Friesland, N Netherlands 53°28′N 05°46′E
154 D6 **Nesbyen** Buskerud, S Norway 60°36′N 09°35′E
65 I6 **Nesconset** New York, USA 40°51′N 73°09′W
218 E6 **Nesher** Israel 32°45′N 35°03′E
152 E2 **Neskaupstadhur** Austurland, E Iceland 65°08′N 13°45′W
152 D6 **Nesna** Nordland, C Norway 66°11′N 12°54′E
172 C3 **Nesperal** Castelo Branco, Portugal 39°49′N 8°10′W
75 C10 **Ness City** Kansas, C USA 38°27′N 99°54′W
Nesselsdorf *see* Kopřivnice
179 D14 **Nesslau** Sankt Gallen, NE Switzerland 47°13′N 09°12′E
156 E5 **Ness, Loch** ◎ N Scotland, United Kingdom
159 L7 **Ness Point** *headland* N England, United Kingdom
Nesterov *see* Zhovkva
159 I10 **Neston** United Kingdom 53°17′N 3°03′W
187 I2 **Néstos** *Bul.* Mesta, *Turk.* Kara Su. ≈ Bulgaria/Greece *see also* Mesta
Néstos *see* Mesta
Nes Tsiyona *see* Nes Ziyyona
154 A7 **Nesttun** Hordaland, S Norway 60°19′N 05°16′E
Nesvizh *see* Nyasvizh
219 D8 **Nes Ziyyona** *var.* Nes Tsiyona. Central, C Israel 31°55′N 34°48′E
218 D7 **Netanya** *var.* Natanya, Nathanya. Central, C Israel 32°20′N 34°51′E
162 H6 **Netherlands** *off.* Kingdom of the Netherlands, *var.* Holland, *Dut.* Koninkrijk der Nederlanden, Nederland. ◆ *monarchy* NW Europe
102 F1 **Netherlands Antilles** *prev.* Dutch West Indies. ◇ *Dutch autonomous region* S Caribbean Sea
Netherlands East Indies *see* Indonesia
Netherlands Guiana *see* Suriname
Netherlands, Kingdom of the *see* Netherlands
Netherlands New Guinea *see* Papua
188 E3 **Netishyn** Khmel'nyts'ka Oblast', W Ukraine 50°20′N 26°38′E
219 D9 **Netivot** Southern, S Israel 31°26′N 34°36′E
175 H11 **Neto** ≈ S Italy
181 E9 **Netphen** Nordrhein-Westfalen, Germany 50°55′E 8°06′N
181 B8 **Nettetal** Nordrhein-Westfalen, Germany 51°19′E 6°17′N
53 L8 **Nettilling Fiord** *coastal sea feature* Nunavut, NE Canada
53 L8 **Nettilling Lake** ◎ Baffin Island, Nunavut, N Canada
74 G2 **Nett Lake** ◎ Minnesota, N USA
159 M10 **Nettleham** United Kingdom 53°16′N 0°29′W
180 H6 **Nettlingen** Niedersachsen, Germany 52°10′E 10°10′N
175 E9 **Nettuno** Lazio, C Italy 41°27′N 12°40′E
Netum *see* Noto
86 A2 **Netzahualcóyotl, Presa** ⊠ SE Mexico
Netze *see* Noteć
Neu Amerika *see* Puławy
Neubetsche *see* Novi Bečej
Neubidschow *see* Nový Bydžov
Neubistritz *see* Nová Bystřice
180 D4 **Neubörger** Niedersachsen, Germany 52°58′E 7°27′N
178 H5 **Neubrandenburg** Mecklenburg-Vorpommern, NE Germany 53°33′N 13°16′E
180 F4 **Neubruchhausen** Niedersachsen, Germany 52°50′E 8°50′N
181 H12 **Neubrunn** Bayern, Germany 49°44′E 9°40′N
180 J6 **Neu Büddenstedt** Niedersachsen, Germany 52°11′E 11°02′N
179 F12 **Neuburg an der Donau** Bayern, S Germany 48°43′N 11°10′E
176 C4 **Neuchâtel** *Ger.* Neuenburg. Neuchâtel, W Switzerland 46°59′N 06°55′E
174 B2 **Neuchâtel** *Ger.* Neuenburg. ⬖ *canton* W Switzerland
176 C4 **Neuchâtel, Lac de** *Ger.* Neuenburger See. ◎ W Switzerland
181 G13 **Neudenau** Baden-Württemberg, Germany 49°18′E 9°16′N
Neudorf *see* Spišská Nová Ves
180 I5 **Neudorf-Platendorf** Niedersachsen, Germany 52°33′E 10°36′N
180 J4 **Neue Elde** *canal* N Germany
Neuenburg *see* Neuchâtel
Neuenburg an der Elbe *see* Nymburk

◆ Country
● Country Capital
◇ Dependent Territory
○ Dependent Territory Capital
⬖ Administrative Regions
✈ International Airport
▲ Mountain
▲▲ Mountain Range
Volcano
≈ River
◎ Lake
⊠ Reservoir

◆ Country   ◇ Dependent Territory   ◈ Administrative Regions   ▲ Mountain   ☈ Volcano   ◎ Lake
● Country Capital   ◉ Dependent Territory Capital   ✕ International Airport   ▲ Mountain Range   ♒ River   ▨ Reservoir

◆ Country ◇ Dependent Territory ◈ Administrative Regions ▲ Mountain ▨ Volcano ◎ Lake
● Country Capital ○ Dependent Territory Capital ✈ International Airport ▲ Mountain Range ♒ River ⊜ Reservoir

| ◆ Country | ◇ Dependent Territory | ■ Administrative Regions | ▲ Mountain | ☷ Volcano | ⊜ Lake |
| ● Country Capital | ○ Dependent Territory Capital | ✕ International Airport | ▲▲ Mountain Range | ♒ River | ■ Reservoir |

◆ Country ◇ Dependent Territory ◈ Administrative Regions ▲ Mountain ✹ Volcano ⊚ Lake
● Country Capital ○ Dependent Territory Capital ✈ International Airport ▲ Mountain Range ᠵ River ⊠ Reservoir

Olbia - Orléans
INDEX
386

175 C9 **Olbia** *prev.* Terranova Pausania. Sardegna, Italy, C Mediterranean Sea *40°55′N 09°30′E*
90 E3 **Old Bahama Channel** *channel* Bahamas/Cuba
Old Bay State/Old Colony State *see* Massachusetts
161 H4 **Oldbury** United Kingdom *52°30′N 2°01′W*
158 C9 **Oldcastle** Meath, Ireland *53°46′N 7°10′W*
65 I2 **Old Chatham** New York, USA *42°26′N 73°34′W*
52 A6 **Old Crow** Yukon Territory, NW Canada *67°34′N 139°55′W*
52 A6 **Old Crow Flats** *Wetland* Yukon Territory, NW Canada
Old Dominion *see* Virginia
Oldeberkeap *see* Oldeberkoop
162 H4 **Oldeberkoop** *Fris.* Oldeberkeap. Friesland, N Netherlands *52°55′N 06°07′E*
162 H6 **Oldebroek** Gelderland, E Netherlands *52°27′N 05°54′E*
162 H4 **Oldemarkt** Overijssel, N Netherlands *52°49′N 05°58′E*
154 B5 **Olden** Sogn Og Fjordane, C Norway *61°52′N 06°44′E*
180 E3 **Oldenbrok** Niedersachsen, Germany *53°17′E 8°24′N*
180 E4 **Oldenburg** Niedersachsen, NW Germany *53°09′N 08°13′E*
180 J1 **Oldenburg** *var.* Oldenburg in Holstein. Schleswig-Holstein, N Germany *54°17′N 10°55′E*
Oldenburg in Holstein *see* Oldenburg
162 I6 **Oldenzaal** Overijssel, E Netherlands *52°19′N 06°53′E*
152 F4 **Olderdalen** Troms, N Norway *69°35′N 20°34′E*
Olderfjord *see* Leaibevuotna
180 D3 **Oldersum** Niedersachsen, Germany *53°20′E 7°20′N*
62 G5 **Old Forge** New York, NE USA *43°42′N 74°59′W*
Old Goa *see* Goa
159 J9 **Oldham** NW England, United Kingdom *53°36′N 02°W*
83 I8 **Old Harbor** Kodiak Island, Alaska, USA *57°12′N 153°18′W*
90 F8 **Old Harbour** C Jamaica *17°56′N 77°06′W*
157 B11 **Old Head of Kinsale** *Ir.* An Seancheann. *headland* SW Ireland *51°37′N 08°33′W*
66 D5 **Old Hickory Lake** ⊠ Tennessee, S USA
181 J8 **Oldisleben** Thüringen, Germany *51°18′E 11°10′N*
Old Line State *see* Maryland
Old North State *see* North Carolina
136 D7 **Ol Doinyo Lengeyo** ▲▲ C Kenya
81 D8 **Old River** California, USA *35°16′N 119°07′W*
57 I6 **Olds** Alberta, SW Canada *51°50′N 114°06′W*
64 K5 **Old Saybrook** Connecticut, NE USA *41°17′N 72°22′W*
63 J4 **Old Speck Mountain** ▲ Maine, NE USA *44°34′N 70°55′W*
63 K3 **Old Town** Maine, NE USA *44°55′N 68°39′W*
57 N8 **Old Wives Lake** ◎ Saskatchewan, S Canada
239 J1 **Öldziyt** *var.* Höshööt. Arhangay, C Mongolia *48°06′N 102°34′E*
239 J2 **Öldziyt** *var.* Ulaan-Uul. Bayanhongor, C Mongolia *46°03′N 100°52′E*
239 L2 **Öldziyt** *var.* Rashaant. Dundgovĭ, C Mongolia *44°54′N 106°32′E*
239 K2 **Öldziyt** *var.* Sangiyn Dalay. Övörhangay, C Mongolia *46°35′N 103°18′E*
Öldziyt *see* Erdenemandal, Arhangay, Mongolia
Öldziyt *see* Sayhandulaan, Dornogovĭ, Mongolia
283 H2 **Oleai** *var.* San Jose. Saipan, S Northern Mariana Islands
64 B3 **Olean** New York, NE USA *42°04′N 78°24′W*
182 I4 **Olecko** *Ger.* Treuburg. Warmińsko-Mazurskie, NE Poland *54°02′N 22°29′E*
172 D3 **Oledo** Castelo Branco, Portugal *39°58′N 7°18′W*
176 E6 **Oleggio** Piemonte, NE Italy *45°36′N 08°37′E*
193 J7 **Olëkma** Amurskaya Oblast', SE Russian Federation *57°00′N 120°27′E*
193 J7 **Olëkma** ≈ C Russian Federation
193 J6 **Olëkminsk** Respublika Sakha (Yakutiya), NE Russian Federation *60°25′N 120°25′E*
189 L5 **Oleksandrivka** Donets'ka Oblast', E Ukraine *48°42′N 36°56′E*
189 I5 **Oleksandrivka** *Rus.* Aleksandrovka. Kirovohrads'ka Oblast', C Ukraine *48°59′N 32°14′E*
189 H6 **Oleksandrivka** Mykolayivs'ka Oblast', S Ukraine *47°42′N 31°17′E*
189 J5 **Oleksandriya** *Rus.* Aleksandriya. Kirovohrads'ka Oblast', C Ukraine *48°42′N 33°07′E*
80 A2 **Olema** California, USA *38°02′N 122°47′W*
154 A7 **Ølen** Hordaland, S Norway *59°36′N 05°48′E*
194 E3 **Olenegorsk** Murmanskaya Oblast', NW Russian Federation *68°06′N 33°15′E*
193 I5 **Olenëk** Respublika Sakha (Yakutiya), NE Russian Federation *68°28′N 112°18′E*
193 I4 **Olenëk** ≈ NE Russian Federation
193 I4 **Olenëkskiy Zaliv** *bay* N Russian Federation
190 J7 **Olenino** Tverskaya Oblast', Russian Federation
194 F4 **Olenitsa** Murmanskaya Oblast', NW Russian Federation *66°27′N 35°21′E*
164 F6 **Oléron, Île d'** *island* W France
168 G9 **Olesa de Montserrat** Cataluña, Spain *41°33′N 1°54′E*
182 E7 **Oleśnica** *Ger.* Oels, Oels in Schlesien. Dolnośląskie, SW Poland *51°13′N 17°20′E*
182 F7 **Olesno** *Ger.* Rosenberg. Opolskie, S Poland *50°53′N 18°23′E*
168 G7 **Olette** Languedoc-Roussillon, France *42°33′N 2°16′E*
188 F2 **Olevs'k** *Rus.* Olevsk. Zhytomyrs'ka Oblast', N Ukraine *51°12′N 27°38′E*
Olevsk *see* Olevs'k
193 L9 **Ol'ga** Primorskiy Kray, SE Russian Federation *43°41′N 135°06′E*
Olga, Mount *see* Kata Tjuṯa
152 C5 **Olgastretet** *strait* E Svalbard
236 D2 **Ölgiy** Bayan-Ölgiy, W Mongolia *48°57′N 89°59′E*
155 C12 **Ølgod** Ribe, W Denmark *55°44′N 08°37′E*
172 C8 **Olhão** Faro, S Portugal *37°01′N 07°50′W*
152 H6 **Olhava** Oulu, C Finland *65°28′N 25°25′E*
171 K3 **Oliana** Cataluña, NE Spain *42°04′N 01°19′E*
184 B4 **Olib** *It.* Ulbo. *island* W Croatia
114 F10 **Oliden** Buenos Aires, Argentina *35°11′S 57°57′W*
173 L1 **Oliete** Aragón, Spain *40°59′N 0°40′W*
138 B3 **Olifa** Kunene, NW Namibia *17°25′S 14°27′E*
140 D3 **Olifants** *var.* Elephant River. ≈ E Namibia
141 J3 **Olifants** ≈ Western Cape, South Africa
Olifants *see* Lepelle
141 I2 **Olifants Drift** *var.* Oliphants Drift. Kgatleng, Botswana *24°11′S 26°52′E*
140 F5 **Olifantshoek** Northern Cape, N South Africa *27°56′S 22°45′E*
141 H9 **Olifantskop** ▲ Eastern Cape, South Africa *32°43′S 25°43′E*
282 E6 **Olimarao Atoll** *atoll* Caroline Islands, C Micronesia
Ólimbos *see* Ólympos
110 F6 **Olímpio Noronha** Minas Gerais, Brazil *22°04′S 45°16′W*
Olimpo *see* Fuerte Olimpo
86 F8 **Olinalá** Guerrero, Mexico *17°50′N 98°51′W*
108 J6 **Olinda** Pernambuco, E Brazil *08°S 34°51′W*
Olinthos *see* Ólynthos
Oliphants Drift *see* Olifants Drift
Olisipo *see* Lisboa
Olita *see* Alytus
171 H2 **Olite** Navarra, N Spain *42°29′N 01°40′W*
112 E8 **Oliva** Córdoba, C Argentina *32°03′S 63°34′W*
171 J6 **Oliva** País Valenciano, E Spain *38°55′N 00°09′W*
Oliva *see* La Oliva
172 D6 **Oliva de la Frontera** Extremadura, W Spain *38°17′N 06°54′W*
Olivares *see* Olivares de Júcar
116 C2 **Olivares, Cerro de** ▲ N Chile *30°25′S 69°52′W*
171 H5 **Olivares de Júcar** *var.* Olivares. Castilla-La Mancha, C Spain *39°45′N 02°21′W*
66 B7 **Olive Branch** Mississippi, S USA *34°58′N 89°49′W*
66 G3 **Olive Hill** Kentucky, S USA *38°18′N 83°10′W*
80 D1 **Olivehurst** California, W USA *39°05′N 121°33′W*
110 F4 **Oliveira** Minas Gerais, Brazil *20°41′S 44°49′W*
172 B1 **Oliveira de Azeméis** Aveiro, N Portugal *40°49′N 08°29′W*
170 D6 **Olivenza** Extremadura, W Spain *38°41′N 07°06′W*
56 F9 **Oliver** British Columbia, SW Canada *49°10′N 119°37′W*
114 D9 **Olivera** Buenos Aires, Argentina *34°38′S 59°15′W*
114 G3 **Olivera** Salto, Uruguay *31°11′S 56°56′W*
114 B6 **Oliveros** Santa Fe, Argentina *32°34′S 60°51′W*
165 H4 **Olivet** Loiret, C France *47°53′N 01°53′E*
74 E6 **Olivet** South Dakota, N USA *43°14′N 97°40′W*
74 F5 **Olivia** Minnesota, N USA *44°46′N 94°59′W*
141 J6 **Oliviershoek Pass** *pass* South Africa
278 B10 **Olivine Range** ▲▲ South Island, New Zealand
176 E5 **Olivone** Ticino, S Switzerland *46°32′N 08°55′E*
244 D4 **Oljoq** Inner Mongolia, China *38°07′N 107°16′E*
Ölkeyek *see* Ol'keyyek
226 F4 **Ol'keyyek** *Kaz.* Ölkeyek; *prev.* Ul'kayak. ≈ C Kazakhstan
197 I5 **Ol'khovka** Volgogradskaya Oblast', SW Russian Federation *49°54′N 44°36′E*
183 G8 **Olkusz** Małopolskie, S Poland *50°18′N 19°33′E*
68 C2 **Olla** Louisiana, S USA *31°54′N 92°14′W*
112 B3 **Ollage, Volcn** ⛰ Chile *21°06′S 68°06′W*
105 H12 **Ollagüe, Volcán** *var.* Oyahue, Volcán Oyahue. ⛰ N Chile *21°25′S 68°10′W*
282 E9 **Ollan** *island* Chuuk, C Micronesia
282 C8 **Ollei** Babeldaob, N Palau *07°43′N 134°37′E*
161 J2 **Ollerton** C England, United Kingdom *53°12′N 01°04′W*
169 I2 **Olliergues** Auvergne, France *45°40′N 3°38′E*
Ollius *see* Oglio
176 C5 **Ollon** Vaud, W Switzerland *46°19′N 07°00′E*
229 I5 **Olmaliq** *Rus.* Almalyk. Toshkent Viloyati, E Uzbekistan *40°51′N 69°39′E*
170 F4 **Olmedo** Castilla-León, N Spain *41°17′N 04°41′W*
104 B4 **Olmos** Lambayeque, W Peru *06°00′S 79°43′W*
Olmütz *see* Olomouc
161 J4 **Olney** United Kingdom *52°09′N 0°42′W*
73 D12 **Olney** Illinois, N USA *38°43′N 88°05′W*
70 G4 **Olney** Texas, SW USA *33°22′N 98°45′W*
173 L2 **Olocau del Rey** Valenciana, Spain *40°38′N 0°20′W*
155 G11 **Olofström** Blekinge, S Sweden *56°16′N 14°33′E*
59 K6 **Olomane River** ≈ Québec, E Canada
281 K2 **Olomburi** Malaita, N Solomon Islands *09°00′S 161°09′E*
190 I3 **Olomna** Leningradskaya Oblast', Russian Federation
183 E9 **Olomouc** *Ger.* Olmütz, *Pol.* Ołomuniec. Olomoucký Kraj, E Czech Republic *49°36′N 17°13′E*
183 E9 **Olomoucký Kraj** ◐ *region* E Czech Republic
Ołomuniec *see* Olomouc
194 E7 **Olonets** Respublika Kareliya, NW Russian Federation *60°58′N 33°01′E*
263 K5 **Olongapo** *off.* Olongapo City. Luzon, N Philippines *14°52′N 120°16′E*
Olongapo City *see* Olongapo
169 H6 **Olonzac** Languedoc-Roussillon, France *43°16′N 2°44′E*
168 D6 **Oloron-Ste-Marie** Pyrénées-Atlantiques, SW France *43°12′N 00°35′W*
285 L2 **Olosega** *island* Manua Islands, E American Samoa
171 K3 **Olot** Cataluña, NE Spain *42°11′N 02°30′E*
228 G6 **Olot** *Rus.* Alat. Buxoro Viloyati, C Uzbekistan *39°22′N 63°42′E*
184 E4 **Olovo** Federacija Bosna I Hercegovina, E Bosnia and Herzegovina *44°08′N 18°35′E*
193 I8 **Olovyannaya** Zabaykalskiy Kray, S Russian Federation *50°59′N 115°24′E*
193 L4 **Oloy** ≈ NE Russian Federation
181 D9 **Olpe** Nordrhein-Westfalen, W Germany *51°02′N 07°51′E*
179 G14 **Olperer** ▲ SW Austria *47°03′N 11°36′E*
181 D13 **Olsbrücken** Rheinland-Pfalz, Germany *49°32′E 7°39′N*
191 I8 **Ol'sha** Smolenskaya Oblast', Russian Federation
Olshanka *see* Vil'shanka
Ol'shany *see* Al'shany
Olsnitz *see* Murska Sobota
162 H6 **Olst** Overijssel, E Netherlands *52°19′N 06°06′E*
182 G4 **Olsztyn** *Ger.* Allenstein. Warmińsko-Mazurskie, N Poland *53°46′N 20°28′E*
182 G4 **Olsztynek** *Ger.* Hohenstein in Ostpreussen. Warmińsko-Mazurskie, N Poland *53°35′N 20°17′E*
188 D8 **Olt** ◐ *county* SW Romania
188 D10 **Olt** *var.* Oltul, *Ger.* Alt. ≈ S Romania
179 C14 **Olten** Solothurn, NW Switzerland *47°22′N 07°55′E*
188 E10 **Oltenița** *prev.* *Eng.* Oltenitsa; *anc.* Constantiola. Călărași, SE Romania *44°05′N 26°40′E*
Oltenitsa *see* Oltenița
188 C9 **Olteț** ≈ S Romania
70 D3 **Olton** Texas, SW USA *34°10′N 102°07′W*
215 J5 **Oltu** Erzurum, NE Turkey *40°34′N 41°59′E*
Oltul *see* Olt
228 D4 **Oltynko'l** Qoraqalpog'iston Respublikasi, NW Uzbekistan *43°04′N 58°51′E*
Ólubló *see* Stará L'ubovňa
215 J5 **Olur** Erzurum, NE Turkey *40°49′N 42°08′E*
170 E8 **Olvera** Andalucía, S Spain *36°56′N 05°15′W*
Ol'viopol' *see* Pervomays'k
Olwanpi, Cape *see* Eluanbi
186 F7 **Olympía** Dytikí Elláda, S Greece *37°39′N 21°36′E*
76 C4 **Olympia** *state capital* Washington, NW USA *47°02′N 122°54′W*
276 F3 **Olympic Dam** South Australia *30°25′S 136°56′E*
76 B3 **Olympic Mountains** ▲▲ Washington, NW USA
218 B2 **Ólympos** *var.* Troodos, *Eng.* Mount Olympus. ▲ C Cyprus *34°55′N 32°49′E*
186 G3 **Ólympos** *var.* Ólimbos, *Eng.* Mount Olympus. ▲ N Greece *40°04′N 22°24′E*
187 K5 **Ólympos** ▲ Lésvos, E Greece *39°03′N 26°20′E*
290 F4 **Olympus Knoll** *undersea feature* N Atlantic Ocean
76 B3 **Olympus, Mount** ▲ Washington, NW USA *47°48′N 123°42′W*
Olympus, Mount *see* Ólympos
187 H3 **Ólynthos** *var.* Olinthos; *anc.* Olynthus. *site of ancient city* Kentrikí Makedonía, N Greece
Olynthus *see* Ólynthos
189 H2 **Olyshivka** Chernihivs'ka Oblast', N Ukraine *51°13′N 31°19′E*
193 N4 **Olyutorskiy, Mys** *headland* E Russian Federation *59°56′N 170°22′E*
193 N4 **Olyutorskiy Zaliv** *bay* E Russian Federation
280 A3 **Om** ≈ W Papua New Guinea
205 J3 **Om'** ≈ N Russian Federation
238 E8 **Oma** Xizang Zizhiqu, W China *32°30′N 83°14′E*
252 D6 **Ōma** Aomori, Honshū, C Japan *41°31′N 140°54′E*
195 H4 **Oma** ≈ NW Russian Federation
251 K2 **Ōmachi** *var.* Ōmati. Nagano, Honshū, S Japan *36°30′N 137°51′E*
251 K5 **Omae-zaki** *headland* Honshū, S Japan *34°36′N 138°12′E*
253 D9 **Ōmagari** Akita, Honshū, C Japan *39°29′N 140°29′E*
158 C6 **Omagh** *Ir.* An Ómaigh. W Northern Ireland, United Kingdom *54°36′N 07°18′W*
75 F8 **Omaha** Nebraska, C USA *41°14′N 95°57′W*
138 D4 **Omaheke** ◐ *district* W Namibia
221 K6 **Oman** *off.* Sultanate of Oman, *Ar.* Salṭanat 'Umān; *prev.* Muscat and Oman. ◆ *monarchy* SW Asia
205 H6 **Oman Basin** *var.* Bassin d'Oman. *undersea feature* N Indian Ocean *23°20′N 63°00′E*
Oman, Bassin d' *see* Oman Basin
205 H6 **Oman, Gulf of** *Ar.* Khalīj 'Umān. *gulf* N Arabian Sea
Oman, Sultanate of *see* Oman
278 F2 **Omapere** Northland, North Island, New Zealand *35°32′S 173°24′E*
278 C11 **Omarama** Canterbury, South Island, New Zealand *44°29′S 169°57′E*
184 C3 **Omarska** ◐ Republika Srpska, NW Bosnia and Herzegovina
138 C5 **Omaruru** Erongo, NW Namibia *21°28′S 15°56′E*
140 A1 **Omaruru** ≈ W Namibia
138 D4 **Omatako** ≈ NE Namibia
Ōmati *see* Ōmachi
138 D5 **Omawewozonyanda** Omaheke, E Namibia *21°30′S 19°34′E*
252 D6 **Ōma-zaki** *headland* Honshū, C Japan *41°32′N 140°53′E*
Omba *see* Ambae
Ombai *see* Alor, Pulau
Ombai, Selat *see* Ombai Strait
260 F8 **Ombai Strait** *var.* Selat Ombai. *strait* Nusa Tenggara, S Indonesia
138 B3 **Ombalantu** Omusati, N Namibia *17°33′S 14°58′E*
134 E5 **Ombella-Mpoko** ◐ *prefecture* S Central African Republic
161 H4 **Ombersley** United Kingdom *52°16′N 2°14′W*
Ombetsu *see* Onbetsu
138 B4 **Ombombo** Kunene, NW Namibia *18°43′S 13°53′E*
135 A8 **Omboué** Ogooué-Maritime, W Gabon *01°38′S 09°20′E*
177 H10 **Ombrone** ≈ C Italy
115 H7 **Ombúes de Oribe** Durazno, Uruguay *33°18′S 56°21′W*
140 G7 **Omdraaisvlei** Northern Cape, South Africa *30°07′S 23°07′E*
136 B2 **Omdurman** *var.* Umm Durmān. Khartoum, C Sudan *15°37′N 32°29′E*
253 B13 **Ōme** Tōkyō, Honshū, S Japan *35°48′N 139°17′E*
176 D6 **Omegna** Piemonte, NE Italy *45°54′N 08°25′E*
277 K7 **Omeo** Victoria, SE Australia *37°09′S 147°36′E*
219 D10 **Omer** Southern, C Israel *31°16′N 34°51′E*
86 F8 **Ometepec** Guerrero, S Mexico *16°39′N 98°23′W*
88 G7 **Ometepe, Isla de** *island* S Nicaragua
Om Hager *see* Om Ḥajer
136 D2 **Om Ḥajer** *var.* Om Hager. SW Eritrea *14°19′N 36°46′E*
251 I4 **Ōmihachiman** Shiga, Honshū, SW Japan *35°08′N 136°04′E*
56 D2 **Omineca Mountains** ▲▲ British Columbia, W Canada
184 C5 **Omiš** *It.* Almissa. Split-Dalmacija, S Croatia *43°27′N 16°41′E*
184 B3 **Omišalj** Primorje-Gorski Kotar, NW Croatia *45°10′N 14°33′E*
250 D5 **Ōmi-shima** *island* SW Japan
140 C1 **Omitara** Khomas, C Namibia *22°18′S 18°01′E*
86 E8 **Omitlán, Río** ≈ S Mexico
83 M8 **Ommaney, Cape** *headland* Baranof Island, Alaska, USA *56°10′N 134°40′W*
162 I5 **Ommen** Overijssel, E Netherlands *52°31′N 06°25′E*
239 L1 **Ömnödelger** *var.* Bayanbulag. Hentiy, C Mongolia *47°54′N 109°51′E*
239 K3 **Ömnögovĭ** ◐ *province* S Mongolia
285 K5 **Omoa** Fatu Hira, NE French Polynesia *10°30′S 138°41′E*
Omo Botego *see* Omo Wenz
Ómoldova *see* Moldova Veche
193 L4 **Omolon** Chukotskiy Avtonomnyy Okrug, NE Russian Federation *65°11′N 160°33′E*
193 M4 **Omolon** ≈ NE Russian Federation
193 J4 **Omoloy** ≈ NE Russian Federation
253 C9 **Omono-gawa** ≈ Honshū, C Japan
80 E2 **Omo Ranch** California, USA *38°35′N 120°34′W*
136 D5 **Omo Wenz** *var.* Omo Botego. ≈ Ethiopia/Kenya
192 E7 **Omsk** Omskaya Oblast', C Russian Federation *55°N 73°22′E*
192 E7 **Omskaya Oblast'** ◐ *province* C Russian Federation
193 L5 **Omsukchan** Magadanskaya Oblast', E Russian Federation *62°25′N 155°22′E*
252 F3 **Ōmu** Hokkaidō, NE Japan *44°36′N 142°55′E*
182 H4 **Omulew** ≈ NE Poland
188 D8 **Omul, Vârful** *prev.* Vîrful Omu. ▲ C Romania *45°24′N 25°26′E*
138 C3 **Omundaungilo** Ohangwena, N Namibia *17°28′S 16°39′E*
250 C7 **Ōmura** Nagasaki, Kyūshū, SW Japan *32°56′N 129°58′E*
138 B3 **Omusati** ◐ *district* N Namibia
250 C7 **Ōmuta** Fukuoka, Kyūshū, SW Japan *33°01′N 130°27′E*
195 J9 **Omutninsk** Kirovskaya Oblast', NW Russian Federation *58°37′N 52°08′E*
Omu, Vîrful *see* Omul, Vârful
74 G4 **Onamia** Minnesota, N USA *46°04′N 93°40′W*
67 M4 **Onancock** Virginia, NE USA *37°42′N 75°45′W*
62 C1 **Onaping Lake** ◎ Ontario, S Canada
73 D10 **Onarga** Illinois, N USA *40°39′N 88°00′W*
84 F4 **Onavas** Sonora, Mexico *28°28′N 109°32′W*
74 F7 **Onawa** Iowa, C USA *42°01′N 96°06′W*
252 G5 **Onbetsu** *var.* Ombetsu. Hokkaidō, NE Japan *42°52′N 143°54′E*
110 F2 **Onça** Minas Gerais, Brazil *19°43′S 44°48′W*
158 G8 **Onchan** E Isle of Man
135 C14 **Oncócua** Cunene, SW Angola *16°37′S 13°23′E*
171 I5 **Onda** País Valenciano, E Spain *39°58′N 00°17′W*
173 M5 **Ondara** Valenciana, Spain *38°50′N 0°01′E*
168 A6 **Ondàrroa** Pais Vasco, Spain *43°19′N 2°25′W*
183 H9 **Ondava** ≈ NE Slovakia
140 E7 **Onderstedorings** Northern Cape, South Africa *30°13′S 20°36′E*
Ondjiva *see* N'Giva
133 J7 **Ondo** Ondo, SW Nigeria *07°07′N 04°50′E*
133 J7 **Ondo** ◐ *state* SW Nigeria
236 G3 **Öndörhaan** *var.* Undur Khan; *prev.* Tsetsen Khan. Hentiy, E Mongolia *47°21′N 110°42′E*
239 L2 **Öndörshil** *var.* Böhöt. Dundgovĭ, C Mongolia *45°13′N 108°12′E*
239 K1 **Öndörshireet** *var.* Bayshint. Töv, C Mongolia *47°22′N 105°04′E*
239 J1 **Öndör-Ulaan** *var.* Teel. Arhangay, C Mongolia *48°01′N 100°30′E*
138 C4 **Ondundazongonda** Otjozondjupa, N Namibia *20°28′S 18°00′E*
80 E5 **O'Neals** California, USA *37°08′N 119°42′W*
235 C13 **One and Half Degree Channel** *channel* S Maldives
280 G9 **Oneata** *island* Lau Group, E Fiji
194 F6 **Onega** Arkhangel'skaya Oblast', NW Russian Federation *63°54′N 37°59′E*
194 F6 **Onega** ≈ NW Russian Federation
Onega Bay *see* Onezhskaya Guba
Onega, Lake *see* Onezhskoye Ozero
64 F1 **Oneida** New York, NE USA *43°05′N 75°39′W*
66 F5 **Oneida** Tennessee, S USA *36°30′N 84°30′W*
64 E1 **Oneida Lake** ◎ New York, NE USA
74 D7 **O'Neill** Nebraska, C USA *42°28′N 98°38′W*
193 N7 **Onekotan, Ostrov** *island* Kuril'skiye Ostrova, SE Russian Federation
66 E8 **Oneonta** Alabama, S USA *33°57′N 86°28′W*
64 G2 **Oneonta** New York, NE USA *42°27′N 75°03′W*
284 G10 **Oneroa** *island* S Cook Islands
188 E8 **Onești** *Hung.* Onyest; *prev.* Gheorghe Gheorghiu-Dej. Bacău, E Romania *46°14′N 26°46′E*
284 E9 **Onevai** *island* Tongatapu Group, S Tonga
176 B5 **Onex** Genève, SW Switzerland *46°12′N 06°04′E*
194 F5 **Onezhskaya Guba** *Eng.* Onega Bay. *bay* NW Russian Federation
194 E7 **Onezhskoye Ozero** *Eng.* Lake Onega. ◎ NW Russian Federation
138 B3 **Ongandjera** Omusati, N Namibia *17°49′S 15°06′E*
278 H6 **Ongaonga** Hawke's Bay, North Island, New Zealand *39°57′S 176°21′E*
140 G7 **Ongers** ≈ Northern Cape, South Africa
Ongi *see* Sayhan-Ovoo, Dundgovĭ, Mongolia
Ongi *see* Uyanga
248 B5 **Ongjin** SW North Korea *37°56′N 125°22′E*
234 F6 **Ongole** Andhra Pradesh, E India *15°33′N 80°03′E*
Ongon *see* Bürd
Ongtüstik Qazaqstan Oblysy *see* Yuzhnyy Kazakhstan
163 F12 **Onhaye** Namur, S Belgium *50°15′N 04°51′E*
256 C6 **Onhne** Bago, SW Myanmar (Burma) *17°02′N 96°28′E*
215 J3 **Oni** N Georgia *42°36′N 43°13′E*
158 F1 **Onich** United Kingdom *56°42′N 5°13′W*
74 C5 **Onida** South Dakota, N USA *44°42′N 100°03′W*
250 E7 **Onigajō-yama** ▲ Shikoku, SW Japan *33°10′N 132°37′E*
250 E6 **Onigajū-yama** ▲ *33°10′N 132°36′E*
139 L9 **Onilahy** ≈ S Madagascar
133 K8 **Onitsha** Anambra, S Nigeria *06°09′N 06°48′E*
251 I3 **Ōno** Fukui, Honshū, SW Japan *35°59′N 136°30′E*
251 H4 **Ono** Hyōgo, Honshū, SW Japan *34°52′N 134°55′E*
280 E9 **Ono** *island* SW Fiji
250 D5 **Onoda** Yamaguchi, Honshū, SW Japan *34°00′N 131°11′E*
281 N8 **Ono-i-lau** *island* SE Fiji
250 C6 **Ōnojō** *var.* Ōnozyô. Fukuoka, Kyūshū, SW Japan *33°34′N 130°29′E*
193 I8 **Onokhoy** Respublika Buryatiya, S Russian Federation *51°51′N 108°17′E*
250 F5 **Onomichi** *var.* Onomiti. Hiroshima, Honshū, SW Japan *34°25′N 133°11′E*
Onomiti *see* Onomichi
237 H2 **Onon Gol** ≈ N Mongolia
Ononte *see* Orontes
102 G3 **Onoto** Anzoátegui, NE Venezuela *09°36′N 65°12′W*
284 B3 **Onotoa** *prev.* Clerk Island. *atoll* Tungaru, W Kiribati
Ōnozyô *see* Ōnojō
140 D6 **Onseepkans** Northern Cape, W South Africa *28°44′S 19°18′E*
141 I2 **Ons Hoop** Limpopo, South Africa *23°34′S 27°43′E*
170 C2 **Ons, Illa de** *island* NW Spain
274 C5 **Onslow** Western Australia *21°42′S 115°08′E*
67 L7 **Onslow Bay** *bay* North Carolina, E USA
162 J4 **Onstwedde** Groningen, NE Netherlands *53°01′N 07°04′E*
250 C8 **On-take** ▲ Kyūshū, SW Japan *31°35′N 130°39′E*
251 J3 **Ontake-san** ▲ Honshū, S Japan *35°54′N 137°28′E*
52 B7 **Ontaratue River** ≈ Northwest Territories, NW Canada
81 E11 **Ontario** California, W USA *34°03′N 117°39′W*
76 F7 **Ontario** Oregon, NW USA *44°01′N 116°57′W*
62 B1 **Ontario** ◐ *province* S Canada
62 E5 **Ontario, Lake** ◎ Canada/USA
42 F6 **Ontario Peninsula** *peninsula* Canada/USA
140 F4 **Ontemoeting** Northern Cape, South Africa *27°03′S 21°34′E*
Onteniente *see* Ontinyent
168 E9 **Ontiñena** Aragón, Spain *41°40′N 0°04′E*
171 I6 **Ontinyent** *var.* Onteniente. País Valenciano, E Spain *38°49′N 00°37′W*
152 I7 **Ontojärvi** ◎ E Finland
72 C4 **Ontonagon** Michigan, N USA *46°52′N 89°18′W*
72 D4 **Ontonagon River** ≈ Michigan, N USA
280 G3 **Ontong Java Atoll** *prev.* Lord Howe Island. *atoll* N Solomon Islands
266 G3 **Ontong Java Rise** *undersea feature* W Pacific Ocean *01°00′N 157°00′E*
173 K5 **Ontur** Castilla-La Manacha, Spain *38°38′N 1°29′W*
Onuba *see* Huelva
103 L5 **Onverwacht** Para, N Suriname *05°36′N 55°12′W*
Onyest *see* Onești
81 E8 **Onyx** California, USA *35°41′N 118°13′W*
Oodeypore *see* Udaipur
276 G4 **Oodla Wirra** South Australia *32°52′S 139°05′E*
276 F2 **Oodnadatta** South Australia *27°34′S 135°27′E*
276 D3 **Ooldea** South Australia *30°29′S 131°50′E*
75 F11 **Oologah Lake** ⊠ Oklahoma, C USA
Oos-Kaap *see* Eastern Cape
Oos-Londen *see* East London
163 C9 **Oostakker** Oost-Vlaanderen, NW Belgium *51°06′N 03°46′E*
163 C9 **Oostburg** Zeeland, SW Netherlands *51°20′N 03°30′E*
162 G5 **Oostelijk-Flevoland** *polder* C Netherlands
163 B9 **Oostende** *Eng.* Ostend, *Fr.* Ostende. West-Vlaanderen, NW Belgium *51°13′N 02°55′E*
163 B9 **Oostende** ✕ West-Vlaanderen, NW Belgium *51°12′N 02°55′E*
162 G7 **Oosterbeek** Gelderland, SE Netherlands *51°59′N 05°51′E*
163 F8 **Oosterhout** Noord-Brabant, S Netherlands *51°38′N 04°51′E*
162 I4 **Oostermoers Vaart** *var.* Hunze. ≈ NE Netherlands
163 D8 **Oosterschelde** *Eng.* Eastern Scheldt. *inlet* SW Netherlands
163 C8 **Oosterscheldedam** *dam* SW Netherlands
162 H4 **Oosterwolde** *Fris.* Easterwâlde. Friesland, N Netherlands *53°01′N 06°15′E*
162 F5 **Oosthuizen** Noord-Holland, NW Netherlands *52°34′N 05°00′E*
163 E9 **Oostmalle** Antwerpen, N Belgium *51°18′N 04°44′E*
Oos-Transvaal *see* Mpumalanga
163 C8 **Oost-Souburg** Zeeland, SW Netherlands *51°28′N 03°36′E*
163 D9 **Oost-Vlaanderen** *Eng.* East Flanders. ◐ *province* NW Belgium
162 F3 **Oost-Vlieland** Friesland, N Netherlands *53°19′N 05°02′E*
162 D7 **Oostvoorne** Zuid-Holland, SW Netherlands *51°55′N 04°06′E*
Ootacamund *see* Udagamandalam
162 I6 **Ootmarsum** Overijssel, E Netherlands *52°25′N 06°55′E*
56 C4 **Ootsa Lake** ⊠ British Columbia, SW Canada
Ooty *see* Udagamandalam
185 L5 **Opaka** Tŭrgovishte, N Bulgaria *43°26′N 26°12′E*
134 G7 **Opala** Orientale, C Dem. Rep. Congo *0°40′S 24°20′E*
195 I8 **Oparino** Kirovskaya Oblast', NW Russian Federation *59°52′N 48°14′E*
184 A2 **Opatija** *It.* Abbazia. Primorje-Gorski Kotar, NW Croatia *45°18′N 14°15′E*
182 H7 **Opatów** Śuiętokrzyskie, C Poland *50°45′N 21°27′E*
183 E8 **Opava** *Ger.* Troppau. Moravskoslezský Kraj, E Czech Republic *49°56′N 17°53′E*
183 E8 **Opava** *Ger.* Oppa. ≈ NE Czech Republic
Ópazova *see* Stara Pazova
Ópécska *see* Pecica
84 E3 **Opedepe** Sonora, Mexico *29°55′N 110°39′W*
72 I3 **Opeepeesway Lake** ◎ Ontario, S Canada
69 I1 **Opelika** Alabama, S USA *32°39′N 85°22′W*
68 C4 **Opelousas** Louisiana, S USA *30°31′N 92°04′W*
280 D3 **Open Bay** *bay* New Britain, E Papua New Guinea
114 D9 **Open Door** Buenos Aires, Argentina *34°30′S 59°05′W*
62 E3 **Opeongo Lake** ◎ Ontario, SE Canada
163 G9 **Opglabbeek** Limburg, NE Belgium *51°04′N 05°39′E*
77 K2 **Opheim** Montana, NW USA *48°50′N 106°24′W*
83 H5 **Ophir** Alaska, USA *63°08′N 156°31′W*
Ophiusa *see* Formentera
134 I7 **Opienge** Orientale, E Dem. Rep. Congo *0°15′N 27°25′E*
278 D10 **Opihi** ≈ South Island, New Zealand
58 G5 **Opinaca** ≈ Québec, C Canada
58 G5 **Opinaca, Réservoir** ⊠ Québec, E Canada
189 J3 **Opishnya** *Rus.* Oposhnya. Poltavs'ka Oblast', NE Ukraine *49°58′N 34°37′E*
181 C9 **Opladen** Nordrhein-Westfalen, Germany *51°04′E 7°01′N*
162 F5 **Opmeer** Noord-Holland, NW Netherlands *52°43′N 04°56′E*
133 K8 **Opobo** Akwa Ibom, S Nigeria *04°36′N 07°37′E*
194 C10 **Opochka** Pskovskaya Oblast', W Russian Federation *56°42′N 28°40′E*
182 G7 **Opoczno** Łodzkie, C Poland *51°24′N 20°18′E*
183 E8 **Opole** *Ger.* Oppeln. Opolskie, S Poland *50°40′N 17°56′E*
182 E7 **Opolskie** ◐ *province* S Poland
Opornyy *see* Borankul
170 C3 **O Porriño** *var.* Porriño. Galicia, NW Spain *42°10′N 08°38′W*
Oporto *see* Porto
Oposhnya *see* Opishnya
278 I5 **Opotiki** Bay of Plenty, North Island, New Zealand *38°02′S 177°18′E*
69 H3 **Opp** Alabama, S USA *31°16′N 86°14′W*
Oppa *see* Opava
154 D4 **Oppdal** Sør-Trøndelag, S Norway *62°36′N 09°41′E*
Oppeln *see* Opole
180 F5 **Oppenwehe** Nordrhein-Westfalen, Germany *52°28′E 8°30′N*
175 H12 **Oppido Mamertina** Calabria, SW Italy *38°17′N 15°58′E*
Oppidum Ubiorum *see* Köln
154 D6 **Oppland** ◐ *county* S Norway
191 F8 **Opsa** Vitsyebskaya Voblasts', NW Belarus *55°32′N 26°50′E*
75 B11 **Optima Lake** ⊠ Oklahoma, C USA
278 F6 **Opunake** Taranaki, North Island, New Zealand *39°27′S 173°52′E*
285 L3 **Opunohu, Baie d'** *bay* Moorea, W French Polynesia
138 B3 **Opuwo** Kunene, NW Namibia *18°03′S 13°54′E*
228 E3 **Oqqal'a** *var.* Akkala, *Rus.* Karakala. Qoraqalpog'iston Respublikasi, NW Uzbekistan *43°43′N 59°25′E*
229 L7 **Oqsu** *Rus.* Oksu. ≈ SE Tajikistan
229 I8 **Oqtogh, Qatorkŭhi** *Rus.* Khrebet Aktau. ▲▲ SW Tajikistan
229 H6 **Oqtosh** *Rus.* Aktash. Samarqand Viloyati, C Uzbekistan *39°23′N 65°46′E*
229 H6 **Oqtov Tizmasi** *var.* Khrebet Aktau. ▲▲ C Uzbekistan
73 B9 **Oquawka** Illinois, N USA *40°56′N 90°56′W*
197 M4 **Or'** *Kaz.* Or. ≈ Kazakhstan/Russian Federation
79 I9 **Oracle** Arizona, SW USA *32°36′N 110°46′W*
172 C5 **Orada** Évora, Portugal *38°53′N 7°28′W*
229 H7 **O'radaryo** *Rus.* Uradar'ya. ≈ S Uzbekistan
188 B6 **Oradea** *prev.* Oradea Mare, *Ger.* Grosswardein, *Hung.* Nagyvárad. Bihor, NW Romania *47°03′N 21°56′E*
Oradea Mare *see* Oradea
168 F1 **Oradour-sur-Glane** Limousin, France *45°56′N 1°02′E*
Orahovac *see* Rahovec
184 D2 **Orahovica** Virovitica-Podravina, NE Croatia *45°33′N 17°54′E*
232 F7 **Orai** Uttar Pradesh, N India *26°00′N 79°26′E*
152 G5 **Orajärvi** Lappi, NW Finland *66°54′N 24°04′E*
218 D7 **Or'Akiva** *prev.* Or 'Aqiva. Haifa, N Israel *32°40′N 34°58′E*
Oral *see* Ural'sk
131 H2 **Oran** *var.* Ouahran, Wahran. NW Algeria *35°42′N 00°37′W*
277 K5 **Orange** New South Wales, SE Australia *33°16′S 149°06′E*
165 J8 **Orange** *anc.* Arausio. Vaucluse, SE France *44°06′N 04°52′E*
81 D11 **Orange** California, USA *33°47′N 117°51′W*
65 J5 **Orange** Connecticut, USA *41°17′N 73°02′W*
71 J7 **Orange** Texas, SW USA *30°05′N 93°43′W*
67 K3 **Orange** Virginia, NE USA *38°14′N 78°07′W*
67 I9 **Orangeburg** South Carolina, SE USA *33°28′N 80°53′W*
103 N6 **Orange, Cabo** *headland* NE Brazil *04°24′N 51°33′W*
74 F6 **Orange City** Iowa, C USA *43°00′N 96°03′W*
Orange Cone *see* Orange Fan
80 E6 **Orange Cove** California, USA *36°37′N 119°19′W*
291 J10 **Orange Fan** *var.* Orange Cone. *undersea feature* SW Indian Ocean *32°00′S 12°00′E*
Orange Free State *see* Free State
70 G8 **Orange Grove** Texas, SW USA *27°57′N 97°56′W*
65 H4 **Orange Lake** New York, NE USA *41°32′N 74°06′W*
69 L5 **Orange Lake** ◎ Florida, SE USA
Orange Mouth/Orangemund *see* Oranjemund
69 L4 **Orange Park** Florida, SE USA *30°10′N 81°42′W*
140 C6 **Orange River** *Afr.* Oranjerivier. ≈ S Africa
62 C4 **Orangeville** Ontario, S Canada *43°55′N 80°06′W*
79 I4 **Orangeville** Utah, W USA *39°14′N 111°03′W*
88 E1 **Orange Walk** Orange Walk, N Belize *18°06′N 88°30′W*
88 D2 **Orange Walk** ◐ *district* NW Belize
140 G6 **Orania** Northern Cape, South Africa *29°49′S 24°24′E*
178 H6 **Oranienburg** Brandenburg, NE Germany *52°46′N 13°15′E*
141 I2 **Oranjefontein** Limpopo, Botswana *23°26′S 27°41′E*
162 I4 **Oranjekanaal** *canal* NE Netherlands
140 B6 **Oranjemund** *var.* Orangemund; *prev.* Orange Mouth. Karas, SW Namibia *28°33′S 16°28′E*
140 G6 **Oranjerivier** Northern Cape, South Africa *29°40′S 24°12′E*
Oranjerivier *see* Orange River
102 E1 **Oranjestad** ○ (Aruba) W Aruba *12°31′N 70°W*
141 J4 **Oranjeville** Free State, South Africa *26°59′S 28°12′E*
Oranje Vrystaat *see* Free State
158 A10 **Oranmore** Galway, Ireland *53°16′N 8°55′W*
261 J4 **Oransbari** Papua, E Indonesia *01°18′S 134°16′E*
Orany *see* Varėna
138 F4 **Orapa** Central, C Botswana *21°16′S 25°22′E*
218 D7 **Or'Aqiva** *var.* 'Aqiva. Israel *32°30′N 34°55′E*
Or 'Aqiva *see* Or'Akiva
184 E3 **Orašje** ◐ Federacija Bosna I Herecegovina, N Bosnia and Herzegovina
188 C8 **Orăștie** *Ger.* Broos, *Hung.* Szászváros. Hunedoara, W Romania *45°50′N 23°11′E*
Orașul Stalin *see* Brașov
183 J11 **Orașu Nou** Satu Mare, N Romania *47°50′N 23°17′E*
111 I4 **Oratórios** Minas Gerais, Brazil *20°26′S 42°48′W*
183 F9 **Orava** *Hung.* Árva, *Pol.* Orawa. ≈ N Slovakia
Oravainen *see* Oravais
153 G8 **Oravais** *Fin.* Oravainen. Länsi-Suomi, W Finland *63°18′N 22°25′E*
Oravicabánya *see* Oravița
188 B9 **Oravița** *Ger.* Orawitza, *Hung.* Oravicabánya. Caraș-Severin, SW Romania *45°02′N 21°43′E*
Orawa *see* Orava
278 B12 **Orawia** Southland, South Island, New Zealand *46°03′S 167°49′E*
Orawitza *see* Oravița
165 I8 **Orb** ≈ S France
176 E8 **Orba** ≈ NW Italy
238 D7 **Orba Co** ◎ W China
169 N3 **Orbassano** Piemonte, NW Italy *45°00′N 07°32′E*
176 C4 **Orbe** Vaud, W Switzerland *46°42′N 06°28′E*
166 E5 **Orbec-en-Auge** Basse-Normandie, France *49°01′N 0°25′E*
174 D7 **Orbetello** Toscana, C Italy *42°28′N 11°15′E*
170 E2 **Orbigo** ≈ NW Spain
277 K7 **Orbost** Victoria, SE Australia *37°44′S 148°28′E*
154 I7 **Örbyhus** Uppsala, C Sweden *60°15′N 17°43′E*
292 E1 **Orcadas** *Argentinian research station* South Orkney Islands, Antarctica *60°37′S 44°48′W*
171 H7 **Orcera** Andalucía, S Spain *38°20′N 02°36′W*
76 G4 **Orchard Homes** Montana, NW USA *46°52′N 114°01′W*
79 J4 **Orchard Mesa** Colorado, C USA *39°02′N 108°33′W*
64 A1 **Orchard Park** New York, NE USA *42°46′N 78°44′W*
Orchid Island *see* Lan Yü
167 I2 **Orchies** Nord-Pas-de-Calais, France *50°28′N 3°14′E*
186 G6 **Orchómenos** *var.* Orhomenos, Orkhómenos, *prev.* Skripón; *anc.* Orchomenus. Stereá Elláda, C Greece *38°29′N 22°58′E*
Orchomenus *see* Orchómenos
174 B4 **Orco** ≈ NW Italy
165 J5 **Or, Côte d'** *physical region* C France
81 B8 **Orcutt** California, USA *34°52′N 120°26′W*
74 D7 **Ord** Nebraska, C USA *41°36′N 98°55′W*
191 I9 **Ordats'** *Rus.* Ordat'. Mahilyowskaya Voblasts', E Belarus *54°10′N 30°42′E*
114 G9 **Ordeig** Uruguay *34°39′S 56°43′W*
79 H5 **Orderville** Utah, W USA *37°16′N 112°38′W*
170 C2 **Ordes** Galicia, NW Spain *43°04′N 08°25′W*
81 F10 **Ord Mountain** ▲ California, W USA *34°41′N 116°46′W*
81 G10 **Ord Mountains** ▲▲ California, USA
244 F3 **Ordos** *prev.* Dongsheng. Nei Mongol Zizhiqu, N China *39°51′N 110°00′E*
Ordos Desert *see* Mu Us Shadi
282 B2 **Ordot** C Guam
214 G5 **Ordu** *anc.* Cotyora. Ordu, N Turkey *41°N 37°52′E*
214 G5 **Ordu** ◐ *province* N Turkey
215 L6 **Ordubad** SW Azerbaijan *38°55′N 46°00′E*
Orduña *see* Urduña
79 M4 **Ordway** Colorado, C USA *38°13′N 103°45′W*
189 J6 **Ordzhonikidze** Dnipropetrovs'ka Oblast', E Ukraine *47°39′N 34°08′E*
Ordzhonikidze *see* Denisovka, Kazakhstan
Ordzhonikidze *see* Vladikavkaz, Russian Federation
Ordzhonikidze *see* Yenakiyeve, Ukraine
Ordzhonikidzeabad *see* Kofarnihon
103 K5 **Orealla** E Guyana *05°13′N 57°17′W*
80 I1 **Oreana** Nevada, USA *40°20′N 118°19′W*
184 D6 **Orebić** *It.* Sabbioncello. Dubrovnik-Neretva, S Croatia *42°58′N 17°12′E*
155 G8 **Örebro** Örebro, C Sweden *59°18′N 15°12′E*
154 G7 **Örebro** ◐ *county* C Sweden
71 I4 **Ore City** Texas, SW USA *32°48′N 94°43′W*
190 H3 **Oredezh** Leningradskaya Oblast', Russian Federation
73 C8 **Oregon** Illinois, N USA *42°00′N 89°19′W*
75 F9 **Oregon** Missouri, C USA *39°59′N 95°08′W*
73 H9 **Oregon** Ohio, N USA *41°38′N 83°29′W*
76 D7 **Oregon** *off.* State of Oregon, *also known as* Beaver State, Sunset State, Valentine State, Webfoot State. ◐ *state* NW USA
76 C5 **Oregon City** Oregon, NW USA *45°21′N 122°36′W*
80 D1 **Oregon House** California, USA *39°21′N 121°17′W*
Oregon, State of *see* Oregon
154 I7 **Öregrund** Uppsala, C Sweden *60°19′N 18°30′E*
Orekhov *see* Orikhiv
196 G2 **Orekhovo-Zuyevo** Moskovskaya Oblast', W Russian Federation *55°46′N 39°01′E*
Orekhovsk *see* Arekhawsk
196 F3 **Orël** Orlovskaya Oblast', W Russian Federation *52°57′N 36°06′E*
Orel *see* Oril'
104 E5 **Orellana** Loreto, N Peru *06°53′S 75°10′W*
102 B8 **Orellana** ◐ *province* NE Ecuador
170 E6 **Orellana, Embalse de** ⊠ W Spain
79 H3 **Orem** Utah, W USA *40°18′N 111°42′W*
Ore Mountains *see* Erzgebirge/Krušné Hory
187 L7 **Ören** Muğla, Turkey *37°02′N 27°57′E*
197 L4 **Orenburg** *prev.* Chkalov. Orenburgskaya Oblast', W Russian Federation *51°46′N 55°12′E*
197 L4 **Orenburg** ✕ Orenburgskaya Oblast', W Russian Federation *51°54′N 55°15′E*
197 K4 **Orenburgskaya Oblast'** ◐ *province* W Russian Federation
187 N4 **Orencik** Kütahya, Turkey *39°16′N 29°33′E*
Orense *see* Ourense
282 C10 **Oreor** *var.* Koror. *island* N Palau
278 B12 **Orepuki** Southland, South Island, New Zealand *46°17′S 167°45′E*
187 K2 **Orestiáda** *prev.* Orestiás. Anatolikí Makedonía kai Thráki, NE Greece *41°30′N 26°31′E*
Orestiás *see* Orestiáda
278 B12 **Oreti** ≈ South Island, New Zealand
278 G3 **Orewa** Auckland, North Island, New Zealand *36°34′S 174°43′E*
261 L7 **Oreyabo** Papua, E Indonesia *06°57′S 139°05′E*
161 M4 **Orford** United Kingdom *52°05′N 1°32′E*
117 G11 **Orford, Cape** *headland* West Falkland, Falkland Islands *52°00′S 61°04′W*
161 N4 **Orford Ness** *cape* E England, United Kingdom
90 B3 **Órganos, Sierra de los** ▲▲ W Cuba
79 L9 **Organ Peak** ▲ New Mexico, SW USA *32°17′N 106°35′W*
170 G5 **Orgaz** Castilla-La Mancha, C Spain *39°39′N 03°52′W*
166 G7 **Orgéres-en-Beauce** Centre, France *48°09′N 1°42′E*
Orgeyev *see* Orhei
Orgil *see* Jargalant
170 G8 **Orgiva** *var.* Orjiva. Andalucía, S Spain *36°54′N 03°25′W*
239 M2 **Örgön** *var.* Senj. Dornogovĭ, SE Mongolia *44°34′N 110°58′E*
Örgön *see* Bayangovĭ
114 F5 **Orgoroso** Paysandú, Uruguay *32°23′S 57°30′W*
Orgraždеn *see* Ograzhden
187 M3 **Orhaneli** Bursa, Turkey *39°54′N 28°59′E*
187 M3 **Orhangazi** Bursa, Turkey *40°29′N 29°19′E*
188 G6 **Orhei** *var.* Orheiu, *Rus.* Orgeyev. N Moldova *47°25′N 28°48′E*
Orheiu *see* Orhei
168 C7 **Orhi** *var.* Orhy, Pico de Orhy, Pic d'Orhy. ▲ France/Spain *42°55′N 01°01′W* *see also* Orhy
Orhi *see* Orhy
Orhomenos *see* Orchómenos
246 E3 **Orhon** ◐ *province* N Mongolia
193 H9 **Orhon Gol** ≈ N Mongolia
168 C6 **Orhy** *var.* Orhi, Pico de Orhy, Pic d'Orhy. ▲ France/Spain *43°00′N 01°00′W* *see also* Orhi
Orhy *see* Orhi
Orhy, Pic d'/Orhy, Pico de *see* Orhi/Orhy
173 J7 **Oria** Andalucía, Spain *37°29′N 2°18′W*
78 A1 **Orick** California, W USA *41°16′N 124°03′W*
76 E2 **Orient** Washington, NW USA *48°51′N 118°14′W*
86 G6 **Oriental** Puebla, Mexico *19°22′N 97°37′W*
98 C4 **Oriental, Cordillera** ▲▲ Bolivia/Peru
98 C4 **Oriental, Cordillera** ▲▲ C Colombia
105 G8 **Oriental, Cordillera** ▲▲ C Peru
116 G6 **Oriente** Buenos Aires, E Argentina *38°45′S 60°37′W*
171 I7 **Orihuela** País Valenciano, E Spain *38°05′N 00°56′W*
173 K2 **Orihuela del Tremedal** Aragón, Spain *40°33′N 1°39′W*
189 K6 **Orikhiv** *Rus.* Orekhov. Zaporiz'ka Oblast', SE Ukraine *47°32′N 35°48′E*
184 F9 **Orikum** *var.* Orikumi. Vlorë, SW Albania *40°20′N 19°28′E*
Orikumi *see* Orikum
189 K4 **Oril'** *Rus.* Orel. ≈ E Ukraine
62 D4 **Orillia** Ontario, S Canada *44°36′N 79°26′W*
153 H9 **Orimattila** Etelä-Suomi, S Finland *60°48′N 25°40′E*
77 M8 **Orin** Wyoming, C USA *42°39′N 105°10′W*
95 J3 **Orinoco, Río** ≈ Colombia/Venezuela
102 D7 **Orinoquía-Amazoniá** *physical region* SW Colombia
280 A4 **Oriomo** Western, SW Papua New Guinea *08°53′S 143°13′E*
73 B9 **Orion** Illinois, N USA *41°21′N 90°22′W*
74 E3 **Oriska** North Dakota, N USA *46°54′N 97°46′W*
234 I4 **Orissa** ◐ *state* NE India
Orissaar *see* Orissaare
190 C4 **Orissaare** *Ger.* Orissaar. Saaremaa, W Estonia *58°34′N 23°05′E*
175 B10 **Oristano** Sardegna, Italy, C Mediterranean Sea *39°54′N 08°35′E*
175 A10 **Oristano, Golfo di** *gulf* Sardegna, Italy, C Mediterranean Sea
102 B8 **Orito** Putumayo, SW Colombia *0°49′N 76°57′W*
153 H9 **Orivesi** Häme, W Finland *61°39′N 24°21′E*
153 I8 **Orivesi** ◎ Länsi-Suomi, SE Finland
107 I2 **Oriximiná** Pará, NE Brazil *01°45′S 55°50′W*
86 G7 **Orizaba** Veracruz-Llave, E Mexico *18°51′N 97°08′W*
86 G7 **Orizaba, Volcán Pico de** *var.* Citlaltépetl. ▲ S Mexico *19°00′N 97°15′W*
86 F5 **Orizabita** Hidalgo, Mexico *20°35′N 99°13′W*
155 E8 **Ørje** Østfold, S Norway *59°28′N 11°40′E*
184 E6 **Orjen** ▲▲ Bosnia and Herzegovina/Montenegro
Orjiva *see* Orgiva
Orjonikidzeobod *see* Kofarnihon
154 D3 **Orkanger** Sør-Trøndelag, S Norway *63°17′N 09°52′E*
154 D4 **Orkdalen** *valley* S Norway
155 F11 **Örkelljunga** Skåne, S Sweden *56°17′N 13°20′E*
Orkhaniye *see* Botevgrad
Orkhómenos *see* Orchómenos
154 D4 **Orkla** ≈ S Norway
141 I4 **Orkney** North West, South Africa *26°59′S 26°40′E*
Orkney *see* Orkney Islands
291 F13 **Orkney Deep** *undersea feature* Scotia Sea/Weddell Sea
156 F2 **Orkney Islands** *var.* Orkney, Orkneys. *island group* N Scotland, United Kingdom
Orkneys *see* Orkney Islands
70 C5 **Orla** Texas, SW USA *31°48′N 103°55′W*
78 B3 **Orland** California, W USA *39°43′N 122°12′W*
110 B4 **Orlândia** São Paulo, Brazil *20°43′S 47°53′W*
69 M6 **Orlando** Florida, SE USA *28°32′N 81°23′W*
69 M6 **Orlando** ✕ Florida, SE USA *28°24′N 81°16′W*
175 G12 **Orlando, Capo d'** *headland* Sicilia, Italy, C Mediterranean Sea *38°10′N 14°44′E*
Orlau *see* Orlová
165 H4 **Orléanais** *cultural region* C France
165 H4 **Orléans** *anc.* Aurelianum. Loiret, C France *47°54′N 01°53′E*

◆ Country
● Country Capital
◇ Dependent Territory
○ Dependent Territory Capital
◐ Administrative Regions
✕ International Airport
▲ Mountain
▲▲ Mountain Range
⛰ Volcano
≈ River
◎ Lake
⊠ Reservoir

◆ Country ◇ Dependent Territory ✕ Administrative Regions ▲ Mountain ≈ Volcano ☺ Lake
● Country Capital ○ Dependent Territory Capital ✕ International Airport ≈ Mountain Range ≈ River ☺ Reservoir

◆ Country	◇ Dependent Territory	✦ Administrative Regions	▲ Mountain	▲ Volcano	⊗ Lake
● Country Capital	○ Dependent Territory Capital	✕ International Airport	▲ Mountain Range	✓ River	⊗ Reservoir

◆ Country   ● Country Capital   ◇ Dependent Territory   ○ Dependent Territory Capital   ◈ Administrative Regions   ✕ International Airport   ▲ Mountain   ▲▲ Mountain Range   ▨ Volcano   ◢ River   ◎ Lake   ▨ Reservoir

Q

◆ Country   ◇ Dependent Territory   ◈ Administrative Regions   ▲ Mountain   ◈ Volcano   ⊚ Lake
● Country Capital   ○ Dependent Territory Capital   ✈ International Airport   ▲ Mountain Range   ♣ River   ⊞ Reservoir

Regina - Rishon LeZiyyon

57 N7 **Regina** ✈ Saskatchewan, S Canada 50°21′N 104°43′W
57 N7 **Regina Beach** Saskatchewan, S Canada 50°44′N 105°03′W
Reginum *see* Regensburg
Région du Haut-Congo *see* Haut-Congo
Registan *see* Rīgestān
113 L4 **Registro** São Paulo, S Brazil 24°30′S 47°50′W
Regium *see* Reggio di Calabria
Regium Lepidum *see* Reggio nell'Emilia
181 J14 **Regnitz** *var.* Rednitz. 〰 SE Germany
85 I8 **Regocijo** Durango, W Mexico 23°35′N 105°11′W
172 C6 **Reguengos de Monsaraz** Évora, S Portugal 38°25′N 07°32′W
218 E6 **REgyptavim** Israel 32°31′N 35°01′E
179 G10 **Rehau** Bayern, E Germany 50°15′N 12°03′E
181 B13 **Rehlingen** Saarland, Germany 49°23′E 6°41′N
140 C2 **Rehoboth** Hardap, C Namibia 23°18′S 17°03′E
64 G10 **Rehoboth Beach** Delaware, NE USA 38°42′N 75°03′W
219 D8 **Reẖovot** Israel 31°53′N 34°49′E
219 D8 **Rehovot** ; *prev.* Reẖovot. Central, C Israel 31°54′N 34°49′E
Reẖovot *see* Rehovot
137 E9 **Rei** *spring/well* S Kenya 03°24′S 39°18′E
181 F12 **Reichelsheim** Hessen, Germany 49°43′E 8°51′N
Reichenau *see* Rychnov nad Kněžnou
Reichenau *see* Bogatynia, Poland
179 G9 **Reichenbach** *var.* Reichenbach im Vogtland. Sachsen, E Germany 50°36′N 12°18′E
Reichenbach *see* Dzierżoniów
Reichenbach im Vogtland *see* Reichenbach
181 D13 **Reichenbach-Steegen** Rheinland-Pfalz, Germany 49°30′E 7°33′N
181 H12 **Reichenberg** Bayern, Germany 49°44′E 9°55′N
Reichenberg *see* Liberec
181 G12 **Reicholzheim** Baden-Württemberg, Germany 49°44′E 9°32′N
276 C4 **Reid** Western Australia 30°49′S 128°24′E
69 L2 **Reidsville** Georgia, SE USA 32°05′N 82°07′W
67 J5 **Reidsville** North Carolina, SE USA 36°21′N 79°39′W
Reifnitz *see* Ribnica
161 K7 **Reigate** SE England, United Kingdom 51°14′N 00°13′W
159 M8 **Reighton** United Kingdom 54°09′N 0°16′W
Reikjavik *see* Reykjavík
164 F6 **Ré, Île de** *island* W France
79 J9 **Reiley Peak** ▲ Arizona, SW USA 32°24′N 110°09′W
219 C9 **Re'im** Israel 31°23′N 34°27′E
165 I3 **Reims** *Eng.* Rheims; *anc.* Durocortorum, Remi. Marne, N France 49°16′N 04°01′E
117 B13 **Reina Adelaida, Archipiélago** *island group* S Chile
102 E1 **Reina Beatrix** ✈ (Oranjestad) C Aruba 12°30′N 69°57′W
176 D4 **Reinach** Aargau, W Switzerland 47°16′N 08°12′E
176 D3 **Reinach** Basel-Land, NW Switzerland 47°30′N 07°36′E
170 A10 **Reina Sofía** ✈ (Tenerife) Tenerife, Islas Canarias, Spain, NE Atlantic Ocean
74 H7 **Reinbeck** Iowa, C USA 42°19′N 92°36′W
180 I3 **Reinbek** Schleswig-Holstein, N Germany 53°31′N 10°15′E
57 N2 **Reindeer** 〰 Saskatchewan, C Canada
57 N1 **Reindeer Lake** ◎ Manitoba/Saskatchewan, C Canada
Reine-Charlotte, Îles de la *see* Queen Charlotte Islands
Reine-Élisabeth, Îles de la *see* Queen Elizabeth Islands
154 C6 **Reineskarvet** ▲ S Norway 60°38′N 07°48′E
278 E1 **Reinga, Cape** *headland* North Island, New Zealand 34°24′S 172°40′E
181 F12 **Reinheim** Hessen, Germany 49°50′E 8°50′N
170 G2 **Reinosa** Cantabria, N Spain 43°01′N 04°09′W
181 C12 **Reinsfeld** Rheinland-Pfalz, Germany 49°41′E 6°53′N
181 F10 **Reiskirchen** Hessen, Germany 50°30′E 8°31′N
179 I14 **Reisseck** ▲ S Austria 46°57′N 13°21′E
181 E8 **Reiste** Nordrhein-Westfalen, Germany 51°16′E 8°15′N
64 D9 **Reisterstown** Maryland, NE USA 39°27′N 76°46′W
Reisui *see* Yeosu
162 H3 **Reitdiep** 〰 NE Netherlands
285 K7 **Reitoru** *atoll* Îles Tuamotu, C French Polynesia
141 J5 **Reitz** Free State, South Africa 27°48′S 28°26′E
155 H8 **Rejmyre** Östergötland, S Sweden 58°49′N 15°55′E
Reka *see* Rijeka
Reka Ili *see* Ile/Ili He
Rekarne *see* Tumbo
Rekhovot *see* Rehovot
118 B8 **Relbun, Río** 〰 Bío-Bío, Chile
54 G4 **Reliance** Northwest Territories, C Canada 62°45′N 109°08′W
77 J9 **Reliance** Wyoming, C USA 41°42′N 109°13′W
131 H2 **Relizane** *var.* Ghelîzâne, Ghilizane. NW Algeria 35°45′N 00°33′E
180 H2 **Rellingen** Schleswig-Holstein, Germany 53°39′E 9°49′N
166 F6 **Rémalard** Basse-Normandie, France 48°26′N 0°46′E
276 G4 **Remarkable, Mount** ▲ South Australia 32°46′S 138°08′E
171 I10 **Remchi** Algeria
181 J10 **Remda** Thüringen, Germany 50°46′E 11°13′N
102 C4 **Remedios** Antioquia, N Colombia 07°02′N 74°42′W
89 J9 **Remedios** Veraguas, W Panama 08°13′N 81°48′W
88 C5 **Remedios, Punta** *headland* SW El Salvador 13°31′N 89°48′W
180 D3 **Remels** Niedersachsen, Germany 53°18′E 7°45′N
Remi *see* Reims
163 I14 **Remich** Grevenmacher, SE Luxembourg 49°33′N 06°23′E
163 F10 **Remicourt** Liège, E Belgium 50°40′N 05°19′E
103 N5 **Rémire** NE French Guiana 04°52′N 52°16′W
167 M7 **Remiremont** Lorraine, France 48°01′N 6°35′E
197 H7 **Remontnoye** Rostovskaya Oblast', SW Russian Federation 46°35′N 43°38′E
261 I6 **Remoon** Pulau Kur, E Indonesia 05°18′S 131°59′E
163 G11 **Remouchamps** Liège, E Belgium 50°29′N 05°43′E
165 J8 **Remoulins** Gard, S France 43°56′N 04°34′E
137 G11 **Rempart, Mont du** *hill* W Mauritius
181 C9 **Remscheid** Nordrhein-Westfalen, W Germany 51°10′N 07°11′E
74 F6 **Remsen** Iowa, C USA 42°48′N 95°58′W
169 K4 **Rémuzat** Rhône-Alpes, France 44°24′N 5°21′E
154 E6 **Rena** Hedmark, S Norway 61°08′N 11°21′E
154 E5 **Renåa** 〰 S Norway
118 B9 **Renaico, Río** 〰 Chile
Renaix *see* Ronse
166 D7 **Renazé** Pays de la Loire, France 47°48′N 1°03′W
190 E5 **Rencēni** Valmiera, N Latvia 57°43′N 25°25′E
190 C6 **Renda** Kuldīga, W Latvia 57°04′N 22°18′E
175 H11 **Rende** Calabria, SW Italy 39°19′N 16°10′E
163 G12 **Rendeux** Luxembourg, SE Belgium 50°15′N 05°28′E
Rendina *see* Rentína
73 C12 **Rend Lake** ⊠ Illinois, N USA
281 H2 **Rendova** *island* New Georgia Islands, NW Solomon Islands
180 H1 **Rendsburg** Schleswig-Holstein, N Germany 54°18′N 09°40′E
176 C5 **Renens** Vaud, SW Switzerland 46°32′N 06°36′E
62 F3 **Renfrew** Ontario, SE Canada 45°28′N 76°44′W
158 G3 **Renfrew** United Kingdom 55°52′N 4°22′W
156 E7 **Renfrew** *cultural region* SW Scotland, United Kingdom
258 E5 **Rengat** Sumatera, W Indonesia 0°26′S 102°38′E
233 M6 **Rengma Hills** ▲▲ NE India
116 B4 **Rengo** Libertador, C Chile 34°24′S 70°50′W
181 D10 **Rengsdorf** Rheinland-Pfalz, Germany 50°30′E 7°30′N
242 C5 **Renhuai** Guizhou, China 27°29′N 106°14′E
188 F8 **Reni** Odes'ka Oblast', SW Ukraine 45°30′N 28°18′E
243 J8 **Renju** Guangdong, SE China 24°49′N 115°53′E
136 B3 **Renk** Upper Nile, NE South Sudan 11°48′N 32°49′E
190 D2 **Renko** Etelä-Suomi, S Finland 60°52′N 24°16′E
162 G7 **Renkum** Gelderland, SE Netherlands 51°58′N 05°43′E
277 H5 **Renmark** South Australia 34°12′S 140°43′E
281 J4 **Rennell** *var.* Mu Nggava. *island* S Solomon Islands
281 I2 **Rennell and Bellona** *prev.* Central. ⬖ *province* S Solomon Islands
275 H3 **Renner Springs Roadhouse** Northern Territory, N Australia 18°12′S 133°48′E
164 F4 **Rennes** *Bret.* Roazon; *anc.* Condate. Ille-et-Vilaine, NW France 48°08′N 01°40′W
293 J8 **Rennick Glacier** *glacier* Antarctica
55 J9 **Rennie** Manitoba, S Canada 49°51′N 95°28′W
80 F2 **Reno** Nevada, W USA 39°32′N 119°49′W
177 H8 **Reno** 〰 N Italy
80 F2 **Reno-Cannon** ✈ Nevada, W USA 39°26′N 119°42′W
141 I5 **Renoster** 〰 Free State, South Africa
138 E9 **Renoster** 〰 SW South Africa
140 F8 **Renosterkop** Western Cape, South Africa 32°12′S 22°51′E
140 E9 **Renosterleegte** 〰 Western Cape, South Africa
63 M1 **Renous** New Brunswick, SE Canada 46°49′N 65°48′W
64 C4 **Renovo** Pennsylvania, NE USA 41°19′N 77°42′W
245 J4 **Renqiu** Hebei, E China 38°49′N 116°02′E
242 A3 **Renshou** Sichuan, C China 30°02′N 104°09′E
73 E10 **Rensselaer** Indiana, N USA 40°57′N 87°09′W
65 H2 **Rensselaer** New York, NE USA 42°38′N 73°44′W
Rentería *see* Errenteria
186 G5 **Rentína** *var.* Rendina. Thessalía, C Greece 39°04′N 21°58′E
74 F5 **Renville** Minnesota, N USA 44°48′N 95°13′W
159 I6 **Renwick** United Kingdom 54°46′N 2°37′W
132 G5 **Réo** W Burkina 12°20′N 02°28′W
63 H3 **Repentigny** Québec, SE Canada 45°42′N 73°28′W
228 F7 **Repetek** Lebap Welaýaty, E Turkmenistan 38°40′N 63°12′E
153 G8 **Replot** *Fin.* Raippaluoto. *island* W Finland
Repola *see* Reboly
Reppen *see* Rzepin
172 C5 **Represa** Évora, Portugal 38°42′N 8°06′W
110 A9 **Represa Armando** *mountains* Sao Paulo, Brazil
110 E4 **Represa de Furnas** *mountains* Minas Gerais, Brazil
110 D4 **Represa dos Peixotos** *mountains* Minas Gerais, Brazil
Reps *see* Rupea
75 H11 **Republic** Missouri, C USA 37°07′N 93°28′W
76 E3 **Republic** Washington, NW USA 48°39′N 118°44′W
75 E9 **Republican River** 〰 Kansas/Nebraska, C USA
53 I9 **Repulse Bay** Northwest Terretories, N Canada 66°35′N 86°20′W
104 F4 **Requena** Loreto, NE Peru 05°05′S 73°52′W
171 I6 **Requena** País Valenciano, E Spain 39°29′N 01°08′W
165 H8 **Réquista** Aveyron, S France 44°00′N 02°31′E
214 G5 **Reşadiye** Tokat, N Turkey 40°24′N 37°19′E
Reschenpass *see* Resia, Passo di
Reschitza *see* Reşiţa
290 C5 **Researcher Seamount** *undersea feature* C Atlantic Ocean
184 G8 **Resen** *Turk.* Resne. SW FYR Macedonia 41°07′N 21°00′E
113 J4 **Reserva** Paraná, S Brazil 24°40′S 50°52′W
55 H9 **Reserve** Saskatchewan, S Canada 52°24′N 102°37′W
79 K8 **Reserve** New Mexico, SW USA 33°42′N 108°45′W
118 D2 **Resguardo de los Patos** Valparaíso, Chile 32°29′S 70°35′W
Reshetilovka *see* Reshetylivka
190 G5 **Reshety** Pskovskaya Oblast', Russian Federation
189 J4 **Reshetylivka** *Rus.* Reshetilovka. Poltavs'ka Oblast', NE Ukraine 49°34′N 34°05′E
Resht *see* Rasht
174 D3 **Resia, Passo di** *Ger.* Reschenpass. *pass* Austria/Italy
Resicabánya *see* Reşiţa
112 F6 **Resistencia** Chaco, NE Argentina 27°27′S 58°56′W
188 B8 **Reşiţa** *Ger.* Reschitza, *Hung.* Resicabánya. Caraş-Severin, W Romania 45°14′N 21°58′E
Resne *see* Resen
118 G5 **Resolana** Mendoza, Argentina 34°32′S 68°06′W
295 I8 **Resolute** *Inuit* Qausuittuq. Cornwallis Island, Nunavut, N Canada 74°41′N 94°54′W
Resolution *see* Fort Resolution
59 I1 **Resolution Island** *island* Nunavut, NE Canada
278 A12 **Resolution Island** *island* SW New Zealand
111 L2 **Resplendor** Minas Gerais, Brazil 19°20′S 41°15′W
111 H5 **Ressaguinha** Minas Gerais, Brazil 21°04′S 43°46′W
167 H4 **Ressons-sur-Matz** Picardie, France 49°33′N 2°45′E
115 L1 **Restinga Sèca** Rio Grande do Sul, Brazil 29°49′S 53°23′W
55 I10 **Reston** Manitoba, S Canada 49°33′N 101°03′W
62 D2 **Restoule Lake** ◎ Ontario, S Canada
102 C6 **Restrepo** Meta, C Colombia 04°20′N 73°29′W
140 F8 **Restvale** Western Cape, South Africa 32°05′S 23°00′E
88 B4 **Retalhuleu** Retalhuleu, SW Guatemala 14°31′N 91°40′W
88 B4 **Retalhuleu** *off.* Departamento de Retalhuleu. ⬖ *department* SW Guatemala
Retalhuleu, Departamento de *see* Retalhuleu
118 F1 **Retamito** San Juan, Argentina 32°06′S 68°36′W
159 L10 **Retford** C England, United Kingdom 53°18′N 00°52′W
165 I2 **Rethel** Ardennes, N France 49°31′N 04°22′E
Rethimno/Réthimnon *see* Réthymno
187 I10 **Réthymno** *prev.* Rethimno, Réthimnon. Kríti, Greece, E Mediterranean Sea 35°21′N 24°29′E
Retiche, Alpi *see* Rhaetian Alps
163 F9 **Retie** Antwerpen, N Belgium 51°18′N 05°05′E
169 I2 **Retournac** Auvergne, France 45°12′N 4°02′E
183 F11 **Rétság** Nógrád, N Hungary 47°57′N 19°08′E
172 G4 **Retuerta de Bullaque** Castilla-La Manacha, Spain 39°27′N 4°24′W
177 L1 **Retz** Niederösterreich, NE Austria 48°46′N 15°58′E
166 G9 **Reuilly** Centre, France 47°05′N 2°03′E
137 I10 **Réunion** *off.* La Réunion. ◇ *French overseas department* W Indian Ocean
204 G10 **Réunion** *island* W Indian Ocean
171 J4 **Reus** Cataluña, E Spain 41°10′N 01°06′E
163 F9 **Reusel** Noord-Brabant, S Netherlands 51°21′N 05°10′E
Reuţel *see* Ciuhuru
179 D12 **Reutlingen** Baden-Württemberg, S Germany 48°30′N 09°13′E
176 G3 **Reutte** Tirol, W Austria 47°30′N 10°44′E
163 H9 **Reuver** Limburg, SE Netherlands 51°17′N 06°05′E
74 B4 **Reva** South Dakota, N USA 45°30′N 103°03′W
Revakha *see* Rewaẖa
Reval/Revel *see* Tallinn
194 F3 **Revda** Murmanskaya Oblast', NW Russian Federation 67°57′N 34°29′E
195 L10 **Revda** Sverdlovskaya Oblast', C Russian Federation 56°48′N 59°42′E
80 J6 **Reveille Range** ▲▲ Nevada, USA
171 K1 **Revel** Haute-Garonne, S France 43°27′N 01°59′E
56 G7 **Revelstoke** British Columbia, SW Canada 51°02′N 118°12′W
89 H8 **Reventazón, Río** 〰 E Costa Rica
176 G7 **Revere** Lombardia, N Italy 45°03′N 11°07′E
159 M10 **Revesby** United Kingdom 53°08′N 0°03′W
167 K5 **Revigny-sur-Ornain** Lorraine, France 48°50′N 4°59′E
83 N8 **Revillagigedo Island** *island* Alexander Archipelago, Alaska, USA
165 J2 **Revin** Ardennes, N France 49°57′N 04°39′E
219 D10 **Revivim** Israel 31°02′N 34°43′E
152 B5 **Revnosa** *headland* C Svalbard 78°03′N 18°52′E
Revolyutsii, Pik *see* Revolyutsiya, Qullai
229 K7 **Revolyutsiya, Qullai** *Rus.* Pik Revolyutsii. ▲ SE Tajikistan 38°40′N 72°26′E
183 G10 **Revúca** *Ger.* Grossrauschenbach, *Hung.* Nagyrőce. Banskobystrický Kraj, C Slovakia 48°40′N 20°10′E
232 G7 **Rewa** Madhya Pradesh, C India 24°32′N 81°18′E
219 D9 **Rewaẖa** *var.* Revakha. Southern, S Israel 31°39′N 34°44′E
232 E5 **Rewāri** Haryāna, N India 28°14′N 76°38′E
77 I7 **Rexburg** Idaho, NW USA 43°49′N 111°47′W
134 C4 **Rey Bouba** Nord, NE Cameroon 08°40′N 14°11′E
152 D2 **Reydharfjördhur** Austurland, E Iceland 65°02′N 14°12′W
106 D9 **Reyes** Beni, NW Bolivia 14°17′S 67°18′W
86 G6 **Reyes de Vallarta** Puebla, Mexico 20°06′N 97°32′W
80 A2 **Reyes, Point** *headland* California, W USA 37°59′N 123°01′W
102 A7 **Reyes, Punta** *headland* SW Colombia 02°44′N 78°08′W
214 G8 **Reyhanlı** Hatay, S Turkey 36°16′N 36°35′E
89 L9 **Rey, Isla del** *island* Archipiélago de las Perlas, SE Panama
152 B2 **Reykhólar** Vestfirdhir, W Iceland 65°28′N 22°12′W
152 D2 **Reykjahlídh** Nordhurland Eystra, NE Iceland 65°37′N 16°54′W
152 B3 **Reykjanes** ⬖ *region* SW Iceland
295 M7 **Reykjanes Basin** *var.* Irminger Basin. *undersea feature* N Atlantic Ocean 62°30′N 33°30′W
295 M7 **Reykjanes Ridge** *undersea feature* N Atlantic Ocean 62°00′N 27°00′W
152 B3 **Reykjavík** *var.* Reikjavik. ● (Iceland) Höfudhborgarsvaedhi, W Iceland 64°08′N 21°54′W
85 J5 **Rey, Laguna del** ◎ Coahuila, Mexico
64 A5 **Reynoldsville** Pennsylvania, NE USA 41°04′N 78°51′W
85 M6 **Reynosa** Tamaulipas, C Mexico 26°03′N 98°19′W
Reẕā'īyeh *see* Orūmīyeh
Reẕā'īyeh, Daryācheh-ye *see* Orūmīyeh, Daryācheh-ye
164 F5 **Rezé** Loire-Atlantique, NW France 47°10′N 01°36′W
190 F7 **Rēzekne** *Ger.* Rositten; *prev. Rus.* Rezhitsa. Rēzekne, SE Latvia 56°31′N 27°22′E
195 M9 **Rezh** Sverdlovskaya Oblasť, Russian Federation
195 M9 **Rezh** 〰 Sverdlovskaya Oblasť, Russian Federation
Rezhitsa *see* Rēzekne
188 G6 **Rezina** NE Moldova 47°44′N 28°58′E
185 M7 **Rezovo** *Turk.* Rezve. Burgas, E Bulgaria 42°00′N 28°00′E
185 M7 **Rezovska Reka** *Turk.* Rezve Deresi. 〰 Bulgaria/Turkey *see also* Rezve Deresi
Rezovska Reka *see* Rezve Deresi
Rezve *see* Rezovo
187 L1 **Rezve Deresi** *Bul.* Rezovska Reka. 〰 Bulgaria/Turkey *see also* Rezovska Reka
Rezve Deresi *see* Rezovska Reka
169 N4 **Rezzo** Liguria, NW Italy 44°01′N 07°52′E
Rhadames *see* Ghadāmis
180 C7 **Rhade** Nordrhein-Westfalen, Germany 51°45′E 6°56′N
Rhaedestus *see* Tekirdağ
176 F5 **Rhaetian Alps** *Fr.* Alpes Rhétiques, *Ger.* Rätische Alpen, *It.* Alpi Retiche. ▲▲ C Europe
176 F4 **Rhätikon** ▲▲ C Europe
181 D12 **Rhaunen** Rheinland-Pfalz, Germany 49°51′E 7°21′N
160 F4 **Rhayader** United Kingdom 52°19′N 3°30′W
180 E7 **Rheda-Wiedenbrück** Nordrhein-Westfalen, W Germany 51°51′N 08°17′E
180 D4 **Rhede** Niedersachsen, Germany 53°04′E 7°16′N
180 B7 **Rhede** Nordrhein-Westfalen, Germany 51°50′E 6°42′N
162 H7 **Rheden** Gelderland, E Netherlands 52°01′N 06°03′E
Rhegion/Rhegium *see* Reggio di Calabria
Rheims *see* Reims
Rhein *see* Rhine
181 C10 **Rheinbach** Nordrhein-Westfalen, W Germany 50°37′N 06°57′E
181 B8 **Rheinberg** Nordrhein-Westfalen, Germany 51°33′E 6°36′N
180 D6 **Rheine** *var.* Rheine in Westfalen. Nordrhein-Westfalen, NW Germany 52°17′N 07°27′E
Rheine in Westfalen *see* Rheine
Rheinfeld *see* Rheinfelden
176 D3 **Rheinfelden** Baden-Württemberg, S Germany 47°34′N 07°46′E
176 D3 **Rheinfelden** *var.* Rheinfeld. Aargau, N Switzerland 47°33′N 07°47′E
181 D10 **Rheinisches Schiefergebirge** *var.* Rhine State Uplands, *Eng.* Rhenish Slate Mountains. ▲▲ W Germany
181 C11 **Rheinland-Pfalz** *Eng.* Rhineland-Palatinate, *Fr.* Rhénanie-Palatinat. ⬖ *state* W Germany
181 F12 **Rhein Main** ✈ (Frankfurt am Main) Hessen, W Germany 50°03′N 08°33′E
181 E14 **Rheinzabern** Rheinland-Pfalz, Germany 49°07′E 8°17′N
Rhénanie du Nord-Westphalie *see* Nordrhein-Westfalen
Rhénanie-Palatinat *see* Rheinland-Pfalz
162 G7 **Rhenen** Utrecht, C Netherlands 52°01′N 06°02′E
Rhenish Slate Mountains *see* Rheinisches Schiefergebirge
181 D11 **Rhens** Rheinland-Pfalz, Germany 50°17′E 7°37′N
Rhétiques, Alpes *see* Rhaetian Alps
181 B9 **Rheydt** Nordrhein-Westfalen, Germany 51°10′E 6°27′N
178 H6 **Rhin** 〰 NE Germany
Rhin *see* Rhine
144 D6 **Rhine** *Dut.* Rijn, *Fr.* Rhin, *Ger.* Rhein. 〰 W Europe
64 H3 **Rhinebeck** New York, NE USA 41°55′N 73°54′W
72 C5 **Rhinelander** Wisconsin, N USA 45°39′N 89°23′W
Rhineland-Palatinate *see* Rheinland-Pfalz
Rhine State Uplands *see* Rheinisches Schiefergebirge
178 H6 **Rhinkanal** *canal* NE Germany
136 B7 **Rhino Camp** NW Uganda 02°58′N 31°24′E
130 D4 **Rhir, Cap** *headland* W Morocco 30°40′N 09°54′W
160 D3 **Rhiw** United Kingdom 52°49′N 4°38′W
176 E6 **Rho** Lombardia, N Italy 45°32′N 09°02′E
158 C10 **Rhode** Offaly, Ireland 53°21′N 7°12′W
65 L4 **Rhode Island** *off.* State of Rhode Island and Providence Plantations, *also known as* Little Rhody, Ocean State. ⬖ *state* NE USA
65 L4 **Rhode Island** *island* Rhode Island, NE USA
65 L4 **Rhode Island Sound** *sound* Maine/Rhode Island, NE USA
Rhodes *see* Ródos
Rhode-Saint-Genèse *see* Sint-Genesius-Rode
144 F9 **Rhodes Basin** *undersea feature* E Mediterranean Sea 35°55′N 28°30′E
Rhodesia *see* Zimbabwe
187 I2 **Rhodope Mountains** *var.* Rodhópi Óri, *Bul.* Rhodope Planina, Rodopi, *Gk.* Orosirá Rodhópis, *Turk.* Dospad Dagh. ▲▲ Bulgaria/Greece
Rhodope Planina *see* Rhodope Mountains
181 H11 **Rhön** ▲▲ C Germany
165 J6 **Rhône** ⬖ *department* E France
148 B7 **Rhône** 〰 France/Switzerland
165 J6 **Rhône-Alpes** ⬖ *region* E France
162 E7 **Rhoon** Zuid-Holland, SW Netherlands 51°52′N 04°25′E
160 F6 **Rhoose** United Kingdom 51°23′N 3°21′W
160 E5 **Rhos** United Kingdom 52°00′N 4°22′W
160 G2 **Rhosllanerchrugog** United Kingdom 53°00′N 3°04′W
160 E6 **Rhossili** United Kingdom 51°34′N 4°17′W
159 H10 **Rhuddlan** United Kingdom 53°17′N 3°28′W
156 D5 **Rhum** *var.* Rum. *island* W Scotland, United Kingdom
181 I8 **Rhumspringe** Niedersachsen, Germany 51°35′E 10°18′N
168 B6 **Rhune** ▲ Spain 43°18′N 1°38′W
Rhuthun *see* Ruthin
160 F1 **Rhyl** NE Wales, United Kingdom 53°19′N 03°28′W
166 C8 **Riaillé** Pays de la Loire, France 47°31′N 1°17′W
109 B9 **Rialma** Goiás, S Brazil 15°22′S 49°35′W
81 E11 **Rialto** California, USA 34°06′N 117°22′W
170 F2 **Riaño** Castilla-León, N Spain 42°59′N 05°00′W
169 L5 **Rians** Provence-Alpes-Côte d'Azur, France 43°37′N 5°45′E
173 I3 **Riansáres** 〰 C Spain
232 D3 **Riāsi** Jammu and Kashmir, NW India 33°03′N 74°51′E
258 E5 **Riau** *off.* Propinsi Riau. ⬖ *province* W Indonesia
Riau Archipelago *see* Riau, Kepulauan
258 F4 **Riau, Kepulauan** *var.* Riau Archipelago, *Dut.* Riouw-Archipel. *island group* W Indonesia
Riau, Propinsi *see* Riau
170 G4 **Riaza** Castilla-León, N Spain 41°17′N 03°29′W
170 G3 **Riaza** 〰 N Spain
136 F7 **Riba** *spring/well* NE Kenya 01°56′N 40°38′E
170 D2 **Ribadavia** Galicia, NW Spain 42°17′N 08°08′W
170 D1 **Ribadeo** Galicia, NW Spain 43°32′N 07°04′W
170 F1 **Ribadesella** Asturias, N Spain 43°27′N 05°04′W
172 A4 **Ribamar** Lisboa, Portugal 39°12′N 9°20′W
168 G8 **Ribas de Freser** Cataluña, Spain 42°18′N 2°10′E
170 C6 **Ribatejo** *former province* C Portugal
139 K2 **Ribáuè** Nampula, N Mozambique 14°56′S 38°19′E
159 I9 **Ribble** 〰 NW England, United Kingdom
159 J9 **Ribchester** United Kingdom 53°48′N 2°32′W
155 C12 **Ribe** Ribe, W Denmark 55°20′N 08°47′E
155 C12 **Ribe** *off.* Ribe Amt, *var.* Ripen. ⬖ *county* W Denmark
Ribe Amt *see* Ribe
167 M6 **Ribeauvillé** Alsace, France 48°12′N 7°19′E
167 H4 **Ribécourt** Picardie, France 49°31′N 2°55′E
Ribeira *see* Sanata Uxía de Ribeira
170 A8 **Ribeira Brava** Madeira, Portugal, NE Atlantic Ocean 32°39′N 17°04′W
172 C10 **Ribeira Grande** São Miguel, Azores, Portugal, NE Atlantic Ocean 37°34′N 25°32′W
110 B7 **Ribeirão Bonito** São Paulo, Brazil 22°04′S 48°10′W
110 A10 **Ribeirão Branco** São Paulo, Brazil 24°13′S 48°47′W
110 D9 **Ribeirão Pires** São Paulo, Brazil 23°43′S 46°25′W
110 B5 **Ribeirão Preto** São Paulo, S Brazil 21°09′S 47°48′W
110 F5 **Ribeirão Vermelho** Minas Gerais, Brazil 21°11′S 45°03′W
113 K4 **Ribeira, Rio** 〰 S Brazil
167 I3 **Ribemont** Picardie, France 49°48′N 3°28′E
175 F12 **Ribera** Sicilia, Italy, C Mediterranean Sea 37°31′N 13°16′E
168 E2 **Ribérac** Aquitaine, France 45°15′N 0°19′E
172 E5 **Ribera del Fresno** Extremadura, Spain 38°33′N 6°14′W
106 D7 **Riberalta** Beni, N Bolivia 11°01′S 66°04′W
110 B4 **Riberão Corrente** São Paulo, Brazil 20°27′S 47°35′W
171 K3 **Ribes de Freser** Cataluña, NE Spain 42°18′N 02°11′E
169 L4 **Ribiers** Provence-Alpes-Côte d'Azur, France 44°14′N 5°52′E
72 C5 **Rib Mountain** ▲ Wisconsin, N USA 44°55′N 89°41′W
177 K6 **Ribnica** *Ger.* Reifnitz. S Slovenia 45°46′N 14°40′E
188 G6 **Rîbniţa** *var.* Râbniţa, *Rus.* Rybnitsa. NE Moldova 47°46′N 29°01′E
178 G4 **Ribnitz-Damgarten** Mecklenburg-Vorpommern, NE Germany 54°14′N 12°25′E
183 C8 **Říčany** *Ger.* Ritschan. Středočesky Kraj, W Czech Republic 49°59′N 14°40′E
85 H3 **Ricardo Flores Magón** Chihuahua, Mexico 29°56′N 106°57′W
114 B6 **Ricardone** Santa Fe, Argentina 32°46′S 60°47′W
81 I12 **Rice** California, USA 34°05′N 114°51′W
74 G4 **Rice** Minnesota, N USA 45°42′N 94°10′W
72 A5 **Rice Lake** Wisconsin, N USA 45°33′N 91°43′W
72 I3 **Rice Lake** ◎ Ontario, S Canada
62 E4 **Rice Lake** ◎ Ontario, SE Canada
67 H8 **Richard B. Russell Lake** ⊠ Georgia, SE USA
52 G6 **Richard Collinson, Cape** *headland* Nunavut, NW Canada 72°46′N 120°47′W
52 F6 **Richard Collinson Inlet** *coastal sea feature* Northwest Territories, NW Canada
141 L6 **Richards Bay** KwaZulu-Natal, South Africa 28°48′S 32°06′E
71 H4 **Richardson** Texas, SW USA 32°55′N 96°44′W
57 J1 **Richardson** 〰 Alberta, C Canada
52 A6 **Richardson Mountains** ▲▲ Yukon Territory, NW Canada
278 B11 **Richardson Mountains** ▲▲ South Island, New Zealand
88 D2 **Richardson Peak** ▲ SE Belize 16°34′N 88°46′W
132 B3 **Richard Toll** N Senegal 16°28′N 15°44′W
74 B3 **Richardton** North Dakota, N USA 46°52′N 102°19′W
64 G7 **Richboro** Pennsylvania, USA 40°13′N 75°01′W
62 C4 **Rich, Cape** *headland* Ontario, S Canada 44°42′N 80°37′W
164 G5 **Richelieu** Indre-et-Loire, C France 47°01′N 00°18′E
181 F14 **Richen** Baden-Württemberg, Germany 49°10′E 8°56′N
76 G8 **Richfield** Idaho, NW USA 43°03′N 114°11′W
79 H4 **Richfield** Utah, W USA 38°45′N 112°05′W
64 G1 **Richfield Springs** New York, NE USA 42°52′N 74°57′W
63 I3 **Richford** Vermont, NE USA 44°59′N 72°37′W
80 D7 **Richgrove** California, USA 35°48′N 119°06′W
158 D7 **Rich Hill** United Kingdom 54°23′N 6°33′W
75 G10 **Rich Hill** Missouri, C USA 38°06′N 94°22′W
63 N1 **Richibucto** New Brunswick, SE Canada 46°42′N 64°54′W
176 E4 **Richisau** Glarus, NE Switzerland 47°00′N 08°54′E
69 J2 **Richland** Georgia, SE USA 32°05′N 84°40′W
75 H10 **Richland** Missouri, C USA 37°51′N 92°24′W
71 H5 **Richland** Texas, SW USA 31°55′N 96°25′W
76 E5 **Richland** Washington, NW USA 46°17′N 119°16′W
72 B7 **Richland Center** Wisconsin, N USA 43°22′N 90°24′W
67 L7 **Richlands** North Carolina, SE USA 34°52′N 77°33′W
67 H5 **Richlands** Virginia, NE USA 37°05′N 81°47′W
70 F6 **Richland Springs** Texas, SW USA 31°16′N 98°56′W
277 L5 **Richmond** New South Wales, SE Australia 33°36′S 150°44′E
56 D9 **Richmond** British Columbia, SW Canada 49°07′N 123°09′W
62 F3 **Richmond** Ontario, SE Canada 45°12′N 75°49′W
63 I3 **Richmond** Québec, SE Canada 45°39′N 72°07′W
279 F8 **Richmond** Tasman, South Island, New Zealand 41°25′S 173°04′E
140 G8 **Richmond** Northern Cape, South Africa 31°25′S 23°56′E
159 K7 **Richmond** United Kingdom 54°24′N 1°44′W
80 B2 **Richmond** California, W USA 37°57′N 122°22′W
73 G11 **Richmond** Indiana, N USA 39°50′N 84°51′W
66 F4 **Richmond** Kentucky, S USA 37°45′N 84°19′W
75 G9 **Richmond** Missouri, C USA 39°15′N 93°59′W
71 I7 **Richmond** Texas, SW USA 29°36′N 95°48′W
79 H1 **Richmond** Utah, W USA 41°55′N 111°51′W
67 L4 **Richmond** *state capital* Virginia, NE USA 37°33′N 77°28′W
62 D5 **Richmond Hill** Ontario, S Canada 43°51′N 79°24′W
279 F8 **Richmond Range** ▲▲ South Island, New Zealand
161 K6 **Richmond upon Thames** United Kingdom 51°26′N 0°18′W
75 G13 **Rich Mountain** ▲ Arkansas, C USA 34°37′N 94°17′W
140 C5 **Richtersveld National Park** Northern Cape, South Africa
73 H10 **Richwood** Ohio, N USA 40°25′N 83°18′W
67 I3 **Richwood** West Virginia, NE USA 38°13′N 80°31′W
180 H1 **Rickling** Schleswig-Holstein, Germany 54°01′E 10°10′N
161 K6 **Rickmansworth** United Kingdom 51°38′N 0°28′W
168 C9 **Ricla** Aragón, Spain 41°31′N 1°24′W
170 E3 **Ricobayo, Embalse de** ⊠ NW Spain
Ricomagus *see* Riom
Ridā' *see* Radā'
227 M3 **Ridder** *Kaz.* Lenīngor *prev.* Leninogorsk. Vostochnyy Kazakhstan, E Kazakhstan 50°20′N 83°34′E
197 K2 **Ridder** Respublika Tatarstan, W Russian Federation 54°34′N 52°27′E
162 E7 **Ridderkerk** Zuid-Holland, SW Netherlands 51°52′N 04°35′E
76 F8 **Riddle** Idaho, NW USA 42°07′N 116°09′W
76 B7 **Riddle** Oregon, NW USA 42°57′N 123°21′W
62 F3 **Rideau** 〰 Ontario, SE Canada
64 J5 **Ridge** New York, NE USA 40°53′N 72°53′W
81 F8 **Ridgecrest** California, W USA 35°37′N 117°40′W
65 I5 **Ridgefield** Connecticut, NE USA 41°16′N 73°30′W
68 E2 **Ridgeland** Mississippi, S USA 32°25′N 90°07′W
67 I10 **Ridgeland** South Carolina, SE USA 32°30′N 80°59′W
66 B5 **Ridgely** Tennessee, S USA 36°15′N 89°29′W
62 B6 **Ridgetown** Ontario, S Canada 42°27′N 81°52′W
67 I8 **Ridgeway** South Carolina, SE USA 34°17′N 80°56′W
Ridgeway *see* Ridgway
161 L5 **Ridgewell** United Kingdom 52°03′N 0°31′E
161 J5 **Ridgmont** United Kingdom 52°00′N 0°35′W
64 A4 **Ridgway** *var.* Ridgeway. Pennsylvania, NE USA 41°24′N 78°40′W
159 J6 **Ridingmill** United Kingdom 54°56′N 1°58′W
55 I9 **Riding Mountain** ▲▲ Manitoba, S Canada
159 J5 **Ridsdale** United Kingdom 55°09′N 2°08′W
141 I5 **Riebeeckstad** Free State, South Africa 27°55′S 26°49′E
140 D9 **Riebeek-Wes** Western Cape, South Africa 33°21′S 18°52′E
Ried *see* Ried im Innkreis
180 F4 **Riede** Niedersachsen, Germany 52°58′E 8°57′N
177 I2 **Ried im Innkreis** *var.* Ried. Oberösterreich, NW Austria 48°13′N 13°29′E
181 C13 **Riegelsberg** Saarland, Germany 49°18′E 6°56′N
177 L4 **Riegersburg** Steiermark, SE Austria 47°03′N 15°52′E
176 D3 **Riehen** Basel-Stadt, NW Switzerland 47°35′N 07°39′E
152 G4 **Riehppegáisá** *var.* Rieppe. ▲ N Norway 69°38′N 21°31′E
180 E6 **Riemsloh** Niedersachsen, Germany 52°11′E 8°25′N
163 G10 **Riemst** Limburg, NE Belgium 50°49′N 05°36′E
181 H11 **Rieneck** Bayern, Germany 50°06′E 9°39′N
Rieppe *see* Riehppegáisá
180 J1 **Riepsdorf** Schleswig-Holstein, Germany 54°14′E 10°58′N
179 H8 **Riesa** Sachsen, E Germany 51°18′N 13°18′E
117 C13 **Riesco, Isla** *island* S Chile
175 F13 **Riesi** Sicilia, Italy, C Mediterranean Sea 37°17′N 14°05′E
180 E5 **Rieste** Niedersachsen, Germany 52°29′E 8°01′N
140 E8 **Riet** 〰 SW South Africa
190 B7 **Rietavas** Telšiai, W Lithuania 55°43′N 21°56′E
180 E7 **Rietberg** Nordrhein-Westfalen, Germany 51°47′E 8°26′N
140 G9 **Rietbron** Eastern Cape, South Africa 32°54′S 23°09′E
140 E1 **Rietfontein** Omaheke, E Namibia 21°58′S 20°58′E
141 J3 **Rietfontein** Gauteng, South Africa 25°42′S 28°13′E
140 E4 **Rietfontein** Northern Cape, South Africa 26°44′S 20°02′E
175 F8 **Rieti** *anc.* Reate. Lazio, C Italy 42°24′N 12°51′E
140 D7 **Rietpoort** Western Cape, South Africa 30°57′S 18°03′E
140 E7 **Riet se Vloer** *salt lake* Northern Cape, South Africa
168 F6 **Rieumes** Midi-Pyrénées, France 43°25′N 1°07′E
168 G4 **Rieupeyroux** Midi-Pyrénées, France 44°18′N 2°14′E
169 L5 **Riez** Provence-Alpes-Côte d'Azur, France 43°49′N 6°06′E
144 B9 **Rif** *var.* Riff, Er Rif, Er Riff. ▲▲ N Morocco
110 C3 **Rifaina** São Paulo, Brazil 20°05′S 47°26′W
Riff *see* Rif
79 K3 **Rifle** Colorado, C USA 39°30′N 107°46′W
72 G6 **Rifle River** 〰 Michigan, N USA
136 D7 **Rift Valley** ⬖ *province* Kenya
Rift Valley *see* Great Rift Valley
190 D6 **Rīga** *Eng.* Riga. ● (Latvia) Rīga, C Latvia 56°57′N 24°08′E
Rigaer Bucht *see* Riga, Gulf of
190 D5 **Riga, Gulf of** *Est.* Liivi Laht, *Ger.* Rigaer Bucht, *Latv.* Rīgas Jūras Līcis, *Rus.* Rizhskiy Zaliv; *prev. Est.* Riia Laht. *gulf* Estonia/Latvia
Rīgas Jūras Līcis *see* Riga, Gulf of
62 G3 **Rigaud** 〰 Ontario/Québec, SE Canada
77 I7 **Rigby** Idaho, NW USA 43°40′N 111°54′W
230 F6 **Rīgestān** *var.* Registan. *desert region* S Afghanistan
76 F6 **Riggins** Idaho, NW USA 45°24′N 116°18′W
168 G4 **Rignac** Midi-Pyrénées, France 44°25′N 2°18′E
59 K4 **Rigolet** Newfoundland and Labrador, NE Canada 51°10′N 58°25′W
133 M4 **Rig-Rig** Kanem, W Chad 14°16′N 14°21′E
190 D4 **Riguldi** Läänemaa, W Estonia 59°07′N 23°34′E
218 F5 **Rīḥāniya** Israel 33°03′N 35°29′E
Riia Laht *see* Riga, Gulf of
153 H9 **Riihimäki** Etelä-Suomi, S Finland 60°45′N 24°45′E
293 K2 **Riiser-Larsen Peninsula** *peninsula* Antarctica
291 J14 **Riiser-Larsen Sea** *sea* Antarctica
Riisser Larsen Ice Shelf *see* Riisser Larsenisen
84 C1 **Riíto** Sonora, NW Mexico 32°06′N 114°57′W
184 A2 **Rijeka** *Ger.* Sankt Veit am Flaum, *It.* Fiume, *Slvn.* Reka; *anc.* Tarsatica. Primorje-Gorski Kotar, NW Croatia 45°20′N 14°26′E
163 F8 **Rijen** Noord-Brabant, S Netherlands 51°35′N 04°55′E
163 E9 **Rijkevorsel** Antwerpen, N Belgium 51°23′N 04°43′E
Rijn *see* Rhine
162 E6 **Rijnsburg** Zuid-Holland, W Netherlands 52°12′N 04°27′E
Rijssel *see* Lille
162 I6 **Rijssen** Overijssel, E Netherlands 52°19′N 06°30′E
162 E7 **Rijswijk** *Eng.* Ryswick. Zuid-Holland, W Netherlands 52°03′N 04°20′E
152 F4 **Riksgränsen** Norrbotten, N Sweden 68°24′N 18°15′E
252 G4 **Rikubetsu** Hokkaidō, NE Japan 43°30′N 143°43′E
253 E9 **Rikuzen-Takata** Iwate, Honshū, C Japan 39°03′N 141°38′E
75 E9 **Riley** Kansas, C USA 39°18′N 96°49′W
163 F10 **Rillaar** Vlaams Brabant, C Belgium 50°58′N 04°58′E
159 L8 **Rillington** United Kingdom 54°09′N 0°42′W
Rí, Loch *see* Ree, Lough
185 I7 **Rilska Reka** 〰 W Bulgaria
133 J5 **Rima** 〰 N Nigeria
222 A9 **Rimah, Wādī ar** *var.* Wādī ar Rummah. *dry watercourse* C Saudi Arabia
169 N1 **Rimasco** Piemonte, NW Italy 45°51′N 08°03′E
Rimaszombat *see* Rimavská Sobota
285 I8 **Rimatara** *island* Îles Australes, SW French Polynesia
183 G10 **Rimavská Sobota** *Ger.* Gross-Steffelsdorf, *Hung.* Rimaszombat. Bankobystrický Kraj, C Slovakia 48°24′N 20°01′E
57 I6 **Rimbey** Alberta, SW Canada 52°39′N 114°10′W
154 I7 **Rimbo** Stockholm, C Sweden 59°44′N 18°21′E
169 N1 **Rimella** Piemonte, NW Italy 45°54′N 08°11′E
155 H9 **Rimforsa** Östergötland, S Sweden 58°06′N 15°40′E
177 I9 **Rimini** *anc.* Ariminum. Emilia-Romagna, N Italy 44°03′N 12°33′E
Rîmnicu-Sărat *see* Râmnicu Sărat
Rîmnicu Vîlcea *see* Râmnicu Vâlcea
231 K3 **Rimo Muztāgh** ▲▲ India/Pakistan
59 I7 **Rimouski** Québec, SE Canada 48°26′N 68°32′W
238 G9 **Rinbung** Xizang Zizhiqu, W China 29°15′N 89°40′E
110 B6 **Rincão** São Paulo, Brazil 21°35′S 48°05′W
115 K6 **Rincón** Uruguay 32°47′S 53°50′W
112 C4 **Rincón, Cerro** ▲ N Chile 24°01′S 67°19′W
85 I10 **Rincón de Guayabitos** Nayarit, Mexico
170 F9 **Rincón de la Victoria** Andalucía, S Spain 36°43′N 04°18′W
115 H6 **Rincón del Bonete** Durazno, Uruguay 32°48′S 56°25′W
Rincón del Bonete, Lago Artificial de *see* Río Negro, Embalse del
114 F6 **Rincón del Cololó** Uruguay 33°05′S 57°26′W
114 B5 **Rincón del Doll** Entre Ríos, Argentina 32°26′S 60°23′W
114 G9 **Rincón del Pino** Uruguay 34°29′S 56°51′W
85 K9 **Rincón de Romos** Aguascalientes, Mexico 22°14′N 102°18′W
171 H3 **Rincón de Soto** La Rioja, N Spain 42°15′N 01°50′W
87 I9 **Rincón Juárez** Oaxaca, Mexico 16°17′N 94°22′W
154 D4 **Rindal** Møre og Romsdal, S Norway 63°02′N 09°09′E
181 H14 **Rindelbach** Baden-Württemberg, Germany 48°59′E 10°08′N
187 I7 **Ríneia** *island* Kykládes, Greece, Aegean Sea
232 E6 **Rīngas** *prev.* Reengus, Rīngus. Rājasthān, N India 27°18′N 75°27′E
155 D13 **Ringe** Fyn, C Denmark 55°14′N 10°30′E
154 D5 **Ringebu** Oppland, S Norway 61°31′N 10°09′E
Ringen *see* Rõngu
159 H6 **Ringford** United Kingdom 54°53′N 4°02′W
281 H2 **Ringgi** Kolombangara, NW Solomon Islands 08°03′S 157°08′E
66 F7 **Ringgold** Georgia, SE USA 34°55′N 85°06′W
68 B2 **Ringgold** Louisiana, S USA 32°19′N 93°16′W
70 G3 **Ringgold** Texas, SW USA 33°47′N 97°56′W
155 C12 **Ringkøbing** Ringkøbing, W Denmark 56°04′N 08°22′E
155 C11 **Ringkøbing** *var.* Ringkøbing Amt. ⬖ *county* W Denmark
Ringkøbing Amt *see* Ringkøbing
155 C12 **Ringkøbing Fjord** *fjord* W Denmark
77 I5 **Ringling** Montana, NW USA 46°15′N 110°48′W
75 E13 **Ringling** Oklahoma, C USA 34°12′N 97°35′W
161 K8 **Ringmer** United Kingdom 50°53′N 0°04′E
154 E6 **Ringsaker** Hedmark, S Norway 60°54′N 10°45′E
158 D5 **Ringsend** United Kingdom 55°02′N 6°45′W
161 L2 **Ringstead** United Kingdom 52°56′N 0°33′E
155 E12 **Ringsted** Vestsjælland, E Denmark 55°28′N 11°48′E
Rīngus *see* Rīngas
152 F3 **Ringvassøya** *Lapp.* Ráneš. *island* N Norway
161 I8 **Ringwood** United Kingdom 50°51′N 1°47′W
65 H5 **Ringwood** New Jersey, NE USA 41°06′N 74°15′W
180 D7 **Rinkerode** Nordrhein-Westfalen, Germany 51°51′E 7°41′N
Rinn Duáin *see* Hook Head
180 G6 **Rinteln** Niedersachsen, NW Germany 52°10′N 09°04′E
186 F6 **Río** Dytikí Elláda, S Greece 38°18′N 21°48′E
Rio *see* Rio de Janeiro
111 H3 **Rio Acima** Minas Gerais, Brazil 20°05′S 43°47′W
104 C2 **Riobamba** Chimborazo, C Ecuador 01°44′S 78°40′W
111 M2 **Rio Bananal** Espírito Santo, Brazil 19°16′S 40°20′W
111 J8 **Rio Bonito** Rio de Janeiro, SE Brazil 22°42′S 42°38′W
106 D6 **Rio Branco** *state capital* Acre, W Brazil 09°59′S 67°49′W
115 L6 **Río Branco** Cerro Largo, NE Uruguay 32°32′S 53°28′W
Rio Branco, Território de *see* Roraima
85 M6 **Río Bravo** Tamaulipas, C Mexico 25°57′N 98°03′W
116 B7 **Río Bueno** Los Lagos, C Chile 40°20′S 72°55′W
106 2B **Rio Caqueta** 〰 Guainia, Colombia
103 H2 **Río Caribe** Sucre, NE Venezuela 10°43′N 63°06′W
111 J3 **Rio Casca** Minas Gerais, Brazil 20°13′S 42°39′W
102 G3 **Río Chico** Miranda, N Venezuela 10°18′N 66°00′W
117 C9 **Río Cisnes** Aisén, S Chile 44°29′S 71°15′W
110 B7 **Rio Claro** São Paulo, S Brazil 22°19′S 47°35′W
91 L8 **Rio Claro** Trinidad, Trinidad and Tobago 10°18′N 61°11′W
102 E3 **Río Claro** Lara, N Venezuela 09°54′N 69°23′W
116 E6 **Rio Colorado** Río Negro, E Argentina 39°01′S 64°05′W
85 H5 **Rio Conchos** 〰 Chihuahua, Mexico
116 E3 **Río Cuarto** Córdoba, C Argentina 33°06′S 64°20′W
111 H7 **Rio das Flores** Rio de Janeiro, Brazil 22°10′S 43°35′W
111 K7 **Rio das Ostras** Rio de Janeiro, Brazil 22°32′S 41°57′W
110 B8 **Rio das Pedras** São Paulo, Brazil 22°50′S 47°36′W
111 I8 **Rio de Janeiro** *var.* Rio. *state capital* Rio de Janeiro, SE Brazil 22°53′S 43°17′W
111 K6 **Rio de Janeiro** *off.* Estado do Rio de Janeiro. ⬖ *state* SE Brazil
Rio de Janeiro, Estado do *see* Rio de Janeiro
89 J10 **Río de Jesús** Veraguas, S Panama 07°58′N 81°01′W
78 A2 **Rio Dell** California, W USA 40°30′N 124°07′W
111 I3 **Rio Doce** Minas Gerais, Brazil 20°15′S 42°54′W
113 K6 **Rio do Sul** Santa Catarina, S Brazil 27°15′S 49°37′W
111 H4 **Rio Espera** Minas Gerais, Brazil 20°51′S 43°29′W
117 D12 **Río Gallegos** *var.* Gallegos, Puerto Gallegos. Santa Cruz, S Argentina 51°40′S 69°21′W
117 D13 **Río Grande** Tierra del Fuego, S Argentina 53°45′S 67°46′W
115 N5 **Rio Grande** *var.* São Pedro do Rio Grande do Sul. Rio Grande do Sul, S Brazil 32°03′S 52°08′W
85 J8 **Río Grande** Zacatecas, C Mexico 23°50′N 103°20′W
88 G5 **Río Grande** León, NW Nicaragua 12°59′N 86°34′W
91 J7 **Río Grande** E Puerto Rico 18°23′N 65°51′W
70 F9 **Rio Grande** 〰 Texas, SW USA
70 F10 **Rio Grande City** Texas, SW USA 26°24′N 98°50′W
108 I4 **Rio Grande do Norte** *off.* Estado do Rio Grande do Norte. ⬖ *state* E Brazil
Rio Grande do Norte, Estado do *see* Rio Grande do Norte
115 K2 **Rio Grande do Sul** *off.* Estado do Rio Grande do Sul. ⬖ *state* S Brazil
Rio Grande do Sul, Estado do *see* Rio Grande do Sul
291 G10 **Rio Grande Fracture Zone** *tectonic feature* C Atlantic Ocean
291 F10 **Rio Grande Gap** *undersea feature* S Atlantic Ocean
Rio Grande Plateau *see* Rio Grande Rise
291 F10 **Rio Grande Rise** *var.* Rio Grande Plateau. *undersea feature* SW Atlantic Ocean 31°00′S 35°00′W
102 D2 **Ríohacha** La Guajira, N Colombia 11°23′N 72°47′W
89 K9 **Río Hato** Coclé, C Panama 08°21′N 80°10′W
70 G10 **Rio Hondo** Texas, SW USA 26°14′N 97°34′W
104 D4 **Rioja** San Martín, N Peru 06°02′S 77°10′W
87 M4 **Río Lagartos** Yucatán, SE Mexico 21°35′N 88°08′W
165 I6 **Riom** *anc.* Ricomagus. Puy-de-Dôme, C France 45°54′N 03°06′E
172 B4 **Rio Maior** Santarém, C Portugal 39°20′N 08°55′W
110 G3 **Rio Manso** Minas Gerais, Brazil 20°16′S 44°19′W
165 H7 **Riom-ès-Montagnes** Cantal, C France 45°15′N 02°39′E
113 K5 **Rio Negro** Paraná, S Brazil 26°06′S 49°46′W
116 D7 **Río Negro** *off.* Provincia de Río Negro. ⬖ *province* C Argentina
114 F6 **Río Negro** ⬖ *department* W Uruguay
95 L7 **Río Negro, Embalse del** *var.* Lago Artificial de Rincón del Bonete. ⊠ C Uruguay
Río Negro, Provincia de *see* Río Negro
175 H9 **Rionero in Vulture** Basilicata, S Italy 40°55′N 15°40′E
215 J3 **Rioni** 〰 W Georgia
111 I5 **Rio Novo** Minas Gerais, Brazil 21°29′S 43°08′W
171 H7 **Riópar** Castilla-La Mancha, C Spain 38°31′N 02°27′W
115 M1 **Rio Pardo** Rio Grande do Sul, S Brazil 29°41′S 52°25′W
111 I3 **Rio Piracicaba** Minas Gerais, Brazil 19°55′S 43°11′W
111 H6 **Rio Prèto** Minas Gerais, Brazil 22°05′S 43°50′W
79 L7 **Rio Rancho Estates** New Mexico, SW USA 35°14′N 106°40′W
88 G7 **Río San Juan** ⬖ *department* S Nicaragua
102 B5 **Ríosucio** Caldas, W Colombia 05°26′N 75°44′W
102 B4 **Ríosucio** Chocó, NW Colombia 07°25′N 77°05′W
114 C8 **Río Tala** Buenos Aires, Argentina 33°45′S 59°38′W
116 E3 **Río Tercero** Córdoba, C Argentina 32°15′S 64°08′W
88 G3 **Río Tinto, Sierra** ▲▲ NE Honduras
102 E3 **Río Tocuyo** Lara, N Venezuela 10°18′N 70°00′W
Riouw-Archipel *see* Riau, Kepulauan
109 A10 **Rio Verde** Goiás, C Brazil 17°50′S 50°55′W
85 L9 **Río Verde** *var.* Rioverde. San Luis Potosí, C Mexico 21°58′N 100°W
Rioverde *see* Río Verde
80 C2 **Rio Vista** California, W USA 38°09′N 121°42′W
167 L8 **Rioz** Franche-Comté, France 47°25′N 6°04′E
184 G4 **Ripanj** Serbia, N Serbia 44°37′N 20°30′E
177 J10 **Ripatransone** Marche, C Italy 43°00′N 13°45′E
Ripen *see* Ribe
161 I2 **Ripley** United Kingdom 53°02′N 1°24′W
81 H13 **Ripley** California, USA 33°32′N 114°39′W
66 C7 **Ripley** Mississippi, S USA 34°43′N 88°57′W
73 H12 **Ripley** Ohio, N USA 38°45′N 83°51′W
66 B6 **Ripley** Tennessee, S USA 35°43′N 89°30′W
67 H3 **Ripley** West Virginia, NE USA 38°49′N 81°44′W
171 K3 **Ripoll** Cataluña, NE Spain 42°12′N 02°12′E
159 K8 **Ripon** N England, United Kingdom 54°07′N 01°31′W
80 C3 **Ripon** California, USA 37°45′N 121°07′W
72 D7 **Ripon** Wisconsin, N USA 43°52′N 88°48′W
175 G12 **Riposto** Sicilia, Italy, C Mediterranean Sea 37°44′N 15°13′E
80 D5 **Ripperdan** California, USA 36°51′N 120°03′W
163 G8 **Rips** Noord-Brabant, SE Netherlands 51°31′N 05°49′E
167 M6 **Riquewihr** Alsace, France 48°10′N 7°18′E
102 B5 **Risaralda** *off.* Departamento de Risaralda. ⬖ *province* C Colombia
Risaralda, Departamento de *see* Risaralda
160 G6 **Risca** United Kingdom 51°37′N 3°06′W
188 F6 **Rîşcani** *var.* Râşcani, *Rus.* Ryshkany. NW Moldova 47°55′N 27°31′E
180 G7 **Rischenau** Nordrhein-Westfalen, Germany 51°53′E 9°17′N
168 D5 **Riscle** Midi-Pyrénées, France 43°40′N 0°05′W
232 F4 **Rishikesh** Uttarakhand, N India 30°06′N 78°16′E
252 E2 **Rishiri-suidō** *strait* E Sea of Japan
252 D2 **Rishiri-tō** *var.* Risiri Tô. *island* NE Japan
252 E2 **Rishiri-yama** ⛰ Rishiri-tō, NE Japan 45°11′N 141°11′E
Rishon Le-Tsiyon *see* Rishon LeẔiyyon
219 D8 **Rishon LeẔiyyon** *var.* Rishon Le-Tsiyon. Central, C Israel 31°57′N 34°48′E

◆ Country
● Country Capital
◇ Dependent Territory
○ Dependent Territory Capital
⬖ Administrative Regions
✈ International Airport
▲ Mountain
▲▲ Mountain Range
⛰ Volcano
〰 River
◎ Lake
⊠ Reservoir

INDEX
397

179 E13 Rot S Germany
170 E9 Rota Andalucía, S Spain 36°39′N 06°20′W
282 E4 Rota island S Northern Mariana Islands
70 E4 Rotan Texas, SW USA 32°51′N 100°28′W
Rotcher Island see Tamana
181 H9 Rotenburg Hessen, Germany 50°59′E 9°43′N
180 G4 Rotenburg Niedersachsen, NW Germany 53°06′N 09°25′E
Rotenburg see Rotenburg an der Fulda
181 H9 Rotenburg an der Fulda var. Rotenburg. Thüringen, C Germany 51°00′N 09°43′E
179 G10 Roter Main E Germany
181 J13 Roth Bayern, SE Germany 49°15′N 11°06′E
181 E9 Rothaargebirge W Germany
159 J5 Rothbury United Kingdom 55°19′N 1°54′W
181 G12 Rothenbuch Bayern, Germany 49°58′E 9°24′N
181 J12 Rothenbühl Bayern, Germany 49°47′E 11°12′N
Rothenburg see Rothenburg ob der Tauber
181 I13 Rothenburg ob der Tauber var. Rothenburg. Bayern, S Germany 49°23′N 10°10′E
181 J14 Rothenstein Bayern, Germany 48°58′E 11°03′N
161 J7 Rother S England, United Kingdom
292 E4 Rothera UK research station Antarctica 67°28′S 68°31′W
161 L7 Rotherfield United Kingdom 51°02′N 0°13′E
279 F9 Rotherham Canterbury, South Island, New Zealand 42°42′S 172°56′E
159 K10 Rotherham N England, United Kingdom 53°26′N 01°20′W
158 F3 Rothesay United Kingdom 55°50′N 5°04′W
158 F3 Rothesay W Scotland, United Kingdom 55°49′N 05°03′W
176 D4 Rothrist Aargau, N Switzerland 47°18′N 07°54′E
292 E4 Rothschild Island island Antarctica
159 K9 Rothwell United Kingdom 53°45′N 1°29′W
260 E9 Roti, Pulau island S Indonesia
260 E9 Roti, Selat strait Nusa Tenggara, S Indonesia
140 B4 Rotkop Karas, Namibia 26°43′S 15°24′E
154 E7 Rotnes Akershus, S Norway 60°08′N 10°45′E
277 J5 Roto New South Wales, SE Australia 33°04′S 145°27′E
278 H5 Rotoiti, Lake ◎ North Island, New Zealand
Rotomagus see Rouen
175 H10 Rotondella Basilicata, S Italy 40°12′N 16°30′E
175 B8 Rotondo, Monte ▲ Corse, France, C Mediterranean Sea 42°15′N 09°03′E
278 E8 Rotoroa, Lake ◎ South Island, New Zealand
278 H5 Rotorua Bay of Plenty, North Island, New Zealand 38°10′S 176°14′E
278 H5 Rotorua, Lake ◎ North Island, New Zealand
179 H12 Rott SE Germany
176 D5 Rotten S Switzerland
181 I14 Rottenbach Bayern, Germany 49°09′E 11°02′N
177 J3 Rottenmann Steiermark, E Austria 47°31′N 14°18′E
162 E7 Rotterdam Zuid-Holland, SW Netherlands 51°55′N 04°30′E
65 H1 Rotterdam New York, NE USA 42°46′N 73°57′W
181 H13 Röttingen Bayern, Germany 49°31′E 9°58′N
181 J8 Röttleberode Sachsen-Anhalt, Germany 51°31′E 10°56′N
155 G11 Rottnen ◎ S Sweden
162 H2 Rottumeroog island Waddeneilanden, NE Netherlands
162 I2 Rottumerplaat island Waddeneilanden, NE Netherlands
179 D13 Rottweil Baden-Württemberg, S Germany 48°10′N 08°38′E
286 F6 Rotuma island NW Fiji Oceania S Pacific Ocean
165 I1 Roubaix Nord, N France 50°42′N 03°10′E
183 B8 Roudnice nad Labem Ger. Raudnitz an der Elbe. Ústecký Kraj, NW Czech Republic 50°25′N 14°14′E
165 H2 Rouen anc. Rotomagus. Seine-Maritime, N France 49°26′N 01°05′E
167 M7 Rouffach Alsace, France 47°58′N 7°17′E
261 L5 Rouffaer Reserves reserve Papua, E Indonesia
167 L8 Rougemont Franche-Comté, France 47°29′N 6°21′E
62 G1 Rouge, Rivière Québec, SE Canada
161 L3 Rougham United Kingdom 52°45′N 0°43′E
80 D1 Rough and Ready California, USA 39°14′N 121°08′W
66 D4 Rough River Kentucky, S USA
66 D4 Rough River Lake ⊠ Kentucky, S USA
161 M2 Roughton United Kingdom 52°53′N 1°18′E
Rouhaïbé see Ar Ruḩaybah
168 E1 Rouillac Charente, W France 45°46′N 00°04′W
165 I9 Roujan Languedoc-Roussillon, France 43°31′N 3°18′E
167 L8 Roulans Franche-Comté, France 47°19′N 6°14′E
Roulers see Roeselare
Roumania see Romania
137 G10 Round Island var. Île Ronde. island NE Mauritius
62 E3 Round Lake ◎ Ontario, SE Canada
80 I2 Round Mountain Nevada, W USA 38°42′N 117°04′W
70 G6 Round Mountain Texas, SW USA 30°25′N 98°20′W
277 M3 Round Mountain ▲ New South Wales, SE Australia 30°22′S 152°13′E
70 G6 Round Rock Texas, SW USA 30°30′N 97°40′W
77 K5 Roundup Montana, NW USA 46°27′N 108°32′W
160 B2 Roundwood Wicklow, Ireland 53°04′N 6°14′W
103 N5 Roura NE French Guiana 04°44′N 52°16′W
Rourkela see Rāulakela
156 F3 Rousay island N Scotland, United Kingdom
Rousselaere see Roeselare
165 H10 Roussillon cultural region S France
163 G14 Rouvroy Luxembourg, SE Belgium 49°33′N 05°28′E
167 J3 Rouvroy-sur-Audry Champagne-Ardenne, France 49°47′N 4°29′E
141 J7 Rouxville Free State, South Africa 30°25′S 26°50′E
58 F7 Rouyn-Noranda Québec, SE Canada 48°16′N 79°03′W
Rouyuan see Huachi
Rouyuanchengzi see Huachi
168 G3 Rouziers Auvergne, France 44°47′N 2°13′E
80 F5 Rovana California, USA 37°25′N 118°37′W
152 H6 Rovaniemi Lappi, N Finland 66°29′N 25°40′E
176 F6 Rovato Lombardia, N Italy 45°34′N 10°03′E
194 G7 Rovdino Arkhangel'skaya Oblast', NW Russian Federation 61°36′N 42°28′E
Roven'ki see Roven'ky
189 N5 Roven'ky var. Roven'ki. Luhans'ka Oblast', E Ukraine 48°05′N 39°20′E
Rovenskaya Oblast' see Rivnens'ka Oblast'
Rovenskaya Sloboda see Rovyenskaya Slabada
176 G6 Rovereto Ger. Rofreit. Trentino-Alto Adige, N Italy 45°53′N 11°03′E
257 H8 Rôviěng Tbong Preăh Vihéar, N Cambodia 13°18′N 105°06′E
Rovigno see Rovinj
177 H7 Rovigo Veneto, NE Italy 45°04′N 11°48′E
184 A3 Rovinj It. Rovigno. Istra, NW Croatia 45°06′N 13°39′E
102 B6 Rovira Tolima, C Colombia 04°15′N 75°15′W
Rovno see Rivne
Rovnoye Saratovskaya Oblast', W Russian Federation 50°43′N 46°03′E
137 D12 Rovuma, Rio var. Ruvuma. Mozambique/Tanzania see also Ruvuma
Rovuma, Rio see Ruvuma
191 I11 Rovyenskaya Slabada Rus. Rovenskaya Sloboda. Homyel'skaya Voblasts', SE Belarus 52°13′N 30°19′E
277 K3 Rowena New South Wales, SE Australia 29°51′S 148°55′E
67 K7 Rowland North Carolina, SE USA 34°32′N 79°17′W
159 K6 Rowlands Gill United Kingdom 54°55′N 1°44′W
53 J7 Rowley Baffin Island, Nunavut, NE Canada
53 J7 Rowley Island island Nunavut, NE Canada
286 B7 Rowley Shelf undersea feature E Indian Ocean
289 J9 Rowley Shoals reef NW Australia
Równe see Rivne
263 L6 Roxas Mindoro, N Philippines 12°36′N 121°29′E
263 L7 Roxas City Panay Island, C Philippines 11°33′N 122°43′E
67 K5 Roxboro North Carolina, SE USA 36°24′N 79°00′W
278 C12 Roxburgh Otago, South Island, New Zealand 45°32′S 169°18′E
156 G7 Roxburgh cultural region SE Scotland, United Kingdom
276 F3 Roxby Downs South Australia 30°29′S 136°56′E
155 H9 Roxen ◎ S Sweden
161 K4 Roxton United Kingdom 52°10′N 0°18′W
71 H4 Roxton Texas, SW USA 33°33′N 95°43′W
63 I3 Roxton-Sud Québec, SE Canada 45°30′N 72°35′W
161 L5 Roxwell United Kingdom 51°45′N 0°22′E
77 J4 Roy Montana, NW USA 47°19′N 108°55′W
79 M6 Roy New Mexico, SW USA 35°56′N 104°12′W
157 D9 Royal Canal Ir. An Chanáil Ríoga. canal C Ireland
72 D2 Royale, Isle island Michigan, N USA
52 D8 Royal Geographical Society Islands island Nunavut, N Canada
79 L4 Royal Gorge valley Colorado, C USA
288 H7 Royalist Bank N Indian Ocean
161 J4 Royal Leamington Spa var. Leamington, Leamington Spa. C England, United Kingdom 52°18′N 01°31′W
161 L7 Royal Tunbridge Wells var. Tunbridge Wells. SE England, United Kingdom 51°08′N 00°16′E
70 D5 Royalty Texas, SW USA 31°21′N 102°51′W
164 F6 Royan Charente-Maritime, W France 45°37′N 01°01′W
169 K2 Roybon Rhône-Alpes, France 45°15′N 5°15′E
117 H11 Roy Cove Settlement West Falkland, Falkland Islands 51°32′S 60°23′W
165 I2 Roye Somme, N France 49°42′N 02°46′E
168 F2 Royère Limousin, France 45°35′N 1°56′E
154 D7 Røyken Buskerud, S Norway 59°47′N 10°21′E
154 F1 Røyrvik Nord-Trøndelag, C Norway 64°53′N 13°30′E
71 H4 Royse City Texas, SW USA 32°58′N 96°19′W
161 K5 Royston E England, United Kingdom 52°05′N 00°01′W
66 G8 Royston Georgia, SE USA 34°17′N 83°06′W
159 J9 Royton United Kingdom 53°34′N 2°07′W
185 L6 Roza prev. Gyulovo. Yambol, E Bulgaria 42°29′N 26°30′E
184 F6 Rožaje E Montenegro 42°51′N 20°11′E
182 H5 Różan Mazowieckie, C Poland 52°36′N 21°27′E
167 H6 Rozay-en-Brie Île-de-France, France 48°41′N 2°58′E
189 H7 Rozdil'na Odes'ka Oblast', SW Ukraine 46°51′N 30°03′E
189 J8 Rozdol'ne Rus. Razdolnoye. Avtonomna Respublika Krym, S Ukraine 45°45′N 33°27′E
Rozhdestvenka see Kabanbay Batyr
188 D4 Rozhnyativ Ivano-Frankivs'ka Oblast', W Ukraine 48°58′N 24°07′E
188 D2 Rozhyshche Volyns'ka Oblast', NW Ukraine 50°54′N 25°16′E
Roznau am Radhost see Rožnov pod Radhoštěm
183 H10 Rožňava Ger. Rosenau, Hung. Rozsnyó. Košický Kraj, E Slovakia 48°41′N 20°32′E
188 E7 Roznov Neamţ, NE Romania 46°47′N 26°33′E
183 F9 Rožnov pod Radhoštěm Ger. Rosenau, Roznau am Radhost. Zlínský Kraj, E Czech Republic 49°28′N 18°09′E
167 J4 Rozoy-sur-Serre Picardie, France 49°43′N 4°08′E
Rózsahegy see Ružomberok
Rozsnyó see Râşnov, Romania
Rozsnyó see Rožňava, Slovakia
184 F7 Rranxë Shkodër, NW Albania 41°58′N 19°27′E
184 F7 Rrëshen var. Rresheni, Rrshen. Lezhë, C Albania 41°46′N 19°54′E
Rresheni see Rrëshen
Rrogozhina see Rrogozhinë
184 F8 Rrogozhinë var. Rogozhina, Rogozhinë, Rrogozhina. Tiranë, W Albania 41°04′N 19°40′E
Rrshen see Rrëshen
185 H5 Rtanj ▲ E Serbia 43°45′N 21°54′E
197 H4 Rtishchevo Saratovskaya Oblast', W Russian Federation 52°16′N 43°46′E
278 H6 Ruahine Range var. Ruarine. ▲ North Island, New Zealand
Ruanda see Rwanda
160 D10 Ruan Minor United Kingdom 49°59′N 5°11′W
278 H6 Ruapehu, Mount North Island, New Zealand 39°15′S 175°33′E
278 C13 Ruapuke Island island SW New Zealand
Ruarine see Ruahine Range
278 I5 Ruatahuna Bay of Plenty, North Island, New Zealand 38°38′S 176°56′E
278 J5 Ruatoria Gisborne, North Island, New Zealand 37°54′S 178°18′E
278 F3 Ruawai Northland, North Island, New Zealand 36°08′S 174°04′E
137 D10 Rubeho Mountains ▲ C Tanzania
252 G3 Rubeshibe Hokkaidō, NE Japan 43°49′N 143°37′E
Rubezhnoye see Rubizhne
168 G9 Rubí Cataluña, Spain 41°29′N 2°02′E
81 E11 Rubidoux California, USA 34°00′N 117°24′W
184 F7 Rubik Lezhë, C Albania 41°46′N 19°48′E
102 D4 Rubio Táchira, W Venezuela 07°42′N 72°23′W
189 M4 Rubizhne Rus. Rubezhnoye. Luhans'ka Oblast', E Ukraine 49°01′N 38°22′E
137 B8 Rubondo Island island N Tanzania
192 F8 Rubtsovsk Altayskiy Kray, S Russian Federation 51°34′N 81°11′E
83 H5 Ruby Alaska, USA 64°44′N 155°29′W
78 F2 Ruby Dome ▲ Nevada, W USA 40°35′N 115°25′W
78 F3 Ruby Lake ◎ Nevada, W USA
78 F2 Ruby Mountains ▲ Nevada, W USA
77 H6 Ruby Range ▲ Montana, NW USA
190 B7 Rucava Liepāja, SW Latvia 56°09′N 21°10′E
243 H7 Rucheng Hunan, SE China 25°32′N 113°39′E
181 J13 Rückersdorf Bayern, Germany 49°16′E 10°44′N
223 I8 Rūdān var. Dehbārez. Hormozgān, S Iran 27°30′N 57°10′E
Rudelstadt see Ciechanowiec
Rudensk see Rudzyensk
181 E9 Rudersdorf Nordrhein-Westfalen, Germany 50°51′E 8°09′N
190 D9 Rūdiškės Vilnius, S Lithuania 54°31′N 24°49′E
155 E13 Rudkøbing Fyn, C Denmark 54°57′N 10°43′E
193 L9 Rudnaya Pristan' Primorskiy Kray, SE Russian Federation 44°19′N 135°42′E
197 J8 Rudnichnyy Kirovskaya Oblast', NW Russian Federation 59°37′N 52°28′E
Rūdnichnyy see Koksu
185 M6 Rudnik Varna, E Bulgaria 42°57′N 27°46′E
Rudny see Rudnyy
196 D2 Rudnya Smolenskaya Oblast', W Russian Federation 54°55′N 31°10′E
197 I5 Rudnya Volgogradskaya Oblast', SW Russian Federation 50°54′N 44°27′E
226 F2 Rudnyy var. Rudny. Kostanay, N Kazakhstan 53°N 63°05′E
192 G1 Rudol'fa, Ostrov island Zemlya Frantsa-Iosifa, NW Russian Federation
Rudolf, Lake see Turkana, Lake
Rudolfswert see Novo mesto
179 F9 Rudolstadt Thüringen, C Germany 50°44′N 11°20′E
243 M1 Rudong Jiangsu, China 32°11′N 121°07′E
159 M8 Rudston United Kingdom 54°05′N 0°19′W
72 G4 Rudyard Michigan, N USA 46°15′N 84°36′W
77 I3 Rudyard Montana, NW USA 48°33′N 110°37′W
191 G10 Rudzyensk Rus. Rudensk. Minskaya Voblasts', C Belarus 53°36′N 27°52′E
170 F4 Rueda Castilla-León, N Spain 41°24′N 04°58′W
161 E1 Ruelle-sur-Touvre Poitou-Charentes, France 45°41′N 0°13′E
185 H7 Ruen ▲ Bulgaria/FYR Macedonia 42°10′N 22°31′E
136 C2 Rufa'a Gezira, C Sudan 14°49′N 33°21′E
164 G6 Ruffec Charente, W France 46°01′N 00°10′E
67 I9 Ruffin South Carolina, SE USA 33°00′N 80°48′W
160 G1 Rufford NW England, United Kingdom 53°38′N 02°55′W
159 I9 Rufford NW England, United Kingdom 53°38′N 02°55′W
137 D11 Rufiji E Tanzania
116 F4 Rufino Santa Fe, C Argentina 34°16′S 62°45′W
132 A4 Rufisque W Senegal 14°44′N 17°18′W
137 H2 Rufunsa Lusaka, C Zambia 15°02′S 29°35′E
190 F6 Rugāji Balvi, E Latvia 57°01′N 27°07′E
243 M1 Rugao Jiangsu, E China 32°27′N 120°35′E
161 J4 Rugby C England, United Kingdom 52°22′N 01°18′W
74 D2 Rugby North Dakota, N USA 48°24′N 100°00′W
161 H3 Rugeley United Kingdom 52°46′N 1°56′W
178 H4 Rügen headland NE Germany 54°25′N 13°21′E
219 D9 Ruḩama var. Ruhama. Southern, S Israel 31°30′N 34°42′E
Ruḩaybeh see Ar Ruḩaybah
241 H3 Ru He C China
162 J5 Ruhen Niedersachsen, Germany 52°29′E 10°53′N
137 A8 Ruhengeri NW Rwanda 01°39′S 29°16′E
Ruhja see Rūjiena
178 G5 Ruhner Berg hill N Germany
190 D5 Ruhnu var. Ruhnu Saar, Swe. Runö. island SW Estonia
Ruhnu Saar see Ruhnu
181 E8 Ruhr W Germany
181 D8 Ruhr Valley industrial region W Germany
243 M5 Rui'an Zhejiang, SE China 27°51′N 120°39′E
243 I3 Ruichang Jiangxi, S China 29°46′N 115°37′E
243 F7 Ruicheng Shanxi, China 34°25′N 110°25′E
70 B6 Ruidosa Texas, SW USA 30°00′N 104°40′W
79 M8 Ruidoso New Mexico, SW USA 33°19′N 105°40′W
243 J7 Ruijin Jiangxi, S China 25°52′N 116°01′E
240 A7 Ruili Yunnan, SW China 24°04′N 97°49′E
162 H5 Ruinen Drenthe, NE Netherlands 52°46′N 06°19′E
163 C9 Ruiselede West-Vlaanderen, W Belgium 51°03′N 03°21′E
170 A8 Ruivo de Santana, Pico ▲ Madeira, Portugal, NE Atlantic Ocean 32°46′N 16°57′W
114 D9 Ruiz Buenos Aires, Argentina 34°25′S 59°15′W
85 I9 Ruiz Nayarit, SW Mexico 22°00′N 105°09′W
102 B5 Ruiz, Nevado del W Colombia 04°53′N 75°22′W
216 D6 Rujaylah, Ḩarrat ar salt lake N Jordan
Rujen see Rūjiena
190 E5 Rūjiena Est. Ruhja, Ger. Rujen. Valmiera, N Latvia 57°54′N 25°22′E
243 C3 Rujigou Ningxia, China 39°01′N 106°04′E
Rukhaima see Ruḩama
134 F7 Ruki W Dem. Rep. Congo
137 B10 Rukwa ◆ region SW Tanzania
137 B11 Rukwa, Lake ◎ SE Tanzania
70 F4 Rule Texas, SW USA 33°10′N 99°53′W
66 B8 Ruleville Mississippi, S USA 33°43′N 90°33′W
Rum see Rhum
184 F3 Ruma Vojvodina, N Serbia 45°02′N 19°51′E
Rumadiya see Ar Ramādī
220 G4 Rumāḩ Ar Riyāḑ, C Saudi Arabia 25°35′N 47°09′E
Rumaitha see Ar Rumaythah
Rumania/Rumänien see Romania
Rumänisch-Sankt-Georgen see Sângeorz-Băi
217 M8 Rumaylah Al Başrah, SE Iraq 30°16′N 47°22′E
217 H2 Rumaylah, Wādī dry watercourse NE Syria
261 J5 Rumbati Papua, E Indonesia 02°44′S 132°04′E
136 A5 Rumbek El Buhayrat, C South Sudan 06°50′N 29°42′E
261 J5 Rumberpon, Pulau island E Indonesia
Rumburg see Rumburk
161 M4 Rumburgh United Kingdom 52°22′N 1°27′E
182 C7 Rumburk Ger. Rumburg. Ústecký Kraj, NW Czech Republic 50°58′N 14°35′E
61 N10 Rum Cay island C Bahamas
163 H14 Rumelange Luxembourg, S Luxembourg 49°28′N 06°02′E
163 B11 Rumes Hainaut, SW Belgium 50°33′N 03°19′E
63 J4 Rumford Maine, NE USA 44°31′N 70°31′W
182 F3 Rumia Pomorskie, N Poland 54°36′N 18°21′E
167 J3 Rumigny Champagne-Ardenne, France 49°48′N 4°16′E
184 E7 Rumija ▲ S Montenegro
165 K6 Rumilly Haute-Savoie, E France 45°52′N 05°57′E
216 G4 Rūmiyah Al Anbār, W Iraq 34°28′N 41°17′E
Rummah, Wādī ar see Rimah, Wādī ar
218 E6 Rummāne Israel 32°47′N 35°18′E
Rummelsburg in Pommern see Miastko
252 E3 Rumoi Hokkaidō, NE Japan 43°57′N 141°40′E
84 B1 Rumorosa Baja California Norte, NW Mexico 32°34′N 116°06′W
137 C12 Rumphi var. Rumpi. Northern, N Malawi 11°00′S 33°51′E
Rumpi see Rumphi
74 G4 Rum River Minnesota, N USA
80 C1 Rumsey California, USA 38°53′N 122°14′W
65 H7 Rumson New Jersey, USA 40°22′N 74°00′W
282 A3 Rumung island Caroline Islands, W Micronesia
Rumuniya/Rumŭniya/Rumunjska see Romania
187 E5 Runabay Head headland United Kingdom 55°10′N 6°02′W
245 I9 Runan Henan, E China 33°0′N 114°21′E
279 D9 Runanga West Coast, South Island, New Zealand 42°25′S 171°15′E
278 I4 Runaway, Cape headland North Island, New Zealand 37°33′S 177°59′E
159 I10 Runcorn C England, United Kingdom 53°20′N 02°44′W
190 G7 Rundāni var. Rundāni. Ludza, E Latvia 56°19′N 27°51′E
Rundāni see Rundāni
139 H4 Runde var. Lundi. SE Zimbabwe
138 D3 Rundu var. Runtu. Okavango, NE Namibia 17°55′S 19°45′E
154 J3 Rundvik Västerbotten, N Sweden 63°31′N 19°22′E
137 C9 Runere Mwanza, N Tanzania 03°06′S 33°18′E
70 G8 Runge Texas, SW USA 28°52′N 97°42′W
262 C7 Rŭng, Kaôh prev. Kas Rong. island SW Cambodia
134 I6 Rungu Orientale, NE Dem. Rep. Congo 03°11′N 27°52′E
118 D3 Rungue Región Metropolitana, Chile 33°01′S 70°54′W
137 B11 Rungwa Rukwa, W Tanzania 07°18′S 31°40′E
137 C10 Rungwa Singida, C Tanzania 06°54′S 33°33′E
154 H7 Runn ◎ C Sweden
65 G8 Runnemede New Jersey, NE USA 39°51′N 75°04′W
70 D3 Running Water Draw valley New Mexico/Texas, SW USA
Runö see Ruhnu
Runtu see Rundu
282 F9 Ruo island Caroline Islands, C Micronesia
238 F5 Ruoqiang var. Jo-ch'iang, Uigh. Charkhlik, Charkhliq, Qarkilik. Xinjiang Uygur Zizhiqu, NW China 38°59′N 88°08′E
239 J4 Ruo Shui N China
152 H3 Ruostekfielbmá var. Rustefjelbma Finnmark. Finnmark, N Norway 70°25′N 28°10′E
153 H9 Ruovesi Länsi-Suomi, W Finland 61°59′N 24°05′E
184 A2 Rupa Primorje-Gorski Kotar, NW Croatia 45°29′N 14°15′E
276 I6 Rupanyup Victoria, SE Australia 36°38′S 142°37′E
258 E4 Rupat, Pulau prev. Roepat. island W Indonesia
258 E4 Rupat, Selat strait Sumatera, W Indonesia
188 D8 Rupea Ger. Reps, Hung. Kőhalom; prev. Cohalm. Braşov, C Romania 46°02′N 25°13′E
163 D9 Rupel N Belgium
Rupella see la Rochelle
77 H8 Rupert Idaho, NW USA 42°37′N 113°40′W
67 I4 Rupert West Virginia, NE USA 37°57′N 80°40′W
58 F6 Rupert Bay coastal sea feature Québec, SE Canada
Rupert House see Waskaganish
58 F6 Rupert, Rivière de Québec, C Canada
292 E7 Ruppert Coast physical region Antarctica
181 D9 Ruppichteroth Nordrhein-Westfalen, Germany 50°51′E 7°29′N
178 H6 Ruppiner Kanal canal NE Germany
167 M7 Rupt-sur-Moselle Lorraine, France 47°56′N 6°40′E
103 J6 Rupununi River S Guyana
181 C8 Rur Dut. Roer. Germany/Netherlands
107 J3 Rurópolis Presidente Medici Pará, N Brazil 04°05′S 55°26′W
285 I8 Rurutu island Îles Australes, SW French Polynesia
Rusaddir see Melilla
139 I3 Rusape Manicaland, E Zimbabwe 18°32′S 32°07′E
Rusayris, Lake see Roseires, Reservoir
Ruschuk/Rusçuk see Ruse
185 K5 Ruse var. Ruschuk, Rustchuk, Turk. Rusçuk. Ruse, N Bulgaria 43°50′N 25°59′E
177 K5 Ruše NE Slovenia 46°31′N 15°30′E
185 K5 Ruse ◆ province N Bulgaria
159 E9 Rush Ir. An Ros. Dublin, E Ireland 53°32′N 06°06′W
245 M5 Rushan var. Xiacun. Shandong, E China 36°55′N 121°26′E
Rushan see Rŭshon
Rushanskiy Khrebet see Rushon, Qatorkŭhi
72 A5 Rush City Minnesota, N USA 45°41′N 92°56′W
79 M4 Rush Creek Colorado, C USA
161 J4 Rushden United Kingdom 52°17′N 0°35′W
74 I5 Rushford Minnesota, N USA 43°48′N 91°45′W
234 H6 Rushikulya E India
72 I3 Rush Lake ◎ Ontario, S Canada
72 D7 Rush Lake ◎ Wisconsin, N USA
74 A5 Rushmore, Mount ▲ South Dakota, N USA 43°52′N 103°27′W
229 J7 Rŭshon Rus. Rushan. S Tajikistan 37°58′N 71°31′E
229 K7 Rushon, Qatorkŭhi Rus. Rushanskiy Khrebet. ▲ SE Tajikistan
75 D13 Rush Springs Oklahoma, C USA 34°46′N 97°57′W
63 I3 Rushville Trinidad, Trinidad and Tobago 10°07′N 61°03′W
73 B10 Rushville Illinois, N USA 40°07′N 90°33′W
91 L8 Rushville Nebraska, C USA 42°41′N 102°28′W
277 I6 Rushworth Victoria, SE Australia 36°36′S 145°03′E
71 I5 Rusk Texas, SW USA 31°49′N 95°11′W
159 M10 Ruskington United Kingdom 53°02′N 0°23′W
154 I1 Rusksele Västerbotten, N Sweden 64°49′N 18°55′E
191 B8 Rusnė Klaipėda, W Lithuania 55°18′N 21°19′E
185 L6 Ruskoastrenska Reka E Bulgaria
Russadir see Melilla
177 L2 Russbach NE Austria
55 I9 Russell Manitoba, S Canada 50°47′N 101°17′W
278 F2 Russell Northland, North Island, New Zealand 35°17′S 174°07′E
75 D9 Russell Kansas, C USA 38°54′N 98°51′W
73 I12 Russell Kentucky, S USA 38°30′N 82°43′W
52 E4 Russell, Cape headland Northwest Territories, NW Canada
64 E4 Russell Hill Pennsylvania, NE USA 41°35′N 76°00′W
52 G5 Russell Island island Nunavut, NW Canada
281 I2 Russell Islands island group C Solomon Islands
66 D5 Russell Springs Kentucky, S USA 37°02′N 85°03′W
66 D7 Russellville Alabama, S USA 34°30′N 87°43′W
75 H12 Russellville Arkansas, C USA 35°17′N 93°06′W
66 D5 Russellville Kentucky, S USA 36°50′N 86°54′W
181 E12 Rüsselsheim Hessen, W Germany 50°00′N 08°25′E
152 G3 Russenes Finnmark, N Norway 70°29′N 24°58′E
Russia see Russian Federation
Russian America see Alaska
195 K6 Russian Federation off. Russian Federation, var. Russia, Latv. Krievija, Rus. Rossiyskaya Federatsiya. ◆ republic Asia/Europe
Russian Federation see Russian Federation
83 G6 Russian Mission Alaska, USA 61°48′N 161°23′W
80 B1 Russian River California, W USA
80 F2 Russkaya Gavan' Novaya Zemlya, Arkhangel'skaya Oblast', N Russian Federation 76°13′N 62°48′E
193 H3 Russkiy, Ostrov island N Russian Federation
Rustaq see Ar Rustāq
215 K4 Rust'avi SE Georgia 41°36′N 45°00′E
67 K4 Rustburg Virginia, NE USA 37°17′N 79°07′W
Rustchuk see Ruse
Rustefjelbma Finnmark see Ruostekfielbmá
141 I3 Rustenburg North-West, N South Africa 25°40′S 27°15′E
141 I5 Rustig Free State, South Africa 29°03′S 26°27′E
68 C1 Ruston Louisiana, S USA 32°31′N 92°38′W
141 I3 Rusverby North-West, South Africa 25°32′S 26°41′E
137 A9 Rutana SE Burundi 04°01′S 30°01′E
137 C3 Rutana, Volcán N Chile 22°43′S 67°52′W
Rutanzige, Lake see Edward, Lake
Rutba see Ar Ruţbah
170 F8 Rute Andalucía, S Spain 37°20′N 04°23′W
260 D8 Ruteng prev. Roeteng. Flores, C Indonesia 08°35′S 120°28′E
292 G5 Rutford Ice Stream ice feature Antarctica
80 K4 Ruth Nevada, W USA 39°15′N 115°00′W
181 E8 Rüthen Nordrhein-Westfalen, W Germany 51°30′N 08°28′E
62 B6 Rutherford Ontario, S Canada 42°39′N 82°06′W
67 H7 Rutherfordton North Carolina, SE USA 35°23′N 81°57′W
158 G3 Rutherglen United Kingdom 55°49′N 4°13′W
160 F2 Ruthin Wel. Rhuthun. NE Wales, United Kingdom 53°05′N 03°18′W
Rutlam see Ratlām
63 H5 Rutland Vermont, NE USA 43°37′N 72°59′W
161 J3 Rutland Water ◎ C England, United Kingdom
66 G6 Rutledge Tennessee, S USA 36°16′N 83°31′W
54 F4 Rutledge Lake ◎ Northwest Territories, C Canada
238 D7 Rutog var. Rutög, Rutok. Xizang Zizhiqu, W China 33°27′N 79°43′E
Rutok see Rutog
135 I8 Rutshuru Nord-Kivu, E Dem. Rep. Congo 01°11′S 29°28′E
162 G4 Rutten Flevoland, N Netherlands 52°49′N 05°44′E
197 J10 Rutul Respublika Dagestan, SW Russian Federation 41°35′N 47°30′E
152 H7 Ruukki Oulu, C Finland 64°40′N 25°35′E
162 I6 Ruurlo Gelderland, E Netherlands 52°04′N 06°27′E
223 H9 Ru'ūs al Jibāl cape Oman/United Arab Emirates
218 I3 Ru'us at Ṭiwāl, Jabal ▲ W Syria
137 D12 Ruvuma ◆ region SE Tanzania
137 E12 Ruvuma var. Rio Rovuma. Mozambique/Tanzania see also Rovuma, Rio
Ruwais see Ar Ruways
218 J2 Ruwāq, Jabal ar ▲ Ḩimş, C Syria
216 D6 Ruwayshid, Wadi ar dry watercourse NE Jordan
221 L5 Ruways, Ra's ar headland E Oman 20°58′N 59°00′E
219 G14 Ruwayyitah, Wādī dry watercourse Jordan
134 J7 Ruwenzori ▲ Dem. Rep. Congo/Uganda
230 B10 Ruwī NE Oman 23°33′N 58°31′E
185 H6 Ruy ▲ Bulgaria/Serbia 42°52′N 22°35′E
Ruya see Luia, Rio
137 A9 Ruyigi E Burundi 03°28′S 30°19′E
197 I3 Ruzayevka Respublika Mordoviya, W Russian Federation 54°04′N 44°56′E
191 D11 Ruzhany Brestskaya Voblasts', SW Belarus 52°52′N 24°53′E
185 J7 Rŭzhevo Konare Plovdiv, C Bulgaria 42°16′N 24°58′E
Ruzhin see Ruzhyn
185 J5 Ruzhintsi Vidin, NW Bulgaria 43°38′N 22°50′E
245 H8 Ruzhou Henan, C China 34°10′N 112°51′E
188 G4 Ruzhyn Rus. Ruzhin. Zhytomyrs'ka Oblast', N Ukraine 49°42′N 29°01′E
183 G9 Ružomberok Ger. Rosenberg, Hung. Rózsahegy. Žilinský Kraj, N Slovakia 49°04′N 19°19′E
183 A8 Ruzyně ✈ (Praha) Praha, C Czech Republic 50°06′N 14°16′E
137 A8 Rwanda off. Rwandese Republic; prev. Ruanda. ◆ republic C Africa
Rwandese Republic see Rwanda
155 D12 Ry Århus, C Denmark 56°06′N 09°46′E
155 F5 Ryan, Loch inlet SW Scotland, United Kingdom
Ryasna see Rasna
196 G2 Ryazan' Ryazanskaya Oblast', W Russian Federation 54°37′N 39°37′E
196 G3 Ryazanskaya Oblast' ◆ province W Russian Federation
196 G3 Ryazhsk Ryazanskaya Oblast', W Russian Federation 53°42′N 40°09′E
191 B8 Rybachiy Ger. Rossitten. Kaliningradskaya Oblast', W Russian Federation 55°09′N 20°49′E
194 E2 Rybachiy, Poluostrov peninsula NW Russian Federation
Rybach'ye see Balykchy
194 F9 Rybinsk prev. Andropov. Yaroslavskaya Oblast', W Russian Federation 58°03′N 38°53′E
194 F9 Rybinskoye Vodokhranilishche Eng. Rybinsk Reservoir, Rybinsk Sea. ⊠ W Russian Federation
Rybinsk Reservoir/Rybinsk Sea see Rybinskoye Vodokhranilishche
183 F8 Rybnik Śląskie, S Poland 50°05′N 18°31′E
Rybnitsa see Rîbniţa
183 D8 Rychnov nad Kněžnou Ger. Reichenau. Královéhradecký Kraj, N Czech Republic 50°10′N 16°17′E
182 F6 Rychwał Wielkopolskie, C Poland 52°04′N 18°10′E
56 G3 Rycroft Alberta, W Canada 55°45′N 118°42′W
155 G11 Ryd Kronoberg, S Sweden 56°27′N 14°44′E
155 G11 Rydaholm Jönköping, S Sweden 56°57′N 14°19′E
292 F5 Rydberg Peninsula peninsula Antarctica
161 J8 Ryde United Kingdom 50°43′N 1°10′W
161 L7 Rye SE England, United Kingdom 50°57′N 00°42′E
77 J5 Ryegate Montana, NW USA 46°21′N 109°12′W
80 I1 Rye Patch Reservoir ⊠ Nevada, W USA
155 E8 Rygge Østfold, S Norway 59°22′N 10°45′E
182 I6 Ryki Lubelskie, E Poland 51°38′N 21°57′E
Rykovo see Yenakiyeve
196 E4 Ryl'sk Kurskaya Oblast', W Russian Federation 51°34′N 34°41′E
277 L4 Rylstone New South Wales, SE Australia 32°48′S 149°58′E
183 E8 Rýmařov Ger. Römerstadt. Moravskoslezský Kraj, E Czech Republic 49°56′N 17°15′E
226 B4 Ryn-Peski desert W Kazakhstan
253 B10 Ryōtsu var. Ryôtu. Niigata, Sado, C Japan 38°06′N 138°28′E
Ryôtu see Ryōtsu
182 G5 Rypin Kujawsko-pomorskie, C Poland 53°03′N 19°25′E
Ryshkany see Rîşcani
Ryssel see Lille
Ryswick see Rijswijk
178 J3 Rytterknægten hill E Denmark
253 C13 Ryūgasaki Ibaraki, Honshū, S Japan 35°51′N 140°12′E
Ryukyu Islands see Nansei-shotō
286 C3 Ryukyu Trench var. Nansei Syotō Trench. undersea feature S East China Sea 24°45′N 128°00′E
182 C6 Rzepin Ger. Reppen. Lubuskie, W Poland 52°20′N 14°48′E
183 I8 Rzeszów Podkarpackie, SE Poland 50°03′N 22°01′E
194 E10 Rzhev Tverskaya Oblast', W Russian Federation 56°17′N 34°22′E
Rzhishchev see Rzhyshchiv
189 H3 Rzhyshchiv Rus. Rzhishchev. Kyyivs'ka Oblast', N Ukraine 49°58′N 31°02′E

S

219 C9 Sa'ad Southern, W Israel 31°27′N 34°31′E
140 F8 Saaifontein Northern Cape, South Africa 31°43′S 21°53′E
177 I3 Saalach W Austria
179 G8 Saale C Germany
179 F9 Saalfeld var. Saalfeld an der Saale. Thüringen, C Germany 50°39′N 11°22′E
Saalfeld see Zalewo
Saalfeld an der Saale see Saalfeld
176 C4 Saane W Switzerland
114 A4 Saa Pereyra Santa Fe, Argentina 31°35′S 61°23′W
181 B13 Saar Fr. Sarre. France/Germany
181 C14 Saarbrücken Fr. Sarrebruck. Saarland, SW Germany 49°13′N 07°01′E
Saarburg see Sarrebourg
181 B12 Saarburg Rheinland-Pfalz, Germany 49°36′E 6°37′N
190 C5 Sääre var. Sjar. Saaremaa, W Estonia 57°57′N 21°53′E
Saare see Saaremaa
190 C4 Saaremaa off. Saare Maakond. ◆ province W Estonia
190 C4 Saaremaa Ger. Oesel, Ösel; prev. Saare. island W Estonia
Saare Maakond see Saaremaa
152 H6 Saarenkylä Lappi, N Finland 66°31′N 25°51′E
Saargemund see Sarreguemines
153 H8 Saarijärvi Länsi-Suomi, C Finland 62°42′N 25°16′E
Saar in Mähren see Žďár nad Sázavou
152 H4 Saariselkä Lapp. Suoločielgi. Lappi, N Finland 68°27′N 27°29′E
152 H4 Saariselkä hill range NE Finland
181 C13 Saarland Fr. Sarre. ◆ state SW Germany
Saarlautern see Saarlouis
181 B13 Saarlouis prev. Saarlautern. Saarland, SW Germany 49°19′N 06°45′E
181 C13 Saarwellingen Saarland, Germany 49°21′E 6°49′N
176 D5 Saaser Vispa S Switzerland
215 M5 Saatlı Rus. Saatly. C Azerbaijan 39°57′N 48°24′E
Saatly see Saatlı
Saaz see Žatec
91 K4 Saba island N Netherlands Antilles
216 D5 Sab' Ābār var. Sab'a Biyar, Sa'b Bi'ār. Ḩimş, C Syria 33°46′N 37°41′E
Sab'a Biyar see Sab' Ābār
184 F3 Šabac Serbia, W Serbia 44°45′N 19°42′E
171 K3 Sabadell Cataluña, E Spain 41°33′N 02°07′E
251 I3 Sabae Fukui, Honshū, SW Japan 36°00′N 136°12′E
259 K2 Sabah prev. British North Borneo, North Borneo. ◆ state East Malaysia
258 D3 Sabak var. Sabak Bernam. Selangor, Peninsular Malaysia 03°45′N 100°59′E
Sabak Bernam see Sabak
82 A9 Sabak, Cape headland Agattu Island, Alaska, USA 52°21′N 173°43′E
137 E9 Sabaki S Kenya
260 C7 Sabalana, Kepulauan var. Kepulauan Liukang Tenggaya. island group C Indonesia
222 D2 Sabalān, Kuhhā-ye ▲ NW Iran 38°21′N 47°47′E
232 E6 Sabalgarh Madhya Pradesh, C India 26°18′N 77°28′E
61 L10 Sabana, Archipiélago de island group C Cuba
88 E5 Sabanagrande var. Sabana Grande. Francisco Morazán, S Honduras 13°48′N 87°15′W
Sabana Grande see Sabanagrande
102 C2 Sabanalarga Atlántico, N Colombia 10°38′N 74°55′W
87 K6 Sabancuy Campeche, SE Mexico 18°58′N 91°11′W
91 H5 Sabaneta NW Dominican Republic 19°30′N 71°21′W
102 E2 Sabaneta Falcón, N Venezuela 11°17′N 70°00′W
283 I1 Sabaneta, Puntan prev. Ushi Point. headland Saipan, S Northern Mariana Islands 15°17′N 145°49′E
261 L6 Sabang Papua, E Indonesia 04°33′S 138°42′E
188 E7 Săbăoani Neamţ, NE Romania 47°01′N 26°51′E
111 H3 Sabará Minas Gerais, Brazil 19°54′S 43°48′W
235 F11 Sabaragamuwa ◆ province C Sri Lanka
Sabaria see Szombathely
232 C8 Sābarmati NW India
260 G3 Sabatai Pulau Morotai, E Indonesia 02°04′N 128°23′E
136 H2 Sab'atayn, Ramlat as desert C Yemen
175 F9 Sabaudia Lazio, C Italy 41°17′N 13°02′E
112 B1 Sabaya Oruro, S Bolivia 19°09′S 68°21′W
Sa'b Bi'ār see Sab' Ābār
Sabbioncello see Orebić
230 D5 Şāberī, Hāmūn-e var. Daryācheh-ye Hāmun, Daryācheh-ye Sīstān. ◎ Afghanistan/Iran see also Sīstān, Daryācheh-ye
Şāberī, Hāmūn-e see Sīstān, Daryācheh-ye
75 F8 Sabetha Kansas, C USA 39°54′N 95°48′W
218 H7 Şabḩā Jordan 32°20′N 36°30′E
128 C4 Sabhā C Libya 27°02′N 14°26′E
121 L8 Sabi var. Save. Mozambique/Zimbabwe see also Save
Sabi see Save
141 K3 Sabie Mpumalanga, South Africa 25°06′S 30°47′E
190 C6 Sabile Ger. Zabeln. Talsi, NW Latvia 57°03′N 22°33′E
219 E14 Sābil, Wādī dry watercourse Jordan
73 H11 Sabina Ohio, N USA 39°29′N 83°38′W
84 G2 Sabinal Chihuahua, N Mexico 30°59′N 107°29′W
70 F7 Sabinal Texas, SW USA 29°19′N 99°28′W
70 F7 Sabinal River Texas, SW USA
171 J2 Sabiñánigo Aragón, NE Spain 42°31′N 00°22′W
85 K5 Sabinas Coahuila, NE Mexico 27°52′N 101°04′W
85 L6 Sabinas Hidalgo Nuevo León, NE Mexico 26°29′N 100°09′W
85 K5 Sabinas, Río NE Mexico
71 J7 Sabine Lake ◎ Louisiana/Texas, S USA
152 B5 Sabine Land physical region C Svalbard
52 F4 Sabine Peninsula Peninsula Nunavut/Northwest Territories, NW Canada
71 I5 Sabine River Louisiana/Texas, SW USA
215 M5 Sabirabad C Azerbaijan 40°00′N 48°27′E
Sabkha see As Sabkhah
219 A10 Sabkhet el Bardawil bay Egypt
263 K6 Sablayan Mindoro, N Philippines 12°48′N 120°48′E
59 N5 Sable, Cape headland Newfoundland and Labrador, SE Canada 43°21′N 65°40′W
69 M10 Sable, Cape headland Florida, SE USA 25°12′N 81°06′W
59 L9 Sable Island island Nova Scotia, SE Canada
166 B5 Sables-d'Or-les-Pins Bretagne, France 48°39′N 2°24′W
62 G2 Sables, Lac des ◎ Québec, SE Canada
62 B1 Sables, Rivière aux Ontario, S Canada
164 G4 Sablé-sur-Sarthe Sarthe, NW France 47°49′N 00°19′W
195 K5 Sablya, Gora ▲ NW Russian Federation 64°46′N 58°52′E
172 B7 Sabóia Beja, Portugal 37°30′N 8°30′W
133 K5 Sabon Birnin Gwari Kaduna, C Nigeria 10°43′N 06°39′E
133 K4 Sabon Kafi Zinder, C Niger 14°37′N 08°46′E
170 D4 Sabor, Rio Portugal
164 F6 Sabres Landes, SW France 44°07′N 00°46′W
293 L7 Sabrina Coast physical region Antarctica
220 E6 Sabt al Ulāyā 'Asīr, SW Saudi Arabia 19°33′N 41°58′E
170 D2 Sabugal Guarda, N Portugal 40°20′N 07°05′W
172 C5 Sabugueiro Évora, Portugal 38°46′N 8°07′W
172 C2 Sabugueiro Guarda, Portugal 40°24′N 7°38′W
250 B1 Sabuk Kangwŏn-do, South Korea 37°14′N 128°49′E
74 I7 Sabula Iowa, C USA 42°04′N 90°10′W
220 F7 Şabyā Jīzān, SW Saudi Arabia 17°50′N 42°50′E
Sabzawar see Sabzevār
Sabzawaran see Jīroft
223 I3 Sabzevār var. Sabzawar. Khorāsān-Razavī, NE Iran 36°13′N 57°38′E
Sabzvārān see Jīroft
Sacajawea Peak see Matterhorn
87 L5 Sacalum Yucatán, Mexico 20°29′N 89°35′W
135 D10 Sacandica Uíge, NW Angola 06°01′S 15°57′E
88 C4 Sacatepéquez off. Departamento de Sacatepéquez. ◆ department S Guatemala
Sacatepéquez, Departamento de see Sacatepéquez
172 A5 Sacavém Lisboa, W Portugal 38°47′N 09°06′W
74 F7 Sac City Iowa, C USA 42°25′N 94°59′W
171 H5 Sacedón Castilla-La Mancha, C Spain 40°29′N 02°44′W
188 D8 Săcele Ger. Vierdörfer, Hung. Négyfalu; prev. Ger. Sieben Dörfer, Hung. Hétfalu. Braşov, C Romania 45°36′N 25°40′E
248 C7 Sacheon Jap. Sansenhō; prev. Sach'ŏn, Samch'ŏnpŏ. S South Korea 34°55′N 128°07′E
58 C4 Sachigo Ontario, C Canada
58 C4 Sachigo Lake Ontario, C Canada 53°52′N 92°16′W
58 C4 Sachigo Lake ◎ Ontario, C Canada
Sach'ŏn see Sacheon
179 H8 Sachsen Eng. Saxony, Fr. Saxe. ◆ state E Germany
178 G7 Sachsen-Anhalt Eng. Saxony-Anhalt. ◆ state C Germany
181 F9 Sachsenberg Hessen, Germany 51°08′E 8°48′N
177 I4 Sachsenburg Salzburg, S Austria 46°49′N 13°23′E
Sachsenfeld see Žalec
52 D5 Sachs Harbour var. Ikaahuk. Banks Island, Northwest Territories, N Canada 72°N 125°14′W
Sächsisch-Reen/Sächsisch-Regen see Reghin
62 F5 Sackets Harbor New York, NE USA 43°57′N 76°06′W
63 N2 Sackville New Brunswick, SE Canada 45°54′N 64°23′W
63 J5 Saco Maine, NE USA 43°32′N 70°25′W
63 J5 Saco River Maine/New Hampshire, NE USA
110 B3 Sacramento Minas Gerais, Brazil 19°53′S 47°27′W
70 E10 Sacramento Coahuila, Mexico 26°05′N 101°20′W
84 E4 Sacramento Sonora, NE Mexico 28°33′N 111°32′W
80 C2 Sacramento state capital California, W USA 38°35′N 121°30′W
80 C2 Sacramento Executive ✈ California, W USA 38°31′N 121°30′W
79 M9 Sacramento Mountains ▲ New Mexico, SW USA
80 C1 Sacramento River California, W USA
80 B1 Sacramento Valley valley California, W USA
172 E10 Sacratif, Cabo headland S Spain 36°41′N 03°30′W
188 B6 Săcueni prev. Săcuieni, Hung. Székelyhíd. Bihor, W Romania 47°20′N 22°05′E
Săcueni see Săcueni
141 I8 Sada Eastern Cape, South Africa 32°12′S 26°49′E
171 I3 Sádaba Aragón, NE Spain 42°15′N 01°16′W
Sá da Bandeira see Lubango
218 J2 Şadad Ḩimş, W Syria 34°19′N 36°52′E
220 F7 Şa'dah NW Yemen 16°59′N 43°45′E
250 E6 Sadamisaki-hantō peninsula Shikoku, SW Japan
260 C6 Sadang, Sungai Sulawesi, C Indonesia
257 E11 Sadao Songkhla, SW Thailand 06°39′N 100°30′E
222 E5 Sadd-e Dez, Daryācheh-ye ◎ W Iran
161 J4 Saddell United Kingdom 55°32′N 5°30′W
63 L2 Saddleback Mountain hill Maine, NE USA
63 J3 Saddleback Mountain ▲ Maine, NE USA 44°57′N 70°27′W
141 K4 Saddleback Pass South Africa
257 H9 Sa Đec Đông Thap, S Vietnam 10°19′N 105°45′E
221 J7 Sadh S Oman 17°11′N 55°08′E
132 C4 Sadiola Kayes, W Mali 13°48′N 11°47′W
231 H7 Sādiqābād Punjab, E Pakistan 28°16′N 70°10′E
233 C1 Sadiya Assam, NE India 27°49′N 95°38′E
217 L6 Sa'dīyah, Hawr as ◎ E Iraq
Sado see Sadoga-shima
253 A10 Sadoga-shima var. Sado. island C Japan
170 B6 Sado, Rio Portugal
185 J5 Sadovets Pleven, N Bulgaria 43°19′N 24°21′E
197 I6 Sadovoye Respublika Kalmykiya, SW Russian Federation 47°51′N 44°34′E
171 K6 Sa Dragonera var. Isla Dragonera. island Islas Baleares, Spain, W Mediterranean Sea
170 G5 Saelices Castilla-La Mancha, C Spain 39°55′N 02°49′W
Saena Julia see Siena
Saetabicula see Alzira
Safad see Tsefat
Şafāqis see Sfax
172 D6 Safara Beja, Portugal 38°06′N 7°13′W
222 G6 Şafashahr var. Deh Bīd. Fārs, C Iran 30°50′N 53°50′E
282 F7 Safata Bay bay Upolo, Samoa, C Pacific Ocean
218 I7 Şafāwī Abū Qudhur, Wādī aş Jordan
Safed see Tsefat
217 L7 Şaffāf, Ḩawr aş marshy lake S Iraq
155 F8 Säffle Värmland, C Sweden 59°08′N 12°55′E
79 J9 Safford Arizona, SW USA 32°46′N 109°41′W
161 L5 Saffron Walden United Kingdom 52°01′N 0°15′E
130 E3 Safi W Morocco 32°19′N 09°14′W
172 B5 Safira Évora, Portugal 38°37′N 8°20′W
218 G1 Şāfītā Syria 34°49′N 36°07′E
196 E2 Safonovo Smolenskaya Oblast', W Russian Federation 55°05′N 33°12′E
214 B9 Safranbolu Karabük, NW Turkey 41°16′N 32°41′E
217 M9 Safwān Al Başrah, SE Iraq 30°06′N 47°44′E
238 E9 Saga var. Gya'gya. Xizang Zizhiqu, W China 29°22′N 85°19′E

◆ Country
● Country Capital
◇ Dependent Territory
○ Dependent Territory Capital
Administrative Regions
✈ International Airport
▲ Mountain
▲ Mountain Range
Volcano
River
◎ Lake
⊠ Reservoir

◆ Country	◇ Dependent Territory	♦ Administrative Regions	▲ Mountain	▲ Volcano	⊜ Lake
● Country Capital	C Dependent Territory Capital	✈ International Airport	▲ Mountain Range	↭ River	▣ Reservoir

Legend

◆ Country | ◇ Dependent Territory | ◆ Administrative Regions | ▲ Mountain | ◈ Volcano | ○ Lake
● Country Capital | ◇ Dependent Territory Capital | ✕ International Airport | ▲ Mountain Range | ♒ River | ☐ Reservoir

◆ Country   ◇ Dependent Territory   ◈ Administrative Regions   ▲ Mountain   ◣ Volcano   ◎ Lake
● Country Capital   ○ Dependent Territory Capital   ✈ International Airport   ◢ Mountain Range   ◢ River   ◙ Reservoir

◆ Country ◇ Dependent Territory ◈ Administrative Regions ▲ Mountain ◉ Volcano ◎ Lake
● Country Capital ○ Dependent Territory Capital ✈ International Airport ▲ Mountain Range ➳ River ⬡ Reservoir

Schleswig-Holstein - Seribu, Kepulauan

180 H2 **Schleswig-Holstein** ◈ *state* N Germany
Schlettstadt *see* Sélestat
176 E4 **Schlieren** Zürich, N Switzerland *47°23´N 08°27´E*
Schlochau *see* Człuchów
Schloppe *see* Człopa
181 J9 **Schlossvippach** Thüringen, Germany *51°06´E 11°08´N*
181 G11 **Schlüchtern** Hessen, C Germany *50°19´N 09°27´E*
181 I10 **Schmalkalden** Thüringen, C Germany *50°42´N 10°26´E*
181 C13 **Schmelz** Saarland, Germany *49°26´N 06°51´E*
177 L1 **Schmida** ~ NE Austria
291 I11 **Schmidt-Ott Seamount** *var.* Schmitt-Ott Seamount, Schmitt-Ott Tablemount. *undersea feature* SW Indian Ocean *39°37´S 13°00´E*
140 G6 **Schmidts Drift** Northern Cape, South Africa *28°42´S 24°04´E*
Schmiegel *see* Śmigiel
Schmitt-Ott Seamount/Schmitt-Ott Tablemount *see* Schmidt-Ott Seamount
179 G10 **Schneeberg** ▲ W Germany *50°03´N 11°51´E*
Schnee-Eifel *see* Schneifel
180 G5 **Schneeren** Niedersachsen, Germany *52°32´E 9°20´N*
180 J4 **Schnega** Niedersachsen, Germany *52°53´E 10°53´N*
Schneidemühl *see* Piła
181 B11 **Schneifel** *var.* Schnee-Eifel. *plateau* W Germany
Schnelle Körös/Schnelle Kreisch *see* Crişul Repede
180 H4 **Schneverdingen** *var.* Schneverdingen (Wümme). Niedersachsen, NW Germany *53°07´N 09°48´E*
Schneverdingen (Wümme) *see* Schneverdingen
Schoden *see* Skuodas
91 M2 **Schœlcher** W Martinique *14°37´N 61°08´W*
141 K3 **Schoemanskloof Pass** Mpumalanga, South Africa
140 F9 **Schoemanspoort** *pass* Western Cape, South Africa
65 H2 **Schoharie** New York, NE USA *42°40´N 74°20´W*
62 G6 **Schoharie Creek** ~ New York, NE USA
187 J8 **Schoinoússa** *island* Kykládes, Greece, Aegean Sea
181 G11 **Schöllkrippen** Bayern, Germany *50°04´E 9°14´N*
178 G7 **Schönebeck** Sachsen-Anhalt, C Germany *52°01´N 11°45´E*
Schöneck *see* Skarszewy
181 B11 **Schönecken** Rheinland-Pfalz, Germany *50°10´E 6°28´N*
178 H7 **Schönefeld** ✈ (Berlin) Berlin, NE Germany *52°23´N 13°29´E*
179 F13 **Schongau** Bayern, S Germany *47°49´N 10°54´E*
180 G7 **Schönhagen** Niedersachsen, Germany *51°41´E 9°34´N*
180 J6 **Schöningen** Niedersachsen, C Germany *52°07´N 10°58´E*
180 C5 **Schoninghsdorf** Niedersachsen, Germany *52°43´E 7°05´N*
Schönlanke *see* Trzcianka
Schönsee *see* Kowalewo Pomorskie
181 F9 **Schönstadt** Hessen, Germany *50°53´E 8°50´N*
181 I11 **Schonungen** Bayern, Germany *50°03´E 10°19´N*
73 F8 **Schoolcraft** Michigan, N USA *42°05´N 85°39´W*
141 H8 **Schoombee** Eastern Cape, South Africa *31°27´S 25°30´E*
162 I5 **Schoonebeek** Drenthe, NE Netherlands *52°39´N 06°57´E*
162 F7 **Schoonhoven** Zuid-Holland, C Netherlands *51°57´N 04°°51´E*
162 E5 **Schoorl** Noord-Holland, NW Netherlands *52°42´N 04°40´E*
Schooten *see* Schoten
179 C13 **Schopfheim** Baden-Württemberg, SW Germany *47°39´N 07°49´E*
181 I14 **Schopfloch** Bayern, Germany *49°07´E 10°18´N*
180 C6 **Schöppingen** Nordrhein-Westfalen, Germany *52°06´E 7°14´N*
179 E12 **Schorndorf** Baden-Württemberg, S Germany *48°48´N 09°31´E*
180 E3 **Schortens** Niedersachsen, NW Germany *53°31´N 07°57´E*
163 E9 **Schoten** *var.* Schooten. Antwerpen, N Belgium *51°15´N 04°30´E*
277 K10 **Schouten Island** *island* Tasmania, SE Australia
280 B2 **Schouten Islands** *island group* NW Papua New Guinea
162 D7 **Schouwen** *island* SW Netherlands
181 G10 **Schrecksbach** Hessen, Germany *50°50´E 9°17´N*
Schreiberhau *see* Szklarska Poręba
177 K1 **Schrems** Niederösterreich, E Austria *48°48´N 15°05´E*
181 F13 **Schriesheim** Baden-Württemberg, Germany *49°29´E 8°40´N*
179 F12 **Schrobenhausen** Bayern, SE Germany *48°33´N 11°14´E*
63 H5 **Schroon Lake** ◎ New York, NE USA
181 H13 **Schrozberg** Baden-Württemberg, Germany *49°21´E 9°59´N*
176 F4 **Schruns** Vorarlberg, W Austria *47°04´N 09°54´E*
Schubin *see* Szubin
180 H6 **Schulenburg** Niedersachsen, Germany *52°12´E 9°47´N*
71 H7 **Schulenburg** Texas, SW USA *29°40´N 96°54´W*
Schuls *see* Scuol
55 I3 **Schultz Lake** ◎ Nunavut, C Canada
167 M8 **Schüpfheim** Luzern, C Switzerland *47°02´N 07°23´E*
80 G3 **Schurz** Nevada, W USA *38°55´N 118°48´W*
179 E13 **Schussen** ~ S Germany
Schüttenhofen *see* Sušice
74 E7 **Schuyler** Nebraska, C USA *41°25´N 97°04´W*
65 I1 **Schuylerville** New York, NE USA *43°05´N 73°34´W*
64 E6 **Schuylkill Haven** Pennsylvania, USA *40°38´N 76°10´W*
181 J13 **Schwabach** Bayern, SE Germany *49°20´N 11°02´E*
Schwabenalb *see* Schwäbische Alb
179 D12 **Schwäbische Alb** *var.* Schwabenalb, *Eng.* Swabian Jura. ▲▲ S Germany
179 E12 **Schwäbisch Gmünd** *var.* Gmünd. Baden-Württemberg, SW Germany *48°49´N 09°48´E*
181 H14 **Schwäbisch Hall** *var.* Hall. Baden-Württemberg, SW Germany *49°07´N 09°45´E*
180 F5 **Schwaförden** Niedersachsen, Germany *52°44´E 8°50´N*
181 G9 **Schwalm** ~ C Germany
177 K4 **Schwanberg** Steiermark, SE Austria *46°46´N 15°12´E*
176 E4 **Schwanden** Glarus, E Switzerland *47°02´N 09°04´E*
179 G11 **Schwandorf** Bayern, SE Germany *49°20´N 12°07´E*
180 J7 **Schwanebeck** Sachsen-Anhalt, Germany *51°58´E 11°07´N*
177 J2 **Schwanenstadt** Oberösterreich, NW Austria *48°03´N 13°47´E*
259 J5 **Schwaner, Pegunungan** ▲▲ Borneo, N Indonesia
180 F3 **Schwanewede** Niedersachsen, Germany *53°14´E 8°36´N*
181 H12 **Schwanfeld** Bayern, Germany *49°55´E 10°08´N*
180 F4 **Schwarme** Niedersachsen, Germany *52°54´E 9°01´N*
180 G5 **Schwarmstedt** Niedersachsen, Germany *52°40´E 9°37´N*
181 I10 **Schwarza** Thüringen, Germany *50°38´E 10°32´N*
177 L3 **Schwarza** ~ E Austria
177 H4 **Schwarzach** ~ S Austria
179 G11 **Schwarzach** *Cz.* Černice. ~ Czech Republic/Germany
Schwarzach *see* Schwarzach im Pongau
177 I4 **Schwarzach im Pongau** *var.* Schwarzach. Salzburg, NW Austria *47°19´N 13°09´E*
Schwarzawa *see* Svratka
178 H7 **Schwarze Elster** ~ E Germany
Schwarze Körös *see* Crişul Negru
180 I3 **Schwarzenbek** Schleswig-Holstein, Germany *53°30´E 10°29´N*
181 G9 **Schwarzenborn** Hessen, Germany *50°55´E 9°27´N*
167 N9 **Schwarzenburg** Bern, W Switzerland *46°51´N 07°28´E*
140 C3 **Schwarzrand** ▲▲ S Namibia
179 C12 **Schwarzwald** *Eng.* Black Forest. ▲▲ SW Germany
Schwarzwasser *see* Wda
83 H4 **Schwatka Mountains** ▲▲ Alaska, USA
177 H4 **Schwaz** Tirol, W Austria *47°21´N 11°44´E*
177 L2 **Schwechat** Niederösterreich, NE Austria *48°09´N 16°29´E*
174 I2 **Schwechat** ✈ (Wien) Wien, E Austria *48°04´N 16°31´E*
178 I6 **Schwedt** Brandenburg, NE Germany *53°04´N 14°16´E*
181 E13 **Schwegenheim** Rheinland-Pfalz, Germany *49°16´E 8°20´N*
180 E3 **Schwei** Niedersachsen, Germany *53°24´E 8°22´N*
181 B12 **Schweich** Rheinland-Pfalz, SW Germany *49°49´N 06°44´E*
Schweidnitz *see* Świdnica
181 I11 **Schweinfurt** Bayern, SE Germany *50°03´N 10°13´E*
Schweiz *see* Switzerland
141 H5 **Schweizer-Reneke** North-West, South Africa *27°11´S 25°20´E*
181 C8 **Schwelm** Nordrhein-Westfalen, Germany *51°17´E 7°17´N*
180 J2 **Schwerin** Mecklenburg-Vorpommern, N Germany *53°38´N 11°25´E*
Schwerin *see* Skwierzyna
178 G5 **Schweriner See** ◎ N Germany
Schwertberg *see* Świecie
181 D8 **Schwerte** Nordrhein-Westfalen, W Germany *51°27´N 07°34´E*
181 F13 **Schwetzingen** Baden-Württemberg, Germany *49°23´E 8°35´N*
Schwiebus *see* Świebodzin
178 I7 **Schwielochsee** ◎ NE Germany
Schwihau *see* Švihov
Schwiz *see* Schwyz
176 E4 **Schwyz** *var.* Schwiz. Schwyz, C Switzerland *47°02´N 08°39´E*
174 C3 **Schwyz** *var.* Schwiz. ◈ *canton* C Switzerland
62 E2 **Schyan** ~ Québec, SE Canada
Schyl *see* Jiu
175 E12 **Sciacca** Sicilia, Italy, C Mediterranean Sea *37°31´N 13°05´E*
Sciasciamana *see* Shashemenē
175 G13 **Scicli** Sicilia, Italy, C Mediterranean Sea *36°48´N 14°43´E*
167 L10 **Sciez** Rhône-Alpes, France *46°20´N 6°23´E*
157 D13 **Scilly, Isles of** *island group* SW England, United Kingdom
182 D7 **Ścinawa** *Ger.* Steinau an der Elbe. Dolnośląskie, SW Poland *51°22´N 16°27´E*
64 B3 **Scio** New York, NE USA *42°10´N 77°58´W*
Scio *see* Chíos
73 H10 **Scioto River** ~ Ohio, N USA
79 H3 **Scipio** Utah, W USA *39°15´N 112°06´W*
65 M3 **Scituate** Massachusetts, USA *42°12´N 70°44´W*
77 L2 **Scobey** Montana, NW USA *48°47´N 105°25´W*
277 L4 **Scone** New South Wales, SE Australia *32°02´S 150°51´E*
169 N1 **Scopello** Piemonte, NW Italy *45°46´N 08°05´E*
53 H7 **Scoresby, Cape** *headland* Nunavut, NW Canada
Scoresby Sound/Scoresbysund *see* Ittoqqortoormiit
Scoresby Sund *see* Kangertittivaq
Scorno, Punta dello *see* Caprara, Punta
159 K7 **Scotch Corner** North Yorkshire, N England, United Kingdom *54°26´N 01°40´W*
65 H4 **Scotchtown** New York, USA *41°29´N 74°22´W*
159 I8 **Scotforth** United Kingdom *54°01´N 2°47´W*
78 A2 **Scotia** California, W USA *40°34´N 124°07´W*
65 H1 **Scotia** New York, USA *42°50´N 73°58´W*
95 M9 **Scotia Plate** *tectonic feature*
95 M9 **Scotia Ridge** *undersea feature* S Atlantic Ocean
292 E2 **Scotia Sea** *sea* SW Atlantic Ocean
74 E6 **Scotland** South Dakota, N USA *43°09´N 97°43´W*
70 G3 **Scotland** Texas, SW USA *33°37´N 98°27´W*
156 E5 **Scotland** ◈ *national region* Scotland, U K
67 L6 **Scotland Neck** North Carolina, SE USA *36°07´N 77°25´W*
158 F1 **Scotstown** United Kingdom *56°43´N 5°34´W*
293 I7 **Scott Base** *NZ research station* Antarctica *77°52´S 167°18´E*
141 K7 **Scottburg** KwaZulu-Natal, South Africa *30°17´S 30°45´E*
141 K7 **Scottburgh** Kwazulu Natal, South Africa *30°17´S 30°45´E*
56 A7 **Scott, Cape** *headland* Vancouver Island, British Columbia, SW Canada *50°43´N 128°24´W*
75 B10 **Scott City** Kansas, C USA *38°28´N 100°55´W*
75 J11 **Scott City** Missouri, C USA *37°13´N 89°31´W*
293 I8 **Scott Coast** *physical region* Antarctica
62 C9 **Scottdale** Pennsylvania, NE USA *40°05´N 79°35´W*
293 M6 **Scott Glacier** *glacier* Antarctica
293 I9 **Scott Island** *island* Antarctica
54 G5 **Scott Lake** ◎ Northwest Territories/Saskatchewan, C Canada
75 D13 **Scott, Mount** ▲ Oklahoma, USA *34°52´N 98°34´W*
76 C8 **Scott, Mount** ▲ Oregon, NW USA *42°53´N 122°06´W*
78 B1 **Scott River** ~ California, W USA
74 A7 **Scottsbluff** Nebraska, C USA *41°52´N 103°40´W*
66 E7 **Scottsboro** Alabama, S USA *34°40´N 86°01´W*
73 F12 **Scottsburg** Indiana, N USA *38°42´N 85°47´W*
277 J9 **Scottsdale** Tasmania, SE Australia *41°13´S 147°30´E*
79 H8 **Scottsdale** Arizona, SW USA *33°31´N 111°54´W*
91 L2 **Scotts Head Village** *var.* Cachacrou. S Dominica *15°12´N 61°22´W*
80 B4 **Scotts Valley** California, USA *37°03´N 122°01´W*
66 E5 **Scottsville** Kentucky, S USA *36°45´N 86°11´W*
80 H6 **Scottys Junction** Nevada, USA *37°18´N 117°03´W*
158 B9 **Scramoge** Ireland *53°46´N 8°03´W*
74 G7 **Scranton** Iowa, C USA *42°01´N 94°33´W*
64 F4 **Scranton** Pennsylvania, NE USA *41°25´N 75°40´W*
280 A2 **Screw** ~ NW Papua New Guinea
74 E7 **Scribner** Nebraska, C USA *41°40´N 96°40´W*
Scrobesbyrig' *see* Shrewsbury
62 D4 **Scugog** ~ Ontario, SE Canada
62 D4 **Scugog, Lake** ◎ Ontario, SE Canada
159 L9 **Scunthorpe** E England, United Kingdom *53°35´N 00°39´W*
176 F4 **Scuol** *Ger.* Schuls. Graubünden, E Switzerland *46°51´N 10°21´E*
Scupi *see* Skopje
Scutari *see* Shkodër
184 F7 **Scutari, Lake** *Alb.* Liqeni i Shkodrës, *SCr.* Skadarsko Jezero. ◎ Albania/Montenegro
Scyros *see* Skýros
Scythopolis *see* Beit She'an
Sde Boker *see* Sedé Bokér
Sde Ilan *see* Sedé Ilan
Sdei Trumot *see* Sedé Terumot
216 B7 **Sderot** *prev.* Sederot. Southern, S Israel *31°31´N 34°35´E*
Sderot *see* Sederot
71 H8 **Seadrift** Texas, SW USA *28°25´N 96°42´W*
161 K8 **Seaford** United Kingdom *50°46´N 0°06´E*
64 F10 **Seaford** *var.* Seaford City. Delaware, NE USA *38°39´N 75°35´W*
Seaford City *see* Seaford
62 B5 **Seaforth** Ontario, S Canada *43°33´N 81°25´W*
70 D4 **Seagraves** Texas, SW USA *32°56´N 102°33´W*
159 K6 **Seaham** United Kingdom *54°50´N 1°20´W*
55 L2 **Seahorse Point** *headland* Nunavut, NE Canada
159 K4 **Seahouses** United Kingdom *55°35´N 1°39´W*
65 G9 **Sea Isle City** New Jersey, NE USA *39°09´N 74°41´W*
55 J5 **Seal** ~ Manitoba, C Canada
277 I6 **Sea Lake** Victoria, SE Australia *35°34´S 142°51´E*
289 D8 **Sealark Fracture Zone** *tectonic feature* W Indian Ocean
81 D11 **Seal Beach** California, USA *33°44´N 118°06´W*
138 F10 **Seal, Cape** *headland* S South Africa *34°06´S 23°18´E*
117 I12 **Sea Lion Islands** *island group* SE Falkland Islands
63 L4 **Seal Island** *island* Maine, NE USA
71 H7 **Sealy** Texas, SW USA *29°46´N 96°09´W*
158 F4 **Seamill** United Kingdom *55°41´N 4°52´W*
161 M3 **Sea Palling** United Kingdom *52°47´N 1°36´E*
80 A1 **Sea Ranch** California, USA *38°43´N 123°27´W*
81 I10 **Searchlight** Nevada, W USA *35°27´N 114°54´W*
75 I12 **Searcy** Arkansas, C USA *35°14´N 91°43´W*
64 J1 **Searsburg** Vermont, NE USA *42°53´N 72°57´W*
63 K4 **Searsport** Maine, NE USA *44°28´N 68°54´W*
159 H7 **Seascale** United Kingdom *54°23´N 3°29´W*
80 A4 **Seaside** California, W USA *36°36´N 121°51´W*
76 B5 **Seaside** Oregon, NW USA *45°57´N 123°55´W*
65 H8 **Seaside Heights** New Jersey, NE USA *39°56´N 74°03´W*
159 K5 **Seaton Delaval** United Kingdom *55°04´N 1°31´W*
76 C3 **Seattle** Washington, NW USA *47°35´N 122°20´W*
76 C4 **Seattle-Tacoma** ✈ Washington, NW USA *47°04´N 122°27´W*
141 H10 **Sea View** Eastern Cape, South Africa *34°01´S 25°22´E*
161 J8 **Seaview** United Kingdom *50°43´N 1°06´W*
279 F9 **Seaward Kaikoura Range** ▲▲ South Island, New Zealand
88 G5 **Sébaco** Matagalpa, W Nicaragua *12°51´N 86°08´W*
63 J5 **Sebago Lake** ◎ Maine, NE USA
261 I6 **Sebakor, Teluk** *bay* Papua, E Indonesia
259 J6 **Sebangan Besar, Sungai** *var.* Sungai Sebangan. ~ Borneo, N Indonesia
Sebangan, Sungai *see* Sebangan Besar, Sungai
259 J6 **Sebangan, Teluk** *bay* Borneo, C Indonesia
258 F5 **Sebangka, Pulau** *island* W Indonesia
Sebaste/Sebastia *see* Sivas
69 M6 **Sebastian** Florida, SE USA *27°55´N 80°31´W*
84 C4 **Sebastían Vizcaíno, Bahía** *bay* NW Mexico
80 E1 **Sebastopol** California, USA *39°22´N 121°07´W*
80 B1 **Sebastopol** California, W USA *38°22´N 122°50´W*
Sebastopol *see* Sevastopol'
259 L3 **Sebatik, Pulau** *island* N Indonesia
63 K3 **Sebec Lake** ◎ Maine, NE USA
132 D5 **Sébékoro** Kayes, W Mali *13°00´N 09°03´W*
Sebenico *see* Šibenik
159 I6 **Sebergham** United Kingdom *54°45´N 2°59´W*
188 C8 **Sebeş** *Ger.* Mühlbach, *Hung.* Szászsebes; *prev.* Sebeşu Săsesc. Alba, W Romania *45°58´N 23°34´E*
Sebes-Körös *see* Crişul Repede
Sebeşu Săsesc *see* Sebeş
72 H7 **Sebewaing** Michigan, N USA *43°43´N 83°27´W*
194 C10 **Sebezh** Pskovskaya Oblast', W Russian Federation *56°19´N 28°31´E*
215 H5 **Şebinkarahisar** Giresun, N Turkey *40°19´N 38°25´E*
188 B7 **Sebiş** *Hung.* Borossebes. Arad, W Romania *46°21´N 22°09´E*
171 I10 **Sebkha El Kebira** ~ Algeria
Sebkra Azz el Matti *see* Azzel Matti, Sebkha
63 K2 **Seboomook Lake** ◎ Maine, NE USA
130 F2 **Sebou** *var.* Sebu. ~ N Morocco
66 D4 **Sebree** Kentucky, S USA *37°34´N 87°30´W*
69 M7 **Sebring** Florida, SE USA *27°30´N 81°26´W*
Sebta *see* Ceuta
Sebu *see* Sebou
259 K6 **Sebuku, Pulau** *island* N Indonesia
259 L3 **Sebuku, Teluk** *bay* Borneo, N Indonesia
261 I5 **Sebyar** ~ Papua, E Indonesia
176 G8 **Secchia** ~ N Italy
141 J2 **Sechego** Limpopo, South Africa *23°50´S 29°22´E*
56 D8 **Sechelt** British Columbia, SW Canada *49°25´N 123°37´W*
104 C6 **Sechin, Río** ~ W Peru
104 B4 **Sechura, Bahía de** *bay* NW Peru
181 G13 **Seckach** Baden-Württemberg, Germany *49°27´E 9°20´N*
167 H2 **Seclin** Nord-Pas-de-Calais, France *50°33´N 3°02´E*
166 D9 **Secondigny** Poitou-Charentes, France *46°37´N 0°25´W*
278 A11 **Secretary Island** *island* SW New Zealand
141 J4 **Secunda** Mpumalanga, South Africa *26°33´S 29°10´E*
234 F5 **Secunderābād** *var.* Sikandarabad. Andhra Pradesh, C India *17°30´N 78°33´E*
106 D9 **Sécure, Río** ~ C Bolivia
190 C7 **Seda** Telšiai, NW Lithuania *56°10´N 22°04´E*
75 H10 **Sedalia** Missouri, C USA *38°42´N 93°15´W*
165 J2 **Sedan** Ardennes, N France *49°42´N 04°56´E*
75 F11 **Sedan** Kansas, C USA *37°07´N 96°11´W*
170 G2 **Sedano** Castilla-León, N Spain *42°43´N 03°43´W*
170 D6 **Seda, Ribeira de** *stream* C Portugal
159 J7 **Sedbergh** United Kingdom *54°19´N 2°31´W*
279 F8 **Seddon** Marlborough, South Island, New Zealand *41°42´S 174°05´E*
279 E8 **Seddonville** West Coast, South Island, New Zealand *41°35´S 171°59´E*
219 D11 **Sedé Bokér** *var.* Sde Boker. Southern, S Israel *30°52´N 34°47´E*
223 I5 **Sedeh** Khorāsān-e Janūbī, E Iran *33°18´N 59°12´E*
218 F6 **Sedé Ilan** *var.* Sde Ilan. Northern, N Israel *32°44´N 35°25´E*
192 E7 **Sedel'nikovo** Omskaya Oblast', C Russian Federation *56°54´N 75°24´E*
218 F5 **Sedé Neḩemya** *var.* Sede Nekhemya. Northern, N Israel *33°11´N 35°21´E*
Sede Nekhemya *see* Sedé Neḩemya
169 K4 **Séderon** Rhône-Alpes, France *44°12´N 5°32´E*
219 D9 **Sederot** *var.* Sderot. Southern, S Israel *31°31´N 34°35´E*
Sederot *see* Sderot
218 F7 **Sedé Terumot** *var.* Sdei Trumot. Northern, N Israel *32°25´N 35°29´E*
161 L2 **Sedgeford** United Kingdom *52°54´N 0°33´E*
117 H10 **Sedge Island** *island* NW Falkland Islands
161 H3 **Sedgley** United Kingdom *52°32´N 2°07´W*
159 I7 **Sedgwick** United Kingdom *54°16´N 2°45´W*
132 B5 **Sédhiou** SW Senegal *12°39´N 15°33´W*
55 H10 **Sedley** Saskatchewan, S Canada *50°06´N 103°51´W*
Sedlez *see* Siedlce
189 H2 **Sedniv** Chernihivs'ka Oblast', N Ukraine *51°39´N 31°34´E*
79 H7 **Sedona** Arizona, SW USA *34°52´N 111°45´W*
218 D6 **Sedot Yam** Israel *32°29´N 34°53´E*
Sedunum *see* Sion
190 D7 **Šeduva** Šiaulai, N Lithuania *55°45´N 23°46´E*
221 K4 **Seeb** *var.* Muscat Sīb Airport. ✈ (Masqaţ) NE Oman *23°36´N 58°27´E*
Seeb *see* As Sīb
176 G4 **Seefeld-in-Tirol** Tirol, W Austria *47°19´N 11°16´E*
181 F12 **Seeheim** Hessen, Germany *49°47´E 8°39´N*
140 C4 **Seeheim Noord** Karas, S Namibia *26°50´S 17°45´E*
140 C1 **Seeis** Khomas, Namibia *22°27´S 17°35´E*
140 F9 **Seekoegat** Western Cape, South Africa *33°03´S 22°30´E*
141 H7 **Seekoei** ~ Eastern Cape, South Africa
Seeland *see* Sjælland
81 G13 **Seeley** California, USA *32°48´N 115°41´W*
292 G5 **Seelig, Mount** ▲ Antarctica *81°45´S 102°15´W*
181 D9 **Seelscheid** Nordrhein-Westfalen, Germany *50°53´E 7°19´N*
180 G6 **Seelze** Niedersachsen, Germany *52°24´E 9°36´N*
161 H6 **Seend** United Kingdom *51°21´N 2°05´W*
Seenu Atoll *see* Addu Atoll
Seeonee *see* Seoni
Seer *see* Dörgön
164 G3 **Sées** Orne, N France *48°36´N 00°11´E*
180 H7 **Seesen** Niedersachsen, C Germany *51°54´N 10°11´E*
Seesker Höhe *see* Szeska Góra
180 H3 **Seevetal** Niedersachsen, N Germany *53°24´N 10°01´E*
177 K3 **Seewiesen** Steiermark, E Austria *47°37´N 15°16´E*
214 F6 **Şefaatli** *var.* Kızılkoca. Yozgat, C Turkey *39°32´N 34°45´E*
187 K6 **Seferihisar** İzmir, Turkey *38°12´N 26°50´E*
223 J6 **Sefīdābeh** Khorāsān-e Janūbī, E Iran *31°05´N 60°30´E*
230 F2 **Sefīd, Darya-ye** *Pash.* Āb-i-safed. ~ N Afghanistan
230 E3 **Sefīd Kūh, Selseleh-ye** *Eng.* Paropamisus Range. ▲▲ W Afghanistan
222 E3 **Sefīd, Rūd-e** ~ NW Iran
141 J1 **Sefophe** Central, Botswana *22°11´S 27°57´E*
130 F2 **Sefrou** N Morocco *33°51´N 04°49´W*
278 C10 **Sefton, Mount** ▲ South Island, New Zealand *43°43´S 169°58´E*
261 H5 **Segaf, Kepulauan** *island group* E Indonesia
259 L2 **Segama, Sungai** ~ East Malaysia
258 E3 **Segamat** Johor, Peninsular Malaysia *02°30´N 102°48´E*
133 I6 **Ségbana** NE Benin *10°56´N 03°42´E*
Segestica *see* Sisak
Segesvár *see* Sighişoara
261 H4 **Seget** Papua, E Indonesia *01°21´S 131°04´E*
Segewold *see* Sigulda
194 E6 **Segezha** Respublika Kareliya, NW Russian Federation *63°39´N 34°24´E*
Seghedin *see* Szeged
171 L9 **Seghouane** Algeria
Segna *see* Senj
175 F8 **Segni** Lazio, C Italy *41°41´N 13°02´E*
Segodunum *see* Rodez
171 I5 **Segorbe** País Valenciano, E Spain *39°51´N 00°30´W*
132 F5 **Ségou** *var.* Segu. Ségou, C Mali *13°26´N 06°12´W*
132 F4 **Ségou** ◈ *region* SW Mali
102 C4 **Segovia** Antioquia, N Colombia *07°08´N 74°39´W*
170 F4 **Segovia** Castilla-León, C Spain *40°57´N 04°07´W*
170 G4 **Segovia** ◈ *province* Castilla-León, N Spain
Segoviao Wangkí *see* Coco, Río
194 E6 **Segozerskoye Vodokhranilishche** *prev.* Ozero Segozero. ◎ NW Russian Federation
164 F4 **Segré** Maine-et-Loire, NW France *47°41´N 00°51´W*
171 J3 **Segre** ~ NE Spain
Segu *see* Ségou
82 D10 **Seguam Island** *island* Aleutian Islands, Alaska, USA
82 D10 **Seguam Pass** *strait* Aleutian Islands, Alaska, USA
133 M2 **Séguédine** Agadez, NE Niger *20°12´N 13°03´E*
132 E7 **Séguéla** W Ivory Coast *07°58´N 06°44´W*
114 C5 **Seguí** Entre Ríos, Argentina *31°57´S 60°08´W*
70 G7 **Seguin** Texas, SW USA *29°34´N 97°58´W*
82 B9 **Segula Island** *island* Aleutian Islands, Alaska, USA
116 E3 **Segundo, Río** ~ C Argentina
171 H7 **Segura** ~ S Spain
172 E6 **Segura de León** Extremadura, Spain *38°07´N 6°31´W*
173 K1 **Segura de los Baños** Aragón, Spain *40°56´N 0°57´W*
171 H7 **Segura , Sierra de** ▲▲ S Spain
Sehfayim *see* Shefayim
138 E4 **Sehithwa** North-West, N Botswana *20°28´S 22°43´E*
141 J6 **Sehlabathebe** Lesotho *29°53´S 29°05´E*
180 I6 **Sehlde** Niedersachsen, Germany *52°03´E 10°16´N*
232 E8 **Sehore** Madhya Pradesh, C India *23°12´N 77°08´E*
280 D4 **Sehulea** Normanby Island, S Papua New Guinea *09°55´S 151°10´E*
230 G8 **Sehwān** Sind, SE Pakistan *26°26´N 67°52´N*
177 K4 **Seiersberg** Steiermark, SE Austria *47°01´N 15°22´E*
158 E2 **Seil** *island* United Kingdom
75 D12 **Seiling** Oklahoma, C USA *36°09´N 98°55´W*
165 J5 **Seille** ~ E France
163 F11 **Seilles** Namur, SE Belgium *50°31´N 05°12´E*
153 G8 **Seinäjoki** *Swe.* Östermyra. Länsi-Suomi, W Finland *62°45´N 22°55´E*
58 C6 **Seine** ~ Ontario, S Canada
165 I3 **Seine** ~ N France
164 F2 **Seine, Baie de la** *bay* N France
Seine, Banc de la *see* Seine Seamount
165 I3 **Seine-et-Marne** ◈ *department* N France
165 H2 **Seine-Maritime** ◈ *department* N France
144 A9 **Seine Plain** *undersea feature* E Atlantic Ocean *34°00´N 12°15´W*
144 A9 **Seine Seamount** *var.* Banc de la Seine. *undersea feature* E Atlantic Ocean *33°45´N 14°25´W*
164 D4 **Sein, Île de** *island* NW France
261 L6 **Seinma** Papua, E Indonesia *04°10´S 138°54´E*
Seisbierrum *see* Sexbierum
168 E6 **Seissan** Midi-Pyrénées, France *43°30´N 0°36´E*
177 K2 **Seitenstetten Markt** Niederösterreich, C Austria *48°03´N 14°41´E*
Seiyo *see* Uwa
Seiyu *see* Chŏnju
155 E12 **Sejerø** *island* E Denmark
182 I3 **Sejny** Podlaskie, NE Poland *54°09´N 23°21´E*
258 F7 **Sekampung, Way** ~ Sumatera, SW Indonesia
137 C9 **Seke** Shinyanga, N Tanzania *03°16´S 33°31´E*
141 K3 **Sekhukhune** Limpopo, South Africa *24°45´S 29°59´E*
251 J4 **Seki** Gifu, Honshū, SW Japan *35°30´N 136°54´E*
187 M8 **Seki** Muğla, Turkey *36°24´N 29°13´E*
241 L6 **Sekibi-sho** *island* China/Japan/Taiwan
252 F4 **Sekihoku-tōge** *pass* Hokkaidō, NE Japan
140 G2 **Sekoma** Southern, Botswana *24°32´S 23°58´E*
Sekondi *see* Sekondi-Takoradi
132 G8 **Sekondi-Takoradi** *var.* Sekondi. S Ghana *04°55´N 01°45´W*
136 E3 **Sek'ot'a** Āmara, N Ethiopia *12°41´N 39°05´E*
Sekseüil *see* Saksaul'skoye
76 D4 **Selah** Washington, NW USA *46°39´N 120°31´W*
258 D3 **Selangor** *var.* Negeri Selangor Darul Ehsan. ◈ *state* Peninsular Malaysia
Selânik *see* Thessaloníki
256 G7 **Selaphum** Roi Et, E Thailand *16°00´N 103°54´E*
261 H8 **Selaru, Pulau** *island* Kepulauan Tanimbar, E Indonesia
261 I5 **Selassi** Papua, E Indonesia *03°16´S 132°50´E*
258 D2 **Selatan, Selat** *strait* Peninsular Malaysia
258 E4 **Selatpanjang** Pulau Rantau, W Indonesia *01°00´N 102°44´E*
82 G4 **Selawik** Alaska, USA *66°36´N 160°00´W*
82 G4 **Selawik Lake** ◎ Alaska, USA
260 D7 **Selayar, Selat** *strait* Sulawesi, C Indonesia
161 J7 **Selborne** United Kingdom *51°05´N 0°56´W*
154 E3 **Selbusjøen** ◎ S Norway
159 L9 **Selby** N England, United Kingdom *53°49´N 01°06´W*
74 C4 **Selby** South Dakota, N USA *45°30´N 100°01´W*
67 N3 **Selbyville** Delaware, NE USA *38°28´N 75°12´W*
214 B6 **Selçuk** *var.* Akıncılar. İzmir, SW Turkey *37°56´N 27°25´E*
83 I7 **Seldovia** Alaska, USA *59°26´N 151°42´W*
175 H10 **Sele** *anc.* Silarius. ~ S Italy
141 I1 **Selebi-Phikwe** Central, Botswana *21°59´S 27°45´E*
138 G5 **Selebi-Phikwe** Central, E Botswana *21°58´S 27°48´E*
88 B3 **Selegua, Río** ~ W Guatemala
205 M4 **Selemdzha** ~ SE Russian Federation
205 L4 **Selenga** *Mong.* Selenge Mörön. ~ Mongolia/Russian Federation
135 E8 **Selenge** Bandundu, W Dem. Rep. Congo *01°58´S 18°11´E*
246 E3 **Selenge** *var.* Ingettolgoy. Bulgan, N Mongolia *49°27´N 103°59´E*
246 F3 **Selenge** ◈ *province* N Mongolia
Selenge *see* Hyalganat, Bulgan, Mongolia
Selenge *see* Ih-Uul, Hövsgöl, Mongolia
Selenge Mörön *see* Selenga
193 I8 **Selenginsk** Respublika Buryatiya, S Russian Federation *52°00´N 106°40´E*
Selenica *see* Selenicë
184 F9 **Selenicë** *var.* Selenica. Vlorë, SW Albania *40°32´N 19°38´E*
193 K4 **Selennyakh** ~ NE Russian Federation
180 I1 **Selent** Schleswig-Holstein, Germany *54°18´E 10°26´N*
180 I1 **Selenter See** ◎ N Germany
Sele Sound *see* Soela Väin
165 K3 **Sélestat** *Ger.* Schlettstadt. Bas-Rhin, NE France *48°16´N 07°28´E*
Seleucia *see* Silifke
152 B3 **Selfoss** Sudhurland, SW Iceland *63°56´N 20°59´W*
74 C4 **Selfridge** North Dakota, N USA *46°01´N 100°52´W*
132 C6 **Seli** ~ N Sierra Leone
132 C4 **Sélibabi** *var.* Sélibaby. Guidimaka, S Mauritania *15°14´N 12°11´W*
Sélibaby *see* Sélibabi
Selidovka/Selidovo *see* Selydove
181 F12 **Seligenstadt** Hessen, Germany *50°03´E 8°59´N*
194 E10 **Seliger, Ozero** ◎ W Russian Federation
79 H7 **Seligman** Arizona, SW USA *35°20´N 112°56´W*
75 G11 **Seligman** Missouri, C USA *36°31´N 93°56´W*
129 H7 **Selima Oasis** *oasis* N Sudan
132 E5 **Sélingué, Lac de** ⊠ S Mali
Selinoús *see* Kréstena
64 D6 **Selinsgrove** Pennsylvania, NE USA *40°47´N 76°51´W*
Selishche *see* Syelishcha
194 E10 **Selizharovo** Tverskaya Oblast', W Russian Federation *56°50´N 33°24´E*
154 A5 **Selje** Sogn Og Fjordane, S Norway *62°02´N 05°22´E*
55 J9 **Selkirk** Manitoba, S Canada *50°10´N 96°52´W*
159 I4 **Selkirk** SE Scotland, United Kingdom *55°36´N 02°48´W*
156 F7 **Selkirk** *cultural region* SE Scotland, United Kingdom
56 G7 **Selkirk Mountains** ▲▲ British Columbia, SW Canada
287 K8 **Selkirk Rise** *undersea feature* SE Pacific Ocean
159 H7 **Sellafield** United Kingdom *54°24´N 3°30´W*
186 G7 **Sellasía** Pelopónnisos, S Greece *37°14´N 22°24´E*
91 H6 **Selle, Pic de la** *var.* La Selle. ▲ SE Haiti *18°18´N 71°55´W*
165 H5 **Selles-sur-Cher** Loir-et-Cher, C France *47°16´N 01°31´E*
167 K9 **Selliéres** Franche-Comté, France *46°50´N 5°34´E*
79 H10 **Sells** Arizona, SW USA *31°54´N 111°52´W*
Sellye *see* Sal'a
180 D7 **Selm** Nordrhein-Westfalen, Germany *51°42´E 7°28´N*
69 H2 **Selma** Alabama, S USA *32°24´N 87°01´W*
80 D6 **Selma** California, W USA *36°33´N 119°37´W*
61 L6 **Selma** North Carolina, SE USA *35°32´N 78°17´W*
66 C7 **Selmer** Tennessee, S USA *35°10´N 88°34´W*
172 C6 **Selmes** Beja, Portugal *38°09´N 7°46´W*
167 K8 **Selongey** Bourgogne, France *47°35´N 5°10´E*
137 I11 **Sel, Pointe au** *headland* W Réunion
Selselehye Kuhe Vākhān *see* Nicholas Range
161 J8 **Selsey** SE England, United Kingdom *50°44´N 00°47´W*
161 J8 **Selsey Bill** *headland* S England, United Kingdom *50°44´N 0°47´W*
180 G3 **Selsingen** Niedersachsen, Germany *53°22´E 9°13´N*
181 F11 **Selters** Hessen, Germany *50°20´E 9°02´N*
181 D10 **Selters** Rheinland-Pfalz, Germany *50°32´E 7°46´N*
195 J10 **Selty** Udmurtskaya Respublika, NW Russian Federation *57°19´N 52°09´E*
Selukwe *see* Shurugwi
112 E7 **Selva** Santiago del Estero, N Argentina *29°46´S 62°02´W*
55 H5 **Selwyn Lake** ◎ Northwest Territories/Saskatchewan, C Canada
54 C3 **Selwyn Mountains** ▲▲ Yukon Territory, NW Canada
275 I4 **Selwyn Range** ▲▲ Queensland, C Australia
190 J7 **Sely** Tverskaya Oblast', Russian Federation
189 L5 **Selydove** *var.* Selidovka, *Rus.* Selidovo. Donets'ka Oblast', SE Ukraine *48°06´N 37°16´E*
Selzaete *see* Zelzate
Seman *see* Semanit, Lumi i
258 F8 **Semangka, Teluk** *bay* Sumatera, SW Indonesia
258 F7 **Semangka, Way** ~ Sumatera, SW Indonesia
184 F9 **Semanit, Lumi i** *var.* Seman. ~ W Albania
259 I8 **Semarang** *var.* Samarang. Jawa, C Indonesia *06°58´S 110°29´E*
259 H4 **Sematan** Sarawak, East Malaysia *01°50´N 109°44´E*
260 E9 **Semau, Pulau** *island* S Indonesia
259 K5 **Semayang, Danau** ◎ Borneo, N Indonesia
259 K3 **Sembakung, Sungai** ~ Borneo, N Indonesia
134 C7 **Sembé** Sangha, NW Congo *01°38´N 14°35´E*
Semberong *see* Semberong, Sungai
258 E4 **Semberong, Sungai** *var.* Semberong. ~ Peninsular Malaysia
259 J6 **Sembulu, Danau** ◎ Borneo, N Indonesia
Semendria *see* Smederevo
189 I1 **Semenivka** Chernihivs'ka Oblast', N Ukraine *52°10´N 32°37´E*
189 J4 **Semenivka** *Rus.* Semenovka. Poltavs'ka Oblast', NE Ukraine *49°36´N 33°10´E*
197 H1 **Semenov** Nizhegorodskaya Oblast', W Russian Federation *56°47´N 44°27´E*
Semenovka *see* Semenivka
259 J9 **Semeru, Gunung** *var.* Mahameru. ▲ Jawa, S Indonesia *08°01´S 112°53´E*
227 L3 **Semey** *prev.* Semipalatinsk. Vostochnyy Kazakhstan, E Kazakhstan *50°26´N 80°16´E*
Semezhevo *see* Syemyezhava
196 G4 **Semiluki** Voronezhskaya Oblast', W Russian Federation *51°46´N 39°00´E*
77 L8 **Seminoe Reservoir** ⊠ Wyoming, C USA
75 E12 **Seminole** Oklahoma, C USA *35°13´N 96°40´W*
70 D4 **Seminole** Texas, SW USA *32°43´N 102°39´W*
69 I4 **Seminole, Lake** ⊠ Florida/Georgia, SE USA
Semiozernoye *see* Auliyekol'
Semipalatinsk *see* Semey
222 F6 **Semīrom** *var.* Samirum. Eşfahān, C Iran *31°20´N 51°50´E*
82 C9 **Semisopochnoi Island** *island* Aleutian Islands, Alaska, USA
258 I4 **Semitau** Borneo, C Indonesia *0°30´N 111°59´E*
134 J7 **Semliki** ~ Uganda/Dem. Rep. Congo
222 G3 **Semnān** *var.* Samnān. Semnān, N Iran *35°37´N 53°21´E*
222 G4 **Semnān** *off.* Ostān-e Semnān. ◈ *province* N Iran
Semnān, Ostān-e *see* Semnān
163 F13 **Semois** ~ SE Belgium
141 I7 **Semonkong** Lesotho *29°51´S 28°06´E*
174 B3 **Sempacher See** ◎ C Switzerland
167 J8 **Semur-en-Auxios** Bourgogne, France *47°29´N 4°20´E*
167 J10 **Semur-en-Brionnais** Bourgogne, France *46°16´N 4°05´E*
Sena *see* Vila de Sena
73 C9 **Senachwine Lake** ◎ Illinois, N USA
110 D7 **Senador Amaral** Minas Gerais, Brazil *22°35´S 46°11´W*
110 D7 **Senador José Bento** Minas Gerais, Brazil *22°10´S 46°10´W*
108 G4 **Senador Pompeu** Ceará, E Brazil *05°30´S 39°25´W*
Sena Gallica *see* Senigallia
106 C6 **Sena Madureira** Acre, W Brazil *09°05´S 68°41´W*
235 H10 **Senanayake Samudra** ◎ E Sri Lanka
138 E2 **Senanga** Western, SW Zambia *16°09´S 23°16´E*
75 J11 **Senath** Missouri, C USA *36°07´N 90°09´W*
66 B7 **Senatobia** Mississippi, S USA *34°37´N 89°58´W*
250 C8 **Sendai** *var.* Satsuma-Sendai. Kagoshima, Kyūshū, SW Japan *31°49´N 130°17´E*
253 D10 **Sendai** Miyagi, Honshū, C Japan *38°16´N 140°52´E*
250 C8 **Sendai-gawa** ~ Kyūshū, SW Japan
253 D10 **Sendai-wan** *bay* E Japan
140 C5 **Sendelingsdrif** Northern Cape, Namibia *28°10´S 16°53´E*
179 E12 **Senden** Bayern, S Germany *48°18´N 10°04´E*
180 D7 **Senden** Nordrhein-Westfalen, Germany *51°51´E 7°30´N*
180 D7 **Sendenhorst** Nordrhein-Westfalen, Germany *51°50´E 7°50´N*
232 D9 **Sendhwa** Madhya Pradesh, C India *21°38´N 75°04´E*
172 E1 **Sendim** Bragança, Portugal *41°23´N 6°26´W*
171 K9 **Sendjas** Algeria
183 E10 **Senec** *Ger.* Wartberg, *Hung.* Szenc; *prev.* Szempcz. Bratislavský Kraj, W Slovakia *48°14´N 17°24´E*
75 F9 **Seneca** Kansas, C USA *39°50´N 96°04´W*
75 G11 **Seneca** Missouri, C USA *36°50´N 94°36´W*
76 E7 **Seneca** Oregon, NW USA *44°06´N 118°57´W*
66 G7 **Seneca** South Carolina, SE USA *34°41´N 82°57´W*
64 D1 **Seneca Falls** New York, USA *42°55´N 76°48´W*
64 D2 **Seneca Lake** ◎ New York, NE USA
73 J11 **Senecaville Lake** ⊠ Ohio, N USA
132 B4 **Senegal** *off.* Republic of Senegal, *Fr.* Sénégal. ◆ *republic* W Africa
132 B3 **Senegal** *Fr.* Sénégal. ~ W Africa
Senegal, Republic of *see* Senegal
141 I5 **Senekal** Free State, South Africa *28°19´S 27°36´E*
72 F4 **Seney Marsh** *wetland* Michigan, N USA
169 L5 **Sénez** Provence-Alpes-Côte d'Azur, France *43°55´N 6°24´E*
179 I8 **Senftenberg** Brandenburg, E Germany *51°31´N 14°01´E*
137 B11 **Senga Hill** Northern, NE Zambia *09°26´S 31°12´E*
238 D8 **Sênggê Zangbo** ~ W China
261 M5 **Senggi** Papua, E Indonesia *03°26´S 140°46´E*
197 J3 **Sengiley** Ul'yanovskaya Oblast', W Russian Federation *53°54´N 48°51´E*
117 C10 **Senguerr, Río** ~ S Argentina
138 G3 **Sengwa** ~ C Zimbabwe
180 E3 **Sengwarden** Niedersachsen, Germany *53°36´E 8°03´N*
111 I4 **Senhora de Oliveira** Minas Gerais, Brazil *20°48´S 43°20´W*
Senia *see* Senj
183 E10 **Senica** *Ger.* Senitz, *Hung.* Szenice. Trnavský Kraj, W Slovakia *48°40´N 17°22´E*
Seniça *see* Sjenica
177 I9 **Senigallia** *anc.* Sena Gallica. Marche, C Italy *43°43´N 13°13´E*
214 C7 **Senirkent** Isparta, SW Turkey *38°07´N 30°34´E*
Senitz *see* Senica
184 B3 **Senj** *Ger.* Zengg, *It.* Segna; *anc.* Senia. Lika-Senj, NW Croatia *44°58´N 14°55´E*
Senj *see* Örgön
152 E4 **Senja** *prev.* Senjen. *island* N Norway
Senjen *see* Senja
237 J8 **Senkaku-shotō** *island group* SW Japan
215 J5 **Şenkaya** Erzurum, NE Turkey *40°33´N 42°17´E*
138 F3 **Senkobo** Southern, S Zambia *17°38´S 25°58´E*
140 G4 **Senlac** North West, South Africa *25°47´S 23°42´E*
165 H3 **Senlis** Oise, N France *49°13´N 02°33´E*
257 I8 **Senmonorom** Môndól Kiri, E Cambodia *12°27´N 107°12´E*
160 C10 **Sennan** United Kingdom *50°04´N 5°42´W*
136 C2 **Sennar** *var.* Sannār. Sinnar, C Sudan *13°31´N 33°38´E*
180 F7 **Senne** Nordrhein-Westfalen, Germany *51°52´E 8°41´N*
180 F7 **Sennestadt** Nordrhein-Westfalen, Germany *51°57´E 8°37´N*
Senno *see* Syanno
160 F5 **Sennybridge** United Kingdom *51°56´N 3°34´W*
166 F6 **Senonches** Centre, France *48°33´N 1°02´E*
167 M6 **Senones** Lorraine, France *48°24´N 6°59´E*
Senones *see* Sens
177 K5 **Senovo** E Slovenia *46°01´N 15°24´E*
141 I7 **Senqu** ~ Lesotho
165 I4 **Sens** *anc.* Agendicum, Senones. Yonne, C France *48°12´N 03°17´E*
Sensburg *see* Mrągowo
257 H8 **Sên, Stœ̆ng** ~ C Cambodia
88 D5 **Sensuntepeque** Cabañas, NE El Salvador *13°52´N 88°38´W*
184 F2 **Senta** *Hung.* Zenta. Vojvodina, N Serbia *45°57´N 20°04´E*
Šent Andraž *see* Sankt Andrä
261 L5 **Sentani, Danau** ◎ Papua, E Indonesia
74 A3 **Sentinel Butte** ▲ North Dakota, N USA *46°52´N 103°50´W*
56 E3 **Sentinel Peak** ▲ British Columbia, W Canada *54°51´N 122°02´W*
108 F6 **Sento Sé** Bahia, E Brazil *09°51´S 41°56´W*
Šent Peter *see* Pivka
Št. Vid *see* Sankt Veit an der Glan
261 M5 **Senu** ~ NW Papua New Guinea
168 F8 **Seo de Urgel** Cataluña, Spain *42°21´N 1°28´E*
Seo de Urgel *see* La Seu d'Urgell
248 B8 **Seogwipo** *prev.* Sŏgwip'o. S South Korea *33°14´N 126°33´E*
232 F6 **Seondha** Madhya Pradesh, C India *26°09´N 78°47´E*
250 A3 **Seongju** *prev.* Sŏngju. *35°54´N 128°17´E*
248 B8 **Seongsan** *prev.* Sŏngsan. S South Korea
232 F9 **Seoni** *prev.* Seeonee. Madhya Pradesh, C India *22°06´N 79°36´E*
250 A2 **Seonsan** *prev.* Sŏnsan. *36°14´N 128°17´E*
248 C5 **Seoul** *off.* Sŏul-t'ŭkpyŏlsi, *Jap.* Keijō; *prev.* Kyŏngsŏng, Sŏul. ● (South Korea) NW South Korea *37°30´N 126°58´E*
138 F4 **Sepako** Central, NE Botswana *19°50´S 26°29´E*
278 F7 **Separation Point** *headland* South Island, New Zealand *40°46´S 172°58´E*
259 L4 **Sepasu** Borneo, N Indonesia *0°44´N 117°38´E*
255 L8 **Sepik** ~ Indonesia/Papua New Guinea
Sepone *see* Muang Xépôn
182 H3 **Sępopol** *Ger.* Schippenbeil. Warmińsko-Mazurskie, N Poland *54°16´N 21°09´E*
188 B7 **Şepreuş** *Hung.* Seprős. Arad, W Romania *46°34´N 21°44´E*
Seprős *see* Şepreuş
Şepşi-Sângeorz/Sepsiszentgyőrgy *see* Sfântu Gheorghe
59 I6 **Sept-Îles** Québec, SE Canada *50°11´N 66°19´W*
170 G4 **Sepúlveda** Castilla-León, N Spain *41°18´N 03°45´W*
258 F7 **Seputih, Way** ~ Sumatera, SW Indonesia
114 G3 **Sequeira** Artigas, Uruguay *31°00´S 56°48´W*
170 E4 **Sequeros** Castilla-León, N Spain *40°31´N 06°04´W*
170 F3 **Sequillo** ~ NW Spain
76 C3 **Sequim** Washington, NW USA *48°04´N 123°06´W*
80 E7 **Sequoia National Park** *national park* California, W USA
215 I6 **Şerafettin Dağları** ▲▲ E Turkey
197 H5 **Serafimovich** Volgogradskaya Oblast', SW Russian Federation *49°34´N 42°43´E*
260 F3 **Serai** Sulawesi, N Indonesia *01°45´N 124°58´E*
163 G11 **Seraing** Liège, E Belgium *50°37´N 05°31´E*
Sêraitang *see* Baima
Serakhs *see* Sarahs
261 K5 **Serami** Papua, E Indonesia *02°11´S 136°46´E*
260 G5 **Seram, Laut** *Eng.* Ceram Sea. *sea* E Indonesia
Serampore/Serampur *see* Shrīrāmpur
260 G5 **Seram, Pulau** *var.* Serang, *Eng.* Ceram. *island* Maluku, E Indonesia
258 G8 **Serang** Jawa, C Indonesia *06°07´S 106°09´E*
Serang *see* Seram, Pulau
259 H3 **Serasan, Pulau** *island* Kepulauan Natuna, W Indonesia
259 H4 **Serasan, Selat** *strait* Indonesia/Malaysia
184 G4 **Serbia** *off.* Federal Republic of Serbia; *prev.* Yugoslavia, *SCr.* Jugoslavija. ◆ *federal republic* SE Europe
184 G5 **Serbia** *Ger.* Serbien, *Serb.* Srbija. ◈ *republic* Serbia
Serbia, Federal Republic of *see* Serbia
Serbien *see* Serbia
Sercq *see* Sark
228 C6 **Serdar** *prev. Rus.* Gyzyrlabat, Kizyl-Arvat. Balkan Welaýaty, W Turkmenistan *39°02´N 56°15´E*
Serdica *see* Sofiya
Serdobol' *see* Sortavala
197 H4 **Serdobsk** Penzenskaya Oblast', W Russian Federation *52°30´N 44°16´E*
227 M3 **Serebryansk** Vostochnyy Kazakhstan, E Kazakhstan *49°44´N 83°16´E*
193 J7 **Serebryanyy Bor** Respublika Sakha (Yakutiya), NE Russian Federation *56°40´N 124°46´E*
183 E10 **Sered'** *Hung.* Szered. Trnavský Kraj, W Slovakia *48°19´N 17°45´E*
190 G5 **Seredka** Pskovskaya Oblast', Russian Federation
189 J1 **Seredyna-Buda** Sums'ka Oblast', NE Ukraine *52°09´N 34°00´E*
191 C8 **Seredžius** Tauragė, C Lithuania *55°04´N 23°24´E*
214 E6 **Şereflikoçhisar** Ankara, C Turkey *38°56´N 33°31´E*
176 E6 **Seregno** Lombardia, N Italy *45°39´N 09°12´E*
165 I4 **Serein** ~ C France
258 E3 **Seremban** Negeri Sembilan, Peninsular Malaysia *02°42´N 101°54´E*
137 C9 **Serengeti Plain** *plain* N Tanzania
139 H1 **Serenje** Central, E Zambia *13°12´S 30°15´E*
Seres *see* Sérres
188 E5 **Seret** ~ W Ukraine
Seret/Sereth *see* Siret
187 I7 **Serfopoúla** *island* Kykládes, Greece, Aegean Sea
197 I2 **Sergach** Nizhegorodskaya Oblast', W Russian Federation *55°31´N 45°29´E*
74 F7 **Sergeant Bluff** Iowa, C USA *42°24´N 96°19´W*
247 H4 **Sergelen** Dornod, NE Mongolia *48°31´N 114°01´E*
Sergelen *see* Tuvshinshiree
258 C3 **Sergeulangit, Pegunungan** ▲▲ Sumatera, NW Indonesia
193 H3 **Sergeya Kirova, Ostrova** *island* N Russian Federation
Sergeyevichi *see* Syarhyeyevichy
227 H2 **Sergeyevka** Severnyy Kazakhstan, N Kazakhstan *53°53´N 67°25´E*
Sergiopol *see* Ayagoz
108 I7 **Sergipe** *off.* Estado de Sergipe. ◈ *state* E Brazil
Sergipe, Estado de *see* Sergipe
196 G1 **Sergiyev Posad** Moskovskaya Oblast', W Russian Federation *56°21´N 38°10´E*
194 F4 **Sergozero, Ozero** ◎ NW Russian Federation
228 F9 **Serhetabat** *prev. Rus.* Gushgy, Kushka. Mary Welaýaty, S Turkmenistan *35°19´N 62°17´E*
258 I4 **Serian** Sarawak, East Malaysia *01°10´N 110°35´E*
258 G8 **Seribu, Kepulauan** *island group* S Indonesia

◆ Country
● Country Capital
◇ Dependent Territory
○ Dependent Territory Capital
◈ Administrative Regions
✈ International Airport
▲ Mountain
▲▲ Mountain Range
Volcano
~ River
◎ Lake
⊠ Reservoir

INDEX

◆ Country   ◇ Dependent Territory   ◈ Administrative Regions   ▲ Mountain   ☼ Volcano   ⊚ Lake
● Country Capital   ○ Dependent Territory Capital   ✈ International Airport   ▲ Mountain Range   ≈ River   ▨ Reservoir

158 A8 **Sligo** *Ir.* Sligeach. *cultural region* NW Ireland
157 B8 **Sligo Bay** *Ir.* Cuan Shligigh. *inlet* NW Ireland
159 L8 **Slingsby** United Kingdom 54°09′N 0°55′W
62 C8 **Slippery Rock** Pennsylvania, NE USA 41°02′N 80°02′W
155 J10 **Slite** Gotland, SE Sweden 57°37′N 18°46′E
185 L6 **Sliven** *var.* Slivno. Sliven, C Bulgaria 42°42′N 26°21′E
185 L6 **Sliven** ♦ *province* C Bulgaria
185 J6 **Slivnitsa** Sofiya, W Bulgaria 42°51′N 23°01′E
Slivno *see* Sliven
185 L4 **Sliva Pole** Ruse, N Bulgaria 43°57′N 26°15′E
74 F7 **Sloan** Iowa, C USA 42°13′N 96°13′W
81 I9 **Sloan** Nevada, W USA 35°56′N 115°13′W
80 E1 **Sloat** California, USA 39°52′N 120°44′W
Slobodka *see* Slabodka
195 H8 **Slobodskoy** Kirovskaya Oblast′, NW Russian Federation 58°43′N 50°12′E
Slobodzeya *see* Slobozia
188 G7 **Slobozia** *Rus.* Slobodzeya. E Moldova 46°45′N 29°42′E
188 F9 **Slobozia** Ialomiţa, SE Romania 44°34′N 27°23′E
62 I3 **Slochteren** Groningen, NE Netherlands 53°13′N 06°48′E
191 E10 **Slonim** *Pol.* Słonim. Hrodzyenskaya Voblasts′, W Belarus 53°06′N 25°19′E
Słonim *see* Slonim
162 G4 **Sloter Meer** ☒ N Netherlands
Slot, The *see* New Georgia Sound
161 I6 **Slough** S England, United Kingdom 51°31′N 00°36′W
183 G10 **Slovakia** *off.* Slovenská Republika, *Ger.* Slowakei, *Hung.* Szlovákia, *Slvk.* Slovensko. ♦ *republic* C Europe
Slovak Ore Mountains *see* Slovenské rudohorie
Slovechna *see* Slavyechna
174 G4 **Slovenia** *off.* Republic of Slovenia, *Ger.* Slowenien, *Slvn.* Slovenija. ♦ *republic* SE Europe
174 G4 **Slovenia, Republic of** *see* Slovenia
Slovenija *see* Slovenia
177 K5 **Slovenj Gradec** *Ger.* Windischgrätz. N Slovenia 46°29′N 15°05′E
177 L5 **Slovenska Bistrica** *Ger.* Windischfeistritz. NE Slovenia 46°21′N 15°27′E
Slovenská Republika *see* Slovakia
177 K5 **Slovenske Konjice** E Slovenia 46°21′N 15°28′E
183 G10 **Slovenské rudohorie** *Eng.* Slovak Ore Mountains, *Ger.* Slowakisches Erzgebirge, Ungarisches Erzgebirge. ▲ C Slovakia
Slovensko *see* Slovakia
189 M5 **Slov″yanoserbs′k** Luhans′ka Oblast′, E Ukraine
189 M4 **Slov″yans′k** *Rus.* Slavyansk. Donets′ka Oblast′, E Ukraine 48°51′N 37°38′E
Slowakei *see* Slovakia
Slowakisches Erzgebirge *see* Slovenské rudohorie
Slowenien *see* Slovenia
182 C6 **Słubice** *Ger.* Frankfurt. Lubuskie, W Poland 52°20′N 14°35′E
191 F11 **Sluch** *Rus.* Sluch′. ♠ C Belarus
188 F2 **Sluch** ♠ NW Ukraine
163 C9 **Sluis** Zeeland, SW Netherlands 51°18′N 03°22′E
184 B3 **Slunj** *Hung.* Szluin. Karlovac, C Croatia 45°06′N 15°35′E
182 E6 **Słupca** Wielkopolskie, C Poland 52°17′N 17°52′E
182 E3 **Słupia** *Ger.* Stolpe. ♠ NW Poland
182 E3 **Słupsk** *Ger.* Stolp. Pomorskie, N Poland 54°28′N 17°01′E
141 H3 **Slurry** North-West, South Africa 25°49′S 25°51′E
191 F10 **Slutsk** Minskaya Voblasts′, S Belarus 53°02′N 27°32′E
191 H10 **Slyedzyuki** *Rus.* Sledyuki. Mahilyowskaya Voblasts′, E Belarus 53°35′N 30°16′E
157 A9 **Slyne Head** *Ir.* Ceann Léime. *headland* W Ireland 53°25′N 10°11′W
193 H8 **Slyudyanka** Irkutskaya Oblast′, S Russian Federation 51°36′N 103°28′E
75 H14 **Smackover** Arkansas, C USA 33°21′N 92°43′W
155 G10 **Småland** *cultural region* S Sweden
155 F10 **Smålandsstenar** Jönköping, S Sweden 57°10′N 13°24′E
161 M3 **Smallburgh** United Kingdom 52°46′N 1°27′E
Small Malaita *see* Maramasike
59 I4 **Smallwood Reservoir** ☒ Newfoundland and Labrador, E Canada
191 H9 **Smalyany** *Rus.* Smolyany. Vitsyebskaya Voblasts′, NE Belarus 54°36′N 30°04′E
191 G9 **Smalyavichy** *Rus.* Smolevichi. Minskaya Voblasts′, C Belarus 54°02′N 28°05′E
130 D5 **Smara** *var.* Es Semara. N Western Sahara 26°45′N 11°44′W
191 F9 **Smarhon′** *Pol.* Smorgonie, *Rus.* Smorgon′. Hrodzyenskaya Voblasts′, W Belarus 54°29′N 26°24′E
140 G7 **Smartt Syndicate Dam** ☒ Northern Cape, South Africa
80 D1 **Smartville** California, USA 39°12′N 121°18′W
184 G4 **Smederevo** *Ger.* Semendria. Serbia, N Serbia 44°41′N 20°56′E
184 G4 **Smederevska Palanka** Serbia, C Serbia 44°24′N 20°56′E
154 H7 **Smedjebacken** Dalarna, C Sweden 60°08′N 15°25′E
188 F9 **Smeeni** Buzău, SE Romania 45°00′N 26°52′E
Smela *see* Smila
175 C9 **Smeralda, Costa** *cultural region* Sardegna, Italy, C Mediterranean Sea
161 M3 **Smethwick** United Kingdom 52°30′N 2°09′W
182 D6 **Śmigiel** *Ger.* Schmiegel. Wielkopolskie, C Poland 52°01′N 16°33′E
189 I4 **Smila** *Rus.* Smela. Cherkas′ka Oblast′, C Ukraine 49°15′N 31°54′E
162 I4 **Smilde** Drenthe, NE Netherlands 52°57′N 06°28′E
57 L6 **Smiley** Saskatchewan, S Canada 51°40′N 109°24′W
70 G7 **Smiley** Texas, SW USA 29°16′N 97°38′W
Smilten *see* Smiltene
190 D6 **Smiltene** *Ger.* Smilten. Valka, N Latvia 57°25′N 25°55′E
193 I3 **Smirnykh** Ostrov Sakhalin, Sakhalinskaya Oblast′, SE Russian Federation 49°43′N 142°48′E
57 I7 **Smith** Alberta, SW Canada 55°06′N 113°57′W
80 D7 **Smith** ♠ California, W USA
52 C8 **Smith Arm** Northwest Territories, NW Canada
54 I4 **Smith Bay** *coastal sea feature* Nunavut, N Canada
83 H7 **Smith Bay** *bay* Alaska, NW USA
53 I2 **Smith, Cape** Québec, NE Canada 60°50′N 78°06′W
74 D9 **Smith Center** Kansas, C USA 39°46′N 98°46′W
56 C5 **Smithers** British Columbia, SW Canada 54°45′N 127°10′W
141 H7 **Smithfield** Free State, South Africa 30°13′S 26°32′E
67 K6 **Smithfield** North Carolina, SE USA 35°30′N 78°21′W
79 H1 **Smithfield** Utah, W USA 41°50′N 111°49′W
67 M5 **Smithfield** Virginia, NE USA 36°41′N 76°38′W
55 M4 **Smith Island** *island* Nunavut, C Canada
Smith Island *see* Sumisu-jima
73 D13 **Smithland** Kentucky, S USA 37°06′N 88°24′W
67 J5 **Smith Mountain Lake** ☒ Virginia, NE USA. Leesville Lake.
67 I5 Virginia, NE USA
78 A1 **Smith River** California, W USA 41°54′N 124°09′W
77 I4 **Smith River** ♠ Montana, NW USA
62 F4 **Smiths Falls** Ontario, SE Canada 44°54′N 76°01′W
76 F6 **Smiths Ferry** Idaho, NW USA 44°20′N 116°04′W
66 G5 **Smiths Grove** Kentucky, S USA 37°03′N 86°12′W
140 G9 **Smithskraal** Eastern Cape, South Africa 33°46′S 24°25′E
53 I3 **Smith Sound** *sound* Nunavut, N Canada
277 J9 **Smithton** Tasmania, SE Australia 40°54′S 145°06′E
65 I6 **Smithtown** Long Island, New York, NE USA 40°52′N 73°13′W
66 E6 **Smithville** Tennessee, S USA 35°59′N 85°49′W
71 H7 **Smithville** Texas, SW USA 30°04′N 97°32′W
Smohor *see* Hermagor
78 D2 **Smoke Creek Desert** *desert* Nevada, USA
56 G4 **Smoky** ♠ Alberta, W Canada
276 I4 **Smoky Bay** South Australia 32°25′S 133°57′E
277 M4 **Smoky Cape** *headland* New South Wales, SE Australia 30°54′S 153°05′E
75 D9 **Smoky Hill River** ♠ Kansas, C USA
75 D9 **Smoky Hills** *hill range* Kansas, C USA
57 I4 **Smoky Lake** Alberta, SW Canada 54°08′N 112°26′W
154 C3 **Smøla** *island* N Norway
195 H8 **Smolensk** Smolenskaya Oblast′, W Russian Federation 54°49′N 32°04′E
196 E2 **Smolenskaya Oblast′** ♦ *province* W Russian Federation
Smolensk-Moscow Upland *see* Smolensko-Moskovskaya Vozvyshennost′
196 E2 **Smolensko-Moskovskaya Vozvyshennost′** *Eng.* Smolensk-Moscow Upland. ▲ W Russian Federation
Smolevichi *see* Smalyavichy
186 H3 **Smólikas** *var.* Smólikás. ▲ W Greece 40°06′N 20°54′E
193 I8 **Smolino** Leningradskaya Oblast′, Russian Federation
185 I8 **Smolyan** *prev.* Pashmakli. Smolyan, S Bulgaria 41°34′N 24°42′E
185 I8 **Smolyan** ♦ *province* S Bulgaria
Smolyany *see* Smalyany
75 E8 **Smoot** Wyoming, C USA 42°37′N 110°55′W
58 H7 **Smooth Rock Falls** Ontario, S Canada
54 G7 **Smoothstone Lake** ☒ Saskatchewan, C Canada
155 F12 **Smygehamn** Skåne, S Sweden 55°19′N 13°25′E
292 H4 **Smyley Island** *island* Antarctica
64 F9 **Smyrna** Delaware, NE USA 39°18′N 75°36′W
66 I1 **Smyrna** Georgia, SE USA 33°52′N 84°31′W
66 E6 **Smyrna** Tennessee, S USA 36°00′N 86°30′W
Smyrna *see* İzmir

261 J5 **Snabai** Papua, E Indonesia 01°45′S 134°14′E
54 I5 **Snaefell** X Isle of Man 54°15′N 04°29′W
152 A2 **Snæfellsjökull** ▲ W Iceland 64°51′N 23°51′W
152 C2 **Snækollur** ▲ C Iceland 64°38′N 19°18′W
159 L9 **Snaith** United Kingdom 53°41′N 1°02′W
54 D5 **Snake** ♠ Yukon Territory, NW Canada
74 D5 **Snake Creek** ♠ South Dakota, N USA
277 J8 **Snake Island** *island* Victoria, SE Australia
78 C4 **Snake Range** ▲ Nevada, W USA
60 **Snake River** ♠ NW USA
77 H7 **Snake River** ♠ Minnesota, N USA
76 B6 **Snake River** ♠ Nebraska, C USA
77 H7 **Snake River Plain** *plain* Idaho, NW USA
54 D10 **Snare** ♠ Northwest Territories, NW Canada
154 F3 **Snare Lakes** Northwest Territories, NW Canada
154 C2 **Snåsa** Nord-Trøndelag, C Norway 64°16′N 12°25′E
65 G5 **Sneedville** Tennessee, S USA 36°31′N 83°13′W
162 G4 **Sneek** Friesland, N Netherlands 53°02′N 05°40′E
162 F4 **Sneekermeer** ☒ N Netherlands
140 F8 **Sneeukraal** Western Cape, South Africa 31°54′S 22°40′E
Sneeuw-gebergte *see* Maoke, Pegunungan
55 C12 **Snefjberg** Ringkøbing, C Denmark 56°08′N 08°55′E
80 D4 **Snelling** California, USA 37°31′N 120°26′W
194 E2 **Snettisham** United Kingdom 52°52′N 0°30′E
192 G5 **Snezhnogorsk** Murmanskaya Oblast′, NW Russian Federation 69°12′N 33°20′E
192 G5 **Snezhnogorsk** Krasnoyarskiy Kray, N Russian Federation 68°06′N 87°37′E
Snezhnoye *see* Snizhne
174 G4 **Snežnik** ▲ SW Slovenia 45°36′N 14°25′E
182 H4 **Śniardwy, Jezioro** *Ger.* Spirdingsee. ☒ NE Poland
Sniečkus *see* Visaginas
189 I7 **Snihurivka** *Rus.* Snigirevka. Mykolayivs′ka Oblast′, S Ukraine 47°05′N 32°48′E
188 D4 **Snilov** X (L'viv) L'vivs'ka Oblast', W Ukraine 49°45′N 23°59′E
183 I9 **Snina** *Hung.* Szinna. Prešovský Kraj, E Slovakia 48°59′N 22°10′E
189 M5 **Snizhne** *Rus.* Snezhnoye. Donets′ka Oblast′, E Ukraine 48°01′N 38°46′E
161 L6 **Snodland** SE England, United Kingdom 51°19′N 00°19′E
154 H3 **Snøhetta** *var.* Snohetta. ▲ S Norway 62°22′N 09°08′E
152 D6 **Snøtinden** ▲ C Norway 66°39′N 13°50′E
55 H5 **Snowbird Lake** ☒ Northwest Territories, C Canada
160 D2 **Snowdon** ▲ NW Wales, United Kingdom 53°04′N 04°04′W
157 H9 **Snowdonia** ▲ NW Wales, United Kingdom
Snøwip'o *see* Lutselk'e
Snowdrift *see* Lutselk'e
79 J4 **Snowflake** Arizona, SW USA 34°30′N 110°04′W
67 M3 **Snow Hill** Maryland, NE USA 38°11′N 75°23′W
67 L8 **Snow Hill** North Carolina, SE USA 35°26′N 77°39′W
292 E3 **Snowhill Island** *island* Antarctica
55 I7 **Snow Lake** Manitoba, C Canada 54°56′N 100°02′W
79 K3 **Snowmass Mountain** ▲ Colorado, C USA 39°07′N 107°04′W
65 I2 **Snow, Mount** ▲ Vermont, USA 42°56′N 72°52′W
78 B3 **Snow Mountain** ▲ California, W USA 39°44′N 123°01′W
76 G3 **Snowshoe Peak** ▲ Montana, NW USA 48°15′N 115°44′W
276 G5 **Snowtown** South Australia 33°49′S 138°13′E
79 H1 **Snowville** Utah, USA 41°59′N 112°42′W
78 F2 **Snow Water Lake** ☒ Nevada, W USA
277 K7 **Snowy Mountains** ▲ New South Wales/Victoria, SE Australia
277 K7 **Snowy River** ♠ New South Wales/Victoria, SE Australia
90 G4 **Snug Corner** Acklins Island, SE Bahamas 22°31′N 73°51′W
257 H9 **Snuol** Krâchéh, E Cambodia 12°04′N 106°26′E
188 F5 **Snyatyn** Ivano-Frankivs′ka Oblast′, W Ukraine 48°27′N 25°34′E
75 D7 **Snyder** Oklahoma, C USA 34°37′N 98°56′W
70 E4 **Snyder** Texas, SW USA 32°43′N 100°54′W
140 F8 **Snyderspoort** *pass* Western Cape, South Africa
136 L9 **Soalala** Mahajanga, W Madagascar 16°05′S 45°21′E
172 D3 **Soalheiras** Castelo Branco, Portugal 39°42′N 7°11′W
139 N6 **Soanierana-Ivongo** Toamasina, E Madagascar 16°53′S 49°35′E
161 I3 **Soar** ♠ United Kingdom
260 G3 **Soasiu** *var.* Tidore. Pulau Tidore, E Indonesia 0°40′N 127°25′E
102 B5 **Soatá** Boyacá, C Colombia 06°23′N 72°40′W
139 L7 **Soavinandriana** *var.* Soavinandriana, C Madagascar 19°09′S 46°43′E
261 L6 **Soba** Papua, E Indonesia 04°18′S 139°11′E
133 K6 **Soba** Kaduna, C Nigeria 10°58′N 08°06′E
248 C6 **Sobaek-sanmaek** ▲ S South Korea
136 B4 **Sobat** ♠ NE South Sudan
261 M6 **Sobger, Sungai** ♠ Papua, E Indonesia
261 J5 **Sobiei** Papua, E Indonesia 02°13′S 134°30′E
196 J3 **Sobinka** Vladimirskaya Oblast′, W Russian Federation 56°00′N 39°55′E
197 K4 **Sobolevo** Orenburgskaya Oblast′, W Russian Federation 53°40′N 51°42′E
Soborsin *see* Săvârşin
257 D7 **Sobo-san** ▲ Kyūshū, SW Japan 32°50′N 131°16′E
182 D7 **Sobótka** Dolnośląskie, SW Poland 50°53′N 16°48′E
108 G6 **Sobradinho, Barragem de** *see* Sobradinho, Represa de
108 F7 **Sobradinho, Represa de** *var.* Barragem de Sobradinho. ☒ E Brazil
108 F3 **Sobral** Ceará, E Brazil 03°45′S 40°20′W
172 B3 **Sobral** Castelo Branco, Portugal 39°57′N 8°01′W
172 D6 **Sobral da Adiça** Beja, Portugal 38°01′N 7°16′W
111 I2 **Sobrália** Minas Gerais, Brazil 19°15′S 42°06′W
118 D2 **Sobrante, Río del** ♠ Valparaíso, Chile
171 I2 **Sobrarbe** *physical region* NE Spain
116 G2 **Socavones, Cañones.** Uruguay 34°41′S 55°51′W
184 A4 **Soča** *It.* Isonzo. ♠ Italy/Slovenia
182 G6 **Sochaczew** Mazowieckie, C Poland 52°15′N 20°15′E
167 M4 **Sochaux** Franche-Comté, France 47°44′N 6°48′E
196 G9 **Sochi** Krasnodarskiy Kray, SW Russian Federation 43°35′N 39°46′E
187 H3 **Sochós** *var.* Sohos, Sokhós. Kentrikí Makedonía, N Greece 40°49′N 23°23′E
285 I7 **Société, Archipel de la** *var.* Archipel de Tahiti, Îles de la Société, *Eng.* Society Islands. *island group* W French Polynesia
Société, Îles de la/Society Islands *see* Société, Archipel de la
67 J7 **Society Hill** South Carolina, SE USA 34°28′N 79°54′W
267 J8 **Society Ridge** *undersea feature* E Pacific Ocean
105 H13 **Socoma, Volcán** X N Chile 24°18′S 68°03′W
54 A3 **Socompa, Volcn** X Chile 24°18′S 68°00′W
110 D7 **Socorro** São Paulo, Brazil 22°35′S 46°32′W
102 B5 **Socorro** Santander, C Colombia 06°30′N 73°16′W
79 L8 **Socorro** New Mexico, SW USA 33°58′N 106°55′W
79 L8 **Socorro, Isla** *island* W Mexico
161 H6 **Socorro** Santander... Sierra
78 A1 **Socorro** Madre, Sierra
79 L8 **Soconusco, Sierra de** *see* Madre, Sierra
173 I8 **Socovos** Castilla-La Mancha, Spain 38°19′N 02°02′W
257 H10 **Soc Trăng** *var.* Khanh Hung. Soc Trăng, S Vietnam 09°36′N 105°58′E
171 H6 **Socuéllamos** Castilla-La Mancha, C Spain 39°18′N 02°48′W
81 L8 **Soda Lake** *salt flat* California, W USA
152 H5 **Sodankylä** Lappi, N Finland 67°26′N 26°35′E
Sodari *see* Sodiri
80 F7 **Soda Springs** California, USA 39°19′N 120°23′W
77 I8 **Soda Springs** Idaho, NW USA 42°39′N 111°35′W
Soddo/Soddu *see* Sodo
66 F7 **Soddy Daisy** Tennessee, S USA 35°16′N 85°11′W
154 I7 **Söderfors** Uppsala, C Sweden 60°23′N 17°14′E
154 H8 **Söderhamn** Gävleborg, C Sweden 61°19′N 17°10′E
155 H9 **Söderköping** Östergötland, S Sweden 58°28′N 16°20′E
154 H7 **Södermanland** *county* C Sweden
154 I8 **Södertälje** Stockholm, C Sweden 59°11′N 17°37′E
136 A2 **Sodiri** *var.* Sawdiri, Sodari. Northern Kordofan, C Sudan
136 C5 **Sodo** *var.* Soddo, Soddu. Southern Nationalities, C Ethiopia 06°49′N 37°43′E
155 H10 **Södra Vi** Kalmar, S Sweden 57°45′N 15°45′E
64 A6 **Sodus Point** *headland* New York, NE USA
141 L5 **Sodwana Bay** *bay* KwaZulu-Natal, South Africa
260 D5 **Soë** Timor, S Indonesia 09°50′S 124°17′E
140 G7 **Soebatsfontein** Northern Cape, South Africa 30°08′S 17°05′E
Soekaboemi *see* Sukabumi
258 I6 **Soekarno-Hatta** X (Jakarta) Jawa, S Indonesia
180 G3 **Soela Väin** *prev.* Sele Sound, *Ger.* Dagden-Sund. Sele Sound, *strait* W Estonia
Soemba *see* Sumba, Pulau
Soembawa *see* Sumbawa
Soemenep *see* Sumenep
Soengaipenoeh *see* Sungaipenuh
Soerabaja *see* Surabaya

181 I8 **Soest** Nordrhein-Westfalen, W Germany 51°34′N 08°06′E
162 E9 **Soest** Utrecht, C Netherlands 52°10′N 05°20′E
180 D4 **Soeste** ♠ NW Germany
162 F6 **Soesterberg** Utrecht, C Netherlands 52°07′N 05°17′E
186 G6 **Sofádes** *var.* Sofádhes. Thessalía, C Greece 39°20′N 22°06′E
Sofádhes *see* Sofádes
139 I3 **Sofala** Sofala, C Mozambique 20°04′S 34°43′E
139 I3 **Sofala** ♦ *province* C Mozambique
139 I3 **Sofala, Baia de** *bay* C Mozambique
139 M5 **Sofia** *seasonal river* NW Madagascar
187 H9 **Sofikó** Pelopónnisos, S Greece 37°46′N 23°04′E
Sofi-Kurgan *see* Sopu-Korgon
185 I6 **Sofiya** *var.* Sophia, *Eng.* Sofia, *Lat.* Serdica. ● (Bulgaria) Sofiya-Grad, W Bulgaria 42°40′N 23°20′E
185 I6 **Sofiya** ♦ *province* W Bulgaria
185 I6 **Sofiya** X Sofiya-Grad, W Bulgaria 42°42′N 23°26′E
185 I6 **Sofiya-Grad** ♦ *municipality* W Bulgaria
Sofiya-Grad *see* Sofiyivka
189 I5 **Sofiyivka** *Rus.* Sofiyevka. Dnipropetrovs′ka Oblast′, E Ukraine 48°04′N 33°53′E
193 K8 **Sofiysk** Khabarovskiy Kray, SE Russian Federation 51°32′N 139°46′E
194 E3 **Sofporog** Respublika Kareliya, NW Russian Federation 65°48′N 31°30′E
187 K9 **Sofraná** *prev.* Záfora. *island* Kykládes, Greece, Aegean Sea
251 M6 **Sōfu-gan** *island* Izu-shotō, SE Japan
238 H4 **Sog** Xizang Zizhiqu, W China 31°52′N 93°40′E
102 D5 **Sogamoso** Boyacá, C Colombia 05°43′N 72°56′W
214 F4 **Soğanlı Çayı** ♠ N Turkey
180 D4 **Sögel** Niedersachsen, NW Germany 52°51′N 7°31′N
154 B3 **Sogn** *physical region* S Norway
154 B3 **Sogndal** *var.* Sogndal. Sogn Og Fjordane, S Norway 61°12′N 07°05′E
Sogndal *see* Sogndalsfjøra
154 B3 **Sogndalsfjøra** *var.* Sogndal. Sogn Og Fjordane, S Norway 61°13′N 07°06′E
154 C5 **Sogne** Vest-Agder, S Norway 58°05′N 07°49′E
154 B3 **Sognefjorden** *fjord* NE North Sea
235 A8 **Sogn Og Fjordane** ♦ *county* S Norway
263 M7 **Sogod** Leyte, C Philippines 10°25′N 125°00′E
239 I8 **Sogo Nur** ☒ N China
239 K7 **Sogruma** Qinghai, W China 32°32′N 100°52′E
Sogwip'o *see* Seogwipo
Sohâg *see* Sawhāj
161 L4 **Soham** United Kingdom 52°20′N 0°21′E
Sohar *see* Şuḩār
290 E7 **Sohm Plain** *undersea feature* NW Atlantic Ocean
178 D3 **Soholmer Au** ♠ N Germany
Sohos *see* Sochós
Sochar *see* Zory
171 C12 **Sohren** Rheinland-Pfalz, Germany 49°56′E 7°19′N
163 D11 **Soignies** Hainaut, SW Belgium 50°35′N 04°04′E
239 I9 **Soila** Xizang Zizhiqu, W China 30°40′N 97°07′E
165 I2 **Soissons** *anc.* Augusta Suessionum, Noviodunum. Aisne, N France 49°23′N 03°20′E
250 G5 **Sōja** Okayama, Honshū, SW Japan 34°40′N 133°42′E
232 D6 **Sojat** Rājasthān, N India 25°55′N 73°47′E
247 L3 **Sŏjosŏn-man** *inlet* W North Korea
188 D3 **Sokal'** *Rus.* Sokal. L'vivs'ka Oblast', NW Ukraine 50°29′N 24°17′E
248 C6 **Sokcho** *prev.* Sokch'o. N South Korea 38°07′N 128°34′E
214 B7 **Söke** Aydın, SW Turkey 37°46′N 27°24′E
283 J1 **Sokehs Island** *island* E Micronesia
135 H11 **Sokela** Katanga, SE Dem. Rep. Congo 09°54′S 24°38′E
229 J6 **Sokh** *Uzb.* Sükh. ♠ Kyrgyzstan/Uzbekistan
Sokh *see* So'x
Sokhós *see* Sochós
215 I5 **Sokhumi** *Rus.* Sukhumi. NW Georgia 43°02′N 41°01′E
185 H5 **Sokobanja** Serbia, E Serbia 43°39′N 21°51′E
133 J7 **Sokodé** C Togo 08°58′N 01°10′E
193 J4 **Sokol** Vologodskaya Oblast′, E Russian Federation 59°51′N 150°56′E
183 H10 **Sokol** Vologodskaya Oblast′, NW Russian Federation 59°26′N 40°09′E
182 J6 **Sokółka** Podlaskie, NE Poland 53°24′N 23°31′E
132 G4 **Sokolo** Ségou, W Mali 14°43′N 06°02′W
183 A8 **Sokolov** *Ger.* Falkenau an der Eger; *prev.* Falknov nad Ohří. Karlovarský Kraj, W Czech Republic 50°12′N 12°38′E
182 I5 **Sokołów Małopolski** NE Poland 50°13′N 22°07′E
182 J5 **Sokołów Podlaski** Mazowieckie, C Poland 52°25′N 22°14′E
132 I3 **Sokone** W Senegal 13°53′N 16°22′W
133 J5 **Sokoto** Sokoto, NW Nigeria 13°05′N 05°16′E
133 J5 **Sokoto** ♦ *state* NW Nigeria
133 J5 **Sokoto** ♠ NW Nigeria
229 K4 **Sokuluk** Chuyskaya Oblast′, N Kyrgyzstan 42°53′N 74°19′E
188 I7 **Sokyryany** Chernivets′ka Oblast′, W Ukraine 48°28′N 27°25′E
155 I1 **Sola** Rogaland, S Norway 58°53′N 05°36′E
281 M1 **Sola** Vanua Lava, N Vanuatu 13°51′S 167°34′E
155 A8 **Sola** X (Stavanger) Rogaland, S Norway 58°53′N 05°38′E
62 E9 **Sola de Vega** Oaxaca, Mexico 16°31′N 96°58′W
137 D8 **Solai** Rift Valley, W Kenya 0°02′N 36°03′E
232 E8 **Solan** Himāchal Pradesh, N India 30°54′N 77°06′E
278 A13 **Solander Island** *island* SW New Zealand
234 D5 **Solāpur** *var.* Sholāpur. Mahārāshtra, W India 17°43′N 75°54′E
13 E8 **Solberg** Västernorrland, C Sweden 63°48′N 17°40′E
158 E8 **Solca** *Ger.* Solka. Suceava, N Romania 47°40′N 25°50′E
176 F5 **Sol, Costa del** *coastal region* S Spain
176 G5 **Solda** *Ger.* Sulden. Trentino-Alto Adige, N Italy
188 G7 **Şoldăneşti** *Rus.* Sholdaneshty. N Moldova 47°49′N 28°45′E
277 F14 **Sölden** Tirol, W Austria 46°58′N 11°01′E
83 I7 **Soldier Creek** ♠ Kansas, C USA
77 B7 **Soldotna** Alaska, USA 60°29′N 151°03′W
79 I8 **Solec Kujawski** Kujawsko-pomorskie, C Poland 53°04′N 18°09′E
114 G6 **Soledad** Santa Fe, C Argentina 30°38′S 60°52′W
102 C2 **Soledad** Atlántico, N Colombia 10°54′N 74°48′W
80 B5 **Soledad** California, USA 36°25′N 121°19′W
113 I6 **Soledade** Rio Grande do Sul, S Brazil 28°50′S 52°30′W
Isla Soledad *see* East Falkland
172 C8 **Soledade** Portugal
161 I6 **Solent, The** *channel* S England, United Kingdom
163 C12 **Solesmes** Nord-Pas-de-Calais, France 50°11′N 3°30′E
Soleure *see* Solothurn
172 C6 **Solgalich** Kostromskaya Oblast′, NW Russian Federation 59°09′N 42°15′E
169 I3 **Soligny-sur-Loire** Auvergne, France 44°58′N 3°53′E
Soligorsk *see* Salihorsk
161 J2 **Solihull** C England, United Kingdom 52°25′N 01°45′W
195 K8 **Solikamsk** Permskaya Oblast′, NW Russian Federation 59°37′N 56°46′E
197 H5 **Sol′-Iletsk** Orenburgskaya Oblast′, W Russian Federation 51°09′N 55°05′E
175 D9 **Soliman** Tunisia
235 H10 **Sölleftea** Västernorrland, C Sweden 63°09′N 17°15′E
168 A8 **Sollentuna** Stockholm, C Sweden 59°26′N 17°56′E
171 H4 **Sóller** Mallorca, Spain, W Mediterranean Sea 39°46′N 02°42′E
154 G5 **Sollerön** Dalarna, C Sweden 60°53′N 14°34′E
154 H5 **Solliès-Pont** Provence-Alpes-Côte d'Azur, France 43°11′N 6°02′E
180 F2 **Solling** *hill range* C Germany
176 D5 **Sondrio** Lombardia, N Italy 46°11′N 09°52′E
230 F9 **Sonepat** *var.* Sonipat. Haryāna, N India
112 G5 **Sonepur** Orissa, E India

88 B4 **Sololá** *off.* Departamento de Sololá. ♦ *department* SW Guatemala
88 B4 **Sololá, Departamento de** *see* Sololá
136 E6 **Sololo** Eastern, N Kenya 03°33′N 38°39′E
88 B3 **Solomá** Huehuetenango, W Guatemala 15°38′N 91°25′W
82 G5 **Solomon** Kansas, C USA 64°33′N 164°00′E
75 E9 **Solomon** Kansas, C USA 38°55′N 97°22′W
281 H4 **Solomon Islands** *prev.* British Solomon Islands Protectorate. ♦ *commonwealth republic* W Solomon Islands N Melanesia W Pacific Ocean
281 J1 **Solomon Islands** *island group* Papua New Guinea/Solomon Islands
75 D9 **Solomon River** ♠ Kansas, C USA
286 D6 **Solomon Sea** *sea* W Pacific Ocean
54 D4 **Solon** Ohio, USA 41°23′N 81°26′W
189 K5 **Solone** Dnipropetrovs′ka Oblast′, E Ukraine 48°12′N 34°49′E
260 E8 **Solor, Kepulauan** *island group* S Indonesia
196 G2 **Solotcha** Ryazanskaya Oblast′, W Russian Federation 54°43′N 39°50′E
176 D4 **Solothurn** *Fr.* Soleure. ♦ *canton* NW Switzerland
176 D4 **Solothurn** *Fr.* Soleure. Solothurn, NW Switzerland 47°13′N 07°32′E
194 F3 **Solovetskiye Ostrova** *island group* NW Russian Federation
184 B3 **Solta** *It.* Solta. *island* S Croatia
Soltānābād *see* Kashmar
222 E3 **Soltāniyeh** Zanjan, N Iran 36°24′N 48°50′E
180 H4 **Soltau** Niedersachsen, NW Germany 52°59′N 09°50′E
180 I4 **Soltendieck** Niedersachsen, Germany 52°52′E 10°46′N
194 D4 **Sol′tsy** Novgorodskaya Oblast′, W Russian Federation 58°09′N 30°23′E
Soltüstik Qazaqstan Oblysy *see* Severnyy Kazakhstan
Solun *see* Thessaloníki
184 G7 **Solunska Glava** ▲ C FYR Macedonia 41°43′N 21°24′E
160 D5 **Solva** United Kingdom 51°52′N 5°12′W
155 G12 **Sölvesborg** Blekinge, S Sweden 56°04′N 14°35′E
159 I9 **Solway Firth** *inlet* England/Scotland, United Kingdom
135 H12 **Solwezi** North Western, NW Zambia 12°11′S 26°23′E
253 D11 **Sōma** Fukushima, Honshū, C Japan 37°49′N 140°52′E
214 B6 **Soma** Manisa, W Turkey 39°10′N 27°31′E
136 I4 **Somalia** *off.* Somali Democratic Republic, *Som.* Jamuuriyada Demuqraadiga Soomaaliyeed, Soomaaliya; *prev.* Italian Somaliland, Somaliland Protectorate. ♦ *republic* E Africa
290 D7 **Somali Basin** *undersea feature* W Indian Ocean 0°00′N 52°00′E
136 I4 **Somali Democratic Republic** *see* Somalia
121 N5 **Somali Plain** *undersea feature* W Indian Ocean 01°00′N 51°50′E
136 I3 **Somaliland** ♦ *disputed territory* N Somalia
136 I4 **Somaliland Protectorate** *see* Somalia
112 J3 **Somaroboro** *prev.* Tweefontein. Mpumalanga, South Africa 25°21′S 28°50′E *see also* Tweefontein
167 J8 **Sombernon** Bourgogne, France 47°18′N 4°42′E
183 H8 **Sombor** *Hung.* Zombor. Vojvodina, NW Serbia 45°46′N 19°07′E
163 E11 **Sombreffe** Namur, S Belgium 50°32′N 04°39′E
85 N8 **Sombrerete** Zacatecas, C Mexico 23°38′N 103°40′W
91 L5 **Sombrero** *island* N Anguilla
257 A10 **Sombrero Channel** *channel* Nicobar Islands, India
188 C6 **Somcuta Mare** *Hung.* Nagysomkút; *prev.* Somcuţa Mare. Maramureş, N Romania 47°29′S 23°28′E
156 G6 **Somdet** Kalasin, E Thailand 16°41′N 103°44′E
163 J9 **Someren** Noord-Brabant, SE Netherlands 51°23′N 05°42′E
153 H10 **Someron** Länsi-Suomi, SW Finland 60°37′N 23°30′E
76 H10 **Somers** Montana, NW USA 48°04′N 114°16′W
67 M10 **Somerset** Somerset Village. ♠ W Bermuda
32°18′N 64°53′E
80 B2 **Somerset** California, USA 38°39′N 120°41′W
79 K4 **Somerset** Colorado, C USA 38°55′N 107°24′W
66 I5 **Somerset** Kentucky, S USA 37°05′N 84°36′W
65 O5 **Somerset** Massachusetts, NE USA 41°46′N 71°07′W
66 B1 **Somerset** *cultural region* SW England, United Kingdom
141 H9 **Somerset East** Eastern Cape, South Africa 32°43′S 25°35′E
Somerset East *see* Somerset-Oos
67 M10 **Somerset Island** *island* W Bermuda
295 **Somerset Island** *island* Queen Elizabeth Islands, Nunavut, N Canada
Somerset Nile *see* Victoria Nile
138 D10 **Somerset-Oos** *var.* Somerset East. Eastern Cape, S South Africa 32°44′S 25°35′E
Somerset Village *see* Somerset
138 D10 **Somerset-Wes** *var.* Somerset West. Western Cape, SW South Africa 34°06′S 18°51′E
140 D10 **Somerset West** Western Cape, South Africa 34°06′S 18°51′E
Somerset West *see* Somerset-Wes
64 G9 **Somers Point** New Jersey, NE USA 39°18′N 74°34′W
63 J5 **Somersworth** New Hampshire, NE USA 43°15′N 70°52′W
79 H14 **Somerton** Arizona, SW USA 32°36′N 114°42′W
65 L2 **Somerville** Massachusetts, NE USA 42°22′N 71°06′W
64 B6 **Somerville** New Jersey, NE USA 40°34′N 74°37′W
71 I3 **Somerville** Tennessee, S USA 35°14′N 89°24′W
71 H6 **Somerville** Texas, SW USA 30°20′N 96°31′W
71 H6 **Somerville Lake** ☒ Texas, SW USA
Somes/Someschul/Someşul *see* Szamos
165 H2 **Somme** ♦ *department* N France
165 H2 **Somme** ♠ N France
155 H9 **Sommen** Jönköping, S Sweden 58°07′N 14°58′E
155 H9 **Sommen** ☒ S Sweden
167 I5 **Sommepy-Tahure** Champagne-Ardenne, France 49°15′N 4°33′E
Sommerfeld *see* Lubsko
181 I10 **Sömmerda** Thüringen, C Germany 51°10′N 11°07′E
167 I4 **Sommesous** Champagne-Ardenne, France 48°44′N 4°12′E
103 N9 **Sommet Tabulaire** *var.* Mont Itoupé. ▲ S French Guiana
169 I5 **Sommières** Languedoc-Roussillon, France 43°47′N 4°05′E
183 E12 **Somogy** *off.* Somogy Megye. ♦ *county* SW Hungary
183 E12 **Somogy Megye** *see* Somogy
173 H2 **Somolinos** Castilla-La Mancha, Spain 41°15′N 3°03′W
173 H1 **Somosierra** ♠ N Spain
170 G3 **Somosierra, Puerto de** *pass* N Spain
280 B4 **Somosomo** Taveuni, N Fiji 16°46′S 179°58′W
88 D5 **Somoto** Madríz, NW Nicaragua 13°29′N 86°36′W
182 F5 **Sompolno** Wielkopolskie, C Poland 52°24′N 18°30′E
168 E7 **Somport, Col du** *var.* Puerto de Somport, *Sp.* Somport; *anc.* Summus Portus. *pass* France/Spain
Somport, Puerto de *see* Somport, Col du
293 J2 **Sør Rondane** ▲ Antarctica
Sør Rondane Mountains *see* Sør Rondane
154 H1 **Sorsele** Västerbotten, N Sweden 65°31′N 17°34′E
175 B9 **Sorso** Sardegna, Italy, C Mediterranean Sea
263 M6 **Sorsogon** Luzon, N Philippines 12°57′N 124°01′E
194 E3 **Sortavala** *prev.* Serdobol′. Respublika Kareliya, NW Russian Federation 61°44′N 30°40′E
175 G13 **Sortino** Sicilia, Italy, C Mediterranean Sea 37°10′N 15°02′E
152 E4 **Sortland** Nordland, C Norway 68°44′N 15°25′E
154 E5 **Sør-Trøndelag** ♦ *county* S Norway
154 E4 **Sørumsand** Akershus, S Norway 59°58′N 11°15′E
154 I2 **Sos** Entre Ríos, E Argentina
152 I2 **Sos del Rey Católico** Aragón, NE Spain

205 L7 **Sông Ma** *Laos, Vam, Nam.* ♠ Laos/Vietnam
248 B4 **Songnim** SW North Korea 38°43′N 125°40′E
135 C10 **Songo** Uíge, NW Angola 07°30′S 14°50′E
135 C9 **Songolo** Bas-Congo, SW Dem. Rep. Congo 05°40′S 14°05′E
239 K7 **Songpan** *var.* Jin'an, *Tib.* Sungpu. Sichuan, C China 32°49′N 103°35′E
Songsan *see* Seongsan
245 H8 **Song Shan** ▲ Henan, C China 34°31′N 113°00′E
243 J6 **Songxi** Fujian, SE China 27°33′N 118°45′E
244 G8 **Songxian** *var.* Song Xian. Henan, C China 34°11′N 112°04′E
243 L4 **Song Xian** *var.* Xiping; *prev.* Songyin. Zhejiang, SE China 27°23′N 120°38′E
247 L5 **Songyuan** *var.* Fu-yü, Petuna; *prev.* Fuyu. Jilin, NE China 45°11′N 124°50′E
242 G3 **Songzi** Hubei, C China 30°06′N 111°28′E
Sonid Youqi *see* SaihanTal
Sonid Zuoqi *see* Mandalt
152 I7 **Sonkajärvi** Itä-Suomi, C Finland 63°40′N 27°30′E
256 G4 **Son La** N Vietnam 21°20′N 103°55′E
230 F9 **Sonmiāni** Baluchistān, S Pakistan 25°24′N 66°37′E
230 F9 **Sonmiāni Bay** *bay* S Pakistan
181 J11 **Sonneberg** Thüringen, C Germany 50°13′E 11°10′E
174 F2 **Sonntagsberg** ▲ Austria/Germany 47°40′N 12°42′E
84 A1 **Sonoita, Río** *var.* Río Sonoyta. ♠ Mexico/USA
80 B2 **Sonoma** California, W USA 38°16′N 122°28′W
84 B6 **Sonoma Peak** ▲ Nevada, W USA 40°50′N 117°34′W
80 C5 **Sonoma Valley** *valley* California, USA
80 D3 **Sonora** California, W USA 37°58′N 120°22′W
70 E6 **Sonora** Texas, SW USA 30°34′N 100°39′W
60 C8 **Sonora** ♦ *state* NW Mexico
60 C7 **Sonoran Desert** *var.* Desierto de Altar. *desert* Mexico/USA *see also* Altar, Desierto de
84 A1 **Sonora, Río** ♠ NW Mexico
84 D2 **Sonoyta** *var.* Sonoita. Sonora, NW Mexico 31°49′N 112°50′W
Sonoyta, Río *see* Sonoita, Río
222 E3 **Sonqor** *var.* Sunqur. Kermānshāhān, W Iran 34°45′N 47°39′E
Sönsan *see* Seonsan
170 C5 **Sonseca** *var.* Sonseca con Casalgordo. Castilla-La Mancha, C Spain 39°40′N 03°59′W
Sonseca con Casalgordo *see* Sonseca
102 B5 **Sonsón** Antioquia, W Colombia 05°45′N 75°18′W
88 C6 **Sonsonate** Sonsonate, W El Salvador 13°44′N 89°43′W
282 A7 **Sonsorol Islands** *island group* S Palau
140 F4 **Sonstraad** Northern Cape, South Africa 27°07′S 22°28′E
184 E2 **Sonta** *Hung.* Szonta. Vojvodina, NW Serbia 45°34′N 19°06′E
256 H4 **Son Tây** *var.* Sontay. Ha Tây, N Vietnam 21°06′N 105°32′E
Sontay *see* Son Tây
179 E13 **Sonthofen** ▲ S Germany 47°31′N 10°16′E
56 B7 **Sooke** Vancouver Island, British Columbia, SW Canada 48°04′N 123°42′W
136 C6 **Sool** Gobolka Sool. ♦ *region* N Somalia
Soomaaliya/Soomaaliyeed, Jamuuriyada Demuqraadiga *see* Somalia
Soome Laht *see* Finland, Gulf of
69 K2 **Soperton** Georgia, SE USA 32°22′N 82°35′W
205 I9 **Sop Hao** Houaphan, N Laos 20°33′N 104°25′E
Sopianae *see* Pécs
261 I5 **Sopinusa** Papua, E Indonesia 02°36′N 128°32′E
261 I5 **Sopi, Tanjung** *headland* Pulau Morotai, N Indonesia 02°34′N 128°18′E
190 C5 **Sopockinie/Sopoćkinie** *see* Sapotskin
185 J6 **Sopot** Plovdiv, C Bulgaria 42°39′N 24°45′E
182 F3 **Sopot** *Ger.* Zoppot. Pomorskie, N Poland 54°26′N 18°32′E
183 D11 **Sopron** *Ger.* Ödenburg. Győr-Moson-Sopron, NW Hungary 47°40′N 16°35′E
229 K6 **Sopu-Korgon** *var.* Sofi-Kurgan. Oshskaya Oblast′, SW Kyrgyzstan 40°03′N 73°30′E
232 D2 **Sopur** Jammu and Kashmir, NW India 34°19′N 74°30′E
175 F9 **Sora** Lazio, C Italy 41°43′N 13°37′E
184 D4 **Sorada** Orissa, E India
175 H9 **Söråker** Västernorrland, C Sweden 62°32′N 17°32′E
105 H9 **Sorata** La Paz, W Bolivia 15°47′N 68°40′W
Sorau/Sorau in der Niederlausitz *see* Zary
171 H5 **Sorbas** Andalucía, S Spain 37°06′N 02°06′W
154 H5 **Sörbygden** C Sweden
154 H5 **Sördelen** ☒ C Sweden
Sörd/Sörd Choluim Chille *see* Swords
168 A5 **Sore** Aquitaine, France 44°19′N 0°35′W
168 A5 **Sorel** Québec, SE Canada 46°03′N 73°06′W
277 J10 **Sorell** Tasmania, SE Australia 42°49′S 147°34′E
277 **Sorell, Lake** ☒ Tasmania, SE Australia
155 B7 **Sørfjorden** *fjord* S Norway
168 C6 **Sörforsa** Gävleborg, C Sweden 61°45′N 17°00′E
168 A9 **Sorgues** Vaucluse, SE France 44°01′N 4°52′E
214 F6 **Sorgun** Yozgat, C Turkey 39°49′N 35°10′E
171 I3 **Soria** Castilla-León, N Spain 41°46′N 02°28′W
171 I3 **Soria** ♦ *province* Castilla-León, N Spain
116 G2 **Soriano** Soriano, SW Uruguay 33°25′S 58°21′W
116 G2 **Soriano** ♦ *department* SW Uruguay
250 A5 **Sori-do** *island* SW South Korea
151 D1 **Sorisdale** United Kingdom 56°31′N 6°17′W
154 G5 **Sørkapp** *headland* SW Svalbard 76°34′N 16°33′E
154 H5 **Sørkappland** *physical region* S Svalbard
197 K3 **Sorochinsk** Orenburgskaya Oblast′, W Russian Federation 52°25′N 53°10′E
Soroki *see* Soroca
188 G6 **Soroca** *Rus.* Soroki. N Moldova 48°10′N 28°18′E
110 D7 **Sorocaba** São Paulo, S Brazil 23°30′S 47°32′W
114 E9 **Sorocaba** Buenos Aires, Argentina 35°02′S 57°37′W
197 K3 **Sorochinsk** Orenburgskaya Oblast′, W Russian Federation 52°25′N 53°10′E
Soroche *see* Sorochy
197 K3 **Sorokino** Pskovskaya Oblast′, Russian Federation
282 B4 **Sorol** *atoll* Caroline Islands, W Micronesia
261 I4 **Sorong** Papua, E Indonesia 0°50′S 131°15′E
136 C7 **Soroti** C Uganda 01°42′N 33°37′E
152 H2 **Sørøya** Sørøy, *Lapp.* Sállan. *island* N Norway
172 B3 **Sorraia, Rio** ♠ C Portugal
155 B8 **Sorreisa** Troms, N Norway 69°08′N 18°09′E
277 J8 **Sorrento** Victoria, SE Australia 38°20′S 144°45′E
152 H3 **Sorsatunturi** ▲ NE Finland
152 E4 **Sorsele** Västerbotten, N Sweden 65°31′N 17°34′E
293 J2 **Sør Rondane Mountains** *see* Sør Rondane
154 H1 **Sorso** Sardegna, Italy
263 M6 **Sorsogon** Luzon, N Philippines 12°57′N 124°01′E
192 E7 **Sort** Jammu and Kashmir, NW India 34°19′N 74°30′E
154 E5 **Sorata** *prev.* Serdobol′. Respublika Kareliya
175 G13 **Sortino** Sicilia, Italy
152 E4 **Sortland** Nordland, C Norway
169 G3 **Sosnovyy Bor** Leningradskaya Oblast′, W Russian Federation

194 E5 **Sosnovka** Murmanskaya Oblast′, NW Russian Federation
195 J10 **Sosnovka** Kirovskaya Oblast′, NW Russian Federation
197 I2 **Sosnovka** Chuvashskaya Respublika, W Russian Federation
194 G3 **Sosnovka** Arkhangel'skaya Oblast′, NW Russian Federation
192 G3 **Sosnogorsk** Respublika Komi, NW Russian Federation

◆ Country   ◇ Dependent Territory   ♦ Administrative Regions   ▲ Mountain   ☒ Volcano   ☒ Lake
● Country Capital   ○ Dependent Territory Capital   X International Airport   ▲ Mountain Range   ♠ River   ☒ Reservoir

Sosnovyy Bor – Stansted
INDEX
410

197 *L1* **Sosnovyy Bor** Respublika Bashkortostan, W Russian Federation *55°51´N 57°09´E*
Sosnovyy Bor *see* Sasnovy Bor
183 *F8* **Sosnowiec** ***Ger.*** Sosnowitz, ***Rus.*** Sosnovets. Śląskie, S Poland *50°16´N 19°07´E*
Sosnowitz *see* Sosnowiec
189 *I2* **Sosnytsya** Chernihivs'ka Oblast', N Ukraine *51°31´N 32°30´E*
169 *N5* **Sospel** Provence-Alpes-Côte d'Azur, France *43°53´N 7°27´E*
140 *B3* **Sossusvlei** *salt lake* Hardap, Namibia
177 *K5* **Šoštanj** N Slovenia *46°23´N 15°03´E*
195 *M8* **Sos'va** Sverdlovskaya Oblast', C Russian Federation *59°13´N 61°58´E*
195 *M8* **Sos'va** Sverdlovskaya Oblast', Russian Federation
102 *B7* **Sotará, Volcán** S Colombia *02°04´N 76°40´W*
132 *B10* **Sotavento, Ilhas de** ***var.*** Leeward Islands. *island group* S Cape Verde
87 *I7* **Soteapan** Veracruz-Llave, Mexico *18°14´N 94°52´W*
152 *I7* **Sotkamo** Oulu, C Finland *64°06´N 28°30´E*
85 *N8* **Soto la Marina** Tamaulipas, C Mexico *23°44´N 98°10´W*
85 *M8* **Soto la Marina, Río** C Mexico
154 *A7* **Sotra** *island* S Norway
180 *G4* **Sottrum** Niedersachsen, Germany *53°07´E 9°14´N*
173 *I5* **Sotuélamos** Castilla-La Manacha, Spain *39°02´N 2°34´W*
87 *L5* **Sotuta** Yucatán, Mexico *20°44´N 89°35´W*
87 *M5* **Sotuta** Yucatán, SE Mexico *20°34´N 89°00´W*
167 *J5* **Souain-Perthes-lés-Hurlus** Champagne-Ardenne, France *49°11´N 4°32´E*
134 *C6* **Souanké** Sangha, NW Congo *02°03´N 14°02´E*
132 *E8* **Soubré** S Ivory Coast *05°50´N 06°35´W*
187 *I9* **Soúda** ***var.*** Soúdha, ***Eng.*** Suda. Kríti, Greece, E Mediterranean Sea *35°29´N 24°04´E*
64 *F7* **Souderton** Pennsylvania, USA *40°19´N 75°20´W*
Soúdha *see* Soúda
Soueida *see* As Suwaydā'
166 *G8* **Souesmes** Centre, France *47°27´N 2°10´E*
167 *N5* **Soufflenheim** Alsace, France *48°50´N 7°58´E*
187 *J2* **Souflí** ***prev.*** Souflíon. Anatolikí Makedonía kai Thráki, NE Greece *41°12´N 26°18´E*
Souflíon *see* Souflí
91 *J3* **Soufrière** W Saint Lucia *13°51´N 61°03´W*
91 *J2* **Soufrière** Basse Terre, S Guadeloupe *16°03´N 61°39´W*
171 *K10* **Sougueur** Algeria
165 *H7* **Souillac** Lot, S France *44°53´N 01°29´E*
137 *G11* **Souillac** S Mauritius *20°31´S 57°31´E*
167 *K5* **Souilly** Lorraine, France *49°01´N 5°17´E*
131 *K1* **Souk Ahras** NE Algeria *36°14´N 08°00´E*
Souk el Arba du Rharb/Souk-el-Arba-du-Rharb/ Souk-el-Arba-el-Rhab *see* Souk-el-Arba-Rharb
130 *F2* **Souk-el-Arba-Rharb** ***var.*** Souk el Arba du Rharb, Souk-el-Arba-du-Rharb, Souk-el-Arba-el-Rhab. NW Morocco *34°38´N 06°00´W*
Soukhné *see* As Sukhnah
Sŏul *see* Seoul
168 *C2* **Soulac-sur-Mer** Gironde, SW France *45°31´N 01°06´W*
167 *J6* **Soulaines-Dhuys** Champagne-Ardenne, France *48°22´N 4°44´E*
Sŏul-t'ŭkpyŏlsi *see* Seoul
163 *G11* **Soumagne** Liège, E Belgium *50°36´N 05°48´E*
65 *J5* **Sound Beach** Long Island, New York, NE USA *40°56´N 72°58´W*
187 *H7* **Soúnio, Akrotírio** *headland* C Greece *37°39´N 24°01´E*
218 *E4* **Soûr** ***var.*** Şūr; ***anc.*** Tyre. SW Lebanon *33°18´N 35°30´E*
218 *E4* **Soûr** Lebanon *33°16´N 35°11´E*
Sources, Mont-aux- *see* Phofung
172 *B3* **Soure** Coimbra, N Portugal *40°04´N 08°38´W*
171 *M9* **Sour El Ghozlane** Algeria
55 *I10* **Souris** Manitoba, S Canada *49°38´N 100°17´W*
59 *K8* **Souris** Prince Edward Island, SE Canada *46°22´N 62°16´W*
74 *B1* **Souris River** ***var.*** Mouse River. Canada/USA
71 *J7* **Sour Lake** Texas, SW USA *30°08´N 94°24´W*
169 *H7* **Sournia** Languedoc-Roussillon, France *42°44´N 2°27´E*
186 *G5* **Soúrpi** Thessalía, C Greece *39°07´N 22°55´E*
172 *C1* **Sousa Rio** Porto, Portugal
168 *G3* **Sousceyrac** Midi-Pyrénées, France *44°52´N 2°02´E*
172 *C5* **Sousel** Portalegre, C Portugal *38°57´N 07°40´W*
131 *K1* **Sousse** ***var.*** Sūsah. NE Tunisia *35°46´N 10°38´E*
168 *C5* **Soustons** Aquitaine, France *43°45´N 1°19´W*
140 *G9* **Sout** Eastern Cape, South Africa
140 *E6* **Sout** Northern Cape, South Africa
140 *D8* **Sout** Western Cape, South Africa
62 *D2* **South** Ontario, S Canada
South *see* Sud
140 *E7* **South Africa** ***off.*** Republic of South Africa, ***Afr.*** Suid-Afrika. ◆ *republic* S Africa
South Africa, Republic of *see* South Africa
161 *K6* **Southall** United Kingdom *51°30´N 0°22´W*
161 *I4* **Southam** United Kingdom *52°15´N 1°23´W*
94 **South America** *continent*
46 *F9* **South American Plate** *tectonic feature*
65 *J2* **South Amherst** Massachusetts, USA *42°20´N 72°30´W*
161 *I8* **Southampton** ***hist.*** Hamwih, ***Lat.*** Clausentum. S England, United Kingdom *50°54´N 01°23´W*
65 *K5* **Southampton** Long Island, New York, NE USA *40°52´N 72°22´W*
55 *L3* **Southampton, Cape** *headland* Nunavut, NE Canada
55 *K2* **Southampton Island** *island* Nunavut, NE Canada
257 *A9* **South Andaman** *island* Andaman Islands, India, NE Indian Ocean
59 *J3* **South Aulatsivik Island** *island* Newfoundland and Labrador, E Canada
276 *F3* **South Australia** ◐ *state* S Australia
South Australian Abyssal Plain *see* South Australian Plain
286 *C8* **South Australian Basin** *undersea feature* SW Indian Ocean *38°00´S 126°00´E*
286 *C8* **South Australian Plain** ***var.*** South Australian Abyssal Plain. *undersea feature* SE Indian Ocean
79 *L8* **South Baldy** ▲ New Mexico, SW USA *33°59´N 107°11´W*
159 *L7* **South Bank** United Kingdom *54°34´N 1°09´W*
158 *G8* **South Barrule** *hill* S Isle of Man
69 *M8* **South Bay** Florida, SE USA *26°39´N 80°43´W*
62 *B3* **South Baymouth** Manitoulin Island, Ontario, S Canada *45°33´N 82°01´W*
73 *C8* **South Beloit** Illinois, N USA *42°29´N 89°02´W*
73 *F9* **South Bend** Indiana, N USA *41°40´N 86°15´W*
70 *G4* **South Bend** Texas, SW USA *32°58´N 98°39´W*
76 *B4* **South Bend** Washington, NW USA *46°38´N 123°48´W*
161 *L6* **South Benfleet** United Kingdom *51°32´N 0°33´E*
South Beveland *see* Zuid-Beveland
South Borneo *see* Kalimantan Selatan
67 *K5* **South Boston** Virginia, NE USA *36°42´N 78°58´W*
276 *E2* **South Branch Neales** *seasonal river* South Australia
64 *A9* **South Branch Potomac River** West Virginia, NE USA
278 *E10* **Southbridge** Canterbury, South Island, New Zealand *43°49´S 172°17´E*
65 *K3* **Southbridge** Massachusetts, NE USA *42°03´N 72°00´W*
141 *K7* **Southbroom** KwaZulu-Natal, South Africa *30°55´S 30°19´E*
277 *K10* **South Bruny Island** *island* Tasmania, SE Australia
63 *H4* **South Burlington** Vermont, NE USA *44°27´N 73°08´W*
64 *I4* **Southbury** Connecticut, NE USA *41°28´N 73°12´W*
91 *H4* **South Caicos** *island* S Turks and Caicos Islands
64 *I3* **South Canaan** Connecticut, NE USA *41°57´N 73°20´W*
South Cape *see* Ka Lae
67 *I8* **South Carolina** ***off.*** State of South Carolina, ***also known as*** The Palmetto State. ◐ *state* SE USA
South Carpathians *see* Carpaţii Meridionalii
159 *L9* **South Cave** United Kingdom *53°46´N 0°36´W*
South Celebes *see* Sulawesi Selatan
161 *H6* **South Cerney** United Kingdom *51°40´N 1°55´W*
67 *H3* **South Charleston** West Virginia, NE USA *38°22´N 81°42´W*
159 *K4* **South Charlton** United Kingdom *55°28´N 1°44´W*
286 *B5* **South China Basin** *undersea feature* SE South China Sea *15°00´N 115°00´E*
286 *B5* **South China Sea** ***Chin.*** Nan Hai, ***Ind.*** Laut Cina Selatan, ***Vtn.*** Biên Đông. *sea* SE Asia
64 *D3* **South Corning** New York, NE USA *42°07´N 77°02´W*
74 *C5* **South Dakota** ***off.*** State of South Dakota, ***also known as*** The Coyote State, Sunshine State. ◐ *state* N USA
69 *M5* **South Daytona** Florida, SE USA *29°09´N 81°01´W*
79 *L7* **South Domingo Pueblo** New Mexico, SW USA *35°28´N 106°24´W*
80 *C5* **South Dos Palos** California, USA *36°58´N 120°39´W*
161 *K7* **South Downs** *hill range* SE England, United Kingdom
138 *F6* **South East** ◐ *district* SE Botswana
132 *C10* **South East Bay** *bay* Ascension Island, C Atlantic Ocean
277 *J10* **South East Cape** *headland* Tasmania, SE Australia *43°36´S 146°52´E*
82 *F5* **Southeast Cape** *headland* Saint Lawrence Island, Alaska, USA *62°56´N 169°39´W*
South-East Celebes *see* Sulawesi Tenggara
286 *C9* **Southeast Indian Ridge** *undersea feature* Indian Ocean/Pacific Ocean *50°00´S 110°00´E*
Southeast Island *see* Tagula Island
276 *A6* **South East Isles** Western Australia, S Australia
287 *J10* **Southeast Pacific Basin** ***var.*** Belling Hausen Mulde. *undersea feature* SE Pacific Ocean *60°00´S 115°00´W*
132 *D10* **South East Point** *headland* SE Ascension Island
285 *N2* **South East Point** *headland* Victoria, S Australia *39°10´S 146°21´E*
61 *N10* **Southeast Point** *headland* Mayaguana, SE Bahamas *22°15´N 72°44´W*
285 *N1* **South East Point** *headland* Kiritimati, NE Kiribati *01°42´N 157°10´W*
South-East Sulawesi *see* Sulawesi Tenggara
57 *N2* **Southend** Saskatchewan, C Canada *56°20´N 103°14´W*
158 *E5* **Southend** United Kingdom *55°19´N 5°38´W*
161 *L6* **Southend-on-Sea** E England, United Kingdom *51°33´N 00°43´E*
138 *F6* **Southern** ***var.*** Bangwaketse, Ngwaketze. ◐ *district* SE Botswana
219 *D11* **Southern** ◐ *district* S Israel
137 *D14* **Southern** ◐ *region* S Malawi
235 *G11* **Southern** ◐ *province* S Sri Lanka
138 *F2* **Southern** ◐ *province* S Zambia
278 *D10* **Southern Alps** ▲▲ South Island, New Zealand
284 *G7* **Southern Cook Islands** *island group* S Cook Islands
274 *E7* **Southern Cross** Western Australia *31°17´S 119°15´E*
134 *H3* **Southern Darfur** ◐ *state* W Sudan
280 *A3* **Southern Highlands** ◐ *province* W Papua New Guinea
55 *I6* **Southern Indian Lake** Manitoba, C Canada
136 *B3* **Southern Kordofan** ◐ *state* C Sudan
280 *G9* **Southern Lau Group** *island group* Lau Group, SE Fiji
136 *D5* **Southern Nationalities** ◐ *region* S Ethiopia
289 *I13* **Southern Ocean** *ocean*
67 *J7* **Southern Pines** North Carolina, SE USA *35°10´N 79°23´W*
159 *H4* **Southern Uplands** ▲▲ S Scotland, United Kingdom
Southern Urals *see* Yuzhnyy Ural
161 *L3* **Southery** United Kingdom *52°31´N 0°22´E*
159 *I1* **South Esk** United Kingdom
277 *J9* **South Esk River** Tasmania, SE Australia
57 *N7* **Southey** Saskatchewan, S Canada *50°53´N 104°27´W*
141 *I8* **Southeyville** Eastern Cape, South Africa *31°47´S 27°27´E*
75 *I8* **South Fabius River** Missouri, C USA
159 *L9* **South Ferriby** United Kingdom *53°40´N 0°30´W*
73 *H8* **Southfield** Michigan, N USA *42°28´N 83°12´W*
286 *F7* **South Fiji Basin** *undersea feature* S Pacific Ocean *26°00´S 175°00´E*
161 *M7* **South Foreland** *headland* SE England, United Kingdom *51°08´N 01°22´E*
80 *E2* **South Fork American River** California, W USA
74 *B4* **South Fork Grand River** South Dakota, N USA
81 *F8* **South Fork Kern River** California, W USA
83 *I4* **South Fork Koyukuk River** Alaska, USA
83 *I6* **South Fork Kuskokwim River** Alaska, USA
75 *B9* **South Fork Republican River** C USA
75 *D9* **South Fork Solomon River** Kansas, C USA
72 *F5* **South Fox Island** *island* Michigan, N USA
66 *C5* **South Fulton** Tennessee, S USA *36°28´N 88°53´W*
81 *D10* **South Gate** California, USA *33°57´N 118°13´W*
293 *J6* **South Geomagnetic Pole** *pole* Antarctica
291 *F12* **South Georgia** *island* South Georgia and the South Sandwich Islands, SW Atlantic Ocean
291 *E12* **South Georgia and the South Sandwich Islands** ◇ *UK Dependent Territory* SW Atlantic Ocean
95 *N9* **South Georgia Ridge** ***var.*** North Scotia Ridge. *undersea feature* SW Atlantic Ocean *54°00´S 40°00´W*
275 *H2* **South Goulburn Island** *island* Northern Territory, N Australia
161 *J7* **South Harting** United Kingdom *50°58´N 0°53´W*
233 *L8* **South Hatia Island** *island* SE Bangladesh
73 *F8* **South Haven** Michigan, N USA *42°24´N 86°16´W*
161 *J8* **South Hayling** United Kingdom *50°47´N 0°58´W*
55 *I4* **South Henik Lake** Nunavut, E Canada
67 *K5* **South Hill** Virginia, NE USA *36°43´N 78°07´W*
South Holland *see* Zuid-Holland
67 *H5* **South Holston Lake** Tennessee/Virginia, S USA
266 *G1* **South Honshu Ridge** *undersea feature* W Pacific Ocean
65 *L1* **South Hooksett** New Hampshire, USA *43°02´N 71°26´W*
75 *D10* **South Hutchinson** Kansas, C USA *38°01´N 97°56´W*
235 *C14* **South Huvadhu Atoll** *atoll* S Maldives
289 *J13* **South Indian Basin** *undersea feature* Indian Ocean/Pacific Ocean *60°00´S 120°00´E*
55 *I6* **South Indian Lake** Manitoba, C Canada *56°48´N 98°56´W*
65 *J4* **Southington** Connecticut, USA *41°36´N 72°53´W*
136 *D7* **South Island** *island* NW Kenya
279 *C9* **South Island** *island* S New Zealand
South Kalimantan *see* Kalimantan Selatan
South Kazakhstan *see* Yuzhnyy Kazakhstan
159 *M9* **South Kelsey** United Kingdom *53°28´N 0°26´W*
55 *J6* **South Knife River** Manitoba, C Canada
248 *C6* **South Korea** ***off.*** Republic of Korea, ***Kor.*** Taehan Min'guk. ◆ *republic* E Asia
80 *F2* **South Lake Tahoe** California, W USA *38°56´N 119°57´W*
70 *E4* **Southland** Texas, SW USA *33°16´N 101°31´W*
278 *B12* **Southland** ***off.*** Southland Region. ◐ *region* South Island, New Zealand
Southland Region *see* Southland
161 *H5* **South Littleton** United Kingdom *52°06´N 1°53´W*
75 *D8* **South Loup River** Nebraska, C USA
235 *C12* **South Maalhosmadulu Atoll** *atoll* N Maldives
62 *B5* **South Maitland** Ontario, S Canada
286 *B6* **South Makassar Basin** *undersea feature* E Java Sea
72 *E5* **South Manitou Island** *island* Michigan, N USA
235 *C11* **South Miladhunmadulu Atoll** ***var.*** Noonu. *atoll* N Maldives
64 *I4* **South Millbrook** New York, NE USA *41°46´N 73°41´W*
67 *M5* **South Mills** North Carolina, SE USA *36°28´N 76°18´W*
160 *F7* **South Molton** United Kingdom *51°01´N 3°50´W*
52 *B10* **South Nahanni** Northwest Territories, NW Canada
83 *H7* **South Naknek** Alaska, USA *58°39´N 157°01´W*
62 *G4* **South Nation** Ontario, SE Canada
89 *L1* **South Negril Point** *headland* W Jamaica *18°14´N 78°21´W*
64 *F2* **South New Berlin** New York, USA *42°32´N 75°23´W*
235 *B13* **South Nilandhe Atoll** ***var.*** Dhaalu Atoll. *atoll* C Maldives
79 *H2* **South Ogden** Utah, W USA *41°09´N 111°58´W*
65 *K5* **Southold** Long Island, New York, NE USA *41°03´N 72°24´W*
292 *E1* **South Orkney Islands** *island group* Antarctica
80 *D1* **South Oroville** California, USA *39°30´N 121°33´W*
South Pacific Basin *see* Southwest Pacific Basin
63 *J4* **South Paris** Maine, NE USA *44°14´N 70°33´W*
282 *F9* **South Pass** *passage* Chuuk Islands, C Micronesia
77 *K8* **South Pass** *pass* Wyoming, C USA
160 *G8* **South Petherton** United Kingdom *50°57´N 2°48´W*
66 *E7* **South Pittsburg** Tennessee, S USA *35°00´N 85°42´W*
79 *N2* **South Platte River** Colorado/Nebraska, C USA
67 *H3* **South Point** Ohio, N USA *38°25´N 82°35´W*
132 *C10* **South Point** *headland* S Ascension Island
72 *H6* **South Point** *headland* Michigan, N USA *44°51´N 83°17´W*
South Point *see* Ka Lae
293 *I5* **South Pole** *pole* Antarctica
277 *J10* **Southport** Tasmania, SE Australia *43°26´S 146°57´E*
159 *I9* **Southport** NW England, United Kingdom *53°39´N 03°01´W*
64 *D3* **Southport** New York, USA *42°03´N 76°49´W*
67 *L8* **Southport** North Carolina, SE USA *33°55´N 78°00´W*
63 *J5* **South Portland** Maine, NE USA *43°38´N 70°14´W*
62 *D2* **South River** Ontario, S Canada *45°50´N 79°23´W*
65 *H6* **South River** New Jersey, USA *40°27´N 74°23´W*
67 *K7* **South River** North Carolina, SE USA
156 *G3* **South Ronaldsay** *island* NE Scotland, United Kingdom
79 *H2* **South Salt Lake** Utah, W USA *40°42´N 111°52´W*
291 *G13* **South Sandwich Fracture Zone** *tectonic feature* S Atlantic Ocean
291 *F13* **South Sandwich Trench** *undersea feature* SW Atlantic Ocean *56°30´S 25°00´W*
80 *B3* **South San Francisco** California, USA *37°39´N 122°24´W*
57 *L7* **South Saskatchewan** Alberta/Saskatchewan, S Canada
291 *E13* **South Scotia Ridge** *undersea feature* S Scotia Sea
55 *I6* **South Seal** Manitoba, C Canada
292 *D3* **South Shetland Islands** *island group* Antarctica
291 *D13* **South Shetland Trough** *undersea feature* Atlantic Ocean/Pacific Ocean *61°00´S 59°30´W*
159 *K5* **South Shields** NE England, United Kingdom *55°N 01°25´W*
286 *E6* **South Solomon Trench** *undersea feature* W Pacific Ocean
277 *N2* **South Stradbroke Island** *island* Queensland, E Australia
136 *B5* **South Sudan** ***off.*** Republic of South Sudan. ◆ *republic* E Africa
South Sudan, Republic off *see* South Sudan
South Sulawesi *see* Sulawesi Selatan
South Sumatra *see* Sumatera Selatan
278 *G6* **South Taranaki Bight** *bight* SE Tasman Sea
South Tasmania Plateau *see* Tasman Plateau
79 *I10* **South Tucson** Arizona, SW USA *32°11´N 110°56´W*
53 *J8* **South Tweedsmuir Island** *Island* Nunavut, NE Canada
58 *F5* **South Twin Island** *island* Nunavut, C Canada
159 *J6* **South Tyne** United Kingdom
156 *C5* **South Uist** *island* NW Scotland, United Kingdom
141 *I9* **Southwell** Eastern Cape, South Africa *31°09´S 25°56´E*
South-West *see* Sud-Ouest
South-West Africa/South West Africa *see* Namibia
132 *C10* **South West Bay** *bay* Ascension Island, C Atlantic Ocean
277 *J10* **South West Cape** *headland* Tasmania, SE Australia *43°34´S 146°01´E*
278 *B13* **South West Cape** *headland* Stewart Island, New Zealand *47°15´S 167°28´E*
82 *E5* **Southwest Cape** *headland* Saint Lawrence Island, Alaska, USA *63°19´N 171°27´W*
263 *H7* **Southwest Cay** *island* NW Spratly Islands
Southwest Indian Ocean Ridge *see* Southwest Indian Ridge
289 *D11* **Southwest Indian Ridge** ***var.*** Southwest Indian Ocean Ridge. *undersea feature* SW Indian Ocean *43°00´S 40°00´E*
287 *H9* **Southwest Pacific Basin** ***var.*** South Pacific Basin. *undersea feature* SE Pacific Ocean *40°00´S 150°00´W*
90 *E2* **Southwest Point** *headland* Great Abaco, N Bahamas *25°50´N 77°12´W*
285 *M2* **South West Point** *headland* Kiritimati, NE Kiribati *01°53´N 157°34´E*
132 *G10* **South West Point** *headland* SW Saint Helena *16°00´S 05°48´W*
70 *F3* **South Wichita River** Texas, SW USA
64 *D5* **South Williamsport** Pennsylvania, USA *41°14´N 77°00´W*
161 *N4* **Southwold** E England, United Kingdom *52°15´N 01°36´E*
65 *N4* **South Yarmouth** Massachusetts, NE USA *41°38´N 70°09´W*
172 *D1* **Souto** Viseu, Portugal *41°01´N 7°21´W*
141 *H6* **Soutpan** Free State, South Africa *28°43´S 26°04´E*
141 *J3* **Soutpan** Gauteng, South Africa *25°24´S 28°06´E*
141 *K1* **Soutpansberg** ▲▲ Limpopo, South Africa
140 *G9* **Soutpansnek** *pass* Eastern Cape, South Africa
167 *I10* **Souvigny** Auvergne, France *46°32´N 3°11´E*
172 *B3* **Souzelas** Coimbra, Portugal *40°06´N 8°43´W*
245 *J5* **Souzhen** Shandong, E China *37°00´N 117°16´E*
188 *D7* **Sovata** ***Hung.*** Szováta. Mureş, C Romania *46°36´N 25°04´E*
175 *H11* **Soverato** Calabria, SW Italy *38°40´N 16°31´E*
216 *A4* **Sovereign Base Area** *uk military installation* S Cyprus
Sovetabad *see* Ghafurov
191 *B8* **Sovetsk** ***Ger.*** Tilsit. Kaliningradskaya Oblast', W Russian Federation *53°04´N 21°52´E*
195 *I9* **Sovetsk** Kirovskaya Oblast', NW Russian Federation *57°37´N 49°02´E*
197 *H6* **Sovetskaya** Rostovskaya Oblast', SW Russian Federation *49°00´N 42°09´E*
193 *L8* **Sovetskaya Gavan'** Khabarovskiy Kray, SE Russian Federation *48°54´N 140°19´E*
195 *M7* **Sovetskiy** Khanty-Mansiyskiy Avtonomnyy Okrug-Yugra, C Russian Federation *61°20´N 63°34´E*
Sovetskoye *see* Ketchenery
228 *E8* **Sovet"yab** ***prev.*** Sovet"yap. Ahal Welaýaty, S Turkmenistan *36°29´N 61°13´E*
Sovet"yap *see* Sovet"yab
189 *K8* **Sovyets'kyy** Avtonomna Respublika Krym, S Ukraine *45°20´N 34°54´E*
138 *F4* **Sowa** ***var.*** Sua. Central, NE Botswana *20°33´S 26°18´E*
138 *F4* **Sowa Pan** ***var.*** Sua Pan. *salt lake* NE Botswana
261 *J4* **Sowek** Papua, E Indonesia *0°46´S 135°31´E*
141 *I4* **Soweto** Gauteng, NE South Africa *26°08´S 27°54´E*
229 *J6* **So'x** ***Rus.*** Sokh. Farg'ona Viloyati, E Uzbekistan *39°56´N 71°10´E*
Sōya-kaikyō *see* La Pérouse Strait
252 *E1* **Sōya-misaki** *headland* Hokkaidō, NE Japan *45°31´N 141°55´E*
194 *G5* **Soyana** NW Russian Federation
228 *A4* **Soye, Mys** ***var.*** Mys Suz. *headland* NW Turkmenistan *41°47´N 52°27´E*
135 *B10* **Soyo** Dem. Rep. Congo, NW Angola *06°07´S 12°18´E*
136 *E2* **Soyra** ▲ C Eritrea *14°46´N 39°29´E*
227 *H7* **Sozak** ***Kaz.*** Sozaq; ***prev.*** Suzak. Yuzhnyy Kazakhstan, S Kazakhstan *44°09´N 68°28´E*
Sozaq *see* Sozak
191 *I11* **Sozh** NE Europe
185 *M6* **Sozopol** ***prev.*** Sizebolu; ***anc.*** Apollonia. Burgas, E Bulgaria *42°25´N 27°42´E*
163 *H11* **Spa** Liège, E Belgium *50°29´N 05°52´E*
292 *F4* **Spaatz Island** *island* Antarctica
226 *G6* **Space Launching Centre** *space station* Kzylorda, S Kazakhstan
170 *F5* **Spain** ***off.*** Kingdom of Spain, ***Sp.*** España; ***anc.*** Hispania, Iberia, ***Lat.*** Hispana. ◆ *monarchy* SW Europe
Spain, Kingdom of *see* Spain
Spalato *see* Split
161 *K3* **Spalding** E England, United Kingdom *52°49´N 00°06´W*
161 *K4* **Spaldwick** United Kingdom *52°20´N 0°20´W*
181 *J14* **Spalt** Bayern, Germany *49°10´E 10°55´N*
62 *B2* **Spanish** Ontario, S Canada *46°12´N 82°21´W*
79 *H3* **Spanish Fork** Utah, W USA *40°09´N 111°40´W*
67 *M10* **Spanish Point** *headland* C Bermuda *32°18´N 64°49´W*
62 *B1* **Spanish River** Ontario, S Canada
90 *F8* **Spanish Town** ***hist.*** St.Iago de la Vega. C Jamaica *18°N 76°57´W*
187 *H9* **Spánta, Ákra** *cape* Kríti, Greece, E Mediterranean Sea
Spánta, Akrotírio *see* Spátha, Akrotírio
141 *I2* **Spanwerk** Limpopo, South Africa *24°01´S 26°55´E*
80 *F1* **Sparks** Nevada, W USA *39°32´N 119°45´W*
Sparnacum *see* Épernay
155 *I8* **Sparreholm** Södermanland, C Sweden *59°04´N 16°51´E*
64 *G4* **Sparrow Bush** New York, NE USA *41°24´N 74°43´W*
66 *G9* **Sparta** Georgia, SE USA *33°16´N 82°58´W*
73 *C12* **Sparta** Illinois, N USA *38°07´N 89°42´W*
72 *F7* **Sparta** Michigan, N USA *43°09´N 85°42´W*
64 *G5* **Sparta** New Jersey, USA *41°02´N 74°38´W*
67 *I5* **Sparta** North Carolina, SE USA *36°30´N 81°07´W*
66 *E6* **Sparta** Tennessee, S USA *35°55´N 85°30´W*
72 *B6* **Sparta** Wisconsin, N USA *43°57´N 90°50´W*
Sparta *see* Spárti
67 *H7* **Spartanburg** South Carolina, SE USA *34°56´N 81°57´W*
130 *F2* **Spartel, Cap** *headland* N Morocco *35°49´N 05°55´W*
186 *G7* **Spárti** ***Eng.*** Sparta. Pelopónnisos, S Greece *37°05´N 22°25´E*
175 *B11* **Spartivento, Capo** *headland* Sardegna, Italy, C Mediterranean Sea *38°52´N 08°50´E*
57 *I8* **Sparwood** British Columbia, SW Canada *49°45´N 114°45´W*
196 *E2* **Spas-Demensk** Kaluzhskaya Oblast', W Russian Federation *54°22´N 34°16´E*
196 *G2* **Spas-Klepiki** Ryazanskaya Oblast', W Russian Federation *55°08´N 40°15´E*
Spasovo *see* Kulen Vakuf
193 *L9* **Spassk-Dal'niy** Primorskiy Kray, SE Russian Federation *44°34´N 132°52´E*
196 *G3* **Spassk-Ryazanskiy** Ryazanskaya Oblast', W Russian Federation *54°25´N 40°21´E*
187 *H9* **Spátha, Akrotírio** ***var.*** Akrotírio Spánta. *headland* Kríti, Greece, E Mediterranean Sea *35°42´N 23°44´E*
Špatrjan *see* Paternion
158 *F1* **Spean Bridge** United Kingdom *56°53´N 4°54´W*
74 *A5* **Spearfish** South Dakota, N USA *44°29´N 103°51´W*
70 *E1* **Spearman** Texas, SW USA *36°12´N 101°13´W*
117 *H11* **Speedwell Island** *island* S Falkland Islands
132 *F10* **Speery Island** *island* S Saint Helena
181 *B12* **Speicher** Rheinland-Pfalz, Germany *49°56´E 6°38´N*
91 *K3* **Speightstown** NW Barbados *13°15´N 59°39´W*
177 *I10* **Spello** Umbria, C Italy *43°00´N 12°41´E*
83 *I6* **Spenard** Alaska, USA *61°09´N 150°03´W*
53 *H8* **Spence Bay** *coastal sea feature* Nunavut, NE Canada
Spence Bay *see* Taloyoak
73 *E11* **Spencer** Indiana, N USA *39°18´N 86°46´W*
74 *F6* **Spencer** Iowa, C USA *43°09´N 95°07´W*
65 *K3* **Spencer** Massachusetts, USA *42°15´N 72°00´W*
74 *D6* **Spencer** Nebraska, C USA *42°52´N 98°42´W*
67 *J6* **Spencer** North Carolina, SE USA *35°41´N 80°26´W*
66 *E6* **Spencer** Tennessee, S USA *35°46´N 85°27´W*
67 *I3* **Spencer** West Virginia, NE USA *38°48´N 81°22´W*
72 *C6* **Spencer** Wisconsin, N USA *44°46´N 90°17´W*
276 *F6* **Spencer, Cape** *headland* South Australia *35°17´S 136°52´E*
83 *L7* **Spencer, Cape** *headland* Alaska, USA *58°12´N 136°39´W*
276 *F5* **Spencer Gulf** *gulf* South Australia
62 *E5* **Spencerport** New York, NE USA *43°11´N 77°48´W*
73 *G10* **Spencerville** Ohio, N USA *40°42´N 84°21´W*
159 *K6* **Spennymoor** United Kingdom *54°41´N 1°36´W*
186 *G5* **Spercheiáda** ***var.*** Sperhiada, Sperkhiás. Stereá Elláda, C Greece *38°54´N 22°07´E*
Sperhiada *see* Spercheiáda
154 *D7* **Sperillen** S Norway
Sperkhiás *see* Spercheiáda
158 *C6* **Sperrin Mountains** ▲▲ United Kingdom
141 *I4* **Spes Bona** Free State, South Africa *27°07´S 27°08´E*
181 *G12* **Spessart** *hill range* C Germany
Spétsai *see* Spétses
187 *H7* **Spétses** ***prev.*** Spétsai. Spétses, S Greece *37°16´N 23°09´E*
187 *H7* **Spétses** *island* S Greece
156 *F5* **Spey** NE Scotland, United Kingdom
181 *E13* **Speyer** ***Eng.*** Spires; ***anc.*** Civitas Nemetum, Spira. Rheinland-Pfalz, SW Germany *49°18´N 08°26´E*
181 *E13* **Speyerbach** W Germany
175 *H10* **Spezzano Albanese** Calabria, SW Italy *39°40´N 16°17´E*
Spice Islands *see* Maluku
53 *J8* **Spicer Islands** *Island group* Nunavut, NE Canada
181 *G14* **Spiegelberg** Baden-Württemberg, Germany *49°02´E 9°27´N*
180 *F2* **Spieka** Niedersachsen, Germany *53°45´E 8°35´N*
180 *D2* **Spiekeroog** *island* NW Germany
177 *L4* **Spielfeld** Steiermark, SE Austria *46°43´N 15°36´E*
167 *N9* **Spiez** Bern, W Switzerland *46°42´N 07°41´E*
162 *E7* **Spijkenisse** Zuid-Holland, SW Netherlands *51°52´N 04°19´E*
83 *J3* **Spike Mountain** ▲ Alaska, USA *67°42´N 141°39´W*
187 *I10* **Spíli** Kríti, Greece, E Mediterranean Sea *35°12´N 24°33´E*
174 *B3* **Spillgerten** ▲ W Switzerland *46°34´N 07°25´E*
159 *M10* **Spilsby** United Kingdom *53°11´N 0°06´E*
190 *D6* **Spilve** (Rīga) Rīga, C Latvia *56°55´N 24°03´E*
175 *H9* **Spinazzola** Puglia, SE Italy *40°58´N 16°06´E*
230 *F6* **Spīn Būldak** Kandahār, S Afghanistan *31°01´N 66°23´E*
167 *K4* **Spincourt** Lorraine, France *49°20´N 5°40´E*
141 *J6* **Spioenkopdam** KwaZulu-Natal, South Africa
Spira *see* Speyer
Spirdingsee *see* Śniardwy, Jezioro
Spires *see* Speyer
56 *G3* **Spirit River** Alberta, W Canada *55°46´N 118°51´W*
57 *L5* **Spiritwood** Saskatchewan, S Canada *53°18´N 107°33´W*
75 *G12* **Spiro** Oklahoma, C USA *35°14´N 94°37´W*
183 *H10* **Spišská Nová Ves** ***Ger.*** Neudorf, Zipser Neudorf, ***Hung.*** Igló. Košický Kraj, E Slovakia *48°58´N 20°35´E*
215 *K5* **Spitak** NW Armenia *40°51´N 44°17´E*
152 *B5* **Spitsbergen** *island* NW Svalbard
160 *D5* **Spittal** United Kingdom *51°52´N 4°57´W*
Spittal *see* Spittal an der Drau
177 *I4* **Spittal an der Drau** ***var.*** Spittal. Kärnten, S Austria *46°48´N 13°30´E*
159 *H1* **Spittal of Glenshee** United Kingdom *56°48´N 3°28´W*
177 *K2* **Spitz** Niederösterreich, NE Austria *48°24´N 15°22´E*
154 *B4* **Spjelkavik** Møre og Romsdal, S Norway *62°28´N 06°22´E*
71 *I6* **Splendora** Texas, SW USA *30°13´N 95°09´W*
184 *C5* **Split** ***It.*** Spalato. Split-Dalmacija, S Croatia *43°31´N 16°27´E*
184 *C5* **Split** ✈ Split-Dalmacija, S Croatia *43°33´N 16°19´E*
184 *C5* **Split-Dalmacija** ***off.*** Splitsko-Dalmatinska Županija. ◐ *province* S Croatia
55 *J7* **Split Lake** Manitoba, C Canada
Splitsko-Dalmatinska Županija *see* Split-Dalmacija
176 *E5* **Splügen** Graubünden, S Switzerland *46°33´N 09°18´E*
Spodnji Dravograd *see* Dravograd
70 *E7* **Spofford** Texas, SW USA *29°10´N 100°24´W*
159 *K8* **Spofforth** United Kingdom *53°57´N 1°27´W*
190 *F7* **Špoģi** Daugvapils, SE Latvia *56°03´N 26°47´E*
76 *F4* **Spokane** Washington, NW USA *47°40´N 117°26´W*
76 *E3* **Spokane River** Washington, NW USA
174 *E7* **Spoleto** Umbria, C Italy *42°44´N 12°44´E*
72 *A4* **Spooner** Wisconsin, N USA *45°51´N 91°49´W*
73 *B10* **Spoon River** Illinois, N USA
67 *L3* **Spotsylvania** Virginia, NE USA *38°12´N 77°35´W*
80 *I7* **Spotted Range** ▲▲ Nevada, USA
76 *E4* **Sprague** Washington, NW USA *47°19´N 117°55´W*
181 *H14* **Spraitbach** Baden-Württemberg, Germany *48°53´E 9°46´N*
180 *D6* **Sprakel** Nordrhein-Westfalen, Germany *52°03´E 7°37´N*
262 *G8* **Spratly Island** *island* SW Spratly Islands
263 *H7* **Spratly Islands** ***Chin.*** Nansha Qundao. ◇ *disputed territory* SE Asia
76 *D6* **Spray** Oregon, NW USA *44°30´N 119°38´W*
184 *E4* **Spreča** N Bosnia and Herzegovina
80 *B5* **Spreckels** California, USA *36°37´N 121°39´W*
178 *I7* **Spree** E Germany
178 *I7* **Spreewald** *wetland* NE Germany
179 *I8* **Spremberg** Brandenburg, E Germany *51°34´N 14°22´E*
181 *F12* **Sprendlingen** Hessen, Germany *50°01´E 8°42´N*
181 *E12* **Sprendlingen** Rheinland-Pfalz, Germany *49°52´E 7°59´N*
159 *M10* **Spridlington** United Kingdom *53°21´N 0°29´W*
71 *I7* **Spring** Texas, SW USA *30°03´N 95°24´W*
73 *G8* **Spring Arbor** Michigan, N USA *42°12´N 84°33´W*
140 *C6* **Springbok** Northern Cape, W South Africa *29°44´S 17°56´E*
64 *F7* **Spring City** Pennsylvania, NE USA *40°10´N 75°33´W*
66 *F6* **Spring City** Tennessee, S USA *35°41´N 84°51´W*
79 *I3* **Spring City** Utah, W USA *39°28´N 111°30´W*
78 *F2* **Spring Creek** Nevada, W USA *40°45´N 115°40´W*
75 *G12* **Springdale** Arkansas, C USA *36°11´N 94°07´W*
73 *G11* **Springdale** Ohio, N USA *39°17´N 84°29´W*
180 *G6* **Springe** Niedersachsen, N Germany *52°13´N 09°33´E*
79 *M6* **Springer** New Mexico, SW USA *36°21´N 104°35´W*
79 *N5* **Springfield** Colorado, C USA *37°24´N 102°36´W*
69 *L2* **Springfield** Georgia, SE USA *32°21´N 81°20´W*
73 *C11* **Springfield** *state capital* Illinois, N USA *39°48´N 89°39´W*
66 *F4* **Springfield** Kentucky, S USA *37°42´N 85°18´W*
65 *J3* **Springfield** Massachusetts, NE USA *42°06´N 72°32´W*
74 *F5* **Springfield** Minnesota, N USA *44°15´N 94°58´W*
75 *H11* **Springfield** Missouri, C USA *37°13´N 93°18´W*
73 *H11* **Springfield** Ohio, N USA *39°55´N 83°49´W*
76 *B6* **Springfield** Oregon, NW USA *44°03´N 123°01´W*
74 *E6* **Springfield** South Dakota, N USA *42°51´N 97°54´W*
66 *D5* **Springfield** Tennessee, S USA *36°30´N 86°54´W*
63 *I5* **Springfield** Vermont, NE USA *43°18´N 72°27´W*
73 *C11* **Springfield, Lake** Illinois, N USA
141 *H7* **Springfontein** Free State, South Africa *30°16´S 25°42´E*
103 *K4* **Spring Garden** NE Guyana *06°58´N 58°34´W*
72 *C7* **Spring Green** Wisconsin, N USA *43°10´N 90°02´W*
72 *A7* **Spring Grove** Minnesota, N USA *43°33´N 91°38´W*
59 *J8* **Springhill** Nova Scotia, SE Canada *45°40´N 64°04´W*
69 *L6* **Spring Hill** Florida, SE USA *28°28´N 82°36´W*
75 *G10* **Spring Hill** Kansas, C USA *38°44´N 94°49´W*
68 *B1* **Springhill** Louisiana, S USA *33°01´N 93°27´W*
66 *D6* **Spring Hill** Tennessee, S USA *35°46´N 86°55´W*
67 *K7* **Spring Lake** North Carolina, SE USA *35°10´N 78°58´W*
70 *D3* **Springlake** Texas, SW USA *34°13´N 102°18´W*
81 *I8* **Spring Mountains** ▲▲ Nevada, W USA
75 *I11* **Spring River** Arkansas/Missouri, C USA
75 *G11* **Spring River** Missouri/Oklahoma, C USA
138 *G6* **Springs** Gauteng, NE South Africa *26°16´S 28°26´E*
279 *E9* **Springs Junction** West Coast, South Island, New Zealand *42°21´S 172°11´E*
275 *K5* **Springsure** Queensland, E Australia *24°09´S 148°06´E*
81 *E13* **Spring Valley** California, USA *32°45´N 117°00´W*
74 *H6* **Spring Valley** Minnesota, N USA *43°41´N 92°23´W*
65 *H5* **Spring Valley** New York, NE USA *41°10´N 73°58´W*
74 *C6* **Springview** Nebraska, C USA *42°49´N 99°45´W*
80 *E7* **Springville** California, USA *36°08´N 118°49´W*
81 *C9* **Springville** California, USA *34°13´N 119°06´W*
64 *A2* **Springville** New York, NE USA *42°27´N 78°52´W*
79 *I3* **Springville** Utah, W USA *40°10´N 111°36´W*
Sprottau *see* Szprotawa
180 *H3* **Sprötze** Niedersachsen, Germany *53°19´E 9°49´N*
159 *J4* **Sprouston** United Kingdom *55°36´N 2°23´W*
57 *I5* **Spruce Grove** Alberta, SW Canada *53°36´N 113°55´W*
67 *J3* **Spruce Knob** ▲ West Virginia, NE USA *38°40´N 79°37´W*
78 *G2* **Spruce Mountain** ▲ Nevada, W USA *40°33´N 114°46´W*
67 *H6* **Spruce Pine** North Carolina, SE USA *35°55´N 82°03´W*
163 *D9* **Spui** SW Netherlands
175 *I10* **Spulico, Capo** *headland* S Italy *39°57´N 16°38´E*
70 *E4* **Spur** Texas, SW USA *33°28´N 100°51´W*
159 *N9* **Spurn Head** *headland* E England, United Kingdom *53°34´N 00°06´E*
163 *E11* **Spy** Namur, S Belgium *50°29´N 04°43´E*
155 *E8* **Spydeberg** Østfold, S Norway *59°36´N 11°04´E*
279 *F9* **Spy Glass Point** *headland* South Island, New Zealand *42°33´S 173°31´E*
140 *G6* **Spytfontein** Northern Cape, South Africa *28°53´S 24°41´E*
56 *D8* **Squamish** British Columbia, SW Canada *49°41´N 123°11´W*
63 *J5* **Squam Lake** New Hampshire, NE USA
63 *L1* **Squa Pan Mountain** ▲ Maine, NE USA *46°36´N 68°09´W*
82 *G9* **Squaw Harbor** Unga Island, Alaska, USA *55°12´N 160°41´W*
62 *C2* **Squaw Island** *island* Ontario, S Canada
80 *E6* **Squaw Valley** California, USA *36°44´N 119°15´W*
175 *I12* **Squillace, Golfo di** *gulf* S Italy
175 *J10* **Squinzano** Puglia, SE Italy *40°26´N 18°03´E*
160 *B2* **Sraghmore** Wicklow, Ireland *53°05´N 6°14´W*
Sráid na Cathrach *see* Milltown Malbay
257 *H8* **Srâlau** Stœng Trêng, N Cambodia *14°03´N 105°46´E*
Srath an Urláir *see* Stranorlar
184 *D3* **Srbac** ◐ Republika Srpska, N Bosnia and Herzegovina
Srbija *see* Serbia
Srbinje *see* Foča
184 *F2* **Srbobran** ***var.*** Bácsszenttamás, ***Hung.*** Szenttamás. Vojvodina, N Serbia *45°33´N 19°46´E*
Srbobran *see* Donji Vakuf
257 *G9* **Srê Âmběl** Kaôh Kông, SW Cambodia *11°07´N 103°46´E*
184 *F4* **Srebrenica** Republika Srpska, E Bosnia and Herzegovina *44°04´N 19°18´E*
184 *E3* **Srebrenik** Federacija Bosna I Hercegovina, NE Bosnia and Herzegovina *44°42´N 18°30´E*
185 *K7* **Sredets** ***prev.*** Syulemeshlii. Stara Zagora, C Bulgaria *42°16´N 25°40´E*
185 *L6* **Sredets** ***prev.*** Grudovo. ◐ Burgas, E Bulgaria
185 *L6* **Sredetska Reka** SE Bulgaria
193 *M5* **Sredinnyy Khrebet** ▲▲ E Russian Federation
185 *M4* **Sredishte** ***Rom.*** Beibunar; ***prev.*** Knyazhevo. Dobrich, NE Bulgaria *43°51´N 27°30´E*
185 *J6* **Sredna Gora** ▲▲ C Bulgaria
193 *L4* **Srednekolymsk** Respublika Sakha (Yakutiya), NE Russian Federation *67°28´N 153°52´E*
196 *F4* **Srednerusskaya Vozvyshennost'** ***Eng.*** Central Russian Upland. ▲▲ W Russian Federation
195 *N7* **Srednesatyginskiy Tuman, Ozero** *lakes* Khanty-Mansiyskiy Avtonomnyy Okrug-Yugra, Russian Federation
193 *H5* **Srednesibirskoye Ploskogor'ye** ***var.*** Central Siberian Uplands, ***Eng.*** Central Siberian Plateau. ▲▲ N Russian Federation
195 *L9* **Sredniy Ural** ▲▲ NW Russian Federation
257 *I9* **Srê Khtŭm** Môndól Kiri, E Cambodia *12°10´N 106°52´E*
182 *E6* **Śrem** Wielkopolskie, C Poland *52°07´N 17°00´E*
184 *F3* **Sremska Mitrovica** ***prev.*** Mitrovica, ***Ger.*** Mitrowitz. Vojvodina, NW Serbia *44°58´N 19°37´E*
257 *G8* **Srêng, Stœng** NW Cambodia
257 *G8* **Srê Noy** Siĕmréab, NW Cambodia *13°47´N 104°03´E*
Srepok, Sông *see* Srêpôk, Tônle
257 *I8* **Srêpôk, Tônle** ***var.*** Sông Srepok. Cambodia/Vietnam
193 *J8* **Sretensk** Zabaykalskiy Kray, S Russian Federation *52°14´N 117°33´E*
258 *I4* **Sri Aman** Sarawak, East Malaysia *01°13´N 111°25´E*
189 *I3* **Sribne** Chernihivs'ka Oblast', N Ukraine *50°40´N 32°55´E*
Sri Jayawardanapura *see* Sri Jayewardenepura Kotte
235 *F11* **Sri Jayewardanepura Kotte** ***var.*** Sri Jayawardanapura. ● (Sri Lanka - legislative capital) Western Province, W Sri Lanka *06°54´N 79°58´E*
234 *H5* **Srīkākulam** Andhra Pradesh, E India *18°18´N 83°54´E*
235 *H10* **Sri Lanka** ***off.*** Democratic Socialist Republic of Sri Lanka; ***prev.*** Ceylon. ◆ *republic* S Asia
208 *B4* **Sri Lanka** *island* S Asia
Sri Lanka, Democratic Socialist Republic of *see* Sri Lanka
233 *L7* **Srimangal** Sylhet, E Bangladesh *24°19´N 91°40´E*
Sri Mohangorh *see* Shri Mohangarh
232 *E2* **Srīnagar** *state capital* Jammu and Kashmir, N India *34°07´N 74°50´E*
256 *E7* **Srinagarind Reservoir** W Thailand
234 *D7* **Sringeri** Karnātaka, W India *13°26´N 75°13´E*
235 *G11* **Sri Pada** ***Eng.*** Adam's Peak. ▲ S Sri Lanka *06°49´N 80°25´E*
Sri Saket *see* Si Sa Ket
182 *D7* **Sroda Śląska** ***Ger.*** Neumarkt. Dolnośląskie, SW Poland *51°10´N 16°30´E*
182 *E6* **Środa Wielkopolska** Wielkopolskie, C Poland *52°13´N 17°17´E*
Srpska Kostajnica *see* Bosanska Kostajnica
184 *D3* **Srpska, Republika** ◐ *republic* Bosnia and Herzegovina
Srpski Brod *see* Bosanski Brod
Ssu-ch'uan *see* Sichuan
Ssu-p'ing/Ssu-p'ing-chieh *see* Siping
Stablo *see* Stavelot
163 *E9* **Stabroek** Antwerpen, N Belgium *51°21´N 04°22´E*
Stackeln *see* Strenči
156 *E3* **Stack Skerry** *island* N Scotland, United Kingdom
180 *G3* **Stade** Niedersachsen, NW Germany *53°36´N 09°29´E*
181 *E12* **Stadecken-Elsheim** Rheinland-Pfalz, Germany *49°55´E 8°08´N*
161 *J6* **Stadhampton** United Kingdom *51°40´N 1°08´W*
177 *J2* **Stadl-Paura** Oberösterreich, NW Austria *48°05´N 13°52´E*
191 *G12* **Stadolichy** ***Rus.*** Stodolichi. Homyel'skaya Voblasts', SE Belarus *51°44´N 28°30´E*
162 *I4* **Stadskanaal** Groningen, NE Netherlands *53°N 06°55´E*
181 *F10* **Stadtallendorf** Hessen, C Germany *50°49´N 09°01´E*
179 *F12* **Stadtbergen** Bayern, S Germany *48°21´N 10°50´E*
180 *G6* **Stadthagen** Niedersachsen, Germany *52°19´E 9°12´N*
181 *I11* **Stadtlauringen** Bayern, Germany *50°11´E 10°22´N*
181 *H10* **Stadtlengsfeld** Thüringen, Germany *50°47´E 10°08´N*
181 *G12* **Stadtprozelten** Bayern, Germany *49°47´E 9°25´N*
158 *D2* **Staffa** *island* United Kingdom
155 *F12* **Staffanstorp** Skåne, S Sweden *55°38´N 13°13´E*
181 *J11* **Staffelstein** Bayern, C Germany *50°05´N 11°00´E*
161 *H3* **Stafford** C England, United Kingdom *52°48´N 02°07´W*
75 *D10* **Stafford** Kansas, C USA *37°57´N 98°36´W*
67 *L3* **Stafford** Virginia, NE USA *38°26´N 77°27´W*
161 *H1* **Staffordshire** *cultural region* C England, United Kingdom
141 *J7* **Stafford's Post** KwaZulu-Natal, South Africa *30°31´S 29°45´E*
65 *K3* **Stafford Springs** Connecticut, NE USA *41°57´N 72°18´W*
80 *G2* **Stagecoach** Nevada, USA *39°22´N 119°22´W*
187 *H3* **Stágira** Kentrikí Makedonía, N Greece *40°31´N 23°46´E*
190 *E5* **Staicele** Limbaži, N Latvia *57°52´N 24°48´E*
Ştaierdorf-Anina *see* Anina
159 *K7* **Staindrop** United Kingdom *54°34´N 1°48´W*
161 *K6* **Staines** United Kingdom *51°26´N 0°31´W*
159 *L9* **Stainforth** United Kingdom *53°36´N 1°02´W*
159 *L7* **Staintondale** United Kingdom *54°22´N 0°28´W*
177 *K4* **Stainz** Steiermark, SE Austria *46°55´N 15°18´E*
159 *L7* **Staithes** United Kingdom *54°33´N 0°47´W*
Stájerlakanina *see* Anina
189 *M5* **Stakhanov** Luhans'ka Oblast', E Ukraine *48°30´N 38°42´E*
161 *H7* **Stalbridge** United Kingdom *50°57´N 2°22´W*
161 *M3* **Stalham** United Kingdom *52°46´N 1°31´E*
Stalin *see* Varna
Stalinabad *see* Dushanbe
Stalingrad *see* Volgograd
Staliniri *see* Ts'khinvali
Stalino *see* Donets'k
Stalinobod *see* Dushanbe
Stalinov Štít *see* Gerlachovský štít
Stalinsk *see* Novokuznetsk
Stalins'kaya Oblast' *see* Donets'ka Oblast'
Stalinski Zaliv *see* Varnenski Zaliv
Stalin, Yazovir *see* Iskŭr, Yazovir
53 *H2* **Stallworthy, Cape** *headland* Nunavut, N Canada
183 *I8* **Stalowa Wola** Podkarpackie, SE Poland *50°35´N 22°02´E*
159 *J9* **Stalybridge** United Kingdom *53°29´N 2°04´W*
185 *J7* **Stamboliyski** Plovdiv, C Bulgaria *42°09´N 24°32´E*
161 *J3* **Stamford** E England, United Kingdom *52°39´N 00°32´W*
65 *I5* **Stamford** Connecticut, NE USA *41°03´N 73°32´W*
64 *G2* **Stamford** New York, USA *42°24´N 74°37´W*
70 *F4* **Stamford** Texas, SW USA *32°55´N 99°49´W*
65 *I1* **Stamford** Vermont, USA *42°45´N 73°04´W*
159 *L8* **Stamford Bridge** N England, United Kingdom *53°59´N 00°49´W*
159 *J5* **Stamfordham** United Kingdom *55°02´N 1°52´W*
70 *F4* **Stamford, Lake** Texas, SW USA
176 *F5* **Stampa** Graubünden, SE Switzerland *46°21´N 09°35´E*
Stampalia *see* Astypálaia
140 *D2* **Stampriet** Hardap, Namibia *24°21´S 18°25´E*
75 *H14* **Stamps** Arkansas, C USA *33°22´N 93°30´W*
152 *E5* **Stamsund** Nordland, C Norway *68°07´N 13°50´E*
75 *G8* **Stanberry** Missouri, C USA *40°12´N 94°33´W*
293 *H3* **Stancomb-Wills Glacier** *glacier* Antarctica
141 *J4* **Standerton** Mpumalanga, E South Africa *26°57´S 29°14´E*
159 *I9* **Standish** United Kingdom *53°35´N 2°40´W*
72 *G7* **Standish** Michigan, N USA *43°59´N 83°58´W*
161 *H2* **Standon** United Kingdom *52°55´N 2°17´W*
66 *F4* **Stanford** Kentucky, S USA *37°30´N 84°40´W*
77 *J4* **Stanford** Montana, NW USA *47°08´N 110°15´W*
161 *L6* **Stanford le Hope** United Kingdom *51°30´N 0°25´E*
155 *J10* **Stånga** Gotland, SE Sweden *57°16´N 18°30´E*
154 *E6* **Stange** Hedmark, S Norway *60°40´N 11°05´E*
139 *H8* **Stanger** KwaZulu/Natal, E South Africa *29°20´S 31°18´E*
Stanger *see* KwaDukuza
159 *J6* **Stanhope** United Kingdom *54°45´N 2°01´W*
Stanimaka *see* Asenovgrad
Stanislau *see* Ivano-Frankivs'k
80 *D3* **Stanislaus River** California, W USA
Stanislav *see* Ivano-Frankivs'k
Stanislavskaya Oblast' *see* Ivano-Frankivs'ka Oblast'
Stanisławów *see* Ivano-Frankivs'k
Stanke Dimitrov *see* Dupnitsa
277 *J9* **Stanley** Tasmania, SE Australia *40°48´S 145°18´E*
117 *J11* **Stanley** ***var.*** Port Stanley, Puerto Argentino. ○ (Falkland Islands) East Falkland, Falkland Islands *51°45´S 57°56´W*
159 *H2* **Stanley** United Kingdom *56°28´N 3°27´W*
76 *G7* **Stanley** Idaho, NW USA *44°12´N 114°58´W*
74 *E2* **Stanley** North Dakota, N USA *48°19´N 102°23´W*
64 *A10* **Stanley** Virginia, NE USA *38°34´N 78°30´W*
72 *B5* **Stanley** Wisconsin, N USA *44°58´N 90°54´W*
135 *D9* **Stanley Pool** ***var.*** Pool Malebo. Congo/Dem. Rep. Congo
235 *E8* **Stanley Reservoir** S India
Stanleyville *see* Kisangani
88 *E2* **Stann Creek** ◐ *district* SE Belize
Stann Creek *see* Dangriga
159 *K5* **Stannington** United Kingdom *55°06´N 1°40´W*
193 *J7* **Stanovoy Khrebet** ▲▲ SE Russian Federation
176 *D4* **Stans** Unterwalden, C Switzerland *46°57´N 08°23´E*
161 *K5* **Stansted** ✈ (London) Essex, E England, United Kingdom *51°53´N 00°16´E*

◆ Country
● Country Capital
◇ Dependent Territory
○ Dependent Territory Capital
◐ Administrative Regions
✈ International Airport
▲ Mountain
▲▲ Mountain Range
Volcano
River
Lake
Reservoir

◆ Country	◇ Dependent Territory	◈ Administrative Regions	▲ Mountain	✦ Volcano	◎ Lake
● Country Capital	◌ Dependent Territory Capital	✈ International Airport	▲ Mountain Range	♣ River	▨ Reservoir

◆ Country ◇ Dependent Territory ◈ Administrative Regions ▲ Mountain ⏦ Volcano ⊚ Lake
● Country Capital ◆ Dependent Territory Capital ✈ International Airport ▲ Mountain Range ♒ River ▨ Reservoir

◆ Country   ◇ Dependent Territory   ◈ Administrative Regions   ▲ Mountain   ▲ Volcano   ⊙ Lake
● Country Capital   ○ Dependent Territory Capital   ✈ International Airport   ▲ Mountain Range   ⟿ River   ▣ Reservoir

♦ Country
● Country Capital
◇ Dependent Territory
○ Dependent Territory Capital
◈ Administrative Regions
✕ International Airport
▲ Mountain
▲▲ Mountain Range
🌋 Volcano
↔ River
◎ Lake
☒ Reservoir

◆ Country
● Country Capital
◇ Dependent Territory
○ Dependent Territory Capital
◈ Administrative Regions
✈ International Airport
▲ Mountain
▲▲ Mountain Range
℞ Volcano
☒ River
⊙ Lake
⊡ Reservoir

◆ Country
● Country Capital
◇ Dependent Territory
◎ Dependent Territory Capital
✦ Administrative Regions
✈ International Airport
▲ Mountain
▲ Mountain Range
▲ Volcano
❖ River
◎ Lake
⊠ Reservoir

◆ Country   **◇** Dependent Territory   **◈** Administrative Regions   **▲** Mountain   **▼** Volcano   **◎** Lake
● Country Capital   **○** Dependent Territory Capital   **✕** International Airport   **▲** Mountain Range   **♦** River   **◎** Reservoir

Tsimlyansk Reservoir - Tzaneen
INDEX
419

Tsimlyansk Reservoir see Tsimlyanskoye Vodokhranilishche
Tsimlyansk Vodoskhovshche see Tsimlyanskoye Vodokhranilishche
Tsinan see Jinan
140 G4 **Tsineng** North-West, South Africa 27°05´S 23°07´E
Tsing Hai see Qinghai Hu, China
Tsinghai see Qinghai, China
Tsingtao/Tsingtau see Qingdao
Tsingyuan see Baoding
Tsinkiang see Quanzhou
Tsintao see Qingdao
138 C3 **Tsintsabis** Otjikoto, N Namibia 18°45´S 17°51´E
139 L10 **Tsiombe** var. Tsihombe. Toliara, S Madagascar
193 I7 **Tsipa** ≈ S Russian Federation
139 L7 **Tsiribihina** ≈ W Madagascar
139 L7 **Tsiroanomandidy** Antananarivo, C Madagascar 18°44´S 46°02´E
282 F9 **Tsis** island Chuuk, C Micronesia
141 J8 **Tsitsa Bridge** Eastern Cape, South Africa 31°14´S 28°50´E
Tsitsihar see Qiqihar
140 G10 **Tsitsikama Mountains** ▲▲ Eastern Cape, South Africa
54 C8 **Tsitsutl Peak** ▲ British Columbia, SW Canada
197 I2 **Tsivil'sk** Chuvashskaya Respublika, W Russian Federation 55°51´N 47°30´E
215 K4 **Ts'khinvali** prev. Staliniri. C Georgia 42°12´N 43°58´E
191 F11 **Tsna** ≈ SW Belarus
194 E9 **Tsna** var. Zna. ≈ W Russian Federation
Tsofar see Zofar
239 I2 **Tsogt** var. Tahilt. Govĭ-Altay, W Mongolia 45°20´N 96°42´E
239 K2 **Tsogt-Ovoo** var. Doloon. Ömnögovĭ, S Mongolia 44°28´N 105°22´E
239 K3 **Tsogttsetsiy** var. Baruunsuu. Ömnögovĭ, S Mongolia 43°46´N 105°28´E
141 J8 **Tsolo** Eastern Cape, South Africa 31°19´S 28°45´E
141 I8 **Tsomo** Eastern Cape, South Africa 32°02´S 27°48´E
141 I8 **Tsomo** ≈ Eastern Cape, South Africa
140 B2 **Tsondalvlei** salt lake Hardap, Namibia
185 M5 **Tsonevo, Yazovir** prev. Yazovir Georgi Traykov. ⊠ NE Bulgaria
Tsoohor see Hürmen
251 I5 **Tsu** var. Tu. Mie, Honshū, SW Japan 34°41´N 136°30´E
253 B11 **Tsubame** var. Tubame. Niigata, Honshū, C Japan 37°40´N 138°56´E
251 J2 **Tsubata** Ishikawa, Honshū, SW Japan 36°33´N 136°42´E
252 G4 **Tsubetsu** Hokkaidō, NE Japan 43°43´N 144°01´E
253 C13 **Tsuchiura** var. Tutiura. Ibaraki, Honshū, S Japan 36°05´N 140°11´E
252 D6 **Tsugaru-kaikyō** strait N Japan
253 C11 **Tsugawa** Niigata, Honshū, C Japan 37°40´N 139°26´E
252 E4 **Tsukigata** Hokkaidō, NE Japan 43°18´N 141°37´E
250 E7 **Tsukumi** var. Tukumi. Ōita, Kyūshū, SW Japan 33°00´N 131°51´E
Tsul-Ulaan see Bayannuur
Tsul-Ulaan see Bayanuur
138 C4 **Tsumeb** Otjikoto, N Namibia 19°13´S 17°42´E
138 D4 **Tsumkwe** Otjozondjupa, NE Namibia 19°37´S 20°30´E
250 D8 **Tsuno** Miyazaki, Kyūshū, SW Japan 32°43´N 131°32´E
250 D5 **Tsuno-shima** island SW Japan
251 I3 **Tsuruga** var. Turuga. Fukui, Honshū, SW Japan 35°38´N 136°01´E
250 G6 **Tsurugi-san** ▲ Shikoku, SW Japan 33°50´N 134°04´E
250 E7 **Tsurumi-zaki** Kyūshū, SW Japan
253 C9 **Tsuruoka** var. Turuoka. Yamagata, Honshū, C Japan 38°44´N 139°48´E
251 J4 **Tsushima** var. Tusima. Aichi, Honshū, SW Japan 35°11´N 136°45´E
250 B5 **Tsushima** var. Tsushima-tō, Tusima. island group SW Japan
Tsushima-tō see Tsushima
250 E5 **Tsuwano** Shimane, Honshū, SW Japan 34°28´N 131°43´E
250 G4 **Tsuyama** var. Tuyama. Okayama, Honshū, SW Japan 35°04´N 134°01´E
140 F1 **Tswaane** Ghanzi, W Botswana 22°21´S 21°52´E
141 H4 **Tswelelang** North West, South Africa 27°13´S 25°58´E
191 H9 **Tsyakhtsin** Rus. Tekhtin. Mahilyowskaya Voblasts', E Belarus 53°51´N 29°44´E
191 I11 **Tsyerakhowka** Rus. Terekhovka. Homyel'skaya Voblasts', SE Belarus 52°13´N 31°24´E
191 E10 **Tsyeshawlya** Rus. Cheshevlya, Tseshevlya. Brestskaya Voblasts', SW Belarus 53°14´N 25°49´E
Tsyurupinsk see Tsyurupyns'k
189 I7 **Tsyurupyns'k** Rus. Tsyurupinsk. Khersons'ka Oblast', S Ukraine 46°35´N 32°43´E
Tu see Tsu
280 B3 **Tua** ≈ C Papua New Guinea
Tuaim see Tuam
278 G4 **Tuakau** Waikato, North Island, New Zealand 37°16´S 174°56´E
158 A9 **Tuam** Ir. Tuaim. Galway, W Ireland 53°31´N 08°50´W
279 F8 **Tuamarina** Marlborough, South Island, New Zealand 41°27´S 174°00´E
Tuamotu, Archipel des see Tuamotu, Îles
287 I6 **Tuamotu Fracture Zone** tectonic feature E Pacific Ocean
285 K6 **Tuamotu, Îles** var. Archipel des Tuamotu, Dangerous Archipelago, Tuamotu Islands. island group N French Polynesia
Tuamotu Islands see Tuamotu, Îles
267 M7 **Tuamotu Ridge** undersea feature C Pacific Ocean
243 I2 **Tuanfeng** Hubei, China 30°23´N 114°31´E
256 G4 **Tuân Giao** Lai Châu, N Vietnam 21°34´N 103°24´E
263 K4 **Tuao** Luzon, N Philippines 17°42´N 121°25´E
285 H9 **Tuapa** NW Niue 18°57´S 169°59´W
89 H4 **Tuapi** Región Autónoma Atlántico Norte, NE Nicaragua 14°10´N 83°20´W
196 G8 **Tuapse** Krasnodarskiy Kray, SW Russian Federation 44°08´N 39°07´E
259 K2 **Tuaran** Sabah, East Malaysia 06°12´N 116°12´E
170 D3 **Tua, Rio** ≈ N Portugal
172 D1 **Tua, Rio** ≈ Portugal
285 I2 **Tuasivi** Savai'i, C Samoa 13°38´S 172°08´W
278 B12 **Tuatapere** Southland, South Island, New Zealand 46°09´S 167°43´E
79 I6 **Tuba City** Arizona, SW USA 36°08´N 111°14´W
216 C7 **Ţūbah, Qaşr aţ** castle 'Ammān, C Jordan
Tubame see Tsubame
259 I8 **Tuban** prev. Toeban. Jawa, C Indonesia 06°55´S 112°01´E
129 N10 **Tuban, Wādī** dry watercourse SW Yemen
113 K6 **Tubarão** Santa Catarina, S Brazil 28°29´S 49°00´W
218 E7 **Ţūbās** West Bank 32°19´N 35°22´E
162 I6 **Tubbergen** Overijssel, E Netherlands 52°25´N 06°46´E
Tubeke see Tubize
179 D12 **Tübingen** var. Tuebingen. Baden-Württemberg, SW Germany 48°32´N 09°04´E
197 M3 **Tubinskiy** Respublika Bashkortostan, W Russian Federation 52°48´N 58°18´E
163 D11 **Tubize** Dut. Tubeke. Walloon Brabant, C Belgium 50°43´N 04°14´E
132 D7 **Tubmanburg** NW Liberia 06°50´N 10°53´W
263 M9 **Tubod** Mindanao, S Philippines 07°58´N 123°46´E
128 F2 **Ţubruq** Eng. Tobruk, It. Tobruch. NE Libya 32°05´N 23°59´E
285 I8 **Tubuai** island Îles Australes, SW French Polynesia
Tubuai, Îles/Tubuai Islands see Australes, Îles
Tubuai-Manu see Maiao
84 E2 **Tubutama** Sonora, NW Mexico 30°51´N 111°31´W
102 F2 **Tucacas** Falcón, N Venezuela 10°50´N 68°22´W
108 H7 **Tucano** Bahia, E Brazil 10°52´S 38°48´W
112 F1 **Tucavaca, Río** ≈ E Bolivia
169 H7 **Tuchan** Languedoc-Roussillon, France 42°53´N 2°43´E
182 E4 **Tuchola** Kujawsko-pomorskie, C Poland 53°36´N 17°50´E
183 H8 **Tuchów** Małopolskie, S Poland 49°53´N 21°04´E
66 F8 **Tucker** Georgia, SE USA 33°53´N 84°10´W
75 I12 **Tuckerman** Arkansas, C USA 35°43´N 91°12´W
67 N10 **Tucker's Town** E Bermuda 32°20´N 64°42´W
65 H8 **Tuckerton** New Jersey, NE USA 39°36´N 74°20´W
Tuckum see Tukums
79 I10 **Tucson** Arizona, SW USA 32°14´N 111°01´W
116 E1 **Tucumán** off. Provincia de Tucumán. ◈ province N Argentina
Tucumán see San Miguel de Tucumán
Tucumán, Provincia de see Tucumán
79 N7 **Tucumcari** New Mexico, SW USA 35°10´N 103°43´W
107 I4 **Tucunaré** Pará, N Brazil 05°15´S 55°49´W
103 I3 **Tucupita** Delta Amacuro, NE Venezuela 09°02´N 62°04´W
108 C4 **Tucuruí, Represa de** ⊠ NE Brazil
182 D5 **Tuczno** Zachodnio-pomorskie, NW Poland 53°12´N 16°08´E
Tuddo see Tudu
171 H3 **Tudela** Basq. Tutera; anc. Tutela. Navarra, N Spain 42°04´N 01°37´W
170 F3 **Tudela de Duero** Castilla-León, N Spain 41°35´N 04°34´W
239 I1 **Tüdevtey** var. Oygon. Dzavhan, N Mongolia 48°57´N 96°33´E
243 H3 **Tuditang** Hubei, E China 30°12´N 114°19´E
216 E4 **Tudmur** var. Tadmur, Tamar, Gk. Palmyra, Bibl. Tadmor. Ḩimş, C Syria 34°36´N 38°15´E
190 F3 **Tudu** Ger. Tuddo. Lääne-Virumaa, NE Estonia 59°12´N 26°52´E
160 D3 **Tudweiliog** United Kingdom 52°54´N 4°37´W
Tuebingen see Tübingen
227 M3 **Tuekta** Respublika Altay, S Russian Federation 50°51´N 85°52´E
170 D3 **Tuela, Rio** ≈ N Portugal
233 M6 **Tuensang** Nāgāland, NE India 26°16´N 94°45´E
214 G7 **Tufanbeyli** Adana, C Turkey 38°15´N 36°13´E
243 J7 **Tufang** Fujian, SE China 25°27´N 116°23´E
Tüffer see Laško
280 C4 **Tufi** Northern, S Papua New Guinea 09°08´S 149°20´S
287 H2 **Tufts Plain** undersea feature N Pacific Ocean
Tugalan see Kolkhozobod
121 L9 **Tugela** ≈ SE South Africa
141 K6 **Tugela** ≈ KwaZulu-Natal, South Africa
67 H4 **Tug Fork** ≈ S USA
83 H8 **Tugidak Island** island Trinity Islands, Alaska, USA
263 L4 **Tuguegarao** Luzon, N Philippines 17°37´N 121°48´E
195 N9 **Tugulym** Sverdlovskaya Oblast', Russian Federation
193 L7 **Tugur** Khabarovskiy Kray, SE Russian Federation 53°43´N 137°00´E
245 K5 **Tuhai He** ≈ E China
170 C3 **Tui** Galicia, NW Spain 42°02´N 08°37´W
132 G5 **Tui** var. Grand Balé. ≈ W Burkina
105 H8 **Tuichi, Río** ≈ W Bolivia
170 B10 **Tuineje** Fuerteventura, Islas Canarias, Spain, NE Atlantic Ocean 28°18´N 14°03´W
140 E6 **Tuins** ≈ Northern Cape, South Africa
89 M9 **Tuira, Río** ≈ SE Panama
Tuisarkan see Tūysarkān
85 I8 **Tuitàn** Durango, Mexico 24°02´N 104°15´W
Tujiabu see Yongxiu
197 M2 **Tukan** Respublika Bashkortostan, W Russian Federation 53°58´N 57°29´E
260 E6 **Tukangbesi, Kepulauan** Dut. Toekang Besi Eilanden. island group C Indonesia
229 L7 **Tŭkhtamish** Rus. Toktomush; prev. Tokhtamyshbek. SE Tajikistan 37°51´N 74°41´E
278 I6 **Tukituki** ≈ North Island, New Zealand
Tu-k'ou see Panzhihua
52 B6 **Tuktoyaktuk** Northwest Territories, NW Canada 69°27´N 133°W
52 B6 **Tuktoyaktuk Peninsula** Isthmus Northwest Territories, NW Canada
258 C3 **Tuktuk** Pulau Samosir, W Indonesia 02°32´N 98°43´E
Tukumi see Tsukumi
190 C6 **Tukums** Ger. Tuckum. Tukums, W Latvia 56°58´N 23°12´E
137 C11 **Tukuyu** prev. Neu-Langenburg. Mbeya, S Tanzania 09°14´S 33°39´E
Tukzār see Tokzār
86 F6 **Tula** var. Tula de Allende. Hidalgo, C Mexico 20°01´N 99°21´W
85 M8 **Tula** Tamaulipas, C Mexico 22°59´N 99°43´W
196 F3 **Tula** Tul'skaya Oblast', W Russian Federation 54°11´N 37°39´E
Tulach Mhór see Tullamore
Tula de Allende see Tula
281 J2 **Tulaghi** var. Tulagi. Florida Islands, C Solomon Islands 09°04´S 160°09´E
Tulagi see Tulaghi
239 H6 **Tulagt Ar Gol** ≈ W China
86 F6 **Tulancingo** Hidalgo, C Mexico 20°34´N 98°25´W
80 D7 **Tulare** California, W USA 36°12´N 119°21´W
74 D5 **Tulare** South Dakota, N USA 44°43´N 98°29´W
80 D6 **Tulare Lake Bed** salt flat California, W USA
79 L9 **Tularosa** New Mexico, SW USA 33°04´N 106°01´W
79 K8 **Tularosa Mountains** ▲▲ New Mexico, SW USA
79 L8 **Tularosa Valley** basin New Mexico, SW USA
138 D10 **Tulbagh** Western Cape, SW South Africa 33°17´S 19°09´E
104 C1 **Tulcán** Carchi, N Ecuador 0°44´N 77°43´W
188 G9 **Tulcea** Tulcea, E Romania 45°11´N 28°49´E
188 G9 **Tulcea** ◈ county SE Romania
Tul'chin see Tul'chyn
188 G5 **Tul'chyn** Rus. Tul'chin. Vinnyts'ka Oblast', C Ukraine 48°40´N 28°49´E
84 C3 **Tule** Chihuahua, N Mexico 29°59´N 114°54´W
Tuléar see Toliara
78 C1 **Tulelake** California, W USA 41°57´N 121°30´W
80 B4 **Tule Lake** ◎ California, USA
80 F3 **Tule Lake** ◎ California, USA
80 F5 **Tule Lake** ◎ California, USA
80 C4 **Tule Lake** ⊠ California, USA
55 I4 **Tulemalu Lake** ◎ Nunavut, C Canada
169 K4 **Tulette** Rhône-Alpes, France 44°17´N 4°56´E
188 E7 **Tulgheş** Hung. Gyergyótölgyes. Harghita, C Romania 46°57´N 25°46´E
141 J1 **Tuli** Zimbabwe 21°55´S 29°12´E
Tuli see Thuli
70 E3 **Tulia** Texas, SW USA 34°22´N 101°46´W
54 D3 **Tulita** prev. Fort Norman, Norman. Northwest Territories, NW Canada 64°55´N 125°25´W
218 E7 **Ţūlkarm** West Bank 32°18´N 35°01´E
66 E6 **Tullahoma** Tennessee, S USA 35°21´N 86°12´W
158 F2 **Tulla, Loch** ◎ United Kingdom
277 I7 **Tullamarine** ✈ (Melbourne) Victoria, SE Australia 37°40´S 144°46´E
277 K4 **Tullamore** New South Wales, SE Australia 32°39´S 147°35´E
158 C10 **Tullamore** Ir. Tulach Mhór. Offaly, C Ireland 53°16´N 07°30´W
165 H7 **Tulle** anc. Tutela. Corrèze, C France 45°16´N 01°46´E
169 K2 **Tullins** Rhône-Alpes, France 45°18´N 5°29´E
177 L2 **Tulln** var. Oberhollabrunn. Niederösterreich, NE Austria 48°20´N 16°02´E
177 L2 **Tulln** ≈ NE Austria
68 C2 **Tullos** Louisiana, S USA 31°48´N 92°19´W
160 A3 **Tullow** Ir. An Tullach. Carlow, SE Ireland 52°48´N 06°44´W
275 J3 **Tully** Queensland, NE Australia 18°03´S 145°56´E
158 B7 **Tully** United Kingdom 54°27´N 7°47´W
194 E2 **Tuloma** ≈ NW Russian Federation
185 K6 **Tulovo** Stara Zagora, C Bulgaria 42°33´N 25°32´E
75 F12 **Tulsa** Oklahoma, C USA 36°09´N 96°W
233 H5 **Tulsipur** Mid Western, W Nepal 28°01´N 82°22´E
158 B9 **Tulsk** Roscommon, Ireland 53°47´N 8°15´W
196 F3 **Tul'skaya Oblast'** ◈ province W Russian Federation
196 G8 **Tul'skiy** Respublika Adygeya, SW Russian Federation 44°26´N 40°12´E
280 C2 **Tulu** Manus Island, N Papua New Guinea 01°58´S 146°50´E
102 B6 **Tuluá** Valle del Cauca, W Colombia 04°01´N 76°16´W
188 F8 **Tuluceşti** Galaţi, E Romania 45°35´N 28°01´E
82 G6 **Tuluksak** Alaska, USA 61°06´N 160°57´W
87 N5 **Tulum** Quintana Roo, Mexico 20°13´N 87°28´W
87 N5 **Tulum, Ruinas de** ruins Quintana Roo, SE Mexico
193 H8 **Tulun** Irkutskaya Oblast', S Russian Federation 54°29´N 100°19´E
259 I9 **Tulungagung** prev. Toeloengagoeng. Jawa, C Indonesia 08°03´S 111°54´E
280 E2 **Tulun Islands** var. Kilinailau Islands; prev. Carteret Islands. island group NE Papua New Guinea
196 G2 **Tuma** Ryazanskaya Oblast', W Russian Federation 55°09´N 40°27´E
102 A7 **Tumaco** Nariño, SW Colombia 01°51´N 78°46´W
102 A7 **Tumaco, Bahía de** bay SW Colombia
118 C4 **Tumán** Región Metropolitana, Chile 34°03´S 71°55´W
Tuman-gang see Tumen
88 G5 **Tuma, Río** ≈ N Nicaragua
155 I8 **Tumba** Stockholm, C Sweden 59°12´N 17°49´E
Tumba, Lac see Ntomba, Lac
258 I5 **Tumbangsenamang** Borneo, C Indonesia 01°17´S 112°21´E
277 K6 **Tumbarumba** New South Wales, SE Australia 35°47´S 148°03´E
104 B3 **Tumbes** Tumbes, NW Peru 03°33´S 80°27´W
104 B3 **Tumbes** off. Departamento de Tumbes. ◈ department NW Peru
Tumbes, Departamento de see Tumbes
118 B7 **Tumbes, Punta** point Bío-Bío, Chile
86 C7 **Tumbiscatio** Michoacán, Mexico 18°31´N 102°21´W
63 J3 **Tumbledown Mountain** ▲ Maine, NE USA 45°27´N 70°28´W
56 F3 **Tumbler Ridge** British Columbia, W Canada 55°06´N 120°51´W
155 H8 **Tumbo** prev. Rekarne. Västmanland, C Sweden 59°25´N 16°04´E
257 G9 **Tumbŏt, Phnum** ▲ W Cambodia 12°23´N 102°57´E
276 F5 **Tumby Bay** South Australia 34°22´S 136°05´E
248 E2 **Tumen** Jilin, NE China 42°56´N 129°47´E
237 K4 **Tumen** Chin. Tumen Jiang, Kor. Tuman-gang, Rus. Tumyn'tszyan. ≈ E Asia
Tumen Jiang see Tumen
103 I4 **Tumeremo** Bolívar, E Venezuela 07°17´N 61°30´W
234 E7 **Tumkūr** Karnātaka, W India 13°20´N 77°06´E
159 H1 **Tummel** ≈ C Scotland, United Kingdom
159 H1 **Tummel Bridge** United Kingdom 56°42´N 4°01´W
159 H1 **Tummel, Loch** ◎ C Scotland, United Kingdom
282 B1 **Tumon Bay** bay W Guam
132 G6 **Tumu** NW Ghana 10°55´N 01°59´W
103 M7 **Tumuc-Humac Mountains** var. Serra Tumucumaque. ▲▲ N South America
Tumucumaque, Serra see Tumuc-Humac Mountains
277 K6 **Tumut** New South Wales, SE Australia 35°20´S 148°14´E
Tumyn'tszyan see Tumen
Tūn see Ferdows
54 D2 **Tunago Lake** ◎ Northwets Territories, NW Canada
91 L7 **Tunapuna** Trinidad, Trinidad and Tobago 10°38´N 61°23´W
113 K5 **Tunas** Paraná, S Brazil 24°57´S 49°05´W
Tunbridge Wells see Royal Tunbridge Wells
187 K1 **Tunca Nehri** Bul. Tundzha. ≈ Bulgaria/Turkey see also Tundzha
Tunca Nehri see Tundzha
215 H6 **Tunceli** var. Kalan. Tunceli, E Turkey 39°07´N 39°34´E
215 H6 **Tunceli** ◈ province C Turkey
232 F6 **Tūndla** Uttar Pradesh, N India 27°13´N 78°14´E
137 D12 **Tunduru** Ruvuma, S Tanzania 11°08´S 37°21´E
185 L7 **Tundzha** Turk. Tunca Nehri. ≈ Bulgaria/Turkey see also Tunca Nehri
Tundzha see Tunca Nehri
246 D3 **Tünel** var. Bulag. Hövsgöl, N Mongolia 49°51´N 100°41´E
172 B8 **Tunes** Faro, S Portugal 37°09´N 08°16´W
234 D7 **Tungabhadra** ≈ S India
234 D6 **Tungabhadra Reservoir** ◎ S India
284 B2 **Tungaru** prev. Gilbert Islands. island group W Kiribati
263 L9 **Tungawan** Mindanao, S Philippines 07°33´N 122°22´E
Tungdor see Mainling
258 E5 **Tungkal** ≈ Sumatera, W Indonesia
T'ung-shan see Xuzhou
241 I9 **Tungsha Tao** Chin. Dongsha Qundao, Eng. Pratas Island. island S Taiwan
243 M8 **Tungshih** Jap. Tôsei. N Taiwan 24°13´N 120°54´E
54 C3 **Tungsten** Northwest Territories, W Canada 62°N 128°09´W
Tung-t'ing Hu see Dongting Hu
104 C2 **Tungurahua** ◈ province C Ecuador
154 C7 **Tunhovdfjorden** ◎ S Norway
66 A7 **Tunica** Mississippi, S USA 34°40´N 90°22´W
131 K1 **Tunis** var. Tūnis. ● (Tunisia) NE Tunisia 36°53´N 10°10´E
131 K1 **Tunis, Golfe de** Ar. Khalīj Tūnis. gulf NE Tunisia
131 K3 **Tunisia** off. Tunisian Republic, Ar. Al Jumhūrīyah at Tūnisīyah, Fr. République Tunisienne. ◆ republic N Africa
Tunisian Republic see Tunisia
Tunisienne, République see Tunisia
Tūnisīyah, Al Jumhūrīyah at see Tunisia
Tūnis, Khalīj see Tunis, Golfe de
102 C5 **Tunja** Boyacá, C Colombia 05°33´N 73°23´W
87 M5 **Tunkàs** Yucatán, Mexico 20°54´N 88°45´W
64 E4 **Tunkhannock** Pennsylvania, USA 41°32´N 75°57´W
154 F2 **Tunnsjøen** Lapp. Dåtnejaevrie. ◎ C Norway
118 C3 **Tunquen, Punta** point Valparaíso, Chile
161 M4 **Tunstall** United Kingdom 52°08´N 1°27´E
82 G7 **Tuntutuliak** Alaska, USA 60°21´N 162°40´W
295 K7 **Tunu** ◈ province E Greenland
229 K4 **Tunuk** Chuyskaya Oblast', C Kyrgyzstan 42°11´N 73°55´E
59 J3 **Tunungayualok Island** island Newfoundland and Labrador, E Canada
116 C3 **Tunuyán** Mendoza, W Argentina 33°35´S 69°00´W
118 G3 **Tunuyán, Río** ≈ W Argentina
Tunxi see Huangshan
243 I8 **Tuocheng** Guangdong, SE China 24°03´N 115°12´E
Tuodian see Shuangbai
Tuoji see Zhongba
Tuokezhake see Shufu
80 E3 **Tuolumne** California, USA 37°58´N 120°14´W
78 C5 **Tuolumne River** ≈ California, W USA
Tuong Buong see Tương Đương
256 G5 **Tương Đương** var. Tuong Buong. Nghệ An, N Vietnam 19°15´N 104°30´E
242 B8 **Tuoniang Jiang** ≈ S China
Tuotiereke see Jeminay
Tuotuo He see Togton He
Tuotuoheyan see Tanggulashan
Tüp see Tyup
113 J3 **Tupã** São Paulo, S Brazil 21°57´S 50°28´W
110 A1 **Tupaciguara** Minas Gerais, Brazil 18°35´S 48°42´W
285 I6 **Tupai** var. Motu Iti. atoll Îles Sous le Vent, W French Polynesia
115 J6 **Tupambaé** E Uruguay 32°50´S 54°46´W
113 I7 **Tupanciretã** Rio Grande do Sul, S Brazil 29°06´S 53°48´W
66 C8 **Tupelo** Mississippi, S USA 34°15´N 88°42´W
193 J8 **Tupik** Zabaykalskiy Kray, S Russian Federation 54°21´N 119°56´E
109 C9 **Tupiraçaba** Goiás, S Brazil 14°33´S 48°40´W
112 C3 **Tupiza** Potosí, S Bolivia 21°27´S 65°45´W
226 B6 **Tupkaragan, Mys** prev. Mys Tyub-Karagan. headland SW Kazakhstan 44°40´N 50°19´E
56 F3 **Tupper** British Columbia, W Canada 55°30´N 119°59´W
62 G4 **Tupper Lake** ◎ New York, NE USA
228 F5 **Tuproqqal'a** Khorazm Viloyati, W Uzbekistan 40°52´N 62°00´E
118 F3 **Tupungata** Mendoza, Argentina 33°22´S 69°08´W
118 E3 **Tupungato, Quebrada del** ≈ Región Metropolitana, Chile
118 E3 **Tupungato, Volcán** ⋀ W Argentina 33°27´S 69°42´W
112 B9 **Tupungato, Volcn** ⋀ Chile 33°06´S 69°42´W
247 K5 **Tuquan** Nei Mongol Zizhiqu, N China 45°21´N 121°36´E
102 A7 **Túquerres** Nariño, SW Colombia 01°06´N 77°37´W
233 K7 **Tura** Meghālaya, NE India 25°33´N 90°14´E
193 H6 **Tura** Krasnoyarskiy Kray, N Russian Federation 64°20´N 100°17´E
195 M8 **Tura** ≈ C Russian Federation
220 E5 **Turabah** Makkah, W Saudi Arabia 22°00´N 42°00´E
103 H4 **Turagua, Cerro** ▲ C Venezuela 06°59´N 64°34´W
278 G6 **Turakina** Manawatu-Wanganui, North Island, New Zealand 40°03´S 175°13´E
279 G8 **Turakirae Head** headland North Island, New Zealand 41°26´S 174°54´E
280 A3 **Turama** ≈ S Papua New Guinea
192 G8 **Turan** Respublika Tyva, S Russian Federation 52°11´N 93°40´E
278 H5 **Turangi** Waikato, North Island, New Zealand 39°01´S 175°47´E
228 E5 **Turan Lowland** var. Turan Plain, Kaz. Turan Oypaty, Rus. Turanskaya Nizmennost', Turk. Turan Pesligi, Uzb. Turan Pasttekisligi. plain C Asia
Turan Oypaty/Turan Pesligi/Turan Plain/Turanskaya Nizmennost' see Turan Lowland
Turan Pasttekisligi see Turan Lowland
216 E5 **Ţurāq al 'Ilab** hill range S Syria
191 G11 **Turaw** Rus. Turov. Homyel'skaya Voblasts', SE Belarus 52°04´N 27°44´E
220 E1 **Ţurayf** Al Ḩudūd ash Shamālīyah, NW Saudi Arabia 31°43´N 38°40´E
Turba see Teruel
102 B3 **Turbaco** Bolívar, N Colombia 10°20´N 75°25´W
230 D9 **Turbat** Baluchistān, SW Pakistan 26°02´N 62°56´E
Turbat-i-Haidari see Torbat-e Ḩeydarīyeh
Turbat-i-Jam see Torbat-e Jām
102 B4 **Turbo** Antioquia, NW Colombia 08°06´N 76°44´W
Turčianský Svätý Martin see Martin
188 C7 **Turda** Ger. Thorenburg, Hung. Torda. Cluj, NW Romania 46°35´N 23°50´E
222 E4 **Ţūreh** Markazī, W Iran
285 L7 **Tureia** atoll Îles Tuamotu, SE French Polynesia
182 F6 **Turek** Wielkopolskie, C Poland 52°01´N 18°30´E
153 H9 **Turenki** Etelä-Suomi, SW Finland 60°55´N 24°38´E
Turfan see Turpan
Turgay see Torgay
Turgay see Torgay
226 G3 **Turgayskaya Stolovaya Strana** Kaz. Torgay Üstirti. plateau Kazakhstan/Russian Federation
Turgel see Türi
185 L5 **Tŭrgovishte** prev. Eski Dzhumaya, Tărgovište. Tŭrgovishte, N Bulgaria 43°15´N 26°34´E
185 L6 **Tŭrgovishte** ◈ province N Bulgaria
214 B6 **Turgutlu** Manisa, W Turkey 38°30´N 27°43´E
214 G5 **Turhal** Tokat, N Turkey 40°23´N 36°05´E
190 E4 **Türi** Ger. Turgel. Järvamaa, N Estonia 58°48´N 25°28´E
171 I6 **Tùria** ≈ E Spain
173 L4 **Turia** ≈ Spain
108 D2 **Turiaçu** Maranhão, E Brazil 01°40´S 45°22´W
Turin see Torino
195 M9 **Turinsk** Sverdlovskaya Oblast', Russian Federation
188 D2 **Turiya** Pol. Turja, Rus. Tur'ya; prev. Tur"ya. ≈ NW Ukraine
248 F1 **Turiy Rog** Primorskiy Kray, SE Russian Federation 45°14´N 131°58´E
188 D2 **Turiys'k** Volyns'ka Oblast', NW Ukraine 51°05´N 24°31´E
Turja see Turiya
188 C4 **Turka** L'vivs'ka Oblast', W Ukraine 49°07´N 23°01´E
136 D6 **Turkana, Lake** var. Lake Rudolf. ◎ N Kenya
238 G4 **Turkem Pendi** depression NW China
Turkestan see Turkistan
229 I6 **Turkestan Range** Rus. Turkestanskiy Khrebet. ▲▲ C Asia
Turkestanskiy Khrebet see Turkestan Range
183 H12 **Túrkeve** Jász-Nagykun-Szolnok, E Hungary 47°06´N 20°42´E
70 E3 **Turkey** Texas, SW USA 34°23´N 100°54´W
214 F6 **Turkey** off. Republic of Turkey, Turk. Türkiye Cumhuriyeti. ◆ republic SW Asia
274 F3 **Turkey Creek** Western Australia 16°54´S 128°12´E
75 D11 **Turkey Creek** ≈ Oklahoma, C USA
79 M6 **Turkey Mountains** ▲▲ New Mexico, SW USA
Turkey, Republic of see Turkey
74 H6 **Turkey River** ≈ Iowa, C USA
197 H4 **Turki** Saratovskaya Oblast', W Russian Federation 52°00´N 43°16´E
218 C1 **Turkish Republic of Northern Cyprus** ◇ disputed territory Cyprus
227 H7 **Turkistan** prev. Turkestan. Yuzhnyy Kazakhstan, S Kazakhstan 43°18´N 68°18´E
Turkistan, Bandi-i see Torkestān, Selseleh-ye Band-e
Türkiye Cumhuriyeti see Turkey
187 K5 **Türkmen** Manisa, Turkey 38°45´N 27°11´E
228 F7 **Türkmenabat** prev. Rus. Chardzhev, Chardzhou, Chardzhui, Lenin-Turkmenski, Turkm. Chärjew. Lebap Welaýaty, E Turkmenistan 39°07´N 63°30´E
228 B6 **Türkmen Aylagy** Rus. Turkmenskiy Zaliv. lake gulf W Turkmenistan
Turkmenbashi see Türkmenbaşy
228 A5 **Türkmenbaşy** Rus. Turkmenbashi; prev. Krasnovodsk. Balkan Welaýaty, W Turkmenistan 40°N 53°04´E
228 A6 **Türkmenbasy Aylagy** prev. Rus. Krasnovodskiy Zaliv, Turkm. Krasnowodsk Aylagy. lake Gulf W Turkmenistan
228 F8 **Türkmengala** Rus. Turkmen-kala; prev. Turkmen-Kala. Mary Welaýaty, S Turkmenistan 37°25´N 62°19´E
228 E7 **Turkmenistan** ; prev. Turkmenskaya Soviet Socialist Republic. ◆ republic C Asia
Turkmen-kala/Turkmen-Kala see Türkmengala
Turkmenskaya Soviet Socialist Republic see Turkmenistan
Turkmenskiy Zaliv see Türkmen Aylagy
214 G7 **Türkoğlu** Kahramanmaraş, S Turkey 37°24´N 36°49´E
91 H4 **Turks and Caicos Islands** ◇ UK dependent territory N West Indies
91 H4 **Turks Islands** island group SE Turks and Caicos Islands
153 G10 **Turku** Swe. Åbo. Länsi-Suomi, SW Finland 60°27´N 22°17´E
136 C7 **Turkwel** seasonal river NW Kenya
75 F12 **Turley** Oklahoma, C USA 36°14´N 95°58´W
80 C4 **Turlock** California, W USA 37°29´N 120°52´W
190 F7 **Turmantas** Utena, NE Lithuania 55°41´N 26°27´E
Turmberg see Wieżyca
102 F3 **Turmero** Aragua, N Venezuela South America 10°14´N 66°40´W
278 I7 **Turnagain, Cape** headland North Island, New Zealand 40°30´S 176°36´E
Turnau see Turnov
158 F5 **Turnberry** United Kingdom 55°20´N 4°51´W
88 E2 **Turneffe Islands** island group E Belize
65 J2 **Turners Falls** Massachusetts, NE USA 42°36´N 72°31´W
57 I7 **Turner Valley** Alberta, SW Canada 50°43´N 114°19´W
163 F9 **Turnhout** Antwerpen, N Belgium 51°19´N 04°57´E
181 C9 **Turnich** Nordrhein-Westfalen, Germany 50°52´E 6°45´N
177 K2 **Türnitz** Niederösterreich, E Austria 47°56´N 15°26´E
57 K2 **Turnor Lake** ◎ Saskatchewan, C Canada
183 C8 **Turnov** Ger. Turnau. Liberecký Kraj, N Czech Republic 50°36´N 15°10´E
Tŭrnovo see Veliko Tŭrnovo
188 D10 **Turnu Măgurele** var. Turnu-Măgurele. Teleorman, S Romania 43°44´N 24°53´E
Turnu Severin see Drobeta-Turnu Severin
Turócszentmárton see Martin
Turoni see Tours
Turov see Turaw
238 G4 **Turpan** var. Turfan. Xinjiang Uygur Zizhiqu, NW China 42°55´N 89°06´E
Turpan Depression see Turpan Pendi
246 A5 **Turpan Pendi** Eng. Turpan Depression. depression NW China
238 G3 **Turpan Zhan** Xinjiang Uygur Zizhiqu, W China 43°10´N 89°06´E
Turpentine State see North Carolina
90 E5 **Turquino, Pico** ▲ E Cuba 19°54´N 76°55´W
75 J12 **Turrell** Arkansas, C USA 35°22´N 90°13´W
89 H8 **Turrialba** Cartago, E Costa Rica 09°56´N 83°40´W
156 G5 **Turriff** NE Scotland, United Kingdom 57°32´N 02°28´W
217 K5 **Tursāq** Diyālá, E Iraq 33°27´N 45°47´E
Turshiz see Kāshmar
195 M7 **Tursuntskiy Tuman, Ozero** lakes Khanty-Mansiyskiy Avtonomnyy Okrug-Yugra, Russian Federation
Tursunzade see Tursunzoda
229 I7 **Tursunzoda** Rus. Tursunzade; prev. Regar. W Tajikistan 38°30´N 68°10´E
Turt see Hanh
Tŭrtkŭl/Turtkul' see To'rtkok'l
81 J14 **Turtleback Mountain** ▲ Nevada, USA 33°08´N 113°24´W
74 D5 **Turtle Creek** ≈ South Dakota, N USA
72 C4 **Turtle Flambeau Flowage** ⊠ Wisconsin, N USA
57 L5 **Turtleford** Saskatchewan, S Canada 53°21´N 108°48´W
74 C2 **Turtle Lake** North Dakota, N USA 47°31´N 100°53´W
152 G6 **Turtola** Lappi, NW Finland 66°39´N 23°55´E
193 H6 **Turu** ≈ N Russian Federation
Turuga see Tsuruga
238 B4 **Turugart Pass** pass China/Kyrgyzstan
229 L5 **Turugart Shankou** var. Pereval Torugart. pass China/Kyrgyzstan
192 G5 **Turukhan** ≈ N Russian Federation
192 G5 **Turukhansk** Krasnoyarskiy Kray, N Russian Federation 65°50´N 87°48´E
216 G2 **Ţurumbah** well NE Syria
Turuoka see Tsuruoka
Turush see Turysh
110 A5 **Turvo, Rio** ≈ S Brazil
Tur"ya see Turiya
226 D6 **Turysh** prev. Turush. Mangistau, SW Kazakhstan 45°24´N 56°02´E
66 D9 **Tuscaloosa** Alabama, S USA 33°13´N 87°34´W
66 D9 **Tuscaloosa, Lake** ◎ Alabama, S USA
Tuscan Archipelago see Toscano, Archipelago
Tuscan-Emilian Mountains see Tosco-Emiliano, Appennino
Tuscany see Toscana
78 F2 **Tuscarora** Nevada, W USA 41°16´N 116°13´W
64 B7 **Tuscarora Mountain** ridge Pennsylvania, NE USA
73 D11 **Tuscola** Illinois, N USA 39°46´N 88°19´W
70 F5 **Tuscola** Texas, SW USA 32°12´N 99°48´W
66 D7 **Tuscumbia** Alabama, S USA 34°43´N 87°42´W
152 B6 **Tusenøyane** island group S Svalbard
226 E6 **Tushchybas, Zaliv** prev. Zaliv Paskevicha. lake gulf SW Kazakhstan
Tusima see Tsushima
261 M7 **Tusirah** Papua, E Indonesia 06°46´S 140°19´E
69 I2 **Tuskegee** Alabama, S USA 32°25´N 85°41´W
154 C3 **Tustna** island S Norway
83 I7 **Tustumena Lake** ◎ Alaska, USA
182 G7 **Tuszyn** Łódzkie, C Poland 51°36´N 19°31´E
215 J6 **Tutak** Ağrı, E Turkey 39°34´N 42°48´E
278 F2 **Tutamoe Range** ▲▲ North Island, New Zealand
Tutasev see Tutayev
194 F9 **Tutayev** var. Tutasev. Yaroslavskaya Oblast', W Russian Federation 57°51´N 39°29´E
Tutela see Tulle, France
Tutela see Tudela, Spain
Tutera see Tudela
235 E10 **Tuticorin** Tamil Nādu, SE India 08°48´N 78°10´E
184 F6 **Tutin** Serbia, S Serbia 43°00´N 20°20´E
278 I6 **Tutira** Hawke's Bay, North Island, New Zealand 39°14´S 176°53´E
Tutiura see Tsuchiura
192 G6 **Tutonchny** Krasnoyarskiy Kray, N Russian Federation 64°12´N 93°52´E
185 L4 **Tutrakan** Silistra, NE Bulgaria 44°03´N 26°38´E
74 C3 **Tuttle** North Dakota, N USA 47°07´N 99°58´W
75 E12 **Tuttle** Oklahoma, C USA 35°17´N 97°48´W
75 F9 **Tuttle Creek Lake** ⊠ Kansas, C USA
179 D13 **Tuttlingen** Baden-Württemberg, S Germany 47°59´N 08°49´E
260 G8 **Tutuala** East Timor 08°23´S 127°12´E
286 F7 **Tutuila** island W American Samoa
138 G4 **Tutume** Central, E Botswana 20°26´S 27°02´E
82 G3 **Tututalak Mountain** ▲ Alaska, USA 67°51´N 161°27´W
66 A8 **Tutwiler** Mississippi, S USA 34°00´N 90°25´W
239 K1 **Tuul Gol** ≈ N Mongolia
153 J8 **Tuupovaara** Itä-Suomi, E Finland 62°30´N 30°40´E
Tuva see Tyva, Respublika
284 C5 **Tuvalu** prev. Ellice Islands. ◆ commonwealth republic SW Pacific Ocean
Tuvinskaya ASSR see Tyva, Respublika
239 M1 **Tuvshinshiree** var. Sergelen. Sühbaatar, E Mongolia 46°12´N 111°48´E
280 G9 **Tuvuca** prev. Tuvutha. island Lau Group, E Fiji
Tuvutha see Tuvuca
213 H7 **Ţuwayq, Jabal** ▲▲ C Saudi Arabia
219 G11 **Ţuwayyil ash Shihāq** desert S Jordan
219 G11 **Ţuwayyil ash Shihāq** ▲▲ Jordan
244 F4 **Tuwei He** ≈ Shaanxi, China
86 C5 **Tuxcueca** Jalisco, Mexico
57 N7 **Tuxford** Saskatchewan, S Canada 50°33´N 105°32´W
159 L10 **Tuxford** United Kingdom 53°13´N 0°53´W
257 I8 **Tu Xoay** Đăc Lăc, S Vietnam 12°18´N 107°33´E
86 C6 **Tuxpan** Jalisco, C Mexico 19°33´N 103°21´W
86 E6 **Tuxpan** Michoacán, Mexico 19°34´N 100°28´W
85 I9 **Tuxpan** Nayarit, C Mexico 21°57´N 105°12´W
86 G5 **Tuxpán** var. Tuxpán de Rodríguez Cano. Veracruz-Llave, E Mexico 20°58´N 97°23´W
Tuxpán de Rodríguez Cano see Tuxpán
87 H7 **Tuxtepec** var. San Juan Bautista Tuxtepec. Oaxaca, S Mexico 18°02´N 96°05´W
87 J8 **Tuxtla** var. Tuxtla Gutiérrez. Chiapas, SE Mexico 16°44´N 93°03´W
Tuxtla see San Andrés Tuxtla
Tuxtla Gutiérrez see Tuxtla
Tuyama see Tsuyama
256 H4 **Tuyên Quang** Tuyên Quang, N Vietnam 21°48´N 105°18´E
257 I9 **Tuy Hoa** Binh Thuân, S Vietnam 11°03´N 108°12´E
257 J8 **Tuy Hoa** Phu Yên, S Vietnam 13°02´N 109°15´E
197 K2 **Tuymazy** Respublika Bashkortostan, W Russian Federation 54°36´N 53°40´E
Tuy Phong see Liên Hương
222 E4 **Tūysarkān** var. Tuisarkan, Tuyserkān. Hamadān, W Iran 34°31´N 48°30´E
Tuyserkān see Tūysarkān
Tuyuk see Tuyyk
227 L7 **Tuyyk** Kaz. Tuyyq; prev. Tuyuk. Taldykorgan, SE Kazakhstan 43°07´N 79°24´E
Tuyyq see Tuyyk
87 K10 **Tuzantàn** Chiapas, Mexico 15°09´N 92°25´W
86 E6 **Tuzantla** Michoacán, Mexico
214 E6 **Tuz Gölü** ◎ C Turkey
195 I9 **Tuzha** Kirovskaya Oblast', NW Russian Federation 57°37´N 48°02´E
184 F7 **Tuzi** S Montenegro 42°22´N 19°21´E
217 J3 **Ţūz Khurmātū** At Ta'mīn, N Iraq 34°56´N 44°38´E
184 E4 **Tuzla** Federacija Bosna I Hercegovina, NE Bosnia and Herzegovina 44°33´N 18°40´E
188 G10 **Tuzla** Constanţa, SE Romania 43°58´N 28°38´E
187 J4 **Tuzla** Çanakkale, Turkey 39°34´N 26°11´E
187 M2 **Tuzla** İstanbul, NW Turkey 40°49´N 29°18´E
215 K5 **Tuzluca** Iğdır, E Turkey 40°02´N 43°39´E
155 F11 **Tvååker** Halland, S Sweden 57°04´N 12°25´E
155 C9 **Tvedestrand** Aust-Agder, S Norway 58°36´N 08°55´E
194 E10 **Tver'** prev. Kalinin. Tverskaya Oblast', W Russian Federation 56°53´N 35°52´E
194 E10 **Tverskaya Oblast'** ◈ province W Russian Federation
194 E10 **Tvertsa** ≈ W Russian Federation
218 F6 **Tverya** var. Tiberias; prev. Teverya. Northern, N Israel 32°48´N 35°32´E
155 C8 **Tvietsund** Telemark, S Norway 59°00´N 08°34´E
190 G3 **Tvorozhkovo** Pskovskaya Oblast', Russian Federation
182 E7 **Twardogóra** Ger. Festenberg. Dolnośląskie, SW Poland 51°21´N 17°27´E
62 E4 **Tweed** Ontario, SE Canada 44°29´N 77°19´W
156 G7 **Tweed** ≈ England/Scotland, United Kingdom
162 I4 **Tweede-Exloërmond** Drenthe, NE Netherlands 52°55´N 06°55´E
277 M2 **Tweed Heads** New South Wales, SE Australia 28°10´S 153°32´E
159 J4 **Tweedmouth** United Kingdom 55°45´N 2°00´W
159 H4 **Tweedsmuir** United Kingdom 55°30´N 3°25´W
141 J3 **Tweefontein** Mpumalanga, South Africa 25°21´S 28°50´E
Tweefontein see Somaroboro
141 J5 **Tweeling** Free State, South Africa 27°33´S 28°31´E
140 D3 **Tweerivier** Hardap, Namibia 25°28´S 19°26´E
140 E4 **Twee Rivieren** Northern Cape, South Africa 33°50´S 23°53´E
141 I6 **Tweespruit** Free State, South Africa 29°11´S 27°02´E
162 H6 **Twello** Gelderland, E Netherlands 52°14´N 06°07´E
81 G11 **Twentynine Palms** California, W USA 34°08´N 116°03´W
59 L6 **Twillingate** Newfoundland and Labrador, SE Canada
70 E5 **Twin Buttes Reservoir** ⊠ Texas, SW USA
76 G8 **Twin Falls** Idaho, NW USA 42°34´N 114°28´W
82 G7 **Twin Hills** Alaska, USA 59°06´N 160°21´W
56 G1 **Twin Lakes** Alberta, W Canada 57°47´N 117°30´W
76 G6 **Twin Peaks** ▲ Idaho, NW USA 44°37´N 114°24´W
279 E8 **Twins, The** ▲ South Island, New Zealand 41°14´S 172°38´E
74 F3 **Twin Valley** Minnesota, N USA 47°15´N 96°15´W
180 C5 **Twist** Niedersachsen, Germany 52°38´E 7°03´N
180 F5 **Twistringen** Niedersachsen, NW Germany 52°48´N 08°39´E
278 C10 **Twizel** Canterbury, South Island, New Zealand 44°04´S 171°12´E
160 E9 **Two Bridges** United Kingdom 50°33´N 3°58´W
72 B3 **Two Harbors** Minnesota, N USA 47°01´N 91°40´W
57 J5 **Two Hills** Alberta, SW Canada 53°40´N 111°43´W
72 E6 **Two Rivers** Wisconsin, N USA 44°10´N 87°33´W
161 I3 **Twycross** United Kingdom 52°38´N 1°30´W
161 I7 **Twyford** United Kingdom 51°01´N 1°19´W
158 G6 **Twynholm** United Kingdom 54°51´N 4°05´W
188 C5 **Tyachiv** Zakarpats'ka Oblast', W Ukraine 48°02´N 23°35´E
Tyan'-Shan' see Tien Shan
233 L8 **Tyao** ≈ Myanmar (Burma)/India
189 I4 **Tyasmin** ≈ N Ukraine
69 M2 **Tybee Island** Georgia, SE USA 32°00´N 80°51´W
Tyborøn see Thyborøn
183 F8 **Tychy** Ger. Tichau. Śląskie, S Poland 50°12´N 19°01´E
183 I8 **Tyczyn** Podkarpackie, SE Poland 49°58´N 22°03´E
154 E4 **Tydal** Sør-Trøndelag, S Norway 63°01´N 11°36´E
187 H10 **Tyflós** ≈ Kríti, Greece, E Mediterranean Sea
67 J2 **Tygart Lake** ⊠ West Virginia, NE USA
193 K8 **Tygda** Amurskaya Oblast', SE Russian Federation 53°07´N 126°12´E
67 H7 **Tyger River** ≈ South Carolina, SE USA
76 C6 **Tygh Valley** Oregon, NW USA 45°15´N 121°12´W
154 C6 **Tyin** ◎ S Norway
74 F5 **Tyler** Minnesota, N USA 44°16´N 96°07´W
71 I5 **Tyler** Texas, SW USA 32°21´N 95°18´W
71 I5 **Tyler, Lake** ⊠ Texas, SW USA
68 E3 **Tylertown** Mississippi, S USA 31°07´N 90°08´W
Tylos see Bahrain
192 F6 **Tym** ≈ C Russian Federation
186 F4 **Týmfi** var. Timfi. ▲ W Greece 39°58´N 20°51´E
186 F5 **Tymfristós** var. Timfristos. ▲ C Greece 38°57´N 21°49´E
187 I10 **Tympáki** var. Timbaki; prev. Timbákion. Kríti, Greece, E Mediterranean Sea 35°04´N 24°47´E
193 J7 **Tynda** Amurskaya Oblast', SE Russian Federation 55°09´N 124°44´E
74 E6 **Tyndall** South Dakota, N USA 42°57´N 97°52´W
158 G2 **Tyndrum** United Kingdom 56°27´N 4°44´W
156 G7 **Tyne** ≈ N England, United Kingdom
159 K5 **Tynemouth** NE England, United Kingdom 55°01´N 01°24´W
154 E4 **Tynset** Hedmark, S Norway 61°45´N 10°49´E
83 I6 **Tyonek** Alaska, USA 61°04´N 151°08´W
Tyôsi see Chōshi
Tyras see Dniester
Tyras see Bilhorod-Dnistrovs'kyy
Tyre see Soûr
154 D7 **Tyrifjorden** ◎ S Norway
155 G12 **Tyringe** Skåne, S Sweden 56°09´N 13°35´E
193 K8 **Tyrma** Khabarovskiy Kray, SE Russian Federation 50°00´N 132°04´E
Tyrnau see Trnava
186 G4 **Týrnavos** var. Tírnavos. Thessalía, C Greece 39°45´N 22°18´E
197 H9 **Tyrnyauz** Kabardino-Balkarskaya Respublika, SW Russian Federation 43°19´N 42°55´E
Tyrol see Tirol
64 B6 **Tyrone** Pennsylvania, NE USA 40°41´N 78°12´W
157 C8 **Tyrone** cultural region W Northern Ireland, United Kingdom
Tyros see Bahrain
277 I6 **Tyrrell, Lake** salt lake Victoria, SE Australia
144 E8 **Tyrrhenian Basin** undersea feature Tyrrhenian Sea, C Mediterranean Sea 39°30´N 13°00´E
175 D10 **Tyrrhenian Sea** It. Mare Tirreno. sea N Mediterranean Sea
Tysa see Tisa/Tisza
188 D5 **Tysmenytsya** Ivano-Frankivs'ka Oblast', W Ukraine 48°54´N 24°50´E
154 A7 **Tysnesøya** island S Norway
154 A7 **Tysse** Hordaland, S Norway 60°23´N 05°46´E
154 B7 **Tyssedal** Hordaland, S Norway 60°07´N 06°36´E
155 I8 **Tystberga** Södermanland, C Sweden 58°51´N 17°15´E
191 C8 **Tytuvėnai** Šiaulai, C Lithuania 55°36´N 23°14´E
Tyub-Karagan, Mys see Tupkaragan, Mys
229 L4 **Tyugel'-Say** Narynskaya Oblast', C Kyrgyzstan 41°57´N 74°40´E
227 I1 **Tyukalinsk** Omskaya Oblast', C Russian Federation 55°56´N 72°02´E
197 L3 **Tyul'gan** Orenburgskaya Oblast', W Russian Federation 52°27´N 56°08´E
195 N9 **Tyumen'** Tyumenskaya Oblast', C Russian Federation 57°11´N 65°29´E
192 E6 **Tyumenskaya Oblast'** ◈ province C Russian Federation
193 J6 **Tyung** ≈ NE Russian Federation
229 M4 **Tyup** Kir. Tüp. Issyk-Kul'skaya Oblast', NE Kyrgyzstan 42°44´N 78°18´E
192 G8 **Tyva, Respublika** prev. Tannu-Tuva, Tuva, Tuvinskaya ASSR. ◈ autonomous republic C Russian Federation
188 F5 **Tyvriv** Vinnyts'ka Oblast', C Ukraine 49°01´N 28°28´E
157 F11 **Tywi** ≈ S Wales, United Kingdom
160 E5 **Tywi, Afon** ≈ United Kingdom
160 E3 **Tywyn** W Wales, United Kingdom 52°35´N 04°06´W
141 K2 **Tzaneen** Limpopo, NE South Africa 23°50´S 30°09´E

◆ Country
● Country Capital
◇ Dependent Territory
○ Dependent Territory Capital
◈ Administrative Regions
✈ International Airport
▲ Mountain
▲▲ Mountain Range
⋀ Volcano
≈ River
◎ Lake
⊠ Reservoir

Tzaneen Dam - Uruguay, Río

141 K2 **Tzaneen Dam** ◎ Limpopo, South Africa
Tzekung see Zigong
187 I7 **Tziá** prev. Kéa, Kéos; anc. Ceos. island Kykládes, Greece, Aegean Sea
87 K9 **Tzimol** Chiapas, Mexico 16°16´N 92°16´W
87 M5 **Tzucacab** Yucatán, SE Mexico 20°04´N 89°03´W

U

135 C12 **Uaco Cungo** var. Waku Kungo, Port. Santa Comba. Cuanza Sul, C Angola 11°21´S 15°04´E
UAE see United Arab Emirates
285 K5 **Ua Huka** island Îles Marquises, NE French Polynesia
103 H6 **Uaiacás** Roraima, N Brazil 03°28´N 63°13´W
Uamba see Wamba
Uanle Uen see Wanlaweyn
285 K5 **Ua Pu** island Îles Marquises, NE French Polynesia
136 F7 **Uar Garas** spring/well SW Somalia 01°19´N 41°22´E
107 H2 **Uatumã, Rio** ≈ C Brazil
Ua Uíbh Fhailí see Offaly
102 F8 **Uaupés, Rio** var. Río Vaupés. ≈ Brazil/Colombia see also Vaupés, Río
111 I5 **Ubá** Minas Gerais, Brazil 21°07´S 42°56´W
Uba see Oba
226 G2 **Ubagan** Kaz. Obagan. ≈ Kazakhstan/Russian Federation
280 D3 **Ubai** New Britain, E Papua New Guinea 05°38´S 150°45´E
114 E4 **Ubajay** Entre Ríos, Argentina 31°47´S 58°18´W
134 E5 **Ubangi** Fr. Oubangui. ≈ C Africa
Ubangi-Shari see Central African Republic
111 J2 **Ubaporanga** Minas Gerais, Brazil 19°38´S 42°06´W
188 F2 **Ubarts'** Ukr. Ubort'. ≈ Belarus/Ukraine see also Ubort'
Ubarts' see Ubort'
102 C5 **Ubaté** Cundinamarca, C Colombia 05°20´N 73°50´W
110 F9 **Ubatuba** São Paulo, S Brazil 23°26´S 45°04´W
231 H7 **Ubauro** Sind, SE Pakistan 28°08´N 69°43´E
263 M7 **Ubay** Bohol, C Philippines 10°02´N 124°29´E
165 K7 **Ubaye** ≈ SE France
Ubayid, Wadi al see Ubayyiḍ, Wādī al
216 F5 **Ubaylah** Al Anbār, W Iraq 33°06´N 40°13´E
216 G7 **Ubayyiḍ, Wādī al** var. Wadi al Ubayid. dry watercourse SW Iraq
162 G7 **Ubbergen** Gelderland, E Netherlands 51°49´N 05°54´E
250 D5 **Ube** Yamaguchi, Honshū, SW Japan 33°57´N 131°15´E
170 G7 **Ubeda** Andalucía, S Spain 38°01´N 03°22´W
177 K4 **Übelbach** var. Markt-Übelbach. Steiermark, SE Austria 47°13´N 15°15´E
110 B3 **Uberaba** Minas Gerais, SE Brazil 19°47´S 47°57´W
107 H10 **Uberaba, Laguna** ◎ E Bolivia
110 A1 **Uberlândia** Minas Gerais, SE Brazil 18°17´S 48°17´W
179 D13 **Überlingen** Baden-Württemberg, S Germany 47°46´N 09°10´E
133 J8 **Ubiaja** Edo, S Nigeria 06°39´N 06°23´E
170 E2 **Ubiña, Peña** ▲ NW Spain 43°01´N 05°58´W
105 G9 **Ubinas, Volcán** 🌋 S Peru 16°16´S 70°49´W
Ubol Rajadhani/Ubol Ratchathani see Ubon Ratchathani
256 F7 **Ubolratna Reservoir** ⊠ C Thailand
141 L5 **Ubombo** KwaZulu-Natal, South Africa 27°34´S 32°05´E
256 H7 **Ubon Ratchathani** var. Muang Ubon, Ubol Rajadhani, Ubol Ratchathani, Udon Ratchathani. Ubon Ratchathani, E Thailand 15°15´N 104°50´E
191 G12 **Ubort'** Bel. Ubarts'. ≈ Belarus/Ukraine see also Ubarts'
Ubort' see Ubarts'
170 E9 **Ubrique** Andalucía, S Spain 36°42´N 05°27´W
181 F14 **Ubstadt-Weiher** Baden-Württemberg, Germany 49°10´E 8°37´N
Ubsu-Nur, Ozero see Uvs Nuur
134 H7 **Ubundu** Orientale, C Dem. Rep. Congo 0°24´S 25°30´E
228 F7 **Üçajy** var. Üchajy, Rus. Uch-Adzhi. Mary Welaýaty, C Turkmenistan 38°06´N 62°44´E
215 M5 **Ucar** Rus. Udzhary. C Azerbaijan 40°31´N 47°40´E
104 F6 **Ucayali** off. Departamento de Ucayali. ◈ department E Peru
Ucayali, Departamento de see Ucayali
104 E4 **Ucayali, Río** ≈ C Peru
Uccle see Ukkel
Uch-Adzhi/Üchajy see Üçajy
197 M2 **Uchaly** Respublika Bashkortostan, W Russian Federation 54°19´N 59°33´E
Ucharal see Usharal
250 D9 **Uchinoura** Kagoshima, Kyūshū, SW Japan 31°16´N 131°04´E
252 D5 **Uchiura-wan** bay NW Pacific Ocean
Uchkuduk see Uchquduq
229 K5 **Uchqo'rg'on** Rus. Uchkurghan. Namangan Viloyati, E Uzbekistan 41°06´N 72°04´E
229 K5 **Uchqo'rg'on** Rus. Uchkurghan. Namangan Viloyati, E Uzbekistan 41°06´N 72°04´E
228 G5 **Uchquduq** Rus. Uchkuduk. Navoiy Viloyati, N Uzbekistan 42°12´N 63°27´E
Uchsay see Uchsoy
228 D3 **Uchsoy** Rus. Uchsay. Qoraqalpog'iston Respublikasi, NW Uzbekistan 43°51´N 58°51´E
Uchtagan Gumy/Uchtagan, Peski see Uçtagan Gumy
193 K7 **Uchur** ≈ E Russian Federation
181 D10 **Uckerath** Nordrhein-Westfalen, Germany 50°44´E 7°22´N
178 I5 **Uckermark** cultural region E Germany
161 K7 **Uckfield** United Kingdom 50°58´N 0°06´E
56 C9 **Ucluelet** Vancouver Island, British Columbia, SW Canada 48°55´N 123°34´W
228 C5 **Uçtagan Gumy** var. Uchtagan Gumy, Rus. Peski Uchtagan. desert NW Turkmenistan
193 K7 **Uda** ≈ E Russian Federation
193 I5 **Udachnyy** Respublika Sakha (Yakutiya), NE Russian Federation 66°27´N 112°18´E
235 E8 **Udagamandalam** var. Ooty, Udhagamandalam; prev. Ootacamund. Tamil Nādu, SW India 11°28´N 76°42´E
232 D7 **Udaipur** prev. Oodeypore. Rājasthān, N India 24°35´N 73°41´E
Udayadhani see Uthai Thani
222 F10 **'Udayd, Khawr al** var. Khor al Udeid. inlet Qatar/Saudi Arabia
184 C4 **Udbina** Lika-Senj, W Croatia 44°33´N 15°46´E
155 E9 **Uddevalla** Västra Götaland, S Sweden 58°20´N 11°56´E
159 H4 **Uddington** C Scotland, United Kingdom
Uddjaur see Uddjaure
152 E6 **Uddjaure** var. Uddjaur. ◎ N Sweden
Udeid, Khor al see 'Udayd, Khawr al
163 G8 **Uden** Noord-Brabant, SE Netherlands 51°40´N 05°37´E
Uden see Udenhout
163 F8 **Udenhout** var. Uden. Noord-Brabant, S Netherlands 51°37´N 05°09´E
181 H8 **Uder** Thüringen, Germany 51°22´E 10°05´N
181 J9 **Udestedt** Thüringen, Germany 51°03´E 11°08´N
234 E5 **Udgīr** Mahārāshtra, C India 18°23´N 77°06´E
Udhagamandalam see Udagamandalam
232 E3 **Udhampur** Jammu and Kashmir, NW India 32°55´N 75°07´E
217 L9 **'Udhaybah, 'Uqlat al** well S Iraq
218 D7 **Udim** Israel 32°16´N 34°50´E
177 I6 **Udine** anc. Utina. Friuli-Venezia Giulia, NE Italy 46°05´N 13°10´E
267 K9 **Udintsev Fracture Zone** tectonic feature S Pacific Ocean
Udipi see Udupi
Udmurtia see Udmurtskaya Respublika
195 J10 **Udmurtskaya Respublika** Eng. Udmurtia. ◈ autonomous republic NW Russian Federation
194 E9 **Udomlya** Tverskaya Oblast', W Russian Federation 57°53´N 34°59´E
Udon Ratchathani see Ubon Ratchathani
256 F6 **Udon Thani** var. Ban Mak Khaeng, Udorndhani. Udon Thani, N Thailand 17°25´N 102°45´E
Udorndhani see Udon Thani
282 E9 **Udot** atoll Chuuk Islands, C Micronesia
193 L7 **Udskaya Guba** bay E Russian Federation
193 K7 **Udskoye** Khabarovskiy Kray, SE Russian Federation 54°32´N 134°26´E
234 D7 **Udupi** var. Udipi. Karnātaka, SW India 13°18´N 74°46´E
Udzhary see Ucar
260 D4 **Uebonti, Teluk** bay Sulawesi, C Indonesia
178 I5 **Uecker** ≈ NE Germany
178 I5 **Ueckermünde** Mecklenburg-Vorpommern, NE Germany 53°43´N 14°03´E
251 K2 **Ueda** var. Uyeda. Nagano, Honshū, S Japan 36°27´N 138°13´E
181 J12 **Uehlfeld** Bayern, Germany 49°40´E 10°44´N
134 G6 **Uele** var. Welle. ≈ NE Dem. Rep. Congo
82 F4 **Uelen** Chukotskiy Avtonomnyy Okrug, Russian Federation 66°12´N 170°00´E
193 N2 **Uelen** Chukotskiy Avtonomnyy Okrug, NE Russian Federation 66°01´N 169°52´W
Uele (upper course) see Kibali, Dem. Rep. Congo
Uele (upper course) see Uolo, Río, Equatorial Guinea/Gabon
180 C5 **Uelsen** Niedersachsen, Germany 52°30´E 6°53´N
180 I4 **Uelzen** Niedersachsen, N Germany 52°58´N 10°34´E
251 I4 **Ueno** Mie, Honshū, SW Japan 34°45´N 136°08´E
180 H2 **Uetersen** Schleswig-Holstein, Germany 53°41´E 9°40´N
180 H5 **Uetze** Niedersachsen, Germany 52°28´E 10°12´N
197 L2 **Ufa** Respublika Bashkortostan, W Russian Federation 54°46´N 56°02´E
197 L2 **Ufa** ≈ W Russian Federation
161 I6 **Uffington** United Kingdom 51°35´N 1°33´W
Ufra see Kenar
138 B4 **Ugab** ≈ C Namibia
190 C6 **Ugāle** Ventspils, NW Latvia 57°16´N 21°58´E
136 B7 **Uganda** off. Republic of Uganda. ◆ republic E Africa
Uganda, Republic of see Uganda
216 C3 **Ugarit** Ar. Ra's Shamrah. site of ancient city Al Lādhiqīyah, NW Syria
118 F3 **Ugarteche** Mendoza, Argentina 33°13´S 68°53´W
83 H8 **Ugashik** Alaska, USA 57°30´N 157°24´W
175 J10 **Ugento** Puglia, SE Italy 39°53´N 18°09´E
141 J8 **Ugie** Eastern Cape, South Africa 31°12´S 28°14´E
170 G8 **Ugíjar** Andalucía, S Spain 36°58´N 03°03´W
169 L1 **Ugine** Savoie, E France 45°45´N 06°25´E
193 L8 **Uglegorsk** Ostrov Sakhalin, Sakhalinskaya Oblast', SE Russian Federation 49°05´N 142°06´E
Ugleural'sk see Ugleural'skiy
195 L8 **Ugleural'skiy** prev. Polovinka, Ugleural'sk. Permskaya Oblast', NW Russian Federation 58°57´N 57°37´E
194 F10 **Uglich** Yaroslavskaya Oblast', W Russian Federation 57°33´N 38°23´E
193 N3 **Ugol'nyye Kopi** Chukotskiy Avtonomnyy Okrug, NE Russian Federation 64°43´N 177°46´E
196 E2 **Ugra** ≈ W Russian Federation
159 L7 **Ugthorpe** United Kingdom 54°29´N 0°46´W
229 L5 **Ugyut** Narynskaya Oblast', C Kyrgyzstan 41°22´N 74°49´E
183 E9 **Uherské Hradiště** Ger. Ungarisch-Hradisch. Zlínský Kraj, E Czech Republic 49°05´N 17°26´E
183 E9 **Uherský Brod** Ger. Ungarisch-Brod. Zlínský Kraj, E Czech Republic 49°01´N 17°40´E
179 H11 **Úhlava** Ger. Angel. ≈ W Czech Republic
Uhorshchyna see Hungary
73 J10 **Uhrichsville** Ohio, N USA 40°23´N 81°21´W
Uhuru Peak see Kilimanjaro
156 D4 **Uig** N Scotland, United Kingdom 57°35´N 06°22´W
135 C10 **Uíge** Port. Carmona, Vila Marechal Carmona. Uíge NW Angola 07°37´S 15°02´E
135 D10 **Uíge** ◈ province N Angola
282 F10 **Uijec** island Chuuk, C Micronesia
248 C5 **Uijeongbu** Jap. Giseifu; prev. Ŭijŏngbu. NW South Korea 37°42´N 127°02´E
Ŭijŏngbu see Uijeongbu
Uil see Oyyl
79 I2 **Uinta Mountains** ▲▲ Utah, W USA
250 A3 **Uiryeong** prev. Ŭiryŏng. 35°18´N 128°17´E
Ŭiryŏng see Uiryeong
138 B5 **Uis** Erongo, NW Namibia 21°08´S 14°49´E
141 H9 **Uitenhage** Eastern Cape, S South Africa 33°44´S 25°27´E
162 E5 **Uitgeest** Noord-Holland, W Netherlands 52°32´N 04°43´E
162 E6 **Uithoorn** Noord-Holland, C Netherlands 52°14´N 04°50´E
162 I3 **Uithuizen** Groningen, NE Netherlands 53°24´N 06°40´E
162 I3 **Uithuizermeeden** Groningen, NE Netherlands 53°25´N 06°43´E
140 D6 **Uitkyk** Northern Cape, South Africa 29°41´S 18°46´E
140 E5 **Uitsakpan** salt lake Northern Cape, South Africa
140 D8 **Uitspankraal** Western Cape, South Africa 32°03´S 19°24´E
283 K5 **Ujae Atoll** var. Wūjae. atoll Ralik Chain, W Marshall Islands
Ujain see Ujjain
183 F8 **Ujazd** Opolskie, S Poland 50°22´N 18°20´E
Új-Becse see Novi Bečej
Ujda see Oujda
283 J5 **Ujelang Atoll** var. Wujlān. atoll Ralik Chain, W Marshall Islands
183 I11 **Újfehértó** Szabolcs-Szatmár-Bereg, E Hungary 47°48´N 21°40´E
Újgradiska see Nova Gradiška
251 I4 **Uji** var. Uzi. Kyōto, Honshū, SW Japan 34°54´N 135°48´E
250 B9 **Uji-guntō** island Nansei-shotō, SW Japan
137 A10 **Ujiji** Kigoma, W Tanzania 04°55´S 29°39´E
232 D8 **Ujjain** prev. Ujain. Madhya Pradesh, C India 23°11´N 75°50´E
Újlak see Ilok
'Ujmān see 'Ajmān
Újmoldova see Moldova Nouă
Újszentanna see Sântana
Ujungpandang see Makassar
Ujung Salang see Phuket
Újvidék see Novi Sad
UK see United Kingdom
232 C9 **Ukāi Reservoir** ⊠ W India
137 B8 **Ukara Island** island N Tanzania
'Ukash, Wādī see 'Akāsh, Wādī
137 C9 **Ukerewe Island** island N Tanzania
141 J6 **uKhahlamba Drakensberg Park** Kwazulu Natal, South Africa
219 I11 **Ukhaiḍir, Wādī** Jordan
217 I6 **Ukhayḍir** Al Anbār, C Iraq 32°28´N 43°36´E
233 M7 **Ukhrul** Manipur, NE India 25°08´N 94°24´E
195 J6 **Ukhta** Respublika Komi, NW Russian Federation 63°31´N 53°48´E
78 A3 **Ukiah** California, W USA 39°07´N 123°14´W
76 E6 **Ukiah** Oregon, NW USA 45°06´N 118°57´W
163 E10 **Ukkel** Fr. Uccle. Brussels, C Belgium 50°47´N 04°19´E
191 D8 **Ukmergė** Pol. Wiłkomierz. Vilnius, C Lithuania 55°16´N 24°46´E
Ukraina see Ukraine
189 I5 **Ukraine** off. Ukraine, Rus. Ukraina, Ukr. Ukrayina; prev. Ukrainian Soviet Socialist Republic, Ukrainskay S.S.R. ◆ republic SE Europe
Ukraine see Ukraine
Ukrainian Soviet Socialist Republic see Ukraine
Ukrainskay S.S.R/Ukrayina see Ukraine
195 M10 **Uksyanskoye** Kurganskaya Oblast, Russian Federation
135 C12 **Uku** Cuanza Sul, NW Angola 11°25´S 14°18´E
250 B6 **Uku-jima** island Gotō-rettō, SW Japan
140 E2 **Ukwi** Kgalagadi, SW Botswana 23°41´S 20°26´E
191 H8 **Ula** Rus. Ulla. Vitsyebskaya Voblasts', N Belarus 55°14´N 29°15´E
214 B7 **Ula** Muğla, SW Turkey 37°08´N 28°25´E
191 H8 **Ula** Rus. Ulla. ≈ N Belarus
236 G3 **Ulaanbaatar** Eng. Ulan Bator; prev. Urga. ● (Mongolia) Töv, C Mongolia 47°55´N 106°57´E
Ulaan-Ereg see Bayanmönh
236 E2 **Ulaangom** Uvs, NW Mongolia 49°56´N 92°06´E
238 G1 **Ulaanhus** var. Bilüü. Bayan-Ölgiy, W Mongolia 48°54´N 89°40´E
Ulaantolgoy see Möst
Ulaan-Uul see Öldziyt, Bayanhongor, Mongolia
Ulaan-Uul see Erdene, Dornogovĭ, Mongolia
244 E3 **Ulan** var. Otog Qi. Nei Mongol Zizhiqu, N China 39°05´N 107°58´E
239 J6 **Ulan** var. Xireg; prev. Xiligou. Qinghai, C China 36°59´N 98°21´E
Ulan Bator see Ulaanbaatar
244 C3 **Ulan Buh Shamo** desert N China
Ulanhad see Chifeng
237 I3 **Ulanhot** Nei Mongol Zizhiqu, N China 46°02´N 122°E
244 G1 **Ulan Hua** Inner Mongolia, China 41°19´N 111°25´E
197 I8 **Ulan Khol** Respublika Kalmykiya, SW Russian Federation 45°27´N 46°48´E
245 H2 **Ulan Qab** var. Jining. Nei Mongol Zizhiqu, N China 40°59´N 113°08´E
244 E2 **Ulansuhai Nur** ◎ N China
193 I8 **Ulan-Ude** prev. Verkhneudinsk. Respublika Buryatiya, S Russian Federation 51°55´N 107°40´E
238 G7 **Ulan Ul Hu** ◎ C China
281 K3 **Ulawa Island** island SE Solomon Islands
218 J3 **'Ulayyānīyah, Bi'r al** var. Al Hilbeh. well S Syria
193 L7 **Ul'banskiy Zaliv** strait E Russian Federation
Ulbo see Olib
159 M10 **Ulceby** United Kingdom 53°13´N 0°07´E
Ulchin see Uljin
184 E7 **Ulcinj** S Montenegro 41°56´N 19°14´E
140 G5 **Ulco** Northern Cape, South Africa 28°19´S 24°13´E
Uldz see Norovlin
Uleåborg see Oulu
Uleälv see Oulujoki
155 D8 **Ulefoss** Telemark, S Norway 59°17´N 09°15´E
173 J8 **Uleila del Campo** Andalucía, Spain 37°11´N 2°12´W
248 D6 **Ulleung-do** prev. Ullŭng-do. island W South Korea
Uleträsk see Oulujärvi
184 F7 **Ulëz** var. Ulëza. Dibër, C Albania 41°42´N 19°52´E
Ulëza see Ulëz
155 C11 **Ulfborg** Ringkøbing, W Denmark 56°16´N 08°21´E
162 H7 **Ulft** Gelderland, E Netherlands 51°53´N 06°23´E
159 K5 **Ulgham** United Kingdom 55°13´N 1°38´W
236 E3 **Uliastay** prev. Jibhalanta. Dzavhan, W Mongolia 47°47´N 96°53´E
282 C9 **Ulimang** Babeldaob, N Palau
121 K6 **Ulindi** ≈ W Dem. Rep. Congo
282 D5 **Ulithi Atoll** atoll Caroline Islands, W Micronesia
250 C1 **Uljin** prev. Ulchin. Kyŏngsang-bukto, South Korea 36°59´N 129°24´E
184 G3 **Uljma** Vojvodina, NE Serbia 45°04´N 21°08´E
Ul'kayak see Ol'keyyek
227 I2 **Ul'ken-Karaoy, Ozero** prev. Ul'ken-Karoy, Ozero. ◎ N Kazakhstan
Ul'ken-Karoy, Ozero see Ul'ken-Karaoy, Ozero
Ülkenözen see Karaozen
Ülkenqobda see Kobda
170 C2 **Ulla** ≈ NW Spain
Ulla see Ula
277 L6 **Ulladulla** New South Wales, SE Australia 35°21´S 150°25´E
233 K7 **Ullapara** Rajshahi, W Bangladesh 24°20´N 89°34´E
156 E4 **Ullapool** N Scotland, United Kingdom 57°54´N 05°10´W
155 F10 **Ullared** Halland, S Sweden 57°07´N 12°45´E
171 J4 **Ulldecona** Cataluña, NE Spain 40°36´N 00°27´E
159 K8 **Ulleskelf** United Kingdom 53°51´N 1°13´W
161 I4 **Ullesthorpe** United Kingdom 52°28´N 1°15´W
250 D1 **Ulleung-do** prev. Ullŭng-do.
152 F3 **Ullsfjorden** fjord N Norway
159 I7 **Ullswater** ◎ NW England, United Kingdom
Ullŭng-do see Ulleung-do
Ullŭng-do see Ulleung-do
179 E12 **Ulm** Baden-Württemberg, S Germany 48°24´N 09°59´E
77 I4 **Ulm** Montana, NW USA 47°27´N 111°32´W
277 M3 **Ulmarra** New South Wales, SE Australia 29°37´S 153°06´E
181 G11 **Ulmbach** Hessen, Germany 50°22´E 9°25´N
181 C11 **Ulmen** Rheinland-Pfalz, Germany 50°13´E 6°59´N
188 E9 **Ulmeni** Buzău, C Romania 45°08´N 26°43´E
188 E10 **Ulmeni** Călăraşi, S Romania 44°08´N 26°43´E
88 G4 **Ulmukhuás** Región Autónoma Atlántico Norte, NE Nicaragua 14°20´N 84°30´W
282 B6 **Ulong** var. Aulong. island Palau Islands, N Palau
139 I2 **Ulonguè** var. Ulongwé. Tete, NW Mozambique 14°34´S 34°21´E
Ulongwé see Ulonguè
159 I7 **Ulpha** United Kingdom 54°19´N 3°14´W
155 F10 **Ulricehamn** Västra Götaland, S Sweden 57°47´N 13°25´E
162 H3 **Ulrum** Groningen, NE Netherlands 53°24´N 06°20´E
248 C7 **Ulsan** Jap. Urusan. SE South Korea 35°33´N 129°19´E
154 B4 **Ulsteinvik** Møre og Romsdal, S Norway 62°21´N 05°53´E
157 C8 **Ulster** ◈ province Northern Ireland, United Kingdom/Ireland
158 C7 **Ulster Canal** canal Ireland/Northern Ireland, United Kingdom
260 F2 **Ulu** Pulau Siau, N Indonesia 02°46´N 125°22´E
193 J6 **Ulu** Respublika Sakha (Yakutiya), NE Russian Federation 60°18´N 127°27´E
88 E3 **Ulúa, Río** ≈ NW Honduras
214 C5 **Ulubat Gölü** ◎ NW Turkey
187 M5 **Ulubey** Uşak, Turkey 38°25´N 29°17´E
214 C5 **Uludağ** ▲ NW Turkey 40°08´N 29°13´E
238 B4 **Ulugqat** Xinjiang Uygur Zizhiqu, W China 39°45´N 74°10´E
214 F7 **Ulukışla** Niğde, S Turkey 37°33´N 34°29´E
282 F6 **Ulul** island Caroline Islands, C Micronesia
87 L6 **Ulumal** Campeche, Mexico 19°16´N 90°38´W
139 H7 **Ulundi** KwaZulu/Natal, E South Africa 28°18´S 31°26´E
238 G2 **Ulungur He** ≈ NW China
238 F2 **Ulungur Hu** ◎ NW China
276 D1 **Uluṟu** var. Ayers Rock. monolith Northern Territory, C Australia
158 E2 **Ulva** island United Kingdom
Ulveah see Lopevi
159 I8 **Ulverston** NW England, United Kingdom 54°13´N 03°08´W
277 J9 **Ulverstone** Tasmania, SE Australia 41°09´S 146°10´E
154 B6 **Ulvik** Hordaland, S Norway 60°34´N 06°53´E
153 G9 **Ulvila** Länsi-Suomi, W Finland 61°26´N 21°55´E
190 H3 **Ul'yanovka** Leningradskaya Oblast', Russian Federation
189 H5 **Ul'yanovka** Kirovohrads'ka Oblast', C Ukraine 48°18´N 30°15´E
197 J3 **Ul'yanovsk** prev. Simbirsk. Ul'yanovskaya Oblast', W Russian Federation 54°17´N 48°21´E
197 I3 **Ul'yanovskaya Oblast'** ◈ province W Russian Federation
Ul'yanovskiy see Botakara
Ul'yanovskiy Kanal see Ul'yanow Kanali
228 G7 **Ul'yanow Kanali** Rus. Ul'yanovskiy Kanal. canal Turkmenistan/Uzbekistan
Ulyshylanshyq see Uly-Zhylanshyk
75 B10 **Ulysses** Kansas, C USA 37°36´N 101°23´W
227 H4 **Ulytau, Gory** ▲▲ C Kazakhstan
193 I8 **Ulyunkhan** Respublika Buryatiya, S Russian Federation 54°48´N 111°01´E
226 G4 **Uly-Zhylanshyk** Kaz. Ulyshylanshyq. ≈ C Kazakhstan
180 H2 **Ulzburg** Schleswig-Holstein, Germany 53°48´E 9°59´N
184 A2 **Umag** It. Umago. Istra, NW Croatia 45°25´N 13°32´E
Umago see Umag
87 L5 **Umán** Yucatán, SE Mexico 20°51´N 89°43´W
189 H5 **Uman'** Rus. Uman. Cherkas'ka Oblast', C Ukraine 48°45´N 30°10´E
282 F9 **Uman** atoll Chuuk Islands, C Micronesia
Uman see Uman'
Umanak/Umanaq see Uummannaq
'Umān, Khalīj see Oman, Gulf of
'Umān, Salṭanat see Oman
261 J6 **Umari** Papua, E Indonesia 04°18´S 135°22´E
232 G8 **Umaria** Madhya Pradesh, C India 23°34´N 80°49´E
231 H9 **Umarkot** Sind, SE Pakistan 25°22´N 69°48´E
282 A2 **Umatac** SW Guam 13°17´N 144°40´E
282 A2 **Umatac Bay** bay SW Guam
217 I4 **Umayqah** Şalāḥ ad Dīn, C Iraq 34°32´N 43°45´E
194 E4 **Umba** Murmanskaya Oblast', NW Russian Federation 66°39´N 34°24´E
216 D5 **Umbāshī, Khirbat al** ruins As Suwaydā', S Syria
134 G3 **Umbelasha** ≈ W Sudan
177 H10 **Umbertide** Umbria, C Italy 43°16´N 12°21´E
114 A3 **Umberto** var. Humberto. Santa Fe, C Argentina 30°52´S 61°19´W
141 K7 **Umbogintwini** KwaZulu-Natal, South Africa 30°02´S 30°55´E
Umbogintwini see eZimbokodweni
280 C3 **Umboi Island** var. Rooke Island. island C Papua New Guinea
194 F3 **Umbozero, Ozero** ◎ NW Russian Federation
174 E7 **Umbria** ◈ region C Italy
Umbrian-Machigian Mountains see Umbro-Marchigiano, Appennino
172 D8 **Umbría, Punta** headland Andalucía, Spain 37°11´N 6°58´W
177 I10 **Umbro-Marchigiano, Appennino** Eng. Umbrian-Machigian Mountains. ▲▲ C Italy
154 J2 **Umeå** Västerbotten, N Sweden 63°50´N 20°15´E
154 I2 **Umeälven** ≈ N Sweden
141 K6 **uMhali** KwaZulu-Natal, South Africa 29°28´S 31°13´E
141 K7 **Umhalnga Rocks** KwaZulu-Natal, South Africa 29°43´S 31°04´E
141 K7 **uMhlanga** prev. Umhlanga Rocks. Kwazulu Natal, South Africa 29°43´S 31°05´E see also Umhlanga Rocks
141 K7 **Umhlanga Rocks** Kwazulu Natal, South Africa 29°43´S 31°05´E
Umhlanga Rocks see uMhlanga
83 I2 **Umiat** Alaska, USA 69°22´N 152°09´W
141 K7 **Umkomaas** ≈ KwaZulu-Natal, South Africa
Umkomaas see eMkhomazi
139 H8 **Umlazi** KwaZulu/Natal, E South Africa 29°58´S 30°50´E
141 K7 **Umlazi** KwaZulu-Natal, South Africa 29°58´S 30°53´E
217 L7 **Umm al Baqar, Hawr** var. Birkat ad Dawaymah. spring S Iraq
217 I4 **Umm al Faṭūr** var. Umm al Tūz. Şalāḥ ad Dīn, C Iraq 34°53´N 42°42´E
221 J7 **Umm al Ḥayt, Wādī** var. Wādī Amilḥayt. seasonal river SW Oman
Umm al Qaiwain see Umm al Qaywayn
221 J4 **Umm al Qaywayn** var. Umm al Qaiwain. Umm al Qaywayn, NE United Arab Emirates 25°43´N 55°55´E
Umm al Tūz see Umm al Faṭūr
216 D2 **Umm 'Āmūd** Ḥalab, N Syria 35°57´N 37°39´E
221 L6 **Umm ar Ruṣāṣ** var. Umm Ruşayş. W Oman 20°26´N 58°48´E
221 K5 **Umm as Samīn** salt flat C Oman
218 H7 **Umm as Sirb** Jordan
221 J5 **Umm az Zumūl** oasis E Saudi Arabia
134 G1 **Umm Buru** Western Darfur, W Sudan 15°01´N 23°36´E
134 G3 **Umm Dafag** Southern Darfur, W Sudan 10°28´N 23°20´E
Umm Durmān see Omdurman
218 E6 **Umm el Fahm** Haifa, N Israel 32°30´N 35°06´E
180 J6 **Ummendorf** Sachsen-Anhalt, Germany 52°09´E 11°11´N
219 F14 **Umm Ḥaraq, Wādī** dry watercourse Jordan
136 B2 **Umm Inderab** Northern Kordofan, C Sudan 15°12´N 31°54´E
134 H2 **Umm Keddada** Northern Darfur, W Sudan 13°36´N 26°42´E
220 D4 **Umm Lajj** Tabūk, W Saudi Arabia 25°02´N 37°19´E
216 E7 **Umm Maḥfur** ≈ N Jordan
217 M9 **Umm Qaṣr** Al Başrah, SE Iraq 30°02´N 47°55´E
218 F6 **Umm Qays** Jordan 32°39´N 35°41´E
Umm Ruṣayṣ see Umm ar Ruşāş
136 B3 **Umm Ruwaba** var. Umm Ruwābah, Um Ruwāba. Northern Kordofan, C Sudan 12°54´N 31°13´E
Umm Ruwābah see Umm Ruwaba
221 I4 **Umm Sa'īd** var. Musay'īd. S Qatar 24°57´N 51°32´E
217 M7 **Umm Sawān, Hawr** ◎ S Iraq
216 E7 **Umm Ṭuways, Wādī** dry watercourse N Jordan
82 E9 **Umnak Island** island Aleutian Islands, Alaska, USA
76 B7 **Umpqua River** ≈ Oregon, NW USA
135 E12 **Umpulo** Bié, C Angola 12°43´S 17°42´E
234 F4 **Umred** Mahārāshtra, C India 20°54´N 79°19´E
Um Ruwāba see Umm Ruwaba
Ŭmsŏng see Eumseong
Umtali see Mutare
141 J8 **Umtata** Eastern Cape, SE South Africa 31°33´S 28°47´E
Umtata see Mthatha
141 K8 **Umtentu** Eastern Cape, South Africa 31°08´S 30°09´E
141 K7 **Umtentweni** KwaZulu-Natal, South Africa 30°43´S 30°28´E
133 K8 **Umuahia** Abia, SW Nigeria 05°30´N 07°33´E
113 I4 **Umuarama** Paraná, S Brazil 23°45´S 53°20´W
Umvuma see Mvuma
141 K7 **Umzimkulu** Eastern Cape, South Africa 30°16´S 29°56´E
141 K1 **Umzingwani** ≈ S Zimbabwe
141 K7 **Umzinto** KwaZulu-Natal, South Africa 30°19´S 30°40´E
173 J3 **Uña** Castilla-La Manacha, Spain 40°13´N 1°58´W
184 C3 **Una** ≈ Bosnia and Herzegovina/Croatia
184 C4 **Unac** ≈ W Bosnia and Herzegovina
69 J2 **Unadilla** Georgia, SE USA 32°15´N 83°44´W
64 F2 **Unadilla** New York, USA 42°20´N 75°19´W
64 F2 **Unadilla River** ≈ New York, NE USA
109 D10 **Unaí** Minas Gerais, SE Brazil 16°24´S 46°49´W
82 G5 **Unalakleet** Alaska, USA 63°52´N 160°47´W
82 F9 **Unalaska Island** island Aleutian Islands, Alaska, USA
279 E8 **Una, Mount** ▲ South Island, New Zealand 42°12´S 172°34´E
137 D13 **Unango** Niassa, N Mozambique 12°45´S 35°28´E
Unao see Unnão
152 H5 **Unari** Lappi, N Finland 67°07´N 25°37´E
219 F12 **'Unayzah** Jordan
220 F3 **'Unayzah** var. Anaiza. Al Qaşīm, C Saudi Arabia 26°03´N 44°00´E
216 F7 **'Unayzah, Jabal** ▲ Jordan/Saudi Arabia 32°09´N 39°11´E
Unci see Almería
112 C1 **Uncía** Potosí, C Bolivia 18°30´S 66°29´W
79 K4 **Uncompahgre Peak** ▲ Colorado, C USA 38°04´N 107°27´W
79 J4 **Uncompahgre Plateau** plain Colorado, C USA
155 G9 **Unden** ◎ S Sweden
141 J7 **Underberg** KwaZulu-Natal, South Africa 29°47´S 29°30´E
74 C3 **Underwood** North Dakota, N USA 47°25´N 101°09´W
261 H6 **Undur** Pulau Seram, E Indonesia 03°41´S 130°38´E
Undur Khan see Öndörhaan
196 E3 **Unecha** Bryanskaya Oblast', W Russian Federation 52°51´N 32°38´E
82 G9 **Unga** Unga Island, Alaska, USA 55°14´N 160°34´W
Ungaria see Hungary
277 J5 **Ungarie** New South Wales, SE Australia 33°39´S 146°54´E
Ungarisch-Brod see Uherský Brod
Ungarisches Erzgebirge see Slovenské rudohorie
Ungarisch-Hradisch see Uherské Hradiště
Ungarn see Hungary
59 I2 **Ungava Bay** bay Québec, E Canada
58 G2 **Ungava, Péninsule d'** peninsula Québec, SE Canada
Ungeny see Ungheni
188 F6 **Ungheni** Rus. Ungeny. W Moldova 47°13´N 27°48´E
Unguja see Zanzibar
228 E5 **Üngüz Angyrsyndaky Garagum** Rus. Zaunguzskiye Garagumy. desert N Turkmenistan
228 E6 **Unguz, Solonchakovyye Vpadiny** salt marsh C Turkmenistan
Ungvár see Uzhhorod
172 C2 **Unhais da Serra** Castelo Branco, Portugal 40°16´N 7°37´W
113 J5 **União da Vitória** Paraná, S Brazil 26°13´S 51°05´W
118 C7 **Unicavén** Maule, Chile 36°05´S 72°01´W
183 E9 **Uničov** Ger. Mährisch-Neustadt. Olomoucký Kraj, E Czech Republic 49°48´N 17°05´E
182 F6 **Uniejów** Łódzkie, C Poland 51°58´N 18°46´E
118 B8 **Unihue** Bío-Bío, Chile 37°07´S 72°55´W
184 A3 **Unije** island W Croatia
82 F9 **Unimak Island** island Aleutian Islands, Alaska, USA
82 F9 **Unimak Pass** strait Aleutian Islands, Alaska, USA
112 D10 **Unión** San Luis, C Argentina 35°09´S 65°55´W
75 I10 **Union** Missouri, C USA 38°27´N 91°01´W
64 G6 **Union** New Jersey, USA 40°40´N 74°55´W
76 E6 **Union** Oregon, NW USA 45°12´N 117°51´W
67 I7 **Union** South Carolina, SE USA 34°42´N 81°37´W
67 I4 **Union** West Virginia, NE USA 37°36´N 80°34´W
116 F7 **Unión, Bahía** bay E Argentina
65 H6 **Union Beach** New Jersey, USA 40°27´N 74°11´W
88 M9 **Unión Chocó** Emberá-Wounaan, Panama 08°07´N 77°32´W
80 B3 **Union City** California, USA 37°36´N 122°01´W
73 G10 **Union City** Indiana, N USA 40°12´N 84°50´W
73 G8 **Union City** Michigan, N USA 42°03´N 85°06´W
65 H6 **Union City** New Jersey, USA 40°47´N 74°01´W
62 C7 **Union City** Pennsylvania, NE USA 41°54´N 79°51´W
66 C5 **Union City** Tennessee, S USA 36°26´N 89°03´W
76 C7 **Union Creek** Oregon, NW USA 42°54´N 122°26´W
138 E10 **Uniondale** Western Cape, SW South Africa 33°40´S 23°07´E
86 B6 **Unión de Tula** Jalisco, SW Mexico 19°58´N 104°16´W
73 D8 **Union Grove** Wisconsin, N USA 42°39´N 88°03´W
87 I9 **Unión Hidalgo** Oaxaca, Mexico 16°28´N 94°50´W
103 I1 **Union Island** island S Saint Vincent and the Grenadines
87 K10 **Unión Juárez** Chiapas, Mexico 15°04´N 92°05´W
Union of Myanmar see Burma
81 J11 **Union Pass** ▲ Nevada, USA 35°13´N 114°23´W
94 F3 **Union Reefs** reef SW Mexico
42 C4 **Union Seamount** undersea feature NE Pacific Ocean 49°35´N 132°45´W
69 I2 **Union Springs** Alabama, S USA 32°08´N 85°43´W
66 D4 **Uniontown** Kentucky, S USA 37°46´N 87°55´W
62 C9 **Uniontown** Pennsylvania, NE USA 39°54´N 79°44´W
75 H8 **Unionville** Missouri, C USA 40°28´N 93°00´W
80 I1 **Unionville** Nevada, USA 40°27´N 118°07´W
221 H5 **United Arab Emirates** Ar. Al Imārāt al 'Arabīyah al Muttaḥidah, abbrev. UAE; prev. Trucial States. ◆ federation SW Asia
United Arab Republic see Egypt
157 G10 **United Kingdom** off. United Kingdom of Great Britain and Northern Ireland, abbrev. UK. ◆ monarchy NW Europe
United Kingdom of Great Britain and Northern Ireland see United Kingdom
United Mexican States see Mexico
United Provinces see Uttar Pradesh
77 J3 **United States of America** off. United States of America, var. America, The States, abbrev. U.S., USA. ◆ federal republic North America
United States of America see United States of America
194 E6 **Unitsa** Respublika Kareliya, NW Russian Federation 62°31´N 34°31´E
57 L6 **Unity** Saskatchewan, S Canada 52°27´N 109°10´W
Unity State see Wahda
173 K2 **Universales, Montes** ▲▲ Aragón, Spain
66 B3 **University City** Missouri, C USA 38°40´N 90°19´W
195 L10 **Unkurda** Chelyabinskaya Oblasť, Russian Federation
281 M3 **Unmet** Malekula, C Vanuatu 16°09´S 167°16´E
181 D8 **Unna** Nordrhein-Westfalen, W Germany 51°32´N 07°41´E
Unnan see Kisuki
232 G6 **Unnão** prev. Unao. Uttar Pradesh, N India 26°32´N 80°30´E
281 N5 **Unpongkor** Erromango, S Vanuatu 18°48´S 169°01´E
Unruhstadt see Kargowa
156 H1 **Unst** island NE Scotland, United Kingdom
179 G8 **Unstrut** ≈ C Germany
Unterdrauburg see Dravograd
181 H14 **Untergröningen** Baden-Württemberg, Germany 48°55´E 9°54´N
Unterlimbach see Lendava
180 I4 **Unterlüss** Niedersachsen, Germany 52°50´E 10°17´N
181 H14 **Untermünkheim** Baden-Württemberg, Germany 49°09´E 9°44´N
179 G12 **Unterschleissheim** Bayern, SE Germany 48°16´N 11°34´E
179 D14 **Untersee** ◎ Germany/Switzerland
181 J11 **Untersiemau** Bayern, Germany 50°12´E 10°58´N
178 H5 **Unterueckersee** ◎ NE Germany
174 B3 **Unterwalden** ◈ canton C Switzerland
181 H13 **Unterwittighausen** Baden-Württemberg, Germany 49°37´E 9°50´N
103 H7 **Unturán, Sierra de** ▲▲ Brazil/Venezuela
239 H7 **Unuli Horog** Qinghai, W China 35°10´N 91°50´E
214 G4 **Ünye** Ordu, W Turkey 41°08´N 37°14´E
Unza see Unzha
195 H9 **Unzha** var. Unza. ≈ NW Russian Federation
134 A7 **Uolo, Río** var. Eyo (lower course), Mbini, Uele (upper course), Woleu; prev. Benito. ≈ Equatorial Guinea/Gabon
103 I6 **Uonán** Bolívar, SE Venezuela 04°33´N 62°10´W
241 L6 **Uotsuri-shima** island China/Japan/Taiwan
251 J2 **Uozu** Toyama, Honshū, SW Japan 36°50´N 137°25´E
88 G7 **Upala** Alajuela, NW Costa Rica 10°52´N 85°W
103 I4 **Upata** Bolívar, E Venezuela 08°02´N 62°25´W
135 H11 **Upemba, Lac** ◎ SE Dem. Rep. Congo
227 I4 **Upenskoye** prev. Uspenskiy. Karaganda, C Kazakhstan 48°45´N 72°46´E
118 D5 **Upeo** Maule, Chile 35°08´S 71°02´W
295 K7 **Upernavik** var. Upernivik. Kitaa, C Greenland 73°06´N 55°42´W
Upernivik see Upernavik
140 E5 **Upington** Northern Cape, W South Africa 28°28´S 21°14´E
Uplands see Ottawa
286 F6 **'Upolu** island SE Samoa
82 D3 **'Upolu Point** var. Upolu Point. headland Hawai'i, USA, C Pacific Ocean 20°15´N 155°51´W
160 G8 **Upottery** United Kingdom 50°52´N 3°08´W
Upper Austria see Oberösterreich
Upper Bann see Bann
62 G4 **Upper Canada Village** tourist site Ontario, SE Canada
160 F5 **Upper Chapel** United Kingdom 52°03´N 3°27´W
64 F8 **Upper Darby** Pennsylvania, NE USA 39°57´N 75°15´W
74 B1 **Upper Des Lacs Lake** ⊠ North Dakota, N USA
278 G7 **Upper Hutt** Wellington, North Island, New Zealand 41°06´S 175°06´E
74 I6 **Upper Iowa River** ≈ Iowa, C USA
76 C8 **Upper Klamath Lake** ◎ Oregon, NW USA
78 B3 **Upper Lake** California, W USA 39°07´N 122°53´W
78 C1 **Upper Lake** ◎ California, W USA
54 C4 **Upper Liard** Yukon Territory, W Canada 60°01´N 128°59´W
157 C8 **Upper Lough Erne** ◎ SW Northern Ireland, United Kingdom
158 C7 **Upper Lough Erne** ◎ United Kingdom
136 B4 **Upper Nile** ◈ state NE South Sudan
159 L8 **Upper Poppleton** United Kingdom 53°58´N 1°09´W
74 F2 **Upper Red Lake** ◎ Minnesota, N USA
73 H10 **Upper Sandusky** Ohio, N USA 40°49´N 83°16´W
Upper Volta see Burkina
161 J3 **Uppingham** United Kingdom 52°35´N 0°43´W
155 I8 **Upplands Väsby** var. Upplandsväsby. Stockholm, C Sweden 59°29´N 18°04´E
Upplandsväsby see Upplands Väsby
154 I7 **Uppsala** Uppsala, C Sweden 59°52´N 17°38´E
154 I7 **Uppsala** ◈ county C Sweden
82 E6 **Upright Cape** headland Saint Matthew Island, Alaska, USA 60°19´N 172°15´W
74 I1 **Upsala** Ontario, S Canada 49°01´N 90°27´W
66 E4 **Upton** Kentucky, S USA 37°25´N 85°53´W
77 M6 **Upton** Wyoming, C USA 44°06´N 104°37´W
220 F4 **'Uqlat aş Şuqūr** Al Qaşīm, W Saudi Arabia 25°51´N 42°13´E
216 F5 **'Uqlat Şawāb** well W Iraq
Uqsuqtuuq see Gjoa Haven
Uqturpan see Wushi
102 B4 **Urabá, Golfo de** gulf NW Colombia
Uracas see Farallon de Pajaros
Uradar'ya see O'radaryo
Urad Qianqi see Xishanzui, N China
253 C14 **Uraga-suidō** strait S Japan
252 G5 **Urahoro** Hokkaidō, NE Japan 42°47´N 143°41´E
252 F5 **Urakawa** Hokkaidō, NE Japan 42°11´N 142°42´E
Ural see Zhayyk
Ural Mountains see Ural'skiye Gory
226 C3 **Ural'sk** Kaz. Oral. Zapadnyy Kazakhstan, NW Kazakhstan 51°12´N 51°17´E
Ural'skaya Oblast' see Zapadnyy Kazakhstan
195 L8 **Ural'skiye Gory** var. Ural'skiy Khrebet, Eng. Ural Mountains. ▲▲ Kazakhstan/Russian Federation
195 L9 **Ural'skiye Gory** mountains Sverdlovskaya Oblasť, Russian Federation
195 L4 **Ural'skiye Gory** mountains Yamalo-Nenetskiy Avtonomnyy Okrug, Russian Federation
Ural'skiy Khrebet see Ural'skiye Gory
216 D2 **Urām aş Şughrá** Ḥalab, N Syria 36°10´N 36°55´E
277 J6 **Urana** New South Wales, SE Australia 35°22´S 146°16´E
114 B7 **Uranga** Santa Fe, Argentina 33°16´S 60°42´W
54 G5 **Uranium City** Saskatchewan, C Canada 59°30´N 108°46´W
103 I6 **Uraricoera** Roraima, N Brazil 03°26´N 60°54´W
95 J3 **Uraricoera, Rio** ≈ N Brazil
Ura-Tyube see Ŭroteppa
253 C13 **Urawa** var. Saitama. Saitama, Honshū, S Japan 35°52´N 139°40´E
195 M7 **Uray** Khanty-Mansiyskiy Avtonomnyy Okrug-Yugra, C Russian Federation 60°07´N 64°38´E
221 H4 **'Uray'irah** Ash Sharqīyah, E Saudi Arabia 25°59´N 48°52´E
73 D10 **Urbana** Illinois, N USA 40°06´N 88°12´W
73 H10 **Urbana** Ohio, N USA 40°04´N 83°46´W
74 G7 **Urbandale** Iowa, C USA 41°37´N 93°42´W
177 I9 **Urbania** Marche, C Italy 43°40´N 12°33´E
261 H4 **Urbinasopon** Papua, E Indonesia 0°19´S 131°12´E
177 I9 **Urbino** Marche, C Italy 43°45´N 12°38´E
161 H7 **Urchfont** United Kingdom 51°18´N 1°56´W
105 G8 **Urcos** Cusco, S Peru 13°40´S 71°38´W
170 G6 **Urda** Castilla-La Mancha, C Spain 39°25´N 03°43´W
Urda see Khan Ordasy
Urdgol see Chandmanĭ
114 D6 **Urdinarrain** Entre Ríos, Argentina 32°41´S 58°53´W
170 G2 **Urduña** var. Orduña. País Vasco, N Spain 43°00´N 03°00´W
Urdunn see Jordan
Urdzhar see Urzhar
159 K8 **Ure** ≈ N England, United Kingdom
191 G11 **Urechcha** Rus. Urech'ye. Minskaya Voblasts', S Belarus 52°57´N 27°54´E
Urech'ye see Urechcha
197 I1 **Uren'** Nizhegorodskaya Oblast', W Russian Federation 57°30´N 45°48´E
192 F5 **Urengoy** Yamalo-Nenetskiy Avtonomnyy Okrug, N Russian Federation 65°52´N 78°42´E
278 G5 **Urenui** Taranaki, North Island, New Zealand 38°59´S 174°25´E
281 M1 **Ureparapara** island Banks Islands, N Vanuatu
84 F4 **Ures** Sonora, NW Mexico 29°26´N 110°24´W
Urfa see Şanlıurfa
Urga see Ulaanbaatar
239 H1 **Urgamal** var. Hungiy. Dzavhan, W Mongolia 48°31´N 94°15´E
228 E5 **Urganch** Rus. Urgench; prev. Novo-Urgench. Xorazm Viloyati, W Uzbekistan 41°40´N 60°32´E
Urgench see Urganch
214 F6 **Ürgüp** Nevşehir, C Turkey 38°39´N 34°55´E
229 H6 **Urgut** Samarqand Viloyati, C Uzbekistan 39°26´N 67°15´E
238 F2 **Urho** Xinjiang Uygur Zizhiqu, W China 46°05´N 84°51´E
232 D2 **Uri** Jammu and Kashmir, NW India 34°05´N 74°03´E
174 C3 **Uri** ◈ canton C Switzerland
102 C6 **Uribe** Meta, C Colombia 03°01´N 74°33´W
114 E10 **Uribelarrea** Buenos Aires, Argentina 35°07´S 58°53´W
102 D2 **Uribia** La Guajira, N Colombia 11°45´N 72°19´W
188 C8 **Uricani** Hung. Hobicaurikány. Hunedoara, SW Romania 45°18´N 23°03´E
219 C10 **Urim** Israel 31°18´N 34°31´E
112 D3 **Uriondo** Tarija, S Bolivia 21°43´S 64°40´W
84 G5 **Urique** Chihuahua, N Mexico 27°16´N 107°51´W
84 G5 **Urique, Río** ≈ N Mexico
104 D3 **Uritiyacu, Río** ≈ N Peru
Uritskiy see Sarykol'
162 G5 **Urk** Flevoland, N Netherlands 52°40´N 05°35´E
187 N7 **Ürkütlü** Burdur, Turkey 37°19´N 30°18´E
214 A6 **Urla** İzmir, W Turkey 38°19´N 26°47´E
188 E9 **Urlaţi** Prahova, SE Romania 44°59´N 26°15´E
197 L2 **Urman** Respublika Bashkortostan, W Russian Federation 54°53´N 56°52´E
229 I6 **Urmetan** W Tajikistan 39°27´N 68°13´E
Urmia see Orūmīyeh
Urmia, Lake see Orūmīyeh, Daryācheh-ye
Urmiyeh see Orūmīyeh
159 J10 **Urmston** United Kingdom 53°27´N 2°21´W
Uroševac see Ferizaj
229 I6 **Ŭroteppa** Rus. Ura-Tyube. NW Tajikistan 39°55´N 68°57´E
172 D4 **Urra** Portalegre, Portugal 39°14´N 7°24´W
102 B5 **Urrao** Antioquia, W Colombia 06°16´N 76°10´W
172 E1 **Urrós** Bragança, Portugal 41°21´N 6°28´W
Ursat'yevskaya see Xovos
181 H12 **Urspringen** Bayern, Germany 49°54´E 9°40´N
Urt see Gurvantes
197 M3 **Urtazym** Orenburgskaya Oblast', W Russian Federation 52°12´N 58°48´E
84 G5 **Uruàchic** Chihuahua, Mexico 27°52´N 108°14´W
109 B9 **Uruaçu** Goiás, C Brazil 14°38´S 49°06´W
86 D6 **Uruapan** var. Uruapan del Progreso. Michoacán, SW Mexico 19°26´N 102°04´W
Uruapan del Progreso see Uruapan
104 F7 **Urubamba, Cordillera** ▲▲ C Peru
104 F7 **Urubamba, Río** ≈ C Peru
111 I3 **Urucânia** Minas Gerais, Brazil 20°22´S 42°45´W
107 H2 **Urucará** Amazonas, N Brazil 02°30´S 57°45´W
114 G1 **Uruguaiana** Rio Grande do Sul, S Brazil 29°45´S 57°05´W
Uruguai, Rio see Uruguay
115 L5 **Uruguay** Cerro Largo, Uruguay 32°29´S 53°31´W
115 H6 **Uruguay** off. Oriental Republic of Uruguay; prev. La Banda Oriental. ◆ republic E South America
114 E8 **Uruguay** var. Rio Uruguai, Río Uruguay. ≈ E South America
Uruguay, Oriental Republic of see Uruguay
Uruguay, Río see Uruguay

◆ Country
● Country Capital
◇ Dependent Territory
○ Dependent Territory Capital
◈ Administrative Regions
✈ International Airport
▲ Mountain
▲▲ Mountain Range
🌋 Volcano
≈ River
◎ Lake
⊠ Reservoir

◆ Country ◇ Dependent Territory ◈ Administrative Regions ▲ Mountain ◢ Volcano ◎ Lake
● Country Capital ○ Dependent Territory Capital ✈ International Airport ▲ Mountain Range ⊗ River ⊠ Reservoir

Vardoúsia - Victoria Strait
INDEX
422

186 G5 **Vardoúsia** ⛰ C Greece
Vareia *see* Logroño
180 E3 **Varel** Niedersachsen, NW Germany 53°24′N 08°07′E
191 D9 **Varėna** *Pol.* Orany. Alytus, S Lithuania 54°13′N 24°35′E
63 H3 **Varennes** Québec, SE Canada 45°42′N 73°25′W
167 K4 **Varennes-en-Argonne** Lorraine, France 49°14′N 5°02′E
165 I6 **Varennes-sur-Allier** Allier, C France 46°17′N 03°24′E
184 E4 **Vareš** Federacija Bosna I Hercegovina, E Bosnia and Herzegovina 44°12′N 18°19′E
176 E6 **Varese** Lombardia, N Italy 45°49′N 08°50′E
Varganzi *see* Warganza
155 F9 **Vårgårda** Västra Götaland, S Sweden 58°00′N 12°49′E
102 G2 **Vargas** *off.* Estado Vargas. ◈ *state* N Venezuela
195 N10 **Vargashi** Kurganskaya Oblast', C Russian Federation 55°22′N 65°39′E
110 D8 **Vargem** São Paulo, Brazil 22°53′S 46°25′W
111 J2 **Vargem Alegre** Minas Gerais, Brazil 19°35′S 42°18′W
111 L4 **Vargem Alta** Espírito Santo, Brazil 20°40′S 41°00′W
110 D3 **Vargem Bonita** Minas Gerais, Brazil 20°20′S 46°22′W
110 C6 **Vargem Grande do Sul** São Paulo, Brazil 21°50′S 46°53′W
110 F6 **Varginha** Minas Gerais, Brazil 21°33′S 45°26′W
155 F9 **Vargön** Västra Götaland, S Sweden 58°21′N 12°22′E
155 A9 **Varhaug** Rogaland, S Norway 58°37′N 05°39′E
168 G6 **Varilhes** Midi-Pyrénées, France 43°03′N 1°38′E
Várjjatvuotna *see* Varangerfjorden
153 I8 **Varkaus** Itä-Suomi, C Finland 62°20′N 27°50′E
152 C2 **Varmahlidh** Nordhurland Vestra, N Iceland 65°32′N 19°33′W
155 F8 **Värmland** ◈ *county* C Sweden
185 M5 **Varna** *prev.* Stalin; *anc.* Odessus. Varna, E Bulgaria 43°14′N 27°56′E
185 M5 **Varna** ◈ *province* E Bulgaria
185 M5 **Varna** ✈ Varna, E Bulgaria 43°16′N 27°52′E
155 G10 **Värnamo** Jönköping, S Sweden 57°11′N 14°03′E
185 M5 **Varnenski Zaliv** *prev.* Stalinski Zaliv. *bay* E Bulgaria
185 M5 **Varnensko Ezero** *estuary* E Bulgaria
190 C7 **Varniai** Telšiai, W Lithuania 55°45′N 22°22′E
Várnjárga *see* Varangerhalvøya
Varnoús *see* Baba
182 C7 **Varnsdorf** *Ger.* Warnsdorf. Ústecký Kraj, NW Czech Republic 50°57′N 14°35′E
183 F12 **Várpalota** Veszprém, W Hungary 47°12′N 18°08′E
180 F5 **Varrel** Niedersachsen, Germany 52°37′E 8°44′N
111 K4 **Varre-Sai** Rio de Janeiro, Brazil 20°56′S 41°54′W
169 M3 **Vars** Provence-Alpes-Côte d'Azur, France 44°37′N 6°41′E
Varshava *see* Warszawa
190 F5 **Värska** Põlvamaa, SE Estonia 57°58′N 27°37′E
162 I7 **Varsseveld** Gelderland, E Netherlands 51°55′N 06°28′E
186 F6 **Vartholomió** *prev.* Vartholomión. Dytikí Elláda, S Greece 37°52′N 21°12′E
Vartholomión *see* Vartholomió
215 I6 **Varto** Muş, E Turkey 39°10′N 41°28′E
155 F9 **Vartofta** Västra Götaland, S Sweden 58°06′N 13°40′E
153 J8 **Värtsilä** Itä-Suomi, E Finland 62°10′N 30°35′E
Värtsilä *see* Vyartsilya
189 I3 **Varva** Chernihivs'ka Oblast', NE Ukraine 50°31′N 32°43′E
64 B1 **Varysburg** New York, NE USA 42°45′N 78°18′W
107 I9 **Várzea Grande** Mato Grosso, SW Brazil 15°39′S 56°08′W
110 D8 **Várzea Paulista** São Paulo, Brazil 23°12′S 46°50′W
176 E7 **Varzi** Lombardia, N Italy 44°51′N 09°13′E
Varzimanor Ayni *see* Ayní
194 F4 **Varzuga** ≈ NW Russian Federation
165 I5 **Varzy** Nièvre, C France 47°22′N 03°22′E
183 D12 **Vas** *off.* Vas Megye. ◈ *county* W Hungary
Vasa *see* Vaasa
284 E2 **Vasafua** *island* Funafuti Atoll, C Tuvalu
183 I10 **Vásárosnamény** Szabolcs-Szatmár-Bereg, E Hungary 48°10′N 22°18′E
172 C7 **Vascão, Ribeira de** ≈ S Portugal
188 B7 **Vaşcău** *Hung.* Vaskoh. Bihor, NE Romania 46°28′N 22°30′E
Vascongadas, Provincias *see* País Vasco
172 C2 **Vasconha** Viseu, Portugal 40°40′N 8°04′W
Vashess Bay *see* Vaskess Bay
195 H5 **Vashka** ≈ NW Russian Federation
Väsht *see* Khāsh
Vasilevichi *see* Vasilyevichy
187 H3 **Vasiliká** Kentrikí Makedonía, NE Greece 40°28′N 23°08′E
186 E5 **Vasilikí** Lefkáda, Iónia Nisiá, Greece, C Mediterranean Sea 38°36′N 20°37′E
187 J10 **Vasilikí** Kríti, Greece, E Mediterranean Sea 35°04′N 25°49′E
191 D10 **Vasilishki** *Pol.* Wasiliszki. Hrodzyenskaya Voblasts', W Belarus 53°47′N 24°51′E
Vasil Kolarov *see* Pamporovo
Vasil'kov *see* Vasyl'kiv
191 H11 **Vasilyevichy** *Rus.* Vasilevichi. Homyel'skaya Voblasts', SE Belarus 52°15′N 29°50′E
190 G5 **Vasil'yevo** Pskovskaya Oblast', Russian Federation
285 M2 **Vaskess Bay** *var.* Vashess Bay. *bay* Kiritimati, E Kiribati
Vaskoh *see* Vaşcău
Vaskohsziklás *see* Ştei
188 F7 **Vaslui** Vaslui, C Romania 46°38′N 27°44′E
188 F7 **Vaslui** ◈ *county* NE Romania
Vas Megye *see* Vas
72 H7 **Vassar** Michigan, N USA 43°22′N 83°34′W
154 B7 **Vassdalsegga** ▲ S Norway 59°47′N 07°07′E
109 E13 **Vassouras** Rio de Janeiro, SE Brazil 22°24′S 43°38′W
166 D5 **Vassy** Basse-Normandie, France 48°51′N 0°40′W
155 H8 **Västerås** Västmanland, C Sweden 59°37′N 16°33′E
154 I1 **Västerbotten** ◈ *county* N Sweden
154 F6 **Västerdalälven** ≈ C Sweden
155 I8 **Västerhaninge** Stockholm, C Sweden 59°07′N 18°06′E
154 I3 **Västernorrland** ◈ *county* C Sweden
155 I10 **Västervik** Kalmar, S Sweden 57°44′N 16°40′E
154 H7 **Västmanland** ◈ *county* C Sweden
175 G8 **Vasto** *anc.* Histonium. Abruzzo, C Italy 42°07′N 14°43′E
155 F9 **Västra Götaland** ◈ *county* S Sweden
155 F8 **Västra Silen** ◎ S Sweden
177 M4 **Vasvár** *Ger.* Eisenburg. Vas, W Hungary 47°03′N 16°48′E
189 K6 **Vasylivka** Zaporiz'ka Oblast', SE Ukraine 47°26′N 35°18′E
189 H3 **Vasyl'kiv** *var.* Vasil'kov. Kyyivs'ka Oblast', N Ukraine 50°12′N 30°18′E
189 L5 **Vasyl'kivka** Dnipropetrovs'ka Oblast', E Ukraine 48°12′N 36°00′E
192 F6 **Vasyugan** ≈ C Russian Federation
165 H5 **Vatan** Indre, C France 47°06′N 01°49′E
Vaté *see* Efate
186 E6 **Vathy** *prev.* Itháki. Itháki, Iónia Nisiá, Greece, C Mediterranean Sea 38°22′N 20°43′E
175 E8 **Vatican City** *off.* Vatican City. ◆ *papal state* S Europe
175 H11 **Vaticano, Capo** *headland* S Italy 38°37′N 15°49′E
Vatilí *see* Vadili
152 D2 **Vatnajökull** *glacier* SE Iceland
154 J7 **Vätö** Stockholm, C Sweden 59°48′N 18°55′E
280 G10 **Vatoa** *island* Lau Group, SE Fiji
139 M7 **Vatomandry** Toamasina, E Madagascar 19°20′S 48°58′E
188 D6 **Vatra Dornei** *Ger.* Dorna Watra. Suceava, NE Romania 47°20′N 25°21′E
188 D6 **Vatra Moldoviţei** Suceava, NE Romania 47°37′N 25°36′E
Vatter, Lake *see* Vättern
155 G9 **Vättern** *Eng.* Lake Vatter; *prev.* Lake Vetter. ◎ S Sweden
280 E8 **Vatukoula** Viti Levu, W Fiji 17°30′S 177°53′E
280 E9 **Vatulele** *island* SW Fiji
189 H5 **Vatutine** Cherkas'ka Oblast', C Ukraine 49°01′N 31°04′E
280 F9 **Vatu Vara** *island* Lau Group, E Fiji
165 J8 **Vaucluse** ◈ *department* SE France
165 J3 **Vaucouleurs** Meuse, NE France 48°37′N 05°38′E
174 A3 **Vaud** *Ger.* Waadt. ◈ *canton* SW Switzerland
63 H3 **Vaudreuil** Québec, SE Canada 45°24′N 74°01′W
79 M7 **Vaughn** New Mexico, SW USA 34°36′N 105°12′W
102 E8 **Vaupés** *off.* Comisaría del Vaupés. ◈ *province* SE Colombia
Vaupés, Comisaría del *see* Vaupés
102 E8 **Vaupés, Río** *var.* Rio Uaupés. ≈ Brazil/Colombia *see also* Uaupés, Rio
169 J5 **Vauvert** Gard, S France 43°42′N 04°16′E
167 L7 **Vauvillers** Franche-Comté, France 47°55′N 6°06′E
57 J8 **Vauxhall** Alberta, SW Canada 50°05′N 112°09′W
163 G13 **Vaux-sur-Sûre** Luxembourg, SE Belgium 49°55′N 05°34′E
139 M6 **Vavatenina** Toamasina, E Madagascar 17°25′S 49°11′E
284 D7 **Vava'u Group** *island group* N Tonga
132 E7 **Vavoua** W Ivory Coast 07°23′N 06°29′W
195 J10 **Vavozh** Udmurtskaya Respublika, NW Russian Federation 56°48′N 51°53′E
235 G10 **Vavuniya** Northern Province, N Sri Lanka 08°45′N 80°30′E
191 D10 **Vawkavysk** *Pol.* Wołkowysk, *Rus.* Volkovysk. Hrodzyenskaya Voblasts', W Belarus 53°10′N 24°28′E
191 D10 **Vawkavyskaye Wzvyshsha** *Rus.* Volkovyskiye Vysoty. *hill range* W Belarus
155 I8 **Vaxholm** Stockholm, C Sweden 59°25′N 18°21′E
155 G11 **Växjö** *var.* Vexiö. Kronoberg, S Sweden 56°52′N 14°50′E
195 K1 **Vaygach, Ostrov** *island* NW Russian Federation
215 L5 **Vayk'** *prev.* Azizbekov. SE Armenia 39°41′N 45°28′E
168 G3 **Vayrac** Midi-Pyrénées, France 44°57′N 1°42′E
187 K1 **Vaysal** Edirne, Turkey 41°57′N 26°52′E
Vazáš *see* Vittangi
195 H6 **Vazhgort** *prev.* Chasovo. Respublika Komi, NW Russian Federation 64°06′N 46°44′E
91 M6 **V. C. Bird** ✈ (St. John's) Antigua, Antigua and Barbuda 17°07′N 61°49′W
74 E4 **Veblen** South Dakota, N USA 45°50′N 97°17′W
180 I6 **Vechelde** Niedersachsen, Germany 52°16′E 10°23′N
162 I5 **Vecht** *Ger.* Vechte. ≈ Germany/Netherlands *see also* Vechte
180 E5 **Vechta** Niedersachsen, NW Germany 52°44′N 08°16′E
180 C5 **Vechte** *Dut.* Vecht. ≈ Germany/Netherlands *see also* Vecht
172 E2 **Vecinos** Castilla y León, Spain 40°47′N 5°52′W
181 G8 **Veckerhagen** Hessen, Germany 51°30′E 9°36′N
190 E6 **Vecpiebalga** Cēsis, C Latvia 57°03′N 25°47′E
190 D6 **Vecumnieki** Bauska, C Latvia 56°36′N 24°30′E
155 A8 **Vedavågen** Rogaland, S Norway 59°18′N 5°13′E
Vedāvati *see* Hagari
155 F10 **Veddige** Halland, S Sweden 57°16′N 12°19′E
188 D10 **Vedea** ≈ S Romania
197 I9 **Vedeno** Chechenskaya Respublika, SW Russian Federation 42°57′N 46°02′E
114 A9 **Vedia** Buenos Aires, Argentina 34°30′S 61°33′W
190 I1 **Vedlozero** Respublika Kareliya, Russian Federation
280 E8 **Ve Drala Reef** *reef* N Fiji
155 A8 **Vedvågen** Rogaland, S Norway 59°18′N 05°13′E
162 I4 **Veendam** Groningen, NE Netherlands 53°05′N 06°53′E
162 G7 **Veenendaal** Utrecht, C Netherlands 52°03′N 05°33′E
163 C8 **Veere** Zeeland, SW Netherlands 51°33′N 03°40′E
70 D2 **Vega** Texas, SW USA 35°14′N 102°26′W
152 D6 **Vega** *island* C Norway
91 I7 **Vega Baja** C Puerto Rico 18°27′N 66°23′W
82 B9 **Vega Point** *headland* Kiska Island, Alaska, USA 51°49′N 177°19′E
155 C8 **Vegår** ◎ S Norway
118 B7 **Vegas de Itata** Bío-Bío, Chile 36°24′S 72°51′W
163 G8 **Veghel** Noord-Brabant, S Netherlands 51°37′N 05°33′E
141 I5 **Vegkop** Free State, South Africa 27°29′S 27°54′E
Veglia *see* Krk
186 G3 **Vegorítida, Límni** *var.* Límni Vegorítis. ◎ N Greece
Vegorítis, Límni *see* Vegorítida, Límni
57 J5 **Vegreville** Alberta, SW Canada 53°30′N 112°02′W
155 F11 **Veinge** Halland, S Sweden 56°33′N 13°04′E
114 C5 **Veinte de Setiembre** Entre Ríos, Argentina 32°23′S 59°40′W
116 G4 **Veinticinco de Mayo** *var.* 25 de Mayo. Buenos Aires, E Argentina 35°27′S 60°11′W
118 G9 **Veinticinco de Mayo** La Pampa, C Argentina 37°45′S 67°40′W
115 H8 **Veinticinco de Mayo** Florida, Uruguay 34°11′S 56°20′W
172 C5 **Veiros** Évora, Portugal 38°57′N 7°30′W
191 D9 **Veisiejai** Alytus, S Lithuania 54°06′N 23°42′E
155 C12 **Vejen** Ribe, W Denmark 55°29′N 09°13′E
170 E9 **Vejer de la Frontera** Andalucía, S Spain 36°15′N 05°58′W
155 D12 **Vejle** Vejle, C Denmark 55°43′N 09°33′E
155 D12 **Vejle** *off.* Vejle Amt. ◈ *county* C Denmark
Vejle Amt *see* Vejle
185 L5 **Vekilski** Shumen, NE Bulgaria 43°33′N 27°19′E
190 I5 **Vekshino** Novgorodskaya Oblast', Russian Federation
102 D2 **Vela, Cabo de la** *headland* NE Colombia 12°14′N 72°13′W
Vela Goa *see* Goa
184 C6 **Vela Luka** Dubrovnik-Neretva, S Croatia 42°57′N 16°43′E
85 J7 **Velardeña** Durango, Mexico 25°04′N 103°44′W
115 K8 **Velázquez** Rocha, E Uruguay 34°05′S 54°16′W
181 C8 **Velbert** Nordrhein-Westfalen, W Germany 51°22′N 07°03′E
140 D9 **Velddrif** Western Cape, South Africa 32°47′S 18°10′E
177 J5 **Velden** Kärnten, S Austria 46°37′N 13°59′E
Veldes *see* Bled
163 G8 **Veldhoven** Noord-Brabant, S Netherlands 51°24′N 05°24′E
184 B4 **Velebit** ⛰ C Croatia
185 M7 **Veleka** ≈ SE Bulgaria
177 K5 **Velenje** *Ger.* Wöllan. N Slovenia 46°22′N 15°07′E
284 A10 **Vele, Pointe** *headland* Île Futuna, S Wallis and Futuna
185 H7 **Veles** *Turk.* Köprülü. C FYR Macedonia 41°43′N 21°49′E
184 G8 **Velešta** SW FYR Macedonia 41°16′N 20°37′E
186 G4 **Velestíno** *prev.* Velestínon. Thessalía, C Greece 39°23′N 22°45′E
Velestínon *see* Velestíno
Velevshchina *see* Vyelyewshchyna
102 C5 **Vélez** Santander, C Colombia 06°02′N 73°43′W
171 H8 **Vélez Blanco** Andalucía, S Spain 37°43′N 02°07′W
173 H8 **Vélez de Benaudalla** Andalucía, Spain 36°50′N 3°31′W
170 F10 **Vélez de la Gomera, Peñon de** *island group* S Spain
170 F9 **Vélez-Málaga** Andalucía, S Spain 36°47′N 04°06′W
171 H8 **Vélez Rubio** Andalucía, S Spain 37°39′N 02°04′W
Velha Goa *see* Goa
Velho *see* Porto Velho
184 C2 **Velika Gorica** Zagreb, N Croatia 45°43′N 16°03′E
177 K6 **Velika Kapela** ⛰ NW Croatia
Velika Kikinda *see* Kikinda
184 C3 **Velika Kladuša** Federacija Bosna I Hercegovina, NW Bosnia and Herzegovina 45°10′N 15°48′E
184 G4 **Velika Morava** *var.* Glavn'a Morava, Morava, *Ger.* Grosse Morava. ≈ C Serbia
184 G4 **Velika Plana** Serbia, C Serbia 44°20′N 21°01′E
193 M3 **Velikaya** ≈ NE Russian Federation
194 C10 **Velikaya** ≈ W Russian Federation
Velikaya Berestovitsa *see* Vyalikaya Byerastavitsa
Velikaya Lepetikha *see* Velyka Lepetykha
Veliki Bečkerek *see* Zrenjanin
185 H4 **Veliki Krš** *var.* Stol. ▲ E Serbia 44°10′N 22°09′E
185 L5 **Veliki Preslav** *prev.* Preslav. Shumen, NE Bulgaria 43°09′N 26°50′E
184 B2 **Veliki Risnjak** ▲ NW Croatia 45°30′N 14°31′E
184 E5 **Veliki Stolac** ▲ E Bosnia and Herzegovina 43°55′N 19°15′E
Velikiy Bor *see* Vyaliki Bor
252 A1 **Velikiye Kema** Primorskiy Kray, SE Russian Federation 45°28′N 137°12′E
194 D10 **Velikiye Luki** Pskovskaya Oblast', W Russian Federation 56°20′N 30°27′E
194 D9 **Velikiy Novgorod** *prev.* Novgorod. Novgorodskaya Oblast', W Russian Federation 58°32′N 31°15′E
195 H8 **Velikiy Ustyug** Vologodskaya Oblast', NW Russian Federation 60°46′N 46°18′E
184 G3 **Veliko Gradište** Serbia, NE Serbia 44°46′N 21°28′E
234 F7 **Velikonda Range** ⛰ SE India
185 K6 **Veliko Tŭrnovo** *prev.* Tirnovo, Trnovo, Tŭrnovo. Veliko Tŭrnovo, N Bulgaria 43°05′N 25°40′E
185 K6 **Veliko Tŭrnovo** ◈ *province* N Bulgaria
Velikovec *see* Völkermarkt
195 I3 **Velikovisochnoye** Nenetskiy Avtonomnyy Okrug, NW Russian Federation 67°13′N 52°00′E
132 B4 **Vélingara** C Senegal 15°00′N 14°39′W
132 B5 **Vélingara** S Senegal 13°12′N 14°05′W
185 J7 **Velingrad** Pazardzhik, C Bulgaria 42°01′N 24°00′E
196 D2 **Velizh** Smolenskaya Oblast', W Russian Federation 55°30′N 31°06′E
183 D8 **Velká Deštná** *var.* Deštná, Grosskoppe, *Ger.* Deschnaer Koppe. ▲ NE Czech Republic 50°18′N 16°25′E
183 D9 **Velké Meziříčí** *Ger.* Grossmeseritsch. Vysočina, C Czech Republic 49°22′N 16°02′E
152 A4 **Velkomstpynten** *headland* NW Svalbard 79°51′N 11°37′E
183 G10 **Vel'ký Krtíš** Banskobystrický Kraj, C Slovakia 48°13′N 19°21′E
180 J3 **Vellahn** Mecklenburg-Vorpommern, Germany 53°24′E 10°58′N
281 H1 **Vella Lavella** *var.* Mbilua. *island* New Georgia Islands, NW Solomon Islands
181 H14 **Vellberg** Baden-Württemberg, Germany 49°05′E 9°53′N
175 E8 **Velletri** Lazio, C Italy 41°41′N 12°47′E
155 F12 **Vellinge** Skåne, S Sweden 55°29′N 13°00′E
235 F8 **Vellore** Tamil Nādu, SE India 12°56′N 79°09′E
Velobriga *see* Viana do Castelo
187 H8 **Velopoúla** *island* S Greece
162 H7 **Velp** Gelderland, SE Netherlands 52°00′N 05°59′E
180 J6 **Velpke** Niedersachsen, Germany 52°24′E 10°56′N
Velsen *see* Velsen-Noord
162 E5 **Velsen-Noord** *var.* Velsen. Noord-Holland, W Netherlands 52°27′N 04°40′E
194 G7 **Vel'sk** *var.* Velsk. Arkhangel'skaya Oblast', NW Russian Federation 61°03′N 42°01′E
Velsuna *see* Orvieto
162 G6 **Veluwemeer** *lake channel* C Netherlands
74 C2 **Velva** North Dakota, N USA 48°03′N 100°55′W
Velvendos/Velvendós *see* Velventós
186 G3 **Velventós** *var.* Velvendos, Velvendós. Dytikí Makedonía, N Greece 40°15′N 22°04′E
189 J4 **Velyka Bahachka** Poltavs'ka Oblast', C Ukraine 49°46′N 33°44′E
189 J7 **Velyka Lepetykha** *Rus.* Velikaya Lepetikha. Khersons'ka Oblast', S Ukraine 47°09′N 33°59′E
188 G7 **Velyka Mykhaylivka** Odes'ka Oblast', SW Ukraine 47°07′N 29°49′E
189 L6 **Velyka Novosilka** Donets'ka Oblast', E Ukraine 47°49′N 36°49′E
189 J6 **Velyka Oleksandrivka** Khersons'ka Oblast', S Ukraine 47°17′N 33°16′E
189 K3 **Velyka Pysarivka** Sums'ka Oblast', NE Ukraine 50°25′N 35°28′E
188 B4 **Velykyy Bereznyy** Zakarpats'ka Oblast', W Ukraine 48°54′N 22°27′E
189 L3 **Velykyy Burluk** Kharkivs'ka Oblast', E Ukraine 50°04′N 37°25′E
Velykyy Tokmak *see* Tokmak
289 E8 **Vema Fracture Zone** *tectonic feature* W Indian Ocean
291 I10 **Vema Seamount** *undersea feature* SW Indian Ocean 31°38′S 08°19′E
154 G4 **Vemdalen** Jämtland, C Sweden 62°26′N 13°50′E
155 H10 **Vena** Kalmar, S Sweden 57°31′N 16°00′E
85 L8 **Venado** San Luis Potosí, C Mexico 22°56′N 101°05′W
86 F5 **Venados** Hidalgo, Mexico 20°28′N 98°40′W
112 E9 **Venado Tuerto** Entre Ríos, E Argentina 33°45′S 61°56′W
116 F4 **Venado Tuerto** Santa Fe, C Argentina 33°46′S 61°57′W
175 F9 **Venafro** Molise, C Italy 41°28′N 14°03′E
103 I5 **Venamo, Cerro** ▲ E Venezuela 05°56′N 61°25′W
167 J8 **Venarey-les-Laumes** Bourgogne, France 47°32′N 4°26′E
176 D7 **Venaria** Piemonte, NW Italy 45°09′N 07°40′E
165 K8 **Vence** Alpes-Maritimes, SE France 43°45′N 07°07′E
170 D3 **Venda Nova** Vila Real, N Portugal 41°40′N 07°58′W
172 C2 **Vendas de Galizes** Coimbra, Portugal 40°19′N 7°54′W
172 B5 **Vendas Novas** Évora, S Portugal 38°41′N 08°27′W
164 F5 **Vendée** ◈ *department* NW France
165 J4 **Vendeuvre-sur-Barse** Aube, NE France 48°08′N 04°17′E
164 G4 **Vendôme** Loir-et-Cher, C France 47°48′N 01°04′E
Venedig *see* Venezia
Vener, Lake *see* Vänern
174 E5 **Veneta, Laguna** *lagoon* NE Italy
Venetia *see* Venezia
83 J3 **Venetie** Alaska, USA 67°00′N 146°25′W
174 E4 **Veneto** *var.* Venezia Euganea. ◈ *region* NE Italy
185 L5 **Venets** Shumen, NE Bulgaria 43°33′N 26°56′E
196 G3 **Venev** Tul'skaya Oblast', W Russian Federation 54°18′N 38°16′E
177 H7 **Venezia** *Eng.* Venice, *Fr.* Venise, *Ger.* Venedig; *anc.* Venetia. Veneto, NE Italy 45°26′N 12°20′E
Venezia Euganea *see* Veneto
Venezia, Golfo di *see* Venice, Gulf of
Venezia Tridentina *see* Trentino-Alto Adige
103 H4 **Venezuela** *off.* Republic of Venezuela; *prev.* Estados Unidos de Venezuela, United States of Venezuela. ◆ *republic* N South America
Venezuela, Cordillera de *see* Costa, Cordillera de la
Venezuela, Estados Unidos de *see* Venezuela
102 E2 **Venezuela, Golfo de** *Eng.* Gulf of Maracaibo, Gulf of Venezuela. *gulf* NW Venezuela
Venezuela, Gulf of *see* Venezuela, Golfo de
290 C6 **Venezuelan Basin** *undersea feature* E Caribbean Sea
Venezuela, Republic of *see* Venezuela
Venezuela, United States of *see* Venezuela
234 C6 **Vengurla** Mahārāshtra, W India 15°55′N 73°39′E
180 D6 **Venhaus** Niedersachsen, Germany 52°22′E 7°27′N
82 G8 **Veniaminof, Mount** ▲ Alaska, USA 56°12′N 159°24′W
69 L7 **Venice** Florida, SE USA 27°06′N 82°27′W
68 E5 **Venice** Louisiana, S USA 29°15′N 89°20′W
Venice *see* Venezia
174 F5 **Venice, Gulf of** *It.* Golfo di Venezia, *Slvn.* Beneški Zaliv. *gulf* N Adriatic Sea
289 H9 **Vening Meinesz Seamounts** *undersea feature* E Indian Ocean
Venise *see* Venezia
154 G6 **Venjan** Dalarna, C Sweden 60°58′N 13°55′E
154 F6 **Venjanssjön** ◎ C Sweden
234 F7 **Venkatagiri** Andhra Pradesh, E India 14°00′N 79°39′E
163 H9 **Venlo** *prev.* Venloo. Limburg, SE Netherlands 51°22′N 06°11′E
Venloo *see* Venlo
155 C9 **Vennesla** Vest-Agder, S Norway 58°15′N 08°00′E
175 H9 **Venosa** *anc.* Venusia. Basilicata, S Italy 40°57′N 15°49′E
Venoste, Alpi *see* Ötztaler Alpen
Venraij *see* Venray
163 H8 **Venray** *var.* Venraij. Limburg, SE Netherlands 51°32′N 05°59′E
190 C7 **Venta** *Ger.* Windau. ≈ Latvia/Lithuania
Venta Belgarum *see* Winchester
84 F8 **Ventana, Punta Arena de la** *var.* Punta de la Ventana. *headland* NW Mexico 24°03′N 109°49′W
Ventana, Punta de la *see* Ventana, Punta Arena de la
116 F6 **Ventana, Sierra de la** *hill range* E Argentina
141 H7 **Venterstad** Eastern Cape, South Africa 30°47′S 25°48′E
Ventia *see* Valence
285 M3 **Vent, Îles du** *var.* Windward Islands. *island group* Archipel de la Société, W French Polynesia
285 H6 **Vent, Îles Sous le** *var.* Leeward Islands. *island group* Archipel de la Société, W French Polynesia
176 D9 **Ventimiglia** Liguria, NW Italy 43°47′N 07°37′E
161 J8 **Ventnor** S England, United Kingdom 50°36′N 01°11′W
64 G9 **Ventnor City** New Jersey, NE USA 39°19′N 74°27′W
169 K4 **Ventoux, Mont** ▲ SE France 44°12′N 05°21′E
190 B6 **Ventspils** *Ger.* Windau. Ventspils, NW Latvia 57°22′N 21°34′E
102 G6 **Ventuari, Río** ≈ S Venezuela
81 C8 **Ventucopa** California, USA 34°50′N 119°28′W
81 C9 **Ventura** California, W USA 34°15′N 119°18′W
158 G2 **Venue, Ben** ▲ United Kingdom 56°13′N 4°27′W
276 E5 **Venus Bay** South Australia 33°15′S 134°42′E
Venusia *see* Venosa
285 M3 **Vénus, Pointe** *var.* Pointe Tataaihoa. *headland* Tahiti, W French Polynesia 17°28′S 149°29′W
87 K9 **Venustiano Carranza** Chiapas, SE Mexico 16°21′N 92°33′W
84 F6 **Venustiano Carranza** Durango, Mexico
85 L5 **Venustiano Carranza, Presa** ▣ NE Mexico
116 G1 **Vera** Santa Fe, C Argentina 29°28′S 60°10′W
171 H8 **Vera** Andalucía, S Spain 37°15′N 01°51′W
117 E9 **Vera, Bahía** *bay* E Argentina
87 H6 **Veracruz** *var.* Veracruz Llave. Veracruz-Llave, E Mexico 19°10′N 96°09′W
Veracruz *see* Veracruz-Llave
172 C6 **Vera Cruz de Marmelar** Évora, Portugal 38°14′N 7°41′W
86 G5 **Veracruz-Llave** *var.* Veracruz. ◈ *state* E Mexico
Veracruz Llave *see* Veracruz
Vera de Bidasoa *see* Bidasoa
89 J9 **Veraguas** *off.* Provincia de Veraguas. ◈ *province* W Panama
Veraguas, Provincia de *see* Veraguas
Veramin *see* Varāmīn
232 B9 **Verāval** Gujarāt, W India 20°54′N 70°22′E
114 B2 **Vera y Pintado** Santa Fe, Argentina 30°09′S 60°21′W
176 E6 **Verbania** Piemonte, NW Italy 45°56′N 08°34′E
167 H4 **Verberie** Picardie, France 49°19′N 2°44′E
175 H10 **Verbicaro** Calabria, SW Italy 39°44′N 15°51′E
176 C5 **Verbier** Valais, SW Switzerland 46°06′N 07°14′E
Vercellae *see* Vercelli
176 D7 **Vercelli** *anc.* Vercellae. Piemonte, NW Italy 45°19′N 08°25′E
169 K4 **Verclause** Rhône-Alpes, France 44°23′N 5°26′E
165 J7 **Vercors** *physical region* E France
Verdal *see* Verdalsøra
154 E3 **Verdalsøra** *var.* Verdal. Nord-Trøndelag, C Norway 63°47′N 11°27′E
Verde, Cabo *see* Cape Verde
90 F3 **Verde, Cape** *headland* Long Island, C Bahamas 22°51′N 75°50′W
170 F1 **Verde, Costa** *coastal region* N Spain
Verde Grande, Río/Verde Grande y de Belem, Río *see* Verde, Río
172 D2 **Verdelhos** Castelo Branco, Portugal 40°22′N 7°28′W
180 G4 **Verden** Niedersachsen, NW Germany 52°55′N 09°14′E
106 D8 **Verde, Río** ≈ Bolivia/Brazil
110 F6 **Verde, Rio** ≈ SE Brazil
86 C5 **Verde, Río** *var.* Río Verde Grande, Río Verde Grande y de Belem. ≈ C Mexico
86 G8 **Verde, Río** ≈ SE Mexico
85 M9 **Verde, Río** ≈ San Luis Potosí, Mexico
Verdhikoúsa/Verdhikoússa *see* Verdikoússa
75 F11 **Verdigris River** ≈ Kansas/Oklahoma, C USA
186 G4 **Verdikoússa** *var.* Verdhikoúsa, Verdhikoússa. Thessalía, C Greece 39°47′N 21°59′E
165 K8 **Verdon** ≈ SE France
63 H3 **Verdun** Québec, SE Canada 45°27′N 73°36′W
165 J3 **Verdun** *var.* Verdun-sur-Meuse; *anc.* Verodunum. Meuse, NE France 49°09′N 05°25′E
115 I6 **Verdún** Durazno, Uruguay 32°40′S 55°27′W
168 F5 **Verdun-sur-Garonne** Midi-Pyrénées, France 43°52′N 1°14′E
167 K9 **Verdun-sur-le-Doubs** Bourgogne, France 46°54′N 5°01′E
Verdun-sur-Meuse *see* Verdun
141 I4 **Vereeniging** Gauteng, NE South Africa 26°41′S 27°56′E
Veremeyki *see* Vyeramyeyki
195 K9 **Vereshchagino** Permskaya Oblast', NW Russian Federation 58°06′N 54°38′E
168 G5 **Verfeil** Midi-Pyrénées, France 43°40′N 1°40′E
132 B6 **Verga, Cap** *headland* W Guinea 10°12′N 14°27′W
115 K6 **Vergara** Treinta y Tres, E Uruguay 32°58′S 53°54′W
140 G3 **Vergeleë** North-West, South Africa 25°46′S 24°12′E
63 H4 **Vergennes** Vermont, NE USA 44°09′N 73°13′W
168 E3 **Vergt** Aquitaine, France 45°01′N 0°43′E
Veria *see* Véroia
170 D3 **Verín** Galicia, NW Spain 41°55′N 07°26′W
Verin T'alin *see* T'alin
190 F5 **Veriora** Põlvamaa, SE Estonia 57°57′N 27°23′E
110 A2 **Veríssimo** Minas Gerais, Brazil 19°42′S 48°18′W
141 I6 **Verkeerdevlei** Free State, South Africa 28°50′S 26°47′E
189 J5 **Verkhivtseve** Dnipropetrovs'ka Oblast', E Ukraine 48°27′N 34°15′E
Verkhnedvinsk *see* Vyerkhnyadzvinsk
192 G6 **Verkhneimbatsk** Krasnoyarskiy Kray, N Russian Federation 63°06′N 88°03′E
195 L6 **Verkhnenil'dina** Khanty-Mansiyskiy Avtonomnyy Okrug-Yugra, Russian Federation
194 E3 **Verkhnetulomskiy** Murmanskaya Oblast', NW Russian Federation 68°37′N 31°46′E
194 E3 **Verkhnetulomskoye Vodokhranilishche** ▣ NW Russian Federation
Verkhneudinsk *see* Ulan-Ude
193 J6 **Verkhnevilyuysk** Respublika Sakha (Yakutiya), NE Russian Federation 63°44′N 119°59′E
195 L9 **Verkh-Neyvinskiy** Sverdlovskaya Oblast', Russian Federation
197 M3 **Verkhniy Avzyan** Respublika Bashkortostan, W Russian Federation 53°31′N 57°26′E
197 I6 **Verkhniy Baskunchak** Astrakhanskaya Oblast', SW Russian Federation 48°14′N 46°43′E
197 M1 **Verkhniye Kigi** Respublika Bashkortostan, W Russian Federation 55°25′N 58°40′E
189 J6 **Verkhniy Rohachyk** Khersons'ka Oblast', S Ukraine 47°16′N 34°16′E
195 L9 **Verkhniy Tagil** Sverdlovskaya Oblast', Russian Federation
195 M10 **Verkhniy Ufaley** Chelyabinskaya Oblast', Russian Federation 56°03′N 60°12′E
193 J6 **Verkhnyaya Amga** Respublika Sakha (Yakutiya), NE Russian Federation 59°34′N 127°07′E
195 K4 **Verkhnyaya Inta** Respublika Komi, NW Russian Federation 65°55′N 60°07′E
195 M9 **Verkhnyaya Pyshma** Sverdlovskaya Oblast', Russian Federation
195 L9 **Verkhnyaya Salda** Sverdlovskaya Oblast', Russian Federation
193 H4 **Verkhnyaya Taymyra** ≈ N Russian Federation
195 H7 **Verkhnyaya Toyma** Arkhangel'skaya Oblast', NW Russian Federation 62°12′N 44°57′E
195 L8 **Verkhotur'ye** Sverdlovskaya Oblast', Russian Federation
190 I3 **Verkhovina** Leningradskaya Oblast', Russian Federation
196 F3 **Verkhov'ye** Orlovskaya Oblast', W Russian Federation 52°49′N 37°20′E
188 D5 **Verkhovyna** Ivano-Frankivs'ka Oblast', W Ukraine 48°09′N 24°48′E
193 J5 **Verkhoyansk** Respublika Sakha (Yakutiya), NE Russian Federation 67°27′N 133°27′E
193 J5 **Verkhoyanskiy Khrebet** ⛰ NE Russian Federation
189 J5 **Verkn'odniprovs'k** Dnipropetrovs'ka Oblast', E Ukraine 48°40′N 34°17′E
180 F7 **Verl** Nordrhein-Westfalen, NW Germany 51°52′N 08°30′E
140 E9 **Verlatekop** ▲ Northern Cape, South Africa 32°33′S 20°38′E
141 H4 **Vermaas** North West, South Africa 26°32′S 26°00′E
167 I3 **Vermand** Picardie, France 49°52′N 3°09′E
135 B10 **Vermelha, Ponta** *headland* NW Angola 05°40′S 12°09′E
111 J3 **Vermelho Novo** Minas Gerais, Brazil 20°01′S 42°17′W
165 I4 **Vermenton** Yonne, C France 47°40′N 03°43′E
57 K5 **Vermilion** Alberta, SW Canada 53°21′N 110°52′W
73 I9 **Vermilion** Ohio, N USA 41°25′N 82°21′W
68 C5 **Vermilion Bay** *bay* Louisiana, S USA
74 H2 **Vermilion Lake** ◎ Minnesota, N USA
62 C1 **Vermilion River** ≈ Ontario, S Canada
73 C9 **Vermilion River** ≈ Illinois, N USA
74 E6 **Vermillion** South Dakota, N USA 42°46′N 96°55′W
74 E6 **Vermillion River** ≈ South Dakota, N USA
63 H1 **Vermillon, Rivière** ≈ Québec, SE Canada
186 G3 **Vérmio** ⛰ N Greece
172 B3 **Vermoil** Leiria, Portugal 39°51′N 8°39′W
63 I4 **Vermont** *off.* State of Vermont, *also known as* Green Mountain State. ◈ *state* NE USA
184 F6 **Vermosh** *var.* Vermoshi. Shkodër, N Albania 42°37′N 19°42′E
Vermoshi *see* Vermosh
79 J2 **Vernal** Utah, W USA 40°27′N 109°31′W
80 C3 **Vernalis** California, USA 37°38′N 121°17′W
62 C2 **Verner** Ontario, S Canada 46°24′N 80°04′W
164 G3 **Verneuil-sur-Avre** Eure, N France 48°44′N 00°55′E
140 E7 **Verneuk pan** *salt lake* Northern Cape, South Africa
186 F3 **Vérno** ⛰ N Greece
56 F8 **Vernon** British Columbia, SW Canada 50°17′N 119°19′W
165 H3 **Vernon** Eure, N France 49°04′N 01°28′E
66 C8 **Vernon** Alabama, S USA 33°45′N 88°06′W
65 J3 **Vernon** Connecticut, USA 41°49′N 72°29′W
73 F12 **Vernon** Indiana, N USA 38°59′N 85°39′W
70 F3 **Vernon** Texas, SW USA 34°11′N 99°17′W
76 B5 **Vernonia** Oregon, NW USA 45°51′N 123°11′W
62 D3 **Vernon, Lake** ◎ Ontario, S Canada
68 B3 **Vernon Lake** ▣ Louisiana, S USA
169 J3 **Vernoux-en-Vivarais** Rhône-Alpes, France 44°54′N 4°39′E
167 L5 **Verny** Lorraine, France 49°01′N 6°12′E
69 N7 **Vero Beach** Florida, SE USA 27°38′N 80°24′W
Verőcze *see* Virovitica
Verodunum *see* Verdun
186 G3 **Véroia** *var.* Veria, Vérroia, *Turk.* Karaferiye. Kentrikí Makedonía, N Greece 40°32′N 22°11′E
176 F7 **Verolanuova** Lombardia, N Italy 45°20′N 10°06′E
62 F4 **Verona** Ontario, SE Canada 44°30′N 76°42′W
176 G7 **Verona** Veneto, NE Italy 45°27′N 11°E
74 E3 **Verona** North Dakota, N USA 46°19′N 98°03′W
72 C7 **Verona** Wisconsin, N USA 42°59′N 89°33′W
112 G10 **Verónica** Buenos Aires, E Argentina 35°25′S 57°16′W
169 N1 **Verres** Valle D'Aosta, NW Italy 45°40′N 07°41′E
68 D4 **Verret, Lake** ◎ Louisiana, S USA
Vérroia *see* Véroia
165 H3 **Versailles** Yvelines, N France 48°48′N 02°08′E
73 F11 **Versailles** Indiana, N USA 39°04′N 85°16′W
66 F4 **Versailles** Kentucky, S USA 38°02′N 84°45′W
75 H10 **Versailles** Missouri, C USA 38°25′N 92°51′W
73 G10 **Versailles** Ohio, N USA 40°13′N 84°28′W
Versecz *see* Vršac
180 C5 **Versen** Niedersachsen, Germany 52°43′E 7°14′N
180 E6 **Versmold** Nordrhein-Westfalen, Germany 52°03′E 8°09′N
176 B5 **Versoix** Genève, SW Switzerland 46°17′N 06°10′E
140 G8 **Verster** Northern Cape, South Africa 31°37′S 23°09′E
168 E2 **Verteillac** Aquitaine, France 45°21′N 0°22′E
183 F11 **Vértes** ⛰ NW Hungary
90 E4 **Vertientes** Camagüey, C Cuba 21°18′N 78°11′W
187 H2 **Vertískos** ⛰ N Greece
164 F5 **Vertou** Loire-Atlantique, NW France 47°10′N 01°28′W
141 K6 **Verulam** KwaZulu-Natal, South Africa 29°39′S 31°03′E
Verulamium *see* St Albans
118 D7 **Vervarco Campos, Lago** ◎ Neuquén, Argentina
163 H11 **Verviers** Liège, E Belgium 50°36′N 05°52′E
167 I3 **Vervins** Picardie, France 49°50′N 3°54′E
141 J4 **Verwoerdburg** South Africa 25°52′S 28°10′E
161 I8 **Verwood** United Kingdom 50°52′N 1°52′W
160 D9 **Veryan** United Kingdom 50°13′N 4°55′W
169 N3 **Verzuolo** Piemonte, NW Italy 44°35′N 07°29′E
167 J5 **Verzy** Champagne-Ardenne, France 49°09′N 4°10′E
174 C7 **Vescovato** Corse, France, C Mediterranean Sea 42°30′N 09°27′E
163 G11 **Vesdre** ≈ E Belgium
189 K7 **Vesele** *Rus.* Veseloye. Zaporiz'ka Oblast', S Ukraine 47°00′N 34°52′E
183 C9 **Veselí nad Lužnicí** *var.* Weseli an der Lainsitz, *Ger.* Frohenbruck. Jihočeský Kraj, S Czech Republic 49°11′N 14°40′E
185 L6 **Veselinovo** Shumen, NE Bulgaria 43°01′N 27°02′E
196 G7 **Veselovskoye Vodokhranilishche** ▣ SW Russian Federation
Veseloye *see* Vesele
189 H6 **Veselynove** Mykolayivs'ka Oblast', S Ukraine 47°21′N 31°15′E
Veseya *see* Vyasyeya
197 H5 **Veshenskaya** Rostovskaya Oblast', SW Russian Federation 49°37′N 41°43′E
197 I3 **Veshkayma** Ul'yanovskaya Oblast', W Russian Federation 54°04′N 47°06′E
Vesisaari *see* Vadsø
Vesontio *see* Besançon
165 K4 **Vesoul** *anc.* Vesulium, Vesulum. Haute-Saône, E France 47°37′N 06°09′E
111 H2 **Vespasiano** Minas Gerais, Brazil 19°40′S 43°55′W
155 F11 **Vessigebro** Halland, S Sweden 56°58′N 12°40′E
155 B9 **Vest-Agder** ◈ *county* S Norway
66 D9 **Vestavia Hills** Alabama, S USA 33°27′N 86°47′W
152 E4 **Vesterålen** *island group* N Norway
152 B2 **Vestfirdhir** ◈ *region* NW Iceland
152 E5 **Vestfjorden** *fjord* C Norway
155 D8 **Vestfold** ◈ *county* S Norway
Vestmanhavn *see* Vestmanna
154 A1 **Vestmanna** *Dan.* Vestmanhavn. Streymoy, N Faeroe Islands 62°09′N 07°11′W
152 B3 **Vestmannaeyjar** Sudhurland, S Iceland 63°26′N 20°14′W
154 B4 **Vestnes** Møre og Romsdal, S Norway 62°39′N 07°00′E
155 E12 **Vestsjælland** *off.* Vestsjællands Amt. ◈ *county* E Denmark
Vestsjællands Amt *see* Vestsjælland
152 B2 **Vesturland** ◈ *region* W Iceland
152 D4 **Vestvågøya** *island* C Norway
Vesulium/Vesulum *see* Vesoul
Vesuna *see* Périgueux
175 G9 **Vesuvio** *Eng.* Vesuvius. ⩚ S Italy 40°48′N 14°29′E
Vesuvius *see* Vesuvio
194 F9 **Ves'yegonsk** Tverskaya Oblast', W Russian Federation 58°40′N 37°13′E
183 E12 **Veszprém** *Ger.* Veszprim. Veszprém, W Hungary 47°06′N 17°54′E
183 E12 **Veszprém** *off.* Veszprém Megye. ◈ *county* W Hungary
Veszprém Megye *see* Veszprém
Veszprim *see* Veszprém
Vetka *see* Vyetka
155 G10 **Vetlanda** Jönköping, S Sweden 57°26′N 15°05′E
197 I1 **Vetluga** Nizhegorodskaya Oblast', W Russian Federation 57°51′N 45°45′E
195 H9 **Vetluga** ≈ NW Russian Federation
195 H9 **Vetluzhskiy** Kostromskaya Oblast', NW Russian Federation 58°21′N 45°25′E
197 I1 **Vetluzhskiy** Nizhegorodskaya Oblast', W Russian Federation 57°10′N 45°07′E
175 E8 **Vetralla** Lazio, C Italy 42°18′N 12°03′E
185 M6 **Vetren** *prev.* Zhitarovo. Burgas, E Bulgaria 42°36′N 27°23′E
185 M5 **Vetrino** Varna, E Bulgaria 43°19′N 27°26′E
Vetrino *see* Vyetryna
193 H4 **Vetrovaya, Gora** ▲ N Russian Federation 73°54′N 95°00′E
181 D10 **Vettelschoss** Rheinland-Pfalz, Germany 50°37′E 7°21′N
Vetter, Lake *see* Vättern
181 B10 **Vettweiss** Nordrhein-Westfalen, Germany 50°44′E 6°36′N
166 F3 **Veules-les-Roses** Haute-Normandie, France 49°52′N 0°48′E
163 A9 **Veurne** *var.* Furnes. West-Vlaanderen, W Belgium 51°04′N 02°40′E
66 F3 **Vevay** Indiana, N USA 38°45′N 85°08′W
176 C5 **Vevey** *Ger.* Vivis; *anc.* Vibiscum. Vaud, SW Switzerland 46°28′N 06°51′E
Vexiö *see* Växjö
165 K7 **Veynes** Hautes-Alpes, SE France 44°33′N 05°51′E
169 H2 **Veyre-Monton** Auvergne, France 45°41′N 3°10′E
167 I8 **Vézelay** Bourgogne, France 47°28′N 3°44′E
167 L6 **Vézelise** Lorraine, France 48°29′N 6°05′E
169 J5 **Vézénobres** Languedoc-Roussillon, France 44°03′N 4°09′E
185 J6 **Vezhen** ▲ C Bulgaria 42°45′N 24°22′E
169 H4 **Vézins-de-Lévézou** Midi-Pyrénées, France 44°17′N 2°57′E
214 F4 **Vezirköprü** Samsun, N Turkey 41°09′N 35°27′E
106 C10 **Viacha** La Paz, W Bolivia 16°40′S 68°17′W
114 C5 **Viale** Entre Ríos, Argentina 31°53′S 60°01′W
75 G12 **Vian** Oklahoma, C USA 35°30′N 94°56′W
Viana de Castelo *see* Viana do Castelo
172 C6 **Viana do Alentejo** Évora, S Portugal 38°20′N 08°00′W
170 D3 **Viana do Bolo** Galicia, NW Spain 42°10′N 07°06′W
170 C3 **Viana do Castelo** *var.* Viana de Castelo; *anc.* Velobriga. Viana do Castelo, NW Portugal 41°41′N 08°50′W
170 D3 **Viana do Castelo** *var.* Viana de Castelo. ◈ *district* N Portugal
162 F7 **Vianen** Utrecht, C Netherlands 52°N 05°06′E
256 F6 **Viangchan** *Eng./Fr.* Vientiane. ● (Laos) C Laos 17°58′N 102°38′E
256 F5 **Viangphoukha** *var.* Vieng Pou Kha. Louang Namtha, N Laos 20°41′N 101°03′E
170 E7 **Viar** ≈ SW Spain
176 F9 **Viareggio** Toscana, C Italy 43°52′N 10°15′E
165 H8 **Viaur** ≈ S France
Vibiscum *see* Vevey
155 D11 **Viborg** Viborg, NW Denmark 56°28′N 09°25′E
155 D11 **Viborg** *off.* Viborg Amt. ◈ *county* NW Denmark
Viborg Amt *see* Viborg
175 H11 **Vibo Valentia** *prev.* Monteleone di Calabria; *anc.* Hipponium. Calabria, SW Italy 38°40′N 16°06′E
166 F7 **Vibraye** Pays de la Loire, France 48°03′N 0°43′E
171 K3 **Vic** *var.* Vich; *anc.* Ausa, Vicus Ausonensis. Cataluña, NE Spain 41°56′N 02°16′E
168 F7 **Vicdessos** Midi-Pyrénées, France 42°46′N 1°30′E
164 G8 **Vic-en-Bigorre** Hautes-Pyrénées, S France 43°23′N 00°04′E
85 J8 **Vicente Guerrero** Durango, C Mexico 23°30′N 104°24′W
86 C4 **Vicente Guerrero** Zacatecas, Mexico 22°20′N 103°27′W
85 M7 **Vicente Guerrero, Presa** *var.* Presa de las Adjuntas. ▣ NE Mexico
114 E9 **Vicente López** Buenos Aires, Argentina 34°32′S 58°28′W
Vicentia *see* Vicenza
177 H6 **Vicenza** *anc.* Vicentia. Veneto, NE Italy 45°32′N 11°31′E
Vich *see* Vic
102 E6 **Vichada** *off.* Comisaría del Vichada. ◈ *province* E Colombia
Vichada, Comisaría del *see* Vichada
102 F5 **Vichada, Río** ≈ E Colombia
115 J4 **Vichadero** Rivera, NE Uruguay 31°45′S 54°41′W
Vichegda *see* Vychegda
194 G10 **Vichuga** Ivanovskaya Oblast', W Russian Federation 57°13′N 41°51′E
118 C5 **Vichuquen, Laguna** ◎ Maule, Chile
165 I6 **Vichy** Allier, C France 46°08′N 03°26′E
75 C12 **Vici** Oklahoma, C USA 36°09′N 99°18′W
155 E10 **Vickan** Halland, S Sweden 57°25′N 12°00′E
159 I8 **Vickerstown** United Kingdom 54°06′N 3°15′W
73 F8 **Vicksburg** Michigan, N USA 42°07′N 85°31′W
68 D2 **Vicksburg** Mississippi, S USA 32°21′N 90°52′W
81 J13 **Vicksburg** Nevada, USA 33°45′N 113°45′W
111 I4 **Viçosa** Minas Gerais, Brazil 20°45′S 42°53′W
165 H7 **Vic-sur-Cère** Cantal, C France 45°00′N 02°36′E
113 I3 **Víctor** Mato Grosso do Sul, SW Brazil 21°39′S 53°21′W
80 C3 **Victor** California, USA 38°08′N 121°12′W
74 H7 **Victor** Iowa, C USA 41°45′N 92°18′W
276 G6 **Victor Harbor** South Australia 35°33′S 138°37′E
114 C6 **Victoria** Entre Ríos, E Argentina 32°40′S 60°10′W
56 D9 **Victoria** *province capital* Vancouver Island, British Columbia, SW Canada 48°25′N 123°22′W
91 N3 **Victoria** NW Grenada 12°12′N 61°42′W
88 E4 **Victoria** Yoro, NW Honduras 15°01′N 87°28′W
175 I13 **Victoria** *var.* Rabat. Gozo, NW Malta 36°02′N 14°14′E
86 E5 **Victoria** Guanajuato, Mexico 21°13′N 100°13′W
188 D8 **Victoria** *Ger.* Viktoriastadt. Braşov, C Romania 45°44′N 24°41′E
137 I9 **Victoria** ● (Seychelles) Mahé, SW Seychelles 04°38′S 28°28′E
71 H8 **Victoria** Texas, SW USA 28°47′N 96°59′W
277 I6 **Victoria** ◈ *state* SE Australia
266 F5 **Victoria** ≈ Western Australia
Victoria *see* Labuan, East Malaysia
Victoria *see* Masvingo, Zimbabwe
53 J2 **Victoria and Albert Mountains** ▲ Nunavut, N Canada
55 J9 **Victoria Beach** Manitoba, S Canada 50°40′N 96°30′W
Victoria de Durango *see* Durango
Victoria de las Tunas *see* Las Tunas
138 F3 **Victoria Falls** Matabeleland North, W Zimbabwe 17°55′S 25°51′E
138 F3 **Victoria Falls** *waterfall* Zambia/Zimbabwe
138 F3 **Victoria Falls** ✈ Matabeleland North, W Zimbabwe 18°03′S 25°48′E
Victoria Falls *see* Iguaçu, Salto do
117 B9 **Victoria, Isla** *island* Archipiélago de los Chonos, S Chile
52 F7 **Victoria Island** *island* Northwest Territories/ Nunavut, NW Canada
277 H5 **Victoria, Lake** ◎ New South Wales, SE Australia
124 E6 **Victoria, Lake** *var.* Victoria Nyanza. ◎ E Africa
293 J8 **Victoria Land** *physical region* Antarctica
280 E9 **Victoria, Mount** ▲ Viti Levu, W Fiji 17°37′S 178°00′E
256 B4 **Victoria, Mount** ▲ W Myanmar (Burma) 21°13′N 93°53′E
280 C4 **Victoria, Mount** ▲ S Papua New Guinea 08°51′S 147°36′E
136 B7 **Victoria Nile** *var.* Somerset Nile. ≈ C Uganda
Victoria Nyanza *see* Victoria, Lake
88 D2 **Victoria Peak** ▲ SE Belize 16°50′N 88°38′W
Victoria Point *see* Kawthoung
279 E8 **Victoria Range** ⛰ South Island, New Zealand
274 G3 **Victoria River** ≈ Northern Territory, N Australia
274 G3 **Victoria River Roadhouse** Northern Territory, N Australia 15°37′S 131°07′E
52 G8 **Victoria Strait** *Sea waterway* Nunavut, N Canada

◆ Country
● Country Capital
◇ Dependent Territory
○ Dependent Territory Capital
◈ Administrative Regions
✈ International Airport
▲ Mountain
⛰ Mountain Range
⩚ Volcano
≈ River
◎ Lake
▣ Reservoir

Vladimir-Volynskiy - Waldo

Vladimir-Volynskiy see Volodymyr-Volyns'kyy
193 L9 Vladivostok Primorskiy Kray, SE Russian Federation 43°09′N 131°53′E
189 K9 Vladyslavivka Avtonomna Respublika Krym, S Ukraine 45°09′N 35°25′E
162 J4 Vlagtwedde Groningen, NE Netherlands 53°02′N 07°07′E
Vlajna see Kukavica
184 E4 Vlasenica ◈ Republika Srpska, E Bosnia and Herzegovina
184 D4 Vlašić ▲ C Bosnia and Herzegovina 44°18′N 17°40′E
183 C9 Vlašim Ger. Wlaschim. Středočesky Kraj, C Czech Republic 49°42′N 14°54′E
185 H6 Vlasotince Serbia, SE Serbia 42°58′N 22°07′E
193 J4 Vlasovo Respublika Sakha (Yakutiya), NE Russian Federation 70°41′N 134°49′E
140 F10 Vleesbaai Western Cape, South Africa 34°17′S 21°55′E
140 F10 Vleesbaai bay Western Cape, South Africa
140 E9 Vleifontein Western Cape, South Africa 33°09′S 21°03′E
162 F6 Vleuten Utrecht, C Netherlands 52°07′N 05°01′E
162 F3 Vlieland Fris. Flylân. island Waddeneilanden, N Netherlands
162 F3 Vliestroom strait NW Netherlands
163 F8 Vlijmen Noord-Brabant, S Netherlands 51°42′N 05°14′E
163 C8 Vlissingen Eng. Flushing, Fr. Flessingue. Zeeland, SW Netherlands 51°26′N 03°34′E
Vlodava see Włodawa
Vlonë/Vlora see Vlorë
184 F9 Vlorë prev. Vlonë, It. Valona, Vlora. Vlorë, SW Albania 40°28′N 19°31′E
184 F9 Vlorë ◈ district SW Albania
184 F9 Vlorës, Gjiri i var. Valona Bay. bay SW Albania
180 F6 Vlotho Nordrhein-Westfalen, Germany 52°10′E 8°51′N
Vlotslavsk see Włocławek
183 B9 Vltava Ger. Moldau. ≈ W Czech Republic
181 B8 Vluyn Nordrhein-Westfalen, Germany 51°26′E 6°32′N
196 F2 Vnukovo ✈ (Moskva) Gorod Moskva, W Russian Federation 55°30′N 36°52′E
228 G6 Vobkent Rus. Vabkent. Buxoro Viloyati, C Uzbekistan 40°01′N 64°25′E
70 F6 Voca Texas, SW USA 30°58′N 99°09′W
177 J2 Vöcklabruck Oberösterreich, NW Austria 48°01′N 13°38′E
184 B5 Vodice Šibenik-Knin, S Croatia 43°46′N 15°46′E
194 F7 Vodlozero, Ozero ◎ NW Russian Federation
184 A3 Vodnjan It. Dignano d'Istria. Istra, NW Croatia 44°57′N 13°51′E
195 J6 Vodnyy Respublika Komi, NW Russian Federation 63°31′N 53°21′E
227 L7 Vodokhranilishche Kapshagay Kaz. Qapshagay Böyeni; prev. Kapchagayskoye Vodokhranilishche. ⊠ SE Kazakhstan
194 E5 Vodokhranilishche, Kumskoye ◎ NW Russian Federation
155 D10 Vodskov Nordjylland, N Denmark 57°07′N 10°02′E
141 H9 Voel ≈ Eastern Cape, South Africa
181 B8 Voerde Nordrhein-Westfalen, Germany 51°36′E 6°41′N
152 B3 Vogar Sudhurland, SW Iceland 63°58′N 22°20′W
Vogelkop see Doberai, Jazirah
133 M7 Vogel Peak prev. Dimlang. ▲ E Nigeria 08°16′N 11°44′E
181 G10 Vogelsberg ▲▲ C Germany
176 E7 Voghera Lombardia, N Italy 44°59′N 09°01′E
184 E4 Vogošća Federacija Bosna I Hercegovina, SE Bosnia and Herzegovina 43°55′N 18°20′E
179 G9 Vogtland historical region E Germany
195 L8 Vogul'skiy Kamen', Gora ▲ NW Russian Federation 60°10′N 58°41′E
280 A9 Voh Province Nord, C New Caledonia 20°57′S 164°41′E
Vohémar see Iharaña
139 L10 Vohimena, Tanjona Fr. Cap Sainte Marie. headland S Madagascar 25°20′S 45°06′E
139 M9 Vohipeno Fianarantsoa, SE Madagascar 22°21′S 47°51′E
190 E4 Võhma Ger. Wöchma. Viljandimaa, S Estonia 58°37′N 25°34′E
137 E9 Voi Coast, S Kenya 03°23′S 38°35′E
167 K5 Void Lorraine, France 48°41′N 5°37′E
132 D7 Voinjama N Liberia 08°25′N 09°42′W
165 J6 Voiron Isère, E France 45°22′N 05°35′E
177 K4 Voitsberg Steiermark, SE Austria 47°04′N 15°09′E
155 D13 Vojens Ger. Woyens. Sønderjylland, SW Denmark 55°15′N 09°19′E
184 F2 Vojvodina Ger. Wojwodina. Vojvodina, N Serbia
Volaterrae see Volterra
89 I9 Volcán var. Hato del Volcán. Chiriquí, W Panama 08°45′N 82°38′W
Volcano Islands see Kazan-rettō
195 L8 Volchansk Sverdlovskaya Oblast', Russian Federation 59°56′N 60°05′E
Volchansk see Vovchans'k
Volchya see Vovcha
154 B5 Volda Møre og Romsdal, S Norway 62°07′N 06°04′E
188 E2 Voldymyerets' Russ. Vladimirets. Rivnens'ka Oblast', NW Ukraine 51°24′N 25°52′E
162 F5 Volendam Noord-Holland, C Netherlands 52°30′N 05°04′E
194 F9 Volga Yaroslavskaya Oblast', W Russian Federation 57°56′N 38°23′E
74 E5 Volga South Dakota, N USA 44°19′N 96°55′W
194 E10 Volga ≈ NW Russian Federation
Volga-Baltic Waterway see Volgo-Baltiyskiy Kanal
Volga Uplands see Privolzhskaya Vozvyshennost'
194 F8 Volgo-Baltiyskiy Kanal var. Volga-Baltic Waterway. canal NW Russian Federation
197 H7 Volgodonsk Rostovskaya Oblast', SW Russian Federation 47°35′N 42°03′E
197 I6 Volgograd prev. Stalingrad, Tsaritsyn. Volgogradskaya Oblast', SW Russian Federation 48°42′N 44°29′E
197 H5 Volgogradskaya Oblast' ◈ province SW Russian Federation
197 I5 Volgogradskoye Vodokhranilishche ⊠ SW Russian Federation
181 I12 Volkach Bayern, C Germany 49°51′N 10°15′E
177 K4 Völkermarkt Slvn. Velikovec. Kärnten, S Austria 46°40′N 14°38′E
194 D8 Volkhov Leningradskaya Oblast', NW Russian Federation 59°56′N 32°19′E
181 C13 Völklingen Saarland, SW Germany 49°15′N 06°51′E
181 G8 Volkmarsen Hessen, Germany 51°24′E 9°07′N
Volkovysk see Vawkavysk
Volkovyskiye Vysoty see Vawkavyskaye Wzvyshsha
141 K5 Volkrust Mpumalanga, South Africa 27°22′S 29°53′E
139 H7 Volksrust Mpumalanga, E South Africa 27°22′S 29°54′E
162 H5 Vollenhove Overijssel, N Netherlands 52°40′N 05°58′E
180 F3 Vollersode Niedersachsen, Germany 53°20′E 8°55′N
191 G10 Volma ≈ C Belarus
Volmari see Valmiera
189 M6 Volnovakha Donets'ka Oblast', SE Ukraine 47°36′N 37°32′E
188 E4 Volochys'k Khmel'nyts'ka Oblast', W Ukraine 49°32′N 26°14′E
188 G4 Volodarka Kyyivs'ka Oblast', N Ukraine 49°31′N 29°55′E
189 L6 Volodars'ke Donets'ka Oblast', E Ukraine 47°11′N 37°19′E
197 J7 Volodarskiy Astrakhanskaya Oblast', SW Russian Federation 46°23′N 48°39′E
Volodarskoye see Saumalkol'
188 G3 Volodars'k-Volyns'kyy Zhytomyrs'ka Oblast', N Ukraine 50°37′N 28°28′E
188 D2 Volodymyr-Volyns'kyy Pol. Włodzimierz, Rus. Vladimir-Volynskiy. Volyns'ka Oblast', NW Ukraine 50°51′N 24°19′E
194 G9 Vologda Vologodskaya Oblast', W Russian Federation 59°10′N 39°55′E
194 G8 Vologodskaya Oblast' ◈ province NW Russian Federation
196 F1 Volokolamsk Moskovskaya Oblast', W Russian Federation 56°03′N 35°57′E
196 F5 Volokonovka Belgorodskaya Oblast', W Russian Federation 50°30′N 37°54′E
169 L4 Volonne Provence-Alpes-Côte d'Azur, France 44°07′N 6°01′E
140 F6 Volop Northern Cape, South Africa 28°54′S 22°27′E
186 G4 Vólos Thessalía, C Greece 39°21′N 22°58′E
194 G7 Voloshka Arkhangel'skaya Oblast', NW Russian Federation 61°19′N 40°06′E
Vološinovo see Novi Bečej
190 G3 Volosovo Leningradskaya Oblast', Russian Federation
190 H5 Volot Pskovskaya Oblast', Russian Federation
188 C5 Volovets' Zakarpats'ka Oblast', W Ukraine 48°42′N 23°12′E
185 K5 Volovo Ruse, N Bulgaria 43°33′N 25°49′E
Volozhin see Valozhyn
169 N2 Volpiano Piemonte, NW Italy 45°12′N 07°46′E
180 J6 Völpke Sachsen-Anhalt, Germany 52°08′E 11°06′N
180 H7 Volpriehausen Niedersachsen, Germany 51°40′E 9°45′N
197 I4 Vol'sk Saratovskaya Oblast', W Russian Federation 52°04′N 47°20′E
140 F7 Volstruispoort pass Northern Cape, South Africa
80 C4 Volta California, USA 37°06′N 120°56′W
133 H8 Volta ≈ SE Ghana
Volta Blanche see White Volta
111 J6 Volta Grande Minas Gerais, Brazil 21°46′S 42°32′W
133 H7 Volta, Lake ⊠ SE Ghana
Volta Noire see Black Volta
110 G7 Volta Redonda Rio de Janeiro, SE Brazil 22°31′S 44°05′W
Volta Rouge see Red Volta
176 G10 Volterra anc. Volaterrae. Toscana, C Italy 43°23′N 10°52′E
175 G9 Volturno ≈ S Italy
184 E5 Volujak ▲▲ NW Montenegro
Volunteer Island see Starbuck Island
64 K4 Voluntown Connecticut, NE USA 41°34′N 71°52′W
187 H3 Vólvi, Límni ◎ N Greece
Volyn see Volyns'ka Oblast'
188 D2 Volyns'ka Oblast' var. Volyn, Rus. Volynskaya Oblast'. ◈ province NW Ukraine
Volynskaya Oblast' see Volyns'ka Oblast'
197 J2 Volzhsk Respublika Mariy El, W Russian Federation 55°53′N 48°21′E
197 I6 Volzhskiy Volgogradskaya Oblast', SW Russian Federation 48°49′N 44°40′E
139 L9 Vondrozo Fianarantsoa, SE Madagascar 22°50′S 47°20′E
185 K6 Voneshta Voda Veliko Tŭrnovo, N Bulgaria 42°55′N 25°40′E
83 H5 Von Frank Mountain ▲ Alaska, USA 63°36′N 154°29′W
186 F5 Vónitsa Dytikí Elláda, W Greece 38°55′N 20°53′E
190 F5 Võnnu Ger. Wendau. Tartumaa, SE Estonia 58°17′N 27°06′E
162 E7 Voorburg Zuid-Holland, W Netherlands 52°04′N 04°22′E
162 E6 Voorschoten Zuid-Holland, W Netherlands 52°08′N 04°26′E
162 H6 Voorst Gelderland, E Netherlands 52°10′N 06°10′E
162 G6 Voorthuizen Gelderland, C Netherlands 52°12′N 05°36′E
152 D2 Vopnafjördhur Austurland, E Iceland 65°45′N 14°51′W
152 D1 Vopnafjördhur bay E Iceland
Vora see Vorë
191 E9 Voranava Pol. Werenów, Rus. Voronovo. Hrodzyenskaya Voblasts', W Belarus 54°09′N 25°19′E
179 E14 Vorarlberg off. Land Vorarlberg. ◈ state W Austria
Vorarlberg, Land see Vorarlberg
162 H6 Vorden Gelderland, E Netherlands 52°07′N 06°18′E
176 E5 Vorderrhein ≈ SE Switzerland
152 C2 Vordhufell ▲ N Iceland 65°42′N 18°45′W
155 E13 Vordingborg Storstrøm, SE Denmark 55°01′N 11°55′E
184 F8 Vorë var. Vora. Tiranë, W Albania 41°23′N 19°37′E
187 H5 Vóreies Sporádes var. Vóreioi Sporádes, Vórioi Sporádhes, Eng. Northern Sporades. island group E Greece
Vóreioi Sporádes see Vóreies Sporádes
187 J5 Vóreion Aigaíon Eng. Aegean North. ◈ region SE Greece
187 H5 Vóreios Evvoïkós Kólpos var. Voreiós Evvoïkós Kólpos. gulf E Greece
169 I2 Vorey Auvergne, France 45°11′N 3°54′E
295 L4 Voring Plateau undersea feature N Norwegian Sea 67°00′N 04°00′E
Vórioi Sporádhes see Vóreies Sporádes
195 L3 Vorkuta Respublika Komi, NW Russian Federation 67°27′N 64°E
190 C4 Vormsi var. Vormsi Saar, Ger. Worms, Swed. Ormsö. island W Estonia
Vormsi Saar see Vormsi
192 G6 Vorogovo Krasnoyarskiy Kray, C Russian Federation 61°01′N 89°25′E
197 H4 Vorona ≈ W Russian Federation
196 G4 Voronezh Voronezhskaya Oblast', W Russian Federation 51°40′N 39°13′E
196 G4 Voronezh ≈ W Russian Federation
196 G4 Voronezhskaya Oblast' ◈ province W Russian Federation
191 J11 Voronok Bryanskaya Oblast', Russian Federation
Voronovitsya see Voronovytsya
Voronovo see Voranava
188 G4 Voronovytsya Rus. Voronovitsya. Vinnyts'ka Oblast', C Ukraine 49°06′N 28°49′E
192 G4 Vorontsovo Krasnoyarskiy Kray, N Russian Federation 71°45′N 83°31′E
194 F3 Voron'ya ≈ NW Russian Federation
Voropayevo see Varapayeva
Voroshilov see Ussuriysk
Voroshilovgrad see Luhans'ka Oblast', Ukraine
Voroshilovgrad see Luhans'k, Ukraine
Voroshilovgradskaya Oblast' see Luhans'ka Oblast'
Voroshilovsk see Stavropol', Russian Federation
Voroshilovsk see Alchevs'k
215 L6 Vorotan Az. Bärguşad. ≈ Armenia/Azerbaijan
197 I2 Vorotynets Nizhegorodskaya Oblast', W Russian Federation 56°06′N 46°06′E
189 J2 Vorozhba Sums'ka Oblast', NE Ukraine 51°10′N 34°15′E
189 J4 Vorskla ≈ Russian Federation/Ukraine
163 F9 Vorst Antwerpen, N Belgium 51°06′N 05°01′E
140 F4 Vorstershoop North-West, N South Africa 25°46′S 22°57′E
190 E5 Võrtsjärv Ger. Wirz-See. ◎ SE Estonia
190 F5 Võru Ger. Werro. Võrumaa, SE Estonia 57°51′N 27°01′E
229 J6 Vorukh N Tajikistan 39°51′N 70°34′E
190 F5 Võrumaa off. Võru Maakond. ◈ province SE Estonia
Võru Maakond see Võrumaa
140 F7 Vosburg Northern Cape, W South Africa 30°35′S 22°52′E
229 I8 Vose' Rus. Vose; prev. Aral. SW Tajikistan 37°51′N 69°31′E
165 J4 Vosges ◈ department NE France
165 K4 Vosges ▲▲ NE France
194 F8 Voskresenkoye Vologodskaya Oblast', NW Russian Federation 59°25′N 37°56′E
196 G2 Voskresensk Moskovskaya Oblast', W Russian Federation 55°19′N 38°42′E
190 J3 Voskresenskoye Leningradskaya Oblast', Russian Federation
197 I1 Voskresenskoye Nizhegorodskaya Oblast', W Russian Federation 57°00′N 45°33′E
197 L3 Voskresenskoye Respublika Bashkortostan, W Russian Federation 53°07′N 56°07′E
154 B6 Voss Hordaland, S Norway 60°38′N 06°25′E
154 B6 Voss physical region S Norway
163 F9 Vosselaar Antwerpen, N Belgium 51°19′N 04°55′E
154 B6 Vosso ≈ S Norway
Vostochno-Kazakhstanskaya Oblast' see Vostochnyy Kazakhstan
193 L3 Vostochno-Sibirskoye More Eng. East Siberian Sea. sea Arctic Ocean
195 M8 Vostochnyy Sverdlovskaya Oblast', Russian Federation
227 L4 Vostochnyy Kazakhstan off. Vostochno-Kazakhstanskaya Oblast', var. East Kazakhstan, Kaz. Shyghys Qazagastan Oblysy. ◈ province E Kazakhstan
Vostochnyy Sayan see Eastern Sayans
Vostock Island see Vostok Island
293 J6 Vostok Russian research station Antarctica 77°18′S 105°32′E
285 I5 Vostok Island var. Vostock Island; prev. Stavers Island. island Line Islands, SE Kiribati
195 K10 Votkinsk Udmurtskaya Respublika, NW Russian Federation 57°04′N 54°00′E
195 K10 Votkinskoye Vodokhranilishche var. Votkinsk Reservoir. ⊠ NW Russian Federation
Votkinsk Reservoir see Votkinskoye Vodokhranilishche
110 C9 Votorantim São Paulo, Brazil 23°33′S 47°26′W
113 K2 Votuporanga São Paulo, S Brazil 20°26′S 49°53′W
172 B2 Vouga, Rio ≈ N Portugal
166 E9 Vouillé Poitou-Charentes, France 46°38′N 0°10′E
186 F3 Voúrinos ▲▲ N Greece
187 H9 Voúxa, Akrotírio headland Kríti, Greece, E Mediterranean Sea 35°37′N 23°34′E
172 C2 Vouzela Viseu, Portugal 40°43′N 8°07′W
165 J2 Vouziers Ardennes, N France 49°24′N 04°42′E
189 K5 Vovcha Rus. Volchya. ≈ E Ukraine
189 L3 Vovchans'k Rus. Volchansk. Kharkivs'ka Oblast', E Ukraine 50°19′N 36°55′E
165 H4 Voves Eure-et-Loir, C France 48°18′N 01°39′E
134 G5 Vovodo ≈ S Central African Republic
154 H6 Voxna Gävleborg, C Sweden 61°21′N 15°35′E
195 L4 Voykar ≈ Yamalo-Nenetskiy Avtonomnyy Okrug, Russian Federation
185 H5 Voynishka Reka ≈ NW Bulgaria
195 J6 Voyvozh Respublika Komi, NW Russian Federation 62°54′N 54°52′E
194 G8 Vozhega Vologodskaya Oblast', NW Russian Federation 60°27′N 40°11′E
194 F8 Vozhe, Ozero ◎ NW Russian Federation
189 H6 Voznesens'k Rus. Voznesensk. Mykolayivs'ka Oblast', S Ukraine 47°34′N 31°21′E
194 E7 Voznesen'ye Leningradskaya Oblast', NW Russian Federation 61°00′N 35°24′E
228 D3 Vozrozhdeniya, Ostrov Uzb. Wozrojdeniye Oroli. island Kazakhstan/Uzbekistan
155 D10 Vrå var. Vraa. Nordjylland, N Denmark 57°21′N 09°57′E
Vraa see Vrå
185 I6 Vrachesh Sofiya, W Bulgaria 42°52′N 23°45′E
186 E6 Vrachíonas ▲ Zákynthos, Iónia Nisiá, Greece, C Mediterranean Sea 37°49′N 20°43′E
189 H6 Vradiyivka Mykolayivs'ka Oblast', S Ukraine 47°51′N 30°37′E
184 D5 Vran ▲ SW Bosnia and Herzegovina 43°35′N 17°30′E
188 E8 Vrancea ◈ county E Romania
229 K8 Vrang SE Tajikistan 37°03′N 72°26′E
193 M2 Vrangelya, Ostrov Eng. Wrangel Island. island NE Russian Federation
184 D4 Vranica ▲ C Bosnia and Herzegovina 43°57′N 17°43′E
185 H6 Vranje Serbia, SE Serbia 42°33′N 21°55′E
Vranov see Vranov nad Topl'ou
183 H10 Vranov nad Topl'ou var. Vranov, Hung. Varannó. Prešovský Kraj, E Slovakia 48°54′N 21°41′E
185 I5 Vratsa Vratsa, NW Bulgaria 43°13′N 23°34′E
185 I5 Vratsa ◈ province NW Bulgaria
185 H7 Vrattsa prev. Mirovo. Kyustendil, W Bulgaria 42°15′N 22°33′E
184 D4 Vrbanja ≈ NW Bosnia and Herzegovina
184 F2 Vrbas Vojvodina, NW Serbia 45°34′N 19°39′E
184 D3 Vrbas ≈ N Bosnia and Herzegovina
184 C2 Vrbovec Zagreb, N Croatia 45°53′N 16°24′E
184 B2 Vrbovsko Primorje-Gorski Kotar, NW Croatia 45°22′N 15°06′E
183 D8 Vrchlabí Ger. Hohenelbe. Královéhradecký Kraj, N Czech Republic 50°38′N 15°35′E
141 J5 Vrede Free State, E South Africa 27°25′S 29°10′E
180 C6 Vreden Nordrhein-Westfalen, NW Germany 52°01′N 06°50′E
140 D9 Vredenburg Western Cape, SW South Africa 32°55′S 18°00′E
140 D8 Vredendal Western Cape, South Africa 31°40′S 18°30′E
180 D4 Vrees Niedersachsen, Germany 52°53′E 7°46′N
163 F13 Vresse-sur-Semois Namur, SE Belgium 49°52′N 04°56′E
155 G8 Vretstorp Örebro, C Sweden 59°03′N 14°51′E
184 D5 Vrgorac prev. Vrhgorac. Split-Dalmacija, SE Croatia 43°10′N 17°24′E
Vrhgorac see Vrgorac
177 J6 Vrhnika Ger. Oberlaibach. W Slovenia 45°57′N 14°18′E
235 F8 Vriddhāchalam Tamil Nādu, SE India 11°33′N 79°18′E
162 I4 Vries Drenthe, NE Netherlands 53°04′N 06°34′E
162 I6 Vriezenveen Overijssel, E Netherlands 52°25′N 06°37′E
155 G10 Vrigstad Jönköping, S Sweden 57°19′N 14°30′E
184 C4 Vrlika Split-Dalmacija, S Croatia 43°54′N 16°24′E
184 G5 Vrnjačka Banja Serbia, C Serbia 43°36′N 20°55′E
140 F5 Vroeggedeel Northern Cape, South Africa 28°01′S 22°26′E
166 G2 Vron Picardie, France 50°19′N 1°45′E
Vrondádhes/Vrondados see Vrontádos
187 J6 Vrontádos var. Vrondados; prev. Vrondádhes. Chíos, E Greece 38°25′N 26°08′E
162 I5 Vroomshoop Overijssel, E Netherlands 52°28′N 06°35′E
140 E5 Vrouenspan Northern Cape, South Africa 27°48′S 20°26′E
184 G3 Vršac Ger. Werschetz, Hung. Versecz. Vojvodina, NE Serbia 45°08′N 21°18′E
184 G3 Vršački Kanal canal N Serbia
141 H4 Vryburg North-West, N South Africa 26°57′S 24°44′E
139 H7 Vryheid KwaZulu/Natal, E South Africa 27°45′S 30°48′E
183 E9 Vsetín Ger. Wsetin. Zlínský Kraj, E Czech Republic 49°21′N 17°57′E
190 H2 Vsevolozhsk Leningradskaya Oblast', Russian Federation
183 F10 Vtáčnik Hung. Madaras, Ptacsnik; prev. Ptačnik. ▲ W Slovakia 48°38′N 18°38′E
Vuadil' see Wodil
Vuanggava see Vuaqava
280 G9 Vuaqava prev. Vuanggava. island Lau Group, SE Fiji
185 J7 Vŭcha ≈ SW Bulgaria
Vučitrn see Vushtrri
163 F8 Vught Noord-Brabant, S Netherlands 51°37′N 05°19′E
189 L6 Vuhledar Donets'ka Oblast', E Ukraine 47°48′N 37°11′E
184 E3 Vuka ≈ E Croatia
184 F6 Vukël var. Vukli. Shkodër, N Albania 42°29′N 19°39′E
Vukli see Vukël
184 E3 Vukovar Hung. Vukovár. Vukovar-Srijem, E Croatia 45°18′N 18°45′E
Vukovarsko-Srijemska Županija see Vukovar-Srijem
184 E3 Vukovar-Srijem off. Vukovarsko-Srijemska Županija. ◈ province E Croatia
195 K5 Vuktyl Respublika Komi, NW Russian Federation 63°49′N 57°07′E
57 J8 Vulcan Alberta, SW Canada 50°27′N 113°12′W
188 C8 Vulcan Ger. Wulkan, Hung. Zsilyvajdevulkán; prev. Crivadia Vulcanului, Vaidei, Hung. Sily-Vajdej, Vajdej. Hunedoara, W Romania 45°22′N 23°16′E
188 F8 Vulcăneşti Rus. Vulkaneshty. S Moldova 45°41′N 28°25′E
175 G12 Vulcano, Isola island Isole Eolie, S Italy
185 I5 Vŭlchedrŭm Montana, NW Bulgaria 43°42′N 23°25′E
185 M5 Vŭlchidol prev. Kurt-Dere. Varna, E Bulgaria 43°25′N 27°33′E
Vulkaneshty see Vulcăneşti
79 H8 Vulture Mountains ▲▲ Arizona, SW USA
257 I9 Vung Tau prev. Fr. Cape Saint Jacques, Cap Saint-Jacques. Ba Ria-Vung Tau, S Vietnam 10°21′N 107°04′E
280 E10 Vunisea Kadavu, SE Fiji 19°04′S 178°10′E
Vuohčču see Vuotso
152 I7 Vuokatti Oulu, C Finland 64°08′N 28°16′E
152 I7 Vuolijoki Oulu, C Finland 64°09′N 27°00′E
Vuolleriebme see Vuollerim
152 F6 Vuollerim Lapp. Vuolleriebme. Norrbotten, N Sweden 66°24′N 20°36′E
Vuonnabahta see Varangerbotn
Vuoreija see Vardø
152 H5 Vuotso Lapp. Vuohčču. Lappi, N Finland 68°04′N 27°05′E
185 K7 Vŭrbitsa prev. Filevo. Khaskovo, S Bulgaria 42°02′N 25°25′E
185 K8 Vŭrbitsa ≈ S Bulgaria
197 I2 Vurnary Chuvashskaya Respublika, W Russian Federation 55°30′N 46°59′E
185 I5 Vŭrshets Montana, NW Bulgaria 43°14′N 23°20′E
Vusan see Busan
184 G6 Vushtrri Serb. Vučitrn. N Kosovo 42°49′N 21°00′E
141 K2 Vuwart Limpopo, South Africa 23°08′S 30°25′E
191 D10 Vyalikaya Byerastavitsa Pol. Brzostowica Wielka, Rus. Bol'shaya Berëstovitsa; prev. Velikaya Berestovitsa. Hrodzyenskaya Voblasts', SW Belarus 53°12′N 24°03′E
191 H12 Vyaliki Bor Rus. Velikiy Bor. Homyel'skaya Voblasts', SE Belarus 52°02′N 29°56′E
191 F11 Vyaliki Rozhan Rus. Bol'shoy Rozhan. Minskaya Voblasts', S Belarus 52°46′N 27°07′E
194 D7 Vyartsilya Fin. Värtsilä. Respublika Kareliya, NW Russian Federation 62°07′N 30°43′E
191 G10 Vyasyeya Rus. Veseya. Minskaya Voblasts', C Belarus 53°04′N 27°41′E
195 I9 Vyatka ≈ NW Russian Federation
Vyatka see Kirov
195 J10 Vyatskiye Polyany Kirovskaya Oblast', NW Russian Federation 56°15′N 51°06′E
193 L8 Vyazemskiy Khabarovskiy Kray, SE Russian Federation 47°28′N 134°39′E
196 E2 Vyaz'ma Smolenskaya Oblast', W Russian Federation 55°09′N 34°20′E
197 H1 Vyazniki Vladimirskaya Oblast', W Russian Federation 56°15′N 42°06′E
197 H5 Vyazovka Volgogradskaya Oblast', SW Russian Federation 50°57′N 43°57′E
191 F9 Vyazyn' Minskaya Voblasts', NW Belarus 54°25′N 27°10′E
190 G5 Vybor Pskovskaya Oblast', Russian Federation
194 D7 Vyborg Fin. Viipuri. Leningradskaya Oblast', NW Russian Federation 60°44′N 28°47′E
195 I7 Vychegda var. Vichegda. ≈ NW Russian Federation
193 H8 Vydrino Respublika Buryatiya, S Russian Federation 51°22′N 104°34′E
191 G9 Vyelyewshchyna Rus. Velevshchina. Vitsyebskaya Voblasts', N Belarus 54°44′N 28°35′E
191 I10 Vyeramyeyki Rus. Veremeyki. Mahilyowskaya Voblasts', E Belarus 53°46′N 31°17′E
190 G7 Vyerkhnyadzvinsk Rus. Verkhnedvinsk. Vitsyebskaya Voblasts', N Belarus 55°47′N 27°56′E
191 I11 Vyetka Rus. Vetka. Homyel'skaya Voblasts', SE Belarus 52°33′N 31°10′E
191 G8 Vyetryna Rus. Vetrino. Vitsyebskaya Voblasts', N Belarus 55°25′N 28°28′E
Vygonovskoye, Ozero see Vyhanashchanskaye, Vozyera
194 F6 Vygozero, Ozero ◎ NW Russian Federation
191 F11 Vyhanashchanskaye, Vozyera prev. Vozyera Vyhanawskaye, Rus. Ozero Vygonovskoye. ◎ SW Belarus
Vyhanawskaye, Vozyera see Vyhanashchanskaye, Vozyera
197 H2 Vyksa Nizhegorodskaya Oblast', W Russian Federation 55°21′N 42°10′E
188 G8 Vylkove Rus. Vilkovo. Odes'ka Oblast', SW Ukraine 45°24′N 29°37′E
195 I6 Vym' ≈ NW Russian Federation
188 C5 Vynohradiv Cz. Sevluš, Hung. Nagyszöllös, Rus. Vinogradov; prev. Sevlyush. Zakarpats'ka Oblast', W Ukraine 48°09′N 23°01′E
190 H3 Vyra Leningradskaya Oblast', Russian Federation
194 D8 Vyritsa Leningradskaya Oblast', NW Russian Federation 59°25′N 30°20′E
157 F10 Vyrnwy Wel. Afon Efyrnwy. ≈ E Wales, United Kingdom
227 M3 Vyshe Ivanovskiy Belak, Gora ▲ E Kazakhstan 50°16′N 83°46′E
190 G5 Vyshgorodok Pskovskaya Oblast', Russian Federation
189 H3 Vyshhorod Kyyivs'ka Oblast', N Ukraine 50°36′N 30°28′E
194 E9 Vyshniy Volochek Tverskaya Oblast', W Russian Federation 57°37′N 34°33′E
183 E9 Vyškov Ger. Wischau. Jihomoravský Kraj, SE Czech Republic 49°17′N 17°01′E
183 C9 Vysočina prev. Jihlavský Kraj. ◈ region N Czech Republic
191 C11 Vysokaye Rus. Vysokoye. Brestskaya Voblasts', SW Belarus 52°20′N 23°18′E
183 D8 Vysoké Mýto Ger. Hohenmauth. Pardubický Kraj, C Czech Republic 49°57′N 16°10′E
189 J6 Vysokopillya Khersons'ka Oblast', S Ukraine 47°28′N 33°30′E
196 F1 Vysokovsk Moskovskaya Oblast', W Russian Federation 56°12′N 36°42′E
Vysokoye see Vysokaye
194 F7 Vytegra Vologodskaya Oblast', NW Russian Federation 60°59′N 36°27′E
188 D5 Vyzhnytsya Chernivets'ka Oblast', W Ukraine 48°14′N 25°10′E

W

132 G6 Wa NW Ghana 10°07′N 02°28′W
Waadt see Vaud
Waag see Váh
Waagbistritz see Považská Bystrica
Waagneustadtl see Nové Mesto nad Váhom
136 G6 Waajid Gedo, SW Somalia 03°37′N 43°19′E
162 G7 Waal ≈ S Netherlands
280 A8 Waala Province Nord, W New Caledonia 19°46′S 163°41′E
163 F8 Waalwijk Noord-Brabant, S Netherlands 51°42′N 05°04′E
163 C9 Waarschoot Oost-Vlaanderen, NW Belgium 51°09′N 03°35′E
280 B3 Wabag Enga, W Papua New Guinea 05°28′S 143°40′E
57 H1 Wabasca ≈ Alberta, SW Canada
73 F10 Wabash Indiana, N USA 40°47′N 85°48′W
74 H5 Wabasha Minnesota, N USA 44°22′N 92°01′W
73 F10 Wabash River ≈ N USA
72 G2 Wabatongushi Lake ◎ Ontario, S Canada
136 F5 Wabē Gestro Wenz ≈ SE Ethiopia
62 A1 Wabos Ontario, S Canada 46°48′N 84°06′W
55 I7 Wabowden Manitoba, C Canada 54°57′N 98°38′W
182 F5 Wąbrzeźno Kujawsko-pomorskie, C Poland 53°18′N 18°55′E
261 N8 Wabuda Island island SW Papua New Guinea
80 G2 Wabuska Nevada, USA 39°09′N 119°11′W
67 K8 Waccamaw River ≈ South Carolina, SE USA
69 K5 Waccasassa Bay bay Florida, SE USA
163 D9 Wachtebeke Oost-Vlaanderen, NW Belgium 51°10′N 03°52′E
181 G11 Wächtersbach Hessen, Germany 50°16′E 9°18′N
180 J6 Wackersleben Sachsen-Anhalt, Germany 52°04′E 11°01′N
71 H5 Waco Texas, SW USA 31°33′N 97°10′W
75 D9 Waconda Lake var. Great Elder Reservoir. ⊠ Kansas, C USA
Wadai see Ouaddaï
Wad Al-Hajarah see Guadalajara
251 H4 Wadayama Hyōgo, Honshū, SW Japan 35°19′N 134°51′E
134 I2 Wad Banda Western Kordofan, C Sudan 13°08′N 27°56′E
128 D3 Waddān NW Libya 29°10′N 16°08′E
162 F3 Waddeneilanden Eng. West Frisian Islands. island group N Netherlands
162 F4 Waddenzee var. Wadden Zee. sea SE North Sea
Wadden Zee see Waddenzee
161 J5 Waddesdon United Kingdom 51°50′N 0°55′W
159 L9 Waddingham United Kingdom 53°27′N 0°31′W
159 L10 Waddington United Kingdom 53°10′N 0°32′W
56 C6 Waddington, Mount ▲ British Columbia, SW Canada 51°17′N 125°16′W
162 E7 Waddinxveen Zuid-Holland, C Netherlands 52°03′N 04°38′E
55 H9 Wadena Saskatchewan, S Canada 51°57′N 103°48′W
74 F3 Wadena Minnesota, N USA 46°27′N 95°07′W
176 E4 Wädenswil Zürich, N Switzerland 47°14′N 08°41′E
181 C13 Wadern Saarland, Germany 49°32′E 6°53′N
67 J7 Wadesboro North Carolina, SE USA 34°59′N 80°03′W
234 E6 Wādi Karnātaka, C India 17°00′N 76°58′E
219 F8 Wādī as Sīr var. Wadi es Sir. 'Ammān, NW Jordan 31°57′N 35°49′E
219 F8 Wādī as Sīr Jordan 31°57′N 35°49′E
Wadi es Sir see Wādī as Sīr
129 I7 Wadi Halfa var. Wādī Ḩalfā'. Northern, N Sudan 21°46′N 31°17′E
219 F12 Wādī Mūsā var. Petra. Ma'ān, S Jordan 30°19′N 35°29′E
219 F12 Wādī Mūsá Jordan 30°19′N 35°29′E
69 K1 Wadley Georgia, SE USA 32°52′N 82°24′W
Wad Madanī see Wad Medani
136 C2 Wad Medani var. Wad Madanī. Gezira, C Sudan 14°24′N 33°30′E
136 B2 Wad Nimr White Nile, C Sudan 14°32′N 32°10′E
251 J9 Wadomari Kagoshima, Okinoerabu-jima, SW Japan 27°25′N 128°40′E
183 G8 Wadowice Małopolskie, S Poland 49°54′N 19°29′E
80 G2 Wadsworth Nevada, W USA 39°39′N 119°16′W
73 I9 Wadsworth Ohio, N USA 41°01′N 81°43′W
159 L9 Wadworth United Kingdom 53°28′N 1°09′W
250 A2 Waegwan 35°59′N 128°24′E
71 H7 Waelder Texas, SW USA 29°42′N 97°16′W
Waereghem see Waregem
245 M3 Wafangdian var. Fuxian, Fu Xian. Liaoning, NE China 39°36′N 122°00′E
260 F5 Waflia Pulau Buru, E Indonesia 03°10′S 126°05′E
Wagadugu see Ouagadougou
140 F8 Wagenaarskraal Northern Cape, South Africa 31°48′S 22°49′E
162 G7 Wageningen Gelderland, SE Netherlands 51°58′N 05°40′E
103 K5 Wageningen Nickerie, NW Suriname 05°44′N 56°45′W
55 J2 Wager Bay inlet Nunavut, N Canada
261 L5 Wageseri Papua, E Indonesia 01°48′S 138°19′E
277 K6 Wagga Wagga New South Wales, SE Australia 35°11′S 147°22′E
180 I6 Waggum Niedersachsen, Germany 52°19′E 10°34′N
274 D8 Wagin Western Australia 33°16′S 117°26′E
74 D6 Wagner South Dakota, N USA 43°04′N 98°17′W
75 F12 Wagoner Oklahoma, C USA 35°58′N 92°23′W
79 M6 Wagon Mound New Mexico, SW USA 36°00′N 104°42′W
76 D7 Wagontire Oregon, NW USA 43°15′N 119°51′W
182 E5 Wągrowiec Wielkopolskie, C Poland 52°49′N 17°11′E
231 I4 Wāh Punjab, NE Pakistan 33°50′N 72°44′E
261 H5 Wahai Pulau Seram, E Indonesia 02°48′S 129°29′E
259 K5 Wahau, Sungai ≈ Borneo, C Indonesia
Wahaybah, Ramlat Al see Wahībah, Ramlat Āl
136 A4 Wahda var. Unity State. ◈ state N South Sudan
82 B2 Wahiawā var. Wahiawa. O'ahu, Hawaii, USA, C Pacific Ocean 21°30′N 158°01′W
Wahībah, Ramlat Ahl see Wahībah, Ramlat Āl
221 L5 Wahībah, Ramlat Āl var. Ramlat Ahl Wahībah, Ramlat Al Wahaybah, Eng. Wahībah Sands. desert N Oman
Wahībah Sands see Wahībah, Ramlat Āl
181 C9 Wahn ✈ (Köln) Nordrhein-Westfalen, W Germany 50°51′N 07°09′E
75 E8 Wahoo Nebraska, C USA 41°12′N 96°37′W
74 E4 Wahpeton North Dakota, N USA 46°16′N 96°36′W
Wahran see Oran
180 I5 Wahrenholz Niedersachsen, Germany 52°37′E 10°36′N
78 G4 Wah Wah Mountains ▲▲ Utah, W USA
82 B2 Wai'anae var. Waianae. O'ahu, Hawaii, USA, C Pacific Ocean 21°26′N 158°11′W
278 J5 Waiapu ≈ North Island, New Zealand
279 F9 Waiau Canterbury, South Island, New Zealand 42°39′S 173°03′E
279 E9 Waiau ≈ South Island, New Zealand
278 B12 Waiau ≈ South Island, New Zealand
179 D12 Waiblingen Baden-Württemberg, S Germany 48°49′N 09°19′E
Waidhofen see Waidhofen an der Ybbs, Niederösterreich, Austria
Waidhofen see Waidhofen an der Thaya, Niederösterreich, Austria
177 K1 Waidhofen an der Thaya var. Waidhofen. Niederösterreich, NE Austria 48°49′N 15°17′E
177 K2 Waidhofen an der Ybbs var. Waidhofen. Niederösterreich, E Austria 47°58′N 14°47′E
244 G8 Waifang Shan ▲▲ Henan, China
261 H4 Waigeo, Pulau island Maluku, E Indonesia
278 G3 Waiheke Island island N New Zealand
278 H4 Waihi Waikato, North Island, New Zealand 37°22′S 175°51′E
278 H4 Waihou ≈ North Island, New Zealand
Waikaboebak see Waikabubak
260 C8 Waikabubak prev. Waikaboebak. Pulau Sumba, C Indonesia 09°40′S 119°25′E
278 C12 Waikaia ≈ South Island, New Zealand
278 C12 Waikaka Southland, South Island, New Zealand 45°55′S 168°59′E
278 G7 Waikanae Wellington, North Island, New Zealand 40°52′S 175°03′E
278 G4 Waikare, Lake ◎ North Island, New Zealand
278 I5 Waikaremoana, Lake ◎ North Island, New Zealand
279 E9 Waikari Canterbury, South Island, New Zealand 42°50′S 172°41′E
278 H5 Waikato off. Waikato Region. ◈ region North Island, New Zealand
278 G4 Waikato ≈ North Island, New Zealand
Waikato Region see Waikato
277 H5 Waikerie South Australia 34°12′S 139°57′E
278 D12 Waikouaiti Otago, South Island, New Zealand 45°36′S 170°39′E
82 D3 Wailea Hawaii, USA, C Pacific Ocean 19°53′N 155°07′W
278 E10 Waimakariri ≈ South Island, New Zealand
279 E8 Waimangaroa West Coast, South Island, New Zealand 41°41′S 171°49′E
278 D11 Waimate Canterbury, South Island, New Zealand 44°44′S 171°03′E
82 D3 Waimea var. Kamuela. Hawaii, USA, C Pacific Ocean 20°02′N 155°20′W
163 H11 Waimes Liège, E Belgium 50°25′N 06°10′E
159 N10 Wainfleet All Saints United Kingdom 53°06′N 0°15′E
232 F9 Wainganga var. Wain River. ≈ C India
Waingapoe see Waingapu
260 C8 Waingapu prev. Waingapoe. Pulau Sumba, C Indonesia 09°40′S 120°16′E
103 J4 Waini ≈ N Guyana
103 J4 Waini Point headland NW Guyana 08°24′N 59°48′W
Wain River see Wainganga
57 K5 Wainwright Alberta, SW Canada 52°50′N 110°51′W
82 G2 Wainwright Alaska, USA 70°38′N 160°02′W
278 G3 Waiotira Northland, North Island, New Zealand 35°56′S 174°11′E
278 H6 Waiouru Manawatu-Wanganui, North Island, New Zealand 39°28′S 175°41′E
261 K6 Waipa Papua, E Indonesia 03°47′S 136°16′E
278 G4 Waipa ≈ North Island, New Zealand
278 I5 Waipaoa ≈ North Island, New Zealand
278 C13 Waipapa Point headland South Island, New Zealand 46°39′S 168°51′E
279 E9 Waipara Canterbury, South Island, New Zealand 43°04′S 172°45′E
278 H6 Waipawa Hawke's Bay, North Island, New Zealand 39°57′S 176°36′E
278 G3 Waipu Northland, North Island, New Zealand 35°58′S 174°25′E
278 H6 Waipukurau Hawke's Bay, North Island, New Zealand 40°01′S 176°34′E
261 I6 Wair Pulau Kai Besar, E Indonesia 05°16′S 133°09′E
Wairakai see Wairakei
278 H5 Wairakei var. Wairakai. Waikato, North Island, New Zealand 38°37′S 176°05′E
279 F8 Wairau ≈ South Island, New Zealand
278 I6 Wairoa Hawke's Bay, North Island, New Zealand 39°03′S 177°26′E
278 I5 Wairoa ≈ North Island, New Zealand
278 F3 Wairoa ≈ North Island, New Zealand
278 H5 Waitahanui Waikato, North Island, New Zealand 38°48′S 176°04′E
278 G4 Waitakaruru Waikato, North Island, New Zealand 37°14′S 175°22′E
278 D11 Waitaki ≈ South Island, New Zealand
278 G5 Waitara Taranaki, North Island, New Zealand 39°01′S 174°14′E
278 H4 Waitoa Waikato, North Island, New Zealand 37°36′S 175°37′E
278 G5 Waitomo Caves Waikato, North Island, New Zealand 38°17′S 175°06′E
278 G6 Waitotara Taranaki, North Island, New Zealand 39°49′S 174°43′E
278 G6 Waitotara ≈ North Island, New Zealand
76 E5 Waitsburg Washington, NW USA 46°16′N 118°09′W
Waitzen see Vác
278 G4 Waiuku Auckland, North Island, New Zealand 37°15′S 174°45′E
251 J1 Wajima var. Wazima. Ishikawa, Honshū, SW Japan 37°23′N 136°53′E
136 E7 Wajir North Eastern, NE Kenya 01°46′N 40°05′E
134 F7 Waka Equateur, NW Dem. Rep. Congo 01°04′N 20°11′E
136 D5 Waka Southern Nationalities, S Ethiopia 07°12′N 37°19′E
72 H3 Wakami Lake ◎ Ontario, S Canada
250 G4 Wakasa Tottori, Honshū, SW Japan 35°18′N 134°25′E
251 H3 Wakasa-wan bay C Japan
278 C11 Wakatipu, Lake ◎ South Island, New Zealand
57 M5 Wakaw Saskatchewan, S Canada 52°40′N 105°45′W
280 E9 Wakaya island C Fiji
251 H5 Wakayama Wakayama, Honshū, SW Japan 34°12′N 135°09′E
251 H6 Wakayama off. Wakayama-ken. ◈ prefecture Honshū, SW Japan
Wakayama-ken see Wakayama
75 C9 Wa Keeney Kansas, C USA 39°02′N 99°53′W
279 F8 Wakefield Tasman, South Island, New Zealand 41°24′S 173°03′E
159 K9 Wakefield N England, United Kingdom 53°42′N 01°29′W
75 E9 Wakefield Kansas, C USA 39°12′N 97°00′W
65 L2 Wakefield Massachusetts, USA 42°30′N 71°04′W
72 C4 Wakefield Michigan, N USA 46°27′N 89°55′W
65 L4 Wakefield Rhode Island, USA 41°26′N 71°30′W
67 K6 Wake Forest North Carolina, SE USA 35°58′N 78°30′W
Wakeham Bay see Kangiqsujuaq
283 N1 Wake Island ◇ US unincorporated territory NW Pacific Ocean
283 N2 Wake Island ✈ NW Pacific Ocean
283 L2 Wake Island atoll NW Pacific Ocean
283 M1 Wake Lagoon lagoon Wake Island, NW Pacific Ocean
256 C6 Wakema Ayeyarwady, SW Myanmar (Burma) 16°36′N 95°11′E
Wakhan see Khandūd
250 G5 Waki Tokushima, Shikoku, SW Japan 34°04′N 134°10′E
252 D7 Wakinosawa Aomori, Honshū, C Japan 41°08′N 140°47′E
252 E2 Wakkanai Hokkaidō, NE Japan 45°25′N 141°39′E
139 H7 Wakkerstroom Mpumalanga, E South Africa 27°21′S 30°10′E
62 A1 Wakomata Lake ◎ Ontario, S Canada
277 I6 Wakool New South Wales, SE Australia 35°30′S 144°22′E
Wakra see Al Wakrah
Waku Kungo see Uaco Cungo
280 E3 Wakunai Bougainville Island, NE Papua New Guinea 05°52′S 155°10′E
Walachei/Walachia see Wallachia
85 H8 Walamo Sinaloa, Mexico 23°07′N 106°15′W
260 C6 Walanae, Sungai ≈ Sulawesi, C Indonesia
219 G9 Wālā, Wādī al dry watercourse Jordan
235 G11 Walawe Ganga ≈ S Sri Lanka
182 D7 Wałbrzych Ger. Waldenburg, Waldenburg in Schlesien. Dolnośląskie, SW Poland 50°45′N 16°20′E
277 L4 Walcha New South Wales, SE Australia 31°01′S 151°38′E
179 F13 Walchensee ◎ SE Germany
163 C8 Walcheren island SW Netherlands
159 M10 Walcot United Kingdom 53°05′N 0°19′W
74 I7 Walcott Iowa, C USA 41°34′N 90°46′W
77 L9 Walcott Wyoming, C USA 41°46′N 106°46′W
163 E12 Walcourt Namur, S Belgium 50°16′N 04°26′E
182 D5 Wałcz Ger. Deutsch Krone. Zachodnio-pomorskie, NW Poland 53°17′N 16°29′E
176 E4 Wald Zürich, N Switzerland 47°17′N 08°56′E
177 K2 Waldaist ≈ N Austria
181 D12 Waldböckelheim Rheinland-Pfalz, Germany 49°49′E 7°43′N
181 D9 Waldbröl Nordrhein-Westfalen, Germany 50°53′E 7°37′N
274 D5 Waldburg Range ▲▲ Western Australia
181 G9 Waldeck Hessen, Germany 51°12′E 9°04′N
79 L2 Walden Colorado, C USA 40°43′N 106°16′W
65 H4 Walden New York, NE USA 41°35′N 74°09′W
64 A1 Walden New York, USA 42°55′N 78°47′W
Waldenburg/Waldenburg in Schlesien see Wałbrzych
57 M5 Waldheim Saskatchewan, S Canada 52°38′N 106°35′W
Waldia see Weldiya
181 H9 Waldkappel Hessen, Germany 51°09′E 9°53′N
179 G12 Waldkraiburg Bayern, SE Germany 48°10′N 12°23′E
181 F13 Wald-Michelbach Hessen, Germany 49°34′E 8°50′N
181 C13 Waldmohr Rheinland-Pfalz, Germany 49°23′E 7°20′N
75 H14 Waldo Arkansas, C USA 33°21′N 93°18′W
69 L4 Waldo Florida, SE USA 29°47′N 82°07′W

◆ Country
● Country Capital
◇ Dependent Territory
○ Dependent Territory Capital
◈ Administrative Regions
✈ International Airport
▲ Mountain
▲▲ Mountain Range
Volcano
≈ River
◎ Lake
⊠ Reservoir

◆ Country
● Country Capital
◇ Dependent Territory
○ Dependent Territory Capital
◆ Administrative Regions
✕ International Airport
▲ Mountain
▲ Mountain Range
♦ Volcano
♂ River
☒ Lake
☒ Reservoir

◆ Country
● Country Capital
◈ Dependent Territory
○ Dependent Territory Capital
◊ Administrative Regions
✈ International Airport
▲ Mountain
▲ Mountain Range
ῶ Volcano
⟠ River
◎ Lake
▢ Reservoir

Williamstown - Xaignabouli
INDEX
427

65 I2 **Williamstown** Massachusetts, NE USA 42°41´N 73°11´W
64 G8 **Williamstown** New Jersey, USA 39°41´N 75°00´W
65 K4 **Willimantic** Connecticut, USA 41°43´N 72°12´W
64 G7 **Willingboro** New Jersey, NE USA 40°01´N 74°52´W
57 J5 **Willingdon** Alberta, SW Canada 53°49´N 112°08´W
161 L8 **Willingdon** United Kingdom 50°47´N 0°15´E
181 F8 **Willingen** Hessen, Germany 51°18´E 8°37´N
71 I6 **Willis** Texas, SW USA 30°25´N 95°28´W
176 D4 **Willisau** Luzern, W Switzerland 47°07´N 08°00´E
140 E8 **Williston** Northern Cape, W South Africa 31°20´S 20°52´E
69 L5 **Williston** Florida, SE USA 29°23´N 82°27´W
74 A2 **Williston** North Dakota, N USA 48°07´N 103°37´W
67 I9 **Williston** South Carolina, SE USA 33°24´N 81°25´W
56 D2 **Williston Lake** ⊠ British Columbia, W Canada
160 F7 **Williton** United Kingdom 51°10´N 3°19´W
78 A3 **Willits** California, W USA 39°24´N 123°22´W
74 F4 **Willmar** Minnesota, N USA 45°07´N 95°02´W
54 B5 **Will, Mount** ▲ British Columbia, W Canada 57°31´N 128°48´W
73 J9 **Willoughby** Ohio, N USA 41°38´N 81°24´W
57 N8 **Willow Bunch** Saskatchewan, S Canada 49°30´N 105°41´W
76 D5 **Willow Creek** 〰 Oregon, NW USA
64 F7 **Willow Grove** Pennsylvania, USA 40°09´N 75°07´W
83 I6 **Willow Lake** Alaska, USA 61°44´N 150°02´W
54 E4 **Willowlake** 〰 Northwest Territories, NW Canada
140 G9 **Willowmore** Eastern Cape, S South Africa 33°18´S 23°30´E
72 C5 **Willow Reservoir** ⊠ Wisconsin, N USA
78 B3 **Willows** California, W USA 39°28´N 122°12´W
75 I11 **Willow Springs** Missouri, C USA 36°59´N 91°58´W
64 E8 **Willow Street** Pennsylvania, USA 39°59´N 76°17´W
141 J8 **Willowvale** Eastern Cape, South Africa 32°16´S 28°31´E
64 E2 **Willseyville** New York, USA 42°17´N 76°23´W
276 G4 **Wilmington** South Australia 32°42´S 138°08´E
64 F8 **Wilmington** Delaware, NE USA 39°45´N 75°33´W
61 I4 **Wilmington** Illinois, N USA North America 41°18′N 88°09′W
67 L8 **Wilmington** North Carolina, SE USA 34°14´N 77°55´W
73 H11 **Wilmington** Ohio, N USA 39°27´N 83°49´W
65 J1 **Wilmington** Vermont, USA 42°52´N 72°52´W
66 F4 **Wilmore** Kentucky, S USA 37°51´N 84°39´W
74 E4 **Wilmot** South Dakota, N USA 45°24´N 96°51´W
159 J10 **Wilmslow** United Kingdom 53°20´N 2°14´W
Wilna/Wilno *see* Vilnius
181 E10 **Wilnsdorf** Nordrhein-Westfalen, W Germany 50°49´N 08°06´E
163 E9 **Wilrijk** Antwerpen, N Belgium 51°11´N 04°25´E
180 I5 **Wilsche** Niedersachsen, Germany 52°31´E 10°29´N
180 H4 **Wilseder Berg** *hill* NW Germany
67 L6 **Wilson** North Carolina, SE USA 35°43´N 77°56´W
70 E4 **Wilson** Texas, SW USA 33°21´N 101°44´W
276 C4 **Wilson Bluff** *headland* South Australia/Western Australia 31°41´S 129°01´E
78 G4 **Wilson Creek Range** ▲▲ Nevada, W USA
66 D7 **Wilson Lake** ⊠ Alabama, S USA
75 D9 **Wilson Lake** ⊠ Kansas, SE USA
79 K5 **Wilson, Mount** ▲ Colorado, C USA 37°50´N 107°59´W
277 J8 **Wilsons Promontory** *peninsula* Victoria, SE Australia
180 G2 **Wilster** Schleswig-Holstein, Germany 53°55´E 9°23´N
180 C5 **Wilsum** Niedersachsen, Germany 52°32´E 6°51´N
181 B12 **Wiltingen** Rheinland-Pfalz, Germany 49°40´E 6°36´N
80 D2 **Wilton** California, USA 38°25´N 121°16´W
65 I5 **Wilton** Connecticut, USA 41°12´N 73°26´W
73 B9 **Wilton** Iowa, C USA 41°35´N 91°01´W
63 J4 **Wilton** Maine, NE USA 44°35´N 70°15´W
74 C3 **Wilton** North Dakota, N USA 47°09´N 100°46´W
161 H7 **Wiltshire** *cultural region* S England, United Kingdom
163 H12 **Wiltz** Diekirch, NW Luxembourg 49°58´N 05°56´E
274 E6 **Wiluna** Western Australia 26°34´S 120°14´E
163 H12 **Wilwerwiltz** Diekirch, NE Luxembourg 49°59´N 06°00´E
74 D3 **Wimbledon** North Dakota, N USA 47°08´N 98°25´W
161 K3 **Wimblington** United Kingdom 52°30´N 0°04´E
161 H8 **Wimborne Minster** United Kingdom 50°47´N 1°59´W
166 G2 **Wimereux** Nord-Pas-de-Calais, France 50°46´N 1°37´E
88 G5 **Wina** *var.* Güina. Jinotega, N Nicaragua 14°00´N 85°14´W
73 E9 **Winamac** Indiana, N USA 41°03´N 86°37´W
137 C8 **Winam Gulf** *var.* Kavirondo Gulf. *gulf* SW Kenya
141 I6 **Winburg** Free State, C South Africa 28°31´S 27°01´E
161 H7 **Wincanton** United Kingdom 51°03´N 2°25´W
161 H5 **Winchcombe** United Kingdom 51°57´N 1°58´W
161 L7 **Winchelsea** United Kingdom 50°55´N 0°43´E
65 K2 **Winchendon** Massachusetts, NE USA 42°41´N 72°01´W
181 B13 **Wincheringen** Rheinland-Pfalz, Germany 49°37´E 6°26´N
62 G3 **Winchester** Ontario, SE Canada 45°07´N 75°19´W
161 I7 **Winchester** *hist.* Wintanceaster, *Lat.* Venta Belgarum. S England, United Kingdom 51°04´N 01°19´W
81 E11 **Winchester** California, USA 33°42´N 117°05´W
76 F5 **Winchester** Idaho, NW USA 46°13´N 116°35´W
73 B11 **Winchester** Illinois, N USA 39°38´N 90°28´W
73 G10 **Winchester** Indiana, N USA 40°11´N 84°57´W
66 G4 **Winchester** Kentucky, S USA 38°00´N 84°10´W
65 J1 **Winchester** New Hampshire, NE USA 42°46´N 72°21´W
66 E7 **Winchester** Tennessee, S USA 35°11´N 86°06´W
64 E9 **Winchester** Virginia, NE USA 39°11´N 78°12´W
163 H12 **Wincrange** Diekirch, NW Luxembourg 50°03´N 05°55´E
54 C1 **Wind** 〰 Yukon Territory, NW Canada
277 L4 **Windamere, Lake** ◎ New South Wales, SE Australia
Windau *see* Ventspils, Latvia
Windau *see* Venta, Latvia/Lithuania
64 A7 **Windber** Pennsylvania, NE USA 40°12´N 78°47´W
66 G8 **Winder** Georgia, SE USA 33°59´N 83°43´W
159 I7 **Windermere** NW England, United Kingdom 54°24´N 02°54´W
72 G3 **Windermere Lake** ◎ Ontario, S Canada
181 D12 **Windesheim** Rheinland-Pfalz, Germany 49°54´E 7°49´N
64 F6 **Wind Gap** Pennsylvania, NE USA 40°50´N 75°17´W
73 J9 **Windham** Ohio, N USA 41°14´N 81°03´W
180 F6 **Windheim** Nordrhein-Westfalen, Germany 52°25´E 9°01´N
140 C1 **Windhoek** *Ger.* Windhuk. ● (Namibia) Khomas, C Namibia 22°34´S 17°06´E
140 C1 **Windhoek** ✕ Khomas, C Namibia 22°31´S 17°04´E
Windhuk *see* Windhoek
Windischfeistritz *see* Slovenska Bistrica
177 J3 **Windischgarsten** Oberösterreich, W Austria 47°42´N 14°21´E
Windischgraz *see* Slovenj Gradec
140 D9 **Windmeul** Western Cape, South Africa 33°39´S 18°55´E
79 M10 **Wind Mountain** ▲ New Mexico, SW USA 32°01´N 105°35´W
74 F5 **Windom** Minnesota, N USA 43°52´N 95°07´W
79 K5 **Windom Peak** ▲ Colorado, C USA 37°37´N 107°35´W
275 J5 **Windorah** Queensland, C Australia 25°25´S 142°41´E
79 J7 **Window Rock** Arizona, SW USA 35°40´N 109°03´W
73 E8 **Wind Point** *headland* Wisconsin, N USA 42°46´N 87°46´W
77 J7 **Wind River** 〰 Wyoming, C USA
59 J9 **Windsor** Nova Scotia, SE Canada 45°00´N 64°09´W
62 A6 **Windsor** Ontario, S Canada 42°18´N 83°W
63 I3 **Windsor** Québec, SE Canada 45°34´N 72°00´W
161 J6 **Windsor** S England, United Kingdom 51°29´N 00°39´W
80 B1 **Windsor** California, USA 38°33´N 122°49´W
79 M2 **Windsor** Colorado, C USA 40°28´N 104°54´W
65 J3 **Windsor** Connecticut, NE USA 41°51´N 72°38´W
65 I2 **Windsor** Massachusetts, USA 42°31´N 73°03´W
75 H10 **Windsor** Missouri, C USA 38°31´N 93°31´W
64 F3 **Windsor** New York, USA 42°05´N 75°38´W
67 L6 **Windsor** North Carolina, SE USA 36°00´N 76°57´W
65 J3 **Windsor Locks** Connecticut, NE USA 41°55´N 72°37´W
140 G5 **Windsorton** Northern Cape, South Africa 28°20´S 24°43´E
141 H5 **Windsorton Road** Northern Cape, South Africa 28°21´S 24°49´E
70 G4 **Windthorst** Texas, SW USA 33°34´N 98°26´W
91 N9 **Windward Islands** *island group* E West Indies
Windward Islands *see* Barlavento, Ilhas de, Cape Verde
Windward Islands *see* Vent, Îles du, Archipel de la Société, French Polynesia
90 G5 **Windward Passage** *Sp.* Paso de los Vientos. *channel* Cuba/Haiti
103 K5 **Wineperu** C Guyana 06°10´N 58°34´W
66 C8 **Winfield** Alabama, S USA 33°55´N 87°49´W
75 I8 **Winfield** Iowa, C USA 41°07´N 91°26´W
75 E11 **Winfield** Kansas, C USA 37°14´N 97°00´W
71 I4 **Winfield** Texas, SW USA 33°10´N 95°06´W
67 H3 **Winfield** West Virginia, NE USA 38°30´N 81°54´W
74 C3 **Wing** North Dakota, N USA 47°06´N 100°16´W
159 K6 **Wingate** United Kingdom 54°44´N 1°23´W
64 I4 **Wingdale** New York, NE USA 41°38´N 73°34´W
277 M4 **Wingham** New South Wales, SE Australia 31°52´S 152°24´E
62 B4 **Wingham** Ontario, S Canada 43°54´N 81°19´W
77 J4 **Winifred** Montana, NW USA 47°33´N 109°26´W
58 D5 **Winisk Lake** ◎ Ontario, C Canada
70 C5 **Wink** Texas, SW USA 31°45´N 103°09´W
79 I9 **Winkelman** Arizona, SW USA 32°59´N 110°46´W
160 E8 **Winkleigh** United Kingdom 50°51´N 3°57´W
55 J10 **Winkler** Manitoba, S Canada 49°12´N 97°55´W
177 I4 **Winklern** Tirol, W Austria 46°54´N 12°54´E
Winkowitz *see* Vinkovci
159 K8 **Winksley** United Kingdom 54°08´N 1°36´W
76 C4 **Winlock** Washington, NW USA 46°29´N 122°56´W
159 I8 **Winmarleigh** United Kingdom 53°55´N 2°49´W
133 H8 **Winneba** SE Ghana 05°22´N 00°38´W
74 G6 **Winnebago** Minnesota, N USA 43°46´N 94°10´W
74 F7 **Winnebago** Nebraska, C USA 42°14´N 96°28´W
72 D6 **Winnebago, Lake** ◎ Wisconsin, N USA
72 D6 **Winneconne** Wisconsin, N USA 44°07´N 88°44´W
80 J1 **Winnemucca** Nevada, W USA 40°59´N 117°44´W
80 G1 **Winnemucca Lake** ◎ Nevada, W USA
181 G14 **Winnenden** Baden-Württemberg, SW Germany 48°52´N 09°22´E
74 C6 **Winner** South Dakota, N USA 43°22´N 99°51´W
77 K4 **Winnett** Montana, NW USA 47°00´N 108°18´W
62 E1 **Winneway** Québec, SE Canada 47°35´N 78°33´W
68 C2 **Winnfield** Louisiana, S USA 31°55´N 92°38´W
74 G3 **Winnibigoshish, Lake** ◎ Minnesota, N USA
71 J7 **Winnie** Texas, SW USA 29°49´N 94°22´W
55 J10 **Winnipeg** *province capital* Manitoba, S Canada 49°53´N 97°10´W
55 J10 **Winnipeg** ✕ Manitoba, S Canada 49°56´N 97°16´W
42 E5 **Winnipeg** 〰 Manitoba, S Canada
55 J9 **Winnipeg Beach** Manitoba, S Canada 50°25´N 96°59´W
55 J8 **Winnipeg, Lake** ◎ Manitoba, C Canada
55 I9 **Winnipegosis** Manitoba, S Canada 51°36´N 99°59´W
55 I8 **Winnipegosis, Lake** ◎ Manitoba, C Canada
63 J5 **Winnipesaukee, Lake** ◎ New Hampshire, NE USA
68 D2 **Winnsboro** Louisiana, S USA 32°09´N 91°43´W
67 I8 **Winnsboro** South Carolina, SE USA 34°22´N 81°05´W
71 I4 **Winnsboro** Texas, SW USA 33°01´N 95°16´W
74 I5 **Winona** Minnesota, N USA 44°03´N 91°37´W
66 B8 **Winona** Mississippi, S USA 33°30´N 89°42´W
75 I11 **Winona** Missouri, C USA 37°00´N 91°19´W
71 I4 **Winona** Texas, SW USA 32°29´N 95°10´W
63 H4 **Winooski River** 〰 Vermont, NE USA
162 J3 **Winschoten** Groningen, NE Netherlands 53°09´N 07°03´E
180 H3 **Winsen** Niedersachsen, N Germany 53°22´N 10°13´E
159 J10 **Winsford** United Kingdom 53°11´N 2°31´W
161 J5 **Winslow** United Kingdom 51°57´N 0°52´W
79 I7 **Winslow** Arizona, SW USA 35°01´N 110°42´W
63 K4 **Winslow** Maine, NE USA 44°33´N 69°35´W
65 I3 **Winsted** Connecticut, NE USA 41°55´N 73°03´W
159 K10 **Winster** United Kingdom 53°08´N 1°39´W
159 K7 **Winston** United Kingdom 54°33´N 1°47´W
76 B7 **Winston** Oregon, NW USA 43°07´N 123°24´W
67 J6 **Winston Salem** North Carolina, SE USA 36°06´N 80°15´W
162 I3 **Winsum** Groningen, NE Netherlands 53°20´N 06°31´E
Wintanceaster *see* Winchester
181 F9 **Winterberg** Nordrhein-Westfalen, Germany 51°12´E 8°32´N
141 H8 **Winterberge** ▲▲ Eastern Cape, South Africa
69 L6 **Winter Garden** Florida, SE USA 28°34´N 81°35´W
56 B7 **Winter Harbour** Vancouver Island, British Columbia, SW Canada 50°28´N 128°03´W
81 H14 **Winterhaven** California, USA 32°44´N 114°38´W
69 L6 **Winter Haven** Florida, SE USA 28°01´N 81°43´W
53 J9 **Winter Island** *Island* Nunavut, NE Canada
69 M6 **Winter Park** Florida, SE USA 28°36´N 81°20´W
80 C2 **Winters** California, USA 38°32´N 121°58´W
70 F5 **Winters** Texas, SW USA 31°57´N 99°57´W
162 I7 **Winterswijk** Gelderland, E Netherlands 51°58´N 06°44´E
176 E3 **Winterthur** Zürich, NE Switzerland 47°30´N 08°43´E
141 J6 **Winterton** KwaZulu-Natal, South Africa 28°48´S 29°32´E
74 G5 **Winthrop** Minnesota, N USA 44°32´N 94°22´W
76 D3 **Winthrop** Washington, NW USA 48°28´N 120°13´W
275 J4 **Winton** Queensland, E Australia 22°22´S 143°04´E
278 B12 **Winton** Southland, South Island, New Zealand 46°08´S 168°20´E
159 J7 **Winton** United Kingdom 54°29´N 2°20´W
80 D4 **Winton** California, USA 37°23´N 120°37´W
67 L5 **Winton** North Carolina, SE USA 36°24´N 76°57´W
181 C12 **Wintrich** Rheinland-Pfalz, Germany 49°53´E 6°57´N
167 M6 **Wintzenheim** Alsace, France 48°04´N 7°17´E
181 J8 **Wipper** 〰 C Germany
Wipper *see* Wieprza
181 I8 **Wipperdorf** Thüringen, Germany 51°27´E 10°40´N
181 D9 **Wipperfürth** Nordrhein-Westfalen, Germany 51°07´E 7°24´N
181 J8 **Wippra** Sachsen-Anhalt, Germany 51°34´E 11°17´N
181 D10 **Wirges** Rheinland-Pfalz, Germany 50°28´E 7°48´N
159 K10 **Wirksworth** United Kingdom 53°05´N 1°34´W
276 F4 **Wirraminna** South Australia 31°10´S 136°13´E
276 E3 **Wirrida** South Australia 29°34´S 134°33´E
276 E4 **Wirrulla** South Australia 32°27´S 134°33´E
Wirz-See *see* Võrtsjärv
161 K3 **Wisbech** E England, United Kingdom 52°39´N 00°08´E
Wisby *see* Visby
63 K4 **Wiscasset** Maine, NE USA 44°01´N 69°41´W
Wischau *see* Vyškov
72 C6 **Wisconsin** *off.* State of Wisconsin, ***also known as*** Badger State. ◐ *state* N USA
72 C7 **Wisconsin Dells** Wisconsin, N USA 43°37´N 89°43´W
72 C7 **Wisconsin, Lake** ⊠ Wisconsin, N USA
72 C6 **Wisconsin Rapids** Wisconsin, N USA 44°24´N 89°50´W
72 B7 **Wisconsin River** 〰 Wisconsin, N USA
77 H5 **Wisdom** Montana, NW USA 45°36´N 113°27´W
67 H5 **Wise** Virginia, NE USA 37°00´N 82°36´W
83 I3 **Wiseman** Alaska, USA 67°24´N 150°06´W
159 H3 **Wishaw** W Scotland, United Kingdom 55°47´N 03°56´W
74 D4 **Wishek** North Dakota, N USA 46°12´N 99°33´W
76 D5 **Wishram** Washington, NW USA 45°40´N 120°53´W
183 F9 **Wisła** Śląskie, S Poland 49°39´N 18°50´E
182 F4 **Wisła** *Eng.* Vistula, *Ger.* Weichsel. 〰 C Poland
Wiślany, Zalew *see* Vistula Lagoon
183 H8 **Wisłoka** 〰 SE Poland
178 F4 **Wismar** Mecklenburg-Vorpommern, N Germany 53°54´N 11°28´E
180 J1 **Wismarbucht** Mecklenburg-Vorpommern, Germany
74 E7 **Wisner** Nebraska, C USA 41°59´N 96°54´W
165 L3 **Wissembourg** *var.* Weissenburg. Bas-Rhin, NE France 49°03´N 07°57´E
161 L3 **Wissey** 〰 United Kingdom
72 B5 **Wissota, Lake** ⊠ Wisconsin, N USA
160 G4 **Wistanstow** United Kingdom 52°28´N 2°51´W
159 H4 **Wiston** United Kingdom 55°34´N 3°38´W
159 L9 **Wistow** United Kingdom 53°49´N 1°06´W
141 J4 **Witbank** Mpumalanga, South Africa 26°29´S 28°46´E
140 E9 **Witberge** ▲▲ Western Cape, South Africa
140 D3 **Witbooisvlei** Hardap, Namibia 25°04´S 18°27´E
140 E4 **Witdraai** Northern Cape, South Africa 26°57´S 20°42´E
161 L5 **Witham** United Kingdom 51°47´N 0°37´E
157 I10 **Witham** 〰 E England, United Kingdom
160 F8 **Witheridge** United Kingdom 50°55´N 3°43´W
159 M9 **Withernsea** E England, United Kingdom 53°46´N 00°01´W
159 M8 **Withernwick** United Kingdom 53°51´N 0°11´W
79 K8 **Withington, Mount** ▲ New Mexico, SW USA 33°52´N 107°29´W
69 K4 **Withlacoochee River** 〰 Florida/Georgia, SE USA
160 F7 **Withypool** United Kingdom 51°06´N 3°39´W
141 I8 **Witkeirivier** 〰 Eastern Cape, South Africa
Witkeirivier *see* Cacadu
141 J4 **Witkleifontein** GautengSA, South Africa 26°52´S 28°14´E
141 I7 **Witkop** Eastern Cape, South Africa 31°08´S 26°37´E
182 E6 **Witkowo** Wielkopolskie, C Poland 52°27´N 17°49´E
141 H8 **Witkransnek** *pass* Eastern Cape, South Africa
141 L5 **Wit-Mfolozi** 〰 KwaZulu-Natal, South Africa
141 J3 **Witnek** Mpumalanga, South Africa 25°21´S 28°54´E
161 I5 **Witney** S England, United Kingdom 51°47´N 01°30´W
140 G5 **Witputs** Northern Cape, South Africa 28°03´S 24°24´E
140 C5 **Witputz** Karas, Namibia 27°36´S 16°42´E
141 I5 **Witteberge** ▲▲ Free State, South Africa
181 D8 **Witten** Nordrhein-Westfalen, W Germany 51°25´N 07°19´E
178 H7 **Wittenberg** Sachsen-Anhalt, E Germany 51°53´N 12°39´E
72 C6 **Wittenberg** Wisconsin, N USA 44°53´N 89°20´W
178 G6 **Wittenberge** Brandenburg, N Germany 52°59´N 11°45´E
165 K4 **Wittenheim** Haut-Rhin, NE France 47°49´N 07°19´E
274 D5 **Wittenoom** Western Australia 22°17´S 118°22´E
181 J9 **Witterda** Thüringen, Germany 51°02´E 10°53´N
161 L7 **Wittersham** United Kingdom 51°00´N 0°42´E
Wittingau *see* Třeboň
180 I5 **Wittingen** Niedersachsen, C Germany 52°42´N 10°43´E
181 C12 **Wittlich** Rheinland-Pfalz, SW Germany 49°59´N 06°54´E
180 D3 **Wittmund** Niedersachsen, NW Germany 53°34´N 07°46´E
178 G5 **Wittstock** Brandenburg, NE Germany 53°10´N 12°29´E
280 C2 **Witu Islands** *island group* E Papua New Guinea
140 D1 **Witvlei** Omaheke, Namibia 22°24´S 18°29´E
140 D7 **Witwater** Northern Cape, South Africa 32°55´S 18°42´E
160 F7 **Wiveliscombe** United Kingdom 51°02´N 3°19´W
161 M5 **Wix** United Kingdom 51°54´N 1°09´E
182 I3 **Wiżajny** Podlaskie, NE Poland 54°22´N 22°51´E
103 L5 **W. J. van Blommesteinmeer** ⊠ E Suriname
182 G5 **Wkra** *Ger.* Soldau. 〰 C Poland
182 F3 **Władysławowo** Pomorskie, N Poland 54°48´N 18°25´E
Wlaschim *see* Vlašim
182 D7 **Wleń** *Ger.* Lähn. Dolnośląskie, SW Poland 51°00´N 15°39´E
182 F5 **Włocławek** *Ger./Rus.* Vlotslavsk. Kujawsko-pomorskie, C Poland 52°39´N 19°03´E
182 J6 **Włodawa** *Rus.* Vlodava. Lubelskie, SE Poland 51°33´N 23°31´E
Włodzimierz *see* Volodymyr-Volyns'kyy
182 G7 **Włoszczowa** Świętokrzyskie, C Poland 50°51´N 19°58´E
140 A1 **Wlotzkasbaken** Erongo, W Namibia 22°26´S 14°30´E
63 J3 **Woburn** Québec, SE Canada 45°22´N 70°52´W
65 L2 **Woburn** Massachusetts, NE USA 42°28´N 71°09´W
Wocheiner Feistritz *see* Bohinjska Bistrica
Wöchma *see* Võhma
229 J6 **Wodil** *var.* Vuadil'. Farg'ona Viloyati, E Uzbekistan 40°10´N 71°43´E
277 J6 **Wodonga** Victoria, SE Australia 36°11´S 146°55´E
183 F8 **Wodzisław Śląski** *Ger.* Loslau. Śląskie, S Poland 49°59´N 18°27´E
162 F6 **Woerden** Zuid-Holland, C Netherlands 52°06´N 04°54´E
167 N6 **Woerth** Alsace, France 48°23´N 7°38´E
81 E8 **Wofford Heights** California, USA 35°42´N 118°27´W
162 F5 **Wognum** Noord-Holland, NW Netherlands 52°40´N 05°01´E
Wohlau *see* Wołów
176 D4 **Wohlen** Aargau, NW Switzerland 47°21´N 08°17´E
293 I2 **Wohlthat Massivet** *Eng.* Wohlthat Mountains. ▲▲ Antarctica
Wohlthat Mountains *see* Wohlthat Massivet
261 J4 **Woinui, Selat** *strait* Papua, E Indonesia
275 K1 **Woitape** Central, S Papua New Guinea 03°86´S 147°15´E
Wojerecy *see* Hoyerswerda
Wōjjā *see* Wotje Atoll
Wojwodina *see* Vojvodina
261 J7 **Wokam, Pulau** *island* Kepulauan Aru, E Indonesia
161 J6 **Woking** SE England, United Kingdom 51°20´N 00°34´W
161 J6 **Wokingham** United Kingdom 51°25´N 0°50´W
Woldenberg Neumark *see* Dobiegniew
159 M9 **Wolds, The** *hill range* E England, United Kingdom
282 E6 **Woleai Atoll** *atoll* Caroline Islands, W Micronesia
Woleu *see* Uolo, Río
134 B7 **Woleu-Ntem** *off.* Province du Woleu-Ntem, *var.* Le Woleu-Ntem. ◐ *province* W Gabon
Woleu-Ntem, Province du *see* Woleu-Ntem
76 B8 **Wolf Creek** Oregon, NW USA 42°40´N 123°22´W
70 E1 **Wolf Creek** 〰 Oklahoma/Texas, SW USA
79 L5 **Wolf Creek Pass** *pass* Colorado, C USA
63 J5 **Wolfeboro** New Hampshire, NE USA 43°34´N 71°10´W
71 H4 **Wolfe City** Texas, SW USA 33°22´N 96°04´W
62 F4 **Wolfe Island** *island* Ontario, SE Canada
179 G8 **Wolfen** Sachsen-Anhalt, E Germany 51°40´N 12°16´E
180 I6 **Wolfenbüttel** Niedersachsen, C Germany 52°10´N 10°33´E
177 J2 **Wolfern** Oberösterreich, N Austria 48°06´N 14°16´E
181 F11 **Wölfersheim** Hessen, Germany 50°24´E 8°49´N
161 L3 **Wolferton** United Kingdom 52°50´N 0°28´E
179 H13 **Wolfgangsee** *var.* Abersee, St Wolfgangsee. ◎ N Austria
181 G8 **Wolfhagen** Hessen, Germany 51°19´E 9°10´N
54 B4 **Wolf Lake** ◎ Yukon Territory, W Canada
83 H4 **Wolf Mountain** ▲ Alaska, USA 65°20´N 154°08´W
77 L3 **Wolf Point** Montana, NW USA 48°05´N 105°40´W
68 E4 **Wolf River** 〰 Mississippi, S USA
72 D6 **Wolf River** 〰 Wisconsin, N USA
177 K4 **Wolfsberg** Kärnten, SE Austria 46°50´N 14°50´E
180 J5 **Wolfsburg** Niedersachsen, N Germany 52°25´N 10°47´E
181 D13 **Wolfstein** Rheinland-Pfalz, Germany 49°35´E 7°36´N
105 B9 **Wolf, Volcán** ♨ Galapagos Islands, Ecuador, E Pacific Ocean 0°01´N 91°22´W
178 I4 **Wolgast** Mecklenburg-Vorpommern, NE Germany 54°04´N 13°47´E
167 N8 **Wolhusen** Luzern, W Switzerland 47°04´N 08°06´E
182 C4 **Wolin** *Ger.* Wollin. Zachodnio-pomorskie, NW Poland 53°52´N 14°35´E
177 L2 **Wolkersdorf** Niederösterreich, NE Austria 48°24´N 16°31´E
Wołkowysk *see* Vawkavysk
181 I8 **Wolkramshausen** Thüringen, Germany 51°25´E 10°45´N
Wöllan *see* Velenje
161 J4 **Wollaston** United Kingdom 52°15´N 0°40´W
52 D6 **Wollaston, Cape** *headland* Victoria Island, Northwest Territories, NW Canada 71°00´N 118°21´W
117 E14 **Wollaston, Isla** *island* S Chile
55 H6 **Wollaston Lake** Saskatchewan, C Canada 58°05´N 103°38´W
55 H6 **Wollaston Lake** ◎ Saskatchewan, C Canada
52 E7 **Wollaston Peninsula** *peninsula* Victoria Island, Northwest Territories/Nunavut NW Canada
Wollin *see* Wolin
277 L5 **Wollongong** New South Wales, SE Australia 34°25´S 150°52´E
181 E12 **Wöllstein** Rheinland-Pfalz, Germany 49°49´E 7°58´N
Wolmar *see* Valmiera
178 G7 **Wolmirstedt** Sachsen-Anhalt, C Germany 52°15´N 11°37´E
182 H6 **Wołomin** Mazowieckie, C Poland 52°20´N 21°11´E
182 D7 **Wołów** *Ger.* Wohlau. Dolnośląskie, SW Poland 51°21´N 16°40´E
Wołożyn *see* Valozhyn
62 C2 **Wolseley Bay** Ontario, S Canada 46°05´N 80°16´W
74 D5 **Wolsey** South Dakota, N USA 44°22´N 98°28´W
159 K6 **Wolsingham** United Kingdom 54°43´N 1°53´W
182 D6 **Wolsztyn** Wielkopolskie, C Poland 52°07´N 16°07´E
245 K3 **Woluogu** Hebei, N China 39°40´N 117°46´E
162 H4 **Wolvega** *Fris.* Wolvegea. Friesland, N Netherlands 52°53´N 06°E
Wolvegea *see* Wolvega
161 H3 **Wolverhampton** C England, United Kingdom 52°36´N 02°08´W
Wolverine State *see* Michigan
163 D10 **Wolvertem** Vlaams Brabant, C Belgium 50°55´N 04°19´E
161 I4 **Wolvey** United Kingdom 52°29´N 1°22´W
141 H9 **Wolwefontein** Eastern Cape, South Africa 33°18´S 24°50´E
141 H6 **Wolwespruit** Free State, South Africa 28°51´S 25°33´E
161 H3 **Wombourne** Staffordshire, C England, United Kingdom
159 K9 **Wombwell** United Kingdom 53°31´N 1°24´W
64 E7 **Womelsdorf** Pennsylvania, USA 40°22´N 76°11´W
163 E9 **Wommelgem** Antwerpen, N Belgium 51°12´N 04°32´E
250 C1 **Wondeok** *prev.* Wŏndŏk. 37°10´N 129°19´E
141 I5 **Wonderkop** Free State, South Africa 29°16´S 27°06´E
261 J5 **Wondiwoi, Pegunungan** ▲▲ Papua, E Indonesia
Wŏndŏk *see* Wondeok
280 B3 **Wonenara** *var.* Wonerara. Eastern Highlands, C Papua New Guinea 06°46´S 145°54´E
Wonerara *see* Wonenara
Wongalara Lake *see* Wongalarroo Lake
277 I4 **Wongalarroo Lake** *var.* Wongalara Lake. *seasonal lake* New South Wales, SE Australia
248 C5 **Wonju** *Jap.* Genshū; *prev.* Wŏnju. N South Korea 37°21´N 127°57´E
Wŏnju *see* Wonju
56 E2 **Wonowon** British Columbia, W Canada 56°46´N 121°54´W
248 C4 **Wŏnsan** SE North Korea 39°11´N 127°21´E
277 J8 **Wonthaggi** Victoria, SE Australia 38°38´S 145°37´E
80 B2 **Woodacre** California, USA 38°01´N 122°39´W
66 C7 **Woodall Mountain** ▲ Mississippi, S USA 34°47´N 88°14´W
69 L3 **Woodbine** Georgia, SE USA 30°58´N 81°43´W
74 F7 **Woodbine** Iowa, C USA 41°44´N 95°42´W
64 G9 **Woodbine** New Jersey, NE USA 39°12´N 74°47´W
161 M4 **Woodbridge** United Kingdom 52°06´N 1°19´E
65 J5 **Woodbridge** Connecticut, USA 41°21´N 73°01´W
64 C9 **Woodbridge** Maryland, USA 39°29´N 77°04´W
65 H6 **Woodbridge** New Jersey, USA 40°33´N 74°17´W
64 C10 **Woodbridge** Virginia, NE USA 38°40´N 77°17´W
277 M3 **Woodburn** New South Wales, SE Australia 29°07´S 153°23´E
76 C5 **Woodburn** Oregon, NW USA 45°08´N 122°51´W
64 F8 **Woodbury** New Jersey, USA 39°50´N 75°09´W
66 E6 **Woodbury** Tennessee, S USA 35°49´N 86°06´W
161 L7 **Woodchurch** United Kingdom 51°04´N 0°46´E
81 E11 **Woodcrest** California, USA 33°53´N 117°21´W
277 M3 **Wooded Bluff** *headland* New South Wales, SE Australia 29°24´S 153°22´E
277 M2 **Woodenbong** New South Wales, SE Australia 28°24´S 152°39´E
160 B3 **Woodenbridge** Wicklow, Ireland 52°50´N 6°14´W
80 F3 **Woodfords** California, USA 38°47´N 119°49´W
159 M10 **Woodhall Spa** United Kingdom 53°09´N 0°13´W
80 E6 **Woodlake** California, W USA 36°24´N 119°06´W
80 C3 **Woodlake** California, USA 38°09´N 121°15´W
80 C2 **Woodland** California, W USA 38°41´N 121°46´W
63 L3 **Woodland** Maine, NE USA 45°10´N 67°25´W
76 C5 **Woodland** Washington, NW USA 45°54´N 122°44´W
64 F9 **Woodland Beach** Delaware, USA 39°20´N 75°28´W
79 M3 **Woodland Park** Colorado, C USA 38°59´N 105°03´W
280 E4 **Woodlark Island** *var.* Murua Island. *island* SE Papua New Guinea
Woodle Island *see* Kuria
54 G10 **Wood Mountain** ▲▲ Saskatchewan, S Canada
73 B11 **Wood River** Illinois, N USA 38°51´N 90°06´W
75 D8 **Wood River** Nebraska, C USA 40°48´N 98°33´W
83 J5 **Wood River** 〰 Alaska, USA
83 H7 **Wood River Lakes** *lakes* Alaska, USA
276 D1 **Woodroffe, Mount** ▲ South Australia 26°19´S 131°42´E
67 H7 **Woodruff** South Carolina, SE USA 34°44´N 82°02´W
72 C4 **Woodruff** Wisconsin, N USA 45°55´N 89°41´W
85 N4 **Woodsboro** Texas, SW USA 28°14´N 97°19´W
73 J11 **Woodsfield** Ohio, N USA 39°45´N 81°07´W
275 H3 **Woods, Lake** ◎ Northern Territory, N Australia
58 B6 **Woods, Lake of the** *Fr.* Lac des Bois. ◎ Canada/USA
70 F4 **Woodson** Texas, SW USA 33°00´N 99°01´W
55 J5 **Woods, Point of the** *headland* Manitoba, C Canada
63 L2 **Woodstock** New Brunswick, SE Canada 46°10´N 67°38´W
62 C5 **Woodstock** Ontario, S Canada 43°07´N 80°46´W
161 I5 **Woodstock** United Kingdom 51°51´N 1°19´W
73 D8 **Woodstock** Illinois, N USA 42°18´N 88°27´W
63 I5 **Woodstock** Vermont, NE USA 43°37´N 72°33´W
64 A10 **Woodstock** Virginia, NE USA 38°55´N 78°31´W
64 F8 **Woodstown** New Jersey, USA 39°39´N 75°20´W
63 I4 **Woodsville** New Hampshire, NE USA 44°08´N 72°02´W
278 H7 **Woodville** Manawatu-Wanganui, North Island, New Zealand 40°22´S 175°59´E
68 D3 **Woodville** Mississippi, S USA 31°06´N 91°18´W
71 J6 **Woodville** Texas, SW USA 30°47´N 94°26´W
75 C11 **Woodward** Oklahoma, C USA 36°26´N 99°25´W
74 D3 **Woodworth** North Dakota, N USA 47°06´N 99°19´W
81 E8 **Woody** California, USA 35°42´N 118°50´W
160 G4 **Woofferton** United Kingdom 52°18´N 2°43´W
261 L6 **Woogi** Papua, E Indonesia 03°59´S 138°45´E
160 G7 **Wookey** United Kingdom 51°13´N 2°42´W
261 J4 **Wool** Papua, E Indonesia 01°38´S 135°34´E
161 H8 **Wool** United Kingdom 50°40´N 2°13´W
160 E7 **Woolacombe** United Kingdom 51°11´N 4°13´W
141 I9 **Wooldridge** Eastern Cape, South Africa 33°13´S 27°14´E
159 J4 **Wooler** United Kingdom 55°33´N 2°00´W
160 E7 **Woolfardisworthy** United Kingdom 50°58´N 4°23´W
277 M3 **Woolgoolga** New South Wales, E Australia 30°04´S 153°09´E
161 K6 **Woolwich** United Kingdom 51°28´N 0°12´E
276 F4 **Woomera** South Australia 31°12´S 136°52´E
65 L3 **Woonsocket** Rhode Island, NE USA 41°58´N 71°27´W
74 D5 **Woonsocket** South Dakota, N USA 44°03´N 98°16´W
73 I10 **Wooster** Ohio, N USA 40°48´N 81°56´W
161 M7 **Wootton** United Kingdom 51°10´N 1°11´E
161 H6 **Wootton Bassett** United Kingdom 51°32´N 1°54´W
Woqooyi Galbeed, Gobolka *see* Gabiley
176 D4 **Worb** Bern, C Switzerland 46°54´N 07°36´E
181 I8 **Worbis** Thüringen, Germany 51°25´E 10°22´N
138 D10 **Worcester** Western Cape, SW South Africa 33°41´S 19°22´E
161 H4 **Worcester** *hist.* Wigorna Ceaster. W England, United Kingdom 52°11´N 02°13´W
65 K2 **Worcester** Massachusetts, NE USA 42°17´N 71°48´W
161 H4 **Worcestershire** *cultural region* C England, United Kingdom
76 C8 **Worden** Oregon, NW USA 42°04´N 121°50´W
177 H3 **Wörgl** Tirol, W Austria 47°29´N 12°04´E
261 J7 **Workai, Pulau** *island* Kepulauan Aru, E Indonesia
159 H6 **Workington** NW England, United Kingdom 54°39´N 03°33´W
159 L10 **Worksop** United Kingdom 53°18´N 1°08´W
162 G4 **Workum** Friesland, N Netherlands 52°58´N 05°25´E
159 M9 **Worlaby** United Kingdom 53°36´N 0°28´W
77 K7 **Worland** Wyoming, C USA 44°01´N 107°57´W
see São João de Cortes
160 F8 **Worlington** United Kingdom 50°55´N 3°45´W
Wormatia *see* Worms
163 I14 **Wormeldange** Grevenmacher, E Luxembourg 49°37´N 06°25´E
162 E5 **Wormer** Noord-Holland, C Netherlands 52°30´N 04°50´E
167 H1 **Wormhout** Nord-Pas-de-Calais, France 50°53´N 2°28´E
181 E13 **Worms** *anc.* Augusta Vangionum, Borbetomagus, Wormatia. Rheinland-Pfalz, SW Germany 49°38´N 08°22´E
Worms *see* Vormsi
181 I14 **Wörnitz** 〰 S Germany
180 F3 **Worpswede** Niedersachsen, Germany 53°13´E 8°56´N
181 I14 **Wört** Baden-Württemberg, Germany 49°02´E 10°16´N
181 G12 **Wörth** Bayern, Germany 49°48´E 9°09´N
71 H5 **Wortham** Texas, SW USA 31°47´N 96°27´W
181 E14 **Wörth am Rhein** Rheinland-Pfalz, SW Germany 49°04´N 08°16´E
174 G3 **Wörther See** ◎ S Austria
161 K8 **Worthing** SE England, United Kingdom 50°48´N 00°23´W
74 F6 **Worthington** Minnesota, N USA 43°37´N 95°37´W
73 H10 **Worthington** Ohio, N USA 40°05´N 83°01´W
80 J6 **Worthington Peak** ▲ Nevada, W USA 37°57´N 115°32´W
261 L6 **Wosi** Papua, E Indonesia 03°55´S 138°54´E
261 J5 **Wosimi** Papua, E Indonesia 02°44´S 134°34´E
283 K5 **Wotho Atoll** *var.* Wōtto. *atoll* Ralik Chain, W Marshall Islands
283 L5 **Wotje Atoll** *var.* Wōjjā. *atoll* Ratak Chain, E Marshall Islands
Wotoe *see* Wotu
Wottawa *see* Otava
Wōtto *see* Wotho Atoll
260 D5 **Wotu** *prev.* Wotoe. Sulawesi, C Indonesia 02°34´S 120°46´E
162 G7 **Woudenberg** Utrecht, C Netherlands 52°05´N 05°25´E
141 J2 **Woudkop** Limpopo, South Africa 23°18´S 28°36´E
162 F7 **Woudrichem** Noord-Brabant, S Netherlands 51°49´N 05°E
89 H5 **Wounta** *var.* Huaunta. Región Autónoma Atlántico Norte, NE Nicaragua 13°30´N 83°32´W
260 E6 **Wowoni, Pulau** *island* C Indonesia
260 E6 **Wowoni, Selat** *strait* Sulawesi, C Indonesia
136 E7 **Woyamdero Plain** *plain* E Kenya
Woyens *see* Vojens
Wozrojdeniye Oroli *see* Vozrozhdeniya, Ostrov
159 M10 **Wragby** United Kingdom 53°17´N 0°18´W
Wrangel Island *see* Vrangelya, Ostrov
83 M7 **Wrangell** Wrangell Island, Alaska, USA 56°28´N 132°22´W
82 A8 **Wrangell, Cape** *headland* Attu Island, Alaska, USA 52°55´N 172°28´E
83 J6 **Wrangell, Mount** ▲ Alaska, USA 62°00´N 144°01´W
83 K6 **Wrangell Mountains** ▲▲ Alaska, USA
294 G5 **Wrangel Plain** *undersea feature* Arctic Ocean
159 M10 **Wrangle** United Kingdom 53°02´N 0°07´E
156 E3 **Wrath, Cape** *headland* N Scotland, United Kingdom 58°37´N 05°01´W
79 N2 **Wray** Colorado, C USA 40°01´N 102°12´W
90 F8 **Wreck Point** *headland* C Jamaica 17°50´N 76°55´W
140 C6 **Wreck Point** *headland* W South Africa 28°52´S 16°17´E
180 F2 **Wremen** Niedersachsen, Germany 53°39´E 8°31´N
67 H9 **Wrens** Georgia, SE USA 33°12´N 82°23´W
161 N4 **Wrentham** United Kingdom 52°23´N 1°41´E
159 L9 **Wressle** United Kingdom 53°46´N 0°56´W
180 I4 **Wrestedt** Niedersachsen, Germany 52°54´E 10°35´N
160 G2 **Wrexham** NE Wales, United Kingdom 53°03´N 03°W
75 G13 **Wright City** Oklahoma, C USA 34°03´N 95°00´W
292 F7 **Wright Island** *island* Antarctica
59 I5 **Wright, Mont** ▲ Québec, E Canada 52°36´N 67°40´W
71 J4 **Wright Patman Lake** ⊠ Texas, SW USA
79 I10 **Wrightson, Mount** ▲ Arizona, SW USA 31°42´N 110°51´W
69 K1 **Wrightsville** Georgia, SE USA 32°43´N 82°43´W
67 L8 **Wrightsville Beach** North Carolina, SE USA 34°12´N 77°48´W
81 E10 **Wrightwood** California, W USA 34°21´N 117°37´W
54 D3 **Wrigley** Northwest Territories, W Canada 63°16´N 123°39´W
160 G6 **Wrington** United Kingdom 51°22´N 2°46´W
182 E7 **Wrocław** *Eng./Ger.* Breslau. Dolnośląskie, SW Poland 51°07´N 17°01´E
182 D5 **Wronki** *Ger.* Fronicken. Wielkopolskie, C Poland 52°42´N 16°22´E
161 L6 **Wrotham** United Kingdom 51°18´N 0°19´E
52 E5 **Wrottesley, Cape** *headland* Northwest Territories, NW Canada
161 M3 **Wroxham** United Kingdom 52°42´N 1°24´E
161 I5 **Wroxton** United Kingdom 52°04´N 1°24´W
182 E6 **Września** Wielkopolskie, C Poland 52°19´N 17°34´E
182 D6 **Wschowa** Lubuskie, W Poland 51°49´N 16°15´E
Wsetin *see* Vsetín
245 H6 **Wu'an** Hebei, E China 36°45´N 114°12´E
274 D7 **Wubin** Western Australia 30°05´S 116°43´E
247 L5 **Wuchang** Heilongjiang, NE China 44°55´N 127°13´E
Wuchang *see* Wuhan
243 J3 **Wuchang Hu** ◎ Anhui, China
243 K3 **Wucheng** Anhui, E China 29°35´N 118°11´E
Wu-chou/Wuchow *see* Wuzhou
240 G8 **Wuchuan** *var.* Meilu. Guangdong, S China 21°28´N 110°49´E
242 D4 **Wuchuan** *var.* Duru, Gelaozu Miaozu Zhizhixian. Guizhou, S China 28°40´N 108°04´E
244 G2 **Wuchuan** Nei Mongol Zizhiqu, N China 41°04´N 111°28´E
244 D3 **Wuda** Nei Mongol Zizhiqu, N China 39°30´N 106°43´E
247 L3 **Wudalianchi** *var.* Qingshan; *prev.* Dedu. Heilongjiang, NE China 48°40´N 126°06´E
242 F1 **Wudang Shan** ▲▲ Hubei, China
239 H7 **Wudaoliang** Qinghai, C China 35°16´N 93°03´E
220 G7 **Wuday'ah** *spring/well* S Saudi Arabia 17°03´N 47°06´E
245 K5 **Wudi** Shandong, China 37°26´N 117°21´E
133 K5 **Wudil** Kano, N Nigeria 11°46´N 08°49´E
240 C6 **Wuding** *var.* Jincheng. Yunnan, SW China 25°30´N 102°21´E
244 F5 **Wuding He** 〰 Shaanxi, China
276 F5 **Wudinna** South Australia 33°06´S 135°30´E
242 B1 **Wudu** Sichuan, C China 31°53´N 104°47´E
Wudu *see* Longnan
242 F3 **Wufeng** Hubei, C China 30°09´N 110°31´E
245 H9 **Wugang** Henan, China 33°10´N 113°18´E
242 F6 **Wugang** Hunan, China 26°26´N 110°22´E
243 H5 **Wugong Shan** ▲▲ S China
244 D3 **Wuhai** *var.* Haibowan. Nei Mongol Zizhiqu, N China 39°40´N 106°48´E
243 H2 **Wuhan** *var.* Han-kou, Han-k'ou, Hanyang, Wuchang, Wu-han; *prev.* Hankow. *province capital* Hubei, C China 30°35´N 114°19´E
Wu-han *see* Wuhan
245 K9 **Wuhe** Anhui, E China 33°05´N 117°55´E
Wuhsien *see* Suzhou
Wuhsi/Wu-his *see* Wuxi
243 K2 **Wuhu** *var.* Wu-na-mu. Anhui, E China 31°23´N 118°25´E
243 I9 **Wuhua** Guangdong, China 23°56´N 115°45´E
Wūjae *see* Ujae Atoll
243 M2 **Wujiang** Jiangsu, China 31°06´N 120°23´E
242 D5 **Wu Jiang** 〰 C China
Wujlān *see* Ujelang Atoll
Wukang *see* Deqing
133 L7 **Wukari** Taraba, E Nigeria 07°51´N 09°49´E
Wulan *see* Jingyuan
232 E2 **Wular Lake** ◎ NE India
245 M5 **Wuleidao Wan** *bay* Shandong, China
180 C7 **Wulfen** Nordrhein-Westfalen, Germany 51°43´E 7°01´N
181 I11 **Wülfershausen** Bayern, Germany 50°20´E 10°20´N
181 C8 **Wülfrath** Nordrhein-Westfalen, Germany 51°17´E 7°03´N
180 H7 **Wulften** Niedersachsen, Germany 51°40´E 10°11´N
245 L6 **Wulian** Shandong, China 35°26´N 119°07´E
242 A5 **Wulian Feng** ▲▲ SW China
240 C7 **Wuliang Shan** ▲▲ SW China
261 H7 **Wuliaru, Pulau** *island* Kepulauan Tanimbar, E Indonesia
242 E5 **Wuling Shan** ▲▲ S China
177 L3 **Wulka** 〰 E Austria
Wulkan *see* Vulcan
177 J1 **Wullowitz** Oberösterreich, N Austria 48°37´N 14°27´E
242 D3 **Wulong** Chongqing Shi, C China 29°11´N 107°26´E
Wu-lu-k'o-mu-shi/Wu-lu-mu-ch'i *see* Ürümqi
134 A5 **Wum** Nord-Ouest, NE Cameroon 06°24´N 10°04´E
242 A5 **Wumeng Shan** ▲▲ SW China
242 D9 **Wuming** Guangxi Zhuangzu Zizhiqu, S China 23°12´N 108°11´E
178 E5 **Wümme** 〰 NW Germany
Wu-na-mu *see* Wuhu
261 L5 **Wunen** Papua, E Indonesia 03°40´S 138°31´E
243 I4 **Wuning** Jiangxi, China 29°09´N 115°03´E
58 D5 **Wunnummin Lake** ◎ Ontario, C Canada
134 I4 **Wun Rog** Warrap, NW South Sudan 09°00´N 28°20´E
179 G10 **Wunsiedel** Bayern, E Germany 50°02´N 12°00´E
180 G5 **Wunstorf** Niedersachsen, NW Germany 52°25´N 09°25´E
256 C3 **Wuntho** Sagaing, N Myanmar (Burma) 23°52´N 95°43´E
243 J7 **Wuping** Fujan, China 25°04´N 116°04´E
181 D9 **Wupper** 〰 W Germany
181 C8 **Wuppertal** *prev.* Barmen-Elberfeld. Nordrhein-Westfalen, W Germany 51°16´N 07°12´E
140 D8 **Wuppertal** Western Cape, South Africa 32°16´S 19°13´E
244 E5 **Wuqi** Shaanxi, C China 36°57´N 108°15´E
245 J5 **Wuqiao** *var.* Sangyuan. Hebei, E China 37°40´N 116°21´E
245 J3 **Wuqing** Tianjin Shi, China 39°13´N 117°02´E
179 F13 **Würm** 〰 SE Germany
133 J5 **Wurno** Sokoto, NW Nigeria 13°15´N 05°24´E
64 G4 **Wurtsboro** New York, NE USA 41°34´N 74°29´W
181 H12 **Würzburg** Bayern, SW Germany 49°48´N 09°56´E
179 H8 **Wurzen** Sachsen, E Germany 51°21´N 12°48´E
243 J1 **Wushan** Anhui, E China 32°04´N 117°03´E
242 E2 **Wushan** Chongqing Shi, C China 31°03´N 109°31´E
244 B7 **Wushan** Gansu, C China 34°42´N 104°53´E
242 E2 **Wu Shan** ▲▲ C China
242 C2 **Wusheng** Sichuan, China 30°14´N 106°10´E
243 H1 **Wusheng Guan** *pass* Hubei, China
238 D4 **Wushi** *var.* Uqturpan. Xinjiang Uygur Zizhiqu, NW China 41°07´N 79°09´E
Wusih *see* Wuxi
243 M1 **Wusong** Shanghai Shi, E China 31°22´N 121°30´E
180 E4 **Wüsting** Niedersachsen, Germany 53°07´E 8°21´N
180 J4 **Wustrow** Niedersachsen, Germany 52°55´E 11°07´N
Wusuli Jiang/Wusuri *see* Ussuri
245 H4 **Wutai** Shanxi, China 38°26´N 113°09´E
245 H4 **Wutai Shan** *var.* Beitai Ding. ▲ C China 39°00´N 114°00´E
245 H4 **Wutai Shan** ▲▲ Shanxi, China
242 A3 **Wutongqiao** Sichuan, C China 29°21´N 103°48´E
239 H4 **Wutongwozi Quan** *spring* NW China
261 M5 **Wutung** Sandaun, NW Papua New Guinea 02°39´S 141°01´E
163 E8 **Wuustwezel** Antwerpen, N Belgium 51°24´N 04°34´E
280 A1 **Wuvulu Island** *island* NW Papua New Guinea
243 K2 **Wuwei** Anhui, China 31°10´N 117°32´E
244 A4 **Wuwei** *var.* Liangzhou. Gansu, C China 37°58´N 102°40´E
242 E2 **Wuxi** Chongqing Shi, C China 31°16´N 109°22´E
243 M1 **Wuxi** *var.* Wuhsi, Wu-hsi, Wusih. Jiangsu, E China 31°35´N 120°19´E
Wuxing *see* Huzhou
242 E9 **Wuxuan** Guangxi Zhuangzu Zizhiqu, S China 23°40´N 109°41´E
243 I3 **Wuxue** Hubei, China 29°31´N 115°20´E
245 H8 **Wuyang** Henan, China 33°16´N 113°21´E
Wuyang *see* Zhenyuan
242 D6 **Wuyang He** 〰 S China
243 L4 **Wuyi** Zhejiang, China 28°32´N 119°29´E
247 M3 **Wuyiling** Heilongjiang, NE China 48°36´N 129°24´E
243 K5 **Wuyishan** *prev.* Chong'an. Fujian, SE China 27°48´N 118°03´E
243 J7 **Wuyi Shan** ▲▲ SE China
245 M8 **Wuyou** Jiangsu, E China 33°18´N 120°14´E
243 K4 **Wuyuan** Jiangxi, China 29°09´N 117°31´E
244 E2 **Wuyuan** Nei Mongol Zizhiqu, N China 41°05´N 108°15´E
262 G2 **Wuzhishan** *prev.* Tongshi. Hainan, S China 18°37´N 109°34´E
240 F10 **Wuzhi Shan** ▲ S China 18°52´N 109°36´E
244 C4 **Wuzhong** Ningxia, N China 37°58´N 106°09´E
242 F9 **Wuzhou** *var.* Wu-chou, Wuchow. Guangxi Zhuangzu Zizhiqu, S China 23°30´N 111°21´E
64 E4 **Wyalusing** Pennsylvania, NE USA 41°40´N 76°13´W
277 J1 **Wyandra** Queensland, Australia
180 C3 **Wybelsum** Niedersachsen, Germany 53°21´E 7°06´N
277 I6 **Wycheproof** Victoria, SE Australia 36°06´S 143°13´E
161 M7 **Wye** United Kingdom 51°11´N 0°55´E
157 G9 **Wye** *Wel.* Gwy. 〰 England/Wales, United Kingdom
Wyłkowyszki *see* Vilkaviškis
161 M3 **Wymondham** E England, United Kingdom 52°29´N 01°10´E
75 E8 **Wymore** Nebraska, C USA 40°07´N 96°39´W
276 E3 **Wynbring** South Australia 30°34´S 133°27´E
274 F3 **Wyndham** Western Australia 15°28´S 128°08´E
74 E4 **Wyndmere** North Dakota, N USA 46°16´N 97°07´W
75 J12 **Wynne** Arkansas, C USA 35°14´N 90°48´W
75 E13 **Wynnewood** Oklahoma, C USA 34°39´N 97°09´W
277 J9 **Wynyard** Tasmania, SE Australia 40°57´S 145°33´E
57 N6 **Wynyard** Saskatchewan, S Canada 51°46´N 104°10´W
77 K6 **Wyola** Montana, NW USA 45°07´N 107°23´W
276 C3 **Wyola Lake** *salt lake* South Australia
73 F8 **Wyoming** Michigan, N USA 42°54´N 85°42´W
77 M8 **Wyoming** *off.* State of Wyoming, ***also known as*** Equality State. ◐ *state* C USA
77 I8 **Wyoming Range** ▲▲ Wyoming, C USA
277 L5 **Wyong** New South Wales, SE Australia 33°18´S 151°27´E
Wysg *see* Usk
182 I5 **Wysokie Mazowieckie** Łomża, E Poland 52°54´N 22°34´E
182 H5 **Wyszków** *Ger.* Probstberg. Mazowieckie, NE Poland 52°36´N 21°28´E
182 G6 **Wyszogród** Mazowieckie, C Poland 52°24´N 20°14´E
67 I5 **Wytheville** Virginia, NE USA 36°57´N 81°07´W
183 G8 **Wyżyna Małopolska** *plateau*

X

136 J4 **Xaafuun** *It.* Hafun. Bari, NE Somalia 10°25´N 51°17´E
136 J3 **Xaafuun, Raas** *var.* Ras Hafun. *cape* NE Somalia
Xabia *see* Jávea
88 C3 **Xaclbal, Río** *var.* Xalbal. 〰 Guatemala/Mexico
215 M4 **Xaçmaz** *Rus.* Khachmas. N Azerbaijan 41°26´N 48°47´E
136 I4 **Xadeed** *var.* Haded. *physical region* N Somalia
239 H8 **Xagquka** Xizang Zizhiqu, W China 31°47´N 92°46´E
Xai *see* Oudômxai
238 C6 **Xaidulla** Xinjiang Uygur Zizhiqu, W China 36°27´N 77°46´E
256 F5 **Xaignabouli** *prev.* Muang Xaignabouri, *Fr.* Sayaboury. Xaignabouli, N Laos 19°16´N 101°43´E

◆ Country
● Country Capital
◇ Dependent Territory
○ Dependent Territory Capital
◐ Administrative Regions
✕ International Airport
▲ Mountain
▲▲ Mountain Range
♨ Volcano
〰 River
◎ Lake
⊠ Reservoir

◆ Country ▲ Mountain ▲ Volcano ⊚ Lake
◇ Dependent Territory ✈ International Airport ▲ Mountain Range ≈ River ⊟ Reservoir
● Country Capital ○ Dependent Territory Capital ✖ Administrative Regions
◇ Dependent Territory Capital

Picture credits

◆ Country
● Country Capital
◇ Dependent Territory
○ Dependent Territory Capital
⬦ Administrative Regions
✕ International Airport
▲ Mountain
▲ Mountain Range
⛰ Volcano
〰 River
⊚ Lake
▨ Reservoir

NORTH AMERICA

CANADA

UNITED STATES OF AMERICA

MEXICO

BELIZE

COSTA RICA

EL SALVADOR

GUATEMALA

HONDURAS

GRENADA

HAITI

JAMAICA

ST KITTS & NEVIS

ST LUCIA

ST VINCENT & THE GRENADINES

TRINIDAD & TOBAGO

SOUTH AMERICA

COLOMBIA

AFRICA

URUGUAY

CHILE

PARAGUAY

ALGERIA

EGYPT

LIBYA

MOROCCO

TUNISIA

LIBERIA

MALI

MAURITANIA

NIGER

NIGERIA

SENEGAL

SIERRA LEONE

TOGO

BURUNDI

DJIBOUTI

ERITREA

ETHIOPIA

KENYA

RWANDA

SOUTH SUDAN

SOMALIA

EUROPE

SOUTH AFRICA

SWAZILAND

ZAMBIA

ZIMBABWE

DENMARK

FINLAND

ICELAND

NORWAY

MONACO

ANDORRA

PORTUGAL

SPAIN

ITALY

SAN MARINO

VATICAN CITY

AUSTRIA

BOSNIA & HERZEGOVINA

CROATIA

KOSOVO (disputed)

MACEDONIA

MONTENEGRO

SERBIA

BULGARIA

GREECE

ASIA

ARMENIA

AZERBAIJAN

GEORGIA

TURKEY

IRAQ

ISRAEL

JORDAN

LEBANON

IRAN

KAZAKHSTAN

KYRGYZSTAN

TAJIKISTAN

TURKMENISTAN

UZBEKISTAN

AFGHANISTAN

Moldova

PAKISTAN

TAIWAN

JAPAN

MYANMAR (BURMA)

CAMBODIA

LAOS

PHILIPPINES

THAILAND

VIETNAM

AUSTRALASIA & OCEANIA

MAURITIUS

SEYCHELLES

AUSTRALIA

NEW ZEALAND

PAPUA NEW GUINEA

FIJI

SOLOMON ISLANDS

VANUATU